# THE ILLUSTRATED ENCYCLOPEDIA
## OF MOVIE
### *Character Actors*

# THE ILLUSTRATED ENCYCLOPEDIA OF MOVIE Character Actors

DAVID QUINLAN

## Harmony Books / New York

Published in the United States in 1986 by Harmony Books,
a division of Crown Publishers, Inc., 225 Park Avenue South,
New York, NY 10003.

Originally published in Great Britain as *The Ilustrated Directory
of Film Character Actors* by B. T. Batsford Ltd.,
4 Fitzhardinge Street, London W1H 0AH.

HARMONY and colophon are trademarks of Crown Publishers, Inc.

Manufactured in Great Britain

Library of Congress Cataloging-in-Publication Data

Quinlan, David.
    The illustrated encyclopedia of movie character actors.
    "Originally published in Great Britain under the title Illustrated
directory of film character actors by B.T. Batsford Ltd.,
London"—T.p. verso.
    Includes filmographies.
    1. Moving-picture actors and actresses—Biography—
Dictionaries.   I. Title.
PN1998.A2Q56   1986       791.43'028'0922  [B]  85–27126
ISBN 0–517–56171–9
        0–517–56172–7 (pbk.)

10 9 8 7 6 5 4 3 2 1

First American Edition

To my wife Shirley, to whom my preoccupation with books has meant a greater share of work in the house – albeit borne with fortitude – than I would have wished.

# Acknowledgements

I would like to offer a special vote of thanks to D. P. Brummell of Farncombe, whose diligent research has added many titles to the filmographies in this book. My thanks also to Bill Ayres, James Cameron-Wilson, Kenneth Thompson, Lionel Perry, Alan Frank and many correspondents for information offered and gladly accepted. I must also mention the staff of the British Film Institute's Information and Stills departments, for snippets and pictures fetched, carried, sought and hunted down. Although the majority of the illustrations in this book are from my own collection, I am greatly indebted to the BFI Stills section who were able to supply scores of 'missing' personalities, often in gratifyingly characteristic poses.

Almost all of the pictures in the book were originally issued to publicize or promote films or TV material made or distributed by the following companies, to whom I gratefully offer acknowledgement: Allied Artists, American-International, Anglo-Amalgamated, Artificial Eye, Associated British-Pathé, ATP, ATV, Avco-Embassy, BIP, Brent-Walker, British and Dominions, Butchers, Cannon-Classic, Cinerama, Columbia, Walt Disney/Buena Vista, Eagle-Lion, Ealing Studios, EMI, Filmmakers Associates, First National, Gainsborough, Gala, Gaumont/Gaumont-British, Goldwyn, Granada TV, Grand National, Hammer, Hemdale, Lippert, London Films, London Weekend TV, Lorimar, Metro-Goldwyn-Mayer, Miracle, Monogram, New World, Orion, Palace Pictures, Paramount, PRC, The Rank Organization, Rediffusion, Republic, RKO/RKO Radio, Hal Roach, Selznick, 20th Century-Fox, UIP, United Artists, Universal/Universal-International, Virgin Films, Warner Brothers and Yorkshire TV.

# Foreword

This book, which many readers have pleaded for as an adjunct to my previous *Illustrated Directory of Film Stars*, is a tribute to those film players whose faces were just as familiar as those of the superstars, but whose names many filmgoers could never quite remember.

There are fewer of these character stars today compared with 30 years ago; yet many are still around, although, if they are good enough, like Harry Dean Stanton, Klaus Kinski, Charles Durning, Thora Hird, M. Emmet Walsh and others, they may eventually wade thigh-deep through a morass of bit parts and supporting cameos to achieve a star status of their own.

For the vast majority of character players, however, there was no stardom – except in the eyes of those cinemagoers who welcomed their every appearance with delighted cries of 'Oh – it's *him* again!' Again was often the operative word, as, especially in Hollywood in the 1930s and 1940s, these priceless people, rushing from set to set and scene to scene, could make appearances in anything up to 20 films in a single year.

Most of the more successful among them soon assumed familiar personae – the slow-witted hoodlum, the fussy hotel manager, the cockney char, the wisecracking blonde, the jovial trickster, the downtrodden little man, the sly hillbilly, the doughty dowager, the snoops and meddlers, the treacherous foreigner, the pompous aristocrat, the redneck bigot and many more besides.

Such 'typing' was part of their attraction; one could rely on well-loved mannerisms and variations on a familiar performance. Most of them became so expert at their own game that they could steal a scene from the star at the flick of an eyelid. If Gale Sondergaard, for example, didn't turn up as the sinister housekeeper but appeared in a sympathetic role, one would feel in some way cheated. One could no more see Elisha Cook without his yellow streak than Kathleen Harrison in tweeds and pearls. And although our favourites tried understandably to take on less familiar characterizations to widen their range, such attempts, although perhaps successful within a single film, did not break the pattern that had been set, any more than they met with the fans' favour.

The pages that follow are both a 'thank you' to 850 of the world's finest character stars past and present (including the many European exiles who found a profitable new home in Hollywood), and an attempt to give them their due by listing all their film appearances, in the filmographies that follow concise details of their personalities and careers.

'Complete' is a contentious word in film circles, and experience has taught that, with apologies to George Orwell, some filmographies will be more complete than others. It is especially difficult with players of often minor roles to gather everything into the net, but a prodigious attempt has been made to list all feature film appearances up to the end of 1984, plus as many short films, guest appearances, narrations-over and films made for television as could be found. Nonetheless, additions are expected – and welcomed – from eagle-eyed readers, although any 1985 film credits should be regarded as a bonus rather than as part of a 'complete' list.

I can say, however, with hand on heart, that almost all of the filmographies within this book are 'more complete' than any listings on these character stars that have ever been published before. Even some of those players transferred rightly from *The Illustrated Directory of Film Stars* (also making more room for newcomers in the next edition of that volume) to this present book have had their listings expanded by a vital few titles which will, it is hoped, bring them closer to true completeness.

References to Academy Awards won, and, in many cases Oscar nominations as well, should be found within the notes on the actor or actress concerned. Any symbols or abbreviations are explained at the foot of the entry, except the single asterisk, which will always indicate a short film, that is one of three reels (about 35 minutes) or less. Photographs are usually taken from a player's most prolific or best-remembered period.

Alphabetical order has been strictly adhered to in the sequence of entries. Thus Le Mesurier follows Lembeck and precedes Leonard, and De Luise comes between Dehner and Demarest. Mc and Mac names are not treated as one. Dates given for films are intended to be those on the credit titles of the film. The original title of a film occurs first in almost every case – American spellings for Hollywood films and British spellings for British pictures. British and American titles for foreign films are given where known.

Although an attempt has been made to include all the cinema's most striking character players, both ancient and modern, and especially from the onset of sound, there will doubtless be omissions that will disappoint some, baffle others and horrify the odd few whose favourite performers may be among the missing.

If you have two or three people you think more deserving than some who appear here, please write to me care of the publishers; every attempt will be made to please all film fans all of the time in any future editions.

It has been difficult to leave out some players whose success has taken them beyond 'character' status to become what might be called 'character superstars', with their names more often than not above the title.

Thus, to take them in convenient pairs, such as Charles Coburn and Edmund Gwenn, Margaret Rutherford and Alastair Sim, Sydney Greenstreet and Peter Lorre, Basil Radford and Naunton Wayne, Lee Marvin and Ernest Borgnine and Kathleen Harrison and Jack Warner, though hardly romantic idols, will continue to find their place, for the present at least, within the pages of our companion *Film Stars* volume.

Meanwhile what you have here is the hardrock foundation of the profession, the players without whom so many films would not have had quite the same flavour. Maybe, as Edward G. Robinson said at the end of *Brother Orchid*, 'this is the *real* class'.

DAVID QUINLAN
*Addington, 1985*

NOTE An asterisk (*) in a filmography designates a 'short film' – that is, one of three reels (about 35 minutes) or less.

1952: The Merry Widow. Rogue's March. 1953: The Steel Lady (GB: The Treasure of Kalifa). Sombrero. 1957: Public Pigeon Number One. 1958: Gigi. 1963: Who's Minding the Store? 1965: The Greatest Story Ever Told. 1966: Gambit. 1967: The Jungle Book (voice only). 1968: Three Guns for Texas (originally TV). 1969: 2,000 Years Later. 1973: The Cat Creature (TV). 1975: The Black Bird. 1976: Sherlock Holmes in New York (TV). 1982: Slapstick (US: Slapstick of Another Kind).

Willis Wayde (TV). The Steel Jungle. 1957: Bernardine. Raintree County. 1958: Handle With Care. 1964: The Confession (GB: TV as Quick! Let's Get Married). 1965: Mirage. 1971: Zora. 1973: Man Without a Country (TV). Silent Night, Bloody Night (later Death House. GB: Night of the Dark Full Moon). 1984: The Ultimate Solution of Grace Quigley (GB: Grace Quigley).

## ACKLAND, Joss 1928-
Fair-haired, heavily-built British stage actor hardly seen in films until the 1970s, when he played a string of characters who often hid various shades of wickedness beneath a florid complexion and a beaming smile. But the stage gave him his biggest hit—as Peròn in the London production of Evita. His mellow tones are frequently used for narrations, voice-overs and commercials.

1950: Seven Days to Noon. 1952: Ghost Ship. 1958: A Midsummer Night's Dream (dubbed voice only). 1965: Rasputin the Mad Monk. 1966: East West Island (narrator only). 1969: Crescendo. 1970: The House That Dripped Blood. 1971: Villain. Mr Forbush and the Penguins (US: Cry of the Penguins). 1972: England Made Me. The Happiness Cage. 1973: Hitler: the Last Ten Days. Penny Gold. The Three Musketeers (The Queen's Diamonds). 1974: S*P*Y*S. The Black Windmill. The Little Prince. 1975: Royal Flash. Great Expectations (TV. GB: cinemas). Operation Daybreak. One of Our Dinosaurs is Missing. The Magic Dream (narrator only). 1976: World within a Ring (narrator only). 1977: Silver Bears. 1978: Watership Down (voice only). Who is Killing the Great Chefs of Europe? (GB: Too Many Chefs). 1979: *The Love Tapes (narrator only). A Nightingale Sang in Berkeley Square (TV). Saint Jack. 1980: Dangerous Davies—the Last Detective (TV). Rough Cut. The Apple (GB: Star Rock). 1985: Lady Jane.

## ACOSTA, Rodolfo 1920-1974
Dark, moustachioed, hawkishly handsome Mexican actor, in Hollywood from 1950, but mostly confined there to playing sneering bandits in huge sombreros. A little cold, perhaps, for bona-fide leading roles,

## ABBOTT, John 1905-
Dishevelled British-born actor with wide-open eyes and drooping lower lip, playing eccentric character roles in Hollywood from 1941. He began his career as a commercial artist, then switched to acting and appeared on the London stage and in a few British films before going permanently to America. Memorable in Jane Eyre and The Woman in White, he had a leading role in one film: London Blackout Murders. Still occasionally glimpsed in films and TV.

1935: Conquest of the Air (released 1940). 1937: Mademoiselle Docteur. The Return of the Scarlet Pimpernel. 1938: This Man is News. Algiers. 1939: Ten Days in Paris (US: Missing Ten Days). The Saint in London. 1941: The Shanghai Gesture. 1942: They Got Me Covered. Mrs Miniver. London Blackout Murders (GB: Secret Motive). Joan of Paris. Nightmare. Get Hep to Love (GB: She's My Lovely). This Above All. 1943: Mission to Moscow. Secret Motive. Gorilla Man. Jane Eyre. 1944: The Mask of Dimitrios. Summer Storm. Cry of the Werewolf. U-Boat Prisoner (GB: Dangerous Mists). Abroad with Two Yanks. The Falcon in Hollywood. 1945: The Vampire's Ghost. Pursuit to Algiers. Saratoga Trunk. 1946: Deception. The Notorious Lone Wolf. One More Tomorrow. Bandit of Sherwood Forest. Anna and the King of Siam. Humoresque. 1947: Navy Bound. The Web. Adventure Island. Time Out of Mind. The Woman in White. 1948: Dream Girl. If Winter Comes. 1949: Madame Bovary. 1950: Her Wonderful Lie. 1951: Thunder on the Hill (GB: Bonaventure). Crosswinds. Thunder in the East.

## ABEL, Walter 1898-1987
Stern-looking, often moustachioed, dark-haired American actor, strangely one of Broadway's foremost exponents of farce before embarking seriously on a movie career that saw him much cast as senior officers, lawyers and chiefs of detectives. Played D'Artagnan in his second sound film, otherwise mainly in supporting roles. Latterly frequently seen as harassed fathers, Abel is at time of writing one of America's oldest working actors.

1918: Out of a Clear Sky. 1920: The North Wind's Malice. 1930: Liliom. 1935: The Three Musketeers. 1936: The Lady Consents. Two in the Dark. The Witness Chair. Fury. We Went to College (GB: The Old School Tie). Second Wife. 1937: Portia on Trial (GB: The Trial of Portia Merriman). Wise Girl. Green Light. 1938: Law of the Underworld. Racket Busters. Men With Wings. 1939: King of the Turf. 1940: Miracle on Main Street. Michael Shayne, Private Detective. Who Killed Aunt Maggie? Dance Girl Dance. Arise, My Love. 1941: Hold Back the Dawn. Skylark. Hearts in Springtime/Glamour Boy. 1942: Beyond the Blue Horizon. Star Spangled Rhythm. Holiday Inn. Wake Island. 1943: So Proudly We Hail! Fired Wife. *The Last Will and Testament of Tom Smith. 1944: Mr Skeffington. Follow the Boys. An American Romance. The Hitler Gang (narrator only). 1945: The Affairs of Susan. Duffy's Tavern. Kiss and Tell. 1946: The Kid from Brooklyn. 13 Rue Madeleine. 1947: The Fabulous Joe. 1948: Dream Girl. That Lady in Ermine. 1953: Island in the Sky. So This Is Love (GB: The Grace Moore Story). 1954: Night People. 1955: The Indian Fighter. 1956: Sincerely,

although he was top-billed once, in *The Tijuana Story*, a minor 'meller'. Then it was back to a whole posse of westerns before his early death. Sometimes billed as Rudy or Rudolfo.

*1946: Rosenda. 1947: The Fugitive. 1949: Salon Mexico. La malquerida. 1950: Victimas de pecado. Pancho Villa Returns. One Way Street. 1951: The Bullfighter and the Lady. 1952: Horizons West. Yankee Buccaneer. 1953: San Antone. Destination Gobi. Wings of the Hawk. Appointment in Honduras. City of Bad Men. Hondo. 1954: Passion. Drum Beat. Night People. 1955: A Life in the Balance. The Littlest Outlaw. 1956: Bandido! The Proud Ones. 1957: The Tijuana Story. Apache Warrior. The Last Stagecoach West. Trooper Hook. 1958: From Hell to Texas (GB: Manhunt). 1960: Flaming Star. Let No Man Write My Epitaph. Walk Like a Dragon. 1961: One-Eyed Jacks. The Last Rebel. Posse from Hell. The Second Time Around. 1962: How the West Was Won. Savage Sam. 1964: Rio Conchos. 1965: The Sons of Katie Elder. The Reward. The Greatest Story Ever Told. 1966: The Return of the Seven. 1967: Valley of Mystery (originally for TV). Stranger on the Run (TV). 1968: Dayton's Devils. Impasse. 1969: Young Billy Young. 1970: Flap (GB: The Last Warrior). The Great White Hope. 1971: Legacy of Blood. 1972: The Magnificent Seven Ride!*

**ADAM, Ronald** 1896-1979
Tall, bushy-browed British actor with round, smily face. He was mostly seen as bureaucrats and administrators; his authority perhaps stemmed from his days as an officer in World War I (he was a prisoner-of-war) and a wing-commander in World War II (wangling his way in despite his age). In between, he gave up a career as a chartered accountant to concentrate on the stage. Film character roles became plentiful as he neared middle age. Also a prolific writer and the author of several plays.

*1936: Song of Freedom. 1938: The Drum (US: Drums). Strange Boarders. 1939: Inspector Hornleigh. Q Planes (US: Clouds Over Europe). The Lion Has Wings. The Missing People. Meet Maxwell Archer (US: Maxwell Archer, Detective). Too Dangerous to Live. At the Villa Rose. 1940: Hell's Cargo. 1941: The Big Blockade. 1942: The Foreman Went to France (US: Somewhere in France). 1943: Escape to Danger. 1945: Pink String and Sealing Wax. 1946: Green for Danger. 1947: The Phantom Shot. Take My Life. 1948: Bonnie Prince Charlie. The Bad Lord Byron. Counterblast. All Over the Town. Christopher Columbus. The Case of Charles Peace. 1949: Under Capricorn. That Dangerous Age (US: If This Be Sin). Helter Skelter. Diamond City. Obsession (US: The Hidden Room). 1950: My Daughter Joy (US: Operation X). Seven Days to Noon. Shadow of the Past. The Adventurers. 1951: Hell Is Sold Out. The Lavender Hill Mob. Laughter in Paradise. The Late Edwina Black. Mr Denning Drives North. Captain Horatio Hornblower RN. I'll Never Forget You (US: The House in the Square). 1952: Angels One Five. Hindle Wakes (US: Holiday Week). Circumstantial Evidence. Top Secret (US: Mr Potts Goes to Moscow). 1953: Thought to Kill. Flannelfoot. Stryker of the Yard. The Beachcomber. The Million Pound Note (US: Man With a Million). 1954: Front Page Story. Escape by Night. Johnny on the Spot. To Dorothy a Son (US: Cash on Delivery). Malta Story. The Black Knight. 1955: The Man Who Never Was. 1956: Reach for the Sky. Assignment Redhead. Tons of Trouble. Private's Progress. Lust for Life. 1957: Sea Wife. The Surgeon's Knife. Kill Me Tomorrow. Woman and the Hunter (GB: Triangle on Safari). Carry On Admiral (US: The Ship Was Loaded). 1958: The Golden Disc. 1959: Carlton-Browne of the FO (US: Man in a Cocked Hat). Sapphire. The Man Who Could Cheat Death. Please Turn Over. 1960: Snowball. And the Same to You. 1961: Shoot to Kill. Offbeat. Three on a Spree. Carry on Regardless. 1962: The Golden Rabbit. Postman's Knock. Two-Letter Alibi. Satan Never Sleeps (GB: The Devil Never Sleeps). 1963: Cleopatra. Heavens Above! The Haunting. 1964: The Tomb of Ligeia. 1966: Who Killed the Cat? 1968: Hellboats. 1970: Song of Norway. 1971: Zeppelin. The Ruling Class. 1973: The Zoo Robbery. 1976: The Man from Nowhere.*

**ADAMS, Casey**
See SHOWALTER, Max

**ADAMS, Dorothy** 1910- *1988*
Dark-haired, weepy-eyed, careworn-looking American actress whose characters wore an expression of permanent dismay and were often pioneer women or work-hard-for-the-kids wives, ground down by life and/or the land. Richly described by one 1950s' correspondent as 'a human wailing wall'. Married to fellow character player Byron Foulger (*qv*). In the early 1960s, she became a lecturer on theatre arts at the University College of Los Angeles, and appeared less often in cinema and television from then on.

*1938: Condemned Women. 1939: The Women. Bachelor Mother. Broadway Musketeers. Calling Dr Kildare. Disputed Passage. Ninotchka. 1940: A Child Is Born. Cross-Country Romance. We Who Are Young. Lucky Partners. Untamed. *The Great Meddler. 1941: Flame of New Orleans. Whistling in the Dark. The Devil Commands. Shepherd of the Hills. Bedtime Story. Affectionately Yours. My Life With Caroline. Penny Serenade. Tobacco Road. 1942: Hi Neighbor! Lady Gangster. 1943: So Proudly We Hail! O My Darling Clementine! 1944: Laura. Since You Went Away. Bathing Beauty. 1945: Captain Eddie. Circumstantial Evidence. Fallen Angel. *Phantom's Inc. The Trouble With Women (released 1947). 1946: The Best Years of Our Lives. Nocturne. Sentimental Journey. The Gangster. The Inner Circle. Miss Susie Slagle's (completed 1944). OSS. 1947: Unconquered. Will Tomorrow Ever Come? The Foxes of Harrow. That's My Man. 1948: Sitting Pretty. He Walked by Night. 1949: Down to the Sea in Ships. Not Wanted. The Sainted Sisters. Samson and Delilah. Montana. 1950: The Cariboo Trail. The Outriders. Paid in Full. The Jackpot. 1951: The First Legion. 1952: Carrie. Fort Osage. Jet Job. The Winning Team. The Greatest Show on Earth. 1955: The Prodigal. 1956: The Man in the Gray Flannel Suit. Three for Jamie Dawn. These Wilder Years. The Ten Commandments. The Killing. Johnny Concho. The Broken Star. 1957: Buckskin Lady. An Affair to Remember. 1958: Gunman's Walk. Unwed Mother. The Big Country. 1960: From the Terrace. 1969: The Good Guys and the Bad Guys. 1974: The Virginia Hill Story (TV). 1975: Peeper.*

**ADDY, Wesley** 1912-
Tall, slim, white-haired American actor, almost entirely on stage, often in productions with his wife (since 1961), former Hollywood star Celeste Holm. His few film roles (often in pictures directed by Robert Aldrich) have been as cold, calculating characters, less showy than the main villain, but less likely to pay the price.

*1951: The First Legion. Scandal Sheet (GB: The Dark Page). 1952: My Six Convicts. Dreamboat. 1955: Kiss Me Deadly. The Big Knife. Timetable. 1956: The Garment Jungle. 1959: Ten Seconds to Hell. 1962: What Ever Happened to Baby Jane? 1963: Four for Texas. 1964: Hush . . . Hush, Sweet Charlotte. 1965: Mister Buddwing (GB: Woman without a Face). 1967: Seconds. Cosa Nostra: an Arch Enemy of the FBI (TV. GB: cinemas). 1970: Tora! Tora! Tora! 1971: The Grissom Gang. Beware! The Blob (GB: Son of Blob). 1976: Network. 1977: The Love Boat II (TV). Tail Gunner Joe (TV). 1979: The Europeans. 1982: The Verdict. 1984: The Bostonians.*

**ADAMS, Edie**
(Elizabeth Edith Enke) 1927-
Vivacious American singer-comedienne, a wisecracking blonde in the Eve Arden tradition, although with a much rounder face. Multi-talented (a graduate of music and drama colleges and a beauty contest

winner as well), she was too often given humourless sexpot roles by Hollywood, even though she livened them up with her personality. Married to comic star Ernie Kovacs from 1955 until his death in a car crash in 1962. She has written a book on beauty.

*1960: The Apartment. 1961: Lover Come Back. 1963: Call Me Bwana. It's a Mad, Mad, Mad, Mad World. Under the Yum Yum Tree. Love With the Proper Stranger. 1964: The Best Man. 1966: Made in Paris. The Oscar. 1967: The Honey Pot. 1972: Evil Roy Slade (TV). 1975: The Return of Joe Forrester (TV). 1978: Up in Smoke. Racquet. 1979: Fast Friends (TV). Superdome (TV). 1980: The Happy Hooker Goes to Hollywood. Box Office. 1983: Shooting Stars (TV). 1984: Ernie Kovacs—Between the Laughs (TV).*

**ADLER, Luther** 1903-1984
Distinguished American stage player—from a famous acting family—whose squat build, olive complexion and heavy-jowled features consigned him mainly to roles as oily villains and kings of the underworld. His film appearances were surprisingly few, although he did crop up on TV's *Hawaii Five-O* in the 1970s with another of his unctuous crime czars. Married (second) to actress Sylvia Sidney from 1938 to 1946. Played Hitler twice.

*1937: Lancer Spy. 1945: Cornered. 1948: Saigon. The Loves of Carmen. Wake of the Red Witch. 1949: House of Strangers. South Sea Sinner (GB: East of Java). D.O.A. (Dead on Arrival). 1950: Under My Skin. Kiss Tomorrow Goodbye. 1951: Rommel—Desert Fox (GB: The Desert Fox). M. The Magic Face. Hoodlum Empire. 1953: The Tall Texan. 1954: The Miami Story. 1955: Crashout. The Girl in the Red Velvet Swing. 1956: Hot Blood. 1958: Last Clear Chance (TV). The Plot to Kill Stalin (TV). 1959: The Last Angry Man. Rank and File (TV). 1966: Cast a Giant Shadow. 1968: Sunshine Patriot (TV). The Brotherhood. 1970: God Bless the Children (TV). 1974: Murph the Surf (GB: Live a Little, Steal a Lot). Crazy Joe. 1975: The Man in the Glass Booth. Mean Johnny Burrows. 1976: Voyage of the Damned. The Three Sisters. 1981: Absence of Malice.*

**ADRIAN, Iris**
(I. A. Hofstadter) 1913- 1994
Fluffy blonde American supporting actress, a chorus girl (and beauty contest winner) in the late 1920s who graduated to play dozens of flea-brained floozies and garrulous gold-diggers, progressing plumply to wisecracking matrons in later years. Turned up in several cameos for the Walt Disney studio from the early 1960s to the late 1970s.

*1930: Paramount on Parade. The Freshman's Goat. College Cuties. 1934: *Raring to Go. 1935: Rhumba/Rumba. Stolen Harmony. The Gay Deception. Murder at Glen Athol (GB: The Criminal Within). Grand Exit. 1936: A Message to Garcia. One Rainy Afternoon. Lady Luck. Our Relations. Stage Struck. Mister Cinderella. Gold Diggers of 1937. 1939: One Third of a Nation. Back Door to Heaven. 1940: Meet the Wildcat. Go West/ Marx Brothers Go West. 1941: Horror Island. The Lady from Cheyenne. Meet the Chump. Too Many Blondes. Road to Zanzibar. Wild Geese Calling. New York Town. Sing Another Chorus. Hard Guy. Swing It, Soldier (GB: Radio Revels of 1942). I Killed That Man. 1942: Roxie Hart. To the Shores of Tripoli. Rings on Her Fingers. Juke Box Jenny. Fingers at the Window. Broadway. Moonlight Masquerade. Orchestra Wives. Highways by Night. The McGuerins from Brooklyn. Calaboose. 1943: Ladies' Day. The Crystal Ball. He's My Guy. Taxi, Mister. Lady of Burlesque (GB: Striptease Lady). Action in the North Atlantic. Hers to Hold. Submarine Base. Spotlight Scandals. Career Girl. 1944: Million Dollar Kid. Shake Hands With Murder. Once Upon a Time. Swing Hostess. The Singing Sheriff. The Woman in the Window. Bluebeard. I'm from Arkansas. Alaska. 1945: It's a Pleasure. Road to Alcatraz. Steppin' in Society. Boston Blackie's Rendezvous. The Stork Club. The Trouble With Women (released 1947). 1946: The Bamboo Blonde. Cross My Heart. Vacation in Reno. 1947: Fall Guy. Love and Learn. Philo Vance Returns. The Wistful Widow of Wagon Gap (GB: The Wistful Widow). 1948: *How to Clean House. Out of the Storm. Smart Women. The Paleface. 1949: Miss Mink of 1949. Flamingo Road. My Dream is Yours. The Lovable Cheat. †Two*

*Knights in Brooklyn/Two Mugs from Brooklyn. Mighty Joe Young. Sky Dragon. Trail of the Yukon. Tough Assignment. I Married a Communist (GB: The Woman on Pier 13). Always Leave Them Laughing. There's a Girl in My Heart. 1950: Blondie's Hero. Joe Palooka in Humphrey Takes a Chance (GB: Humphrey Takes a Chance). Once a Thief. Sideshow. Hi-Jacked. *Foy Meets Girl. 1951: Stop That Cab. GI Jane. Varieties on Parade. The Racket. My Favorite Spy. 1952: Carson City. The Big Trees. 1953: Take the High Ground. 1954: Crime Wave (GB: The City is Dark). Highway Dragnet. The Fast and the Furious. *So You Want to Know Your Relatives. 1956: *So You Want to be Pretty. 1957: The Helen Morgan Story (GB: Both Ends of the Candle). Carnival Rock. 1958: The Buccaneer. 1961: Blue Hawaii. The Errand Boy. 1964: Fate is the Hunter. That Darn Cat! 1967: The Odd Couple. 1968: The Love Bug. 1970: The Barefoot Executive. 1972: Scandalous John. 1974: The Apple Dumpling Gang. 1976: Gus. Freaky Friday. The Shaggy DA. No Deposit, No Return. 1978: Getting Married (TV). 1980: Herbie Goes Bananas.*

† Alternative GB titles for combined version of The McGuerins from Brooklyn/ Taxi, Mister

**AHN, Philip** 1911-1978
Sombre-faced Hollywood oriental cast from the mid-1930s as an assorted collection of inscrutable types, mostly sympathetic until the war years, when his thin, unsmiling expression turned quite readily to nastiness. These roles carried bitter irony as Ahn's father was a Korean diplomat who died in a wartime Japanese prison camp. Found a secure niche in the 1970s with his running role as the old man in the series *Kung Fu*.

*1936: Klondike Annie. The General Died at Dawn. Stowaway. 1937: Tex Rides With the Boy Scouts. Something to Sing About. Daughter of Shanghai (GB: Daughter of the Orient). China Passage. Roaring Timber. Thank You, Mr Moto. 1938: Red Barry (serial). Hawaii Calls. Charlie Chan in Honolulu. 1939: Barricade. Disputed Passage. King of Chinatown. 1940: Passage from Hong Kong. 1941:*

*They Met in Bombay. 1942: China Girl. We Were Dancing. A Yank on the Burma Road (GB: China Caravan). Across the Pacific. Let's Get Tough. They Got Me Covered. 1943: Adventures of Smilin' Jack (serial). The Amazing Mrs Holliday. 1944: The Keys of the Kingdom. Forever Yours/They Shall Have Faith (GB: The Right to Live). Dragon Seed. The Story of Dr Wassell. The Purple Heart. 1945: Back to Bataan. They Were Expendable. Blood on the Sun. China's Little Devils. God Is My Co-Pilot. Betrayal from the East. China Sky. 1947: Singapore. The Chinese Ring. Intrigue. Women in the Night. 1948: The Cobra Strikes. The Miracle of the Bells. Rogues' Regiment. The Creeper. 1949: State Department—File 649 (GB: Assignment in China). Boston Blackie's Chinese Venture (GB: Chinese Adventure). Impact. 1950: The Big Hangover. Halls of Montezuma. 1951: China Corsair. The Sickle or the Cross. I Was an American Spy. 1952: Japanese War Bride. Macao. Target—Hong Kong. Red Snow. Battle Zone. 1953: China Venture. Battle Circus. His Majesty O'Keefe. Fair Wind to Java. 1954: The Shanghai Story. Hell's Half Acre. 1955: Love is a Many-splendored Thing. The Left Hand of God. 1956: Around the World in 80 Days. 1957: The Way to the Gold. Battle Hymn. 1958: Hong Kong Confidential. 1959: Never So Few. Yesterday's Enemy. 1960: The Great Impostor. 1962: A Girl Named Tamiko. Confessions of an Opium Eater (GB: Evils of Chinatown). Diamond Head. 1963: Shock Corridor. 1965: Paradise, Hawaiian Style. 1967: Thoroughly Modern Millie. The Karate Killers (TV. GB: cinemas). 1971: Voodoo Heartbeat. 1972: Kung Fu (TV). 1973: Jonathan Livingstone Seagull (voice only). The World's Greatest Athlete. 1976: The Killer Who Wouldn't Die (TV).*

**AKED, Muriel** 1887-1955
Bony-faced British actress who tended to play sourpusses, easily shocked spinsters, gossipy neighbours and grasping landladies. She hit her stride in British films with the coming of sound, trooping on and off in handfuls of scene-stealing cameos, noticeably in *Rome Express*, *Trouble* and *The Happiest Days of Your Life*, and played a running leading role, through 26 years, in the four screen versions of that old comedy chestnut *A Sister to Assist 'Er*.

*1922: A Sister to Assist 'Er. 1926: Bindle's Cocktail. 1930: Bed and Breakfast. The Middle Watch. 1931: A Sister to Assist 'Er (remake). 1932: Her First Affaire. Rome Express. Goodnight Vienna (US: Magic Night). The Mayor's Nest. Indiscretions of Eve. 1933: The Good Companions. Friday the Thirteenth. No Funny Business. Yes, Madam. Trouble. 1934: The Queen's Affair (US: Runaway Queen). Evensong. Autumn Crocus. The Night of the Party. Josser on the Farm. 1935: Can You Hear Me Mother? 1936: Don't Rush Me. Fame. Public Nuisance*

*Number One. Royal Eagle. 1937: Mr Stringfellow Says No. 1938: A Sister to Assist 'Er (second remake). 1939: The Girl Who Forgot. The Silent Battle (US: Continental Express). 1941: Cottage to Let (US: Bombsight Stolen). Kipps (US: The Remarkable Mr Kipps). 1942: The Demi-Paradise (US: Adventure for Two). 1943: The Life and Death of Colonel Blimp (US: Colonel Blimp). 1944: Two Thousand Women. 1945: The Wicked Lady. They Knew Mr Knight. 1946: The Years Between. 1947: Just William's Luck. 1948: A Sister to Assist 'Er (third remake). So Evil My Love. It's Hard to be Good. 1949: William Comes to Town. The Blue Lamp. 1950: The Happiest Days of Your Life. 1951: The Wonder Kid. Flesh and Blood. 1953: The Story of Gilbert and Sullivan (US: The Great Gilbert and Sullivan).*

**AKINS, Claude** 1918-1994
Burly, surly-looking American actor in the Ernest Borgnine tradition who, after a late start in films, almost inevitably found himself cast as villains. Equally inevitably, it seemed, his later career brought better and more sympathetic roles, and his cheerful grin was also to be seen in leading roles in TV series.

*1953: Seminole. From Here to Eternity. 1954: The Caine Mutiny. Bitter Creek. Down Three Dark Streets. The Human Jungle. The Raid. Shield for Murder. 1955: The Man With a Gun (GB: The Trouble Shooter). The Sea Chase. Battle Stations. 1956: The Proud and Profane. Johnny Concho. Hot Summer Night. The Burning Hills. The Sharkfighters. 1957: Joe Dakota. The Lonely Man. The Kettles on Old McDonald's Farm. 1958: The Defiant Ones. Onionhead. 1959: Porgy and Bess. Don't Give Up the Ship. Yellowstone Kelly. Hound Dog Man. Rio Bravo. 1960: Inherit the Wind. Comanche Station. 1961: Claudelle Inglish (GB: Young and Eager). 1962: How the West Was Won. Black Gold. Merrill's Marauders. 1964: The Killers. A Distant Trumpet. 1965: Incident at Phantom Hill. 1966: Return of the Seven. Ride Beyond Vengeance. 1967: First to Fight. Waterhole Number Three (GB: Waterhole Three). 1968: The Devil's Brigade. 1969: The Great Bank Robbery. 1970: River of Mystery (TV). Sledge (GB: A Man Called Sledge). Lock, Stock and Barrel (TV). Flap (GB: The Last Warrior). 1971: The Night Stalker (TV). 1972: Skyjacked. 1973: The Timber Tramp. Battle for the Planet of the Apes. Death Squad (TV). The Norliss Tapes (TV). 1974: In Tandem (TV). Shadow of Fear (TV). 1975: Eric (TV). Medical Story (TV). 1976: Tentacles. Kiss Me, Kill Me (TV). 1977: Yesterday's Child (TV). 1978: BJ and the Bear (TV). Little Mo (TV). The Broken Badge (TV). Killer on Board (TV). Ebony, Ivory and Jade (TV). Murder in Music City (TV). 1979: The Concrete Cowboys (TV). 1980: Tarantulas: the Deadly Cargo (TV). 1983: Desperate Intruder (TV).*

ABOVE Muriel **Aked** (left) at the beginning of her film career, in *Bed and Breakfast* (1930), here as a vicar's wife from whom Jane Baxter and Richard Cooper seem to have had a narrow escape. The vicar is Frederick Volpe

RIGHT Claude **Akins** manages a rare smile as a trucker trying to become a country 'n' western star in an episode from his successful television series *Movin' On*, which ran in 1974 and 1975

## ALBERTSON, Jack 1907-1981

Plum-nosed, sandy-haired American actor, often cast as grouchy old men. Started as a dancer and straight man to comedians in vaudeville. Won a Best Supporting Actor Academy Award in 1968 for *The Subject is Roses*, although his triumph was barely seen outside the United States. Probably won his greatest popularity in old age on television in the comedy series *Chico and the Man*. Died from cancer.

1947: *Miracle on 34th Street (GB: The Big Heart)*. 1952: *Top Banana*. 1955: *Bring Your Smile Along*. 1956: *The Unguarded Moment. Over-Exposed. The Eddy Duchin Story. The Harder They Fall. You Can't Run Away from It*. 1957: *Don't Go Near the Water. Monkey on My Back. Man of a Thousand Faces*. 1958: *Teacher's Pet*. 1959: *The Shaggy Dog. Never Steal Anything Small*. 1961: *Convicts Four (GB: Reprieve!). The George Raft Story (GB: Spin of a Coin). Lover Come Back*. 1962: *Period of Adjustment. Days of Wine and Roses. Who's Got the Action?* 1963: *A Tiger Walks. Son of Flubber*. 1964: *Kissin' Cousins. The Patsy. Roustabout*. 1965: *How to Murder Your Wife*. 1967: *The Flim Flam Man (GB: One Born Every Minute). How to Save a Marriage—and Ruin Your Life*. 1968: *Changes. The Subject Was Roses*. 1969: *The Monk (TV). Squeeze a Flower. Justine. A Clear and Present Danger (TV)*. 1970. *Rabbit Run. Lock, Stock and Barrel (TV)*. 1971: *Willy Wonka and the Chocolate Factory. The Showdown (TV). Time to Every Purpose. Congratulations, It's a Boy (TV)*. 1972: *The Late Liz. The Poseidon Adventure. Pick Up on 101 (GB: Echoes of the Road)*. 1978: *The Comedy Company (TV). Charlie's Balloon (TV. GB: Charlie and the Great Balloon Chase)*. 1979: *Valentine (TV)*. 1980: *Marriage is Alive and Well (TV)*. 1981: *The Fox and the Hound (voice only). Dead and Buried*. 1982: *My Body, My Child (TV)*.

## ALEXANDER, Terence 1923-

Round-faced, pushy-looking, London-born actor with dark hair. In repertory at 16, he started a regular film career in the 1950s, and usually appeared in light roles—as smooth upper-class charmers, beguiling rogues or amiable oafs. He was a natural for

a part in *The League of Gentlemen*—and it was probably his best film role.

1947: *Comin' Thro' the Rye*. 1950: *The Elusive Pimpernel (US: The Fighting Pimpernel). The Woman With No Name (US: Her Panelled Door)*. 1951: *Death is a Number. A Tale of Five Cities (US: A Tale of Five Women)*. 1952: *The Gentle Gunman. Top Secret (US: Mr Potts Goes to Moscow). *The First Elizabeth (narrator only). *The Stately Home of Kent (narrator only). *Just a Drop (narrator only)*. 1953: *Glad Tidings. Park Plaza 605 (US: Norman Conquest)*. 1954: *The Runaway Bus. Dangerous Cargo. The Green Scarf. Hands of Destiny*. 1955: *Portrait of Alison (US: Postmark for Danger). Out of the Clouds*. 1956: *The Green Man*. 1957: *The One That Got Away*. 1958: *The Square Peg. *Death Was a Passenger. Danger Within (US: Breakout)*. 1959: *Breakout (different GB film from preceding entry). Don't Panic Chaps! The Doctor's Dilemma. The Price of Silence*. 1960: *The League of Gentlemen. The Bulldog Breed*. 1961: *Carry on Regardless. Man at the Carlton Tower*. 1962: *The Gentle Terror. She Always Gets Their Man. On the Beat. The Fast Lady*. 1963: *The Mind Benders. The VIPs. Bitter Harvest*. 1964: *\*All in Good Time. The Intelligence Men*. 1965: *Judith*. 1967: *The Long Duel. \*The Spare Tyres*. 1968: *Only When I Larf*. 1969: *What's Good for the Goose. Run a Crooked Mile (TV). The Magic Christian. All the Way Up*. 1970: *Waterloo*. 1973: *Vault of Horror. The Day of the Jackal*. 1974: *The Internecine Project*. 1978: *Ike (TV)*. 1979: *The Boy Who Never Was*.

## ALISON, Dorothy 1925- *1992*

Cool, capable Australian actress with sympathetic, faintly motherly personality. A doll-like, dark-haired beauty in her early days, she came to England in 1949 and worked as a secretary until acting jobs became more frequent. Her career reached its zenith when she played Nurse Brace in *Reach for the Sky*. Thereafter, it declined somewhat into careworn roles, but she re-emerged in chirpier cameos in the 1980s. British films should have made more use of her than they did.

1948: *Eureka Stockade*. 1949: *Sons of Matthew (GB and US: The Rugged O'Rior-

dans)*. 1952: *Mandy (US: Crash of Silence)*. 1953: *Turn the Key Softly*. 1954: *The Maggie (US: High and Dry). The Purple Plain. Child's Play. Companions in Crime*. 1956: *The Long Arm (US: The Third Key). The Feminine Touch (US: The Gentle Touch). Reach for the Sky. The Silken Affair*. 1957: *The Scamp. Interpol (US: Pickup Alley)*. 1958: *The Man Upstairs*. 1959: *The Nun's Story. Life in Emergency Ward 10*. 1961: *Two Living, One Dead*. 1962: *The Prince and the Pauper*. 1966: *Georgy Girl*. 1967: *Pretty Polly (US: Loss of Innocence)*. 1971: *Blind Terror (US: See No Evil). Doctor Jekyll and Sister Hyde*. 1972: *Baxter! (US: The Boy). The Amazing Mr Blunden*. 1978: *En vandring i solen*. 1980: *\*The Errand*. 1982: *The Return of the Soldier*. 1983: *Invitation to the Wedding. The Winds of Jarrah*.

## ALLEN, Patrick 1927-

Tall, long-jawed, light-haired, tough-looking, Nyasaland-born, Canadian-raised leading man and (often villainous) character player whose inimitable resonant voice guaranteed him a juicy income from voice-overs in TV commercials after a long and varied career in British films and television. Married to actress Sarah Lawson since 1956.

1954: *Dial M for Murder*. 1955: *\*Dead on Time*. 1984. *Confession (US: The Deadliest Sin)*. 1956: *Wicked As They Come*. 1957: *High Tide at Noon. The Long Haul. Accused (US: Mark of the Hawk)*. 1958: *The Man

Who Wouldn't Talk. High Hell. Tread Softly, Stranger. Dunkirk. I Was Monty's Double (US: Monty's Double). 1959: Jet Storm. 1960: Never Take Sweets from a Stranger (US: Never Take Candy from a Stranger). 1961: The Sinister Man. 1962: The Traitors. Captain Clegg (US: Night Creatures). Flight from Singapore. 1966: The Night of the Generals. 1967: The Life and Times of John Huston Esquire (narrator only). Night of the Big Heat (US: Island of the Burning Damned). 1969: The Body Stealers. When Dinosaurs Ruled the Earth. 1970: Puppet on a Chain. The World at Their Feet (narrator only). 1971: Erotic Fantasies (voice only). The Sword and the Geisha (narrator only). *Winter With Dracula (narrator only). 1972: Diamonds on Wheels. 1973: *Way Out East (narrator only). 1974: Persecution. The Wilby Conspiracy. 1976: The Domino Principle (GB: The Domino Killings. Released 1978). 1978: The Wild Geese. 1980: The Sea Wolves. 1981: Murder Is Easy (TV). 1982: Who Dares Wins.

How Green Was My Valley. 1942: Roxie Hart. This Above All. It Happened in Flatbush. The War Against Mrs Hadley. Life Begins at 8.30 (GB: The Light of Heart). 1943: Forever and a Day. City Without Men. Jane Eyre. 1944: The Lodger. Between Two Worlds. The Keys of the Kingdom. 1945: The Strange Affair of Uncle Harry (GB: Uncle Harry). Kitty. 1946: The Spiral Staircase. Cluny Brown. 1947: The Fabulous Dorseys. Ivy. Mother Wore Tights. Mourning Becomes Electra. My Wild Irish Rose. 1948: The Girl from Manhattan. One Touch of Venus. The Man from Texas. The Accused. 1949: Challenge to Lassie. 1950: Sierra. Cheaper by the Dozen.

### ALLISTER, Claud
(William C. Palmer) 1891-1970
Monocled, long-nosed, weak-chinned British comedy actor with light-brown hair smarmed across, large eyes and asinine smile that showed off his big teeth. His upper-class voice was well in keeping with the 'silly ass' nature of the characters he played, and he remained in demand on both sides of the Atlantic until his retirement in 1955. A former clerk who swapped the Stock Exchange for the stage, he went on to make a splendidly well-cast Algy in several Bulldog Drummond films.

1929: Bulldog Drummond. The Trial of Mary Dugan. Charming Sinners. Three Live Ghosts. 1930: Monte Carlo. The Florodora Girl (GB: The Gay Nineties). The Czar of Broadway. Slightly Scarlet. In the Next Room. Such Men Are Dangerous. Murder Will Out. Ladies Love Brutes. Reaching for the Moon. 1931: I Like Your Nerve. Platinum Blonde. *On the Loose. Captain Applejack. Meet the Wife. *Roughhouse Rhythm. Papa Loves Mama. 1932: The Midshipmaid (US: Midshipmaid Gob). Two White Arms (US: Wives Beware). Diamond Cut Diamond (US: Blame the Woman). The Return of Raffles. The Unexpected Father. Medicine Man. 1933: The Private Life of Henry VIII. Excess Baggage. That's My Wife. Sleeping Car. 1934: The Lady is Willing. Those Were the Days. The Return of Bulldog Drummond. The Private Life of Don Juan. 1935: The Dark Angel. Three Live Ghosts (and 1929 film). 1936: Dracula's Daughter. Yellowstone. 1937: Bulldog Drummond at

Bay. Let's Make a Night Of It. The Awful Truth. Danger—Love at Work. Radio Parade of 1937. 1938: Men Are Such Fools. Storm Over Bengal. Kentucky Moonshine (GB: Three Men and a Girl). The Blonde Cheat. 1939: Arrest Bulldog Drummond! Captain Fury. 1940: Lillian Russell. 1941: Charley's Aunt. The Reluctant Dragon. Confirm or Deny. A Yank in the RAF. Never Give a Sucker an Even Break (GB: What a Man!). 1943: Forever and a Day. The Hundred Pound Window. 1944: Kiss the Bride Goodbye. 1945: Don Chicago. Dumb Dora Discovers Tobacco (US: Fag End). 1946: Gaiety George. 1948: Quartet. The First Gentleman (US: Affairs of a Rogue). 1949: The Adventures of Ichabod and Mr Toad (voice only). 1951: Hong Kong. 1952: Down Among the Sheltering Palms (filmed 1950). 1953: Kiss Me, Kate! 1954: The Black Shield of Falworth.

### AMBLER, Joss 1900-1959
Stocky little British actor with wispy brown hair, heavily employed by the British cinema from 1937 to 1947. He spent a great deal of his younger days in Australia, where he made his screen début but, on his return to Britain, was soon much in demand for lawyers, doctors and other professional advisers, all of which he bumbled through in his customary buzzy manner.

1933: Waltzing Matilda. 1937: Captain's Orders. The Last Curtain. 1938: The Citadel. Break the News. Premiere (US: One Night in Paris). Keep Smiling. Meet Mr Penny. The Claydon Treasure Mystery. Murder in Soho (US: Murder in the Night). 1939: Secret Journey (US: Among Human Wolves). Come On, George. Trouble Brewing. 1940: Contraband (US: Blackout). Fingers. The Briggs Family. 1941: Atlantic Ferry (US: Sons of the Sea). Once a Crook. The Black Sheep of Whitehall. Break the News. The Prime Minister. Jeannie. Penn of Pennsylvania (US: The Courageous Mr Penn). The Big Blockade. 1942: Flying Fortress. Next of Kin. The Peterville Diamond. Much Too Shy. Gert and Daisy Clean Up. 1943: Happidrome. Headline. Rhythm Serenade. The Silver Fleet. Battle for Music. Somewhere in Civvies. 1944: Give Me the Stars. A Canterbury Tale. Candles at

### ALLGOOD, Sara 1883-1950
Dublin-born actress whose memorable sprinkling of mother roles—most of them involved in tragedy of some kind or other—was topped by the one in How Green Was My Valley, for which she received an Oscar nomination. She made her first film appearance in Australia, and later worked for Alfred Hitchcock, whom she considered a 'cheap, second-rate director'! In Hollywood from 1940. Died from Bright's Disease.

1918: Just Peggy. 1929: Blackmail. To What Red Hell. 1930: Juno and the Paycock (US: The Shame of Mary Boyle). 1932: The World, the Flesh and the Devil. 1933: The Fortunate Fool. 1934: Lily of Killarney (US: Bride of the Lake). Irish Hearts (US: Norah O'Neale). 1935: Peg of Old Drury. Riders to the Sea. Lazybones. The Passing of the Third Floor Back. 1936: Pot Luck. Sabotage (US: The Woman Alone). It's Love Again. Southern Roses. 1937: Kathleen Mavourneen (US: Kathleen). Storm in a Teacup. The Sky's the Limit. The Londonderry Air. 1939: On the Night of the Fire (US: The Fugitive). 1940: That Hamilton Woman (GB: Lady Hamilton). 1941: Dr Jekyll and Mr Hyde. Lydia.

Nine. *The Halfway House.* 1945: *They Were Sisters. I'll Be Your Sweetheart. The World Owes Me a Living. The Agitator. Here Comes the Sun.* 1946: *The Years Between. Under New Management.* 1947: *Mine Own Executioner.* 1950: *The Magnet. Her Favourite Husband* (US: *The Taming of Dorothy*). 1952: *Ghost Ship. Who Goes There!* (US: *The Passionate Sentry*). *Something Money Can't Buy.* 1953: *The Captain's Paradise. Background.* 1954: *The Harassed Hero.* 1955: *Miss Tulip Stays the Night.* 1956: *The Long Arm* (US: *The Third Key*). *The Feminine Touch* (US: *The Gentle Touch*). *Aunt Clara. Soho Incident* (US: *Spin a Dark Web*). 1958: *Dunkirk.*

**AMES, Leon**
(L. Wycoff) 1903- *1993*
Stocky, moustachioed American actor who began his career in semi-leading roles, but never seemed quite at home in them, and moved from dapper, man-about-town types in the 1930s to faintly harassed fathers in later years. His two most successful television series reflected this: *Life with Father* and *Father of the Bride.* At time of writing, Ames is still active in his early eighties, having returned from retirement in 1970. Acted as Leon Waycoff in all his early films, up to and including *Reckless* in 1935.

1932: *The Murders in the Rue Morgue. 13 Women. Stowaway. The Famous Ferguson Case. State's Attorney* (GB: *Cardigan's Last Case*). *A Successful Calamity. Silver Dollar. Cannonball Express. Uptown New York.* 1933: *Parachute Jumper. Alimony Madness. The Man Who Dared. Ship of Wanted Men. Forgotten.* 1934: *The Count of Monte Cristo. I'll Tell the World. Now I'll Tell* (GB: *When New York Sleeps*). 1935: *The Crosby Case* (GB: *The Crosby Murder Case*). *Reckless. Strangers All. Get That Man. Mutiny Ahead.* 1936: *Stowaway* (and 1932 version). 1937: *Dangerously Yours. Death in the Air. Charlie Chan on Broadway. Murder in Greenwich Village. 45 Fathers.* 1938: *International Settlement. Bluebeard's Eighth Wife. Walking Down Broadway. Island in the Sky. Come On Leathernecks. The Mysterious Mr Moto. Strange Faces. Cipher Bureau. Suez. Secrets of a Nurse.* 1939: *The Spy Ring. Risky Business.*

*I Was a Convict. Pack Up Your Troubles* (GB: *We're in the Army Now*). *Mr Moto in Danger Island* (GB: *Mr Moto on Danger Island*). *Man of Conquest. Panama Patrol. Fugitive at Large. Code of the Streets. Legion of Lost Flyers. Calling All Marines. Thunder Afloat. Help Wanted.* 1940: *Marshal of Mesa City. East Side Kids.* 1941: *No Greater Sin* (GB: *Social Enemy No. 1*). *Ellery Queen and the Murder Ring* (GB: *The Murder Ring*). 1943: *The Crime Doctor. The Iron Major. Thirty Seconds Over Tokyo.* 1944: *Meet Me in St Louis. The Thin Man Goes Home.* 1945: *Son of Lassie. Anchors Aweigh.* *Fall Guy. Week-End at the Waldorf. They Were Expendable.* 1946: *The Postman Always Rings Twice. Yolanda and the Thief. Lady in the Lake. No Leave, No Love. The Great Morgan. The Show-Off. The Cockeyed Miracle* (GB: *Mr Griggs Returns*). 1947: *Undercover Maisie* (GB: *Undercover Girl*). *Song of the Thin Man. The Amazing Mr Nordill. Merton of the Movies.* 1948: *Alias a Gentleman. On an Island With You. A Date with Judy. The Velvet Touch.* 1949: *Any Number Can Play. Little Women. Scene of the Crime. Battleground.* 1950: *Ambush. The Big Hangover. Dial 1119* (GB: *The Violent Hour*). *Watch the Birdie. The Skipper Surprised His Wife. The Happy Years. Crisis.* 1951: *Cattle Drive. On Moonlight Bay. It's a Big Country.* 1952: *Angel Face. By the Light of the Silvery Moon.* 1953: *Let's Do It Again. Sabre Jet.* 1957: *Peyton Place.* 1959: *The Raider* (TV). 1960: *From the Terrace.* 1961: *The Absent-Minded Professor.* 1963: *Son of Flubber.* 1964: *The Misadventures of Merlin Jones.* 1966: *The Monkey's Uncle.* 1970: *On a Clear Day You Can See Forever. Tora! Tora! Tora!* 1971: *Toklat. A Capitol Affair* (TV). 1972: *Cool Breeze. Hammersmith is Out. Brother of the Wind* (and narrator). 1973: *The Timber Tramp.* 1974: *The Meal.* 1976: *Sherlock Holmes in New York* (TV). 1977: *Claws.* 1979: *Just You and Me, Kid. The Best Place To Be* (TV). 1983: *Testament.*

**ANDERSON, Eddie 'Rochester'**
1905-1977
Bronchial-voiced, bulging-eyed, stocky, concerned-looking American comic actor, the son of a minstrel and a high-wire artist. His own career in show business was

nothing special until he signed up as radio manservant to comedian Jack Benny in 1937, a role which gave him his nickname and which he played, on and off, for almost 30 years. He was a popular figure in wartime films, and had the star role in the all-black musical *Cabin in the Sky* in 1943.

1932: *Hat Check Girl* (GB: *Embassy Girl*). *What Price Hollywood?* 1935: *Transient Lady* (GB: *False Witness*). 1936: *Two in a Crowd. Green Pastures. Rainbow on the River. Three Men on a Horse. Show Boat.* 1937: *Melody for Two. Bill Cracks Down* (GB: *Men of Steel*). *On Such a Night. White Bondage. Over the Goal. One Mile from Heaven.* 1938: *Kentucky. Reckless Living. You Can't Take It With You. Gold Diggers in Paris* (GB: *The Great Impostors*). *Jezebel. Thanks for the Memory. Going Places. Exposed.* 1939: *Honolulu. You Can't Cheat an Honest Man. Gone With the Wind. Man About Town.* 1940: *Buck Benny Rides Again. Love Thy Neighbor.* 1941: *Topper Returns. Birth of the Blues. Kiss the Boys Goodbye.* 1942: *Tales of Manhattan. Star-Spangled Rhythm.* 1943: *The Meanest Man in the World. Cabin in the Sky. What's Buzzin' Cousin?* 1944: *Broadway Rhythm.* 1945: *Brewster's Millions. I Love a Bandleader* (GB: *Memory for Two*). 1946: *The Show-Off. The Sailor Takes a Wife.* 1957: *Green Pastures* (TV remake). 1963: *It's a Mad, Mad, Mad, Mad World.*

**ANDERSON, Jean** 1908-
Kindly-looking, dark-haired British player with prominent nose, small features and smiling mouth, an actress from an early age who did repertory work in Cambridge and Dublin before coming to the London stage. Almost always in sympathetic rôles to which she brought a benevolent force of personality: nurses, policewomen, teachers, social workers and various senior officials. Made fewer films than one imagined, and became entrenched in television from the early 1970s in two long-running series, *The Brothers* and *Tenko.*

1947: *The Mark of Cain.* 1949: *The Romantic Age* (US: *Naughty Arlette*). *Elizabeth of Ladymead.* 1950: *The Franchise Affair.* 1951: *Out of True. Life in Her Hands. White Corridors.* 1952: *The Brave Don't Cry.*

1953: *Street Corner* (US: *Both Sides of the Law*). *The Kidnappers* (US: *The Little Kidnappers*). *Johnny on the Run.* 1954: *The Dark Stairway. Lease of Life.* 1956: *Secret Tent. A Town Like Alice.* 1957: *Heart of a Child. Robbery Under Arms. Lucky Jim. The Barretts of Wimpole Street.* 1959: *Solomon and Sheba. SOS Pacific.* 1961: *Spare the Rod.* 1962: *The Inspector* (US: *Lisa*). *The Waltz of the Toreadors.* 1963: *The Silent Playground. The Three Lives of Thomasina.* 1967: *Half a Sixpence.* 1969: *Country Dance* (US: *Brotherly Love*). *Run a Crooked Mile* (TV). 1971: *The Night Digger.* 1979: *The Lady Vanishes.*

**ANDERSON, John** 1922- 1992

Lean, laconic, lantern-jawed, fair-haired American actor who looked a certainty for fanatical Confederate colonels and powers behind the thrones of western towns. In his early years, he spent more than three years acting on a Mississippi showboat, only leaving to serve with the Coast Guard during World War II. He appeared fairly regularly in films from the late 1950s, mainly in westerns, but was most prolific on television.

1952: *Against All Flags.* 1955: *Target Zero.* 1958: *The True Story of Lynn Stuart.* 1959: *Last Train from Gun Hill.* 1960: *Psycho.* 1961: *Ride the High Country* (GB: *Guns in the Afternoon*). 1962: *Geronimo. A Walk on the Wild Side.* 1964: *The Satan Bug.* 1965: *The Hallelujah Trail.* 1966: *Scalplock* (TV. GB: *cinemas*). *Namu the Killer Whale. A Covenant With Death. Welcome to Hard Times* (GB: *Killer on a Horse*). 1968: *Massacre Harbor. Five Card Stud. Day of the Evil Gun. A Man Called Gannon. Heaven With a Gun.* 1969: *Set This Town on Fire* (TV. released 1973). *The Great Bank Robbery.* 1970: *Soldier Blue. Cotton Comes to Harlem. The Animals* (GB: *Five Savage Men*). 1972: *Man and Boy. The Stepmother.* 1973: *Call to Danger* (TV). *Brock's Last Case* (TV). *Il consigliore* (GB: *The Counsellor*). *Executive Action.* 1974: *The Dove. Heatwave* (TV). *Smile Jenny, You're Dead* (TV). *Manhunter* (TV). 1975: *Dead Man on the Run* (TV). *The Specialist. Death Among Friends* (TV). 1976: *The Dark Side of Innocence* (TV). *The Hancocks* (TV). *Bridger: The 40th Day* (TV). *Once an Eagle* (TV). 1977: *Tail Gunner Joe*

(TV). *Peter Lundy and the Medicine Hat Stallion* (TV). *The Last Hurrah* (TV). *The Lincoln Conspiracy.* 1978: *Donner Pass: The Road to Survival* (TV). *The Deerslayer* (TV). 1980: *Smokey and the Bandit II* (GB: *Smokey and the Bandit Ride Again*). 1982: *Missing Children: A Mother's Story* (TV). 1983: *Lone Wolf McQuade.*

**ANDERSON, Dame Judith**

(Frances Anderson) 1898- 1992

Formidable, dark-haired, strong-featured Australian-born actress who played Mrs Danvers in the 1940 *Rebecca*, a role that brought her an Academy Award nomination, and set her up for a good run of generally malevolent matrons in the *cinema noir* of the 1940s. Perfect casting for Lady Macbeth: a pity she did not play the rôle on film until she was 62. Created a Dame in 1960.

1930: *Madame of the Jury.* 1932: *Judith Anderson.* 1933: *Blood Money.* 1940: *Forty Little Mothers. Rebecca.* 1941: *Lady Scarface. Free and Easy.* 1942: *All Through the Night. Kings Row.* 1943: *Edge of Darkness. Stage Door Canteen.* 1944: *Laura.* 1945: *And Then There Were None* (GB: *Ten Little Niggers*). *The Diary of a Chambermaid.* 1946: *The Specter of the Rose. The Strange Love of Martha Ivers. Pursued.* 1947: *The Red House. Tycoon.* 1950: *The Furies.* 1953: *Salome.* 1954: *Come of Age.* 1956: *The Ten Commandments.* 1957: *The Clouded Image* (TV). 1958: *Cat on a Hot Tin Roof.* 1960: *To the Sounds of Trumpets* (TV). *Cinderfella. Macbeth.* 1961: *Don't Bother to Knock!* (US: *Why Bother to Knock?*). 1970: *A Man Called Horse.* 1974: *The Borrowers* (TV). *Inn of the Damned. The Underground Man* (TV). 1984: *Star Trek III: The Search for Spock.*

**ANDERSON, Richard** 1926-

Lean-faced, sleekly dark-haired, brainy-looking American 'second lead' who found a niche as senior officers and wise counsellors in successful TV series (most notably *The Six Million Dollar Man*) after his days as an M-G-M contract player were over.

1949: *Twelve O'Clock High.* 1950: *The Vanishing Westerner. The Magnificent Yankee* (GB: *The Man With 30 Sons*). *Payment on*

Demand. *A Life of Her Own.* 1951: *Cause for Alarm. No Questions Asked. The Unknown Man. Across the Wide Missouri. The People Against O'Hara. Rich, Young and Pretty.* 1952: *Just This Once. Scaramouche. Holiday for Sinners. Fearless Fagan.* 1953: *The Story of Three Loves. I Love Melvin. Dream Wife.* 1954: *Escape from Fort Bravo. Give a Girl a Break.* 1955: *The Student Prince. Hit the Deck. It's a Dog's Life.* 1956: *Forbidden Planet. The Search for Bridey Murphy. A Cry in the Night.* 1957: *Three Brave Men. Paths of Glory. The Buster Keaton Story.* 1958: *Gunfight at Dodge City. The Long, Hot Summer. Curse of the Faceless Man.* 1959: *Compulsion.* 1960: *The Wackiest Ship in the Army.* 1963: *Johnny Cool. A Gathering of Eagles.* 1964: *Seven Days in May. Kitten With a Whip.* 1966: *The Ride to Hangman's Tree. Seconds.* 1969: *Along Came a Spider* (TV). 1970: *Tora! Tora! Tora! Macho Callahan.* 1971: *The Astronaut* (TV). *Doctors' Wives. Dead Men Tell No Tales* (TV). 1972: *Menace on the Mountain* (TV. GB: *cinemas*). *The Honkers. The Longest Night* (TV). *The Night Strangler* (TV). *Play It As It Lays. Say Goodbye, Maggie Cole* (TV). 1973: *Black Eye. Jarrett* (TV). *Partners in Crime* (TV). 1979: *Sharks! Murder by Natural Causes* (TV). 1981: *Rally.*

**ANDERSON, Warner** 1911-1976

Dependable, grave-looking American supporting actor who enjoyed a good run of doctors, judges, senior officers and attorneys until the mid 1950s, after which he was lost almost entirely to long-running television series, latterly as editor Matthew Swain in *Peyton Place.* He made one appearance in a silent film as a child, and played in vaudeville and legitimate theatre before coming to the screen.

*1916: Sunbeam. 1943: \*Oklahoma Outlaws. This Is the Army. 1944: Destination Tokyo (shown in 1943). \*Trial by Trigger. 1945: Her Highness and the Bellboy. Objective Burma. Bud Abbott and Lou Costello in Hollywood. My Reputation. Dangerous Partners. Week-End at the Waldorf. 1946: Bad Baskomb. Three Wise Fools. Faithful in My Fashion. 1947: The Arnelo Affair. Dark Delusion (GB: Cynthia's Secret). The Beginning or the End? Song of the Thin Man. High Wall. 1948: Command Decision. Tenth Avenue Angel. Alias a Gentleman. 1949: The Lucky Stiff. The Doctor and the Girl. 1950: Destination Moon. 1951: Santa Fé. Detective Story. The Blue Veil. Go For Broke. Only the Valiant. \*The Guest. Bannerline. 1952: The Star. 1953: A Lion Is in the Streets. The Last Posse. 1954: The Caine Mutiny. Drum Beat. Yellow Tomahawk. 1955: Blackboard Jungle. The Violent Men (GB: Rough Company). A Lawless Street. 1958: The Line-Up. 1961: Armored Command. 1964: Rio Conchos. 1969: Gidget Grows Up (TV).*

*West. 1959: Night of the Quarter Moon. 1960: Elmer Gantry. 1961: The Absent-Minded Professor. The Young Savages. Advise and Consent. Love in a Goldfish Bowl. 1962: Son of Flubber. 40 Pounds of Trouble. 1963: The Man from Galveston (TV. GB: cinemas). The Thrill of It All. A Tiger Walks. 1964: The Brass Bottle. Good Neighbor Sam. Kisses for My President. Send Me No Flowers. Young-blood Hawke. 1965: Fluffy. 1966: The Glass Bottom Boat. Birds Do It. 1969: The Over-the-Hill Gang (TV). 1970: The Intruders (TV). Tora! Tora! Tora! The Trouble With Girls. 1971: Million Dollar Duck. How to Frame a Figg. Travis Logan DA (TV). 1972: Now You See Him, Now You Don't. Avanti! 1973: Charley and the Angel. 1975: The Photographer. 1976: How to Break Up a Happy Divorce (TV). 1977: Don't Push, I'll Charge When I'm Ready (TV. Originally filmed in 1969). 1978: Seniors. Lacy and the Mississippi Queen (TV). 1979: Supertrain (TV. Later: Express to Terror). 1984: Gremlins.*

**ANDREWS, Harry** 1911- *1989*
Craggy, stern-faced British actor, a top supporting player much in demand for sergeant-majors, martinet figures and similar forbidding rôles, after he swapped a largely Shakespearian stage career for films. He graduated to fanatics of various shapes and shades, with one or two gentler rôles for welcome relief.

*1953: The Red Beret (US: Paratrooper). 1954: The Black Knight. The Man Who Loved Redheads. Helen of Troy. 1956: A Hill in Korea (US: Hell in Korea). Alexander the Great. Moby Dick. 1957: Saint Joan. 1958: I Accuse! Ice-Cold in Alex (US: Desert Attack). 1959: Solomon and Sheba. The Devil's Disciple. A Touch of Larceny. In the Nick. 1960: Circle of Deception. 1961: The Best of Enemies. Barabbas. 1962: Lisa (GB: The Inspector). 55 Days at Peking. Reach for Glory. Nine Hours to Rama. 1963: Cleopatra. The Informers. 1964: Nothing But the Best (shown 1963). The System. The Truth About Spring. 633 Squadron. 1965: The Hill. The Agony and the Ecstasy. Sands of the Kalahari. 1966: The Jokers. Modesty Blaise. The Deadly Affair.*

*The Night of the Generals. 1967: Danger Route. The Long Duel. I'll Never Forget What's 'Is Name. 1968: The Charge of the Light Brigade. Play Dirty. The Night They Raided Minsky's. A Dandy in Aspic. 1969: The Sea Gull. A Nice Girl Like Me. Battle of Britain. Too Late the Hero. The Southern Star. Destiny of a Spy/The Gaunt Woman (TV). Country Dance (US: Brotherly Love). 1970: Wuthering Heights. Entertaining Mr Sloane. 1971: Nicholas and Alexandra. Burke and Hare. I Want What I Want. Night Hair Child. The Ruling Class. The Nightcomers. 1972: Man of La Mancha. 1973: Theatre of Blood. The Final Programme (US: The Last Days of Man on Earth). Man at the Top. The Mackintosh Man. 1974: The Internecine Project. Valley Forge (TV). The Story of Jacob and Joseph (TV). 1976: The Bluebird. The Passover Plot. Sky Riders. 1977: The Prince and the Pauper (US: Crossed Swords). The Medusa Touch. Equus. 1978: The Big Sleep. Death on the Nile. The Four Feathers (TV. GB: cinemas). Watership Down (voice only). Superman. 1979: SOS Titanic. 1980: †Second to the Right and On Till Morning. Hawk the Slayer. 1984: Mesmerized.*

† Unreleased

**ANDREWS, Edward** 1914-1985
Avuncular, heftily-built American actor whose big, beaming, bespectacled features could adapt just as easily to comic panic or coldly genuine menace. It was in the latter vein that he broke into films (in *The Phenix City Story*) after years of solid work on Broadway, but he was soon instantly identifiable in a series of characters whose hale-and-hearty exteriors hid a wide variety of characteristics beneath. An incorrigible stealer of the stars' limelight in his peak (1955-66) years. Died from a heart attack.

*1955: The Phenix City Story (GB: The Phoenix City Story). 1956: Tea and Sympathy. The Harder They Fall. These Wilder Years. The Unguarded Moment. Tension at Table Rock. 1957: Hot Summer Night. Three Brave Men. The Tattered Dress. Trooper Hook. 1958: The Fiend That Walked the*

**ANKRUM, Morris**
(M. Nussbaum) 1896-1964
Tall, small-eyed, ferret-featured, grey-moustached, slightly stooping American actor who rarely looked happy on screen and played villains in low-budget westerns and townsfolk of one kind or another in bigger films. Originally an economics professor, he became interested in acting while teaching in California, beginning his screen career as 'Stephen Morris'. Later he balanced accounts a little by playing judges and officers in 1950s' films. Died from trichinosis.

*1933: †Reunion in Vienna. 1936: †Hopalong Cassidy Returns. †Trail Dust. 1937: †Borderland. †Hills of Old Wyoming. †North of the Rio Grande. †Rustlers' Valley. 1939: Three Texas Steers (GB: Danger Rides the Range). 1940: The Showdown. Cherokee Strip (GB: Fighting Marshal). Three Men from Texas. Buck Benny Rides Again. Light of*

Western Stars. Knights of the Range. 1941: This Woman is Mine. The Roundup. Doomed Caravan. In Old Colorado. Pirates on Horseback. Border Vigilantes. Wide Open Town. The Bandit Trail. I Wake Up Screaming (GB: Hot Spot). Road Agent. 1942: Roxie Hart. Ride 'Em Cowboy. Ten Gentlemen from West Point. The Loves of Edgar Allan Poe. Tales of Manhattan. The Omaha Trail. Reunion|Reunion in France (GB: Mademoiselle France). Tennessee Johnson (GB: The Man on America's Conscience). Time to Kill. 1943: Let's Face It. Dixie Dugan. Swing Fever. The Human Comedy. Best Foot Forward. The Heavenly Body. 1944: Rationing. Meet the People. Barbary Coast Gent. Marriage is a Private Affair. The Thin Man Goes Home. Gentle Annie. *Radio Bugs. *Dark Shadows. *Return from Nowhere. 1945: The Hidden Eye. Adventure. The Harvey Girls. 1946: Courage of Lassie. Little Mr Jim. The Cockeyed Miracle (GB: Mr Griggs Returns). The Postman Always Rings Twice. Lady in the Lake. The Mighty McGurk. 1947: Undercover Maisie (GB: Undercover Girl). Cynthia (GB: The Rich, Full Life). The Sea of Grass. Desire Me. High Wall. Good News. 1948: Joan of Arc. For the Love of Mary. *The Fabulous Fraud. Bad Men of Tombstone. Fighting Back. 1949: We Were Strangers. Colorado Territory. Slattery's Hurricane. 1950: In a Lonely Place. Rocketship X-M. The Damned Don't Cry. Chain Lightning. Borderline. Short Grass. The Redhead and the Cowboy. Southside 1-1000 (GB: Forgery). 1951: The Lion Hunters (GB: Bomba and the Lion Hunters). Fighting Coast Guard. Along the Great Divide. My Favorite Spy. Tomorrow is Another Day. Flight to Mars. 1952: Son of Ali Baba. And Now Tomorrow. Red Planet Mars. Mutiny. The Raiders. Hiawatha. The Man Behind the Gun. Fort Osage. 1953: Mexican Manhunt. Arena. Invaders from Mars. Devil's Canyon. Fort Vengeance. Sky Commando. The Moonlighter. 1954: Southwest Passage (GB: Camels West). Apache. Vera Cruz. Three Young Texans. Taza, Son of Cochise. Silver Lode. Two Guns and a Badge. Drums Across the River. The Saracen Blade. The Outlaw Stallion. The Steel Cage. Cattle Queen of Montana. 1955: Jupiter's Darling. The Silver Star. Chief Crazy Horse (GB: Valley of Fury). Abbott and Costello Meet the Mummy. The Eternal Sea. Tennessee's Partner. Crashout. No Man's Woman. Jujin Yukiotoko (GB and US: Half Human). 1956: Fury at Gunsight Pass. When Gangland Strikes. Earth vs the Flying Saucers. Walk the Proud Land. Death of a Scoundrel. Quincannon, Frontier Scout (GB: Frontier Scout). 1957: Drango. Zombies of Mora-Tau (GB: The Dead That Walk). The Badge of Marshal Brennan. Kronos. Hell's Crossroads. The Giant Claw. The Beginning of the End. Omar Khayyam. 1958: Badman's Country. Young and Wild. Twilight for the Gods. Tarawa Beachhead. The Saga of Hemp Brown. From the Earth to the Moon. Frontier Gun. How to Make a Monster. Giant from the Unknown. Most Dangerous Man Alive (released 1961).

1960: The Little Shepherd of Kingdom Come. 1963: 'X'—The Man with the X-Ray Eyes (GB: The Man with the X-Ray Eyes).

†As Stephen Morris

**ANSARA, Michael** 1922-
Back in the 1950s, American-born (of Lebanese ancestry) Ansara vied with the Australian Michael Pate (qv) as the actor most likely to be found in action pictures as Red Indians or ruthless, bearded, Middle Eastern despots. Ever ready with a sword or an arrow, his handsome, olive-complexioned, rather cruel-looking features saw him into a whole run of powerful villains, and it was no surprise when he turned up as Cochise in a TV series based on the film Broken Arrow. Married to actress Barbara Eden from 1958 to 1973; earlier married to actress Jean Byron.

1944: Action in Arabia. 1951: Only the Valiant. Soldiers Three. Bannerline. 1952: Yankee Buccaneer. Diplomatic Courier. Brave Warrior. Road to Bali. The Lawless Breed. 1953: White Witch Doctor. Julius Caesar. Serpent of the Nile. The Robe. Slaves of Babylon. The Diamond Queen. 1954: Sign of the Pagan. The Egyptian. Three Young Texans. Princess of the Nile. The Saracen Blade. Bengal Brigade (GB: Bengal Rifles). 1955: Diane. New Orleans Uncensored (GB: Riot on Pier 6). Abbott and Costello Meet the Mummy. Jupiter's Darling. 1956: Pillars of the Sky (GB: The Tomahawk and the Cross). The Ox-Bow Incident (TV. GB: cinemas). The Lone Ranger. Gun Brothers. 1957: Last of the Badmen. The Tall Stranger. The Sad Sack. Quantez. 1959: The Killers of Mussolini (TV). 1961: The Comancheros. Voyage to the Bottom of the Sea. 1962: Five Weeks in a Balloon. 1964: A Truce to Terror (TV). The Confession (GB: TV, as Quick! Let's Get Married). 1965: Harum Scarum (GB: Harem Holiday). The Greatest Story Ever Told. 1966: ... And Now Miguel. The Destructors. Texas Across the River. How I Spent My Summer Vacation (TV. GB: cinemas, as Deadly Roulette). 1967: The Pink Jungle. Sol Madrid (GB: The Heroin Gang). 1968: Daring Game. 1969: Guns of the Magnificent Seven. The Phynx. How to Make It (GB: Target Harry). 1971: Powderkeg

(TV. GB: cinemas). 1972: Stand Up and Be Counted. 1973: The Doll Squad. Call to Danger (TV). Ordeal (TV). 1974: Shootout in a One-Dog Town (TV). The Bears and I. 1975: Dear Dead Delilah. Barbary Coast (TV. GB: In Old San Francisco). 1976: Day of the Animals. The Message|Mohammed—Messenger of God. 1977: The Manitou. 1981: The Guns and the Fury. 1983: The Fantastic World of DC Collins (TV).

**ARCHARD, Bernard** 1922-
Gaunt, angular-faced, serious-looking, cold-eyed, tight-lipped British actor with high forehead and dark hair who gave incisive performances and was often cast as prosecutors, interrogators and religious fanatics. He was 'about to emigrate to Canada' when given the rôle that won him his greatest popular success, in the long-running TV series Spycatcher, in 1959, and has been busy in all media ever since.

1958: The Secret Man. 1960: Village of the Damned. 1961: Clue of the New Pin. Man Detained. 1962: Flat Two. Two-Letter Alibi. A Woman's Privilege. 1963: The Silent Playground. The List of Adrian Messenger. 1964: Face of a Stranger. 1966: The Spy With a Cold Nose. 1967: Son of the Sahara. 1968: The Mini Affair. File of the Golden Goose. Play Dirty. 1969: Run a Crooked Mile (TV). 1970: Fragment of Fear. The Horror of Frankenstein. Song of Norway. 1971: Macbeth. Dad's Army. 1972: Madigan: The Lisbon Beat (TV). 1973: The Day of the Jackal. 1979: The Purple Twilight (TV). 1980: The Sea Wolves. 1983: Krull.

**ARDEN, Eve**
(Eunice Quedens) 1912- 1990
Ziegfeld Follies dancer who became the archetypal wisecracking Hollywood blonde of the 1940s. After playing a fistful of heroines' friends—one of which, in Mildred Pierce, earned her an Academy Award nomination in the Best Supporting Actress category—she enjoyed huge success on television in the 1950s.

1929: †Song of Love. 1933: †Dancing Lady. 1937: Oh Doctor. Stage Door. 1938: Coconut Grove. Letter of Introduction. Having Wonderful Time. Women in the Wind. 1939: Big Town Czar. The Forgotten Women. Eternally

Yours. At the Circus. 1940: A Child Is Born. Slightly Honorable. Comrade X. No, No, Nanette. 1941: Ziegfeld Girl. That Uncertain Feeling. She Couldn't Say No. She Knew All the Answers. San Antonio Rose. Sing for Your Supper. Manpower. Whistling in the Dark. 1942: Last of the Duanes. Obliging Young Lady. Bedtime Story. 1943: Hit Parade of 1943. Let's Face It. 1944: Cover Girl. The Doughgirls. My Reputation (released 1946). 1945: Pan Americana. Earl Carroll's Vanities. Mildred Pierce. 1946: The Kid from Brooklyn. Night and Day. 1947: Song of Scheherazade. The Arnelo Affair. The Unfaithful. 1948: The Voice of the Turtle. One Touch of Venus. Whiplash. 1949: My Dream Is Yours. The Lady Takes a Sailor. 1950: Paid in Full. Curtain Call at Cactus Creek (GB: Take the Stage). Tea for Two. Three Husbands. 1951: Goodbye My Fancy. 1952: We're Not Married. 1953: The Lady Wants Mink. 1954: *Hollywood Life. 1956: Our Miss Brooks. 1959: Anatomy of a Murder. 1960: The Dark at the Top of the Stairs. 1965: Sergeant Deadhead. 1969: In Name Only (TV). 1971: A Very Missing Person. 1972: All My Darling Daughters (TV). 1973: Mother of the Bride (TV). 1975: The Strongest Man in the World. 1978: A Guide for the Married Woman (TV). Grease. 1981: Under the Rainbow. 1982: Grease 2.

†As Eunice Quedens

**ARMETTA, Henry** 1888-1945
Short, stocky, moustachioed Italian-born Hollywood actor who cornered the market

in harassed, excitable, voluble foreigners, from the beginnings of sound. His early death from a heart attack robbed him of the well-deserved opportunity of carrying a film-filled career through to the end of the studio era. Stowed away on a ship to come to America in 1902.

1915: The Nigger. 1918: My Cousin. 1923: The Silent Command. 1925: The Desert's Price. 1927: Seventh Heaven. 1928: Street Angel. Love Song. Alias Jimmy Valentine. 1929: Lady of the Pavements (GB: Lady of the Night). In Old Arizona. Homesick. The Trespasser. Love, Live and Laugh. Jazz Heaven. 1930: A Lady to Love. *Society Goes Spaghetti. The Climax. *Razored in Old Kentucky. Little Accident. Lovin' the Ladies. *Hey Diddle-Diddle. Romance. *Moonlight and Monkey Business. Sons of the Children. Die Sehnsucht jeder Frau. *He Loved Her Not. 1931: Strangers May Kiss. Five and Ten (GB: Daughter of Luxury). A Tailor Made Man. Hush Money. The Wife o' Riley. The Unholy Garden. Laughing Sinners. Speak Easy. 1932: Scarface. Arsène Lupin. The Passionate Plumber. The Doomed Battalion. Weekends Only. Central Park. Cauliflower Alley. Steady Company. Huddle (GB: Impossible Lover). They Just Had To Get Married. Prosperity. A Farewell to Arms. Uptown New York. Okay, America (GB: Penalty of Fame). Men of America (GB: Great Decision). 1933: The Devil's Brother (GB: Fra Diavolo). *Pick Me Up. The Cohens and the Kellys in Trouble. Her First Mate. Too Much Harmony. Laughing at Life. Reception. *The Trial of Vince Barnett. What! No Beer? *Hello Pop. So This Is Africa. *Open Sesame. Don't Bet on Love. 1934: The Cat and the Fiddle. Cross Country Cruise. One Night of Love. Viva Villa! Poor Rich. *Full Coverage. The Hide-Out. Embarrassing Moments. Gift of Gab. *Ceiling Whacks. The Black Cat. Two Heads on a Pillow. Wake Up and Dream. Imitation of Life. The Merry Widow. The Man Who Reclaimed His Head. Kiss and Make Up. Cheating Cheaters. Romance in the Rain. Let's Talk It Over. 1935: Straight from the Heart. Vanessa, Her Love Story. Night Life of the Gods. After Office Hours. I've Been Around. Dinky. *Social Splash. Princess O'Hara. Unknown Woman. Three Kids and a Queen (GB: The Baxter Millions). The Show Goes On. *Old Age Pension. Manhattan Moon (GB: Sing Me a Love Song). 1936: Magnificent Obsession. Let's Sing Again. The Crime of Dr Forbes. Poor Little Rich Girl. The Magnificent Brute. Two in a Crowd. 1937: Top of the Town. Make a Wish. Manhattan Merry-Go-Round (GB: Manhattan Music Box). Seventh Heaven. 1938: Everybody Sing. Speed to Burn. Submarine Patrol. Road Demon. *My Pop. 1939: Fisherman's Wharf. The Lady and the Mob. Winner Take All. *Home Cheap Home. I Stole a Million. 1940: The Outsider. Dust Be My Destiny. Escape. Three Cheers for the Irish. We Who Are Young. You're Not So Tough. The Man Who Talked Too Much. 1941: Caught in the Act. The Big Store. Slick Chick.

1942: Stage Door Canteen. Good Luck Mr Yates. 1943: Thank Your Lucky Stars. 1944: Allergic to Love. Ghost Catchers. Once Upon a Time. 1945: Penthouse Rhythm. A Bell for Adano. Anchors Aweigh. Col Effingham's Raid (GB: Man of the Hour).

**ARMSTRONG, R. G.** 1917-
Big, balding, glowering American supporting actor who became one of Hollywood's few really distinctive character players in the post-1960 era, often in menacing or bigoted roles. A frustrated writer, the 6 foot 3 inch Armstrong turned to acting in 1952, when he enrolled at The Actors' Studio. Entering Hollywood films in 1957, he soon became a man in demand, especially for portraits of mid-west rednecks. The initials stand for Robert Golden.

1957: The Garden of Eden. 1958: From Hell to Texas (GB: Manhunt). Never Love a Stranger. No Name on the Bullet. 1959: The Fugitive Kind. 1960: Ten Who Dared. 1961: Ride the High Country (GB: Guns in the Afternoon). 1962: Six Gun Law (TV. GB: cinemas). 1963: He Rides Tall. 1964: Major Dundee. 1966: El Dorado. 1968: Tiger by the Tail. 80 Steps to Jonah. 1969: The McMasters ... Tougher Than the West Itself! 1970: The Ballad of Cable Hogue. The Great White Hope. Angels Die Hard. 1971: The Great Northfield Minnesota Raid. J W Coop. 1972: The Century Turns/Hec Ramsey (TV). 1973: My Name is Nobody. Pat Garrett and Billy the Kid. White Lightning. 1974: Manhunter (TV). Boss Nigger (GB: The Black Bounty Killer). Reflections of Murder (TV). Who Fears the Devil/The Legend of Hillbilly John. 1975: White Line Fever. Race with the Devil. 1976: Kingston: The Power Play (TV). Stay Hungry. Dixie Dynamite. 1977: Mr Billion. The Car. The Pack. 1978: Heaven Can Wait. Devil Dog: The Hound of Hell (TV). Fast Charlie—the Moonbeam Rider. The Time Machine (TV). Texas Detour. Good Luck, Miss Wyckoff. 1979: Steel. The Villain (GB: Cactus Jack). The Legend of the Golden Gun (TV). 1980: Hammett (released 1982). Where the Buffalo Roam. 1981: Reds. Raggedy Man. The Pursuit of D. B. Cooper/Pursuit. Evilspeak. 1982: The Beast Within. The Shadow Riders

(TV). 1983: Lone Wolf McQuade. 1984: Children of the Corn. 1985: Road Trip. The Best of Times.

## ARNE, Peter
(P. A. Albrecht) 1922-1983
Dark, tight-lipped, furtive-looking, narrow-eyed, incisive Malaya-born British actor who had some good roles as cruel, half-smiling villains in British action films of the 1950s and early 1960s before his career disappointingly dipped into minor supporting parts, sometimes verging on the comic. Perhaps the oiliness was piled on a bit thickly, but he was always good value for money. Victim of an unsolved murder.

1944: For Those in Peril. 1948: Saraband for Dead Lovers (GB: Saraband). 1953: You Know What Sailors Are. 1954: Mystery on Bird Island. The Purple Plain. The Dam Busters. 1955: Timeslip (US: The Atomic Man). *Murder Anonymous. Cockleshell Heroes. 1957: High Tide at Noon. Strangers' Meeting. Tarzan and the Lost Safari. 1958: The Moonraker. Ice Cold in Alex (US: Desert Attack). Intent to Kill. Danger Within (US: Breakout). 1960: Conspiracy of Hearts. Sands of the Desert. A Story of David. Scent of Mystery (GB: Holiday in Spain). 1961: The Hellfire Club. The Treasure of Monte Cristo (GB: The Secret of Monte Cristo). The Pirates of Blood River. 1963: The Victors. Girl in the Headlines (US: The Model Murder Case). 1964: The Black Torment. The Secret of Blood Island. 1966: Khartoum. The Sandwich Man. 1967: Battle Beneath the Earth. 1968: Chitty Chitty Bang Bang. 1969: The Oblong Box. 1970: House of Evil. 1971: When Eight Bells Toll. Nobody Ordered Love. Straw Dogs. Murders in the Rue Morgue. 1972: Antony and Cleopatra. Pope Joan. 1974: The Return of the Pink Panther. 1977: Providence. 1978: The Passage. Agatha. 1982: Victor/Victoria. Trail of the Pink Panther. 1983: Curse of the Pink Panther.

## ARNO, Sig
(Siegfried Aron) 1895-1975
German-born comic actor who had both lightweight and dramatic leading roles in German films (in all of which he was billed as Siegfried Arno) before fleeing the country in 1933. Like so many Continental refugees, Arno, after travelling (and acting) through several countries, ended up in Hollywood, where he contributed a delightful series of cameos as over-eager men-on-the-make whose fractured English made the hero instantly suspicious. Died from Parkinson's Disease.

1923: Schicksal. 1924: Eine Frau von vierzig Jahren. 1926: Der Panzergewolbe. Manon Lescaut. Schatz mach Kasse. 1927: Die Liebe der Jeanne Ney (GB and US: The Love of Jeanne Ney). Beef und Steak. Moral. Bigoudis. 1928: Sigi, der Matrose. Leise flehen meine Lieder. Der schönste Mann im Staate. Um eine Nasenlänge. Tragödie im Zirkus Royale. Geschichten aus dem Wienerwald. Rutschbahn. Moderne Piraten. 1929: Aufruhr im Junggesellenheim. Die Buchse der Pandora (GB and US: Pandora's Box). Ihr dunkler Punkt. Das Tagebuch einer Verlorenen (GB and US: Diary of a Lost Girl). Wir halten fest und treu zusammen. 1930: Die vom Rummelplatz. Wien du Stadt der Lieder. Heute Nacht—eventuell. 1931: Schuberts Frühlingstraum. Keine Feier ohne Meyer. Schritzenfest im Schilda. Das Geheimnis der roten Katze. Im Kampf mit der Unterwelt. Eine Freundin so goldig wie Du. Schachmatt (GB: Checkmate). Die Nacht ohne Pause (GB: Night Without End). Der Storch streikt. Ein ausgekochter Junge. Mortiz macht sein Glück. Die grosse Attraktion. 1933: Zapfenstreich am Rhein. 1939: The Star Maker. Bridal Suite. 1940: The Mummy's Hand. Diamond Frontier. The Great Dictator. Dark Streets of Cairo. A Little Bit of Heaven. 1941: This Thing Called Love. New Wine (GB: The Great Awakening). It Started With Eve. Two Latins from Manhattan. Gambling Daughters. 1942: Pardon My Sarong. Juke Box Jenny. Two Yanks in Trinidad. Tales of Manhattan. The Palm Beach Story. The Devil With Hitler. 1943: The Crystal Ball. Larceny with Music. Taxi, Mister. Passport to Suez. Let's Have Fun. His Butler's Sister. 1944: Once Upon a Time. Up in Arms. Standing Room Only. Song of the Open Road. 1945: Bring on the Girls. Roughly Speaking. A Song to Remember. 1946: One More Tomorrow. 1949: The Great Lover. Holiday in Havana. 1950: Nancy Goes to Rio. Duchess of Idaho. The Toast of New Orleans. 1951: On Moonlight Bay, 1952: Diplomatic Courier. 1953: Fast Company. The Great Diamond Robbery.

## ASKEW, Luke 1937-
Tall, rangy, brown-haired American actor who came to Hollywood after a varied early career (television announcer, manager of a waste-paper plant, off-Broadway acting work) and played mostly unkempt villains, often in westerns.

1966: Hurry Sundown. The Happening. 1967: Cool Hand Luke. Will Penny. 1968: The Green Berets. The Devil's Brigade. 1969: Easy Rider. Flare-Up. 1971: The Great Northfield Minnesota Raid. 1972: The Glass House (TV. GB: cinemas). The Magnificent Seven Ride! The Culpepper Cattle Co. 1973: Pat Garrett and Billy the Kid. 1974: Manhunter (TV). Night Games (TV). This Was the West That Was (TV). 1975: Posse. Part 2 Walking Tall (GB: Legend of the Lawman). Attack on Terror: the FBI vs the Ku Klux Klan (TV). 1976: A Matter of Wife ... or Death (TV). The Quest (TV). The Invasion of Johnson County (TV). 1977: Rolling Thunder. 1978: Wanda Nevada. 1982: The Beast Within. 1983: White Star. 1984: The Warrior and the Sorceress.

## ASKIN, Leon 1910-
Tubby, swarthy, often moustachioed Austrian actor who started his career on the German stage, but fled the Nazis in 1933, came to New York in 1940 and became an American citizen in 1943. From 1952, he began a spasmodic flirtation with the Hollywood and (from 1959) international film scenes, appearing in very on-and-off fashion down through the years, mostly as Slavic villains—both comic and dramatic. Also directs, teaches and lectures on drama.

1952: Assignment—Paris! Road to Bali. 1953: Desert Legion. The Robe. The Veils of Bagdad. South Sea Woman. 1954: China Venture. Knock on Wood. Secret of the Incas. Valley of the Kings. 1955: Son of Sinbad. 1956: Spy Chasers. 1958: My Gun is Quick. 1959: Abschied von den Wolken (GB: Rebel Flight to Cuba). 1961: One, Two, Three. 1962: The Testament of Dr Mabuse. Sherlock Holmes und das Halsband des Todes (GB and US: Sherlock Holmes and the Deadly Necklace). 1964: John Goldfarb, Please Come Home. Do Not Disturb. 1966: Carnival of Thieves (US: The Caper of the Golden Bulls). What Did You Do in the War, Daddy? 1967: Guns for San Sebastian. Double Trouble. The Perils of Pauline. 1968: Lucrezia. A Fine Pair. The Wicked Dreams of Paula Schultz. 1969: The Maltese Bippy. 1972: Hammersmith is Out. 1973: Doctor Death: Seeker of Souls. The World's Greatest Athlete. Genesis II (TV). 1974: Young Frankenstein. 1975: Death Knocks Twice. 1979: Going Ape! 1982: Airplane II The Sequel. 1985: First Strike.

## ASLAN, Gregoire
(Krikor Aslanian) 1908-1982
Alarmed-looking, dark-haired (balding), big-nosed actor with large face and full,

ABOVE Posing as a maid, Deanne Durbin is courted by five other 'menials' – Sig **Arno** (second from right), Akim Tamiroff, Hans Conreid, Alan Mowbray (all *qv*), and Frank Jenks, in *His Butler's Sister* (1943)

BELOW Luke **Askew** (foreground) keeps his eye (and gun) on the saloon bad guys, while Gary Grimes guns down bartender Ted Gehring, in *The Culpepper Cattle Co.* (1972)

usually pursed lips. Born in Istanbul, he began his career at 18 as a vocalist and drummer with a dance band in Paris. He also did vaudeville and cabaret work before beginning to turn to acting. In post-war years, his thick Gallic accent and double-takes became a familiar part of the film scene in British studios, and he tackled both comic and dramatic roles. Billed as Coco Aslan throughout the earlier part of his career, a nickname he gradually discarded after the 1950s. Died from a heart attack.

1938: Feu de joie. 1948: Hans le marin (GB: The Wicked City). Sleeping Car to Trieste. 1949: Occupe-toi d'Amélie (GB: Keep an Eye on Amelia. US: Oh Amelia!). 1950: Last Holiday. Cairo Road. Cage of Gold. The Adventurers (US: The Great Adventure). 1951: L'auberge rouge (GB and US: The Red Inn). 1953: Act of Love. Innocents in Paris. 1955: Oasis. Confidential Report (US: Mr Arkadin). Joe Macbeth. 1957: Celui qui doit mourir (US: He Who Must Die). 1958: The Snorkel. The Roots of Heaven. Windom's Way. Sea Fury. 1959: Killers of Kilimanjaro. Our Man in Havana. The Three Worlds of Gulliver. 1960: Under Ten Flags. The Criminal (US: The Concrete Jungle). 1961: The Rebel (US: Call Me Genius). King of Kings. The Devil at Four O'Clock. The Happy Thieves. Invasion Quartet. Village of Daughters. 1963: Cleopatra. 1964: The Fabulous Adventures of Marco Polo (US: Marco the Magnificent). Aimez-vous les femmes? (GB: Do You Like Women?). The Main Chance. The Yellow Rolls Royce. Paris When It Sizzles. 1965: The High Bright Sun (US: McGuire, Go Home!). Une ravissante idiote (GB: A Ravishing Idiot. US: Adorable Idiot). Moment to Moment. 1966: Lost Command. Our Man in Marrakesh. A Man Could Get Killed. 1967: The 25th Hour. 1968: Mazel Tov ou le mariage (GB and US: Marry Me! Marry Me!). A Flea in Her Ear. 1970: You Can't Win 'Em All. 1972: Sex Shop. 1973: The Girl from Hong Kong. The Golden Voyage of Sinbad. 1974: The Girl from Petrovka. The Return of the Pink Panther. QB VII (TV). Bon baisers de Hong Kong. 1976: The Killer Who Wouldn't Die (TV). 1977: Blood-Relations. 1978: Meetings With Remarkable Men.

## ASNER, Ed(ward) 1929-

Thick-set, gruff-voiced, balding, aggressive American actor in Hollywood films cast as tough characters after long theatre training. His career really took off in the 1970s with his long-running TV portrait of hard-nosed, soft-hearted newspaper editor Lou Grant in a series of that name. But his career received a severe setback in the early 1980s when, as militant president of the Screen Actors' Guild, he clashed showily with President Reagan (himself a former president of SAG). The Lou Grant series nosedived in the ratings and was promptly cancelled.

1964: The Satan Bug. 1965: The Slender Thread. 1966: The Venetian Affair. El Dorado. The Doomsday Flight (TV. GB: cinemas). 1967: Gunn. 1969: Daughter of the Mind (TV). Change of Habit. 1970: They Call Me MISTER Tibbs! The Todd Killings. Halls of Anger. The House on Greenapple Road (TV). The Old Man Who Cried Wolf (TV). 1971: The Last Child (TV). They Call It Murder (TV). Skin Game. 1972: Haunts of the Very Rich. 1973: Police Story (TV. GB: cinemas). The Girl Most Likely To … (TV). 1974: The Wrestler. 1975: The Imposter (TV). Death Scream (TV). Hey! I'm Alive (TV). 1976: Gus. 1977: The Life and Assassination of the Kingfish (TV). The Gathering (TV). 1981: Fort Apache the Bronx. O'Hara's Wife. A Small Killing (TV). 1983: Daniel. 1984: Anatomy of an Illness (TV).

## ATES, Roscoe 1892-1962

Bug-eyed, sawn-off, scrawny-necked American comedy actor who often seemed to be wearing funny clothes and hats the wrong way round, and cashed in by re-creating a childhood stutter and making it part of his many nervous characters. Escaped being browbeaten by heroes and henpecked by screen wives when he became the comic sidekick of cowboy star Eddie Dean in 15 1940s' westerns. He had begun his career as a concert violinist. Died from lung cancer.

1929: South Sea Rose. 1930: The Lone Star Ranger. Reducing. Caught Short. The Big House. City Girl. Billy the Kid. Love in the

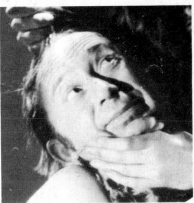

Rough. 1931: The Great Lover. Cracked Nuts. The Big Shot (GB: The Optimist). The Champ. A Free Soul. Cimarron. Politics. Too Many Cooks. 1932: *Shampoo the Magician. Freaks. Ladies of the Jury. The Rainbow Trail. Young Bride/Love Starved/Veneer. Roadhouse Murder. Hold 'Em, Jail! Come On, Danger. Deported. 1933: Renegades of the West. The Past of Mary Holmes. The Cheyenne Kid. Golden Harvest. Alice in Wonderland. What! No Beer? Scarlet River. Lucky Devils. 1934: Woman in the Dark. She Made Her Bed. The Merry Wives of Reno. 1935: The People's Enemy. 1936: God's Country and the Woman. Fair Exchange. 1938: Riders of the Black Hills. The Great Adventures of Wild Bill Hickok (serial). 1939: Three Texas Steers (GB: Danger Rides the Range). Gone with the Wind. Rancho Grande. 1940: *Fireman, Save My Choo-Choo. Cowboy from Sundown. Captain Caution. Untamed. I Want a Divorce. Chad Hanna. 1941: I'll Sell My Life. Birth of the Blues. Mountain Moonlight (GB: Moving in Society). She Knew All the Answers. Sullivan's Travels. Robin Hood of the Pecos. Reg'lar Fellers. Bad Men of Missouri. One Foot in Heaven. 1942: The Palm Beach Story. The Affairs of Jimmy Valentine. 1944: Can't Help Singing. 1946: Colorado Serenade. Down Missouri Way. Driftin' River. Tumbleweed Trail. Stars over Texas. Wild West. 1947: Wild Country. Range Beyond the Blue. West to Glory. Black Hills. Shadow Valley. 1948: Check Your Guns. Tornado Range. Inner Sanctum. The Westward Trail. The Hawk of Powder River. Prairie Outlaws. The Tioga Kid. Thunder in the Pines. 1950: The Hills of Oklahoma. Father's Wild Game. 1951: Honeychile. 1952: The Blazing Forest. 1953: Those Redheads from Seattle. The Stranger Wore a Gun. 1955: Lucy Gallant. Abbott and Costello Meet the Keystone Kops. 1956: Come Next Spring. The Birds and the Bees. The Kettles in the Ozarks. Meet Me in Las Vegas (GB: Viva Las Vegas!). 1957: Run of the Arrow. The Big Caper. Short Cut to Hell. 1958: The Sheepman. 1961: The Silent Call. The Errand Boy.

## ATWILL, Lionel 1885-1946

Suave, usually moustachioed British-born actor of impeccable diction and an air of

faintly seedy sophistication. His characters suppurated corruption under their skins of suavity. He went to Hollywood, where he was soon busy playing dozens of mad professors, crooked lawyers and staring-eyed scientists, but made a memorable Moriarty to Basil Rathbone's Sherlock Holmes. His career survived a rather po-faced scandal in the early 1940s over the showing of 'blue movies' at his home. Died from pneumonia.

1918: Eve's Daughter. For Sale. The Marriage Price. 1921: The Highest Bidder. Indiscretion. 1928: *The White-Faced Fool. *The Actor's Advice to His Son. 1932: The Silent Witness. Doctor X. 1933: The Vampire Bat. Secret of Madame Blanche. The Mystery of the Wax Museum. Murders in the Zoo. The Secret of the Blue Room. Song of Songs. The Sphinx. Solitaire Man. 1934: Nana. Beggars in Ermine. Stamboul Quest. One More River (GB: Over the River). The Age of Innocence. The Firebird. The Man Who Reclaimed His Head. 1935: Mark of the Vampire. The Devil Is a Woman. Murder Man. Rendezvous. Captain Blood. 1936: Lady of Secrets. Till We Meet Again. Absolute Quiet. 1937: The High Command. The Road Back. Last Train from Madrid. The Wrong Road. Lancer Spy. The Great Garrick. 1938: The Great Waltz. Three Comrades. 1939: Son of Frankenstein. The Three Musketeers. The Hound of the Baskervilles. The Mad Empress (GB: Carlotta, the Mad Empress). The Gorilla. The Sun Never Sets. Mr Moto Takes a Vacation. The Secret of Dr Kildare. Balalaika. 1940: Johnny Apollo. Charlie Chan in Panama. The Girl in 313. Boom Town. Charlie Chan's Murder Cruise. 1941: The Great Profile. Man Made Monster (GB: The Electric Man). The Ghost of Frankenstein. 1942: Junior G-Men of the Air (serial). The Strange Case of Dr RX. To Be or Not To Be. Pardon My Sarong. Cairo. Night Monster (GB: The Hammond Mystery). The Mad Doctor of Market Street. Sherlock Holmes and the Secret Weapon. 1943: Frankenstein Meets the Wolf Man. Captain America (serial). 1944: Lady in the Death House. Secrets of Scotland Yard. Raiders of Ghost City (serial). House of Frankenstein. 1945: Fog Island. Crime Inc. House of Dracula. 1946: Lost City of the Jungle (serial). Genius at Work.

**AUER, Mischa**
(M. Ounskowsky) 1905-1967
Pop-eyed, pencil-moustached, anxious-looking Russian-born comedy actor who came to Hollywood with the advent of sound, and stayed to create a memorable gallery of eccentric comic characters, usually flapping over some fresh disaster. He was at his peak in the late 1930s, but continued working until his death, in Italy, from a heart attack. Oscar Nominee for My Man Godfrey.

1928: Something Always Happens. The Mighty. Marquis Preferred. 1929: Fame and the Devil. The Studio Murder Mystery. 1930: The Benson Murder Case. Inside the Lines. The Lady from Nowhere. Just Imagine. Paramount on Parade. Women Love Once. The Unholy Garden. 1931: Drums of Jeopardy. The Yellow Ticket (GB: The Yellow Passport). King of the Wild (serial). Delicious. No Limit. The Midnight Patrol. Command Performance. 1932: Last of the Mohicans (serial). The Intruder. Mata Hari. Sinister Hands. Murder at Dawn (GB: The Death Ray). No Greater Love (GB: Divine Love). Drifting Souls. Scarlet Dawn. Arsène Lupin. The Unwritten Law. The Monster Walks. Call Her Savage. Western Code. Beauty Parlor. 1933: Rasputin and the Empress (GB: Rasputin the Mad Monk). Dangerously Yours. Sucker Money (GB: Victims of the Beyond). Tarzan the Fearless (serial). Infernal Machine. Corruption. The Flaming Signal. After Tonight (GB: Sealed Lips). Cradle Song. Girl without a Room. Storm at Daybreak. 1934: Wharf Angel. The Crosby Case (GB: The Crosby Murder Case). Viva Villa! Bulldog Drummond Strikes Back. Change of Heart. Stamboul Quest. Student Tour. Woman Condemned. 1935: Mystery Woman. Lives of a Bengal Lancer. Clive of India. The Adventures of Rex and Rinty (serial). Condemned to Live. Anna Karenina. Biography of a Bachelor Girl. The Crusades. I Dream Too Much. 1936: Murder in the Fleet. The House of 1000 Candles. One Rainy Afternoon. The Princess Comes Across. Winterset. The Gay Desperado. We're Only Human. Here Comes Trouble. Tough Guy. Sons o' Guns. 1937: My Man Godfrey. That Girl from Paris. Three Smart Girls. Top of the Town. We Have Our Moments. Pick a Star.

Vogues of 1938. Marry the Girl. Merry-Go-Round. Prescription for Romance. 1938: 100 Men and a Girl. Service De Luxe. It's All Yours. The Rage of Paris. You Can't Take It With You. Little Tough Guys in Society. Sweethearts. 1939: East Side of Heaven. Unexpected Father (GB: Sandy Takes a Bow). Destry Rides Again. *Three and a Day. 1940: Alias the Deacon. Sandy is a Lady. Public Deb Number One. Margie. Spring Parade. Trail of the Vigilantes. Seven Sinners. 1941: Flame of New Orleans. Cracked Nuts. Hold That Ghost! Moonlight in Hawaii. Hellzapoppin. Sing Another Chorus. 1942: Don't Get Personal. Twin Beds. 1943: Around the World. 1944: Lady in the Dark. Up in Mabel's Room. 1945: A Royal Scandal (GB: Czarina). Brewster's Millions. And Then There Were None (GB: Ten Little Niggers). 1946: Sentimental Journey. She Wrote the Book. 1947: For You I Die. 1948: Sofia. 1949: Al diavolo la celebrita. 1951: The Sky is Red. 1952: Song of Paris (US: Bachelor in Paris). 1954: Mr Arkadin (GB: Confidential Report). Escalier de service. 1955: Frou-Frou. Treize à table. L'impossible M. Pipelet. Futures vedettes (GB: Sweet Sixteen). Cette sacrée gamine (GB and US: Mam'zelle Pigalle). 1956: Mannequins de Paris. La polka des menottes. En effeuillant la marguerite (GB: Mam'selle Striptease. US: Please, Mr Balzac). 1957: Le tombeur. The Monte Carlo Story. 1958: Nathalie, agent secret (GB and US: The Foxiest Girl in Paris). Tabarin. Sacrée jeunesse. A pied, à cheval et en spoutnik (GB: Hold Tight for the Satellite. (US: A Dog, a Mouse and a Sputnik). 1962: We Joined the Navy. Les femmes d'abord (US: Ladies First). *The King's Breakfast. 1964: What Ever Happened to Baby Toto? Queste pazze, pazze, pazze donne. 1966: The Christmas That Almost Wasn't. Drop Dead, Darling (US: Arrivederci, Baby). Par amore... per magia...

**AYLMER, Sir Felix**
(F. A. Jones) 1889-1979
Distinguished, beady-eyed, balding British actor, adept at fussy or incisive characters, who was for many years president of the British actors' association Equity. He only had one leading role of real importance in the British cinema, in Mr Emmanuel, but produced a typically fine performance for

the occasion. He was also amusing in a semi-lead in *The Ghosts of Berkeley Square*. Knighted in 1965.

*1930: Escape. The Temporary Widow. 1932: The Lodger (US: The Phantom Fiend). The World, the Flesh and the Devil. 1933: The Ghost Camera. Home Sweet Home. The Wandering Jew. 1934: Night Club Queen. The Path of Glory. My Old Dutch. Doctor's Orders. The Soul of a Nation (narrator only). Evergreen. The Iron Duke. 1935: The Ace of Spades. Hello Sweetheart. The Divine Spark/Casta Diva. Old Roses. The Price of a Song. The Clairvoyant. Checkmate. Her Last Affaire. She Shall Have Music. Improper Duchess. 1936: Jack of All Trades. Rhodes of Africa (US: Rhodes). In the Soup. Tudor Rose (US: Nine Days a Queen). Royal Eagle. Seven Sinners (US: Doomed Cargo). As You Like It. Dusty Ermine (US: Hideout in the Alps). The Man in the Mirror. Sensation. The Mill on the Floss. 1937: Dreaming Lips. The Frog. Glamorous Night. The Vicar of Bray. Action for Slander. Victoria the Great. The Live Wire. The Rat. Bank Holiday (US: Three on a Weekend). South Riding. 1938: Just Like a Woman. Kate Plus Ten. Break the News. I've Got a Horse. Sixty Glorious Years (US: Queen of Destiny). The Citadel. 1939: Spies of the Air. Young Man's Fancy. Laugh It Off. Dr O'Dowd. 1940: Quiet Wedding. The Briggs Family. Charley's (Big-Hearted) Aunt. Night Train to Munich (US: Night Train). Saloon Bar. The Case of the Frightened Lady (US: The Frightened Lady). The Girl in the News. Spellbound (US: The Spell of Amy Nugent). 1941: The Ghost of St Michael's. Kipps (US: The Remarkable Mr Kipps). The Saint's Vacation. Major Barbara. Atlantic Ferry (US: Sons of the Sea). Once a Crook. I Thank You. The Seventh Survivor. The Black Sheep of Whitehall. Hi Gang! South American George. The Young Mr Pitt. 1942: Sabotage at Sea. The Peterville Diamond. Thursday's Child. 1943: The Life and Death of Colonel Blimp (US: Colonel Blimp). Escape to Danger. Bell Bottom George. \*Welcome to Britain. The Demi-Paradise (US: Adventure for Two). Time Flies. 1944: English Without Tears (US: Her Man Gilbey). Mr Emmanuel. Henry V. 1945: \*Julius Caesar. The Way to the Stars (US: Johnny in the Clouds). Caesar and Cleopatra. The Wicked Lady. 1946: The Years Between. The Magic Bow. The Laughing Lady. 1947: Green Fingers. The Man Within (US: The Smugglers). A Man About the House. The October Man. The Ghosts of Berkeley Square. 1948: The Calendar. Escape. Hamlet. Quartet. Alice in Wonderland (voice only). 1949: Prince of Foxes. Edward My Son. Christopher Columbus. 1950: Your Witness (US: Eye Witness). So Long at the Fair. Trio. She Shall Have Murder. 1951: The Lady With a Lamp. The House in the Square (US: I'll Never Forget You). 1952: Ivanhoe. The Man Who Watched Trains Go By (US: Paris Express). Quo Vadis? 1953: The Master of Ballantrae. The Triangle. The Love Lottery. Knights of the Round Table. 1954: The Angel Who Pawned Her Harp. 1956: Loser Takes All. Anastasia. 1957: Saint Joan. 1958: Separate Tables. I Accuse! The Two-Headed Spy. 1959: The Doctor's Dilemma. The Mummy. 1960: Never Take Sweets from a Stranger (US: Never Take Candy from a Stranger). The Hands of Orlac. Exodus. From the Terrace. 1961: Macbeth. 1962: The Road to Hong Kong. The Boys. 1963: The Running Man. 1964: The Chalk Garden. Becket. Masquerade. 1968: Decline and Fall ... of a birdwatcher! Hostile Witness.*

**BACKUS, Jim** 1913- *1989*
Well-built American comedy actor, seen either beaming or scowling—there were few half-measures with Backus characters. After military service in World War II, he became a familiar part of the cinema for 20 years, playing grouchy growlers and over-hearty businessmen. Also popular as the long-suffering husband of Joan Davis in TV's *I Married Joan*, and as the rasping tones of cartoonland's short-sighted Mr Magoo.

*1942: The Pied Piper. 1949: One Last Fling. Father Was a Fullback. Easy Living. The Great Lover. A Dangerous Profession. Ma and Pa Kettle Go to Town (GB: Going to Town). 1950: Customs Agent. Emergency Wedding (GB: Jealousy). The Hollywood Story. Bright Victory (GB: Lights Out). The Killer That Stalked New York (GB: The Frightened City). 1951: I Want You. Iron Man. Half Angel. The Man With a Cloak. M. His Kind of Woman. I'll See You in My Dreams. 1952: Pat and Mike. Deadline USA (GB: Dead-*
line). *Here Come the Nelsons. The Rose Bowl Story. Don't Bother to Knock. Androcles and the Lion. Above and Beyond. Angel Face. 1953: I Love Melvin. Geraldine. 1954: Deep in My Heart. 1955: Francis in the Navy. Rebel Without a Cause. The Square Jungle. 1956: Meet Me in Las Vegas (GB: Viva Las Vegas!). The Naked Hills. You Can't Run Away from It. The Opposite Sex. 1957: Top Secret Affair (GB: Their Secret Affair). Man of a Thousand Faces. Eighteen and Anxious. The Pied Piper of Hamelin (TV. GB: cinemas). 1958: The High Cost of Loving. Free Week-End (TV). Macabre. 1959: Ask Any Girl. 1960: Ice Palace. 1962: The Horizontal Lieutenant. Boys' Night Out. Zotz! The Wonderful World of the Brothers Grimm. Critic's Choice. 1963: Sunday in New York. Johnny Cool. The Wheeler Dealers (GB: Separate Tables). It's a Mad, Mad, Mad, Mad World. Operation Bikini. My Six Loves. Advance to the Rear (GB: Company of Cowards). 1964: John Goldfarb, Please Come Home. 1965: Fluffy. Billie. 1966: Hurry Sundown. 1967: Don't Make Waves. 1968: Hello Down There. Where Were You When the Lights Went Out? 1969: The Cockeyed Cowboys of Calico County (GB: TV as A Woman for Charlie). Wake Me When the War is Over (TV). 1970: Myra Breckinridge. 1971: Getting Away from It All (TV). The Magic Carpet (TV). 1972: Now You See Him Now You Don't. 1973: The Girl Most Likely To (TV). 1974: Miracle on 34th Street (TV). 1975: The Return of Joe Forrester (TV). Friday Foster. Crazy Mama. 1976: The Feather and Father Gang (TV). 1977: Pete's Dragon. 1978: Good Guys Wear Black. Rescue from Gilligan's Island (TV). 1979: Seven from Heaven. Chomps. There Goes the Bride. Angels' Brigade. 1981: Jayne Mansfield—an American Tragedy. 1982: Slapstick (US: Slapstick of Another Kind). 1984: Prince Jack.*

**BACON, Irving** 1892-1965
Soft-spoken, open-faced, sandy-haired, genial American mid-westerner. Usually cast as a solid citizen, Bacon could project honesty, friendliness and perplexity with equal ease, sometimes all three together, as with his long-running characterization of

the mailman in the Blondie films. Sometimes his 'honesty' was turned into gullibility with equal success. This filmography does not cover fleeting appearances Bacon is said to have made in Sennett shorts in pre-World War I days.

1923: *Anna Christie.* 1927: *California or Bust.* \**The Girl from Everywhere.* 1928: *The Goodbye Kiss. The Head Man. The Three Sinners.* 1929: *Half Way to Heaven.* \**The Old Barn. Side Street* (GB: *Three Brothers*). *The Saturday Night Kid. All at Sea. China Bound. The Duke Steps Out. Stark Mad. Hot Stuff. Hard to Get. Two Sisters.* 1930: *Spring is Here. Wide Open. Free and Easy. Street of Chance.* 1931: *Alias the Bad Man. Branded Men. Fighting Caravans, Newly Rich.* 1932: *File No. 113. This Is the Night. Million Dollar Legs. No One Man. Union Depot* (GB: *Gentleman for a Day*). *Central Park. The Match King. I Am a Fugitive from a Chain Gang. If I Had a Million. Lawyer Man. Madame Racketeer* (GB: *The Sporting Widow*). 1933: *He Learned About Women. Hello, Everybody! Private Detective 62. Big Executive. Lone Cowboy. Lady for a Day. The Bowery. Sitting Pretty. The Keyhole. Ann Vickers.* 1934: *Miss Fane's Baby is Stolen* (GB: *Kidnapped*). *Six of a Kind. The Hell Cat. It Happened One Night. No Ransom. Shadows of Sing Sing. You Belong to Me. Hat, Coat and Glove. The Pursuit of Happiness. Ready for Love. Now I'll Tell* (GB: *When New York Sleeps*). *George White's Scandals. Broadway Bill* (GB: *Strictly Confidential*). *Romance in Manhattan. The House of Mystery.* 1935: *Here Comes Cookie* (GB: *The Plot Thickens*). *Millions in the Air. West of the Pecos. Powdersmoke Range. Private Worlds. Goin' to Town. The Virginia Judge. The Glass Key. Two Fisted. Ship Café. It's a Small World. Diamond Jim. Manhattan Moon* (GB: *Sing Me a Love Song*). *Bright Lights. It's a Great Life. Page Miss Glory. The Farmer Takes a Wife. Men Without Names. Murder Man. She Couldn't Take It* (GB: *Woman Tamer*). *Bad Boy.* \**Tuned Out.* 1936: *Love on a Bet. Three Cheers for Love. Murder With Pictures. The Texas Rangers. Petticoat Fever. Earthworm Tractors* (GB: *A Natural Born Salesman*). *Hollywood Boulevard. Drift Fence. Lady, Be Careful. Wives Never Know. Valiant is the Word for Carrie. The Big Broadcast of 1937. Let's Make a Million. Hopalong Cassidy Returns. Arizona Mahoney. San Francisco. Mr Deeds Goes to Town. The Plainsman. Trail of the Lonesome Pine. China Clipper. Big Town Girl.* 1937: *It's Love I'm After. Internes Can't Take Money* (GB: *You Can't Take Money*). *Exclusive. Seventh Heaven. The Big City. Marry the Girl. Angel's Holiday. Sing and Be Happy. A Star is Born. Passport Husband.* 1938: *Midnight Intruder. Professor Beware. The Cowboy and the Lady. You Can't Take It With You. Exposed. The Big Broadcast of 1938. The First Hundred Years. The Texans. The Chaser. Tip-Off Girls. The Arizona Wildcat. Sing, You Sinners. Spawn of the North. There Goes My Heart. Kentucky Moonshine* (GB: *Three Men and a Girl*). *The*

*Amazing Dr Clitterhouse. The Sisters. City Girl. Mr Moto's Gamble. Racket Busters. The Mad Miss Manton. Strange Faces. Swing Your Lady. Hard to Get. Letter of Introduction. Sweethearts. Man-Proof. Blondie. Every Day's a Holiday.* 1939: *Too Busy to Work. The Adventures of Huckleberry Finn. Tail Spin. The Gracie Allen Murder Case. Lucky Night. Second Fiddle. I Stole a Million. Hollywood Cavalcade. Gone With the Wind. Blondie Takes a Vacation. Rio. The Oklahoma Kid. Blondie Brings Up Baby. Torchy Runs for Mayor. Indianapolis Speedway* (GB: *Devil on Wheels*). *Heaven with a Barbed Wire Fence. The Lone Wolf Spy Hunt* (GB: *The Lone Wolf's Daughter*). *They Made Me a Criminal. Big Town Czar. At the Circus. Blondie Meets the Boss. The Housekeeper's Daughter. Bachelor Mother.* \**Hollywood Slaves. Invisible Stripes.* 1940: *The Grapes of Wrath. The Man Who Wouldn't Talk. Star Dust. You Can't Fool Your Wife. Dr Ehrlich's Magic Bullet* (GB: *The Story of Dr Ehrlich's Magic Bullet*). *Young People. Blondie on a Budget. Manhattan Heartbeat. The Return of Frank James. Gold Rush Maisie. The Howards of Virginia* (GB: *The Tree of Liberty*). *Blondie Has Servant Trouble. Dreaming Out Loud. Michael Shayne, Private Detective. Lillian Russell. Blondie Plays Cupid. Brother Rat and a Baby* (GB: *Baby Be Good*). *Broadway Melody of 1940. His Girl Friday. The Doctor Takes a Wife. Sailor's Lady. Love, Honor and Oh Baby! Jennie. Western Union. Edison the Man.* 1941: *Meet John Doe. Great Guns. Cadet Girl. Henry Aldrich for President. A Girl, a Guy and a Gob* (GB: *The Navy Steps Out*). *Tobacco Road. Blondie Goes Latin* (GB: *Conga Swing*). *She Couldn't Say No. Ride On, Vaquero. Caught in the Draft. Accent on Love. Too Many Blondes. Moon Over Her Shoulder. It Started with Eve. Never Give a Sucker an Even Break* (GB: *What a Man!*). *Blondie in Society* (GB: *Henpecked*). *Remember the Day. The Lone Wolf Takes a Chance. Barnacle Bill. Skylark. Our Wife. Million Dollar Baby. Back Street. They Died with Their Boots On. Wild Man of Borneo.* 1942: *The Bashful Bachelor. Through Different Eyes. Juke Girl. Young America. Pardon My Sarong. Holiday Inn. Footlight Serenade. Give Out, Sisters. Blondie for Victory* (GB: *Troubles Through Billets*). *Between Us Girls. Get Hep to Love* (GB: *She's My Lovely*). *Star Spangled Rhythm. The Great Man's Lady. Lady in a Jam. Sweetheart of the Fleet. Blondie's Blessed Event* (GB: *A Bundle of Trouble*). 1943: *The Desperados. Dixie Dugan. The Amazing Mrs Holliday. A Stranger in Town. Shadow of a Doubt. Johnny Come Lately* (GB: *Johnny Vagabond*). *Hers to Hold. Follow the Band. King of the Cowboys. Two Weeks to Live. Happy Go Lucky. The Good Fellows. So's Your Uncle. In Old Oklahoma* (GB: *War of the Wildcats*). *Action in the North Atlantic. Girl Crazy. Gung Ho! It's a Great Life* (and *1935 version*). *Footlight Glamour. This is the Army. What a Woman!* (GB: *The Beautiful Cheat*). *A Guy Named Joe.* 1944: *Pin-Up Girl. Weekend Pass. Wing and a Prayer. Chip Off the Old Block. Her Primitive Man. Since You Went Away.*

*Heavenly Days. The Thin Man Goes Home. Can't Help Singing. The Story of Dr Wassell. Casanova Brown. Knickerbocker Holiday.* 1945: *Roughly Speaking. Patrick the Great. Out of This World. Guest Wife. Under Western Skies. Hitchhike to Happiness. One Way to Love. Week-End at the Waldorf. Spellbound.* 1946: *Night Train to Memphis. Wake Up and Dream. My Brother Talks to Horses.* 1947: *Saddle Pals. Monsieur Verdoux. The Bachelor and the Bobby-Soxer* (GB: *Bachelor Knight*). *Dear Ruth. The High Wall.* 1948: *Moonrise. State of the Union* (GB: *The World and His Wife*). *Albuquerque* (GB: *Silver City*). *The Velvet Touch. Adventures in Silverado. Good Sam. Rocky. Family Honeymoon. Words and Music.* 1949: *John Loves Mary. Dear Wife. The Green Promise* (GB: *Raging Waters*). *Night unto Night. The Big Cat. Dynamite. It's a Great Feeling. Manhandled. Woman in Hiding. Down Memory Lane.* 1950: *Born To Be Bad. Wabash Avenue. Emergency Wedding* (GB: *Jealousy*). *Sons of New Mexico* (GB: *The Brat*). *Riding High. Never a Dull Moment.* 1951: *Honeychile. Cause for Alarm. Two Weeks to Live. Katie Did It. Desert of Lost Men. Here Comes the Groom.* 1952: *O Henry's Full House* (GB: *Full House*). *It Grows on Trees. Room for One More. Rose of Cimarron.* 1953: *Devil's Canyon. Kansas Pacific. Sweethearts on Parade. Fort Ti. The Glenn Miller Story.* 1954: *Ma and Pa Kettle at Home. Black Horse Canyon. Duffy of San Quentin* (GB: *Men Behind Bars*). *A Star is Born.* 1955: *Run for Cover. At Gunpoint* (GB: *Gunpoint!*). 1956. *Hidden Guns. Dakota Incident.* 1958: *Ambush at Cimarron Pass. Fort Massacre.*

**BADDELEY, Hermione**
(H. Clinton-Baddeley) 1906- 1986
Jolly-looking, fair-haired, full-faced British actress who could be both sophisticated and blowzy, and contributed a rich range of characters to the screen (after a long stage career), most of them 'below stairs', but some of which, like the vengeful Ida in *Brighton Rock*, she turned memorably into semi-leads. The younger sister of actress Angela Baddeley (1904-1976), who was seen mainly on stage and television. Nominated for an Oscar in *Room at the Top*.

1926: *A Daughter in Revolt.* 1927: *The Guns of Loos.* 1930: *Caste.* 1934: *Love, Life and Laughter.* 1935: *Royal Cavalcade* (US:

Regal Cavalcade). 1941: Kipps (US: The Remarkable Mr Kipps). 1947: It Always Rains on Sunday. Brighton Rock. 1948: No Room at the Inn. Quartet. 1949: Passport to Pimlico. Dear Mr Prohack. 1950: The Woman in Question (US: Five Angles on Murder). There is Another Sun (US: Wall of Death). 1951: Hell is Sold Out. Scrooge (US: A Christmas Carol). Tom Brown's Schooldays. 1952: Song of Paris (US: Bachelor in Paris). Time Gentlemen Please! The Pickwick Papers. Cosh Boy (US: The Slasher). 1953: Counterspy (US: Undercover Agent). The Amazing Mr Canasta. 1954: The Belles of St Trinian's. 1956: Women Without Men (US: Blonde Bait). 1958: Room at the Top. 1959: Jet Storm. Expresso Bongo. 1960: Midnight Lace. Let's Get Married. 1961: Rag Doll. Information Received. 1964: Mary Poppins. The Unsinkable Molly Brown. 1965: Do Not Disturb. Harlow. The Adventures of Bullwhip Griffin. Marriage on the Rocks. 1967: The Happiest Millionaire. 1970: The Aristocats (voice only). 1972: Up the Front. 1974: The Black Windmill. 1979: There Goes the Bride. Chomps. 1982: The Secret of NIMH (voice only). I Take These Men (TV). 1983: This Girl for Hire (TV).

**BAINTER, Fay** 1891-1968
Dark-haired, dark-eyed American actress with soothing smile, an expert at motherly types. Her attractively husky voice and sympathetic nature made her a top featured attraction throughout the late 1930s and early 1940s. Her double nomination as Best Actress and Best Supporting Actress in 1938 (she won the latter Oscar for Jezebel) led to a change in the Academy rules. Her other Oscar nomination was for The Children's Hour in 1962.

1934: This Side of Heaven. 1937: The Soldier and the Lady (GB: Michael Strogoff). Quality Street. Make Way for Tomorrow. 1938: Jezebel. White Banners. Mother Carey's Chickens. The Arkansas Traveller. The Shining Hour. 1939: Yes, My Darling Daughter. The Lady and the Mob. Daughters Courageous. 1940: Our Neighbors, the Carters. Young Tom Edison. Our Town. Maryland. A Bill of Divorcement. 1941: Babes on Broadway. 1942: Woman of the Year. The War Against Mrs Hadley. Journey for Margaret. Mrs Wiggs

of the Cabbage Patch. 1943: The Human Comedy. Salute to the Marines. Presenting Lily Mars. Cry Havoc. The Heavenly Body. 1944: Dark Waters. Three is a Family. 1945: State Fair. 1946: The Kid from Brooklyn. The Virginian. 1947: Deep Valley. The Secret Life of Walter Mitty. 1948: Give My Regards to Broadway. June Bride. 1951: Close to My Heart. 1953: The President's Lady. 1962: The Children's Hour (GB: The Loudest Whisper). Bon Voyage!

**BALDWIN, Walter** 1896- 1977
Light-haired, open-mouthed, eager-looking American, often seen with rimless spectacles. Baldwin played friendly small-town men—storekeepers, farmers and the like, sometimes oppressed by the bad guys, but more often just part of a realistic rustic background. Came to Hollywood in early middle age after extensive Broadway experience.

1940: Angels over Broadway. Arizona. 1941: All That Money Can Buy (GB: The Devil and Daniel Webster). They Died With Their Boots On. Harvard, Here I Come (GB: Here I Come). I'm Nobody's Sweetheart Now. The Devil Commands. Look Who's Laughing. Miss Polly. Barnacle Bill. Kings Row. 1942: Scattergood Rides High. After Midnight With Boston Blackie (GB: After Midnight). In This Our Life. 1943: A Stranger in Town. Always a Bridesmaid. Happy Land. 1944: Arms and the Woman. Together Again. Tall in the Saddle. Louisiana Hayride. I'm from Arkansas. 1945: Trail to Vengeance (GB: Vengeance). Bring On the Girls. Murder He Says. Rhythm Round-Up (GB: Honest John). State Fair. The Lost Weekend. Why Girls Leave Home. Christmas in Connecticut (GB: Indiscretion). Colonel Effingham's Raid (GB: Man of the Hour). 1946: Young Widow. Sing While You Dance. The Time of Their Lives. To Each His Own. The Bride Wore Boots. Cross My Heart. The Strange Love of Martha Ivers. Claudia and David. The Best Years of Our Lives. The Perfect Marriage. 1947: The Unsuspected. Mourning Becomes Electra. Framed (GB: Paula). 1948: Winter Meeting. Hazard. Return of the Badmen. Rachel and the Stranger. A Miracle Can Happen (later and GB: On Our Merry Way). Cry of the City. Albuquerque (GB: Silver City). The Man from Colorado. 1949: Special Agent. Come to the Stable. Calamity Jane and Sam Bass. Thieves' Highway. Flamingo Road. 1950: Cheaper by the Dozen. Stella. Storm Warning. The Jackpot. 1951: Rough Riders of Durango. The Racket. I Want You. A Millionaire for Christy. 1952: Carrie. The Winning Team. Something for the Birds. Scandal at Scourie. 1953: Ride, Vaquero! 1954: The Long, Long Trailer. Living It Up. Destry. 1955: Interrupted Melody. Glory. The Desperate Hours. 1956: You Can't Run Away from It.

**BALFOUR, Michael** 1918-
Thick-lipped, pudgy, rosy-cheeked American-born actor who came to British films after a varied career in circuses, burlesque

and stock companies. Minor British films kept him very busy and his stocky figure, often clad in dark shirts and light ties or bow ties, was to be seen as minor crooks, taxi-drivers and slow-witted sidekicks of the hero. Rarely out of the studios from 1947 to 1972, then mainly on TV.

1947: Just William's Luck. 1948: Sleeping Car to Trieste. No Orchids for Miss Blandish. William Comes to Town. The Small Voice (US: Hideout). Obsession (US: The Hidden Room). 1949: Stop Press Girl. Don't Ever Leave Me. Melody Club. 1950: Her Favourite Husband (US: The Taming of Dorothy). *Help Yourself. Prelude to Fame. Helter Skelter. Cage of Gold. 1951: The Quiet Woman. A Case for PC 49. 1952: 13 East Street. Top Secret (US: Mr Potts Goes to Moscow). Hot Ice. Venetian Bird (US: The Assassin). 1953: Genevieve. The Red Beret (US: Paratrooper). Johnny on the Run. Albert RN. The Captain's Paradise. Moulin Rouge. Recoil. Small Town Story. Park Plaza 605 (US: Norman Conquest). Black 13. Three Steps to the Gallows (released 1955. US: White Fire). The Steel Key. 1954: The Sea Shall Not Have Them. The Scarlet Web. River Beat. Meet Mr Callaghan. Delayed Action. The Diamond (US: Diamond Wizard). Devil's Point (US: Devil's Harbor). The Belles of St Trinian's. One Good Turn. Track the Man Down. The Delavine Affair. Secret Venture. 1955: Dust and Gold. Double Jeopardy. The Reluctant Bride (US: Two Grooms for a Bride). Gentlemen Marry Brunettes. Barbados Quest (US: Murder on Approval). 1956: Breakaway. Secret of the Forest. The Big Money (released 1958). It's a Great Day. Reach for the Sky. 1957: The Steel Bayonet. Quatermass II (US: Enemy from Space). Man from Tangier. Hour of Decision/Table in the Corner. 1958: Fiend without a Face. 1959: Look Back in Anger. The Flesh and the Fiends (US: Mania). 1960: Carry on Constable. Make Mine Mink. Sink the Bismarck! Too Hot to Handle. 1961: The Monster of Highgate Ponds. The Hellfire Club. Pit of Darkness. The Treasure of Monte Cristo (US: The Secret of Monte Cristo). 1962: Design for Loving. She Always Gets Their Man. The Fast Lady. 1963: The Rescue Squad. Echo of Diana. 1964: The Sicilians. Beware of the Dog. Five Have a Mystery to Solve. 1966: Strangler's Web. Fahrenheit 451. Kaleidoscope. Where the Bullets Fly. Press for Time. The Sandwich Man. 1969: The Oblong Box. *The Undertakers. 1970: The Private Life of Sherlock Holmes. Hoverbug. The Adventurers. Man of Violence/The Sex Racketeers. 1971: Macbeth. The Magnificent Six and a Half (third series). The Canterbury Tales. 1972: Wreck Raisers. Madigan: The London Beat (TV). 1976: The 'Copter Kids. Joseph Andrews. 1977: Candleshoe. Come Play with Me. 1978: The Stick-Up. 1979: The Prisoner of Zenda. *Resting Rough. 1985 The Holcroft Covenant.

**BALL, Vincent** 1924-
Cheerful, long-faced Australian actor with fair curly hair, who worked his passage to

ABOVE Walter **Baldwin** (seated) has bad news for Maude Eburne in *I'm from Arkansas* (1944). Gathered round are Iris Adrian (*qv*), Bruce Bennett, Paul Newlan and Harry Hayden. A wealth of character players...

BELOW 'So dis little thing is worth all dat money?' Michael **Balfour** (right) gets a little lesson in stamp-collecting from his boss (Tom Conway) in *Barbados Quest* (1955)

England as a deck hand on a tramp steamer, then won a scholarship to RADA. He got some quite nice supporting roles in British films, but was a bit colourless starring in B features of the early 1960s. In the mid-1970s, Ball returned to Australia, where he proved a reliable character star.

*1948: The Blue Lagoon (stunt double only). Warning to Wantons. 1949: The Interrupted Journey. Stop Press Girl. 1950: Come Dance With Me. 1951: Talk of a Million (US: You Can't Beat the Irish). London Entertains. 1953: * The Drayton Case. 1954: * The Dark Stairway. Dangerous Voyage (US: Terror Ship). Devil's Point (US: Devil's Harbor). The Black Rider. 1955: John and Julie. The Big Fish (narrator only). Stolen Time (US: Blonde Blackmailer). The Blue Peter (US: Navy Heroes). 1956: A Town Like Alice. The Baby and the Battleship. The Secret of the Forest. 1957: Face in the Night (US: Menace in the Night). Robbery under Arms. 1958: Blood of the Vampire. Sea of Sand (US: Desert Patrol). Danger Within (US: Breakout). 1960: Dentist in the Chair. Identity Unknown. Dead Lucky. Summer of the Seventeenth Doll (US: Season of Passion). 1961: Feet of Clay. Nearly a Nasty Accident. Very Important Person. Highway to Battle. The Middle Course. A Matter of WHO. 1962: Carry on Cruising. 1963: Echo of Diana. The Mouse on the Moon. 1967: Follow That Camel. 1968: Where Eagles Dare. 1969: Oh! What a Lovely War. 1971: Not Tonight Darling! Clinic Xclusive. 1977: Demolition (TV). 1978: The Irishman. 1979: Alison's Birthday. 1980: Breaker Morant. 1981: Deadline. 1982: Southern Cross (GB: The Highest Honor). 1983: Phar Lap.*

## BALSAM, Martin 1919- |996

Versatile, pug-faced, balding American actor, originally of 'The Method' school. Although vividly remembered as the doomed detective in *Psycho*, and in brilliant form opposite Joanne Woodward in *Summer Wishes, Winter Dreams*, this native New Yorker, who switches easily from character roles to leads and back, has never quite realized his full potential in the cinema. But he did win an Oscar in 1965 for *A Thousand Clowns*.

*1954: On the Waterfront. 1957: 12 Angry Men. Time Limit. 1958: Bomber's Moon (TV). Marjorie Morningstar. 1959: Al Capone. Free Week-End (TV). Middle of the Night. 1960: Psycho. Tutti a casa. 1961: Ada. Breakfast at Tiffany's. 1962: Cape Fear. La citta prigioniera (GB: The Captive City. US: The Conquered City). 1963: Who's Been Sleeping in My Bed? The Carpetbaggers. 1964: Youngblood Hawke. Seven Days in May. 1965: A Thousand Clowns. Harlow. The Bedford Incident. 1966: After the Fox. Hombre. The Paths to Eden. 1969: Me, Natalie. Trilogy. The Good Guys and the Bad Guys. 1970: Tora! Tora! Tora! Hunters Are For Killing (TV). Catch 22. The Old Man Who Cried Wolf (TV). Little Big Man. 1971: Imputazione di omicidio per uno studente (US: Suspected of Murder). The Anderson Tapes. The True and the False. Confessione di un commissario di polizia al procuratore della republica (US: Confessions of a Police Commissioner). 1972: The Stone Killer. The Man. Night of Terror (TV). 1973: Summer Wishes, Winter Dreams. A Brand New Life (TV). Death of a Snow Queen. Six Million Dollar*

*Man (TV). A Complete State of Death. The Counsellor. Trapped Beneath the Sea (TV). 1974: The Taking of Pelham 1-2-3. Money to Burn (TV). Murder on the Orient Express. Miles to Go Before I Sleep (TV). Corruzione al Palazzo di Giustizia. 1975: Mitchell. Death Among Friends (TV). Cry Onion. The Time of the Assassin. 1976: All the President's Men. The Lindbergh Kidnapping Case (TV). Raid on Entebbe (TV. GB: cinemas). The Sentinel. Con la rabbia agli occhi (GB: Anger in His Eyes). Two-Minute Warning. 1977: Silver Bears. The Storyteller (TV). Contract on Cherry Street (TV). Shadow of a Killer. Death Rage. Occhi dalle stelle. 1978: Rainbow (TV). Diamanti rosso sangue. The Millionaire (TV). Siege. 1979: Gardenia. The House on Garibaldi Street (originally for TV). Cuba. Aunt Mary (TV). The Seeding of Sarah Burns/ Sanctuary of Fear (TV). There Goes the Bride. 1980: The Love Tapes (TV). 1981: The Salamander. 1982: Little Gloria—Happy at Last (TV). 1983: The Goodbye People. I Want to Live! (TV). The People Vs Jean Harris (TV). 1984: Innocent Prey. Fratelli dello spazio. 1985: St Elmo's Fire. Death Wish 3.*

## BANNER, John
(Johann Banner) 1910-1973

Chubby Austrian actor who led a very spotty Hollywood film career after fleeing from the Nazis in 1938, but from 1965 to 1970 found enormous success on television playing the would-be-menacing but comically hapless Sergeant Schultz in *Hogan's Heroes*, an act imitated by other comedians for many years. It did not, however, lead to success in films, and, on his 63rd birthday, he died from an intestinal haemorrhage.

*1942: Once Upon a Honeymoon. Seven Miles from Alcatraz. The Moon is Down. 1943: Tonight We Raid Calais. The Fallen Sparrow. 1946: Black Angel. Rendezvous. 1948: To Victor. The Argyle Secrets. My Girl Tisa. 1950: Guilty of Treason (GB: Treason). 1953: The Juggler. 1955: The Rains of Ranchipur. 1958: The Beast of Budapest. 1959: The Blue Angel. 1960: The Story of Ruth. 1961: 20,000 Eyes. Operation Eichmann. Hitler. 1962: The Interns. 1963: The Yellow Canary. 1964: 36 Hours. 1968: The Wicked Dreams of Paula Schultz. 1970: Togetherness.*

## BARCROFT, Roy
(Howard Ravenscroft) 1902-1969

The tall, solid western villain who always looked as if he meant business, Barcroft's florid features were probably punched more often by cowboy heroes, especially in 'B' features of the 1940s, than those of any other actor. After service in World War I, the man from Crab Orchard, Nebraska or Weeping Water, Texas (according to which biographer you believe) tried a career as a clarinettist before settling into scores of films. In later years, he grew a bushy white beard for more sympathetic character roles. An infected leg wound led to his death from cancer.

1931: Mata Hari. 1932: A Woman Commands. 1937: SOS Coastguard (serial). Dick Tracy. Join the Marines. Night Key. Rosalie. 1938: Heroes of the Hills. The Crowd Roars. Blondes at Work. Stranger from Arizona. The Frontiersman. Flaming Frontiers (serial). Mexicali Rose. Silver on the Sage. Renegade Trail. Yukon Flight. They All Come Out. Crashing Thru. The Phantom Creeps (serial). Daredevils of the Red Circle (serial). Another Thin Man. The Oregon Trail. Rancho Grande. 1940: Hidden Gold. Bad Man from Red Butte. Stage to Chino. Winners of the West (serial). Ragtime Cowboy Joe. East of the River. Santa Fé Trail. Flash Gordon Conquers the Universe (serial). Deadwood Dick (serial). The Green Hornet Strikes Again (serial). Abe Lincoln in Illinois (GB: Spirit of the People). Trailing Double Trouble. The Showdown. 1941: Pals of the Pecos. The Bandit Trail. Wide Open Town. Jesse James at Bay. Outlaws of the Cherokee Trail. The Masked Rider. King of the Texas Rangers (serial). West of Cimarron. Riders of Death Valley (serial). Riders of the Badlands. Sky Raiders (serial). They Died With Their Boots On. White Eagle. Sheriff of Tombstone. 1942: Stardust on the Sage. Romance on the Range. Sunset on the Desert. Pirates of the Prairie. Land of the Open Range. The Lone Rider in Cheyenne. West of the Law. The Valley of Vanishing Men (serial). Dawn on the Great Divide. Nazi Agent. Northwest Rangers. Sunset Serenade. Tennessee Johnson (GB: The Man on America's Conscience). Below the Border. 1943: The Old Chisholm Trail. Hoppy Serves a Writ. Cheyenne Roundup. Calling Wild Bill Elliott. Carson City Cyclone. The Stranger from Pecos. False Colors. Bordertown Gun Fighters. Wagon Tracks West. Riders of the Rio Grande. The Masked Marvel (serial). Dr Gillespie's Criminal Case. Chatterbox. Hands Across the Border. Idaho. In Old Oklahoma (later and GB: War of the Wildcats). The Man from Music Mountain. Overland Mail Robbery. Raiders of Sunset Pass. Sagebrush Law. Six-Gun Gospel. 1944: Call of the South Seas. The Laramie Trail. Hidden Valley Outlaws. Code of the Prairie. The Girl Who Dared. Lights of Old Santa Fé. Stagecoach to Monterey. Firebrands of Arizona. Sheriff of Sundown. Cheyenne Wildcat. The Big Bonanza. The Fighting Seabees. Haunted Harbor (serial). Man from Frisco. Rosie the Riveter (GB: In Rosie's Room). Storm over Lisbon. Tucson Raiders. 1945: The Vampire's Ghost. Bells of Rosarita. Sunset in El Dorado. Along the Navajo Trail. Dakota. Marshal of Laredo. Manhunt of Mystery Island (serial). Wagon Wheels Westward. The Purple Monster Strikes (serial). Santa Fé Saddlemates. Colorado Pioneers. Trail of Kit Carson. The Lone

Texas Ranger. Topeka Terror. Corpus Christi Bandits. 1946: Home on the Range. Daughter of Don Q (serial). Alias Billy the Kid. Sun Valley Cyclone. My Pal Trigger. Night Train to Memphis. Traffic in Crime. The Phantom Rider (serial). Stagecoach to Denver. Plainsman and the Lady. Crime of the Century (voice only). The Last Frontier Uprising. 1947: Oregon Trail Scouts. The Web of Danger. Vigilantes of Boomtown. Rustlers of Devil's Canyon. Spoilers of the North. Springtime in the Sierras. Wyoming. Marshal of Cripple Creek. Blackmail. Along the Oregon Trail. The Wild Frontier. Bandits of Dark Canyon. Son of Zorro (serial). The Fabulous Texan. 1948: The Bold Frontiersman. Old Los Angeles. G-Men Never Forget (serial). Madonna of the Desert. The Main Street Kid. Lightnin' in the Forest. Oklahoma Badlands. Secret Service Investigator. Trail to Alcatraz. The Timber Trail. Out of the Storm. Eyes of Texas. Sons of Adventure. Grand Canyon Trail. Renegades of Sonora. Desperadoes of Dodge City. Marshal of Amarillo. Sundown in Santa Fé. The Far Frontier. The Gallant Legion. Montana Belle (released 1952). 1949: The Duke of Chicago. The Ghost of Zorro (serial). Sheriff of Wichita. Prince of the Plains. Frontier Investigator. Law of the Golden West. Federal Agents vs Underworld Inc (serial). South of Rio. Down Dakota Way. San Antone Ambush. Ranger of Cherokee Strip. Outcasts of the Trail. Powder River Rustlers. Pioneer Marshal. 1950: The James Brothers of Missouri (serial). Desperadoes of the West. Vigilante Hideout. The Vanishing Westerner. The Savage Horde. Federal Agent at Large. Under Mexicali Stars. Salt Lake Raiders. Surrender. Rustlers on Horseback. Gunmen of Abilene. Rock Island Trail (GB: Transcontinent Express). Radar Patrol vs Spy King (serial. Voice only). Woman from Headquarters (voice only). The Arizona Cowboy. Code of the Silver Sage. North of the Great Divide. Tyrant of the Sea. The Missourians. 1951: Wells Fargo Gunmaster. In Old Amarillo. Don Daredevil Rides Again (serial). Insurance Investigator. Night Riders of Montana. The Dakota Kid. Rodeo King and the Senorita. Utah Wagon Train. Fort Dodge Stampede. Arizona Manhunt. Street Bandits. Honeychile. Government Agents vs Phantom Legion (serial. Voice only). Pals of the Golden West. Desert of Lost Men. Rhythm Inn. Flying Disc Men from Mars (serial). Hoodlum Empire. 1952: Oklahoma Annie. Radar Men from the Moon (serial). Border Saddlemates. Wild Horse Ambush. Thundering Caravans. Old Oklahoma Plains. Black Hills Ambush. Ride the Man Down. Desperadoes' Outpost. The WAC from Walla Walla (GB: Army Capers). South Pacific Trail. Captive of Billy the Kid. Tropical Heat Wave. 1953: Marshal of Cedar Rock. Down Laredo Way. Iron Mountain Trail. Bandits of the West. Savage Frontier. Old Overland Trail. El Paso Stampede. Shadows of Tombstone. 1954: Rogue Cop. Man With the Steel Whip (serial). The Desperado. Two Guns and a Badge. 1955: Man without a Star. Oklahoma! The Spoilers. The Cobweb. Commando Cody (serial). 1956:

Gun Brothers. The Last Hunt. 1957: The Kettles on Old McDonald's Farm. Gun Duel in Durango. The Domino Kid. Last Stagecoach West. Band of Angels. Gunfire at Indian Gap. 1958: The Plunderers of Painted Flats. 1959: Escort West. 1960: Freckles. Ten Who Dared. 1961: When the Clock Strikes. Six Black Horses. 1964: He Rides Tall. 1965: Billy the Kid vs Dracula. 1966: Destination Inner Space. Gunpoint. Texas Across the River. 1967: The Way West. 1968: Rosemary's Baby. Bandolero! 1969: Gaily, Gaily (GB: Chicago, Chicago). The Reivers. 1970: Monte Walsh.

**BARKER, Eric** 1912-1990

Small, dark-haired, bespectacled British radio comedian who, after success in such post-war series as Merry-Go-Round and Just Fancy, in partnership with his wife Pearl Hackney, took on a whole new career at 45 as a film character comedian, often playing busybodies or petty officials. Boulting Brothers comedies gave him a good start and he was a semi-regular in British films for the next 10 years. Catchphrase (and the title of his autobiography): 'Steady Barker!'

1936: Carry On London. 1937: West End Frolics. Concert Party. 1938: On Velvet. 1957: Brothers in Law. Happy is the Bride! 1958: Blue Murder at St Trinian's. Carry On Sergeant. *A Clean Sweep. Bachelor of Hearts. 1959: Left, Right and Centre. 1960: Carry On Constable. Dentist in the Chair. Watch Your Stern. The Pure Hell of St Trinian's. 1961: Dentist on the Job (US: Get On with It!). Raising the Wind. On the Fiddle (US: Operation Snafu). 1962: Carry On Cruising. The Fast Lady. On the Beat. 1963: The Mouse on the Moon. Heavens Above! Father Came Too. 1964: The Bargee. Carry On Spying. Ferry 'Cross the Mersey. 1965: Three Hats for Lisa. Those Magnificent Men in Their Flying Machines. 1966: Doctor in Clover. The Great St Trinian's Train Robbery. Maroc 7. 1969: Twinky (US: Lola). 1970: There's a Girl in My Soup. Cool It Carol! 1972: That's Your Funeral. 1978: The Chiffy Kids (second series). Carry On Emmannuelle.

**BARKER, Ronnie** 1929-

Bespectacled, affable, portly British comedy actor of faintly furtive and foxy aspect

who has enjoyed enormous popularity in situation comedy series and comedy variety shows on television in the 1970s and 1980s (latterly in harness with diminutive Ronnie Corbett), proving himself no mean actor in the process and tackling complicated and clever monologues at the gallop. His film appearances, alas, have made something less than a splash, the first of them being a sadly inapt comment on the rest.

1958: Wonderful Things! 1962: Kill or Cure. 1963: The Cracksman. Doctor in Distress. Father Came Too. 1964: The Bargee. A Home of Your Own. 1965: Runaway Railway. 1967: The Man Outside. A Ghost of a Chance. 1968: Two Off the Cuff (voice only). 1970: Futtock's End. 1976: Robin and Marian. 1979: Porridge.

**BARNARD, Ivor** 1887-1953
Slightly built, dark-haired (balding) British actor with weasel-like, secretive features that could turn furtive, frightened or plain mean. Ideally cast as Wemmick in Great Expectations, he was involved in many of the best British films of the 1938-48 period. Just before his death, John Huston used him as one of his cargo of grotesques—a worthy companion for Peter Lorre and Robert Morley—in Beat the Devil.

1920: The Skin Game. 1931: Sally in Our Alley. 1932: Illegal. Blind Spot. 1933: The Good Companions. The Wandering Jew. The Crime at Blossom's. Sleeping Car. The Roof. Waltz Time. 1934: Love, Life and Laughter.

Princess Charming. Death at Broadcasting House. Brides to Be. 1935: The Price of Wisdom. The 39 Steps. The Village Squire. Some Day. Foreign Affaires. 1936: Dreams Come True. The House of the Spaniard. The Man Behind the Mask. 1937: What a Man. The Frog. Storm in a Teacup. The Mill on the Floss. Victoria the Great. Farewell to Cinderella. Double Exposures. 1938: Pygmalion. Everything Happens to Me. 1939: Eye Witness. *Oh Dear Uncle! Cheer Boys Cheer. The Stars Look Down. 1940: The House of the Arrow (US: Castle of Crimes). 1941: The Saint's Vacation. Quiet Wedding. 1943: The Silver Fleet. Undercover (US: Underground Guerillas). Escape to Danger. 1944: Hotel Reserve. Don't Take It to Heart. English Without Tears (US: Her Man Gilbey). 1945: Caesar and Cleopatra. The Wicked Lady. Perfect Strangers (US: Vacation from Marriage). Murder in Reverse. Great Day. 1946: Great Expectations. Appointment With Crime. 1947: So Well Remembered. Mrs Fitzherbert. 1948: Oliver Twist. London Belongs to Me (US: Dulcimer Street). Esther Waters. So Evil, My Love. The Queen of Spades. 1949: Paper Orchid. 1950: Madeleine. 1952: Hot Ice. The Importance of Being Earnest. Time Gentlemen Please! 1953: Malta Story. Sea Devils. Beat the Devil.

**BARNETT, Vince** 1902-1977
Short, jaunty, pale-eyed, bald, fast-talking American actor with wispy moustache who played runts, weasels and whining Runyonesque gangsters, often comic ones. One of life's losers on screen, but a well-liked and ubiquitous figure off it as an inveterate wisecracker and practical joker. In his twenties, Barnett was an airmail pilot who pioneered trans-American routes.

1930: All Quiet on the Western Front. Night Work. Dancing Sweeties. Queen of Scandal. Wide Open. 1931: One Heavenly Night. *Scratch As Catch Can. 1932: Tiger Shark. Rackety Rax. Night Mayor. Flesh. The Big Cage. Horse Feathers. The Death Kiss. Scarface—Shame of a Nation. 1933: *The Trial of Vince Barnett. Made on Broadway (GB: The Girl I Made). The Prizefighter and the Lady (GB: Everywoman's Man). Sunset Pass. The Girl in 419. Men of the Forest. Tugboat Annie. Heritage of the Desert. Fast Workers. Madame

Spy. 1934: The Ninth Guest. Air Maniacs. Now I'll Tell (GB: When New York Sleeps). No Ransom (GB: Bonds of Honour). Registered Nurse. Take the Stand (GB: The Great Radio Mystery). The Crimson Romance. Hell in the Heavens. Young and Beautiful. She Loves Me Not. Thirty-Day Princess. The Affairs of Cellini. The Secret Bride (GB: Concealment). 1935: Princess O'Hara. Black Fury. Don't Bet on Blondes. The Silk Hat Kid. Streamline Express. Champagne for Breakfast. Riff Raff. I Cover the Waterfront. I Live My Life. 1936: San Francisco. After the Thin Man. The Rest Cure. Dancing Feet. Down to the Sea. *Pirate Party on Catalina Isle. Yellow Cargo. Captain Calamity. I Cover Chinatown. 1937: The Woman I Love (GB: The Woman Between). A Star is Born. Boots of Destiny. *The Bank Alarm. 1938: Little Miss Broadway. Water Rustlers. The Headleys at Home (GB: Among Those Present). 1939: Exile Express. Overland Mail. The Singing Cowgirl. 1940: East Side Kids. Boys of the City. Seven Sinners. The Ghost Creeps. Heroes of the Saddle. 1941: Gangs Incorporated. Sierra Sue. A Girl, a Guy and a Gob (GB: The Navy Steps Out). A Dangerous Game. Paper Bullets. Jungle Man. Puddin' Head (GB: Judy Goes to Town). 1 Killed That Man. 1942: Klondike Fury. Girls' Town. The Corpse Vanishes. My Favorite Spy. Baby Face Morgan. X Marks the Spot. Foreign Agent. Stardust on the Sage. Bowery at Midnight. Prison Girls. The Phantom Plainsmen. Queen of Broadway. 1943: Tornado. The Crime Smasher. Kid Dynamite. Danger—Women at Work! High Explosive. Captive Wild Woman. Thundering Trails. Petticoat Larceny. 1944: The Mask of Dimitrios. Leave It to the Irish. Sweethearts of the USA (GB: Sweethearts on Parade). 1945: River Gang (GB: Fairy Tale Murder). High Powered. Thrill of a Romance. 1946: No Leave, No Love. The Virginian. Sensation Hunters. Swell Guy. The Killers. The Falcon's Alibi. Bowery Bombshell. 1947: I Cover Big Town. Little Miss Broadway (and 1938 film). Big Town after Dark. The Trespasser. Shoot to Kill. Brute Force. High Wall. Gas House Kids Go West. The Flame. 1948: Big Town Scandal. Joe Palooka in The Knockout. 1949: Knock on Any Door. Big Jack. Loaded Pistols. Deputy Marshal. Thunder in the Pines. 1950: Mule Train. Border Treasure. 1951: On Dangerous Ground. Kentucky Jubilee. I'll See You in My Dreams. 1952: Carson City. Red Planet Mars. Springfield Rifle. 1953: Charade. 1954: The Human Jungle. 1957: The Quiet Gun. Girl on the Run. Outlaw Queen. 1959: The Rookie. 1965: Zebra in the Kitchen. Dr Goldfoot and the Bikini Machine (GB: Dr G and the Bikini Machine). 1966: The Spy in the Green Hat (TV. GB: cinemas). 1967: The Big Mouth. 1975: Crazy Mama.

**BARRAT, Robert** 1891-1970
Big, powerful, banana-nosed, sandy-haired American actor, often seen as imposing, sometimes harsh figures of authority, but equally at ease as strong, nasty villains or benign, pipe-smoking officials. Resident at

Warners through the 1930s, he had some spectacular fights on screen, notably the one with Joel McCrea in *Union Pacific*.

1933: The Mayor of Hell. Picture Snatcher. Baby Face. King of the Jungle. The Silk Express. Lilly Turner. Captured! Heroes for Sale. Wild Boys of the Road (GB: Dangerous Days). The Kennel Murder Case. I Loved a Woman. From Headquarters. Ann Carver's Profession. The Secret of the Blue Room. 1934: I Sell Anything. Fog Over Frisco. Dames. Dark Hazard. A Very Honorable Guy. Massacre. Wonder Bar. Midnight Alibi. Hi, Nellie! Gambling Lady. Upper World. Friends of Mr Sweeney. The Dragon Murder Case. Here Comes the Navy. Housewife. Return of the Terror. Big-Hearted Herbert. The St Louis Kid (GB: A Perfect Weekend). The Fire Bird. I Am a Thief. 1935: The Florentine Dagger. While the Patient Slept. Dressed to Thrill. Captain Blood. Devil Dogs of the Air. Border-town. Stranded. Special Agent. Dr Socrates. Moonlight on the Prairie. A Village Tale. The Murder Man. 1936: The Country Doctor. Exclusive Story. Trail of the Lonesome Pine. I Married a Doctor. Sons o' Guns. The Last of the Mohicans. Mary of Scotland. Draegerman Courage (GB: The Cave-In). The Charge of the Light Brigade. God's Country and the Woman. Trailin' West (GB: On Secret Service). Black Legion. 1937: The Life of Emile Zola. Souls at Sea. Confession. Love is on the Air (GB: The Radio Murder Mystery). The Barrier. Mountain Justice. Bad Man of Brimstone. 1938: Penitentiary. Forbidden Valley. Marie Antoinette. The Buccaneer. The Texans. Charlie Chan in Honolulu. Breaking the Ice. Shadows over Shanghai. 1939: Colorado Sunset. Allegheny Uprising (GB: The First Rebel). Union Pacific. Bad Lands. Conspiracy. The Cisco Kid and the Lady. Man of Conquest. Heritage of the Desert. Return of the Cisco Kid. 1940: Northwest Passage. Go West/The Marx Brothers Go West. Captain Caution. The Man from Dakota (GB: Arouse and Beware). Fugitive from a Prison Camp. Laddie. 1941: Riders of the Purple Sage. Parachute Battalion. They Met in Argentina. 1942: The Girl from Alaska. American Empire (GB: My Son Alone). Fall In. 1943: They Came to Blow Up America. Bomber's Moon. Johnny Come Lately (GB: Johnny

Vagabond). A Stranger in Town. 1944: Enemy of Women. The Adventures of Mark Twain. 1945: Grissly's Millions. They Were Expendable. Road to Utopia. The Great John L (GB: A Man Called Sullivan). Dakota. Strangler of the Swamp. San Antonio. Wan-derer of the Wasteland. 1946: Dangerous Millions. Magnificent Doll. Just Before Dawn. The Time of Their Lives. Sunset Pass. 1947: Road to Rio. The Sea of Grass. The Fabulous Texan. 1948: I Love Trouble. Relentless. Bad Men of Tombstone. Joan of Arc. 1949: Canadian Pacific. Song of India. The Lone Wolf and His Lady. Riders of the Range. The Doolins of Oklahoma (GB: The Great Man-hunt). The Kid from Texas (GB: Texas Kid—Outlaw). 1950: An American Guerilla in the Philippines (GB: I Shall Return). The Baron of Arizona. Davy Crockett—Indian Scout. Double Crossbones. 1951: Pride of Maryland. Flight to Mars. Darling, How Could You? (GB: Rendezvous). Distant Drums. 1952: Denver and Rio Grande. Son of Ali Baba. 1953: Cow Country. 1955: Tall Man Riding.

**BASS, Alfie** 1920- *1987*

Chunky, diminutive Londoner with juicy lips and distinctively squashed features beneath a mop of black hair. Often seen in cockney and/or Jewish 'cloth cap' roles, he lurked under a cloak of anonymity until his co-starring part as one of *The Lavender Hill Mob* brought his name to the public's attention. Later he tackled weightier roles, although almost always in the same vein as that in which he had started. Less often seen in films after 1958, following his creation of the malingering soldier 'Bootsie' who ap-peared in two long-running TV series, *The Army Game* and *Bootsie and Snudge*.

1943: The Bells Go Down. 1945: Johnny Frenchman. Perfect Strangers (US: Vacation from Marriage). Brief Encounter. 1947: Holiday Camp. It Always Rains on Sunday. 1948: Vice Versa. The Monkey's Paw. *They Gave Him the Works. Man on the Run. 1949: The Hasty Heart. Boys in Brown. 1950: Stage Fright. Pool of London. 1951: Talk of a Million (US: You Can't Beat the Irish). The Galloping Major. The Lavender Hill Mob. High Treason. Brandy for the Parson. 1952: Treasure Hunt. Derby Day (US: Four Against

Fate). The Planter's Wife (US: Outpost in Malaya). Made in Heaven. 1953: Top of the Form. The Square Ring. 1954: To Dorothy a Son (US: Cash on Delivery). The Angel Who Pawned Her Harp. The Passing Stranger. Time is My Enemy. Make Me an Offer. Svengali. 1955: The Night My Number Came Up. Murder by Proxy. A Kid for Two Farthings. *The Bespoke Overcoat. King's Rhapsody. 1956: Jumping for Joy. Tiger in the Smoke. A Child in the House. Behind the Headlines. A Touch of the Sun. Sailor Beware! (US: Panic in the Parlor). No Road Back. 1957: Carry On Admiral (US: The Ship Was Loaded). Hell Drivers. 1958: A Tale of Two Cities. I Was Monty's Double (US: Monty's Double). I Only Arsked! 1960: The Million-airess. 1965: Help! 1966: Doctor in Clover. Alfie. The Sandwich Man. A Funny Thing Happened on the Way to the Forum. 1967: Dance of the Vampires (US: The Fearless Vampire Killers). A Challenge for Robin Hood. Up the Junction. Bindle (One of Them Days). 1968: The Fixer. 1971: The Magnificent Seven Deadly Sins. 1976: The Chiffy Kids (series). 1977: Come Play With Me. 1978: Revenge of the Pink Panther. 1979: Moon-raker. 1980: High Rise Donkey.

**BASSERMAN, Albert** 1867-1952

Prominent on the German stage for many years, Basserman became a big star in sombre Teutonic dramas of the early silent days. His appearances became less regular after the mid-twenties, and he ultimately fled the Nazi regime and ended up in Hollywood, where he crammed a large number of films into a few years, mostly as heavy-set avuncular types. Died from a heart attack. Basserman spelt with two 'n's in German films. Nominated for an Oscar in *Foreign Correspondent*.

1912: Der Andere. 1913: Der König. Der letzte Tag. 1914: Das Erteil des Arztes. 1917: Der eiserne Wille. Du sollst keine anderen Götte haben. Herr und Diener. 1918: Die Brüder von Zaarden. Dr Schotte. Lorenzo Burghardt. Vater und Sohn. 1919: Das Werk seines Lebens. Der letzte Zeuge. Die Duplizität der Ereignisse. Eine schwache Stunde. Puppen des Todes. 1920: Die Sohne des Grafen Dossy. Die Stimme. Masken. 1921: Das Weib des Pharao (US: Loves of Pharaoh). Die kleine Dagmar.

*Die Nächte des Cornelis Brouwer. 1922:
Christopher Columbus. Frauenopfer, Lucrezia
Borgia. Erdgeist. 1924: Helena. 1925: Briefe,
die ihn nicht erreichten. Der Herr Generaldirek-
tor. 1926: Wenn des Herz der Jugend spricht,
1929: Fräulein Else. Napoleon auf St Helena.
1930: Alraune. Dreyfus. 1931: Gefahren der
Liebe. Kadetten. 1914: Voruntersuchung. Zum
goldenen Anker. 1933: Ein gewisser Herr
Gran. 1938: Letzte Liebe. 1939: La Famille
Lefrançais (US: Heroes of the Marne). 1940:
Dr Ehrlich's Magic Bullet. Foreign Correspon-
dent. A Dispatch from Reuter's (GB: This Man
Reuter). Moon Over Burma. Knute Rockne,
All American (GB: A Modern Hero). Escape.
1941: The Shanghai Gesture. A Woman's
Face. New Wine. (GB: The Great Awaken-
ing). 1942: The Moon and Sixpence. Invisible
Agent. Once Upon a Honeymoon. Fly By Night.
Reunion in France (GB: Mademoiselle
France). 1943: Desperate Journey. Good Luck
Mr Yates. Passport to Heaven. 1944:
Madame Curie. Since You Went Away.
1945: Rhapsody in Blue. 1946: Strange
Holiday. The Searching Wind. 1947: The
Private Affairs of Bel Ami. Escape Me Never.
1948: The Red Shoes.*

*Racket Man. Tahiti Nights. Tonight and Every
Night. 1945: Saratoga Trunk. San Antonio.
Out of This World. 1946: Claudia and David.
Cluny Brown. The Diary of a Chambermaid.
Whistle Stop. The Time, the Place and the Girl.
1947: The Brasher Doubloon (GB: The High
Window). Love and Learn. Desire Me. The
Secret Life of Walter Mitty. 1948: Texas,
Brooklyn and Heaven (GB: The Girl from
Texas). Winter Meeting. The Inside Story.
River Lady. My Dear Secretary. Portrait of
Jennie (GB: Jennie). I Remember Mama. A
Letter to Three Wives. 1949: The Judge Steps
Out. The Girl from Jones Beach. On the Town.
1950: Belle of Old Mexico. County Fair. The
Second Woman (GB: Ellen). 1951: Lullaby
of Broadway. The Tall Target. Havana Rose.
The Whistle at Eaton Falls (GB: Richer Than
the Earth). Father Takes the Air. 1952: The
San Francisco Story. Les Misérables. 1953:
Paris Model. Main Street to Broadway.*

**BEATTY, Ned** 1937-
Round-faced, weighty American actor with
brown, rumpled hair, usually in sweaty
roles: can play comic, dramatic, sympathetic or silly. Gained wide-ranging theatrical
experience (he played Big Daddy in a
production of *Cat on a Hot Tin Roof* at 21)
before heading for Hollywood and landing a
good variety of parts following his debut in
*Deliverance.* Oscar Nominee for *Network.*

*1972: Deliverance. The Life and Times of
Judge Roy Bean. Footsteps (TV). 1973: The
Marcus-Nelson Murders (TV). Dying Room
Only (TV). The Last American Hero. White
Lightning. The Thief Who Came to Dinner.
1974: The Execution of Private Slovik (TV).
1975: W W and the Dixie Dancekings.
Nashville. Attack on Terror: The FBI versus
the Ku Klux Klan (TV). The Deadly Tower
(TV). 1976: Mikey and Nicky. The Big Bus.
All the President's Men. Network. Silver
Streak. 1977: Exorcist II: The Heretic.
Remember Those Poker-Playing Monkeys?
Gray Lady Down. The Great Georgia Bank
Hoax/Shenanigans. Tail Gunner Joe (TV).
Lucan (TV). 1978: A Question of Love (TV).
Superman. 1979: Promises in the Dark. 1941.
Wise Blood. Alambrista! The American Suc-
cess Company (later $uccess). Friendly Fire
(TV). 1980: Hopscotch. Superman II. Guy-
ana Tragedy: The Story of Jim Jones (TV).
All God's Children (TV). 1981: The Incred-
ible Shrinking Woman. Splendor in the Grass
(TV). 1982: The Toy. The Ballad of Gregorio
Cortez. 1983: Kentucky Woman (TV).
Stroker Ace. Touched. Denmark Vesey (TV).
1984: The Last Days of Pompeii (TV). 1985:
Some Sunny Day. Trouble at the Royal
Rose/Trouble with Spys. Alfred Hitchcock
Presents (TV).*

**BATES, Florence**
**(F. Rabe) 1888-1954**
Formidable was about the only word for
this dominant, galleon-shaped American
actress much in demand in the 1940s: her
matrons were meddlesome and her matriarchs monstrous. She was once a lawyer
(how the opposition must have suffered),
but her Edythe Van Hopper in Alfred
Hitchcock's *Rebecca* set her galloping
through a gallery of gorgons and gargoyles.
Died from a heart attack.

*1937: The Man in Blue. 1940: Rebecca.
Calling All Husbands. Son of Monte Cristo.
Hudson's Bay. Kitty Foyle. 1941: Road Show.
Love Crazy. The Chocolate Soldier. Strange
Alibi. 1942: The Devil and Miss Jones. The
Tuttles of Tahiti. My Heart Belongs to Daddy.
The Moon and Sixpence. We Were Dancing.
They Got Me Covered. Mexican Spitfire at
Sea. 1943: Slightly Dangerous. His Butler's
Sister. Mister Big. Heaven Can Wait. Mr
Lucky. 1944: The Mask of Dimitrios. Kismet.
Since You Went Away. Belle of the Yukon. The*

**BAYLDON, Geoffrey** 1924-
Tall, fair-haired, scarecrow-like British
actor whose name became familiar to the
public only after his starring role in the
television series *Catweazle* when he was well
into his forties. Extensive stage work,
especially in Shakespearian roles, preceded
his entry into feature-film roles in 1958,
after which he wandered skeletally through
some 50 movies—never better cast than as
one of the emaciated prisoners-of-war in
*King Rat.*

*1953: *The Stranger Left No Card. 1958: A
Night to Remember. Dracula (US: The Horror
of Dracula). The Two-Headed Spy. 1959:
Whirlpool. Idle on Parade (US: Idol on
Parade). The Rough and the Smooth (US:
Portrait of a Sinner). Libel. 1960: The Day
They Robbed the Bank of England. Cone of
Silence (US: Trouble in the Sky). Greyfriars
Bobby. 1961: Bomb in the High Street. The
Webster Boy. 1962: The Prince and the
Pauper. The Amorous Prawn. Jigsaw. 55 Days
at Peking. 1964: Becket. A Jolly Bad Fellow.
1965: King Rat. Dead Man's Chest. Life at the
Top. Where the Spies Are. Sky West and
Crooked (US: Gypsy Girl). 1966: To Sir with
Love. 1967: Assignment K. Two a Penny.
Casino Royale. 1968: A Dandy in Aspic.*

*Inspector Clouseau. The Bush Baby. Otley.
1969: Frankenstein Must Be Destroyed.
1970: The Raging Moon (US: Long Ago
Tomorrow). Scrooge. Say Hello to Yesterday.
The House That Dripped Blood. 1971: The
Magnificent Seven Deadly Sins. 1972: Asylum. Au Pair Girls. Tales from the Crypt.
1973: Gawain and the Green Knight. Steptoe
and Son Ride Again. 1976: The Slipper and
the Rose. The Pink Panther Strikes Again.
1979: Porridge. 1983: Bullshot.*

**BEAVERS, Louise** 1898-1962

Squarely-built, benign black American actress whose cooks, housekeepers and lady's maids proved a great comfort to movie heroines in times of trouble. Once a member of an all-girl minstrel show, she came to Hollywood in 1924 as a dresser to the stars, but bit parts in silent films soon led to regular featured roles in talkies. Best remembered as Claudette Colbert's servant/confidante in *Imitation of Life* (1934), this most perfect of Hollywood housekeepers in real life hated cooking. Died from heart failure after a long struggle against diabetes.

*1923: Gold Diggers. 1927: Uncle Tom's Cabin. 1929: Barnum Was Right. The Glad Rag Doll. Coquette. Nix on Dames. Wall Street. Gold Diggers of Broadway. 1930: Manslaughter. Our Blushing Brides. Second Choice. She Couldn't Say No. Wide Open. Back Pay. Recaptured Love. Safety in Numbers. 1931: Party Husbands. Ladies of the Big House. Millie. Heaven on Earth. Annabelle's Affairs. Up for Murder. Don't Bet on Women. Girls About Town. Sundown Trail. Good Sport. Six Cylinder Love. Reckless Living. 1932: The Expert. *Old Man Minick. *You're Telling Me. Freaks. Night World. It's Tough to be Famous. Midnight Lady (GB: Dream Mother). Young America (GB: We Humans). Street of Women. Wild Girl (GB: Salomy Jane). What Price Hollywood? Unashamed. Divorce in the Family. The Strange Love of Molly Louvain. Hell's Highway. Pick Up. Too Busy to Work. 1933: 42nd Street. She Done Him Wrong. Girl Missing. What Price Innocence? A Shriek in the Night. Hold Your Man. Her Bodyguard. The Big Cage. Bombshell (GB: Blonde Bombshell). Notorious But Nice. Her Splendid Folly. In the Money. 1934: Glamour. I Believed in You. Palooka (GB: The Great Schnozzle). Bedside. I've Got Your Number. The Cheaters. Hat, Coat and Glove. The Merry Frinks (GB: The Happy Family). Imitation of Life. West of the Pecos. The Merry Wives of Reno. A Modern Hero. Registered Nurse. 1935: Dr Monica. Annapolis Farewell (GB: Gentlemen of the Navy). 1936: General Spanky. Bullets or Ballots. Wives Never Know. Rainbow on the River. The Gorgeous Hussy. 1937: Wings over Honolulu. Make Way for Tomorrow. Love in a Bungalow. The Last Gangster. 1938: Life Goes On. Scandal Street. Brother Rat. The Headleys at Home (GB: Among Those Present). Peck's Bad Boy with the Circus. Reckless Living (remake). 1939: Made for Each Other. The Lady's from Kentucky. Reform School. 1940: Women without Names. Parole Fixer. I Want a Divorce. No Time for Comedy. 1941: Virginia. Belle Starr. Sign of the Wolf. Shadow of the Thin Man. The Vanishing Virginian. Kisses for Breakfast. 1942: Reap the Wild Wind. Holiday Inn. The Big Street. Seven Sweethearts. Tennessee Johnson (GB: The Man on America's Conscience). Young America (remake). 1943: Good Morning, Judge! All by Myself. DuBarry Was a Lady. Top Man. Jack London. There's Something About a Soldier. 1944: Follow the Boys. Dixie Jamboree. Barbary Coast Gent. South of Dixie. 1945: Delightfully Dangerous. 1946: Lover Come Back. Young Widow. 1947: Banjo. 1948: Good Sam. Mr Blandings Builds His Dream House. For the Love of Mary. 1949: Tell It to the Judge. 1950: Girls' School (GB: Dangerous Inheritance). My Blue Heaven. The Jackie Robinson Story. 1951: Colorado Sundown. 1952: I Dream of Jeanie. Never Wave at a WAC (GB: Army Capers). 1956: Goodbye, My Lady. You Can't Run Away from It. Teenage Rebel. 1957: The Hostess With the Mostest (TV). Tammy and the Bachelor (GB: Tammy). 1958: The Goddess. 1960: The Facts of Life. All the Fine Young Cannibals.*

**BECKWITH, Reginald** 1908-1965

Bumbling, curly-haired, chubby British actor of the 'Oh-dear-what's-to-become-of-us' school. He started as a successful playwright with acting as the second string to his bow; but, after 1948, these roles began to be reversed (although he continued to write—*Boys in Brown* was one of his earliest hit plays) and he was to be found wringing his hands in the background of numerous British comedies. He could also tackle comic businessmen and straight dramatic roles with equal conviction. His writing talents also led him to try film and theatre criticism and from 1941 to 1945 he was a war correspondent for the BBC.

*1940: Freedom Radio (US: A Voice in the Night). 1946: This Man is Mine. 1948: My Brother's Keeper. Scott of the Antarctic. 1949: Miss Pilgrim's Progress. 1950: The Body Said No! Mr Drake's Duck. 1951: Circle of Danger. Another Man's Poison. Brandy for the Parson. 1952: Whispering Smith Hits London (US: Whispering Smith versus Scotland Yard). Penny Princess. You're Only Young Twice! 1953: Genevieve. The Titfield Thunderbolt. Innocents in Paris. Don't Blame the Stork! The Million Pound Note (US: Man with a Million). 1954: Fast and Loose. The Runaway Bus. Lease of Life. Dance Little Lady. Aunt Clara. Men of Sherwood Forest. 1955: The Lyons in Paris. Break in the Circle. They Can't Hang Me! A Yank in Ermine. Dust and Gold. Charley Moon. 1956: The March Hare. It's a Wonderful World. A Touch of the Sun. Jumping for Joy. 1957: Carry on Admiral (US: The Ship Was Loaded). These Dangerous Years (US: Dangerous Youth). Lucky Jim. Night of the Demon (US: Curse of the Demon). Light Fingers. 1958: Up the Creek. Law and Disorder. Next to No Time! Rockets Galore (US: Mad Little Island). Further Up the Creek. The Captain's Table. 1959: The 39 Steps. The Horse's Mouth. The Ugly Duckling. Upstairs and Downstairs. The Navy Lark. Friends and Neighbours. Desert Mice. Expresso Bongo. 1960: Bottoms Up! Dentist in the Chair. Doctor in Love. There Was a Crooked Man. The Night We Got the Bird. The Girl on the Boat. 1961: Five Golden Hours. Double Bunk. Dentist on the Job (US: Get on with It!) The Day the Earth Caught Fire. 1962: Night of the Eagle (US: Burn, Witch, Burn). Hair of the Dog. The Prince and the Pauper. The Password is Courage. *The King's Breakfast. Lancelot and Guinevere. 1963: Just for Fun. The VIPs. Doctor in Distress. Never Put It in Writing. 1964: The Yellow Rolls Royce. A Shot in the Dark. Gonks Go Beat. 1965: The Amorous Adventures of Moll Flanders. Thunderball. The Secret of My Success. The Big Job. How to Undress in Public Without Undue Embarrassment. Where the Spies Are. Mister Moses.*

**BEDDOE, Don** 1888-1979

Apple-cheeked, auburn-haired American actor with small, twinkling blue eyes, seen as impish confederates, excitable reporters or defective detectives. Although he was 50 when he came to Hollywood from Broadway, his cherubic, butter-innocent looks allowed him a good variety of middle-range roles before he moved into old codgers, and, in one delightful instance, a leprechaun trapped in a bottle. Had the lead in 1961's **Saintly Sinners**. Married for the first time at the age of 86, Beddoe was obviously a believer that life begins any time you choose.

*1938: There's That Woman Again (GB: What a Woman). 1939: The Lone Wolf Spy Hunt (GB: The Lone Wolf's Daughter). Good Girls Go to Paris. Flying G-Men (serial). Outside These Walls. Mandrake the Magician (serial). Romance of the Redwoods. Golden Boy. Missing Daughters. Taming of the West. The*

Man They Could Not Hang. Blondie Meets the Boss. Those High, Gray Walls (GB: The Gates of Alcatraz). Beware Spooks! My Son is Guilty (GB: Crime's End). The Amazing Mr Williams. *Three Sappy People. Konga, the Wild Stallion (GB: Konga). 1940: The Doctor Takes a Wife. Texas Stagecoach (GB: Two Roads). Beyond the Sacramento (GB: Power of Justice). The Lone Wolf Strikes. Scandal Sheet. Charlie Chan's Murder Cruise. Blondie on a Budget. Men Without Souls. Island of Doomed Men. The Man from Tumbleweeds. Manhattan Heartbeat. Girls of the Road. West of Abilene. Before I Hang. Military Academy. Beyond the Sacramento. The Secret Seven. Glamour for Sale. 1941: The Lone Wolf Keeps a Date. The Face Behind the Mask. Texas. Unholy Partners. Sing for Your Supper. Under Age. The Big Boss. The Blonde from Singapore. Sweetheart of the Campus (GB: Broadway Ahead). The Lone Wolf Takes a Chance. Two Latins from Manhattan. She Knew All the Answers. This Thing Called Love (GB: Married But Single). Submarine Zone. Harvard, Here I Come (GB: Here I Come). 1942: Meet the Stewarts. Shut My Big Mouth. The Talk of the Town. Tales of Manhattan. Sabotage Squad. Honolulu Lu. Lucky Legs. Junior Army. Not a Ladies' Man. The Boogie Man Will Get You. Smith of Minnesota. 1943: Power of the Press. 1944: Winged Victory. 1945: Getting Gertie's Garter. Midnight Manhunt. 1946: Behind Green Lights. O.S.S. The Well-Groomed Bride. The Notorious Lone Wolf. The Best Years of Our Lives. California. 1947: Buck Privates Come Home (GB: Rookies Come Home). Blaze of Noon. The Farmer's Daughter. Welcome Stranger. They Won't Believe Me. The Bachelor and the Bobby-Soxer (GB: Bachelor Knight). Calcutta. 1948: If You Knew Susie. Another Part of the Forest. An Act of Murder. Black Bart (GB: Black Bart—Highwayman). 1949: Bride of Vengeance. Flame of Youth. Hideout. The Lady Gambles. Once More, My Darling. Easy Living. Dancing in the Dark. Dear Wife. Gun Crazy. Woman in Hiding. The Crime Doctor's Diary. 1950: The Great Rupert. Caged. Young Daniel Boone. Tarnished. Beyond the Purple Hills. Cyrano de Bergerac. Emergency Wedding (GB: Jealousy). The Company She Keeps. Gasoline Alley. The Enforcer (GB: Murder Inc). 1951: As Young As You Feel. The Racket. Starlift. Three Guys Named Mike. Francis Goes to the Races. Million Dollar Pursuit. Rodeo King and the Senorita. Belle le Grand. Corky of Gasoline Alley (GB: Corky). Man in the Saddle (GB: The Outcast). The Unknown Man. The Narrow Margin. Hoodlum Empire. Scandal Sheet (GB: The Dark Page). 1952: The Big Sky. Room for One More. Washington Story (GB: Target for Scandal). Carrie. Don't Bother to Knock. The Iron Mistress. Blue Canadian Rockies. Stop, You're Killing Me! The Clown. 1953: The System. Cow Country. 1954: Loophole. A Star is Born. River of No Return. The Steel Cage. Jubilee Trail. 1955: Wyoming Renegades. Tarzan's Hidden Jungle. The Night of the Hunter. 1956: Behind the

High Wall. The Rawhide Years. 1957: Shootout at Medicine Bend. 1958: Toughest Gun in Tombstone. Bullwhip! 1959: Warlock. Pillow Talk. 1960: The Wizard of Baghdad. 1961: The Boy Who Caught a Crook. Jack the Giant Killer. Saintly Sinners. 1962: Papa's Delicate Condition. 1965: A Very Special Favor. 1966: Texas Across the River. 1968: The Impossible Years. 1969: Generation (GB: A Time for Giving). 1970: How Do I Love Thee?

## BEERY, Noah Jnr 1913- 1994

Stocky, dark-haired American supporting actor with small, round face, slow smile and easy-going air, son of Noah and nephew of Wallace. He never quite rose to the ranks of co-star, but pursued his career tenaciously, mostly in westerns as sidekicks, good or bad, at first headstrong, later philosophical. In later years, a welcome part of television's *The Rockford Files*, playing James Garner's father. Married to Maxine, daughter of cowboy star Buck Jones, from 1940 to 1966 (first of two).

1920: The Mark of Zorro. 1922: Penrod. 1923: Penrod and Sam. 1929: Father and Son. 1932: Heroes of the West (serial). The Jungle Mystery (serial). 1933: The Three Mesquiteers (serial). Fighting With Kit Carson (serial). Rustlers' Roundup. 1934: The Trail Beyond. Tailspin Tommy (serial). Tailspin Tommy in the Great Air Mystery (serial). 1935: Call of the Savage (serial). Stormy. Five Bad Men. Devil's Canyon. 1936: Parole. Ace Drummond (serial). 1937: The Road Back. Some Blondes Are Dangerous. The Mighty Treve. 1938: Girls' School. Trouble at Midnight. Outside the Law. Forbidden Valley. 1939: Only Angels Have Wings. Flight at Midnight. Of Mice and Men. *Glove Slingers. Parents on Trial. Bad Lands. 1940: Twenty-Mule Team. A Little Bit of Heaven. The Carson City Kid. The Light of Western Stars. Passport to Alcatraz. 1941: Sergeant York. Tanks a Million. Riders of Death Valley (serial). All-American Co-Ed. Two in a Taxi. 1942: Overland Mail (serial). Dudes Are Pretty People. 'Neath Brooklyn Bridge. Hay Foot. 1943: Calaboose. What a Woman! (GB: The Beautiful Cheat). Prairie Chickens. Corvette K-225 (GB: The Nelson Touch). Pardon My Gun. Gung Ho! We've Never Been Licked (GB: Texas to Tokyo). Top Man. Frontier Badmen. 1944: See My Lawyer. Follow the Boys. Week-end Pass. Allergic to Love. Hi, Beautiful! (GB: Pass to Romance). 1945: Under Western Skies. Her Lucky Night. The Daltons Ride Again. The Beautiful Cheat (GB: What a Woman! Also 1943 films of reverse titles!). The Crimson Canary. 1946: The Cat Creeps. 1948: Red River. Indian Agent. 1949: The Doolins of Oklahoma (GB: The Great Manhunt). 1950: Two Flags West. Davy Crockett—Indian Scout (GB: Indian Scout). Rocketship X-M. The Savage Horde. 1951: The Last Outpost. The Texas Rangers. 1952: The Story of Will Rogers. Wagons West. The Cimarron Kid. 1953: Wings of the Hawk.

War Arrow. Tropic Zone. 1954: The Black Dakotas. Yellow Tomahawk. 1955: White Feather. 1956: Jubal. The Fastest Gun Alive. 1957: Decision at Sundown. 1958: Escort West. 1960: Guns of the Timberland. Inherit the Wind. 1964: The Seven Faces of Dr Lao. 1965: Incident at Phantom Hill. 1966: Hondo and the Apaches. 1969: Heaven with a Gun. Little Fauss and Big Halsy. The Cockeyed Cowboys of Calico County (GB: TV as A Woman for Charlie). 1973: The Alpha Caper (TV. GB: cinemas as Inside Job). The Petty Story/Smash-Up Alley (TV. GB: cinemas). Walking Tall. 1974: The Spikes Gang. Savages (TV). 1976: Part Two, Walking Tall (GB: Legend of the Lawman). 1977: Francis Gary Powers—the True Story of the U-2 Incident (TV). 1980: The Great American Traffic Jam (TV). 1981: The Capture of Grizzly Adams (TV). 1982: The Best Little Whorehouse in Texas. 1983: Waltz Across Texas.

## BEERY, Noah Snr 1883-1946

Bluff and burly, often moustachioed American actor of ruddy complexion, a rough, tough, swarthy villain of strong personality who was at his best in silent days—although his crackling tones adapted well to sound. Killed by a heart attack at exactly the same age as his slightly more prestigious brother Wallace, with whom he had worked as a chorus boy in musicals at the turn of the century.

1917: The Hostage. The Spirit of '76. Sacrifice. The Mormon Maid. 1918: Hidden Pearls. The White Man's Law. His Robe of Honor. Less Than Kin. Believe Me, Xanthippe. The Whispering Chorus. The Squaw Man. The Source. 1919: In Mizzoura. The Woman Next Door. The Red Lantern. The Valley of the Giants. Louisiana. 1920: The Fighting Shepherdess. Go Get It. The Mark of Zorro. Dinty. Everywoman. The Sea Wolf. 1921: Bob Hampton of Placer. The Scoffer. Beach of Dreams. Bits of Life. Lotus Blossom. Call of the North. 1922: Tillie. Belle of Alaska. Wild Honey. Penrod. Good Men and True. I Am the Law. The Lying Truth. Crossroads of New York. The Heart Specialist. Flesh and Blood. The Power of Love. Youth to Youth. Omar the Tentmaker. Ebb Tide. 1923: Stormswept. The

ABOVE Don **Beddoe** (with gun) seems to have the 'goods' on Eric Blore and Gerald Mohr (both *qv*) as disguised detectives, in *The Notorious Lone Wolf* (1946)

BELOW Bad guys Noah **Beery** Jr (right) and Gary Merrill step out for a showdown in the 1954 Western, *The Black Dakotas*

*Spider and the Rose. Dangerous Trails. Soul of the Beast. Quicksands. Main Street, Wandering Daughters. The Spoilers. Forbidden Lover. Tipped Off. When Law Comes to Hades. Hollywood. To the Last Man. The Destroying Angel. His Last Race. Stephen Steps Out. The Call of the Canyon.* 1924: *The Heritage of the Desert. The Fighting Coward. Wanderer of the Wasteland. Lily of the Dust. Female. Welcome, Stranger. North of 36.* 1925: *East of Suez. The Thundering Herd. The Light of Western Stars. The Spaniard* (GB: *Spanish Lore). Contraband. Old Shoes. Wild Horse Mesa. Lord Jim. The Coming of Amos. The Vanishing American.* 1926: *The Enchanted Hill. The Crown of Lies. Padlocked. Beau Geste. Paradise.* 1927: *The Rough Riders* (GB: *The Trumpet Calls). The Love Mart. Evening Clothes. The Dove.* 1928: *Noah's Ark. Beau Sabreur. Two Lovers. Hell Ship Bronson.* 1929: *Passion Song. Linda. Careers. The Isle of Lost Ships. The Four Feathers. Love in the Desert. The Godless Girl. The Show of Shows. Glorifying the American Girl. Two O'Clock in the Morning. False Feathers.* 1930: *Murder Will Out. Song of the Flame. The Way of All Men* (GB: *Sin Flood). Golden Dawn. Big Boy. Under a Texas Moon. Isle of Escape. Feet First. The Love Trader. Mammy. Renegades. Tol'able David. Oh Sailor, Behave. Bright Lights. A Soldier's Plaything* (GB: *A Soldier's Pay).* 1931: *The Millionaire. Honeymoon Lane. In Line of Duty. Homicide Squad* (GB: *The Lost Men). Shanghaied Love. Riders of the Purple Sage.* 1932: *The Drifter. The Kid from Spain. Out of Singapore. Stranger in Town. The Stoker. No Living Witness. The Big Stampede. Cornered. The Devil Horse* (serial). 1933: *Fighting With Kit Carson* (serial). *The Flaming Signal. Sunset Pass. To the Last Man. She Done Him Wrong. Laughing at Life. The Woman I Stole. Man of the Forest. Easy Millions. The Thundering Herd* (remake). 1934: *David Harum. Kentucky Kernels* (GB: *Triple Trouble). Madame Spy. Mystery Liner. Cock-eyed Cavaliers. Happy Landing. The Trail Beyond. Caravan.* 1935: *Sweet Adeline. King of the Damned.* 1936: *The Crimson Circle. Live Again. Someone at the Door. The Avenging Hand. The Marriage of Corbal* (US: *The Prisoner of Corbal). Strangers on a Honeymoon.* 1937: *Our Fighting Navy* (US: *Torpedoed!). The Frog. Glamorous Night. Zorro Rides Again* (serial). 1938: *Bad Man of Brimstone. The Girl of the Golden West. Panamint's Best Man.* 1939: *Mexicali Rose. Mutiny on the Blackhawk.* 1940: *Pioneers of the West. Grandpa Goes to Town. Adventures of Red Ryder* (serial). *A Little Bit of Heaven. The Tulsa Kid.* 1941: *A Missouri Outlaw.* 1942: *Overland Mail* (serial). *The Devil's Trail. Outlaws of Pine Ridge. The Isle of Missing Men. Tennessee Johnson* (GB: *The Man on America's Conscience). Pardon My Gun.* 1943: *Mr Muggs Steps Out. The Clancy Street Boys. Carson City Cyclone. Salute to the Marines.* 1944: *Block Busters. The Million Dollar Kid. Gentle Annie. Barbary Coast Gent.* 1945: *This Man's Navy. Sing Me a Song of Texas* (GB: *Fortune Hunter).*

**BEGLEY, Ed** 1901-1970
Blustering, barrel-like, aggressive American character star who had few peers in the portrayal of tyranny in all its many forms. His best performance was probably in *Patterns* (1956), although he won his Academy Award six years later in *Sweet Bird of Youth.* Died of a heart attack.

1947: *Big Town. The Web. Boomerang.* 1948: *Deep Waters. Sitting Pretty. The Street With No Name.* 1949: *Sorry Wrong Number. Tulsa. It Happens Every Spring. The Great Gatsby.* 1950: *Backfire. Stars in My Crown. Wyoming Mail. Convicted. Saddle Tramp. Dark City. You're in the Navy Now* (originally: *USS Teakettle).* 1951: *The Lady from Texas. On Dangerous Ground.* 1952: *Deadline, USA* (GB: *Deadline). Boots Malone. The Turning Point. What Price Glory? Lone Star.* 1956: *Patterns* (GB: *Patterns of Power).* 1957: *Twelve Angry Men.* 1959: *Odds Against Tomorrow.* 1961: *The Green Helmet.* 1962: *Sweet Bird of Youth.* 1964: *The Unsinkable Molly Brown.* 1966: *The Oscar.* 1967: *Warning Shot. Billion Dollar Brain. Firecreek.* 1968: *A Time to Sing. Hang 'Em High.* 1969: *The Monitors. Wild in the Streets. The Violent Enemy. The Dunwich Horror.* 1970: *The Silent Gun* (TV). *Road to Salina.*

**BELLAVER, Harry** 1905- 1993
Chubby-faced, concerned-looking, 'average Joe' American actor, often seen polishing the bar, but sometimes as shabby policeman, chatty cab-driver or threadbare

minion. Hollywood could have kept him a busy man, but he preferred theatre, drama teaching and television work. In the last-named field, he spent five years with the popular series *Naked City* in the late 1950s and early 1960s.

1939: *Another Thin Man.* 1945: *The House on 92nd Street.* 1950: *Side Street. No Way Out. Stage to Tucson* (GB: *Lost Stage Valley). Perfect Strangers* (GB: *Too Dangerous to Love).* 1951: *The Lemon Drop Kid. The Tanks Are Coming.* 1952: *Something to Live For.* 1953: *From Here to Eternity. The Great Diamond Robbery. Miss Sadie Thompson.* 1955: *Love Me or Leave Me.* 1956: *The Birds and the Bees. Serenade.* 1957: *Slaughter on 10th Avenue. The Brothers Rico.* 1958: *The Old Man and the Sea.* 1960: *A Death of Princes* (TV. GB: *cinemas).* 1964: *One Potato, Two Potato.* 1966: *A Fine Madness.* 1968: *Madigan.* 1972: *The Hot Rock* (GB: *How to Steal a Diamond in Four Uneasy Lessons).* 1976: *God Told Me To* (GB: *Demon).* 1978: *Blue Collar. Murder in Music City* (TV). 1979: *Hero at Large.*

**BENCHLEY, Robert** 1889-1945
One of the great Hollywood wits of the 1920s, 1930s and 1940s, dark-haired, smooth-faced Benchley possessed impeccable comic timing, and his appearances as a supporting actor in feature films, often in the character of a well-meaning busybody, were almost always occasions to savour. He also instigated and presented a brilliant series of comedy shorts, most of which began *How to* ..... One of these bumbling diatribes, *How to Sleep* (1935), won an Oscar. Died from a cerebral haemorrhage.

1928: *\*The Treasurer's Report. \*The Sex Life of the Polyp. \*The Spellbinder.* 1929: *\*Furnace Trouble. \*Lesson Number One. \*Stewed, Fried and Boiled.* 1933: *Headline Shooter* (GB: *Evidence in Camera). Rafter Romance. \*Your Technocracy and Mine. Dancing Lady.* 1934: *The Social Register.* 1935: *China Seas. \*How to Sleep. \*How to Break 90 at Croquet.* 1936: *\*How to Behave. \*How to Train a Dog. \*How to Vote. \*How to be a Detective. Piccadilly Jim.* 1937: *Live, Love and Learn. \*The Romance of Digestion. Broadway Melody of 1938. \*How to Start the Day. \*A Night at* the Movies. 1938: *Music Made Simple. *How to Figure Income Tax. *An Evening Alone. *The Courtship of the Newt. *Opening Day. *Mental Poise. *An Hour for Lunch. *How to Raise a Baby. *How to Read. *How to Watch Football. *How to Sub-Let. 1939: *How to Eat. *Dark Magic. *Home Early. *The Day of Rest. *See Your Doctor. 1940: *Home Movies. *That Inferior Feeling. *The Trouble with Husbands. Foreign Correspondent. Hired Wife. 1941: Bedtime Story. Nice Girl? The Reluctant Dragon. Three Girls about Town. You'll Never Get Rich. *How to Take a Vacation. *Waiting for Baby. *Crime Control. *The Forgotten Man. 1942: *Nothing But Nerves. *The Witness. *Keeping in Shape. *The Man's Angle. I Married a Witch. The Major and the Minor. Take a Letter, Darling (GB: The Green-Eyed Woman). 1943: Flesh and Fantasy. The Sky's the Limit. Song of Russia. Young and Willing. *My Tomato. *No News is Good News. 1944: *Important Business. *The National Barn Dance. *Why, Daddy? Her Primitive Man. Janie. Practically Yours. See Here, Private Hargrove. It's in the Bag! (GB: The Fifth Chair). 1945: Duffy's Tavern. Kiss and Tell. Pan-American. Snafu (GB: Welcome Home). Week-End at the Waldorf. *Hollywood Victory Caravan. *I'm a Civilian Here Myself. Road to Utopia. *Boogie Woogie. 1946: Janie Gets Married. The Bride Wore Boots.

**BENNETT, Jill** 1929-1990
Attractive, fair-haired Malayan-born British actress with gargoyle-like features. Played one or two unusual heroines in her early days, pixie-like creatures with backbones of steel. Her later characters tended to run to the neurotic, but she never really made her mark in British films, despite some telling performances, and her greatest successes have been on the stage. Married for some years to the playwright John Osborne, but later divorced.

1951: The Long Dark Hall. 1952: Moulin Rouge. 1953: Hell Below Zero. 1954: Aunt Clara. 1955: *Murder Anonymous. 1956: Lust for Life. The Extra Day. 1960: The Criminal (US: The Concrete Jungle). 1965: The Nanny. The Skull. 1968: Inadmissible Evidence. The Charge of the Light Brigade.

1970: Julius Caesar. 1971: I Want What I Want. 1974: Mister Quilp. 1976: Full Circle. 1981: For Your Eyes Only. 1982: Britannia Hospital. 1985: Paradise Postponed.

**BENSON, George** 1911-
Fidgety, apologetic, brown-haired Welshborn actor in British films, whose characters, like those of America's Elisha Cook Jr (qv) were life's losers. Benson's, though, were not mean or vindictive; rather they were shy, ineffectual or menial—or the hero's inconspicuous friend, his pleasant features usually taking on a perplexed air at some stage of the film, at which his well-rounded tones would express distress. Trained at RADA and was playing Shakespeare at 18. For such a familiar and welcome face, he has made surprisingly few films.

1932: Holiday Lovers. 1937: Keep Fit. 1938: Break the News. 1940: Convoy. 1947: The October Man. 1949: Helter Skelter. The Lost People. 1950: The Happiest Days of Your Life. Cage of Gold. Highly Dangerous. Pool of London. 1951: The Man in the White Suit. Appointment With Venus (US: Island Rescue). 1952: Mother Riley Meets the Vampire (US: Vampire over London). 1953: The Captain's Paradise. The Broken Horseshoe. Three's Company. 1954: Doctor in the House. Aunt Clara. 1955: Value for Money. 1957: The Naked Truth (US: Your Past is Showing!). 1958: Dracula (US: The Horror of Dracula). 1959: Model for Murder. Left, Right and Centre. 1960: The Pure Hell of St Trinians. 1964: A Jolly Bad Fellow. A Home of Your Own. 1966: The Great St Trinian's Train Robbery. 1968: The Strange Affair. 1971: What Became of Jack and Jill? (US: Romeo and Juliet '71). 1972: The Creeping Flesh.

**BENSON, Martin** 1918-
Smooth and oily big-time crooks were the province of this dark, menacing British actor, one of the prime villains from British 'Bs' of the 1950s. Often moustachioed, his faintly oriental features got their biggest break on the other side of the Atlantic, as the chancellor in Yul Brynner's Siamese court in The King and I. Then it was back to untrustworthy types of all nations for

British films, often with one of the excellent foreign accents which were another Benson speciality.

1948: The Blind Goddess. But Not in Vain. 1949: Trapped by the Terror. The Adventures of PC 49. 1951: I'll Get You for This (US: Lucky Nick Cain). Night Without Stars. Assassin for Hire. Mystery Junction. The Dark Light. Judgment Deferred. 1952: The Frightened Man. Wide Boy. The Gambler and the Lady. 1953: Top of the Form. Black 13. Always a Bride. Wheel of Fate. Recoil. Escape by Night. 1954: Knave of Hearts (US: Lovers, Happy Lovers). West of Zanzibar. The Death of Michael Turbin. 1955: Passage Home. Doctor at Sea. 1956: The King and I. 23 Paces to Baker Street. Soho Incident (US: Spin a Dark Web). 1957: The Man from Tangier. Interpol (US: Pickup Alley). Doctor at Large. The Flesh is Weak. Istanbul. 1958: Windom's Way. The Strange World of Planet X (US: Cosmic Monsters). The Two-Headed Spy. 1959: Killers of Kilimanjaro. The Three Worlds of Gulliver. Make Mine a Million. 1960: Exodus. Once More with Feeling. Sands of the Desert. Oscar Wilde. The Pure Hell of St Trinian's. The Gentle Trap. 1961: Five Golden Hours. Gorgo. Village of Daughters. 1962: Captain Clegg (US: Night Creatures). The Silent Invasion. The Fur Collar. The Devil Never Sleeps (US: Satan Never Sleeps). A Matter of WHO. The Secret Door (released 1964). 1963: Cleopatra. Behold a Pale Horse. 1964: A Shot in the Dark. Goldfinger. Mozambique. 1965: The Secret of My Success. A Man Could Get Killed. 1967: The Magnificent Two. Battle Beneath the Earth. 1972: Pope Joan. 1973: Tiffany Jones. 1976: The Omen. The Message/Mohammed, Messenger of God. Jesus of Nazareth (TV). 1978: Meetings with Remarkable Men. 1979: The Human Factor. 1980: The Sea Wolves. Sphinx. 1985: Arch of Triumph (TV).

**BERKELEY, Ballard** 1904-
Tall, rangy, brown-haired, long-lasting British actor, handsome in a rather old-fashioned kind of way, with a pronounced chin. Took up acting in his mid-twenties and brought his military bearing to films, in leading roles at first, before stage experience. Later played affable types and

ABOVE Matheson Lang's Mandarin is about to try (unsuccessfully) to poison his wife's lover (Ballard **Berkeley**) in the 1930 version of *The Chinese Bungalow*

BELOW Willie **Best** (left) has that about-to-turn-and-run look, with Helen Westley, Alexis Smith and Roland Drew in the 1941 film *The Smiling Ghost*

dogged investigative policemen. In more recent times seen as randy old men and old soldiers with courtly manners and barking voices—but most memorably as the hotel's resident major in the hit television series *Fawlty Towers*.

*1930: London Melody. The Chinese Bungalow. 1933: Trouble. 1934: White Ensign. 1936: East Meets West. 1937: The Last Adventurers. Jennifer Hale. 1938: The Outsider. 1939: The Saint in London. 1942: In Which We Serve. 1946: Quiet Weekend. 1947: They Made Me a Fugitive (US: I Became a Criminal). 1949: Third Time Lucky. 1950: Stage Fright. Blackmailed. 1951: The Long Dark Hall. 1952: Circumstantial Evidence. The Night Won't Talk. 1953: The Blue Parrot. Operation Diplomat. Three Steps to the Gallows (released 1955. US: White Fire). 1954: Delayed Action. Dangerous Cargo. Child's Play. Men of Sherwood Forest. 1955: See How They Run. The Stolen Airliner. 1956: My Teenage Daughter (US: Teenage Bad Girl). Passport to Treason. 1957: After the Ball. \*Bullet from the Past. The Betrayal. Just My Luck. The Man Who Wouldn't Talk. 1958: Chain of Events. Life is a Circus. Further Up the Creek. 1960: Cone of Silence (US: Trouble in the Sky). 1963: Impact. A Matter of Choice. 1965: The Murder Game. The Night Caller. 1968: Star! Hostile Witness. 1970: Concerto per pistole solista (GB: Weekend Murders). 1976: Confessions of a Driving Instructor. 1978: The Playbirds. 1979: Confessions from the David Galaxy Affair. Queen of the Blues. 1980: The Wildcats of St Trinian's. Little Lord Fauntleroy. 1983: Bullshot.*

## BEST, Willie 1913-1962

Stocky, stoop-shouldered, rather downcast-looking performer who became the epitome of the 'Yes, massa' black servant who panicked at the slightest provocation. The image was much castigated in later years, but Best, who was initially billed as 'Sleep 'n' Eat', after a character he played, milked it to great effect, especially in comic chillers, when his drooping lower lip quivered in fright at the swish of a curtain. Busy in television after his film career until he became terminally ill with the cancer that killed him at 48.

*1930: †Feet First. 1931: †Up Pops the Devil. 1932: †The Monster Walks (GB: The Monster Walked). 1934: †Little Miss Marker (GB: Girl in Pawn). †Kentucky Kernels (GB: Triple Trouble). †David Harum. †West of the Pecos. 1935: †Murder on a Honeymoon. The Nitwits. Jalna. The Arizonian. The Littlest Rebel. Hot Tip. 1936: Murder on a Bridle Path. The Bride Walks Out. Mummy's Boys. Racing Lady. Make Way for a Lady. Thank You, Jeeves. General Spanky. Down the Stretch. Two in Revolt. 1937: Breezing Home. Merrily We Live. The Lady Fights Back. Super Sleuth. Meet the Missus. Saturday's Heroes. 1938: Youth Takes a Fling. Blondie. Gold is Where You Find It. Spring Madness.*

*Everybody's Doing It. Goodbye Broadway. I'm from the City. Vivacious Lady. 1939: Nancy Drew, Trouble Shooter. At the Circus. The Covered Trailer. Mr Moto Takes a Vacation. 1940: I Take This Woman. The Ghost Breakers. Slightly Honorable. Money and the Woman. Who Killed Aunt Maggie? 1941: Road Show. High Sierra. Kisses for Breakfast. The Lady from Cheyenne. Flight from Destiny. Scattergood Baines. The Body Disappears. Highway West. Nothing But the Truth. The Smiling Ghost. 1942: Whispering Ghosts. Juke Girl. A-Haunting We Will Go. Busses Roar. Maisie Gets Her Man (GB: She Got Her Man). The Hidden Hand. Scattergood Survives a Murder. 1943: The Powers Girl (GB: Hi! Beautiful). Cabin in the Sky. Dixie. The Kansan (GB: Wagon Wheels). Thank Your Lucky Stars. Cinderella Swings It. 1944: The Adventures of Mark Twain. The Girl Who Dared. Home in Indiana. 1945: The Monster and the Ape (serial). Hold That Blonde. Pillow to Post. Red Dragon. 1946: Dangerous Money. The Bride Wore Boots. She Wouldn't Say Yes. The Face of Marble. 1947: Suddenly It's Spring. The Red Stallion. 1948: Smart Woman. Half Past Midnight. The Shanghai Chest. 1949: Jackpot Jitters (GB: Jiggs and Maggie in Jackpot Jitters). \*The Hidden Hand. 1950: \*High and Dizzy. 1951: South of Caliente.*

†As *Sleep 'n' Eat*

## BEVANS, Clem
(C. Blevins) 1879-1963

Gaunt, massively white-bearded (often disguising a surprisingly small chin), beak-nosed and beady-eyed, Bevans, jaws moving up and down from his sidewalk rocking-chair as he surveyed the newest arrival in town, was one of the most recognizable old-timers in Hollywood films—mostly westerns. 'Discovered' for films at 56, Bevans still managed to creak his grasshopper frame through close to 100 of them before retiring at 77.

*1935: Way Down East. 1936: Rhythm on the Range. Come and Get It. The Phantom Rider (serial). 1937: Dangerous Number. Toast of New York. Idol of the Crowds. Riding on Air. The Big City. 1938: Mr Chump. Of Human Hearts. Valley of the Giants. Young Fugitives.*

*Comet over Broadway. Tom Sawyer, Detective. \*Miracle Money. Hold That Co-Ed (GB: Hold That Girl). Boy Meets Girl. 1939: Ambush. Maisie. Zenobia (GB: Elephants Never Forget). \*Help Wanted. Hell's Kitchen. Idiot's Delight. Night Work. Outside These Walls. Thunder Afloat. Main Street Lawyer (GB: Small Town Lawyer). Undercover Doctor. They Made Me a Criminal. Dodge City. Stand Up and Fight. Cowboy Quarterback. The Kid from Kokomo (GB: Orphan of the Ring). King of the Underworld. The Oklahoma Kid. Young Tom Edison. 1940: Abe Lincoln in Illinois. (GB: Spirit of the People). Gold Rush Maisie. Twenty-Mule Team. Go West/The Marx Brothers Go West. The Captain is a Lady. Untamed. The Girl from God's Country. Calling All Husbands. Granny Get Your Gun. Half a Sinner. 1941: Sergeant York. Pacific Blackout. She Couldn't Say No. The Parson of Panamint. The Smiling Ghost. Wyoming (GB: Bad Man of Wyoming). 1942: Saboteur. Tombstone the Town Too Tough to Die. The Forest Rangers. This Gun for Hire. Captains of the Clouds. Mrs Wiggs of the Cabbage Patch. Lucky Jordan. 1943: The Human Comedy. Lady Bodyguard. The Kansan (GB: Wagon Wheels). Happy Go Lucky. The Woman of the Town. 1944: Night Club Girl. Tall in the Saddle. 1945: Grissly's Millions. Captain Eddie. 1946: The Yearling. Gallant Bess. Wake Up and Dream. 1947: Yankee Fakir. The Millerson Case. Mourning Becomes Electra. 1948: Texas, Brooklyn and Heaven (GB: The Girl from Texas). Portrait of Jennie (GB: Jennie). The Paleface. Moonrise. Relentless. Highway 13. 1949: Loaded Pistols. Big Jack. Streets of Laredo. Rim of the Canyon. Deputy Marshal. The Gal Who Took the West. Tell It to the Judge. 1950: Joe Palooka Meets Humphrey. Harvey. 1951: Gold Raiders (GB: Stooges Go West). Silver City Bonanza. Man in the Saddle (GB: The Outcast). 1952: Captive of Billy the Kid. Hangman's Knot. 1953: The Stranger Wore a Gun. 1954: The Boy from Oklahoma. Hurricane at Pilgrim Hill. 1955: Ten Wanted Men. The Kentuckian. 1956: Davy Crockett and the River Pirates.*

## BIBERMAN, Abner 1909-1977

Slit-eyed, Polynesian-looking, chunky American actor with dark hair, quizzical eyebrows and set expression. Originally a journalist, he turned to acting in the 1930s, coming to Hollywood in 1939 and soon qualifying for all kinds of foreign menaces. In the 1950s he doubled up as a drama coach at Universal-International (as it then was), the studio that gave him the chance to direct films in 1955, after which he gave up acting. From the end of that decade, Biberman worked solidly in TV, directing episodes of drama series.

*1936 : Soak the Rich. 1939 : The Rains Came. Gunga Din. Each Dawn I Die. Panama Patrol. Another Thin Man. The Roaring Twenties. Panama Lady. Balalaika. 1940 : Zanzibar. Ski Patrol. South of Pago-Pago. His Girl Friday. Golden Gloves. The Girl from Havana. Enemy Agent. South to Karanga. 1941 : Singapore Woman. South of Tahiti (GB : White Savage). The Monster and the Girl. This Woman is Mine. The Gay Vagabond. The Devil Pays Off. 1942 : Beyond the Blue Horizon. Broadway. Whispering Ghosts. Little Tokyo USA (GB : East of Chinatown). King of the Mounties (Serial). 1943 : The Leopard Man. Submarine Alert. Behind the Rising Sun. Bombardier. 1944 : Dragon Seed. The Bridge of San Luis Rey. The Keys of the Kingdom. Two-Man Submarine. 1945 : Back to Bataan. Captain Kidd. Betrayal from the East. Salome, Where She Danced. 1946 : Strange Conquest. 1950 : Winchester 73. 1951 : Roaring City. 1952 : Viva Zapata! 1954 : Elephant Walk. Knock on Wood. The Golden Mistress.*

**As director :**
*1955 : The Looters. Running Wild. 1956 : The Price of Fear. Behind the High Wall. 1957 : Gun for a Coward. The Night Runner. Flood Tide (GB : Above All Things).*

**BIKEL, Theodore** 1924-
Swarthy, black-haired, heavy-set, Austrian-born actor and entertainer, a beefier version of Topol. Fled to Palestine before World War II and moved to England in post-war years, where he was seen in films, mainly as sweaty, threatening foreigners. Latterly in Hollywood playing characters of more kindly disposition. Also sings, plays guitar and is keenly interested in local (New York)

politics. Was nominated for an Oscar as the sheriff in *The Defiant Ones.*

*1951 : The African Queen. 1952 : Moulin Rouge. 1953 : Never Let Me Go. Melba. Desperate Moment. A Day to Remember. 1954 : The Love Lottery. The Kidnappers (US : The Little Kidnappers). The Young Lovers (US : Chance Meeting). The Divided Heart. Forbidden Cargo. 1956 : The Pride and the Passion. 1957 : The Vintage. The Enemy Below. 1958 : Fraulein. I Want to Live! I Bury the Living. The Defiant Ones. 1959 : The Blue Angel. A Woman Obsessed. The Angry Hills. 1960 : A Dog of Flanders. 1964 : My Fair Lady. 1965 : Sands of the Kalahari. Who Has Seen the Wind? (TV). 1966 : The Russians Are Coming, the Russians Are Coming. The Last Chapter (narrator only). 1967 : Festival. 1968 : Sweet November. The Desperate Ones. My Side of the Mountain. 1970 : Flap (GB : The Last Warrior). Darker Than Amber. 1971 : 200 Motels. The Little Ark. 1972 : Killer By Night (TV). 1975 : Murder on Flight 502 (TV). 1976 : Victory at Entebbe (TV. GB : cinemas). 1984 : Prince Jack.*

**BING, Herman** 1889-1947
Bulky, pigeon-cheeked, purse-lipped, round-eyed, red-nosed German who came to Hollywood in the 1920s as assistant to the director F. W. Murnau, but soon became a comedy character relief in dozens of (especially light) films, typically as an easily flustered Viennese shopkeeper or official who minced words in more senses than one. Found work extremely hard to get in wartime, and shot himself at 57.

*1927 : Sunrise—a Song of Two Humans (GB : Sunrise). 1929 : A Song of Kentucky. Married in Hollywood. 1930 : Menschen hinter Gettern. The Three Sisters. 1931 : The Great Lover. The Guardsman. Women Love Once. 1932 : The Tenderfoot. Jewel Robbery. Hypnotized. Silver Dollar. Flesh. 1933 : After Tonight. The Nuisance (GB : Accidents Wanted). *Fits in a Fiddle. Lady Killer. The Bowery. Dinner at Eight. My Lips Betray. The Great Jasper. College Coach (GB : Football Coach). Footlight Parade. 1934 : The Hide-Out. The Black Cat (GB : The House of Doom). Mandalay. Melody in Spring. The Merry*

*Widow. Manhattan Love Song. I'll Tell the World. The Mighty Barnum. Embarrassing Moments. Twentieth Century. Love Time. Crimson Romance. When Strangers Meet. 1935 : It Happened in New York. The Great Hotel Murder. Call of the Wild. Redheads on Parade. The Florentine Dagger. Don't Bet on Blondes. Calm Yourself. In Caliente. Three Kids and a Queen (GB : The Baxter Millions). Every Night at Eight. His Family Tree. Fighting Youth. $1,000 a Minute. The Night is Young. Hands Across the Table. Thunder in the Night. *The Misses Stooge. 1936 : Laughing Irish Eyes. Rose Marie. Three Wise Guys. Human Cargo. Dimples. The Great Ziegfeld. The King Steps Out. Adventure in Manhattan (GB : Manhattan Madness). That Girl from Paris. The Music Goes Round. Tango. Come Closer, Folks. The Champagne Waltz. 1937 : Maytime. Beg, Borrow or Steal. 1938 : Every Day's a Holiday. Paradise for Three. Vacation from Love. The Great Waltz. Sweethearts. Bluebeard's Eighth Wife. Four's a Crowd. 1940 : Bitter Sweet. 1942 : The Devil With Hitler. 1945 : Where Do We Go from Here? 1946 : Rendezvous 24. Night and Day.*

**BIRCH, Paul** 1908-1969
Craggy, fair-haired American actor, a sort of strait-laced version of Jay C. Flippen (*qv*). Entirely a Broadway actor until 1952, he was kept in routine rugged character roles by Hollywood—sheriffs, attorneys and the like—apart from two fine performances much treasured by fantasy film fans in the leading roles of *The Beast with 1,000,000 Eyes* and *Not of This Earth*, both from the Roger Corman stable.

*1952 : Assignment—Paris! 1953 : The War of the Worlds. Ride Clear of Diablo. 1955 : Apache Woman. Five Guns West. Man Without a Star. The Fighting Chance. Rebel Without a Cause. Strange Lady in Town. 1956 : The Fastest Gun Alive. The Beast with 1,000,000 Eyes. When Gangland Strikes. The White Squaw. Everything But the Truth. Not of This Earth. 1957 : Gun for a Coward. The 27th Day. Joe Dakota. The Tattered Dress. 1958 : The World Was His Jury. Queen of Outer Space. Gunman's Walk. Wild Heritage. The Gun Runners. 1959 : Gunmen from Laredo. 1960 : Too Soon to Love. The Dark at* the Top of the Stairs. Pay or Die! Portrait in Black. 1961: Two Rode Together. 1962: A Public Affair. The Man Who Shot Liberty Valance. 1963: It's a Mad, Mad, Mad, Mad World. The Raiders. 1966: Welcome to Hard Times (GB: Killer on a Horse). A Covenant With Death.

## BIRD, Norman 1924-

Light-haired, doleful-looking British actor with man-in-the-street air, usually sporting a toothbrush moustache. Refers to himself as 'the man with the cardigan' and has played numerous henpecked, inadequate, interfering or tentatively friendly little men. Busiest in films in the 1960s.

1954: An Inspector Calls. 1960: The League of Gentlemen. The Angry Silence. 1961: The Man in the Moon. Very Important Person. The Secret Partner. Whistle Down the Wind. Victim. Cash on Demand. 1962: Night of the Eagle (US: Burn Witch Burn). Term of Trial. Maniac. The Punch and Judy Man. 1963: The Mind Benders. Bitter Harvest. 80,000 Suspects. The Cracksman. Hot Enough for June (US: Agent 8¾). 1964: The Bargee. The Beauty Jungle (US: Contest Girl). The Black Torment. 1965: The Hill. Sky West and Crooked (US: Gypsy Girl). 1966: The Wrong Box. 1968: A Dandy in Aspic. The Limbo Line. 1969: Run a Crooked Mile (TV). All at Sea. 1970: The Rise and Rise of Michael Rimmer. The Virgin and the Gypsy. The Raging Moon (US: Long Ago Tomorrow). 1971: Hands of the Ripper. Please Sir! 1972: Young Winston. Doomwatch. Ooh ... You Are Awful (US: Get Charlie Tully). 1976: The Slipper and the Rose. The Chiffy Kids (series). 1978: The Medusa Touch. The Lord of the Rings (voice only). 1981: The Final Conflict (later Omen III The Final Conflict).

## BISSELL, Whit(ner) 1919-1981

Fair-haired, pear-faced, inquisitive-looking American actor who rarely played sympathetic characters, but rather those whose ostensible interest in the community cloaked self-enriching schemes. His do-gooders were no-gooders, his solid citizens usually revealed a yellow streak and sometimes he was just the weak victim of his oppressors. On stage as a child, he briefly

started a Hollywood career before war service intervened. Had one leading role, as a mad professor in I Was a Teenage Frankenstein.

1943: Holy Matrimony. Destination Tokyo. 1946: It Shouldn't Happen to a Dog. Cluny Brown. Somewhere in the Night. 1947: The Sea of Grass. Night Song. Brute Force. The Senator Was Indiscreet (GB: Mr Ashton Was Indiscreet). 1948: A Double Life. Another Part of the Forest. Canon City. He Walked by Night. Raw Deal. That Lady in Ermine. Chicken Every Sunday. 1949: Anna Lucasta. The Crime Doctor's Diary. Tokyo Joe. 1950: Perfect Strangers (GB: Too Dangerous to Love). When Willie Comes Marching Home. The Killer That Stalked New York (GB: The Frightened City). Convicted. For Heaven's Sake. Wyoming Mail. The Great Missouri Raid. A Life of Her Own. 1951: Red Mountain. The Family Secret. The Sellout. Night into Morning. Sealed Cargo. The Red Badge of Courage. Tales of Robin Hood. The Lost Continent. Hoodlum Empire. Boots Malone. 1952: The Turning Point. Skirts Ahoy! 1953: Devil's Canyon. It Should Happen to You. 1954: The Shanghai Story. The Caine Mutiny. Riot in Cell Block 11. Three Hours to Kill. Target Earth. The Atomic Kid. The Creature from the Black Lagoon. 1955: The Big Combo. The Desperate Hours. Not As a Stranger. The Naked Street. Shack Out on 101. At Gunpoint! GB: Gunpoint!). 1956: Miracle on 34th Street (TV. GB: cinemas). Invasion of the Body Snatchers. The Proud Ones. Dakota Incident. The Man from Del Rio. Gunfight at the OK Corral. 1957: The Young Stranger. Johnny Tremain. I Was a Teenage Werewolf. The Wayward Girl. The Tall Stranger. I Was a Teenage Frankenstein (GB: Teenage Frankenstein). 1958: Monster on the Campus. No Name on the Bullet. The Defiant Ones. Gang War. 1959: The Black Orchid. Warlock. Never So Few. 1960: The Time Machine. The Magnificent Seven. 1961: Bird Man of Alcatraz. One Third of a Man. The Manchurian Candidate. The Final Hour (TV. GB: cinemas). Hemingway's Adventures of a Young Man (GB: Adventures of å Young Man). Trauma. 1963: Advance to the Rear (GB: Company of Cowards). Spencer's Mountain. Hud. 1964: Seven Days in May. Where

Love Has Gone. 1965: The Hallelujah Trail. 1966: A Covenant with Death. 1968: Five Card Stud. 1969: ... And Sudden Death. Airport. 1970: City Beneath the Sea (TV. GB: cinemas, as One Hour to Doomsday). 1971: A Tattered Web (TV). In Broad Daylight (TV). 1972: The Salzburg Connection. Pete 'n' Tillie. 1973: Soylent Green. Cry Rape! (TV). 1974: The FBI vs Alvin Karpis, Public Enemy No. One (TV). 1975: Psychic Killer. 1976: Flood! (TV. GB: cinemas). 1977: The Lincoln Conspiracy. Last of the Mohicans (TV). The Incredible Rocky Mountain Race (TV). Casey's Shadow. 1978: Donner Pass: The Road to Survival (TV). The Time Machine (TV. And cinema version). 1979: Night Rider (TV). Strangers: The Story of a Mother and Daughter (TV).

## BLACKMER, Sidney 1894-1973

Suave, elegant American actor, good at upper-class sneers and often seen as society crooks with a weakness for women. Began his career in Pearl White serials, then didn't film again for 12 years. He was married to actresses Lenore Ulric (from 1928 to 1939) and Suzanne Kaaren (from 1942 to 1973), both of whom had successful minor careers. Died from cancer.

1914: The Perils of Pauline (serial). 1915: The Romance of Elaine (serial). 1927: Million Dollar Mystery (serial). 1929: A Most Immoral Lady. 1930: The Love Racket (GB: Such Things Happen). Strictly Modern. The Bad Man. Kismet. Little Caesar. Mothers Cry. Sweethearts and Wives. 1931: Woman Hungry (GB: The Challenge). It's a Wise Child. The Lady Who Dared. One Heavenly Night. Daybreak. Once a Sinner. 1933: The Cocktail Hour. The Wrecker. From Hell to Heaven. The Deluge. 1934: Goodbye Love. Transatlantic Merry-Go-Round. This Man is Mine. The Count of Monte Cristo. Down to Their Last Yacht (GB: Hawaiian Nights). 1935: The Great God Gold. The President Vanishes (GB: Strange Conspiracy). A Notorious Gentleman. The Little Colonel. Behind the Green Lights. Streamline Express. Smart Girl. False Pretenses. The Girl Who Came Back. Forced Landing. Fire Trap. 1936: The Florida Special. Missing Girls. The President's Mystery (GB: One for All). Heart of the West.

Early to Bed. Woman Trap. 1937 : Shadows of the Orient. House of Secrets. A Doctor's Diary. This is My Affair (GB : His Affair). Thank You Mr Moto. Women Men Marry. Girl Overboard. Michael O'Halloran. The Last Gangster. Charlie Chan at Monte Carlo. Wife, Doctor and Nurse. Heidi. John Meade's Woman. 1938 : In Old Chicago. Straight, Place and Show (GB : They're Off). Sharpshooters. Speed to Burn. Suez. Orphans of the Storm. Trade Winds. While New York Sleeps. 1939 : The Convict's Code. Fast and Loose. It's a Wonderful World. Unmarried (GB : Night Club Hostess). Law of the Pampas. Hotel for Women/Elsa Maxwell's Hotel for Women. Within the Law. Trapped in the Sky. 1940 : Maryland. I Want a Divorce. Framed. Third Finger, Left Hand. Dance, Girl, Dance. 1941 : Cheers for Miss Bishop. Rookies on Parade. The Great Swindle. Love Crazy. The Obliging Young Lady. Ellery Queen and the Perfect Crime (GB : The Perfect Crime). Angels with Broken Wings. Murder Among Friends. Down Mexico Way. The Feminine Touch. The Officer and the Lady. 1942 : Always in My Heart. Nazi Agent. Gallant Lady. Quiet Please, Murder. The Panther's Claw. The Sabotage Squad. 1943 : I Escaped from the Gestapo (GB : No Escape). Murder in Times Square. In Old Oklahoma (later and GB : War of the Wildcats). 1944 : Buffalo Bill. Broadway Rhythm. The Lady and the Monster (GB : The Lady and the Doctor). Wilson. 1946 : Duel in the Sun. 1948 : My Girl Tisa. A Song is Born (narrator only). 1949 : The Hero (narrator only). 1950 : Farewell to Yesterday (narrator only). 1951 : People Will Talk. Saturday's Hero (GB : Idols in the Dust). 1952 : Washington Story (GB : Target for Scandal). The San Francisco Story. 1954 : Johnny Dark. The High and the Mighty. 1956 : The View from Pompey's Head (GB : Secret Interlude). High Society. Beyond a Reasonable Doubt. Accused of Murder. 1957 : Tammy and the Bachelor (GB : Tammy). 1959 : Stampede at Bitter Creek (TV. GB : cinemas). 1965 : Joy in the Morning. How to Murder Your Wife. 1967 : A Covenant with Death. 1968 : Rosemary's Baby. 1970 : Do You Take This Stranger? (TV). 1973 : Revenge is My Destiny (TV).

**BLAKELY, Colin** 1930-1987
Talented, aggressive British leading character actor, equally adept at harassed fathers, loyal friends, ruthless gangsters or professional men—in fact will have a go at anything. Born in Northern Ireland, Blakely did not make his debut on stage until he was 27, but his abrasive approach soon made him a leading figure in the London theatre world and, despite a number of sterling film performances, he is still best known in that medium.

1960 : Saturday Night and Sunday Morning. 1961 : The Hellions. 1962 : The Password is Courage. 1963 : This Sporting Life. The Informers. Never Put It in Writing. The Long Ships. 1965 : The Legend of Young Dick Turpin. 1966 : The Spy With a Cold Nose. A Man for All Seasons. 1967 : Charlie Bubbles. The Day the Fish Came Out. 1968 : Decline and Fall … of a Birdwatcher! The Vengeance of She. 1969 : Alfred the Great. 1970 : The Private Life of Sherlock Holmes. 1971 : Young Winston. Something to Hide. 1973 : The National Health. 1974 : Love Among the Ruins (TV). Murder on the Orient Express. Galileo. 1976 : The Pink Panther Strikes Again. It Shouldn't Happen to a Vet. 1977 : Equus. 1978 : The Big Sleep. 1979 : Nijinsky. Meetings with Remarkable Men. 1980 : The Dogs of War. Little Lord Fauntleroy (TV. GB : cinemas). 1981 : The Day Christ Died (TV). Evil Under the Sun. 1982 : Don Camillo. 1983 : Red Monarch (TV).

**BLORE, Eric** 1887-1959
Inimitable, unctuous, balding actor-comedian who would have made an ideal Uriah Heep but, after going to Hollywood in the 1920s from his native Britain, settled down to performing invaluable service in the Astaire-Rogers musicals and, later, in the Lone Wolf movies. Probably the cinema's best-known butler (no-one excelled him at the pained look) and capable of giving as good as he got in the wisecrack stakes. Died from a heart attack.

1920 : *A Night Out and a Day In. 1926 : The Great Gatsby. 1929 : Laughter. 1930 : My Sin. 1931 : Tarnished Lady. 1933 : Flying Down to Rio. 1934 : The Gay Divorcee (GB : The Gay Divorce). Limehouse Blues. 1935 : Behold My Wife. Folies Bergère (GB : The Man from the Folies Bergère). The Casino Murder Case. Top Hat. Diamond Jim. Old Man Rhythm. I Live My Life. I Dream Too Much. To Beat the Band. Seven Keys to Baldpate. The Good Fairy. 1936 : Two in the Dark. The Ex-Mrs Bradford. Sons o' Guns. Piccadilly Jim. Swing Time. Smartest Girl in Town. Quality Street. 1937 : The Soldier and the Lady (GB : Michael Strogoff). Shall We Dance? It's Love I'm After. Breakfast for Two. Hitting a New High. 1938 : The Joy of Living. Swiss Miss. A Desperate Adventure (GB : It Happened in Paris). 1939 : $1,000 a Touchdown. Island of Lost Men. A Gentleman's Gentleman. 1940 : The Man Who Wouldn't Talk. The Lone Wolf Strikes. Music in My Heart. Till We Meet Again. The Boys from Syracuse. The Lone Wolf Meets a Lady. Earl of Puddlestone (GB : Jolly Old Higgins). South of Suez. 1941 : The Lone Wolf Keeps a Date. The Lady Eve. The Lone Wolf Takes a Chance. Road to Zanzibar. Red Head. Lady Scarface. New York Town. Three Girls About Town. Confirm or Deny. The Shanghai Gesture. 1942 : Sullivan's Travels. Secrets of the Lone Wolf (GB : Secrets). The Moon and Sixpence. 1943 : Forever and a Day. *Heavenly Music. Happy Go Lucky. Submarine Base. Holy Matrimony. One Dangerous Night. Passport to Suez. The Sky's the Limit. 1944 : San Diego, I Love You. 1945 : Penthouse Rhythm. Easy to Look At. 1946 : Two Sisters from Boston. Kitty. Men in Her Diary. The Notorious Lone Wolf. Abie's Irish Rose. 1947 : The Lone Wolf in Mexico. Winter Wonderland. The Lone Wolf in London. 1948 : Romance on the High Seas (GB : It's Magic). 1949 : Love Happy (later Kleptomaniacs). Adventures of Ichabod and Mr Toad (voice only). 1950 : Fancy Pants. 1952 : Babes in Baghdad. 1955 : Bowery to Baghdad.

**BLUE, Ben**
(Benjamin Bernstein) 1900-1975
Mainly on the Broadway stage, this thin, mournful American indiarubber comedian cheered up many a dull film by wandering on, doing a drunk act or running mime gag, and usually bringing the house down. A cartoon of a man from a vaudeville family, he was on the musical-comedy stage at 15, then starred in some film sound shorts and one or two minor romps before settling for cameo appearances. Notable among these cameos was his apartment man trying to

complete a shave in the New York blackout in *Where Were You When the Lights Went Out?*

1927: *The Arcadians/Land of Heart's Desire.* 1932: *\*Strange Inner-tube.* *\*What Price Taxi?* 1933: *\*Wreckety Wreck.* *\*Call Her Sausage.* 1934: *College Rhythm.* 1936: *Follow Your Heart.* *College Holiday.* 1937: *Turn Off the Moon.* *Top of the Town.* *High, Wide and Handsome.* *Artists and Models.* *Thrill of a Lifetime.* 1938: *College Swing* (GB: *Swing, Teacher, Swing*). *The Big Broadcast of 1938.* *Cocoanut Grove.* 1939: *Paris Honeymoon.* 1942: *Panama Hattie.* *For Me and My Gal* (GB: *For Me and My Girl*). 1943: *Thousands Cheer.* 1944: *Two Girls and a Sailor.* *Broadway Rhythm.* 1945: *\*Badminton.* 1946: *Two Sisters from Boston.* *Easy to Wed.* 1947: *My Wild Irish Rose.* 1948: *One Sunday Afternoon.* 1963: *It's a Mad, Mad, Mad, Mad World.* 1966: *The Russians Are Coming, the Russians Are Coming.* *The Busy Body.* 1967: *A Guide for the Married Man.* 1968: *Where Were You When the Lights Went Out?*—his last film role.

**BLUE, Monte** 1890-1963
Moon-faced American romantic lead with sleek brown hair, popular in silent and early sound light dramas before moving into scores of character roles until his retirement in 1955, following a brief period working for a circus. Part Cherokee Indian, Blue began his career as a stuntman for director D. W. Griffith. Died from a coronary attack.

1915: *The Birth of a Nation.* *Ghosts.* 1916: *The Microscope Mystery.* *Intolerance.* 1917: *Wild and Woolly.* *Hands Up!* *The Man from Painted Post.* *Betrayed.* 1918: *Till I Come Back to You.* *The Squaw Man.* *The Romance of Tarzan.* *Johanna Enlists.* *M'Liss.* 1919: *In Mizzoura.* *Pettigrew's Girl.* *Every Woman.* 1920: *Something to Think About.* *The Thirteenth Commandment.* *A Cumberland Romance.* *Too Much Johnson.* *Jucklins.* 1921: *The Kentuckians.* *Moonlight and Honeysuckle.* *The Affairs of Anatol.* *A Perfect Crime.* *Orphans of the Storm.* *A Broken Doll.* 1922: *Peacock Alley.* *My Old Kentucky Home.* *Loving Lies.* *Broadway Rose.* 1923: *Main Street.* *Brass.* *The Tents of Allah.* *The Purple Highway.* *Defying Destiny.* *Lucretia Lombard.*

1924: *How to Educate a Wife.* *Daughters of Pleasure.* *The Marriage Circle.* *Revelation.* *Mademoiselle Midnight.* *Her Marriage Vow.* *The Lover of Camille.* *Being Respectable.* *The Dark Swan* (GB: *The Black Swan*). 1925: *Red Hot Tires.* *Hogan's Alley.* *Kiss Me Again.* *The Limited Mail.* *Recompense.* 1926: *The Man Upstairs.* *Across the Pacific.* *So This is Paris.* *Other Women's Husbands.* 1927: *Bitter Apples.* *Wolf's Clothing.* *Brass Knuckles.* *The Black Diamond Express.* *The Brute.* *The Bush Leaguer.* *One Round Hogan.* 1928: *Across the Atlantic.* *White Shadows in the South Seas.* 1929: *Conquest.* *Tiger Rose.* *From Headquarters.* *Greyhound Limited.* *No Defense.* *Skin Deep.* *The Show of Shows.* 1930: *Isle of Escape.* *Those Who Dance.* 1931: *The Flood.* 1932: *The Stoker.* *The Valley of Adventure.* *The Thundering Herd.* 1933: *The Nectors.* *Her Forgotten Past.* *Officer 13.* *The Intruder.* 1934: *Come on Marines!* *The Last Round-Up.* *Student Tour.* *Wagon Wheels.* *College Rhythm.* 1935: *The Lives of a Bengal Lancer.* *Hot Off the Press.* *Trails of the Wild.* *G Men.* *Nevada.* *Wanderer of the Wasteland.* *On Probation.* 1936: *Undersea Kingdom* (serial). *Mary of Scotland.* *Ride, Ranger, Ride.* *Treachery Rides the Range.* *Song of the Gringo.* *Desert Gold.* 1937: *Souls at Sea.* *Rootin' Tootin' Rhythm* (GB: *Rhythm on the Ranch*). *The Outcasts of Poker Flat.* *High, Wide and Handsome.* *Thunder Trail.* 1938: *Hawk of the Wilderness* (serial). *Tom Sawyer, Detective.* *Spawn of the North.* *The Mysterious Rider.* *Illegal Traffic.* *The Great Adventures of Wild Bill Hickok* (serial). *Born to the West.* *Rebellious Daughters.* *Cocoanut Grove.* *The Big Broadcast of 1938.* *King of Alcatraz* (GB: *King of the Alcatraz*). 1939: *Juarez.* *Dodge City.* *Union Pacific.* *Frontier Pony Express.* *Geronimo.* *Days of Jesse James.* *\*Port of Hats.* *Our Leading Citizen.* 1940: *North West Mounted Police.* *Mystery Sea Raider.* *A Little Bit of Heaven.* *Road to Singapore.* *Young Bill Hickok.* *Texas Rangers Ride Again.* 1941: *King of the Texas Rangers* (serial). *Riders of Death Valley* (serial). *Treat 'Em Rough.* *The Great Train Robbery.* *Arkansas Judge* (GB: *False Witness*). *Law of the Timber.* *Scattergood Pulls the Strings.* *New York Town.* *Sunset in Wyoming.* *Bad Man of Deadwood.* *North to the Klondike.* *Sullivan's Travels.* 1942: *Across the Pacific.* *The Palm Beach Story.* *Gentleman Jim.* *Road to Morocco.* *Secret Enemies.* *Panama Hattie.* *Reap the Wild Wind.* *I Married a Witch.* *The Great Man's Lady.* *My Favorite Blonde.* *The Forest Rangers.* *The Remarkable Andrew.* *Casablanca.* 1943: *Northern Pursuit.* *Mission to Moscow.* *Edge of Darkness.* *Truck Busters.* *Thank Your Lucky Stars.* *Thousands Cheer.* 1944: *Passage to Marseille* (GB: *Passage to Marseilles*). *The Mask of Dimitrios.* *The Conspirators.* *The Adventures of Mark Twain.* *Janie.* 1945: *San Antonio.* *Saratoga Trunk.* *Danger Signal.* *The Horn Blows at Midnight.* 1946: *Janie Gets Married.* *Cinderella Jones.* *Shadow of a Woman.* *Two Sisters from Boston.* *Easy to Wed.* *Humoresque.* *A Stolen Life.* *Two Guys from Milwaukee* (GB: *Royal Flush*). *The Man I Love.* 1947: *Bells of*

San Fernando. *Speed to Spare.* *Life With Father.* *Cheyenne.* *Possessed.* *My Wild Irish Rose.* *That Way With Women.* *The Unfaithful.* *Stallion Road.* 1948: *Two Guys from Texas* (GB: *Two Texas Knights*). *Silver River.* *Key Largo.* *Johnny Belinda.* 1949: *South of St Louis.* *Ranger of Cherokee Strip.* *The Younger Brothers.* *Flaxy Martin.* *Homicide.* *Colorado Territory.* 1950: *Dallas.* *This Side of the Law.* *Iroquois Trail* (GB: *The Tomahawk Trail*). *The Blonde Bandit.* *Backfire.* *Montana.* 1951: *Warpath.* *Snake River Desperadoes.* *Gold Raiders* (GB: *Stooges Go West*). *Three Desperate Men.* *The Sea Hornet.* 1952: *Rose of Cimarron.* *The Will Rogers Story* (GB: *The Story of Will Rogers*). *Hangman's Knot.* 1953: *The Last Posse.* *Ride, Vaquero!* 1954: *Apache.*

**BLYTHE, John** 1921-
In view of the fact that his screen characters were those most likely to sell you black market goods, it was rather surprising that a lot of this British actor's career in the 1950s was taken up introducing advertising magazines on television. A stagehand at 16, he got going in films in post-war years, at first in minor leads as fast-talking reporters but soon, trilby tipped even further back over those round, butter-wouldn't-melt-in-my-mouth features, as bow-tied smoothies on the make.

1939: *Goodbye Mr Chips!* 1944: *The Way Ahead.* *This Happy Breed.* 1947: *Holiday Camp.* *Easy Money.* *Dear Murderer.* *Crime Reporter.* 1948: *River Patrol.* *Good Time Girl.* *Here Come the Huggetts.* *Portrait from Life* (US: *The Girl in the Painting*). 1949: *Vote for Huggett.* *A Boy, a Girl and a Bike.* *Diamond City.* *It's a Wonderful Day.* *The Huggetts Abroad.* *Boys in Brown.* 1950: *Lilli Marlene.* 1951: *Worm's Eye View.* 1952: *The Frightened Man.* 1953: *Out of the Bandbox.* *The Wedding of Lilli Marlene.* *It's a Grand Life.* *Three Steps to the Gallows* (released 1955. US: *White Fire*). 1954: *The Gay Dog.* *Meet Mr Malcolm.* 1955: *As Long As They're Happy.* 1956: *Doublecross.* *They Never Learn.* 1984. 1960: *Foxhole in Cairo.* *Doctor in Love.* 1961: *No Love for Johnnie.* *No, My Darling Daughter.* 1962: *The Devil's Daffodil* (US: *The Daffodil Killer*) *Gaolbreak.* *On the Beat.*

1963: *A Stitch in Time. Call Me Bwana.*
1969: *The Bed Sitting Room.* 1974: *Love Among the Ruins (TV).* 1975: *The Ups and Downs of a Handyman.* 1976: *Keep It Up Downstairs.*

## BODDEY, Martin 1908-

Burly British actor, often moustachioed, with dark hair sleekly brushed across his head and dark, almost choleric complexion. Mostly he played solid types, like police sergeants and inspectors, but occasionally let the solidity slip into wronged husbands, or even out-and-out villains—these roles having an intensity missing in his other work.

1948: *A Song for Tomorrow.* 1949: *The Third Man. The Dancing Years.* 1950: *State Secret* (US: *The Great Manhunt*). *Seven Days to Noon. Cage of Gold. The Franchise Affair. The Adventurers* (US: *The Great Adventure*). *Cairo Road.* 1951: *Laughter in Paradise. Valley of Eagles. Appointment with Venus* (US: *Island Rescue*). *The Magic Box. Cloudburst.* 1952: *Top Secret* (US: *Mr Potts Goes to Moscow*). *Venetian Bird* (US: *The Assassin*). *Folly to be Wise.* 1953: *Single-Handed* (US: *Sailor of the King*). *Personal Affair. Park Plaza 605* (US: *Norman Conquest*). *Rob Roy the Highland Rogue.* 1954: *Doctor in the House. Face the Music* (US: *The Black Glove*). *Forbidden Cargo. Up to His Neck. Svengali. The Yellow Robe. Mad About Men. Secret Venture.* 1955: *You Can't Escape.* 1956: *The Silken Affair. Escape in the Sun. Up in the World. The Iron Petticoat. Eyewitness. The Last Man to Hang?* 1957: *There's Always a Thursday. How to Murder a Rich Uncle. Not Wanted on Voyage. These Dangerous Years* (US: *Dangerous Youth*). *Cat Girl. I Accuse!* 1958: *Carry on Sergeant. Violent Moment. The Two-Headed Spy. Chain of Events. I Only Arsked! The Square Peg. The Duke Wore Jeans. No Time to Die!* (US: *Tank Force*). 1959: *The Boy and the Bridge. The Siege of Pinchgut. Killers of Kilimanjaro. I'm All Right, Jack.* 1960: *Moment of Danger* (US: *Malaga*). *Sands of the Desert. Circle of Deception. Too Hot to Handle.* 1961: *The Kitchen. The Naked Edge. Gorgo.* 1962: *The Wrong Arm of the Law. The Man Who Finally Died.* 1963: *Girl in the Headlines* (US: *The Model Murder Case*). \**Business Connections.* 1966: *A Man for All Seasons.* 1967: *Bedazzled.* 1972: *Tales from the Crypt. Psychomania.* 1973: *Dark Places.*

## BOLAND, Mary 1880-1965

Round-faced, fair-haired American actress who turned from drama on the stage to comedy on the screen, scoring a resounding success opposite Charlie Ruggles in a whole series of films in the thirties, usually playing his harassed (sometimes domineering) wife.

1915: *The Edge of the Abyss.* 1916: *The Stepping Stone. The Price of Happiness. Big Jim Garrity.* 1918: *His Temporary Wife. The Prodigal Wife. A Woman's Experience.* 1931: *Personal Maid. Secrets of a Secretary.* 1932:

*The Night of June 13th. Trouble in Paradise. Evenings for Sale. If I Had a Million. Night After Night.* 1933: *Three-Cornered Moon. The Solitaire Man. Mama Loves Papa.* 1934: *Six of a Kind. Four Frightened People. Melody in Spring. Stingaree. Down to Their Last Yacht* (GB: *Hawaiian Nights*). *The Pursuit of Happiness. Here Comes the Groom.* 1935: *People Will Talk. Two for Tonight. Ruggles of Red Gap. The Big Broadcast of 1936.* 1936: *Wives Never Know. Early to Bed. College Holiday. A Son Comes Home.* 1937: *Marry the Girl. Mama Runs Wild. There Goes the Groom. Danger - Love at Work.* 1938: *Little Tough Guys in Society. Artists and Models Abroad* (GB: *Stranded in Paris*). 1939: *The Magnificent Fraud. Boy Trouble. The Women.* 1940: *Night Work. He Married His Wife. One Night in the Tropics. New Moon. Pride and Prejudice. Hit Parade of 1941.* 1944: *Nothing But Trouble. In Our Time. Forever Yours. They Shall Have Faith* (GB: *The Right to Live*). 1948: *Julia Misbehaves.* 1950: *Guilty Bystander.*

## BOND, Ward 1903-1960

Chunky, aggressive, light-haired American actor with jutting lower lip. At first in small roles (after a youthful career in American football), he was often cast as Irish policeman or boxers, but also employed by director John Ford in progressively juicier parts, usually as rugged, warm-hearted westerners. Was enjoying his greatest success as the wagonmaster in TV's *Wagon Train* when a heart attack in his shower struck him down at 57.

1929: *Salute. Words and Music.* 1930: *The Big Trail. Born Reckless.* 1931: *Arrowsmith.* 1932: *Virtue. Hello, Trouble. Rackety Rax. White Eagle. High Speed. Air Mail. The Trial of Vivienne Ware.* 1933: *Heroes for Sale. Wild Boys of the Road* (GB: *Dangerous Days*). *When Strangers Marry. College Coach* (GB: *Football Coach*). *The Wrecker. Police Car No. 17. Whirlpool. The Sundown Rider. Unknown Valley. Obey the Law.* 1934: *Straightaway. Most Precious Thing in Life. The Poor Rich. Frontier Marshal. Broadway Bill* (GB: *Strictly Confidential*). *It Happened One Night. The Defense Rests. Fighting Ranger. Here Comes the Groom. Chained. The Affairs of Cellini. The*

*Fighting Code. A Voice in the Night. A Man's Game. The Crime of Helen Stanley. Kid Millions. Against the Law. Girl in Danger. The Human Side. Tall Timber. The Crimson Trail.* 1935: *Western Courage. Devil Dogs of the Air. She Gets Her Man. His Night Out. Black Fury. Fighting Shadows. Little Big Shot. The Last Days of Pompeii. G-Men. Go Into Your Dance. Calm Yourself. The Informer. Guard That Girl. Murder in the Fleet. Waterfront Lady. The Headline Woman. Justice of the Range. Men of the Night. Too Tough to Kill.* 1936: *Cattle Thief. Muss 'Em Up* (GB: *House of Fate*). *The Bride Walks Out. Second Wife. Without Orders. Crash Donovan. They Met in a Taxi. The Legion of Terror. Conflict. The Man Who Lived Twice. Fury. The Leathernecks Have Landed* (GB: *The Marines Have Landed*). *Avenging Waters. Pride of the Marines. The Gorgeous Hussy. Colleen. Fatal Lady. White Fang.* 1937: *You Only Live Once. Dead End. The Devil's Playground. A Fight to the Finish. The Wildcatter. 23½ Hours' Leave. Escape by Night. Night Key. Park Avenue Logger* (GB: *Millionaire Playboy*). *The Go-Getter. Mountain Music. The Singing Marine. Music for Madame.* 1938: *Born to be Wild. The Law West of Tombstone. Reformatory. Professor Beware. Gun Law. Hawaii Calls. Flight into Nowhere. Mr Moto's Gamble. The Amazing Dr Clitterhouse. Over the Wall. Numbered Woman. Prison Break. Bringing Up Baby. You Can't Take It With You. Of Human Hearts. Penitentiary. The Adventures of Marco Polo. Going Places. Fugitives for a Night. Submarine Patrol.* 1939: *Dodge City. Made for Each Other. Son of Frankenstein. They Made Me a Criminal. Waterfront. Trouble in Sundown. The Return of the Cisco Kid. Gone With the Wind. Young Mr Lincoln. Frontier Marshal. The Kid from Kokomo* (GB: *The Orphan of the Ring*). *The Oklahoma Kid. The Girl from Mexico. Drums Along the Mohawk. Dust Be My Destiny. Heaven With a Barbed-Wire Fence. Mr Moto in Danger Island* (GB: *Mr Moto on Danger Island*). *Confessions of a Nazi Spy. Pardon Our Nerve.* 1940: *Santa Fé Trail. Buck Benny Rides Again. Little Old New York. Virginia City. The Cisco Kid and the Lady. The Grapes of Wrath. The Mortal Storm. The Long Voyage Home. Sailor's Lady. Kit Carson.* 1941: *The Shepherd of the Hills. A Man Betrayed* (GB: *Citadel of Crime*). *Tobacco Road. Swamp Water* (GB: *The Man Who Came Back*). *Sergeant York. Manpower. Doctors Don't Tell. Wild Bill Hickok Rides. The Maltese Falcon.* 1942: *In This Our Life. Gentleman Jim. The Falcon Takes Over. Sin Town. Ten Gentlemen from West Point. A Night to Remember.* 1943: *A Guy Named Joe. They Came to Blow Up America. Hitler—Dead or Alive. Cowboy Commandos. Hello, Frisco, Hello. Slightly Dangerous.* 1944: *Home in Indiana. The Sullivans. Tall in the Saddle.* 1945: *Dakota. They Were Expendable.* 1946: *Canyon Passage. It's a Wonderful Life! My Darling Clementine.* 1947: *The Fugitive. Unconquered.* 1948: *Fort Apache. Three Godfathers. The Time of Your Life. Joan of Arc. Tap Roots.* 1950: *Wagonmaster. Rid*

ABOVE Stars Martin **Boddey** (extreme right), John Bentley and Vera Fusek relax in the African heat off the set of the 1956 jungle thriller *Escape in the Sun*

BELOW Mary **Boland** (centre) obviously finds the wiles of Lilyan Tashman more resistible than does Charlie Ruggles in 1933's *Mama Loves Papa*

High. Singing Guns. Kiss Tomorrow Goodbye. 1951: The Great Missouri Raid. Operation Pacific. Only the Valiant. On Dangerous Ground. 1952: The Quiet Man. Thunderbirds. Hellgate. 1953: Blowing Wild. The Moon-lighter. Hondo. 1954: Gypsy Colt. The Bob Mathias Story (GB: The Flaming Torch). Johnny Guitar. The Long Gray Line. 1955: Mr Roberts. A Man Alone. 1956: The Searchers. Dakota Incident. Pillars of the Sky (GB: The Tomahawk and the Cross). 1957: The Wings of Eagles. The Halliday Brand. 1958: China Doll. 1959: Rio Bravo. Alias Jesse James.

The Snake Pit. The Sainted Sisters. 1949: So Dear to My Heart. The Life of Riley. Reign of Terror (GB: The Black Book). Mr Soft Touch (GB: House of Settlement). The Baron of Arizona. 1950: The Furies. 1951: Lone Star. 1953: Latin Lovers. 1954: Track of the Cat. 1956: Back from Eternity. 1957: The Unholy Wife. 1959: The Big Fisherman. A Summer Place. 1960: Tomorrow (TV). 1961: Tammy, Tell Me True. 1962: The Wonderful World of the Brothers Grimm. 1963: Tammy and the Doctor. 1971: She Waits (TV). 1976: Crossing Fox River (TV).

## BONDI, Beulah
(B. Bondy) 1888-1981

Sharp-faced, dark-featured, penetrating American actress who, after a highly successful stage career, spent almost her whole Hollywood life playing widows, mothers, dowagers and grandmothers—in real life she never married—who were usually practical types. Twice nominated for an Academy Award, she travelled around the world twice after officially 'retiring' in 1962. Died following a severe fall.

1931: Street Scene. Arrowsmith. 1932: Rain. 1933: Christopher Bean (GB: The Late Christopher Bean). The Stranger's Return. Finishing School. 1934: The Painted Veil. Two Alone. Ready for Love. 1935: Registered Nurse. Bad Boy. The Good Fairy. 1936: The Invisible Ray. Trail of the Lonesome Pine. The Moon's Our Home. The Case Against Mrs Ames. Hearts Divided. The Gorgeous Hussy. 1937: Maid of Salem. Make Way for Tomorrow. 1938: The Buccaneer. Of Human Hearts. Vivacious Lady. The Sisters. 1939: On Borrowed Time. Mr Smith Goes to Washington. The Under-Pup. Remember the Night. 1940: Our Town. The Captain is a Lady. 1941: Penny Serenade. Shepherd of the Hills. One Foot in Heaven. 1943: Watch on the Rhine. Tonight We Raid Calais. 1944: I Love a Soldier. Our Hearts Were Young and Gay. The Very Thought of You. And Now Tomorrow. She's a Soldier, Too. 1945: The South-erner. Back to Bataan. Breakfast in Hollywood (GB: The Mad Hatter). Sister Kenny. It's a Wonderful Life! 1947: High Conquest. 1948:

## BORG, Veda Ann 1915-1973

Fluffy blonde (brunette until 1939) Holly-wood actress with a cynical air, who worked hard through the 1930s and 1940s as a succession of sluts, double-crossers, gang-sters' molls, blowzy waitresses, faithless wives and generally blondes who had seen better days but were often optimistic of something turning up. Career disrupted in 1939 by a car crash, her injuries from which entailed plastic surgery and 10 operations. Married (second) to director Andrew V. McLaglen from 1946 to 1958.

1936: Three Cheers for Love. 1937: Men in Exile. Kid Galahad. San Quentin. The Case of the Stuttering Bishop. Public Wedding. The Singing Marine. Confession. Back in Circula-tion. Marry the Girl. It's Love I'm After. Varsity Show. Submarine D-1. Alcatraz Is-land. Missing Witness. 1938: She Loved a Fireman. Over the Wall. Café Hostess. 1939: The Law Comes to Texas. 1940: A Miracle on Main Street. Melody Ranch. I Take This Oath. Dr Christian Meets the Women. The Shadow (serial). Laughing at Danger. Glamour for Sale. Bitter Sweet. Behind the News. 1941: The Arkansas Judge (GB: False Witness). The Penalty. The Pittsburgh Kid. The Getaway. Honky Tonk. Down in San Diego. The Corsican Brothers. 1942: About Face. Duke of the Navy. She's in the Army. Two Yanks in Trinidad. I Married an Angel. Lady in a Jam. 1943: Murder in Times Square. Isle of Forgotten Sins. Revenge of the Zombies (GB: The Corpse Vanished). The Girl from Monte-rey. The Unknown Guest. False Faces (GB: The Attorney's Dilemma). Something to Shout About. 1944: Smart Guy (GB: You Can't

Beat the Law). Standing Room Only. Detective Kitty O'Day. Irish Eyes Are Smiling. Marked Trails. The Girl Who Dared. The Big Noise. The Falcon in Hollywood. 1945: What a Blonde. Fog Island. Jungle Raiders (serial). Rough, Tough and Ready (GB: Men of the Deep). Bring on the Girls. Scared Stiff. Nob Hill. Don Juan Quilligan. Dangerous Intruder. Love, Honor and Goodbye. Mildred Pierce. 1946: Life with Blondie. Avalanche. Wife Wanted (GB: Shadow of Blackmail). Accom-plice. The Fabulous Suzanne. *I Love My Husband, But! 1947: The Pilgrim Lady. Big Town. Mother Wore Tights. 1948: The Bachelor and the Bobby Soxer (GB: Bachelor Knight). Blonde Savage. Chicken Every Sun-day. Julia Misbehaves. 1949: Mississippi Rhythm. One Last Fling. Forgotten Women. 1950: Rider from Tucson. Kangaroo Kid. 1951: Aaron Slick from Punkin Crick (GB: Marshmallow Moon). 1952: Big Jim McLain. Hold That Line. 1953: A Perilous Journey. Mr Scoutmaster. Hot News. Three Sailors and a Girl. 1954: Bitter Creek. 1955: You're Never Too Young. Guys and Dolls. Love Me Or Leave Me. I'll Cry Tomorrow. 1956: The Naked Gun. Frontier Gambler. 1957: The Wings of Eagles. 1958: The Fearmakers. 1959: Thunder in the Sun. 1960: The Alamo.

## BOUCHEY, Willis 1895-1977

Solidly built, ambivalent-looking American supporting player with greying brown hair. He left the security of a Broadway career to try his luck in the still film-filled Hollywood of the early 1950s and stayed in steady employ there for the remainder of his career, often in westerns as bankers, ageing sheriffs, judges or town big-shots. Some-times billed as Willis B. Bouchey.

1951: Elopement. 1952: Red Planet Mars. Carbine Williams. Just for You. Assignment—Paris! Don't Bother to Knock! Million Dollar Mermaid (GB: The One-Piece Bathing Suit). Deadline USA (GB: Deadline). 1953: Gun Belt. The Big Heat. The 'I Don't Care' Girl. The President's Lady. Pick-Up on South Street. From Here to Eternity. Dangerous Crossing. 1954: Battle of Rogue River. The Bridges at Toko-Ri. Suddenly! Drum Beat. The Long Gray Line. The Violent Men (GB: Rough Company). Executive Suite. Fireman, Save My

Child. A Star is Born. 1955: I Cover the Underworld. Battle Cry. The Spoilers. The McConnell Story (GB: Tiger in the Sky). Hell on Frisco Bay. The Man on the Ledge (TV. GB: cinemas). Big House USA. 1956: Pillars of the Sky (GB: The Tomahawk and the Cross). Forever Darling. Johnny Concho. Magnificent Roughnecks. 1957: Mister Cory. The Garment Jungle. The Night Runner. The Wings of Eagles. Last of the Badmen. Beau James. Zero Hour! Last Stagecoach West. Darby's Rangers (GB: The Young Invaders). 1958: The Sheepman. The Last Hurrah. No Name on the Bullet. 1959: The Horse Soldiers. 1960: Sergeant Rutledge. 1961: Saintly Sinners. Five Guns to Tombstone. Two Rode Together. You Have to Run Fast. Man Missing (GB: Pocketful of Miracles). 1962: Incident in an Alley. The Man Who Shot Liberty Valance. Panic in Year Zero. How the West Was Won. 1964: Cheyenne Autumn. Where Love Has Gone. Apache Rifles. 1965: McHale's Navy Joins the Air Force. 1966: Return of the Gunfighter. Follow Me, Boys! 1968: Support Your Local Sheriff. 1969: Young Billy Young. The Love God? 1970: Dirty Dingus Magee. The Intruders (TV). 1971: Support Your Local Gunfighter.

## BOXER, John
(Cyril J. Boxer) 1909-
Squarely built, black-haired, pugnacious-looking British actor who played rural figures of authority—aldermen, squires, country policemen and the like—and almost made a career out of playing Petty Officer Herbert in several stage productions of Seagulls over Sorrento. He swapped a stockbroking for an acting career at 19, and has remained largely a man of the theatre, despite a busy period of film activity in the 1940s.

1935: Royal Cavalcade (US: Regal Cavalcade). 1940: Convoy. George and Margaret. 1942: In Which We Serve. The Foreman Went to France (US: Somewhere in France). Flying Fortress. 1943: The Flemish Farm. Millions Like Us. The Adventures of Tartu (US: Tartu). The Demi-Paradise (US: Adventure for Two). San Demetrio London. 1944: Waterloo Road. The Halfway House. 1947: The October Man. The White Unicorn

(US: Bad Sister). 1948: My Brother's Keeper. London Belongs to Me (US: Dulcimer Street). The Blue Lagoon. Man on the Run. 1949: It's Not Cricket. Stop Press Girl. 1950: Mr Drake's Duck. The Happiest Days of Your Life. The Woman in Question (US: Five Angles on Murder). Highly Dangerous. 1951: Encore. 1953: The Red Beret (US: Paratrooper). 1954: Secret Venture. Diplomatic Passport. Three Cases of Murder. 1956: Brothers in Law. 1957: Undercover Girl. The Bridge on the River Kwai. The Tommy Steele Story (US: Rock Around the World). 1958: Heart of a Child. 1962: Emergency. 1963: Hide and Seek. 1966: *The Haunted Man. 1972: Frenzy. For the Love of Ada.

## BRAMBELL, Wilfrid 1912-1985
Scraggy Irish-born actor of skeletal aspect, specializing in toothless old codgers, but virtually unknown to the public at large until his gigantic success as the horrendous Albert Steptoe, rag-and-bone merchant, in television's Steptoe and Son, in which he alternated between pop-eyed horror, cronish cackling and lascivious leers. The series was unsuccessfully transferred to the cinema screen; a sequel was equally disastrous. Died from cancer.

1935: The 39 Steps. 1948: Another Shore. 1956: Dry Rot. 1957: The Story of Esther Costello (US: Golden Virgin). 1958: The Long Hot Summer. 1959: Serious Charge (US: A Touch of Hell). 1960: Urge to Kill. 1961: The Sinister Man. Flame in the Streets. What a Whopper! *The Grand Junction Case. 1962: In Search of the Castaways. The Boys. The Fast Lady. 1963: The Small World of Sammy Lee. Crooks in Cloisters. The Three Lives of Thomasina. Go Kart Go! 1964: A Hard Day's Night. 1965: San Ferry Ann. 1966: Where the Bullets Fly. Mano di velluto. 1968: Witchfinder-General (US: The Conqueror Worm). Lionheart. Cry Wolf. 1969: *The Undertakers. Carry on Again, Doctor. 1970: Some Will, Some Won't. 1972: Steptoe and Son. 1973: Steptoe and Son Ride Again. Holiday on the Buses. 1978: The Adventures of Picasso. 1980: High Rise Donkey. 1983: *Death and Transfiguration. Sword of the Valiant.

## BRANDON, Henry
(H. Kleinbach) 1912-
Dark-haired German-born actor in American films, with eternally young, if slightly cruel-looking features. He had a leading role in his first film, a Laurel and Hardy comedy, as 'the meanest man in Toyland', but star billing eluded him through 40 years of films until he appeared as the tiger-taming man of the wild in the big money-spinning When the North Wind Blows in 1975, looking so little older one could barely credit it was the same actor who had threatened Buck Rogers with destruction in the 1930s.

1934: †Babes in Toyland. 1936: †The Preview Murder Mystery. †Big Brown Eyes. Killer at Large. The Garden of Allah. Black Legion. Trail of the Lonesome Pine. Poker Faces. 1937: Jungle Jim (serial). Secret Agent X-9 (serial). I Promise to Pay. Island Captives. Last Train from Madrid. Conquest (GB: Marie Walewska). West Bound Limited. Wells Fargo. 1938: Spawn of the North. Three Comrades. If I Were King. The Last Warning. 1939: Conspiracy. Buck Rogers (serial). Pirates of the Skies. Nurse Edith Cavell. Beau Geste. Marshal of Mesa City. Geronimo. 1940: The Ranger and the Lady. Half a Sinner. Under Texas Skies. Ski Patrol. The Son of Monte Cristo. Dark Streets of Cairo. Drums of Fu Manchu (serial). Half a Winner. 1941: Bad Man of Deadwood. Shepherd of the Hills. Underground. Hurricane Smith. Two in a Taxi. 1943: Edge of Darkness. 1947: Northwest Outpost (GB: End of the Rainbow). 1948: Old Los Angeles. Canon City. Joan of Arc. The Paleface. Hollow Triumph (GB: The Scar). 1949: The Fighting O'Flynn. Tarzan's Magic Fountain. 1951: Cattle Drive. The Golden Horde (GB: The Golden Horde of Genghis Khan). Flame of Araby. 1952: Harem Girl. Scarlet Angel. Wagons West. Hurricane Smith (and 1941 film). 1953: Tarzan and the She-Devil. War Arrow. The War of the Worlds. Pony Express. Raiders of the Seven Seas. Scared Stiff. The Caddy. Casanova's Big Night. 1954: Vera Cruz. Knock on Wood. 1955: Silent Fear. 1956: The Ten Commandments. The Searchers. Comanche. Bandido! 1957: Hell's Crossroads. Omar Khayyam. The Land Unknown. 1958: Auntie

Mame. The Buccaneer. 1959: The Big Fisherman. Okefenokee (GB: Indian Killer). 1961: Two Rode Together. 1963: Captain Sindbad. 1967: Search for the Evil One. 1973: So Long, Blue Boy. 1974: When the North Wind Blows. 1975: The Manhandlers. 1976: Assault on Precinct 13. 1983: To Be or Not to Be.

†As Harry Kleinbach

### BRENDEL, El 1890-1964

Dark, skinny comedy performer who spoke in splintered Scandinavian but in fact hailed from Philadelphia. A vaudeville veteran, he starred in short comedies and 'B' features throughout Hollywood's golden era, and was a popular guest 'fool' in main features. Married to his ex-vaudeville partner, he died from a heart attack. The 'El' was short for Elmer.

1926: The Campus Flirt. You Never Know Women. Man of the Forest. 1927: Arizona Bound. Rolled Stockings. Too Many Crooks. Wings. Ten Modern Commandments. 1929: Sunny Side Up. The Cock-Eyed World. Hot for Paris. Frozen Justice. *Beau Night. 1930: The Golden Calf. Just Imagine. Happy Days. The Big Trail. New Movietone Follies of 1930. 1931: Mr Lemon of Orange. Women of All Nations. Delicious. The Spider. Six Cylinder Love. *The Stolen Jools (GB: The Slippery Pearls). 1932: West of Broadway. Handle With Care. Disorderly Conduct. 1933: Hot Pepper. My Lips Betray. The Last Trail. Olsen's Big Moment. 1934: The Meanest Gal in Town. 1935: *Broadway Brevities. 1936: *Lonesome Trailer. Career Woman. God's Country and the Woman. 1937: The Holy Terror. Blonde Trouble. 1938: Little Miss Broadway. Happy Landing. Valley of the Giants. 1939: Code of the Streets. Risky Business. House of Fear. Spirit of Culver (GB: Man's Heritage). Call a Messenger. 1940: If I Had My Way. Captain Caution. Gallant Sons. 1944: Machine Gun Mama. *Defective Detectives. *Mopey Dope. I'm from Arkansas. 1945: *Pistol-Packin' Nitwits. *Snooper Service. 1949: The Beautiful Blonde from Bashful Bend. 1953: Paris Model. 1956: The She-Creature.

### BRENNAN, Eileen 1936-

Abrasive, light-haired American comedy actress, with broad, if somewhat strained smile, pitched somewhere between Gladys George and Thelma Ritter (qv). She was nominated for a Best Supporting Actress Oscar in Private Benjamin, but her career was disrupted when she was severely injured in a car accident in 1982, spending some time in a wheelchair.

1967: Divorce American Style. 1971: The Last Picture Show. 1972: Playmates (TV). 1973: Scarecrow. The Blue Knight (TV. GB: cinemas). The Sting. 1974: Daisy Miller. My Father's House (TV). 1975: At Long Last Love. Hustle. The Night That Panicked America (TV). 1976: Murder by Death. 1977: The Last of the Cowboys (later The Great Smokey Roadblock). The Death of Ritchie (TV). 1978: The Cheap Detective. Black Beauty (TV). FM. 1980: Private Benjamin. 1982: My Old Man (TV). Pandemonium. 1985: Clue.

### BRENNAN, Michael 1912-

Solidly built, brown-haired, hopeful- but slightly dim-looking London-born actor who played tough mugs both straight and comic. Once John Gielgud's stage manager, Brennan brought his wide-apart eyes and long, grinning mouth into the acting scene in the mid-1930s and, in the post-war years, became a familiar, if sporadic visitor to films, between TV and stage assignments. Enjoyed one of his most effective roles as the inept store detective in Norman Wisdom's Trouble in Store.

1947: They Made Me a Fugitive (US: I Became a Criminal). Blanche Fury. Captain Boycott. 1948: Noose (US: The Silk Noose). Cardboard Cavalier. 1949: For Them That Trespass. The Chiltern Hundreds (US: The Amazing Mr Beecham). 1950: Waterfront (US: Waterfront Women). The Clouded Yellow. Morning Departure (US: Operation Disaster). They Were Not Divided. Blackout. No Trace. Paul Temple's Triumph. 1951: Circle of Danger. Tom Brown's Schooldays. The Lady with a Lamp. 1952: Emergency Call (US: Hundred-Hour Hunt). 13 East Street. Made in Heaven. Ivanhoe. Something Money Can't Buy. 1953: Trouble in Store. Personal Affair. It's a Grand Life. 1954: Up to His Neck. 1955: See How They Run. 1956: Up in the World. The Big Money (released 1958). 1957: Just My Luck. Not Wanted on Voyage. 1958: Law and Disorder. Girls at Sea. 1959: The 39 Steps. 1960: The Day They Robbed the Bank of England. Watch Your Stern. 1961: Johnny Nobody. On the Fiddle (US: Operation Snafu). Ambush in Leopard Street. 1962: The Waltz of the Toreadors. The Devil's Agent. Live Now—Pay Later. 1963: Tom Jones. 1964: Act of Murder. 1965: Three Hats for Lisa. Cuckoo Patrol. The Amorous Adventures of Moll Flanders. Thunderball. 1966: Death is a Woman. The Deadly Affair. 1968: The Great Pony Raid. 1970: Lust for a Vampire. 1971: Fright. 1972: Doomwatch. The Trouble with 2B (series). Up the Front. Nothing But the Night.

### BRENNAN, Walter 1894-1974

Brennan was born in a town called Swampscott, Massachusetts, a name exactly suited to the assortment of veteran westerners for which his career will largely be remembered. Usually seen on screen in clothes as battered as his face, Brennan's distinctive voice sounded as though it were issuing through a plug of chaw tobaccy. The man who had started in films as an extra and stuntman, then played dozens of tiny roles, went on to win Best Supporting Actor Oscars in 1936 (Come and Get It), 1938 (Kentucky) and 1940 (The Westerner) and was actually nominated again in 1941! Died from an emphysema.

1927: The Ridin' Rowdy. Tearin' into Trouble. 1928: The Ballyhoo Buster. The

*Lariat Kid. Silks and Saddles (GB: Thoroughbreds). One Hysterical Night. 1929: The Long, Long Trail. The Shannons of Broadway. Smiling Guns. 1930: King of Jazz. \*Scratch As Scratch Can. 1931: Dancing Dynamite. Neck and Neck. 1932: Law and Order. Texas Cyclone. Two-Fisted Law. The All-American (GB: Sport of a Nation). Miss Pinkerton. The Airmail Mystery (serial). The Fourth Horseman. Parachute Jumper. \*The Iceman's Ball. 1933: One Year Later. Man of Action. The Invisible Man. The Phantom of the Air (serial). Saturday's Millions. The Kiss Before the Mirror. Fighting for Justice. The Keyhole. Baby Face. Lilly Turner. Female. Sing, Sinner, Sing. From Headquarters. Strange People. 1934: The Life of Vergie Winters. Whom the Gods Destroy. Death on the Diamond. Rustlers' Roundup. Silent Men. \*Woman Haters. Good Dame (GB: Good Girl). Half a Sinner. Desirable. Housewife. Stamboul Quest. Riptide. The Painted Veil. 1935: The Wedding Night. \*Restless Knights. Lady Tubbs (GB: The Gay Lady). Northern Frontier. The Mystery of Edwin Drood. We're in the Money. Public Hero No. One. The Man on the Flying Trapeze (GB: The Memory Expert). Seven Keys to Baldpate. Barbary Coast. Bride of Frankenstein. Law Beyond the Range. Metropolitan. \*Bric-a-Brac. 1936: Three Godfathers. Fury. These Three. Come and Get It. Banjo on My Knee. The Moon's Our Home. The Prescott Kid. 1937: She's Dangerous. When Love is Young. Wild and Woolly. The Affairs of Cappy Ricks. 1938: The Adventures of Tom Sawyer. The Buccaneer. Kentucky. The Texans. Mother Carey's Chickens. The Cowboy and the Lady. 1939: Stanley and Livingstone. The Story of Vernon and Irene Castle. They Shall Have Music (GB: Melody of Youth). Joe and Ethel Turp Call on the President. 1940: The Westerner. Northwest Passage. Maryland. 1941: Meet John Doe. Sergeant York. Swamp Water (GB: The Man Who Came Back). Nice Girl? This Woman is Mine. Rise and Shine. 1942: Pride of the Yankees. Stand By for Action! (GB: Cargo of Innocents). 1943: Slightly Dangerous. Hangmen Also Die. North Star. \*The Last Will and Testament of Tom Smith. 1944: The Princess and the Pirate. To Have and Have Not. Home in Indiana. 1945: Dakota. 1946: Nobody Lives Forever. My Darling Clementine. A Stolen Life. Centennial Summer. 1947: Driftwood. 1948: Red River. Scudda Hoo! Scudda Hay! (GB: Summer Lightning). Blood on the Moon. 1949: Brimstone. Task Force. The Great Dan Patch. The Green Promise (GB: Raging Waters). 1950: Singing Guns. Curtain Call at Cactus Creek (GB: Take the Stage). Surrender. A Ticket to Tomahawk. The Showdown. 1951: The Wild Blue Yonder (GB: Thunder Across the Pacific). Along the Great Divide. Best of the Bad Men. 1952: Return of the Texan. Lure of the Wilderness. 1953: Sea of Lost Ships. 1954: Drums Across the River. Four Guns to the Border. Bad Day at Black Rock. The Far Country. 1955: At Gunpoint! (GB: Gunpoint!). 1956: The Proud Ones. Glory. Come*

*Next Spring. Goodbye, My Lady. 1957: Tammy and the Bachelor (GB: Tammy). The Way to the Gold. God Is My Partner. 1959: Rio Bravo. 1962: How the West Was Won. 1963: Shoot Out at Big Sag. 1964: Those Calloways. 1966: The Oscar. Who's Minding the Mint? 1967: The Gnome-Mobile. 1968: The One and Only Genuine Original Family Band. 1969: Support Your Local Sheriff. The Over-the-Hill Gang (TV). 1970: The Young Country. The Over-the-Hill Gang Rides Again (TV). 1971: Smoke in the Wind. Two for the Money (TV). 1972: Home for the Holidays (TV).*

**BRESSART, Felix** 1880-1949
Sad-eyed, wild-haired refugee from German films (actually born in what was then East Prussia), whose receding chin and five o'clock shadow emphasized his big nose and made his head seem to nod as he offered fractured advice to his fellows. He came to Hollywood in 1939 and hovered about the fringes of a fistful of films, looking mostly doleful but not tragic, before leukaemia struck him down in 1949.

*1928: Liebe im Kuhstall. 1930: Die Drei von der Tankstelle (GB: Three Men and Lillian). 1931: Der wahre Jakob. Das alte Lied. Nie wieder Liebe (US: No More Love). Eine Freundin so goldig wie Du. 1932: Der Schrecken der Garnison. Hirsekorn greift ein. Der Herr Bürovorsteher. 1933: Holzapfel weiss alles. Drei Tage Mittelarrest. Der Sohn der weissen Berg. 1934: Der Glückzylinder. Und wer küsst mich? 1939: Three Smart Girls Grow Up. Bridal Suite. Swanee River. Ninotchka. 1940: Edison the Man. The Shop around the Corner. It All Came True. Third Finger, Left Hand. Bitter Sweet. Comrade X. Escape. 1941: Ziegfeld Girl. Blossoms in the Dust. Married Bachelor. Kathleen. Mr and Mrs North. 1942: To Be or Not to Be. Crossroads. Iceland (GB: Katina). 1943: Above Suspicion. Song of Russia. Three Hearts for Julia. 1944: The Seventh Cross. Blonde Fever. Greenwich Village. Secrets in the Dark. 1945: Dangerous Partners. Without Love. Ding Dong Williams (GB: Melody Maker). 1946: I've Always Loved You (GB: Concerto). The Thrill of Brazil. Her Sister's Secret. 1948: Portrait of Jennie (GB: Jennie). A Song is Born. 1949: Take One False Step.*

**BRESSLAW, Bernard** 1933-
Giant-sized British cockney comedy actor specializing in gormless types, who scored an overwhelming personal success in TV's *The Army Game* as a witless, kiss-curled private called Popeye. But subsequent starring roles in films were not well chosen (also his hair was disappearing rapidly) and his career suffered a lull until he became a regular in the Carry On Series.

*1954: Men of Sherwood Forest. 1955: The Glass Cage (US: The Glass Tomb). 1956: Up in the World. 1957: High Tide At Noon. 1958: Blood of the Vampire. I Only Arsked! 1959: Too Many Crooks. The Ugly Duckling. 1963: It's All Happening. 1965: Carry On Cowboy. Morgan - a Suitable Case for Treatment. 1966: \*Round the Bend. Carry On Screaming. 1967: Follow That Camel. Carry On Doctor. 1968: Carry On Up the Khyber. 1969: Carry On Camping. Moon Zero Two. Carry On Up the Jungle. Spring and Port Wine. 1970: Carry On Loving. 1971: Up Pompeii. The Magnificent Seven Deadly Sins. Carry On at Your Convenience. Blinker's Spy Spotter. 1972: Carry On Matron. Carry On Abroad. 1973: Carry On Girls. 1974: Carry On Dick. Vampira (US: Old Dracula). 1975: One of Our Dinosaurs is Missing. 1976: Joseph Andrews. 1977: Jabberwocky. Behind the Iron Mask (GB: The Fifth Musketeer). 1980: Hawk the Slayer. 1983: Krull.*

**BRIMLEY, (A.) Wilford** 1935-
Barrel-like, moustachioed American actor with blinky eyes who almost always plays characters older than his real age. Brimley was a farm worker and rodeo rider who gained weight and became a blacksmith, then determined to become a film actor and gradually got a toehold after years of extra work. Nowadays giving fine performances in fat (!) character roles and seems a certainty for a Best Supporting Actor Oscar nomination at some time or other in the future.

*1971: Lawman. 1976: The Oregon Trail (TV). 1978: The China Syndrome. 1979: The Wild, Wild West Revisited (TV). The Electric Horseman. 1980: Brubaker. Borderline. 1981: Rodeo Girl. Death Valley. Absence of Malice. 1982: The Thing. Tender Mercies.*

*1983: 10 to Midnight. High Road to China. 1984: Harry & Son. The Hotel New Hampshire. The Natural. The Stone Boy. Country. 1985: Cocoon. Murder in Space (TV). Remo Williams and the Secret of Sinanju. Jackals.*

**BROCCO, Peter** 1913- *1993*
Scrawny, sharp-featured, often dishevelled American actor with dark, thinning hair and 'continental villain' looks. After star roles in local repertory, he toured French, Italian, Spanish and Swiss theatres before war service. From 1947, he started playing vicious or frightened little men in Hollywood films, actually once appearing as a character called 'Short and Thin'; although 5 feet 9 inches, his slight build made him seem less. Still around, in roles both large and small, he had his first film lead in 1973 in *Homebodies*.

*1947: The Swordsman. Alias Mr Twilight. The Lone Wolf in Mexico. 1948: The Gallant Blade. The Boy with Green Hair. The Saxon Charm. 1949: Post Office Investigator. The Undercover Man. Flaming Fury. Jolson Sings Again. Search for Danger. Boston Blackie's Chinese Venture (GB: Chinese Adventure). Miss Grant Takes Richmond (GB: Innocence is Bliss). The Reckless Moment. 1950: Black Hand. The Killer That Stalked New York (GB: The Frightened City). The Breaking Point. 1951: Flame of Stamboul. The Great Caruso. Sirocco. The Tall Target. Francis Goes to the Races. His Kind of Woman. Drums in the Deep South. The Whip Hand. The Fat Man. Belle le Grand. 1952: Ma and Pa Kettle on Vacation (GB: Ma and Pa Kettle Go to Paris). Harem Girl. Woman in the Dark. Cripple Creek. The Prisoner of Zenda. Mutiny. The Ring. 1953: El Alamein (GB: Desert Patrol). The Story of Three Loves. 1954: Duffy of San Quentin (GB: Men Behind Bars). Rogue Cop. 1955: The Racers (GB: Such Men Are Dangerous). Thrill of the Ring. The Big Knife. I'll Cry Tomorrow. 1956: Superman Flies Again (TV. GB: cinemas). He Laughed Last. 1958: Black Patch. 1960: Spartacus. 1962: The Three Stooges in Orbit. 1964: The Pleasure Seekers. 1965: Our Man Flint. 1967: Games. 1969: A Time for Dying. Then Came Bronson (TV. GB: cinemas). 1971: Alias Smith and Jones (TV). Johnny Got His Gun. The Priest Killer (TV). What's the Matter with Helen? 1973: Homebodies. 1974: The Family Kovack (TV). 1975: One Flew Over the Cuckoo's Nest. 1976: Raid on Entebbe (TV. GB: Cinemas). 1977: The One and Only. 1979: Butch and Sundance The Early Days. 1980: Cruising. 1982: Fighting Back (GB: Death Vengeance). 1983: The Twilight Zone (GB: Twilight Zone The Movie). Jekyll and Hyde Together Again. Night Partners (TV).*

**BROMBERG, J. Edward** 1903-1951
Plump-chinned, bespectacled, Hungarian-born actor, in America from childhood. Prematurely-greying hair saw him cast in

character roles from his 1936 début, often as doctors and professors, but in a generally satisfying variety of types. His services were less in demand in the post-war years and he was in London when he collapsed and died 'of natural causes' just days short of his 48th birthday.

*1936: Sins of Man. The Crime of Dr Forbes. Under Two Flags. Girls' Dormitory. Ladies in Love. Star for a Night. Stowaway. Reunion (GB: Hearts in Reunion). 1937: Fair Warning. Seventh Heaven. Charlie Chan on Broadway. That I May Live. Second Honeymoon. 1938: The Baroness and the Butler. Mr Moto Takes a Chance. Four Men and a Prayer. Suez. Sally, Irene and Mary. Rebecca of Sunnybrook Farm. I'll Give a Million. 1939: Jesse James. Hollywood Cavalcade. Wife, Husband and Friend. Three Sons. 1940: The Mark of Zorro. Strange Cargo. The Return of Frank James. 1941: Dance Hall. The Devil Pays Off. Hurricane Smith. Pacific Blackout. 1942: Invisible Agent. Life Begins at Eight-Thirty (GB: The Light of Heart). Tennessee Johnson (GB: The Man on America's Conscience). Reunion/Reunion in France (GB: Mademoiselle France). Half-Way to Shanghai. 1943: Lady of Burlesque (GB: Striptease Lady). Son of Dracula. Phantom of the Opera. 1944: A Voice in the Wind. Chip Off the Old Block. 1945: Salome, Where She Danced. The Missing Corpse. Easy to Look At. Pillow of Death. 1946: Cloak and Dagger. Tangier. The Walls Came Tumbling Down. Queen of the Amazons. 1948: Arch of Triumph. A Song is Born. 1949: I Shot Jesse James. 1950: Guilty Bystander.*

**BROMLEY, Sydney** 1919-
Wiry, gimlet-eyed, quick-moving, ginger-bearded British actor, mostly in very minor film roles as toothless hayseeds or rural sages. In the theatre, however, he built up a very different reputation as a formidable interpreter of eccentric Shakespearian roles. Always highly distinctive.

*1944: Demobbed. 1945: Brief Encounter. 1946: Loyal Heart. 1947: The Mark of Cain. The Dark Road. 1954: The Love Match. 1955: Stolen Time (US: Blonde Blackmailer). 1957: Saint Joan. 1960: The Criminal (US: The Concrete*

*Jungle). 1961: The Piper's Tune. 1962: Paranoiac. Captain Clegg (US: Night Creatures). 1965: Monster of Terror (US: Die, Monster, Die). 1966: Operation Third Form. The Christmas Tree. Slave Girls. 1967: Smashing Time. Dance of the Vampires (US: The Fearless Vampire Killers). 1971: Macbeth. 1973: No Sex Please—We're British. Frankenstein and the Monster from Hell. 1974: Professor Popper's Problem (serial). 1975: Robin Hood Junior. 1977: The Prince and the Pauper (US: Crossed Swords). Candleshoe. 1980: Dangerous Davies—the Last Detective (TV). 1981: An American Werewolf in London. Dragonslayer. 1984: The Neverending Story. 1985: Pirates.*

**BROOK-JONES, Elwyn** 1911-1962
Chubby British actor with round face, small features and dark, receding hair, often to be found playing blue-jowled, sweaty types, usually on the disreputable side. Born in Sarawak, he studied music as a child and was a concert pianist at 11. After a career in concert-halls and cabaret, he turned to acting in the late 1930s, and played many Shakespearian roles, as well as in a number of films—most notably as Tober in *Odd Man Out*.

*1941: Dangerous Moonlight (US: Suicide Squadron). Pimpernel Smith (US: Mister V). 1942: Tomorrow We Live (US: At Dawn We Die). 1943: The Night Invader. 1946: Odd Man Out. 1948: The Three Weird Sisters. Good Time Girl. Bonnie Prince Charlie. It's Hard to Be Good. 1949: Dear Mr*

LEFT By sheer girth, Wilford **Brimley** (extreme right) dominates this family group from *Country* (1984). Also there are Levi Knebel, Sam Shepard, Therese Graham, Jessica Lange and a baby

BELOW Peter **Brocco** (with cap, at left) tries to look inconspicuous, as usual, here in *The Whip Hand* (1951). The others are Raymond Burr, Elliott Reid and Michael Steele

*Prohack. 1951: Life in Her Hands. I'll Get You for This (US: Lucky Nick Cain). The Wonder Kid. Judgment Deferred. 1952: The Night Won't Talk. 1953: Three Steps in the Dark. 1954: The Harassed Hero. The Case of the Bogus Count. The Gilded Cage. Beau Brummell. 1956: Assignment Redhead (US: Million Dollar Manhunt). Rogue's Yarn. 1958: The Duke Wore Jeans. 1959: Passport to Shame (US: Room 43). The Ugly Duckling. Mystery in the Mine. 1960: The Pure Hell of St Trinian's.*

**BROPHY, Edward/Ed** 1895-1960
Thick-set, podgy-faced, bald American actor in aggressive parts. His speak-first-think-later roles included several thick detectives who embarrassed their superiors, and a rather bizarre collection of valets, blustering politicians and cheap chisellers. His bald head often concealed under a bowler hat, Brophy remains one of the best examples of the recognizable face to which it is hard to put a name.

*1920: Yes or No. 1928: West Point (GB: Eternal Youth). The Cameraman. 1930: Doughboys (GB: Forward March). Our Blushing Brides. Remote Control. Paid (GB: Within the Law). Those Three French Girls. Free and Easy. 1931: A Free Soul. Parlor, Bedroom and Bath (GB: Romeo in Pyjamas). The Champ. A Dangerous Affair. The Big Shot (GB: The Optimist). 1932: Speak Easily. Freaks. Flesh. 1933: Broadway to Hollywood (GB: Ring Up the Curtain). What, No Beer? 1934: Death on the Diamond. The Thin Man. Paris Interlude. The Hide-Out. I'll Fix It. Evelyn Prentice. 1935: The Whole Town's Talking (GB: Passport to Fame). Naughty Marietta. Shadow of Doubt. Mad Love (GB: The Hands of Orlac). China Seas. People Will Talk. I Live My Life. Remember Last Night? She Gets Her Man. Show Them No Mercy (GB: Tainted Money). 1936: Strike Me Pink. Woman Trap. Spend-thrift. Wedding Present. The Case Against Mrs Ames. Kelly the Second. All-American Chump (GB: Country Bumpkin). Here Comes Trouble. Great Guy. Career Woman. Mr Cinderella. 1937: Varsity Show. The Soldier and the Lady (GB: Michael Strogoff). Hideaway Girl. The Great Gambini. Blossoms on Broadway. Jim Hanvey, Detective. The Hit Parade. Oh,*

*Doctor! The Last Gangster. The Girl Said No. Trapped by G-Men (GB: River of Missing Men). 1938: A Slight Case of Murder. Gambling Ship. Romance on the Run. Hold That Kiss. Passport Husband. Vacation from Love. Come On, Leathernecks. Pardon Our Nerve. Gold Diggers in Paris (GB: The Gay Impostors). 1939: For Love or Money. Society Lawyer. You Can't Cheat an Honest Man. The Amazing Mr Williams. The Kid from Kokomo (GB: The Orphan of the Ring). Kid Nightingale. Golden Boy. 1940: Calling Philo Vance. The Big Guy. A Dangerous Game. Sandy Gets Her Man. Dance, Girl, Dance. The Great Profile. Alias the Deacon. Golden Gloves. 1941: The Invisible Woman. Sleepers West. Dumbo (voice only). Thieves Fall Out. The Bride Came COD. Buy Me That Town. The Gay Falcon. Steel Against the Sky. Nine Lives Are Not Enough. 1942: All Through the Night. Broadway. Larceny Inc. Madame Spy. One Exciting Night. Air Force. 1943: Lady Bodyguard. Destroyer. 1944: A Night of Adventure. It Happened Tomorrow. Cover Girl. The Thin Man Goes Home. 1945: I'll Remember April. Wonder Man. See My Lawyer. Penthouse Rhythm. The Falcon in San Francisco. 1946: Swing Parade of 1946. Sweetheart of Sigma Chi. Girl on the Spot. The Falcon's Adventure. Renegade Girl. 1947: It Happened on Fifth Avenue. 1949: Arson Inc. 1951: Roaring City. Danger Zone. Pier 23. 1956: Bundle of Joy. 1958: The Last Hurrah.*

**BROUGH, Mary** 1863-1934
Probably the first great character actress of British sound films. This fierce, chunky little woman brought her haranguing approach from the stage to screen, most notably in her last few years, as a formidable adversary for the Aldwych farceurs. You felt that anyone hit by Mary Brough's umbrella would stay hit. Brown-haired and pugnacious, she was a stage actress for more than 50 years. Died from a heart ailment.

*1914: The Brass Bottle. *Lawyer Quince. *Beauty and the Barge. *The Bo'sun's Mate. A Christmas Carol. *Mrs Scrubs' Discovery. 1915: His Lordship. 1917: Masks and Faces. 1920: The Amazing Quest of Mr Ernest Bliss (serial). London Pride. Enchantment. Judge Not. The Law Divine. The Fordington Twins.*

*John Forrest Finds Himself. 1921: The Will. The Tainted Venus. The Diamond Necklace. Squibs. Demos (US: Why Men Forget). The Bachelor's Club. All Sorts and Conditions of Men. The Golden Dawn. The Night Hawk. The Adventures of Mr Pickwick. The Old Wives' Tale. 1922: Squibs Wins the Calcutta Sweep. Tit for Tat. A Sister to Assist 'Er. 1923: Lily of the Alley. Lights of London. Married Love. The School for Scandal. 1924: Miriam Rozella. Tons of Money. His Grace Gives Notice. The Passionate Adventure. The Alley of Golden Hearts. Not for Sale. 1925: The Only Way. 1926 *John Henry Calling (series). Safety First. 1927: A Sister to Assist 'Er (and 1922 version). 1928: Dawn. Sailors Don't Care. Wait and See. The Physician. The Passing of Mr Quin. *Nursery Chairs. *The King's Breakfast. 1929: Master and Man. The Broken Melody. 1930: Rookery Nook (US: One Embarrassing Night). On Approval. 1931: Tons of Money (and 1924 version). Plunder. 1932: A Night Like This. Thark. 1933: A Cuckoo in the Nest. Up to the Neck. Turkey Time.*

**BRUCE, Nigel**
(William N. Bruce) 1895-1953
British actor (born in Mexico) who carved a whole corner for himself in well-meaning bumbler-fumblers and cuckolded husbands. His Doctor Watson in the Sherlock Holmes films of the thirties and forties, although excellent at first, tended to drift into caricature in later films. In British films from 1929, Hollywood from 1934. Died from a heart attack.

*1929: Red Aces. 1930: The Squeaker. Escape. Birds of Prey (US: The Perfect Alibi). 1931: The Calendar (US: Bachelor's Folly). 1932: The Midshipmaid. Lord Camber's Ladies. 1933: I Was a Spy. Channel Crossing. The Lady is Willing. 1934: The Scarlet Pimpernel. Springtime for Henry. Stand Up and Cheer. Coming Out Party. Murder in Trinidad. Treasure Island. 1935: Becky Sharp. Jalna. She. The Man Who Broke the Bank at Monte Carlo. 1936: Thunder in the City. The Trail of the Lonesome Pine. The Charge of the Light Brigade. Under Two Flags. The White Angel. Make Way for a Lady. Follow Your Heart. The Man I Marry. 1937: The Last of Mrs Cheyney. 1938: The Baroness and the Butler. Kidnapped. Suez. 1939: The*

*Hound of the Baskervilles. The Adventures of Sherlock Holmes (GB: Sherlock Holmes). The Rains Came. 1940: Adventure in Diamonds. Rebecca. The Bluebird. Lillian Russell. Hudson's Bay. Susan and God (GB: The Gay Mrs Trexel). A Dispatch from Reuter's (GB: This Man Reuter). 1941: Playgirl. The Chocolate Soldier. Free and Easy. This Woman is Mine. Suspicion. 1942: Roxie Hart. Eagle Squadron. Sherlock Holmes and the Voice of Terror (GB: The Voice of Terror). This Above All. Journey for Margaret. Sherlock Holmes and the Secret Weapon. 1943: Forever and a Day. Sherlock Holmes in Washington. Sherlock Holmes Faces Death. Crazy House. Lassie Come Home. 1944: Follow the Boys. The Pearl of Death. Gypsy Wildcat. The Scarlet Claw. Frenchman's Creek. Sherlock Holmes and the Spider Woman (GB: The Spider Woman). 1945: The Corn is Green. Son of Lassie. The Woman in Green. Pursuit to Algiers. The House of Fear. 1946: Terror by Night. Dragonwyck. Dressed to Kill (GB: Sherlock Holmes and the Secret Code). 1947: The Two Mrs Carrolls. The Exile. 1948: Julia Misbehaves. 1950: Vendetta. 1951: Hong Kong. 1952: Limelight. Othello. 1953: Bwana Devil. 1954: World for Ransom.*

## BRYAN, Dora
(D. Broadbent) 1923-

Fluffy blonde British actress, with pixieish smile, nearly always seen as maids or strumpets. Originally from Lancashire, she could vary her high nasal tones effectively enough to suggest the backstreets of Soho or the sidestreets of Southport. A British Academy Award for her fine performance in *A Taste of Honey* did not produce further leading roles for the cinema; indeed her output diminished considerably thereafter.

*1946: Odd Man Out. 1948: The Fallen Idol. No Room at the Inn. 1949: Now Barabbas was a robber ... Adam and Evelyne (US: Adam and Evelyn). Once Upon a Dream. The Perfect Woman. The Interrupted Journey. Traveller's Joy (released 1951). The Blue Lamp. The Cure for Love. 1950: No Trace. Something in the City. 1951: Files from Scotland Yard. The Quiet Woman. Circle of Danger. Scarlet Thread. No Highway (US: No Highway in the Sky). High Treason. Lady Godiva Rides*

*Again. Whispering Smith Hits London (US: Whispering Smith versus Scotland Yard). 1952: 13 East Street. Gift Horse (US: Glory at Sea). Time Gentlemen Please! Mother Riley Meets the Vampire (US: Vampire Over London). Made in Heaven. The Ringer. Miss Robin Hood. Women of Twilight (US: Twilight Women). 1953: Street Corner (US: Both Sides of the Law). The Fake. The Intruder. You Know What Sailors Are. 1954: Fast and Loose. The Crowded Day. *Harmony Lane. Mad About Men. 1955: As Long As They're Happy. See How They Run. You Lucky People. Cockleshell Heroes. 1956: The Green Man. Child in the House. 1957: The Man Who Wouldn't Talk. 1958: Hello London! Carry On Sergeant. 1959: Operation Bullshine. Desert Mice. 1960: Follow That Horse! The Night We Got the Bird. 1961: A Taste of Honey. 1966: The Great St Trinian's Train Robbery. The Sandwich Man. 1968: Two a Penny. 1971: Hands of the Ripper. 1972: Up the Front. 1983: Screamtime (V).*

(V) Video

## BUCHANAN, Edgar
(William E. Buchanan) 1902-1979

Light-haired, often bewhiskered American actor of chubby build. Appeared mainly in westerns, as veteran sheriffs, boozy bankers, crooked judges, or just as the hero's sidekick. A former dentist, he started alternating acting with dentistry in the 1930s before becoming a full-time actor and making close to 100 films, his distinctive growling voice matching his round 'country-boy' features. Died following brain surgery.

*1939: My Son is Guilty (GB: Crime's End). Tear Gas Squad. 1940: Three Cheers for the Irish. Too Many Husbands. The Doctor Takes a Wife. When the Daltons Rode. Arizona. Escape to Glory. The Sea Hawk. 1941: Penny Serenade. Submarine Zone. Her First Beau. Richest Man in Town. Texas. You Belong to Me (GB: Good Morning, Doctor). 1942: Tombstone, the Town Too Tough to Die. The Talk of the Town. 1943: City Without Men. The Desperadoes. Good Luck, Mr Yates. Destroyer. *Mr Smug. 1944: Buffalo Bill. The Impatient Years. Bride By Mistake. 1945: Strange Affair. The Fighting Guardsman. Abilene Town. 1946: The Bandit of Sherwood*

*Forest. The Walls Came Tumbling Down. Perilous Holiday. If I'm Lucky. Renegades. 1947: The Sea of Grass. Framed (GB: Paula). 1948: The Swordsman. Wreck of the Hesperus. Adventures in Silverado. Best Man Wins. The Black Arrow (GB: The Black Arrow Strikes). The Untamed Breed. Coroner Creek. The Man from Colorado. 1949: The Walking Hills. Red Canyon. Any Number Can Play. Lust for Gold. 1950: Cheaper by the Dozen. Cargo to Capetown. The Big Hangover. Devil's Doorway. 1951: The Great Missouri Raid. Cave of Outlaws. Rawhide (GB: Desperate Siege). Silver City (GB: High Vermilion). 1952: Flaming Feather. The Big Trees. Wild Stallion. Toughest Man in Arizona. 1953: It Happens Every Thursday. Shane. Make Haste to Live. She Couldn't Say No (GB: Beautiful But Dangerous). 1954: Dawn at Socorro. Human Desire. Destry. 1955: Rage at Dawn. Wichita. The Silver Star. The Lonesome Trail. 1956: Come Next Spring. 1957: Spoilers of the Forest. 1958: Day of the Bad Man. The Sheepman. 1959: King of the Wild Stallions. It Started With a Kiss. Hound Dog Man. Edge of Eternity. 1960: Four Fast Guns. Stump Run. Chartroose Caboose. 1961: Cimarron. The Devil's Partner. Tammy Tell Me True. The Comancheros. Ride the High Country (GB: Guns in the Afternoon). 1963: Donovan's Reef. Move Over, Darling. McLintock! A Ticklish Affair. 1964: The Man from Button Willow (voice only). 1965: The Rounders. 1966: Gunpoint. Welcome to Hard Times (GB: Killer on a Horse). 1969: Angel in My Pocket. Something for a Lonely Man. The Over-the-Hill Gang (TV). 1970: The Over-the-Hill Gang Rides Again (TV). 1971: Yuma (TV). 1974: Benji.*

## BULL, Peter 1912-1984

Corpulent British actor with frog-like features, a hobgoblin of a man usually cast as arrogant, aristocratic nasties who sometimes came to a sticky end. Also enjoyed himself in snooty comedy roles. In private life the most affable of men, he wrote several books, ran an astrological shop and was the world's leading authority on teddy bears. At one time he ran his own repertory company, and won the DSC with the Royal

Navy during World War II. A formidable wit and genuine English eccentric.

1936: *As You Like It. Sabotage (US: The Woman Alone)*. 1937: *Dreaming Lips. Non-Stop New York*. 1938: *The Ware Case*. 1939: *Dead Man's Shoes. Young Man's Fancy*. 1940: *Contraband (US: Blackout)*. 1941: *Quiet Wedding*. 1946: *The Grand Escapade*. 1947: *The Turners of Prospect Road*. 1948: *Saraband for Dead Lovers (US: Saraband). Cardboard Cavalier. Oliver Twist*. 1949: *The Lost People*. 1950: *The Reluctant Widow*. 1951: *I'll Get You for This (US: Lucky Nick Cain). Salute the Toff. The African Queen. The Six Men. Scrooge (US: A Christmas Carol). The Lavender Hill Mob*. 1952: *The Second Mrs Tanqueray*. 1953: *Strange Stories. Malta Story. The Captain's Paradise. Saadia*. 1954: *Beau Brummell*. 1955: *Footsteps in the Fog*. 1956: *The Green Man*. 1958: *tom thumb*. 1959: *The Scapegoat. The Three Worlds of Gulliver*. 1960: *The Girl on the Boat*. 1961: *Goodbye Again/Aimez-vous Brahms? Follow That Man. The Rebel (US: Call Me Genius)*. 1962: *The Old Dark House*. 1963: *Tom Jones*. 1964: *Dr Strangelove, or: How I Learned to Stop Worrying and Love the Bomb*. 1965: *Licensed to Kill (US: The Second Best Secret Agent in the Whole, Wide World). The Intelligence Men*. 1967: *Doctor Dolittle*. 1969: *Lock Up Your Daughters!* 1970: *The Executioner*. 1971: *Girl Stroke Boy*. 1972: *Up the Front. Alice's Adventures in Wonderland. Lady Caroline Lamb*. 1975: *Great Expectations (TV. GB: cinemas)*. 1976: *Joseph Andrews*. 1978: *Rosie Dixon Night Nurse. The Brute*. 1979: *The Tempest*. 1983: *Yellowbeard*.

### BUONO, Victor 1938-1982

It's a pity Victor Buono pointed his massive, heavyweight frame towards comedy, for he could have been a latter-day Laird Cregar. But there are some reminders of what a good, suave, straight villain he could have made, especially in *What Ever Happened to Baby Jane?* (which brought him an Oscar nomination), *The Strangler* and *Goodnight My Love*, the latter a TV movie in which, as the white-suited gourmet villain, he could well be a younger Sydney Greenstreet.

1962: *What Ever Happened to Baby Jane?* 1963: *Four for Texas. My Six Loves*. 1964:

*The Strangler. Robin and the Seven Hoods*. 1965: *Hush… Hush, Sweet Charlotte. The Greatest Story Ever Told. Young Dillinger*. 1966: *The Silencers. Who's Minding the Mint? No Place for the Dead*. 1968: *In the Name of Our Father*. 1969: *Beneath the Planet of the Apes. How to Make It (later Target Harry). La collina degli stivali (US: Boot Hill)*. 1970: *Savage Season*. 1971: *L'uomo dagli occhi di ghiaccio/The Man with Ice in His Eyes. Mother*. 1972: *The Wrath of God. Goodnight My Love (TV). The Crime Club (TV). Der Würger kommt auf leisen Socken (US: The Mad Butcher). Northeast to Seoul*. 1973: *Arnold*. 1974: *Moon Child. Brenda Starr, Girl Reporter (TV)*. 1975: *Big Daddy*. 1976: *High Risk (TV)*. 1977: *Savage in the City. Cyclone*. 1978: *The Evil*. 1979: *The Return of the Mod Squad (TV). Better Late Than Never (TV). The Man With Bogart's Face*. 1980: *Murder Can Hurt You! (TV)*. 1981: *More Wild, Wild West (TV)*.

### BURKE, Alfred 1918-

Lean, brown-haired British actor with world-weary look and faintly desperate and dangerous air. Started in British films as villains, then scored a big personal success as a very down-at-heel detective in the long-running TV series *Public Eye*. Later roles revealed the serious actor behind the grubby raincoat and occasional flourish of a revolver.

1955: *The Constant Husband*. 1956: *Touch and Go (US: The Light Touch)*. 1957: *Bitter Victory. Interpol (US: Pickup Alley). Let's Be Happy. Yangtse Incident (US: Battle Hell)*. 1958: *The Man Inside. The Man Upstairs. Law and Disorder*. 1959: *Model for Murder*. 1960: *The Angry Silence. Moment of Danger (US: Malaga). The Trials of Oscar Wilde (US: The Man with the Green Carnation). Dead Lucky*. 1961: *She Knows Y'Know. Man at the Carlton Tower*. 1962: *Backfire. The Pot Carriers. The Man Who Finally Died. Locker 69. Mix Me a Person. The Small World of Sammy Lee*. 1963: *The £20,000 Kiss. Farewell Performance*. 1964: *Children of the Damned*. 1965: *The Nanny. The Night Caller*. 1968: *Guns in the Heather*. 1971: *One Day in the Life of Ivan Denisovitch*. 1979: *The House on Garibaldi Street (TV. GB: cinemas)*.

### BURKE, Billie (Mary William Burke) 1885-1970

Pretty American stage star, a silky blonde (daughter of a circus clown) who had leading roles in a few silents after her marriage to showman Florenz Ziegfeld in 1914 (he died in 1932). After his death, she consolidated the Hollywood comeback she had begun in character roles as nice aunts and fluttery matrons. Probably best remembered today as Mrs Topper in the 'Topper' ghost comedies, and as the Blue Fairy in *The Wizard of Oz*. Academy Award nomination for *Merrily We Live*.

1915: *Peggy*. 1916: *Gloria's Romance (serial)*. 1917: *The Land of Promise. The Mysterious Miss Terry. Arms and the Girl*. 1918: *Eve's Daughter. In Pursuit of Polly. The Make Believe Wife. Let's Get a Divorce*. 1919: *Good Gracious, Annabelle. The Misleading Widow. Wanted—a Husband*. 1920: *Sadie Love. Away Goes Prudence*. 1921: *The Education of Elizabeth. The Frisky Mrs Johnson*. 1929: *Glorifying the American Girl*. 1930: *Ranch House Blues*. 1932: *A Bill of Divorcement*. 1933: *Christopher Strong. Dinner at Eight. Only Yesterday*. 1934: *Finishing School. Where Sinners Meet (GB: The Dover Road). We're Rich Again. Forsaking All Others. Only Eight Hours*. 1935: *Becky Sharp. Doubting Thomas. A Feather in Her Hat. Society Doctor. She Couldn't Take It (GB: Woman Tamer). Splendor. After Office Hours*. 1936: *Piccadilly Jim. My American Wife. Craig's Wife*. 1937: *Parnell. Topper. Navy Blue and Gold. The Bride Wore Red*. 1938: *Everybody Sing. The Young in Heart. Merrily We Live*. 1939: *Topper Takes a Trip. The Wizard of Oz. The Bridal Suite. Eternally Yours. Remember? Zenobia (GB: Elephants Never Forget)*. 1940: *And One Was Beautiful. Irene. Dulcy. Hullabaloo. The Ghost Comes Home. The Captain is a Lady*. 1941: *Topper Returns. One Night in Lisbon. The Man Who Came to Dinner*. 1942: *The Wild Man of Borneo. What's Cookin'? (GB: Wake Up and Dream). They All Kissed the Bride. Girl Trouble*. 1943: *Hi Diddle Diddle. So's Your Uncle. Gildersleeve on Broadway. You're a Lucky Fellow, Mr Smith*. 1944: *Laramie Trail*. 1945: *Swing Out, Sister. The Cheaters*. 1946: *Breakfast in Hollywood (GB: The Mad Hatter). The Bachelor's Daughters.*

*1948: \*Silly Billy. \*Billie Gets Her Man. 1949: The Barkleys of Broadway. 1950: And Baby Makes Three. Father of the Bride. Three Husbands. The Boy from Indiana (GB: Blaze of Glory). 1951: Father's Little Dividend. Darling How Could You? (GB: Rendezvous). 1953: Small Town Girl. 1957: The Star-Wagon (TV). 1958: Rumors of Evening (TV). 1959: The Young Philadelphians (GB: The City Jungle). 1960: Sergeant Rutledge. Pepe.*

**BURNABY, Davy** 1881-1949
Plump, monocled, light-haired British music-hall comedian, a forerunner of Fred Emney (qv). More addle-brained and less irascible than Emney, Burnaby brought his ingratiating comedy style to numerous comedy films in the 1930s. Ill-health limited his later appearances and he died from a heart attack on the same day as his friend and fellow character comedian Will Hay. Also wrote songs and humorous books.

*1929: The Devil's Maze. The Co-Optimists. 1933: Just My Luck. The Wishbone. That's My Wife. Cleaning Up. Three Men in a Boat. The Right to Live. Strike It Rich. A Shot in the Dark. 1934: \*Screen Vaudeville No. 1. On the Air. Murder at the Inn. The Man I Want. Keep It Quiet. How's Chances? Are You a Mason? Radio Parade of 1935 (US: Radio Follies). 1935: \*Equity Musical Revue (series). Dandy Dick. We've Got to Have Love. \*When the Cat's Away. Boys Will Be Boys. While Parents Sleep. 1936: The Marriage of Corbal (US: Prisoner of Corbal). 1937: Song of the Road. Feather Your Nest. Calling All Stars. Song of the Forge. Talking Feet. Leave It to Me. 1938: Second Best Bed. Chips. Many Thanks Mr Atkins. Kicking the Moon Around (US: The Playboy). 1939: Come On George.*

**BURNETTE, Smiley**
**(Lester Burnette) 1911-1967**
In the days when every 'B' western star had comic-books devoted to their imaginary adventures, only two 'sidekicks' were awarded the accolade of a comic to themselves. One of these was George 'Gabby' Hayes (qv); the other was tubby Smiley Burnette, with his flapjack black stetson, and manic humour. Living up to his

nickname by always grinning, Burnette came on like a chubbier version of Eddie Bracken, coming into films with his friend Gene Autry (whose radio vocals he had backed on guitar). He remained one of the most popular 'B'-westerners, with a number of partners, through the 1930s and 1940s, sticking with the genre until it petered out in 1953. When appearing as a regular on the TV comedy series *Petticoat Junction*, Burnette learned he had leukaemia, the disease that killed him at 55. Also a prolific songwriter.

*1934: In Old Santa Fé. Mystery Mountain (serial). 1935: The Phantom Empire (serial). Tumbling Tumbleweeds. Waterfront Lady. Melody Trail. The Sagebrush Troubador. The Singing Vagabond. The Adventures of Rex and Rinty (serial). Streamline Express. Harmony Lane. 1936: Hitch Hike Lady (GB: Eventful Journey). Doughnuts and Society (GB: Stepping into Society). Red River Valley. Comin' Round the Mountain. The Singing Cowboy. Guns and Guitars. Oh, Susannah! Ride, Ranger, Ride. The Big Show. The Old Corral (GB: Texas Serenade). Hearts in Bondage. A Man Betrayed. The Border Patrolman. 1937: Round-Up Time in Texas. Rootin' Tootin' Rhythm (GB: Rhythm on the Ranch). Git Along Little Dogies (GB: Serenade of the West). Yodelin' Kid from Pine Ridge (GB: The Hero of Pine Ridge). Public Cowboy No. 1. Boots and Saddles. Manhattan Merry-Go-Round (GB: Manhattan Music Box). Springtime in the Rockies. Larceny on the Air. Dick Tracy (serial). Meet the Boy Friend. 1938: The Old Barn Dance. Gold Mine in the Sky. Man from Music Mountain. Prairie Moon. Rhythm of the Saddle. Western Jamboree. The Hollywood Stadium Mystery. Under Western Stars. Billy the Kid Returns. 1939: Home on the Prairie. Mexicali Rose. Blue Montana Skies. Mountain Rhythm. Colorado Sunset. In Old Monterey. Rovin' Tumbleweeds. South of the Border. 1940: Rancho Grande. Gaucho Serenade. Carolina Moon. Ride, Tenderfoot, Ride. Men with Steel Faces (GB: Couldn't Possibly Happen). 1941: Ridin' on a Rainbow. Back in the Saddle. The Singing Hills. Sunset in Wyoming. Under Fiesta Stars. Down Mexico Way. Sierra Sue. 1942: Cowboy Serenade (GB: Serenade of the West). Heart of the Rio*

*Grande. Home in Wyoming. Stardust on the Sage. Call of the Canyon. Bells of Capistrano. Heart of the Golden West. 1943: Idaho. Beyond the Last Frontier. King of the Cowboys. Silver Spurs. 1944: Beneath Western Skies. Call of the Rockies. The Laramie Trail. Code of the Prairie. Pride of the Plains. Bordertown Trail. Firebrands of Arizona. 1946: Roaring Rangers (GB: False Hero). Galloping Thunder (GB: On Boot Hill). Frontier Gun Law (GB: Menacing Shadows). Two-Fisted Stranger. Heading West (GB: The Cheat's Last Throw). Terror Trail (GB: Hands of Menace). Gunning for Vengeance (GB: Jail Break). The Desert Horseman (GB: Checkmate). Landrush (GB: The Claw Strikes). The Fighting Frontiersman (GB: Golden Lady). 1947: The Lone Hand Texan (GB: The Cheat). Prairie Raiders (GB: The Forger). Riders of the Lone Star. The Buckaroo from Powder River. West of Dodge City (GB: The Sea Wall). Law of the Canyon (GB: The Price of Crime). The Stranger from Ponca City. The Last Days of Boot Hill. 1948: Whirlwind Raiders (GB: State Police). Phantom Valley. Blazing Across the Pecos (GB: Under Arrest). El Dorado Pass (GB: Desperate Men). West of Sonora. Six Gun Law. Trail to Laredo (GB: Sign of the Dagger). Quick on the Trigger (GB: Condemned in Error). 1949: Desert Vigilante. Challenge of the Range (GB: Moonlight Raid). Horsemen of the Sierras (GB: Remember Me). Bandits of El Dorado (GB: Tricked). The Blazing Trail (GB: The Forged Will). South of Death Valley (GB: River of Poison). Laramie. Renegades of the Sage (GB: The Fort). 1950: Trail of the Rustlers (GB: Lost River). Outcasts of Black Mesa (GB: The Clue). Across the Badlands (GB: The Challenge). Raiders of Tomahawk Creek (GB: Circle of Fear). Texas Dynamo (GB: Suspected). Streets of Ghost Town. Lightning Guns (GB: Taking Sides). Frontier Outpost. 1951: Whirlwind. Fort Savage Raiders. Prairie Roundup. Bonanza Town (GB: Two-Fisted Agent). The Kid from Amarillo (GB: Silver Chains). Riding the Outlaw Trail. Snake River Desperadoes. Cyclone Fury. Pecos River (GB: Without Risk). 1952: Junction City. Smoky Canyon. The Hawk of Wild River. The Rough, Tough West. Laramie Mountains (GB: Mountain Desperadoes). The Kid from Broken Gun. 1953: Winning of the West. On Top of Old Smoky. Goldtown Ghost Riders. Saginaw Trail. Last of the Pony Riders.*

**BUTTERWORTH, Charles** 1896-1946
Twittering timidity was doleful-looking Charles Butterworth's stock-in-trade. A former law graduate and reporter, he turned to acting and brought his uniquely nervous manner to films with the coming of sound, together with a perennially dubious expression and a streak of fair hair that threatened to disappear from the top of his head. Often cast as vacillating rich bachelors who didn't get the girl. Killed in a car crash.

*1930: The Life of the Party. Illicit. 1931: Side Show. The Bargain. The Mad Genius. *The Stolen Jools (GB: The Slippery Pearls). 1932: Beauty and the Boss. Love Me Tonight. Manhattan Parade. 1933: The Nuisance (GB: Accidents Wanted). Penthouse (GB: Crooks in Clover). My Weakness. 1934: Student Tour. Hollywood Party. The Cat and the Fiddle. Forsaking All Others. Bulldog Drummond Strikes Back. 1935: Ruggles of Red Gap. The Night is Young. Baby Face Harrington. Orchids to You. Magnificent Obsession. 1936: Half Angel. We Went to College. Rainbow on the River. The Moon's Our Home. 1937: Swing High, Swing Low. Every Day's a Holiday. 1938: Thanks for the Memory. 1939: Let Freedom Ring. 1940: The Boys from Syracuse. Second Chorus. 1941: Road Show. Blonde Inspiration. *There's Nothing to It. Sis Hopkins. 1942: What's Cookin'? (GB: Wake Up and Dream). Night in New Orleans. Give Out, Sisters. 1943: Always a Bridesmaid. The Sultan's Daughter. This is the Army. 1944: Follow the Boys. Bermuda Mystery. Dixie Jamboree.*

**BUTTERWORTH, Peter** 1919-1979
Tubby, brown-haired British light comedian and comic supporting actor, often as querulous incompetents or bungling minor officials. In very minor post-war film roles before bumbling his way to success on children's television, Butterworth was later a valuable member of the 'Carry On' team. Long married to star impressionist Janet Brown. Died from a heart attack.

*1948: William Comes to Town. 1949: The Adventures of Jane. Murder at the Windmill (US: Murder at the Burlesque). Miss Pilgrim's Progress. 1950: Night and the City. Paul Temple's Triumph. Mr Drake's Duck. The Body Said No! 1951: The Case of the Missing Scene. Old Mother Riley's Jungle Treasure. Appointment with Venus (US: Island Rescue). Saturday Island (US: Island of Desire). 1952: Penny Princess. 1953: *Watch Out! *A Good Pull-Up. Will Any Gentleman? 1954: *Five O'Clock Finish. The Gay Dog. 1955: Playground Express. Fun at St Fanny's. *Black in the Face. *That's an Order. 1958: Blow Your Own Trumpet. tom thumb. 1960: The Spider's Web. Escort for Hire. 1961: The Day the Earth Caught Fire. Murder She Said. 1962: Fate Takes a Hand. The Prince and the Pauper. She'll Have to Go (US: Maid for Murder). Live Now—Pay Later. Kill or Cure. 1963: The Horse Without a Head. The Rescue Squad. Doctor in Distress. 1964: Never Mention Murder. A Home of Your Own. 1965: Carry On Cowboy. The Amorous Adventures of Moll Flanders. 1966: Carry On Screaming. 1967: Don't Lose Your Head. Follow That Camel. Danny and the Dragon. *Ouch! 1968: Carry On Doctor. Prudence and the Pill. Carry On Up the Khyber. 1969: Carry On Camping. Carry On Again, Doctor. 1970: Carry On Henry. 1972: Carry On Abroad. 1973: Carry On Girls. 1974: Carry On Dick. 1975: Carry On Behind. 1976: Carry On England. The Ritz. Robin and Marian. 1977: What's Up Nurse? 1978: Carry On Emmannuelle. The First Great Train Robbery.*

**BYINGTON, Spring** 1886-1971
From the moment Spring Byington appeared on screen as Marmee in *Little Women* (1933), there was no competition for the title of Hollywood's favourite mother. That, and her bewitching sense of comedy, kept her in dozens of similar roles from the mid-thirties to the early fifties. Strangely, this queen of homely matriarchs (she began on stage in 1900) was a divorcee who never re-married. Oscar nominee for *You Can't Take It With You.*

*1931: *Papa's Slay Ride. 1933: Little Women. 1935: Werewolf of London. Love Me Forever. Orchids to You. Way Down East. Ah,*

*Wilderness! Mutiny on the Bounty. Broadway Hostess. 1936: The Charge of the Light Brigade. The Great Impersonation. Every Saturday Night. The Voice of Bugle Ann. Educating Father. Back to Nature. Palm Springs (GB: Palm Springs Weekend). Stage Struck. The Girl on the Front Page. Dodsworth. Theodora Goes Wild. 1937: The Green Light. Penrod and Sam. Off to the Races. Big Business. Hot Water. Hotel Haywire. The Road Back. Borrowing Trouble. It's Love I'm After. Clarence. A Family Affair. 1938: Love on a Budget. A Trip to Paris. Safety in Numbers. The Buccaneer. Penrod and his Twin Brother. Jezebel. You Can't Take It With You. The Adventures of Tom Sawyer. Down on the Farm. 1939: The Jones Family in Hollywood. The Story of Alexander Graham Bell (GB: The Modern Miracle). Everybody's Baby. Quick Millions. Chicken Wagon Family. Too Busy to Work. The Jones Family at the Grand Canyon. 1940: A Child is Born. The Blue Bird. On Their Own. The Ghost Comes Home. My Love Came Back. Lucky Partners. Laddie. Young As You Feel. 1941: Arkansas Judge (GB: False Witness). Meet John Doe. The Devil and Miss Jones. When Ladies Meet. Ellery Queen and the Perfect Crime (GB: The Perfect Crime). The Vanishing Virginian. 1942: Rings on Her Fingers. Roxie Hart. The Affairs of Martha. The War Against Mrs Hadley. Once Upon a Thursday. 1943: Presenting Lily Mars. Heaven Can Wait. The Heavenly Body. 1944: I'll Be Seeing You. 1945: Thrill of a Romance. Captain Eddie. Salty O'Rourke. The Enchanted Cottage. A Letter for Evie. 1946: Dragonwyck. Faithful in My Fashion. Meet Me on Broadway. Little Mr Jim. My Brother Talks to Horses. 1947: Singapore. It Had to Be You. Cynthia (GB: The Rich Full Life). Living in a Big Way. 1948: B.F.'s Daughter (GB: Polly Fulton). 1949: In the Good Old Summertime. The Big Wheel. 1950: Please Believe Me. Devil's Doorway. Louisa. Walk Softly, Stranger. The Reformer and the Redhead (voice only). The Skipper Surprised His Wife. 1951: Angels in the Outfield (GB: Angels and the Pirates). Bannerline. According to Mrs Hoyle. 1952: No Room for the Groom. Because You're Mine. 1954: The Rocket Man. 1960: Please Don't Eat the Daisies.*

**BYRNE, Eddie** 1911-1981
Crinkly-haired Irish character actor, in British films after winning attention both as a variety star and straight actor at the Abbey Theatre, Dublin. Had one or two leading roles in the early fifties, a decade when he seemed to be turning up in every third British film. Returned to Ireland in the mid-sixties.

*1946: Odd Man Out. I See a Dark Stranger (US: The Adventuress). Hungry Hill. 1947: Captain Boycott. 1949: Saints and Sinners. 1951: Lady Godiva Rides Again. 1952: Time Gentlemen Please! The Gentle Gunman. 1953: The Square Ring. Albert R.N. (US: Break to Freedom). 1954: Trouble in the Glen.*

*Happy Ever After (US: Tonight's the Night). Beautiful Stranger (US: Twist of Fate). Aunt Clara. The Divided Heart. Children Galore. The Sea Shall Not Have Them. 1955: A Kid for Two Farthings. Three Cases of Murder. Stolen Assignment. One Way Out. 1956: The Extra Day. It's Great to be Young. Reach for the Sky. The Man in the Sky (US: Decision Against Time). Zarak. 1957: Seven Waves Away (US: Abandon Ship!). The Admirable Crichton (US: Paradise Lagoon). Face in the Night (US: Menace in the Night). These Dangerous Years (US: Dangerous Youth). 1958: Rooney. Dunkirk. Wonderful Things! Floods of Fear. 1959: Jack the Ripper. The Bridal Path. The Mummy. The Scapegoat. The Shakedown. 1960: Jackpot. The Bulldog Breed. 1961: Johnny Nobody. The Mark. 1962: The Break. Mutiny on the Bounty. The Pot Carriers. Locker 69. The Punch and Judy Man. 1963: The Running Man. The Cracksman. 1964: Devils of Darkness. 1966: Island of Terror. 1968: \*Gold is Where You Find It. 1969: Sinful Davey. Where's Jack? Guns in the Heather. I Can't ... I Can't (GB: Wedding Night). 1971: All Coppers Are ... 1972 Never Mind the Quality Feel the Width. 1973: The Mackintosh Man. 1977: A Portrait of the Artist as a Young Man. Star Wars. 1979: The Outsider.*

**CABOT, Sebastian** 1918–1977
Beefy, brown-bearded British actor with small, deep-set eyes who, after years of supporting roles in big films, and villains in minor ones, went to America in 1955 and achieved unexpected success, popularity and recognition there, chiefly on television as pompous but loveable buffoons. Had a leading role (the old Edmund Gwenn part as Kris Kringle) in his last film, a TV version of *Miracle on 34th Street*. Died after a stroke.

*1935: Foreign Affaires. 1936: Secret Agent. 1941: Love on the Dole. Jeannie. Pimpernel Smith (US: Mister V). 1942: Old Mother Riley Detective. 1943: Old Mother Riley Overseas. 1944: The Agitator. 1946: Othello. 1947: Dual Alibi. Teheran (US: The Plot to Kill Roosevelt). They Made Me a Fugitive (US: I Became a Criminal). 1948: Third Time Lucky. 1949: Dick Barton Strikes Back. Old Mother Riley's New Venture. The Spider and the Fly. The Adventures of Jane. 1950: Midnight Episode. 1951: Laughter in Paradise. Old Mother Riley's Jungle Treasure. The Wonder Kid. 1952: Ivanhoe. Babes in Bagdad. Alf's Baby. 1953: Heights of Danger. The Case of the Marriage Bureau. The Captain's Paradise. Always a Bride. The Blakes Slept Here. The Love Lottery. The Case of Soho Red. 1954: Romeo and Juliet. I cavalieri della regina/Knights of the Queen. 1955: The Adventures of Quentin Durward (US: Quentin Durward). Kismet. 1956: Rommel's Treasure. Westward Ho! The Wagons. 1957: Johnny Tremain. Black Patch. Omar Khayyam. So Soon to Die (TV). Dragoon Wells Massacre. 1958: Terror in a Texas Town. In Love and War. 1959: Say One for Me. The Angry Hills. 1960: The Time Machine. Seven Thieves. 1963: The Sword in the Stone (voice only). Twice Told Tales. 1965: The Family Jewels. 1967: The Jungle Book (voice only). 1969: Foreign Exchange (TV). The Spy Killer (TV). 1974: Miracle on 34th Street (TV).*

**CADELL, Jean** 1884–1967
Red-headed Scottish actress with inquisitive features and piercing blue eyes. She played a few 'wee lassies' in silent films, but her career in movies really got under way with the coming of sound, in numerous roles as housekeepers, busybodies, maids and mothers. The Barbara Mullen of her day, although perhaps in less good-humoured parts. Her penultimate feature film brought her first starring role.

*1912: David Garrick. 1915: The Man Who Stayed at Home. 1920: Anna the Adventuress. Alf's Button. 1923: The Naked Man. 1930: The Loves of Robert Burns. Escape. 1932: Two White Arms (US: Wives Beware). Fires of Fate. 1933: Timbuctoo. 1934: Little Friend. The Luck of a Sailor. 1935: David Copperfield. 1936: Whom the Gods Love (US: Mozart). Love from a Stranger. 1937: South Riding. 1938: Pygmalion. 1939: Confidential Lady. 1941: Quiet Wedding. The Young Mr Pitt. 1943: Dear Octopus (US: The Randolph Family). 1944: Soldier, Sailor. 1945: I Know Where I'm Going. 1947: Jassy. 1949: Marry Me. Whisky Galore! (US: Tight Little Island). That Dangerous Age (US: If This Be Sin). No Place for Jennifer. 1950: Madeleine. The Reluctant Widow. 1951: The Late Edwina Black. 1952: I'm a Stranger. 1953: Meet Mr Lucifer. Three's Company. 1956: Keep It Clean. 1957: Let's Be Happy. The Surgeon's Knife. The Little Hut. 1958: Rockets Galore (US: Mad Little Island). 1959: Upstairs and Downstairs. Serious Charge (US: A Touch of Hell). 1960: A Taste of Money. 1961: \*Like Unto You. Very Important Person.*

**CALHERN, Louis**
(Carl Vogt) 1895–1956
Affable Hollywood character who moved easily from swindlers and roués to avuncular figures as his hair turned from black to silver. But he had an interesting relapse into villainy in *The Asphalt Jungle* and was an unexpectedly impressive Julius Caesar.

Died from a heart attack. Two of his four wives (all divorced) were actresses Ilka Chase and Natalie Schafer.

*1921: The Blot. Too Wise Wives. What's Worth While. Woman, Wake Up! 1923: The Last Moment. 1931: Stolen Heaven. Road to Singapore. Blonde Crazy (GB: Larceny Lane). 1932: Okay, America (GB: Penalty of Fame). They Call It Sin (GB: The Way of Life). Night After Night. Afraid to Talk. 1933: 20,000 Years in Sing Sing. Strictly Personal. Frisco Jenny. The Woman Accused. Diplomaniacs. Duck Soup. The World Gone Mad (GB: The Public Be Hanged). 1934: The Affairs of Cellini. The Count of Monte Cristo. The Man with Two Faces. 1935: The Arizonian. The Last Days of Pompeii. Sweet Adeline. Woman Wanted. 1936: The Gorgeous Hussy. 1937: Her Husband Lies. The Life of Emile Zola. 1938: Fast Company. 1939: Juarez. Fifth Avenue Girl. Charlie McCarthy, Detective. 1940: Doctor Ehrlich's Magic Bullet. I Take This Woman. 1943: Nobody's Darling. Heaven Can Wait. 1944: Up in Arms. The Bridge of San Luis Rey. 1946: Notorious. 1948: Arch of Triumph. 1949: The Red Danube. The Red Pony. 1950: Nancy Goes to Rio. Two Weeks with Love. Annie Get Your Gun. The Asphalt Jungle. A Life of Her Own. Devil's Doorway. 1951: The Man with a Cloak. The Magnificent Yankee (GB: The Man with Thirty Sons). It's a Big Country (narrator only). 1952: Invitation. The Washington Story (GB: Target for Scandal). The Prisoner of Zenda. We're Not Married. The Bad and the Beautiful (voice only). 1953: Confidentially Connie. Julius Caesar. Remains to be Seen. Main Street to Broadway. Latin Lovers. 1954: Rhapsody. Executive Suite. The Student Prince. Men of the Fighting Lady. Athena. 1955: Blackboard Jungle. The Prodigal. 1956: High Society. Forever, Darling.*

## CALLEIA, Joseph
(J. Spurin-Calleja) 1897-1975
Dark-haired, moustachioed, somewhat shifty-eyed Hollywood actor, born and raised in Malta (where he also died), who forsook an operatic career to play dozens of swarthy, greasy, smiling and almost always untrustworthy types in gangster films and westerns. His sharp voice was often to be heard in films over a tuxedo, running nightclubs or saloons.

*1931: His Woman. 1935: Public Hero No. 1. Riffraff. 1936: Exclusive Story. Sworn Enemy. Tough Guy. His Brother's Wife. Sinner Take All. After the Thin Man. 1937: Man of the People. 1938: Algiers. Marie Antoinette. Four's a Crowd. Bad Man of Brimstone. 1939: Juarez. The Gorilla. Five Game Back. Golden Boy. Full Confession. 1940: My Little Chickadee. Wyoming (GB: Bad Man of Wyoming). 1941: The Monster and the Girl. Sundown. 1942: The Glass Key. Jungle Book. 1943: For Whom the Bell Tolls. The Cross of Lorraine. 1944: The Conspirators. 1946:*

*Gilda. Deadline at Dawn. 1947: The Beginning or the End. Lured (GB: Personal Column). 1948: The Noose Hangs High. Noose (US: The Silk Noose). Four Faces West (GB: They Passed This Way). 1949: Captain Carey USA (GB: After Midnight). 1950: Branded. The Palomino (GB: Hills of the Brave). Vendetta. 1951: Valentino. The Light Touch. 1952: Yankee Buccaneer. The Iron Mistress. When in Rome. 1953: The Caddy. 1955: Underwater. The Treasure of Pancho Villa. 1956: The Littlest Outlaw. Hot Blood. Serenade. 1958: Touch of Evil. The Light in the Forest. 1959: Cry Tough. 1960: The Alamo. 1963: Johnny Cool.*

## CALTHROP, Donald 1888-1940
Slightly built, fuzzy-haired British actor whose distinctive diction and electrifying presence came into their own with sound, in a vivid selection of men who wouldn't quite meet your gaze: vindictive cowards, uncertain menaces and characters generally living on the edges of their nerves. He was in three Hitchcock films and other big British movies of the early 1930s, but an alcohol problem limited later appearances. Died from a heart attack.

*1916: Wanted a Widow. Altar Chains. 1917: Masks and Faces. The Gay Lord Quex. 1918: Goodbye. Nelson. 1925: *Stage Stars Off Stage. 1927: Shooting Stars. 1928: The Flying Squad. 1929: Clue of the New Pin. Blackmail. *Up the Poll. Atlantic. Juno and the Paycock (US: The Shame of Mary Boyle). 1930: *The Cockney Spirit in the War—1. *All Riot on the Western Front. *The Cockney Spirit in the War—2. Song of Soho. The Night Porter. Loose Ends. Two Worlds. Elstree Calling. Murder. Spanish Eyes. *We Take Off Our Hats. Almost a Honeymoon. *Star Impersonations. Cape Forlorn (US: The Love Storm). 1931: Uneasy Virtue. The Ghost Train. The Bells. Many Waters. Money for Nothing. 1932: Number Seventeen. Fires of Fate. Rome Express. 1933: FP1. Orders Is Orders. Early to Bed. I Was a Spy. Sorrell and Son. The Night Watchman's Story. Friday the Thirteenth. This Acting Business. 1934: Red Ensign (US: Strike!). It's a Cop. Nine Forty-Five. The Phantom Light. 1935: The Divine Spark/Casta Diva. The Clairvoyant. Scrooge. Man of the Moment. 1936: The Man Behind the Mask. Broken Blossoms. The Man Who Changed His Mind (US: The Man Who Lived Again). Love from a Stranger. Fire Over England. Café Colette (US: Danger in Paris). 1937: Dreaming Lips. Cotton Queen. 1938: Shadow of Death. 1939: Band Waggon. *Tommy Atkins. *Tommy Atkins No 2. *The Sound of Death. 1940: Let George Do It. Charley's (Big-Hearted) Aunt. 1941: Major Barbara.*

## CANNON, Esma 1896-1972
Diminutive Australian-born actress with red-gold hair, narrow eyes and set lips which frequently saw her cast in spinsterly or busybody roles. Arriving in Britain in the

early 1930s, she built a theatrical career there before entering films in 1937 and contributing dozens of invaluable cameos as maids, maiden aunts, village gossips and (latterly) strong-minded little old ladies. The 'Carry On' series would probably have kept her busy into her seventies had she not decided to retire in 1963.

*1937: The £5 Man. The Last Adventurers. 1938: It's in the Air. I See Ice. 1939: Trouble Brewing. Poison Pen. I Met a Murderer. The Spy in Black (US: U-Boat 29). 1940: The Briggs Family. 1941: The Big Blockade. Quiet Wedding. The Young Mr Pitt. 1942: Asking for Trouble. 1943: It's in the Bag. 1944: The Way Ahead. English Without Tears (US: Her Man Gilbey). A Canterbury Tale. Don't Take It to Heart. 1946: The Years Between. 1947: Jassy. Holiday Camp. 1948: Here Come the Huggetts. Vote for Huggett. 1949: Fools Rush In. Marry Me! Helter Skelter. The Huggetts Abroad. 1950: Guilt is My Shadow. Double Confession. Last Holiday. 1952: Crow Hollow. 1953: The Steel Key. Trouble in Store. Noose for a Lady. The Case of Soho Red. 1954: The Sleeping Tiger. Out of the Clouds. The Dam Busters. 1956: A Touch of the Sun. Sailor Beware! (US: Panic in the Parlor). Three Men in a Boat. 1958: Further Up the Creek. 1959: Jack the Ripper. I'm All Right, Jack. Inn for Trouble. The Flesh and the Fiends (US: Mania). Expresso Bongo. 1960: No Kidding (US: Beware of Children). Carry on Constable. Doctor in Love. 1961: Carry on Regardless. What a Carve Up! (US: No Place Like Homicide). Raising the Wind. Over the Odds. In the Doghouse. 1962: We Joined the Navy. The Fast Lady. 1963: Nurse on Wheels. Hide and Seek. Carry on Cabby.*

## CAREY, Harry Jnr 1921-
American actor with gingery fair hair and apple cheeks, the son of Harry Carey Snr (1878–1947) and totally unlike his father in looks. He began in semi-leading roles as young soldiers or westerners undergoing ordeals by fire, often in films directed by John Ford, a great friend of his father. But he had moved down to character roles by the early 1950s, and was playing western old-timers at a remarkably early age.

RIGHT Joseph **Calleia**, unusually well dressed for once, played a saloon owner who is also an amorous masked bandit, in *My Little Chickadee* (1940). Here he and Mae West size each other up

BELOW Donald **Calthrop** (centre) looks unconvinced, as Ann Harding is taken in by Basil Rathbone's treacherous charm in *Love from a Stranger* (1936)

1946: Rolling Home. 1947: Pursued. 1948: Red River. So Dear to My Heart. Blood on the Moon. Three Godfathers. 1949: She Wore a Yellow Ribbon. 1950: Wagonmaster. Rio Grande. Copper Canyon. 1951: Warpath. The Wild Blue Yonder (GB: Thunder Across the Pacific). 1952: Monkey Business. 1953: San Antone. Beneath the 12-Mile Reef. Sweethearts on Parade. Island in the Sky. Niagara. Gentlemen Prefer Blondes. 1954: The Outcast (GB: The Fortune Hunter). Silver Lode. The Long Gray Line. 1955: Mister Roberts. House of Bamboo. 1956: The Searchers. The Great Locomotive Chase. The Seventh Cavalry. Gun the Man Down. 1957: The River's Edge. Kiss Them for Me. Island in the Sky. 1958: From Hell to Texas (GB: Manhunt). 1959: Rio Bravo. Escort West. 1960: Noose for a Gunman. 1961: The Great Impostor. Two Rode Together. Geronimo's Revenge (TV. GB: cinemas). The Comancheros. 1964: Cheyenne Autumn. The Raiders. Taggart. 1965: Shenandoah. Billy the Kid vs Dracula. The Rare Breed. 1966: Alvarez Kelly. 1967: The Way West. Cyborg 2087 (GB: Man from Tomorrow). 1968: The Devil's Brigade. Bandolero! The Ballad of Josie. 1969: The Undefeated. Death of a Gunfighter. One More Time. 1970: Dirty Dingus Magee. The Moonshine War. 1971: Trinity is Still My Name. Big Jake. Something Big. One More Train to Rob. 1972: Seeta, the Mountain Lion (GB: Run, Cougar, Run). E poi lo chiamarono il Magnifico (GB: Man of the East). 1973: Cahill: United States Marshal (GB: Cahill). 1975: Take a Hard Ride. 1976: Nickelodeon. 1978: Kate Bliss and the Tickertape Kid (TV). 1980: The Long Riders. 1982: Endangered Species. The Shadow Riders (TV). 1984: Gremlins. 1985: Mask.

**CAREY, Joyce** (J. Lawrence) 1898-
Serious-looking, dark-haired British actress, the daughter of Dame Lilian Braithwaite, a distinguished stage player. She made her own start in the theatre at 18, and remained almost entirely in that medium until World War II, after which she began to make occasional film appearances, usually in either shrewish or careworn roles. Remained active in the theatrical world into her eighties.

1918: God and the Man. Because. 1920: Colonel Newcome the Perfect Gentleman. 1942: In Which We Serve. 1945: Blithe Spirit. The Way to the Stars (US: Johnny in the Clouds). Brief Encounter. 1947: The October Man. 1948: London Belongs To Me (US: Dulcimer Street). It's Hard To Be Good. 1949: The Chiltern Hundreds (US: The Amazing Mr Beecham). 1950: The Astonished Heart. Happy Go Lovely. 1951: Cry the Beloved Country (US: African Fury). 1953: Street Corner (US: Both Sides of the Law). 1954: The End of the Affair. 1955: Stolen Assignment. 1956: Loser Takes All. 1958: Alive and Kicking. 1959: Libel. The Rough and the Smooth (US: Portrait of a Sinner). 1960: Let's Get Married. Greyfriars Bobby. 1961: Nearly a Nasty Accident. The Naked Edge. 1963: The VIPs. The Eyes of Annie Jones. 1964: A Jolly Bad Fellow. 1969: A Nice Girl Like Me. 1972: Father Dear Father. 1974: The Black Windmill.

**CARNEY, George** 1887-1947
Chunky, brown-haired British actor, round of face and short of stature, usually seen in braces and boots as the 'common bloke'. A popular music-hall comedian in his younger days, he proved popular as soon as he entered sound films in 1933 and, a natural, relaxed actor, was often the best thing in some poor films. Probably now best remembered as John Mills's father from In Which We Serve.

1916: Some Waiter! 1933: Television Follies. Commissionaire. 1934: Say It With Flowers. Night Club Queen. Music Hall. Lest We Forget. Easy Money. A Glimpse of Paradise. Hyde Park. Flood Tide. 1935: The Small Man. A Real Bloke. Variety. The City of Beautiful Nonsense. Cock o' the North. Windfall. 1936: It's in the Bag. Land Without Music (US: Forbidden Music). Tomorrow We Live. 1937: Beauty and the Barge. Dreaming Lips. Father Steps Out. Little Miss Somebody. Lancashire Luck. 1938: Easy Riches. Paid in Error. Kicking the Moon Around (US: The Playboy). Weddings Are Wonderful. Consider Your Verdict. Miracles Do Happen. The Divorce of Lady X. 1939: Where's That Fire? A Window in London (US: Lady in Distress). Young Man's Fancy. Come on George. The Stars Look Down. 1940: The Briggs Family. 1941: Kipps (US: The Remarkable Mr Kipps). Love on the Dole. The Common Touch. 1942: Hard Steel. Thunder Rock. In Which We Serve. Unpublished Story. Rose of Tralee. 1943: The Night Invader. When We Are Married. Schweik's New Adventures. 1944: Tawny Pipit. Welcome Mr Washington. Soldier, Sailor. Waterloo Road. 1945: The Agitator. I Know Where I'm Going! 1946: Spring Song (US: Springtime). Wanted for Murder. Woman to Woman. 1947: The Root of All Evil. The Little Ballerina. Brighton Rock (US: Young Scarface). Fortune Lane. 1948: Good Time Girl.

**CARNOVSKY, Morris** 1897- 1992
Round-faced American actor of long stage experience and smooth, urbane manner; he was just as likely to be malevolent as benevolent in films and was building up a useful list of credits as a Hollywood character player when his film career was destroyed after he was blacklisted by the House Un-American Activities Committee. Now best remembered as the villain in Bogart's Dead Reckoning. A poor man's Luther Adler (qv).

1937: The Life of Emile Zola. Tovarich. 1943: Edge of Darkness. 1944: Address Unknown. The Master Race. 1945: Our Vines Have Tender Grapes. Rhapsody in Blue. Cornered. 1946: Miss Susie Slagle's (completed 1944). Dead Reckoning. 1947: Dishonored Lady. Joe Palooka in The Knockout. 1948: Saigon. Man-Eater of Kumaon. Siren of

Atlantis. 1949: Gun Crazy. Thieves' Highway. 1950: Western Pacific Agent. Cyrano de Bergerac. The Second Woman (GB: Ellen). 1961: Vu du pont (GB and US: A View from the Bridge). 1974: The Gambler.

**CARRADINE, John**

(Richmond Carradine) 1906- 1988

Tall, dark, cadaverous, thin-lipped American actor with deep, cultured voice. Just as likely to turn up as Arab, westerner or Englishman, he had some good featured roles in the 1930s and 1940s—several of them for John Ford—but later made a great number of cheap horror films. Probably no non-star has been so consistently busy from the beginnings of sound to the present day. Three of his five sons, David, Keith and Robert, have followed him profitably into the acting profession.

1930: †Tol'able David. 1931: †Bright Lights. †Heaven on Earth. 1932: †Forgotten Commandments. †The Sign of the Cross. 1933: †This Day and Age. †The Invisible Man. †The Story of Temple Drake. †To the Last Man. 1934: †The Black Cat (GB: House of Doom). Cleopatra. †The Meanest Gal in Town. †Of Human Bondage. 1935: The Man Who Broke the Bank at Monte Carlo. Bride of Frankenstein. Les Miserables. She Gets Her Man. Clive of India. Transient Lady (GB: False Witness). Cardinal Richelieu. Alias Mary Dow. Bad Boy. The Crusades. 1936: Anything Goes. Captain January. Winterset. The Garden of Allah. Daniel Boone. Ramona. Under Two Flags. Mary of Scotland. A Message to Garcia (voice only). White Fang. Half Angel. Prisoner of Shark Island. Laughing at Death (GB: Laughing at Trouble). Dimples. 1937: Nancy Steele Is Missing. Ali Baba Goes to Town. Captains Courageous. The Last Gangster. The Hurricane. This Is My Affair (GB: His Affair). Love Under Fire. Danger—Love at Work. Thank You, Mr Moto. 1938: Alexander's Ragtime Band. Of Human Hearts. International Settlement. Four Men and a Prayer. Gateway. Kentucky Moonshine (GB: Four Men and a Girl). I'll Give a Million. Kidnapped. Submarine Patrol. 1939: Drums Along the Mohawk. Frontier Marshal. Stagecoach. Jesse James. The Three Musketeers (GB: The Singing Musketeer).

Five Came Back. Mr Moto's Last Warning. The Hound of the Baskervilles. Captain Fury. 1940: Brigham Young—Frontiersman (GB: Brigham Young). The Return of Frank James. The Grapes of Wrath. Chad Hanna. 1941: Western Union. Blood and Sand. Swamp Water (GB: The Man Who Came Back). Man Hunt. King of the Zombies. 1942: Northwest Rangers. Whispering Ghosts. Reunion/Reunion in France (GB: Mademoiselle France). Son of Fury. The Black Swan. 1943: Hitler's Madman. I Escaped from the Gestapo (GB: No Escape). The Isle of Forgotten Sins. Silver Spurs. Gangway for Tomorrow. Revenge of the Zombies (GB: The Corpse Vanished). Captive Wild Woman. 1944: Bluebeard. The Mummy's Ghost. Barbary Coast Gent. The Adventures of Mark Twain. The Black Parachute. Waterfront. The Invisible Man's Revenge. Alaska. Voodoo Man. The Return of the Ape Man. House of Frankenstein. It's in the Bag (GB: The Fifth Chair). 1945: Captain Kidd. House of Dracula. 1946: Fallen Angel. The Face of Marble. Down Missouri Way. 1947: The Private Affairs of Bel Ami. 1949: C-Man. 1953: Casanova's Big Night. 1954: Thunder Pass. The Egyptian. Johnny Guitar. 1955: Desert Sands. The Kentuckian. Stranger on Horseback. Dark Venture. Half Human. 1956: The Black Sleep. The Female Jungle. The Ten Commandments. Around the World in 80 Days. Hidden Guns. The Court Jester. 1957: The True Story of Jesse James (GB: The James Brothers). The Unearthly. Shoes (TV). Hell Ship Mutiny. The Story of Mankind. 1958: The Cosmic Man. The Proud Rebel. The Last Hurrah. Showdown at Boot Hill. 1959: The Oregon Trail. Invisible Invaders. The Incredible Petrified World. 1960: The Adventures of Huckleberry Finn. Tarzan the Magnificent. Sex Kittens Go to College. 1962: Invasion of the Animal People. The Man Who Shot Liberty Valance. 1964: Curse of the Stone Hand. The Patsy. Cheyenne Autumn. The Wizard of Mars. 1965: Broken Sabre (TV. GB: cinemas). House of the Black Death. Billy the Kid vs Dracula. They Ran for Their Lives (released 1968). 1966: Night of the Beast. Munster Go Home! Night Train to Mundo Fine. 1967: Blood of Dracula's Castle. The Helicopter Spies (TV. GB: cinemas). Hillbillys in the Haunted House. The Hostage. Creatures of the Red Planet. The Fiend with the Electronic Brain. Lonely Man. Dr Terror's Gallery of Horrors. 1968: The Astro Zombies. La senora muerte (GB: The Death Woman. US: Mrs Death). Las vampiras (GB: The Vampires). The Hostage. Genesis (narrator only). The Fakers (later Hell's Bloody Devils). Pact With the Devil. 1969: Smashing the Crime Syndicate (released 1973). Man With the Synthetic Brain. Blood of the Iron Maiden. Bigfoot. Vampire Men of the Lost Planet. Daughter of the Mind (TV). The Good Guys and the Bad Guys. The Trouble With Girls. The McMasters ...Tougher Than the West Itself! 1970: Crowhaven Farm (TV). Myra Breckinridge. Blood of Frankenstein. Five Bloody Graves. Death Corps (later Shock Waves. GB: Almost Human). Horror of the

Blood Monsters (Vampire Men of the Lost Planet with added footage). 1971: Shinbone Alley (voice only). The Seven Minutes. Threshold. Decisions! Decisions! Legacy of Blood. 1972: Blood of Ghastly Horror. The Night Strangler (TV). Boxcar Bertha. House of the Seven Corpses. Everything You Always Wanted to Know About Sex* *But Were Afraid to Ask. Portnoy's Complaint. The Gatling Gun. Richard. Shadow House. 1973: House of Dracula's Daughter. Superchick. 1,000,000 AD. Bad Charleston Charlie. Hex. Terror in the Wax Museum. Silent Night, Bloody Night (later Death House. GB: Night of the Dark Full Moon). The Cat Creature (TV). 1974: Moon Child. Stowaway to the Moon (TV). 1975: Won Ton Ton, the Dog Who Saved Hollywood. Mary, Mary, Bloody Mary. The Killer Inside Me. 1976: Crash. The Last Tycoon. Death at Love House (TV). The Shootist. The Sentinel. 1977: Tail Gunner Joe (TV). The White Buffalo. Golden Rendezvous. The Christmas Coal Mine Miracle (TV). The Mouse and His Child (voice only). Satan's Cheerleaders. Journey into the Beyond (narrator only). 1978: Missile X. Nocturna. Sunset Cove. Vampire Hookers. The Bees. The Mandate of Heaven. 1979: Monster. The Seekers (TV). Americathon. Teheran Incident/Teheran 1943. The Nesting. 1980: Carradines in Concert. The Long Riders. The Monster Club. Phobia. The Howling. The Boogey Man (GB: The Bogey Man). 1981: Zorro the Gay Blade. The Scarecrow. Dark Eyes (later Satan's Mistress). 1982: The Secret of NIMH (voice only). House of the Long Shadows. 1983: Boogeyman II. Evils of the Night. 1984: The Ice Pirates. 1985: The Tomb.

†As John Peter Richmond

**CARRILLO, Leo** 1880-1961

Plumpish, moustachioed, dark-haired former vaudeville comedian of Spanish-American background who gradually became familiar in Hollywood films for fractured-English character roles. A more benevolent version of Akim Tamiroff (qv); like Tamiroff, he could also give strong performances in minor leading assignments. Latterly played Pancho in the Cisco Kid series that transferred to TV. Died from cancer.

1927: *Italian Humorist. *At the Ball Game. 1928: *The Hell Gate of Soissons. *The Foreigner. The Dove. 1929: Mr Antonio. 1931: Lasca of the Rio Grande. Guilty Generation. Hell Bound. Homicide Squad (GB: The Lost Men). 1932: Broken Wing. Second Fiddle. Cauliflower Alley. Girl of the Rio (GB: The Dove. And 1928 title). Deception. Men Are Such Fools. *Screen Snapshots No. 15. 1933: Parachute Jumper. City Streets. Moonlight and Pretzels (GB: Moonlight and Melody). Obey the Law. Racetrack. Before Morning. 1934: Viva Villa! The Barretts of Wimpole Street. The Gay Bride. Four Frightened People. The Band Plays On. Manhattan Melodrama. 1935: The Winning Ticket. In Caliente. *La Fiesta de Santa Barbara. If You Could Only Cook. Love Me Forever. 1936: It Had to Happen. Moonlight Murder. The Gay Desperado. 1937: I Promise to Pay. History Is Made at Night. Hotel Haywire. Manhattan Merry-Go-Round (GB: Manhattan Music Box). 52nd Street. The Barrier. 1938: Arizona Wildcat. Girl of the Golden West. City Streets. Little Miss Roughneck. Too Hot to Handle. Blockade. Flirting With Fate. 1939: The Girl and the Gambler. Society Lawyer. The Chicken Wagon Family. Rio. Fisherman's Wharf. 1940: Twenty-Mule Team. Wyoming (GB: Bad Man of Wyoming). One Night in the Tropics. Lillian Russell. Captain Caution. 1941: Horror Island. Barnacle Bill. Riders of Death Valley (serial). Tight Shoes. The Kid from Kansas. What's Cookin'? (GB: Wake Up and Dream). 1942: Unseen Enemy. Escape from Hong Kong. Men of Texas (GB: Men of Destiny). Top Sergeant. Danger in the Pacific. Timber. Sin Town. American Empire. 1943: Crazy House. *Screen Snapshots No. 105. Frontier Bad Men. Larceny With Music. Follow the Band. Phantom of the Opera. 1944: Babes on Swing Street. Bowery to Broadway. Gypsy Wildcat. Ghost Catchers. Merrily We Sing. Moonlight and Cactus. 1945: Crime Inc. Under Western Skies. Mexicana. 1947: The Fugitive. 1948: The Valiant Hombre. 1949: The Gay Amigo. The Daring Caballero. Satan's Cradle. 1950: The Girl from San Lorenzo. Pancho Villa Returns.

**CARROLL, Leo G.** 1892-1972
Beetle-browed, black-haired, English-born (of Irish parents) actor with deep-set eyes and deliberate speech who came to Hollywood via the English stage (debut 1911) and Broadway. He continued to show a preference for the stage, but will be remembered by moviegoers as the villain in Hitchcock's Spellbound and by televiewers as Mr Waverly in the long-running UNCLE series. Was just as likely to be kindly or villainous.

1934: What Every Woman Knows. Sadie McKee. Outcast Lady (GB: A Woman of the World). The Barretts of Wimpole Street. Stamboul Quest. 1935: Murder on a Honeymoon. The Right to Live (GB: The Sacred Flame). Clive of India. The Casino Murder Case. 1937: Captains Courageous. London By Night. 1938: A Christmas Carol. 1939: Bulldog Drummond's Secret Police. Charlie Chan in City in Darkness (GB: City in Darkness). Wuthering Heights. The Private Lives of Elizabeth and Essex. Tower of London. 1940: Charlie Chan's Murder Cruise. Waterloo Bridge. Rebecca. 1941: Scotland Yard. Suspicion. Bahama Passage. This Woman Is Mine. 1945: The House on 92nd Street. Spellbound. 1947: Forever Amber. Time Out of Mind. Song of Love. 1948: The Paradine Case. Enchantment. So Evil My Love. 1950: The Happy Years. Father of the Bride. 1951: The First Legion. Strangers on a Train. The Desert Fox (GB: Rommel—Desert Fox). 1952: The Snows of Kilimanjaro. Rogue's March. The Bad and the Beautiful. 1953: Treasure of the Golden Condor. Young Bess. 1954: We're No Angels. 1955: Tarantula! 1956: The Swan. 1959: North by Northwest. 1961: One Plus One (GB: The Kinsey Report). The Parent Trap. 1963: The Prize. 1964: To Trap a Spy (TV. GB: cinemas). The Spy With My Face. 1965: That Funny Feeling. One Spy Too Many (TV. GB: cinemas). 1966: One of Our Spies is Missing! (TV. GB: cinemas). The Spy in the Green Hat (TV. GB: cinemas). 1967: The Karate Killers (TV. GB: cinemas). The Helicopter Spies (TV. GB: cinemas). 1968: How to Steal the World (TV. GB: cinemas). 1969: From Nashville With Music.

**CARSON, Charles** 1885-1977
Stern-faced, moustachioed British actor who, after deciding to swop civil engineering for an acting career in his early thirties, soon proved himself one of London's most reliable Shakespeare performers of the 1920s. From the mid-1930s onwards, in the cinema, he played a lot of senior officers, solicitors and statesmen, as well as other strong-willed figures of authority; he was acting regularly on stage and screen until 1961. Directed ENSA plays during World War II.

1931: Dreyfus (US: The Dreyfus Case). Ariane. Many Waters. 1932: Men of Tomorrow. The Chinese Puzzle. Marry Me. Leap Year. There Goes the Bride. 1933: The Blarney Stone. Early to Bed. 1934: Trouble in Store. Whispering Tongues. No Escape. Father and Son. The Perfect Flaw. Blossom Time (US: April Romance). Hyde Park. Blind Justice. The Broken Melody. 1935: D'Ye Ken John Peel? (US: Captain Moonlight). Sanders of the River (US: Bosambo). Abdul the Damned. Invitation to the Waltz. Scrooge. Moscow Nights (US: I Stand Condemned). 1936: Head Office. Secret Agent. Forget-Me-Not (US: Forever Yours). Talk of the Devil. The Beloved Vagabond. Once in a Million. Things to Come. Café Colette (US: Danger in Paris). Fire Over England. 1937: Dark Journey. Victoria the Great. The Frog. Dreaming Lips. Who Killed Fen Markham?/The Angelus. Saturday Night Revue. Old Mother Riley. Glamorous Night. 1938: Sixty Glorious Years. Oh Boy. No Parking. We're Going to Be Rich. The Return of the Frog. 1939: The Saint in London. The Gang's All Here (US: The Amazing Mr Forrest). The Lion Has Wings. 1940: Spare a Copper. 1941: The Common Touch. Penn of Pennsylvania (US: The Courageous Mr Penn). Quiet Wedding. They Flew Alone. 1943: Battle for Music. The Dummy Talks. 1945: Pink String and Sealing Wax. 1951: The Lady With a Lamp. Cry the Beloved Country (US: African Fury). 1952: Moulin Rouge. 1953: The Master of Ballantrae. 1954: The Dam Busters. Beau Brummell. Duel in the Jungle. 1955: An Alligator Named Daisy. 1956: The Silken Affair. Reach for the Sky. 1959: Bobbikins. A Touch of Larceny. 1960: The Trials of Oscar Wilde (US: The Man with the Green Carnation). Sands of the Desert. A Story of David. 1961: Macbeth. 1965: Curse of the Fly. 1972: Lady Caroline Lamb.

**CARUSO, Anthony** 1915-
Tall, solidly built, dark-haired, Italian-looking American actor with 'mobster'-style handsomeness. After abandoning a career as a singer, he broke into Hollywood films in 1940, but rarely achieved more than minor hoodlums and gunmen. He got his first leading role in the 1976 film, The Zebra Force, his last to date.

1940: Johnny Apollo. Northwest Mounted Police. Catman of Paris (released 1946). 1941: Tall, Dark and Handsome. The Bride Came COD. 1942: Always in My Heart. Sunday Punch. Across the Pacific. Lucky Jordan. 1943: The Ghost and the Guest. Above Suspicion. The Girl From Monterey. Watch on the Rhine. 1944: The Racket Man. And Now Tomorrow. The Conspirators. The Story of Dr Wassell. 1945: Don Juan Quilligan. That Night With You. Crime Doctor's Courage (GB: The Doctor's Courage). Pride of the Marines (GB: Forever in Love). Objective Burma! Isle of Tabu. The Stork Club. *Star in the Night. 1946: Monsieur Beaucaire. Night Editor (GB: The Trespasser). Tarzan and the Leopard Woman. Don't Gamble With Strangers. The Last Crooked Mile. The Blue Dahlia. To Each His Own. 1947: News Hounds. Devil Ship. The Trespasser (and 1946 film). Wild Harvest. To the Victor. My Favourite Brunette. The Gangster. They Won't Believe Me.

ABOVE **Charles Carson** (in pinstripes) seems to have sprouted a halo in this scene from *No Parking* (1938). With him are Gordon Harker, Irene Ware and Leslie Perrins (*qv*)

BELOW Anthony **Caruso** (in bow-tie) and Paul Stewart (*qv*) seem to have the drop on upright Howard Duff in this scene from 1949's *Illegal Entry*

1948: Incident. The Loves of Carmen. 1949:
Song of India. The Undercover Man. Bride of
Vengeance. Anna Lucasta. The Threat. Illegal
Entry. Scene of the Crime. 1950: Tarzan and
the Slave Girl. The Asphalt Jungle. Prisoners in
Petticoats. 1951: According to Mrs Hoyle. His
Kind of Woman. Pals of the Golden West. Boots
Malone. 1952: The Iron Mistress. Blackbeard
the Pirate. The Man Behind the Gun. Desert
Pursuit. 1953: Raiders of the Seven Seas.
Desert Legion. Fighter Attack. The Steel Lady
(GB: Treasure of Kalifa). Fort Algiers. 1954:
Phantom of the Rue Morgue. The Boy from
Oklahoma. Drum Beat. Cattle Queen of
Montana. Saskatchewan (GB: O'Rourke of the
Royal Mounted). Passion. 1955: Jail Busters.
Santa Fé Passage. Thrill of the Ring. City of
Shadows. The Magnificent Matador (GB: The
Brave and the Beautiful). Tennessee's Partner.
The Toughest Man Alive. Hell on Frisco Bay.
1956: A Cry in the Night. Walk the Proud
Land. Crashing Las Vegas. When Gangland
Strikes. 1957: Baby Face Nelson. The Big
Land (GB: Stampeded!) The Lawless Eight-
ies. The Oklahoman. Joe Dakota. 1958: Never
Steal Anything Small. Most Dangerous Man
Alive (released 1961). Fort Massacre. The
Badlanders. Legion of the Doomed. 1959: The
Wonderful Country. 1961: Escape from Zah-
rain. 1964: Where Love Has Gone. Sylvia.
Young Dillinger. 1967: Never a Dull
Moment. 1968: Desperate Mission/Joaquin
Murieta (shown 1975). 1970: Flap (GB: The
Last Warrior). 1974: Lenny. 1975: The
Legend of Earl Durand. Mean Johnny
Barrows. 1976: The Zebra Force.

**CATLETT, Walter** 1889-1960
Flap-eared American character comedian
specializing in bespectacled, fussy types
whose imperious façade tended to go to
pieces under pressure. He gave valiant
support to the stars for years before
belatedly starring in a short comedy series
himself in the late 1940s and early 1950s.
Once sang in opera. Died following a stroke.

1924: Second Youth. 1926: Summer Bache-
lors. 1927: The Music Master. 1929: Why
Leave Home? Married in Hollywood. 1930:
The Florodora Girl (GB: The Gay Nineties).
The Big Party. The Golden Calf. Happy Days.

Let's Go Places. *Aunts in the Pants. *Camp-
ing Out. 1931: The Front Page. Platinum
Blonde. Palmy Days. The Maker of Men.
Yellow. Goldfish Bowl. 1932: The Expert.
Cock of the Air. Big City Blues. It's Tough to be
Famous. Back Street. Rain. Rockabye. Okay,
America (GB: Penalty of Fame). Free, White
and 21. Sport Parade. 1933: Mama Loves
Papa. *Private Wives. Private Jones. Only
Yesterday. *Caliente Love. Arizona to Broad-
way. 1934: Olsen's Big Moment. Lightning
Strikes Twice. Unknown Blonde. The Captain
Hates the Sea. 1935: A Tale of Two Cities.
Every Night at Eight. The Affair of Susan.
1936: We Went to College (GB: The Old
School Tie). I Loved a Soldier. Follow Your
Heart. Sing Me a Love Song. Cain and Mabel.
Banjo on My Knee. Mr Deeds Goes to Town.
1937: Four Days' Wonder. On the Avenue.
Wake Up and Live. Love Is News. Love Under
Fire. Varsity Show. Every Day's a Holiday.
Danger—Love at Work. Come Up Smiling.
1938: Bringing Up Baby. Going Places.
1939: Kid Nightingale. Zaza. Exile Express.
1940: Pop Always Pays. Li'l Abner (GB:
Trouble Chaser). Remedy for Riches. Comin'
Round the Mountain. Spring Parade. Half a
Sinner. The Quarterback. Pinocchio (voice
only). 1941: You're the One. Honeymoon for
Three. Horror Island. Sing Another Chorus.
Wild Bill Hickok Rides. Wild Man of Borneo.
Million Dollar Baby. It Started with Eve. Hello
Sucker. Manpower. Bad Men of Missouri.
Unfinished Business. Steel Against the Sky.
1942: Star Spangled Rhythm. My Gal Sal.
They Got Me Covered. Between Us Girls.
Maisie Gets Her Man (GB: She Gets Her
Man). Yankee Doodle Dandy. Give Out,
Sisters. Hearts of the Golden West. 1943: Hit
Parade of 1943. West Side Kid. How's About
It? Fired Wife. His Butler's Sister. Cowboy in
Manhattan. Get Going. 1944: I Love a
Soldier. Hat Check Honey. Pardon My
Rhythm. Up In Arms. The Ghost Catchers.
Lady, Let's Dance! Hi, Beautiful (GB: Pass to
Romance). My Gal Loves Music. Three Is a
Family. Her Primitive Man. Lake Placid
Serenade. 1945: I Love a Bandleader (GB:
Memory for Two). The Man Who Walked
Alone. 1946: Riverboat Rhythm. Slightly
Scandalous. 1947: I'll Be Yours. 1948: Mr
Reckless. Are You With It? The Boy with
Green Hair. 1949: Henry the Rainmaker.
Look for the Silver Lining. The Inspector
General. Dancing in the Dark. Leave It to
Henry. 1950: Father's Wild Game. Father
Makes Good. 1951: Here Comes the Groom.
Honeychile. Father Takes the Air. 1956: Davy
Crockett and the River Pirates. Friendly
Persuasion. 1957: Beau James.

**CAVANAGH, Paul** 1895-1964
Suave, debonair, moustachioed, slightly
gaunt British leading man of the 1920s who
went to Hollywood and became an equally
suave and debonair character player and
villain, latterly often in costume. He returned to Britain for a few starring parts in
the middle 1930s, but then settled in
America for good. Cavanagh enjoyed his

showiest part as Mae West's leading man in
Goin' to Town, a role in which, as always, he
was immaculately dressed and radiated
class. Died from a heart attack.

1928: Tesha. Two Little Drummer Boys.
1929: A Woman in the Night (sound remake
of Tesha). The Runaway Princess. 1930:
Grumpy. The Storm. The Virtuous Sin (GB:
Cast Iron). The Devil to Pay. Strictly Uncon-
ventional. 1931: Unfaithful. Always Goodbye.
Born to Love. The Squaw Man (GB: The
White Man). Transgression. Menace. Heart-
break. 1932: The Crash. The Devil's Lottery.
A Bill of Divorcement. 1933: Tonight is Ours.
In the Money. The Sin of Nora Moran. The
Kennel Murder Case. 1934: Shoot the Works
(GB: Thank Your Stars). Curtain at Eight.
Menace (remake). The Notorious Sophie Lang.
Tarzan and His Mate. Uncertain Lady.
Escapade. One Exciting Adventure. 1935:
Goin' to Town. Without Regret. Thunder in
the Night. Splendor. 1936: Crime over
London. Cafe Colette (US: Danger in Paris).
1937: Romance in Flanders (US: Lost on the
Western Front). 1939: The Under-Pup. Reno.
Within the Law. 1940: I Take This Woman.
The Case of the Black Parrot. 1941: Maisie
Was a Lady. Shadows on the Stairs. Passage
from Hong Kong. 1942: The Strange Case of
Dr RX. Captains of the Clouds. Eagle
Squadron. Pacific Rendezvous. The Hard
Way. The Gorilla Man. 1943: Adventure in
Iraq. 1944: Maisie Goes to Reno (GB: You
Can't Do That to Me). Marriage is a Private
Affair. The Scarlet Claw. The Man in Half-
Moon Street. 1945: The House of Fear. The
Woman in Green. Club Havana. This Man's
Navy. 1946: Night in Paradise. Night and
Day. The Verdict. Humoresque. Wife Wanted
(GB: Shadow of Blackmail). 1947: Dis-
honored Lady. Ivy. 1948: The Black Arrow
(GB: The Black Arrow Strikes). The Babe
Ruth Story. The Secret Beyond the Door. You
Gotta Stay Happy. 1949: Madame Bovary.
1950: The Iroquois Trail (GB: The Toma-
hawk Trail). Rogues of Sherwood Forest. Hit
Parade of 1951. Hi-Jacked. 1951: Hollywood
Story. The Desert Fox (GB: Rommel—Desert
Fox). The Strange Door. The Son of Dr Jekyll.
Bride of the Gorilla. All That I Have. The
Highwayman. Tales of Robin Hood. 1952:
The Golden Hawk. Plymouth Adventure.

1953: Charade. Mississippi Gambler. House of Wax. Port Sinister. The Bandits of Corsica (GB: Return of the Corsican Brothers). Flame of Calcutta. The All-American (GB: The Winning Way). Casanova's Big Night. 1954: Khyber Patrol. The Iron Glove. The Raid. The Law vs Billy the Kid. Magnificent Obsession. 1955: The Purple Mask. Diane. The Prodigal. The Scarlet Coat. The King's Thief. 1956: Francis in the Haunted House. Blonde Bait. 1957: She Devil. God is My Partner. The Man Who Turned to Stone. 1958: In the Money. 1959: The Four Skulls of Jonathan Drake. The Beat Generation.

## CAVANAUGH, Hobart 1886-1950

Stocky, balding, brush-moustached American actor whose tiny eyes frequently blinked in bewildered or cowed fashion from behind large glasses. Almost always cast as the little man done down by life, wife or enemies, Cavanaugh was usually a bank clerk or something similar, forever worried about his own adequacy. One of his first films, a short called The Poor Fish, summed up the pattern of his career, although he also (too rarely) played malevolent minions to great effect.

1928: San Francisco Nights. 1929: *Sympathy. 1930: *The Poor Fish. *The Headache Man. 1932: *Close Friends. 1933: The Devil's Mate (GB: He Knew Too Much). Headline Shooter (GB: Evidence in Camera). Goodbye Again. Mary Stevens MD. Private Detective 62. The Kennel Murder Case. The Mayor of Hell. From Headquarters. I Cover the Waterfront. Broadway Through a Keyhole. Lilly Turner. Havana Widows. Convention City. No Marriage Ties. My Woman. Footlight Parade. Study in Scarlet. Picture Snatcher. Gold Diggers of 1933. Death Watch. 1934: Now I'll Tell (GB: When New York Sleeps). Dark Hazard. Moulin Rouge. Mandalay. Hi, Nellie! Wonder Bar. Easy to Love. I've Got Your Number. Harold Teen (GB: The Dancing Fool). Jimmy the Gent. The Merry Wives of Reno. The Key. The St Louis Kid (GB: A Perfect Weekend). A Very Honorable Guy. A Modern Hero. The Firebird. I Sell Anything. Housewife. I Am a Thief. Fashions/Fashions of 1934. Madame du Barry. A Lost Lady. Kansas City Princess. 1935: *Broad-way Brevities. Bordertown. Wings in the Dark. Captain Blood. While the Patient Slept. Don't Bet on Blondes. We're in the Money. Broadway Gondolier. Page Miss Glory. Dr Socrates. Steamboat 'Round the Bend. A Midsummer Night's Dream. I Live for Love (GB: I Live for You). 1936: Here Comes Carter (GB: The Voice of Scandal). The Lady Consents. Love Letters of a Star. Colleen. Love Begins at Twenty. Hearts Divided. Two Against the World (GB: The Case of Mrs Pembrook). Sing Me a Love Song. Cain and Mabel. The Golden Arrow. Stage Struck. Wife vs Secretary. 1937: The Great O'Malley. The Mighty Treve. Mysterious Crossing. Three Smart Girls. Night Key. Girl Overboard. Love in a Bungalow. Reported Missing. 1938: That's My Story. Cowboy from Brooklyn (GB: Romance and Rhythm). Orphans of the Street. 1939: Rose of Washington Square. Zenobia (GB: Elephants Never Forget). *The Day of Rest. *See Your Doctor. Career. Idiot's Delight. Tell No Tales. Chicken Wagon Family. Reno. Broadway Serenade. The Adventures of Jane Arden. That's Right, You're Wrong. The Covered Trailer. The Honeymoon's Over. I Stole a Million. Naughty But Nice. 1940: *Home Movies. A Child is Born. You Can't Fool Your Wife. An Angel from Texas. Stage to Chino. Shooting High. Hired Wife. Public Deb No. 1. The Great Plane Robbery. Santa Fé Trail. Charter Pilot. Love, Honor and Oh, Baby! The Ghost Comes Home. Street of Memories. 1941: There's Magic in Music. Horror Island. Playmates. I Wanted Wings. Thieves Fall Out. Meet the Chump. Our Wife. Land of the Open Range. Skylark. 1942: A Tragedy at Midnight. My Favorite Spy. Tarzan's New York Adventure. Lady in a Jam. The Magnificent Dope. Jackass Mail. Pittsburgh. Her Cardboard Lover. Whistling in Dixie. Stand By for Action! (GB: Cargo of Innocents). 1943: The Meanest Man in the World. Sweet Rosie O'Grady. Dangerous Blondes. The Man from Down Under. The Kansan (GB: Wagon Wheels). Gildersleeve on Broadway. Jack London. The Human Comedy. What a Woman! (GB: The Beautiful Cheat). 1944: *The Immortal Blacksmith. San Diego, I Love You. Kismet. Louisiana Hayride. Together Again. 1945: I'll Remember April. Don Juan Quilligan. Roughly Speaking. House of Fear. Lady on a Train. 1946: Black Angel. Margie. Cinderella Jones. Spider Woman Strikes Back. Night and Day. Faithful in My Fashion. Easy Come, Easy Go. Margie. Little Iodine. 1947: Driftwood. 1948: You Gotta Stay Happy. Best Man Wins. Up in Central Park. The Inside Story. 1949: A Letter to Three Wives. 1950: Stella.

## CELI, Adolfo 1922-

Heftily built, grey-haired, black-eyebrowed, pudgy-faced, Sicilian character actor, popular in international roles since playing Largo (the villain) in the James Bond film Thunderball. After a promising start in post-war Italian films, he went to South America in 1949, and worked in Argentina and Brazil as a director for the

theatre, films and TV. A French film made in Brazil brought him back to Europe and he worked busily there, mostly as conspirators of one kind or another. Mostly occupied with TV since 1977, recently gaining a nationwide following in Britain for his performance in The Borgias.

1946: Un Americano in vacanza. 1948: Natale al campo 119 (US: Escape into Dreams). Proibito rubare. 1949: Emigrés/Emigrantes. 1964: L'homme de Rio (GB and US: That Man from Rio). Un monsieur de compagnie. E venne un uomo (GB: A Man Named John. US: And There Came a Man). Tre notti d'amore. 1965: Thunderball. Von Ryan's Express. The Agony and the Ecstasy. Slalom. Rapina al sole. Le belle famiglie. 1966: Le roi de coeur (GB and US: King of Hearts). El Greco. Grand Prix. El Yankee. The Honey Pot. Le piacevoli notti. 1967: The Bobo. Grand Slam. Operation Kid Brother. Colpo maestro al servizio di sua maesta Britannica. Tiro a segno per uccidere. Diabolik (GB and US: Danger: Diabolik). 1968: Il padre di famiglia. U atraco de ita y unetta. Dalle Ardenne all' inferno (GB: From Hell to Glory. US: The Dirty Heroes). Death Sentence. La donna, il sesso e il superuomo. In Search of Gregory. 1969: Midas Run (GB: A Run on Gold). Detective Belli. L'alibi. Sette volte Sette/Seven against Seven. L'arcangelo. Blonde Köder für den Mörder. Io Emanuelle. 1970: Fragment of Fear. Brancaleone alle crociate. The Man from Chicago. Hanna cambiato faccia. Murders in the Rue Morgue. 1972: Brother Sun, Sister Moon. La 'mala' ordina/The Italian Connection/Mafia Boss/Manhunt in Milan. L'occhio nel labirinto. Chi l'ha vista morire? Una chica casi decente. Una ragazza tutta nuda assassinata nel parco. Terza ipotesi su un caso di perfetta strategia criminale. 1973: Hitler: The Last 10 Days. Piazza pulita (GB: Pete, Pearl and the Pole). La villeggiatura. Le mataf. Il sorriso del grande tentatore (GB: The Tempter). 1974: And Then There Were None (US: Ten Little Indians). Libera amore mio. Le fantôme de la liberté (GB and US: The Phantom of Liberty). 1975: Amici miei. The Devil is a Woman. 1976: Le grand escogriffe. Sandokan (originally for TV). Signore a signori—buonanotte. The Next Man. Uomini si nasce poliziotti si muore (GB: Live Like a Cop, Die Like a

Man). 1977: Les passagers. 1979: Café Express. 1982: Monsignor.

**As director:**
1951: Ciacara. 1952: Aliba. 1953: Tico tico no fuba. 1969: †L'alibi.

†Co-directed

**CHAMBERLAIN, Cyril** 1909-
Big, tall British actor with distinctive receding dark hair, slightly shifty look and lived-in, 'working-class' profile. He began in minor juvenile leads just before war service, but in post-war years settled down to playing a fistful of policemen, fathers and second-string crooks. An aptitude for tongue-in-cheek comedy made him one of the cast in 'Carry On' films from 1958 to 1963.

1939: This Man in Paris. Poison Pen. Jail Birds. What Would You Do, Chums? 1940: Old Mother Riley in Society. Crook's Tour. 1941: *Night Watch. The Common Touch. The Black Sheep of Whitehall. The Big Blockade. 1945: India Strikes (narrator only). 1947: The Dark Road. Dancing With Crime. The Upturned Glass. 1948: London Belongs to Me (US: Dulcimer Street). The Calendar. The Blind Goddess. Quartet. Portrait from Life (US: The Girl in the Painting). It's Not Cricket. A Boy, a Girl and a Bike. Once a Jolly Swagman (US: Maniacs on Wheels). The Bad Lord Byron. 1949: Marry Me! Don't Ever Leave Me. Helter Skelter. Stop Press Girl. Boys in Brown. The Chiltern Hundreds (US: The Amazing Mr Beecham). 1950: The Clouded Yellow. Stage Fright. The Adventurers (US: The Great Adventure). Blackmailed. 1951: Old Mother Riley's Jungle Treasure. The Lavender Hill Mob. Scarlet Thread. Lady Godiva Rides Again. 1952: Sing Along With Me. Folly to be Wise. 1953: The Net (US: Project M-7). *Out of the Bandbox. Trouble in Store. Hell Below Zero. You Know What Sailors Are. 1954: Doctor in the House. The Diamond (US: Diamond Wizard). The Embezzler. Companions in Crime. 1955: Impulse. Raising a Riot. Man of the Moment. Tiger by the Tail. Windfall. Simon and Laura. Above Us the Waves. Doctor at Sea. Dial 999 (US: The Way Out). Lost (US: Tears for Simon). The Gamma People. 1956: *Wall of Death.

The Green Man. 1957: The Tommy Steele Story (US: Rock Around the World). Doctor at Large. After the Ball. No Time for Tears. Blue Murder at St Trinian's. The Man Who Wouldn't Talk. The One That Got Away. 1958: The Duke Wore Jeans. Chain of Events. Carry On Sergeant. A Night to Remember. Wonderful Things! Man with a Gun. 1959: Carry On Nurse. Carry On Teacher. Operation Bullshine. The Ugly Duckling. Upstairs and Downstairs. Please Turn Over. 1960: Carry On Constable. No Kidding (US: Beware of Children). The Bulldog Breed. Two-Way Stretch. *The Dover Road Mystery. The Pure Hell of St Trinian's. 1961: A Pair of Briefs. Dentist on the Job (US: Get On With It!). Carry On Regardless. Nearly a Nasty Accident. Raising the Wind (US: Roommates). Flame in the Streets. 1962: Carry On Cruising. On the Beat. 1963: Carry On Cabby. Two Left Feet. Ring of Spies. 1964: Carry On Spying. 1965: Joey Boy. Sky West and Crooked (US: Gypsy Girl). 1966: The Great St Trinian's Train Robbery. The Yellow Hat.

**CHANDLER, John Davis** 1937-
Pale-eyed, pale-haired, short, stocky American 'bad guy' actor, who looks like a mole blinking weakly in the sunlight, whined at a fistful of western heroes and was almost always neurotic and dangerous. Started in modern clothes in the title role of Mad Dog Coll, his snarling, lily-livered style of bravado being exactly right for the part. He failed to find a wider range and was consequently seen in too few films, although finding richer pastures in TV westerns. Sometimes billed as John Chandler in later roles.

1961: Mad Dog Coll. The Young Savages. Ride the High Country (GB: Guns in the Afternoon). 1962: The Brazen Bell (TV. GB: cinemas). 1964: Those Calloways. Major Dundee. 1965: Once a Thief. 1966: Return of the Gunfighter. 1969: The Good Guys and the Bad Guys. 1970: Barquero. 1971: Shoot Out. 1972: Moon of the Wolf (TV). 1973: Pat Garrett and Billy the Kid. Chase (TV). 1974: The Take. 1975: Capone. Part 2 Walking Tall (GB: Legend of the Lawman). The Desperate Miles (TV). 1976: The Jaws of Death. Chesty Anderson, US Navy. Scorchy.

1977: Whiskey Mountain. The Shadow of Chikara/Wishbone Cutter. 1982: The Sword and the Sorcerer. 1984: Triumphs of a Man Called Horse.

**CHAPMAN, Edward** 1901-1977.
One of Britain's most solid, dependable and prolific leading character actors through several decades. Chapman looked more like a bank manager than an actor and his film career produced a stream of businessmen, mill owners, politicians, shop managers, worried fathers, citizens variously solid and irate and the occasional villain. Died from a heart attack.

1929: Juno and the Paycock (US: The Shame of Mary Boyle). 1930: Murder. Caste. 1931: The Skin Game. Tilly of Bloomsbury. 1932: The Flying Squad. Happy Ever After. 1934: The Queen's Affair (US: Runaway Queen). Guest of Honour. The Church Mouse. Blossom Time (US: April Romance). Girls Will Be Boys. Mister Cinders. 1935: Royal Cavalcade (narrator only. US: Regal Cavalcade). The Divine Spark. Things to Come. 1936: The Man Who Could Work Miracles. Someone at the Door. Rembrandt. 1937: Who Killed John Savage? 1938: I've Got a Horse. Marigold. Premiere (US: One Night in Paris). The Citadel. 1939: The Nursemaid Who Disappeared. The Four Just Men (US: The Secret Four). There Ain't No Justice. Poison Pen. Inspector Hornleigh on Holiday. The Proud Valley. 1940: *Now You're Talking. The Briggs Family. Convoy. Law and Disorder. *Goofer Trouble. 1941: Inspector Hornleigh Goes to It (US: Mail Train). *Eating Out with Tommy. Turned Out Nice Again. Jeannie. Ships with Wings. They Flew Alone (US: Wings and the Woman). 1947: It Always Rains on Sunday. The October Man. 1948: Mr Perrin and Mr Traill. 1949: The History of Mr Polly. Man on the Run. The Spider and the Fly. Madeleine. 1950: Night and the City. Gone to Earth (US: The Wild Heart). 1951: The Magic Box. His Excellency. 1952: The Card (US: The Promoter). Mandy (US: Crash of Silence). Folly to be Wise. 1953: The Intruder. Point of No Return. A Day to Remember. 1954: The End of the Road. The Crowded Day. 1955: The Love Match. A Yank in Ermine. 1956: Bhowani Junction.

*X the Unknown. Lisbon. 1957: Doctor at Large. Just My Luck. 1958: Innocent Sinners. The Young and the Guilty. The Square Peg. 1959: The Rough and the Smooth (US: Portrait of a Sinner). 1960: School for Scoundrels. Oscar Wilde. The Bulldog Breed. 1963: Hide and Seek. A Stitch in Time. 1965: Joey Boy. The Early Bird. 1970: The Man Who Haunted Himself.*

### CHITTY, Erik 1907-1977

Small, shuffling, grey-haired, round-faced, worried-looking British actor who cornered the market in doddering old fools as soon as he looked old enough and retained a firm grip on it for 20 years. The main body of his work has been for television (more than 200 appearances) especially in the school series *Please Sir!*, but he happily contrived to totter in and out of more than 30 films as well.

*1940: Contraband (US: Blackout). 1948: All Over the Town. Forbidden. 1950: Your Witness (US: Eye Witness). Chance of a Lifetime. 1952: King of the Underworld. 1954: Time is My Enemy. 1955: Raising a Riot. 1957: After the Ball. Zoo Baby (released 1960). 1959: Left, Right and Centre. The Devil's Disciple. 1960: The Day They Robbed the Bank of England. 1963: The Horror of It All. 1964: First Men in the Moon. 1965: Doctor Zhivago. 1967: *Ouch! Bedazzled. 1969: A Nice Girl Like Me. Twinky (US: Lola). 1970: Anne of the Thousand Days. Lust for a Vampire. Song of Norway. The Statue. The Railway Children. 1971: Please Sir! 1973: Vault of Horror. 1974: The Flying Sorcerer. 1975: Great Expectations (TV. GB: cinemas). One of Our Dinosaurs is Missing. The Bawdy Adventures of Tom Jones. 1976: The Seven-Per-Cent Solution. 1977: A Bridge Too Far. Jabberwocky.*

### CHRISTINE, Virginia 1917-

Blonde, baby-faced American actress of Swedish extraction, somewhere between Kathleen Freeman (*qv*) and Nancy Olson, and generally seen as maids or downtrodden housewives. There were a few notable exceptions to this, especially an Egyptian princess (in black wig) in *The Mummy's Curse* and a gangster's moll in *The Invisible*

*Wall.* More recently, she spent 11 years advertising coffee (as a character called Mrs Olson) on television. Married since 1940 to fellow character player Fritz Feld (also *qv*).

*1942: Women at War. 1943: Truck Busters. Edge of Darkness. Mission to Moscow. 1944: The Mummy's Curse. The Old Texas Trail (GB: Stagecoach Line). 1945: Counter-Attack (GB: One Against Seven). Phantom of the Plains. Girls of the Big House. 1946: Idea Girl. The Inner Circle. Murder is My Business. The Killers. The Wife of Monte Cristo. The Mysterious Mr Valentine. 1947: The Gangster. The Invisible Wall. Women in the Night. 1948: Night Wind. 1949: Special Agent. Cover Up. 1950: Cyrano de Bergerac. The Men. 1952: Never Wave at a WAC (GB: The Private Wore Skirts). The First Time. High Noon. 1953: The Woman They Almost Lynched. 1954: Dragnet. 1955: Not As a Stranger. The Cobweb. Good Morning Miss Dove. 1956: Invasion of the Body Snatchers. Nightmare. 1957: Three Brave Men. Johnny Tremain. The Careless Years. Spirit of St Louis. 1960: Flaming Star. 1961: Judgment at Nuremberg. 1962: Incident in an Alley. 1963: Cattle King (GB: Guns of Wyoming). Four for Texas. The Prize. 1964: One Man's Way. A Rage to Live. 1966: Billy the Kid vs Dracula. 1967: In Enemy Country. Guess Who's Coming to Dinner. 1969: Hail Hero. Daughter of the Mind (TV). 1970: The Old Man Who Cried Wolf (TV). 1976: Woman of the Year (TV).*

### CHURCHILL, Berton 1876-1940

Hardly anyone today remembers Berton Churchill for anything other than the embezzling banker in the 1939 *Stagecoach*, a memorable performance in the mood of his plumper successor, Sydney Greenstreet. Yet the white-haired, stoat-faced Canadian actor played in dozens of other films as businessmen, judges and fathers, and worked prolifically through the 1930s before uraemic poisoning killed him at 64.

*1923: Six Cylinder Love. 1924: Tongues of Flame. 1929: Nothing But the Truth. 1930: *Five Minutes from the Station. 1931: Secrets of a Secretary. Air Eagles. A Husband's Holiday. 1932: The Rich Are Always With Us. Cabin in the Cotton. The Dark Horse.*

*Taxi! Impatient Maiden. Two Seconds. Scandal for Sale. Week-Ends Only. American Madness. Madame Butterfly. The Crooked Circle. I Am a Fugitive from a Chain Gang. The Wet Parade. The Mouthpiece. Information Kid/Fast Companions. Faith. If I Had a Million. Common Ground. Forgotten Million. False Faces (GB: What Price Beauty). Washington Parade. Laughter in Hell. Okay America (GB: Penalty of Fame). It's Tough to be Famous. The Big Stampede. Afraid to Talk. Silver Dollar. 1933: Ladies Must Love. From Hell to Heaven. So This Is Africa. Elmer the Great. Private Jones. Hard to Handle. Her First Mate. Only Yesterday. The Little Giant. The Big Brain (GB: Enemies of Society). Heroes for Sale. Golden Harvest. Master of Men. Ladies Must Love. The Avenger. Dr Bull. College Coach (GB: Football Coach). Employees' Entrance. The Mysterious Rider. Billion Dollar Scandal. King of the Ritz. The Girl Is Mine. 1934: Judge Priest. Hi, Nellie. Menace. Babbitt. Half a Sinner. Frontier Marshal. Helldorado. Sing Sing Nights (GB: Reprieved!). Strictly Dynamite. Bachelor Brat. Red Head. Murder in the Private Car (GB: Murder on the Runaway Train). Men in White. Let's Be Ritzy (GB: Millionaire for a Day). Dames. Bachelor of Arts. Take the Stand. Friends of Mr Sweeney. Kid Millions. Life Is Worth Living. If I Was Rich. Lillies of Broadway. 1935: Ten Dollar Raise (GB: Mr Faintheart). The County Chairman. Steamboat 'Round the Bend. Page Miss Glory. I Live for Love (GB: I Live for You). Vagabond Lady. A Night at the Ritz. Speed Devils. The Rainmakers. The Spanish Cape Mystery. Coronado. 1936: You May Be Next! Colleen. Dizzy Dames. Three of a Kind. Parole! Panic On the Air. Dimples. Under Your Spell. Bunker Bean (GB: His Majesty Bunker Bean). The Dark Hour. 1937: Racing Lady. You Can't Beat Love. Parnell. Wild and Woolly. The Singing Marine. Sing and Be Happy. Public Wedding. Quick Money. He Couldn't Say No. 1938: In Old Chicago. Four Men and a Prayer. Kentucky Moonshine (GB: Three Men and a Girl). Meet the Mayor. Wide Open Faces. The Cowboy and the Lady. Sweethearts. Ladies in Distress. Danger On the Air. Down in Arkansas. 1939: Daughters Courageous. Angels Wash Their Faces. Should Husbands Work? Stagecoach. Hero for a Day. On Your*

Toes. 1940: Brother Rat and a Baby (GB: Baby Be Good). I'm Nobody's Sweet-heart Now. Saturday's Children. Twenty Mule Team. Turnabout. The Way of All Flesh. Cross Country Romance. Public Deb No 1. Alias the Deacon.

**CIANNELLI, Eduardo** 1887-1969
Italian-born character actor who moved from opera singing to acting and became a Hollywood regular from 1937 to 1948, after which he began to commute between America and Italy. His deeply lined features, as menacing as a snake's head, conveyed all kinds of manic masterminds and Mafia mobsters. His sharp and grating accent was inimitable and his impeccable manners increased the menace beneath. He died from cancer, back in his beloved Rome.

1933: Reunion in Vienna. 1935: The Scoundrel. 1936: Winterset. 1937: Hitting a New High. Criminal Lawyer. A Night of Mystery. On Such a Night. The Girl from Scotland Yard. The League of Frightened Men. Super Sleuth. Marked Woman. 1938: Law of the Underworld. Blind Alibi. 1939: Angels Wash Their Faces. Gunga Din. Society Lawyer. Risky Business. Bulldog Drummond's Bride. 1940: Forgotten Girls. Outside the Three-Mile Limit (GB: Mutiny on the Seas). Foreign Correspondent. Zanzibar. Strange Cargo. Mysterious Dr Satan (serial). The Mummy's Hand. Kitty Foyle. 1941: Ellery Queen's Penthouse Mystery. They Met in Bombay. I Was a Prisoner on Devil's Island. Sky Raiders (serial). Paris Calling. 1942: Dr Broadway. You Can't Escape Forever. Cairo. They Got Me Covered. 1943: For Whom the Bell Tolls. Adventures of the Flying Cadets (serial). Flight for Freedom. The Constant Nymph. 1944: The Mask of Dimitrios. Passage to Marseille. Storm Over Lisbon. The Conspirators. Dillinger. 1945: Incendiary Blonde. A Bell for Adano. The Crime Doctor's Warning (GB: The Doctor's Warning). 1946: Gilda. Wife of Monte Cristo. Joe Palooka—Champ. Heartbeat. Perilous Holiday. California. 1947: Seven Keys to Baldpate. Rose of Santa Rosa. The Crime Doctor's Gamble (GB: The Doctor's Gamble). 1948: I Love Trouble. The Lost Moment. To the Victor. The Creeper. A Miracle Can Happen (later On Our Merry Way). Patto con

diavolo. 1949: In estase/Rapture. Fugitive Lady. Volcano. Prince of Foxes. 1950: Gli inesorabili. 1951: E l'amor che mi rovina. The People Against O'Hara. 1952: Lt Giorgio. Sul ponti dei sospiri. I vinti. Prigioniere delle tenebre. I nostri figli. La voce del silenzio. 1953: La nave delle donne maledette (US: Ship of Condemned Women). Attila the Hun. The City Stands Trial. 1954: The Stranger's Hand. Mambo. Helen of Troy. 1955: Proibito. Uomini ombra (US: Shadow Men). 1956: Il riccato di un padre. 1957: Lost Slaves of the Amazon (US: Love Slaves of the Amazon). The Monster from Green Hell. 1958: Houseboat. 1959: The Killers of Mussolini (TV). 1962: 40 Pounds of Trouble. 1963: I pascoli rossi. 1964: The Visit. 1965: The Chase. Massacre at Grand Canyon. 1966: Dr Satan's Robot (feature version of 1940 serial). The Spy in the Green Hat (TV. GB: cinemas). 1968: The Brotherhood. Mackenna's Gold. 1969: The Secret of Santa Vittoria. Stiletto. Colpo rovente. La collina degli stivali (US: Boot Hill). The Syndicate. Mission Impossible Versus the Mob (TV. GB: cinemas).

**CLARE, Mary** 1894-1970
Gracious, fair-haired British actress of strong and distinctive personality. A much-respected figure on the London stage after a debut there at 16, she became one of the cinema's best villainesses in the 1930s. She possessed a wide range, and was more than capable of carrying a play or film on her own shoulders, as with the title role in Mrs Pym of Scotland Yard.

1920: The Black Spider. The Skin. 1922: A Prince of Lovers (US: The Life of Lord Byron). A Gipsy Cavalier (US: My Lady April). Foolish Monte Carlo. 1923: Becket. The Lights of London. 1927: *Packing Up. 1928: The Constant Nymph. The Princes in the Tower. 1929: The Feather. 1931: Hindle Wakes. Many Waters. Keepers of Youth. Bill's Legacy. Gypsy Blood (US: Carmen). Shadows. The Outsider. 1933: The Constant Nymph. 1934: Say it With Flowers. Jew Süss (US: Power). Night Club Queen. 1935: Lorna Doone. A Real Bloke. The Clairvoyant. The Passing of the Third Floor Back. Line Engaged. The Guv'nor (US: Mister Hobo). 1937: The Mill on the Floss. The Rat. Young and Innocent

(US: The Girl Was Young). 1938: Our Royal Heritage. The Challenge. The Lady Vanishes. Climbing High. The Citadel. 1939: A Girl Must Live. There Ain't No Justice. On the Night of the Fire (US: The Fugitive). Mrs Pym of Scotland Yard. 1940: The Briggs Family. *Miss Grant Goes to the Door. Old Bill and Son. 1941: The Big Blockade. The Patient Vanishes (later and US: This Man is Dangerous). 1942: Next of Kin. The Night Has Eyes (US: Terror House). 1943: The Hundred Pound Window. 1944: One Exciting Night (US: You Can't Do Without Love). Fiddlers Three. 1946: London Town (US: My Heart Goes Crazy). 1947: Mrs Fitzherbert. 1948: Oliver Twist. My Brother Jonathan. Esther Waters. 1949: Cardboard Cavalier. 1950: Portrait of Clare. The Black Rose. 1952: Penny Princess. Hindle Wakes (remake. US: Holiday Week). Moulin Rouge. 1953: The Beggar's Opera. 1955: Mambo. 1959: The Price of Silence.

**CLARENCE, O. B.** 1868–1955
Cheerful, round-faced, sturdily built British actor who, after one or two stronger roles in his earlier days, played genial old buffers from the start of his entry into British sound films—often bespectacled, cloth-capped working-class types—and went on doing so until he finally retired at 80. Excellent as the Aged Parent in David Lean's Great Expectations. Long stage experience made him one of the most reliable and versatile of supporting players. The 'O' stood for Oliver.

1914: Liberty Hall. 1920: London Pride. The Little Hour of Peter Wells. 1930: The Man from Chicago. 1931: Keepers of Youth. The Bells. 1932: Where Is This Lady? The Barton Mystery. The Flag Lieutenant. Goodnight Vienna (US: Magic Night). Perfect Understanding. 1933: Discord. The Only Girl (US: Heart Song). Excess Baggage. Soldiers of the King (US: The Woman in Command). Falling for You. His Grace Gives Notice. A Shot in the Dark. Eyes of Fate. I Adore You. Friday the Thirteenth. 1934: The Silver Spoon. The Double Event. Song at Eventide. Father and Son. The Great Defender. Lady in Danger. The King of Paris. The Feathered Serpent. The Scarlet Pimpernel. 1935: The

*Private Secretary. Squibs. Barnacle Bill. Captain Bill. No Monkey Business. 1936: East Meets West. All In. Seven Sinners (US: Doomed Cargo). The Cardinal. 1937: The Return of the Scarlet Pimpernel. The Mill on the Floss. 1938: Old Iron. Pygmalion. It's in the Air (US: George Takes the Air). 1939: Me and My Pal. Jamaica Inn. Black Eyes. 1940: Saloon Bar. Return to Yesterday. Spy for a Day. Old Mother Riley in Business. 1941: Inspector Hornleigh Goes To It (US: Mail Train). Quiet Wedding. Turned Out Nice Again. Major Barbara. Old Mother Riley's Circus. Penn of Pennsylvania (US: The Courageous Mr Penn). 1942: Front Line Kids. 1944: On Approval. 1945: A Place of One's Own. The Way to the Stars (US: Johnny in the Clouds). 1946: Great Expectations. The Magic Bow. Meet Me at Dawn. While the Sun Shines. School for Secrets (US: Secret Flight). 1947: Uncle Silas (US: The Inheritance). 1948: The Calendar. No Room at the Inn.*

**CLARK, Ernest** 1912-
Smooth, aristocratic-looking, brown-haired British actor whose mouth seemed to set naturally in an expression of disapproval and who found himself cast as martinets, civil servants, obstructive officials and strait-laced, humourless, sometimes treacherous types in general. Clark was a reporter on a provincial newspaper at 25 when offered the chance to join a local repertory company; London stage appearances followed from 1939, and films in post-war years. Well in character as Professor Loftus in the long-running 'Doctor' series on TV. Married (third) to actress Julia Lockwood (daughter of Margaret).

*1949: Private Angelo. 1950: The Mudlark. 1954: Father Brown (US: The Detective). Doctor in the House. Beau Brummell. The Dam Busters. 1956: 1984. The Baby and the Battleship. 1957: Time Without Pity. Man in the Sky (US: Decision Against Time). I Accuse! The Birthday Present. The Safecracker. 1958: A Tale of Two Cities. Woman of Mystery. Blind Spot. 1959: A Touch of Larceny. 1960: Sink the Bismarck! 1961: Partners in Crime. Three on a Spree. 1962: Time to Remember. Tomorrow at Ten. A Woman's Privilege. 1963: Master Spy. Billy*

*Liar! A Stitch in Time. The Devil-Ship Pirates. 1964: *Boy With a Flute. Masquerade. Nothing But the Best. 1965: Cuckoo Patrol. 1966: Finders Keepers. Arabesque. It (US: Return of the Golem). 1967: Attack on the Iron Coast. 1968: Salt and Pepper. 1969: Run a Crooked Mile (TV). 1970: The Executioner. Song of Norway. 1982: Gandhi. 1983: Memed My Hawk.*

**CLARK, Fred** 1914-1968
Bald, waspish, apoplectic-mannered American supporting star with coat-hanger shoulders. Usually the victim of the star comedian—or his own nefarious schemes. He only came to films in his thirties, but quickly established himself as a familiar and popular face. Married to actress Benay Venuta from 1952 to 1963, the first of two wives. Died from a liver ailment.

*1947: The Unsuspected. Ride the Pink Horse. 1948: Hazard. Fury at Furnace Creek. Cry of the City. Mr Peabody and the Mermaid. Two Guys from Texas (GB: Two Texas Knights). 1949: Flamingo Road. The Younger Brothers. Alias Nick Beal (GB: The Contact Man). The Lady Takes a Sailor. White Heat. Task Force. 1950: Sunset Boulevard. The Eagle and the Hawk. The Jackpot. Dynamite Pass. Mrs O'Malley and Mr Malone. Return of the Frontiersman. 1951: The Lemon Drop Kid. Meet Me After the Show. A Place in the Sun. Hollywood Story. Dreamboat. Three for Bedroom C. 1953: The Stars Are Singing. The Caddy. How to Marry a Millionaire. Here Come the Girls. 1954: Living It Up. 1955: How To Be Very, Very Popular. Abbott and Costello Meet the Keystone Kops. Daddy Long Legs. The Court-Martial of Billy Mitchell (GB: One Man Mutiny). 1956: The Solid Gold Cadillac. Miracle in the Rain. Back from Eternity. The Birds and the Bees. 1957: Joe Butterfly. The Fuzzy Pink Nightgown. Don't Go Near the Water. 1958: Mardi Gras. Auntie Mame. 1959: The Mating Game. It Started with a Kiss. 1960: Risate di gioia (GB and US: The Passionate Thief). Visit to a Small Planet. Bells Are Ringing. A porte chiuse (GB: Behind Closed Doors). 1962: Zotz! Boys' Night Out. Hemingway's. Adventures of a Young Man (GB: Adventures of a Young Man). Les saints nitouches (GB: Wild Living).*

*1963: Move Over, Darling. 1964: John Goldfarb, Please Come Home. The Curse of the Mummy's Tomb. 1965: Sergeant Deadhead. Dr Goldfoot and the Bikini Machine (GB: Dr G and the Bikini Machine). When the Boys Meet the Girls (GB: When the Girls Meet the Boys). War Italian Style. 1967: I Sailed to Tahiti with an All-Girl Crew. 1968: Skidoo. The Horse in the Gray Flannel Suit. The Face of Eve (US: Eve).*

**CLARKE-SMITH, D. A.** 1888-1959
Light-haired, moustachioed, pale-eyed, roguish-looking Scottish actor, often as moustache-twirling lotharios fond of the booze. He brought an infectious sense of humour to many of his stage portrayals from his 1913 debut on and, with sound, found a career in films as well, although he was mainly back on stage after 1939. In private life, this most courtly of screen gentlemen had an unusual hobby: pig-breeding. The 'D' stood for Douglas.

*1929: Atlantic. 1931: Shadows. Bracelets. The Old Man. Peace and Quiet. Michael and Mary. 1932: A Letter of Warning. A Voice Said Goodnight. Help Yourself. Illegal. White Face. The Frightened Lady (US: Criminal at Large). 1933: The Laughter of Fools. *Skipper of the Osprey. I'm an Explosive. Friday the Thirteenth. Head of the Family. Mayfair Girl. The Good Companions. The Thirteenth Candle. High Finance. Follow the Lady. Smithy. Waltz Time. The Ghoul. Turkey Time. Flat No. 3. 1934: Sabotage (US: When London Sleeps). Warn London! The Man Who Knew Too Much. Keep It Quiet. Designing Woman. A Cup of Kindness. Passing Shadows. The Perfect Flaw. Money Mad. The Feathered Serpent. 1935: Lorna Doone. Key to Harmony. Royal Cavalcade (US: Regal Cavalcade). 1936: The Happy Family. Murder by Rope. Southern Roses. Café Colette (US: Danger in Paris). 1937: Splinters in the Air. Little Miss Somebody. Dangerous Fingers (US: Wanted by Scotland Yard). 1938: I've Got a Horse. 1939: Flying Fifty Five. 1947: Frieda. 1951: Quo Vadis? 1952: Something Money Can't Buy. The Pickwick Papers. 1953: The Sword and the Rose. 1955: The Man Who Never Was. 1956: The Baby and the Battleship.*

**CLEESE, John 1939-**

Tall, thin, dark-haired British comedian with grasshopper legs, pained expression and, latterly, moustache—a master of sarcasm and one of the screen's great escalating panickers. Came into show business via university revue, and became a member of Monty Python's Flying Circus, where his deadpan expression and cutting, upperclass tones soon made him a national figure. Film roles were mostly cameos until the Python pictures came along; then he did several cameos—all in the same film. Most successful of all in the TV series *Fawlty Towers*.

*1968: Interlude (shown 1967). The Bliss of Mrs Blossom. The Best House in London. 1969: The Magic Christian. 1970: The Rise and Rise of Michael Rimmer. The Statue. 1971: And Now for Something Completely Different. 1972: The Love Ban (originally It's a Two-Foot-Six-Inch-Above-the-Ground World). 1974: Romance With a Double Bass. 1975: Monty Python and the Holy Grail. 1976: Pleasure at Her Majesty's (US: Monty Python Meets Beyond the Fringe). 1979: Monty Python's Life of Brian. †\*Away from It All (narrator only). The Secret Policeman's Ball. 1980: The Taming of the Shrew (TV). 1981: The Great Muppet Caper. Time Bandits. Monty Python Live at the Hollywood Bowl. 1982: The Secret Policeman's Other Ball. Privates on Parade. 1983: Monty Python's Meaning of Life. Yellowbeard. 1985: Silverado. Clockwise.*

†And co-directed.

**CLEMENTS, Stanley 1926-1981**

Stocky American actor with dark hair, sharp, pointy-chinned features and hunted, aggressive look. He played roles in the Frankie Darro (*qv*) tradition—punks, street youths and bullying wise guys who whined and snivelled in the end. Associated on and off with the Bowery Boys; replaced Leo Gorcey for their final few comedy films. War service badly hit the progress of his career. Died from an emphysema, 11 days after the death of his first wife, actress Gloria Grahame (married 1945-8).

*1941: Accent on Love. Down in San Diego. Tall, Dark and Handsome. I Wake Up Screaming (GB: Hot Spot). 1942: Right to the Heart. Smart Alecks. On the Sunny Side. 'Neath Brooklyn Bridge. They Got Me Covered. 1943: The More the Merrier. Ghosts on the Loose. Sweet Rosie O'Grady. You're a Lucky Fellow, Mr Smith. Thank Your Lucky Stars. 1944: Girl in the Case (GB: The Silver Key). Going My Way. Cover Girl. 1945: Salty O'Rourke. See My Lawyer. 1947: Variety Girl. 1948: Hazard. Big Town Scandal. Canon City. Joe Palooka in Winner Take All (GB: Winner Take All). The Babe Ruth Story. Racing Luck. 1949: Mr Soft Touch (GB: House of Settlement). Bad Boy. Johnny Holiday. Red Light. 1950: Military Academy With That Tenth Avenue Gang (GB: Sentence Suspended). Destination Murder. 1951: Pride of Maryland. Boots Malone. 1952: Jet Job. Army Bound. Off Limits (GB: Military Policemen). 1953: White Lightning. Hot News. 1954: The Rocket Man. 1955: Robber's Roost. Last of the Desperadoes. Fort Yuma. 1956: Wiretapper. Fighting Trouble. Hot Shots. Hold That Hypnotist. 1957: Spook Chasers. Looking for Danger. Up in Smoke. Air Strike. 1958: In the Money. A Nice Little Bank That Should Be Robbed. 1961: Sniper's Ridge. Saintly Sinners. 1963: Tammy and the Doctor. It's a Mad, Mad, Mad, Mad World. 1965: That Darn Cat! 1968: Panic in the City. 1973: The Timber Tramp.*

**CLEVELAND, George 1883-1957**

One of the great grandpas of the Hollywood scene. Cleveland's round, twinkling features exuded kindliness and he was very rarely cast as a shady character. Born in Nova Scotia, he began working on stage in 1903 and, when he came to Hollywood in 1934, he was immediately kept frantically busy playing veterans of all descriptions—but mostly in westerns from 1940, where he could be found holding down (never up) the stage line, prospecting for gold, or offering the hero wheezily wise advice. Died from a heart attack.

*1934: Monte Carlo Nights. The Star Packer (GB: He Wore a Star). The Man from Utah. Blue Steel. Girl o' My Dreams. School for Girls. City Limits. Mystery Liner (GB: The Ghost of John Holling). 1935: Make Mine a Million. The Spanish Cape Mystery. Keeper of the Bees. His Night Out. Forced Landing. 1936: \*Foolproof. I Conquer the Sea. The Plainsman. Revolt of the Zombies. Robinson Crusoe of Clipper Island (GB: SOS Clipper Island). Flash Gordon (serial). Don't Get Personal. North of Nome. Brilliant Marriage. Rio Grande Romance. Put on the Spot (GB: Framed). 1937: The Man in Blue. Swing It Professor! (GB: Swing It Buddy). Boy of the Streets. Paradise Express. Trapped by G-Men/River of Missing Men. Prescription for Romance. Adventure's End. 1938: Rose of the Rio Grande. Under the Big Top (GB: The Circus Comes to Town). The Lone Ranger (serial). Valley of the Giants. Port of Missing Girls. Romance of the Limberlost. Ghost Town Riders. 1939: \*The Sap Takes a Rap. Streets of New York. Dick Tracy's G-Men (serial).*

*Wolf Call. Stunt Pilot. Home on the Prairie. The Phantom Stage. Mutiny in the Big House. Overland Mail. Konga, the Wild Stallion (GB: Konga). 1940: Midnight Limited. West of Abilene (GB: The Showdown). Tomboy. The Haunted House. The Ol' Swimmin' Hole (GB: When Youth Conspires). Pioneers of the West. Drums of Fu Manchu (serial). Blazing Six Shooters (GB: Stolen Wealth). One Man's Law. Chasing Trouble. Pioneers of the West. The Ape. Hi-Yo Silver! (feature version of The Lone Ranger). Queen of the Yukon. 1941: A Girl, a Guy and a Gob (GB: The Navy Steps Out). All That Money Can Buy/The Devil and Daniel Webster. Sunset in Wyoming. Two in a Taxi. Man at Large. The Obliging Young Lady. Riders of the Purple Sage. Look Who's Laughing. Playmates. 1942: The Big Street. \*Hold 'Em Jail. \*Mail Trouble. The Spoilers. My Favorite Spy. The Mexican Spitfire's Elephant. The Falcon Takes Over. Army Surgeon. The Traitor Within. Highways By Night. Powder Town. Seven Miles from Alcatraz. Call Out the Marines. Valley of the Sun. Here We Go Again. 1943: The Woman of the Town. Klondike Kate. Cowboy in Manhattan. Johnny Come Lately (GB: Johnny Vagabond). Ladies' Day. The Man from Music Mountain. 1944: Yellow Rose of Texas. Home in Indiana. My Best Gal. It Happened Tomorrow. Man from Frisco. Abroad With Two Yanks. Alaska. When the Lights Go On Again. Can't Help Singing. My Pal Wolf. It's in the Bag! (GB: The Fifth Chair). 1945: Song of the Sarong. Dakota. Senorita from the West. Pillow of Death. Sunbonnet Sue. Her Highness and the Bellboy. She Wouldn't Say Yes. 1946: Courage of Lassie. Little Giant (GB: On the Carpet). Wake Up and Dream. The Runaround. Angel on My Shoulder. Step by Step. Wild Beauty. The Show-Off. 1947: Mother Wore Tights. I Wonder Who's Kissing Her Now. The Wistful Widow of Wagon Gap (GB: The Wistful Widow). Easy Come, Easy Go. My Wild Irish Rose. 1948: Albuquerque (GB: Silver City). Fury at Furnace Creek. Miraculous Journey. The Plunderers. A Date With Judy. 1949: Home in San Antone (GB: Harmony Inn). Kazan. Miss Grant Takes Richmond (GB: Innocence is Bliss). Rimfire. 1950: Boy from Indiana (GB: Blaze of Glory). Please Believe Me. Frenchie. Trigger Jr. 1951: Fort Defiance. Flaming Feather. 1952: The WAC from Walla Walla (GB: Army Capers). Carson City. Cripple Creek. 1953: San Antone. Affair With a Stranger. Walking My Baby Back Home. 1954: The Outlaw's Daughter. Fireman, Save My Child. Untamed Heiress. Racing Blood.*

**CLIVE, E. E. 1878-1940**

Sturdy, sour-looking, sandy-haired Welsh actor, often cast as spoilsport sobersides or humourless figure of authority—though he could also be amusing when playing the hero's butler or drily dubious friend. He only spent seven years in Hollywood films, before his death from a heart attack, but in that short span racked up over 80 movies, latterly becoming best known as Bulldog

ABOVE It was rare that Stanley **Clements** got the girl or played a leading role in a serious film. But he did both in 1952, albeit in a minor entry called *Jet Job*. The girl is the perennial Elena Verdugo

BELOW George **Cleveland** shares a chuckle with Marjorie Main (*qv*) as she plays the title role in *The Wistful Widow Wagon Gap* in 1947

Drummond's manservant Tenny. Clive would certainly have been profitably involved in Universal's Briton-packed Sherlock Holmes series had not early death intervened.

*1933: The Invisible Man. Looking Forward (GB: Service). 1934: One More River (GB: Over the River). The Poor Rich. The Gay Divorcee (GB: The Gay Divorce). Tin Pants. Riptide. Bulldog Drummond Strikes Back. Charlie Chan in London. Long Lost Father. 1935: The Mystery of Edwin Drood. A Feather in Her Hat. Bride of Frankenstein. Remember Last Night? We're in the Money. Gold Diggers of 1935. Stars Over Broadway. A Tale of Two Cities. Widow from Monte Carlo. Atlantic Adventure. Captain Blood. Father Brown, Detective. Sylvia Scarlett. Clive of India. The Man Who Broke the Bank at Monte Carlo. 1936: Little Lord Fauntleroy. Love Before Breakfast. The King Steps Out. Dracula's Daughter. All American Chump (GB: Country Bumpkin). Palm Springs (GB: Palm Springs Affair). The Unguarded Hour. Trouble for Two (GB: The Suicide Club). Piccadilly Jim. Libeled Lady. Tarzan Escapes! Camille. The Golden Arrow. The Charge of the Light Brigade. Isle of Fury. Cain and Mabel. Ticket to Paradise. Lloyds of London. The Dark Hour. Show Boat. 1937: They Wanted to Marry. The Great Garrick. Live, Love and Learn. Bulldog Drummond Escapes! Maid of Salem. Ready, Willing and Able. Bulldog Drummond's Revenge. It's Love I'm After. On the Avenue. Love Under Fire. Danger—Love at Work. Personal Property. The Emperor's Candlesticks. Night Must Fall. Beg, Borrow or Steal. Bulldog Drummond Comes Back. 1938: Arsene Lupin Returns. Bulldog Drummond's Peril. The First Hundred Years. The Last Warning. Bulldog Drummond in Africa. Kidnapped. Submarine Patrol. Gateway. Arrest Bulldog Drummond! 1939: I'm from Missouri. The Little Princess. Bulldog Drummond's Secret Police. Mr Moto's Last Warning. Man About Town. The Hound of the Baskervilles. Rose of Washington Square. Bulldog Drummond's Bride. The Adventures of Sherlock Holmes. Bachelor Mother. The Honeymoon's Over. 1939/40: Raffles. 1940: The Earl of Chicago. Congo Maisie. Pride and Prejudice. Foreign Correspondent.*

## COLEMAN, Dabney 1934-

Tall, dark, strongly-spoken, usually moustachioed American actor with wolfish smile and dark, curly, receding hair. Abandoning law studies to become an actor, he has only very gradually come through to better roles (notably in the recent TV series *Buffalo Bill*), with a series of decisive, often neurotically edged performances in often insignificant material. Stalwart in drama, but probably most attractive in comedy.

*1965: The Slender Thread. 1966: This Property Is Condemned. 1968: The Scalphunters. 1969: The Trouble With Girls. Downhill Racer. 1970: The Brotherhood of the Bell (TV). I Love My Wife. 1973: Cinderella Liberty. Savage (TV). Dying Room Only (TV). The President's Plane is Missing (TV). 1974: Bad Ronald (TV). The Dove. 1975: Attack on Terror: The FBI versus the Ku Klux Klan (TV). Returning Home (TV). The Other Side of the Mountain (GB: A Window to the Sky). Bite the Bullet. Kiss Me, Kill Me (TV). 1977: Viva Knievel. Rolling Thunder. Black Fist. The Amazing Howard Hughes (TV). 1978: Maneaters Are Loose! (TV). More Than Friends (TV). 1979: North Dallas Forty. When She Was Bad (TV). 1980: How to Beat the High Cost of Living. Melvin and Howard. 9 to 5. 1981: On Golden Pond. Modern Problems. Callie and Son (TV). 1982: Young Doctors in Love. Tootsie. 1983: WarGames. 1984: Cloak and Dagger. The Muppets Take Manhattan. 1985: Mischief/ The Man With the One Red Shoe.*

## COLLIER, Constance

(Laura C. Hardie) 1875-1955

Impassive British-born stage star who turned to Hollywood in the 1930s (initially as a drama coach) to portray a series of *grandes dames* with varying degrees of eccentricity about them. Her alabaster features could convey every emotion from scorn to sorrow with the minimum of movement. Some filmographies credit her with an appearance in *Our Betters* (1933), but it appears this may be a confusion with Constance Bennett.

*1916: Intolerance. The Code of Marcia Gray. Macbeth. Tongues of Men. 1919: The Impossible Woman. 1920: Bleak House. 1922: The*

*Bohemian Girl. 1933: Dinner at Eight. 1934: Peter Ibbetson. 1935: Shadow of Doubt. Anna Karenina. Professional Soldier. 1936: Girls' Dormitory. Little Lord Fauntleroy. Thunder in the City. 1937: Stage Door. A Damsel in Distress. She Got What She Wanted. Wee Willie Winkie. Clothes and the Woman. 1939: Zaza. 1940: Susan and God (GB: The Gay Mrs Trexel). Half a Sinner. 1945: Week-End at the Waldorf. Kitty. 1946: Monsieur Beaucaire. The Dark Corner. 1947: The Perils of Pauline. 1948: Rope. An Ideal Husband. The Girl from Manhattan. 1949: Whirlpool.*

## COLLINS, Ray 1888-1965

Affable, avuncular type who came to Hollywood in his early fifties as a member of the Orson Welles company, and stayed to exude solid benevolence for nearly 20 years. Universally recognized in the latter stages of his career as the dogged Lieutenant Tragg of the *Perry Mason* series on television. Died from an emphysema.

*1940: The Grapes of Wrath. 1941: Citizen Kane. 1942: The Big Street. Highways by Night. Commandos Strike at Dawn. The Magnificent Ambersons. The Navy Comes Through. 1943: The Crime Doctor. Madame Curie (narrator only). The Human Comedy. Slightly Dangerous. Salute to the Marines. Whistling in Brooklyn. 1944: The Eve of St Mark. See Here, Private Hargrove. Barbary Coast Gent. The Seventh Cross. Can't Help Singing. The Hitler Gang. Shadows in the Night. Miss Susie Slagle's (released 1946).*

1945: *Roughly Speaking. The Hidden Eye. Leave Her to Heaven. Up Goes Maisie* (GB: *Up She Goes*). 1946: *Badman's Territory. Boys' Ranch. Crack-Up. Three Wise Fools. Two Years Before the Mast. The Return of Monte Cristo* (GB: *Monte Cristo's Revenge*). *The Best Years of Our Lives. A Night in Paradise.* 1947: *The Bachelor and the Bobby Soxer* (GB: *Bachelor Knight*). *The Red Stallion. The Swordsman. The Senator Was Indiscreet* (GB: *Mr Ashton Was Indiscreet*). 1948: *Homecoming. Good Sam. The Man from Colorado. A Double Life. Command Decision. For the Love of Mary.* 1949: *Red Stallion in the Rockies. Hideout. It Happens Every Spring. The Fountainhead. The Heiress. Free for All. Francis.* 1950: *Paid in Full. Kill the Umpire. Summer Stock* (GB: *If You Feel Like Singing*). *The Reformer and the Redhead. USS Teakettle* (later *You're in the Navy Now*). 1951: *Ma and Pa Kettle Back on the Farm. I Want You. Reunion in Reno. The Racket. Vengeance Valley.* 1952: *Invitation. Dreamboat. Young Man With Ideas.* 1953: *The Desert Song. Column South. Ma and Pa Kettle at the Fair. Ma and Pa Kettle on Vacation* (GB: *Ma and Pa Kettle Go to Paris*). *Bad for Each Other. The Kid from Left Field.* 1954: *Rose Marie. Athena.* 1955: *The Desperate Hours. Texas Lady.* 1956: *Invitation to a Gunfighter* (TV). *Never Say Goodbye. Gun in His Hand* (TV. GB: cinemas). *The Solid Gold Cadillac.* 1957: *Spoilers of the Forest.* 1958: *Touch of Evil.* 1961: *I'll Give My Life.*

**COLONNA, Jerry**
(Gerald Colonna) 1904- *1986*
Beaming, round-faced, bulge-eyed American musician and comedian who had a black moustache that almost rivalled Groucho Marx's fake one, and an ability to hold a note until it sounded as though it were bouncing around in an echo chamber. He was a trombone player at 14, and later led his own band, but his raucous voice and sense of ridiculous led him into comedy and, after a regular stint on Bob Hope's radio show, he made engagingly lunatic cameo appearances in film frolics featuring Hope and others.

1937: *52nd Street. Rosalie.* 1938: *College Swing* (GB: *Swing, Teacher, Swing*). *Little*

Miss Broadway. Garden of the Moon. Valley of the Giants. 1939: *Naughty But Nice. Sweepstakes Winner.* 1940: *Road to Singapore. Comin' Round the Mountain.* 1941: *Melody and Moonlight. You're the One. Sis Hopkins. Ice-Capades.* 1942: *True to the Army. Priorities on Parade. Ice-Capades Revue* (GB: *Rhythm Hits the Ice*). 1943: *Star-Spangled Rhythm.* 1944: *It's in the Bag!* (GB: *The Fifth Chair*). *Atlantic City.* 1946: *Make Mine Music.* 1947: *Road to Rio.* 1950: *Alice in Wonderland* (voice only). 1951: *Kentucky Jubilee.* 1956: *Meet Me in Las Vegas* (GB: *Viva Las Vegas!*). 1958: *Andy Hardy Comes Home.* 1961: *The Road to Hong Kong.*

**COMPTON, Joyce**
(Eleanor Hunt) 1907-
Fair-haired American actress with twinkling eyes and a cheeky smile who was one of the Wampas Baby Stars in the peak year of 1926, and went on to play zany or scatterbrained blondes for 25 years. She is best recalled as an enchanting female detective called Chris Cross in 1940's *Sky Murder.* Carried on her busy life in the 1950s by combining (mostly television) acting with part-time nursing work.

1925: *What Fools Men. Broadway Lady.* 1926: *Syncopating Sue.* 1927: *Border Cavalier. Ankles Preferred.* 1928: *Soft Living.* 1929: *The Wild Party. Salute. Dangerous Curves. The Sky Hawk.* 1930: *High Society Blues. Three Sisters. Wild Company. Lightnin'.* 1931: *Three Girls Lost. Up Pops the Devil. Women of All Nations. Not Exactly Gentlemen. Good Sport. Annabelle's Affairs.* 1932: *Lena Rivers. Under Eighteen. Westward Passage. Beauty Parlor. Unholy Love. Lady and Gent. False Faces* (GB: *What Price Beauty*). *A Parisian Romance. If I had a Million. Afraid to Talk. Hat Check Girl* (GB: *Embassy Girl*). 1933: *Clip Joint* (GB: *Sing, Sinner, Sing*). *Fighting for Justice. *Dream Stuff. *Daddy Knows Best. *Knockout Kisses. *Caliente Love. *The Plumber and the Lady. Only Yesterday. Roadhouse Queen.* 1934: *The Trumpet Blows. Imitation of Life. *Everything's Ducky. King Kelly of the USA* (GB: *Irish and Proud Of It*). *Affairs of a Gentleman. Million Dollar Ransom. The White Parade.* 1935: *Rustlers of Red Dog* (serial).

*Let 'Em Have It!* (GB: *False Faces*). *Manhattan Monkey Business. Go Into Your Dance* (GB: *Casino de Paree*). *Mr Dynamite, *Public Ghost No 1. College Scandal. Magnificent Obsession.* 1936: *Valley of the Lawless. Love Before Breakfast. *Life Hesitates at 40. The Harvester. Under Your Spell. Trapped By Television. Star for a Night. Ellis Island. Sitting on the Moon. Country Gentleman. Murder with Pictures.* 1937: *Top of the Town. China Passage. We Have Our Moments. Pick a Star. Wings Over Honolulu. Kid Galahad. Rhythm in the Clouds. The Toast of New York. Small Town Boy. Born Reckless. The Awful Truth. Sea Racketeers. She Asked For It.* 1938: *You and Me. Love on a Budget. Manproof. The Last Warning. Women Are Like That. Trade Winds. Spring Madness. Going Places. Artists and Models Abroad* (GB: *Stranded in Paris*). *How to Watch Football.* 1939: *Rose of Washington Square. The Flying Irishman. Reno. Balalaika. Hotel for Women/ Elsa Maxwell's Hotel for Women.* 1940: *Honeymoon Deferred. Turnabout. Sky Murder. The Villain Still Pursued Her. I Take This Woman. City for Conquest. Who Killed Aunt Maggie? Let's Make Music. They Drive by Night* (GB: *The Road to Frisco*). 1941: *Scattergood Meets Broadway. Bedtime Story. Moon Over Her Shoulder. Manpower. Blues in the Night. Ziegfeld Girl.* 1942: *Too Many Women. Thunderbirds.* 1943: *Silver Skates. Swing Out the Blues. Let's Face It. Silver Spurs.* 1945: *Roughly Speaking. Pillow to Post. Christmas in Connecticut* (GB: *Indiscretion*). *Danger Signal. Mildred Pierce.* 1946: *Behind the Mask. The Best Years of Our Lives. Rendezvous with Annie. Night and Day. Dark Alibi.* 1947: *Scared to Death. Exposed. Linda Be Good.* 1948: *A Southern Yankee* (GB: *My Hero*). *Incident. Sorry, Wrong Number.* 1949: *Mighty Joe Young. Grand Canyon.* 1950: *Jet Pilot* (released 1957). 1957: *The Persuader.* 1958: *Girl in the Woods.*

**CONNOLLY, Walter** 1887-1940
Heavyweight American stage actor who came to the screen in the thirties and proved his talent in screwball comedy. Usually with thick, black moustache and prince-nez and at his wits' end, but also a

solid performer in dramatic roles. Film-goers would have been happy to see him go on stealing scenes through the 1940s, but a stroke killed him at only 53.

*1930: \*Many Happy Returns. 1931: Plain-clothes Man. 1932: No More Orchids. Wash-ington Merry-Go-Round (GB: Invisible Power). Man Against Woman. 1933: The Bitter Tea of General Yen. Lady for a Day. Paddy the Next Best Thing. Master of Men. East of Fifth Avenue (GB: Two in a Million). Man's Castle. 1934: Eight Girls in a Boat. It Happened One Night. Once to Every Woman. Twentieth Century. Whom the Gods Destroy. Servants' Entrance. Lady by Choice. Broadway Bill (GB: Strictly Confidential). The Captain Hates the Sea. White Lies. Many Happy Returns. 1935: Father Brown. Detective. She Couldn't Take It. So Red the Rose. One Way Ticket. 1936: Soak the Rich. The King Steps Out. The Music Goes Round. Libeled Lady. 1937: Nancy Steele is Missing. Let's Get Married. The League of Frightened Men. The Good Earth. First Lady. Nothing Sacred. 1938: Start Cheering. Penitentiary. Four's a Crowd. Too Hot To Handle. 1939: Girl Downstairs, Good Girls Go to Paris. Bridal Suite. Those High Gray Walls (GB: The Gates of Alcatraz). Fifth Avenue Girl. Coastguard. The Great Victor Herbert. The Adventures of Huckleberry Finn.*

### CONNOR, Kenneth 1918- 1993

Wiry little British comedian, a specialist in hurt bewilderment, fierce indignation and, latterly, impotent lechery. His career hardly got started before World War II service but, afterwards, he became radio's man of many comic voices in Peter Sellers' footsteps and, later one of the Carry On gang, to which series of films he returned, with lower billing, after a mid-sixties sabbatical in the theatre.

*1939: Poison Pen. 1950: Don't Say Die. 1952: Elstree Story (voice only). There Was a Young Lady. 1953: Marilyn (later Roadhouse Girl). 1954: The Black Rider. 1955: The Ladykillers. 1957: Davy. 1958: Carry On Sergeant. 1959: Make Mine a Million. Carry On Nurse. Carry On Teacher. 1960: Carry On Constable. Dentist in the Chair. Watch Your Stern. His and Hers. 1961: Carry On*

*Regardless. A Weekend with Lulu. Nearly a Nasty Accident. Dentist on the Job (US: Get On With It!). What a Carve Up! (US: No Place like Homicide). 1962: Carry On Cruising. 1963: Carry On Cabby. 1964: Gonks Go Beat. Carry On Cleo. 1965: How to Undress in Public without Undue Embarrass-ment. Cuckoo Patrol. 1966: Danny the Dragon (serial, voice only). 1968: Captain Nemo and the Underwater City. 1969: Carry On Up the Jungle. 1970: Rhubarb. Carry On Henry. 1972: Carry On Matron. Carry On Abroad. 1973: Carry On Girls. 1974: Carry On Dick. 1975: Carry On Behind. 1976: Carry On England. 1978: Carry On Emmannuelle.*

### CONRIED, Hans 1917-1982

You might find it hard to put a name to the face, but you really couldn't miss Hans Conried in a film. Lanky and sharp-faced, with startled eyes, this American character comedian was forever popping up in lunatic supporting roles as professors, waiters or photographers, often with nonsensical dia-logue that sounded as though he wrote it himself. He might have become a star in *The 5,000 Fingers of Dr T*, but front-office interference made it a box-office flop. Died from a heart ailment.

*1938: Dramatic School. 1939: It's a Wonder-ful World. On Borrowed Time. Never Say Die. 1940: Dulcy. Bitter Sweet. The Great Dictator. 1941: Maisie Was a Lady. Unexpected Uncle. Underground. The Gay Falcon. Weekend for Three. A Date with the Falcon. 1942: Joan of Paris. Saboteur. The Wife Takes a Flyer (GB: A Yank in Dutch). The Greatest Gift. The Falcon Takes Over. Pacific Rendezvous. Blondie's Blessed Event (GB: A Bundle of Trouble). Journey into Fear. Underground Agent. The Big Street. Once Upon a Honey-moon. Nightmare. 1943: Hostages. Crazy House. Hitler's Children. A Lady Takes a Chance. His Butler's Sister. 1944: Passage to Marseille. Mrs Parkington. 1947: The Sena-tor Was Indiscreet. 1948: Design for Death (narrator only). 1949: The Barkleys of Broadway. My Friend Irma. Bride for Sale. On the Town. 1950: Jet Pilot (released 1957). Nancy Goes to Rio. Summer Stock (GB: If You Feel Like Singing). 1951: Rich, Young and Pretty. Texas Carnival. The Light Touch.*

*Too Young to Kiss. Behave Yourself! New Mexico. 1952: Three for Bedroom C. The World in His Arms. Big Jim McLain. 1953: Peter Pan (voice only). Siren of Bagdad. The Affairs of Dobie Gillis. The Twonky. The 5,000 Fingers of Dr T. 1955: Davy Crockett, King of the Wild Frontier. You're Never Too Young. 1956: The Birds and the Bees. Bus Stop. Miracle on 34th Street (TV. GB: cinemas). 1957: The Monster That Challenged the World. 1958: The Big Beat. Rock-a-Bye Baby. 1959: Juke Box Rhythm. 1001 Arabian Nights (voice only). 1963: My Six Loves. 1964: The Patsy. Robin and the Seven Hoods. 1968: The Jay Ward Intergalactic Film Festival (voice only). 1969: Wake Me When the War is Over (TV). \*Up is Down (narrator only). 1970: The Phantom Tollbooth (voice only). 1973: The Brothers O'Toole (GB: TV). 1976: The Shaggy DA. 1978: The Cat from Outer Space. 1980: Oh, God! Book II. 1981: \*Once Upon a Mouse (narrator only). Ameri-can Dream (TV).*

### COOK, Elisha Jnr 1906- 1995

The man who seems to be many people's favourite American character actor, Cook played losers: short, shifty, nervous guys living on life's edge. They made a bluster of bravado, but were always found wanting, or just out of luck. Shot in *Shane*, knifed in *The Black Bird*, strangled in *Phantom Lady*, poisoned in *The Big Sleep*—Cook Got His in a score of different ways. It comes as a surprise to find that he has only made about 100 films. Some sources give his birthdate as 1902, but this seems to be erroneous.

*1930: Her Unborn Child. 1936: Two in a Crowd. Pigskin Parade (GB: The Harmony Parade). Bullets or Ballots. 1937: Wife, Doctor and Nurse. They Won't Forget. The Devil is Driving. Life Begins in College (GB: The Joy Parade). 1937: Love is News. Breezing Home. Danger—Love at Work. 1938: Submarine Patrol. Three Blind Mice. My Lucky Star. 1939: Grand Jury Secrets. Newsboys' Home. 1940: Stranger on the Third Floor. He Married His Wife. Public Deb Number One. Tin Pan Alley. 1941: Man at Large. Love Crazy. Sergeant York. The Maltese Falcon. I Wake Up Screaming (GB: Hot Spot). Hellza-poppin'. Ball of Fire. 1942: A Gentleman at*

Heart. In This Our Life. A-Haunting We Will Go. Sleepytime Gal. Manila Calling. 1943: Phantom Lady. 1944: Up in Arms. Casanova Brown. Dark Waters. Dillinger. Dark Mountain. 1945: Why Girls Leave Home. 1946: Blonde Alibi. The Big Sleep. Cinderella Jones. Two Smart People. Joe Palooka—Champ. The Falcon's Alibi. 1947: Born to Kill (GB: Lady of Deceit). The Long Night. The Fall Guy. The Gangster. 1949: Flaxy Martin. The Great Gatsby. 1951: Behave Yourself! 1952: Don't Bother To Knock. 1953: Shane. Thunder Over the Plains. I, the Jury. 1954: Superman's Peril. The Outlaw's Daughter. Drum Beat. 1955: Timberjack. The Indian Fighter. Trial. 1956: The Killing. Accused of Murder. 1957: The Lonely Man. Voodoo Island. Plunder Road. Baby Face Nelson. 1958: Chicago Confidential. The House on Haunted Hill. 1959: Day of the Outlaw. 1960: College Confidential. Platinum High School (GB: Rich, Young and Deadly). 1961: One Eyed Jacks. 1962: Papa's Delicate Condition. 1963: Black Zoo. The Haunted Palace. Johnny Cool. 1964: Blood on the Arrow. The Glass Cage. 1966: The Spy in the Green Hat (TV. GB: cinemas). Welcome to Hard Times (GB: Killer on a Horse). 1968: Rosemary's Baby. 1969: The Great Bank Robbery. 1970: El Condor. The Movie Murderer. Night Chase (TV). 1971: The Night Stalker (TV). 1972: Blacula. The Great Northfield Minnesota Raid. 1973: Emperor of the North Pole (GB: Emperor of the North). Electra Glide in Blue. †Pat Garrett and Billy the Kid. The Outfit. 1974: Messiah of Evil. 1975: The Black Bird. Winterhawk. 1976: St Ives. 1977: Mad Bull (TV). Dead of Night (TV). 1979: 1941. The Champ. 1980: Carny. Tom Horn. Harry's War. 1981: Leave 'Em Laughing (TV). 1982: Hammett. The Escape Artist. 1983: This Girl for Hire (TV). 1984: It Came Upon the Midnight Clear (TV).

†Scenes deleted from final release print, but shown in some TV versions.

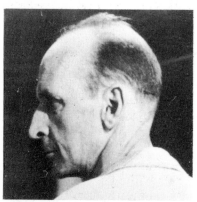

**COOLIDGE, Philip** 1908-1967
Dark, lanky, stoop-shouldered American actor of hangdog aspect. Only really a visitor to films from television and the stage, he was notable in one or two, especially *I Want to Live!* and *The Tingler*,

and considerably under-used by Hollywood. Died from cancer.

1947: Boomerang. 1956: The Sharkfighters. 1957: Slander. 1958: I Want to Live! 1959: The Tingler. It Happened to Jane. The Mating Game. North by Northwest. 1960: Inherit the Wind. The Bramble Bush. Because They're Young. 1962: Bon Voyage! 1964: Hamlet. 1965: The Greatest Story Ever Told. The Russians Are Coming, the Russians Are Coming. 1967: Never a Dull Moment.

**COOPER, George A.** 1916-
There were few sympathetic roles for this tough-looking little British actor with snub nose, small eyes and a fuzz of disappearing fair hair, a grouchy-looking, wiry ferret of a man who looked as though he would tear the throat out of any weak hero, and nearly did that very thing to Albert Finney's *Tom Jones* as the incensed Mr Fitzpatrick. Fewer than 30 films though; maybe the image was too hard and unvarying.

1954: The Passing Stranger. 1956: Fortune is a Woman (US: She Played With Fire). Sailor Beware! (US: Panic in the Parlour). 1957: Miracle in Soho. The Secret Place. 1958: Violent Playground. 1959: Follow That Horse! Hell is a City. 1962: The Wild and the Willing. Vengeance (US: The Brain). 1963: The Cracksman. Tom Jones. Nightmare. 1964: The Bargee. Ferry 'Cross the Mersey. 1965: Life at the Top. 1967: Smashing Time. 1968: The Strange Affair. Dracula Has Risen from the Grave. 1969: On Her Majesty's Secret Service. Start the Revolution Without Me. 1970: The Rise and Rise of Michael Rimmer. 1971: What Became of Jack and Jill? (US: Romeo and Juliet '71). 1974: The Black Windmill. 1976: The Chiffy Kids (series). 1985: Reunion at Fairborough (TV).

**COOPER, Dame Gladys** 1888-1971
Fair-haired, gracious-looking English actress, one of the loveliest leading ladies on the London stage from the early 1900s on. She went to Hollywood late in her career and stayed for many years playing mainly likeable ladies of the aristocracy. Three times nominated for an Academy Award: for *Now, Voyager* (probably her best

performance), *The Song of Bernadette* and *My Fair Lady*.

1913: The Eleventh Commandment. 1914: Dandy Donovan, the Gentleman Cracksman. 1916: *The Real Thing at Last. 1917: The Sorrows of Satan. Masks and Faces. My Lady's Dress. 1920: Unmarried. 1922: Headin' North. The Bohemian Girl. 1923: Bonnie Prince Charlie. 1935: The Iron Duke. 1940: Kitty Foyle. Rebecca. 1941: That Hamilton Woman (GB: Lady Hamilton). The Black Cat. The Gay Falcon. 1942: This Above All. Eagle Squadron. Now, Voyager. 1943: Forever and a Day. The Song of Bernadette. Mr Lucky. Princess O'Rourke. 1944: The White Cliffs of Dover. Mrs Parkington. 1945: Valley of Decision. Love Letters. 1946: The Cockeyed Miracle (GB: Mr Griggs Returns). The Green Years. 1947: Beware of Pity. Green Dolphin Street. The Bishop's Wife. 1948: Homecoming. The Pirate. 1949: The Secret Garden. Madame Bovary. 1951: Thunder on the Hill (GB: Bonaventure). 1952: At Sword's Point (GB: Sons of the Musketeers). 1955: The Man Who Loved Redheads. 1957: Circle of the Day (TV). The Mystery of 13 (TV). 1958: Separate Tables. Verdict of Three (TV). 1963: The List of Adrian Messenger. 1964: My Fair Lady. 1967: The Happiest Millionaire. 1969: A Nice Girl Like Me.

**COOPER, Melville** 1896-1973
Plump-faced, droop-eyed, dark-haired British actor who went to Hollywood in 1935 and played ineffectual villains pumped up by their own pomposity. Seemingly ideally

cast as a nose-in-the-air butler, he actually succeeded in playing a laudable variety of characters within his range, notably Romney in *The Scarlet Pimpernel*, the Sheriff of Nottingham in *The Adventures of Robin Hood*, a con-man in *The Lady Eve* and Mr Collins in *Pride and Prejudice*. Died from cancer.

1930: *All Riot on the Western Front. 1931: Black Coffee. The Calendar (US: Bachelor's Folly). 1932: Two White Arms (US: Wives Beware). 1933: Forging Ahead. Leave It to Me. To Brighton With Gladys. 1934: The Private Life of Don Juan. The Scarlet Pimpernel. 1935: The Bishop Misbehaves (GB: The Bishop's Misadventures). 1936: The Gorgeous Hussy. 1937: The Last of Mrs Cheyney. Thin Ice (GB: Lovely to Look At). The Great Garrick. Tovarich. 1938: Women Are Like That. The Adventures of Robin Hood. Hard to Get. Gold Diggers in Paris (GB: The Gay Imposters). Four's a Crowd. The Dawn Patrol. Comet Over Broadway. Dramatic School. The Garden of the Moon. 1939: I'm from Missouri. Two Bright Boys. The Sun Never Sets. Blind Alley. 1940: Pride and Prejudice. Too Many Husbands. Rebecca. Murder Over New York. 1941: Scotland Yard. Submarine Zone. Flame of New Orleans. The Lady Eve. You Belong to Me (GB: Good Morning, Doctor). 1942: This Above All. The Affairs of Martha (GB: Once Upon a Thursday). Life Begins at 8:30 (GB: The Light of Heart). 1943: Hit Parade of 1943. The Immortal Sergeant. Holy Matrimony. My Kingdom for a Cook. 1946: The Imperfect Lady (GB: Mrs Loring's Secret). Heartbeat. 13 Rue Madeleine. 1948: Enchantment. 1949: The Red Danube. And Baby Makes Three. Love Happy (later Kleptomaniacs). 1950: Father of the Bride. The Underworld Story. The Petty Girl (GB: Girl of the Year). Let's Dance. 1953: It Should Happen to You. The Story of Gilbert and Sullivan (US: The Great Gilbert and Sullivan). 1954: Moonfleet. 1955: The King's Thief. Diane. 1956: Bundle of Joy. Around the World in 80 Days. 1957: The Story of Mankind. 1958: From the Earth to the Moon.*

**COOTE, Robert** 1909-1982
Plumpish, ruddy-cheeked, moustachioed English actor largely in Hollywood films

(after screen starts in Britain and Australia), usually as an affable cove, an RAF officer or the hero's best friend. He was a real-life squadron-leader in World War II, with the Royal Canadian Air Force. After decades of semi-anonymity, he became known worldwide in the 1960s as one of the stars of a television series called *The Rogues*.

1931: Sally in Our Alley. 1936: Rangle River. 1937: The Thirteenth Chair. The Sheik Steps Out. 1938: The Girl Downstairs. Blonde Cheat. A Yank at Oxford. Mr Moto's Last Warning. 1939: Gunga Din. Bad Lands. The House of Fear. Nurse Edith Cavell. The Girl Downstairs. Vigil in the Night. 1940: You Can't Fool Your Wife. 1942: Commandos Strike at Dawn. 1943: Forever and a Day. 1946: A Matter of Life and Death (US: Stairway to Heaven). Cloak and Dagger. 1947: The Ghost and Mrs Muir. Forever Amber. Lured (GB: Personal Column). 1948: The Exile. Bonnie Prince Charlie. Berlin Express. The Three Musketeers. 1949: The Red Danube. 1950: The Elusive Pimpernel (US: The Fighting Pimpernel). 1951: Soldiers Three. The Desert Fox (GB: Rommel—Desert Fox). 1952: Scaramouche. The Prisoner of Zenda. The Merry Widow. 1955: The Constant Husband. Othello. 1956: The Swan. 1958: Merry Andrew. Hello London. The Horse's Mouth. 1960: The League of Gentlemen. 1963: The VIPs. 1964: The Golden Head. 1966: A Man Could Get Killed. The Swinger. 1967: The Cool Ones. 1968: Prudence and the Pill. 1970: Kenner. 1972: Up the Front. 1973: Theatre of Blood. 1975: Target Risk (TV). 1978: Institute for Revenge.*

**COPLEY, Peter** 1915-
One thinks of this British actor—bald, bespectacled and far from benign—as if through a fish-eye lens. As psychiatrists, magistrates and interrogators he displayed a civilized menace to those under his microscope. A stage actor since 1932, when he finally abandoned thoughts of a naval career. Married (first of three) to actress Pamela Brown. Copley was also a legal expert who was called to the bar in 1963: opponents beware! Not many films, but well-remembered from most of them.

1934: *Tell Me If It Hurts. 1949: Golden Salamander. 1950: The Elusive Pimpernel (US: The Fighting Pimpernel). 1952: The Card (US: The Promoter). The Hour of 13. 1953: The Sword and the Rose. 1956: Peril for the Guy. Foreign Intrigue. 1957: Time Without Pity. Man Without a Body. Just My Luck. 1959: Mystery in the Mine. Follow That Horse! 1961: Victim. 1964: The Third Secret. King and Country. 1965: Help! The Knack ... and how to get it. 1967: Quatermass and the Pit (US: Five Million Miles to Earth). 1968: The Shoes of the Fisherman. 1969: Frankenstein Must Be Destroyed. All at Sea. Walk a Crooked Path. 1970: The Engagement. Jane Eyre (TV. GB: cinemas). 1971: What Became of Jack and Jill? (US: Romeo and Juliet '71). 1972: That's Your Funeral. 1973: Gawain and the Green Knight. 1975: Hennessey. 1976: Shout at the Devil. 1977: The Black Panther. 1980: Little Lord Fauntleroy.*

**CORBY, Ellen** (née Hansen) 1913-1999
American actress of Scandinavian origins who, after World War II, switched from being a script girl and quickly cornered the market in nosey neighbours, bigoted townswomen, starchy schoolma'ams, repressed spinsters and dowdy servants. Her tight, dark hair and pinched features added character to dozens of films before she turned to television and became Grandma (and sometime scriptwriter) of *The Waltons*, a series for which she took two Emmy Awards to add to her Oscar nomination for *I Remember Mama* in 1948.

1933: *Twisted Rails. 1945: Cornered. 1946: The Dark Corner. It's a Wonderful Life! From This Day Forward. Bedlam. The Locket. In Old Sacramento. The Spiral Staircase. Till the End of Time. The Scarlet Horseman (serial). Cuban Pete (GB: Down Cuba Way). Crack-Up. Sister Kenny. Lover Come Back. The Truth About Murder. 1947: Hal Roach Comedy Carnival/The Fabulous Joe. Beat the Band. Forever Amber. Railroaded! Born to Kill (GB: Lady of Deceit). They Won't Believe Me. Driftwood. The Bachelor and the Bobby Soxer (GB: Bachelor Knight). 1948: Strike It Rich. I Remember Mama. Fighting Father*

*Dunne. The Dark Past. The Noose Hangs
High. If You Knew Susie. 1949: Little
Women. Mighty Joe Young. Rusty Saves a
Life. The Judge Steps Out. A Woman's Secret.
Madame Bovary. Ma and Pa Kettle Go to
Town (GB: Going to Town). Captain China.
1950: The Gunfighter. Caged. Peggy. Edge of
Doom (GB: Stronger Than Fear). 1951:
Harriet Craig. Goodbye, My Fancy. Angels in
the Outfield (GB: Angels and the Pirates).
Here Comes the Groom. The Mating Season.
The Sea Hornet. The Barefoot Mailman. On
Moonlight Bay. 1952: Monsoon. The Big
Trees. Fearless Fagan. 1953: The Woman
They Almost Lynched. Shane. The Vanquished.
A Lion is in the Streets. 1954: About Mrs
Leslie. The Bowery Boys Meet the Monsters.
Sabrina (GB: Sabrina Fair). Susan Slept
Here. Untamed Heiress. 1955: Illegal. 1956:
Slightly Scarlet. Stagecoach to Fury. 1957:
The Seventh Sin. Night Passage. God is My
Partner. Rockabilly Baby. All Mine to Give
(GB: The Day They Gave Babies Away).
1958: Macabre. Vertigo. As Young As We
Are. 1960: Visit to a Small Planet. 1961: A
Pocketful of Miracles. Saintly Sinners. 1963:
The Caretakers (GB: Borderlines). 1964:
Hush ... Hush, Sweet Charlotte. The Strangler.
1965: The Family Jewels. The Ghost and Mr
Chicken. 1966: The Night of the Grizzly. The
Glass Bottom Boat. The Gnome-Mobile. 1968:
Ruba al prossimo tuo (GB and US: A Fine
Pair). The Legend of Lylah Clare. 1969: A
Quiet Couple (TV). Angel in My Pocket.
1971: A Tattered Web (TV). Support Your
Local Gunfighter. The Homecoming (TV).
1972: Napoleon and Samantha. 1974: Pretty
Boy Floyd (TV). 1982: A Day of Thanks on
Walton's Mountain (TV). 1983: A Wedding
on Walton's Mountain (TV).*

**COREY, Jeff** 1914–
Thin- and bony-faced American actor, with
dark eyes and unruly black wavy hair, often
seen as men not to be trusted. After quitting
his job as a salesman for an acting career,
he came to Hollywood in 1941, playing
shabbily clothed, sometimes psychotic
types. Absent from the screen for 11 years
from 1951 after McCarthy blacklisting,
Corey established himself as one of
Hollywood's leading drama coaches, then

returned in much the same (though better
dressed) types of role as before.

*1941: All That Money Can Buy/The Devil
and Daniel Webster. North to the Klondike.
Small Town Deb. Petticoat Politics. Paris
Calling. 1942: The Man Who Wouldn't Die.
The Postman Didn't Ring. Girl Trouble. The
Moon is Down. 1943: My Friend Flicka.
1946: The Killers. Somewhere in the Night. It
Shouldn't Happen to a Dog. 1947: Ramrod.
Hoppy's Holiday. Miracle on 34th Street (GB:
The Big Heart). Brute Force. The Flame.
1948: The Wreck of the Hesperus. Alias a
Gentleman. Let's Live Again. Kidnapped.
Wake of the Red Witch. Joan of Arc. I, Jane
Doe. City Across the River. 1949: Roughshod.
Follow Me Quietly. The Hideout. Baghdad.
Home of the Brave. 1950: The Outriders. Rock
Island Trail (GB: Transcontinent Express).
The Nevadan (GB: The Man from Nevada).
Singing Guns. The Next Voice You Hear.
Bright Leaf. Rawhide/Desperate Siege. The
Prince Who Was a Thief. 1951: Red
Mountain. Superman and the Mole-Men
(GB: Superman and the Strange People).
Fourteen Hours. Only the Valiant. New
Mexico. Never Trust a Gambler. 1963: The
Balcony. The Yellow Canary. 1964: Lady in a
Cage. 1965: Once a Thief. The Cincinnati
Kid. Mickey One. 1966: Seconds. 1967: In
Cold Blood. 1968: The Boston Strangler.
Impasse. 1969: True Grit. Butch Cassidy and
the Sundance Kid. Set This Town on Fire (TV.
Not Shown until 1973). Beneath the Planet of
the Apes. 1970: The Movie Murderer (TV). A
Clear and Present Danger (TV). Getting
Straight. They Call Me MISTER Tibbs!
Little Big Man. 1971: Shoot-Out. Catlow.
Clay Pigeon (GB: Trip to Kill). 1972:
Something Evil (TV). 1974: Paper Tiger. The
Gun and the Pulpit (TV). 1976: Banjo
Hackett: Roamin' Free (TV). The Premoni-
tion. The Last Tycoon. 1977: Oh, God!
Moonshine County Express. Curse of the Black
Widow (TV). Captains Courageous (TV).
1978: The Pirate (TV). Jennifer (TV). The
Wild Geese. 1979: Butch and Sundance The
Early Days. 1980: Battle Beyond the Stars.
1982: The Sword and the Sorcerer. 1984:
Conan the Destroyer. 1985: Hell Town (TV).*

**CORRIGAN, Lloyd** 1900–1969
Podgy American actor, best remembered
from mainly light films in fussy, jovial or
panicky roles. An actor until 1925, he
worked as a screenwriter from 1926 to 1930
(and occasionally later), a director from
1930 to 1938 and an actor again from 1939
on, working mainly in television from 1955.
The son of another popular character star,
Lillian Elliott (1875-1959).

*1925: The Splendid Crime. 1939: The Great
Commandment. 1940: High School. The Ghost
Breakers. *Jack Pot. Queen of the Mob.
Sporting Blood. Captain Caution. The Return
of Frank James. Dark Streets of Cairo. The
Lady in Question. Two Girls on Broadway.
Public Deb No. 1. 1941: Young Tom Edison.*

*Men to Boys' Town. Mexican Spitfire's Baby.
North of the Klondike. Whistling in the Dark.
Kathleen. A Girl, a Guy and a Gob (GB: The
Navy Steps Out). 1942: Confessions of Boston
Blackie (GB: Confessions). Tennessee Johnson
(GB: The Man on America's Conscience). The
London Blackout Murders (GB: Secret Mo-
tive). Alias Boston Blackie. Bombay Clipper.
Treat 'Em Rough. The Great Man's Lady. The
Wife Takes a Flyer. Boston Blackie Goes
Hollywood (GB: Blackie Goes Hollywood).
The Mystery of Marie Roget. Lucky Jordan.
The Mantrap. Maisie Gets Her Man (GB:
She Got Her Man). 1943: Captive Wild
Woman. Hitler's Children. After Midnight with
Boston Blackie (GB: After Midnight). Stage
Door Canteen. Nobody's Darling. Tarzan's
Desert Mystery. Secrets of the Underworld.
King of the Cowboys. Song of Nevada. 1944:
Since You Went Away. Rosie the Riveter (GB:
In Rosie's Room). Passport to Adventure.
Gambler's Choice. Lights of Old Santa Fé.
Goodnight, Sweetheart. Reckless Age. The Thin
Man Goes Home. 1945: Bring on the Girls.
Boston Blackie Booked on Suspicion (GB:
Booked on Suspicion). The Fighting Guards-
man. Lake Placid Serenade. Crime Doctor's
Courage (GB: The Doctor's Courage). 1946:
She-Wolf of London (GB: The Curse of the
Allenbys). The Bandit of Sherwood Forest.
Lady Luck. Two Smart People. The Chase.
Alias Mr Twilight. 1947: Blaze of Noon.
Stallion Road. The Ghost Goes Wild. Shad-
owed. 1948: A Date With Judy. Adventures of
Casanova. The Return of October (GB: Date
With Destiny). Mr Reckless. The Bride Goes
Wild. Strike It Rich. The Big Clock. Homicide
for Three. 1949: Blondie Hits the Jackpot
(GB: Hitting the Jackpot). Home in San
Antone. Dancing in the Dark. The Girl from
Jones Beach. 1950: Father is a Bachelor. And
Baby Makes Three. My Friend Irma Goes
West. Cyrano de Bergerac. When Willie Comes
Marching Home. 1951: The Last Outpost.
Sierra Passage. Her First Romance (GB: Girls
Never Tell). New Mexico. Ghost Chasers.
1952: Rainbow 'Round My Shoulder. Son of
Paleface. Sound Off. 1953: Marry Me Again.
The Stars Are Singing. 1954: Return from the
Sea. The Bowery Boys Meet the Monsters.
1955: Paris Follies of 1956. 1956: Hidden
Guns. 1962: The Manchurian Candidate.
1963: It's a Mad, Mad, Mad, Mad World.*

**As director:**

*1930: †Follow Thru. †Along Came Youth.
1931: Daughter of the Dragon. The Beloved
Bachelor. 1932: The Broken Wing. No One
Man. 1933: He Learned about Women.
1934: *La Cucuracha. 1935: Murder on a
Honeymoon. 1936: The Dancing Pirate.
1937: Night Key. 1938: Lady Behave.*

†Co-directed

## COULOURIS, George 1903- 1989

British actor with staring eyes and tightly-
clamped lips that got him cast in mean,
villainous or even madman roles. He went
to America in 1930, but his biggest impact
came 11 years later, as Walter Parks
Thatcher in *Citizen Kane*, which set him up
for eight years of good character parts, often
in eccentric roles. His familiar mournful
features have been back in British films
since 1950.

*1933: Christopher Bean (GB: The Late
Christopher Bean). 1940: All This and
Heaven Too. The Lady in Question. 1941:
Citizen Kane. 1943: Assignment in Brittany.
This Land Is Mine. For Whom the Bell Tolls.
Watch on the Rhine. 1944: Between Two
Worlds. Mr Skeffington. The Master Race.
None But the Lonely Heart. A Song to
Remember. 1945: Hotel Berlin. Lady on a
Train. Confidential Agent. 1946: Nobody
Lives Forever. The Verdict. California. 1947:
Mr District Attorney. Where There's Life.
1948: Sleep My Love. Beyond Glory. Joan of
Arc. A Southern Yankee (GB: My Hero).
1951: Appointment With Venus (US: Island
Rescue). Outcast of the Islands. 1952: Venetian
Bird (US: The Assassin). 1953: The Heart of
the Matter. A Day to Remember. The Dog and
the Diamonds. The Runaway Bus. 1954:
Doctor in the House. Duel in the Jungle. The
Teckman Mystery. Mask of Dust (US: Race
for Life). 1955: Doctor at Sea. 1956:
Private's Progress. 1957: Doctor at Large. The
Man Without a Body. Kill Me Tomorrow.
Seven Thunders (US: The Beasts of Mar-
seilles). Tarzan and the Lost Safari. I Accuse!
1958: Spy in the Sky. Womaneater. No
Time to Die! (US: Tank Force). Law and
Disorder. Son of Robin Hood. 1960: Conspir-
acy of Hearts. Bluebeard's 10 Honeymoons.
Surprise Package. 1961: King of Kings. Fury
at Smuggler's Bay. The Boy Who Stole a
Million. 1964: The Crooked Road. 1965: The
Skull. Too Many Thieves (TV. GB: cinemas).
1966: Arabesque. 1968: The Assassination
Bureau. 1969: Land Raiders. 1970: No
Blade of Grass. 1971: Blood from the
Mummy's Tomb. 1972: Tower of Evil (US:
Horror of Snape Island). The Stranger (TV).
1973: The Suicide Club (TV). The Final
Programme (US: The Last Days of Man on
Earth). Coffee, Tea or Me? (TV). 1974:
Mahler. Papillon. Percy's Progress. Murder on
the Orient Express. 1976: The Antichrist (US:
The Tempter). Shout at the Devil. The Ritz.
1979: The Long Good Friday.*

## COWAN, Jerome 1897-1972

Dapper, moustachioed American actor with
foxy smile who was nearly 40 when he came
to films, but certainly made up for lost time
in the next 15 years. His lack of inches
confined him to just a few leading roles in
the mid-forties, but his character work
includes such memorable roles as the
doomed Miles Archer in *The Maltese Falcon*,
and Dagwood's boss in the *Blondie* films.

*1936: Beloved Enemy. 1937: New Faces of
1937. You Only Live Once. Shall We Dance?
The Hurricane. Vogues of 1938. 1938:
There's Always a Woman. The Goldwyn
Follies. 1939: The Saint Strikes Back. St
Louis Blues. The Gracie Allen Murder Case.
The Great Victor Herbert. East Side of Heaven.
She Married a Cop. The Old Maid. Exile
Express. 1940: Wolf of New York. Framed.
Castle on the Hudson (GB: Years Without
Days). Meet the Wildcat. Ma, He's Making
Eyes at Me. Torrid Zone. The Quarterback.
City for Conquest. Street of Memories. Victory.
Melody Ranch. 1941: High Sierra. Rags to
Riches. The Roundup. Affectionately Yours.
One Foot in Heaven. Kisses for Breakfast. Kiss
the Boys Goodbye. Too Many Blondes. Mr and
Mrs North. Singapore Woman. Out of the Fog.
The Bugle Sounds. The Maltese Falcon. The
Great Lie. 1942: Frisco Lil. The Girl from
Alaska. Joan of Ozark (GB: Queen of Spies).
Moontide. Thru Different Eyes. Who Done It?
A Gentleman at Heart. Street of Chance.
1943: The Song of Bernadette. Ladies' Day.
Hi Ya, Sailor (GB: Everything Happens to
Us). The Crime Doctor's Strangest Case (GB:
The Strangest Case). Silver Spurs. Mission to
Moscow. No Place for a Lady. Find the
Blackmailer. 1944: Sing a Jingle (GB: Lucky
Days). South of Dixie. Guest in the House.
Crime by Night. Mr Skeffington. The Minstrel
Man. 1945: Fog Island. Divorce. Getting
Gertie's Garter. The Crime Doctor's Courage
(GB: The Doctor's Courage). Hitchhike to
Happiness. GI Honeymoon. Blonde Ransom.
One Way to Love. Behind City Lights. Jungle
Captive. 1946: My Reputation. Claudia and
David. Murder in the Music Hall. The Kid
from Brooklyn. Flight to Nowhere. One Exciting
Week. Blondie Knows Best. Mr Ace. Deadline
at Dawn. A Night in Paradise. Deadline for
Murder. 1947: Blondie's Holiday. Driftwood.
The Perfect Marriage. Riffraff. Miracle on 34th
Street (GB: The Big Heart). The Unfaithful.
Cry Wolf. Dangerous Years. Blondie's Anni-
versary. Blondie's Big Moment. Blondie in the
Dough. 1948: So This is New York. Wall-
flower. Blondie's Reward. Arthur Takes Over.
Night Has a Thousand Eyes. June Bride.
1949: Scene of the Crime. Blondie's Secret.
Blondie Hits the Jackpot (GB: Hitting the
Jackpot). Blondie's Big Deal (GB: The Big
Deal). Always Leave Them Laughing. The
Fountainhead. The Girl from Jones Beach.
1950: The West Point Story (GB: Fine and
Dandy). Young Man with a Horn (GB: Young
Man of Music). The Fuller Brush Girl
(GB: The Affairs of Sally). Joe Palooka Meets
Humphrey. Peggy. When You're Smiling.*

*Dallas. 1951: Disc Jockey. The Fat Man.
Criminal Lawyer. 1952: The Magnificent
Adventure. 1953: The System. 1959: Have
Rocket, Will Travel. 1960: Visit to a Small
Planet. Private Property. 1961: All in a
Night's Work. Pocketful of Miracles. 1963:
Critic's Choice. Black Zoo. 1964: The Patsy.
John Goldfarb, Please Come Home. 1965:
Frankie and Johnny. 1966: Penelope. The
Gnome-Mobile. 1969: The Comic.*

## CRAVAT, Nick 1911- 1994

Diminutive (five feet two), black-bearded,
dark-eyed, narrow-faced, acrobatic American actor, for many years the trapeze
partner of Burt Lancaster in an act (Lang
and Cravat) that toured circuses, nightclubs
and vaudeville. After Lancaster was discovered for films, Cravat also headed for
Hollywood, and they devised some spectacular stunts together for swashbuckling
adventures of the early 1950s. He continued
to pop up occasionally in pictures until his
retirement in 1977. Often played mutes.

*1949: My Friend Irma. 1950: Thelma
Jordon (GB: The File on Thelma Jordon). The
Flame and the Arrow. 1952: The Crimson
Pirate. 1953: The Veils of Baghdad. 1954:
King Richard and the Crusaders. Three-Ring
Circus. 1955: Davy Crockett—King of the
Wild Frontier. Kiss Me Deadly. 1957: The
Story of Mankind. 1958: Run Silent Run
Deep. 1967: The Way West. 1968: The
Scalphunters. 1970: Valdez is Coming. 1972:
Ulzana's Raid. 1974: The Midnight Man.
1977: The Island of Dr Moreau.*

## CRAVEN, Frank 1875-1945

Kindly-looking, apple-cheeked American
actor who was a distinguished playwright
before becoming a Hollywood character
star in late middle age, chiefly as nice old
sticks with an effective line in wise philos-
ophy and sometimes as put-upon fathers.
While doing this work, he also worked on
screenplays and had leading roles in some
minor 'family' films. Like the more acerbic
Charles Coburn, Craven might well have
acted on into his eighties had a heart
ailment not intervened.

*1928: We Americans (GB: The Heart of a
Nation). 1929: The Very Idea. 1932: *The*

LEFT George **Coulouris** goes into his mad scientist act in a scene from a television series called *Pathfinders to Mars*, made in 1973

BELOW Jerome **Cowan** (centre) turns the pitying look on Gracie Allen in *The Gracie Allen Murder Case* (1939). Kent Taylor looks as though he doesn't quite know what to believe

*Putter. 1933: State Fair. 1934: That's Gratitude. City Limits. Funny Thing Called Love. He Was Her Man. Let's Talk It Over. 1935: Car 99. Vagabond Lady. Barbary Coast. 1936: Small Town Girl. The Harvester. 1937: Penrod and Sam. Blossoms on Broadway. 1938: You're Only Young Once. Penrod and His Twin Brother. 1939: Miracles for Sale. Our Neighbors, the Carters. 1940: Our Town. City for Conquest. Dreaming Out Loud. 1941: The Lady from Cheyenne. The Richest Man in Town. 1942: In This Our Life. Pittsburgh. Thru Different Eyes. Girl Trouble. Keeper of the Flame. 1943: Son of Dracula. Harrigan's Kid. Jack London. The Human Comedy. 1944: Destiny. My Best Gal. They Shall Have Faith/Forever Yours (GB: The Right to Live). 1945: Colonel Effingham's Raid (GB: Man of the Hour).*

**As director**
*1934: That's Gratitude.*

**CRAWFORD, John** 1926-
Powerfully built, brown-haired American actor of pudgy-faced handsomeness who, despite a not unlimited talent, has clung to his acting career with commendable tenacity, and widened his range in succeeding years. He progressed slowly to minor leading roles in Hollywood by 1957, then crossed to Britain and did some of his best work before returning to America in 1964 and taking on some tough, sometimes villainous character parts. Not to be confused with actors John Robert Crawford (of

*Red Line 7000)* or Johnny Crawford (of *Indian Paint).*

*1944: Thoroughbreds. 1945: The Phantom of 42nd Street. 1946: The Time of Their Lives. 1948: Sons of Adventure. 1949: Ghost of Zorro (serial). 1950: Radar Patrol vs Spy King (serial). A Life of Her Own. Mystery Street. Union Station. Cyrano de Bergerac. Raton Pass (GB: Canyon Pass). Lonely Hearts Bandits. 1951: Northwest Territory. I Was a Communist for the FBI. 1952: Actors and Sin. Old Oklahoma Plains. 1953: Marshal of Cedar Rock. Salome. The Big Heat. Conquest of Cochise. Rebel City. Serpent of the Nile. Slaves of Babylon. Star of Texas. Man Crazy. 1954: Battle of Rogue River. Captain Kidd and the Slave Girl. 1956: The Man in the Gray Flannel Suit. 1957: Courage of Black Beauty. 1958: Satan's Satellites. The Space Children. Graft and Corruption. Orders to Kill. The Key. Intent to Kill. Floods of Fear. Blind Spot. 1959: John Paul Jones. Solomon and Sheba. Hell is a City. 1960: Exodus. Piccadilly Third Stop. The Man Who Was Nobody. I Aim at the Stars. 1961: The Lion of Sparta. The Impersonator. The Long Shadow. 1962: Come Fly with Me. The 300 Spartans. The Longest Day. 1963: Jason and the Argonauts. Captain Sindbad. The Victors. 1964: The Americanization of Emily. 1965: Duel at Diablo. 1966: Return of the Gunfighter. 1967: El Dorado. 1969: La cattura (GB: The Ravine). 1971: J W Coop. 1972: Trouble Man. The Poseidon Adventure. Killer by Night (TV). 1973: The Severed Arm. 1974: Strange Homecoming (TV). 1975: The Swiss Family Robinson (TV). Night Moves. Guilty or Innocent: The Sam Sheppard Murder Case (TV). 1976: The Macahans (TV). The Enforcer. 1977: Outlaw Blues. 1978: The Two-Five (TV). Desperate Women (TV). Tilt. 1979: Dreamer. The Apple Dumpling Gang Rides Again. 1981: The Boogens.*

**CRIBBINS, Bernard** 1928-
Long-faced, curly-haired British leading comedy character star, a stalwart of British comedies of the early 1960s, a period when he almost became a star—and made some very popular recordings of silly songs. His distinctive voice, adaptable to all sorts of timbres and accents, made him a favourite

storyteller on radio and television in the 1970s.

*1957: Yangtse Incident (US: Battle Hell). Davy. 1958: Dunkirk. 1959: Make Mine a Million. Tommy the Toreador. 1960: Two Way Stretch. Visa to Canton (US: Passport to China). The World of Suzie Wong. The Girl on the Boat. 1961: Nothing Barred. The Best of Enemies. 1962: The Wrong Arm of the Law. 1963: The Mouse on the Moon. Crooks in Cloisters. Carry On Jack. 1964: Carry On Spying. Allez France (US: The Counterfeit Constable). A Home of Your Own. 1965: She. You Must Be Joking! Cup Fever. 1966: The Sandwich Man. Daleks—Invasion Earth 2150 AD. 1967: Casino Royale. A Ghost of a Chance. 1968: Don't Raise the Bridge, Lower the River. 1969: *The Undertakers. 1970: The Railway Children. 1972: Frenzy. 1976: Night Ferry. 1978: The Water Babies. The Adventures of Picasso. 1980: Dangerous Davies—the Last Detective (TV).*

**CRISP, Donald** 1880-1974
It's impossible to think of Donald Crisp as anything other than a crusty old shepherd, rancher or patriarch, the collective image from a fistful of 1940s' films. But this Scottish-born actor who never lost his burr was a multi-talented man who began his career with D. W. Griffith in the early silent days, and directed many silent films, including some classics from the 1920s, when he also made films in Britain. Won an Oscar in 1941 for *How Green Was My Valley* and, in his nineties and retired, took to haranguing interviewers with splendidly cantankerous views on 'modern' movies. A grand old man indeed.

*1907: *The French Maid. 1910: *The Two Paths. *Fate's Turning. *Winning Back His Love. *Sunshine Sue. 1911: *The Battle. *The Failure. *What Shall We Do With Our Old? *A Wreath of Orange Blossoms. *The Primal Call. *The Diving Girl. *Out from the Shadow. *The Adventures of Billy. 1912: *When Kings Were the Law. *The Best Man Wins. 1913. *Pirate Gold. *The Sheriff's Baby. *Drinks Lure. *Two Men of the Desert. *Black and White. *The Daytime Burglar. *The Blue or the Gray. *By Man's Law. *In the Elemental World. 1914: *The Different*

Man. The Battle of the Sexes. The Escape. Home, Sweet Home. The Mountain Rat. *The Tavern of Tragedy. *The Sisters. *The Mysterious Shot. The Avenging Conscience. *The Newer Woman. *The Warning. 1915: The Birth of a Nation. The Love Route. The Commanding Officer. A Girl of Yesterday. The Foundling. May Blossom. Such a Little Queen. Bred in the Bone. 1916: Intolerance. Joan the Woman. Ramona. 1917: The Countess Charming. 1918: One More American. 1919: Broken Blossoms. 1921: Beside the Bonnie Brier Bush (US: The Bonnie Brier Bush). 1925: Don Q, Son of Zorro. 1926: The Black Pirate. 1928: The Viking. Stand and Deliver. The River Pirate. 1929: Trent's Last Case. The Pagan. The Return of Sherlock Holmes. 1930: Scotland Yard (GB: Detective Clive, Bart). 1931: Svengali. Kick In. 1932: A Passport to Hell (GB: Burnt Offering). Red Dust. 1933: Broadway Bad (GB: Her Reputation). 1934: The Crime Doctor. The Little Minister. The Key. The Life of Vergie Winters. What Every Woman Knows. 1935: Vanessa, Her Love Story. Laddie. Mutiny on the Bounty. Oil for the Lamps of China. 1936: Mary of Scotland. The Charge of the Light Brigade. The White Angel. A Woman Rebels. The Great O'Malley. Beloved Enemy. 1937: Parnell. The Life of Emile Zola. That Certain Woman. Confession. Sergeant Murphy. 1938: Jezebel. The Amazing Dr Clitterhouse. Valley of the Giants. The Beloved Brat (GB: A Dangerous Age). The Sisters. The Dawn Patrol. Comet over Broadway. 1939: Juarez. The Old Maid. Wuthering Heights. The Oklahoma Kid. Daughters Courageous. The Private Lives of Elizabeth and Essex. 1940: The Story of Dr Ehrlich's Magic Bullet (GB: Dr Ehrlich's Magic Bullet). Brother Orchid. The Sea Hawk. City for Conquest. Knute Rockne—All-American (GB: A Modern Hero). 1941: Dr Jekyll and Mr Hyde. Shining Victory. How Green Was My Valley. 1942: The Gay Sisters. *The Battle of Midway (narrator only). 1943: Forever and a Day. Lassie Come Home. 1944: The Uninvited. The Adventures of Mark Twain. National Velvet. 1945: Son of Lassie. The Valley of Decision. 1947: Ramrod. 1948: Whispering Smith. Hills of Home (GB: Master of Lassie). 1949: Challenge to Lassie. 1950: Bright Leaf. 1951: Home Town Story. 1954: Prince Valiant. The Long Gray Line. 1955: The Man from Laramie. 1957: Drango. 1958: Saddle the Wind. The Last Hurrah. 1959: The Raider (TV). A Dog of Flanders. 1960: Pollyanna. 1961: Greyfriars Bobby. 1963: Spencer's Mountain.

**As director:**

1914: *The Dawn. *The Mysterious Shot. *The Newer Woman. *The Idiot. *The Tavern of Tragedy. *The Milkfed Boy. *Her Father's Silent Partner. *Her Birthday Present. *Their First Acquaintance, *Her Mother's Necklace. *Down the Hill to Creditville. *The Warning. *His Mother's Trust. *Sands of Fate. *The Availing Prayer. *His Lesson. *Frenchy. 1915: *An Old-Fashioned Girl. 1916:

Ramona. 1917: His Sweetheart. The Bond Between. A Roadside Impresario. The Marcellini Millions. The Cook of Canyon Camp. Lost in Transit. The Clever Mrs Carfax. The Countess Charming. 1918: Jules of the Strong Heart. The House of Silence. Less Than Kin. Venus in the East. Under the Top. Believe Me Xanthippe. The Firefly of France. The Goat. The Way of a Man with a Maid. Rimrock Jones. 1919: Johnny Get Your Gun. Poor Boob. Why Smith Left Home. Love Insurance. Too Much Johnson. Something to Do. Putting It Over. A Very Good Young Man. It Pays to Advertise. 1920: Miss Hobbs. The Six Best Cellars. Held by the Enemy. 1921: The Barbarian. Appearances. The Princess of New York. Beside the Bonnie Brier Bush (US: The Bonnie Brier Bush). 1922: Tell Your Children. 1923: Ponjola. 1925: Don Q Son of Zorro. 1926: Young April. Man Bait. Sunny Side Up (GB: Footlights). 1927: Vanity. Dress Parade. Nobody's Widow. The Fighting Eagle (GB: Brigadier Gerard). 1928: The Cop. Stand and Deliver. 1930: The Runaway Bride.

**As co-director:**

1924: The Navigator.

**CRONYN, Hume**
(H. C. Blake) 1911-
Short, skinny, waspish Canadian actor with reedy voice, narrow face and frowning brows, often as nosey parkers, henpecked husbands or sadistic pint-size villains. He was little seen in pictures after the 1940s, preferring stage work with his wife Jessica Tandy (married 1942), although he contributed to the scripts of a couple of Hitchcock films in the late 1940s. Never seemed to alter much in aspect on his infrequent appearances thereafter, despite the loss of an eye in 1970. Oscar nomination for The Seventh Cross.

1943: Shadow of a Doubt. Phantom of the Opera. The Cross of Lorraine. 1944: Lifeboat. The Seventh Cross. Blonde Fever. An American Romance. Main Street After Dark. Ziegfeld Follies (released 1946). 1945: A Letter for Evie. The Sailor Takes a Wife. 1946: The Green Years. The Postman Always Rings Twice. The Secret Heart (narrator only). 1947: The Beginning or the End? Brute Force. 1948: The Bride Goes Wild. 1949: Top o' the

Morning. 1951: People Will Talk. 1956: Crowded Paradise. 1960: Sunrise at Campobello. 1963: Cleopatra. 1964: *Miracle in Minnesota. Hamlet. 1969: The Arrangement. Gaily, Gaily (GB: Chicago, Chicago). 1970: There Was a Crooked Man. 1974: The Parallax View. Conrack. 1981: Honky Tonk Freeway. Roll-Over. 1982: The World According to Garp. 1984: Impulse. 1985: Brewster's Millions. Cocoon.

**CROSSLEY, Syd** 1885-1960
Gangling London-born comic actor, a popular favourite of the British music-halls (where he was billed as 'The Long Comic') who went to America and worked in vaudeville before a brief visit to Hollywood. Back in England from 1929, he slipped quickly into cockney character roles in a fistful of cheap comedies, giving yeoman support to most of the British cinema's comedy stars of the period. Began his stage career as a boy of 14 singing comedy songs.

1925: Keep Smiling. North Star. 1926: The Unknown Soldier. The Golden Web. One Hour Married. 1927: The Gorilla. Ain't Love Funny? Jewels of Desire. The Romantic Rogue. Play Safe. The Blood Ship. 1928: Fangs of the Wild. The Circus Kid. A Perfect Gentleman. The Cowboy Kid. That Certain Thing. Into No Man's Land (GB: The Secret Lie). 1929: The Younger Generation. The Hate Ship. Atlantic. The Fatal Warning (serial). Pride of Donegal. Just for a Song. 1930: Suspense. The Man from Chicago. *The Musical Beauty Shop. The Middle Watch. 1931: The Flying Fool. Never Trouble Trouble. The Professional Guest. Men Like These. Tonight's the Night—Pass It On. 1932: The Mayor's Nest. High Society. *On the Air. For the Love of Mike. Lucky Ladies. The Last Coupon. 1933: The King's Cup. Letting in the Sunshine. Leave It to Me. Excess Baggage. The Medicine Man. The Umbrella. Meet My Sister. You Made Me Love You. The Bermondsey Kid. 1934: Master and Man. Night Club Queen. Those Were the Days. Gay Love. It's a Bet. Eighteen Minutes. Dandy Dick. Radio Parade of 1935 (US: Radio Follies). Bagged. Over the Garden Wall. Give Her a Ring. 1935: Me and Marlborough. The Deputy Drummer. Honeymoon for Three. Royal Cavalcade (US: Regal Cavalcade). Jimmy Boy. Music Hath Charms. One Good Turn. The Ghost Goes West. Public Nuisance No. 1. 1936: The Man behind the Mask. Everything is Rhythm. Cheer Up. Queen of Hearts. Two's Company. Paybox Adventure. Keep Your Seats, Please. The Limping Man. Sporting Love. Double Alibi. Full Speed Ahead. The Man in the Mirror. 1937: Silver Blaze. Sensation. The Gang Show. The Dark Stairway. The Squeaker (US: Murder on Diamond Row). Lucky Jade. Feather Your Nest. Pearls Bring Tears. Boys Will Be Girls. Old Mother Riley. Racketeer Rhythm. Cotton Queen. Young and Innocent (US: The Girl Was Young). Sweet Devil. 1938: The Return of Carol Deane. Everything Happens to Me. His Lordship Goes to Press. *Peter's Pence.

ABOVE Grasping relatives Syd **Crossley** (right) and Ethel
Coleridge are fended off by pools millionaire Edmund Gwenn
in the 1938 comedy *Penny Paradise*

BELOW Scatman **Crothers** performs his own introduction as
Doc Lynch, ringmaster of a travelling Wild West show in
*Broncho Billy* (1980)

Save a Little Sunshine. Little Dolly Daydream. We're Going to be Rich. Penny Paradise. 1939: *Oh Dear Uncle. Meet Maxwell Archer (US: Maxwell Archer, Detective). Come On George! 1940: *Open House. 1941: Old Mother Riley's Circus. 1942: Let the People Sing.

## CROTHERS, Scatman
(Benjamin Crothers) 1909-
Engaging black American musician and spare-time actor of stringy build. A singer-drummer-musician at local speakeasies when only 14, Crothers had formed his own band by the 1930s, and has since written hundreds of tunes. He briefly visited films in the early 1950s but, after supplying the voice for Scatcat in Disney's *The Aristocats*, he brought his infectious grin and husky tones to a good range of screen veteran characterizations. His name derives from the jazz word 'scatting'—improvising nonsense syllables to a melody.

1952: Meet Me at the Fair. 1953: Walking My Baby Back Home. East of Sumatra. 1956: Between Heaven and Hell. 1963: Lady in a Cage. 1969: Hello, Dolly! 1970: The Aristocats (voice only). The Great White Hope. 1971: Chandler. 1972: Lady Sings the Blues. 1973: Detroit 9000 (GB: Call Detroit 9000). 1974: The Fortune. 1975: Friday Foster. Man on the Outside (TV). One Flew Over the Cuckoo's Nest. 1976: Silver Streak. The Shootist. 1978: The Cheap Detective. Mean Dog Blues. Vega$ (TV). 1979: Scavenger Hunt. 1980: Bronco Billy. The Shining. 1981: Deadly Eyes. 1982: Zapped! Missing Children: A Mother's Story (TV). 1983: Twilight Zone The Movie/The Twilight Zone. Two of a Kind.

## CROWDEN, Graham 1922-
Very tall, rangy, fair-haired British actor with gleefully ghoulish grin. An experienced Shakespearian performer, he came to film prominence playing eccentric roles in films directed by Lindsay Anderson. His mournfully mirthful self in too few other films, sometimes as mad professors or priests who should probably be defrocked. Would make a wonderful Marley's Ghost.

1961: Don't Bother to Knock! (US: Why Bother to Knock?) 1968: If ... 1969: The Virgin Soldiers. 1970: The Rise and Rise of Michael Rimmer. 1971: Percy (shown 1970). Up the Chastity Belt. Something to Hide. 1973: O Lucky Man! The Final Programme (US: The Last Days of Man on Earth). 1974: The Abdication. The Little Prince. Romance With a Double Bass. 1977: Hardcore (US: Fiona). Jabberwocky. 1981: For Your Eyes Only. 1982: Britannia Hospital. The Missionary. 1984: The Company of Wolves.

## CRUTCHLEY, Rosalie 1921-
Probably the British actress you would most expect to find behind the creaking door of a haunted house, this slim, black-haired, gloomy-looking lady was a dyed-in-the-wool stage player who made her theatrical debut at 17. She played a violinist who gets bumped off in her first film, a touch of gloom and doom which set the pattern for her movie career. Theatre gave her a better range of roles; it's a medium in which she still remains busy.

1947: Take My Life. 1949: Give Us This Day. 1950: Prelude to Fame. 1951: The Lady With a Lamp. Quo Vadis? 1953: Malta Story. The Sword and the Rose. 1954: Make Me an Offer. The Flame and the Flesh. 1956: The Spanish Gardener. The Gamma People. 1957: Miracle in Soho. Seven Thunders (US: The Beasts of Marseilles). No Time for Tears. 1958: A Tale of Two Cities. 1959: Beyond This Place (US: Web of Evidence). The Nun's Story. 1960: Sons and Lovers. Greyfriars Bobby. 1961: *Frederic Chopin. No Love for Johnnie. 1962: Freud/Freud—the Secret Passion. 1963: Girl in the Headlines (US: The Model Murder Case). The Haunting. 1964: Behold a Pale Horse. 1970: Wuthering Heights. 1971: Creatures the World Forgot. Blood from the Mummy's Tomb. Whoever Slew Auntie Roo? (US: Who Slew Auntie Roo?). 1972: Man of La Mancha. Au Pair Girls. 1973: ...And Now the Screaming Starts. *The Return. 1974: Mahler. 1976: The Message/Mohammed, Messenger of God. 1983: Memed My Hawk. The Keep.

## CULVER, Roland 1900-1984
Good-looking English actor with good-natured features that turned owlish in later life, usually seen in drily humorous upper-crust roles. He unspectacularly built up one of the longest careers in the English cinema: a visit to Hollywood from 1946 to 1949 brought a few good roles, but came too late to make him a star name in America. Died from a heart attack.

1930: Flat Number Nine. 1931: 77 Park Lane. Fascination. 1932: COD. A Voice Said Goodnight. There Goes the Bride. Love on Wheels. Her First Affaire. Puppets of Fate (US: Wolves of the Underground). 1933: Head of the Family. Her Imaginary Lover. Mayfair Girl. 1934: Lucky Loser. Two Hearts in Waltztime. The Scoop. Nell Gwyn. Borrow a Million. 1935: Oh, What a Night! 1936: Accused. 1937: Paradise for Two (US: The Gaiety Girls). 1939: French Without Tears. Blind Folly. 1940: The Girl in the News. *Dangerous Comment. Night Train to Munich (US: Night Train). Fingers. Old Bill and Son. 1941: This England. Quiet Wedding. 1942: One of Our Aircraft is Missing. Unpublished Story. The Day Will Dawn (US: The Avengers). Talk About Jacqueline. The First of the Few (US: Spitfire). Secret Mission. Dear Octopus (US: The Randolph Family). 1943: The Life and Death of Colonel Blimp (US: Colonel Blimp). 1944: On Approval. Give Us the Moon. English Without Tears (US: Her Man Gilbey). 1945: Perfect Strangers (US: Vacation from Marriage). Dead of Night. 1946: Wanted for Murder. To Each His Own. 1947: Down to Earth. 1948: The Emperor Waltz. Isn't it Romantic? 1949: The Great Lover. 1950: Trio. 1951: The Late Edwina Black (US: Obsessed). The Magic Box. Encore. Hotel Sahara. 1952: The Holly and the Ivy. The Hour of 13. 1953: Rough Shoot (US: Shoot First). 1954: Betrayed. The Teckman Mystery. The Man Who Loved Redheads. 1955: The Ship That Died of Shame (US: PT Raiders). An Alligator Named Daisy. Touch and Go (US: The Light Touch). 1956: Safari. 1957: The Hypnotist (US: Scotland Yard Dragnet). Light Fingers. The Vicious Circle (US: The Circle). 1958: The Truth About Women. Bonjour Tristesse. Rockets Galore (US: Mad Little Island). Next *to No Time. 1962: A Pair of Briefs. Term of Trial. The Iron Maiden. 1964: The Yellow Rolls Royce. 1965: Thunderball. 1966: A Man Could Get Killed. 1969: In Search of Gregory. 1970: The Rise and Rise of Michael Rimmer. Fragment of Fear. 1973: Bequest to the Nation (US: The Nelson Affair). The Legend of Hell House. The Mackintosh Man. 1977: The Uncanny. 1978: The Greek Tycoon. No Longer Alone. 1980: †Second to the Right and on till Morning. Rough Cut. 1982: Britannia Hospital. The Missionary.*

†Unreleased.

**CURRIE, Finlay**
(F. Jefferson) 1878-1968
Dour, craggy, heavily built Scottish actor with powerful, distinctive features. A former organist and music-hall singer, he broke into films with the coming of sound, often playing Americans. Continued playing rugged action roles (typically as the convict Magwitch in *Great Expectations*) into his sixties and seventies.

*1931: The Old Man. 1932: The Frightened Lady (US: Criminal at Large). Rome Express. 1933: Excess Baggage. Orders is Orders. The Good Companions. 1934: Princess Charming. Little Friend. Mister Cinders. Gay Love. In Town Tonight. My Old Dutch. 1935: The Big Splash. The Improper Duchess. 1936: The Gay Adventure. 1937: Wanted. Catch As Catch Can. Glamorous Night. Command Performance. The Edge of the World. Paradise for Two (US: The Gaiety Girls). 1938: The Claydon Treasure Mystery. Around the Town. Follow Your Star. 1939: \*Hospital Hospitality. 1941: 49th Parallel. 1942: The Day Will Dawn (US: The Avengers). Thunder Rock. 1943: The Bells Go Down. Undercover (US: Underground Guerillas). Warn That Man. They Met in the Dark. Theatre Royal. The Ship-builders. 1945: Don Chicago. I Know Where I'm Going. The Trojan Brothers. 1946: Spring Song (US: Springtime). Woman to Woman. Great Expectations. School for Secrets. 1947: The Brothers. 1948: Sleeping Car to Trieste. My Brother Jonathan. So Evil My Love. Mr Perrin and Mr Traill. Bonnie Prince Charlie. 1949: The History of Mr Polly. Whisky Galore (US: Tight Little Island). (narrator only). 1950: The Black Rose.*

*Treasure Island. My Daughter Joy (US: Operation X). Trio. The Mudlark. 1951: People Will Talk. Quo Vadis? 1952: Kangaroo. Stars and Stripes Forever (GB: Marching Along). Ivanhoe. Walk East on Beacon (GB: Crime of the Century). 1953: Rob Roy the Highland Rogue. \*Prince Philip (narrator only). Treasure of the Golden Condor. 1954: The End of the Road. Beau Brummell. Captain Lightfoot. Make Me an Offer. 1955: Third Party Risk (US: The Deadly Game). Footsteps in the Fog. King's Rhapsody. 1956: Around the World in 80 Days. Zarak. 1957: The Little Hut. Seven Waves Away (US: Abandon Ship!). Saint Joan. Campbell's Kingdom. Dangerous Exile. 1958: Tempest. The Naked Earth. Six-Five Special. Corridors of Blood. Rockets Galore (US: Mad Little Island) (narrator only). 1959: Ben Hur. Solomon and Sheba. 1960: Kidnapped. Hand in Hand. The Adventures of Huckleberry Finn. The Angel Wore Red. Giuseppe vendito dai fratelli (GB: Sold into Egypt. US: The Story of Joseph and His Brethren). 1961: Five Golden Hours. Francis of Assisi. Clue of the Silver Key. 1962: Go to Blazes. The Amorous Prawn (US: The Playgirl and the War Minister). The Inspector (US: Lisa). 1963: Billy Liar! The Cracksman. West 11. The Three Lives of Thomasina. The Fall of the Roman Empire. Cleopatra. Murder at the Gallop. 1964: Who Was Maddox? 1965: The Battle of the Villa Fiorita. Bunny Lake is Missing.*

**CUSACK, Cyril** 1910-1993
South Africa-born, Ireland-bred character star best known for fey, whimsical or scruffy roles, but capable of a wide range of characterization. Stocky, thin-lipped and mischievous-looking, he has made films all over the world, whether as menace, semi-lead or comic relief. Father of actresses Sinead and Sorcha Cusack.

*1918: Knocknagow. 1935: The Man Without a Face. 1936: Servants All. 1941: Inspector Hornleigh Goes to It (US: Mail Train). Once a Crook. 1946: Odd Man Out. 1948: Esther Waters. Escape. Once a Jolly Swagman (US: Maniacs on Wheels). The Small Back Room. All Over the Town. 1949: The Blue Lagoon. Christopher Columbus. 1950: Gone to Earth (US: The Wild Heart). The Elusive Pimpernel (US: The Fighting*

*Pimpernel). 1951: Soldiers Three. The Secret of Convict Lake. The Blue Veil. 1953: Saadia. 1954: The Last Moment. Destination Milan. 1955: Passage Home. The Man Who Never Was. 1956: Jacqueline. The Man in the Road. The March Hare. The Spanish Gardener. 1957: Ill-Met by Moonlight (US: Night Ambush). The Rising of the Moon. Miracle in Soho. 1958: Floods of Fear. Gideon's Day (US: Gideon of Scotland Yard). 1959: Shake Hands With the Devil. 1960: A Terrible Beauty (US: Night Fighters). 1961: The Power and the Glory (TV. GB: cinemas). Johnny Nobody. 1962: Waltz of the Toreadors. I Thank a Fool. Lawrence of Arabia. 1963: 80,000 Suspects. 1965: The Spy Who Came in from the Cold. Where the Spies Are. I Was Happy Here (US: Time Lost and Time Remembered). 1966: Fahrenheit 451. The Taming of the Shrew. 1967: Oedipus the King. 1968: Galileo. 1969: David Copperfield (TV. GB: cinemas). Country Dance (US: Brotherly Love). 1970: King Lear. 1971: Harold and Maude. Tam Lin (GB: The Devil's Widow). La polizia ringrazia (GB: The Law Enforcers). Sacco and Vanzetti. 1972: The Hands of Cormac Joyce (TV). La 'mala' ordina (GB: Manhunt in Milan). Più forte ragazzi (GB: All the Way Boys). 1973: Catholics (TV). The Day of the Jackal. The Homecoming. La mano spietata della lege (GB: The Bloody Hands of the Law. US: Execution Squad). 1974: The Abdication. Juggernaut. Run Run Joe. 1975: The Last Circus Show. 1977: Children of Rage. 1978: Les Misérables (TV). Poitín. Cry of the Innocent (TV). 1979: Tristan and Isolt (unreleased). 1981: True Confessions. The Outcasts. 1984: 1984.*

**CUTHBERTSON, Allan** 1920-1988
Tall, very fair-haired, moustachioed Australian-born actor of occasional crocodile smile and icily imperious demeanour. Almost always in unsympathetic roles, whether as coward, traitor, snob, wrong-headed administrator, vindictive officer or killer. It was mostly on television, though, that he revealed the other side of his talent, as a (very) straight-faced foil for some top comedians.

*1953: The Million Pound Note (US: Man with a Million). 1954: Carrington VC (US: Court-Martial). 1955: Portrait of Alison*

*(US: Postmark for Danger). The Man Who Never Was. Cloak Without Dagger (US: Operation Conspiracy). 1956: Anastasia. On Such a Night. \*Dick Turpin—Highwayman. Eyewitness. Doublecross. 1957: Barnacle Bill (US: All at Sea). Yangtse Incident (US: Battle Hell). The Passionate Stranger (US: A Novel Affair). 1958: Law and Disorder. Ice Cold in Alex (US: Desert Attack). I Was Monty's Double (US: Monty's Double). Room at the Top. 1959: The Crowning Touch. Shake Hands with the Devil. The Stranglers of Bombay. Killers of Kilimanjaro. 1960: Tunes of Glory. 1961: The Guns of Navarone. On the Double. The Malpas Mystery. Man at the Carlton Tower. 1962: The Boys. Solo for Sparrow. The Fast Lady. Term of Trial. Vengeance (US: The Brain). Nine Hours to Rama. 1963: The Informers. Tamahine. Bitter Harvest. The Mouse on the Moon. The Running Man. 1964: The Seventh Dawn. 1965: Life at the Top. Cast a Giant Shadow. Operation Crossbow (US: The Great Spy Mission). Game for Three Losers. 1966: Press for Time. 1967: Half a Sixpence. Jules Verne's Rocket to the Moon (US: Those Fantastic Flying Fools). The Trygon Factor. 1968: Captain Nemo and the Underwater City. 1969: The Body Stealers. 1970: The Adventurers. The Firechasers. One More Time. Performance. 1971: The Railway Children. 1972: Diamonds on Wheels. 1974: In the Devil's Garden. 1976: The Chiffy Kids (series). 1979: The Outsider. 1980: Hopscotch. The Sea Wolves. The Mirror Crack'd. 1983: Invitation to the Wedding.*

# D

## DALBY, Amy 1888-1969

Small, sturdy, sweet-faced, light-haired British supporting actress who came to films after a long theatrical career, to play a few spinster aunts and the like. Almost unbelievable that she wasn't one of Katie Johnson's (*qv*) gang of little old ladies in *The Ladykillers*: she must have had the 'flu. In her last film, *Smashing Time*, she played 'demolished old lady'!

*1941: Quiet Wedding. 1942: The Great Mr Handel. 1943: The Gentle Sex. Dear Octopus (US: The Randolph Family). 1944: Waterloo Road. 1945: The Wicked Lady. 1947: The*

*White Unicorn (US: Bad Sister). 1948: My Sister and I. 1951: Home to Danger. Brandy for the Parson. 1953: The Straw Man. 1958: Further Up the Creek. The Man Upstairs. 1962: The Lamp in Assassin Mews. 1963: The Haunting. 1964: Topkapi. 1965: The Secret of My Success. 1966: The Spy With a Cold Nose. Who Killed the Cat? Money-Go-Round. 1967: Smashing Time.*

## DALEY, Cass
### (Catherine Daley) 1915-1975

Gawky, loose-limbed, buck-toothed, brunette American singer-comedienne whose jitterbugging comedy routines enlivened a few 1940s' musicals, but who was really just too exuberant to stay on the film scene for long. She came out of retirement in 1966 to do nightclubs, nostalgia shows and the occasional film, but died in a freak accident when glass pierced her neck in a fall at home.

*1942: The Fleet's In. Star Spangled Rhythm. 1943: Riding High (GB: Melody Inn). Crazy House. 1945: Duffy's Tavern. Out of This World. 1947: Ladies' Man. Variety Girl. 1951: Here Comes the Groom. 1966: The Spirit is Willing. 1969: The Phynx. 1970: Norwood.*

## DALIO, Marcel
### (Israel Bleuschild) 1900-1983

Short, dark, dapper, incisive French actor who appeared with distinction in films from many countries. Never quite a star,

even in his native France, where he started in revue and music-hall, but a much-respected craftsman who brought all his roles, however small, briskly to life and created instantly identifiable characters.

*1933: Mon chapeau. 1934: Les affaires publiques. Turandot. 1935: Une nuit à l'hôtel. 1936: Quand minuit sonnera. Cargaison blanche. L'or. Pépé-le-Moko. Un grand amour de Beethoven. 1937: La grande illusion. Les perles de la Couronne. Gribouille. Alibi. L'homme à abattre. Les pirates du Rail. Naples où baiser de feu. Miarke la fille à l'ours. Marthe Richard. Sarati-le-Terrible. Troïka. 1938: Mollenard. Entrée des artistes (US: The Curtain Rises). Conflit. Chéri-Bibi. La maison du Maltais. 1939: La tradition de minuit. Les quatres jambes. La règle du jeu. L'esclave blanche. Le bois sacré. Tempête sur Paris. Le corsaire. 1941: Joan of Paris. One Night in Lisbon. The Shanghai Gesture. 1942: Unholy Partners. The Pasha's Wives. Flight Lieutenant. Casablanca. The Pied Piper. 1943: Paris After Dark. Tonight We Raid Calais. The Song of Bernadette. The Constant Nymph. 1944: The Conspirators. To Have and Have Not. Pin-Up Girl. Wilson. Action in Arabia. The Desert Song. 1945: The Night is Ending. A Bell for Adano. 1946: Pétrus. Son dernier rôle. Les maudits (GB: The Wicked City). Le bataillon du ciel. 1947: Dédée d'Anvers. Erreur judiciare. Temptation Harbour. 1948: Snowbound. Hans le marin. Sombre dimanche. Les amants de Vérone. 1949: Maya. Black Jack. Ménace de mort. Portrait d'un assassin. Adventure à Pigalle. 1950: Porte d'orient. 1951: On the Riviera. Nous irons à Monte Carlo (GB: Monte Carlo Baby). Rich, Young and Pretty. 1952: The Happy Time. Lovely to Look At. The Snows of Kilimanjaro. The Merry Widow. 1953: Scrupule, gangster. Gentlemen Prefer Blondes. Flight to Tangier. 1954: Sabrina (GB: Sabrina Fair). Lucky Me. Razzia sur la chnouf. La patrouille des Sables. 1955: Les Amants du tage (GB: Girls for the Summer). Jump into Hell. 1956: Hand of Fate (TV. GB: cinemas). Miracle in the Rain. Istanbul. 1957: China Gate. The Sun Also Rises. 10,000 Bedrooms. Tip on a Dead Jockey (GB: Time for Action). 1958: Lafayette Escadrille (GB: Hell Bent for Glory). The Perfect Furlough (GB: Strictly for*

Pleasure). 1959: Pillow Talk. The Man Who Understood Women. Classé tous risques (GB: The Big Risk). 1960: Can-Can. Song without End. 1961: The Devil at Four O'Clock. Le petit garçon et l'ascenseur. Jessica. 1962: The Devil and the 10 Commandments. Cartouche (GB: Swords of Blood). L'abominable homme des douanes. 1963: Donovan's Reef. The List of Adrian Messenger. A couteaux tirés (US: Daggers Drawn). 1964: Wild and Wonderful. Un monsieur de compagnie. Le monocle rit jaune. 1965: Le dix-septième ciel. Made in Paris. Lady L. 1966: How to Steal a Million. Tendre Voyou (GB: Simon the Swiss). The Oldest Profession. 1967: The 25th Hour. 1968: How Sweet It Is! L'amour c'est gai, l'amour c'est triste. 1969: Justine. 1970: Du blé en liasses. Catch 22. The Great White Hope. 1971: Papa, les petits bâteaux. Les yeux fermés. 1972: Dédée la tendresse. La punition. 1973: Les aventures de Rabbi Jacob (GB: The Mad Adventures of "Rabbi" Jacob). Ursule et Grétu. 1974: Trop c'est trop. Que la fête commence. 1975: Le faux cul. The Beast. 1976: L'aile ou la cuisse. 1977: L'ombre des châteaux. La communion solonelle. Le paradis des riches. L'honorable société. 1978: Une page d'amour. 1980: Brigade mondaine. 1981: Vaudou aux Caraïbes.

**DALY, Mark** 1887-1957
Fair-haired, tubby little Scottish-born actor of ruddy complexion, receding chin, beaky nose and watery eyes, a cheerful character who was once a music-hall comic and member of Fred Karno's troupe. Came to films with sound and soon settled into playing a string of amiable old bumblers. Daly had the leading role in 1953's *Alf's Baby* and was the old junk shop man who sold Tommy Steele his first guitar in *The Tommy Steele Story.*

1931: East Lynne on the Western Front. The Beggar Student. 1932: The Third String. 1933: Up for the Derby. Doss House. The Private Life of Henry VIII. A Cuckoo in the Nest. Say It With Flowers. 1934: The River Wolves. By-Pass to Happiness. Music Hall. There Goes Susie (US: Scandals of Paris). Flood Tide. 1935: That's My Uncle. The Small Man. A Real Bloke. Jubilee Window.

The Ghost Goes West. 1936: The Man Who Could Work Miracles. Shipmates o' Mine. Murder at the Cabaret. Hearts of Humanity. The Captain's Table. 1937: Good Morning, Boys (US: Where There's a Will). Wanted! Command Performance. Captain's Orders. Wings of the Morning. Knight Without Armour. 1938: Follow Your Star. Lassie from Lancashire. Break the News. 1939: Q Planes (US: Clouds over Europe). Hoots Mon! Ten Days in Paris (US: Missing Ten Days). 1940: The Farmer's Wife. 1941: The Big Blockade. 1942: Next of Kin. 1946: The Voyage of Peter Joe (serial). 1947: Stage Frights. 1948: Bonnie Prince Charlie. 1949: The Romantic Age (US: Naughty Arlette). Three Bags Full. 1953: Alf's Baby. 1954: Don't Blame the Stork! Lease of Life. The Delavine Affair. 1955: Footsteps in the Fog. Keep It Clean. 1956: The Gelignite Gang (US: The Dynamiters). The Feminine Touch (US: The Gentle Touch). You Pay Your Money. 1957: The Shiralee. The Tommy Steele Story (US: Rock Around the World). Soap-Box Derby.

**DAMPIER, Claude**
(C. Cowan) 1879-1955
Light-haired, bespectacled, idiotically beaming British character comedian who spoke through his buck teeth with a gurgly voice that sounded as though he were operating through a gullet-full of marmalade. A music-hall comedian who made his first two films in Australia, he later proved an enjoyably asinine foil in British films of the 1930s and an ear-stealing part of the post-war Jewel and Warriss radio shows (catchphrase: 'It's me-ee') although he joined them in only one of their (abortive) film forays.

1924: Hello Marmaduke. 1925: The Adventures of Algy. 1930: *Claude Deputises. 1934: Radio Parade of 1935 (US: Radio Follies). 1935: Boys Will Be Boys. So You Won't Talk. White Lilac. She Shall Have Music. No Monkey Business. 1936: King of the Castle. Public Nuisance No. 1. She Knew What She Wanted. Such Is Life. All In. Valiant Is the Word for Carrie. 1937: Wanted! Mr Stringfellow Says No. Sing As You Swing. Riding High. 1940: *The Backyard Front. 1944:

Don't Take It to Heart. 1946: Wot! No Gangsters? 1950: Let's Have a Murder. 1953: Meet Mr Malcolm.

**DANIELL, Henry**
(Charles H. Daniell) 1894-1963
British-born Hollywood actor with hard, unsmiling face and rat-trap mouth, a villain par excellence, who could also project sympathy in off-beat leading roles. Probably run through by more swashbuckling stars than any other villain except Basil Rathbone.

1929: Jealousy. The Awful Truth. 1930: Last of the Lone Wolf. 1934: The Path of Glory. 1936: The Unguarded Hour. Camille. 1937: The Thirteenth Chair. The Firefly. Madame X. Under Cover of Night. 1938: Holiday. Marie Antoinette. 1939: We Are Not Alone. The Private Lives of Elizabeth and Essex. 1940: The Sea Hawk. The Great Dictator. The Philadelphia Story. All This and Heaven Too. 1941: Four Jacks and a Jill. The Feminine Touch. Dressed to Kill. A Woman's Face. 1942: Sherlock Holmes and the Voice of Terror. Reunion/Reunion in France (GB: Mademoiselle France). Nightmare. Random Harvest. Castle in the Desert. The Great Impersonation. 1943: Mission to Moscow. Sherlock Holmes in Washington. Watch on the Rhine. 1944: Jane Eyre. 1945: The Suspect. Captain Kidd. The Body Snatcher. The Woman in Green. Hotel Berlin. The Chicago Kid. 1946: The Bandit of Sherwood Forest. 1947: The Exile. Song of Love. 1948: Wake of the Red Witch. Siren of Atlantis. 1949: Secret of St Ives. 1950: Buccaneer's Girl. 1954: The Egyptian. 1955: The Prodigal. Diane. 1956: The Man in the Gray Flannel Suit. Lust for Life. Around the World in 80 Days. Confession (TV). 1957: Les Girls. The Sun Also Rises. The Story of Mankind. Mister Cory. Witness for the Prosecution. 1958: From the Earth to the Moon. The Wings of the Dove (TV). 1959: The Four Skulls of Jonathan Drake. 1961: Voyage to the Bottom of the Sea. The Comancheros. The Chapman Report. 1962: The Notorious Landlady. Madison Avenue. Mutiny on the Bounty. Five Weeks in a Balloon. 1964: My Fair Lady.

**DANO, Royal** 1922- *1994*

Somehow, this tall, dark, grim-looking American actor always seems to be playing harbingers of doom in one way or another. His jaws always clamped tightly together, you felt he would have been happy delivering telegrams of bereavement or finding a nice, damp grave in which to bed down for the night. Sometimes he was a sheriff, sometimes a fire-breathing evangelist, sometimes just the bad guy's henchman: there certainly hasn't been much humour in Dano's 35 years of scattered screen roles. A killjoy, that's him.

1950: Undercover Girl. Under the Gun. 1951: The Red Badge of Courage. Flame of Araby. 1952: Bend of the River (GB: Where the River Bends). Carrie. 1954: Johnny Guitar. The Far Country. 1955: The Trouble with Harry. Tribute to a Bad Man. 1956: Moby Dick. Santiago (GB: The Gun Runner). Tension at Table Rock. 1957: All Mine To Give (GB: The Day They Gave Babies Away). Man in the Shadow (GB: Pay the Devil). Crime of Passion. Trooper Hook. 1958: Saddle the Wind. Handle with Care. Man of the West. 1959: Never Steal Anything Small. These Thousand Hills. Hound Dog Man. The Boy and the Bridge. Face of Fire. 1960: The Adventures of Huckleberry Finn. Cimarron. 1961: King of Kings. Posse from Hell. 1962: The Brazen Bell (TV. GB: cinemas). Savage Sam. 1964: The Seven Faces of Dr Lao. 1965: Gunpoint. 1966: The Dangerous Days of Kiowa Jones (TV. GB: cinemas). Welcome to Hard Times (GB: Killer on a Horse). 1967: The Last Challenge (GB: The Pistolero of Red River). 1968: The Manhunter (TV). Day of the Evil Gun. If He Hollers, Let Him Go. 1969: The Undefeated. Backtrack. 1970: Run, Simon, Run (TV). Machismo (40 Graves for 40 Guns) (GB: Forty Graves for Forty Guns). 1971: Chandler. Skin Game. The Great Northfield Minnesota Raid. 1972: The Culpepper Cattle Co. Moon of the Wolf (TV). Howzer. 1973: Ace Eli and Rodger of the Skies. Cahill, United States Marshal (GB: Cahill). Electra Glide in Blue. 1974: Big Bad Mama. The Wild Party. 1975: Huckleberry Finn (TV). Messiah of Evil. Capone. The Killer Inside Me. 1976: Drum. Manhunter (TV). The Outlaw Josey Wales. 1977: Bad Georgia Road. Murder in Peyton Place (TV). 1978: A Love Affair: The Eleanor and Lou Gehrig Story (TV). Donner Pass: The Road to Survival (TV). 1979: Strangers: The Story of a Mother and Daughter (TV). 1980: Hammett (released 1982). In Search of Historic Jesus (GB: Jesus). 1981: Take This Job and Shove It. 1982: Something Wicked This Way Comes. 1983: The Right Stuff. Will There Really Be a Morning? (TV). 1984: Teachers.

**DARRO, Frankie**
(F. Johnson) 1917-1976

Slim, whippy, sawn-off, aggressive-looking American actor with a mop of dark, unruly hair. In films from boyhood, he was the prototype of the Dead End Kids, Stanley Clements (qv) and every kid from the wrong side of the big-city tracks who never got the breaks. His best role came early, in Wild Boys of the Road. Thereafter, he seemed to be forever playing runts, jockeys and minor leads. It comes as no surprise to find that he actually made a film called Tough Kid. Died from a heart attack. Billed as 'Darrow' until 1930.

1923: Judgment of the Storm. 1924: Roaring Rails. The Signal Tower. So Big. 1925: Memory Lane. Confessions of a Queen. The People versus Nancy Preston. Bustin' Through (GB: Broke to the Wide). 1926: Kiki. The Cowboy Cop. Flaming Waters. Flesh and the Devil. Hearts and Spangles. Her Husband's Secret. 1927: Long Pants. Lightning Lariats. Cyclone of the Range. Judgment of the Hills. Her Father Said No. Flying U Ranch. Little Mickey Grogan. Moulders of Men. 1928: The Texas Tornado. Tyrant of Red Gulch (GB: The Sorcerer). When the Law Rides. The Circus Kid. The Avenging Rider. Phantom of the Range. Terror Mountain (GB: Tom's Vacation). Mystery Valley. 1929: The Pride of Pawnee. Trail of the Horse Thieves. The Rainbow Man. Gun Law. The Red Sword. Blaze of Glory. Idaho Red. 1931: The Mad Genius. The Vanishing Legion (serial). Way Back Home (GB: Old Greatheart). Public Enemy (GB: Enemies of the Public). 1932: Cheyenne Cyclone. Amateur Daddy. The Lightning Warrior (serial). Three on a Match. 1933: The Big Brain (GB: Enemies of Society). Tugboat Annie. Wild Boys of the Road (GB: Dangerous Days). Laughing at Life. Mayor of Hell. The Wolf Dog (serial). The Big Race (GB: Raising the Wind). 1934: Little Men. The Devil Horse (serial). The Merry Frinks (GB: The Happy Family). No Greater Glory. Broadway Bill (GB: Strictly Confidential). Stranded. Burn 'Em Up Barnes (serial. GB: Devils on Wheels). 1935: Men of Action. Valley of Wanted Men (GB: Wanted Men). The Phantom Empire (serial). Three Kids and a Queen (GB: The Baxter Millions). The Unwelcome Stranger. Red Hot Tires/ Racing Luck. The Pay Off. 1936: The Ex Mrs Bradford. Racing Blood. Mind Your Own Business. The Devil Diamond. 1937: Charlie Chan at the Race Track. Headline Crasher. Tough to Handle. Saratoga. Anything for a Thrill. Thoroughbreds Don't Cry. Young Dynamite. 1938: Reformatory. Wanted by the Police. Juvenile Court. 1939: The Great Adventures of Wild Bill Hickok. Tough Kid (GB: The Fifth Round). Boys' Reformatory. Irish Luck (GB: Amateur Detective). 1940: Chasing Trouble. On the Spot. Laughing at Danger. Up in the Air. Men with Steel Faces (GB: Couldn't Possibly Happen). 1941: The Gang's All Here (GB: In the Night). You're Out of Luck. Let's Go Collegiate (GB: Farewell to Fame). Tuxedo Junction (GB: The Gang Made Good). 1946: Her Sister's Secret. Freddie Steps Out. High School Hero. Junior Prom. 1947: That's My Man (GB: Will Tomorrow Never Come?). Vacation Days. Sarge Goes to College. 1948: Smart Politics. Angels' Alley. Heart of Virginia. Trouble Makers. Hold That Baby. 1949: Fighting Fools. 1950: A Life of Her Own. Riding High. Wyoming Mail. Sons of New Mexico (GB: The Brat). 1951: Pride of Maryland. Across the Wide Missouri. 1954: The Lawless Rider. 1956: The Ten Commandments. 1960: Operation Petticoat. 1964: The Carpetbaggers. 1969: Hook, Line and Sinker. 1974: The Girl on the Late, Late Show (TV).

**DARWELL, Jane**
(Patti Woodward) 1879-1967

Stout, homely American stage actress who, after a false start in silent films, came back to Hollywood with sound and chalked up a long and impressive portrait gallery of dominating, albeit soft-centred matrons and matriarchs. For one of the most famous, Ma Joad in *The Grapes of Wrath*, she won an Academy Award as Best Supporting Actress. Bid a sentimental farewell to the screen as the old bird-woman in *Mary Poppins*. Died from a heart attack.

*1913*: *The Capture of Aquinaldo*. *1914*: *Rose of the Rancho*. *The Only Son*. *After Five*. *Master Mind*. *Brewster's Millions*. *1920*: *The Mastermind*. *1930*: *Tom Sawyer*. *1931*: *Huckleberry Finn*. *Fighting Caravans*. *Ladies of the Big House*. *1932*: *Back Street*. *Hot Saturday*. *Murders in the Zoo*. *No One Man*. *1933*: *Bondage*. *Jennie Gerhardt*. *Bed of Roses*. *Ann Vickers*. *Only Yesterday*. *Air Hostess*. *One Sunday Afternoon*. *Before Dawn*. *\*Good Housewrecking*. *Women Won't Tell*. *Design for Living*. *Emergency Call*. *Child of Manhattan*. *He Couldn't Take It*. *Roman Scandals*. *1934*: *Once to Every Woman*. *Finishing School*. *Wake Up and Dream*. *Desirable*. *The Scarlet Empress*. *Heat Lightning*. *The Firebird*. *Fashions (GB: Fashion Follies of 1934)*. *Let's Talk It Over*. *Happiness Ahead*. *Wonder Bar*. *Change of Heart*. *Most Precious Thing in Life*. *Blind Date*. *Embarrassing Moments*. *Journal of a Crime*. *Gentlemen Are Born*. *Jimmy the Gent*. *Million Dollar Ransom*. *The White Parade*. *One Night of Love*. *Bright Eyes*. *1935*: *Beauty's Daughter (later Navy Wife)*. *Life Begins at 40*. *Paddy O'Day*. *Curly Top*. *Tomorrow's Youth*. *McFadden's Flats*. *One More Spring*. *Metropolitan*. *1936*: *Captain January*. *Little Miss Nobody*. *The Country Doctor*. *White Fang*. *Ramona*. *Private Number*. *Star for a Night*. *Poor Little Rich Girl*. *We're Only Human*. *The First Baby*. *Craig's Wife*. *1937*: *The Great Hospital Mystery*. *Dead Yesterday*. *Dangerously Yours*. *Wife, Doctor and Nurse*. *The Singing Marine*. *Nancy Steele is Missing*. *Slave Ship*. *Love Is News*. *Laughing at Trouble*. *Fifty Roads to Town*. *1938*: *The Jury's Secret*. *Five of a Kind*. *Change of Heart (remake)*. *Time Out for Murder*. *Little Miss Broadway*. *Three Blind Mice*. *Inside Story*. *Battle of Broadway*. *Up the River*. *1939*: *Jesse James*. *Unexpected Father (GB: Sandy Takes a Bow)*. *Zero Hour*. *The Rains Came*. *Gone With the Wind*. *Grand Jury Secrets*. *20,000 Men a Year*. *1940*: *The Grapes of Wrath*. *Chad Hanna*. *Brigham Young—Frontiersman (GB: Brigham Young)*. *Youth Will Be Served*. *Untamed*. *Miracle on Main Street*. *1941*: *All That Money Can Buy*. *Here Is a Man*. *Thieves Fall Out*. *Small Town Deb*. *Private Nurse*. *1942*: *Young America*. *The Loves of Edgar Allan Poe*. *Men of Texas (GB: Men of Destiny)*. *It Happened in Flatbush*. *The Great Gildersleeve*. *All Through the Night*. *On the Sunny Side*. *Highways by Night*. *The Ox-Bow Incident (GB: Strange Incident)*. *1943*: *Battle of Midway*. *Tender Comrade*. *Gildersleeve's Bad Day*. *\*A Family Feud*. *Government Girl*. *Stage Door Canteen*. *1944*: *Sunday Dinner for a Soldier*. *She's a Sweetheart*. *Music in Manhattan*. *Double Indemnity*. *Reckless Age*. *The Impatient Years*. *1945*: *Captain Tugboat Annie*. *I Live in Grosvenor Square (US: A*

*Yank in London)*. *1946*: *Three Wise Fools*. *My Darling Clementine*. *Dark Horse*. *1947*: *Red Stallion*. *Keeper of the Bees*. *1948*: *Three Godfathers*. *The Time of Your Life*. *Train to Alcatraz*. *1949*: *Red Canyon*. *1950*: *Wagonmaster*. *The Daughter of Rosie O'Grady*. *Caged*. *Redwood Forest Trail*. *Surrender*. *Three Husbands*. *The Second Face*. *Father's Wild Game*. *1951*: *The Lemon Drop Kid*. *Excuse My Dust*. *Journey into Light*. *Fourteen Hours*. *1952*: *We're Not Married*. *1953*: *The Sun Shines Bright*. *It Happens Every Thursday*. *Affair With a Stranger*. *The Bigamist*. *1955*: *Hit the Deck*. *A Life at Stake*. *1956*: *There's Always Tomorrow*. *Sincerely, Willis Wayde (TV)*. *Girls in Prison*. *The Greer Case (TV)*. *1957*: *Three Men on a Horse (TV)*. *1958*: *The Last Hurrah*. *1959*: *Hound Dog Man*. *1964*: *Mary Poppins*.

**DA SILVA, Howard**
(Harold Silverblatt) 1909- 1986

Fair-haired, surly-looking, Broadway-trained American actor, a very useful off-centre villain whose career was stopped in its tracks by the McCarthy blacklist. He was fired from the film (*Slaughter Trail*, 1951) on which he was working, and spent 11 years in the wilderness. Unsurprisingly, his film career failed to recover, although he has made sporadic returns to movies, mainly in biting cameo roles, since 1962.

*1936*: *Once in a Blue Moon*. *1939*: *Golden Boy*. *1940*: *Abe Lincoln in Illinois (GB: Spirit of the People)*. *I'm Still Alive*. *\*A Day in the Orchard*. *1941*: *The Sea Wolf*. *Steel Against the Sky*. *Strange Alibi*. *Navy Blues*. *Sergeant York*. *Bad Men of Missouri*. *Nine Lives Are Not Enough*. *Wild Bill Hickok Rides*. *1942*: *Bullet Scars*. *Native Land*. *Juke Girl*. *The Big Shot*. *Reunion/Reunion in France (GB: Mademoiselle France)*. *The Omaha Trail*. *Keeper of the Flame*. *1943*: *Tonight We Raid Calais*. *Five Were Chosen*. *Duffy's Tavern*. *The Lost Weekend*. *1946*: *The Blue Dahlia*. *Two Years Before the Mast*. *1947*: *Variety Girl*. *Blaze of Noon*. *Unconquered*. *1949*: *The Great Gatsby*. *They Live By Night*. *Border Incident*. *1950*: *The Underworld Story*. *Wyoming Mail*. *Tripoli*. *1951*: *Fourteen Hours*. *Three Husbands*. *1962*: *David and Lisa*. *1963*: *It's a Mad, Mad, Mad, Mad*

*World*. *1964*: *The Outrage*. *1966*: *Nevada Smith*. *1972*: *1776*. *1974*: *The Great Gatsby (remake)*. *The Missiles of October (TV)*. *Smile Jenny, You're Dead (TV)*. *1977*: *The Private Files of J. Edgar Hoover*. *1981*: *Mommie Dearest*. *1984*: *Garbo Talks!*

**DAVENPORT, Harry** 1866-1949
From a long line of actors (his two wives and four children were all in the profession), this tall, distinguished American player brought his own distinctive sense of humour to bear on many of the Hollywood roles he graced. Played Grandpa in 'The Higgins Family' comedy series (1938-1940) and Grandpa again in *Meet Me in St Louis*. Also directed a few films in the silent era. Died from a heart attack, his last film still to be shown.

*1914*: *Fogg's Millions*. *1915*: *Father and the Boy*. *1916*: *One Night*. *1917*: *The False Friend*. *A Man's Law*. *The Planter*. *Sowers and Reapers*. *1919*: *A Girl at Bay*. *The Unknown Quantity*. *1930*: *Her Unborn Child*. *1931*: *My Sin*. *His Woman*. *1933*: *Get That Venus*. *1935*: *The Scoundrel*. *1936*: *Three Men on a Horse*. *The Case of the Black Cat*. *Legion of Terror*. *Three Cheers for Love*. *King of Hockey (GB: King of the Ice Rink)*. *1937*: *Fly Away Baby*. *The Life of Emile Zola*. *Under Cover of Night*. *Her Husband's Secretary*. *White Bondage*. *They Won't Forget*. *Four Days' Wonder*. *Maytime*. *Radio Patrol (serial)*. *The Great Garrick*. *Mountain Justice*. *Mr Dodd Takes the Air*. *First Lady*. *The Perfect Specimen*. *Paradise Express*. *Wells Fargo*. *As Good As Married*. *Armored Car*. *Fit for a King*. *1938*: *The Sisters*. *Saleslady*. *Gold Is Where You Find It*. *Long Shot*. *The First Hundred Years*. *Marie Antoinette*. *The Cowboy and the Lady*. *Young Fugitives*. *The Rage of Paris*. *Reckless Living*. *You Can't Take It With You*. *\*Screen Snapshots No 75*. *The Higgins Family*. *Tail Spin*. *1939*: *Juarez*. *Orphans of the Street*. *My Wife's Relatives*. *Made for Each Other*. *Should Husbands Work?* *The Covered Trailer*. *Money to Burn*. *Exile Express*. *Gone With the Wind*. *The Story of Alexander Graham Bell (GB: The Modern Miracle)*. *Death of a Champion*. *The Hunchback of Notre Dame*. *1940*: *Granny Get Your Gun*. *Too Many Husbands*. *Grandpa Goes to*

Town. All This and Heaven Too. Lucky Partners. Foreign Correspondent. Earl of Puddlestone (GB : Jolly Old Higgins). I Want a Divorce. The Story of Dr Ehrlich's Magic Bullet (GB : Dr Ehrlich's Magic Bullet). 1941 : That Uncertain Feeling. I Wanted Wings. Hurricane Smith. The Bride Came COD. One Foot in Heaven. Kings Row. Meet John Doe. 1942 : Son of Fury. The Ox-Bow Incident (GB : Strange Incident). Larceny Inc. Ten Gentlemen from West Point. Tales of Manhattan. 1943 : Shantytown. Headin' for God's Country. We're Never Been Licked (GB : Texas to Tokyo). Jack London. Government Girl. Princess O'Rourke. The Amazing Mrs Holliday. Gangway for Tomorrow. 1944 : Meet Me in St Louis. The Impatient Years. The Thin Man Goes Home. Kismet. Music for Millions. 1945 : The Enchanted Forest. This Love of Ours. Too Young to Know. Adventure. She Wouldn't Say Yes. A Boy, a Girl and a Dog (GB : Lucky). 1946 : Pardon My Past. Courage of Lassie. Blue Skies. Faithful in My Fashion. Three Wise Fools. Claudia and David. Lady Luck. GI War Brides (GB : War Brides). 1947 : The Farmer's Daughter. Stallion Road. Keeper of the Bees. The Bachelor and the Bobby-Soxer (GB : Bachelor Knight). That Hagen Girl. Sport of Kings (GB : Heart Royal). The Fabulous Texan. 1948 : Three Daring Daughters (GB : The Birds and the Bees). For the Love of Mary. The Man from Texas. That Lady in Ermine. The Decision of Christopher Blake. 1949 : That Forsyte Woman (GB : The Forsyte Saga). Down to the Sea in Ships. Tell It to the Judge. Little Women. 1950 : Riding High.

## As director:

1915 : *Mr Jarr and the Lady Reformer. *Mr Jarr and the Visiting Firemen. *Mr Jarr Brings Home a Turkey. *Mr Jarr Takes a Night Off. *Mr Jarr Visits His Home Town. *Mr Jarr's Big Vacation. *Mr Jarr's Magnetic Friend. *Mrs Jarr and the Beauty Treatment. *Mrs Jarr and the Society Circus. *Mrs Jarr's Auction Bridge. *The Closing of the Circuit. *The Enemies. For a Woman's Fair Name. *The Jarr Family Discover Harlem. *The Jarrs Visit Arcadia. The Making Over of Geoffrey Manning. *Mr Jarr and Circumstantial Evidence. *Mr Jarr and Gertrude's Beaux. *Mr Jarr and Love's Young Dream. *Mr Jarr and the Captive Maiden. *Mr Jarr and the Dachshund. *Mr Jarr and the Ladies' Cup. 1916 : *Myrtle, the Manicurist. *The Resurrection of Hollis. *The Accusing Voice.

## DAVIES, Betty Ann 1910-1955

Brunette (occasionally blonde) English actress with small, bird-like face and busy acting style, seen mainly as chirpy maids and carefree young heroines until 1941. After a six-year absence, she returned to films in much darker roles, as shrews (notably Miriam in The History of Mr Polly), faithless wives, prostitutes and murder victims. She died at 44 from complications following an operation for appendicitis. One of the original Cochran Young Ladies.

Billed in her earliest films as Betty Davies.

1933 : Oh! What a Duchess. 1934 : Death at Broadcasting House. Youthful Folly. 1935 : Joy Ride. Play Up the Band. 1936 : She Knew What She Wanted. Excuse My Glove. Chick. Tropical Trouble. Radio Lover. 1937 : Lucky Jade. Under a Cloud. Silver Top. 1938 : Mountains o' Mourne. 1941 : Kipps (US : The Remarkable Mr Kipps). *I Bet. 1947 : It Always Rains on Sunday. 1948 : Escape. To the Public Danger. 1949 : Now Barabbas was a robber...(US : Barabbas the Robber). The Man in Black. The Blue Lamp. Which Will You Have? The History of Mr Polly. The Passionate Friends (US : One Woman's Story). 1950 : Trio. The Woman With No Name (US : Her Panelled Door). 1951 : Outcast of the Islands. 1952 : Meet Me Tonight. Cosh Boy (US : The Slasher). 1953 : Grand National Night (US : Wicked Wife). Gilbert Harding Speaking of Murder. 1954 : The Belles of St Trinian's. Children Galore. 1955 : Murder by Proxy (US : Blackout). 1956 : *Ring of Greed. Alias John Preston.

## DAVIES, Rupert 1916-1976

Burly, crinkle-haired, affable British actor with small features set in a large face. His film career gained momentum in the late 1950s, but almost came to a halt after he won the title role in the TV series Maigret, continuing as Georges Simenon's pipe-smoking sleuth for several seasons. Most of his remaining film roles were in horror films, mostly as comforting peripheral figures.

1949 : Private Angelo. 1955 : The Dark Avenger (US : The Warriors). 1957 : The Traitor (US : The Accused). 1958 : Next to No Time! Sea Fury. The Key. 1959 : Sapphire. John Paul Jones. Breakout. Life in Emergency Ward 10. Idle on Parade (US : Idol on Parade). Violent Moment. Devil's Bait. Bobbikins. 1960 : The Criminal (US : Hell is a City). Danger Tomorrow. 1965 : The Spy Who Came in from the Cold. The Uncle. 1966 : Five Golden Dragons. Das Geheimnis der gelben Mönche (GB : Target for Killing). Brides of Fu Manchu. 1967 : House of a Thousand Dolls. Submarine X-1. 1968 : Curse of the Crimson Altar (US : Crimson Cult). Dracula Has Risen from the Grave. Witchfinder-General. 1969 : The Oblong Box. 1970 : The Firechasers. Waterloo. 1971 : Zeppelin. Danger Point! The Night Visitor. 1976 : Frightmare.

## DAWSON, Anthony 1916-

Long, lean, gaunt, dark, moustachioed, sinister British actor who looked as though he would throttle his grandmother for a handful of silver, and slunk famously into film history as the disgraced ex-army officer hired to kill Grace Kelly in Dial M for Murder. Dawson brought his disreputable scowl effectively to a similar part in Midnight Lace, but his other film roles have been largely unworthy of his talent. Despite the impeccable accent, he was born in Edinburgh.

1944 : The Way Ahead. 1945 : The Way to the Stars (US : Johnny in the Clouds). 1946 : School for Secrets (US : Secret Flight). Beware of Pity. 1948 : The Queen of Spades. 1950 : They Were Not Divided. The Woman in Question (US : Five Angles on Murder). The Wooden Horse. 1951 : The Long Dark Hall. I'll Get You for This (US : Lucky Nick Cain). Valley of Eagles. 1954 : Dial M for Murder. 1955 : That Lady. 1957 : Action of the Tiger. Hour of Decision/Table in the Corner. 1958 : Grip of the Strangler (US : The Haunted Strangler). 1959 : Tiger Bay. Libel. 1960 : Midnight Lace. 1961 : Curse of the Werewolf. Offbeat. Follow That Man. 1962 : Dr No. Seven Seas to Calais. 1965 : The Amorous Adventures of Moll Flanders. Change Partners. 1966 : Triple Cross. 1967 : Hell is Empty (completed 1963). L'avventurio (GB and US :

*The Rover). Operation Kid Brother. Dalle Ardenne all' inferno (GB: The Dirty Heroes). 1970: The Battle of Neretva/The Battle for Neretva. 1972: Cool Million (TV). The Big Game. 1973: Massacre in Rome. 1974: The Count of Monte Cristo (TV. GB: cinemas). 1981: Inchon!*

### DEACON, Richard 1922-1984

Tall, bald-headed, bespectacled American comic actor who walked as though there were eggs all over the ground and played self-righteous employees eager to shop the hero or heroine to the boss. He became popular in television series (*Mister Ed, Leave It to Beaver, The Dick Van Dyke Show, Mothers-in-Law*) and in his fifties started a programme on microwave cookery. Died from a heart attack.

*1954: Desiree. Rogue Cop. 1955: Abbott and Costello Meet the Mummy. My Sister Eileen. Lay That Rifle Down. Good Morning, Miss Dove. Hot Blood. Blackboard Jungle. 1956: Francis in the Haunted House. My Man Godfrey. The Kettles in the Ozarks. The Scarlet Hour. The Proud Ones. The Solid Gold Cadillac. The Power and the Prize. 1957: Affair in Reno. Decision at Sundown. Spring Reunion. 1958: The Last Hurrah. A Nice Little Bank That Should Be Robbed (GB: How to Rob a Bank). 1959: The Remarkable Mr Pennypacker. The Young Philadelphians (GB: The City Jungle). 1961: All in a Night's Work. Everything's Ducky. 1962: That Touch of Mink. Critic's Choice. 1963: The Raiders. The Birds. 1964: John Goldfarb, Please Come Home. The Patsy. Dear Heart. The Disorderly Orderly. 1965: That Darn Cat! Billie. 1966: Don't Worry, We'll Think of a Title. The Gnome-Mobile. 1967: Blackbeard's Ghost. The King's Pirate. Enter Laughing. 1968: Lady in Cement. The One and Only Genuine Original Family Band. 1978: Piranha. Getting Married (TV). 1980: The Happy Hooker Goes to Hollywood.*

### DE CAMP, Rosemary 1913- 2001

Dark-haired American actress with warm smile and heart-shaped face, whose sympathetic voice matched her screen personality, and had made her a popular actress on radio before she came to Hollywood in 1941.

Almost from the very start of her screen career, she appeared in mother roles, having teenage 'daughters' while still in her late twenties and early thirties. Television work from the 1950s to the 1970s stretched her career as a screen mother over 30 years.

*1941: Cheers for Miss Bishop. The Wagons Roll at Night. Hold Back the Dawn. 1942: Jungle Book. Yankee Doodle Dandy. Eyes in the Night. Commandos Strike at Dawn. Smith of Minnesota. 1943: This is the Army. 1944: The Merry Monahans. Bowery to Broadway. Practically Yours. 1945: Pride of the Marines (GB: Forever in Love). Rhapsody in Blue. Danger Signal. Week-End at the Waldorf. Too Young to Know. Blood on the Sun. 1946: From This Day Forward. Two Guys from Milwaukee (GB: Royal Flush). 1947: Nora Prentiss. Night unto Night (released 1949). 1949: The Life of Riley. Look for the Silver Lining. 1950: The Story of Seabiscuit (GB: Pride of Kentucky). The Big Hangover. 1951: On Moonlight Bay. Night into Morning. Scandal Sheet (GB: The Dark Page). 1952: Treasure of Lost Canyon. 1953: So This is Love (GB: The Grace Moore Story). By the Light of the Silvery Moon. Main Street to Broadway. 1955: Many Rivers to Cross. Strategic Air Command. 1960: 13 Ghosts. 1978: The Time Machine (TV). 1981: Saturday the 14th.*

### DE CASALIS, Jeanne
(J. de Casalis de Pury) 1896-1966
Dark, twittery, pencil-slim, Basutoland-born entertainer in British show business.

She began as a straight dramatic actress, but developed into a top music-hall and radio comedienne, inventing the famous gossipy character Mrs Feather and continuing to make eccentric appearances in British films until 1949. At one time married to the actor Colin Clive.

*1925: Settled Out of Court (US: Evidence Enclosed). 1927: The Glad Eye. The Arcadians/Land of Heart's Desire. 1928: Zero. 1930: Infatuation. Knowing Men. 1932: Nine Till Six. 1933: Radio Parade. Mixed Doubles. 1934: Nell Gwyn. 1938: Just Like a Woman. 1939: Jamaica Inn. The Girl Who Forgot. 1940: Sailors Three (US: Three Cockeyed Sailors). Charley's (Big-Hearted) Aunt. 1941: Cottage To Let (US: Bombsight Stolen). * The Fine Feathers. Pathetone Parade of 1941. 1942: Those Kids from Town. Pathetone Parade of 1942: 1943: They Met in the Dark. 1944: Medal for the General. 1946: This Man Is Mine! 1947: The Turners of Prospect Road. 1948: Woman Hater. 1949: The Twenty Questions Murder Mystery.*

### DECKERS, Eugene 1917-1977
Dark-haired, sharp-faced little French actor, in Britain from World War II times. In post-war years, he became one of the British cinema's regular 'continentals' much in demand for both straight-faced villainy and comic relief. Demands for his services in films slackened in the late 1950s, as studio production ground almost to a halt, and he turned to other media.

*1946: Woman to Woman. Dual Alibi. 1947: Mrs Fitzherbert. 1948: Sleeping Car to Trieste. Against the Wind. 1949: Golden Salamander. 1950: The Elusive Pimpernel (US: The Fighting Pimpernel). Highly Dangerous. Madeleine. Tony Draws a Horse. So Long at the Fair. 1951: The Lavender Hill Mob. Hotel Sahara. Captain Horatio Hornblower RN. Night without Stars. 1953: The Love Lottery. 1954: Father Brown (US: The Detective). The Colditz Story. 1955: Doctor at Sea. Man of the Moment. 1956: Port Afrique. House of Secrets (US: Triple Deception). 1957: Let's Be Happy. Seven Thunders (US: The Beasts of Marseilles). 1959: Northwest Frontier (US: Flame Over India). 1961: A Weekend With Lulu. 1963: Hell is Empty (released 1967). 1965: Lady L. 1967: The Last Safari. 1968: The Limbo Line. The Assassination Bureau.*

### DE CORSIA, Ted 1903-1973
Chunky, thick-necked, black-haired American actor from Brooklyn, mostly on radio until he began a belated film career at 45, after which he still managed to scowl and bluster his way through more than 50 films. His raucous voice, set features and slitted eyes made him a favourite for aggressive gangster roles, and he is best remembered as the bad guy who falls from the bridgework in *The Naked City*—his first role in front of the camera.

ABOVE Ted **de Corsia** (extreme left) adopts a typically
phlegmatic stance in *The Midnight Story* (1957). With him are
Jay C. Flippen (*qv*), Russ Conway, John Cliff and Tony Curtis

BELOW French-born character actor Eugene **Deckers** here
shown in a British TV documentary film from 1966

1947: *Brooklyn USA (narrator only). 1948: *Brooklyn Makes Capital (narrator only). The Naked City. The Lady from Shanghai. 1949: It Happens Every Spring. Neptune's Daughter. The Life of Riley. Mr Soft Touch (GB: House of Settlement). 1950: The Outriders. Cargo to Capetown. Three Secrets. The Enforcer (GB: Murder Inc.). 1951: Vengeance Valley. New Mexico. Inside the Walls of Folsom Prison. A Place in the Sun. 1952: Captain Pirate (GB: Captain Blood, Fugitive). The Turning Point. The Savage. 1953: Ride Vaquero! Man in the Dark. Hot News. 1954: Crime Wave (GB: The City is Dark). 20,000 Leagues under the Sea. 1955: The Big Combo. The Man With the Gun (GB: The Trouble Shooter). Kismet. 1956: The Kettles in the Ozarks. The Conqueror. The Steel Jungle. Mohawk. The Killing. Showdown at Abilene. Dance with Me, Henry. Slightly Scarlet. Gunfight at the OK Corral. 1957: The Lawless Eighties. The Midnight Story (GB: Appointment with a Shadow). The Joker is Wild. Man on the Prowl. Gun Battle at Monterey. Baby Face Nelson. 1958: Handle with Care. Enchanted Island. Violent Road. The Buccaneer. 1959: South Seas Adventure (narrator only). Inside the Mafia. Noose for a Gunman. Oklahoma Territory. 1960: From the Terrace. Spartacus. 1961: The Crimebusters. 1962: It's Only Money. 1964: Blood on the Arrow. The Quick Gun. 1966: Nevada Smith. 1967: The King's Pirate. 1968: Five Card Stud. 1970: The Delta Factor. 1972: Un homme est mort (US: The Outside Man).

## DEHNER, John
(J. Forkum) 1915-1992

Stern-faced, dark-haired, often moustachioed American actor with skin strung tautly over his features—characteristics which have seen him playing sundry martinets, sadistic villains or humourless upholders of the law. He has done well in the occasional lead role, but probably a lack of warmth has kept him from becoming a name above the title. Still busy, though now mainly in television.

1944: Lake Placid Serenade. 1945: Captain Eddie. State Fair. The Corn is Green. Christmas in Connecticut (GB: Indiscretion). Club Havana. She Went to the Races. 1946: O.S.S. Catman of Paris. The Undercover Woman. The Last Crooked Mile. Out California Way. 1947: Golden Earrings. Vigilantes of Boomtown. Dream Girl. Blonde Savage. 1948: Let's Live a Little. He Walked by Night. Prejudice. 1949: Secret of St Ives. Bandits of El Dorado (GB: Tricked). Tulsa. *Riders of the Pony Express. Horsemen of the Sierras (GB: Remember Me). Feudin' Rhythm (GB: Ace Lucky). Kazan. Barbary Pirate. 1950: Captive Girl. Backfire. Dynamite Pass. David Harding—Counterspy. Rogues of Sherwood Forest. Mary Ryan, Detective. Bodyhold. Destination Murder. Texas Dynamo (GB: Suspected). Last of the Buccaneers. Counterspy meets Scotland Yard. 1951: Al Jennings of Oklahoma. China Corsair. When the Redskins Rode. The Texas Rangers. Lorna Doone. Corky of Gasoline Alley (GB: Corky). Fort Savage Raiders. Hot Lead. Ten Tall Men. 1952: California Conquest. Scaramouche. Aladdin and His Lamp. Cripple Creek. Plymouth Adventure. Desert Passage. Harem Girl. Junction City. Bad Men of Marysville (TV. GB: cinemas). 1953: Man on a Tightrope. Powder River. The Steel Lady (GB: Treasure of Kalifa). Vicki. Gun Belt. Fort Algiers. 1954: Southwest Passage (GB: Camels West). The Bowery Boys Meet the Monsters. Apache. The Cowboy (narrator only). 1955: The Man from Bitter Ridge. The Prodigal. The King's Thief. Tall Man Riding. Duel on the Mississippi. Top Gun. The Scarlet Coat. 1956: A Day of Fury. Carousel. The Fastest Gun Alive. Please Murder Me. Terror at Midnight. Tension at Table Rock. 1957: Revolt at Fort Laramie. The Girl in Black Stockings. Trooper Hook. The Iron Sheriff. 1958: Man of the West. Apache Territory. The Left-Handed Gun. 1959: Cast a Long Shadow. Timbuktu. 1960: The Sign of Zorro. 1961: The Canadians. The Chapman Report. 1963: Critic's Choice. 1964: Youngblood Hawke. 1965: The Hallelujah Trail (narrator only). 1967: The Helicopter Spies (TV. GB: cinemas). Winchester 73 (TV). 1969: Stiletto. Something for a Lonely Man. 1970: Quarantined (TV). 1971: Support Your Local Gunfighter. 1972: Slaughterhouse-Five. 1973: The Day of the Dolphin. 1974: Honky Tonk (TV). 1975: The Killer Inside Me. 1976: Guardian of the Wilderness. Fun With Dick and Jane. The New Daughters of Joshua Cabe (TV). 1977: The Lincoln Conspiracy. Danger in Paradise (TV). 1978: The Boys from Brazil. 1979: The Young Maverick (TV). 1980: California Gold Rush (TV). 1982: Airplane II The Sequel. 1983: The Right Stuff. 1985: Ragged Edge.

## DeLUISE, Dom 1933-

Plump, giggling, mischievous (and later bearded) American comedian who gradually built up a reputation on television, then became a familiar film face through his appearances in films by Mel Brooks and those associated with him. In recent time, has become equally associated with the comedies of Burt Reynolds. At first he

played dupes and bunglers, but later diversified to include rogues and charlatans, all in the same broad vein. Married actress Carol Arthur.

1963: Diary of a Bachelor. 1964: Fail Safe. The Ordeal of Thomas Moon (unreleased). 1966: The Glass Bottom Boat. The Busy Body. 1968: What's So Bad About Feeling Good? 1969: Norwood. 1970: The Twelve Chairs. 1971: Who is Harry Kellerman and Why Is He Saying These Terrible Things about Me? 1972: Evil Roy Slade (TV). Every Little Crook and Nanny. 1974: Only With Married Men (TV). Blazing Saddles. 1975: The Adventure of Sherlock Holmes' Smarter Brother. 1976: Silent Movie. 1977: The World's Greatest Lover. 1978: The Cheap Detective. The End. 1979: The Muppet Movie. †Hot Stuff. The Last Married Couple in America. Diary of a Young Comic (TV). 1980: Wholly Moses! Smokey and the Bandit II (GB: Smokey and the Bandit Ride Again). The Cannonball Run. Fatso. 1981: History of the World Part I. 1982: The Secret of NIMH (voice only). The Best Little Whorehouse in Texas. 1983: Cannonball Run II. Happy (TV). 1984: Johnny Dangerously.

†And directed

## DEMAREST, William 1892-1983

Craggy, grizzled veteran of well over 100 films, who became, from the 1930s to the 1960s, one of Hollywood's best-known and best-loved familiar faces. He began in vaudeville as a song-and-dance act with his brother Rubin (1886-1962), but moved into films right at the beginning of sound and, after a hiatus from 1929 to 1933, established himself with dozens of Brooklynese character studies. Although often a soft-hearted and slightly dense policeman, he also excelled at brooding suspicion and tight-lipped sarcasm. Oscar nomination for *The Jolson Story*.

*1926: When the Wife's Away. 1927: \*A Night at Coffee Dan's. Don't Tell the Wife. Fingerprints. Simple Sis. A Million Bid. In Old San Francisco. The Bush Leaguer. A Sailor's Sweetheart. The Jazz Singer. Matinee Ladies. The Gay Old Bird. What Happened to Father. The Black Diamond Express. The First Auto. A Reno Divorce. 1928: Five and Ten Cent Annie (GB: Ambitious Annie). The Butter and Egg Man (GB: Actress and Angel). \*Papa's Vacation. †A Girl in Every Port. The Escape. Sharp Shooters. The Crash. Pay As You Enter. 1932: \*The Runaround. 1934: White Lies. Circus Clown. Fog Over Frisco. Fugitive Lady. Many Happy Returns. 1935: The Murder Man. The Casino Murder Case. After Office Hours. Diamond Jim. Bright Lights (GB: Funny Face). Hands Across the Table. 1936: The Great Ziegfeld. Love on the Run. Wedding Present. Charlie Chan at the Opera. Mind Your Own Business. 1937: Don't Tell Your Wife. The Great Hospital Mystery. The Big City. Rosalie. Blonde Trouble. The Great Gambini. Oh Doctor! The Hit Parade. Easy Living. Time Out for Romance. Wake Up and Live. 1938: Rebecca of Sunnybrook Farm. Josette. One Wild Night. While New York Sleeps. Romance on the Run. Peck's Bad Boy With the Circus. 1939: King of the Turf. The Gracie Allen Murder Case. Mr Smith Goes to Washington. The Great Man Votes. The Cowboy Quarterback. Miracles for Sale. Laugh It Off (GB: Lady Be Gay). 1940: Tin Pan Alley. Little Men. Wolf of New York. The Great McGinty (GB: Down Went McGinty). The Farmer's Daughter. Christmas in July. Comin' Round the Mountain. 1941: Ride On, Vaquero. Glamour Boy. Dressed to Kill. Rookies on Parade. The Lady Eve. Country Fair. The Devil and Miss Jones. 1942: Pardon My Sarong. Sullivan's Travels. All Through The Night. True to the Army. My Favorite Spy. The Palm Beach Story. Life Begins at 8.30 (GB: The Light of Heart). Behind the Eight Ball (GB: Off the Beaten Track). Johnny Doughboy. 1943: Stage Door Canteen. True to Life. Dangerous Blondes. 1944: Hail the Conquering Hero. The Great Moment. Nine Girls. Once Upon a Time. The Miracle of Morgan's Creek. 1945: Duffy's Tavern. \*Hollywood Victory Caravan. Along Came Jones. Salty O'Rourke. Pardon My Past. 1946: Our Hearts Were Growing Up. The Jolson Story. 1947: Variety Girl. The Perils of Pauline. 1948: The Sainted Sisters. Night Has a Thousand Eyes. A Miracle Can Happen (later On Our Merry Way). Whispering Smith. 1949: Jolson Sings Again. Sorrowful Jones. Red, Hot and Blue. 1950: Never a Dull Moment. When Willie Comes Marching Home.*

*Riding High. He's a Cockeyed Wonder. 1951: The First Legion. Excuse My Dust. The Strip. Behave Yourself! 1952: The Blazing Forest. What Price Glory? 1953: Dangerous When Wet. Here Come the Girls. The Lady Wants Mink. Escape from Fort Bravo. 1954: The Yellow Mountain. 1955: Jupiter's Darling. The Far Horizons. The Private War of Major Benson. Lucy Gallant. Sincerely Yours. Hell on Frisco Bay. 1956: The Mountain. The Rawhide Years. 1960: Pepe. 1961: King of the Roaring Twenties (GB: The Big Bankroll). Twenty Plus Two (GB: It Started in Tokyo). 1962: Son of Flubber. 1963: It's a Mad, Mad, Mad, Mad World. 1964: Viva Las Vegas (GB: Love in Las Vegas). That Darn Cat! 1973: Don't Be Afraid of the Dark (TV). 1975: The Wild McCullochs. Won Ton Ton—the Dog Who Saved Hollywood. 1978: The Millionaire (TV).*

† Scenes deleted from final release print

**DENHAM, Maurice** 1909-
Quizzical, intelligent-looking, bald British actor who made his name as sundry comic characters in such 1940s' radio shows as *ITMA* and *Much-Binding-in-the-Marsh*. His move into films coincided with a shift to more varied character studies and he remained very busy in that medium until the 1970s, when he became accepted as a penetrating portrayer of heavy personality drama on television, and a formidable protagonist on stage.

*1946: \*Home and School. Daybreak. 1947: Fame is the Spur. The Man Within (US: The Smugglers). They Made Me a Fugitive (US: I Became a Criminal). Take My Life. The Upturned Glass. Holiday Camp. Jassy. Captain Boycott. The End of the River. Easy Money. Dear Murderer. Blanche Fury. 1948: Escape. Miranda. Oliver Twist. The Peaceful Years (narrator only). My Brother's Keeper. London Belongs to Me (US: Dulcimer Street). The Blind Goddess. Here Come the Huggetts. Look Before You Love. The Bad Lord Byron. The Blue Lagoon. 1949: It's Not Cricket. Once Upon a Dream. Poet's Pub. A Boy, a Girl and a Bike. Traveller's Joy (released 1951). Landfall. Scrapbook for 1933 (voice only). The Spider and the Fly. Don't Ever Leave Me. Madness of the Heart. 1951: No Highway (US: No*

*Highway in the Sky). 1952: The Net (US: Project M-7). 1953: Time Bomb (US: Terror on a Train). Street Corner (US: Both Sides of the Law). \*Prince Philip (narrator only). Eight O'Clock Walk. The Million Pound Note (US: Man with a Million). Malta Story (voice only). 1954: The Purple Plain. Carrington VC (US: Court Martial). Animal Farm (all voices). 1955: Doctor at Sea. Simon and Laura. 1956: 23 Paces to Baker Street. Checkpoint. 1957: Night of the Demon (US: Curse of the Demon). Barnacle Bill (US: All at Sea). 1958: \*Man with a Dog. The Captain's Table. 1959: Our Man in Havana. Campbell's Kingdom. 1960: Sink the Bismarck! Two Way Stretch. Ali and the Camel (serial. Voice only). 1961: The Greengage Summer (US: Loss of Innocence). Invasion Quartet. The Mark. The Last Rhino (voice only). 1962: The Set-Up. HMS Defiant (US: Damn the Defiant!) \*The King's Breakfast. Paranoiac. 1963: The Very Edge. Downfall. 1964: The Seventh Dawn. The Uncle. Hysteria. 1965: The Legend of Young Dick Turpin. Those Magnificent Men in Their Flying Machines, or: How I flew from London to Paris in 11 Hours and 25 Minutes. The Alphabet Murders. The Heroes of Telemark. The Nanny. Operation Crossbow (US: The Great Spy Mission). The Night Caller (US: Blood Beast from Outer Space). 1966: After the Fox. 1967: Torture Garden. The Long Duel. Danger Route. Attack on the Iron Coast. 1968: Negatives. The Best House in London. 1969: A Touch of Love (US: Thank You All Very Much). Some Girls Do. Midas Run (GB: A Run on Gold). 1970: The Virgin and the Gypsy. Countess Dracula. 1971: Sunday, Bloody Sunday. Nicholas and Alexandra. 1973: The Day of the Jackal. Luther. 1976: Shout at the Devil. 1977: Julia. 1979: \*Recluse. 1981: From a Far Country. 1985: The Chain. Young Sherlock Holmes. Mr Love.*

**DENNEHY, Brian** 1940-
Thick-necked, hard-driving, fair-haired American actor who came to films and TV late in his career, but quickly made his mark with a series of fierce and abrasive performances that augur well for a long stay. Had the lead in the television series *Big Shamus, Little Shamus*.

*1977: Johnny, We Hardly Knew Ye (TV).
Semi-Tough. Looking for Mr Goodbar. It
Happened at Lakewood Manor (TV. GB:
Panic at Lakewood Manor). 1978: Foul Play.
Ruby and Oswald (TV). A Death in Canaan
(TV). A Real American Hero (TV). 1979:
Silent Victory: The Kitty O'Neal Story (TV).
Dummy (TV). Pearl (TV). Butch and Sun-
dance The Early Days. The Jericho Mile (TV.
GB: cinemas). '10'. 1980: Little Miss
Marker. A Rumor of War (TV). 1981:
Captured! (later Split Image). 1982: First
Blood. I Take These Men (TV). 1983: Never
Cry Wolf. Gorky Park. Blood Feud (TV).
1984: Finders Keepers. Hunter (TV). The
River Rat. 1985: Cocoon. Silverado. F/X. The
Check is in the Mail.*

## DESNY, Ivan
(I. Desnitzky) 1922-

Dark, suave, baby-faced, moustachioed
Continental charmer, ideally cast in his first
international success as the blackmailing
lover in *Madeleine*, but afterwards more
often seen in supporting roles. Born in
Peking to a Russian father and French
mother (refugees from the Russian revolution), he was educated in France, but sent to
a German labour camp in 1940. He escaped
but was recaptured. Appearing much in
European theatres and films from many
nations, he is one of those actors who has
cropped up time and again after one had
thought his film career might be over.

*1947: †La fleur de l'âge. 1948: Le bonheur en
location. 1949: Madeleine. 1950: Dangerous
Mission. †Les trois mousquetaires. 1952: La
p... respectueuse. 1953: Corps sans âme. La
signore senza camelie (GB: The Lady without
Camelias). Le bon Dieu sans confession. Weg
ohne Umkehr. 1954: Act of Love. Die goldene
Pest. 1955: Frou-Frou. Lola Montès. 1956:
Anastasia. Ballerina. 1957: Une vie (US:
End of Desire). Is Anna Anderson Anastasia?
1958: Der Satan lockt mit Liebe. The Mirror
Has Two Faces. 1960: Song Without End.
1961: The Magnificent Rebel. 1962: Bon
Voyage! 1964: I misteri della giungla nera
(GB: The Mystery of Thug Island. US:
Mysteries of the Black Jungle). 1965: Das
Liebeskarussel (GB: Who Wants to Sleep?).*

*1966: Tendre voyou (GB: Simon the Swiss.
US: Tender Scoundrel). Captain from Toledo.
Da Berlino l'apocalisse (GB: The Spy Pit).
1967: I Killed Rasputin. Liebesnächte in der
Taiga (GB: Code Name Kill). 1968: Guns
for San Sebastian. Mayerling. 1970: The
Adventures of Gérard. 1972: Little Mother/
Don't Cry for Me, Little Mother. Nocturno.
1974: Paper Tiger. Who? 1975: Faustrecht
der Freiheit (GB: Fox. US: Fox and His
Friends). Falsche Bewegung (GB: Wrong
Movement). 1976: Die Eroberung der Zita-
delle. 1977: Halbe-Halbe. 1978: Die Ehe der
Maria Braun (GB: The Marriage of Maria
Braun). Enigma rosso (GB: Red Rings of
Fear). 1979: Bloodline/Sidney Sheldon's
Bloodline. 1980: Malou. La dame sans
camélias. 1981: Lola. 1985: L'Avenir
d'Emilie (GB: The Future of Emily).*

†Unfinished

## DEVINE, Andy 1905-1977

Jolly, roly-poly American actor with unruly
light brown hair and unique, croakingly
raucous, high-pitched voice—the comic
sidekick of many a western. He got into
films through being a college football star,
liked it, overcame objections to the effec-
tiveness of his voice in sound films and
stayed to cheer up more than 150 of them.
Death caused by cardiac arrest.

*1928: We Americans (GB: The Heart of a
Nation). Lonesome. Red Lips. 1929: Hot Stuff.
Naughty Baby (GB: Reckless Rosie). 1930:
The Spirit of Notre Dame (GB: Vigour of
Youth). 1931: The Criminal Code. Danger
Island (serial). 1932: Law and Order. The
Man from Yesterday. The Impatient Maiden.
Destry Rides Again. Three Wise Girls. Radio
Patrol. Tom Brown of Culver. Fast Compan-
ions/Information Kid. The All-American
(GB: Sport of a Nation). 1933: Saturday's
Millions. The Cohens and Kellys in Trouble.
Midnight Mary. Horse Play. Chance at
Heaven. Song of the Eagle. The Big Cage. Dr
Bull. 1934: The Poor Rich. Let's Talk It Over.
Upper World. Gift of Gab. Wake Up and
Dream. Million Dollar Ransom. Stingaree.
Hell in the Heavens. 1935: *La Fiesta de
Santa Barbara. The President Vanishes (GB:
Strange Conspiracy). Hold 'Em Yale (GB:
Uniform Lovers). Chinatown Squad. Straight*

*from the Heart. The Farmer Takes a Wife.
Way Down East. Fighting Youth. Coronado.
1936: Flying Hostess. Romeo and Juliet. The
Big Game. Yellowstone. Small Town Girl.
1937: Mysterious Crossing. A Star Is Born.
Double or Nothing. You're a Sweetheart. The
Road Back. 1938: Yellow Jack. Swing That
Cheer. Personal Secretary. Strange Faces. The
Storm. Men With Wings. In Old Chicago. Dr
Rhythm. 1939: Never Say Die. The Spirit of
Culver (GB: Man's Heritage). Mutiny on the
Blackhawk. Stagecoach. Tropic Fury. Legion of
Lost Flyers. Geronimo. The Man from Mon-
treal. 1940: Little Old New York. Black
Diamonds. Hot Steel. Torrid Zone. Margie.
Danger on Wheels. The Leather Pushers. When
the Daltons Rode. Trail of the Vigilantes. Buck
Benny Rides Again. The Devil's Pipeline.
1941: A Dangerous Game. South of Tahiti
(GB: White Savage). Lucky Devils. Road
Agent. Men of the Timberland. The Kid from
Kansas. The Flame of New Orleans. Mutiny in
the Arctic. Badlands of Dakota. Raiders of the
Desert. 1942: Top Sergeant. North to the
Klondike. Timber. Unseen Enemy. Sin Town.
*Keeping Fit. Danger in the Pacific. Between
Us Girls. Escape from Hong Kong. 1943:
Rhythm of the Islands. Frontier Badmen.
Corvette K-225 (GB: The Nelson Touch).
Crazy House. Ali Baba and the 40 Thieves.
1944: Follow the Boys. The Ghost Catchers.
Babes on Swing Street. Bowery to Broadway.
1945: Sudan. Frontier Gal (GB: The Bride
Wasn't Willing). That's the Spirit. Frisco Sal.
1946: Canyon Passage. 1947: The Michigan
Kid. The Vigilantes Return (GB: The Return
of the Vigilantes). Bells of San Angelo.
Springtime in the Sierras. The Marauders. On
the Old Spanish Trail. The Fabulous Texan.
Slave Girl. 1948: The Gallant Legion. The
Gay Ranchero. Montana Belle (released 1952).
Under California Skies. Old Los Angeles.
Grand Canyon Trail. The Far Frontier. Eyes of
Texas. Nighttime in Nevada. 1949: The Last
Bandit. The Traveling Saleswoman. 1950:
Never a Dull Moment. 1951: Slaughter Trail.
‡The Red Badge of Courage. †Border City
Rustlers (TV). †Two Gun Marshal (TV). †Six
Gun Decision (TV). †Arrow in the Dust (TV).
†Behind Southern Lines (TV). 1952: †The
Ghost of Crossbones Canyon (TV). 1953:
Island in the Sky. The Yellow Haired Kid.
†Secret of Outlaw Flats (TV). 1954: Thunder
Pass. †Marshals in Disguise (TV). †Outlaw's
Son (TV). †Titled Tenderfoot (TV). †Timber
County Trouble (TV). †Two Gun Teacher
(TV). †Phantom Trouble (TV). 1955: Pete
Kelly's Blues. †The Match Making Marshal
(TV). 1956: Around the World in 80 Days.
1960: The Adventures of Huckleberry Finn.
1961: Two Rode Together. 1962: How the
West Was Won. The Man Who Shot Liberty
Valance. 1963: It's a Mad, Mad, Mad, Mad
World. 1965: Zebra in the Kitchen. 1968:
The Ballad of Josie. The Road Hustlers. 1969:
Ride a Northbound Horse (TV. GB: cinemas).
The Over-the-Hill Gang (TV). The Phynx.
1970: Myra Breckinridge. The Over-the-Hill
Gang Rides Again (TV). Smoke (TV. GB:
cinemas). 1973: Robin Hood (voice only).*

*1975: Won Ton Ton, the Dog Who Saved Hollywood. 1976: A Whale of a Tale. 1977: The Mouse and His Child (voice only).*

‡ Scenes deleted from final release print
† Released as films in some countries.

**DE WOLFE, Billy**

(William Jones) 1907–1974

Dark-haired, moustachioed American comedian, much underused by the cinema, but seen to hilarious effect in several Paramount and Warners romps, mainly as prissy suitors destined not to win the heroine. At his best, though, in stage and night-club routines. Spent his early childhood in Wales. Died of lung cancer.

*1943: Dixie. 1944: Miss Susie Slagle's (released 1946). 1945: Duffy's Tavern. 1946: Blue Skies. Our Hearts Were Growing Up. 1947: The Perils of Pauline. Dear Ruth. Variety Girl. 1948: Isn't It Romantic? 1949: Dear Wife. 1950: Tea for Two. 1951: Dear Brat. Lullaby of Broadway. 1953: Call Me Madam. 1965: Billie. 1973: The World's Greatest Athlete.*

**DE WOLFF, Francis** 1913–

Huge, fearsome, thickly bearded British actor. With his stern expression, fierce eyebrows and immense bulk, he made a formidable villain, but was difficult to cast in a wider variety of roles. He would have made a magnificent Beadle in *Oliver Twist* if Francis L. Sullivan (*qv*) hadn't got there

first; as it was, his distinctive, RADA-trained tones made him a favourite voice in radio drama.

*1935: Flame in the Heather. 1936: Fire Over England. 1949: Adam and Evelyne (US: Adam and Evalyn). Trottie True (US: Gay Lady). Under Capricorn. 1950: Treasure Island. The Naked Heart/Maria Chapdelaine /The Naked Earth. She Shall Have Murder. 1951: Flesh and Blood. Tom Brown's Schooldays. Scrooge (US: A Christmas Carol). 1952: Ivanhoe. Miss Robin Hood. Moulin Rouge. 1953: The Master of Ballantrae. The Kidnappers (US: The Little Kidnappers). 1954: The Diamond (US: Diamond Wizard). The Seekers (US: Land of Fury). 1955: Geordie (US: Wee Geordie). King's Rhapsody. 1956: Moby Dick. 1957: The Smallest Show on Earth. Saint Joan. Odongo. 1958: The Roots of Heaven. Sea Fury. Corridors of Blood. 1959: The Hound of the Baskervilles. The Savage Innocents. Tommy the Toreador. The Man Who Could Cheat Death. 1960: The Two Faces of Dr Jekyll (US: House of Fright). Clue of the Twisted Candle. 1961: The Silent Invasion. 1962: The Durant Affair. 1963: The World Ten Times Over (US: Pussycat Alley). Siege of the Saxons. Devil Doll. The Three Lives of Thomasina. From Russia With Love. 1964: The Black Torment. Carry On Cleo. 1965: Licensed to Kill (US: The Second Best Secret Agent in the Whole Wide World). 1966: The Liquidator. Triple Cross. 1968: The Fixer. 1969: Sinful Davey. 1973: The Three Musketeers (The Queen's Diamonds). 1976: Jesus of Nazareth (TV).*

**DEXTER, Brad** 1917–

Big, muscular, lightish-haired, blue-eyed, square-cut, stiff-moving American actor who looked as though he had wandered in from a Russ Meyer movie, but tended to play grating villains who had as much brain as brawn. A talented amateur boxer, he became more interested in acting and did well for a while in the Hollywood of the early 1950s. Later turned producer, sometimes of films starring Frank Sinatra, a personal friend whose life Dexter once saved in a swimming mishap. The only one of the 'The Magnificent Seven' not to become a major star. At one time married to singer Peggy Lee.

*1950: The Asphalt Jungle. 1951: Fourteen Hours. 1952: The Las Vegas Story. Macao. 1953: 99 River Street. 1955: Untamed. Violent Saturday. House of Bamboo. 1956: The Bottom of the Bottle (GB: Beyond the River). Between Heaven and Hell. 1957: The Oklahoman. 1958: Run Silent, Run Deep. 1959: Vice Raid. Last Train from Gun Hill. 1960: Thirteen Fighting Men. The Magnificent Seven. 1961: Twenty Plus Two (GB: It Started in Tokyo). The George Raft Story (GB: Spin of a Coin). 1962: Taras Bulba. 1963: Johnny Cool. Kings of the Sun. 1964: Invitation to a Gunfighter. 1965: Bus Riley's Back in Town. None But the Brave. Von Ryan's Express. 1966: Blindfold. 1973: Jory. 1975: Shampoo. Vigilante Force. 1977: The Private Files of J. Edgar Hoover. 1978: House Calls.*

**DIERKES, John** 1905–1975

Since this American actor always looked a bit like a scarecrow, it was no surprise to find him as The Gaunt Man, looming out of the mist like a phantom in one of his early films, *The Red Badge of Courage*. Tall (6ft 4in), fair-haired and craggy, with coathanger shoulders, Dierkes was an economist who worked for the US government before becoming so interested in acting that, in post-war years, he decided to make a career of it. Hollywood welcomed the latecomer, and cast him as detectives, fanatics, prospectors and bandits, to all of which he lent a lived-in look. Died from an emphysema.

*1948: Macbeth. 1950: Three Husbands. 1951: The Red Badge of Courage. Silver City (GB: High Vermilion). The Thing … from Another World. 1952: Les Miserables. Plymouth Adventure. 1953: The Moonlighter. Shane. The Vanquished. Abbott and Costello Meet Dr Jekyll and Mr Hyde. A Perilous Journey. 1954: The Naked Jungle. Prince Valiant. Hell's Outpost. Silver Lode. Passion. The Desperado. The Raid. 1955: The Vanishing American. Betrayed Women. 1956: Jubal. 1957: Valerie. The Halliday Brand. Buckskin Lady. The Daughter of Dr Jekyll. Duel at Apache Wells. 1958: Blood Arrow. The Buccaneer. The Left-Handed Gun. The Rawhide Trail. 1959: The Oregon Trail. The*

*Hanging Tree. 1960: The Alamo. 1961: The Comancheros. One-Eyed Jacks. 1962: Convicts Four (GB: Reprieve!) The Premature Burial. 1963: The Haunted Palace. 'X'—the Man with the X-Ray Eyes (GB: The Man with the X-Ray Eyes). Johnny Cool. 1971: The Omega Man. 1973: Oklahoma Crude.*

## DIGGES, Dudley 1879-1947

Small, dapper, often moustachioed Irish actor much in demand in the Hollywood of the 1930s. Could be downtrodden, downright evil (as in the 1931 *The Maltese Falcon*), wise, shifty, dogged or devoted—few escaped typecasting more effectively. Perhaps because of this, however, his career in films faded by the end of the decade. Died after a stroke.

*1929: Condemned (GB: Condemned to Devil's Island). 1930: Outward Bound. Upper Underworld. 1931: Alexander Hamilton. The Maltese Falcon. The Ruling Voice. Devotion. 1932: The Hatchet Man (GB: The Honourable Mr Wong). The First Year. Roar of the Dragon. Tess of the Storm Country. The Strange Case of Clara Deane. 1933: The Narrow Corner. The Mayor of Hell. The King's Vacation. The Emperor Jones. The Invisible Man. The Silk Express. Before Dawn. 1934: Fury of the Jungle. The World Moves On. Caravan. Massacre. I Am a Thief. What Every Woman Knows. 1935: Notorious Gentleman. China Seas. Mutiny on the Bounty. The Bishop Misbehaves (GB: The Bishop's Misadventures). Three Live Ghosts. Kind Lady (later House of Menace). 1936: The Voice of Bugle Ann. The Unguarded Hour. The General Died at Dawn. Valiant Is the Word for Carrie. 1937: Love Is News. 1939: The Light That Failed. 1939/40: Raffles. 1940: The Fight for Life. 1942: Son of Fury. 1946: The Searching Wind.*

## DIGNAM, Basil 1905-1979

Round-faced, grey-haired, squarely built, earnest- and slightly worried-looking British actor who played small roles as professional men in 'A' grade films and top supporting roles in minor thrillers. In his mid-forties before coming to films after long theatrical experience, he quickly built up a list of credits twice as long as his actor

brother Mark Dignam (1909-), who remained busier in the theatre. Married to character actress Mona Washbourne (*qv*). Once a lumberjack in Canada.

*1951: The Lady with a Lamp. Appointment with Venus (US: Island Rescue). His Excellency. 1952: Hammer the Toff. There Was a Young Lady. 1953: Albert RN (US: Break to Freedom). 1954: Carrington VC (US: Court Martial). 1955: Touch and Go (US: The Light Touch). Port of Escape. The Quatermass Experiment (US: The Creeping Unknown). They Can't Hang Me! The Narrowing Circle. 1956: The Intimate Stranger (US: Finger of Guilt). Private's Progress. The Counterfeit Plan. The Weapon. Reach for the Sky. Brothers in Law. 1957: Three Sundays to Live. Son of a Stranger. Yangtse Incident (US: Battle Hell). Man in the Shadow. You Pay Your Money. I Accuse! 1958: Up the Creek. Carry on Sergeant. Corridors of Blood. Them Nice Americans. The Spaniard's Curse. Carlton-Browne of the FO (US: Man in a Cocked Hat). A Cry from the Streets. Room at the Top. Further Up the Creek. 1959: A Touch of Larceny. I'm All Right, Jack. Sapphire. 1960: Sentenced for Life. The Pure Hell of St Trinian's. The Spider's Web. Suspect (US: The Risk). 1961: Gorgo. The Court Martial of Major Keller. The Fourth Square. The Secret Partner. Victim. 1962: Master Spy. Fate Takes a Hand. Seven Seas to Calais. Lawrence of Arabia. 1963: Life for Ruth (US: Walk in the Shadow). Ring of Spies. 80,000 Suspects. Heavens Above! 1965: Rotten to the Core. Cuckoo Patrol. Operation Crossbow (US: The Great Spy Mission). Joey Boy. The Amorous Adventures of Moll Flanders. Where the Spies Are. 1966: Naked Evil. 1967: Assignment K. The Jokers. 1968: Twisted Nerve. 1969: Laughter in the Dark. The Games. 1970: The Great White Hope. 10 Rillington Place. 1972: Young Winston. 1973: Soft Beds, Hard Battles (US: Undercovers Hero).*

## DONNELL, Jeff
(Jean Donnell) 1921-*1988*

Happy-looking, red-haired American actress who played bobby-soxers, kid sisters, prairie flowers, best friends, secretaries, shopgirls and other second-leads for 15 years, only graduating to mothers when she

turned 40. Her cheery, chirpy personality was always welcome; in latter days, she was too seldom seen. Married (second of four) to actor Aldo Ray from 1954 to 1956.

*1942: My Sister Eileen. The Boogie Man Will Get You. A Night to Remember. 1943: City Without Men. What's Buzzin' Cousin? There's Something About a Soldier. Doughboys in Ireland. *Mr Smug. 1944: She's a Soldier, Too. Nine Girls. Stars on Parade. Carolina Blues. Mr Winkle Goes to War (GB: Arms and the Woman). Cowboy Canteen (GB: Close Harmony). Three Is a Family. Once Upon a Time. 1945: Power of the Whistler. Dancing in Manhattan. Edie Was a Lady. Song of the Prairie (GB: Sentiment and Song). Over 21. He's My Guy. 1946: Throw a Saddle on a Star. Night Editor (GB: The Trespasser). The Phantom Thief. The Unknown. That Texas Jamboree (GB: Medicine Man). Cowboy Blues (GB: Beneath the Starry Skies). Singing on the Trail (GB: Lookin' for Someone). It's Great To Be Young. Tars and Spars. 1947: Mr District Attorney. *My Pal Ringeye. 1949: Stagecoach Kid. Outcasts of the Trail. Roughshod. Post Office Investigator. Easy Living. 1950: Hoedown. In a Lonely Place. Tall Timber (GB: Big Timber). Walk Softly Stranger. The Fuller Brush Girl (GB: The Affairs of Sally). Redwood Forest Trail. 1951: Three Guys Named Mike. 1952: Skirts Ahoy! Thief of Damascus. The First Time. Because You're Mine. 1953: Flight Nurse. So This Is Love (GB: The Grace Moore Story). The Blue Gardenia. 1954: Massacre Canyon. 1956: Magnificent Roughnecks. Sincerely, Willis Wayde (TV). 1957: The Guns of Fort Petticoat. Destination 60,000. Sweet Smell of Success. My Man Godfrey. 1961: Gidget Goes Hawaiian. 1962: The Iron Maiden (US: The Swingin' Maiden). 1963: Gidget Goes to Rome. 1969: The Comic. 1970: Love Hate Love (TV). Tora! Tora! Tora! 1971: Congratulations, It's a Boy (TV). 1972: Stand Up and Be Counted. 1976: McNaughton's Daughter. 1977: Spiderman (TV. GB: cinemas). 1978: Murder by Natural Causes (TV).*

## DONNELLY, Ruth 1896-1982

Light-haired, square-built, sharp-eyed American actress with strong chin. Usually cast as ladies who dished out verbal

1940: In the Nick of Time. 1948; Once a Jolly Swagman (US: Maniacs on Wheels). All Over the Town. 1949: Train of Events. A Run for Your Money. The Blue Lamp. 1950: Blackout. Highly Dangerous. 1951: Appointment with Venus (US: Island Rescue). Calling Bulldog Drummond. The Lavender Hill Mob. The Man in the White Suit. High Treason. 1952: I'm a Stranger. Gift Horse (US: Glory at Sea). The Gentle Gunman. The Net (US: Project M7). 1953: Wheel of Fate. The Red Beret (US: Paratrooper). The Case of Gracie Budd. 1954: What Every Woman Wants. Seagulls Over Sorrento (US: Crest of the Wave). 1955: John and Julie. Cockleshell Heroes.

witticisms to the discomfort of their menfolk; sometimes as dowagers who flirted with gigolos. Soon became the Thelma Ritter of the middle-class bracket, but after the death of her husband in the late 1950s, she left films and turned to song-writing.

1927: Rubber Heels. 1931: Transatlantic. Wicked. The Spider. 1932: Make Me a Star. Blessed Event. The Rainbow Trail. Jewel Robbery. 1933: Ladies They Talk About. Hard to Handle. Lilly Turner. Goodbye Again. Ever in My Heart. Private Detective 62. 42nd Street. Female. Convention City. Bureau of Missing Persons. Sing, Sinner, Sing. Havana Widows. Footlight Parade. Employees' Entrance. 1934: Wonder Bar. Romance in the Rain. Happiness Ahead. Housewife. Heat Lightning. Mandalay. The Merry Wives of Reno. You Belong to Me. 1935: The White Cockatoo. Maybe It's Love. Hands Across the Table. Personal Maid's Secret. Metropolitan. Red Salute (GB: Arms and the Girl). Alibi Ike. Traveling Saleslady. 1936: Mr Deeds Goes to Town. The Song and Dance Man. 13 Hours By Air. Fatal Lady. Cain and Mabel. More Than a Secretary. 1937: Portia on Trial (GB: The Trial of Portia Merriman). Roaring Timber. 1938: The Affairs of Annabel. Meet the Girls. A Slight Case of Murder. Annabel Takes a Tour. Army Girl. Personal Secretary. Holiday (GB: Free to Live/Unconventional Linda). 1939: Mr Smith Goes to Washington. The Family Next Door. The Amazing Mr Williams. 1940: My Little Chickadee. Meet the Missus. Scatterbrain. 1941: Model Wife. The Roundup. Sailors on Leave. You Belong to Me (GB: Good Morning, Doctor). Petticoat Politics. Rise and Shine. The Gay Vagabond. 1942: Johnny Doughboy. 1943: Thank Your Lucky Stars. This Is the Army. Sleepy Lagoon. 1945: Pillow to Post. The Bells of St Mary's. 1946: Cross My Heart. Cinderella Jones. In Old Sacramento. 1947: The Fabulous Texan. Little Miss Broadway. The Ghost Goes Wild. Millie's Daughter. 1948: The Snake Pit. Fighting Father Dunne. 1950: Where the Sidewalk Ends. 1951: I'd Climb the Highest Mountain. The Secret of Convict Lake. The Wild Blue Yonder (GB: Thunder Across the Pacific). 1955: A Lawless Street. The Spoilers. 1956: Autumn Leaves. 1957: The Way to the Gold.

**DOOLEY, Paul** 1928-
Chunky, florid, versatile American actor with receding dark hair. He originally planned to become a cartoonist, then spent a period as a comedy writer for television. Roles in films by Robert Altman in particular have brought him to the fore as an actor and, although sometimes seen as a father or friend, he is perfectly capable of handling a leading role, as he proved in A Perfect Couple.

1968: What's So Bad About Feeling Good? 1969: The Out-of-Towners. 1972: Up the Sandbox. 1974: Death Wish. The Dion Brothers (TV. GB: cinemas, as Gravy Train). 1976: Slap Shot. 1977: Raggedy Ann and Andy (voice only). 1978: A Wedding. 1979: A Perfect Couple. Rich Kids. Breaking Away. Health (shown 1982). 1980: Popeye. 1981: Paternity. 1982: Endangered Species. Kiss Me Goodbye. 1983: Strange Brew. 1984: Sixteen Candles. Big Trouble.

**DOONAN, Patric** 1925-1958
Fair, wavy-haired British actor (son of music-hall comedian George Doonan), with a hunted, shifty look. After numerous roles as secondary crooks, other ranks and the occasional hero's friend, his film career petered out. He might have played hard-nosed police inspectors, but the opportunity seemed to escape him. Committed suicide by gassing himself. Married actress Aud Johansen in 1953.

**DRAKE, Charles**
(C. Ruppert) 1914- *1994*
Very tall, well-built, mild-mannered American actor with fair, wavy hair and vaguely bemused expression, in very small roles during the war years, then as 'second lead' in films from the mid-1940s to the early 1960s; his best roles came in movies with his real-life friend Audie Murphy. Could be colourless as juvenile lead, much more absorbing as characters with an interest on either side of the fence.

1939: Career. 1941: Affectionately Yours. Nine Lives Are Not Enough. Sergeant York. Navy Blues. Out of the Fog. You're in the Army Now. I Wanted Wings. The Man Who Came to Dinner. The Maltese Falcon. Million Dollar Baby. Dive Bomber. The Body Disappears. 1942: The Male Animal. Now, Voyager. Busses Roar. Across the Pacific. The Gay Sisters. Yankee Doodle Dandy. Larceny Inc. Dangerously They Live. 1943: Air Force. 1944: Mr Skeffington. 1945: Conflict. You Came Along. 1946: Whistle Stop. A Night in Casablanca. 1947: Winter Wonderland. The Pretender. 1948: The Tender Years. Bowie Knife. 1949: Johnny Stool Pigeon. Tarzan's Magic Fountain. 1950: I Was a Shoplifter. Comanche Territory. Winchester '73. Peggy. Harvey. 1951: Little Egypt (GB: Chicago Masquerade). Air Cadet (GB: Jet Men of the Air). You Never Can Tell (GB: You Never Know). Treasure of Lost Canyon. 1952: Bonzo Goes to College. Red Ball Express. 1953: Gunsmoke! The Lone Hand. It Came from Outer Space. War Arrow. The Glenn Miller Story. 1954: Tobor the Great. Four Guns to the Border. 1955: Female on the Beach. All That Heaven Allows. To Hell and Back. 1956: Walk the Proud Land. The Price of Fear. The Night Runner. Gun in His Hand (TV. GB: cinemas). 1957: Jeanne Eagels. Until They Sail. 1958: Step Down to Terror (GB: The Silent Stranger). Reunion (TV). No Name on the Bullet. 1961: Tammy Tell Me True. Back Street. 1963: Showdown. 1964: Dear Heart. The Lively Set. 1965: The Third Day. 1967: Valley of the Dolls. The Counterfeit Killer (TV. GB: cinemas). 1968: The Swimmer. The Smugglers (TV). The Money Jungle. 1969: The Arrangement. Hail Hero. 1971: The Seven Minutes. The Screaming Woman (TV). 1973: Partners in Crime (TV). Scream Pretty Peggy (TV). 1975: The Return of Joe Forrester (TV). The Lives of Jenny Dolan (TV).

**DRAYTON, Alfred**
(A. Varick) 1881-1949
Big, broad-shouldered, bald, barnstorming, husky-voiced, often beaming British actor, equally at home in drama or farce. He made his reputation on stage and never deserted the theatre, although a powerful and very popular member of film casts from 1930 onwards.

1915: Iron Justice. 1919: A Little Bit of Fluff. 1920: The Honeypot. The Winning Goal. A Temporary Gentleman. 1921: *A Scandal in Bohemia. Love Maggy. 1930: The 'W' Plan. The Squeaker. 1931: The Calendar (US: Bachelor's Folly). The Happy Ending. Brown Sugar. 1932: Lord Babs. 1933: The Little Damozel. Friday the Thirteenth. It's a Boy. Falling for You. 1934: Red Ensign (US: Strike!) Jack Ahoy! Lady in Danger. Radio Parade of 1935 (US: Radio Follies). 1935: Look Up and Laugh. Me and Marlborough. First a Girl. The Dictator (US: The Loves of a Dictator). Oh Daddy! 1936: Tropical Trouble. The Crimson Circle. Aren't Men Beasts! 1938: A Spot of Bother. 1939: So This Is London. 1941: Banana Ridge. The Big Blockade. 1942: Women Aren't Angels. 1944: Don't Take It to Heart. Halfway House. 1945: They Knew Mr Knight. 1947: Nicholas Nickleby. 1948: Things Happen at Night.

**DRESDEL, Sonia**
(Lois Obee, later legally changed) 1909-1976
Stern-looking, dark-haired English actress who made a formidable villainess—the woman you loved to hate. She preferred a stage career but, even so, some of her film roles were so memorable, especially the evil wife in The Fallen Idol, that it's amazing her films were so few and far between. In full flight, she would have made a memorable Lady Macbeth.

1944: The World Owes Me a Living. 1947: While I Live. 1948: This Was a Woman. The Fallen Idol. 1950: The Clouded Yellow. 1951: The Third Visitor. 1956: Now and Forever. The Secret Tent. 1957: Death over my Shoulder. 1960: The Trials of Oscar Wilde (US: The Man with the Green Carnation). 1962: The Break. 1972: Lady Caroline Lamb.

**DUGGAN, Andrew** 1923-1988
Strong-jawed, fair-haired, reliable-looking American actor who frequently made a mockery of such looks by playing villainous or even comic roles. His characters were usually smartly dressed, and had a persuasive charm—not always to the hero or heroine's advantage. A prolific TV guest star in drama series.

1956: Patterns (GB: Patterns of Power). 1957: Three Brave Men. The Domino Kid. Decision at Sundown. 1958: Return to Warbow. The Bravados. 1959: Westbound.

1961: The Chapman Report. 1962: House of Women. Merrill's Marauders. FBI Code 98. 1963: The Incredible Mr Limpet. Palm Springs Weekend. 1964: Seven Days in May. 1965: The Glory Guys. 1967: The Secret War of Harry Frigg. 1968: Hawaii Five-O (TV). 1971: Skin Game. The Forgotten Man (TV). Two on a Bench (TV). The Homecoming (TV). 1972: Jigsaw (TV). The Streets of San Francisco (TV). Bone (GB: Dial Rat for Terror). 1973: Firehouse (TV). 1974: The Last Angry Man (TV). Panic on the 5:22 (TV). The Bears and I. 1975: Attack on Terror: The FBI Versus the Ku Klux Klan (TV). 1977: Tail Gunner Joe (TV). The Private Files of J. Edgar Hoover. The Deadliest Season (TV). Pine Canyon is Burning (TV). The Hunted Lady (TV). 1978: It Lives Again. Overboard (TV). The Time Machine (TV). A Fire in the Sky (TV). 1979: The Incredible Journey of Dr Meg Laurel (TV). 1980: M Station: Hawaii (TV).

**DUMBRILLE, Douglass** 1888-1974
Stiff-necked, eagle-eyed, saturnine, moustachioed Canadian actor whose smile was that of a conspirator, and whose villains could be stuffy or sadistic, farcical or for real. A good foil for the Marx Brothers, Bob Hope and Abbott and Costello, a fine sophisticated menace for a fistful of 'B' feature detectives to overcome. Sometimes billed as 'Douglas' in the 1930s. Died from a heart attack.

1916: What 80 Million Women Want. 1931: Monkey Business. His Woman. 1932: That's My Boy. The Wiser Sex. Blondie of the Follies. Laughter in Hell. I Am a Fugitive from a Chain Gang. 1933: The Working Man. Female. The World Changes. The Pride of the Legion. Elmer the Great. Smoke Lightning. The Big Brain. The Man Who Dared. The Way to Love. Baby Face. Heroes for Sale. Silk Express. Rustlers' Roundup. Convention City. Lady Killer. King of the Jungle. Voltaire. 1934: Massacre. Operator 13 (GB: Spy 13). Fog over Frisco. Hide-Out. Treasure Island. Harold Teen (GB: The Dancing Fool). Hi, Nellie! Journal of a Crime. Broadway Bill (GB: Strictly Confidential). The Secret Bride (GB: Concealment). 1935: Lives of a Bengal Lancer. Naughty Marietta. Love Me Forever.

Peter Ibbetson. Air Hawks. Cardinal Richelieu. Crime and Punishment. The Public Menace. Unknown Woman. 1936: The Lone Wolf Returns. The Music Goes Round. Mr Deeds Goes to Town. The Calling of Dan Matthews. End of the Trail. You May Be Next! (GB: Panic on the Air). M'Liss. The Witness Chair. The Princess Comes Across. 1937: A Day at the Races. The Firefly. Ali Baba Goes to Town. Woman in Distress. Counterfeit Lady. The Emperor's Candlesticks. 1938: The Buccaneer. Storm Over Bengal. Crime Takes a Holiday. Sharpshooters. Fast Company. Stolen Heaven. Kentucky. The Mysterious Rider. 1939: Thunder Afloat. Charlie Chan at Treasure Island. The Three Musketeers (GB: The Singing Musketeer). Tell No Tales. Captain Fury. Rovin' Tumbleweeds. Charlie Chan in City of Darkness. Mr Moto in Danger Island (GB: Mr Moto on Danger Island). 1940: Slightly Honorable. South of Pago Pago. Virgina City. Catman of Paris (released 1946). 1941: Michael Shayne, Private Detective. The Big Store. Ellery Queen and the Perfect Crime (GB: The Perfect Crime). The Roundup. Murder Among Friends. Washington Melodrama. 1942: Stand By for Action! (GB: Cargo of Innocents). Ride 'Em Cowboy. Castle in the Desert. Ten Gentlemen from West Point. A Gentleman After Dark. I Married an Angel. DuBarry Was a Lady. King of the Mounties (serial). 1943: False Colors. 1944: Lumberjack. Uncertain Glory. Lost in a Harem. Jungle Woman. Gypsy Wildcat. Forty Thieves. 1945: Road to Utopia. Jungle Queen (serial). The Frozen Ghost. The Daltons Ride Again. Flame of the West. A Medal for Benny. 1946: The Cat Creeps. Spook Busters. Night in Paradise. Monsieur Beaucaire. Pardon My Past. Under Nevada Skies. 1947: Christmas Eve. It's a Joke, Son! The Fabulous Texan. The Dragnet. Dishonored Lady. Blonde Savage. 1948: Last of the Wild Horses. 1949: Tell It to the Judge. Alimony. Dynamite. Joe Palooka in the Counterpunch. The Lone Wolf and His Lady. Riders of the Whistling Pines. 1950: Buccaneer's Girl. Her Wonderful Lie. The Kangaroo Kid. Abbott and Costello in the Foreign Legion. Riding High. The Savage Horde. Rapture. 1951: A Millionaire for Christy. 1952: Son of Paleface. Apache War Smoke. Sky Full of Moon. Scaramouche. Sound Off. 1953: Julius Caesar. Plunder of the Sun. Captain John Smith and Pocahontas (GB: Burning Arrows). 1954: World for Ransom. Lawless Rider. 1955: Jupiter's Darling. A Life at Stake. 1956: The Ten Commandments. Shake, Rattle and Rock. 1958: The Buccaneer (remake). 1960: High Time. 1962: Air Patrol. 1963: Johnny Cool. 1964: Shock Treatment. What a Way to Go!

### DUMKE, Ralph 1899-1964

Truculent-looking, heavyweight, brown-haired American supporting actor, a minor-league Sydney Greenstreet. Most often seen in white trilbies and suits, mopping his brow in the approved Greenstreet fashion. He came to Hollywood in middle age after a long stage career, much of it spent singing

in light opera, and played almost entirely villains, entrepreneurs and corrupt businessmen. Occasionally allowed to play a blusterer in the Thurston Hall (qv) tradition. His voice became well-known in the 1930s on a popular American radio comedy show called Sisters of the Skillet.

1942: Lucky Jordan. 1949: All the King's Men. 1950: Where Danger Lives. Mystery Street. The Fireball. The Breaking Point. 1951: When I Grow Up. The Law and the Lady. The Mob (GB: Remember That Face). Boots Malone. 1952: The San Francisco Story. Carbine Williams. Holiday for Sinners. We're Not Married. Hurricane Smith. 1953: Hannah Lee/Outlaw Territory. Mississippi Gambler. Lili. Count the Hours (GB: Every Minute Counts). It Should Happen to You. Massacre Canyon. The President's Lady. She Couldn't Say No (GB: Beautiful But Dangerous). Alaska Seas. 1954: They Rode West. Rails into Laramie. Daddy Long Legs. 1955: Artists and Models. Violent Saturday. Hell's Island. 1956: When Gangland Strikes. Francis in the Haunted House. Forever Darling. Invasion of the Body Snatchers. The Solid Gold Cadillac. 1957: The Buster Keaton Story. Loving You. 1960: Wake Me When It's Over. 1961: All in a Night's Work.

### DUMONT, Margaret

(Daisy Baker) 1889-1965

Tall, stately American actress, built along dowager duchess lines, who started her career as a singer, but became the world's best-loved comedy foil when she started working, at first on stage, then in films, with the Marx Brothers. Groucho always insisted that she didn't understand the jokes. Died from a heart attack a few days after a TV sketch with Groucho.

1917: A Tale of Two Cities. 1929: The Cocoanuts. 1930: Animal Crackers. 1931: The Girl Habit. 1933: Duck Soup. 1934: Gridiron Flash (GB: Luck of the Game). Kentucky Kernels (GB: Triple Trouble). Fifteen Wives (GB: The Man with the Electric Voice). 1935: A Night at the Opera. Orchids to You. Rendezvous. 1936: Anything Goes. The Song and Dance Man. 1937: A Day at the Races. Wise Girl. Youth on Parole. High Flyers. The Life of the Party. 1938: Dramatic School.

1939: The Women. At the Circus. 1941: For Beauty's Sake. The Big Store. Never Give a Sucker an Even Break. 1942: Born To Sing. About Face. Rhythm Parade. Sing Your Worries Away. 1943: The Dancing Masters. 1944: Seven Days Ashore. Up in Arms. Bathing Beauty. 1945: Sunset in El Dorado. Billy Rose's Diamond Horseshoe (GB: Diamond Horseshoe). The Horn Blows at Midnight. 1946: Little Giant (GB: On the Carpet). Susie Steps Out. 1952: Three for Bedroom C. Stop, You're Killing Me. 1956: Shake, Rattle and Rock. 1958: Auntie Mame. 1962: Zotz! 1964: What a Way To Go!

### DUNN, Michael

(Gary Miller) 1934-1973

The most successful dwarf actor in Hollywood's history, Dunn was forced to abandon a career as a concert pianist because of the congenital chondrodystrophy which eventually brought about his death. After being nominated for an Academy Award in Ship of Fools, he tackled an amazing variety of roles, although none so rewarding as the private eye in the TV movie Goodnight My Love.

1960: Pity Me Not. 1961: Without Each Other. 1965: Ship of Fools. 1966: You're a Big Boy Now. 1967: No Way to Treat a Lady. 1968: Madigan. Boom! Kampf um Rom (GB: The Struggle for Rome). 1969: Justine. Kampf um Rom II. Too Small Ticky. 1971: Murders in the Rue Morgue. You Think You've Got Problems (TV). 1972: *The Swan Song. Goodnight My Love (TV). 1973: The Mutations. The Werewolf of Washington. Frankenstein's Castle of Freaks. 1974: La loba y la paloma. The Abdication.

### DUNNOCK, Mildred 1900- 1991

Black-haired, thin-featured, birdlike American actress, adept at spinsters, whether fey, warm-hearted or waspish. Exceptionally busy on television in the 1950s. Film appearances were relatively few, but often memorable. Her strong acting style took her to two Oscar nominations, for Death of a Salesman (1951) and Baby Doll (1956), and there might well have been others for The Corn is Green (1945, a

ABOVE The dowager duchess of comedy, Margaret **Dumont**, is propositioned not, for once, by Groucho Marx, but by Charlie Ruggles in *The Girl Habit* (1931)

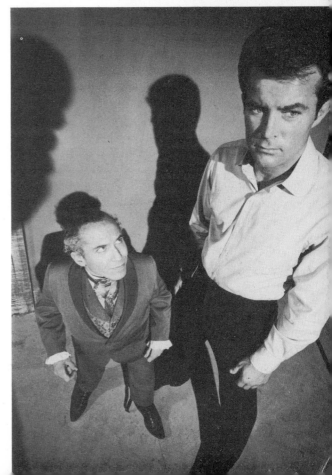

RIGHT Besides his film roles, Michael **Dunn** (left) made some 10 appearances in the TV series *The Wild, Wild West*. Here he is in a 1966 episode with series star Robert Conrad

repeat of her stage role) and *Sweet Bird of Youth* in 1962.

*1945: The Corn Is Green. 1947: Kiss of Death. 1951: I Want You. Death of a Salesman. 1952: The Girl in White (GB: So Bright the Flame). Viva Zapata! 1953: The Jazz Singer. Bad for Each Other. 1954: Hansel and Gretel (voice only). 1955: The Trouble With Harry. 1956: Baby Doll. Love Me Tender. 1957: Peyton Place. Winter Dreams (TV). The Play Room (TV). 1959: The Nun's Story. Diary of a Nurse (TV). The Story on Page One. 1960: Butterfield 8. 1961: Something Wild. 1962: Sweet Bird of Youth. 1964: Beyond a Pale Horse. Youngblood Hawke. 1965: Seven Women. 1969: Whatever Happened to Aunt Alice? 1975: The Spiral Staircase. 1976: One Summer Love (TV). 1979: And Baby Makes Six (TV). 1980: Baby Comes Home (TV). 1981: Miracle of Love (TV).*

### DURNING, Charles 1933-

Heavily built, big-faced, piggy-eyed, amiable-looking American actor who developed into one of the few star character players of the 1970s. The son of an Army officer, and himself a Korean War veteran who won the Silver Star, Durning tried an amazing variety of jobs—boxer, buttonfactory operator, bouncer, liftman, ballroom-dancing instructor, construction worker, cabbie and waiter, before settling on acting. An experienced Shakespearian by the time he came to the screen, he gradually rose in prominence from the early 1970s, at first in abrasive and often unpleasant parts, but later in a variety of roles, some of which showed off his talent for comedy.

*1965: Harvey Middleman, Fireman, 1970: Hi Mom! I Walk the Line. The Pursuit of Happiness. 1971: Dealing: Or, The Berkeleyto-Boston-Forty-Bricks-Lost-Bag Blues. 1972: Sisters (GB: Blood Sisters). Madigan: The Midtown Beat (TV). Deadhead Miles. 1973: Connection (TV. GB: The Connection). The Sting. 1974: The Front Page. 1975: The Rivalry (TV). The Trial of Chaplain Jensen (TV). Queen of the Stardust Ballroom (TV). Switch (TV). Dog Day Afternoon. Breakheart Pass. The Hindenberg.* -

*1976: Harry and Walter Go to New York. 1977: Twilight's Last Gleaming. The Choirboys. An Enemy of the People. 1978: The Greek Tycoon. The Fury. Tilt. Special Olympics (TV). 1979: North Dallas Forty. Starting Over. When a Stranger Calls. The Muppet Movie. 1980: Die Laughing. Crisis at Central High (TV). Attica: The Story of a Prison Riot (TV). The Final Countdown. A Perfect Match (TV). 1981: The Best Little Girl in the World (TV). Sharky's Machine. True Confessions. Dark Night of the Scarecrow (TV). 1982: Tootsie. The Best Little Whorehouse in Texas. Hadley's Rebellion. 1983: To Be or Not to Be. Two of a Kind. 1984: Mass Appeal. Stick. Mister Roberts (TV). Big Trouble. 1985: Mischief (The Man With One Red Shoe).*

### DWYER, Leslie 1906-

Pugnacious, shortish, brown-haired cockney character star in prominent supporting roles and semi-leads in British films throughout the 1940s and 1950s. Stockily built, he was typically seen as fast-talking, aggressive 'ordinary blokes', mainly in comedy although he could be likeable in drama too, and rarely overplayed his hand. From a theatrical family, he studied at a stage school, took to the boards at 10 and made his film debut at 15. A lifetime cricket enthusiast.

*1921: The Fifth Form at St Dominic's. 1932: The Flag Lieutenant. 1934: Badger's Green. It's a Cop. 1935: Some Day. 1938: Housemaster. 1941: The Young Mr Pitt. The Goose Steps Out. They Flew Alone (US: Wings and the Woman). 1942: In Which We Serve. 1943: The Lamp Still Burns. The Bells Go Down. The Yellow Canary. 1944: The Way Ahead. 1945: Perfect Strangers (US: Vacation from Marriage). Great Day. 1946: I See a Dark Stranger (US: The Adventuress). This Man Is Mine! Piccadilly Incident. Night Boat to Dublin. 1947: The Little Ballerina. When the Bough Breaks. *Christmas Weekend. Temptation Harbour. 1948: Bond Street. The Calendar. The Bad Lord Byron. A Boy, a Girl and a Bike. 1949: It's Not Cricket. Poet's Pub. Now Barabbas was a robber ... 1950: Lilli Marlene. Double Confession. Midnight Episode. 1951: There Is Another Sun (US: Wall of Death). Laughter in Paradise. Smart Alec.*

*Judgment Deferred. 1952: Hindle Wakes (US: Holiday Week). The Hour of Thirteen. My Wife's Lodger. 1953: Marilyn (later Roadhouse Girl). 1954: Act of Love. The Good Die Young. The Black Rider. 1955: Where There's a Will. Not So Dusty. Room in the House. 1956: *Death of a Ham. *The Milkman. Clock without Dagger (US: Operation Conspiracy). Eyewitness. Face in the Night (US: Menace in the Night). 1958: Stormy Crossing (US: Black Tide). 1959: The 39 Steps. Left, Right and Centre. 1961: Rendezvous. 1964: Seventy Deadly Pills. I've Gotta Horse. 1965: Monster of Terror (US: Die, Monster, Die). 1968: Lionheart. Up in the Air. Crooks and Coronets (US: Sophie's Place). 1970: *A Hole Lot of Trouble. 1975: One of Our Dinosaurs is Missing. 1978: Dominique.*

### DYALL, Valentine 1908-1985

Very dark and tall, cadaverous, disgruntledlooking British actor, vaguely reminiscent in aspect and voice of Raymond Massey. The son of actor Franklin Dyall (1874-1950), he was an emaciated black beetle of a man whose early career was sharply divided between plays (1930-41) and the cinema (1942-54), later combining the two. In the 1940s, his dark-brown voice gained him a million fans who listened to him each week on radio as the narrator of a long series of chillers (opening words: 'This is your storyteller—the man in black'). He was less personable than one expected in films, looking as though he would be happier if he could find a nice, damp crypt to which to slip away. His voice in narrations, however, has continued to be as unmistakeable as it is unmatchable.

*1942: Much Too Shy. 1943: The Life and Death of Colonel Blimp (US: Colonel Blimp). The Yellow Canary. The Silver Fleet. 1944: Henry V. Hotel Reserve. 1945: Latin Quarter. I Know Where I'm Going! Pink String and Sealing Wax. Caesar and Cleopatra. Night Boat to Dublin. Brief Encounter. 1946: Prisoners of the Tower (narrator only). *The Clock Strikes Eight. *The Gong Cried Murder. *The House in Rue Rapp. 1947: The Dover Road (narrator only). The White Unicorn (US: Bad Sister). 1948: Corridor of Mirrors. The Story of Shirley Yorke. Night Comes Too*

Soon. Woman Hater. Man on the Run. Vengeance Is Mine. The Queen of Spades. Christopher Columbus (narrator only). The Case of Charles Peace. 1949: Filming for Fun (narrator only). Helter Skelter. Dr Morelle— The Case of the Missing Heiress. For Them That Trespass. Golden Salamander. Miss Pilgrim's Progress. 1950: Room to Let. The Body Said No! The Man in Black. Stranger at My Door. 1951: Salute the Toff. 1952: Ivanhoe. Hammer the Toff. Paul Temple Returns. 1953: The Final Test. Strange Stories (narrator only). 1954: The Devil's Jest. Johnny on the Spot. 1956: Suspended Alibi. 1959: Night Train for Inverness. 1960: Identity Unknown. City of the Dead (US: Horror Hotel). 1962: Fate Takes a Hand. 1963: The Haunting. *The Money Makers (narrator only). The Horror of It All. 1965: The Naked World of Harrison Marks (narrator only). 1966: Our Incredible World (narrator only). The Wrong Box. 1967: Casino Royale. 1974: The Great McGonagall. 1976: The Slipper and the Rose. 1977: Come Play With Me. 1978: *A Child's Voice (narrator only). 1982: Britannia Hospital.

**EDWARDS, Glynn** 1931-
Brawny, Malaya-born British actor with homely face, receding dark hair and deep, rumbling voice. He studied agriculture, then worked in Trinidad managing a sugar plantation before turning to acting. Once married to fellow character star Yootha Joyce (qv; first of three). Success in the TV

series *Minder* enabled him to give more time to his hobby: sailing.

1957: The Heart Within. 1961: A Prize of Arms. 1962: Sparrows Can't Sing. 1963: The Hi-Jackers. 1964: Smokescreen. Zulu. 1965: The Ipcress File. 1967: Robbery. The Blood Beast Terror. 1968: The Bofors Gun. 1970: Get Carter! Fragment of Fear. 1971: Burke and Hare. Under Milk Wood. All Coppers Are... 1973: Shaft in Africa. 1974: 11 Harrowhouse. 1978: The Stick-Up. The Playbirds. 1979: Confessions from the David Galaxy Affair. 1980: Rising Damp. 1983: Champions.

**EDWARDS, Meredith** 1917-
Balding, wistful-looking, slightly built Welsh actor who formed a drama company for the firm in Wales where he worked, then turned professional and quickly gained radio and theatrical assignments. Came to films through Ealing Studios and played canny Welshmen, kindly policemen and well-meaning advisers throughout the 1950s. A bright and lively part of any film.

1949: A Run for Your Money. The Blue Lamp. 1950: Midnight Episode. The Magnet. 1951: There Is Another Sun (US: Wall of Death). The Lavender Hill Mob. Where No Vultures Fly. 1952: The Last Page (US: Manbait). Girdle of Gold. The Gambler and the Lady. Gift Horse (US: Glory at Sea). 1953: The Cruel Sea. The Great Game. A Day To Remember. 1954: Meet Mr Malcolm. Devil on Horseback. Burnt Evidence. The Red Dress. Final Appointment. To Dorothy a Son (US: Cash on Delivery). Mask of Dust (US: Race for Life). 1955: Lost (US: Tears for Simon). 1956: The Long Arm (US: The Third Key). Peril for the Guy. Circus Friends. Town on Trial! 1957: Escapement (US: Zex/The Electronic Monster). 1958: Dunkirk. Law and Disorder. The Supreme Secret. 1959: Tiger Bay. 1960: Doctor in Love. The Trials of Oscar Wilde (US: The Man with the Green Carnation). 1961: Flame in the Streets. Mix Me a Person. 1962: Go to Blazes! Only Two Can Play. 1963: This Is My Street. 1966: The Great St Trinian's Train Robbery. 1976: Gulliver's Travels.

**ELAM, Jack** 1916-
Dark-haired, scowling American actor with sightless left eye, who gained steady employment in the 1950s (after switching to acting from accountancy) as a mean *hombre* always ready to shoot the hero in the back. Mainly seen in westerns, Elam could also play sympathetic characters and comedy, but was later encouraged to guy his own image rather too much. Gained weight dramatically in more recent times.

1949: *Trailin' West. The Sundowners (GB: Thunder in the Dust). 1950: One Way Street. Quicksand. High Lonesome. Key to the City. An American Guerilla in the Philippines (GB: I Shall Return). Love That Brute. A Ticket to Tomahawk. 1951: Bird of Paradise. Rawhide/ Desperate Siege. Finders Keepers. The Frogmen. The Bushwhackers (GB: The Rebel). 1952: Kansas City Confidential (GB: The Secret Four). The Battle at Apache Pass. My Man and I. The Ring. High Noon. Rancho Notorious. Montana Territory. Lure of the Wilderness. 1953: Gun Belt. The Moonlighter. Count the Hours (GB: Every Minute Counts). Ride, Vaquero! Appointment in Honduras. Ride Clear of Diablo. 1954: Jubilee Trail. Princess of the Nile. Vera Cruz. Cattle Queen of Montana. The Far Country. 1955: Moonfleet. Tarzan's Hidden Jungle. The Man from Laramie. Kiss Me Deadly. Wichita. Artists and Models. Man Without a Star. Kismet. 1956: Jubal. Thunder over Arizona. Pardners. Gunfight at the OK Corral. 1957: Dragoon Wells Massacre. Baby Face Nelson. Night Passage. Lure of the Swamp. 1958: The Gun Runners. 1959: Edge of Eternity. The Girl in Lovers' Lane. 1961: The Last Sunset. Pocketful of Miracles. The Comancheros. 1963: Four for Texas. 1965: The Rare Breed. 1966: Night of the Grizzly. 1967: The Last Challenge (GB: The Pistolero of Red River). Never a Dull Moment. The Way West. Firecreek. 1968: Once Upon a Time...in the West. Sonora. Support Your Local Sheriff. 1969: Ride a Northbound Horse (TV. GB: cinemas). The Over-the-Hill Gang (TV). The Cockeyed Cowboys of Calico County (GB: TV, as A Woman for Charlie). 1970: Dirty Dingus Magee. Rio Lobo. The Wild Country. 1971: Support Your Local Gunfighter. Hannie Caulder. The Last Rebel. 1972: The Daughters of *Joshua Cabe* (TV). *1973: The Red Pony* (TV. GB: cinemas). *Shootout in a One-Dog Town* (TV). *Pat Garrett and Billy the Kid*. *1974: A Knife for the Ladies. Sidekicks* (TV). *Huckleberry Finn* (TV). *1976: The New Daughters of Joshua Cabe* (TV). *The Winds of Autumn. Pony Express Rider. The Creature from Black Lake. Hawmps. 1977: Grayeagle*. *1978: The Norsemen. Hot Lead and Cold Feet. Lacy and the Mississippi Queen* (TV). *1979: The Villain* (GB: *Cactus Jack*). *The Apple Dumpling Gang Rides Again. The Sacketts* (TV). *1980: Soggy Bottom USA*. *1981: The Cannonball Run. 1982: Jinxed! Sacred Ground* (revised version of *Grayeagle*). *The Girl, the Watch and Dynamite* (TV). *1983: Silent Sentence. Cannonball Run II*.

**ELPHICK, Michael** 1946–
Dark-haired, shadow-jowled, round-faced, rough-voiced Londoner, one of the few outstanding British character actors to emerge in recent times, and an embryonic Long John Silver if ever there were one—though just as effective in quieter roles. Elphick's career is symptomatic of the virtual demise of the film character actor in Britain—almost all of it spent in the theatre and television.

*1968: Fräulein Doktor. Where's Jack? 1970: The Buttercup Chain. Cry of the Banshee. 1971: Blind Terror* (US: *See No Evil*). *1973: O Lucky Man! 1977: Star Wars. 1978: The Odd Job. The First Great Train Robbery. Black Island. 1979: Quadrophenia. 1980: The Elephant Man. 1982: Privates on Parade. 1983: Curse of the Pink Panther. Memed My Hawk. Gorky Park. 1984: Forbrydelsens Element/The Element of Crime. 1985: Hitler's SS: Portrait in Evil* (TV. GB: cinemas).

**ELSOM, Isobel**
(I. Reed) 1893–1981
Fair-haired, regal leading lady from the English stage who enjoyed a very good run in British films of the silent and early sound era, before finding her way to Hollywood where she played self-righteous upper-crust matrons whose pomposity was made to be punctured. Married/divorced British director Maurice Elvey.

*1915: A Prehistoric Love Story. 1916: Milestones. The Way of an Eagle. 1918: The Elder Miss Blossom* (US: *Wanted a Wife*). *Tinker, Tailor, Soldier, Sailor. Onward Christain Soldiers. God Bless Our Red, White and Blue. The Man Who Won. 1919: Quinney's. Hope. Linked by Fate. A Member of Tattersall's. Mrs Thompson. Edge o' Beyond. 1920: Aunt Rachel. Nance. 1921: For Her Father's Sake. 1922: Dick Turpin's Ride to York. A Debt of Honour. The Game of Life. The Harbour Lights. Broken Shadows. 1923: Just a Mother. The Sign of Four. The Wandering Jew. 1924: The Love Story of Aliette Brunton. Who is the Man? 1925: The Last Witness. *Glamis Castle. *The Tower of London. 1926: Human Law. Tragödie einer Ehe. 1927: Dance Magic. 1931: Stranglehold. The Other Woman. 1932: The Crooked Lady. Illegal. 1933: The Thirteenth Candle. 1934: The Primrose Path. 1941: Ladies in Retirement. 1942: Eagle Squadron. The War Against Mrs Hadley. Seven Sweethearts. You Were Never Lovelier. 1943: Forever and a Day. First Comes Courage. My Kingdom for a Cook. 1944: The White Cliffs of Dover. Between Two Worlds. Casanova Brown. 1945: The Unseen. 1946: Of Human Bondage. Two Sisters from Boston. 1947: The Ghost and Mrs Muir. The Two Mrs Carrolls. Ivy. Monsieur Verdoux. Love from a Stranger* (GB: *A Stranger Walked In*). *Escape Me Never. The Paradine Case. 1948: Smart Woman. 1949: The Secret Garden. 1950: Her Wonderful Lie. 1954: Desirée. Deep in My Heart. 1955: The King's Thief. Love is a Many-Splendored Thing. 1956: 23 Paces to Baker Street. Lust for Life. Over-Exposed. 1957: The Guns of Fort Petticoat. 1958: Rock-a-Bye Baby. 1959: The Miracle. The Young Philadelphians* (GB: *The City Jungle*). *1960: The Bellboy. 1961: The Second Time Around. 1962: The Errand Boy. 1963: Who's Minding the Store? 1964: My Fair Lady. The Pleasure Seekers*.

**EMERSON, Hope** 1897–1960
You really couldn't miss Hope Emerson in films. About as wide as a barn door and with eagle-like features, she was also 6ft 2in tall. A vaudeville and Broadway star of the 1920s and 1930s, she was commandeered by the cinema in post-war years and

sometimes cast as fearless pioneering frontier western women (Indians beware!), but even more effective as the death-dealing masseuse in *Cry of the City* and the pitiless prison matron in *Caged*. She was nominated for an Oscar for this last performance, but ironically lost to *Harvey's* Josephine Hull, one of the screen's tiniest actresses. Died from a liver ailment.

*1932: Smiling Faces. 1948: Cry of the City. That Wonderful Urge. 1949: House of Strangers. Dancing in the Dark. Adam's Rib. Roseanna McCoy. Thieves' Highway. 1950: Caged. Copper Canyon. Double Crossbones. 1951: Belle le Grand. Westward the Women. 1953: The Lady Wants Mink. Champ for a Day. A Perilous Journey. Casanova's Big Night. 1955: Untamed. 1957: The Guns of Fort Petticoat. All Mine to Give* (GB: *The Day They Gave Babies Away*). *1958: Rock-a-Bye Baby*.

**EMERY, Dick** 1918–1983
Cheerful British comedian with dark (later nearly white) hair, a wolfish smile and barking, upper-class voice, in supporting roles for years before TV success came along in the 1960s. Often seen in drag, he excelled at funny voices and bizarre disguises, but did not impress as a star personality on the bigger screen. Died from respiratory problems associated with gout and blood poisoning.

*1953: *The Super Secret Service. 1955: *The Case of the Mukkinese Battlehorn. 1960:*

*Light Up the Sky. A Taste of Money. 1962: Mrs Gibbons' Boys. Crooks Anonymous. The Wrong Arm of the Law. *The Plain Man's Guide to Advertising (voice only). The Fast Lady. 1963: Just for Fun. 1965: The Big Job. 1966: The Wrong Box. 1967: River Rivals (serial). Yellow Submarine (voice only). 1968: Baby Love. 1970: Loot. 1972: Ooh...You Are Awful (US: Get Charlie Tully).*

### EMERY, Gilbert
(G. E. Pottle) 1875–1945

American-born, British-raised, well-travelled, very tall actor of shamblingly aristocratic bearing. He acted all over the world before settling in Hollywood with the coming of sound, where (between taking a sabbatical for stage work in 1932 and 1933) he quickly established himself as craggy figures of authority. His juiciest role came with third billing (as Winslow, Mae West's business manager) in *Goin' to Town.* Although it seems fairly certain that the Australian and American silents listed below are his work and not that of another acting Gilbert Emery (1882-1934), they are included only in square brackets. A poor man's C. Aubrey Smith (*qv*).

*[1919: The Sentimental Bloke. 1920: Ginger Mick. 1921: Where the Billy Boils. Cousin Kate. 1922: Any Wife. A Daughter of Australia. A Rough Passage. Lust for Gold.] 1929: Behind That Curtain. The Sky Hawk. 1930: A Lady's Morals (GB: Jenny Lind). Sarah and Son. Let Us Be Gay. The Prince of Diamonds. The Soul Kiss. The Royal Bed (GB: The Queen's Husband). 1931: Scandal Sheet. The Lady Refuses. Party Husband. The Ruling Voice. Rich Man's Folly. Ladies' Man. Upper Underworld. 1932: A Man Called Back. A Farewell to Arms. 1934: All of Me. Gallant Lady. Coming-Out Party. The House of Rothschild. Where Sinners Meet. I Believed in You. One More River (GB: Over the River). Grand Canary. Now and Forever. Whom the Gods Destroy. The Man Who Reclaimed His Head. 1935: Clive of India. Night Life of the Gods. Cardinal Richelieu. Goin' to Town. Harmony Lane. Reckless Roads. Let's Live Tonight. Ladies Crave Excitement. Without Regret. Peter Ibbetson. Magnificent Obsession. 1936: Girl on the Front*

*Page. Little Lord Fauntleroy. Dracula's Daughter. Wife vs Secretary. Bullets or Ballots. 1937: The Great Barrier (US: Silent Barriers). The Life of Emile Zola. Double or Nothing. Souls at Sea. 1938: The House of Mystery. Making the Headlines. The Buccaneer. Lord Jeff (GB: The Boy from Barnardo's). Always Goodbye. A Man to Remember. Storm Over Bengal. 1939: The Saint Strikes Back. The Lady's from Kentucky. Juarez. Nurse Edith Cavell. 1939-40: Raffles. 1940: Anne of Windy Poplars (GB: Anne of Windy Willows). The House of the Seven Gables. River's End. South of Suez. 1941: That Hamilton Woman (GB: Lady Hamilton). New Wine (GB: The Great Awakening). Rage in Heaven. Adam Had Four Sons. Scotland Yard. A Woman's Face. Singapore Woman. Sundown. 1942: The Remarkable Andrew. Escape from Hong Kong. The Loves of Edgar Allan Poe. 1943: Sherlock Holmes in Washington. The Return of the Vampire. 1944: Between Two Worlds. 1945: The Brighton Strangler.*

### EMHARDT, Robert 1903-1994

Versatile, fat, tiny-eyed, droop-cheeked American actor whose sheer bulk and presence joined forces to grab the attention in his every scene. Hollywood made too little use of this one-time understudy to Sydney Greenstreet, especially in view of the fact that he could project villainy, kindliness or just plain eccentricity with equal perception.

*1952: The Iron Mistress. 1955: The Big Knife. 1957: 3:10 to Yuma. 1958: The Badlanders. 1960: Wake Me When It's Over. 1961: Underworld USA. The Intruder (GB: The Stranger). 1962: The Mooncussers (TV. GB: cinemas). Kid Galahad. 1966: The Group. 1967: Hostile Guns. 1968: Where Were You When the Lights Went Out? 1969: Rascal. Change of Habit. Operation Heartbeat (TV). Suppose They Gave a War and Nobody Came? 1970: Lawman. 1971: Lock, Stock and Barrel (TV). 1972: Scorpio. 1973: The Stone Killer. 1974: It's Alive. Night Games (TV). The FBI versus Alvin Karpis, Public Enemy No. One (TV). 1976: Alex and the Gypsy. 1977: Fraternity Row. It Happened One Christmas (TV). 1978: Seniors. Pleasure Cove (TV). 1979: Institute for Revenge (TV).*

### EMNEY, Fred 1900-1980

Enormous British comic actor, comedian, circus ringmaster and raconteur, unmistakeable with grouchy growl, monocle, cigar almost as fat as himself and (usually) top hat as well. In London pantomime at 16 (he played the squire in *Puss in Boots*), he stayed in America from 1920 to 1931, but returned to the British music-hall and to bring his wheezing apoplectics to film character roles from 1934.

*1934: Brewster's Millions. 1935: Come Out of the Pantry. 1937: Let's Make a Night of It. The Lilac Domino. 1938: Just Like a Woman. Jane Steps Out. Hold My Hand. Yes, Madam? 1939: Just William. She Couldn't Say No. The Middle Watch. 1940: *Goofer Trouble. 1942: Let the People Sing. 1955: Fun at St Fanny's. 1962: The Fast Lady. 1963: Father Came Too. 1964: A Home of Your Own. I've Gotta Horse. 1965: San Ferry Ann. Bunny Lake is Missing. Those Magnificent Men in Their Flying Machines. 1966: The Sandwich Man. 1968: Oliver! 1969: Lock Up Your Daughters! The Italian Job. The Magic Christian. Under the Table You Must Go. 1970: Doctor in Trouble. 1971: Up the Chastity Belt. 1973: Mistress Pamela. 1974: The Amorous Milkman. 1977: Adventures of a Private Eye.*

### ERDMAN, Richard
(John R. Erdman) 1925-

Snub-nosed, eager-looking American supporting actor with a shock of fair hair. He proved perfect casting for 'GI Joes' in war films, but, as the 1950s drew to a close, he began to diversify, directing comedy shows for television (including many segments of *The Dick Van Dyke Show*) as well as drama segments and a couple of feature films. Still busy on one thing and another, but these days only rarely seen in front of the camera.

*1944: Hollywood Canteen. The Very Thought of You. Janie. 1945: Danger Signal. Objective Burma! Too Young To Know. 1946: Janie Gets Married. Deception. Nobody Lives Forever. Shadow of a Woman. 1947: That Way With Women. Wild Harvest. 1948: The Time of Your Life. 1949: Easy Living. Four Days' Leave. 1950: The Admiral Was a Lady. The Men. USS Teakettle (later and GB: You're in the Navy Now). 1951: Cry Danger. The Wild Blue Yonder (GB: Thunder across the Pacific). The Stooge. 1952: The San Francisco Story. Aladdin and His Lamp. The Happy Time. Jumping Jacks. 1953: Stalag 17. The Blue Gardenia. Mission Over Korea (GB: Eyes of the Skies). The Steel Lady (GB: The Treasure of Kalifa). 1955: Francis in the Navy. Bengazi. 1956: Anything Goes. The Power and the Prize. 1957: Bernadine. 1958: The Rawhide Trail. Saddle the Wind. 1959: Face of Fire. 1963: The Brass Bottle. 1966: Namu the Killer Whale. 1969: The Great Man's Whiskers (TV. Not shown until 1973). Rascal. 1970: Tora! Tora! Tora! 1972: Visions (TV). 1982: Heidi's Song (voice only). 1984: Trancers. 1985: Tomboy.*

**As director:**
*1971: Bleep. 1973: The Brothers O'Toole.*

**ERICKSON, Leif**
(William Anderson) 1911- 1986
Big, broad, blond, benign American actor who sweated away for years in stiffish 'second lead' roles before finding his niche in the 1960s as the father-figure in the TV western series *High Chaparral*. He began as a band singer and trombonist, but hit more headlines for his stormy marriages to Frances Farmer and Margaret (Maggie) Hayes until TV came along. Later married a non-professional; they're still married.

*1933: The Sweetheart of Sigma Chi (GB: Girl of My Dreams). 1935: Wanderer of the*

Wasteland. Nevada. 1936: Desert Gold. Drift Fence. Girl of the Ozarks. College Holiday. *1937: Conquest (GB: Marie Walewska). Waikiki Wedding. The Thrill of a Lifetime. 1938: The Big Broadcast of 1938. Ride a Crooked Mile. 1939: Crisis (narrator only). One Third of a Nation. Escape from Yesterday. 1941: H. M. Pulham Esq. Nothing But the Truth. The Blonde from Singapore (GB: Hot Pearls). 1942: Are Husbands Necessary? The Fleet's In. Night Monster (GB: House of Mystery). Arabian Nights. Eagle Squadron. Pardon My Sarong. 1947: The Gangster. Blonde Savage. 1948: The Gay Intruders. Sorry, Wrong Number. Miss Tatlock's Millions. Joan of Arc. The Snake Pit. 1949: Partners in Crime. Johnny Stool Pigeon. The Lady Gambles. 1950: Stella. Three Secrets. Dallas. Mother Didn't Tell Me. Love That Brute. The Showdown. 1951: The Tall Target. Reunion in Reno. The Cimarron Kid. Sailor Beware! Show Boat. 1952: With a Song in My Heart. Carbine Williams. My Wife's Best Friend. Abbott and Costello Meet Captain Kidd. Never Wave at a WAC (GB: The Private Wore Skirts). 1953: Trouble Along the Way. Fort Algiers. Perilous Journey. Paris Model. Invaders from Mars. Captain Scarface. 1954: On the Waterfront. 1956: Star in the Dust. Tea and Sympathy. The Fastest Gun Alive. 1957: The Vintage. One Coat of White (TV). Istanbul. Kiss Them for Me. Panic Button (TV). 1958: Twilight for the Gods. The Young Lions. Once Upon a Horse. 1959: The Raider (TV). 1960: The Shape of the River (TV). 1962: A Gathering of Eagles. 1963: The Carpetbaggers. 1964: Strait-Jacket. Roustabout. 1965: I Saw What You Did. Mirage. 1971: Terror in the Sky (TV). The Deadly Dream (TV). 1972: Man and Boy. The Family Rico (TV). The Daughters of Joshua Cabe (TV). 1975: Winterhawk. Abduction. 1977: Twilight's Last Gleaming. 1981: Hunter's Moon. 1983: Wild Times (TV).*

**ERWIN, Stuart** 1902-1967
Fair-haired American actor with open, puzzled face, the Eddie Bracken of his day in roles of hapless innocence, first as fresh college kids, then as honest Joes. Very successful in television from 1949 onwards, initially in his own show with his wife,

actress June Collyer (1907-1968). Oscar nominee for *Pigskin Parade*.

*1928: Mother Knows Best. 1929: Speakeasy. Happy Days. The Exalted Flapper. New Year's Eve. Thru Different Eyes. Sweetie. The Cock-eyed World. The Trespasser. This Thing Called Love. Dangerous Curves. The Sophomore. 1930: Men without Women. Paramount on Parade. Young Eagles. Dangerous Nan McGrew. Only Saps Work. Playboy of Paris. Love Among the Millionaires. Maybe It's Love. Along Came Youth. 1931: No Limit. Up Pops the Devil. The Magnificent Lie. Dude Ranch. Working Girls. 1932: *Hollywood on Parade No. 2. Two Kinds of Women. Make Me a Star. The Big Broadcast. The Misleading Lady. Strangers in Love. 1933: Face in the Sky. The Crime of the Century. International House. Hold Your Man. The Stranger's Return. Day of Reckoning. Before Dawn. Going Hollywood. He Learned About Women. Under the Tonto Rim. 1934: Viva Villa! Palooka (GB: The Great Schnozzle). Chained. Have a Heart. Bachelor Bait. The Band Plays On. The Party's Over. 1935: Ceiling Zero. After Office Hours. 1936: Exclusive Story. Absolute Quiet. Women Are Trouble. Pigskin Parade (GB: The Harmony Parade). All American Chump (GB: The Country Bumpkin). 1937: Dance, Charlie, Dance. Second Honeymoon. Slim. I'll Take Romance. Checkers. Small Town Boy. 1938: Three Blind Mice. Mr Boggs Steps Out. Passport Husband. 1939: It Could Happen to You. Back Door to Heaven. Hollywood Cavalcade. The Honeymoon's Over. 1940: When the Daltons Rode. Our Town. Sandy Gets Her Man. A Little Bit of Heaven. 1941: Cracked Nuts. The Bride Came COD. 1942: The Adventures of Martin Eden. Blondie for Victory (GB: Trouble Through Billets). Drums of the Congo. 1943: He Hired the Boss. 1944: The Great Mike. 1945: Pillow to Post. 1947: Killer Dill. Heaven Only Knows. Heading for Heaven. 1948: Strike It Rich. 1950: Father is a Bachelor. 1953: Main Street to Broadway. 1956: †Snow Shoes (TV). 1958: †The Right Hand Man (TV). 1959: †A Diamond is a Boy's Best Friend (TV). 1960: †Wrong Way Mooche (TV). †For the Love of Mike (GB: None But the Brave). 1963: †Son of Flubber. 1964: †The Misadventures of Merlin Jones. 1968: Shadow Over Elveron (TV).*

†As Stu Erwin

**ESMOND, Carl**
(Willy Eichberger) 1905-
Dark, handsome, often moustachioed Austrian who began his career as a bank clerk in Vienna, then switched to acting, but was forced to flee the Nazis in the early 1930s. After one or two films in Britain as romantic singing lead, he ended up in Hollywood (later becoming an American citizen) where, after the war was over, he had an increasingly sporadic film career, despite quite charismatic performances, sometimes in villainous parts. Much on TV till 1974.

1934: *Blossom Time* (US: *April Romance*). *Evensong*. 1935: *Invitation to the Waltz*. 1938: *The Dawn Patrol*. 1939: *Little Men*. *Thunder Afloat*. 1940: *The Catman of Paris* (released 1946). 1941: *Sundown. Sergeant York*. 1942: *Pacific Rendezvous. Panama Hattie. Seven Sweethearts. The Navy Comes Through*. 1943: *First Comes Courage. Margin for Error. Ministry of Fear*. 1944: *Address Unknown. The Story of Dr Wassell. The Master Race. Experiment Perilous*. 1945: *Without Love. This Love of Ours. Her Highness and the Bellboy*. 1946: *Lover Come Back*. 1947: *Smash-Up, the Story of a Woman* (GB: *A Woman Destroyed*). *Slave Girl*. 1948: *Walk a Crooked Mile*. 1950: *Mystery Submarine. The Desert Hawk*. 1952: *The World in His Arms*. 1955: *Lola Montès. The Racers* (GB: *Such Men Are Dangerous*). 1958: *From the Earth to the Moon*. 1959: *Thunder in the Sun*. 1961: *Hitler. Brushfire!* 1962: *Kiss of the Vampire* (TV version only). 1965: *Agent for HARM. Morituri* (GB: *The Saboteur, Code Name Morituri*). 1984: *My Wicked, Wicked Ways: The Legend of Errol Flynn* (TV).

**EVANS, Gene** 1922-
Red-haired, blue-eyed, unhandsome, huskily built, hard-driving American actor with gruff voice, usually in tough or brutish roles, but occasionally effective in leads. The cinema underestimated his versatility, but television allowed him to show his more benevolent side in the series *My Friend Flicka*.

1947: *Under Colorado Skies*. 1948: *Assigned to Danger. Criss Cross. Larceny. Berlin Express*. 1949: *Mother is a Freshman* (GB: *Mother Knows Best*). *It Happens Every Spring*. 1950: *Jet Pilot* (released 1957). *Never a Dull Moment. Dallas. The Asphalt Jungle. Wyoming Mail. Storm Warning. Armored Car Robbery*. 1951: *Sugarfoot. Steel Helmet. I Was an American Spy. The Big Carnival* (later and GB: *Ace in the Hole*). *Fixed Bayonets! Force of Arms*. 1952: *Park Row. Thunderbirds. Mutiny*. 1953: *Donovan's Brain. The Golden Blade*. 1954: *Cattle Queen of Montana. The Long Wait. Hell and High Water*. 1955: *Crashout. Wyoming Renegades*. 1957: *The Helen Morgan Story* (GB: *Both Ends of the Candle*). *The Sad Sack. Damn Citizen!* 1958: *Money, Women and Guns. Revolt in the Big House. Young and Wild. The Bravados. Behemoth the Sea Monster* (US: *The Giant Behemoth*). 1959: *The Hangman. Operation Petticoat*. 1961: *Gold of the Seven Saints*. 1963: *Shock Corridor*. 1965: *Apache Uprising*. 1966: *Nevada Smith. Waco*. 1967: *The War Wagon*. 1968: *Support Your Local Sheriff*. 1969: *Dragnet* (TV. GB: *The Big Dragnet*). 1970: *The Ballad of Cable Hogue. The Intruders* (TV). *There Was a Crooked Man*. 1971: *Support Your Local Gunfighter*. 1972: *The Bounty Man* (TV). 1973: *Pat Garrett and Billy the Kid. Walking Tall*. 1974: *Shootout in a One-Dog Town* (TV). *Sidekicks* (TV). *People Toys. Devil Times Five*. 1975: *The Last Day* (TV). *Matt Helm* (TV). 1976: *The Macahans* (TV). *Sourdough*. 1977: *Fire!* (TV. GB: *cinemas*). 1978: *The Magic of Lassie. Kate Bliss and the Ticker Tape Kid* (TV). 1979: *The Sacketts* (TV). *The Last Ride of the Dalton Gang* (TV). 1982: *Travis McGee* (TV). *The Shadow Riders* (TV).

**EVEREST, Barbara** 1890-1968
Plump-cheeked, kind-eyed, dark-haired British actress who found herself cast as wives, mothers and housekeepers after returning to films to play character roles following a session as a leading lady in silent days. She worked solidly but unobtrusively in British films of the 1930s, then surprisingly went to Hollywood in 1941 and gave some of her most striking performances (especially those in *The Uninvited* and *Jane Eyre*), winning co-star billing. On her return to Britain, she was magnificent as Eric Portman's domineering mother in *Wanted for Murder*, but then slipped back into smaller roles.

1916: *The Hypocrites. Man Without a Soul* (US: *I Believe*). 1919: *Whosoever Will Offend. Not Guilty. The Lady Clare. Till Our Ship Comes In* (series). 1920: *The Joyous Adventures of Aristide Pujol. Calvary. Testimony*. 1921: *The Bigamist*. 1922: *Fox Farm. The Persistent Lovers. A Romance of Old Bagdad*. 1932: *Lily Christine. There Goes the Bride. The Lodger* (US: *The Phantom Fiend*). *The World, the Flesh and the Devil. When London Sleeps*. 1933: *The Roof. The Umbrella. Love's Old Sweet Song. The Wandering Jew. She Was Only a Village Maiden. The River Wolves. Home Sweet Home. The Lost Chord*. 1934: *Passing Shadows. Song at Eventide. The Warren Case*. 1935: *Scrooge. The Lad. The Passing of the Third Floor Back*. 1936: *Love in Exile. Men of Yesterday. The Man Behind the Mask*. 1937: *Death Croons the Blues. Jump for Glory* (US: *When Thief Meets Thief*). *Old Mother Riley*. 1939: *Discoveries. Inquest. Trunk Crime. Meet Maxwell Archer* (US: *Maxwell Archer, Detective*). 1940: *Tilly of Bloomsbury. The Second Mr Bush. *Bringing It Home*. 1941: *Telefootlers. The Prime Minister. This Man is Dangerous/The Patient Vanishes. He Found a Star*. 1942: *Commandos Strike at Dawn*. 1943: *Phantom of the Opera. Forever and a Day. Mission to Moscow. The Uninvited. Jane Eyre*. 1944: *Gaslight* (GB: *The Murder in Thornton Square*). 1945: *The Valley of Decision*. 1946: *Wanted for Murder*. 1947: *Frieda*. 1949: *Children of Chance. Madeleine*. 1950: *Tony Draws a Horse*. 1954: *An Inspector Calls*. 1957: *The Safecracker*. 1959: *Upstairs and Downstairs*. 1961: *The Damned* (US: *These Are the Damned*). *Dangerous Afternoon. El Cid*. 1962: *The Man Who Finally Died*. 1963: *Nurse on Wheels*. 1965: *Rotten to the Core*. 1967: *Franchette*.

**FAIRBROTHER, Sydney**
(S. Tapping) 1872-1941
Petite, fair-haired British actress, attractive even in old age, who had a strong personality and played mostly indomitable and independent cockney ladies in comedy films, occasionally in leading roles. On stage at 17, she had a few indeterminate character roles in silent films, but came into her own in British films of the 1930s; her personal popularity boosted several minor comedies and added zest to major ones. Retired in 1938.

1915: *Iron Justice*. 1916: *The Mother of Dartmoor. Frailty/Temptation's Hour. The Game of Liberty. Me and Me Moke* (US: *Me and M' Pal*). *Mother. A Mother's Influence*. 1917: *Auld Lang Syne*. 1919: *In Bondage*. 1920: *A Temporary Gentleman. Laddie. The Children of Gibeon*. 1921: *The Bachelors'*

ABOVE Barbara Everest (seated) puts on her 'anxious' look as
Mother Riley (Arthur Lucan) turns up selling matches at a
stately home in *Old Mother Riley* (1937). Patrick Ludlow looks on

BELOW Diminutive but dominant British actress Sydney
**Fairbrother** looks to have taken director Thornton Freeland's
measure in this script conference for *Brewster's Millions* (1934)

Club. The Rotters. The Golden Dawn. 1923: Married Love (US: Maisie's Marriage). Heartstrings. Love, Life and Laughter. The Beloved Vagabond. The Rest Cure. Don Quixote. Sally Bishop. 1924: Reveille. The Happy Prisoner. *Wanted, a Boy. 1925: *Mrs May (series). 1926: Nell Gwynne. 1927: The Silver Lining. Confetti. My Lord the Chauffeur. 1928: *The Market Square. 1931: The Other Mrs Phipps. Murder on the Second Floor. The Temperance Fete. 1932: The Third String. *Postal Orders. A Letter of Warning. Double Dealing. Down Our Street. Insult. Lucky Ladies. The Return of Raffles. 1933: Excess Baggage. Home Sweet Home. *Dora. 1934: *A Touching Story. The Crucifix. Chu Chin Chow. Gay Love. Brewster's Millions. 1935: The Private Secretary. The Last Journey. 1936: Fame. All In. 1937: Dreaming Lips. Rose of Tralee. King Solomon's Mines. Paradise for Two (US: The Gaiety Girls). 1938: Make It Three. Little Dolly Daydream.

**FARNSWORTH, Richard** 1920-2000
Although many of his 'roles' in films were stuntwork and are not recorded here, this lean, grey, twinkle-eyed, droop-moustached American player deserves his place in this book for sheer durability. An ex-rodeo rider, he was stunting at 16, before becoming regular stunt man for Roy Rogers and an 'occasional' for other cowboy stars. 'I'd go out and drive my head into the ground and get a bigger cheque than they would,' he says. Eventually, he 'just got tired of doing stunt work. The ground was gettin' kinda hard.' Small parts came along ('I'd be drivin' a coach or something that needed lines') and escalated in recent years to the point where he was nominated for an Oscar in Comes a Horseman and won a Canadian Oscar for The Grey Fox.

1937: A Day at the Races. 1938: The Adventures of Marco Polo. 1944: This Is the Army. 1948: Red River. 1953: The Wild One. 1957: The Tin Star. 1960: Spartacus. 1965: Duel at Diablo. 1966: Texas Across the River. 1971: The Cowboys. Pocket Money. 1972: The Life and Times of Judge Roy Bean. 1975: Strange New World (TV). 1976: The Duchess and the Dirtwater Fox. 1977: Un

autre homme, une autre chance (GB: Another Man, Another Woman. US: Another Man, Another Chance). 1978: Comes a Horseman. 1980: Tom Horn. Ruckus. Resurrection. 1981: The Legend of the Lone Ranger. 1982: Independence Day. The Grey Fox. Travis McGee (TV). 1983: Ghost Dancing (TV). 1984: The Natural. Rhinestone. 1985: Sylvester. The Last Frontier.

**FAYLEN, Frank**
(F. Ruf) 1907- 1985
Thin, wiry, tough-looking American supporting player with a shock of fairish curly hair and a face you couldn't trust, often half-concealed beneath tip-tilted trilby. He had his best roles in the mid-1940s, notably as the male nurse, Bim, in The Lost Weekend. On stage in his parents' vaudeville act at 18 months, he switched from song-and-dance on stage to tough guys on film in his twenties. Married to actress Carol Hughes (1921-) since 1936.

1935: Thanks a Million. 1936: Down the Stretch. King of Hockey (GB: King of the Ice Rink). Bullets or Ballots. The Golden Arrow. Night Waitress. Smart Blonde. China Clipper. Gold Diggers of 1937. Border Flight. 1937: Wine, Women and Horses. The Cherokee Strip (GB: Strange Laws). That Certain Woman. Marked Woman. Kid Galahad. Talent Scout. The Case of the Stuttering Bishop. They Won't Forget. Headin' East. Dance, Charlie, Dance. Mr Dodd Takes the Air. Public Wedding. San Quentin. Ever Since Eve. Back in Circulation. 1938: The Invisible Menace. *Crime Rave. Too Hot to Handle. 1939: Five Came Back. Thunder Afloat. Waterfront. Reno. Nick Carter—Master Detective. No Place to Go. The Star Maker. It's a Wonderful World. Gone With the Wind. The Story of Vernon and Irene Castle. Lucky Night. Women in the Wind. Edison the Man. 1940: Curtain Call. Margie. Married and In Love. No Time for Comedy. The Grapes of Wrath. The Fighting 69th. Brother Orchid. Castle on the Hudson (GB: Years without Days). They Drive By Night (GB: The Road to Frisco). Pop Always Pays. 1941: Come Live With Me. Thieves Fall Out. City Limits. Knockout/Right to the Heart. Let's Go Collegiate (GB: Farewell to Fame). Top Sergeant Mulligan. Father Steps Out. No

Hands on the Clock. Affectionately Yours. International Squadron. Model Wife. Johnny Eager. Sergeant York. Unholy Partners. Footsteps in the Dark. The Reluctant Dragon. 1942: Across the Pacific. Star Spangled Rhythm. The Palm Beach Story. Dudes Are Pretty People. Fall In. Maisie Gets Her Man (GB: She Got Her Man). Somewhere I'll Find You. Wake Island. The Hard Way. Yankee Doodle Dandy. About Face. A-Haunting We Will Go. Joe Smith—American (GB: Highway to Freedom). Whispering Ghosts. The McGuerins from Brooklyn. 1943: Thank Your Lucky Stars. Silver Skates. She's for Me. Taxi, Mister. Mission To Moscow. That Nazty Nuisance. Good Morning, Judge. Yanks Ahoy. Prairie Chickens. Get Going. The Mystery of the 13th Guest. Salute for Three. Three Hearts for Julia. Corvette K-225 (GB: The Nelson Touch). The Gang's All Here (GB: The Girls He Left Behind). Tarzan's Desert Mystery. The Falcon Strikes Back. Follow the Band. A Guy Named Joe. Slightly Dangerous. 1944: The Canterville Ghost. Address Unknown. And the Angels Sing. Standing Room Only. An American Romance. See Here, Private Hargrove. 1945: The Affairs of Susan. Duffy's Tavern. You Came Along. The Lost Weekend. *Boogie Woogie. Bring on the Girls. The Incendiary Blonde. Masquerade in Mexico. The Blue Dahlia. 1946: Our Hearts Were Growing Up. To Each His Own. The Well-Groomed Bride. Blue Skies. It's a Wonderful Life! Two Years Before the Mast. Cross My Heart. California. 1947: Welcome Stranger. Variety Girl. Road to Rio. Easy Come, Easy Go. The Perils of Pauline. Suddenly It's Spring. The Trouble with Women. 1948: Hazard. Race Street. Blood on the Moon. Whispering Smith. 1949: Francis. †Two Mugs from Brooklyn/Two Knights from Brooklyn. 1950: Copper Canyon. The Eagle and the Hawk. Convicted. The Nevadan (GB: The Man from Nevada). 1951: Detective Story. My Favorite Spy. Father's Little Dividend. Fourteen Hours. Passage West (GB: High Venture). 1952: The Sniper. The Lusty Men. Hangman's Knot. 1953: 99 River Street. 1954: The Lone Gun. Red Garters. Riot in Cell Block 11. 1955: The Looters. The McConnell Story (GB: Tiger in the Sky). 1956: Away All Boats. Seventh Cavalry. Everything But the Truth. Terror at Midnight (GB: And Suddenly You Run). 1957: Three Brave Men. Dino (GB: Killer Dino). 1960: North to Alaska. 1965: Fluffy. When the Boys Meet the Girls. The Monkey's Uncle. 1968: Funny Girl.

†Combined GB version of 1942/3 films The McGuerins from Brooklyn and Taxi, Mister

**FELD, Fritz** 1900- 1993
Tall, usually moustachioed, lisping German-born comic actor, in U.S. from 1922 (with the director Max Reinhardt), and soon in sound films as the archetypal, fussy, sardonic head waiter. His leaning stance, foreign accent and the champagne-cork noise he made with his cheek soon made him an unmistakeable part of the Hollywood scene. He was busy with stage

work and promoting his writing career through most of the 1930s, but from 1937 settled in to provide dozens of amusing cameos for the cinema. Married to equally successful character player Virginia Christine (*qv*) since 1940. A co-founder of the Hollywood Playhouse.

*1917: Der Golem und die Tänzerin. 1928: The Last Command. A Ship Comes In (GB: His Country). Blindfold. 1929: One Hysterical Night. The Charlatan. Broadway. Black Magic. 1937: Expensive Husbands. I Met Him in Paris. Hollywood Hotel. Tovarich. True Confession. Lancer Spy. 1938: Go Chase Yourself. Campus Confessions (GB: Fast Play). Romance in the Dark. Bringing Up Baby. The Affairs of Annabel. Artists and Models Abroad (GB: Stranded in Paris). Gold Diggers in Paris (GB: The Gay Impostors). I'll Give a Million. 1939: Idiot's Delight. At the Circus. When Tomorrow Comes. Little Accident. Everything Happens at Night. 1940: It's a Date. Millionaire Playboy. Victory. Little Old New York. Ma, He's Making Eyes at Me. I Was an Adventuress. Sandy Is a Lady. 1941: Four Jacks and a Jill. World Premiere. Mexican Spitfire's Baby. Three Sons o' Guns. You Belong to Me (GB: Good Morning, Doctor!). Skylark. 1942: Shut My Big Mouth. Sleepytime Gal. Maisie Gets Her Man (GB: She Gets Her Man). Iceland (GB: Katina). 1943: Henry Aldrich Swings It (GB: Henry Swings It). Phantom of the Opera. Holy Matrimony. 1944: Four Jills in a Jeep. Knickerbocker Holiday. Passport to Adventure. Take It Big. Ever Since Venus. 1945: The Great John L (GB: A Man Called Sullivan). George White's Scandals. Captain Tugboat Annie. 1946: Catman of Paris (filmed 1940). Wife of Monte Cristo. Her Sister's Secret. Gentleman Joe Palooka. 1947: Carnival in Costa Rica. The Secret Life of Walter Mitty. Fun on a Weekend. 1948: If You Knew Susie. The Noose Hangs High. Julia Misbehaves. Trouble Makers. My Girl Tisa. You Gotta Stay Happy. Mexican Hayride. 1949: The Lovable Cheat. Appointment With Danger (released 1951). 1950: The Jackpot. Belle of Old Mexico. 1951: Missing Women. Rhythm Inn. Kentucky Jubilee. Sky High. Little Egypt (GB: Chicago Masquerade). 1952: Aaron Slick from Punkin Crick (GB: Marshmallow Moon). O Henry's Full House (GB: Full House). Has Anybody Seen My Gal? 1953: Casanova's Big Night. Call Me Madam. 1954: Riding Shotgun. Living It Up. Crime Wave (GB: The City Is Dark). 1955: Jail Busters. 1957: Up in Smoke. 1959: Juke Box Rhythm. Don't Give Up the Ship. 1961: Pocketful of Miracles. Ladies' Man. The Errand Boy. 1963: Wives and Lovers. Who's Minding the Store? Four for Texas. 1964: The Patsy. 1965: Harlow. The Miracle of Santa's White Reindeer. 1966: Three on a Couch. 1967: Caprice. Barefoot in the Park. 1968: The Wicked Dreams of Paula Schultz. 1969: The Comic. Hello, Dolly! The Computer Wore Tennis Shoes. The Phynx. 1970: Which Way to the Front? (GB: Ja! Ja! Mein General, But Which Way to the Front?). 1972: Call Her Mom (TV). 1973: Herbie Rides Again. 1974: Only with Married Men (TV). 1975: The Strongest Man in the World. The Sunshine Boys. Won Ton Ton, the Dog Who Saved Hollywood. 1976: Silent Movie. Freaky Friday. 1977: The World's Greatest Lover. 1980: Herbie Goes Bananas. 1981: History of the World Part I. 1982: Heidi's Song (voice only). 1983: Last of the Great Survivors (TV).*

**FELL, Norman** 1924–1998
Sad-eyed, worried-looking, light-haired American actor who started to mix films with TV and theatre from the late 1950s, and proved as adept with a throwaway gag as a straight dramatic role. Mostly, though (and especially on TV), he played superiors who did the fretting while the hero went his own sweet way. Was an Air Force aerial gunner during World War II.

*1959: Pork Chop Hill. 1960: The Rat Race. Inherit the Wind. Ocean's 11. 1962: PT 109. 1963: It's a Mad, Mad, Mad, Mad World. Sergeant Ryker (TV. Later issued to cinemas). 1964: The Killers. The Hanged Man (TV. GB: cinemas). Quick, Before It Melts. 1966: The Young Warriors. 1967: The Secret War of Harry Frigg. Fitzwilly (GB: Fitzwilly Strikes Back). The Movie Maker (TV). The Graduate. 1968: Bullitt. The Young Runaways. 1969: Three's a Crowd (TV). If It's Tuesday, This Must Be Belgium. 1970: Rabbit Test. The Boatniks. Catch 22. 1972: The Heist (TV). 1973: The Stone Killer. Charley Varrick. 1974: Thursday's Game* (made for cinemas but shown only on TV). *Airport 1975. 1975: Death Stalk (TV). Cleopatra Jones and the Casino of Gold. 1976: Richie Brockelman: The Missing 24 Hours (TV). Guardian of the Wilderness. 1978: The End. 1981: Paternity. On the Right Track. Kinky Coaches and the Pom Pom Pussycats. 1983: Uncommon Valor (TV).*

**FERGUSON, Frank** 1899–1978
Light-haired American actor whose bedraggled toothbrush moustache gave him a faintly gloomy look. Mostly just a townsman, but seen down the years in dozens of different kinds of role, although usually a professional man on either side of the law. Came to Hollywood from Broadway with the shortage of acting talent in the wartime years and stayed for more than two decades, gradually improving the quality of his roles, and later settling in a niche in TV's *Peyton Place*. Died from cancer.

*1940: Father is a Prince. *Sockaroo. Gambling on the High Seas. 1941: They Died With Their Boots On. You'll Never Get Rich. The Body Disappears. 1942: Spy Ship. You Were Never Lovelier. City of Silent Men. Boss of Big Town. My Gal Sal. Broadway. Reap the Wild Wind. Ten Gentlemen from West Point. This Gun for Hire. 1943: Truck Busters. Mission to Moscow. Pilot No. 5. 1945: The Dolly Sisters. Rhapsody in Blue. 1946: Little Miss Big (GB: The Baxter Millions). Swell Guy. Night and Day. Canyon Passage. Cross My Heart. The Searching Wind. Lady Chasers. Secrets of a Sorority Girl (GB: Secret of Linda Hamilton). If I'm Lucky. Blonde for a Day. The Perfect Marriage. OSS. The Man I Love. California. 1947: They Won't Believe Me. T-Men. Variety Girl. The Beginning or the End? The Farmer's Daughter. The Perils of Pauline. Blaze of Noon. Cass Timberlane. The Fabulous Texan. Welcome Stranger. Road to Rio. Killer at Large. 1948: Fort Apache. They Live by Night. Abbott and Costello Meet Frankenstein (GB: Abbott and Costello Meet the Ghosts). The Hunted. Miracle of the Bells. The Vicious Circle. The Walls of Jericho. Walk a Crooked Mile. The Inside Story. The Wonderful Urge. Rachel and the Stranger. Fighting Father Dunne. 1949: Caught. The Barkleys of Broadway. Follow Me Quietly. Free for All. State Department—File 649 (GB: Assignment in China). Slightly French. Dynamite.*

Shockproof. Roseanna McCoy. Dancing in the Dark. 1950: He's a Cockeyed Wonder. The West Point Story (GB: Fine and Dandy). Frenchie. Under Mexicali Skies. Tyrant of the Sea. The Good Humor Man. The Great Missouri Raid. The Furies. Right Cross. Key to the City. Louisa. 1951: Thunder in God's Country. Santa Fé. Elopement. Warpath. The People Against O'Hara. On Dangerous Ground. The Barefoot Mailman. The Cimarron Kid. The Model and the Marriage Broker. Boots Malone. 1952: Rancho Notorious. Wagons West. Rodeo. It Grows on Trees. The Lone Hand. Bend of the River (GB: Where the River Bends). Has Anybody Seen My Gal? Ma and Pa Kettle at the Fair. The Marrying Kind. Oklahoma Annie. The Winning Team. Million Dollar Mermaid (GB: The One-Piece Bathing Suit). Stars and Stripes Forever (GB: Marching Along). Models Inc (GB: That Kind of Girl). Room for One More. 1953: Main Street to Broadway. The Beast from 20,000 Fathoms. Big Leaguer. The Marksman. Star of Texas. The Woman They Almost Lynched. Wicked Woman. Trouble along the Way. House of Wax. Powder River. Outlaw Territory/Hannah Lee. Texas Badman. The Blue Gardenia. 1954: Johnny Guitar. A Star Is Born. The Shanghai Story. The Outcast (GB: The Fortune Hunter). Young at Heart. Drum Beat. Moonfleet. The Violent Men (GB: Rough Company). Riding Shotgun. 1955: Battle Cry. New York Confidential. A Lawless Street. The Eternal Sea. The McConnell Story (GB: Tiger in the Sky). At Gunpoint! (GB: Gunpoint!). City of Shadows. 1956: Tribute to a Bad Man. 1957: This Could Be the Night. The Phantom Stagecoach. The Iron Sheriff. Gun Duel in Durango. The Lawless Eighties. 1958: The Light in the Forest. Cole Younger, Gunfighter. Andy Hardy Comes Home. Terror in a Texas Town. Man of the West. 1959: The Big Night. 1960: Sunrise at Campobello. Raymie. 1961: Pocketful of Miracles. 1964: Those Calloways. Hush ... Hush, Sweet Charlotte. The Quick Gun. 1965: The Great Sioux Massacre. 1969: Along Came a Spider (TV).

**FETCHIT, Stepin**
(Lincoln Perry) 1898- 1985
Gloomy-looking black actor who, after beginning his career in minstrel shows, had

a great success as the slow-moving Gummy in Hearts in Dixie (1929) and repeated it over and over again. Although reviled in later years over his 'Yas'm; Iza Comin' image, Fetchit became the first great black Hollywood star, at one time owning six houses and a fleet of limousines (including a pink one)—but went bankrupt in 1945. Tried a comeback in the 1950s, but his image was passé.

1927: In Old Kentucky. 1928: Nameless Men. The Tragedy of Youth. The Devil's Skipper. 1929: Show Boat. Hearts in Dixie. Big Time. Salute. Fox Movietone Follies of 1929. Thru Different Eyes. The Kid's Clever. The Ghost Talks. 1930: Cameo Kirby. Swing High. The Big Fight. 1931: Neck and Neck. The Wild Horse. The Prodigal. 1934: David Harum. The World Moves On. Stand Up and Cheer. Carolina (GB: The House of Connelly). Judge Priest. Bachelor of Arts. Marie Galante. 1935: Helldorado. One More Spring. The Virginia Judge. The County Chairman. Steamboat 'Round the Bend. Charlie Chan in Egypt. 1936: 36 Hours to Kill. Dimples. 1937: On the Avenue. Love Is News. Fifty Roads to Town. 1938: His Exciting Night. 1939: Zenobia (GB: Elephants Never Forget). 1947: Miracle in Harlem. 1952: Sudden Fear. Bend of the River (GB: Where the River Bends). 1953: The Sun Shines Bright. 1974: Amazing Grace. 1975: Won Ton Ton, the Dog Who Saved Hollywood.

**FIELDING, Fenella** 1932-
Plummy-voiced, doe-eyed, dark-haired British comedy actress with extravagant figure. After she sprang to fame in West End revue, British films decided she was too good to miss, and they were right. The only trouble was that they never figured out what to do with her. In the mid-1960s they came close, but, alas, she was allowed to go back to the stage.

1959: Follow a Star. 1960: Doctor in Love. Foxhole in Cairo. No Love for Johnnie. 1961: Carry on Regardless. In the Doghouse. 1962: The Old Dark House. 1963: Doctor in Distress. 1965: How to Undress in Public Without Undue Embarrassment (narrator only). 1966: Doctor in Clover. *Road to St Tropez (narrator only). Carry On Screaming. Drop Dead

Darling (US: Arrivederci, Baby!) 1969: Lock Up Your Daughters! 1970: Dougal and the Blue Cat (voice only).

**FINLAYSON, James** 1887-1953
Scrawny Scotsman with bald head, walrus moustache and wizened features, imperishably associated with Laurel and Hardy through the 33 shorts and features he made with them, almost entirely with the Hal Roach studio where Finlayson got his own first starring opportunities in the early 1920s. Although no great actor, Finlayson had an amazing facial range, squeezing one eye almost closed while widening the other, as part of his famous 'double take and fade away'. In 1934/5, he made a series of small comedy features in England, but soon returned to America—and Stan and Ollie. Died from a heart attack.

1920: Married Life. 1921: A Small Town Idol. Home Talent. 1922: The Crossroads of New York. Home-Made Movies. 1923: Hollywood. 1925: Welcome Home. 1927: *With Love and Hisses. *Love 'Em and Weep. *Do Detectives Think? *Hats Off. *Flying Elephants. * Sugar Daddies. *The Call of the Cuckoos. *The Second Hundred Years. No Man's Law. 1928: Lady Be Good. Ladies' Night in a Turkish Bath (GB: Ladies' Night). Show Girl. Bachelor's Paradise. 1929: *Big Business. *Liberty. *Men o' War. *The Hoose Gow. Two Weeks Off. Hard To Get. Wall Street. 1930: *Dollar Dizzy. *Night Owls. *Another Fine Mess. For the Defense. Young Eagles. Flight Commander. The Dawn Patrol. 1931: Big Business (and 1929 short). *One of the Smiths. *False Roomers. *A Melon-Drama. *Catch As Catch Can. *Oh! Oh! Cleopatra. *Scratch As Catch Can. *One Good Turn. *Our Wife. *Chickens Come Home. *The Hasty Marriage. Pardon Us (GB: Jailbirds). Stout Hearts and Willing Hands. 1932: *The Chimp. *Boy, Oh, Boy. †*Any Old Port. *The Iceman's Ball. Pack Up Your Troubles. Thunder Below. *The Millionaire Cat. *Jitters the Butler. 1933: The Devil's Brother (GB: Fra Diavolo). *Mush and Milk. *Me and My Pal. *His Silent Racket. *Hokus Fokus. *The Druggist's Dilemma. *The Gay Nighties. The Girl in Possession. Dick Turpin. 1934: What Happened to Harkness. Oh! No, Doctor. Big

Business (and 1931 feature and 1929 short). Father and Son. Nine Forty Five. 1935: Handle with Care. Who's Your Father? *Thicker Than Water. Bonnie Scotland. *Manhattan Monkey Business. 1936: The Bohemian Girl. Our Relations. *Life Hesitates at 40. 1937: All Over Town. Pick a Star. Way Out West. Angel. 1938: Block-Heads. Wise Girl. 1939: The Great Victor Herbert. The Flying Deuces. Hollywood Cavalcade. 1939-40: Raffles. 1940: A Chump at Oxford. Saps at Sea. 1942: To Be or Not To Be. 1943: Yanks Ahoy! 1946: Till the Clouds Roll By. 1947: The Perils of Pauline. Thunder in the Valley (GB: Bob, Son of Battle). 1948: Grand Canyon Trail. 1950: Royal Wedding (GB: Wedding Bells). 1951: Here Comes the Groom.

†Scenes deleted from final release print

**FITZGERALD, Walter**
(W. Bond) 1896-1976
Square-faced, reliable-looking, solidly built British actor who projected honesty and integrity with gritty conviction. He abandoned a career on the Stock Exchange for studies at RADA and, after a late start to his film career, enjoyed a particularly good run of roles from 1942 to 1950. Also very busy in the theatre and on TV.

1932: Murder at Covent Garden. 1941: This England. 1942: In Which We Serve. Squadron Leader X. 1943: San Demetrio London. 1944: Strawberry Roan. 1945: Great Day. 1947: Mine Own Executioner. Blanche Fury. 1948: This Was a Woman. The Fallen Idol. The Winslow Boy. The Small Back Room. 1949: Edward My Son. 1950: Treasure Island. 1951: Flesh and Blood. 1952: The Pickwick Papers. The Ringer. The Net (US: Project M7). Appointment in London. 1953: The Cruel Sea. Twice Upon a Time. Personal Affair. Front Page Story. Our Girl Friday (US: The Adventures of Sadie). 1954: Lease of Life. 1955: Cockleshell Heroes. 1956: The Man in the Sky (US: Decision Against Time). 1957: The Birthday Present. 1958: The Camp on Blood Island. Something of Value. Darby O'Gill and the Little People. 1959: Third Man on the Mountain. 1962: HMS Defiant (US: Damn the Defiant!). We Joined the Navy. 1963: Decision at Midnight.

**FIX, Paul**
(P. F. Morrison) 1901-1983
Wry-faced American actor with light brown hair. He only fenced with films until the 1930s when he became a Hollywood fixture, one of many players whose faces were more familiar than their names, at first often in unsympathetic roles such as cowardly crooks. Later Fix film characters pursued a policy of non-aggression and a succession of sheriffs, taxi-drivers, judges, seamen, ranchers and priests established him well on the right side of the law. His mild-mannered, dry-humoured approach made him something of a lesser Barry Fitzgerald.

1920: The Adventuress. 1926: Hoodoo Ranch. 1927: Chicago. 1928: The First Kiss. 1929: Lucky Star. Trial Marriage. 1930: Ladies Love Brutes. Man Trouble. 1931: Bad Girl. Three Girls Lost. The Fighting Sheriff. Good Bad Girl. 1932: The Last Mile. Dancers in the Dark. Scarface (The Shame of a Nation). *Free Eaters. South of the Rio Grande. Back Street. Fargo Express. The Racing Strain. Sky Devils. 1933: Zoo in Budapest. Hard to Handle. The Sphinx. The Avenger. The Mad Game. Gun Law. Somewhere in Sonora. Emergency Call. The Devil's Mate (GB: He Knew Too Much). 1934: Little Man, What Now? Rocky Rhodes. The Woman Who Dared. Flirtation Walk. The Count of Monte Cristo. 1935: The Desert Trail. The Eagle's Brood. Let 'Em Have It (GB: False Faces). Men Without Names. Bar-20 Rides Again. Miss Pacific Fleet. The Crimson Trail. The World Accuses. His Fighting Blood. The Throwback. Mutiny Ahead. Living on Velvet. Valley of Wanted Men. Bulldog Courage. Millions in the Air. Don't Bet on Blondes. Reckless. 1936: Road to Glory. Charlie Chan at the Race Track. The Phantom Patrol. Yellowstone. Straight from the Shoulder. The Prisoner of Shark Island. The Ex-Mrs Bradford. Winterset. The Plot Thickens (GB: The Swinging Pearl Mystery). Two in a Crowd. After the Thin Man. The Bridge of Sighs. 1937: Souls at Sea. Western Gold (GB: The Mysterious Stranger). Armored Car. Paid to Dance. King of Gamblers. The Game That Kills. Woman in Distress. Daughter of Shanghai. Border Café. On Such a Night. 1938: King of Alcatraz

(GB: King of the Alcatraz). Gun Law. The Buccaneer. Mannequin. Penitentiary. When G-Men Step In. Crime Ring. Mr Moto's Gamble. The Saint in New York. Smashing the Rackets. The Night Hawk. Crime Takes a Holiday. 1939: Mutiny on the Blackhawk. Two Thoroughbreds. Disbarred. Wall Street Cowboy. They All Come Out. The Girl and the Gambler. News is Made at Night.*Heritage of the Desert. Those High Gray Walls (GB: The Gates of Alcatraz). Star Reporter. Behind Prison Gates. Code of the Streets. Undercover Doctor. 1940: The Ghost Breakers. Outside the Three-Mile Limit (GB: Mutiny on the Seas). The Crooked Road. Black Friday. Dr Cyclops. Triple Justice. Black Diamonds. Virginia City. Glamour for Sale. Queen of the Mob. Strange Cargo. The Fargo Kid. Trail of the Vigilantes. The Great Plane Robbery. 1941: A Missouri Outlaw. Citadel of Crime (GB: Outside the Law). Down Mexico Way. H. M. Pulham Esq. Unfinished Business. Public Enemies. The Roar of the Press. 1942: Pittsburgh. Highways by Night. That Other Woman. South of Santa Fé. Sherlock Holmes and the Secret Weapon. Jail House Blues. Escape from Crime. Kid Glove Killer. Youth on Parade. Sleepytime Gal. Dr Gillespie's New Assistant. 1943: Hitler—Dead or Alive. Mug Town. Captive Wild Woman. Bombardier. In Old Oklahoma (later War of the Wildcats). The Unknown Guest. 1944: The Fighting Seabees. Tall in the Saddle. 1945: Flame of the Barbary Coast. Grissly's Millions. Back to Bataan. Dakota. 1947: Tycoon. 1948: Wake of the Red Witch. Angel in Exile. Red River. Strange Gamble. Force of Evil. The Plunderers. 1949: The Fighting Kentuckian. She Wore a Yellow Ribbon. Hellfire. Fighting Man of the Plains. 1950: California Passage. Surrender. Jet Pilot (released 1957). The Great Missouri Raid. 1951: Warpath. 1952: What Price Glory? Ride the Man Down. Denver and Rio Grande. 1953: Star of Texas. Fair Wind to Java. Island in the Sky. Devil's Canyon. 1954: Hondo. Johnny Guitar. Ring of Fear. The High and the Mighty. 1955: Top of the World. The Sea Chase. Blood Alley. 1956: Giant. Santiago (GB: The Gun Runner). Toward the Unknown (GB: Brink of Hell). Man in the Vault. The Bad Seed. Stagecoach to Fury. 1957: Night Passage. The Devil's Hairpin. Man in the Shadow (GB: Pay the Devil). 1958: Guns, Girls and Gangsters. Lafayette Escadrille (GB: Hell Bent for Glory). The Notorious Mr Monks. 1962: To Kill a Mockingbird. 1963: Mail Order Bride (GB: West of Montana). 1964: The Outrage. 1965: Baby, the Rain Must Fall. The Sons of Katie Elder. Shenandoah. 1966: Nevada Smith. An Eye for an Eye. Ride Beyond Vengeance. Incident at Phantom Hill. Welcome to Hard Times (GB: Killer on a Horse). 1967: El Dorado. The Ballad of Josie. Winchester '73 (TV). 1968: The Day of the Evil Gun. 1969: The Undefeated. The Profane Comedy/Set This Town on Fire (TV). Young Billy Young. Zabriskie Point. 1970: Dirty Dingus Magee. The House on Greenapple Road (TV). 1971: Something Big. Shoot Out. 1972: Night of the

*Lepus. 1973: Cahill, US Marshal (GB: Cahill). Pat Garrett and Billy the Kid. Guilty or Innocent: the Sam Sheppard Murder Case (TV). 1977: Grayeagle. The City (TV). 1978: Just Me and You. Wanda Nevada. 1979: Hanging by a Thread (TV).*

## FLEMING, Ian 1888-1969

Diffident, dogged, self-effacing, reliable-looking Australian-born actor in British films; his acting career spanned more than 60 years. On stage in Australia at 16, he came to Britain in 1914, then made his name in films at the beginning of sound as an excellent Dr Watson to Arthur Wontner's Sherlock Holmes in several Conan Doyle adventures. After that he was kept busy for 30 years, often as professional men offering level-headed advice.

*1926: Second to None. 1928: The Ware Case. 1929: The Devil's Maze. 1930: The School for Scandal. 1931: The Sleeping Cardinal (US: Sherlock Holmes' Fatal Hour). 1932: The Missing Rembrandt. Lucky Girl. After Dark. 1933: Called Back. Paris Plane. 1934: The Third Clue. Passing Shadows. 1935: The Riverside Murder. The Triumph of Sherlock Holmes. School for Stars. Sexton Blake and the Mademoiselle. The Crouching Beast. 1936: 21 Today. Prison Breaker. 1937: Darby and Joan. Racing Romance. Jump for Glory (US: When Thief Meets Thief). Silver Blaze (US: Murder at the Baskervilles). 1938: Almost a Honeymoon. Ghost Tales Retold. Dial 999. Bad Boy. The Reverse Be My Lot. Quiet Please. The Return of Carol Deane. Double or Quits. If I Were Boss. 1939: The Nursemaid Who Disappeared. Men without Honour. Shadowed Eyes. The Lion Has Wings. The Good Old Days. 1940: Gentleman of Venture (US: It Happened to One Man). The Briggs Family. Tilly of Bloomsbury. Night Train to Munich (US: Night Train). 1941: Hatter's Castle. Jeannie (US: Girl in Distress). They Flew Alone (US: Wings and the Woman). 1942: Next of Kin. Sabotage at Sea. Let the People Sing. Salute John Citizen. Soldiers Without Uniform. Talk About Jacqueline. 1943: Up With the Lark. They Met in the Dark. The Yellow Canary. Bell Bottom George. The Butler's Dilemma. 1944: Tawny Pipit. He Snoops to Conquer. 1945: I Didn't Do It.*

*They Knew Mr Knight. 1946: George in Civvy Street. Appointment With Crime. 1947: Captain Boycott. 1948: Quartet. 1949: For Them That Trespass. What a Carry On. A Matter of Murder. School for Randle. 1950: The Woman in Question (US: Five Angles on Murder). Shadow of the Past. 1951: Chelsea Story. Salute the Toff. 1952: Circumstantial Evidence. Come Back Peter. Hammer the Toff. Crow Hollow. Deadly Nightshade. The Voice of Merrill (US: Murder Will Out). 1953: Recoil. The Saint's Return (US: The Saint's Girl Friday). It's a Grand Life. Stryker of the Yard. Park Plaza 605 (US: Norman Conquest). 1954: The Seekers (US: Land of Fury). The Embezzler. Delayed Action. Companions in Crime. What Every Woman Wants. 1955: Police Dog. 1957: High Flight. 1958: A Woman Possessed. Innocent Meeting. 1959: Web of Suspicion. Man Accused. Crash Drive. Your Money or Your Wife. The Flesh and the Fiends (US: Mania). 1960: Make Mine Mink. Bluebeard's Ten Honeymoons. The Trials of Oscar Wilde (US: The Man with the Green Carnation). Too Hot to Handle (US: Playgirl after Dark). 1961: No, My Darling Daughter! Return of a Stranger. 1962: The Lamp in Assassin Mews. The Boys. 1963: Tamahine. Crooks in Cloisters. 1964: Seventy Deadly Pills. 1965: The Return of Mr Moto. 1967: River Rivals (serial).*

## FLETCHER, Louise 1936-

Tall, square-built, light-haired American actress of forthright manner. Born to deaf parents, she acted steadily in TV series of the late 1950s and early 1960s, but retired in 1964, re-emerging 10 years later with two excellent portrayals of treacherous, unsmiling women in *Thieves Like Us* and *One Flew over the Cuckoo's Nest*, for the second of which she won a Best Actress Oscar. But her height and style possibly limited further appearances, and she has been seen only sporadically since.

*1974: Thieves Like Us. 1975: One Flew Over the Cuckoo's Nest. Russian Roulette. 1977: Exorcist II: The Heretic. 1978: The Cheap Detective. Thou Shalt Not Commit Adultery (TV). 1979: Natural Enemies. The Magician of Lublin. The Lady in Red. 1980: The Lucky Star. Mama Dracula. 1981: Dead Kids.*

*Brainstorm (released 1983). 1983: Strange Invaders. \*Overnight Sensation. 1984: Firestarter. 1985: A Summer to Remember (TV).*

## FLIPPEN, Jay C. 1898-1971

Bulldog-faced, craggy, thick-set American actor with thick, grey curly hair and beetle brows that expressed doubt or incredulity. For years he was a minstrel and comic in travelling shows and made a couple of early two-reeler comedy films. He returned to films in 1947 as a character actor, to play hard eggs who could be comic or genuinely tough, and was much in demand until the end of the fifties. Lost a leg in later years. Died from an aneurysm (swollen artery).

*1928: \*†The Ham What Am. 1929: \*†The Home Edition. 1934: Million Dollar Ransom. Marie Galante. 1947: Brute Force. Intrigue. 1948: They Live By Night. 1949: Down to the Sea in Ships. A Woman's Secret. Oh, You Beautiful Doll. 1950: The Yellow Cab Man. Love That Brute. Winchester 73. Jet Pilot (released 1957). Two Flags West. Buccaneer's Girl. 1951: The Lemon Drop Kid. Flying Leathernecks. The People Against O'Hara. The Lady from Texas. The Model and the Marriage Broker. 1952: Bend of the River (GB: Where the River Bends). The Las Vegas Story. Woman of the North Country. 1953: Thunder Bay. East of Sumatra. Devil's Canyon. The Wild One. 1954: Carnival Story. The Far Country. 1955: Six Bridges to Cross. Man Without a Star. Strategic Air Command. It's Always Fair Weather. Oklahoma! 1956: Kismet. The Killing. The Seventh Cavalry. The King and Four Queens. The Halliday Brand. 1957: Night Passage. Hot Summer Night. Public Pigeon Number One. The Restless Breed. The Deerslayer. The Midnight Story (GB: Appointment With a Shadow). Run of the Arrow. Lure of the Swamp. 1958: Escape from Red Rock. Before I Die (TV). From Hell to Texas (GB: Manhunt). 1960: Wild River. Where the Boys Are. Studs Lonigan. The Plunderers. 1962: Six-Gun Law (TV. GB: cinemas). How the West Was Won. 1964: Looking for Love. 1965: Cat Ballou. 1966: Fame is the Name of the Game (TV). 1967: The Spirit is Willing. Firecreek. 1968: The Sound of Anger (TV). Hellfighters. 1970: The Old Man Who Cried*

Wolf (TV). 1971: Sam Hill—Who Killed the Mysterious Mr Foster? (TV). The Seven Minutes.

†as J. C. Flippin

**FORD, Paul**
(P. F. Weaver) 1901–1976
Lugubrious, balding, bloodhound-jowled American comic actor specializing in outrage and despair. He made his name as the hapless colonel in Phil Silvers' TV 'Bilko' series You'll Never Get Rich in the 1950s. Subsequently Ford, once a puppeteer at the onset of a belated showbusiness career, was a delight in several leading character roles.

1945: The House on 92nd Street. 1948: Naked City. 1949: Lust for Gold. All the King's Men. The Kid from Texas (GB: Texas Kid—Outlaw). 1950: Perfect Strangers (GB: Too Dangerous to Love). 1956: The Teahouse of the August Moon. 1958: The Missouri Traveler. The Matchmaker. 1960: The Right Man (TV). 1961: The Music Man. Advise and Consent. 1962: Who's Got the Action? 1963: It's a Mad, Mad, Mad, Mad World. 1965: Never Too Late. 1966: The Russians Are Coming, the Russians Are Coming. A Big Hand for the Little Lady (GB: Big Deal at Dodge City). The Spy With a Cold Nose. 1967: The Comedians. 1969: In Name Only (TV). 1971: Journey Back to Oz (voice only). 1973: Lola.

**FORD, Wallace**
(Samuel Grundy) 1897–1966
Broad-shouldered, tow-haired, British-

born Hollywood actor who played good-hearted, affable types, tough heroes, Irishmen and gangsters with a soft streak. He hit the headlines in the mid-1930s when seeking (and finding) his long-lost parents in England. His acting improved in stocky character roles, after a few leads in the 1930s, and he remained in films and TV until his death from a heart ailment.

1930: *Absent-Minded. *Fore! The Swellhead (GB: Counted Out). 1931: Possessed. Skyscraper Souls. X Marks the Spot. 1932: Freaks. Beast of the City. Prosperity. Hypnotized. Central Park. Are You Listening? The Wet Parade. The Big Cage. City Sentinel. 1933: Goodbye Again. East of Fifth Avenue (GB: Two in a Million). Employees' Entrance. Headline Shooter (GB: Evidence in Camera). My Woman. Night of Terror. Three Cornered Moon. She Had to Say Yes. 1934: Money Means Nothing. A Woman's Man. Men in White. The Man Who Reclaimed His Head. I Hate Women. The Lost Patrol. The Whole Town's Talking (GB: Passport to Fame). 1935: Another Face (GB: It Happened in Hollywood). The Nut Farm. The Informer. Swell Head (and 1930 film). In Spite of Danger. She Couldn't Take It. Men of the Hour. Get That Man. Mary Burns—Fugitive. One Frightened Night. The Mysterious Mr Wong. Sanders of the River. 1936: OHMS (US: You're in the Army Now). Rogues' Tavern. Two in the Dark. Absolute Quiet. A Son Comes Home. 1937: Jericho (US: Dark Sands). Mad About Money (US: He Loved an Actress). Swing It Sailor. Exiled to Shanghai. 1939: Back Door to Heaven. 1940: Isle of Destiny. Two Girls on Broadway (GB: Change Your Partner). Love, Honor and Oh! Baby. Give Us Wings. The Mummy's Hand. Scatterbrain. 1941: A Man Betrayed (GB: Citadel of Crime). The Roar of the Press. Blues in the Night. Murder by Invitation. 1942: Scattergood Survives a Murder. Inside the Law. X Marks the Spot (and earlier version). All Through the Night. Seven Days' Leave. The Mummy's Tomb. 1943: The Marines Come Through. Shadow of a Doubt. The Cross of Lorraine. The Ape Man. 1944: Secret Command. Machine Gun Mama. 1945: The Woman Who Came Back. The Great John L (GB: A Man Called Sullivan). Spellbound. They Were Expendable. Blood on the Sun. On Stage, Everybody. 1946: The Green Years. A Guy Could Change. Rendezvous with Annie. Crack-Up. The Black Angel. Lover Come Back. Dead Reckoning. 1947: Magic Town. T-Men. 1948: Shed No Tears. Coroner Creek. The Man from Texas. Embraceable You. Bell Starr's Daughter. 1949: Red Stallion in the Rockies. The Set-Up. 1950: The Breaking Point. Dakota Lil. The Furies. Harvey. 1951: Warpath. He Ran All the Way. Painting the Clouds with Sunshine. 1952: Flesh and Fury. Rodeo. 1953: She Couldn't Say No (GB: Beautiful But Dangerous). The Nebraskan. The Great Jesse James Raid. 1954: The Boy from Oklahoma. Destry. Three Ring Circus. 1955: The Man from

Laramie. The Spoilers. Lucy Gallant. A Lawless Street. Wichita. The Ox-Bow Incident (TV. GB: cinemas). 1956: Johnny Concho. The Maverick Queen. The First Texan. Snow Shoes (TV). Stagecoach to Fury. Thunder Over Arizona. The Rainmaker. 1957: The Last Man (TV). 1958: The Last Hurrah. The Matchmaker. Twilight for the Gods. 1959: Warlock. 1961: Tess of the Storm Country. 1965: A Patch of Blue.

**FOSTER, Dudley** 1925–1973
Dark, cadaverous English actor who played scheming and untrustworthy types in British films, alternating leads in second features with characters parts in bigger films. He was particularly good in one minor thriller, Never Mention Murder (1964) but, after four years off screen, he was seen in smaller roles and, in January 1973, committed suicide.

1959: The Two-Headed Spy. 1962: Term of Trial. 1963: Ricochet. 1964: Never Mention Murder. 1965: The Little Ones. A Study in Terror (US: Fog). 1969: Where's Jack? Foreign Exchange (TV). Moon Zero Two. 1970: The Rise and Rise of Michael Rimmer. Wuthering Heights. 1971: Quest for Love. Dulcima. Follow Me (US: The Public Eye). 1972: That's Your Funeral. 1973: Mistress Pamela.

**FOULGER, Byron** 1900–1970
Squat, dark, square-faced, close-cropped, often bespectacled American actor, generally seen as unpleasant characters who

might be treacherous, cringing, servile, edgy or all four. Shuffled his way almost apologetically through scores of roles in the 1930s, 1940s and 1950s, his rat-trap jaws almost inevitably coming into demand for TV series after that, usually as narrow-minded spoilsports. Married to equally prolific character actress Dorothy Adams (qv). Died from a heart condition.

1937: True Confession. The Duke Comes Back (GB: The Call of the Ring). Larceny on the Air. A Day at the Races. Dick Tracy (serial). The Prisoner of Zenda. The Awful Truth. Make Way for Tomorrow. The Luck of Roaring Camp. 1938: I Am a Criminal. Lady in the Morgue (GB: The Case of the Missing Blonde). Fools of Desire/It's All in Your Mind. Born to Be Wild. Tenth Avenue Kid. Delinquent Parents. Tarnished Angel. I Am the Law. You Can't Take It With You. Say It in French. King of the Newsboys. Test Pilot. Gangster's Boy. Listen Darling. The Spider's Web (serial). 1939: At the Circus/Marx Brothers at the Circus. In Name Only. Union Pacific. Let Us Live! Mutiny on the Blackhawk. Exile Express. The Girl from Rio. The Man They Could Not Hang. Television Spy. The Secret of Dr Kildare. Andy Hardy Gets Spring Fever. Mr Smith Goes to Washington. Million Dollar Legs. Some Like It Hot. 1940: Flash Gordon Conquers the Universe (serial). Heroes of the Saddle. The Great McGinty (GB: Down Went McGinty). The Man With Nine Lives (GB: Behind the Door). Edison, the Man. Sky Murder. Ellery Queen, Master Detective. Arizona. Untamed. Dr Kildare's Crisis. Golden Gloves. Boom Town. I Want a Divorce. Parole Fixer. The Saint's Double Trouble. Abe Lincoln in Illinois (GB: Spirit of the People). Opened by Mistake. *Good Bad Guys. 1941: Man-Made Monster (GB: The Electric Man). Remember the Day. Ridin' on a Rainbow. The Gay Vagabond. Sweetheart of the Campus (GB: Broadway Ahead). Mystery Ship. Dude Cowboy. Sullivan's Travels. Harvard, Here I Come (GB: Here I Come). The Penalty. Sis Hopkins. Meet Boston Blackie. You Belong to Me (GB: Good Morning Doctor). She Knew All the Answers. Bedtime Story. H.M. Pulham Esq. *Helping Hands. *Come Back Miss Pipps. 1942: The Panther's Claw. The Tuttles of Tahiti. Man from Headquarters. Reap the Wild Wind. The Palm Beach Story. Quiet Please, Murder. Stand By for Action! (GB: Cargo of Innocents). The Magnificent Dope. Pacific Rendezvous. The Sabotage Squad. Miss Annie Rooney. *Keep 'Em Sailing. 1943: The Human Comedy. So Proudly We Hail! Sweet Rosie O'Grady. The Adventures of a Rookie. In Old Oklahoma (later War of the Wildcats). Hi Diddle Diddle. Hoppy Serves a Writ. Dixie Dugan. Coney Island. Silver Spurs. The Black Raven. Hangmen Also Die. The Falcon strikes Back. What a Woman! (GB: The Beautiful Cheat). Appointment in Berlin. Margin for Error. First Comes Courage. Ministry of Fear. The Power of God. 1944: Enemy of Women. Summer Storm. Roger Touhy—Gangster (GB: The Last Gangster). The Miracle of

Morgan's Creek. The Whistler. Henry Aldrich's Little Secret. Since You Went Away. Dark Mountain. Beautiful But Broke. Swing in the Saddle (GB: Swing and Sway). Marriage is a Private Affair. *He Forgot to Remember. Girl Rush. Three Men in White. Maisie Goes to Reno (GB: You Can't Do That to Me). Casanova Brown. Mrs Parkington. Take It Big. The Great Moment. An American Romance. And Now Tomorrow. Barbary Coast Gent. Ladies of Washington. Music in Manhattan. Ever Since Venus. Lady in the Death House. 1945: The Master Key (serial). Grissly's Millions. Circumstantial Evidence. The Hidden Eye. The Adventures of Kitty O'Day. Arson Squad. The Blonde from Brooklyn. Snafu (GB: Welcome Home). Sensation Hunters. Week-End at the Waldorf. The Lost Weekend. Don Juan Quilligan. Adventure. Nob Hill. Wonder Man. *Purity Squad. The Cheaters. Brewster's Millions. It's in the Bag (GB: The Fifth Chair). Let's Go Steady. Cornered. Scarlet Street. 1946: Sentimental Journey. Just Before Dawn. The Postman Always Rings Twice. The Mysterious Mr M (serial). Till the Clouds Roll By. The French Key. Dick Tracy vs Cueball. The Plainsman and the Lady. House of Horrors (GB: Joan Medford is Missing). The Show Off. Courage of Lassie. The Hoodlum Saint. The Magnificent Doll. Suspense. Deadline at Dawn. Blonde Alibi. Dead Reckoning. 1947: The Michigan Kid. Hard-Boiled Mahoney. The Bells of San Fernando. The Adventures of Don Coyote. Too Many Winners. Stallion Road. The Red Hornet. The Chinese Ring. The Trouble with Women. Unconquered. The Long Night. Easy Come, Easy Go. They Won't Believe Me. Song of Love. Linda Be Good. 1948: The Hunted. Arch of Triumph. Out of the Storm. The Return of October (GB: Date with Destiny). I Surrender Dear. The Three Musketeers. Relentless. Best of the Badmen. A Southern Yankee (GB: My Hero). The Kissing Bandit. The Bride Goes Wild. Let's Live a Little. He Walked by Night. They Live By Night. 1949: Samson and Delilah. I Shot Jesse James. Arson, Inc. The Inspector General. The Dalton Gang. Satan's Cradle. Dancing in the Dark. Red Desert. Streets of Laredo. 1950: The Girl from San Lorenzo. Salt Lake Raiders. The Return of Jesse James. Champagne for Caesar. Experiment Alcatraz. Dark City. Union Station. Riding High. Key to the City. To Please a Lady. 1951: Lightning Strikes Twice. FBI Girl. Footlight Varieties. Gasoline Alley. The Home Town Story. A Millionaire for Christy. The Sea Hornet. Best of the Badmen. Superman and the Mole-Men (GB: Superman and the Strange People). *Hollywood Honeymoon. 1952: Apache Country. My Six Convicts. Cripple Creek. The Steel Fist. Confidentially Connie. Hold That Line. We're Not Married. Skirts Ahoy. The Sniper. The Sword of D'Artagnan. 1953: Paris Model. The Magnetic Monster. Cruisin' Down the River. Bandits of the West. A Perilous Journey. 1954: Cattle Queen of Montana. Silver Lode. 1955: At Gunpoint (GB: Gunpoint!). The Scarlet Coat. The Spoilers. 1956: You Can't

Run Away from It. 1957: The River's Edge. Sierra Stranger. Dino (GB: Killer Dino). The Buckskin Lady. Gun Battle at Monterey. Up In Smoke. 1958: Going Steady. Man from God's Country. The Long, Hot Summer. Onionhead. 1959: King of the Wild Stallions. 1960: Twelve Hours to Kill. Ma Barker's Killer Brood/Bloody Brood. 1961: The Devil's Partner. Pocketful of Miracles. Ride the High Country (GB: Guns in the Afternoon). 1963: Son of Flubber. Who's Minding the Store? 1965: Marriage on the Rocks. 1966: The Gnome-Mobile. The Spirit is Willing. 1969: The Cockeyed Cowboys of Calico County (GB: TV as A Woman for Charlie). 1970: The Love War (TV). There Was a Crooked Man.

**FOWLER, Harry** 1926–
Jaunty British actor with brashly cheerful manner and shovel-shaped face. A former newspaper boy, his distinctive cockney voice got him wartime parts on radio before a film debut in 1942. Enjoyed his finest hour as the leader of the street kids in Hue and Cry, after which he was seen in a long series of character roles, from fat to tiny. Moustachioed from 1970, and latterly starring in TV series. Married to actress Joan Dowling from 1951 to her death in 1954.

1942: Salute John Citizen. Those Kids from Town. Went the Day Well? (US: 48 Hours). 1943: The Demi-Paradise (US: Adventure for Two). Get Cracking. 1944: Give Us the Moon. Don't Take It to Heart. Champagne Charlie. 1945: Painted Boats (US: The Girl on the Canal). 1947: Hue and Cry. 1948: Trouble in the Air. A Piece of Cake. 1949: Landfall. For Them That Trespass. Now Barabbas was a robber ... 1950: Trio. Once a Sinner. She Shall Have Murder. 1951: *Introducing the New Worker. There is Another Sun. The Dark Man. Scarlet Thread. High Treason. Madame Louise. 1952: *A Spot of Bother. I Believe in You. *Food for Thought. Angels One Five. *The Paper Chase. The Last Page (US: Manbait). *Height of Ambition. The Pickwick Papers. *Shedding the Load. Top of the Form. *A Sweeping Statement. 1953: A Day to Remember. Don't Blame the Stork! 1954: Conflict of Wings. Up to His Neck. 1955: Stock Car. The Blue Peter

(US: Navy Heroes). 1956: Fire Maidens from Outer Space. Behind the Headlines. Home and Away. Town on Trial! 1957: The Supreme Secret. West of Suez (US: Fighting Wildcats). Booby Trap. Lucky Jim. The Birthday Present. Soapbox Derby. 1958: I Was Monty's Double (US: Monty's Double). Diplomatic Corpse. 1959: Idle on Parade (US: Idol on Parade). The Heart of a Man. The Dawn Killer (serial). Don't Panic Chaps! 1962: Lawrence of Arabia. The Golliwog. Flight from Singapore. Crooks Anonymous. Tomorrow at Ten. The Longest Day. 1963: Just for Fun. Clash by Night (US: Escape by Night). Ladies Who Do. 70 Deadly Pills. 1965: Life at the Top. Joey Boy. The Nanny. 1966: Doctor in Clover. Secrets of a Windmill Girl. 1968: Two by Two. 1969: Start the Revolution Without Me. 1975: GREAT: Isambard Kingdom Brunel (voice only). 1977: The Prince and the Pauper (US: Crossed Swords). 1980: High Rise Donkey. Sir Henry at Rawlinson End. George and Mildred. 1983: Fanny Hill.

**FOWLEY, Douglas (V)**
(Daniel Fowley). 1911-
Tall, thin-lipped, strong-voiced, dark-eyed American actor who was soon typecast as a villain when he decided to make acting his career after trying various other occupations in the early 1930s. As age tempered his characterizations, they tended to become bemused rather than plain mean; he was notable as the bellowing movie director in *Singin' in the Rain*, and subsequently found ready employers in many TV series.

1933: The Mad Game. 1934: The Gift of Gab. Operator 13 (GB: Spy 13). The Thin Man. The Woman Who Dared. Student Tour. I Hate Women. Let's Talk It Over. The Girl from Missouri (GB: 100 Per Cent Pure). 1935: Miss Pacific Fleet. Straight from the Heart. Transient Lady (GB: False Witness). Night Life of the Gods. Two for Tonight. Old Man Rhythm. 1936: Ring Around the Moon. Dimples. Small Town Girl. Big Brown Eyes. Navy Born. Crash Donovan. Sing, Baby, Sing. Thirty-Six Hours to Kill. 15 Maiden Lane. 1937: Woman Wise. Time Out for Romance. On the Avenue. Fifty Roads to Town. Wake Up and Live. This Is My Affair (GB: His Affair).

One Mile from Heaven. Wild and Woolly. Charlie Chan on Broadway. She Had to Eat. Love and Kisses. City Girl. Passport Husband. 1938: Mr Moto's Gamble. Walking Down Broadway. Alexander's Ragtime Band. Keep Smiling. Time Out for Murder. Inside Story. Submarine Patrol. Arizona Wildcat. 1939: Lucky Night. Dodge City. The Boy Friend. It Could Happen to You. Charlie Chan at Treasure Island. Slightly Honorable. Henry Goes Arizona (GB: Spats to Spurs). 1940: Café Hostess. Twenty-Mule Team. Wagons Westward. Pier 13. The Leather Pushers. Cherokee Strip (GB: Fighting Marshal). East of the River. Ellery Queen, Master Detective. 1941: The Great Swindle. The Parson of Panamint. Tanks a Million. Doctors Don't Tell. Dangerous Lady. Secrets of the Wasteland. Mr District Attorney in the Carter Case (GB: The Carter Case). 1942: Mississippi Gambler. *For the Common Defense. The Devil with Hitler. Pittsburgh. Sunset on the Desert. Somewhere I'll Find You. Mr Wise Guy. Hay Foot. So's Your Aunt Emma. I Live on Danger. The Man in the Trunk. Stand By for Action! (GB: Cargo of Innocents). 1943: Jitterbugs. Johnny Doesn't Live Here Any More. Gildersleeve's Bad Day. Chance of a Lifetime. Bar 20. Minesweeper. Colt Comrades. The Kansan (GB: Wagon Wheels). Sleepy Lagoon. Riding High (GB: Melody Inn). Lost Canyon. 1944: Racket Man. Rationing. One Body Too Many. See Here, Private Hargrove. Shake Hands with Murder. And the Angels Sing. Detective Kitty O'Day. Lady in the Death House. 1945: Don't Fence Me In. Life With Blondie. Along the Navajo Trail. 1946: Chick Carter, Detective. 'Neath Canadian Skies. Her Sister's Secret. Driftin' Along. In Fast Company. The Glass Alibi. Rendezvous 24. North of the Border. Larceny in Her Heart. Freddie Steps Out. Blonde Alibi. High School Hero. 1947: Wild Country. Undercover Maisie (GB: Undercover Girl). Backlash. Three on a Ticket. Yankee Fakir. The Sea of Grass. Jungle Flight. Desperate. The Hucksters. The Trespasser. Gas House Kids in Hollywood. Fall Guy. Scared to Death. Ridin' Down the Trail. Roses Are Red. Merton of the Movies. Rose of Santa Rosa. 1948: Docks of New Orleans. Waterfront at Midnight. If You Knew Susie. The Dude Goes West. Black Bart (GB: Black Bart—Highwayman). Coroner Creek. Joe Palooka in Winner Take All (GB: Winner Take All). Behind Locked Doors. Gun Smugglers. The Denver Kid. Badmen of Tombstone. 1949: Flaxy Martin. Massacre River. Battleground. Susanna Pass. Arson. Search for Danger. Mighty Joe Young. Take Me Out to the Ball Game (GB: Everybody's Cheering). Satan's Cradle. Renegades of the Sage. Joe Palooka in the Counter-Punch. 1950: Bunco Squad. Rider from Tucson. Armored Car Robbery. Hoedown. Edge of Doom (GB: Stronger Than Fear). Killer Shark. He's a Cockeyed Wonder. Mrs O'Malley and Mr Malone. Rio Grande Patrol. Stage to Tucson (GB: Lost Stage Valley). Beware of Blondie. 1951: Chain of Circumstance. Tarzan's Peril (GB: Tarzan and the Jungle Queen). Callaway Went

Thataway (GB: The Star Said No). Across the Wide Missouri. Criminal Lawyer. South of Caliente. 1952: Just This Once. Singin' in the Rain. This Woman is Dangerous. Room for One More. Horizons West. The Man Behind the Gun. 1953: A Slight Case of Larceny. The Band Wagon. Cruisin' Down the River. Kansas Pacific. Casanova's Big Night. 1954: Deep in My Heart. The Naked Jungle. Catwomen of the Moon. The Lone Gun. The High and the Mighty. Three Ring Circus. Untamed Heiress. 1955: The Girl Rush. Texas Lady. 1956: Bandido! The Broken Star. The Man from Del Rio. Rock Pretty Baby. 1957: Bayou. Kelly and Me. The Badge of Marshal Brennan. Raiders of Old California. 1959: These Thousand Hills. 1960: Desire in the Dust. 1961: Barabbas. 1962: Miracle of the White Stallions (GB: Flight of the White Stallions). 1963: Who's Been Sleeping in My Bed? 1964: The Seven Faces of Dr Lao. Guns of Diablo. 1969: The Good Guys and the Bad Guys. 1972: Seeta the Mountain Lion (GB: Run, Cougar, Run). 1973: Walking Tall. Homebodies. 1975: Starsky and Hutch (TV). 1976: Black Oak Conspiracy. The Oregon Trail (TV). 1977: From Noon Till Three. Sunshine Christmas (TV). The White Buffalo. 1978: The North Avenue Irregulars (GB: Hill's Angels).

**As director:**
1960: Macumba Love.

**FRANCEN, Victor** 1888-1977
Suave Belgian actor with lined face and heavy eyebrows. He filmed extensively in France before World War II, then fled to Hollywood, where he settled in happily at Warners to play cunning charmers, often effete millionaires with cigarette holder and silk dressing gown. At his best in the mid-1940s.

1921: Crépuscule d'épouvante. 1922: Le logis de l'horreur. 1923: La neige sur les pas. 1924: La doute. 1930: La fin du monde. 1931: Après l'amour. L'aiglon. 1932: Les ailes brisées. 1933: Le voleur. Mélo. 1934: L'aventurier. Ariane, jeune fille Russe. 1935: Le chemineau. Veille d'armes. 1936: L'appel de la vie. La porte du large. Nuits de feu. Le roi. 1937: Double crime sur la Ligne Maginot.

*Feu! Tamara la Complaisante. Forfaiture.*
*1938: J'accuse. Sacrifice d'honneur. La vierge*
*falle. 1939: La fin du jour. Entente cordiale.*
*L'homme du Niger. 1940: The Living Corpse.*
*The Open Road. 1941: Hold Back the Dawn.*
*1942: The Tuttles of Tahiti. Ten Gentlemen*
*from West Point. Tales of Manhattan. 1943:*
*Mission to Moscow. The Desert Song. Madame*
*Curie. Devotion (released 1946). 1944: In*
*Our Time. Passage to Marseille (GB: Passage*
*to Marseilles). The Mask of Dimitrios. Holly-*
*wood Canteen Follow the Boys. The Conspira-*
*tors. 1945: Confidential Agent. San Antonio.*
*1946: Night and Day. The Beast With Five*
*Fingers. 1947: The Beginning or the End? La*
*revoltée. To the Victor. 1949: La nuit s'achève.*
*1950: The Adventures of Captain Fabian.*
*1954: Hell and High Water. Boulevard de*
*Paris. 1955: Bedevilled. 1957: A Farewell to*
*Arms. 1961: Fanny. 1967: Top Crack.*

### FRANZ, Eduard 1902-1983

Grey-haired, benevolent-looking American
actor who dispensed kindness and wisdom
to many a hot-headed young hero during
his 37-year tenure of films and television.
Played fathers, uncles, counsellors, doctors,
elders and pyschiatrists and once claimed to
have perfected '14 different wise looks'.

*1947: Killer at Large. 1948: The Iron*
*Curtain. Hollow Triumph (GB: The Scar).*
*Wake of the Red Witch. 1949: Madame*
*Bovary. The Doctor and the Girl. Outpost in*
*Morocco. Francis. Oh, You Beautiful Doll.*
*Whirlpool. 1950: The Vicious Years (GB:*
*The Gangster We Made). Tarnished. Molly.*
*The Magnificent Yankee (GB: The Man With*
*Thirty Sons). Emergency Wedding (GB:*
*Jealousy). 1951: The Great Caruso. The*
*Thing ... from another world. The Desert Fox*
*(GB: Rommel—Desert Fox). The Unknown*
*Man. Shadow in the Sky. 1952: Because*
*You're Mine. One Minute to Zero. Everything*
*I Have is Yours. 1953: Dream Wife. Latin*
*Lovers. Sins of Jezebel. The Jazz Singer.*
*1954: Sign of the Pagan. Broken Lance.*
*Beachhead. 1955: Lady Godiva (GB: Lady*
*Godiva of Coventry). The Last Command.*
*White Feather. The Indian Fighter. Man on the*
*Ledge (TV. GB: cinemas). 1956: The Ten*
*Commandments. Three for Jamie Dawn. The*
*Burning Hills. 1957: Man Afraid. 1958:*

*Day of the Bad Man. Last of the Fast Guns. A*
*Certain Smile. 1959: The Miracle. The Four*
*Skulls of Jonathan Drake. 1960: The Story of*
*Ruth. 1961: Francis of Assisi. The Fiercest*
*Heart. 1962: Hatari! Beauty and the Beast.*
*1966: Cyborg 2087. 1967: The President's*
*Analyst. 1970: The Brotherhood of the Bell*
*(TV). 1971: Johnny Got His Gun. 1974:*
*Panic on the 5.22 (TV). The Sex Symbol (TV).*
*1983: Twilight Zone—The Movie.*

### FRASER, Liz

(Elizabeth Winch) 1933-
Big, busty, bouncy British comedy actress
who cornered the market in dumb cockney
blondes, especially in Peter Sellers comedies and the Carry On series, before
showing that she could tackle the odd
dramatic role as well. Drifted back into
broad film comedies in the 1970s after a
long period away; television and the theatre
have offered her more rewarding roles in
recent times. A prolific worker for charities.

*1955: ‡Touch and Go (US: The Light*
*Touch). 1957: † The Smallest Show on Earth.*
*†Not Wanted on Voyage. †Davy. 1958:*
*†Wonderful Things! 1959: †Top Floor Girl.*
*I'm All Right, Jack. The Night We Dropped a*
*Clanger. Desert Mice. 1960: Two Way*
*Stretch. Doctor in Love. The Night We Got the*
*Bird. The Pure Hell of St Trinian's. The*
*Bulldog Breed. 1961: The Rebel (US: Call*
*Me Genius). Fury at Smuggler's Bay. Double*
*Bunk. Carry On Regardless. Watch It Sailor!*
*Raising the Wind. A Pair of Briefs. The*
*Painted Smile. 1962: Carry On Cruising. The*
*Amorous Prawn. Live Now—Pay Later.*
*1963: Carry On Cabby. 1964: Every Day's a*
*Holiday (US: Seaside Swingers). The Ameri-*
*canization of Emily. 1966: The Family Way.*
*1967: Up the Junction. 1971: Dad's Army.*
*1972: Hide and Seek. 1974: Three for All.*
*1975: Carry On Behind. Adventures of a Taxi*
*Driver. 1976: Confessions of a Driving*
*Instructor. Under the Doctor. 1977: Adven-*
*tures of a Private Eye. Confessions from a*
*Holiday Camp. 1978: Rosie Dixon Night*
*Nurse. 1980: The Great Rock 'n' Roll*
*Swindle.*

‡As Elizabeth Winch
†As Elizabeth Fraser

### FRASER, Ronald 1930-

British character star with rumpled hair,
small, piggy features and inimitable breathless delivery. Rarely looking smart on
screen, he swiftly made his mark as a
specialist in pugnacity and pomposity who
could sometimes give remarkably self-
effacing portrayals. At his best in the mid-
1960s, when he was briefly in leading roles,
he is still capable of lifting inferior material
and a delight on the stage in restoration
comedy.

*1957: Black Ice. 1959: Bobbikins. 1960: The*
*Sundowners. There Was a Crooked Man. The*
*Girl on the Boat. The Long and the Short and*
*the Tall (US: Jungle Fighters). 1961: The*
*Best of Enemies. Don't Bother to Knock! (US:*
*Why Bother to Knock?) The Hellions. 1962:*
*The Pot Carriers. In Search of the Castaways.*
*Private Potter. The Punch and Judy Man.*
*1963: The VIPs. Girl in the Headlines (US:*
*The Model Murder Case). Crooks in Cloisters.*
*1964: The Beauty Jungle (US: Contest Girl).*
*Victim Five (US: Code Seven, Victim Five).*
*Allez France (US: The Counterfeit Constable).*
*Daylight Robbery. 1965: The Flight of the*
*Phoenix. 1966: The Whisperers. 1967: Fath-*
*om. Sebastian. 1968: The Killing of Sister*
*George. 1969: Sinful Davey. The Bed Sitting*
*Room. Too Late the Hero. 1970: The Rise and*
*Rise of Michael Rimmer. 1971: The Magnifi-*
*cent Seven Deadly Sins. Rentadick. 1972: Ooh*
*... You Are Awful (US: Get Charlie Tully).*
*1974: Swallows and Amazons. Percy's Pro-*
*gress. Paper Tiger. 1977: Hardcore. Come*
*Play with Me. 1978: The Wild Geese. 1982:*
*Trail of the Pink Panther. 1983: Tangier.*

### FRAWLEY, William 1887-1966

Lovable, cherubic, balding American character actor who vies with Allen Jenkins and
Jesse White in the memory as cigar-
chewing gangsters with tough exteriors and
soft centres. Overcame an alcohol problem
to become a TV star of the early fifties as
the irascible Fred Mertz in *In Love Lucy*
then, in the sixties, as Bub in another long-
running TV series, *My Three Sons*. Died
from a heart attack.

*1915: *Cupid Beats Father. 1916: Lord*
*Loveland Discovers America. 1929: *Fancy*

That. *Turkey for Two. 1931: Surrender. 1933: Hell and High Water (GB: Cap'n Jericho). Moonlight and Pretzels (GB: Moonlight and Melody). 1934: Miss Fane's Baby is Stolen (GB: Kidnapped!). Bolero. Shoot the Works (GB: Thank Your Stars). Here Is My Heart. The Crime Doctor. The Witching Hour. The Lemon Drop Kid. 1935: Ship Café. Car 99. Alibi Ike. Harmony Lane. Welcome Home. Hold 'em, Yale (GB: Uniform Lovers). College Scandal (GB: The Clock Strikes Eight). 1936: Strike Me Pink. The Princess Comes Across. The General Died at Dawn. Three Married Men. Three Cheers for Love. Desire. F-Man. Rose Bowl (GB: O'Riley's Luck). 1937: Blossoms on Broadway. Double or Nothing. Something to Sing about. High, Wide and Handsome. 1938: Mad About Music. Professor, Beware! Crime Takes a Holiday. Sons of the Legion. Touchdown Army (GB: Generals of Tomorrow). 1939: Persons in Hiding. Ambush. St Louis Blues. Grand Jury Secrets. Night Work. Rose of Washington Square. The Adventures of Huckleberry Finn. Ex-Champ. Stop, Look and Love. 1940: Untamed. The Quarterback. Rhythm on the River. Golden Gloves. Opened by Mistake. The Farmer's Daughter. One Night in the Tropics. Sandy Gets Her Man. Those Were the Days. 1941: The Bride Came C.O.D. Blondie in Society (GB: Henpecked). Cracked Nuts. Six Lessons from Madame La Zonga. Footsteps in the Dark. Public Enemies. 1942: Treat 'em Rough. Roxie Hart. It Happened in Flatbush. Give Out, Sisters. Wildcat. Moonlight in Havana. Gentleman Jim. 1943: We've Never Been Licked (GB: Texas to Tokyo). Whistling in Brooklyn. Larceny With Music. 1944: Minstrel Man. Ziegfeld Follies (released 1946). The Fighting Seabees. Going My Way. 1945: Flame of the Barbary Coast. Hitchhike to Happiness. Lady on a Train. 1946: The Virginian. Rendezvous With Annie. The Inner Circle. The Crime Doctor's Manhunt. 1947: Miracle on 34th Street (GB: The Big Heart). Down to Earth. I Wonder Who's Kissing Her Now? Monsieur Verdoux. My Wild Irish Rose. Mother Wore Tights. Hit Parade of 1947. Blondie's Anniversary. 1948: Texas, Brooklyn and Heaven (GB: The Girl from Texas). Good Sam. The Babe Ruth Story. Chicken Every Sunday. Joe Palooka in Winner Take All (GB: Winner Take All). The Girl from

Manhattan. 1949: The Lady Takes a Sailor. Red Light. Home in San Antone (GB: Harmony Inn). East Side, West Side. The Lone Wolf and His Lady. 1950: Blondie's Hero. Kill the Umpire. Kiss Tomorrow Goodbye. Pretty Baby. 1951: The Lemon Drop Kid. Rhubarb. Abbott and Costello Meet the Invisible Man. 1952: Rancho Notorious. 1962: Safe at Home.

### FREED, Bert 1919- 1994

Of medium height, but heftily built, this thick-necked, crop-haired, tough-looking American actor played top sergeants, crooks and policemen. A semi-regular in films from 1950 to 1954 and again from 1963 to 1971, but at other times only a rare migrant from heavy schedules in television and the theatre. His characters licked more than one raw recruit into shape in their time.

1949: Ma and Pa Kettle Go to Town (GB: Going to Town). 1950: Key to the City. Black Hand. No Way Out. 711 Ocean Drive. Halls of Montezuma. 1951: The Company She Keeps. Where the Sidewalk Ends. Detective Story. 1952: The Atomic City. The Snows of Kilimanjaro. 1953: Tangier Incident. 1954: Take the High Ground. The Long, Long Trailer. Men of the Fighting Lady. 1957: Paths of Glory. 1958: The Goddess. 1959: The Gazebo. 1960: The Subterraneans. Why Must I Die? (GB: 13 Steps to Death). 1963: Twilight of Honor (GB: The Charge is Murder). 1964: Invitation to a Gunfighter. Shock Treatment. Fate is the Hunter. 1966: Nevada Smith. The Swinger. 1967: PJ (GB: New Face in Hell). Hang 'em High. 1968: Madigan. Wild in the Streets. 1969: Then Came Bronson (TV. GB: cinemas). 1970: There Was a Crooked Man. Breakout (TV). 1971: Billy Jack. Evel Knievel. 1975: Death Scream (TV). 1977: Till Death. In the Matter of Karen Ann Quinlan (TV). Barracuda (The Lucifer Project). 1979: Norma Rae.

### FREEMAN, Kathleen 1922- 2001

Cheerful, chubby, round-faced, light-haired American supporting actress whose 'farm-girl' features were first seen as bobbysoxers and college girls. She played small roles and occasional minor leads

(Lonely Hearts Bandits) for more than a decade, before her raucous tones, expressive face and now aggressive manner made her an inveterate scene-stealer of the 1960s, especially in Jerry Lewis comedies. A kindlier version of Brtain's Peggy Mount. Had a rare tough leading part in Wild Harvest (1961).

1948: *Annie Was a Wonder. The Naked City. The Saxon Charm. Casbah. Behind Locked Doors. 1949: Mr Belvedere Goes to College. The House by the River. 1950: A Life of Her Own. Lonely Hearts Bandits (GB: Lonely Heart Bandits). The Reformer and the Redhead. Once a Thief. No Man of Her Own. 1951: Appointment with Danger (filmed 1949). A Place in the Sun. Cause for Alarm. The Wild Blue Yonder (GB: Thunder Across the Pacific). Kid Monk Baroni (GB: Young Paul Baroni). The Company She Keeps. Love is Better than Ever (GB: The Light Fantastic). Let's Make It Legal. 1952: Talk About a Stranger. Singin' in the Rain. The Bad and the Beautiful. O Henry's Full House (GB: Full House). The Greatest Show on Earth. The Prisoner of Zenda. Monkey Business. Bonzo Goes to College. 1953: She's Back on Broadway. The Magnetic Monster. Half a Hero. The Glass Web. The Affairs of Dobie Gillis. Dream Wife. The Glass Wall. A Perilous Journey. 1954: Athena. Three-Ring Circus. The Far Country. 1955: Artists and Models. 1956: Hollywood or Bust. 1957: The Midnight Story (GB: Appointment With a Shadow). Kiss Them for Me. Pawnee (GB: Pale Arrow). 1958: The Fly. Houseboat. Too Much, Too Soon. The Buccaneer. The Missouri Traveler. 1959: Don't Give Up the Ship. 1960: North to Alaska. 1961: The Ladies' Man. The Errand Boy. Wild Harvest. 1962: Madison Avenue. 1963: The Nutty Professor. Mail Order Bride (GB: West of Montana). 1964: The Rounders. The Disorderly Orderly. 1965: Marriage on the Rocks. 1966: Three on a Couch. 1967: Point Blank. The Helicopter Spies (TV. GB: cinemas). 1968: Hook, Line and Sinker. 1969: The Good Guys and the Bad Guys. Death of a Gunfighter. 1970: But I Don't Want to Get Married (TV). Myra Breckinridge. Hitched (TV. GB: Westward the Wagon). The Ballad of Cable Hogue. Which Way to the Front? (GB: Ja, Ja, Mein

General! But Which Way to the Front?).
1971: Support Your Local Gunfighter. Head
On. Where Does It Hurt? 1972: Stand Up
and Be Counted. Call Her Mom (TV). 1973:
Unholy Rollers. Your Three Minutes Are Up.
1974: The Daughters of Joshua Cabe Return
(TV). 1975: The Strongest Man in the World.
1978: The Norseman. 1980: The Blues
Brothers.

**FRÖBE, Gert** 1912- 1988
Squat, thick-set, small-eyed, sandy-haired,
menacing German actor who moved from
untrustworthy little men to international
menaces, when he put on weight and
triumphed in the title role of *Goldfinger*
(1964). Since then he has been more
selective about his appearances.

1948: Berliner Ballade. 1949: Nach Regen
scheint Sonne. 1952: Der Tag vor der
Hochzeit. 1953: Arlette erobert Paris. Salto
mortale. Man on a Tightrope. Ein Herz spielt
falsch. Hochzeit auf Reisen. 1954: Mannequins
für Rio. Das zweite Leben/Double destin.
Ewiger Walzer. Die kleine Stadt will schlafen
gehn. Morgengrauen. Das Kreuz am Jägerstag.
1955: Der Postmeister (GB: Her Crime Was
Love). Der dunkle Stern. Vom Himmel
Gefallen/Special Delivery. Confidential Report
(US: Mr Arkadin). Das Forsthaus in Tirol.
The Heroes Are Tired/Les héros sont fatigués.
They Were So Young. Ich weiss, wofür ich liebe.
Ein Mädchen aus Flandern. 1956: Wald-
winter. Ein Herz schlägt für Erika. Celui qui
doit mourir. Der tolle Bomberg. Typhoon over
Nagasaki. Das Herz von St Pauli. 1957:
Robinson soll nicht sterben. El Hakim. Echec au
porteur. Charmants garçons. 1958: Grafatigués.
I batellieri di Volga (GB: The Boatmen. US:
The Volga Boatman). Es geschah am hellichten
Tag (GB: Assault in Broad Daylight). The
Girl Rosemarie. Nasse Asphalt. Der Pauker.
Das Mädchen mit den Katzenaugen. Nick
Knattertons Abenteuer. Grabenplatz 17 (US:
17 Sinister Street). 1959: Jons und Erdman.
Und ewig singen die Wälder (GB: Vengeance
in Timber Valley). Schüsse im Morgengrauen.
Douze heures d'horloge. Old Heidelberg. Am
Tag, als der Regen kam. Menschen im Hotel.
1960: Le bois des amants (GB: Between Love
and Duty). Der Gauner und der lieber Gott. Bis
dass das Geld euch scheidet. Das kunstseidene
Mädchen. Soldatensender Calais. 12 Stunden
Angst. 1961: The Green Archer. The Return
of Dr Mabuse. Via mada. 1962: Auf
Wiedersehen. Heute kündigt mir mein Mann.
The Longest Day. Die Rote. The Testament of
Dr Mabuse. The Threepenny Opera. 1963:
Der Mörder (GB: Enough Rope). Karussell
der Leidenschaften. Peau de banane (GB:
US: Banana Peel). 1964: Goldfinger.
$100,000 au soleil. Tonio Kröger. 1965: Is
Paris Burning? Those Magnificent Men in
Their Flying Machines. A High Wind in
Jamaica. Du Rififi à Paname (GB: Rififi in
Paris). Ganoversehre. Eschappement libre (US:
Backfire). Das Liebeskarussell (GB and US:
Who Wants to Sleep?). 1966: Triple Cross.
1967: Rocket to the Moon (US: Those

Fantastic Flying Fools). Caroline Chérie. I
Killed Rasputin. 1968: Chitty Chitty Bang
Bang. 1969: Monte Carlo or Bust (US: Those
Daring Young Men in Their Jaunty Jalopies).
1971: $ (GB: The Heist). 1972: Ludwig.
1973: Nuits rouges (GB: Shadowman).
1974: Der räuber Hotzenplotz. And Then
There Were None. L'homme sans visage.
1975: Mein Onkel Theodor. Dr Justice.
Profezia per un delitto. 1977: The Serpent's
Egg. Das Gesetz des Clans. Tod oder Freiheit.
1978: Der Tiefstapler. Der Schimmelreiter.
1979: Bloodline/Sidney Sheldon's Bloodline.
1980: Le coup du parapluie. The Falcon.
1981: Daisy Chain.

**FRYE, Dwight** 1899-1943
Small, dapper American actor whose dark-
haired, fresh-faced looks seemed to qualify
him for lounge lizards. But there was a hint
of anguish about the features that drew
directors of horror films and bizarre thrillers to cast him in featured roles. The
grotesques that resulted were often genuinely frightening, and his pathetic, chilling
Renfield in the 1930 *Dracula* has never been
bettered. Died from a heart attack.

1927: The Night Bird. 1930: The Doorway to
Hell. Man to Man. Dracula. 1931: The
Maltese Falcon. The Black Camel. Franken-
stein. 1932: A Strange Adventure. Attorney
for the Defense. By Whose Hand? The Western
Code. 1933: The Invisible Man. The Vampire
Bat. The Circus Queen Murder. 1934: King
Solomon of Broadway. 1935: Bride of Franken-
stein. Atlantic Adventure. The Crime of Dr
Crespi. The Great Impersonation. 1936: Florida
Special. Alibi for Murder. Beware of Ladies.
1937: The Man Who Found Himself. Sea
Devils. Great Guy (GB: Pluck of the Irish).
The Road Back. Something to Sing About.
Renfrew of the Royal Mounted. The Shadow.
1938: The Invisible Enemy. *Think It Over.
Who Killed Gail Preston? Sinners in Paradise.
Fast Company. Adventure in the Sahara.
The Night Hawk. 1939: The Man in the
Iron Mask. The Cat and the Canary. Son
of Frankenstein. Conspiracy. I Take This
Woman. 1940: Drums of Fu Manchu (serial).
Gangs of Chicago. Phantom Raiders. Son of
Monte Cristo. Sky Bandits. 1941: The People
Versus Dr Kildare (GB: My Life is Yours).
The Blonde from Singapore. The Devil Pays
Off. The Ghost of Frankenstein. Mystery Ship.
1942: Danger in the Pacific. Prisoner of
Japan. Sleepytime Gal. 1943: Dead Men
Walk. Hangmen Also Die. Frankenstein Meets
the Wolf Man. Submarine Alert. Dangerous
Blondes.

**FURSE, Judith** 1912-
Gargantuan, circular-faced, dark-haired
British supporting actress frequently called
upon to express bigotry, ruthlessness or
outrage. A formidable matron or school
governor. On stage at 12, she is the sister of
the lighter-haired Jill Furse, a budding
leading lady of the late 1930s who suffered
from ill-health and died tragically young.
Has also produced and directed on stage.

1939: Goodbye Mr Chips! 1944: English
Without Tears (US: Her Man Gilbey). A
Canterbury Tale. 1945: Johnny Frenchman.
1946: Quiet Weekend. While the Sun Shines.
1947: Black Narcissus. 1948: One Night
With You. 1949: Dear Mr Prohack. Helter
Skelter. Marry Me! The Romantic Age (US:
Naughty Arlette). 1951: The Browning Ver-
sion. The Man in the White Suit. I Believe in
You. 1952: Mother Riley Meets the Vampire
(US: Vampire Over London). 1953: The
Heart of the Matter. 1954: Mad About Men.
1955: Cockleshell Heroes. 1957: Doctor at
Large. 1958: Blue Murder at St Trinian's.
Further Up the Creek. 1959: Serious Charge
(US: A Touch of Hell). 1960: Scent of
Mystery (GB: Holiday in Spain). Sands of the
Desert. Not a Hope in Hell. 1961: In the
Doghouse. Carry On Regardless. A Weekend
With Lulu. 1962: Postman's Knock. The Iron
Maiden (US: The Swingin' Maiden). Live
Now—Pay Later. 1963: Carry On Cabby.
1964: A Jolly Bad Fellow (shown 1963).
Carry On Spying. 1965: The Amorous
Adventures of Moll Flanders. Sky West and
Crooked (US: Gypsy Girl). 1969: Twinky
(US: Lola). 1972: The Adventures of Barry
McKenzie.

**GALLAGHER, Skeets**
(Richard Gallagher) 1891-1955
Round-faced, cheery-looking American
song-and-dance man, occasional romantic
lead and oft-time quipster from the side-
lines, silver-haired from his late thirties. A
vaudevillian of long standing, in comedy

RIGHT Gert **Frobe** in the role that shot him to international fame: *Goldfinger* (1964)

BELOW Dwight **Frye**'s hunchback (right) awaits further orders from Frankenstein (Colin Clive) as he tries to bring his creation to life in the 1931 *Frankenstein*

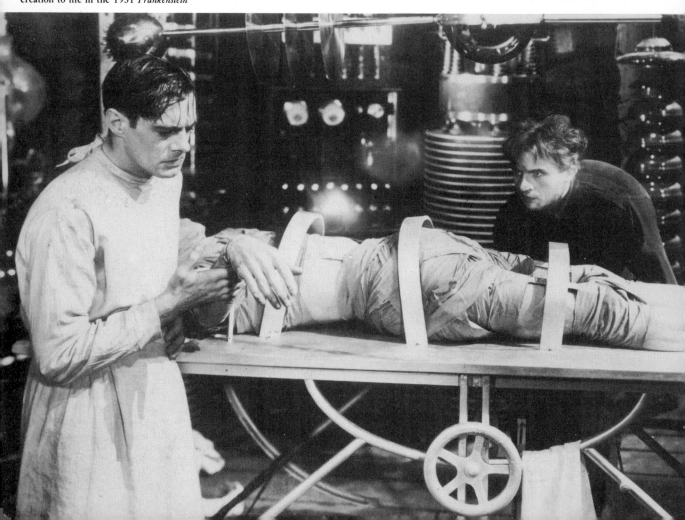

acts with various female partners, his live-wire (occasionally over-the-top) performances made him a popular attraction in Hollywood films from 1929 to 1934. Thereafter his career dipped into smaller roles, and he enjoyed the better successes of his later years back on stage. The 'Skeets' was a childhood nickname: mosquito, describing the way he zipped around. Died from a heart attack.

1923: The Daring Years. 1927: The Potters. New York. For the Love of Mike. 1928: Stocks and Blondes (GB: Blondes and Bonds). Alex the Great. Three-Ring Marriage. The Racket. 1929: Pointed Heels. Close Harmony. Fast Company. The Dance of Life. 1930: Honey. Paramount on Parade. Her Wedding Night. Love Among the Millionaires. The Social Lion. Let's Go Native. 1931: Possessed. It Pays to Advertise. Up Pops the Devil. Road to Reno. 1932: Merrily We Go to Hell (GB: Merrily We Go to —). The Phantom of Crestwood. The Unwritten Law. Night Club Lady. The Sport Parade. The Conquerors. Bird of Paradise. *Hollywood on Parade. The Trial of Vivienne Ware. 1933: Reform Girl. The Past of Mary Holmes. Too Much Harmony. Easy Millions. Alice in Wonderland. *Private Wives. 1934: The Crosby Case (GB: The Crosby Murder Case). In The Money. Bachelor Bait. The Meanest Gal in Town. Riptide. Woman Unafraid. Lightning Strikes Twice. 1935: The Perfect Clue. 1936: Polo Joe. Yours for the Asking. Hats Off. The Man I Marry. 1937: Espionage. 1938: Danger in the Air. Mr Satan. 1939: Idiot's Delight. 1941: Citadel of Crime (GB: Outside the Law). Zis Boom Bah! 1942: Brooklyn Orchid. 1945: The Duke of Chicago. 1952: Three for Bedroom C.

## GARDENIA, Vincent
(Vincente Scognamiglio) 1922-1992
Bulky, full-faced Italian-born actor, in America from childhood and usually seen as the trilbied, forehead-mopping police chief, Mafia boss or city official. First acted at five with his father's Italian theatre in Manhattan, but didn't get a foothold in films until he was nearly 50, around the same time as he received a Tony for The Prisoner of Second Avenue on stage, and an Oscar nomination

for Bang the Drum Slowly. Best known as the detective trying to keep tabs on Charles Bronson in the Death Wish films.

1945: The House on 92nd Street. 1958: Cop Hater. 1960: Murder Inc. 1961: The Hustler. Mad Dog Coll. A View from the Bridge. 1965: The Third Day. 1969: Jenny. 1970: The Pursuit of Happiness. Where's Poppa? Cold Turkey. 1972: Hickey and Boggs. 1973: Bang the Drum Slowly. Lucky Luciano. 1974: Death Wish. The Front Page. 1975: The Manchu Eagle Murder Caper Mystery. 1976: Il grande rocket. 1977: Fire Sale. Greased Lightning. 1978: Heaven Can Wait. 1979: Firepower. 1980: Home Movies (shown 1979). The Last Flight of Noah's Ark. 1981: Death Wish II. 1984: Dark Mirror (TV). 1985: Movers and Shakers.

## GARDINER, Reginald
(William R. Gardiner) 1903-1980
Dark-haired, moustachioed, owlish-looking British comic actor, raconteur and recording artist, chiefly remembered for the 'silly ass' characterizations he created when he went to Hollywood in the mid-thirties, but in fact capable of a much wider range. His record of train noises remains a collector's item: so do some of his performances. Died from pneumonia.

1931: *My Old China. Aroma of the South Seas. *Bull Rushes. The Perfect Lady. 1932: Flat No. 9. Lovelorn Lady. Josser on the River. 1933: Radio Parade. Just Smith (US: Leave It to Smith). 1934: How's Chances? Borrow a

Million. Virginia's Husband. 1935: Opening Night. A Little Bit of Bluff. Royal Cavalcade (US: Regal Cavalcade). 1936: Born to Dance. 1937: A Damsel in Distress. 1938: Everybody Sing. Sweethearts. Marie Antoinette. 1939: The Night of Nights. The Flying Deuces. The Girl Downstairs. 1940: The Great Dictator. Dulcy. The Doctor Takes a Wife. 1941: My Life with Caroline. A Yank in the R.A.F. Sundown. The Man Who Came to Dinner. 1942: Captains of the Clouds. 1943: Forever and a Day. The Immortal Sergeant. Sweet Rosie O'Grady. Claudia. 1944: Molly and Me. 1945: Christmas in Connecticut (US: Indiscretion). The Horn Blows At Midnight. The Dolly Sisters. 1946: Do You Love Me? Cluny Brown. One More Tomorrow. 1947: I Wonder Who's Kissing Her Now. 1948: That Wonderful Urge. Fury at Furnace Creek. That Lady in Ermine. 1950: Wabash Avenue. I'll Get By. Halls of Montezuma. 1951: Elopement. 1952: Androcles and the Lion. 1954: The Barefoot Contessa. Black Widow. 1955: Ain't Misbehavin'. 1956: The Birds and the Bees. Around the World in 80 Days. 1957: The Story of Mankind. 1958: Rock-a-Bye Baby. No Time at All (TV). 1961: Back Street. 1962: Mr Hobbs Takes a Vacation. 1964: What a Way to Go! 1965: Do Not Disturb. Sergeant Deadhead.

## GARFIELD, Allen
(A. Goorwitz) 1939-
Mournful-looking, dark, balding, plump (until recent times) American actor who played greasy and often obnoxious types during the first decade of his film career. He looked a different kind of character actor when he reappeared, trimmed and toupeed, in the early 1980s. Garfield was a Golden Gloves boxer and a journalist before turning to acting at 26. His first job on the New York stage, as a spear carrier, lasted only a few days—he caught chickenpox! Now plays high-pressure types prone to anxiety attacks.

1968: Greetings. Orgy Girls '69. 1969: Roommates/March of the Spring Hare. Putney Swope. 1970: Hi Mom! The Commitment. The Owl and the Pussycat. 1971: Taking Off. Bananas. Cry Uncle (GB: Super Dick). Believe in Me. You've Got to Walk It Like You

*Talk It or You'll Lose That Beat. The Organization. 1972: Get to Know Your Rabbit. Footsteps (TV). The Candidate. 1973: The Marcus-Nelson Murders (TV). Slither. Busting. 1974: The Virginia Hill Story (TV). The Conversation. The Front Page. Mother, Jugs and Speed (released 1976). 1975: Nashville. 1976: Serpico: The Deadly Game (TV). The Million Dollar Rip-Off (TV). Gable and Lombard. Paco. 1977: The Stunt Man (released 1980). 1978: Skateboard. Nowhere to Run (TV). Ring of Passion (TV). †The Brink's Job. 1980: †One Trick Pony. †National Lampoon Goes to the Movies. 1981: †Continental Divide. †One from the Heart. 1982: †Der Stand der Dinge/The State of Things. 1983: The Black Stallion Returns. Get Crazy. 1984: Teachers. Irreconcilable Differences. The Cotton Club. 1985: Desert Bloom.*

†As Allen Goorwitz

## GAUGE, Alexander 1914-1960

Corpulent, brown-haired British actor usually seen in faintly disreputable roles: his best was probably his first, as the vengeful husband in *The Interrupted Journey*. His film career, largely confined to petty crooks, practically dried up altogether after he was cast as Friar Tuck in the long-running *Robin Hood* series on TV with Richard Greene. Died from a heart attack. Born in Wenchow, China.

*1949: The Interrupted Journey. 1951: Flesh and Blood. 1952: Murder in the Cathedral. The Pickwick Papers. Penny Princess. 1953: Counterspy (US: Undercover Agent). Will Any Gentleman?... Martin Luther. House of Blackmail. The Great Game. The Square Ring. 1954: Fast and Loose. Double Exposure. Dance Little Lady. The Golden Link. \* The Blazing Caravan. Mystery on Bird Island. 1955: Before I Wake (US: Shadow of Fear). Tiger by the Tail (US: Crossup). The Reluctant Bride (US: Two Grooms for a Bride). The Hornet's Nest. No Smoking. 1956: Port of Escape. Breakaway. The Green Man. The Iron Petticoat. The Passionate Stranger (US: A Novel Affair). 1960: Les canailles (US: The Ruffians). 1961: Nothing Barred.*

## GAWTHORNE, Peter 1884-1962

Heavily built, large-headed, fiercely blustering, silver-haired, Irish-born supporting actor who returned from Hollywood in 1932 to become a stalwart of the British cinema, especially in comedies (several with Will Hay) as top-ranking figures of authority doomed to deflation.

*1929: Behind That Curtain. Sunny Side Up. His Glorious Night. 1930: Temple Tower. One Hysterical Night. Those Three French Girls. 1931: Charlie Chan Carries On. The Man Who Came Back. 1932: The Flag Lieutenant. Jack's the Boy (US: Night and Day). C.O.D. His Lordship. The Lodger (US: The Phantom Fiend). Perfect Understanding. 1933: The Blarney Stone (US: The Blarney Kiss). Just*

*Smith (US: Leave It to Smith). Prince of Arcadia. The House of Trent. 1934: Two Hearts in Waltztime. Grand Prix. Girls Please. Something Always Happens. The Camels Are Coming. Money Mad. My Old Dutch. Dirty Work. Murder at Monte Carlo. 1935: The Iron Duke. Boys Will Be Boys. Who's Your Father? Me and Marlborough. Crime Unlimited. Stormy Weather. The Crouching Beast. Man of the Moment. No Limit. 1936: Wolf's Clothing. The Man Behind the Mask. Pot Luck. Windbag the Sailor. The Amazing Quest of Ernest Bliss (US: Romance and Riches). A Woman Alone (US: Two Who Dared). Everybody Dance. 1937: Ticket of Leave Man. Good Morning, Boys! (US: Where There's a Will). Gangway. Mr Stringfellow Says No. Father Steps Out. Brief Ecstasy. Under a Cloud. The Last Adventurers. Riding High. \*George Bizet, Composer of Carmen. 1938: Alf's Button Afloat. Easy Riches. Convict 99. Scruffy. Hey! Hey! USA. 1939: Dead Men Are Dangerous. Ask a Policeman. Home from Home. Flying Fifty-Five. Sword of Honour. Secret Journey (US: Among Human Wolves). Where's That Fire? What Would You Do Chums? Traitor Spy (US: The Torso Murder Mystery). Laugh It Off. Band Waggon. 1940: Three Silent Men. They Came by Night. Two for Danger. Gasbags. Crooks' Tour. 1941: Inspector Hornleigh Goes to It (US: Mail Train). Love on the Dole. Pimpernel Smith (US: Mister V). Old Mother Riley's Ghosts. 1942: Let the People Sing. Women Aren't Angels. Much Too Shy. 1943: Bell Bottom George. The Hundred Pound Window. 1945: Murder in Reverse. 1946: This Man is Mine! 1948: Nothing Venture. The Case of Charles Peace. 1949: High Jinks in Society. 1950: Soho Conspiracy. 1951: Death is a Number. 1952: Paul Temple Returns. 1954: Five Days (US: Paid to Kill). A Tale of Three Women.*

## GEER, Will
(W. Ghere) 1902-1978

Abrasively distinctive American actor whose career in shifty middle-aged roles was abruptly halted by the McCarthy blacklist. He returned in the 1960s to play a variety of ratty, crafty and lovable old men, culminating in his western patriarch in TV's long-running outdoor soap opera *The*

*Waltons.* Got his first leading role at the age of 75 in *The Billion Dollar Hobo.* Died from a respiratory ailment.

*1932: The Misleading Lady. 1935: The Mystery of Edwin Drood. 1940: Fight for Life (narrator only). 1948: Deep Waters. 1949: Anna Lucasta. Lust for Gold. Johnny Allegro (GB: Hounded). Intruder in the Dust. 1950: It's a Small World. Convicted. The Kid from Texas (GB: Texas Kid—Outlaw). To Please a Lady. Broken Arrow. Winchester 73. Double Crossbones. Comanche Territory. 1951: The Tall Texan. The Barefoot Mailman. Bright Victory (GB: Lights Out). 1954: Salt of the Earth. 1955: Mobs Inc. (TV. GB: cinemas). 1962: Advise and Consent. 1964: Black Like Me. 1966: Seconds. 1967: In Cold Blood. The President's Analyst. 1968: Bandolero! 1970: Pieces of Dreams. The Moonshine War. The Reivers. Brother John. 1971: The Brotherhood of the Bell (TV). Sam Hill: Who Killed the Mysterious Mr Foster? (TV). Napoleon and Samantha. 1972: Jeremiah Johnson. The Rowdyman. Dear Dead Delilah. Brock's Last Case (TV). 1973: Executive Action. The Memory of Us. Savage (TV). Isn't It Shocking? (TV). 1974: The Hanged Man (TV). Hurricane (TV). Honky Tonk (TV). 1975: The Silence (TV). The Manchu Eagle Murder Caper Mystery. The Night That Panicked America (TV). 1976: The Blue Bird. Moving Violation. Law and Order (TV). 1977: The Billion Dollar Hobo. 1978: A Woman Called Moses. The Mafu Cage.*

## GEORGE, Chief Dan
(Geswanouth Slahoot) 1899-1981

Aged Canadian Indian who only came to films at 70, but showed an amazing aptitude for acting in his few appearances, even upstaging Clint Eastwood in *The Outlaw Josey Wales.* Academy Award nominee for *Little Big Man.*

*1969: Smith! 1970: Little Big Man. 1974: Harry and Tonto. The Bears and I. 1975: Alien Thunder. 1976: The Outlaw Josey Wales. Shadow of the Hawk. 1979: Americathon. 1980: Spirit of the Wind.*

## GEORGE, Muriel 1883-1965

Dumpy, homely, brown-haired British actress, usually seen with shopping basket,

ABOVE Friar Tuck (Alexander **Gauge**) is taken unawares as denizens of Sherwood Forest make him see their point in a scene from the long-running British TV series of the 1950s, *The Adventures of Robin Hood*

BELOW Millionaire Peter **Gawthorne** and daughter Margaret Lockwood learn that her suitor has run off to Monte Carlo with a working-girl in *Man of the Moment* (1935)

Me Madam. The Golden Blade. Gentlemen Prefer Blondes. The Great Diamond Robbery. The Story of Three Loves. Royal African Rifles (GB: Storm Over Africa). 1954: Knock on Wood. Tobor the Great. The French Line. Paris Playboys. 1955: A Bullet for Joey. New York Confidential. To Catch a Thief. Daddy Long Legs. Artists and Models. 1956: The Birds and the Bees. Attack! Stagecoach to Fury. 1958: A Certain Smile. 1959: Verboten. Count Your Blessings. 1963: Dime With a Halo. 1964: Wild and Wonderful. 1965: Ship of Fools. Jesse James Meets Frankenstein's Daughter. 1966: The Swinger.

heavy coat and old-fashioned hat. Once a character performer in music-hall and variety, her cheerfully tired, round-faced looks slotted well into a whole gallery of lower-class ladies in the British cinema— landladies, mothers, chars, cleaners and maiden aunts. Married/divorced fellow character player Ernest Butcher (1885-1965). Semi-retired in post-war years.

1932: His Lordship. Yes, Mr Brown. 1933: Cleaning Up. 1934: My Song for You. Something Always Happens. Nell Gwyn. 1935: Wedding Eve. Key to Harmony. Mr What's His Name. Old Faithful. 1936: Limelight (US: Backstage). The Happy Family. Whom the Gods Love (US: Mozart). Busman's Holiday. Not So Dusty. King of Hearts. 1937: Song of the Road. Merry Comes to Town (US: Merry Comes to Stay). Dr Syn. Overcoat Sam. Talking Feet. Lancashire Luck. Who's Your Lady Friend? 21 Days (US: 21 Days Together). Bank Holiday. 1938: A Sister to Assist 'Er. Darts Are Trumps. Crackerjack (US: Man with a Hundred Faces). 1940: Pack Up Your Troubles. The Briggs Family. *Food for Thought. You Will Remember. 1941: Quiet Wedding. Freedom Radio (US: A Voice in the Night). *Lady Be Kind. *Telefootlers. *Mr Proudfoot Shows a Light. South American George. Cottage to Let (US: Bombsight Stolen). Love on the Dole. *Rush Hour. The Young Mr Pitt. They Flew Alone (US: Wings and the Woman). 1942: Unpublished Story. Went the Day Well? (US: 48 Hours). Alibi. 1943: The Bells Go Down. Dear Octopus (US: The Randolph Family). 1944: Kiss the Bride Goodbye. The Man from Scotland Yard. 1945: A Place of One's Own. For You Alone. Perfect Strangers (US: Vacation from Marriage). I'll Be Your Sweetheart. 1946: The Years Between. 1947: When the Bough Breaks. 1948: A Sister to Assist 'Er (remake). 1950: The Dancing Years. Last Holiday. 1953: The Triangle. 1955: Simon and Laura.

## GERAY, Steven
(Stefan Gyergay) 1899-1973

Born on Uzhgorod, on the Russian-Czech border, diminutive, sometimes moustachioed Geray made his name in the Hungarian theatre, and seems to have made

no films before coming to London in 1934. He moved on to Hollywood in 1940, and quickly entered the most rewarding phase of his career there, sneaking scenes from the stars and playing leading roles in The Moon and Sixpence and So Dark the Night.

1935: Dance Band. The Student's Romance. 1936: A Star Fell from Heaven. 1937: The High Command. Let's Make a Night of It. 1938: Premiere (US: One Night in Paris). Lightning Conductor. 1939: Inspector Hornleigh. 1940: Dark Streets of Cairo. 1941: Blue, White and Perfect. Man at Large. 1942: Secret Agent of Japan. Castle in the Desert. A Gentleman at Heart. The Moon and Sixpence. Eyes in the Night. The Wife Takes a Flyer (GB: A Yank in Dutch). 1943: Hostages. *To My Unborn Son. *Heavenly Music. Henry Aldrich Swings It (GB: Henry Swings It). Night Plane from Chungking. Pilot No. 5. The Phantom of the Opera. Above Suspicion. Assignment in Brittany. Background to Danger. Whistling in Brooklyn. Appointment in Berlin. 1944: Meet the People. The Seventh Cross. In Society. The Conspirators. The Mark of Dimitrios. *Easy Life. 1945: Tarzan and the Amazons. Hotel Berlin. Spellbound. Cornered. The Crimson Canary. Mexicana. 1946: Gilda. So Dark the Night. The Return of Monte Cristo (GB: Monte Cristo's Revenge). Deadline at Dawn. Blondie Knows Best. 1947: The Crime Doctor's Gamble (GB: The Doctor's Gamble). Mr District Attorney. Blind Spot. Gunfighters (GB: The Assassin). The Unfaithful. When a Girl's Beautiful. 1948: I Love Trouble. Port Said. 1949: The Dark Past. Ladies of the Chorus. El Paso. Sky Liner. Once More, My Darling. Tell It to the Judge. Holiday in Havana. The Lone Wolf and His Lady. 1950: A Lady Without Passport. Woman on the Run. Harbor of Missing Men. Under My Skin. In a Lonely Place. All About Eve. Pygmy Island. The Second Woman (GB: Ellen). 1951: I Can Get It for You Wholesale (GB: This Is My Affair). Target Unknown. My Favorite Spy. The House on Telegraph Hill. Little Egypt (GB: Chicago Masquerade). Savage Drums. 1952: A Lady Possessed. Bal Tabarin. The Big Sky. Affair in Trinidad. O Henry's Full House (GB: Full House). Night Without Sleep. 1953: Tonight We Sing. Call

## GILBERT, Billy 1893-1971

Tall, dark, portly, ruddy-complexioned, usually moustachioed, explosive American comic and 'straight' support, whose frequent cameos filled the screen (he weighed 280 lbs) in more ways than one. Often a pince-nez'd, short-tempered, smartly-dressed businessman confounded by the likes of Laurel and Hardy, the Marx Brothers or, in many shorts, the all-female combination of Thelma Todd and ZaSu Pitts. Sometimes seen as an easily exasperated foreigner, he could also handle a song-and-dance routine and directed productions on Broadway. Died following a stroke. The voice/sneeze of Sneezy in Snow White and the Seven Dwarfs.

1916: Bubbles of Trouble. 1921: Dynamite Allen. 1929: Noisy Neighbors. Woman from Hell. *The Woman Tamer. 1930: *The Doctor's Wife. *The Beauties. 1931: *Dogs Is Dogs. *War Mamas. *Shiver My Timbers. *The Panic Is On. *The Hasty Marriage. *One Good Turn. *A Melon-Drama. *Catch As Catch Can. Chinatown after Dark. *The Pajama Party. 1932: *Free Eats. *Spanky. *The Taxi Boys. *The Tabasco Kid. Pack Up Your Troubles. *The Nickel Nurser. *In Walked Charley. Blondie of the Follies. Million Dollar Legs. *First In War. *You're Telling Me. *County Hospital. *Their First Mistake. *The Chimp. *Strictly Unreliable. *The Music Box. *Seal Skins. *Sneak Easily. *On the Loose. *Red Noses. *Towed in a Hole. 1933: This Day and Age. *Fallen Arches. *Luncheon at Twelve. *Maids à la Mode. *The Bargain of the Century. *Asleep in the Fleet. *One Track

Minds. Sons of the Desert (GB: Fraternally
Yours. Voice only). 1934: Happy Landing
(GB: Air Patrol). Peck's Bad Boy. Eight Girls
in a Boat. Cockeyed Cavaliers. The Merry
Widow. Evelyn Prentice. *Another Wild Idea
(voice only). *The Cracked Iceman. *Them
Thar Hills. *Men in Black. *Soup and Fish.
1935: A Night at the Opera. Millions in the
Air. Mad Love (GB: The Hands of Orlac).
Escapade. *Just Another Murder. *Nurse to
You. *His Bridal Sweet. *Pardon My Scotch.
*Hail Brother. Here Comes the Band. I Dream
Too Much. 1936: Sutter's Gold. Parole! Love
on the Run. Three of a Kind. Dangerous
Waters. The Bride Walks Out. Grand Jury.
The Big Game. Early to Bed. Night Waitress.
Kelly the Second. *The Brain Busters. Hi,
Gaucho! Give Us This Night. The First Baby.
F-Man. Poor Little Rich Girl. Devil Doll. My
American Wife. One Rainy Afternoon. 1937:
The Man Who Found Himself. The Outcasts of
Poker Flat. Live, Love and Learn. Rosalie.
We're on the Jury. Sea Devils. Music for
Madame. China Passage. The Toast of New
York. The Life of the Party. The Firefly. On the
Avenue. Espionage. Broadway Melody of
1938. One Hundred Men and a Girl. Captains
Courageous. Maytime. Fight for Your Lady.
When You're in Love. Snow White and the
Seven Dwarfs (voice only). 1938: Mr Doodle
Kicks Off. She's Got Everything. My Lucky
Star. The Girl Downstairs. Maid's Night Out.
Joy of Living. Block-Heads. Angels with Dirty
Faces. Happy Landing (and 1934 film).
Breaking the Ice. Peck's Bad Boy with the
Circus. Army Girl (GB: The Last of the
Cavalry). The Great Waltz. 1939: Forged
Passport. Destry Rides Again. Rio. The Under-
Pup. The Star Maker. Million Dollar Legs.
1940: Sing, Dance, Plenty Hot (GB: Melody
Girl). The Great Dictator. His Girl Friday.
Women in War. Scatterbrain. Safari. A Night
at Earl Carroll's. Sandy is a Lady. Seven
Sinners. A Little Bit of Heaven. Queen of the
Mob. Cross Country Romance. The Villain Still
Pursued Her. Tin Pan Alley. No, No, Nanette.
1941: *Crazy Like a Fox. Reaching for the
Sun. New Wine (GB: The Great Awakening).
One Night in Lisbon. Angels With Broken
Wings. Model Wife. Week-End in Havana.
Our City. 1942: Mr Wise Guy. Sleepytime
Gal. Valley of the Sun. Song of the Islands. Ara-
bian Nights. 1943: Shantytown. Crazy House.
Spotlight Scandals. Always a Bridesmaid.
Stage Door Canteen. 1944: Three of a Kind.
Ghost Catchers. Ghost Crazy. Crazy Knights.
Ever Since Venus. Three's a Family. 1945:
Anchors Aweigh. Trouble Chasers. 1947: Fun
and Fancy Free (voice only). 1948: The
Kissing Bandit. The Counterfeiters. 1949:
Bride of Vengeance. 1952: Down Among the
Sheltering Palms. 1961: Paradise Alley.
1962: Five Weeks in a Balloon.

## GILCHRIST, Connie
(Rose C. Gilchrist) 1901-
Fair-haired, formidably-built, strong-fea-
tured, Brooklyn-born actress. If you met
Connie Gilchrist behind the bar, you knew

she'd stand no nonsense. Even her below-
stairs characters were inclined to speak
their minds. A stage actress from 1917, she
was signed by M-G-M in 1940, forming the
third point of the triangle in the Marjorie
Main-Wallace Beery roughhouse comedies,
and duetting delightfully with Judy Gar-
land in Presenting Lily Mars. Later a match
for Robert Newton in his Long John Silver
TV series, playing Purity Pinker.

1940: Hullabaloo. 1941: Down in San Diego.
Dr Kildare's Wedding Day (GB: Mary
Names the Day). H. M. Pulham Esq. Billy the
Kid. The Wild Man of Borneo. Two-Faced
Woman. Johnny Eager. Barnacle Bill. A
Woman's Face. 1942: This Time for Keeps.
We Were Dancing. Born to Sing. Tortilla Flat.
Sunday Punch. The War Against Mrs Hadley.
Grand Central Murder. Apache Trail. 1943:
Swing Shift Maisie (GB: The Girl in
Overalls). Presenting Lily Mars. Cry Havoc!
The Heavenly Body. Thousands Cheer. The
Human Comedy. 1944: Rationing. Music for
Millions. See Here, Private Hargrove. Nothing
But Trouble. The Seventh Cross. The Thin
Man Goes Home. 1945: The Valley of
Decision. Junior Miss. 1946: Bad Bascomb.
Faithful in My Fashion. Young Widow.
Merton of the Movies. Cloak and Dagger.
1947: Good News. Song of the Thin Man. The
Hucksters. 1948: Big City. Tenth Avenue
Angel. Chicken Every Sunday. An Act of
Violence. Luxury Liner. The Bride Goes Wild.
A Letter to Three Wives. 1949: Little Women.
The Story of Molly X. 1950: Stars in My
Crown. A Ticket to Tomahawk. Buccaneer's
Girl. Peggy. Undercover Girl. Tripoli. The
Killer That Stalked New York (GB: Fright-
ened City). 1951: Here Comes the Groom.
Thunder on the Hill (GB: Bonaventure).
Chain of Circumstance. Flesh and Fury. 1952:
One Big Affair. The Half-Breed. 1953:
Houdini. The Great Diamond Robbery. It
Should Happen to You. 1954: Long John
Silver. The Far Country. 1955: Under the
Black Flag (TV. GB: cinemas). 1956: The
Man in the Gray Flannel Suit. 1958: Auntie
Mame. Some Came Running. 1959: Machine
Gun Kelly. Say One for Me. 1960: The
Schnook (GB: Double Trouble). 1962: The
Interns. Swingin' Along (revised version of [The
Schnook). 1963: A Tiger Walks. 1964: The

Misadventures of Merlin Jones. A House is Not
a Home. Two on a Guillotine. Fluffy. The
Monkey's Uncle. 1965: Sylvia. Tickle Me.
1969: Some Kind of a Nut. 1972: Fuzz.

## GILLINGWATER, Claude 1870-1939
Lofty, balding American actor with craggy
features and caterpillar eyebrows. He came
to Hollywood to play the recalcitrant earl
finally converted by Little Lord Fauntleroy in
the 1921 version, and found himself consistently typed in the same sort of role, his
crotchety old codgers several times falling
victim to Shirley Temple's wiles in the
1930s. At the age of 69, Gillingwater shot
himself.

1921: Little Lord Fauntleroy. My Boy. 1922:
The Dust Flower. Fools First. Remembrance.
The Stranger's Banquet. 1923: Alice Adams.
Three Wise Fools. The Christian. Souls for Sale.
Crinoline and Romance. Dulcy. A Chapter in
Her Life. Tiger Rose. 1924: Daddies. How to
Educate a Wife. Idle Tongues. Madonna of the
Streets. 1925: Seven Sinners. Cheaper to
Marry. A Thief in Paradise. Winds of Chance.
We Moderns. Wages for Wives. 1926: Into
Her Kingdom. For Wives Only. That's My
Baby. 1927: Barbed Wire. The Gorilla. Fast
and Furious. Naughty But Nice. Husbands for
Rent. 1928: Women They Talk About. Stark
Mad. The Little Shepherd of Kingdom Come.
Oh, Kay! Remember? 1929: The Great
Divide. So Long, Letty. Stolen Kisses. Glad
Rag Doll. Smiling Irish Eyes. 1930: The
Flirting Widow. Dumbbells in Ermine. Toast of
the Legion. 1931: Gold Dust Gertie (GB:
Why Change Your Husband?). Illicit. The
Conquering Horde. Kiss Me Again. Daddy
Long Legs. *Oh! Oh! Cleopatra. Compromised
(GB: We Three). 1932: Tess of the Storm
Country. 1933: Ann Carver's Profession. The
Avenger. Ace of Aces. Skyway. Before Mid-
night. 1934: Broadway Bill (GB: Strictly
Confidential). The Show-Off. City Limits. You
Can't Buy Everything. The Unknown Blonde.
In Love with Life (GB: Re-Union). Green
Eyes. The Back Page. The Captain Hates the
Sea. 1935: Calm Yourself. Mississippi. Baby
Face Harrington. The Woman in Red. A Tale
of Two Cities. 1936: Florida Special. The
Prisoner of Shark Island. Poor Little Rich Girl.
Ticket to Paradise. Wives Never Know. Can

*This Be Dixie? Counterfeit. 1937: Conquest (GB: Marie Walewska). Top of the Town. A Yank at Oxford. 1938: Just Around the Corner. There Goes My Heart. Little Miss Broadway. 1939: Café Society.*

**GINGOLD, Hermione** 1897-*1987*
Red-headed British comic actress with wonderfully unique tones, adept at dragons, grotesques and eccentric aunts. Remembered by many for her revue roles and radio characters including the long-running Mrs Doom. Her best two film roles, in *Gigi* and *Bell, Book and Candle,* came in the same year: 1958.

*1936: Someone at the Door. 1937: Merry Comes to Town. 1938: Meet Mr Penny. 1943: The Butler's Dilemma. 1952: The Pickwick Papers. Cosh Boy (US: The Slasher). 1953: Our Girl Friday (US: The Adventures of Sadie). 1956: Around the World in 80 Days. 1958: Gigi. Bell, Book and Candle. 1961: The Naked Edge. The Music Man. 1962: Gay Purr-ee (voice only). 1964: I'd Rather Be Rich. 1965: Harvey Middleman, Fireman. Promise Her Anything. 1966: Munster Go Home! 1967: Jules Verne's Rocket to the Moon (US: Those Fantastic Flying Fools). 1971: Banyon (TV). 1976: A Little Night Music. 1984: Garbo Talks!*

**GLEASON, James** 1886-1959
Wiry, thin-faced American actor with pencil moustache, a wisp of hair and rasping Brooklyn accent—a familiar face from the onset of sound in scores of films as

policemen, editors, army sergeants, taxi drivers and cynically wisecracking best friends. He never failed to build an identifiable and usually likeable character. He was a long-term sufferer from asthma, eventually the cause of his death at 72. Also wrote—plays for theatre and screenplays for the cinema. Academy Award nominee for *Here Comes Mr Jordan.*

*1922: Polly of the Follies. 1928: The Count of Ten. 1929: \*The Garden of Eatin'. High Voltage. Oh, Yeah! (GB: No Brakes). The Shannons of Broadway. His First Command. The Broadway Melody. \*Fairways and Foul. 1930: The Swellhead (GB: Counted Out). \*Don't Believe It. Big Money. What a Widow! Dumbbells in Ermine. The Matrimonial Bed (GB: A Matrimonial Problem). \*No Brakes (and 1929 feature). Her Man. Big Money. Puttin' on the Ritz. 1931: A Free Soul. \*Where Canaries Sing Bass. Sweepstakes. The Big Gamble. Suicide Fleet. \*Slow Poison. \*Doomed to Win. It's a Wise Child. Beyond Victory. 1932: \*Lights Out. \*Battle Royal. \*High Hats and Low Brows. \*Stealin' Home. \*Yoo Hoo. The Penguin Pool Murder (GB: The Penguin Pool Mystery). Fast Companions/Information Kid. The Crooked Circle. \*Rule 'em and Weep. The All-American (GB: Sport of a Nation). Lady and Gent. Blondie of the Follies. The Devil is Driving. 1933: Orders is Orders. Hoopla. Clear All Wires. Billion Dollar Scandal. \*Alias the Professor. \*Mister Mugg. \*Gleason's New Deal. 1934: Search for Beauty. Murder on the Blackboard. Change of Heart. The Meanest Gal In Town. \*Pie for Two. 1935: Helldorado. Murder on a Honeymoon. Hot Tip. West Point of the Air. 1936: Murder on a Bridle Path. The Ex-Mrs Bradford. Don't Turn 'em Loose. The Plot Thickens (GB: The Swinging Pearl Mystery). The Big Game. Yours for the Asking. We're Only Human. 1937: Manhattan Merry-Go-Round (GB: Manhattan Music Box). Forty Naughty Girls. 1938: Army Girl (GB: The Last of the Cavalry). The Higgins Family. 1939: Should Husbands Work? The Covered Trailer. My Wife's Relatives. On Your Toes. 1940: Earl of Puddlestone (GB: Jolly Old Higgins). Grandpa Goes to Town. Money to Burn. 1941: Affectionately Yours. Meet John Doe. Nine Lives Are Not Enough. Here Comes Mr Jordan. Tanks a Million. Babes on Broadway. A Date With the Falcon. 1942: My Gal Sal. Hayfoot. Tales of Manhattan. Footlight Serenade. Manila Calling. The Falcon Takes Over. Tramp, Tramp, Tramp. All Through the Night. 1943: Crash Dive. A Guy Named Joe. Arsenic and Old Lace. 1944: The Keys of the Kingdom. Once Upon a Time. 1945: The Clock (GB: Under the Clock). Captain Eddie. A Tree Grows in Brooklyn. This Man's Navy. 1946: The Hoodlum Saint. Lady Luck. The Well-Groomed Bride. Home Sweet Homicide. 1947: Down to Earth. The Homestretch. Tycoon. The Bishop's Wife. 1948: When My Baby Smiles at Me. The Return of October (GB: Date with Destiny). Smart Woman. The Dude Goes West. 1949:*

*The Life of Riley. Bad Boy. Take One False Step. Miss Grant Takes Richmond (GB: Innocence is Bliss). 1950: Riding High. \*Screen Snapshots No. 182. The Yellow Cab Man. Key to the City. The Jackpot. Joe Palooka in the Squared Circle (GB: The Squared Circle). 1951: Come Fill the Cup. Joe Palooka in the Triple Cross (GB: The Triple Cross). Two Gals and a Guy. I'll See You in My Dreams. 1952: What Price Glory? We're Not Married. The Story of Will Rogers. 1953: Movie Stuntmen (GB: Hollywood Thrill Makers). Forever Female. 1954: Suddenly! 1955: The Night of the Hunter. The Girl Rush. 1956: Star in the Dust. 1957: Spring Reunion. Loving You. Man in the Shadow (GB: Pay the Devil). 1958: The Female Animal. Once Upon a Horse. Man or Gun. Rockabye Baby. Money, Women and Guns. The Last Hurrah. The Time of Your Life (TV).*

**GODDARD, Alf** 1897-*1981*
Big, tough, hearty, brown-haired, hook-nosed British actor, a bargain-basement Victor McLaglen who looked like the ex-boxer he was and got into films via stuntwork in the silent days. Played manual workers, soldiers, crooks and, especially in comedy, anyone not averse to kicking sand in the weakling hero's face.

*1923: The Sign of Four. 1925: Battling Bruisers. 1926: Every Mother's Son. White Heat. Mademoiselle from Armentières. Second to None. 1927: Downhill (US: When Boys Leave Home). Hindle Wakes (US: Holiday Week). Remembrance. A Sister to Assist 'Er. The Flight Commander. Carry On. 1928: Sailors Don't Care. Mademoiselle Parley-Voo. What Money Can Buy. Smashing Through. You Know What Sailors Are. Balaclava (US: Jaws of Hell). The Last Post. 1929: Down Channel. High Treason. Rough Seas. 1930: \*The Cockney Spirit in the War No. 2. Alf's Button. The Brat. Bed and Breakfast. 1931: Old Soldiers Never Die. East Lynne on the Western Front. The Happy Ending. Splinters in the Navy. 1932: The Third String. 1933: Too Many Wives. Pride of the Force. Enemy of the Police. 1934: Lost in the Legion. Strictly Illegal. 1935: It's a Bet. No Limit. 1936: Song of Freedom. The Amazing Quest of Ernest*

*Bliss (US: Romance and Riches).* 1937: *Farewell Again (US: Troopship). The Squeaker (US: Murder on Diamond Row). Action for Slander. King Solomon's Mines. Non Stop New York. The Green Cockatoo (US: Four Dark Hours). Bank Holiday (US: Three on a Weekend). Owd Bob (US: To the Victor).* 1938: *The Drum (US: Drums). Convict 99. St Martin's Lane (US: Sidewalks of London). Luck of the Navy. Night Journey. The Ware Case.* 1939: *Murder in Soho (US: Murder in the Night). Young Man's Fancy. Let's Be Famous. A Window in London (US: Lady in Distress). Return to Yesterday.* 1940: *Spy for a Day.* 1941: *South American George. The Young Mr Pitt.* 1942: *Much Too Shy.* 1943: *They Met in the Dark. The Butler's Dilemma.* 1944: *The Way Ahead.* 1945: *The Way to the Stars (US: Johnny in the Clouds). I'll Be Your Sweetheart. They Knew Mr Knight. Perfect Strangers (US: Vacation from Marriage).* 1953: *Innocents in Paris.*

### GOLDBLUM, Jeff 1953-

Dark, spare, cynical-looking American actor who broke with tradition by sticking to his obviously-Jewish real-life surname and, from a start as callow youths, soon built up a reputation in a wide variety of roles, though usually with a streak of humour somewhere in them. 'Anyway,' he says, 'Jewish can be exciting. Maybe I'll get to do Cohen the Barbarian.' With his build, it isn't likely.

1974: *Death Wish. California Split.* 1975: *Nashville. Next Stop Greenwich Village.* 1976: *The Sentinel. St Ives. Special Delivery.* 1977: *Between the Lines. Annie Hall.* 1978: *Thank God It's Friday. Remember My Name. Invasion of the Body Snatchers.* 1979: *The Legend of Sleepy Hollow (TV).* 1980: *Tenspeed and Brownshoe (TV).* 1981: *Threshhold.* 1982: *The Big Chill. Rehearsal for Murder (TV).* 1983: *The Right Stuff.* 1984: *Ernie Kovacs: Between the Laughter (TV). The Adventures of Buckaroo Banzai: Across the Eighth Dimension.* 1985: *Silverado. Into the Night. Transylvania 6-5000.*

### GOMEZ, Thomas

(Sabino Tomas Gomez) 1905-1971
Although well into his thirties before he tried films, this heavy-jowled, scowling American actor whose greasy black hair

fitted his oily characters, was soon a staple part of villainy in numerous forties' Hollywood thrillers. The fifties only proved that he was less effective when used as comic relief, and he faded from the scene. Billed as S. Tomas Gomez in some early films. Academy Award nomination for *Ride the Pink Horse.*

1942: *Sherlock Holmes and the Voice of Terror. Arabian Nights. Pittsburgh. Who Done It?* 1943: *Corvette K-225 (GB: The Nelson Touch). Crazy House. White Savage. (GB: White Captive). Frontier Badmen.* 1944: *The Climax. Phantom Lady. Dead Man's Eyes. In Society. Can't Help Singing. Bowery to Broadway. Follow the Boys.* 1945: *Patrick the Great. I'll Tell the World. Frisco Sal. The Daltons Ride Again.* 1946: *A Night in Paradise. Swell Guy. The Dark Mirror.* 1947: *Singapore. Captain from Castile. Johnny O'Clock. Ride the Pink Horse.* 1948: *Angel in Exile. Key Largo. Casbah.* 1949: *Come to the Stable. Force of Evil. That Midnight Kiss. Sorrowful Jones. I Married a Communist (GB: The Woman on Pier 13).* 1950: *Kim. The Eagle and the Hawk. The Furies. The Toast of New Orleans. Dynamite Pass. Macao (released 1952).* 1951: *The Sellout. Anne of the Indies. The Harlem Globetrotters. The Merry Widow. Pony Soldier (GB: MacDonald of the Canadian Mounties).* 1953: *Sombrero.* 1954: *The Gambler from Natchez. The Adventures of Hajji Baba.* 1955: *The Looters. Night Freight. Las Vegas Shakedown. The Magnificent Matador (GB: The Brave and the Beautiful).* 1956: *Trapeze. The Conqueror.* 1959: *John Paul Jones. But Not for Me.* 1961: *Summer and Smoke. The Power and the Glory (TV. GB: Cinemas).* 1968: *Stay Away Joe. Shadow over Elveron (TV).* 1969: *Beneath the Planet of the Apes.*

### GOODLIFFE, Michael 1914-1976

Thin-faced, very dark-eyed, alert-looking British actor of shadowed aspect and black hair stretching forward from receding temples. A vicar's son, he learned his craft at Stratford's Shakespeare Theatre, but war service (including five years in a P.O.W camp) interrupted his career. He entered films from 1948 in featured roles as policemen, soldiers, relatives or sympathetic figures of authority, often giving better

performances than those billed above him. Never quite a star, despite success in a couple of TV series towards the end of his too-short career, he committed suicide (by leaping from a height) while in hospital.

1948: *The Small Back Room.* 1949: *Stop Press Girl.* 1950: *The Wooden Horse.* 1951: *Captain Horatio Hornblower RN. Cry the Beloved Country (US: African Fury).* 1952: *The Hour of 13. Sea Devils.* 1953: *Rob Roy the Highland Rogue.* 1954: *Front Page Story. The End of the Affair.* 1955: *The Adventures of Quentin Durward (US: Quentin Durward). Dial 999 (US: The Way Out). Double Jeopardy.* 1956: *The Battle of the River Plate (US: Pursuit of the Graf Spee). Wicked As They Come.* 1957: *The One That Got Away. Fortune is a Woman (US: She Played with Fire).* 1958: *A Night to Remember. The Camp on Blood Island. Carve Her Name With Pride. Up the Creek. Further Up the Creek.* 1959: *The Battle of the Sexes. The White Trap. Peeping Tom.* 1960: *Sink the Bismarck! The Trials of Oscar Wilde (US: The Man with the Green Carnation). Conspiracy of Hearts.* 1961: *No Love for Johnnie. The Day the Earth Caught Fire.* 1962: *Number Six. Jigsaw.* 1963: *80,000 Suspects. The £20,000 Kiss.* 1964: *The Seventh Dawn. Man in the Middle. The Gorgon. Troubled Waters. 633 Squadron.* 1965: *Von Ryan's Express.* 1966: *The Night of the Generals. The Jokers.* 1970: *Cromwell.* 1971: *The Johnstown Monster.* 1972: *Henry VIII and His Six Wives.* 1973: *Hitler: The Last Ten Days.* 1974: *The Man With the Golden Gun.*

### GOODWIN, Harold 1917-

Yorkshire-born small-part player in British films. After three years in repertory at Liverpool, he used his slight stature and gormless expression to propel himself into dozens of 'innocent' roles of low intelligence—sidekicks, straight men, friends, soldiers and workers in low-paid jobs. One can still see his small mournful features and slick of dark hair beneath some enormous flat cap.

1938: *The Ware Case.* 1950: *Dance Hall. The Happiest Days of Your Life. The Magnet.* 1951: *Appointment With Venus (US: Island Rescue). The Man in the White Suit. Green*

Grow the Rushes. Judgment Deferred. 1952: Angels One Five. The Last Page (US: Manbait). The Card (US: The Promoter). 1953: The Cruel Sea. Grand National Night (US: Wicked Wife). The Case of Gracie Budd. The Million Pound Note (US: Man with a Million). 1954: The Harassed Hero. One Good Turn. The Gay Dog. The Dam Busters. 1955: A Kid for Two Farthings. The Ship That Died of Shame (US: PT Raiders). You Lucky People. The Ladykillers. Josephine and Men. 1956: Now and Forever. Charley Moon. The Long Arm (US: The Third Key). Zarak. The Last Man to Hang? Three Men in a Boat. 1957: Barnacle Bill (US: All at Sea). The Prince and the Showgirl. The Bridge on the River Kwai. Seawife. 1958: Girls at Sea. The Square Peg. Law and Disorder. Sea of Sand. 1959: The Mummy. The Bandit of Zhobe. The Ugly Duckling. Wrong Number. 1960: Sink the Bismarck! Spartacus. Operation Cupid. The Bulldog Breed. 1961: The Terror of the Tongs. Nearly a Nasty Accident. On the Fiddle (US: Operation Snafu). *The Square Mile Murder. Never Back Losers. 1962: The Traitors. Hair of the Dog. Number Six. Phantom of the Opera. The Longest Day. Crooks Anonymous. The Fast Lady. 1963: The Hi-Jackers. The Comedy Man. 1964: Curse of the Mummy's Tomb. *All in Good Time. 1965: Monster of Terror (US: Die, Monster, Die). 1967: Don't Raise the Bridge, Lower the River. 1969: Frankenstein Must Be Destroyed. Some Will, Some Won't. 1970: Hoverbug. 1974: All Creatures Great and Small. 1976: The Chiffy Kids (series). 1977: Jabberwocky.

## GORDON, Colin 1911-1972

Fair-haired, moustachioed, bespectacled, aristocratic-looking British actor (born in Sri Lanka, then Ceylon); he played characters whose air of cynical and snooty authority could turn to harassed bewilderment—teachers, lawyers and especially civil servants. Made his West End stage debut as the hind legs of a horse.

1947: Jim the Penman. 1948: Bond Street. It's Hard to be Good. The Winslow Boy. 1949: Helter Skelter. Traveller's Joy (released 1951). Golden Arrow (US: Three Men and a Girl. Released 1952). Edward My Son. 1951: The

Third Visitor. The Long Dark Hall. Green Grow the Rushes. Circle of Danger. Laughter in Paradise. The Man in the White Suit. The Lady with a Lamp. 1952: Folly to be Wise. The Hour of 13. Mandy (US: Crash of Silence). 1953: The Heart of the Matter. Grand National Night (US: Wicked Wife). Innocents in Paris. 1954: Up to His Neck. Escapade. Little Red Monkey (US: The Case of the Red Monkey). 1955: John and Julie. Jumping for Joy. Keep It Clean. 1956: The Extra Day. A Touch of the Sun. Up in the World. The Green Man. 1957: The Key Man. The One That Got Away. The Safecracker. 1958: Alive and Kicking. Virgin Island (US: Our Virgin Island). The Doctor's Dilemma. The Key. The Crowning Touch. 1959: The Mouse That Roared. Please Turn Over. Bobbikins. 1960: Make Mine Mink. His and Hers. The Big Day. Carry on Constable. The Day They Robbed the Bank of England. 1961: Don't Bother to Knock! (US: Why Bother to Knock?). Three on a Spree. The Horsemasters.

House of Mystery. In the Doghouse. Very Important Person. 1962: Night of the Eagle (US: Burn, Witch, Burn). Crooks Anonymous. The Devil's Agent. The Boys. Strongroom. Seven Keys. 1963: Bitter Harvest. The Running Man. Heavens Above! The Pink Panther. 1964: Allez France! (US: The Counterfeit Constable). 1965: The Liquidator. 1966: The Great St Trinian's Train Robbery. The Psychopath. The Family Way. 1967: The Trygon Factor. Casino Royale. 1968: Subterfuge. Don't Raise the Bridge, Lower the River. 1969: Mischief.

## GORDON, Hal 1894-1946

Short, thick-set, dark-haired, ever-smiling British comic actor, an ex-music-hall performer who got into British films with the coming of sound. The cheerful, rather dim-witted personality he projected made him an ideal partner for some broad comedians of the 1930s, especially big, bluff Leslie Fuller. From 1939 onwards, Gordon combined acting with running a pub.

1928: Adam's Apple. 1929: When Knights Were Bold. 1930: The Windjammer. *The Cockney Spirit in the War No. 2. *The Cockney Spirit in the War No. 3. 1931: Out of the Blue. Old Soldiers Never Die. Poor Old Bill. Up for

the Cup. Bill and Coo. Money for Nothing. Tonight's the Night—Pass It On. 1932: Partners Please. The New Hotel. The Strangler. Old Spanish Customers. Help Yourself. The Indiscretions of Eve. The Bad Companions. Brother Alfred. Strip, Strip, Hooray! Lucky Girl. The Last Coupon. Josser in the Army. His Wife's Mother. Money Talks. For the Love of Mike. Sleepless Nights. Lord Camber's Ladies. Let Me Explain, Dear. 1933: Their Night Out. Hawleys of High Street. Facing the Music. The Pride of the Force. Crime on the Hill. A Southern Maid. 1934: Master and Man. Happy. A Political Party. The Outcast. Sometimes Good. My Song Goes Round the World. Lost in the Legion. Wishes. 1935: Dance Band. Captain Bill. Eighteen Minutes. Dandy Dick. Lend Me Your Wife. The Deputy Drummer. Invitation to the Waltz. Play Up the Band. 1936: No Escape/No Exit. Queen of Hearts. The Man Behind the Mask. One Good Turn. The Amazing Quest of Ernest Bliss (US: Romance and Riches). Keep Your Seats, Please. It's in the Bag. Dusty Ermine (US: Hideout in the Alps). Southern Roses. 1937: Keep Fit. East of Ludgate Hill. 1938: Father o' Nine. We're Going to Be Rich. It's in the Air (US: George Takes the Air). Break the News. St Martin's Lane (US: Sidewalks of London). 1939: Come on George. 1940: Let George Do It. *Food for Thought. Spare a Copper. 1943: Old Mother Riley, Detective. 1944: Give Me the Stars. Heaven is Round the Corner. Welcome Mr Washington. It Happened One Sunday. Kiss the Bride Goodbye. 1946: I'll Turn to You.

## GORDON, Leo 1922- 2000

One of the few striking Hollywood uglies of the 1950s not to make stardom. In any case, Gordon, a dark-haired, square-faced, mean-looking actor usually cast as sullen, loud-mouthed, aggressive heavies, has preferred to work on his second-string career as a writer, contributing several screenplays, before returning sporadically to acting in recent times.

1953: All the Brothers Were Valiant. Gun Fury. Hondo. City of Bad Men. China Venture. 1954: Riot in Cell Block 11. The Yellow Mountain. Sign of the Pagan. The Bamboo Prison. 1955: Ten Wanted Men. Santa Fé Passage. Seven Angry Men. Soldier of Fortune. Robbers' Roost. The Man With the Gun (GB: The Trouble Shooter). Tennessee's Partner. 1956: Red Sundown. The Conqueror. Great Day in the Morning. Johnny Concho. The Outlander (TV. GB: cinemas). The Steel Jungle. The Man Who Knew Too Much. Great Day in the Morning. The 7th Cavalry. 1957: The Restless Breed. Black Patch. Lure of the Swamp. The Tall Stranger. Baby Face Nelson. Man in the Shadow (GB: Pay the Devil). 1958: The Notorious Mr Monks. Quantrill's Raiders. Ride a Crooked Trail. Apache Territory. Cry Baby Killer. Texas John Slaughter (TV. GB: cinemas). 1959: The Big Operator. Escort West. The Jayhawkers. 1960: Noose for a Gunman. 1961: The Intruder (GB: The

ABOVE Hal **Gordon** (right) provided loyal support to a number of British film comedians. Here are Gordon and Leslie Fuller in suits that speak louder than words in *The Outcast* (1934)

BELOW Villains Leo **Gordon** (right) and Phil Carey are quick to show their true colours in *Gun Fury* (1953)

Stranger). 1962: The Nun and the Sergeant. Tarzan Goes to India. 1963: The Haunted Palace. Kings of the Sun. McLintock! 1964: L'arme à gauche. The Dictator's Guns (GB: Guns for the Dictator). Kitten With a Whip. 1965: Girls on the Beach. 1966: Tobruk. Night of the Grizzly. Beau Geste. 1967: The Devil's Angels. Hostile Guns. The St Valentine's Day Massacre. 1968: Buckskin. 1970: You Can't Win 'em All. 1971: The Trackers (TV). 1972: Bonnie's Kids. 1973: My Name is Nobody. 1975: Barbary Coast (TV. GB: In Old San Francisco). 1976: Nashville Girl. 1978. Hitler's Son. Bog. 1980: Rage (TV). 1982: Fire and Ice (voice only). 1985: Savage Dawn.

### GORDON, Mary
(M. Gilmour) 1882-1963

Diminutive but heftily built Scottish-born actress in Hollywood films from 1925 after coming to America with a touring company. She could be kindly, truculent, or down-to-earth, and played scores of small supporting roles as mothers, housekeepers, washerwomen and landladies before her bun-like features found their perfect niche as Mrs Hudson, Basil Rathbone's housekeeper, in the Sherlock Holmes films (and on radio). Later played Leo Gorcey's much put-upon mother in the Bowery Boys films.

1925: Tessie. The People vs Nancy Preston. The Home Maker. 1926: Black Paradise. 1927: Clancy's Kosher Wedding. Naughty Nanette. 1928: The Old Code. 1929: Madame X. Dynamite. The Saturday Kid. One of the Bravest. Sunny Side Up. 1930: Oh, for a Man! *When the Wind Blows. Dance With Me. 1931: The Black Camel. Subway Express. 1932: The Texas Cyclone. Almost Married. Dancers in the Dark. Call Her Savage. Blonde Venus. The Trial of Vivienne Ware. Wild Girl (GB: Salomy Jane). Pack Up Your Troubles. 1933: *Nature in the Wrong. My Woman. Design for Living. She Done Him Wrong. The Whirlwind. Lucky Dog. 1934: Beloved. The Little Minister. The Whole Town's Talking (GB: Passport to Fame). 1935: *I'm a Father. Vanessa—Her Love Story. Bonnie Scotland. Bride of Frankenstein. The Irish in Us. Waterfront Lady. Mutiny on the Bounty. 1936: *Share the Wealth. Laughing Irish Eyes. Forgotten Faces. Stage Struck.

Mary of Scotland. Yellowstone. The Plough and the Stars. After the Thin Man. Bullets or Ballots. 1937: Great Guy (GB: Pluck of the Irish). The Man in Blue. Meet the Boy Friend. Nancy Steele Is Missing. Pick a Star. Double Wedding. The Great O'Malley. A Damsel in Distress. Way Out West. Toast of New York. You Can't Have Everything. One-Man Justice. Married Before Breakfast. 1938: Lady Behave. Kidnapped. Gateway. Angels with Dirty Faces. City Streets. The Cowboy from Brooklyn (GB: Romance and Rhythm). Blonde Cheat. Tail Spin. 1939: The Jones Family in Hollywood. Wings of the Navy. Day Time Wife. My Son Is Guilty (GB: Crime's End). The Hound of the Baskervilles. Parents on Trial. Captain Fury. She Married a Cop. The Adventures of Sherlock Holmes (GB: Sherlock Holmes). Rulers of the Sea. Joe and Ethel Turp Call on the President. Marshal of Mesa City. Code of the Streets. Broadway Serenade. Mr Smith Goes to Washington. The Night of Nights. Off the Record. Tell No Tales. Racketeers of the Range. 1940: My Son, My Son. Tear Gas Squad. The Last Alarm. I Take This Oath. Kitty Foyle. No, No, Nanette. When the Daltons Rode. Queen of the Mob. Nobody's Children. Saps at Sea. The Doctor Takes a Wife. Brother Orchid. Women Without Names. Public Deb No. 1. The Invisible Man Returns. 1941: How Green Was My Valley. The Invisible Woman. Pot o' Gold (GB: The Golden Hour). Flight from Destiny. Borrowed Hero. It Started With Eve. Riot Squad. Appointment for Love. Unfinished Business. Sealed Lips. Unexpected Uncle. Four Jacks and a Jill. Bombay Clipper. 1942: Sherlock Holmes and the Voice of Terror. Fly by Night. Dr Broadway. Gentleman Jim. Powder Town. Meet the Stewarts. It Happened in Flatbush. Sherlock Holmes and the Secret Weapon. The Mummy's Tomb. Boss of Big Town. Half-Way to Shanghai. The Strange Case of Dr RX. The Pride of the Yankees. 1943: Sherlock Holmes Faces Death. Two Tickets to London. Forever and a Day. Sweet Rosie O'Grady. Here Comes Kelly. Keep 'em Slugging. Sarong Girl. Sherlock Holmes in Washington. Smart Guy. Whispering Footsteps. You're a Lucky Fellow, Mr Smith. Sherlock Holmes and the Spider Woman (GB: Spider Woman). 1944: Ever Since Venus. Million Dollar Kid. Pearl of Death. The Last Ride. Follow the Leader. The Hour before the Dawn. Hollywood Canteen. Hat Check Honey. The Racket Man. Secrets of Scotland Yard. Irish Eyes Are Smiling. The Scarlet Claw. 1945: Divorce. The Woman in Green. Strange Confession. See My Lawyer. Captain Eddie. Kitty. Pillow of Death. The House of Fear. The Body Snatcher. Pursuit to Algiers (GB: Sherlock Holmes in Pursuit to Algiers). 1946: Little Giant (GB: On the Carpet). Sentimental Journey. The Dark Horse. The Hoodlum Saint. Terror by Night. In Fast Company. Sing While You Dance. Dressed to Kill (GB: Sherlock Holmes and the Secret Code). Shadows Over Chinatown. Sister Kenny. Singin' in the Corn (GB: Give and Take). 1947: The Secret Life of Walter Mitty. Stallion Road. Exposed. The Invisible Wall. The Long Night. Angels' Alley.

1948: The Strange Mrs Crane. Highway 13. Fort Apache. 1949: Mighty Joe Young. Deputy Marshal. Shamrock Hill. Haunted Trails. The File on Thelma Jordon (GB: Thelma Jordon). 1950: West of Wyoming.

### GORDON, Nora(h) 1894-1970

Pudding-faced British small-part actress with red-gold hair and honest if severe features. She followed her character-actor husband Leonard Sharp (1890-1958) into films and appeared sporadically in mother roles in British films over a 20-year period. Her daughter, Dorothy Gordon (1924-) is also an actress. The spelling of her Christian name varies from film to film.

1941: Danny Boy. Facing the Music. Old Mother Riley's Circus. Sheepdog of the Hills. South American George. Somewhere in Camp. 1942: Front Line Kids. Old Mother Riley, Detective. 1947: Death in High Heels. Green Fingers. Journey Ahead. The Mark of Cain. My Brother Jonathan. 1948: The Fallen Idol. 1949: Floodtide. 1950: The Woman in Question (US: Five Angles on Murder). Blackmailed. 1951: Circle of Danger. Night Was Our Friend. 1952: The Woman's Angle. Sing Along with Me. 1953: Murder at 3 am. Murder by Proxy (released 1955. US: Blackout). Twice Upon a Time. 1954: Radio Cab Murder. 1955: The Glass Cage (US: The Glass Tomb). A Kid for Two Farthings. The Constant Husband. Police Dog. 1957: Woman in a Dressing Gown. 1958: High Jump. 1959: Horrors of the Black Museum. Sentenced for Life. Top Floor Girl. 1960: Compelled. Sons and Lovers. 1961: The Grass Is Greener. The Rebel (US: Call Me Genius). Victim. The Young Ones. The Piper's Tune. 1962: Twice Round the Daffodils. Postman's Knock. 1964: Carry on Spying. 1965: The Nanny.

### GORDON, Ruth
(Ruth G. Jones) 1896-

Tiny, sharp-faced American actress and writer who played a couple of leading roles in silents, mothers in the 1940s and aged eccentrics in recent times. She turned the early part of her life into a play: it was filmed, as The Actress, in 1953. Long married to writer/director Garson Kanin, with whom she wrote several screenplays

for Spencer Tracy and Katharine Hepburn. Academy Award (best supporting actress) in 1968 for *Rosemary's Baby*. Oscar nominee for *Inside Daisy Clover*.

1915: *Camille.* 1916: *The Wheel of Life.* 1939: **Information Please* (series 1, number 8). 1940: *Abe Lincoln in Illinois (GB: Spirit of the People). Dr Ehrlich's Magic Bullet (GB: The Story of Dr Ehrlich's Magic Bullet).* **Information Please* (series 2, number 2). 1941: *Two-Faced Woman.* 1943: *Edge of Darkness. Action in the North Atlantic.* 1966: *Lord Love a Duck. Inside Daisy Clover.* 1968: *Rosemary's Baby.* 1969: *Whatever Happened to Aunt Alice?* 1970: *Where's Poppa?* 1972: *Harold and Maude.* 1973: *Isn't It Shocking?* 1975: *The Prince of Central Park (TV).* 1976: *The Big Bus.* 1977: *The Great Houdinis (TV). Look What's Happened to Rosemary's Baby (TV). Perfect Gentlemen (TV).* 1978: *Every Which Way But Loose.* 1979: *Scavenger Hunt. Boardwalk.* 1980: *Any Which Way You Can. My Bodyguard. Smokey and the Bandit II (GB: Smokey and the Bandit Ride Again).* 1982: *Don't Go to Sleep (TV). Jimmy the Kid.* 1984: *Mugsy's Girls/Delta Pi.* 1985: *Trouble with Spys. Voyage of the Rock Aliens.*

**GOSS, Helen** 1903-
Pleasantly plump, red-haired, full-faced, high-cheekboned, cheerful-looking British actress who played a few barmaids and servants in between concentrating on her other career as a drama coach, notably in charge of the acting side of the Rank 'Charm School' for starlets in post-war years.

1932: *Bachelor's Baby.* 1934: *Important People.* 1936: *Hail and Farewell.* 1937: *The Reverse Be My Lot.* 1943: *Dear Octopus (US: The Randolph Family).* 1945: *A Place of One's Own. The Wicked Lady. Pink String and Sealing Wax. They Were Sisters.* 1947: *The Mark of Cain.* 1948: *My Sister and I. The Weaker Sex.* 1950: *The Woman in Question (US: Five Angles on Murder). Blackmailed. Stage Fright.* 1951: *Cheer the Brave. Appointment with Venus (US: Island Rescue). Honeymoon Deferred.* 1952: *Something Money Can't Buy. The Pickwick Papers. The Planter's Wife (US: Outpost in Malaya).* 1953: *The Sword and the Rose.* 1954: *Three Cornered Fate.* 1957: *Action of the Tiger.* 1959: *The Hound of the Baskervilles.* 1960: *Moment of Danger (US: Malaga). The Two Faces of Dr Jekyll (US: House of Fright).* 1970: *Jane Eyre (TV. GB: cinemas).*

**GOSSETT, Lou(is)** 1936-
Slim, tall, whippy black American actor, balding, then shaven-headed, who struggled for years to make an impact in worthwhile roles while 'wearing loincloths' in TV series set in Africa. Notice began to be taken of his powerful presence in the 1970s, and the big breakthrough came when he took the Best Supporting Actor Oscar for 1981's *An Officer and a Gentleman*, in a typically forthright role. Sometimes billed as Lou(is) Gossett Jnr.

1961: *A Raisin in the Sun.* 1968: *The Bush Baby. Companions in Nightmare (TV).* 1970: *The Landlord.* 1971: *Skin Game.* 1972: *Travels With My Aunt.* 1973: *The Laughing Policeman (GB: An Investigation of Murder).* 1974: *The White Dawn. It's Good to Be Alive (TV). Sidekicks (TV).* 1975: *Delancey Street: The Crisis Within (TV).* 1976: *The River Niger (completed 1972). J.D.'s Revenge.* 1977: *Little Ladies of the Night (TV). The Deep. The Choirboys.* 1978: *To Kill a Cop (TV). The Critical List (TV).* 1979: *The Man Who Stands Alone/This Man Stands Alone (TV).* 1981: *Don't Look Back (TV). An Officer and a Gentleman.* 1982: *Benny's Place (TV).* 1983: *Jaws 3-D. Sadat (TV).* 1984: *Finders Keepers. The Guardian (TV).* 1985: *Enemy Mine. The Iron Eagle.*

**GOTELL, Walter** 1924-
Bald, severe-looking British actor with crooked smile who uniquely combines acting, farming and business careers. Acting was the first of these and he broke into films briefly as a young man straight from repertory. Later returned in more 'senior' roles as figures of authority—headmasters, superintendents and an assortment of martinets, a range which also stood him in good stead on television. Is managing director of a group of engineering companies.

1943: *We Dive at Dawn.* 1944: *2,000 Women.* 1950: *The Wooden Horse. Lilli Marlene. Cairo Road.* 1951: *The African Queen.* 1953: *Desperate Moment. The Red Beret (US: Paratrooper). Stryker of the Yard.* 1954: *Duel in the Jungle.* 1955: *Dial 999 (US: The Way Out).* 1956: *The Man Who Knew Too Much.* 1958: *Ice-Cold in Alex (US: Desert Attack). I Was Monty's Double (US: Monty's Double). No Safety Ahead.* 1959: *Solomon and Sheba. The Bandit of Zhobe. The Treasure of San Teresa. Shake Hands With the Devil.* 1960: *Conspiracy of Hearts. Moment of Danger (US: Malaga). Circle of Deception.* 1961: *The Guns of Navarone. The Devil's Daffodil (US: The Daffodil Killer). The Damned (US: These Are the Damned).* 1962: *55 Days at Peking. Lancelot and Guinevere (US: Sword of Lancelot). The Road to Hong Kong. The Devil's Agent.* 1963: *From Russia With Love. The Million Dollar Collar.* 1964: *Lord Jim.* 1965: *The Spy Who Came In from the Cold.* 1967: *Attack on the Iron Coast.* 1968: *Cry Wolf.* 1969: *The File of the Golden Goose.* 1971: *Endless Night.* 1972: *Our Miss Fred.* 1976: *Black Sunday.* 1977: *The Spy Who Loved Me. March or Die.* 1978: *The Stud. The Boys from Brazil.* 1979: *Moonraker. The London Connection (US: TV, as The Omega Connection). Cuba.* 1981: *For Your Eyes Only.* 1983: *Memed My Hawk. Octopussy.* 1984: *KGB: The Secret War.* 1985: *A View to a Kill. Up the Military.*

**GRAPEWIN, Charley** 1869-1956
Solidly built American actor, playwright, composer and author who came to Hollywood when he was past 60, and must have delighted himself, as well as audiences, by prolonging his career for a further 15 years

as the prototype of wise, wheezy, elderly relations. Remembered by most as Grandpa Joad in *The Grapes of Wrath*, but also by series fans as Inspector Queen in the Ellery Queen crime thrillers of the early 1940s.

*1902: Above the Limit. 1929: \*Ladies' Choice. \*That Red-Headed Hussy. The Shannons of Broadway. \*Jed's Vacation. 1930: Only Saps Work. 1931: The Millionaire. Gold Dust Gertie (GB: Why Change Your Husband?). 1932: Hell's House. No Man of Her Own. Disorderly Conduct. Lady and Gent. The Woman in Room 13. The Night of June 13th. Wild Horse Mesa. Big Timer. 1933: Hello, Everybody! The Kiss Before the Mirror. Midnight Mary. Beauty for Sale. Don't Bet on Love. Pilgrimage. Wild Boys of the Road (GB: Dangerous Days). Heroes for Sale. Torch Singer (GB: Broadway Singer). Hell and High Water (GB: Cap'n Jericho). 1934: Anne of Green Gables. Judge Priest. The Quitter. The Loudspeaker (GB: The Radio Star). Caravan. She Made Her Bed. Two Alone. Return of the Terror. 1935: The President Vanishes (GB: Strange Conspiracy). King Solomon of Broadway. Alice Adams. Shanghai. Eight Bells. Party Wire. In Spite of Danger. One Frightened Night. Ah, Wilderness! Superspeed. Rendezvous. 1936: The Petrified Forest. Sinner Take All. Small Town Girl. The Voice of Bugle Ann. Libeled Lady. Without Orders. 1937: The Good Earth. A Family Affair. Captains Courageous. Between Two Women. Bad Man of Brimstone. The Big City. Broadway Melody of 1938. Bad Guy. 1938: Three Comrades. Girl of the Golden West. Of Human Hearts. Three Loves Has Nancy. Listen, Darling. Artists and Models Abroad (GB: Stranded in Paris). 1939: Stand Up and Fight. The Wizard of Oz. Burn 'em Up O'Connor. Sabotage (GB: Spies at Work). Hero for a Day. The Man Who Dared. Sudden Money. Dust Be My Destiny. I Am Not Afraid. 1940: Texas Rangers Ride Again. Ellery Queen, Master Detective. Johnny Apollo. Earthbound. The Grapes of Wrath. Rhythm on the River. 1941: Ellery Queen's Penthouse Mystery. Ellery Queen and the Murder Ring (GB: The Murder Ring). Ellery Queen and the Perfect Crime (GB: The Perfect Crime). They Died with Their Boots On. Tobacco Road. 1942: Enemy Agents Meet Ellery Queen*

*(GB: The Lido Mystery). A Close Call for Ellery Queen (GB: A Close Call). Crash Dive. A Desperate Chance for Ellery Queen (GB: A Desperate Chance). 1944: Follow the Boys. Atlantic City. The Impatient Years. 1947: Gunfighters (GB: The Assassin). 1948: The Enchanted Valley. 1949: Will James' Sand (GB: Sand). 1951: When I Grow Up.*

## GRAY, Charles
(Donald Gray) 1928- 2000
Fair-haired British actor with large, square head and fruity tones, a dab hand at smug and supercilious characters who sometimes progressed to top-grade villainy (as with his Blofeld in *Diamonds Are Forever*). Even when he was affable and hearty, you felt he was faking, and the lack of further film roles for his distinctive personality was the cinema's loss. Also the 'voice' for Jack Hawkins in several films after he had lost the use of his own.

*1957: I Accuse! 1959: Tommy the Toreador. Follow a Star. The Desperate Man. 1960: The Entertainer. 1961: Man in the Moon. 1965: Masquerade. 1966: The Night of the Generals. 1967: You Only Live Twice. The Man Outside. The Secret War of Harry Frigg. 1968: The Devil Rides Out (US: The Devil's Bride). The File of the Golden Goose. Mosquito Squadron. 1970: The Excutioner. Cromwell. 1971: Diamonds Are Forever. 1974: The Beast Must Die! 1975: The Rocky Horror Picture Show. 1976: Seven Nights in Japan. The Seven Per Cent Solution. 1977: Silver Bears. 1978: The Legacy. 1979: The House on Garibaldi Street (TV: GB: cinemas). 1980: The Mirror Crack'd. 1981: Shock Treatment. 1982: Charles and Diana, a Royal Love Story (TV). 1983: The Jigsaw Man.*

## GREEN, Danny 1903-
Thickly built, balding, tough-looking British actor. Born in the East End of London (within the sound of Bow Bells; a true cockney), he was typecast as hulking thugs and few cinemagoers ever knew his name until, in his early fifties, he was cast as One Round in the famous black comedy *The Ladykillers*. After that, he went back to playing mainly small roles until his retirement in 1968. Spent several years in America as a boy, and is said to have appeared in a couple of silent films there.

*1929: Atlantic. The Silent House. The Crooked Billet. 1934: Things Are Looking Up. 1936: Crime Over London. 1937: Gangway. Midnight Menace. Non Stop New York. Jericho (US: Dark Sands). 1940: 'Bulldog' Sees It Through. 1944: Fiddlers Three. Welcome Mr Washington. Madonna of the Seven Moons. 1945: The Echo Murders. 1947: The Man Within (US: The Smugglers). 1948: Good Time Girl. No Orchids for Miss Blandish. 1949: Helter Skelter. 1950: Someone at the Door. State Secret (US: The Great Manhunt). The Lady Craved Excitement. Her Favourite Husband (US: The*

*Taming of Dorothy). 1951: A Tale of Five Cities (US: A Tale of Five Women). Whispering Smith Hits London (US: Whispering Smith versus Scotland Yard). 1952: Little Big Shot. 1953: Laughing Anne. 1955: A Kid for Two Farthings. Jumping for Joy. The Ladykillers. 1956: Assignment Redhead (US: Requirement for a Redhead). Interpol (US: Pickup Alley). Seven Waves Away (US: Abandon Ship!). 1958: The Seventh Voyage of Sinbad. 1959: Beyond This Place (US: Web of Evidence). Hidden Homicide. 1960: Girls of Latin Quarter. The Man in the Moon. Surprise Package. 1961: In the Wake of a Stranger. 1962: The Fast Lady. The Old Dark House. 1963: A Stitch in Time. 1967: Smashing Time.*

## GREEN, Nigel 1924-1972
South Africa-born dark-haired actor of smooth, saturnine, superior features, in British films from the early 1950s after theatrical experience. He began playing much larger roles after *Zulu* (1963), and came close to becoming a star in the late 1960s. Died from an accidental overdose of sleeping pills.

*1953: Meet Mr Malcolm. 1954: Stranger from Venus (US: Immediate Decision). The Sea Shall Not Have Them. 1955: As Long As They're Happy. 1956: Reach for the Sky. Find the Lady. 1957: Bitter Victory. The Gypsy and the Gentleman. 1958: Corridors of Blood (released 1961). 1959: Witness in the Dark. Beat Girl (US: Wild for Kicks). 1960: The Criminal (US: The Concrete Jungle). Sword of Sherwood Forest. Gorgo. The Queen's Guards. 1961: The Man at the Carlton Tower. Pit of Darkness. The Spanish Sword. 1962: The Durant Affair. Mysterious Island. Playback. The Man Who Finally Died. Mystery Submarine (US: Decoy). The Prince and the Pauper. 1963: Jason and the Argonauts. Zulu. Saturday Night Out. 1964: The Masque of the Red Death. 1965: The Ipcress File. The Face of Fu Manchu. The Skull. 1966: Khartoum. Deadlier Than the Male. Let's Kill Uncle. Tobruk. 1967: Africa—Texas Style! 1968: Play Dirty. Fräulein Doktor. The Pink Jungle. The Wrecking Crew. 1969: The Kremlin Letter. 1970: Countess Dracula. 1971: The Ruling Class. 1973: Gawain and the Green Knight.*

ABOVE Charles **Gray** in his most supercilious form as a judge in
the 1981 satirical musical *Shock Treatment*. With him is Ruby
Wax

BELOW Danny **Green** (centre) in his most famous role: One-
Round in Ealing Studios' *The Ladykillers* (1955). With him in
this unholy quintet: Alec Guinness, Peter Sellers, Herbert Lom
and Cecil Parker

## GREENWOOD, Charlotte

(Frances C. Greenwood) 1890-1978

Tall, horsey-faced but happy-looking American actress and eccentric dancer, with hearty, no-nonsense voice. She played plain Janes in her early days, then moved on to character roles in comedies and musicals and became internationally known for her long-legged, high-kicking dance routines. At her best while under contract to Fox in the early 1940s, but also notable as Aunt Eller in *Oklahoma!* One could hardly believe her when she boomed 'That's about as far as I can go' at the end of one of her routines.

1915: *Jane.* 1928: *Baby Mine.* 1929: *So Long, Letty.* 1931: *Parlor, Bedroom and Bath (GB: Romeo in Pyjamas). Palmy Days. Stepping Out. Flying High (GB: Happy Landing). The Man in Possession.* 1932: *Cheaters at Play.* 1933: *Orders Is Orders.* 1940: *Young People. Star Dust. Down Argentine Way.* 1941: *Moon Over Miami. Tall, Dark and Handsome.* 1942: *The Perfect Snob. Springtime in the Rockies.* 1943: *Dixie Dugan. The Gang's All Here (GB: The Girls He Left Behind).* 1944: *Up in Mabel's Room. Home in Indiana.* 1946: *Wake Up and Dream. Driftwood.* 1949: *The Great Dan Patch. Oh, You Beautiful Doll.* 1950: *Peggy.* 1953: *Dangerous When Wet.* 1955: *Oklahoma!* 1956: *Glory. The Opposite Sex.*

## GREGG, Everley 1898-1959

Very dark-haired, moon-faced British actress of strong personality. After long theatrical experience, she made a striking film debut as the nagging Catherine Parr, the king's last wife in *The Private Life of Henry VIII.* Films called her back from time to time in more routine roles, but a tally of only 39 feature films in 25 years speaks volumes of her affection for the theatre.

1933: *The Private Life of Henry VIII.* 1935: *The Scoundrel. The Ghost Goes West.* 1936: *Thunder in the City.* 1938: *Blondes for Danger. Pygmalion.* 1939: *Spies of the Air.* 1941: *Major Barbara.* 1942: *Uncensored. In Which We Serve. The First of the Few (US: Spitfire).* 1943: *The Demi-Paradise (US: Adventure for Two). The Gentle Sex.* 1944: *\*The Two Fathers. This Happy Breed.* 1945:

*Brief Encounter.* 1946: *Gaiety George (US: Showtime). Great Expectations. I See a Dark Stranger (US: The Adventuress). Piccadilly Incident.* 1947: *The Woman in the Hall.* 1949: *Marry Me! The Huggetts Abroad.* 1950: *The Astonished Heart. Stage Fright. The Woman in Question (US: Five Angles on Murder). The Franchise Affair.* 1951: *The Magic Box. Worm's Eye View.* 1952: *Moulin Rouge. Stolen Face. \*A Spot of Bother. \*The Paper Chase. \*A Sweeping Statement. \*Shedding the Load. \*Food for Thought. \*Height of Ambition.* 1954: *The Night of the Full Moon. Father Brown (US: The Detective).* 1955: *Lost (US: Tears for Simon). The Man Who Never Was.* 1956: *Brothers in Law.* 1957: *Carry on Admiral (US: The Ship Was Loaded). \*Danger List.* 1958: *Room at the Top.* 1959: *Deadly Record.*

## GREGORY, James 1911-

American actor with distinctive, receding dark, wavy hair, slightly reminiscent of Joseph Cotten. His film career was slow to start after he switched from stockbroking to acting in the post-war years, but in latter days he became one of television's most frequent and efficient guest stars in drama series. His gruff voice and soothing manner often concealed villainous instincts, but he also played friendly advisers and unbending superiors. Has made up for his late start by notching up almost 40 years as an actor.

1948: *The Naked City.* 1951: *The Frogmen.* 1956: *Nightfall. The Scarlet Hour. The Big*

*Caper.* 1957: *Gun Glory. The Young Stranger.* 1958: *Underwater Warrior. Onionhead.* 1959: *Al Capone. Hey Boy! Hey Girl!* 1961: *X-15.* 1962: *Two Weeks in Another Town. The Manchurian Candidate. PT 109.* 1963: *Twilight of Honor (GB: The Charge is Murder). The Great Escape. Captain Newman MD.* 1964: *A Distant Trumpet. Quick, Before it Melts. A Rage to Live.* 1965: *The Sons of Katie Elder.* 1966: *The Silencers. Murderers' Row.* 1967: *The Secret War of Harry Frigg. The Ambushers. Clambake.* 1968: *Hawaii Five-O (TV).* 1969: *The Love God? Beneath the Planet of the Apes.* 1970: *The Hawaiians (GB: Master of the Islands).* 1971: *Shoot Out. Million Dollar Duck.* 1972: *The Late Liz. A Very Missing Person (TV). The Weekend Nun (TV).* 1973: *Miracle on 34th Street (TV).* 1975: *The Strongest Man in the World. The Abduction of Saint Anne/They've Kidnapped Anne Benedict (TV).* 1976: *Francis Gary Powers: The True Story of the U-2 Spy Incident (TV).* 1979: *The Main Event.* 1981: *Goldie and the Boxer Go to Hollywood.* 1983: *Wait 'Til Your Mother Gets Home (TV).*

## GRENFELL, Joyce

(J. Phipps) 1910-1979

Toothy, engaging, dark-haired British monologuist, originally from stage revue. Once described herself as 'about eight feet tall with a face like a reflection in a spoon'. Her crisp, fruity upper-class voice and ability to create a delightful range of ever-so-English characters was much underused by the cinema. Died from cancer.

1943: *The Lamp Still Burns. The Demi-Paradise (US: Adventure for Two).* 1946: *While the Sun Shines.* 1948: *\*Designing Women. Alice in Wonderland (voice only).* 1949: *Poet's Pub. Scrapbook for 1933 (voice only). A Run for Your Money.* 1950: *The Happiest Days of Your Life. Stage Fright.* 1951: *The Galloping Major. Laughter in Paradise. The Magic Box.* 1952: *The Pickwick Papers.* 1953: *Genevieve. The Million Pound Note (US: Man With a Million).* 1954: *Forbidden Cargo. The Belles of St Trinian's.* 1957: *The Good Companions. Blue Murder at St Trinian's.* 1958: *Happy is the Bride.* 1960: *The Pure Hell of St Trinian's.*

1962: *The Old Dark House.* 1964: *The Yellow Rolls Royce. The Americanization of Emily.*

## GRIFFIES, Ethel
(E. Woods) 1878-1975

Severe-looking, tight-lipped, brown-haired, often bespectacled British actress, mainly in Hollywood since 1924 with sporadic intervals for appearances in British and American theatres. On stage at two, she was still treading the boards at 87. She could play frail and vulnerable, or fierce and disapproving; made several stage appearances as the ill-fated Mrs Bramson in *Night Must Fall*, but did not take the role in either film version. Died following a stroke.

1917: *The Cost of a Kiss.* 1930: *Old English. Chances/Changes. Stepdaughters.* 1931: *Manhattan Parade. Once a Lady. The Road to Singapore. Waterloo Bridge. Millionaire.* 1932: *Love Me Tonight. The Impatient Maiden. Westward Passage. Are You Listening? Union Depot (GB: Gentleman for a Day). Lovers Courageous. Devil's Lottery. Payment Deferred.* 1933: *Tonight Is Ours. A Lady's Profession. Alice in Wonderland. Midnight Club. Torch Singer. White Woman. Doctor Bull. Bombshell (GB: Blonde Bombshell). Looking Forward. Horseplay.* 1934: *Bulldog Drummond Strikes Back. The House of Rothschild. We Live Again. Of Human Bondage. Jane Eyre. Olsen's Big Moment. Sadie McKee. Fog. Four Frightened People. The Painted Veil. Call It Luck.* 1935: *Vanessa: Her Love Story. Hold 'Em Yale (GB: Uniform Lovers). The Werewolf of London. Anna Karenina. The Return of Peter Grimm. Enchanted April. The Mystery of Edwin Drood. Twice Branded.* 1936: *Guilty Melody. Not So Dusty.* 1937: *Kathleen Mavourneen (US: Kathleen). Over the Moon (released 1940).* 1938: *Crackerjack (US: The Man With A Hundred Faces).* 1939: *The Star Maker. I'm from Missouri. We Are Not Alone.* 1940: *Vigil in the Night. Anne of Windy Poplars (GB: Anne of Windy Willows). The Stranger on the Third Floor. Irene. Waterloo Bridge (and 1931 version).* 1941: *Great Guns. Dead Men Tell. Time to Kill. A Yank in the RAF. How Green Was My Valley. Billy the Kid. Man at Large. Remember the Day.*

*Knockout/Right to the Heart.* 1942: *Between Us Girls. Mrs Wiggs of the Cabbage Patch. Castle in the Desert. Son of Fury. The Postman Didn't Ring.* 1943: *Forever and a Day. Holy Matrimony. First Comes Courage. Jane Eyre (and 1934 version).* 1944: *Music for Millions. The White Cliffs of Dover. Pardon My Rhythm. The Keys of the Kingdom.* 1945: *The Thrill of a Romance. Molly and Me. The Horn Blows at midnight. Uncle Harry/The Strange Affair of Uncle Harry. Saratoga Trunk.* 1946: *Devotion (completed 1943). Sing While You Dance.* 1947: *Millie's Daughter. The Homestretch. Forever Amber. The Brasher Doubloon (GB: The High Window).* 1963: *Billy Liar! The Birds.* 1965: *Bus Riley's Back in Town.*

## GRIFFITH, Hugh 1912-1980

Fiercely-staring, bushy-browed, chubby-cheeked Welsh actor noted for extravagantly scene-stealing character portraits on both British and international scenes. A former bank clerk, he switched to acting in his middle-twenties. Won an Academy Award (best supporting actor) in 1959 for his portrayal of the Sheikh in *Ben-Hur.* Also Oscar nominated for *Tom Jones.*

1940: *Neutral Port.* 1947: *The Silver Darlings.* 1948: *So Evil My Love. The Three Weird Sisters. The First Gentleman (US: Affairs of a Rogue). London Belongs to Me (US: Dulcimer Street).* 1949: *The Last Days of Dolwyn (US: Woman of Dolwyn). Kind Hearts and Coronets. A Run for Your Money. Scrapbook for 1933 (voice only).* 1950: *Gone to Earth (US: The Wild Heart).* 1951: *The Galloping Major. Laughter in Paradise.* 1953: *The Million Pound Note (US: Man with a Million). The Beggar's Opera. The Titfield Thunderbolt.* 1954: *The Sleeping Tiger.* *Outpost.* 1955: *Passage Home.* 1957: *The Good Companions. Lucky Jim.* 1959: *Ben-Hur.* 1960: *Exodus. The Story on Page One. The Day They Robbed the Bank of England.* 1961: *The Counterfeit Traitor.* 1962: *Mutiny on the Bounty. Term of Trial. The Inspector (US: Lisa).* 1963: *Hide and Seek. Tom Jones.* 1964: *The Bargee.* 1965: *The Amorous Adventures of Moll Flanders.* 1966: *Dare I Weep, Dare I Mourn. The Evil Eye. How to Steal a Million. Oh Dad, Poor Dad, Mama's Hung You in the Closet and I'm Feeling So*

*Sad. The Poppy Is Also a Flower (GB: Danger Grows Wild).* 1967: *The Chastity Belt. Sailor from Gibraltar. Il marito è mio e l'ammazzo quando mi pare.* 1968: *Oliver! The Fixer.* 1969: *Cry of the Banshee. Start the Revolution without Me.* 1970: *Wuthering Heights.* 1971: *The Abominable Dr Phibes. Whoever Slew Auntie Roo? (US: Who Slew Auntie Roo?). The Canterbury Tales.* 1972: *What?* 1973: *Take Me High. Craze. The Final Programme (US: The Last Days of Man on Earth). Crescete e moltiplicatavi. Luther.* 1974: *Legend of the Werewolf. Cugini carnali (GB: The Visitor).* 1975: *Bridges to Heaven.* 1976: *Joseph Andrews. The Passover Plot.* 1977: *The Hound of the Baskervilles. The Last Remake of Beau Geste. Casanova & Co (GB: The Rise and Rise of Casanova).* 1980: *The Biggest Bank Robbery (TV).*

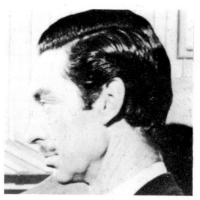

## GRIFFITH, James 1919-

Lean, laconic, slack-jawed, black-haired, drawling American actor who got his best roles in the early 1950s, when, playing a series of true-life westerners, he stole scenes from the stars and edged up to third place on the cast list. Griffith's talent was too unusual to succeed at this level for long, however, and he slipped back into smaller roles.

1944: *Pardon My Rhythm.* 1948: *Blonde Ice. Appointment with Murder. Every Girl Should Be Married.* 1949: *Search for Danger. Daughter of the West. Fighting Man of the Plains. Oh, You Beautiful Doll! Alaska Patrol.* 1950: *The Breaking Point. Indian Territory. Bright Leaf. The Cariboo Trail. Double Deal. The Great Missouri Raid. In a Lonely Place.* 1951: *As Young as You Feel. Apache Drums. The Lady Pays Off. Rhubarb. Al Jennings of Oklahoma. Chain of Circumstance. Inside the Walls of Folsom Prison.* 1952: *Eight Iron Men. Ma and Pa Kettle at the Fair. Wait 'Til the Sun Shines, Nellie.* 1953: *No Escape. Kansas Pacific.* 1954: *The Boy from Oklahoma. Jesse James vs the Daltons. The Black Dakotas. The Law vs Billy the Kid. The Shanghai Story. Masterson of Kansas. Dragnet. Day of Triumph. Rails into Laramie.* 1955: *Son of Sinbad. I Cover the Underworld. Apache Ambush. Count Three and Pray. At Gunpoint! (GB: Gunpoint!).* 1956: *The Killing. Anything Goes. Tribute to a Bad Man. The First*

*Texan. Rebel in Town. Domino Kid. Overnight Haul (TV. GB: cinemas). 1957: Raintree County. The Guns of Fort Petticoat. The Vampire. Omar Khayyam. 1958: Return to Warbow. The Man from God's Country. Bullwhip. Seven Guns to Mesa. 1959: Frontier Gun. The Big Fisherman. The Amazing Transparent Man. 1960: Spartacus. 1962: How the West Was Won. 1963: Advance to the Rear (GB: Company of Cowards). 1966: A Big Hand for the Little Lady (GB: Big Deal at Dodge City). 1968: The Face of Eve (US: Eve). Day of the Evil Gun. Heaven With a Gun. 1969: Seven in Darkness (TV). 1970: Dial Hot Line (TV). 1971: Vanishing Point. 1974: Seven Alone. Hitchhike! (TV). 1975: Babe (TV). 1976: Flood! (TV. GB: cinemas). 1977: Speedtrap. 1978: Desperate Women (TV). 1979: The Main Event.*

### GRIFFITH, Kenneth 1921-

Small, dark Welsh actor who has often played weasels, or shiftless young men who coveted the heroine but couldn't have her. He had a series of meaty top supporting roles in the immediate post-war years, but from 1954 was seen in much smaller parts. His characters have remained largely unsympathetic, if more effete, and he has also gained a reputation as a TV historian on famous battles.

*1940: The Farmer's Wife. 1941: Love on the Dole. Hard Steel. The Black Sheep of Whitehall. 1946: The Shop at Sly Corner (US: The Code of Scotland Yard). 1947: Fame Is the Spur. 1948: Bond Street. Forbidden. 1949: Blue Scar. Helter Skelter. 1950: Waterfront (US: Waterfront Women). The Starfish. 1951: High Treason. 1954: 36 Hours (US: Terror Street). The Green Buddha. Track the Man Down. 1955: The Prisoner. 1984. 1956: Private's Progress. The Baby and the Battleship. Tiger in the Smoke. Brothers in Law. 1957: Lucky Jim. Blue Murder at St Trinian's. The Naked Truth (US: Your Past is Showing!). 1958: A Night to Remember. The Man Upstairs. Chain of Events. The Two-Headed Spy. 1959: Tiger Bay. Carlton-Browne of the FO (US: Man in a Cocked Hat). I'm All Right, Jack. Libel. Expresso Bongo. 1960: Circus of Horrors. Snowball. A French Mistress. 1961: Rag Doll. Payroll. The Frightened City. Only Two Can Play. The Painted Smile. 1962: We Joined the Navy. 1963: Heavens Above! 1965: Rotten to the Core. 1966: The Whisperers. 1967: Great Catherine. The Bobo. 1968: Decline and Fall ... of a Birdwatcher! The Lion in Winter. The Assassination Bureau. 1969: The Gamblers. 1970: Jane Eyre (TV. GB: Cinemas). 1971: Revenge. 1973: The House in Nightmare Park. 1974: Callan. S\*P\*Y\*S. 1976: Sky Riders. Why Shoot the Teacher? 1978: The Wild Geese. 1980: The Sea Wolves. 1982: Who Dares Wins. Remembrance.*

### GUILFOYLE, Paul 1902-1961

Sinewy, dark-haired American actor whose close-set, unfriendly-looking features consigned him to playing whining runts and treacherous, lily-livered hoodlums. Two typical roles at either end of his career were Louie the Weasel in *You Can't Beat Love* and an Indian called Worm in *Chief Crazy Horse*. Came to Hollywood in 1935 after an extensive Broadway career, and had already made almost 50 films before the end of 1940.

*1935: Special Agent. The Crime of Dr Crespi. 1936: Wanted: Jane Turner. Roaming Lady. Winterset. Two-Fisted Gentleman. 1937: The Soldier and the Lady (GB: Michael Strogoff). The Woman I Love (GB: The Woman Between). Behind the Headlines. You Can't Beat Love. You Can't Buy Luck. Hideaway. Super-Sleuth. Fight for Your Lady. Flight from Glory. Danger Patrol. 1938: \*Stage Fright. Double Danger. Crashing Hollywood. Law of the Underworld. Quick Money. The Saint in New York. This Marriage Business. I'm from the City. Sky Giant. Blind Alibi. Fugitives for a Night. Tarnished Angel. The Mad Miss Manton. The Law West of Tombstone. Pacific Liner. 1939: \*Money to Loan. \*The Story of Alfred Nobel. Society Lawyer. Heritage of the Desert. Unexpected Father (GB: Sandy Takes a Bow). News is Made at Night. Our Leading Citizen. One Hour to Live. Sabotage (GB: Spies at Work). Boy Slaves. 1940: Thou Shalt Not Kill. Remember the Night. The Saint Takes Over. The Grapes of Wrath. East of the River. Brother Orchid. Millionaires in Prison. One Crowded Night. Wildcat Bus. 1941: The Saint in Palm Springs. 1942: \*Madero of Mexico. \*The Incredible Stranger. Who Is Hope Schuyler? Time to Kill. The Man Who Returned to Life. 1943: North Star (later Armored Attack). Petticoat Larceny. White Savage (GB: White Captive). Three Russian Girls. 1944: The Seventh Cross. It Happened Tomorrow. Mark of the Whistler. The Master Race. \*Dark Shadows. \*Thou Shalt Not Kill. 1945: The Missing Corpse. Why Girls Leave Home. 1946: The Virginian. Sweetheart of Sigma Chi. 1947: Sinbad the Sailor. Roses Are Red. The Millerson Case. Second Chance. 1948: The Judge (GB: The Gamblers). 1949: Follow Me Quietly. Mighty Joe Young. I Married a Communist (GB: The Woman on Pier 13). Miss Mink of 1949. There's a Girl in My Heart. Trouble Preferred. White Heat. 1950: Messenger of Peace. Davy Crockett— Indian Scout (GB: Indian Scout). Bomba and the Hidden City. 1951: When I Grow Up. Japanese War Bride. 1952: Actors and Sin. Confidence Girl. 1953: Julius Caesar. Torch Song. 1954: Apache. The Golden Idol. A Life at Stake. 1955: Chief Crazy Horse (GB: Valley of Fury). 1960: The Boy and the Pirates.*

**As director:**

*1953: Captain Scarface. 1954: A Life at Stake. 1960: Tess of the Storm Country.*

### GULAGER, Clu 1934-

Throatily spoken, prematurely grey-haired, baby-faced American actor from theatrical background. He attracted some attention with his sporadic film performances (especially those in *The Killers* and *The Last Picture Show*), but has divided his time primarily between television and the theatre. Had ambitions to give up acting for direction, but this seems to have been sidelined for the present.

*1960: Temple of the Swinging Doll. 1962: The Sam Spicer Story. 1964: The Killers. 1965: ...And Now Miguel. 1967: Sullivan's Empire. 1969: Winning. 1970: Company of Killers. San Francisco International Airport (TV). 1971: The Last Picture Show. 1972: Call to Danger (TV). Footsteps (TV). The Glass House (TV. GB: cinemas). 1973: Chant of Silence (TV). Gangsterfilmen. 1974: En Främling Steg av Tåget. McQ. Hit Lady (TV). Houston, We've Got a Problem (TV). Smile*

Jenny, You're Dead (TV). Heart in Hiding (TV). 1976: The Killer Who Wouldn't Die (TV). 1977: Charlie Cobb: Nice Night for a Hanging (TV). The Other Side of Midnight. 1978: A Force of One. Lawman without a Gun (TV). A Question of Love (TV). Willa (TV). Stickin' Together (TV). This Man Stands Alone (TV). Ski Lift to Death (TV). 1979: Black Beauty (TV). 1980: Touched by Love. Kenny Rogers as The Gambler (TV. GB: The Gambler). Skyward (TV). 1982: Living Proof: The Hank Williams Jr Story (TV). 1983: Lies. 1984: The Imitation. 1985: Return of the Living Dead. Into the Night. Prime Risk.

**As director:**
1969: *A Day With the Boys.

**HAADE, William** 1903–1966
Tall, tow-haired, tough-looking American actor of ruddy complexion. Visually a cross between Harry Carey and Bruce Cabot, Haade made his debut as the boxing champion managed by Humphrey Bogart in Kid Galahad. After getting himself knocked out by Wayne Morris in the climactic bout, Haade, who was of Dutch extraction, spent the next 20 years being slugged by other movie heroes, mostly in minor westerns, before quitting films for television.

1937: Kid Galahad. Without Warning. The Missing Witness. He Couldn't Say No. 1938: The Invisible Menace. The Stadium Murders. Boy Meets Girl. The Amazing Dr Clitterhouse. Sing You Sinners. Three Comrades. Down on the Farm. The Texans. If I Were King. Shadows Over Shanghai. 1939: The Gracie Allen Murder Case. Island of Lost Men. Union Pacific. $1,000 a Touchdown. Full Confession. Unmarried (GB: Night Club Hostess). Tom Sawyer, Detective. Night Work. Kid Nightingale. Reno. Geronimo. Invisible Stripes. 1940: The Man from Dakota (GB: Arouse and Beware). The Earl of Chicago. Lillian Russell. The Saint's Double Trouble. One Crowded Night. Cherokee Strip (GB: Fighting Marshal). Knute Rockne—All-American (GB: A Modern Hero). Bullet Code. Stage to Chino. Flowing Gold. Johnny Apollo. The Grapes of Wrath. Who Killed Aunt Maggie? They Drive by Night (GB: The Road to Frisco). 1941: The Roundup. The Shepherd of the Hills. The Penalty. Honky Tonk. Dance Hall. Sergeant York. Sailors on Leave. Rise and Shine. You're in the Army Now. Pirates on Horseback. Knockout/Right to the Heart. Robin Hood of the Pecos. Kansas Cyclone. In Old Cheyenne. Man Hunt. Affectionately Yours. 1942: Juke Girl. Jackass Mail. I Married a Witch. Gang Busters (serial). You're Telling Me. To the Shores of Tripoli. Just Off Broadway. Shepherd of the Ozarks (GB: Susanna). Star Spangled Rhythm. Heart of the Rio Grande. Iceland (GB: Katina). Pittsburgh. Hearts of the Golden West. Man from Cheyenne. The Spoilers. A Gentleman After Dark. 1943: The Dancing Masters. Action in the North Atlantic. Hangmen Also Die. Daredevils of the West (serial). Thank Your Lucky Stars. Song of Texas. Scream in the Dark. There's Something About a Sailor. You're a Lucky Fellow, Mr Smith. Sing a Jingle (GB: Lucky Days). 1944: Buffalo Bill. Seven Days Ashore. Here Come the Waves. Timber Queen. Roger Touhy, Gangster (GB: The Last Gangster). Man from Frisco. The Yellow Rose of Texas. Sheriff of Las Vegas. The Adventures of Mark Twain. 1945: I'll Tell the World. Honeymoon Ahead. The Trouble with Women (released 1947). Nob Hill. Incendiary Blonde. Dakota. Fallen Angel. Phantom of the Plains. A Guy Could Change. 1946: Affairs of Geraldine. In Old Sacramento. Renegades. The Well Groomed Bride. Sentimental Journey. Fallen Angel. My Pal Trigger. The Pilgrim Lady. 1947: Lady Chaser. Where There's Life. Night Unto Night (released 1949). Buck Privates Come Home (GB: Rookies Come Home). The Web. The Secret Life of Walter Mitty. Deep Valley. Magic Town. Unconquered. Under Colorado Skies. Down to Earth. It Happened in Brooklyn. Exposed. 1948: The Inside Story. April Showers. Good Sam. Michael O'Halloran. A Song Is Born. The Night Has a Thousand Eyes. Tap Roots. Key Largo. Lulu Belle. Strike It Rich. 1949: Scene of the Crime. The Fountainhead. The Wyoming Bandit. I Married a Communist (GB: The Woman on Pier 13). The Bribe. Alaska Patrol. Flamingo Road. The Gal Who Took the West. *Prairie Pirates. Malaya (GB: East of the Rising Sun). Last of the Wild Horses. 1950: Rawhide/Desperate Siege. Trial Without Jury. No Man of Her Own. Outcast of Black Mesa (GB: The Clue). The Old Frontier. Buckaroo Sheriff of Texas. Caged. Father of the Bride. Joe Palooka in The Squared Circle (GB: The Squared Circle). 1951: Leave It to the Marines. Santa Fé. Oh! Susanna. The Sea Hornet. Stop That Cab. Three Desperate Men. A Yank in Korea. 1952: Skirts Ahoy! Carson City. Here Come the Nelsons. Come Back, Little Sheba. Rancho Notorious. 1953: Red River Shore. Secret of Outlaw Flats (TV. GB: cinemas). 1954: Untamed Heiress. Silver Lode. Kansas City Confidential (GB: The Secret Four). Jubilee Trail. 1955: Many Rivers to Cross. Abbott and Costello Meet the Keystone Kops. 1957: Spoilers of the Forest.

**HADEN, Sara** 1897–1981
Plain-faced, dark-haired American supporting player, a former child actress who came to Hollywood in her late thirties and played nosey neighbours, spinster aunts, dragon-like secretaries, no-nonsense parole officers and frozen-faced, strait-laced do-gooders in general. Switched to films after a long theatre career, was nasty (on film) to Shirley Temple, then established herself as maiden aunt Milly in the Andy Hardy series.

1934: Spitfire. The Life of Vergie Winters. Anne of Green Gables. The White Parade. Affairs of a Gentleman. Music in the Air. The Fountain. Finishing School. Hat, Coat and Glove. 1935: Mad Love (GB: Hands of Orlac). O'Shaughnessy's Boy. Way Down East. Magnificent Obsession. Black Fury. 1936: Little Miss Nobody. Captain January. Reunion (GB: Hearts in Reunion). Everybody's Old Man. Half Angel. Can This Be Dixie? Poor Little Rich Girl. The Crime of Dr Forbes. 1937: Under Cover of Night. Laughing at Trouble. A Family Affair. First Lady. The Barrier. The Last of Mrs Cheyney. 1938: Out West with the Hardys. Four Girls in White. You're Only Young Once. The Hardys Ride High. 1939: Tell No Tales. The Secret of Dr Kildare. Andy Hardy Gets Spring Fever. Remember? Judge Hardy and Son. 1940: The Shop Around the Corner. Boom Town. Andy Hardy Meets Debutante. 1941: Hullabaloo. The Trial of Mary Dugan. Washington Melodrama. Andy Hardy's Private Secretary. Love Crazy. *Come Back, Miss Pipps. Barnacle Bill. Life Begins for Andy Hardy. Keeping

Company. H. M. Pulham Esq. 1942: The Courtship of Andy Hardy. The Affairs of Martha (GB: There's Always a Thursday). Andy Hardy's Double Life. 1943: The Youngest Profession. Lost Angel. Above Suspicion. Thousands Cheer. Best Foot Forward. 1944: Bathing Beauty. Andy Hardy's Blonde Trouble. 1945: Our Vines Have Tender Grapes. 1946: Bad Bascomb. Mr Ace. Love Laughs at Andy Hardy. She-Wolf of London (GB: The Curse of the Allenbys). She Wouldn't Say Yes. Our Hearts Were Growing Up. So Goes My Love (GB: A Genius in the Family). 1947: The Bishop's Wife. 1948: Rachel and the Stranger. 1949: The Big Cat. Roughshod. 1950: A Life of Her Own. The Great Rupert. 1952: Wagons West. Rodeo. 1953: A Lion Is in the Streets. 1954: The Outlaw's Daughter. 1955: Betrayed Women. 1958: Andy Hardy Comes Home.

**HALE, Alan**

(Rufus A. MacKahn) 1892-1950

Tall, burly American actor with fair, crinkly hair, who played Rochester in a silent *Jane Eyre* at 23, then settled down to 35 years as a top Hollywood character star, mostly in bluff, likeable, slow-witted roles (his real first name suited him ideally), but occasionally as a strong villain. Early death at 57 (from a liver ailment and virus infection) robbed him of a deserved 200 films before retirement. Once trained as an opera singer.

1911: The Cowboy and the Lady. 1913: The Prisoner of Zenda. By Man's Law. 1914: Martin Chuzzlewit. Masks and Faces. Strongheart. Men and Women. Adam Bede. The Cricket on the Hearth. A Scrap of Paper. The Power of the Press. 1915: Dora Thorne. East Lynne. Jane Eyre. After the Storm. The Americano. Under Two Flags. 1916: Pudd'nhead Wilson. The Purple Lady. Rolling Stones. The Love Thief. The Scarlet Oath. The Woman in the Case. 1917: The Price She Paid. Life's Whirlpool. One Hour. The Eternal Temptress. 1918: Masks and Faces (remake). Moral Suicide. The Whirlpool. 1919: Love Hunger. The Trap. The Blue Bonnet. 1921: A Wise Fool. The Four Horsemen of the Apocalypse. Over the Wire. The Fox. The Great Impersonation. The Barbarian. A Voice in the Dark.

1922: Shirley of the Circus. One Glorious Day. The Dictator. The Trap (and 1919 film. GB: Heart of a Wolf). Robin Hood. A Doll's House. 1923: The Covered Wagon. Cameo Kirby. Hollywood. The Eleventh Hour (GB: The Purple Phial). Quicksands. Main Street. Long Live the King. The Cricket. 1924: Black Oxen. Code of the Wilderness. Girls Men Forget. Troubles of a Bride. One Night in Rome. For Another Woman. 1925: Dick Turpin. The Scarlet Honeymoon. Braveheart. The Crimson Runner. Flattery. Ranger of the Big Pines. The Wedding Song. Rolling Stones. 1926: Forbidden Waters. †Risky Business. Hearts and Fists. The Sporting Lover. Redheads Preferred. 1927: †Rubber Tires (GB: Ten Thousand Reward). *Life in Hollywood No 4. Vanity. The Wreck of the Hesperus. 1928: The Cop. Oh, Kay! Skyscraper. The Leopard Lady. Sal of Singapore. Power. The Spieler (GB: The Spellbinder). 1929: Sailor's Holiday. Red Hot Rhythm. The Leatherneck. The Sap. 1930: She Got What She Wanted. A Bachelor's Secret. Up and at 'em. 1931: Aloha. Susan Lenox, Her Fall and Rise (GB: The Rise of Helga). Rebound. Night Angel. The Sin of Madelon Claudet (GB: The Lullaby). The Sea Ghost. 1932: Union Depot (GB: Gentleman for a Day). So Big. Rebecca of Sunnybrook Farm. The Match King. 1933: Picture Brides. What Price Decency? Destination Unknown. The Eleventh Commandment. 1934: Of Human Bondage. The Little Minister. Imitation of Life. The Lost Patrol. It Happened One Night. Fog Over Frisco. Great Expectations. Little Man, What Now? Broadway Bill (GB: Strictly Confidential). Miss Fane's Baby is Stolen (GB: Kidnapped). The Scarlet Letter. There's Always Tomorrow. Babbitt. 1935: Grand Old Girl. The Last Days of Pompeii. The Crusades. The Good Fairy. Another Face (GB: It Happened in Hollywood). 1936: Two in the Dark. A Message to Garcia. Yellowstone. Our Relations. God's Country and the Woman. Parole! The Country Beyond. 1937: Jump for Glory (US: When Thief Meets Thief). High, Wide and Handsome. Stella Dallas. The Prince and the Pauper. Thin Ice (GB: Lovely to Look At). Music for Madame. 1938: The Adventures of Robin Hood. Algiers. Four Men and a Prayer. Valley of the Giants. Listen, Darling. The Adventures of Marco Polo. The Sisters. Dodge City. The Man in the Iron Mask. Dust Be My Destiny. Pacific Liner. The Private Lives of Elizabeth and Essex. On Your Toes. 1940: Virginia City. Three Cheers for the Irish. The Fighting 69th. They Drive By Night (GB: The Road to Frisco). Santa Fé Trail. Tugboat Annie Sails Again. The Sea Hawk. Green Hell. 1941: Strawberry Blonde. Manpower. Thieves Fall Out. The Great Mr Nobody. The Smiling Ghost. Footsteps in the Dark. 1942: Juke Girl. Captains of the Clouds. Gentleman Jim. Desperate Journey. 1943: Action in the North Atlantic. Destination Tokyo. Thank Your Lucky Stars. This is the Army. 1944: The Adventures of Mark Twain. Make Your Own Bed. Hollywood Canteen. Janie. 1945: Roughly Speaking. Hotel Berlin. God is My Co-Pilot. Escape in the Desert. 1946: Perilous

Holiday. The Time, the Place and the Girl. Night and Day. The Man I Love. Pursued. 1947: Cheyenne. My Wild Irish Rose. That Way with Women. 1948: My Girl Tisa. Whiplash. The Adventures of Don Juan. 1949: South of St Louis. The Younger Brothers. The Inspector General. Always Leave Them Laughing. The House Across the Street. 1950: Colt .45. Stars in My Crown. Rogues of Sherwood Forest.

†And directed

**HALE, Alan Jnr**

(A. MacKahn) 1918- 1990

Burly, robust, cheerful, fair-haired American actor, the son of Alan Hale. His tousled mop could be seen in leading roles—if only in minor features—in the late 1940s, but he did not quite equal his father's standing in the cinema, and his greatest success has been in such TV series as *Casey Jones* (a perennial children's favourite) and *Gilligan's Island*.

1933: Wild Boys of the Road (GB: Dangerous Days). 1941: I Wanted Wings. Dive Bomber. All American Co-Ed. 1942: Top Sergeant. Wake Island. To the Shores of Tripoli. Rubber Racketeers. Eagle Squadron. 1943: No Time for Love. Watch on the Rhine. 1944: And Now Tomorrow. 1946: The Sweetheart of Sigma Chi. Monsieur Beaucaire. 1947: It Happened on Fifth Avenue. Sarge Goes to College. Spirit of West Point. 1948: One Rainy Afternoon. The Music Man. Homecoming. 1949: Rim of the Canyon. Riders in the Sky. The Blazing Trail. It Happens Every Spring. 1950: The Blazing Sun. Kill the Umpire! Short Grass. The Gunfighter. Four Days' Leave. The Underworld Story. The West Point Story (GB: Fine and Dandy). Sierra Passage. 1951: The Hometown Story. Honeychile. At Sword's Point (GB: Sons of the Musketeers). 1952: Springfield Rifle. Lady in the Iron Mask. The Big Trees. Wait 'Til the Sun Shines, Nellie. Mr Walkie Talkie. Arctic Flight. The Man Behind the Gun. 1953: The Yellow-Haired Kid. The Trail Blazers. Captain John Smith and Pocahontas (GB: Burning Arrows). 1954: Captain Kidd and the Slave Girl. Silver Lode. The Iron Glove. Destry. The Law vs Billy the Kid. Rogue Cop. Young at Heart. 1955: Many Rivers to Cross. The Sea Chase. A Man

Alone. Man on the Ledge (TV. GB: cinemas). The Indian Fighter. 1956: All Mine to Give (GB: The Day They Gave Babies Away). The Killer is Loose. Canyon River. The Cruel Tower. The Three Outlaws. Affair in Reno. 1957: Battle Hymn. The True Story of Jesse James (GB: The James Brothers). The Lady Takes a Flyer. 1958: Up Periscope! 1960: Thunder in Carolina. 1961: The Long Rope. 1962: The Iron Maiden (GB: The Swingin' Maiden). 1963: Advance to the Rear (GB: Company of Cowards). The Crawling Hand. 1964: Bullet for a Badman. 1966: Dead Heat on a Merry-Go-Round. 1967: Hang 'Em High. 1968: Tiger by the Tail. 1970: There Was a Crooked Man. 1975: The Giant Spider Invasion. 1977: Behind the Iron Mask (GB: The Fifth Musketeer). 1978: The North Avenue Irregulars (GB: Hill's Angels). Rescue from Gilligan's Island (TV). 1979: The Great Monkey Rip-Off. Angels' Brigade. 1983: Hambone and Hillie (GB: The Adventures of Hambone). 1985: The Red Fury.

## HALL, Porter
(Clifford P. Hall) 1888-1953

Small, dark-haired, shifty-eyed, moustachioed American actor, the epitome of the double-dealing businessman or (often corrupt) public figure. Following beginnings with a travelling Shakespeare company, he became a considerable figure in the theatrical world before succumbing late in life to the lure of Hollywood. Died from a heart attack.

1931: Secrets of a Secretary. 1934: The Thin Man. Murder in the Private Car (GB: Murder on the Runaway Train). 1935: The Case of the Lucky Legs. The Petrified Forest. 1936: Too Many Parents. And Sudden Death. The Princess Comes Across. The Story of Louis Pasteur. The General Died at Dawn. Saan Met a Lady. Snowed Under. The Plainsman. 1937: Souls at Sea. Make Way for Tomorrow. Wild Money. True Confession. Let's Make a Million. Bulldog Drummond Escapes. King of the Gamblers. Hotel Haywire. This Way, Please. Wells Fargo. 1938: Scandal Street. Dangerous to Know. Prison Farm. Stolen Heaven. Bulldog Drummond's Peril. King of Alcatraz (GB: King of the Alcatraz). Tom Sawyer—Detective. The Arkansas Traveler. Men with Wings. 1939: Grand Jury

Secrets. They Shall Have Music (GB: Melody of Youth). Mr Smith Goes to Washington. 1940: His Girl Friday. Arizona. Dark Command. Trail of the Vigilantes. 1941: The Parson of Panamint. Mr and Mrs North. Sullivan's Travels. 1942: Butch Minds the Baby. The Remarkable Andrew. Tennessee Johnson (GB: The Man on America's Conscience). 1943: A Stranger in Town. Woman of the Town. The Desperadoes. The Great Moment. 1944: Standing Room Only. Going My Way. The Miracle of Morgan's Creek. Double Indemnity. Mark of the Whistler (GB: The Marked Man). 1945: Blood on the Sun. Bring on the Girls. Kiss and Tell. Murder, He Says. Week-End at the Waldorf. Mad Wednesday/ The Sin of Harold Diddlebock. 1947: Miracle on 34th Street (GB: The Big Heart). Singapore. 1948: You Gotta Stay Happy. Unconquered. That Wonderful Urge. 1949: Chicken Every Sunday. The Beautiful Blonde from Bashful Bend. Intruder in the Dust. 1951: The Big Carnival (GB: Ace in the Hole). 1952: Carbine Williams. Holiday for Sinners. The Half-Breed. 1953: Vice Squad (GB: The Girl in Room 17). Pony Express. 1954: Return to Treasure Island.

## HALL, Thurston 1882-1958

Large, hearty, generously built American actor. He acted on stages all over the world in his youth, including England, South Africa and New Zealand, before trying his luck in Hollywood, initially as a powerful leading man (his first role was as Marc Antony). When he returned as a character player in the 1930s, producers soon detected the roguish glint in the eye that caused him to be cast as dozens of smilingly affable, but crooked businessmen, who would wriggle out of a jam and launch some fresh scheme at a bluster of confusion or a clearing of the throat. Died from a heart attack.

1917: Cleopatra. 1918: We Can't Have Everything. The Squaw Man (GB: The White Man). Tyrant Fear. Brazen Beauty. The Kaiser's Shadow. 1919: The Unpainted Woman. 1921: Idle Hands. The Iron Trail. Mother Eternal. 1922: Fair Lady. Wilderness of Youth. 1923: The Royal Oak. 1924: The Great Well (US: Neglected Women). 1930: *Absent Minded. 1935: Metropolitan. Crime

and Punishment. The Girl Friend. Too Tough to Kill. The Black Room. Love Me Forever (GB: On Wings of Song). Public Menace. One Way Ticket. The Case of the Missing Man. A Feather in Her Hat. Hooray for Love. Guard That Girl. After the Dance. 1936: The Lone Wolf Returns. Theodora Goes Wild. Don't Gamble With Love. The Man Who Lived Twice. Killer at Large. The King Steps Out. The Devil's Squadron. Trapped by Television (GB: Caught by Television). Shakedown. Three Wise Guys. Pride of the Marines. Roaming Lady. Two-Fisted Gentleman. Lady from Nowhere. 1937: Penitentiary. Paid to Dance. I Promise to Pay. All American Sweetheart. Women of Glamour. Don't Tell the Wife. Parole Racket. It Can't Last Forever. Venus Makes Trouble. Counsel for Crime. Murder in Greenwich Village. We Have Our Moments. Oh, Doctor. 1938: Professor Beware. The Amazing Dr Clitterhouse. No Time to Marry. Women in Prison. The Main Event. There's Always a Woman. Little Miss Roughneck. Extortion. Campus Confessions (GB: Fast Play). The Affairs of Annabel. Women Are Like That. Squadron of Honor. Hard to Get. Fast Company. Going Places. Out West With the Hardys. 1939: You Can't Cheat an Honest Man. Each Dawn I Die. Dodge City. Three Smart Girls Grow Up. Stagecoach. First Love. Ex-Champ (GB: Golden Gloves). Our Neighbors—the Carters. Hawaiian Nights. Million Dollar Legs. Mutiny on the Blackhawk. Jeepers Creepers (GB: Money Isn't Everything). The Star Maker. Dancing Co-Ed (GB: Every Other Inch a Lady). The Day the Bookies Wept. 1940: *Kiddie Cure. The Blue Bird. City for Conquest. Blondie on a Budget. Sued for Libel. Alias the Deacon. In Old Missouri. The Lone Wolf Meets a Lady. Millionaires in Prison. The Great McGinty (GB: Down Went McGinty). Friendly Neighbors. The Golden Fleecing. Virginia City. 1941: The Great Lie. The Lone Wolf Takes a Chance. Where Did You Get That Girl? Washington Melodrama. In the Navy. She Knew All the Answers. Repent at Leisure. Accent on Love. Design for Scandal. Secrets of the Lone Wolf (GB: Secrets). Hold That Ghost! Tuxedo Junction. Pacific Blackout/Midnight Angel. Remember the Day. Swing It Soldier (GB: Radio Revels of 1942). The Invisible Woman. Flight from Destiny. The Lone Wolf Keeps a Date. Nine Lives Are Not Enough. Life With Henry. 1942: Sleepytime Gal. Counter Espionage. The Night Before the Divorce. The Hard Way. Rings on Her Fingers. Shepherd of the Ozarks (GB: Susanna). The Great Man's Lady. Hello Annapolis (GB: Personal Honour). Call of the Canyon. Her Cardboard Lover. The Great Gildersleeve. We Were Dancing. Crash Dive. 1943: This Land Is Mine! One Dangerous Night. The Youngest Profession. I Dood It (GB: By Hook or By Crook). Footlight Glamour. Sherlock Holmes in Washington. Hoosier Holiday (GB: Farmyard Follies). Here Comes Elmer. He Hired the Boss. 1944: Cover Girl. Wilson. The Adventures of Mark Twain. Goodnight, Sweetheart. The Great Moment. Something for the Boys. In

Society. Follow the Boys. Ever Since Eve. Song of Nevada. 1945: Brewster's Millions. Bring on the Girls. The Blonde from Brooklyn. Don Juan Quilligan. The Gay Señorita. Lady on a Train. West of the Pecos. Colonel Effingham's Raid (GB: Man of the Hour). Song of the Prairie (GB: Sentiment and Song). Saratoga Trunk. Thrill of a Romance. 1946: Dangerous Business. One More Tomorrow. Three Little Girls in Blue. She Wrote the Book. Two Sisters from Boston. Without Reservations. 1947: The Secret Life of Walter Mitty. The Farmer's Daughter. Morning Becomes Electra. Swing the Western Way (GB: The Schemer). Son of Rusty. Welcome Stranger. Black Gold. The Unfinished Dance. It Had to Be You. 1948: Three Daring Daughters (GB: The Sun Comes Up). Up in Central Park. King of Gamblers. Miraculous Journey. Blondie's Secret. Blondie's Reward. 1949: Manhattan Angel. The Stagecoach Kid. Rim of the Canyon. Square Dance Jubilee. Bride for Sale. Rusty Saves a Life. Tell It to the Judge. 1950: Girls' School (GB: Dangerous Inheritance). Belle of Old Mexico. Federal Agent at Large. Bright Leaf. Chain Gang. Bandit Queen. 1951: One Too Many (GB: Killer with a Label). Whirlwind. Belle le Grand. Texas Carnival. 1952: One Big Affair. Night Stage to Galveston. Skirts Ahoy! Woman of the North Country. Carson City. The WAC from Walla Walla (GB: Army Capers). It Grows on Trees. 1956: Affair in Reno.

### HALLIDAY, John 1880-1947

This native New Yorker, who must have played more cuckolded husbands than most, was a tall, elegant man with neat moustache. He trained as a mining engineer in Scotland, served with the British army in the Boer War, and went to Cambridge, before taking up an engineering career in the Nevada mining territory. Amateur performances in Gilbert and Sullivan led him to switch careers to acting and he became a respected Broadway figure before trying Hollywood at the beginning of the sound era. Now best remembered as Katharine Hepburn's wayward dad in The Philadelphia Story, he retired to Honolulu, where he died from a heart ailment.

1920: The Woman Gives. 1929: East Side Sadie. 1930: Father's Son. Recaptured Love. Scarlet Pages. Captain Applejack. 1931: The Ruling Voice. Consolation Marriage (GB: Married in Haste). Fifty Million Frenchmen. Smart Woman. Transatlantic. Millie. The Spy. Once a Sinner. 1932: The Impatient Maiden. Week-Ends Only. Men of Chance. Bird of Paradise. The Age of Consent. The Man Called Back. Perfect Understanding. 1933: The Woman Accused. Terror Aboard. Bed of Roses. The House on 56th Street. 1934: Happiness Ahead. A Woman's Man. Return of the Terror. Housewife. Desirable. Finishing School. The Witching Hour. Registered Nurse. 1935: The Dark Angel. Mystery Woman. Peter Ibbetson. The Melody Lingers On. 1936: Desire. Fatal Lady. Hollywood Boulevard. Three Cheers for Love. 1938: Arsene Lupin Returns. That Certain Age. Blockade. 1939: Elsa Maxwell's Hotel for Women (GB: Hotel for Women). Intermezzo—A Love Story (GB: Escape to Happiness). The Light That Failed. 1940: The Philadelphia Story. 1941: Submarine Zone. Lydia.

### HALTON, Charles 1876-1959

Small, sharp-faced American actor with pasted-across grey hair and rimless spectacles; played businessmen, bank managers, doctors and even spies. His characters were suspicious of intentions and generally nobody's fools; you could almost see their noses twitch. A late arrival to the film world, Halton became one of Hollywood's most prolific actors. From 1938 to 1940 alone, he appeared in more than 50 films, often giving incisive cameos; he was at his interfering best in the war years, notably in such films as To Be or Not To Be. Died from hepatitis.

1931: *The Strange Case. Honor Among Lovers. 1934: Twenty Million Sweethearts. 1936: Sing Me a Love Song. Stolen Holiday. Come and Get It. Dodsworth. More Than a Secretary. Gold Diggers of 1937. 1937: Penrod and Sam. Black Legion. Ready, Willing and Able. Pick a Star. Woman Chases Man. Blossoms on Broadway. Dead End. The Road Back. The Prisoner of Zenda. Partners in Crime. Talent Scout (GB: Studio Romance). 1938: Penrod's Double Trouble. Bluebeard's Eighth Wife. Stolen Heaven. The Saint in New York. Room Service. The Mad Miss Manton. A Man to Remember. Trouble at Midnight. Penrod and His Twin Brother. I'll Give a Million. I Am the Law. Gold Is Where You Find It. Penitentiary. Federal Man Hunt (GB: Flight from Justice). 1939: Nancy Drew—Reporter. Swanee River. No Place to Go. Young Mr Lincoln. Jesse James. Golden Boy. Bachelor Mother. News Is Made at Night. Indianapolis Speedway (GB: Devil on Wheels). I'm from Missouri. Dodge City. Charlie Chan at Treasure Island. Juarez. Sabotage (GB: Spies at Work). They Asked for It. Reno. Sudden Money. They Made Her a Spy. Ex-Champ (GB: Golden Gloves). 1940: Stranger on the Third Floor. Behind the News. Gangs of Chicago. Foreign Correspondent. Lillian Russell. The Shop Around the Corner. Dr Ehrlich's Magic Bullet (GB: The Story of Dr Ehrlich's Magic Bullet). Dr Cyclops. They Drive by Night (GB: The Road to Frisco). Young People. Twenty-Mule Team. Lucky Partners. The Doctor Takes a Wife. Tugboat Annie Sails Again. The Westerner. Virginia City. Calling All Husbands. Brigham Young—Frontiersman (GB: Brigham Young). Little Nellie Kelly. 1941: Lady Scarface. Meet the Chump. One Foot in Heaven. Mr District Attorney. Mr and Mrs Smith. I Was a Prisoner on Devil's Island. Tobacco Road. Footlight Fever. Three Girls About Town. A Very Young Lady. H. M. Pulham Esq. Dance Hall. The Smiling Ghost. Million Dollar Baby. Look Who's Laughing. Unholy Partners. Three Sons o' Guns. The Body Disappeared. 1942: Juke Box Jenny. Whispering Ghosts. To Be or Not To Be. The Spoilers. They All Kissed the Bride. In Old California. The Lady Is Willing. Priorities on Parade. There's One Born Every Minute. Across the Pacific. Saboteur. You Can't Escape Forever. That Other Woman. Henry Aldrich, Editor. Captains of the Clouds. 1943: My Kingdom for a Cook. †The Private Life of Dr Paul Joseph Goebbels. Jitterbugs. Lady Bodyguard. Heaven Can Wait. Flesh and Fantasy. Government Girl. Whispering Footsteps. 1944: Shadows in the Night. Address Unknown. Wilson. Up in Arms. It Happened Tomorrow. Rationing. The Town Went Wild. The Thin Man Goes Home. Enemy of Women. A Tree Grows in Brooklyn. 1945: Rhapsody in Blue. The Fighting Guardsman. She Went to the Races. Mama Loves Papa. Midnight Manhunt. 1946: One Exciting Week. Singin' in the Corn (GB: Give and Take). Because of Him. Three Little Girls in Blue. The Best Years of Our Lives. It's a Wonderful Life! Sister Kenny. 1947: The Ghost Goes Wild. The Bachelor and the Bobby Soxer (GB: Bachelor Knight). 1948: Three Godfathers. If You Knew Susie. *Bet Your Life. My Dear Secretary. 1949: The Hideout. The Sickle or the Cross. The Daring Caballero. 1950: The Nevadan (GB: The Man from Nevada). When Willie Comes Marching Home. The Traveling Saleswoman. Stella. Joe Palooka in the Squared Circle (GB: The Squared Circle). 1951: Gasoline Alley. Here Comes the Groom. 1952: Carrie. 1953: The Moonlighter. A Slight Case of Larceny. 1954: A Star is Born. 1956: Friendly Persuasion.

†Unreleased

## HAMILTON, Margaret 1902-1985

Beaky-nosed, beady-eyed, bony-featured American character actress with very dark hair, unforgettable as the Wicked Witch of the West in *The Wizrd of Oz*. Remained very much a working actress into her late seventies, and in private life an avid worker for charity. Died from a heart attack.

*1933: Another Language. 1934: Hat, Coat and Glove. There's Always Tomorrow. Broadway Bill (GB: Strictly Confidential). By Your Leave. 1935: The Farmer Takes a Wife. The Wedding Night. Way Down East. People Will Talk. 1936: These Three. Chatterbox. The Trail of the Lonesome Pine. The Witness Chair. The Moon's Our Home. 1937: Laughing at Trouble. When's Your Birthday? You Only Live Once. Nothing Sacred. Mountain Justice. The Good Old Soak. I'll Take Romance. Saratoga. 1938: Mother Carey's Chickens. Four's a Crowd. A Slight Case of Murder. Breaking the Ice. Stablemates. 1939: Angels Wash Their Faces. The Wizard of Oz. Main Street Lawyer (GB: Small Town Lawyer). Babes in Arms. 1940: My Little Chickadee. I'm Nobody's Sweetheart Now. The Villain Still Pursued Her. 1941: Playgirl. The Invisible Woman. The Gay Vagabond. The Shepherd of the Hills. Babes on Broadway. 1942: Twin Beds. Meet the Stewarts. The Affairs of Martha (GB: Once Upon a Thursday). Journey for Margaret. The Ox-Bow Incident (GB: Strange Incident). 1943: City Without Men. Johnny Come Lately (GB: Johnny Vagabond). 1944: Guest in the House. 1945: George White's Scandals. 1946: Janie Gets Married. Faithful in My Fashion. Mad Wednesday/The Sin of Harold Diddlebock. 1947: Dishonored Lady.* Pet Peeves. Driftwood. 1948: State of the Union (GB: The World and His Wife). On Our Merry Way (GB: A Miracle Can Happen). Texas, Brooklyn and Heaven (GB: The Girl from Texas). Bungalow 13. 1949: The Red Pony. The Sun Comes Up. The Beautiful Blonde from Bashful Bend. 1950: Wabash Avenue. Riding High. The Great Plane Robbery. 1951: People Will Talk. Comin' Round the Mountain. 1957: Paradise Alley (released 1962). 1959: The Silver Whistle (TV). 1960: 13 Ghosts. 1963: The Cardinal. 1966: The Daydreamer. 1967: Rosie! Ghostbreaker (TV). 1969: Angel in*

*My Pocket. 1970: Brewster McCloud. 1971. The Anderson Tapes. Journey Back to Oz (voice only). 1973: The Night Strangler (TV). 1978: A Last Cry for Help (TV). Donovan's Kid (TV). 1979: Letters from Frank.*

## HAMILTON, Murray 1923-*1986*

Tousle-haired, crumple-faced, stockily-built American actor who started his career playing straight-down-the-line types, but, as the lines increased, gained recognition as connivers and men of straw, or officials more concerned with city hall than the people. Notable in this vein were his portraits of the mayor, forever willing to ignore dangers to cram in more tourists, in the *Jaws* films.

*1950: Bright Victory (GB: Lights Out). 1951: The Whistle at Eaton Falls (GB: Richer Than the Earth). 1956: Toward the Unknown (GB: Brink of Hell). The Girl He Left Behind. 1957: Jeanne Eagels. The Spirit of St Louis. Darby's Rangers (GB: The Young Invaders). 1958: Too Much Too Soon. No Time for Sergeants. Houseboat. Girl in the Subway (TV. GB: cinemas). 1959: Anatomy of a Murder. The FBI Story. 1960: Tall Story. 1961: The Hustler. 1962: Papa's Delicate Condition. 1963: The Cardinal. 13 Frightened Girls! Sergeant Ryker (TV. GB: cinemas). 1966: Danger Has Two Faces. An American Dream (GB: See You in Hell, Darling). Seconds. 1967: The Graduate. No Way to Treat a Lady. 1968: The Brotherhood. The Boston Strangler. 1969: If It's Tuesday, This Must Be Belgium. 1971: Vanished (TV). Cannon (TV). A Tattered Web (TV). The Harness (TV). The Failing of Raymond (TV). 1972: Deadly Harvest (TV). Madigan: The Manhattan Beat (TV). 1973: The Way We Were. Incident on a Dark Street (TV). Murdock's Gang (TV). 1975: Jaws. The Drowning Pool. 1976: Midway (GB: Battle of Midway). 1977: Casey's Shadow. Murder at the World Series (TV). Killer on Board (TV). 1978: Jaws 2. 1979: 1941. The Amityville Horror. A Last Cry for Help (TV). 1980: Brubaker. 1982: Mazes and Monsters (TV). Hysterical. 1983: Summer Girl (TV).*

## HANCOCK, Sheila 1933-

Wide-mouthed, gawky, long-legged, British blonde comedienne and actress, from

revue. She has never really seemed at home in films, and her greatest successes have been on stage and in television comedy series. Married to actors Alec Ross (died 1971) and John Thaw (since 1973).

*1960: Doctor in Love. The Bulldog Breed. Light Up the Sky. The Girl on the Boat. 1962: Twice Round the Daffodils. 1963: Night Must Fall. 1964: The Moon-Spinners. Carry On Cleo. 1967: How I Won the War. The Anniversary. 1969: The Magnificent Six and a Half. Take a Girl Like You. 1979: The Lion, the Witch and the Wardrobe (TV. Voice only, GB version). 1980: The Wildcats of St Trinian's.*

## HANDL, Irene 1901-*1987*

Plump-faced British comedy actress with brown, curly hair, plaintive, mewling, ingratiatingly friendly tones and unique way of haranguing her fellow players. She came late to the theatre via an acting course in her early thirties, but was an immediate success as the to-the-rescue maid in *George and Margaret*, a role that also set her up for a film career of mothers, cooks and landladies, to all of which she lent her own touch of eccentricity. After appearing with a number of top comedians, she became a star in her own right in TV series of the 1960s. A loveable human puffin.

*1937: Missing—Believed Married. 1938: Strange Boarders. 1939: Mrs Pym of Scotland Yard. On the Night of the Fire (US: The Fugitive). Dr O'Dowd. 1940: The Girl in the*

News. *Night Train to Munich* (US: *Night Train*). *George and Margaret*. *Gasbags*. *Spellbound* (US: *The Spell of Amy Nugent*). 1941: *Pimpernel Smith* (US: *Mister V*). *\*Mr Proudfoot Shows a Light*. 1942: *\*Partners in Crime*. *Uncensored*. 1943: *I'll Walk Beside You*. *Rhythm Serenade*. *Get Cracking*. *The Flemish Farm*. *Millions Like Us*. *It's in the Bag*. *Dear Octopus* (US: *The Randolph Family*). 1944: *Welcome Mr Washington*. *Mr Emmanuel*. *English Without Tears* (US: *Her Man Gilbey*). *Kiss the Bride Goodbye*. *Give Us the Moon*. *Medal for the General*. 1945: *For You Alone*. *Great Day*. *Brief Encounter*. *The Shop at Sly Corner* (US: *The Code of Scotland Yard*). 1946: *I'll Turn to You*. 1947: *Temptation Harbour*. *The Hills of Donegal*. 1948: *Woman Hater*. *The Fool and the Princess*. *Silent Dust*. *The History of Mr Polly*. *Cardboard Cavalier*. 1949: *Adam and Evelyne* (US: *Adam and Evalyn*). *For Them That Trespass*. *The Perfect Woman*. *Dark Secret*. 1950: *Stage Fright*. 1951: *One Wild Oat*. *Young Wives' Tale*. 1952: *Top Secret* (US: *Mr Potts Goes to Moscow*). *Treasure Hunt*. 1953: *The Wedding of Lilli Marlene*. *Meet Mr Lucifer*. *The Weak and the Wicked*. *Stryker of the Yard*. *The Accused*. 1954: *Burnt Evidence*. *The Case of the Second Shot*. *The Belles of St Trinian's*. *Mad About Men*. 1955: *A Kid for Two Farthings*. *Now and Forever*. 1956: *It's Never Too Late*. *The Silken Affair*. *Brothers in Law*. 1957: *Small Hotel*. *Happy is the Bride!* 1958: *The Key*. *Law and Disorder*. *Next to No Time!* *Carlton-Browne of the F O* (US: *Man in a Cocked Hat*). 1959: *The Crowning Touch*. *Carry On Nurse*. *Inn for Trouble*. *I'm All Right, Jack*. *Desert Mice*. *Upstairs and Downstairs*. *Left, Right and Centre*. 1960: *School for Scoundrels*. *Two-Way Stretch*. *Carry on Constable*. *Make Mine Mink*. *Doctor in Love*. *A French Mistress*. *The Night We Got The Bird*. *No Kidding* (US: *Beware of Children*). *The Pure Hell of St Trinian's*. 1961: *Double Bunk*. *The Rebel* (US: *Call Me Genius*). *A Weekend With Lulu*. *Watch It Sailor!* *Nothing Barred*. 1963: *Heavens Above!* *Just for Fun*. 1965: *You Must Be Joking*. 1966: *Morgan—a Suitable Case for Treatment* (US: *Morgan*). *The Wrong Box*. 1967: *Smashing Time*. 1968: *Lionheart*. *Wonderwall*. 1969: *The Italian Job*. 1970: *Doctor in Trouble*. *The Private Life of Sherlock Holmes*. *On a Clear Day You Can See Forever*. 1972: *For the Love of Ada*. 1976: *Confessions of a Driving Instructor*. *The Chiffy Kids* (series). 1977: *Come Play With Me*. *The Last Remake of Beau Geste*. *Adventures of a Private Eye*. *The Hound of the Baskervilles*. *Stand Up, Virgin Soldiers*. 1979: *The Great Rock 'n' Roll Swindle*. 1980: *Riding High*.

## HANRAY, Lawrence 1874-1947

This British supporting player was such an actor of the old school and bore himself with such dignity that one always expected to see him in a winged collar and black tie. However, if the characters he played were solicitors, physicians, bankers and noblemen, they were not always sympathetic.

Made a first-rate Archbishop Cranmer in *The Private Life of Henry VIII*, one of only several important Korda pictures in which he was cast.

1923: *The Pipes of Pan*. 1930: *Beyond the Cities*. 1931: *Her Reputation*. 1932: *That Night in London* (US: *Overnight*). *Love on Wheels*. *There Goes the Bride*. *The Faithful Heart* (US: *Faithful Hearts*). *Leap Year*. *The Man from Toronto*. 1933: *The Good Companions*. *The Private Life of Henry VIII*. *Loyalties*. *This Week of Grace*. *\*A Dickensian Fantasy*. *His Grace Gives Notice*. 1934: *Catherine the Great/The Rise of Catherine the Great*. *Those Were the Days*. *What Happened Then?* *The Great Defender*. *Chu Chin Chow*. *Adventure Limited*. *Easy Money*. *The Scarlet Pimpernel*. *Brewster's Millions*. *Murder at Monte Carlo*. 1935: *Expert's Opinion*. *Mimi*. *Lorna Doone*. *Street Song*. 1936: *Whom the Gods Love* (US: *Mozart*). *The Lonely Road* (US: *Scotland Yard Commands*). *Someone at the Door*. *As You Like It*. *The Three Maxims* (US: *The Show Goes On*). *Rembrandt*. *The Man Who Could Work Miracles*. *Fire Over England*. *Beloved Imposter*. 1937: *The Show Goes On* (different from 1936 one). *Knight Without Armour*. *Moonlight Sonata*. *Knights for a Day*. *It's Never Too Late to Mend*. *Action for Slander*. *Midnight Menace*. *The Girl in the Taxi*. *The Last Chance*. *Smash and Grab*. *Over the Moon* (released 1940). *21 Days* (released 1940. US: *21 Days Together*). 1938: *A Royal Divorce*. 1941: *Hatter's Castle*. *Quiet Wedding*. *Old Mother Riley's Circus*. *Penn of Pennsylvania* (US: *The Courageous Mr Penn*). 1943: *My Learned Friend*. 1944: *Love Story* (US: *A Lady Surrenders*). *On Approval*. *Hotel Reserve*. 1947: *Nicholas Nickleby*. *Mine Own Executioner*.

## HARDING, Lyn

(David Llewellyn Harding) 1867-1952
Enormous, bushy-browed, Welsh-born actor, equivalent in build to Hollywood's Scottish-born comic heavy Eric Campbell (1879-1917). He made a formidable villain, even well into his sixties, but a sojourn in America, although taking in a couple of film roles, didn't lead to a Hollywood career. Alleged to have made his film debut in 1914.

1920: *The Barton Mystery*. *A Bachelor Husband*. 1922: *\*Les Misérables* (extract). *When Knighthood Was in Flower*. 1924: *Yolanda*. 1927: *Further Adventures of the Flag Lieutenant*. *Land of Hope and Glory*. 1930: *Sleeping Partners*. 1931: *The Speckled Band*. 1932: *The Barton Mystery* (remake). 1933: *The Constant Nymph*. 1934: *The Man Who Changed His Name*. *Wild Boy*. *The Lash*. 1935: *The Triumph of Sherlock Holmes*. *Escape Me Never*. *The Invader* (US: *An Old Spanish Custom*). 1936: *The Man Who Changed His Mind* (US: *The Man Who Lived Again*). *Spy of Napoleon*. *Fire Over England*. *Please Teacher*. 1937: *Underneath the Arches*. *Knight Without Armour*. *Silver Blaze* (US: *Murder at the Baskervilles*). *The*

*Mutiny of the Elsinore*. 1938: *The Pearls of the Crown*. 1939: *The Missing People*. *Goodbye Mr Chips!* 1941: *The Prime Minister*.

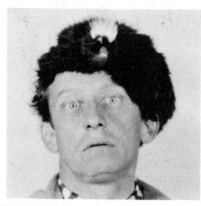

## HATTON, Raymond 1887-1971

Cross-looking American actor with unruly dark hair. A leading star of early silents, he formed a comedy team with big Wallace Beery in the late 1920s, Beery's bulk contrasting hilariously with short, skinny Hatton. Despite facial features that seemed to qualify him for villain roles, he got a wide variety of parts before, in the late 1930s, becoming the scruffy sidekick of numerous western stars, latterly Johnny Mack Brown. Died from a heart attack.

1914: *The Circus Man*. *The Making of Bobby Burnit*. 1915: *The Arab*. *The Golden Chance*. *The Woman*. *The Immigrant* (not the Chaplin). *The Unknown*. *The Wild Goose Chase*. *Chimmie Fadden*. *The Unafraid*. *Temptation*. *The Girl of the Golden West*. *Armstrong's Wife*. *Kindling*. 1916: *Tennessee's Partner*. *Joan the Woman*. *Oliver Twist*. *Public Opinion*. *To Have and to Hold*. *Chimmie Fadden Out West*. *The Sowers*. *The Love Mask*. *The Lash*. *The Honorable Friend*. 1917: *The Woman God Forgot*. *The Little American*. *The American Consul*. *What Money Can't Buy*. *Hashimura Togo*. *The Devil Stone*. *Nan of Music Mountain*. *Crystal Gazer*. *Sandy*. *The Secret Game*. *Romance of the Redwoods*. 1918: *The Whispering Chorus*. *We Can't Have Everything*. *The Source*. *Arizona*. *The Goat*. *The Firefly of France*. *Cruise of the Make-Believe*. *Less Than Kin*. *Jules of the Stronghcart*. 1919: *You're Fired!* *Male and Female* (GB: *The Admirable Crichton*). *Everywoman*. *The Love Burglar*. *For Better, For Worse*. *The Dub* (GB: *The Fool*). *The Squaw Man*. *Maggie Pepper*. *The Wild Goose Chase*. *Experimental Marriage*. *Poor Boob*. *Secret Service*. *The Dancin' Fool*. 1920: *Jes' Call Me Jim*. *Officer 666*. *Stop, Thief!* 1921: *The Affairs of Anatol*. *The Ace of Hearts*. *Doubling for Romeo*. *Salvage*. *The Concert*. *Bunty Pulls the Strings*. *Peck's Bad Boy*. *All's Fair in Love*. *Pilgrims of the Night*. 1922: *To Have and to Hold*. *The Hottentot*. *Pink Gods*. *Manslaughter*. *Ebb Tide*. *His Back Against the Wall*. *Head Over Heels*. 1923: *The Virginian*. *The Barefoot Boy*. *Java Head*. *Three Wise Fools*. *Big Brother*. *Enemies*

ABOVE Lawrence **Hanray** (extreme right) gives his skinflint lawyer the full treatment in *It's Never Too Late to Mend* (1937). With him: D. J. Williams, another redoubtable British character player, Tod Slaughter and Marjorie Taylor

BELOW Racetrack bad guys: Lyn **Harding** (right) and Leonora Corbett in *Wild Boy* (1934)

of Children. The Tie That Binds. A Man of Action. Trimmed in Scarlet. The Hunchback of Notre Dame. 1924: True As Steel. Triumph. Three Women. The Mine with the Iron Door. Half-a-Dollar Bill. The Fighting American. Cornered. 1925: Adventure. Contraband. In the Name of Love. The Devil's Cargo. The Thundering Herd. A Son of His Father. The Top of the World. The Lucky Devil. Tomorrow's Love. 1926: Lord Jim. Behind the Front. Born to the West. Silence. Forlorn River. We're in the Navy Now. 1927: Fashions for Women. Now We're in the Air. Fireman, Save My Child. 1928: Partners in Crime. The Big Killing. Wife Savers. 1929: Her Unborn Child (GB: Her Child). The Office Scandal. Trent's Last Case. Dear Vivien. Hell's Heroes. *When Caesar Ran a Newspaper. The Mighty. 1930: The Silver Horde. Murder on the Roof. Rogue of the Rio Grande. The Road to Paradise. Midnight Mystery. *Pineapples. 1931: The Squaw Man (GB: The White Man). Woman Hungry (GB: The Challenge). Honeymoon Lane. The Lion and the Lamb. Arrowsmith. 1932: Polly of the Circus. The Fourth Horseman. Drifting Souls. Exposed. The Crooked Circle. Law and Order. Uptown New York. Malay Nights (GB: Shadows of Singapore). Stranger in Town. Vanishing Frontier. Alias Mary Smith. Cornered (and 1924 film of same title). Vanity Street. *Divorce à la Mode. *Long Loop Laramie. 1933: Terror Trail. Hidden Gold. The Big Cage. Penthouse (GB: Crooks in Clover). The Three Musketeers (serial). Lady Killer. The Thundering Herd. State Trooper. Under the Tonto Rim. The Women in His Life. Alice in Wonderland. *Tom's in Town. Day of Reckoning. 1934: Lazy River. Fifteen Wives (GB: The Man with the Electric Voice). Straight Is the Way. The Defense Rests. Red Morning. Wagon Wheels. Once to Every Bachelor. 1935: Times Square Lady. Murder in the Fleet. The Daring Young Man. *Desert Death. Wanderer of the Wasteland. Steamboat 'Round the Bend. Nevada. Stormy. Rustlers of Red Gap (serial). Calm Yourself. G-Men. 1936: Arizona Raiders. Desert Gold. Undersea Kingdom (serial). Laughing Irish Eyes. Timothy's Quest. Yellowstone. Fury. The Vigilantes Are Coming (serial). Mad Holiday. Exclusive Story. Women Are Trouble. 1937: Jungle Jim (serial). Marked Woman. San Quentin. Bad Men of Brimstone. Fly-Away Baby. The Adventurous Blonde. Roaring Timber. Public Wedding. Over the Goal. The Missing Witness. Love is On the Air (GB: The Radio Murder Mystery). 1938: Love Finds Andy Hardy. Tom Sawyer, Detective. Touchdown, Army! (GB: Generals of Tomorrow). The Texans. Over the Wall. He Couldn't Say No. Come On, Rangers. I'm from Missouri. Ambush. Wall Street Cowboy. Paris Honeymoon. Undercover Doctor. Six Thousand Enemies. Cowboys from Texas. The New Frontier/Frontier Horizon. Kansas Terror. Career. Frontier Pony Express. Wyoming Outlaw. Rough Riders' Roundup. 1940: Oklahoma Renegades. Kit Carson. Rocky Mountain Rangers. Covered Wagon Days. Heroes of the Saddle. Queen of the Mob.

Pioneers of the West. 1941: Texas. Gunman from Bodie. White Eagle (serial). Arizona Bound. Forbidden Trails. 1942: Down Texas Way. Dawn on the Great Divide. Cadets on Parade. Riders of the West. Ghost Town Law. West of the Law. The Affairs of Martha (GB: Once Upon a Tuesday). The Girl from Alaska. Below the Border. Her Cardboard Lover. Reap the Wild Wind. 1943: Outlaws of Stampede Pass. Six Gun Gospel. Stranger from Pecos. Prairie Chickens. The Ghost Rider. The Texas Kid. 1944: Raiders of the Border. Tall in the Saddle. Range Law. West of the Rio Grande. Law of the Valley. Land of the Outlaws. Ghost Guns. Partners of the Trail. Law Men. 1945: Flame of the West. Frontier Flame. Gun Smoke. Navajo Trail. Sunbonnet Sue. Rhythm Round-up (GB: Honest John). The Lost Trail. Frontier Feud. Stranger from Santa Fé. Northwest Trail. 1946: Fool's Gold. Drifting Along. Under Arizona Skies. Border Bandits. Gentleman from Texas. The Haunted Mine. Shadows on the Range. Silver Range. Raiders of the South. Trigger Fingers. Rolling Home. 1947: Trailing Danger. Land of the Lawless. Valley of Fear. Black Gold. Code of the Saddle. The Law Comes to Gunsight. Unconquered. Flashing Guns. Paririe Express. Gun Talk. 1948: Back Trail. Overland Trail. Trigger-man. Crossed Trails. White Eagle. Frontier Agent. The Sheriff of Medicine Bow. Silver River. The Fighting Ranger. Gunning for Justice. Hidden Danger. 1950: Hostile Country. Fast on the Draw. West of the Brazos. County Fair. Crooked River. Marshal of Heldorado. Operation Haylift. Colorado Ranger. 1951: Skipalong Rosenbloom. Kentucky Jubilee. 1952: The Daltons' Women. †Arrow in the Dust (TV). †Two-Gun Marshal (TV). The Golden Hawk. 1953: Cow Country. 1954: Thunder Pass. 1955: The Twinkle in God's Eye. The Treasure of Ruby Hills. The Day the World Ended. 1956: Dig That Uranium. Flesh and the Spur. Shake, Rattle and Rock. Girls in Prison. 1957: Invasion of the Saucer Men (GB: Invasion of the Hell Creatures). Motorcycle Gang. Pawnee (GB: Pale Arrow). 1959: Alaska Passage. 1964: The Quick Gun. 1965: Requiem for a Gunfighter. 1967: In Cold Blood.

†Shown in cinemas in some countries

## HATTON, Rondo 1894-1946

Thanks to the congenital acromegaly that distorted his body and facial features, this American actor was unmistakeable. It also confined him to playing villainous or horrific roles. In 1946, Universal spun an entire film around him, The Brute Man. But in the same year, he was dead from a heart attack.

1930: Hell Harbor. 1938: In Old Chicago. Alexander's Ragtime Band. 1939: The Hunchback of Notre Dame. Captain Fury. The Big Guy. 1940: Chad Hanna. Moon Over Burma. 1942: The Cyclone Kid. The Moon and Sixpence. The Ox-Bow Incident (GB: Strange Incident). 1943: Sleepy Lagoon.

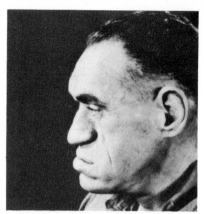

1944: Raiders of Ghost City (serial). Pearl of Death. The Princess and the Pirate. Johnny Doesn't Live Here Anymore. 1945: The Royal Mounted Rides Again (serial). Jungle Captive. 1946: House of Horrors (GB: Joan Medford is Missing). Spider Woman Strikes Back. The Brute Man.

## HAWTREY, Charles
(George C. Hartree) 1914-

Bespectacled, goggle-eyed, thin-lipped, dry-voiced, skinny comic actor who made a whole career out of snooty schoolboys, especially in Will Hay comedies. Dark-haired Hawtrey, from a theatrical family, started in show business as a child: on radio, he was the voice of Norman Bones, boy detective in children's programmes, for many years. Later one of the Carry On comedy gang.

1922: †Tell Your Children. 1923: †This Freedom. 1932: †Marry Me. 1933: †The Melody Maker. 1935: *Kiddies on Parade. 1936: Sabotage (US: The Woman Alone). Well Done Henry. Good Morning, Boys! 1937: East of Ludgate Hill. 1939: Where's That Fire? Jailbirds. 1941: The Ghost of St Michael's. The Black Sheep of Whitehall. 1942: Let the People Sing. The Goose Steps Out. Much Too Shy. 1944: A Canterbury Tale. 1946: Meet Me at Dawn. 1947: The End of the River. 1948: The Story of Shirley Yorke. 1949: Passport to Pimlico. Dark Secret. 1950: Room to Let. 1951: Smart Alec. The Galloping Major. Brandy for the Parson.

*1952: Hammer the Toff. You're Only Young Twice! 1954: Five Days (US: Paid to Kill). To Dorothy a Son (US: Cash on Delivery). 1955: As Long As They're Happy. Man of the Moment. Timeslip (US: The Atomic Man). Simon and Laura. Jumping for Joy. 1956: Who Done It? The March Hare. 1958: Carry On Sergeant. 1959: I Only Arsked! Carry On Nurse. Carry On Teacher. Please Turn Over. 1960: Carry On Constable. Inn for Trouble. 1961: Carry On Regardless. Dentist on the Job (US: Get On with It!) What a Whopper! 1963: Carry On Cabby. Carry On Jack. 1964: Carry On Spying. 1965: Carry On Cowboy. 1966: Carry On Screaming. Don't Lose Your Head. 1967: The Terrornauts. Follow That Camel. Carry On Doctor. 1968: Carry On Up the Khyber. 1969: Carry On Camping. Carry On Again, Doctor. Zeta One. 1970: Carry On Up the Jungle. Carry On Henry. Grasshopper Island (TV). 1971: Carry On at Your Convenience. 1972: Carry On Matron. Carry On Abroad.*

**As director:**
*1945: What Do We Do Now? Dumb Dora Discovers Tobacco.*

†As Charles Hawtrey Jr

**HAYDN, Richard** 1905-1985
Tall, angular, aloof-looking English character actor who cornered the market in prissy professors in the Hollywood of the forties. A former dancer and revue artist, he became an inveterate scene-stealer in comic cameos, and also scored in the occasional serious role, such as his schoolmaster in *The Green Years*. Has also directed.

*1941: Charley's Aunt (GB: Charley's American Aunt). Ball of Fire. 1942: Are Husbands Necessary? Thunder Birds. 1943: Forever and a Day. No Time for Love. 1945: Tonight and Every Night. And Then There Were None (GB: Ten Little Niggers). Adventure. 1946: Cluny Brown. The Green Years. 1947: The Late George Apley. The Beginning or the End? Singapore. Forever Amber. The Foxes of Harrow. 1948: Sitting Pretty. Miss Tatlock's Millions. The Emperor Waltz. 1949: Dear Wife. 1950: Mr Music. 1951: Alice in Wonderland (voice only). 1952: The Merry Widow. 1953: Never Let Me Go. Money from* Home. *1954: Her Twelve Men. 1955: Jupiter's Darling. 1956: Toy Tiger. 1958: Twilight for the Gods. 1960: Please Don't Eat the Daisies. The Lost World. 1962: Mutiny on the Bounty. Five Weeks in a Balloon. 1965: The Sound of Music. Clarence the Cross-Eyed Lion. The Adventures of Bullwhip Griffin. 1974: Young Frankenstein.*

**As director:**
*1948: Miss Tatlock's Millions. 1949: Dear Wife. 1950: Mr Music.*

**HAYES, George 'Gabby'** 1885-1969
Many western heroes had comic sidekicks in the 1930s and 1940s. But bewhiskered (from 1935) George 'Gabby' Hayes was not only about the most popular, but perhaps the only one who was also a star in the public eye. A vaudevillian of long experience, he joined films with the coming of sound, and soon assumed the all-round white whiskers and flapped-back stetson that, together with such expressions as 'Consarn it!' or 'You're durn tootin' built an unforgettable westerner. Died from a heart ailment.

*1923: Why Women Marry. 1929: The Rainbow Man. Smiling Irish Eyes. Big News. 1930: For the Defense. 1931: Nevada Buckaroo. God's Country and the Man. Rose of the Rio Grande. Big Business Girl. Cavalier of the West. Dragnet Patrol (GB: Love Redeemed). 1932: Night Rider. Border Devils. Texas Buddies. From Broadway to Cheyenne (GB: Broadway to Cheyenne). *The Stolen Jools (GB: The Slippery Pearls). Hidden Valley. Winner Take All. Without Honor. Love Me Tonight. Klondike. The Boiling Point. Wild Horse Mesa. The Fighting Champ. The Man from Hell's Edges. Riders of the Desert. 1933: The Gallant Fool. Sagebrush Trail. Skyway. The Fugitive. Crashing Broadway. The Sphinx. Galloping Romeo. The Phantom Broadcast (GB: Phantom of the Air). Riders of Destiny. Devil's Mate (GB: He Knew Too Much). Breed of the Border. (GB: Speed Brent Wins). The Return of Casey Jones. The Ranger's Code. The Fighting Texans (GB: Randy Strikes Oil). Trailing North. Self Defense. 1934: Monte Carlo Nights. The Star Packer (GB: He Wore a Star). The Man from* Utah. *In Old Santa Fé. The Lucky Texan. 'Neath Arizona Skies. West of the Divide. Blue Steel. Randy Rides Alone. The Man from Hell. Mystery Liner. The Lost Jungle (serial). House of Mystery. Beggars in Ermine. City Limits. Brand of Hate. 1935: The Throwback. Smokey Smith. Justice of the Range. $1,000 a Minute. Hop-a-Long Cassidy. Texas Terrors. Rainbow Valley. Thunder Mountain. Tumbling Tumbleweeds. The Hoosier Schoolmaster (GB: The Schoolmaster). Tombstone Terror. Bar 20 Rides Again. The Eagle's Brood. Welcome Home. The Outlaw Tamer. Ladies Crave Excitement. Hitchhike Lady. Death Flies East. Lawless Frontier. Honeymoon Limited. Headline Woman. The Lost City (serial). 1936: The Plainsman. Silver Spurs. Song of the Trail. Swifty. Call of the Prairie. Hopalong Cassidy Returns. Valiant is the Word for Carrie. Mr Deeds Goes to Town. The Lawless Nineties. Three on the Trail. I Married a Doctor. Hearts in Bondage. The Texas Rangers. Hearts of the West. Trail Dust. Valley of the Lawless. Glory Parade. 1937: Hills of Old Wyoming. Mountain Music. North of the Rio Grande. Rustler's Valley. Borderland. Hopalong Rides Again. Texas Trail. 1938: Forbidden Music. Gold is Where You Find It. Bar 20 Justice. Heart of Arizona. The Frontiersman. In Old Mexico. Pride of the West. Sunset Trail. 1939: In Old Caliente. In Old Monterey. Southward Ho! Man of Conquest. Wall Street Cowboy. Fighting Thoroughbreds. Saga of Death Valley. Days of Jesse James. Renegade Trail. Silver on the Sage. The Arizona Kid. Let Freedom Ring. 1940: Wagons Westward. Young Buffalo Bill. Dark Command. Melody Ranch. Young Bill Hickok. The Carson City Kid. The Ranger and the Lady. Colorado. Border Legion. 1941: In Old Cheyenne. Robin Hood of the Pecos. Nevada City. Sheriff of Tombstone. Jesse James at Bay. Red River Valley. Bad Men of Deadwood. *Meet Roy Rogers. 1942: Man from Cheyenne. Sunset on the Desert. South of Santa Fé. Hearts of the Golden West. Ridin' Down the Canyon. Romance on the Range. Sons of the Pioneers. Sunset Serenade. 1943: Calling Wild Bill Elliott. Bordertown Gunfighters. Death Valley Manhunt. Overland Mail Robbery. Wagon Tracks West. In Old Oklahoma (GB: War of the Wildcats). The Man from Thunder River. 1944: Lights of Old Santa Fé. Tucson Raiders. Mojave Firebrand. The Big Bonanza. Tall in the Saddle. Marshal of Reno. Hidden Valley Outlaws. Leave It to the Irish. 1945: Bells of Rosarita. The Man from Oklahoma. Along the Navajo Trail. Utah. Don't Fence Me In. Sunset in Eldorado. Out California Way. 1946: Home in Oklahoma. My Pal Trigger. Song of Arizona. Badman's Territory. Roll On, Texas Moon. Rainbow over Texas. Under Nevada Skies. Heldorado. 1947: Trail Street. Wyoming. 1948: Albuquerque (GB: Silver City). The Untamed Breed. Return of the Bad Men. 1949: El Paso. 1950: The Cariboo Trail.*

**HAYES, Patricia** 1911-
Diminutive, brown-haired actress with rather forlorn features, one of Britain's

most popular character players, although actually in amazingly few films. Her voice became familiar to young radio fans in the 1940s as that of Henry Bones, *boy* detective on *Children's Hour*! Later she made a speciality of disreputable working-class characters and won a British TV Oscar in 1971 for *Edna the Inebriate Woman*. Reckoned to have worked with more top British comedians than any other actress.

*1943: The Dummy Talks. 1944: Candles at Nine. Hotel Reserve. 1945: Great Day. 1947: Nicholas Nickleby. 1948: To the Public Danger. 1949: Skimpy in the Navy. 1954: The Love Match. 1959: The Battle of the Sexes. 1963: Saturday Night Out. 1964: The Sicilians. 1967: The Terrornauts (released 1971). 1969: Goodbye, Mr Chips. Carry On Again, Doctor. 1970: Fragment of Fear. 1971: Raising the Roof. 1973: Love Thy Neighbour. Servizio di scorta (GB: Blue Movie Blackmail). 1974: The Best of Benny Hill. 1979: *Film. The Corn is Green (TV). 1980: Danger on Dartmoor. 1984: The Neverending Story.*

**HAYTER, James** 1907-1983
Short, smiley, chubby-cheeked, round-faced, India-born British stalwart, much in demand for supporting roles from the time he decided to try films in 1936. Briefly a star in the early 1950s (at the time he played Friar Tuck and Mr Pickwick), he stayed in good roles for the rest of the decade. Could be comic—or quite touching

in more serious roles. Busy in TV series of the 1970s, a time when he was also a popular voice-over for commercials.

*1936: Aren't Men Beasts! Sensation. 1937: Big Fella. 1938: Marigold. Murder in Soho (US: Murder in the Night). 1939: Come On George. Band Waggon. 1940: Sailors Three (US: Three Cockeyed Sailors). 1946: The Laughing Lady. The Captive Heart. School for Secrets (US: Secret Flight). 1947: Nicholas Nickleby. The End of the River. Vice Versa. Captain Boycott. The Ghosts of Berkeley Square. The Mark of Cain. The October Man. My Brother Jonathan. 1948: Quartet. A Song for Tomorrow. The Fallen Idol. Bonnie Prince Charlie. No Room at the Inn. Once a Jolly Swagman (US: Maniacs on Wheels). All Over the Town. Silent Dust. The Blue Lagoon. 1949: For Them That Trespass. Helter Skelter. Don't Ever Leave Me. Scrapbook for 1933 (voice only). Passport to Pimlico. Dear Mr Prohack. The Spider and the Fly. Morning Departure (US: Operation Disaster). 1950: Your Witness (US: Eye Witness). Night and the City. Waterfront (US: Waterfront Women). Trio. The Woman With No Name (US: Her Panelled Door). 1951: Flesh and Blood. Tom Brown's Schooldays. Calling Bulldog Drummond. 1952: The Story of Robin Hood and His Merrie Men. I'm a Stranger. The Crimson Pirate. The Pickwick Papers. The Great Game. 1953: Four-Sided Triangle. Will Any Gentleman?... The Triangle. Always a Bride. A Day to Remember. 1954: *The Journey. For Better, For Worse (US: Cocktails in the Kitchen). Beau Brummell. 1955: See How They Run. Touch and Go (US: The Light Touch). Land of the Pharaohs. 1956: Keep It Clean. Port Afrique. It's a Wonderful World. The Big Money (released 1958). 1957: Seven Waves Away (US: Abandon Ship!). The Heart Within. Carry On Admiral (US: The Ship Was Loaded). Sail into Danger. 1958: Gideon's Day (US: Gideon of Scotland Yard). The Key. I Was Monty's Double. The Captain's Table. 1959: The 39 Steps. The Boy and the Bridge. 1961: Go to Blazes. 1962: Out of the Fog. 1967: Stranger in the House (US: Cop-Out). A Challenge for Robin Hood. 1968: Oliver! 1969: David Copperfield (TV. GB: cinemas). 1970: Blood on Satan's Claw. Scramble. The Firechasers. Song of Norway. 1971: Not Tonight Darling! 1975: The Bawdy Adventures of Tom Jones.*

**HEATHCOTE, Thomas** 1917-
Scowling British actor with dark hair and dented cheeks, usually in downbeat or 'countrified' roles. Born in India, he was taken under the wing of Laurence Olivier, who helped him get into films via a small role in *Hamlet*. Despite a distinctive style, he played only smallish parts after that, and gained more popularity in television and the theatre.

*1948: Hamlet. 1950: Dance Hall. 1951: Cloudburst. 1953: Malta Story. The Red Beret (US: Paratrooper). The Large Rope. The*

*Sword and the Rose. Blood Orange. 1954: The Seekers (US: Land of Fury). 1955: Above Us the Waves. Doctor at Sea. 1956: The Iron Petticoat. The Last Man to Hang? Eyewitness. Tiger in the Smoke. 1958: A Night to Remember. Tread Softly, Stranger. 1960: Village of the Damned. 1961: On the Fiddle (US: Operation Snafu). 1966: A Man for All Seasons. 1967: Quatermass and the Pit (US: Five Million Miles to Earth). 1968: The Fixer. 1970: Julius Caesar. 1971: The Abominable Dr Phibes. Burke and Hare. Demons of the Mind. 1973: Luther. 1976: A Choice of Weapons (later Trial by Combat. US: Dirty Knights' Work). 1983: The Sword of the Valiant. 1984: The Shooting Party.*

**HECKART, Eileen**
(Anna E. Herbert) 1919-
Thin-faced American actress with dark, tautly curly hair. When she arrived in Hollywood in 1956, after success on Broadway, Heckart looked set to become a regular part of the cinema scene. But she soon returned to stage work, reappearing in 1970s' films only long enough to snatch an Oscar for *Butterflies Are Free*, having already bagged an Emmy in 1967 for *Win Me a Place at Forest Lawn*. Most of her characters were only happy when haranguing their fellows. Also nominated for an Academy Award for *The Bad Seed*.

*1956: Miracle in the Rain. The Bad Seed. Bus Stop. Somebody Up There Likes Me. 1958: The Blue Men (TV). Hot Spell. 1959: A Corner of the Garden (TV). 1960: Heller in*

*Pink Tights. 1963: My Six Loves. 1967: Up the Down Staircase. No Way to Treat a Lady. 1969: The Tree. 1972: Butterflies Are Free. The Victim (TV). 1974: Zandy's Bride. The Hiding Place (released 1977). The FBI versus Alvin Karpis, Public Enemy Number One (TV). 1976: Burnt Offerings. 1977: Sunshine Christmas (TV). 1978: Suddenly, Love (TV). 1980: FDR: The Last Year (TV). White Mama (TV). The Black Pill (TV). 1982: Games Mother Never Taught You (TV). 1984: Fifty Fifty.*

### HEGGIE, O. P. 1879-1936

Square-faced, apprehensive-looking, large-eyed, pear-nosed Australian-born actor with a scrap of light-brown hair who was equally at home with authority, sincerity and querulousness and is undoubtedly best recalled by most nostalgia fans as the blind hermit in *Bride of Frankenstein*. But he was also a resourceful Nayland Smith battling Warner Oland's Fu Manchu in two early sound adventures of the oriental master-fiend. Heggie looked set for a typically busy 1930s' career as a Hollywood character player when a midwinter bout of pneumonia killed him at only 56.

*1928: The Actress. The Letter. 1929: The Mysterious Dr Fu Manchu. The Mighty. The Wheel of Life. 1930: The Vagabond King. One Romantic Night. The Return of Dr Fu Manchu. The Bad Man. Playboy of Paris. Sunny. Broken Dishes. 1931: The Woman Between (GB: Madame Julie). East Lynne. Too Young to Marry. Devotion. 1932: Smilin' Through. 1933: The King's Vacation. Zoo in Budapest. 1934: Midnight. Peck's Bad Boy. The Count of Monte Cristo. Anne of Green Gables. 1935: Chasing Yesterday. Bride of Frankenstein. A Dog of Flanders. Ginger. 1936: The Prisoner of Shark Island.*

### HEINZ, Gerard
(Gerhard Hinze) 1903-1972
Smooth, saturnine German actor in British films, often menacing, but occasionally effective in more sympathetic roles. On stage at 18, he led his own travelling company before he was 30, but was thrown in a Nazi concentration camp in 1934, escaping to Czechoslovakia and thence to Switzerland. Arriving in England just before World War II, he found his film career largely confined to shady foreigners.

*1942: Thunder Rock. Went the Day Well? (US: 48 Hours). 1944: English Without Tears (US: Her Man Gilbey). 1946: Caravan. 1947: Frieda. Broken Journey. 1948: Portrait from Life (US: The Girl in the Painting). The Fallen Idol. The First Gentleman (US: Affairs of a Rogue). Sleeping Car to Trieste. The Bad Lord Byron. 1949: That Dangerous Age (US: If This Be Sin).*

*Traveller's Joy (released 1951). The Lost People. 1950: State Secret (US: The Great Manhunt). The Clouded Yellow. 1951: White Corridors. His Excellency. 1952: Private Information. Top Secret (US: Mr Potts Goes to Moscow). 1953: Desperate Moment. The Accused. 1955: The Prisoner. 1956: You Pay Your Money. 1957: The Traitor (US: The Accused. And 1953 title). Seven Thunders (US: The Beasts of Marseilles). Accused (And 1953 and 1957 films. US: Mark of the Hawk). The Man Inside. Carlton-Browne of the F O (US: Man in a Cocked Hat). 1959: The House of the Seven Hawks. 1960: Offbeat. I Aim at the Stars. 1961: The Guns of Navarone. Highway to Battle. 1962: Operation Snatch. The Password Is Courage. 1963: The Cardinal. 1964: Devils of Darkness. \*Boy with a Flute. 1965: The Heroes of Telemark. 1966: Where the Bullets Fly. The Projected Man. 1967: The Dirty Dozen.*

### HENSON, Gladys
(nee Gunn) 1897-1983
Brown-haired, Ireland-born supporting actress in British films. On stage at 13, she was a Hippodrome chorus girl who grew up to look plump and motherly with macaw-like features which seemed to suit a lifetime of working-class motherhood. Thus, without previous film experience, she came quickly into demand in post-war years, appearing more than once as the wife of Jack Warner, forever doing the washing and cooking the tea. Married to actor-comedian Leslie Henson from 1926 to 1943; never remarried.

*1946: The Captive Heart. 1947: Frieda. Temptation Harbour. It Always Rains on*

*Sunday. 1948: Counterblast. The Weaker Sex. London Belongs to Me (US: Dulcimer Street). The History of Mr Polly. 1949: Train of Events. The Blue Lamp. The Cure for Love. 1950: Dance Hall. Highly Dangerous. The Magnet. The Happiest Days of Your Life. Cage of Gold. Happy Go Lovely. 1951: Lady Godiva Rides Again. I Believe in You. 1952: Derby Day (US: Four Against Fate). 1953: Those People Next Door. Meet Mr Lucifer. 1955: Cockleshell Heroes. 1957: Davy. Doctor at Large. The Prince and the Showgirl. 1960: Clue of the Twisted Candle. The Trials of Oscar Wilde (US: The Man With the Green Carnation). Double Bunk. Dangerous Afternoon. No Love for Johnnie. Stork Talk. 1962: Death Trap. 1963: The Leather Boys. 1964: Go Kart Go! First Men in the Moon. 1965: The Legend of Young Dick Turpin. 1975: The Bawdy Adventures of Tom Jones.*

### HERBERT, Holmes
(Edward Sanger) 1882-1956
Tall, dark, imposing English-born actor with solid features and resounding tones. He made no films in his native country but, once in America, he became a stalwart leading man in silents, often as stern and unrelenting characters. The 'Holmes' in his stage name was taken from Sherlock Holmes, his favourite character. In his younger days, he would have been ideal for the role. As it was, he had to be content with minor roles in the Universal 'Holmes' films of the 1940s, all of which he handled with

his customary dignity. Married (second) character actress Beryl Mercer (1882-1939).

*1917: A Doll's House. 1918: The Whirlpool. 1919: The White Heather. Market of Souls. 1920: My Lady's Garter. Black Is White. His House in Order. Lady Rose's Daughter. The Right to Love. Dead Men Tell No Tales. 1921: Heedless Moths. The Inner Chamber. The Wild Goose. The Truth About Husbands. His Lord and Master. The Family Closet. 1922: Divorce Coupons. Evidence. Any Wife. Moonshine Valley. A Woman's Woman. A Stage Romance. 1923: I Will Repay. Toilers of the Sea. 1924: The Enchanted Cottage. Sinners in Heaven. Love's Wilderness. His Own Free Will. Another Scandal. Week-End Husbands. 1925: Daddy's Gone a-Hunting. Wreckage. A Woman of the World. Wildfire. Up the Ladder. 1926: Honeymoon Express. The Wanderer. Josselyn's Wife. The Passionate Quest. The Fire Brigade. 1927: East Side, West Side. Mr Wu. Lovers? The Heart of Salome. The Gay Retreat. The Silver Slave. The Nest. One Increasing Purpose. Slaves of Beauty. When a Man Loves. 1928: The Terror. Gentlemen Prefer Blondes. The Sporting Age. Their Hour. Through the Breakers. On Trial. 1929: The Charlatan. Untamed. Careers. Madame X. Her Private Life. The Thirteenth Chair. Say It with Songs. The Kiss. The Careless Age. 1930: The Ship from Shanghai. 1931: The Single Sin. The Hot Heiress. Broadminded. Chances. Daughter of the Dragon. Dr Jekyll and Mr Hyde. 1932: Shop Angel. Miss Pinkerton. Central Park. 1933: Sister to Judas. The Mystery of the Wax Museum. The Invisible Man. 1934: The House of Rothschild. The Curtain Falls. Beloved. One in a Million. The Pursuit of Happiness. The Count of Monte Cristo. 1935: Accent on Youth. Sons of Steel. Mark of the Vampire. Captain Blood. Cardinal Richelieu. 1936: The Country Beyond. 15 Maiden Lane. Brilliant Marriage. Lloyds of London. Gentleman from Louisiana. The Charge of the Light Brigade. Wife Versus Secretary. The Prince and the Pauper. 1937: The Girl Said No. Slave Ship. House of Secrets. Love Under Fire. Lancer Spy. Here's Flash Casey. The Thirteenth Chair (remake). 1938: The Adventures of Robin Hood. The Black Doll. Mystery of Mr Wong. Marie Antoinette. The Buccaneer. Say It in French. 1939: The Little Princess. Stanley and Livingstone. Everything Happens at Night. The Adventures of Sherlock Holmes (GB: Sherlock Holmes). Juarez. Wolf Call. Bad Boy (GB: Perilous Journey). We Are Not Alone. Trapped in the Sky. The Sun Never Sets. The Mystery of the White Room. Mr Moto's Last Warning. Hidden Power. 1940: British Intelligence (GB: Enemy Agent). Foreign Correspondent. Angel from Texas. South of Suez. 1941: Man Hunt. International Squadron. The Ghost of Frankenstein. 1942: This Above All. Invisible Agent. Lady in a Jam. Sherlock Holmes and the Secret Weapon. The Undying Monster (GB: The Hammond Mystery). 1943: Corvette K-225*

*(GB: The Nelson Touch). Sherlock Holmes in Washington. Two Tickets to London. Calling Doctor Death. 1944: Pearl of Death. The Bermuda Mystery. Our Hearts Were Young and Gay. The Uninvited. Enter Arsène Lupin. The Mummy's Curse. 1945: House of Fear. Uncle Harry/The Strange Affair of Uncle Harry. Confidential Agent. Jealousy. George White's Scandals. 1946: The Verdict. Three Strangers. Dressed to Kill (GB: Sherlock Holmes and the Secret Code). 1947: Over the Santa Fé Trail (GB: No Escape). Singapore. Bulldog Drummond Strikes Back. Bulldog Drummond at Bay. This Time for Keeps. The Swordsman. 1948: Johnny Belinda. The Wreck of the Hesperus. Jungle Jim. Sorry, Wrong Number. 1949: The Stratton Story. Barbary Pirate. Post Office Investigator. 1950: Iroquois Trail (GB: The Tomahawk Trail). 1951: David and Bathsheba. The Unknown Man. The Law and the Lady. Anne of the Indies. At Sword's Point (GB: Sons of the Musketeers). 1952: The Brigand.*

**HERBERT, Hugh 1887-1952**

Black-haired, ruddy-cheeked, cheerful-looking American comic actor, writer and director. From the beginning of sound, he cropped up in dozens of 'excitable' cameo roles, almost all of them characterized by his raising fluttering hands, doing a double-take and crying 'Woo Woo!' Brought a touch of farcical anarchy to nearly everything he tackled. Died from a heart attack.

*1927: *Realisation. *Solomon's Children. Husbands for Rent. 1928: *The Lemon. *On the Air. Lights of New York. *Mind Your Business. *The Prediction. *Miss Information. Caught in the Fog. 1929: *She Went for a Tramp. 1930: Danger Lights. Hook, Line and Sinker. Second Wife. The Sin Ship. 1931: Traveling Husbands. Laugh and Get Rich. Cracked Nuts. Friends and Lovers. 1932: The Lost Squadron. *Shampoo the Magician. Faithless. Million Dollar Legs. 1933: Goldie Gets Along. *It's Spring. Diplomaniacs. Convention City. College Coach (GB: Football Coach). From Headquarters. Footlight Parade. Bureau of Missing Persons. Goodbye Again. Strictly Personal. She Had to Say Yes. 1934: Easy to Love. Dames. Fashions of 1934. Wonder Bar. Harold Teen (GB: The Dancing*

*Fool). Kansas City Princess. The Merry Frinks (GB: The Happy Family). Sweet Adeline. The Merry Wives of Reno. Fog over Frisco. 1935: Gold Diggers of 1935. *A Trip thru a Hollywood Studio. The Traveling Saleslady. A Midsummer Night's Dream. We're in the Money. To Beat the Band. Miss Pacific Fleet. 1936: Colleen. Love Begins at 20 (GB: All One Night). Sing Me a Love Song. One Rainy Afternoon. We Went to College (GB: The Old School Tie). Mind Your Own Business. 1937: Sh! The Octopus. That Man's Here Again. Marry the Girl. The Perfect Specimen. Hollywood Hotel. Top of the Town. The Singing Marine. 1938: The Great Waltz. Men Are Such Fools. Four's a Crowd. Gold Diggers in Paris. 1939: The Little Accident. The Family Next Door. *Dad for a Day. Eternally Yours. The Lady's from Kentucky. 1940: La Conga Nights. Slightly Tempted. A Little Bit of Heaven. Hit Parade of 1941. The Villain Still Pursued Her. Private Affairs. 1941: The Black Cat. Hello Sucker. Hellzapoppin. Meet the Chump. Nobody's Fool. Badlands of Dakota. Mrs Wiggs of the Cabbage Patch. 1942: There's One Born Every Minute. You're Telling Me. Don't Get Personal. 1943: It's a Great Life. *Who's Hugh? *Pitchin' in the Kitchen. Stage Door Canteen. Beauty for Sale. 1944: Ever Since Venus. Music for Millions. *Woo Woo. Kismet. 1945: One Way to Love. *The Mayor's Husband. *When the Wife's Away. *Honeymoon Blues. 1947: *Should Husbands Marry? Carnegie Hall. Blondie in the Dough. 1948: A Miracle Can Happen (later On Our Merry Way). So This is New York. One Touch of Venus. A Song is Born. The Girl from Manhattan. 1949: *Trapped by a Blonde. *Super Wolf. The Beautiful Blonde from Bashful Bend. 1950: *A Slip and a Miss. 1951: *Woo Woo Blues. Havana Rose. *Trouble-in-Laws. *The Gink at the Sink.*

**HERBERT, Percy 1925- 1992**

Pugnacious, light-haired, wide-nosed portrayer of cockney characters in British films, a self-confessed 'East End [of London] tearaway' who got into acting via the good offices of Dame Sybil Thorndike, and soon became a staple of the British cinema, whether as soldier, crook, blue-collar worker or comedy relief. Went to America for a while in the late 1960s, incongruously to play a Scot in the TV western series *Cimarron Strip.*

*1953: The Case of Express Delivery. 1954: The Green Buddha. One Good Turn. 1955: The Prisoner. The Night My Number Came Up. Confession (US: The Deadliest Sin). Cockleshell Heroes. 1956: Child in the House. The Baby and the Battleship. A Hill in Korea (US: Hell in Korea). 1957: Quatermass II (US: Enemy from Space). The Steel Bayonet. Night of the Demon (US: Curse of the Demon). The Bridge on the River Kwai. Barnacle Bill (US: All at Sea). 1958: The Safecracker. Dunkirk. No Time to Die! (US: Tank Force). Sea Fury. Sea of Sand (US: Desert Patrol). 1959: Yesterday's Enemy. Serious Charge (US: A Touch of Hell). Don't Panic Chaps! Deadly Record. Idle on Parade (US: Idol on Parade). A Touch of Larceny. 1960: The Challenge. There Was a Crooked Man. Tunes of Glory. 1961: The Guns of Navarone. 1962: Mutiny on the Bounty. Mysterious Island. The Cracksman. La citta prigioniera (GB: The Captive City. US: The Conquered City). 1963: Dr Syn Alias the Scarecrow. Carry On Jack. Becket. 1964: Guns at Batasi. Allez France! (US: The Counterfeit Constable). 1965: Joey Boy. Bunny Lake is Missing. Carry On Cowboy. 1966: Tobruk. One Million Years BC. 1967: The Viking Queen. Casino Royale. Mister Ten Per Cent. Night of the Big Heat. 1969: Too Late the Hero. The Royal Hunt of the Sun. One More Time. 1971: Captain Apache. Man in the Wilderness. The Fiend. 1972: Doomwatch. Up the Front. 1973: The Mackintosh Man. Blacksnake (GB: Slaves). Craze. 1975: One of Our Dinosaurs is Missing. 1977: Hardcore. Valentino. 1978: The Wild Geese. 1979: The London Connection (US: The Omega Connection). 1980: The Sea Wolves.*

**HEYDT, Louis Jean** 1905-1960
Stocky, flaxen-haired American supporting actor of Dutch extraction whose hunted, mistrustful look and reliability of performance got him cast in some good thrillers, mostly as little men on the wrong side of the law, or with shady pasts. Also remembered as the barfly to whom Brian Donlevy tells the story in *The Great McGinty* (1940). The quality of his roles diminished after the 1940s—although he had a juicier part in 1957's *The Wings of Eagles*—and he was struck down by a heart attack at 54.

*1937: SOS Coastguard (serial). Make Way for Tomorrow. 1938: Test Pilot. I Am the Law. *They're Always Caught. 1939: *Dad for a Day. Let Freedom Ring. They Made Her a Spy. Charlie Chan at Treasure Island. Gone With the Wind. Reno. Mr Smith Goes to Washington. Each Dawn I Die. They Made Me a Criminal. 1940: Abe Lincoln in Illinois (GB: Spirit of the People). The Great McGinty (GB: Down Went McGinty). A Child is Born. Irene. The Man Who Talked Too Much. Let's Make Music. *All About Hash. Santa Fé Trail. *The Hidden Master. Johnny Apollo. Joe and Ethel Turp Call on the President. Dr Ehrlich's Magic Bullet (GB: The Story of Dr Ehrlich's Magic Bullet). Pier 13. 1941: Sleepers West. How Green Was My Valley. Power Dive. High Sierra. Dive Bomber. Midnight Angel. 1942: Tortilla Flat. Ten Gentlemen from West Point. Commandos Strike at Dawn. Pacific Blackout. Captains of the Clouds. Manila Calling. Triumph over Pain. 1943: Mission to Moscow. Gung Ho! The Iron Major. One Dangerous Night. Stage Door Canteen. First Comes Courage. 1944: The Great Moment. The Story of Dr Wassell. See Here, Private Hargrove. Her Primitive Man. Thirty Seconds over Tokyo. Betrayal from the East. 1945: They Were Expendable. Zombies on Broadway (GB: Loonies on Broadway). Our Vines Have Tender Grapes. 1946: Gentleman Joe Palooka. The Big Sleep. The Hoodlum Saint. 1947: Sinbad the Sailor. I Cover Big Town. Spoilers of the North. 1948: *California's Golden Beginning. 1949: Bad Men of Tombstone. Make Believe Ballroom. Come to the Stable. The Kid from Cleveland. 1950: Paid in Full. The Furies. The Great Missouri Raid. 1951: Al Jennings of Oklahoma. Rawhide. Raton Pass (GB: Canyon Pass). Drums in the Deep South. Two of a Kind. Criminal Lawyer. Close to My Heart. Flesh and Fury. Road Block. Sailor Beware. 1952: Models Inc. (later Call Girl. GB: That Kind of Girl). The Old West. Mutiny. 1953: Island in the Sky. The Vanquished. 1954: The Boy from Oklahoma. A Star Is Born. 1955: Ten Wanted Men. The Eternal Sea. No Man's Woman. 1956: Stranger at My Door. Wet-backs. 1957: Raiders of Old California. The Wings of Eagles. 1958: The Badge of Marshal Brennan. The Man Who Died Twice. 1959: Inside the Mafia.*

**HICKSON, Joan** 1906- *1998*
Inconspicuous, light-haired British actress with open, hopeful face, in a wide variety of stage and film roles since her theatrical debut in 1927. Excellent in comedy cameos as middle-class working women or addle-pated relations. In 1983, she completed 50 years in films with her role in *The Wicked Lady* and at the end of 1984 she became the world's oldest spinster detective as Agatha Christie's Miss Marple in a TV series.

*1933: Trouble in Store. 1934: Widows Might. 1936: The Man Who Could Work Miracles. Love from a Stranger. 1937: The Lilac Domino. 1938: Second Thoughts. 1944: Don't Take It to Heart. 1945: The Trojan Brothers. 1946: I See a Dark Stranger (US: The Adventuress). 1947: This Was a Woman. 1948: The Guinea Pig (US: The Outsider). 1949: Celia. 1950: Seven Days to Noon. The Magnet. 1951: High Treason. Hell Is Sold Out. Hunted (US: The Stranger in Between). 1952: No Haunt for a Gentleman. Tall Headlines. Hindle Wakes (US: Holiday Week). Come Back Peter. The Card (US: The Promoter). Rough Shoot (US: Shoot First). Curtain Up. 1953: Deadly Nightshade. The Million Pound Note (US: Man With a Million). 1954: Doctor in the House. The House Across the Lake (US: Heatwave). Mad About Men. What Every Woman Wants. To Dorothy a Son (US: Cash on Delivery). Dance Little Lady. The Crowded Day. 1955: As Long as They're Happy. Doctor at Sea. Value for Money. The Woman for Joe. Simon and Laura. A Time to Kill. Lost (US: Tears for Simon). Jumping for Joy. The Man Who Never Was. 1956: The Extra Day. Port of Escape. The Last Man to Hang? Child in the House. 1957: Carry On Admiral (US: The Ship Was Loaded). No Time for Tears. Happy is the Bride! Barnacle Bill (US: All at Sea). 1958: Law and Disorder. 1959: Upstairs and Downstairs. Please Turn Over. The 39 Steps. 1960: Carry On Constable. No Kidding (US: Beware of Children). 1961: His and Hers. Carry On Regardless. Raising the Wind. In the Doghouse. Murder She Said. 1963: Nurse on Wheels. Heavens Above! 1965: The Secret of My Success. 1968: Mrs Brown, You've Got a Lovely Daughter. 1970: Carry on Loving. 1971: Friends. A Day in the Death of Joe Egg. 1973: Theatre of Blood. Carry On Girls. 1974: Confessions of a Window Cleaner. 1975: One of Our Dinosaurs is Missing. 1978: Yanks. 1983: The Wicked Lady. 1985: Clockwise.*

**HINDS, Samuel S.** 1875-1948
Although one's abiding memory of Hinds remains an image of him stretched out on the slab beneath Bela Lugosi's pendulum in *The Raven*, in fact he played scores of solid citizens through the 1930s and 1940s. Ironically, fair-haired (turning to silver), affable-looking Hinds was often cast as an attorney—his own profession before turning his hobby of acting into a profitable career in the early 1930s. Occasionally, his honest looks hid a streak of crookedness, a break he no doubt enjoyed after so much kindliness and wisdom.

*1932: If I Had a Million. 1933: The Nuisance (GB: Accidents Wanted). The House on 56th Street. Penthouse (GB: Crooks in Clover). The World Changes. The Crime of the Century. Gabriel over the White House. Day of Reckoning. Bed of Roses. Lady for a Day. Berkeley Square. The Deluge. Little Women. One Man's Journey. Hold the Press. This Day and Age. Son of a Sailor. Female. Women in*

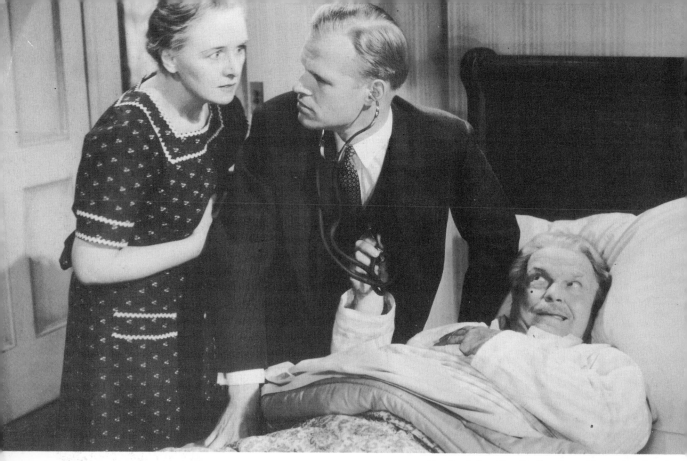

ABOVE Louis Jean **Heydt**'s listening to his own heartbeat in *Make Way for Tomorrow* (1937), thanks to rascally Victor Moore. The lady's another redoubtable Hollywood character player, British-born Elisabeth Risdon (E. Evans, 1887–1958)

LEFT Joan **Hickson** puts on an unusually stern expression for her role in *Carry On Nurse* (1959)

His Life. Convention City. 1934: A Wicked
Woman. Operator 13 (GB: Spy 13). Sadie
McKee. Fog. The Big Shakedown. Manhattan
Melodrama. Most Precious Thing in Life. He
Was Her Man. Evelyn Prentice. The Ninth
Guest. No Greater Glory. Sisters under the Skin
(GB: The Romantic Age). Massacre. Men in
White. The Crime Doctor. Straightaway. The
Defense Rests. Have a Heart. Sequoia. A Lost
Lady (GB: Courageous). Hat, Coat and
Glove. The Cat's Paw. 1935: Devil Dogs of the
Air. Bordertown. Black Fury. Wings in the
Dark. West of the Pecos. Strangers All. She. In
Person. College Scandal (GB: The Clock
Strikes Eight). Annapolis Farewell (GB:
Gentlemen of the Navy). Mills of the Gods.
Behind the Evidence. Dr Socrates. Rumba/
Rhumba. Private Worlds. Accent on Youth.
The Big Broadcast of 1936. The Secret Bride
(GB: Concealment). Two-Fisted. Living on
Velvet. The Raven. Millions in the Air. Shadow
of Doubt. Rendezvous. 1936: Timothy's Quest.
Woman Trap. The Trail of the Lonesome Pine.
Fatal Lady. Border Flight. Rhythm on the
Range. Sworn Enemy. His Brother's Wife. The
Gorgeous Hussy. Love Letters of a Star. The
Longest Night. Black Legion. 1937: The
Mighty Treve. The Lady Fights Back. Top of
the Town. Night Key. Wings Over Honolulu.
The Road Back. A Girl With Ideas. Prescrip-
tion for Romance. Double or Nothing. She's
Dangerous. Navy Blue and Gold. Stage Door.
1938: Wives Under Suspicion. The Jury's
Secret. The Devil's Party. The Rage of Paris.
The Road to Reno. Pirates of the Skies. Swing
That Cheer. Secrets of a Nurse. The Storm. Test
Pilot. You Can't Take It with You. Double
Danger. Forbidden Valley. Young Dr Kildare.
Personal Secretary. 1939: Ex-Champ (GB:
Golden Gloves). Calling Dr Kildare. Hawaiian
Nights. The Under-Pup. Within the Law.
Destry Rides Again. One Hour to Live.
Newsboys' Home. Career. Charlie McCarthy,
Detective. Tropic Fury. Rio. Hero for a Day.
First Love. The Secret of Dr Kildare. You're a
Sweetheart. No Greater Glory. 1940: Zanzi-
bar. Dr Kildare's Strange Case. It's a Date. Ski
Patrol. I'm Nobody's Sweetheart Now. The
Boys from Syracuse. Spring Parade. Dr
Kildare Goes Home. Seven Sinners. Trail of the
Vigilantes. 1941: Adventure in Washington
(GB: Female Correspondent). The Lady from
Cheyenne. Buck Privates (GB: Rookies).
Man-Made Monster (GB: The Electric Man).
Back Street. Tight Shoes. Blossoms in the Dust.
The Shepherd of the Hills. Dr Kildare's
Wedding Day (GB: Mary Names the Day).
Unfinished Business. Badlands of Dakota. Keep
'em Flying. Mob Town. Road Agent. 1942:
Ride 'em Cowboy. Frisco Lil. Saboteur. Jail
House Blues. The Strange Case of Dr RX. Kid
Glove Killer. The Spoilers. Lady in a Jam.
Grand Central Murder. Pardon My Sarong.
Pittsburgh. Don Winslow of the Navy (serial).
1943: Mr Big. Top Man. Fired Wife. He's
My Guy. Larceny with Music. Keep 'em
Slugging. Don Winslow of the Coast Guard
(serial). Son of Dracula. It Ain't Hay (GB:
Money for Jam). Good Morning, Judge. Hers to
Hold. Follow the Band. We've Never Been

Licked (GB: Texas to Tokyo). Sing a Jingle
(GB: Lucky Days). Hi, Buddy. 1944: The
Great Alaskan Mystery (serial). Chip Off the
Old Block. Weird Woman. South of Dixie.
Jungle Woman. Ladies Courageous. Cobra
Woman. The Singing Sheriff. Murder in the
Blue Room. Follow the Boys. 1945: Swing Out,
Sister. Frisco Sal. Escape in the Desert. I'll
Remember April. Secret Agent X-9 (serial).
The Strange Affair of Uncle Harry/Uncle
Harry. Week-End at the Waldorf. Lady on a
Train. Scarlet Street. Men in Her Diary.
1946: Inside Job. White Tie and Tails. It's a
Wonderful Life! Strange Conquest. The Run-
around. Little Miss Big (GB: The Baxter
Millions). Danger Woman. Blonde Alibi.
1947: The Egg and I. Time Out of Mind.
Slave Girl. Call Northside 777. 1948: Perilous
Waters. The Return of October (GB: Date with
Destiny). The Boy with Green Hair. 1949:
The Bribe.

**HINGLE, Pat**
(Martin Patterson Hingle) 1923-
Thickly-set, light-haired American actor
with natural scowl. A former construction
worker, he enrolled at the Actors' Studio
and broke into the theatre in 1950, TV and
films in 1954. At first cast as surly, edgy
types—apart from a role as one of the 'eight
new stars' in Fox's No Down Payment—he
has taken increasingly sympathetic, if still
grouchy parts in recent times, while still
never quite finding his niche in the cinema.

1954: On the Waterfront. The Long Gray
Line. 1957: End as a Man (GB: The Strange
One). No Down Payment. 1960: Wild River
(narrator only). 1961: Splendor in the Grass.
Black Monday (TV). 1963: The Ugly
American. All the Way Home. 1964: Carol for
Another Christmas (TV). Invitation to a
Gunfighter. 1966: Nevada Smith. 1967:
Hang 'em High. Sol Madrid (GB: The Heroin
Gang). 1968: Jigsaw (TV. Originally for
cinemas). 1969: The Ballad of Andy Crocker
(TV). Bloody Mama. Norwood. 1970: A
Clear and Present Danger (TV). WUSA.
1971: The City (TV). Sweet Sweet Rachel
(TV). If Tomorrow Comes (TV). 1972: The
Carey Treatment. 1973: Happy As the Grass
Was Green. Trouble Comes to Town (TV). One
Little Indian. The Super Cops. Running Wild.
1974: The Last Angry Man (TV). Deadly

Honeymoon. 1975: Deliver Us from Evil
(TV). 1976: The Secret Life of John Chapman
(TV). *Independence. 1977: Escape from
Bogen County (TV). The Gauntlet. Sunshine
Christmas (TV). Tarantulas: The Deadly
Cargo (TV). 1979: Elvis (TV. GB: cinemas).
Stone/Killing Stone (TV). Norma Rae. When
You Comin' Back, Red Ryder? 1980: The
Legend of John Hammer (TV). 1981: Wash-
ington Mistress (TV). Of Mice and Men (TV).
When Hell Was in Session (TV). Off the
Minnesota Strip (TV). 1982: The Act. 1983:
Running Brave (completed 1980). Sudden
Impact. The Fighter. 1984: Going Berserk.
1985: The Falcon and the Snowman. Brew-
ster's Millions. The Lady from Yesterday (TV).
The Rape of Richard Beck (TV).

**HIRD, Thora** 1913-
Slightly built, dynamic British actress with
goggle-eyed, purse-lipped looks, ear-
crunching voice and personality as bright as
her hair. Although from the coast of
Lancashire, she proved adept at a variety of
terrace-row accents, and played maids,
landladies, cleaners, shopwomen and forthright parents. Also popular in TV series;
mother of former child star Janette Scott.

1940: Spellbound (US: The Spell of Amy
Nugent). 1941: The Big Blockade. The Black
Sheep of Whitehall. 1942: Next of Kin. Went
the Day Well? (US: 48 Hours). The Foreman
Went to France (US: Somewhere in France).
1944: 2,000 Women. 1947: The Courtneys of
Curzon Street (US: The Courtney Affair). My
Brother Jonathan. 1948: Corridor of Mirrors.
The Weaker Sex. The Blind Goddess. Portrait
from Life (US: The Girl in the Painting). Once
a Jolly Swagman (US: Maniacs on Wheels). A
Boy, a Girl and a Bike. Fools Rush In. 1949:
Madness of the Heart. Maytime in Mayfair.
Boys in Brown. Conspirator. The Cure for Love.
1950: The Magnet. Once a Sinner. 1951:
The Galloping Major. 1952: The Frightened
Man. Emergency Call (US: Hundred Hour
Hunt). Time Gentlemen Please! The Lost
Hours (US: The Big Frame). 1953: The
Great Game. Background (US: Edge of
Divorce). Turn the Key Softly. The Long
Memory. Personal Affair. Street Corner (US:
Both Sides of the Law). A Day to Remember.
1954: Don't Blame the Stork! For Better, For

Worse (US: Cocktails in the Kitchen). The Crowded Day. One Good Turn. The Love Match. 1955: The Quatermass Experiment (US: The Creeping Unknown). Tiger by the Tail (US: Crossup). Lost (US: Tears for Simon). 1956: Women without Men (US: Blonde Bait). Sailor Beware! (US: Panic in the Parlor). Home and Away. 1957: The Good Companions. These Dangerous Years (US: Dangerous Youth). 1958: *A Clean Sweep. Further Up the Creek. 1950: The Entertainer. 1961: Over the Odds. 1962: A Kind of Loving. Term of Trial. 1963: Bitter Harvest. 1964: Rattle of a Simple Man. 1970: Some Will, Some Won't. 1971. The Nightcomers. 1985: Uncle of the Bride (TV).

**HOBART, Rose**
(R. Kefer) 1906-
Brown-haired American leading lady with angular features. Called to Holywood to repeat a stage success (in *Liliom*), she had a few more starring roles in the early 1930s—including Muriel in *Dr Jekyll and Mr Hyde*—then returned in the 1940s to play character roles throughout the decade, often as spiteful, vindictive women, in contrast to her earlier, gentle heroines.

1930: Liliom. A Lady Surrenders. 1931: East of Borneo. Chances. Compromised. Dr Jekyll and Mr Hyde. 1932: Scandal for Sale. 1933: Shadow Laughs. 1934: Convention Girl (GB: Atlantic City Romance). 1939: Tower of London. 1940: Wolf of New York. Susan and God (GB: The Gay Mrs Trexel). A Night at Earl Carroll's. 1941: Singapore Woman. Lady Be Good. Ziegfeld Girl. I'll Sell My Life. Hands on the Clock. Mr and Mrs North. Nothing But the Truth. 1942: Adventures of Smilin' Jack (serial). A Gentleman at Heart. Who Is Hope Schuyler? Dr Gillespie's New Assistant. Prison Girls. 1943: Swing Shift Maisie (GB: The Girl in Overalls). Salute to the Marines. The Mad Ghoul. Crime Doctor's Strangest Case (GB: The Strangest Case). 1944: Song of the Open Road. Soul of a Monster. 1945: Conflict. The Brighton Strangler. 1946: The Cat Creeps. Canyon Passage. Claudia and David. 1947: The Farmer's Daughter. The Trouble with Women. Cass Timberlane. 1948: Mickey. 1949: Bride of Vengeance.

**HOBBES, Halliwell**
(Herbert H. Hobbes) 1877-1962
Big, bald British actor whose strong features and powerful build were belied by a soft voice and gentle manner. He began his career in 1898 on the London stage, but made no films until the sound era in Hollywood (having come to America in 1923). Cast as a butler in one of his earliest films, *Grumpy*, he very soon became one of the film capital's most solid and reliable manservants, most prominently in *The Masquerader*. He also had a keen sense of comedy, used to best advantage as the eccentric De Pinna in *You Can't Take It With You*. Died from a heart attack.

1929: Jealousy. Lucky in Love. 1930: Grumpy. Charley's Aunt. Scotland Yard (GB: 'Detective Clive', Bart). 1931: The Sin of Madelon Claudet (GB: The Lullaby). Five and Ten (GB: Daughter of Luxury). Bachelor Father. Platinum Blonde. The Right of Way. The Woman Between (GB: Madame Julie). Dr Jekyll and Mr Hyde. 1932: The Devil's Lottery. Forbidden. Lovers Courageous. The Menace. Man About Town. Weekends Only. Six Hours to Live. Love Affair. Payment Deferred. 1933: Lady for a Day. Midnight Mary. Looking Forward. Should Ladies Behave? A Study in Scarlet. Captured! The Masquerader. 1934: I Am Suzanne! All Men Are Enemies. British Agent. Mandalay. The Key. Riptide. Double Door. Menace. Madame Du Barry. Bulldog Drummond Strikes Back. 1935: Folies Bergere (GB: The Man from the Folies Bergere). Cardinal Richelieu. Whipsaw. The Right to Live (GB: The Sacred Flame). Charlie Chan in Shanghai. The Story of Louis Pasteur. Millions in the Air. Jalna. Father Brown, Detective. 1936: Here Comes Trouble. Dracula's Daughter. Love Letters of a Star. The White Angel. Hearts Divided. Give Me Your Heart. Spendthrift. 1937: Varsity Show. Maid of Salem. The Prince and the Pauper. Fit for a King. 1938: The Jury's Secret. Service De Luxe. You Can't Take It With You. Kidnapped. Bulldog Drummond's Peril. Storm Over Bengal. 1939: Nurse Edith Cavell. Pacific Liner. Naughty But Nice. Tell No Tales. The Hardys Ride High. The Light That Failed. Remember? 1940: The Earl of Chicago. The Sea Hawk. Third Finger, Left

Hand. 1941: That Hamilton Woman (GB: Lady Hamilton). Here Comes Mr Jordan. 1942: To Be or Not To Be. The War Against Mrs Hadley. Journey for Margaret. Son of Fury. The Undying Monster (GB: The Hammond Mystery). 1943: Sherlock Holmes Faces Death. Forever and a Day. 1944: The Invisible Man's Revenge. Gaslight. Mr Skeffington. Casanova Brown. 1946: Canyon Passage. 1947: If Winter Comes. 1948: You Gotta Stay Happy. The Black Arrow (GB: The Black Arrow Strikes). 1949: That Forsyte Woman (GB: The Forsyte Saga). 1956: Miracle in the Rain.

**HOEY, Dennis**
(Samuel Hyams) 1893-1960
Dark, taciturn, bulky British actor with increasingly receding hair and often with pencil moustache. After a spotty eight-year slog in British sound films, he went to America in 1940 and created a plank-thick and totally memorable version of Conan Doyle's Inspector Lestrade in the Basil Rathbone Sherlock Holmes films. A Universal regular through the war years.

1927: Tiptoes. 1930: The Man from Chicago. 1931: Tell England (US: The Battle of Gallipoli). Never Trouble Trouble. Love Lies. 1932: Life Goes On. Baroud (US: Love in Morocco). The Maid of the Mountains. 1933: The Good Companions. Maid Happy. Oh What a Duchess! I Spy. The Wandering Jew. Facing the Music. 1934: Jew Süss (US: Power). Lily of Killarney (US: Bride of the Lake). Chu Chin Chow. Brewster's Millions. 1935: Maria Marten, or: the Murder in the Red Barn. Immortal Gentleman. Honeymoon for Three. The Mystery of the Mary Celeste (US: Phantom Ship). 1936: Did I Betray? Faust. Uncivilized. 1941: How Green Was My Valley. 1942: Son of Fury. Cairo. This Above All. Sherlock Holmes and the Secret Weapon. 1943: Forever and a Day. They Came to Blow Up America. Bomber's Moon. Sherlock Holmes and the Spider Woman (GB: Spider Woman). Frankenstein Meets the Wolf Man. Sherlock Holmes Faces Death. 1944: The Keys of the Kingdom. Uncertain Glory. Pearl of Death. National Velvet. 1945: House of Fear. A Thousand and One Nights. 1946: Terror by Night. Roll On, Texas Moon. Kitty. Anna and the King of Siam. She-Wolf of London (GB: The Curse of the Allenbys). The Strange Woman. Tarzan and the Leopard Woman. 1947: Second Chance. The Crimson Key. Where There's Life. Golden Earrings. Christmas Eve. If Winter Comes. The Foxes of Harrow. 1948: Ruthless. Wake of the Red Witch. Joan of Arc. 1949: Bad Men of Tombstone. The Secret Garden. The Kid from Texas (GB: Texas Kid—Outlaw). 1951: David and Bathsheba. 1952: Plymouth Adventure. Caribbean (GB: Caribbean Gold). 1953: Ali Baba Nights.

## HOLBROOK, Hal 1925-

Long-faced American actor with special, wistful qualities, and one of the most attractive American speaking voices since Henry Fonda. Played a few, often gloomy leading roles in films, but was always more interesting in support, especially as 'Deep Throat' in All the President's Men. A prolific stage performer, particularly in one-man shows as Mark Twain, and a frequent TV guest star.

1966: The Group. 1968: Wild in the Streets. 1969: The Whole World Is Watching (TV). 1970: A Clear and Present Danger (TV). The Great White Hope. The People Next Door. 1971: Travis Logan DA (TV). Suddenly Single (TV). Goodbye Raggedy Ann (TV). 1972: That Certain Summer (TV). They Only Kill Their Masters. 1973: Magnum Force. Jonathan Livingstone Seagull (voice only). 1974: The Girl from Petrovka. 1976: All the President's Men. Midway (GB: Battle of Midway). 1977: Julia. Capricorn One. 1978: Rituals. 1979: The Fog. Murder by Natural Causes (TV). The Kidnapping of the President. The Legend of the Golden Gun (TV). Natural Enemies. 1980: The Killing of Randy Webster (TV). 1982: Creepshow. Girls' Nite Out. 1983: The Star Chamber. 1984: The Three Wishes of Billy Grier (TV).

## HOLDEN, Gloria 1908-

Dark, straight-backed, austere and rather sinister-looking English actress who made an enormous impact in the title role of her first Hollywood film, Dracula's Daughter, then waited for offers of other leading roles

that never materialized. She returned sporadically in smaller parts from the late 1930s, often proving a formidable adversary for the leading lady.

1936: Dracula's Daughter. Wife Versus Secretary. 1937: The Life of Emile Zola. 1938: Test Pilot. Hawaii Calls. Girls' School. 1939: Dodge City. Miracles for Sale. 1940: A Child is Born. 1941: Passage from Hong Kong. This Thing Called Love. The Corsican Brothers. 1942: Miss Annie Rooney. A Gentleman After Dark. Apache Trail. 1943: Behind the Rising Sun. 1945: Having Wonderful Crime. The Adventures of Rusty. Strange Holiday (GB: The Day After Tomorrow). The Girl of the Limberlost. 1946: Hit The Hay. Sister Kenny. 1947: The Hucksters. Undercover Maisie (GB: Undercover Girl). Killer McCoy. 1948: Perilous Waters. 1949: A Kiss for Corliss. 1951: The Sickle and the Cross. 1953: Dream Wife. 1956: The Eddy Duchin Story. 1958: This Happy Feeling.

## HOLLOWAY, Sterling 1905-1992

Strangely enough, Hollywood's butter-haired, blue eyed, whisper-voiced, freckle-faced country bumpkin didn't actually make the hundreds of films one imagines. But there was a whole string of yokels and bellboys—often with some nice one-liners—in the 1930s, and later Holloway was heard as the voice of many Disney characters. His voice was once described as like a rusty nail being pulled slowly out of a piece of wood.

1927: Casey at the Bat. 1928: *The Girl from Nowhere. 1932: American Madness. Blonde Venus. Lawyer Man. Faithless. Rockabye. 1933: Elmer the Great. International House. Hell Below. Gold Diggers of 1933. Dancing Lady. Professional Sweetheart (GB: Imaginary Sweetheart). Blondie Johnson. Wild Boys of the Road (GB: Dangerous Days). Female. Hard to Handle. Picture Snatcher. Going Hollywood. *One Track Minds. Alice in Wonderland. Advice to the Lovelorn. Fast Workers. 1934: The Merry Widow. Gift of Gab. Down to Their Last Yacht (GB: Hawaiian Nights). A Wicked Woman. Adorable. Strictly Dynamite. Tomorrow's Children (GB: The Unborn). Back Page. Girl o' My Dreams. *Bring 'em Back A'Lie. Operator 13 (GB: Spy 13). The Cat and the Fiddle. *Heartburn. Murder in the Private Car (GB: Murder on the Runaway Train). The Whole Town's Talking (GB: Passport to Fame). 1935: $1,000 a Minute. Lottery Lover. Life Begins at 40. Rendezvous. Doubting Thomas. 1936: Avenging Waters. Career Woman. Palm Springs (GB: Palm Springs Affair). 1937: Behind the Mike. Join the Marines. Maid of Salem. The Woman I Love. When Love is Young. Varsity Show. 1938: Spring Madness. Dr Rhythm. Professor, Beware! Of Human Hearts. 1939: St Louis Blues. Nick Carter, Master Detective. 1940: The Blue Bird. Remember the Night. Street of Memories. Hit Parade of 1941. Little Men. 1941: Cheers for Miss Bishop. New Wine (GB: The Great Awakening). Top Sergeant Mulligan. Dumbo (voice only). Meet John Doe. Look Who's Laughing. 1942: Don't Get Personal. Iceland (GB: Katina). Bambi (voice only). The Lady Is Willing. Star Spangled Rhythm. 1943: Saludos Amigos (voice only). 1944: The Three Cabelleros (voice only). 1945: Wildfire (GB: Wildfire: the story of a Horse). A Walk in the Sun. 1946: Sioux City Sue. Make Mine Music (voice only). Death Valley. 1947: Twilight on the Rio Grande. Saddle Pals. Robin Hood of Texas. Trail to San Antone. 1949: The Beautiful Blonde from Bashful Bend. 1950: Her Wonderful Lie. Alice in Wonderland (voice only). 1956: Kentucky Rifle. 1960: The Adventures of Huckleberry Finn. 1961: Alakazam the Great (voice only). 1963: My Six Loves. It's a Mad, Mad, Mad, Mad World. 1965: *Winnie the Pooh and the Honey Tree (voice only). 1966: Batman. 1967: The Jungle Book (voice only). 1968: *Winnie the Pooh and the Blustery Day (voice only). Live a Little, Love a Little. 1970: The Aristocats (voice only). 1975: Won Ton Ton, the Dog Who Saved Hollywood. *Winnie the Pooh and Tigger Too (voice only). 1976: Super Seal. 1977: Thunder on the Highway. Thunder and Lightning. 1983: *Winnie the Pooh and a Day for Eeyore (voice only).

## HOLMES, Taylor 1872-1959

Stocky American actor whose fresh features (dark hair, blue eyes) enabled him to keep going in romantic roles of stage and screen until well into his forties. He played a few indeterminate character parts in the 1930s,

then came back to Hollywood in the post-war period for a busy few years of sharply etched studies, notably lawyers and businessmen, both corrupt and incorruptible, having developed baggy eyes that gave him a cunning look. Father of actors Phillip Holmes and Ralph Holmes, both of whom predeceased him, the former in an air crash, the latter a suicide.

*1917: Efficiency Edgar's Courtship. Two-Bit Seats. Fools for Luck. Small-Town Guy. Uneasy Money. 1918: Ruggles of Red Gap. 1919: Taxi. It's a Bear. A Regular Fellow. Upside Down. 1920: Nothing But the Truth. 1924: Twenty Dollars a Week. 1925: Borrowed Finery. The Crimson Runner. The Verdict. Her Market Value. 1927: One Hour of Love. 1929: \*He Loved the Ladies. \*He Did His Best. 1930: \*Dad Knows Best. 1931: An American Tragedy. 1933: Before Morning. Dinner at Eight. 1934: Nana. Great Expectations. 1936: The First Baby. The Crime of Dr Forbes. Make Way for a Lady. 1946: Boomerang! 1947: In Self Defense. Kiss of Death. Nightmare Alley. The Egg and I. Time Out of Mind. 1948: Hazard. Smart Woman. Let's Love Again. The Plunderers. An Act of Murder. That Wonderful Urge. Joan of Arc. 1949: Woman in Hiding. Joe Palooka in The Big Fight. Once More, My Darling. Mr Belvedere Goes to College. 1950: Caged. Copper Canyon. Bright Leaf. Double Deal. Father of the Bride. Quicksand. 1951: The First Legion. Two Tickets to Broadway. Drums in the Deep South. Hoodlum Empire. 1952: Hold That Line. Beware My Lovely. Woman of the North Country. Ride the Man Down. 1953: Gentlemen Prefer Blondes. 1954: The Outcast (GB: The Fortune Hunter). Tobor the Great. Untamed Heiress. 1955: Hell's Outpost. The Fighting Chance. 1956: The Maverick Queen. The Peacemaker. 1958: Wink of an Eye.*

## HOPE, Vida 1918-1962

Strong-looking British actress with rather wild dark hair, often cast in slatternly or vixenish roles, which she took by the scruff of the neck and shook into life. A multi-talented woman—she also directed plays and designed clothes—her careers came to an abrupt end when she was killed in a car crash two days before Christmas. She was married to British film director Derek Twist.

*1944: English Without Tears (US: Her Man Gilbey). Champagne Charlie. 1945: The Way to the Stars (US: Johnny in the Clouds). 1946: School for Secrets (US: Secret Flight). While the Sun Shines. Beware of Pity. 1947: Nicholas Nickleby. It Always Rains on Sunday. Hue and Cry. They Made Me a Fugitive (US: I Became a Criminal). 1948: The Mark of Cain. Vice Versa. Woman Hater. 1949: For Them That Trespass. The Interrupted Journey. Paper Orchid. 1950: Double Confession. The Woman in Question (US: Five Angles on Murder). 1951: Cheer the Brave. The Man in the White Suit. Green Grow the Rushes. 1952: Emergency Call (US: Hundred Hour Hunt). Angels One Five. Women of Twilight (US: Twilight Women). The Long Memory. 1953: The Broken Horseshoe. Marilyn (later Roadhouse Girl). 1954: The Case of Diamond Annie. Fast and Loose. Lease of Life. 1956: Charley Moon. 1958: Family Doctor (US: RX Murder). 1961: In the Doghouse.*

## HOPPER, William 1915-1970

Tall, dark, clean and sympathetic-looking American actor, the son of actress/columnist Hedda Hopper (Elda Furry, 1890-1966) and stage actor William DeWolf Hopper (1868-1935). Played many very small roles before war service from 1944 to 1946, always listed (when billed) as DeWolf Hopper. Then, after stage experience, he returned, prematurely greying, to the cinema as William Hopper, and enjoyed better roles before becoming a national figure as Paul Drake in the long-running *Perry Mason* TV series. Died, like his mother, from pneumonia.

*1916: Sunshine Dad. 1936: Sissy. The Big Broadcast of 1937. 1937: Over the Goal. Mr Dodd Takes the Air. Public Wedding. Back in Circulation. The Adventurous Blonde/Torchy Blane the Adventurous Blonde. Footloose Heiress. Love Is on the Air (GB: The Radio Murder Mystery). Women Are Like That. 1938: Mystery House. The Patient in Room 18. Daredevil Drivers. 1939: Angels Wash Their Faces. Espionage Agent. The Old Maid. Stagecoach. Nancy Drew and the Hidden Staircase. The Return of Dr X. The Cowboy Quarterback. Invisible Stripes. 1940: Knute Rockne—All American (GB: A Modern Hero). The Lady With Red Hair. The Fighting Sixty-Ninth. Castle on the Hudson (GB: Years without Days). Ladies Must Live. Till We Meet Again. The Man Who Talked Too Much. Tear Gas Squad. Gambling on the High Seas. Brother Orchid. Flight Angels. \*Sockaroo. Santa Fé Trail. Calling Philo Vance. Virginia City. 1941: Flight from Destiny. Footsteps in the Dark. Dive Bomber. The Maltese Falcon. High Sierra. Navy Blues. They Died with Their Boots On. Manpower. Affectionately Yours. The Bride Came C.O.D. International Squadron. Here Comes Happiness. The Body Disappears. Bullets for O'Hara. Right to the Heart (GB: Knockout). Pride of the Blue Grass. 1942: Lady Gangster. Desperate Journey. Gentleman Jim. Secret Enemies. Juke Girl. Larceny Inc. The Male Animal. Across the Pacific. Yankee Doodle Dandy. 1943: Murder on the Waterfront. The Mysterious Doctor. Air Force. 1944: The Last Ride. 1954: Track of the Cat. The High and the Mighty. This Is My Love. Sitting Bull. 1955: Conquest of Space. One Desire. One Life (TV. GB: cinemas). Robbers' Roost. Rebel without a Cause. 1956: The First Texan. Goodbye, My Lady. The Bad Seed. 1957: The Deadly Mantis. Slim Carter. 20,000,000 Miles to Earth. 1970: Myra Breckinridge.*

## HORDERN, Sir Michael 1911- 1995

Balding, long-faced British actor who gave up teaching for acting and, after World War II service, became one of Britain's most reliable film players. His resonant tones, mournful expression and watery eyes brought life to a series of harassed officials, both comic and serious, although he was also seen in a wide variety of other parts. His roles grew justifiably larger in the 1960s, while the 1970s saw perhaps his best part, the seedy reporter in *England Made Me*. Knighted in 1983.

*1939: Band Waggon. A Girl Must Live. 1940: The Girl in the News. 1946: The Years Between. A Girl in a Million. Great Expectations. School for Secrets (US: Secret Flight). 1947: Mine Own Executioner. 1948: Third Time Lucky. Night Beat. Portrait from Life (GB: The Girl in the Painting). The Small Voice (US: Hideout). Good Time Girl. 1949: Train of Events. Passport to Pimlico. 1950: The Astonished Heart. Trio. Highly Dangerous. 1951: Flesh and Blood. The Magic Box. Tom Brown's Schooldays. Scrooge (US: A Christmas Carol). 1952: The Card (US: The Promoter). The Story of Robin Hood and His Merrie Men. The Hour of 13. 1953: Street Corner (US: Both Sides of the Law). Grand National Night (US: Wicked Woman). The Heart of the Matter. Personal Affair. You Know What Sailors Are. 1954: The Beachcomber. Forbidden Cargo. 1955: The Night My Number Came Up. The Constant Husband. The Dark Avenger (US: The Warriors). Storm Over the Nile. 1956: Alexander the Great. The Man Who Never Was. Pacific Destiny. The Baby and the Battleship. The Spanish Gardener. 1957: No Time for Tears. I Accuse! Windom's Way. 1958: The Spaniard's Curse. I Was Monty's Double (US: Monty's Double). Girls at Sea. 1960: Sink the Bismarck! Moment of Danger (US: Malaga). The Man in the Moon. 1961: El Cid. Macbeth. First Left Past Aden (narrator only). 1963: Cleopatra. The VIPs. Dr Syn Alias the Scarecrow. 1964: The Yellow Rolls Royce. 1965: The Spy Who Came In from the Cold. Genghis Khan. Cast a Giant Shadow. 1966: Khartoum. The Taming of the Shrew. A Funny Thing Happened on the Way to the Forum. The Jokers. 1967: How I Won the War. I'll Never Forget What's 'is Name ... 1968: Where Eagles Dare. 1969: The Bed Sitting Room. 1970: Futtock's End. Anne of the Thousand Days. Some Will, Some Won't. 1971: Up Pompeii. Girl Stroke Boy. The Pied Piper. The Possession of Joel Delaney. Demons of the Mind. 1972: Alice's Adventures in Wonderland. England Made Me. 1973: Theatre of Blood. The Mackintosh Man. 1974: Juggernaut. Mister Quilp. 1975: Royal Flash. Barry Lyndon (narrator only). Lucky Lady. 1976: The Slipper and the Rose. Joseph Andrews. 1977: \*Mr Brit—the Man Who Made Miracles (narrator only). 1978: The Medusa Touch. Watership Down (voice only). Gauguin—the Savage. 1980: Wildcats of St Trinian's. Shogun (TV. GB: cinemas in abridged version). 1982: Gandhi. Oliver Twist. Ivanhoe (TV). The Missionary. 1983: Yellowbeard. 1984: Boxer (narrator only). 1985: Lady Jane. Paradise Postponed.*

**HORNE, David** 1898-1970
Rotund, balding British actor with genial, upper-crust voice, skilful at unctuous self-importance. A Grenadier Guards officer who turned to acting in his late twenties, he found himself cast largely as officers, noblemen and, latterly, senior clubmen, although the cinema gave him a wider variety of parts, sometimes as ruthless figures of authority.

*1933: Lord of the Manor. General John Regan. 1934: Badger's Green. The Case for the Crown. 1935: That's My Uncle. The Village Squire. Late Extra. Gentleman's Agreement. 1936: It's Love Again. Under Proof. Seven Sinners (US: Doomed Cargo). The Cardinal. A Touch of the Moon. Debt of Honour. Interrupted Honeymoon. The House of the Spaniard. The Mill on the Floss. 1937: 21 Days (US: 21 Days Together. Released 1940). Farewell Again (US: Troopship). The Green Cockatoo (US: Four Dark Hours). 1938: The Wrecker. 1939: Blind Folly. The Stars Look Down. Return to Yesterday. 1940: Crimes at the Dark House. The Door with Seven Locks (US: Chamber of Horrors). Night Train to Munich (US: Night Train). 1941: Breach of Promise (US: Adventure in Blackmail). Inspector Hornleigh Goes to It (US: Mail Train). They Flew Alone (US: Wings and the Woman). 1942: The First of the Few (US: Spitfire). The Day Will Dawn (US: The Avengers). 1943: San Demetrio London. The Yellow Canary. The Hundred Pound Window. 1944: Don't Take It to Heart. 1945: The Seventh Veil. The Rake's Progress (US: Notorious Gentleman). The Wicked Lady. They Were Sisters. The Man from Morocco. 1946: Spring Song (US: Spring Time). Men of Two Worlds (US: Kisenga—Man of Africa). Gaiety George (US: Showtime). Caravan. The Magic Bow. 1947: The Man Within (US: The Smugglers). Easy Money. 1948: It's Hard to be Good. The Winslow Boy. Saraband for Dead Lovers (US: Saraband). Once Upon a Dream. The History of Mr Polly. 1949: Madeleine. 1950: Cage of Gold. 1951: Appointment with Venus (US: Island Rescue). 1953: Spaceways. Thought to Kill. Street Corner (US: Both Sides of the Law). The Intruder. Martin Luther. 1954: A Tale of Three Women. Beau Brummell. 1955: Three*

*Cases of Murder. 1956: Lust for Life. The Last Man to Hang? 1957: The Prince and the Showgirl. The Safecracker. 1958: The Sheriff of Fractured Jaw. 1959: The Devil's Disciple. 1961: Goodbye Again/Aimez-vous Brahms? Dentist on the Job (US: Get on with It!). Clue of the New Pin. 1963: Nurse on Wheels. 1965: The Big Job. 1968: Diamonds for Breakfast. A Flea in Her Ear.*

**HORSLEY, John** 1920-
Sympathetic-looking, heftily-built British actor with large, kindly features and fair, thinning hair. A light leading man, especially on television, a medium in which he worked prodigiously through the 1950s, he later switched from playing police sergeants, inspectors and superintendents (progressively, he says) to doctors, lawyers and other senior professional men, looking dubiously at clients over the tops of their spectacles.

*1950: Blackmailed. Highly Dangerous. The Quiet Woman. 1951: Appointment with Venus (US: Island Rescue). Encore. 1952: The Frightened Man. The Long Memory. Deadly Nightshade. 1953: Recoil. Time Bomb (US: Terror on a Train). Single-Handed (US: Sailor of the King). Wheel of Fate. 1954: Meet Mr Malcolm. The Runaway Bus. Delayed Action. Destination Milan. Mad About Men. The Brain Machine. Father Brown (US: The Detective). Night People. Double Exposure. Little Red Monkey (US: The Case of the Red Monkey). 1955: Above Us the Waves. Impulse. Barbados Quest. A Time to Kill. They Can't Hang Me. 1956: The Weapon. Breakaway. Circus Friends. Bond of Fear. 1957: Stranger in Town. Hell Drivers. Man in the Shadow. Yangtse Incident (US: Battle Hell). 1958: Operation Amsterdam. Dunkirk. 1959: Carry On Nurse. Wrong Number. A Touch of Larceny. 1960: Let's Get Married. Sink the Bismarck! 1961: The Sinister Man. The Secret Ways. 1962: Jigsaw. Night of the Prowler. Serena. 1963: The Comedy Man. Return to Sender. Panic. 1965: \*Material Witness. 1966: Where the Bullets Fly. 1968: The Limbo Line.*

**HORTON, Edward Everett** 1886-1970
Small, dapper American comic actor who took his worried penguin act through scores

of films. His crooked, uncertain leer and crackling delivery created a series of characters from all walks of life so liable to flap and fluster that one could imagine them, like Woody Allen 'at home, having an anxiety attack on the floor'. Especially memorable, and valuable, in the Astaire-Rogers musicals. Just before he died (from cancer) he told an interviewer: 'I've had a grand time'. So did his audiences.

1920: Leave It to Me. 1922: The Ladder Jinx. Too Much Business. A Front Page Story. 1923: Ruggles of Red Gap. To the Ladies. Try and Get It. 1924: Flapper Wives. The Man Who Fights Alone. Helen's Babies. 1925: Marry Me. The Business of Love. Beggar on Horseback. The Nut-Cracker (GB: You Can't Fool Your Wife). 1926: The Whole Town's Talking. Poker Faces. La Bohème. 1927: Taxi! Taxi! *No Publicity. *Find the King. *Dad's Choice. 1928: *Miss Information. *Behind the Counter. *Horse Shy. *Vacation Waves. *Call Again. *Scrambled Weddings. The Terror. 1929: Sonny Boy. The Hottentot. The Sap. The Aviator. *Trusting Wives. *Ask Dad. *Prince Gabby. *The Eligible Mr Bangs. *Good Medicine. 1930: *The Right Bed. *The Great Junction Hotel. Take the Heir. Wide Open. Holiday. Once a Gentleman. 1931: Reaching for the Moon. Lonely Wives. The Age for Love. Kiss Me Again (GB: Toast of the Legion). Six Cylinder Love. Smart Woman. The Front Page. 1932: Trouble in Paradise. But the Flesh is Weak. Roar of the Dragon. 1933: Soldiers of the King (US: The Woman in Command). It's a Boy! A Bedtime Story. The Way to Love. Design for Living. Alice in Wonderland. 1934: The Gay Divorcee (GB: The Gay Divorce). Poor Rich. Ladies Should Listen. The Merry Widow. Kiss and Make Up. Easy to Love. Success at Any Price. Uncertain Lady. Sing and Like It. Smarty (GB: Hit Me Again). 1935: The Night is Young. In Caliente. Biography of a Bachelor Girl. Top Hat. $10 Raise (GB: Mr Faintheart). The Devil is a Woman. Going Highbrow. Little Big Shot. The Private Secretary. His Night Out. All the King's Horses. Your Uncle Dudley. 1936: The Man in the Mirror. The Singing Kid. Her Master's Voice. Hearts Divided. Nobody's Fool. 1937: Let's Make a Million. The King and the Chorus Girl (GB:

Romance Is Sacred). Lost Horizon. Shall We Dance? The Great Garrick. Hitting a New High. Oh Doctor! Wild Money. Angel. The Perfect Specimen. Danger - Love at Work. 1938: Holiday (later Unconventional Linda. GB: Free to Live). College Swing (GB: Swing, Teacher, Swing). Bluebeard's Eighth Wife. Little Tough Guys in Society. 1939: The Gang's All Here (US: The Amazing Mr Forrest). That's Right - You're Wrong. Paris Honeymoon. 1941: Ziegfeld Girl. You're the One. Bachelor Daddy/Sandy Steps Out. Here Comes Mr Jordan. Sunny. Week-End for Three. The Body Disappeared. 1942: I Married an Angel. The Magnificent Dope. Springtime in the Rockies. 1943: Forever and a Day. Thank Your Lucky Stars. The Gang's All Here (GB: The Girls He Left Behind). Arsenic and Old Lace. 1944: Her Primitive Man. Summer Storm. San Diego, I Love You. The Town Went Wild. Brazil. 1945: Steppin' in Society. Lady on a Train. 1946: Cinderella Jones. Faithful in My Fashion. Earl Carroll Sketchbook (GB: Hats Off to Rhythm). 1947: The Ghost Goes Wild. Down to Earth. Her Husband's Affairs. 1948: All My Sons. 1957: The Story of Mankind. Three Men on a Horse (TV). 1961: Pocketful of Miracles. 1963: It's a Mad, Mad, Mad, Mad World. 1964: Sex and the Single Girl. 1967: The Perils of Pauline. 1969: 2000 Years Later. 1970: Cold Turkey.

## HOUSMAN, Arthur 1888-1942

One of Hollywood's most engaging 'drunks'; in real life, like his only challenger Jack Norton (qv), short, florid, darkly moustachioed Housman never took a drop. He was encountered from time to time by Laurel and Hardy, most notably in Scram! and Our Relations, and could always be relied upon to ruin the best-laid plans at the drop of a cork. In the winter of 1941/2, however, he contracted the pneumonia that killed him at only 53.

1921: Clay Dollars. The Way of a Maid. Room and Board. Worlds Apart. The Fighter. Is Life Worth Living? 1922: *The Snitching Hour. Man Wanted. Love's Masquerade. Destiny's Isle. Shadows of the Sea. The Prophet's Paradise. Why Announce Your Marriage? 1923: Under the Red Robe. Wife

in Name Only. Male Wanted. 1924: Nellie (the Beautiful Cloak Model). Manhandled. 1925: Thunder Mountain. A Man Must Live. The Necessary Evil. The Coast of Folly. The Desert's Price. Night Life of New York. 1926: Braveheart. Whispering Wires. The Bat. The Midnight Kiss. Early to Wed. 1927: Publicity Madness. Bert̲ ̲ ̲e Sewing Machine Girl. Rough H̲ ̲ ̲ ̲unrise - A Song of Two H̲ ̲ ̲ ̲unrise). The Spotlight. Love ̲ ̲ ̲ ̲ Wild. 1928: The Singing Fool. ̲artners in Crime. Fools for Luck. Sins of the Fathers. 1929: Side Street (GB: Three Brothers). Queen of the Night Clubs. Broadway. Times Square (GB: The Street of Jazz). Fast Company. The Song of Love. 1930: Officer O'Brien. The Squealer. Feet First. Girl of the Golden West. 1931: Five and Ten (GB: Daughter of Luxury). Anybody's Blonde (GB: When Blonde Meets Blonde). Bachelor Girl. Night Life in Reno. Caught Plastered. Bachelor Apartment. 1932: Hat Check Girl (GB: Embassy Girl). No More Orchids. Movie Crazy. *Parlor, Bedroom and Wrath. Afraid to Talk. *Scram! *Any Old Port. 1933: She Done Him Wrong. The Intruder. Her Bodyguard. Sing, Sinner, Sing, The Way to Love. *Good Housewrecking. 1934: Mrs Wiggs of the Cabbage Patch. Here is My Heart. Kansas City Princess. The Merry Widow. *The Chases of Pimple Street. *Something Simple. *The Live Ghost. *Babes in the Goods. *Done in Oil. *Punch Drunks. 1935: Hold 'Em Yale (GB: Uniform Lovers). Two for Tonight. Riffraff. Paris in Spring (GB: Paris Love Song). Here Comes Cookie (GB: The Plot Thickens). *The Fixer-Uppers. Diamond Jim. The Fire Trap. *Treasure Blues. *Sing, Sister, Sing. 1936: Our Relations. Wives Never Know. Show Boat. With Love and Kisses. Racing Blood. *Am I Having Fun! 1937: Step Lively, Jeeves! 1938: Hard to Get. 1939: Navy Secrets. Broadway Serenade. 1940: Go West (GB: The Marx Brothers Go West). 1941: Public Enemies.

## HOUSTON, Glyn 1926-

Taciturn, dark-haired, self-effacing Welsh actor whose cosmopolitan image gave him a much wider variety of parts in British films than his more famous older brother Donald. Glyn progressed gradually to semi-leading roles by the early 1960s, but was thereafter more seen in theatre and TV. With his solid, low-key approach, it seemed he might make an ideal police inspector in a TV series - instead he popped up in another series playing detective Lord Peter Wimsey's manservant.

*1949: The Blue Lamp. 1950: The Clouded Yellow. Trio. 1951: Home to Danger. I Believe in You. 1952: Girdle of Gold. Wide Boy. Gift Horse (US: Glory at Sea). The Great Game. 1953: The Cruel Sea. Hell below Zero. Turn the Key Softly. Stryker of the Yard. 1954: The Rainbow Jacket. River Beat. The Sea Shall Not Have Them. The Sleeping Tiger. The Happiness of Three Women. Betrayed. 1955: Passage Home. Lost (US: Tears for Simon). 1956: Private's Progress. The Long Arm (US: The Third Key). 1957: High Flight. The One That Got Away. 1958: A Cry from the Streets. 1959: Tiger Bay. Follow a Star. Jet Storm. 1960: The Bulldog Breed. Sink the Bismarck! There Was a Crooked Man. 1961: Payroll. The Green Helmet. The Wind of Change. Flame in the Streets. 1962: Phantom of the Opera. Emergency. Solo for Sparrow. Mix Me a Person. 1963: Panic. A Stitch in Time. 1964: One Way Pendulum. 1965: The Brigand of Kandahar. The Secret of Blood Island. 1966: Invasion. 1968: Headline Hunters. 1977: Are You Being Served? 1980: The Sea Wolves.*

## HOWARD, Arthur (A. Stainer) 1910-

Lugubrious, donkey-faced, bald British actor with a fine line in dithering, hand-wringing panic which completely broke up his normal dignity. The 20-years-younger brother of acting superstar Leslie Howard, Arthur was always the journeyman actor of the Howard clan but was only seized by the cinema in post-war years. At the same time, he assumed his best-remembered role, at first on radio, then on TV and in a film - that of Pettigrew, the deputy headmaster to 'Professor' Jimmy Edwards's rascally and incompetent headmaster in the *Whack-O!* series. Now in small cameos, but still busy.

*1933: The Lady is Willing. 1947: Frieda. The Mark of Cain. 1948: London Belongs to Me (US: Dulcimer Street). The Passionate Friends (US: One Woman's Story). Passport to Pimlico. 1949: Private Angelo. 1950: The Happiest Days of Your Life. State Secret (US: The Great Manhunt). Stage Fright. Last Holiday. Cage of Gold. The Undefeated. 1951: The Man in the White Suit. Lady Godiva Rides Again. Laughter in Paradise. 1952: Never Look Back. Cosh Boy (US: The Slasher). 1953: Glad Tidings. The Intruder. Grand National Night (US: Wicked Wife). Will Any Gentleman?... Albert RN. 1954: The Belles of St Trinian's. Knave of Hearts (US: Lovers, Happy Lovers). Out of the Clouds. 1955: The Constant Husband. The Glass Cage (US: The Glass Tomb). One Way Out. Touch and Go (US: The Light Touch). 1956: One Wish Too Many. Guilty? 1957: I Accuse! 1958: Nowhere to Go. I Only Arsked! Law and Disorder. Rockets Galore*

(US: Mad Little Island). *1959: Libel. Friends and Neighbours. 1960: Bottoms Up! 1961: Watch It Sailor! 1962: Kill or Cure. 1963: Ladies Who Do. 1964: Les félins (GB: The Love Cage. US: Joy House). 1965: Lady L. 1966: The Ghost Goes Gear. 1968: The Shoes of the Fisherman. The Best House in London. 1969: My Lover, My Son. 1970: Jane Eyre (TV. GB: cinemas). Hoverbug. 1971: Zeppelin. The Magnificent Seven Deadly Sins. Blinker's Spy Spotter. 1972: Steptoe and Son. 1975: One of Our Dinosaurs is Missing. The Bawdy Adventures of Tom Jones. 1976: Full Circle. 1977: Hardcore (US: Fiona). 1979: The Prisoner of Zenda. Moonraker. 1982: Trail of the Pink Panther. The Missionary. 1983: Curse of the Pink Panther. 1984: Another Country.*

## HOWLETT, Noel 1901-1984

Alphabetical order places close together Britain's two most prominent portrayers of querulous, pupil-beset schoolteachers. The studious-looking Howlett was in real life a schoolmaster who wavered between teaching and acting in his twenties before deciding on the latter career. Although mostly a man of the theatre (he was major-in-charge of ENSA shows in World War II), he made quite a number of minor film appearances as teachers, doctors, solicitors and company executives before winning national recognition as testy headmaster Cromwell in the popular TV series *Please, Sir!*

*1936: Men Are Not Gods. Such Men Are Dangerous. 1937: A Yank at Oxford. 1940: George and Margaret. 1947: When the Bough Breaks. Fortune Lane. This Was a Woman. The White Unicorn (US: Bad Sister). Jassy. 1948: The Calendar. Scott of the Antarctic. The Blind Goddess. The Winslow Boy. Saraband for Dead Lovers (US: Saraband). Once Upon a Dream. 1950: Your Witness (US: Eye Witness). The Reluctant Widow. 1951: Laughter in Paradise. Cloudburst. Scrooge (US: A Christmas Carol). 1954: Father Brown (US: The Detective). 1955: Handcuffs London. 1956: Lust for Life. 1958: The Scapegoat. 1959: The Battle of the Sexes. Serious Charge (US: A Touch of Hell). You'll Never See Me Again. 1960: Let's Get Married. 1961: Victim. Mary Had a Little ... 1962: Kiss of the Vampire. Tomorrow at Ten. Lawrence of Arabia. 1964: Woman of Straw. 1965: The Amorous Adventures of Moll Flanders. 1967: Quatermass and the Pit (US: Five Million Miles to Earth). 1968: The Bush Baby. 1969: Some Will, Some Won't. 1971: Please, Sir! 1978: Mr Selkie.*

## HOYT, John (J. Hoysradt) 1905- [1991]

Tall, gaunt-faced, light-haired American actor, a former historian and drama teacher who only became a full-time actor after World War II. Played scientists, period aristocrats, Nazi officers, prison wardens and upper-class crooks, as well as a few mad professors in horror films. Has also done impressions in nightclubs.

*1946: OSS. 1947: My Favorite Brunette. Brute Force. The Unfaithful. 1948: Winter Meeting. To the Ends of the Earth. Sealed Verdict. The Decision of Christopher Blake. 1949: Trapped. The Bribe. The Great Dan Patch. The Lady Gambles. Everybody Does It. 1950: The Lawless. The Company She Keeps. The Dividing Line. Outside the Wall. 1951: Quebec. Inside Straight. New Mexico. When Worlds Collide. The Desert Fox (GB: Rommel - Desert Fox). 1952: Loan Shark. The Black Castle. Androcles and the Lion. 1953: Julius Caesar. Sins of Jezebel. Casanova's Big Night. 1954: The Student Prince. Moonfleet. Desiree. 1955: The Big Combo. Blackboard Jungle. The Purple Mask. The Girl in the Red Velvet Swing. Trial. 1956: The Conqueror. Forever, Darling. The Come-On. Mohawk. Death of a Scoundrel. Wetbacks. 1957: Sierra Stranger. God is My Partner. Baby-Face Nelson. Fighting Trouble. The Beast of Budapest. 1958: Attack of the Puppet People (GB: Six Inches Tall). 1959: Never So Few. Riot in Juvenile Prison. Curse of the Undead. 1960: Spartacus. 1962: Merrill's Marauders. 1963: Cleopatra. X - The Man with the X-Ray Eyes (GB: The Man With the X-Ray Eyes). 1964: The Glass Cage. The Time Travelers. Two on a Guillotine. Young Dillinger. 1965: Duel at Diablo. 1966: Fame Is the Name of the Game (TV). 1967: Winchester '73 (TV). 1970: The Intruders (TV). 1972: Welcome Home, Johnny Bristol (TV). 1974: Flesh Gordon. 1975: The Turning Point of Jim Malloy (TV). 1978: The Winds of Kitty Hawk (TV).*

## HUBER, Harold 1904-1959

With his dark, slick hair, swarthily ruddy complexion, trim moustache and white-toothed smile, this American actor was something of a cut-price Cesar Romero. Typed in villainous roles, as crooked nightclub owners and the like, in the early part of his film career, he was later much on the side of the law, especially in Mr Moto and Charlie Chan thrillers, where he played sharpish inspectors. The war changed the direction of his career and he virtually quit films in post-war years after return from service abroad. In 1950, he became a TV regular in the series *I Cover Times Square* and continued working steadily in the

ABOVE A clutch of schoolmasters . . . Arthur **Howard** (right)
prepares to go into his 'Oh, headmaster! . . .' routine in *Bottoms
Up!* (1960) with Jimmy Edwards and Vanda Hudson . . .

. . . while Noel **Howlett** is for once in calmer mood away from
his headmaster Cromwell of TV's *Please, Sir!* He's pictured
(RIGHT) in a 1970 television play called *The Trap*

## HUGHES, Roddy 1891-

Roly-poly, balding Welsh actor who looked like the man in the moon. A fine singer, he began in musical comedy when first on the London stage during World War I, but soon came into demand for straight character roles. Theatrical commitments continued to limit his film appearances, but he was never better cast than as Mr Fezziwig in the 1951 *Scrooge*; with his pudgy but mobile features, few players could better express extremes of joy and sorrow without resource to words.

medium up to his early death. Started as an attorney.

*1932: The Match King. Central Park. Lawyer Man. 1933: Frisco Jenny. Parachute Jumper. 20,000 Years in Sing Sing. Girl Missing. Central Airport. Midnight Mary. Ladies They Talk About. The Life of Jimmy Dolan (GB: The Kid's Last Fight). The Silk Express. The Mayor of Hell. Mary Stevens MD. The Bowery. Police Car 17. 1934: Hi, Nellie! No More Women. The Crosby Case (GB: The Crosby Murder Case). The Line-Up. A Very Honorable Guy. Fury of the Jungle. He Was Her Man. The Thin Man. Hide-Out. The Defense Rests. Cheating Cheaters. Port of Lost Dreams. The Merry Frinks (GB: The Happy Family). 1935: Mad Love (GB: The Hands of Orlac). One New York Night (GB: The Trunk Mystery). Naughty Marietta. Pursuit. G Men. 1936: The Devil Is a Sissy (GB: The Devil Takes the Count). Kelly the Second. Muss 'Em Up (GB: House of Fate). We're Only Human. San Francisco. Women Are Trouble. The Gay Desperado. Klondike Annie. 1937: The Good Earth. Midnight Taxi. Trouble in Morocco. Angel's Holiday. You Can't Beat Love. Charlie Chan at Monte Carlo. Outlaws of the Orient. Charlie Chan on Broadway. Love Under Fire. 1938: International Settlement. Mr Moto's Gamble. A Slight Case of Murder. The Adventures of Marco Polo. Gangs of New York. Passport Husband. Going Places. A Trip to Paris. Mysterious Mr Moto. Little Tough Guys in Society. While New York Sleeps. 1939: Mr Moto in Danger Island (GB: Mr Moto on Danger Island). You Can't Get Away with Murder. King of the Turf. Chasing Danger. 60,000 Enemies. The Lady and the Mob. Main Street Lawyer (GB: Small Town Lawyer). Beau Geste. Charlie Chan in City in Darkness. Charlie McCarthy, Detective. 1940: The Ghost Comes Home. Dance, Girl, Dance. Kit Carson. 1941: A Man Betrayed (GB: Citadel of Crime). Country Fair. Charlie Chan in Rio. Down Mexico Way. 1942: Pardon My Stripes. A Gentleman After Dark. Sleepytime Gal. Little Tokyo USA. Manila Calling. The Lady from Chungking. Ice Capades Revue (GB: Rhythm Hits the Ice). 1943: The Crime Doctor. 1950: My Friend Irma Goes West. Let's Dance.*

*1934: How's Chances? A Glimpse of Paradise. Kentucky Minstrels. Lest We Forget. The Old Curiosity Shop. 1935: Breakers Ahead. The Small Man. The Mad Hatters. A Real Bloke. Cock o' the North. The River House Mystery. 1936: Cheer Up. Men of Yesterday. Twelve Good Men. 1937: The House of Silence. Captain's Orders. La mort du Sphinx. Little Miss Somebody. 1938: \*Confidence Tricksters. \*In Your Garden. 1939: The Stars Look Down. Poison Pen. 1940: Saloon Bar. The Girl in the News. Old Mother Riley in Business. 1941: Pimpernel Smith (US: Mister V). The Ghost of St Michael's. Atlantic Ferry (US: Sons of the Sea). Hatter's Castle. Quiet Wedding. Hard Steel. 1944: Meet Sexton Blake. 1945: Here Comes the Sun. 1946: George in Civvy Street. 1947: Nicholas Nickleby. Green Fingers. The Silver Darlings. So Well Remembered. 1948: The Dark Road. The Small Black Room. Mr Perrin and Mr Traill. Blanche Fury. Obsession (US: The Hidden Room). 1949: The Last Days of Dolwyn (US: Woman of Dolwyn). Poet's Pub. 1950: The Reluctant Widow. 1951: The Man in The White Suit. Old Mother Riley's Jungle Treasure. Scrooge (US: A Christmas Carol). Salute the Toff. 1952: The Great Game. Hammer the Toff. Escape Route (US: I'll Get You). 1953: Alf's Baby. Meet Mr Lucifer. Trouble in Store. 1954: The Lark Still Sings. Mystery on Bird Island. 1955: One Jump Ahead. See How They Run. 1956: Not So Dusty. 1957: Sea Wife. 1958: The Spaniard's Curse. 1960: The House on Marsh Road.*

## HULL, Henry 1890-1977

Dark, gauntly handsome American actor, a thin-faced Henry Fonda in his youth who

strayed all too rarely from the stage in silent days and was well into his forties before becoming a regular cinema performer. After a couple of leads, including a haunting portrayal of *The Werewolf of London*, he settled into character roles as crusty types with barking voices, often in period drama, and just as likely to pop up on one side of the law as the other.

*1916: The Man Who Came Back. 1917: The Volunteer. 1919: Little Women. 1922: One Exciting Night. 1923: The Last Moment. A Bride for a Knight. 1924: The Hoosier School Master (GB: The School Master). For Women's Favor. Roulette. 1925: The Wrongdoers. Wasted Lives. 1928: Matinee Idol. 1931: The Man Who Came Back. 1933: The Story of Temple Drake. 1934: Great Expectations. Midnight. 1935: The Werewolf of London. Transient Lady (GB: False Witness). 1938: Yellow Jack. Boys' Town. Three Comrades. Paradise for Three (GB: Romance for Three). The Great Waltz. 1939: Judge Hardy and Son. Babes in Arms. Spirit of Culver (GB: Man's Heritage). Bad Little Angel. Stanley and Livingstone. The Return of the Cisco Kid. Miracles for Sale. Nick Carter, Master Detective. Jesse James. 1940: The Return of Frank James. The Ape. My Son, My Son. 1941: High Sierra. 1942: Queen of Broadway. 1943: What a Man. The Woman of the Town. The West Side Kid. 1944: Lifeboat. Goodnight, Sweetheart. Voodoo Man. 1945: Objective, Burma! 1947: High Barbaree. Deep Valley. Mourning Becomes Electra. 1948: Scudda Hoo! Scudda Hay! (GB: Summer Lightning). The Walls of Jericho. Belle Starr's Daughter. Portrait of Jennie (GB: Jennie). Fighter Squadron. 1949: Song of Surrender. El Paso. The Fountainhead. Rimfire. The Great Dan Patch. Colorado Territory. The Great Gatsby. 1950: The Return of Jesse James. The Hollywood Story. 1951: The Treasure of Lost Canyon. 1952: The Mad Monster. 1953: The Last Posse. Inferno. Thunder Over the Plains. 1955: The Man With the Gun (GB: The Trouble Shooter). 1956: Kentucky Rifle. 1957: The Buckskin Lady. 1958: The Sheriff of Fractured Jaw. The Buccaneer. Face of a Hero (TV). The Proud Rebel. 1959: The Oregon Trail. 1961: Master of the World. 1965: The Fool Killer.*

*1966: The Chase. A Covenant With Death.*

## HUNNICUTT, Arthur 1911-1979

It seems appropriate that Hunnicutt should have been born in a town called Gravelly. For the gruff, 'countrified' voice and bearded features of this distinctive American player, a sort of backwoods Walter Brennan who chewed dialogue rather than spoke it, were seen in many a western, through the forties, fifties and sixties. In the middle of this period he was a top character star billed above the title. Nominated for an Oscar in *The Big Sky*. Died from cancer.

*1940: Northwest Passage. 1942: Wildcat. Silver Queen. Hay Foot. Fall In. 1943: Fighting Buckaroo. Riding Thro' Nevada. Pardon My Gun. Frontier Fury. Johnny Come Lately (GB: Johnny Vagabond). Chance of a Lifetime. Law of the Northwest. Robin Hood of the Range. Hail to the Rangers (GB: Illegal Rights). 1944: Abroad with Two Yanks. Riding West. 1949: Lust for Gold. The Great Dan Patch. Pinky. Border Incident. 1950: Stars in My Crown. A Ticket to Tomahawk. The Furies. Two Flags West. Broken Arrow. 1951: Passage West (GB: High Venture). Sugarfoot. The Red Badge of Courage. Distant Drums. 1952: The Big Sky. The Lusty Men. 1953: Split Second. Devil's Canyon. She Couldn't Say No (GB: Beautiful But Dangerous). The French Line. 1955: The Last Command. 1956: The Kettles in the Ozarks. 1957: The Tall T. 1959: Born Reckless. 1963: The Cardinal. A Tiger Walks. 1965: Cat Ballou. The Adventures of Bullwhip Griffin. 1966: Apache Uprising. 1967: El Dorado. 1971: The Trackers (TV). Million Dollar Duck. 1972: The Revengers. Climb an Angry Mountain (TV). The Bounty Man (TV). 1973: Shoot-Out. Mrs Sundance (TV). 1974: The Spikes Gang. Harry and Tonto. The Daughters of Joshua Cabe Return (TV). 1975: Moonrunners. Winterhawk.*

## HUNT, Martita 1900-1969

Formidable Argentine-born actress with rich voice who made her name on the British stage and screen and used her horsey features and dominant plainness to create a colourful gallery of villainesses and (later) eccentric dowagers. Perhaps most memorable as Miss Havisham in the 1946 *Great Expectations.*

*1920: A Rank Outsider. 1931: Service for Ladies (US: Reserved for Ladies). 1932: Love on Wheels. 1933: I Was a Spy. Friday the Thirteenth. 1934: Too Many Millions. 1935: The Case of Gabriel Perry. First a Girl. Mr What's-His-Name. 1936: When Knights Were Bold. Pot Luck. Tudor Rose (US: Nine Days a Queen). Sabotage (US: The Woman Alone). Good Morning, Boys. The Interrupted Honeymoon. The Mill on the Floss. 1937: Farewell Again (US: Troopship). Second Best Bed. 1938: Prison Without Bars. Strange Boarders. Everything Happens to Me. 1939: Trouble Brewing. A Girl Must Live. The Nursemaid Who Disappeared. The Good Old Days. At the Villa Rose (US: House of Mystery). Young Man's Fancy. The Middle Watch. Old Mother Riley Joins Up. 1940: \*Miss Grant Goes to the Door. Tilly of Bloomsbury. East of Piccadilly (US: The Strangler). 1941: Freedom Radio (US: A Voice in the Night). Quiet Wedding. The Seventh Survivor. They Flew Alone (US: Wings and the Woman). 1942: Lady from Lisbon. Talk About Jacqueline. 1943: The Man in Grey. 1944: Welcome Mr Washington. 1945: The Wicked Lady. 1946: Great Expectations. 1947: The Little Ballerina. The Ghosts of Berkeley Square. 1948: So Evil My Love. Anna Karenina. My Sister and I. 1949:*

*The Fan (GB: Lady Windermere's Fan). 1952: The Story of Robin Hood and His Merrie Men. Treasure Hunt. Meet Me Tonight. It Started in Paradise. Folly to be Wise. 1953: Melba. 1955: King's Rhapsody. 1956: The March Hare. Three Men in a Boat. Anastasia. 1957: Les Espions. The Admirable Crichton (US: Paradise Lagoon). Dangerous Exile. The Prince and the Showgirl. 1958: Me and the Colonel. La prima notte/Les noces Venetiennes. Bonjour Tristesse. 1960: Bottoms Up! The Brides of Dracula. Song Without End. 1961: Mr Topaze (US: I Like Money). 1962: The Wonderful World of the Brothers Grimm. 1963: Becket. 1964: The Unsinkable Molly Brown. 1965: Bunny Lake is Missing. 1968: The Best House in London.*

## HUNTLEY, Raymond 1904- 1990

Slight British character actor with black hair and moustache and indifferent air. Usually cast as vicious, underhand villains

and, with the war years, sneaky, evil Nazis. As he grew older, the features turned from sinister to cynical, and he enjoyed a good run as pompous civil servants and other supercilious types in British comedies of the fifties and sixties.

*1934: What Happens then? 1935: Can You Hear Me, Mother? 1936: Rembrandt. Whom the Gods Love (US: Mozart). 1937: Dinner at the Ritz. Knight Without Armour. 1940: Bulldog Sees It Through. Night Train to Munich (US: Night Train). 1941: The Ghost Train. Inspector Hornleigh Goes to It (US: Mail Train). Once a Crook. Pimpernel Smith (US: Mister V). Freedom Radio (US: A Voice in the Night). The Ghost of St Michael's. 1943: When We Are Married. 1944: The Way Ahead. They Came to a City. 1946: I See A Dark Stranger (US: The Adventuress). School for Secrets. 1947: Broken Journey. 1948: \*They Gave Him the Works. Mr Perrin and Mr Traill. So Evil My Love. It's Hard to Be Good. 1949: Passport to Pimlico. Trio. 1951: The Long Dark Hall. The House in the Square (US: I'll Never Forget You). Mr Denning Drives North. 1952: The Last Page (US: Manbait). 1953: Laxdale Hall (US: Scotch on the Rocks). Meet Mr Lucifer. Glad Tidings. 1954: The Teckman Mystery. Aunt Clara. Hobson's Choice. Orders Are Orders. 1955: The Dam Busters. The Constant Husband. Doctor at Sea. The Prisoner. Geordie (US: Wee Geordie). 1956: The Green Man. The Last Man to Hang? Town on Trial. 1957: Brothers in Law. 1958: Next to No Time. Room at the Top. 1959: Carlton-Browne of the FO (US: Man in a Cocked Hat). Innocent Meeting. The Mummy. I'm All Right Jack. Our Man in Havana. 1960: Bottoms Up! Make Mine Mink. Follow That Horse! Sands of the Desert. A French Mistress. Suspect. The Pure Hell of St Trinian's. 1961: Only Two Can Play. 1962: Waltz of the Toreadors. On the Beat. Crooks Anonymous. Nurse on Wheels. 1963: The Yellow Teddybears. Father Came Too. 1964: The Black Torment. 1965: Rotten to the Core. 1966: The Great St Trinian's Train Robbery. 1968: Hostile Witness. Hot Millions. 1959: The Adding Machine. Destiny of a Spy (TV). 1971: Young Winston. 1972: That's Your Funeral. 1974: Symptoms.*

**HURST, Paul** 1888-1953

Big, tough-looking American actor with slow smile and Irish features, including red hair and twinkling eyes. Played breezy but none-too-bright characters on screen, but was nothing like that in real life, starting as an innovative star of early silent serials who occasionally co-directed material he had written himself. His cowboys then were rather in the Guinn 'Big Boy' Williams (*qv*) tradition, but, with the coming of sound, Hurst settled in to countless cameos, many of them as thick-skulled cops ready to step in and arrest the framed hero before their superiors could advise caution. Made nearly 250 films, one of the longest lists in this book, before committing suicide in 1953.

*1912: Red Wing and the Paleface. The Stolen Invention. Driver of the Deadwood Coach (GB: Deadwood Stagecoach Driver). The Mayor's Crusade. When Youth Meets Youth. 1913: The Big Horn Massacre/The Little Big Horn Massacre. The Last Blockhouse. Redemption. On the Brink of Ruin. The Struggle. Daughter of the Underworld. 1914: In the Days of the Thundering Herd. The Smugglers of Lone Isle. Why the Sheriff is a Bachelor. The Rajah's Vow. The Barrister of Ignorance. 1915: Whispering Smith. Social Pirates. The Pitfall. The Parasite. The Corsican Sisters. 1916: The Manager of the B & A. \*Lass of the Lumberland (serial). Medicine Bend. Judith of the Cumberlands. The Missing Millionaire. The Moth and the Star. The Taking of Stingaree. A Voice in the Wilderness. To the Vile Dust. The Millionaire Plunger. The Black Hole of Glenranald. 1917: A Race for a Fortune (serial). The Further Adventures of Stingaree. The Railroad Riders (serial). The Jackaroo. The Tracking of Stingaree. 1918: Smashing Through. †The Tiger's Trail (serial). Play Straight or Fight. 1919: †Lightning Bryce (serial). 1920: Shadows of the West. 1921: The Black Sheep. The Crow's Nest. 1922: The Heart of a Texan. Rangeland. The King Fischer's Roost. Table Top Ranch. Golden Silence. 1924: Branded a Bandit. The Courageous Coward. The Passing of Wolf MacLean. Battling Bunyan. 1925: The Fighting Cub. 1926: The High Hand. The Outlaw Express. 1927: The Valley of the Giants. Buttons. The Man from Hard Pan. The Red Raiders. The Devil's Saddle. Overland Stage. The Range Riders. 1928: The Cossacks. 1929: Oh, Yeah! (GB: No Brakes). The California Mail. The Lawless Legion. The Rainbow. The Racketeer (GB: Love's Conquest). Tide of Empire. Sailor's Holiday. 1930: The Swellhead (GB: Counted Out). Mountain Justice. Borrowed Wives. Hot Curves. Lucky Larkin. Officer O'Brien. The Runaway Bride. Paradise Island. Shadow of the Law. His First Command. The Third Alarm. 1931: The Public Defender. The Single Sin. The Secret Six. Kick In. Sweepstakes. Secret Witness. Bad Company. 1932: The Phantom President. Panama Flo. The Thirteenth Guest. Dancers in the Dark. The Big Stampede. Hold 'Em Jail. My Pal, the King. Island of Lost Souls. 1933: Hold Your Man. Men Are Such Fools. Terror Abroad. Tugboat Annie. Day of Reckoning. The Sphinx. Saturday's Millions. Women in His Life. The Big Race (GB: Raising the Wind). Scarlet River. 1934: Take the Stand (GB: The Great Radio Mystery). Midnight Alibi. The Line-Up. Among the Missing. Sequoia. \*There Ain't No Justice. 1935: Tomorrow's Youth. Wilderness Mail. Shadow of Doubt. Mississippi. Star of Midnight. Public Hero No. 1. Calm Yourself. Carnival (GB: Carnival Nights). The Gay Deception. Riffraff. The Case of the Curious Bride. 1936: San Francisco. The Blackmailer. Robin Hood of Eldorado. The Gay Desperado. I'd Give My Life. To Mary - with Love. It Had to Happen. North of Nome (GB: The Lawless North). We Who Are About To Die. 1937: Fifty Roads to Town. You Can't Beat Love. Trouble in Morocco. The Lady Fights Back. Wake Up and Live. Angel's Holiday. This is My Affair (GB: His Affair). Super-Sleuth. Slave Ship. She's No Lady. Wife, Doctor and Nurse. Small Town Boy. Danger - Love at Work. Ali Baba Goes to Town. Second Honeymoon. You Can't Have Everything. 1938: Rebecca of Sunnybrook Farm. In Old Chicago. No Time to Marry. Josette. Alexander's Ragtime Band. Island in the Sky. Prison Break. My Lucky Star. The Last Express. Hold That Co-Ed (GB: Hold That Girl). Secrets of a Nurse. Thanks for Everything. 1939: Topper Takes a Trip. Café Society. Broadway Serenade. It Could Happen to You. Each Dawn I Die. Remember? The Kid from Kokomo (GB: The Orphan of the Ring). Quick Millions. Bad Lands. Gone With the Wind. On Your Toes. Heaven with a Barbed-Wire Fence. Edison the Man. 1940: Torrid Zone. South to Karanga. The Westerner. Tugboat Annie Sails Again. They Drive by Night (GB: The Road to Frisco). Star Dust. Men Against the Sky. \*Goin' Fishing. 1941: Tall, Dark and Handsome. Petticoat Politics. Virginia. Bowery Boy. The Parson of Panamint. Caught in the Draft. Ellery Queen and the Murder Ring (GB: The Murder Ring). This Woman Is Mine. The Great Mr Nobody. 1942: Dudes Are Pretty People. A Night in New Orleans. Sundown Jim. Pardon My Stripes. The Ox-Bow Incident (GB: Strange Incident). Hi'Ya Chum (GB: Everything Happens to Us). 1943: Calaboose. Jack London. Coney Island. Young and Willing. The Sky's the Limit. 1944: Barbary Coast Gent. The Ghost That Walks Alone. Girl Rush. Summer Storm. Greenwich Village. Something for the Boys. 1945: One Exciting Night. The Big Show-Off. Dakota. The Dolly Sisters. Penthouse Rhythm. Her Lucky Night. Nob Hill. Midnight Manhunt. Scared Stiff. Steppin' in Society. 1946: In Old Sacramento. Death Valley. Murder in the Music Hall. The Virginian. The Plainsman and the Lady. 1947: Angel and the Badman. Under Colorado Skies. 1948: The Arizona Ranger. Heart of Virginia. Son of God's Country. Gun Smugglers. California Firebrand. Yellow Sky. On Our Merry Way/A Miracle Can Happen. Old Los Angeles. Madonna of the Desert. 1949: Law of the Golden West. Prince of the Plains. Outcasts of the Trail. South of Rio. Ranger of Cherokee Strip. San Antone Ambush. 1950: Pioneer Marshal. The Vanishing Westerner. The Missourians. The Old Frontier. 1951: Million Dollar Pursuit. 1952: Big Jim McLain. Toughest Man in Arizona. 1953: The Sun Shines Bright.*

†And co-directed

**HUTCHESON, David** 1905-1976

Cheerful Scottish actor of the 'I say, old chap' school, with long, equine features and sunny nature. He played a few dashing heroes in minor films of the 1930s, then settled down to portraits of asinine friends, mostly in comedy. Almost entirely on stage after 1952, Hutcheson made something of a habit of playing Colonel Pickering in *My Fair Lady* in numerous touring performances of the 1960s.

*1930: Fast and Loose. 1934: Romance in Rhythm. 1935: The Love Test. 1936: Wedding Group (US: Wrath of Jealousy). This'll Make You Whistle. 1937: The Sky's the Limit. 1939: A Gentleman's Gentleman. She Couldn't Say No. Lucky to Me. The Middle Watch. 1940: 'Bulldog' Sees It Through. Convoy. 1942: Next of Kin. Sabotage at Sea. 1943: The Life and Death of Colonel Blimp (US: Colonel Blimp). The Hundred Pound Window. 1945: The Trojan Brothers. 1946: School for Secrets (US: Secret Flight). 1947: Vice Versa. 1948: The Small Back Room. Woman Hater. Sleeping Car to Trieste. 1949: Madness of the Heart. 1950: My Daughter Joy*

(US: Operation X). The Elusive Pimpernel (US: The Fighting Pimpernel). 1951: Circle of Danger. No Highway (US: No Highway in the Sky). Encore. 1952: Something Money Can't Buy. 1953: The Blakes Slept Here. 1958: Law and Disorder. 1964: The Evil of Frankenstein. 1969: The Magic Christian. 1970: Every Home Should Have One. 1971: Follow Me (US: The Public Eye). The Abominable Dr Phibes. 1973: The National Health.

**HYDE WHITE, Wilfrid** 1903- 1991
Roguishly avuncular British actor, with spade-shaped face and inimitable sly, drawling tones. Almost always cast as affable upper-class coves, but sometimes with a cunning streak. He has now shuffled his way with deceptive casualness through 50 years of films. Billed in some of his 1930s' films simply as 'Hyde White'.

1934: Josser on the Farm. 1935: Admirals All. Night Mail. Alibi Inn. Smith's Wives. 1936: Murder By Rope. Rembrandt. Servants All. The Scarab Murder Case. 1937: Elephant Boy. Bulldog Drummond at Bay. Change for a Sovereign. 1938: Keep Smiling. Meet Mr Penny. I've Got a Horse. 1939: The Lambeth Walk. Poison Pen. 1941: Turned Out Nice Again. 1942: Lady from Lisbon. Back Room Boy. Asking for Trouble. 1943: The Butler's Dilemma. The Demi-Paradise (US: Adventure for Two). 1945: Night Boat to Dublin. 1946: Appointment with Crime. While the Sun Shines. Wanted for Murder. 1947: Meet Me at Dawn. The Ghosts of Berkeley Square. My Brother Jonathan. 1948: My Brother's Keeper. Quartet. The Winslow Boy. Bond Street. The Bad Lord Byron. 1949: Britannia Mews (US: Forbidden Street). The Man on the Eiffel Tower. Adam and Evelyne (US: Adam and Evalyn). The Passionate Friends (US: One Woman's Story). That Dangerous Age (US: If This Be Sin). Helter Skelter. The Third Man. Conspirator. Golden Salamander. 1950: Last Holiday. Trio. The Angel with the Trumpet (and German version). Midnight Episode. Highly Dangerous. The Mudlark. Mr Drake's Duck. Blackmailed. 1951: No Highway (US: No Highway in the Sky). The Browning Version. Mr Denning Drives North. Outcast of the Islands. 1952: The Card (US:

The Promoter). Top Secret (US: Mr Potts Goes to Moscow). 1953: The Story of Gilbert and Sullivan (US: The Great Gilbert and Sullivan). The Triangle. The Million Pound Note (US: Man with a Million). 1954: The Rainbow Jacket. Duel in the Jungle. Betrayed. To Dorothy a Son (US: Cash on Delivery). *The Journey. 1955: John and Julie. See How They Run. The Adventures of Quentin Durward (US: Quentin Durward). 1956: The March Hare. My Teenage Daughter (US: Teenage Bad Girl). The Silken Affair. That Woman Opposite (US: City After Midnight). The Vicious Circle (US: The Circle). Tarzan and the Lost Safari. The Truth about Women. 1958: Wonderful Things! Up the Creek. 1959: Life in Emergency Ward 10. Carry On Nurse. The Lady Is a Square. Libel. North West Frontier (US: Flame over India). 1960: Two Way Stretch. Let's Make Love. His and Hers. 1961: On the Fiddle (US: Operation Snafu). On the Double. Ada. 1962: Aliki. In Search of the Castaways. Crooks Anonymous. 1963: A Jolly Bad Fellow. 1964: John Goldfarb, Please Come Home. My Fair Lady. 1965: Ten Little Indians. The Liquidator. You Must Be Joking! 1966: Our Man in Marrakesh (US: Bang Bang You're Dead). The Sandwich Man. Chamber of Horrors. 1967: Sumuru (US: The 1,000,000 Eyes of Sumuru). P.J. (US: New Face in Hell). 1968: Sunshine Patriot (TV). 1969: Run a Crooked Mile (TV). The Magic Christian. Skullduggery. Gaily, Gaily (GB: Chicago Chicago). Fear No Evil (TV). Ritual of Evil (TV). 1970: Fragment of Fear. 1972: The Cherry Picker. A Brand New Life (TV). 1977: The Great Houdini (TV). 1978: No Longer Alone. King Solomon's Treasure. The Cat and the Canary. Battlestar Galactica (TV. GB: cinemas). 1979: In God We Trust. 1980: Dick Turpin (TV. US: cinemas). Xanadu (voice only). Damien, the Leper Priest (TV). Oh, God! Book II. Scout's Honor (TV). 1981: Tarzan the Ape-Man. The Letter (TV). 1982: The Toy. 1983: Fanny Hill.

**HYMER, Warren** 1906-1948
Snub-nosed, square-chinned, dark-haired New Yorker kept very busy in Hollywood from 1929 to 1942, his close-set eyes and fast delivery of a line lending themselves

ideally to dim-witted but generally good-natured characters on either side of the law. The demand for 'big palookas', however, decreased in post-war years and ill-health also hit his career. He died in hospital 'after a long illness' at only 42. Son of the playwright John B. Hymer.

1929: The Far Call. Fox Movietone Follies of 1929. Frozen Justice. The Girl from Havana. Speak-Easy. 1930: The Lone Star Ranger. Born Reckless. Men without Women. Oh, for a Man! Up the River. Sinners' Holiday. Men on Call. 1931: The Seas Beneath. Goldie. Charlie Chan Carries On. The Spider. The Unholy Garden. The Cockeyed World. 1932: Hold 'Em, Jail! One Way Passage. The Night Mayor. Madison Square Garden. Love Is a Racket. 1933: My Woman. Her First Mate. I Love That Man. Midnight Mary. 20,000 Years in Sing Sing. The Billion Dollar Scandal. A Lady's Profession. In the Money. The Mysterious Rider. 1934: Woman Unafraid. *The Gold Ghost. George White's Scandals. The Cat's Paw. She Loves Me Not. Young and Beautiful. Kid Millions. King for a Night. The Crosby Case (GB: The Crosby Murder Case). Belle of the Nineties. One is Guilty. Little Miss Marker (GB: Girl in Pawn). 1935: Hold 'Em Yale (GB: Uniform Lovers). Straight from the Heart. Our Little Girl. The Daring Young Man. The Silk Hat Kid. Navy Wife. Hong Kong Nights. The Gilded Lily. The Case of the Curious Bride. She Gets Her Man. Confidential. Show Them No Mercy (GB: Tainted Money). 1936: Hitch Hike Lady (GB: Eventful Journey). Tango. The Widow from Monte Carlo. The Leavenworth Case. Desert Justice (GB: Crime's Highway). Laughing Irish Eyes. Everybody's Old Man. Mr Deeds Goes to Town. San Francisco. Rhythm on the Range. Nobody's Fool. Love Letters of a Star. Thirty-Six Hours to Kill. 1937: Join the Marines. You Only Live Once. We Have Our Moments. Meet the Boy Friend. Navy Blues. Sea Racketeers. Wake Up and Live. Ali Baba Goes to Town. Bad Guy. Married Before Breakfast. She's Dangerous. 1938: Arson Gang Busters. Lady Behave. Joy of Living. Submarine Patrol. Gateway. Telephone Operator. Thanks for Everything. You and Me. Bluebeard's Eighth Wife. 1939: The Boy Friend. The Lady and the Mob. Coast Guard. Calling All Marines. Charlie McCarthy, Detective. Mr Moto in Danger Island (GB: Mr Moto on Danger Island). Destry Rides Again. 1940: I Can't Give You Anything But Love, Baby. Love, Honor and Oh, Baby! 1941: Buy Me That Town. Meet John Doe. Birth of the Blues. Skylark. 1942: Mr Wise Guy. Henry and Dizzy. Jail House Blues. Girl's Town. Dr Broadway. So's Your Aunt Emma. One Thrilling Night. Lure of the Islands. Baby Face Morgan. Police Bullets. Phantom Killer. She's in the Army. 1943: Hitler - Dead or Alive. Danger - Women at Work. Gangway for Tomorrow. 1944: Since You Went Away. Three is a Family. 1945: The Affairs of Susan. 1946: Gentleman Joe Palooka. Joe Palooka - Champ.

The Battle of the River Plate (US: Pursuit of the Graf Spee). Zarak. Passport to Treason. Loser Takes All. 1957: Man in the Shadow. Miracle in Soho. Interpol (US: Pickup Alley). Fire Down Below. A Farewell to Arms. Manuela (US: Stowaway Girl). Campbell's Kingdom. I Accuse! 1958: Escapement (US: Zex/The Electronic Monster). 1959: The Angry Hills. Jet Storm. The Wreck of the Mary Deare. Friends and Neighbours. Whirlpool. 1960: Moment of Danger (US: Malaga). Sands of the Desert. Bluebeard's Ten Honeymoons. 1961: The Middle Course. The Secret Partner. The Happy Thieves. Village of Daughters. 1962: The Devil's Daffodil (US: The Daffodil Killer). The Secret Door (released 1964). Nine Hours to Rama. 1963: Echo of Diana. The VIPs. 1964: Devils of Darkness. 1965: A Man Could Get Killed. 1967: The 25th Hour.

### ILLING, Peter 1899-1966

Stocky, staring-eyed Austrian actor (of Turkish parentage), of rather dangerous appearance, with receding, unruly dark hair, often moustachioed. He appeared on the Berlin stage for 13 years before fleeing to Britain in 1937. In World War II his became known as the German-speaking voice that translated Sir Winston Churchill's speeches for broadcast overseas; but, with peace, the heroic image vanished, and he played mainly unkempt and sometimes powerful villains in British films; on occasion his foreigners were less evil but no less irascible.

*1947: The Silver Darlings. The End of the River. 1948: Eureka Stockade (US: Massacre Hill). Against the Wind. 1949: Madness of the Heart. The Huggetts Abroad. Floodtide. Children of Chance. Traveller's Joy (released 1951). 1950: State Secret (US: The Great Manhunt). My Daughter Joy (US: Operation X). Her Favourite Husband (US: The Taming of Dorothy). 1951: I'll Get You For This (US: Lucky Nick Cain). Outcast of the Islands. 1952: The Woman's Angle. 24 Hours of a Woman's Life (US: Affair in Monte Carlo). 1953: Never Let Me Go. Innocents in Paris. 1954: West of Zanzibar. The House Across the Lake (US: Heatwave). Flame and the Flesh. Mask of Dust (US: Race for Life). The Glass Slipper. The Young Lovers (US: Chance Meeting). Svengali. 1955: That Lady. As Long As They're Happy. Born for Trouble. 1956: It's Never Too Late. Bhowani Junction.*

### INESCORT, Frieda
(F. Wightman) 1900-1976

Tall, dark, Scottish-born actress with faintly forbidding good looks. The daughter of actress Elaine Inescort (only film: 1933's *Rolling in Money*), she began her film career in America, where she had lived and worked – first as a secretary, then as a stage actress – since 1921. In the 1930s, she appeared as society wives, scheming women and aristocratic cousins. After a break of five years, she played out the remainder of her career in older character roles. Died from multiple sclerosis.

*1935: The Dark Angel. If You Could Only Cook. 1936: Hollywood Boulevard. The King Steps Out. Give Me Your Heart. The Garden Murder Case. Mary of Scotland. 1937: Portia on Trial (GB: The Trial of Portia Merriman). The Great O'Malley. Another Dawn. Call It a Day. 1938: Beauty for the Asking. 1939: Zero Hour. Woman Doctor. Tarzan Finds a Son! A Woman Is the Judge. 1940: Pride and Prejudice. Convicted Woman. The Letter. 1941: The Trial of Mary Dugan. Sunny. Father's Son. You'll Never Get Rich. Remember the Day. Shadows on the Stairs. 1942: It Comes Up Love (GB: A Date with an Angel). The Courtship of Andy Hardy. Street of Chance. Sweater Girl. 1943: The Amazing Mrs Holliday. Mission to Moscow. The Return*

*of the Vampire. 1944: Heavenly Days. 1945: *Young and Beautiful. 1948: The Judge Steps Out (GB: Indian Summer). 1950: The Underworld Story. 1951: A Place in the Sun. 1952: Never Wave at a WAC (GB: The Private Wore Skirts). 1953: Casanova's Big Night. 1955: Foxfire. Flame of the Islands. 1956: The Eddy Duchin Story. 1957: Darby's Rangers (GB: The Young Invaders). 1958: Senior Prom. 1959: The Alligator People. Juke Box Rhythm. 1960: The Crowded Sky.*

### INGRAM, Rex 1895-1969

Formidable black American actor with powerful features, born on a riverboat but later an honours medical graduate. He succumbed to the lure of an acting career soon afterwards, but it was years before he gained recognition in films, with his starring performance as De Lawd in *Green Pastures*. He was also impressive as the genie in the 1940 version of *The Thief of Bagdad* (having had a very minor assignment in the silent version), but most of his other roles were unworthy of his talents. He died from a heart attack.

*1915: Snatched from a Burning Death. 1918: Salome. Tarzan of the Apes. 1923: Scaramouche. The Ten Commandments. 1924: Thief of Bagdad. 1925: The Wanderer. The Big Parade. 1926: Lord Jim. Beau Geste. 1927: King of Kings. 1928: The Four Feathers. 1929: Hearts in Dixie. 1932: The Sign of the Cross. 1933: King Kong. The Emperor Jones. Love in Morocco. 1934: Harlem After Midnight. 1935: Captain Blood. 1936: Green Pastures. 1939: The Adventures of Huckleberry Finn. 1940: The Thief of Bagdad. 1942: The Talk of the Town. 1943: Cabin in the Sky. Sahara. Fired Wife. 1944: Dark Waters. 1945: A Thousand and One Nights. Adventure. 1948: Moonrise. 1950: King Solomon's Mines. 1955: Tarzan's Hidden Jungle. 1956: The Ten Commandments (and earlier film). Congo Crossing. 1957: Hell on Devil's Island. 1958: Anna Lucasta. God's Little Acre. 1959: Escort West. Watusi. 1960: Elmer Gantry. Desire in the Dust. 1964: Your Cheatin' Heart. 1966: Hurry Sundown. 1967: Journey to Shiloh. How to Succeed in Business Without Really Trying.*

**IVAN, Rosalind** 1881-1959

Though in real life a bright, amusing, charming, multi-talented person, this red-haired English-born actress's disagreeable-looking facial features clearly doomed her to playing shrikes and shrews in drama, which she did to great effect. Dubbed 'Ivan the Terrible' by some after her performance as the termagant wife of Charles Laughton in *The Suspect*, she returned to the stage in the late 1940s and to a career as an acting coach. Died from heart failure.

*1936: The Garden Murder Case. 1944: None But the Lonely Heart. 1945: The Suspect. The Corn is Green. Pursuit to Algiers. Scarlet Street. Pillow of Death. 1946: That Brennan Girl. Three Strangers. The Verdict. Alias Mr Twilight. 1947: Ivy. 1948: Johnny Belinda. 1953: The Robe. 1954: Elephant Walk.*

**JACKSON, Freda** 1909- *1990*

Forbidding-faced, dark-haired British character actress who created some memorably grim portraits, women that made her the Sonia Dresdel of the lower classes. Started as a singer, but turned to acting in her middle twenties. Film appearances are fewer than one would have liked, but she was really too ferocious for supporting roles.

*1938: Mountains o' Mourne. 1944: A Canterbury Tale. Henry V. 1946: Great Expectations. Beware of Pity. 1948: No Room at the Inn. 1951: Flesh and Blood. Mr Denning Drives North. 1952: Women of Twilight (US: Twilight Women). 1954: The*

*Crowded Day. The Good Die Young. 1956: Bhowani Junction. The Last Man to Hang? 1957: The Flesh is Weak. 1958: A Tale of Two Cities. 1960: The Brides of Dracula. 1961: The Shadow of the Cat. Greyfriars Bobby. Attempt to Kill. 1963: West 11. Tom Jones. 1964: The Third Secret. \*Boy with a Flute. 1965: Monster of Terror (US: Die, Monster, Die). 1966: The Jokers. 1968: The Valley of Gwangi. 1981: Clash of the Titans.*

**JACQUES, Hattie**
(Josephine Jacques) 1924-1980

Tall, plumply beaming, dark-haired British character actress, in vivid supporting roles from her early twenties. A radio comedienne from 1947, but did not get into her film comedy stride until the 'Carry On' series came along. Later a notable foil for Eric Sykes in his long-running television show. Married to actor John le Mesurier (qv) from 1949 to 1965. Died from a heart attack.

*1946: Green for Danger. 1947: Nicholas Nickleby. 1948: Oliver Twist. 1949: Trottie True (US: Gay Lady). The Spider and the Fly. 1950: Waterfront (US: Waterfront Women). Chance of a Lifetime. 1951: Scrooge. 1952: No Haunt for a Gentleman. Mother Riley Meets the Vampire (US: Vampire over London). The Pickwick Papers. 1953: Our Girl Friday (US: The Adventures of Sadie). All Hallowe'en. 1954: The Love Lottery. Up to His Neck. 1955: As Long As They're Happy. 1958: Carry On Sergeant. The Square Peg. 1959: Carry On Nurse. Carry On Teacher. Left, Right and Centre. The Night We Dropped a Clanger. The Navy Lark. Follow a Star. 1960: Carry On Constable. Make Mine Mink. Watch Your Stern. School for Scoundrels. 1961: Carry On Regardless. In the Doghouse. 1962: She'll Have to Go (US: Maid for Murder). The Punch and Judy Man. 1963: Carry On Cabby. 1967: The Bobo. The Plank. Carry On Doctor. 1968: Crooks and Coronets (US: Sophy's Place). 1969: Carry On Again, Doctor. Carry On Camping. The Magic Christian. Monte Carlo or Bust! (US: Those Daring Young Men in Their Jaunty Jalopies). 1970: Rhubarb. Carry On Loving. 1971: Danger Point. Carry On at Your Convenience. 1972: Carry On Matron. Carry On Abroad. 1974: Carry On Dick. Three for All.*

**JAECKEL, Richard** 1926- *1997*

Sturdy American actor with baby face and shock of fair hair who was plucked from the 20th Century-Fox mail room to portray a teenage soldier in *Guadalcanal Diary* and, apart from serving in the US Navy from mid-1944 to mid-1948, has been playing little tough guys ever since. Star roles between 1952 and 1954 should perhaps have led to something better, but he has been largely confined to soldiers and outlaws since then. Never seems to age. Nominated for an Oscar in *Sometimes a Great Notion*.

*1943: Guadalcanal Diary. 1944: Wing and a Prayer. 1948: Jungle Patrol. 1949: City Across the River. Sands of Iwo Jima. Battleground. 1950: The Gunfighter. Wyoming Mail. 1951: Fighting Coast Guard. The Sea Hornet. Hoodlum Empire. 1952: My Son John. Come Back, Little Sheba. 1953: The Big Leaguer. Sea of Lost Ships. 1954: The Shanghai Story. The Violent Men (GB: Rough Company). 1955: Apache Ambush. 1956: Attack! Smoke Jumpers (TV). 1957: 3:10 to Yuma. Ain't No Time for Glory (TV). 1958: Cowboy. The Line-Up. The Naked and the Dead. When Hell Broke Loose. The Gun Runners. 1960: The Gallant Hours. Platinum High School. Flaming Star. 1961: Town Without Pity. 1963: The Young and the Brave. Four for Texas. Nightmare in the Sun. 1965: Town Tamer. 1966: Once Before I Die. 1967: The Dirty Dozen. 1968: The Devil's Brigade. The Green Slime. 1969: Latitude Zero. 1970: Gold Seekers. Chisum. 1971: Sometimes a Great Notion (GB: Never Give an Inch). The Deadly Dream (TV). 1972: Ulzana's Raid. 1973: †The Red Pony (TV. GB: cinemas in abridged version). Firehouse (TV). Partners in Crime (TV). Pat Garrett and Billy the Kid. The Outfit. 1974: Chosen Survivors. Born Innocent (TV). 1975: The Last Day (TV). The Drowning Pool. Part Two Walking Tall (GB: Legend of the Lawman). 1976: Delta Fox. The Jaws of Death. Day of the Animals. Grizzly. 1977: Champions, a Love Story (TV). Twilight's Last Gleaming. Speedtrap. Assault on Paradise (GB: Maniac). 1978: The Falcon's Ultimatum. Go West Young Girl (TV). The Dark. 1979: Salvage (TV. GB: Salvage One). Champions: a Love Story (TV). Cold River (released 1982). 1980: Herbie Goes Bananas. Reward (TV). The $5.20 an Hour Dream (TV). 1981: All the Marbles ... (GB: The California Dolls). 1982: Airplane II The Sequel. 1984: Starman. 1985: The Dirty Dozen: Next Mission (TV). Pacific Inferno (filmed 1977). Black Moon Rising.*

*†Scenes deleted from final release print*

**JAFFE, Sam** 1893-1984

Talented little American actor who looked wizened even in early middle age, and specialized in obscure foreign characterizations: Tibetan, Indian, Russian, Israeli and

ABOVE Freda **Jackson** in rampaging form as the vicious Mrs Voray in *No Room at the Inn* (1948), here offering a wolfish smile to her sailor boyfriend (Niall MacGinnis, *qv*)

LEFT Hattie **Jacques** appearing as Grace Short in *Carry On Teacher* (1960)

Mexican were only a few. Film appearances were limited by his prolific stage work, but they have often been memorable, notably his native water-carrier in *Gunga Din* and his High Lama in *Lost Horizon*. Married to actress Bettye Ackerman (1928-) since 1955; she appeared with him during his years as Dr Zorba in television's *Ben Casey*. Died from cancer. Nominated for an Oscar in *The Asphalt Jungle*.

1934: We Live Again. The Scarlet Empress. 1937: Lost Horizon. 1939: Gunga Din. 1943: Stage Door Canteen. 1946: 13 Rue Madeleine. 1947: Gentleman's Agreement. 1948: The Accused. 1949: Rope of Sand. 1950: Under the Gun. The Asphalt Jungle. 1951: I Can Get It for You Wholesale (GB: This is My Affair). The Day the Earth Stood Still. 1956: All Mine to Give (GB: The Day They Gave Babies Away). 1957: Les espions. 1958: The Barbarian and the Geisha. 1959: Ben-Hur. The Dingaling Girl (TV). 1960: The Sound of Trumpets (TV). In the Presence of Mine Enemies (TV). 1967: A Guide for the Married Man. Guns for San Sebastian. 1969: The Great Bank Robbery. Night Gallery (TV). 1970: The Dunwich Horror. The Kremlin Letter. Quarantined (TV). The Old Man Who Cried Wolf (TV). 1971: Bedknobs and Broomsticks. Sam Hill - Who Killed the Mysterious Mr Foster? (TV). 1974: QB VII (TV). 1980: Battle Beyond the Stars. Gideon's Trumpet (TV). 1981: Jayne Mansfield - An American Tragedy (TV). 1984: Nothing Lasts Forever. On the Line.

## JAMES, Clifton 1921-

Fat, pink-faced, throaty-toned American actor, briefly popular in the mid-1970s (after a hard climb up the acting ladder) as redneck, cigar-chewing sheriffs and villains, but less frequently seen in films since 1976. Another graduate of the Actors' Studio.

1954: On the Waterfront. 1957: End As a Man (GB: The Strange One). 1958: The Last Mile. 1962: Experiment in Terror (GB: The Grip of Fear). David and Lisa. 1964: Black Like Me. Invitation to a Gunfighter. 1965: The Chase. 1966: The Happening. The Caper of the Golden Bulls (GB: Carnival of Thieves). 1967: Cool Hand Luke. Will Penny. 1969: The Reivers. ...tick...tick...tick.

1970: WUSA. 1971: The Biscuit Eater. 1972: The New Centurions (GB: Precinct 45 - Los Angeles Police). 1973: Kid Blue/Dime Box. The Iceman Cometh. The Laughing Policeman (GB: An Investigation of Murder). The Last Detail. The Werewolf of Washington. Live and Let Die. Buster and Billie. 1974: Bank Shot. Juggernaut. The Man With the Golden Gun. Rancho de Luxe. 1976: Silver Streak. The November Plan (originally for TV). 1977: The Bad News Bears in Breaking Training. 1979: CaboBlanco. 1980: Superman II. 1985: Where Are the Children?

## JAMESON, Joyce 1932- 1987

Glamorous, buxom American blonde actress with wide mouth and corncrake voice. She played mostly dames and broads in comedy roles; at her best in two Gothic horror films of the early 1960s when she showed she could be just as effective playing for chuckles and chills. Otherwise mainly on television and in shamefully small roles in films.

1951: The Strip. Show Boat. 1953: Veils of Bagdad. Problem Girls. The French Line. 1954: Phffft! Son of Sinbad. 1955: Gang Busters. 1956: Crime Against Joe. 1957: Tip on a Dead Jockey (GB: Time for Action). 1960: The Apartment. 1962: Poe's Tales of Terror (GB: Tales of Terror). 1963: The Balcony. Comedy of Terrors. 1964: Good Neighbor Sam. 1966: Boy, Did I Get a Wrong Number! 1968: The Split. 1970: Company of Killers. Run, Simon, Run (TV). 1971:

Crosscurrent (TV). 1972: Women in Chains (TV). 1975: Death Race 2000. The First 36 Hours of Dr Durant (TV). Promise Him Anything (TV). 1976: The Outlaw Josey Wales. The Love Boat (TV). Scorchy. 1978: Crash (TV). Every Which Way But Loose. 1979: The Wild, Wild West Revisited (TV). Leo and Loree.

## JEAYES, Allan 1885-1963

Solidly built, dark-haired, sometimes moustachioed British actor who tackled a good range of aggressive semi-leads when he came to films at the beginning of sound, then settled down with Korda's London Films to play inspectors, judges and even the occasional oriental. His splendid, resonant voice was used to good effect as the storyteller in *The Thief of Bagdad*. Retired in 1950, but came back for a couple of 'old man' roles just before his death from a heart attack.

1918: Nelson. 1921: A Gentleman of France. The Solitary Cyclist. 1922: The Hound of the Baskervilles. The Missioner. 1925: Bulldog Drummond's Third Round (US: The Third Round). 1929: The Hate Ship. 1931: The Ghost Train. Stranglehold. 1932: Above Rubies. The Impassive Footman (US: Woman in Bondage/Woman in Chains). 1933: Anne One Hundred. Little Napoleon. Purse Strings. Paris Plane. Ask Beccles. Song of the Plough. Eyes of Fate. Colonel Blood. 1934: Red Ensign (US: Strike!). Catherine the Great/The Rise of Catherine the Great. The Scarlet Pimpernel. The Camels Are Coming. 1935: Koenigsmark. Sanders of the River (US: Bosambo). Drake of England (US: Drake the Pirate). King of the Damned. 1936: His Lordship (US: Man of Affaires). Forget-Me-Not (US: Forever Yours). Things to Come. Seven Sinners (US: Doomed Cargo). Rembrandt. The House of the Spaniard. Crown v Stevens. Public Nuisance. 1937: Elephant Boy. The High Command. Knight without Armour. Action for Slander. The Squeaker (US: Murder on Diamond Row). The Green Cockatoo (US: Four Dark Hours). 1938: The Return of the Scarlet Pimpernel. A Royal Divorce. Everything Happens to Me. They Drive by Night. Thirteen Men and a Gun. Dangerous Medicine. 1939: The Good Old Days. The Spider. The Four

Feathers. The Stars Look Down. The Proud Valley. 1940: The Thief of Bagdad. Spy for a Day. Sailors Three (US: Three Cockeyed Sailors). Convoy. You Will Remember. The Girl in the News. The Flying Squad. Old Bill and Son. 1941: Pimpernel Smith (US: Mister V). 1942: Tomorrow We Live (US: At Dawn We Die). Uncensored. Talk about Jacqueline. 1943: The Shipbuilders. 1945: Perfect Strangers (US: Vacation from Marriage). Dead of Night. 1946: Lisbon Story. 1947: The Man Within (US: The Smugglers). Blanche Fury. 1948: Saraband for Dead Lovers (US: Saraband). Obsession (US: The Hidden Room). 1950: Waterfront (US: Waterfront Women). The Reluctant Widow. 1961: Attempt to Kill. 1962: Reach for Glory.

**JEFFRIES, Lionel 1926–**
Bewhiskered British comedy actor, bald since his twenties. He began as nosey types and men in the street, progressed to inept, would-be malevolent figures of authority and finally put on a little weight to arrive at eccentric blunderers and benevolent benefactors. Jeffries became a force in the British cinema of the early 1970s for his direction of children, but later ventures behind the camera were less successful. An inveterate scene-stealer in his peak period of comic invention.

1949: Stage Fright. 1953: Will Any Gentleman? 1954: The Colditz Story. The Black Rider. 1955: Windfall. No Smoking. The Quatermass Experiment (US: The Creeping Unknown). All for Mary. 1956: Jumping for Joy. Eyewitness. Bhowani Junction. Lust for Life. The Baby and the Battleship. Up in the World. The High Terrace. The Man in the Sky (US: Decision Against Time). 1957: The Vicious Circle (US: The Circle). Hour of Decision. Doctor at Large. Barnacle Bill (US: All at Sea). Blue Murder at St Trinian's. 1958: Law and Disorder. Orders to Kill. Dunkirk. Up the Creek. The Revenge of Frankenstein. Girls at Sea. The Nun's Story. Behind the Mask. Nowhere to Go. Further Up the Creek. Life is a Circus. 1959: Idle on Parade (US: Idol on Parade). Please Turn Over. Bobbikins. 1960: Two Way Stretch. The Trials of Oscar Wilde (US: The Man in the Green Carnation). Jazzboat. Let's Get

Married. Tarzan the Magnificent. 1961: The Hellions. Fanny. 1962: Operation Snatch. Mrs Gibbons' Boys. Kill or Cure. The Notorious Landlady. The Wrong Arm of the Law. 1963: Call Me Bwana. The Scarlet Blade (US: The Crimson Blade). The Long Ships. 1964: First Men in the Moon. The Truth About Spring. Murder Ahoy. 1965: You Must Be Joking! The Secret of My Success. 1966: Drop Dead, Darling (US: Arrivederci Baby!). Oh Dad, Poor Dad, Mama's Hung You in the Closet and I'm Feeling So Sad. The Spy With a Cold Nose. 1967: Jules Verne's Rocket to the Moon (US: Those Fantastic Flying Fools). Camelot. 1968: Chitty Chitty Bang Bang. 1969: Twinky (US: Lola). Twelve Plus One/The Twelve Chairs. 1970: Eyewitness (and 1956 film). 1971: Whoever Slew Auntie Roo? (US: Who Slew Auntie Roo?). 1974: Royal Flash. What Changed Charley Farthing? 1977: Wombling Free (voice only). 1978: The Water Babies (voice only). The Prisoner of Zenda. 1982: Ménage à Trois/Better Late Than Never.

**As director:**
1970: The Railway Children. 1972: The Amazing Mr Blunden. Baxter! 1977: Wombling Free. 1978: The Water Babies.

**JENKINS, Allen**
(Alfred McGonegal) 1890–1974
Brown-haired, bag-eyed, hook-nosed American actor whose ugly mug might have come straight from a Damon Runyan story, and proved to be his fortune. In the 1930s and 1940s, matchstick often dangling from a drooping lower lip, he was ever ready with a leering remark and played dozens of dim-witted but by and large friendly penny-ante crooks and ne'er-do-wells. Largely retired after 1957, but still played a few cameo roles in his last years. Died from complications following surgery.

1931: The Girl Habit. 1932: Rackety Rax. Blessed Event. I Am a Fugitive from a Chain Gang. Three on a Match. *The Stolen Jools (GB: The Slippery Pearls). Lawyer Man. 1933: 42nd Street. Ladies They Talk About. The Mayor of Hell. Employees' Entrance. The Keyhole. Tomorrow at Seven. Professional Sweetheart (GB: Imaginary Sweetheart). The Mind Reader. Havana Widows. Hard to Handle. The Silk Express. Bureau of Missing

Persons. Blondie Johnson. 1934: I've Got Your Number. Twenty Million Sweethearts. Happiness Ahead. The Merry Frinks (GB: The Happy Family). The St Louis Kid (GB: A Perfect Weekend). The Case of the Howling Dog. Bedside. The Big Shakedown. Whirlpool. Jimmy the Gent. 1935: A Night at the Ritz. Miss Pacific Fleet. The Case of the Curious Bride. Page Miss Glory. The Irish in Us. Sweet Music. While the Patient Slept. The Case of the Lucky Legs. Broadway Hostess. I Live for Love (GB: I Live for You). 1936: The Singing Kid. Sing Me a Love Song. Three Men on a Horse. Sins of Man. Cain and Mabel. 1937: There Goes My Girl. Dance, Charlie, Dance. The Singing Marine. Marry the Girl. Dead End. Talent Scout. Ready, Willing and Able. Marked Woman. Ever Since Eve. The Perfect Specimen. Sh! The Octopus. 1938: A Slight Case of Murder. Swing Your Lady. Racket Busters. Heart of the North. Going Places. Gold Diggers in Paris (GB: The Gay Imposters). The Amazing Dr Clitterhouse. Hard to Get. Fools for Scandal. *For Auld Lang Syne. 1939: Sweepstakes Winner. Five Came Back. Torchy Plays with Dynamite. Naughty But Nice. Destry Rides Again. 1940: Oh, Johnny, How You Can Love. Meet the Wildcat. Brother Orchid. Margie. Tin Pan Alley. 1941: The Gay Falcon. Time Out for Rhythm. Footsteps in the Dark. Dive Bomber. Ball of Fire. Go West, Young Lady. A Date with the Falcon. 1942: Maisie Gets Her Man (GB: She Got Her Man). The Falcon Takes Over. Tortilla Flat. Eyes in the Night. They All Kissed the Bride. 1943: Stage Door Canteen. 1945: Wonder Man. Lady on a Train. 1946: Singin' in the Corn (GB: Give and Take). The Dark House. Meet Me on Broadway. 1947: The Case of the Babysitter. Fun on a Week-End. Easy Come, Easy Go. Wild Harvest. The Senator Was Indiscreet (GB: Mr Ashton Was Indiscreet). The Hat Box Mystery. 1948: The Inside Story. 1949: The Big Wheel. 1950: Bodyhold. 1951: Let's Go Navy. Crazy over Horses. Behave Yourself! 1952: The WAC from Walla Walla (GB: Army Capers). Oklahoma Annie. 1957: Three Men on a Horse (remake. TV). 1959: Pillow Talk. Chained for Life. 1963: It's a Mad, Mad, Mad, Mad World. 1964: I'd Rather Be Rich. Robin and the Seven Hoods. For Those Who Think Young. 1966: The Spy in the Green Hat (TV. GB: cinemas). 1967: Doctor, You've Got to Be Kidding! 1971: Getting Away from It All (TV). 1974: The Front Page.

**JEWELL, Isabel 1909–1972**
Petite American platinum blonde actress who never quite made it as a star name after coming to Hollywood from Broadway success in 1932. Later played hard-bitten or world-weary dames before falling on hard times when acting roles dried up. There were several brushes with the law before her death 'from natural causes' at 62. Best remembered as Gloria Stone (who decides to stay in Shangri-La) in the 1937 Lost Horizon.

*1932: Blessed Event. 1933: Bombshell (GB: Blonde Bombshell). Bondage. Design for Living. Counsellor-at-Law. Day of Reckoning. Advice to the Lovelorn. The Women in His Life. 1934: Evelyn Prentice. She Had to Choose. Manhattan Melodrama. Here Comes the Groom. Let's Be Ritzy. 1935: Times Square Lady. Shadow of Doubt. Mad Love (GB: The Hands of Orlac). The Casino Murder Case. I've Been Around. A Tale of Two Cities. Ceiling Zero. 1936: The Leathernecks Have Landed (GB: The Marines Have Landed). Valiant is the Word for Carrie. Small Town Girl. Big Brown Eyes. The Man Who Lived Twice. Go West Young Man. Dancing Feet. Career Woman. Thirty-Six Hours to Kill.*

*1937: Marked Woman. Swing It, Sailor. Lost Horizon. 1938: The Crowd Roars. Love on Toast. 1939: They Asked for It. Missing Daughters. Gone With the Wind. 1940: Scatterbrain. Oh, Johnny, How You Can Love. Northwest Passage. Marked Men. Babies for Sale. Little Men. Irene. 1941: High Sierra. For Beauty's Sake. 1943: Danger - Women at Work! The Falcon and the Co-Eds. The Leopard Man. Calling Doctor Death. The Seventh Victim. 1944: The Merry Monaghans. 1945: Steppin' in Society. 1946: Sensation Hunters. Badman's Territory. 1947: Born to Kill (GB: Lady of Deceit). The Bishop's Wife. 1948: Michael O'Halloran. The Snake Pit. Unfaithfully Yours. Belle Starr's Daughter. 1949: The Story of Molly X. 1954: Drum Beat. The Man in the Attic. 1957: Bernadine.*

### JOHNS, Stratford 1925-

Portly South Africa-born actor with large, round face, small features and distinctive 'half head' of dark hair. He seemed destined to play sweaty, unsavoury minor characters until cast as a police inspector in British TV's *Z Cars*; this catapulted him to national stardom and led to another series, *Softly, Softly*, with Johns' character promoted to superintendent. After this was over, his bulky figure proved difficult to cast, but he has latterly won some interesting roles on stage.

*1955: The Ladykillers. The Night My Number Came Up. The Ship That Died of Shame (US: PT Raiders). Who Done It? 1956: The Long Arm (US: The Third Key).*

*Tiger in the Smoke. 1957: The One That Got Away. 1958: Law and Disorder. No Trees in the Street. 1960: The Professionals. Hand in Hand. 1961: The Naked Edge. The Valiant. 1962: Two-Letter Alibi. 1966: The Great St Trinian's Train Robbery. 1967: Jules Verne's Rocket to the Moon (US: Those Fantastic Flying Fools). The Plank. 1970: Cromwell. 1980: George and Mildred. The Fiendish Plot of Dr Fu Manchu. 1984: Dance with a Stranger. 1985: Wild Geese II. Hitler's SS: Portrait in Evil (TV. GB: cinemas). Car Trouble.*

### JOHNSON, Katie
(Katherine Johnson) 1878-1957

In her latter days seen almost entirely as sweet little old ladies, this British actress with the kindly, rather noble (prominent nose, narrow forehead) features slaved away at minor roles for almost her entire career until given the leading role of Mrs Wilberforce, the landlady who accidentally confounds a gang of robbers and would-be murderers in Ealing Studios' *The Ladykillers*. For it, she won a British Oscar as best actress, and a second plum role, in *How to Murder a Rich Uncle*: her last.

*1932: After Office Hours. 1933: Strictly in Confidence. 1934: A Glimpse of Paradise. 1936: Laburnum Grove. Dusty Ermine (US: Hideout in the Alps). 1937: Farewell Again (US: Troopship). The Last Adventurers. The*

*Dark Stairway. Sunset in Vienna (US: Suicide Legion). The Rat. 1938: Marigold. 1940: Two for Danger. 1941: The Black Sheep of Whitehall. Jeannie (US: Girl in Distress). Freedom Radio (US: A Voice in the Night). 1942: Talk about Jacqueline. 1944: He Snoops to Conquer. Tawny Pipit. 1946: The Years Between. The Shop at Sly Corner (US: The Code of Scotland Yard). Meet Me at Dawn. I See a Dark Stranger (US: The Adventuress). 1951: I Believe in You. Death of an Angel. 1952: Lady in the Fog (US: Scotland Yard Inspector). 1953: Three Steps in the Dark. The Large Rope. 1954: The Delavine Affair. The Rainbow Jacket. Out of the Clouds. 1955: John and Julie. The Ladykillers. 1956: How to Murder a Rich Uncle.*

### JOHNSON, Tor
(T. Johansson) 1903-1971

Massive, shaven-headed, outraged-looking Swedish ex-wrestler with pouched cheeks and deep-set eyes who brought his chilling and sometimes ghoulish appearance to occasional Hollywood films from 1934, many of them horror cheapies. Remembered especially as the police inspector turned into a zombie in the ghastly *Plan 9 from Outer Space*; as an actor, he was no Mike Mazurki (*qv*), but was nonetheless unmistakeable whenever he appeared. Died from a heart condition.

*1934: Kid Millions. 1935: Man on the Flying Trapeze (GB: The Memory Expert). 1936: Under Two Flags. 1943: Swing Out the Blues. 1944: The Canterville Ghost. Lost in a Harem. Ghost Catchers. 1945: Sudan. 1947: Road to Rio. 1948: State of the Union (GB: The World and His Wife). Behind Locked Doors. 1949: Alias the Champ. 1950: Abbott and Costello in the Foreign Legion. The Reformer and the Redhead. 1951: Dear Brat. The Lemon Drop Kid. 1952: The San Francisco Story. Lady in the Iron Mask. Houdini. 1954: Bride of the Monster. 1956: Carousel. The Black Sleep. 1957: The Unearthly. Journey to Freedom. 1958: Plan 9 from Outer Space. 1959: Night of the Ghouls (GB: Revenge of the Dead). 1961: The Beast of Yucca Flats.*

**JOHNSTON, Oliver 1888-1966**
Diffident, apologetic, small-faced, latterly white-haired British actor who, at the age when most people are thinking of slipping into retirement, started a busy film and televison career. By the age of 76, he had progressed to fourth billing, with a prime role in *The Tomb of Ligeia!*

*1938: Kate Plus Ten. Stolen Life. 1953: The Good Beginning. 1954: Dangerous Voyage (US: Terror Ship). A Tale of Three Women. 1955: Room in the House. You Can't Escape. 1956: The Girl in the Picture. Circus Friends. 1957: A King in New York. The Hypnotist (US: Scotland Yard Dragnet). 1958: Hello London. Son of Robin Hood. Indiscreet. 1959: Beyond This Place (US: Web of Evidence). A Touch of Larceny. Kidnapped. The Night We Dropped a Clanger (US: Make Mine a Double). 1961: Francis of Assisi. Raising the Wind. 1962: Dr Crippen. The Fast Lady. Backfire. 1963: Cleopatra. The Three Lives of Thomasina. Island of Love. 1964: The Tomb of Ligeia. 1965: You Must Be Joking! 1966: It (US: Return of the Golem). A Countess from Hong Kong.*

**JONES, Barry 1893-1981**
Bald British character actor, often seen looking harassed or dishevelled, who suddenly found himself in leading roles, and even making a run of films in Hollywood, after his eye-catching performance, at the age of 57, as the demented scientist in *Seven Days to Noon.* Born in Guernsey, he had a few mild leading roles in British films of the 1930s.

*1932: Women Who Play. Number Seventeen. Arms and the Man. 1936: The Gay Adventure. 1938: Murder in the Family. 1942: Squadron Leader X. 1947: Dancing with Crime. Frieda. 1948: The Calendar. Uneasy Terms. The Bad Lord Byron. 1949: That Dangerous Age (US: If This Be Sin). Madeleine. 1950: Seven Days to Noon. The Clouded Yellow. 1951: White Corridors. The Magic Box. Appointment With Venus (US: Island Rescue). 1952: Return to Paradise. Plymouth Adventure. 1954: Prince Valiant. Demetrius and the Gladiators. Brigadoon. The Glass Slipper. 1956: Alexander the Great. War and Peace. 1957: Saint Joan. The Safecracker. 1959: The 39 Steps. 1965: The Heroes of Telemark. A Study in Terror (US: Fog).*

**JONES, Freddie 1927-**
One of the few British character players to come to prominence in recent times, the crafty-looking Jones, with rolling eyes and wildly unruly (disappearing) hair, began life as a laboratory technician, but a belated drama scholarship set him on the path to an acting career. He quickly cornered the British market in twitching, volatile eccentrics and was the best 'monster' since Boris Karloff, in *Frankenstein Must Be Destroyed.* Won numerous awards for his performance as Claudius in the TV series *The Caesars.*

*1966: The Persecution and Assassination of Jean Paul Marat ... (The Marat/Sade). 1967: Accident. Far from the Madding Crowd. Deadfall. 1968: The Bliss of Mrs Blossom. Otley. 1969: Frankenstein Must Be Destroyed. 1970: The Man Who Haunted Himself. Doctor in Trouble. Goodbye Gemini. 1971: Kidnapped. Mr Horatio Knibbles. Antony and Cleopatra. 1972: Sitting Target. 1973: The Satanic Rites of Dracula (US: Dracula and His Vampire Bride). Gollocks! There's Plenty of Room in New Zealand. 1974: All Creatures Great and Small. In the Devil's Garden. Juggernaut. Vampira (US: Old Dracula). Romance with a Double-Bass. 1975: Appointment with a Killer (TV). Never Too Young To Rock. 1978: The Nativity (TV). 1979: Zulu Dawn. 1980: The Elephant Man. 1981: Murder Is Easy (TV). 1982: Captain Stirrick. Firefox. 1983: Krull.*

*E la nave va/And the Ship Sails On ... 1984: Firestarter. Dune. 1985: Young Sherlock Holmes. Eleanor, First Lady of the World (TV).*

**JONES, Henry 1912- 1999**
Short, roly-poly, round-faced American actor who can just as easily be meek or malevolent, henpecked or horrible. If ever an actor were born for the role of Mole in an adaptation of *The Wind in the Willows*, Henry Jones is surely that man. To date, he's had to be content with stealing scenes in a variety of colourful roles.

*1943: This Is the Army. 1951: The Lady Says No! 1956: The Bad Seed. The Girl He Left Behind. The Girl Can't Help It. 1957: Will Success Spoil Rock Hunter? (GB: Oh! For a Man!). 3:10 to Yuma. The Mystery of 13 (TV). 1958: Vertigo. 1959: The Sounds of Eden (TV). 1960: Cash McCall. The Bramble Bush. Angel Baby. 1965: Never Too Late. 1966: Le scandale/The Champagne Murders. 1967: Project X. 1968: Support Your Local Sheriff. Stay Away Joe. 1969: Butch Cassidy and the Sundance Kid. The Cockeyed Cowboys of Calico Country (GB: TV as A Woman for Charlie). Rascal. Angel in My Pocket. 1970: Rabbit Run. The Movie Murderer (TV). Love Hate Love (TV). Dirty Dingus Magee. 1971: The Skin Game. Support Your Local Gunfighter. 1972: The Daughters of Joshua Cabe (TV). The Letters (TV). Pete 'n' Tillie. 1973: Tom Sawyer. The Outfit. Shootout in a One-Dog Town (TV). Letters from Three Lovers (TV). 1974: Roll, Freddy, Roll (TV). 1975: Please Call It Murder (TV). Who Is the Black Dahlia? (TV). 1980: 9 to 5. California Gold Rush (TV). 1982: Deathtrap.*

**JONES, L. Q.**
(Justus McQueen) 1927-
Tall, fair-haired American actor with lived-in face and coat-hanger shoulders, a former horse- and cattle-rancher brought to Hollywood in 1954; he took his screen name from the character he played in his first film. In later years also made forays into production and direction. His powerful, rangy figure was generally seen as an assortment of hardened and/or unkempt westerners.

1954: Battle Cry. 1955: Target Zero. Annapolis Story (GB: The Blue and the Gold). 1956: Santiago (GB: The Gun Runner). Toward the Unknown (GB: Brink of Hell). Between Heaven and Hell. Love Me Tender. 1957: Men in War. Operation Mad Ball. 1958: Border Showdown (TV. GB: cinemas). The Young Lions. Mountain Fortress (TV. GB: cinemas). The Naked and the Dead. Buchanan Rides Alone. Julesberg (TV. GB: cinemas). Torpedo Run. 1959: Warlock. Hound Dog Man. Battle of the Coral Sea. 1960: Ten Who Dared. Cimarron. Flaming Star. 1961: Ride the High Country (GB: Guns in the Afternoon). 1962: The Deadly Companions. Hell Is for Heroes! 1963: Showdown. The Lady Is My Wife (TV). 1964: Apache Rifles. Major Dundee. Iron Angel. 1966: Noon Wine (TV). 1967: Hang 'em High. 1968: The Counterfeit Killer (TV. GB: cinemas). Stay Away Joe. 1969: The Wild Bunch. 1970: The Ballad of Cable Hogue. The McMasters...tougher than the west itself! The Brotherhood of Satan. 1971: The Hunting Party. 1972: Fireball Forward (TV). The Bravos (TV). 1973: Pat Garrett and Billy the Kid. The Petty Story/73: The Petty Story/Smash-Up Alley (TV. GB: cinemas). 1974: Mrs Sundance (TV). Manhunter (TV). Mother, Jugs and Speed (released 1976). The Strange and Deadly Occurrence (TV). 1975: White Line Fever. Winterhawk. Attack on Terror: The FBI Versus the Ku Klux Klan (TV). Winner Take All (TV). 1976: Banjo Hackett – Roamin' Free (TV). 1978: Fast Charlie. The Moonbeam Rider. Standing Tall (TV). 1979: The Sacketts (TV). 1982: The Beast Within. Timerider – The Adventure of Lyle Swann. Melanie. Sacred Ground. 1983: Lone Wolf McQuade.

**As director:**
1974: A Boy and His Dog.

## JONES, Peter 1920–

Tall, often bespectacled, brown-haired British actor and playwright. In his comedy cameos for films, his liquidly cultivated tones have specialized in men from the ministry, civil servants and any bumblers subject to benevolent bewilderment. Also a radio and television panel game whiz. The

Peter Jones in *Vice Versa* (1947) and *The Blue Lagoon* (1948) is a child player.

1944: Fanny by Gaslight (US: Man of Evil). 1945: Dead of Night. 1946: I See a Dark Stranger (US: The Adventuress). 1950: Chance of a Lifetime. The Franchise Affair. 1951: Home to Danger. The Magic Box. The Browning Version. 1952: Miss Robin Hood. Time Gentlemen Please! 24 Hours of a Woman's Life (US: Affair in Monte Carlo). Angels One Five. Elstree Story. The Yellow Balloon. The Long Memory. 1953: Albert RN (US: Break to Freedom). Always a Bride. Innocents in Paris. The Good Beginning. A Day to Remember. 1954: The Red Dress. For Better, For Worse (US: Cocktails in the Kitchen). 1955: John and Julie. 1956: Private's Progress. Charley Moon. 1957: Blue Murder at St Trinian's. 1958: Danger Within (US: Breakout). 1959: Operation Bullshine. 1960: Never Let Go. The Bulldog Breed. School for Scoundrels. 1961: Nearly a Nasty Accident. Romanoff and Juliet. 1963: A Stitch in Time. Father Came Too. 1966: Press for Time. Just Like a Woman. 1967: Smashing Time. 1968: Hot Millions. Carry on Doctor. 1974: The Return of the Pink Panther. 1976: Carry on England. 1977: *Marcia.

## JOSLYN, Allyn 1901–1981

Light-haired, moustachioed, pawky American actor with distinctive grey-green eyes. His round, indiarubber features could express handsomeness, prissiness, or pompousness, as the role required, but rather too often he was slated to play the suitor who was only in the film as a chopping-block for the hero. His sharply distinctive voice was also heard in thousands of radio programmes over a period of 40 years. Died from cardiac failure.

1937: They Won't Forget. Expensive Husbands. Hollywood Hotel. 1938: The Shining Hour. Sweethearts. 1939: Café Society. Only Angels Have Wings. Fast and Furious. 1940: If I Had My Way. The Great McGinty (GB: Down Went McGinty). Spring Parade. No Time for Comedy. 1941: This Thing Called Love. Bedtime Story. Hot Spot (GB: I Wake Up Screaming). 1942: The Wife Takes a Flyer (GB: A Yank in Dutch). My Sister Eileen. The Affairs of Martha (GB: Once

Upon a Thursday). 1943: Young Ideas. The Immortal Sergeant. Heaven Can Wait. Dangerous Blondes. 1944: Bride by Mistake. Sweet and Low Down. The Imposter. Strange Affair. 1945: The Horn Blows at Midnight. Junior Miss. Colonel Effingham's Raid (GB: Man of the Hour). 1946: It Shouldn't Happen to a Dog. Thrill of Brazil. The Shocking Miss Pilgrim. 1948: If You Knew Susie. Moonrise. 1949: The Lady Takes a Sailor. 1950: Harriet Craig. 1951: As Young As You Feel. 1953: Island in the Sky. Titanic. I Love Melvin. The Jazz Singer. 1956: The Fastest Gun Alive. You Can't Run Away from It. 1957: Public Pigeon No. One. 1963: Nightmare in the Sun. 1972: The Brothers O'Toole.

## JOYCE, Yootha 1927–1980

Toothy blonde British actress with raucous tones and predatory look. She contributed a number of acerbic cameos, both nasty and nice, to British films of the 1960s, usually as working-class women with pretensions. Soon, though, she became a comedy star in the Peggy Mount tradition with her creation of an amorous ogress called Mildred on British television. At one time married (divorced 1968) to actor Glynn Edwards (q.v.). Died from cirrhosis of the liver.

1962: Sparrows Can't Sing. 1963: A Place to Go. 1964: Fanatic (US: Die, Die, My Darling). The Pumpkin Eater. 1965: Catch Us If You Can (US: Having a Wild Weekend). 1966: Kaleidoscope. A Man for All Seasons. 1967: Our Mother's House. Stranger in the House (US: Cop-Out). Charlie Bubbles. 1968: *Twenty Nine. 1969: All the Right Noises. 1970: Fragment of Fear. 1971: Burke and Hare. The Night Digger. 1972: Nearest and Dearest. Never Mind the Quality, Feel the Width. 1973: Frankenstein: the True Story (TV. GB: cinemas in abbreviated version). Steptoe and Son Ride Again. 1974: Man About The House. 1980: George and Mildred.

## JUNKIN, John 1930–

Dark-haired, balding British writer and comic actor, with thick London accent and 'ordinary bloke' looks. He began his career as a schoolteacher until scriptwriting took over his life and gradually led him into

ABOVE Allyn **Joslyn** (right) and Wendell Corey in the 1950 film *Harriet Craig*

LEFT Yootha **Joyce** adopts a typically trenchant pose in the feature film version, made in 1974, of the successful television comedy series, *Man About the House*

acting, at first with Joan Littlewood's Theatre Workshop. Subsequently he wrote hundreds of comedy scripts for TV and had his own series as well. Film appearances usually minor cameos. In private life a great Scrabble enthusiast.

*1962: Sparrows Can't Sing. The Wrong Arm of the Law. The Break. Vengeance (US: The Brain). 1963: The Primitives. Hot Enough for June (Agent 8¾). 1964: A Hard Day's Night. The Pumpkin Eater. 1966: The Wrong Box. The Sandwich Man. Kaleidoscope. 1967: The Plank. How I Won the War. 1970: \*Simon, Simon. 1976: Confessions of a Driving Instructor. 1977: Confessions from a Holiday Camp. \*Marcia. 1978: Rosie Dixon Night Nurse. Brass Target. 1979: That Summer! Licensed to Love and Kill.*

**JUSTICE, James Robertson**
**1905-1975**
Glowering, red-bearded, large Scottish actor who was a naturalist and journalist before turning full-time actor in the 1940s and quickly becoming an essential part of the British cinema scene. He made several figures of history, including Henry VIII, larger than life, enlivening dozens of films before his retirement in 1970 - but never more so than as the irascible Sir Lancelot Spratt in the 'Doctor' comedies.

*1944: †Champagne Charlie. †Fiddlers Three. †For Those in Peril. 1946: †Hungry Hill. †Appointment With Crime. 1947: Vice Versa. My Brother Jonathan. 1948: Against the Wind. Quartet. Scott of the Antarctic. Whisky Galore! (US: Tight Little Island). 1949: Christopher Columbus. Stop Press Girl. Poet's Pub. Private Angelo. 1950: Prelude to Fame. My Daughter Joy (US: Operation X). ‡The Magnet. The Black Rose. Blackmailed. 1951: Pool of London. David and Bathsheba. Anne of the Indies. The Lady Says No! Captain Horatio Hornblower RN. Circle of Danger. 1952: The Story of Robin Hood and His Merrie Men. Miss Robin Hood. The Voice of Merrill (US: Murder Will Out). Les Miserables. 1953: The Sword and the Rose. Rob Roy the Highland Rogue. 1954: Doctor in the House. 1955: Out of the Clouds. \*Challenge of the North (narrator only). Above Us the Waves. Doctor at Sea. Land of the Pharaohs. An Alligator Named*

*Daisy. Storm Over the Nile. 1956: The Living Idol. The Iron Petticoat. Moby Dick. Checkpoint. 1957: Doctor at Large. Souvenir d'Italie/It Happened in Rome. Seven Thunders (US: The Beasts of Marseilles). Campbell's Kingdom. Thérèse Etienne. 1958: Orders to Kill. The Revenge of Frankenstein. 1959: Upstairs and Downstairs. 1960: Doctor in Love. Die Botschafterin. A French Mistress. Foxhole in Cairo. 1961: Very Important Person. The Guns of Navarone. Murder She Said. Raising the Wind (US: Roommates). 1962: A Pair of Briefs. Crooks Anonymous. Guns of Darkness. Dr Crippen. Le repos du guerrier (GB: Warrior's Rest). Mystery Submarine. The Fast Lady. 1963: Father Came Too. Das Feuerschiff. Doctor in Distress. Hell Is Empty (released 1967). 1965: You Must Be Joking! The Face of Fu Manchu. Up from the Beach. Those Magnificent Men in Their Flying Machines (narrator only). 1966: Doctor in Clover. 1967: The Trygon Factor. Two Weeks in September. Histoires extraordinares (GB: Tales of Mystery). Lange Beine, lange Finger. 1968: Chitty Chitty Bang Bang. Mayerling. 1969: Zeta One. 1970: Some Will, Some Won't. Doctor in Trouble.*

†As James Robertson
‡As Seamus Mor Na Feasag

**K**

**KAHN, Madeline** 1942- *1999*
Big-chinned, purse-lipped American comic actress with copper-coloured hair and a unique way of chewing round a line before

spitting it out. She was popular for a while in escapist satires of the 1970s, notably those of Mel Brooks. Trained as an opera singer and started her career in the chorus of *Kiss Me Kate* on stage in the mid-1960s. In 1983 she started her own television show. Nominated for best supporting actress Oscars in *Paper Moon* and *Blazing Saddles*.

*1968: \*The Dove. 1972: What's Up, Doc? 1973: Paper Moon. From the Mixed-Up Files of Mrs Basil E Frankweiler (GB: The Hideaways). 1974: Blazing Saddles. Young Frankenstein. 1975: At Long Last Love. Won Ton Ton, the Dog Who Saved Hollywood. The Adventure of Sherlock Holmes' Smarter Brother. 1977: High Anxiety. 1978: The Cheap Detective. 1979: The Muppet Movie. Simon. 1980: Happy Birthday, Gemini. Wholly Moses! First Family (GB: TV). 1981: History of the World Part I. 1982: Slapstick (US: Slapstick of Another Kind). 1983: Yellowbeard. 1985: Clue.*

**KARLIN, Miriam**
**(M. Samuels) 1925-**
Thin, plain-looking, corncrake-voiced British actress with dark hair, wide smile and strong personality. She started her career entertaining wartime troops in ENSA shows, then brought her talents to stage revue, films and television, where she became a nationally known figure as the militant shop steward in *The Rag Trade* comedy series. Films never really made the most of her, and she later toured in one-woman shows.

*1952: Down Among the Z Men. 1955: The Deep Blue Sea. The Woman for Joe. Fun at St Fanny's. 1956: A Touch of the Sun. 1958: Room at the Top. 1960: The Millionairess. The Entertainer. Hand in Hand. Crossroads to Crime. 1961: On the Fiddle (US: Operation Snafu). 1962: The Phantom of the Opera. I Thank a Fool. 1963: The Small World of Sammy Lee. Heavens Above! Ladies Who Do. 1964: The Bargee. 1971: A Clockwork Orange. 1975: Barry Lyndon. Mahler. Dick Deadeye (voice only).*

**KARNS, Roscoe** 1893-1970
Red-haired light relief of dozens of Hollywood films of the 1930s and 1940s - a sort

of straighter Red Skelton. Of Irish heritage, Karns took to the stage at 15, coming to films in silent days to play characters who looked on the brighter side of life. Sometimes he was a sidekick of the hero, at others a fast-talking reporter. He left films in the post-war years, working steadily in television until 1961. His son, Todd Karns (Roscoe Karns Jr), much more ruggedly handsome than his father, also appeared in pictures.

*1913: A Western Governor's Humanity. 1920: The Life of the Party. 1921: The Man Turner. Too Much Married. 1922: Conquering the Woman. Her Own Money. Afraid to Fight. The Trooper. 1923: Other Men's Daughters. 1924: Bluff. The Midnight Express. The Foolish Virgin. 1925: Dollar Down. Headlines. Overland Limited. 1926: Ritzy. 1927: Ten Modern Commandments. The Jazz Singer. 1928: Beggars of Life. Jazz Mad. Beau Sabreur. Object - Alimony. Win That Girl. Warming Up. The Desert Bride. Moran of the Marines. Something Always Happens. 1929: This Thing Called Love. New York Nights. Shopworn Angel. 1930: Man Trouble. Troopers Three. Safety in Numbers. The Costello Case (GB: The Costello Murder Case). Little Accident. Lights of New York. 1931. Laughing Sinners. Leftover Ladies (GB: Broken Links). The Gorilla. Dirigible. Many a Slip. 1932: Ladies of the Big House. Pleasure. Rockabye. Week-End Marriage (GB: Working Wives). Lawyer Man. Night After Night. I Am a Fugitive from a Chain Gang. Two against the World. Roadhouse Murder. The Crooked Circle. One Way Passage. If I Had a Million. Undercover Man. The Stowaway. 1933: One Sunday Afternoon. Today We Live. Gambling Ship. Alice in Wonderland. A Lady's Profession. 20,000 Years in Sing Sing. 1934: Come on, Marines. Search for Beauty. Shoot the Works. Elmer and Elsie. I Sell Anything. Twentieth Century. It Happened One Night. The Women in His Life. 1935: Red Hot Tires (GB: Racing Luck). Two-Fisted. Stolen Harmony. Four Hours to Kill. Wings in the Dark. Alibi Ike. Front Page Woman. 1936: Border Flight. Woman Trap. Three Cheers for Love. Three Married Men. Cain and Mabel. 1937: Murder Goes to College. Clarence. A Night of Mystery. On Such*

*a Night. Partners in Crime. 1938: Tip-Off Girls. You and Me. Scandal Street. Dangerous to Know. Thanks for the Memory. 1939: Everything's On Ice. That's Right - You're Wrong. King of Chinatown. Dancing Co-Ed (GB: Every Other Inch a Lady). 1940: Double Alibi. His Girl Friday. Ladies Must Live. Saturday's Children. Meet the Missus. They Drive by Night (GB: The Road to Frisco). 1941: Footsteps in the Dark. Petticoat Politics. The Gay Vagabond. Woman of the Year. 1942: The Road to Happiness. A Tragedy at Midnight. Yokel Boy (GB: Hitting the Headlines). You Can't Escape Forever. 1943: His Butler's Sister. Stage Door Canteen. Old Acquaintance. My Son, the Hero. 1944: The Navy Way. Minstrel Man. Hi, Good Lookin'. 1945: I Ring Doorbells. One Way to Love. 1946: The Kid from Brooklyn. It's a Wonderful Life! Avalanche. Down Missouri Way. 1947: That's My Man. Vigilantes of Boomtown. Will Tomorrow Ever Come? 1948: Texas, Brooklyn and Heaven (GB: The Girl from Texas). The Devil's Cargo. The Inside Story. Speed to Spare. 1958: Onionhead. 1963: Man's Favorite Sport?*

**KASKET, Harold** 1916-

Chubby British actor with thick black moustache, plus hair and horn-rimmed glasses to match. Originally a comedy impressionist, he came to British films in post-war years and was almost always seen as unctuous foreigners, rubbing their hands, beaming an oily beam, and giving out with such familiar lines as 'You like the English girl, sir? She weel be on again after the next show!' Busy in films until 1961, but much more often seen on TV from then on.

*1948: No Orchids for Miss Blandish. 1949: Children of Chance. 1951: Hotel Sahara. 1952: Made in Heaven. 1953: Moulin Rouge. Saadia. The House of the Arrow. 1954: Up to His Neck. One Good Turn. Beau Brummell. Out of the Clouds. 1955: The Dark Avenger (US: The Warriors). Doctor at Sea. Born for Trouble. Dust and Gold. Man of the Moment. 1956: Bhowani Junction. 1957: Interpol (US: Pickup Alley). The Key Man. Naked Earth. 1958: Life Is a Circus. The Lady Is a Square. Wonderful Things! The*

*Scapegoat. 1959: The Navy Lark. SOS Pacific. Whirlpool. The Mouse That Roared. The Heart of a Man. Tommy the Toreador. 1960: Sands of the Desert. 1961: The Roman Spring of Mrs Stone. The Boy Who Stole a Million. The Green Helmet. A Weekend with Lulu. The Greengage Summer (US: Loss of Innocence). Village of Daughters. The Fourth Square. 1965: The Return of Mr Moto. 1966: Arabesque. 1969: Where's Jack? 1982: Trail of the Pink Panther. 1983: Curse of the Pink Panther.*

**KASZNAR, Kurt**

(K. Serwischer) 1912-1979

Plumpish, flat-faced Austrian-born actor with strikingly dark hair and eyes, around on the Hollywood (mostly M-G-M) scene quite a bit in the 1950s, following long stage experience in Europe and (from 1936) America. He ambled amiably through a succession of sub-S. Z. Sakall (qv) roles in musicals, comedies and adventures, providing some attractively fractured English. Married/divorced actress Leora Dana, second of two. Made film debut as a child. Died from cancer.

*1920: Max, King of the Circus. 1951: The Light Touch. 1952: Glory Alley. The Happy Time. Anything Can Happen. Lovely to Look At. Talk about a Stranger. 1953: Give a Girl a Break. Sombrero. Ride, Vaquero! Lili. All the Brothers Were Valiant. The Great Diamond Robbery. Kiss Me Kate. 1954: Valley of the Kings. The Last Time I Saw Paris. 1955: Jump Into Hell. My Sister Eileen. Flame of the Islands. 1956: Fanny. Anything Goes. 1957: Legend of the Lost. The Customs of the Country (TV). A Farewell to Arms. 1958: The Journey. The Bridge of San Luis Rey (TV). 1959: For the First Time. Thieves' Carnival (TV). 1960: Volpone (TV). 1961: Waiting for Godot (TV). 1962: Helden (US: Arms and the Man). 55 Days at Peking. 1963: The Thrill of It All. 1967: Code Name: Heraclitus (TV). Casino Royale. The Perils of Pauline. The Ambushers. The King's Pirate. 1968: The Smugglers (TV). 1971: Once Upon a Dead Man (TV). 1972: The Female Instinct (TV. GB: The Snoop Sisters). 1978: Suddenly, Love.*

**KATCH, Kurt** (Isser Kac) 1896-1958
This Polish-born actor was a shaven-headed gremlin who was handy to have around in evil-cohort roles of Hollywood's wartime years, following his flight from the Nazis in 1937. His little eyes plotted all kinds of dire deeds then, but he found film work hard to get in the post-war years. His career picked up a bit in the 1950s, but at 62 he died during an operation for cancer.

*1938: Tkies Khaf/The Vow. 1941: Man at Large. The Wolf-Man. 1942: Counter Espionage. They Came to Blow Up America. Secret Agent of Japan. The Wife Takes a Flyer. Quiet Please, Murder. Berlin Correspondent. Edge of Darkness. 1943: Mission to Moscow. Background to Danger. Watch on the Rhine. Ali Baba and the 40 Thieves. The Purple V. 1944: Make Your Own Bed. The Conspirators. The Purple Heart. The Mask of Dimitrios. The Seventh Cross. The Mummy's Curse. 1945: Salome, Where She Danced. 1946: Angel on My Shoulder. Rendezvous 24. 1947: Strange Journey. Song of Love. 1954: Secret of the Incas. The Adventures of Hajji Baba. 1955: Abbott and Costello Meet the Keystone Kops. Abbott and Costello Meet the Mummy. 1956: Hot Cars. 1957: The Girl in the Kremlin. The Beast of Budapest. The Pharaoh's Curse. 1958: The Young Lions.*

**KAYE, Stubby** 1918-1997
Roly-poly American comedian, singer, actor and entertainer with easy-going personality, in vaudeville after winning a talent contest at 21, and in the theatre from 1950 when he created Nicely-Nicely Johnson in *Guys and Dolls*, a role he would later repeat for his screen musical debut. His hit song from that show, *Sit Down You're Rockin' the Boat*, remains his best-remembered number, but the cinema has made only infrequent use of his throaty-voiced talents. His is one of the few 'real names' I haven't been able to pin down, but it is assuredly neither Stubby nor Kaye.

*1953: Taxi. 1955: Guys and Dolls. 1956: You Can't Run Away from It. 1962: 40 Pounds of Trouble. 1963: The Cool Mikado. 1964: Sex and the Single Girl. 1965: Cat Ballou. 1967: The Way West. 1968: Sweet Charity. Can Hieronymus Merkin Ever Forget Mercy Humppe and Find True Happiness? 1969: The Cockeyed Cowboys of Calico County (GB: TV, as A Woman for Charlie). 1970: Cool It Carol! 1973: The Dirtiest Girl I Ever Met. 1975: Six Pack Annie. 1981: Goldie and the Boxer Go Hollywood (TV).*

**KEEN, Geoffrey** 1918-
Adaptable, tetchy-looking British player with receding dark hair and cultured, deliberate speech guaranteed to annoy subordinates of the characters he played. At first in helpful roles, but later as grouchy bosses - would have made a good 'M' in the Bond films if Bernard Lee (*qv*) hadn't got the job first, and indeed eventually assumed Lee's mantle after his death. Son of distinguished stage player Malcolm Keen (1887-1970), who also played some film roles.

*1946: Riders of the New Forest. Odd Man Out. 1948: The Fallen Idol. The Small Back Room (US: Hour of Glory). It's Hard to be Good. 1949: The Third Man. *Call-Up. 1950: Treasure Island. Seven Days to Noon. The Clouded Yellow. 1951: Chance of a Lifetime. Cheer the Brave. High Treason. Green Grow the Rushes. His Excellency. Cry the Beloved Country (US: African Fury). 1952: Hunted (US: The Stranger in Between). Lady in the Fog (US: Scotland Yard Inspector). Angels One Five. The Long Memory. 1953: Rob Roy the Highland Rogue. Malta Story. Genevieve. Turn the Key Softly. 1954: Face the Music (US: The Black Glove). The 'Maggie' (US: High and Dry). Doctor in the House. The Divided Heart. Carrington VC (US: Court-Martial). 1955: Passage Home. Doctor at Sea. The Glass Cage (US: The Glass Tomb). Portrait of Alison (US: Postmark for Danger). Storm Over the Nile. The Man Who Never Was. 1956: A Town Like Alice. The Long Arm (US: The Third Key). House of Secrets (US: Triple Deception). Yield to the Night (US: Blonde Sinner). Loser Takes All. Zarak. The Spanish Gardener. Sailor Beware! (US: Panic in the Parlor). Town on Trial! Fortune Is a Woman (US: She Played with Fire). 1957: The Scamp. The Birthday Present. Doctor at Large. The Secret Place. 1958: Nowhere to Go. The Scapegoat. 1959: Horrors of the Black Museum. Beyond This Place (US: Web of Evidence). Devil's Bait. The Boy and the Bridge. Deadly Record. 1960: *The Dover Road Mystery. Sink the Bismarck! The Angry Silence. 1961: No Love for Johnnie. Spare the Rod. *The Silent Weapon. The Malpas Mystery. Raising the Wind (US: Roommates). 1962: The Spiral Road. Live Now - Pay Later. A Matter of WHO. The Inspector (US: Lisa). The Prince and the Pauper. The Mind Benders. Torpedo Bay/Finche dura la tempesta. 1963: The Cracksman. Return to Sender. Dr Syn Alias the Scarecrow. 1965: Doctor Zhivago. The Heroes of Telemark. 1966: Born Free. 1967: Berserk! 1968: Thunderbird 6 (voice only). 1970: Cromwell. Taste the Blood of Dracula. 1971: Sacco and Vanzetti. 1972: Living Free. Doomwatch. 1974: QB VII (TV). 1977: The Spy Who Loved Me. Holocaust 2000 (US: The Chosen). No. 1 of the Secret Service. 1979: Licensed to Love and Kill. Moonraker. 1980: The Rise and Fall of Idi Amin. 1981: For Your Eyes Only. 1983: Octopussy. 1985: A View to a Kill.*

**KEIR, Andrew** 1926-
Big, bluff, often bearded Scottish actor whose early films included whimsical comedies but who, from the late 1950s on, both in the cinema and TV, was almost always seen as towers of strength. Seemingly a certainty for the role of Little John in Robin Hood, he somehow managed to steer clear of it, but there were an awful lot of costume dramas as professional soldiers and the like, plus success in a couple of television series in the 1970s.

1950: The Lady Craved Excitement. 1952: The Brave Don't Cry. Laxdale Hall (US: Scotch on the Rocks). 1954: The 'Maggie' (US: High and Dry). 1956: Suspended Alibi. 1958: Heart of a Child. A Night To Remember. Tread Softly Stranger. 1960: The Day They Robbed the Bank of England. 1961: The Pirates of Blood River. 1962: Torpedo Bay/Finche dura la tempesta. 1963: The Fall of the Roman Empire. Cleopatra. The Devil-Ship Pirates. 1964: Lord Jim. 1966: Dracula Prince of Darkness. Daleks Invasion Earth 2150 AD. The Fighting Prince of Donegal. 1967: The Long Duel. The Viking Queen. Quatermass and the Pit (US: Five Million Miles to Earth). Attack on the Iron Coast. 1969: The Royal Hunt of the Sun. 1970: The Last Grenade. 1971: Zeppelin. Blood from the Mummy's Tomb. The Night Visitor. Mary Queen of Scots. 1973: Catholics (TV). 1978: Meetings with Remarkable Men. The Thirty-Nine Steps. 1980: Lion of the Desert. 1984: Haunters of the Deep.

### KEITH, Robert 1896-1966

Worried-looking, darting-eyed, skull-faced American supporting actor with receding brown hair. He began his career as a singer, then took up straight acting roles; but this main occupation in pre-war years was writing, penning the occasional play in between working as a dialogue writer for Universal and Columbia Studios. In post-war years, he made quick strides towards the top of cast lists, often in tense, nervous roles. Father of film star Brian Keith.

1924: The Other Kind of Love. 1930: Just Imagine. 1931: Bad Company. 1939: Spirit of Culver (GB: Man's Heritage). 1947: Boomerang! Kiss of Death. 1949: My Foolish Heart. 1950: Edge of Doom (GB: Stronger Than Fear). Woman on the Run. Branded. The Reformer and the Redhead. 1951: Fourteen Hours. Here Comes the Groom. I Want You. 1952: Just Across the Street. Somebody Loves Me. 1953: Battle Circus. The Wild One. Small Town Girl. Devil's Canyon. 1954: Drum Beat. Young at Heart. 1955: Underwater! Guys and Dolls. Love Me or Leave Me. 1956: Ransom! Written on the Wind. Between Heaven and Hell. 1957: Men in War. My Man Godfrey. 1958: The Lineup. Tempest.

1959: They Came to Cordura. 1960: Cimarron. 1961: Posse from Hell. Duel of Champions.

### KELLAWAY, Cecil 1891-1973

Jolly, round-faced, plump-cheeked Hollywood actor with silvery hair. Although born in South Africa, initiating his acting career in Australia and not all that short of stature, he soon became Hollywood's favourite leprechaun. His characters were often wise, sometimes mischievous (notably as the centuries-old warlock in I Married a Witch) and occasionally magic. Went on acting until illness forced his retirement in 1970. Oscar nominee for The Luck of the Irish.

1933: The Hayseeds. 1936: It Isn't Done. 1938: Mr Chedworth Steps Out. Double Danger. Everybody's Doing It. Annabel Takes a Tour. Law of the Underworld. This Marriage Business. Maid's Night Out. Night Spot. Wise Girl. Blonde Cheat. Tarnished Angel. 1939: We Are Not Alone. The Sun Never Sets. Intermezzo (GB: Escape to Happiness). Wuthering Heights. Gunga Din. Mexican Spitfire. The Under-Pup. 1940: The Invisible Man Returns. Adventure in Diamonds. Phantom Raiders. Brother Orchid. The Mummy's Hand. The House of the Seven Gables. Mexican Spitfire Out West. The Letter. South of Suez. Diamond Frontier. The Lady With Red Hair. 1941: West Point Widow. The Night of January 16th. A Very Young Lady. Birth of the Blues. New York Town. Burma Convoy. Small Town Deb. Bahama Passage. Appointment for Love. 1942: The Lady Has Plans. Take a Letter, Darling (GB: The Green-Eyed Woman). I Married a Witch. Are Husbands Necessary? Star-Spangled Rhythm. My Heart Belongs to Daddy. Night in New Orleans. 1943: The Crystal Ball. Forever and a Day. It Ain't Hay (GB: Money for Jam). The Good Fellows. 1944: Frenchman's Creek. Mrs Parkington. And Now Tomorrow. Practically Yours. 1945: Bring on the Girls. Love Letters. Kitty. 1946: Monsieur Beaucaire. The Cock-eyed Miracle (GB: Mr Griggs Returns). The Postman Always Rings Twice. Easy to Wed. 1947: Unconquered. Variety Girl. Always Together. 1948: The Decision of Christopher Blake. The Luck of the Irish. Joan of Arc. Portrait of Jennie (GB: Jennie). 1949: Down

to the Sea in Ships. 1950: The Reformer and the Redhead. Kim. 1951: Harvey. Half Angel. Francis Goes to the Races. Katie Did It. Thunder in the East. 1952: Just Across the Street. My Wife's Best Friend. 1953: Young Bess. Cruisin' Down the River. The Beast from 20,000 Fathoms. Paris Model. Hurricane at Pilgrim Hill. 1955: Interrupted Melody. Female on the Beach. The Prodigal. 1956: Toy Tiger. 1957: Johnny Trouble. 1958: The Proud Rebel. Verdict of Three (TV). 1959: The Shaggy Dog. 1960: The Private Lives of Adam and Eve. Cage of Evil. 1961: Tammy Tell Me True. Francis of Assisi. 1962: Zotz! 1963: The Cardinal. 1964: Hush ... Hush, Sweet Charlotte. The Confession (GB: TV, as Quick! Let's Get Married). 1965: The Adventures of Bullwhip Griffin. 1966: Spinout (GB: California Holiday). 1967: Fitzwilly (GB: Fitzwilly Strikes Back). Guess Who's Coming to Dinner. 1968: A Garden of Cucumbers. 1970: The Wacky Zoo of Morgan City (TV). Getting Straight.

### KELLEY, Barry 1908-

Expansive (6 ft 2 in; 230 lb), brown-haired, deep-voiced American actor, an ace at corrupt figures in high places. Born in Chicago of Irish parents, he made his theatrical debut in 1930 and remained in that medium until 1947, when brought to Hollywood by director Elia Kazan for a role in Boomerang! Subsequently stayed to play grafters, judges and tough policemen until his early retirement in 1968.

1947: Boomerang! 1948: Force of Evil. 1949: Mr Belvedere Goes to College. Red, Hot and Blue. Fighting Man of the Plains. Too Late for Tears. Knock on Any Door. The Undercover Man. Johnny Stool Pigeon. Thelma Jordon (GB: The File on Thelma Jordon). Ma and Pa Kettle. 1950: The Killer That Stalked New York (GB: The Frightened City). The Asphalt Jungle. 711 Ocean Drive. Southside 1-1000 (GB: Forgery). Love That Brute. The Captive. Black Hand. Wabash Avenue. Right Cross. The Great Missouri Raid. Singing Guns. 1951: Flying Leathernecks. Francis Goes to the Races. 1952: Carrie. The Well. Back at the Front (GB: Willie and Joe in Tokyo). 1953: Law and Order. Remains to be Seen. South Sea Woman. 1954: The Shanghai Story. The Long Wait. 1955: Women's Prison. New York Confidential. 1956: Accused of Murder. 1957: The Wings of Eagles. Monkey on My Back. Gunfire at Indian Gap. 1958: The Buccaneer. The Tall Stranger. Buchanan Rides Alone. 1960: The Police Dog Story. 1961: Secret of Deep Harbor. The Clown and the Kid. Jack the Giant Killer. 1962: The Manchurian Candidate. 1964: Rio Conchos. 1968: The Extraordinary Seaman. The Love Bug.

### KELLY, Patsy (Sarah Kelly) 1910-1981

Dynamic little dark-haired, plump-jowled American actress who forsook a career as a dancing teacher to come to Hollywood as star comedienne in two-reelers, and play

ABOVE Judge Barry **Kelley** (in bow-tie) presides, while John Derek sits in the dock and Humphrey Bogart addresses the jury. George Macready (*qv*, left) can obviously see the funny side. From *Knock on Any Door* (1949)

BELOW A little unusual accompaniment from Patsy **Kelly** (left) to Frances Langford's number in *Hit Parade of 1941* (1940)

supporting roles in features, often as wisecracking maids, or gutsy, lower-class girlfriends. She left show business in the wartime years, but returned in 1960 for some welcome cameo roles. Died from cancer. Never married.

*1929: A Single Man. 1931: *Unidentified short. 1933: Going Hollywood. *Beauty and the Bus. *Air Fright. *Backs to Nature. 1934: *Maid in Hollywood. The Countess of Monte Cristo. Party's Over. *Babes in the Goods. *I'll Be Suing You. The Girl from Missouri (GB: 100 Per Cent Pure). *Three Chumps Ahead. Transatlantic Merry-Go-Round. *Opened by Mistake. *One Horse Farmers. *Done in Oil. *Bum Voyage (GB: Bon Voyage). 1935: *Treasure Blues. *The Tin Man. *Sing, Sister, Sing. Go into Your Dance (GB: Casino de Paree). Every Night at Eight. Page Miss Glory. Thanks a Million. *The Misses Stooge. *Slightly Static. *Top Flat. *Hot Money. *Twin Triplets. *All American Toothache. 1936: Private Number. Kelly the Second. Sing, Baby, Sing. Pigskin Parade (GB: Harmony Parade). *Pan Handlers. *Hill-Tillies. *At Sea Ashore. 1937: Nobody's Baby. Wake Up and Live. Pick a Star. Ever Since Eve. 1938: Merrily We Live. There Goes My Heart. The Cowboy and the Lady. 1939: The Gorilla. 1940: Hit Parade of 1941. *The Happiest Man on Earth. Road Show. 1941: Topper Returns. Broadway Limited. 1942: Playmates. Sing Your Worries Away. In Old California. *Screen Snapshots No. 99. 1943: My Son, the Hero. Ladies' Day. Danger! Women at Work. 1960: Please Don't Eat the Daisies. The Crowded Sky. 1964: The Naked Kiss. 1966: Ghost in the Invisible Bikini. 1967: C'mon Let's Live a Little. 1968: Rosemary's Baby. 1969: The Pigeon (TV). The Phynx. 1976: Freaky Friday. 1978: North Avenue Irregular. (GB: Hill's Angels).

**KENNEDY, Edgar** 1890-1948
Pinkly bald, round-faced, head-scratching, rotund American comedian whose featured roles in big films were usually over the top (often as dim detectives), but who proved a useful sounding-board for Laurel and Hardy, popping up in their world mostly as baffled cops, but perhaps most memorably

as the gouty uncle crammed into the back seat of a car in *Perfect Day*. He called his double-take reaction to their antics a 'slow burn' and, in between using it, directed them once or twice as well. The 'Mr Average Man' series of shorts in which he starred ran from 1931 until his death from cancer of the throat.

*1912: Hoffmeyer's Legacy. 1914: *The Star Boarder. *Twenty Minutes of Love. *Caught in a Cabaret. *The Knockout. Tillie's Punctured Romance. *Our Country Cousin. *The Noise of Bombs. *Getting Acquainted. 1915: *A Game Old Knight. *The Great Vacuum Robbery. *Fatty's Tin Type Tangle. *Fickle Fatty's Fall. 1916: *His Hereafter. *His Bitter Pill. *Madcap Ambrose. *A Scoundrel's Toll. *Bombs. *Ambrose's Cup of Woe. *Bucking Society. 1917: *Her Fame and Shame. *Her Torpedoed Love. *Oriental Love. 1918: *She Loved Him Plenty. 1921: Skirts. 1922: The Leather Pushers. 1924: The Night Message. The Battling Fool. 1925: Proud Heart/His People. The Golden Princess. *The Marriage Circus. 1926: *My Old Dutch. The Better 'Ole. Across the Pacific. Going Crooked. Oh! What a Nurse. 1927: *Wedding Bills. *The Wrong Mr Right. Finger Prints. The Chinese Parrot. 1928: *A Pair of Tights. *Two Tars. *The Finishing Touch. *Leave 'Em Laughing. *Should Married Men Go Home? 1929: *Moan and Groan Inc. *Great Gobs. *Hotter Than Hot. *Bacon Grabbers. *Dad's Day. *Hurdy-Gurdy. *Unaccustomed As We Are. *Perfect Day. *Angora Love. Trent's Last Case. They Had to See Paris. The Gay Old Bird. Going Crooked (and 1926 film). 1930: *Night Owls. *The First Seven Years. *Shivering Shakespeare. *When the Wind Blows. *The Real McCoy. *All Teed Up. *Fifty Million Husbands. *Dollar Dizzy. *Girl Shock. *Looser Than Loose. *The Head Guy. *The Big Kick. *Bigger and Better. *Doctor's Orders. *Ladies Last. 1931: Bad Company. *The Midnight Patrol. *High Gear. *Love Fever. *Lemon Meringue. *Rough House Rhythm. *Thanks Again. *Camping Out. 1932: *Parlor, Bedroom and Wrath. *Mother-in-Law's Day. *Bon Voyage. *Giggle Water. *The Golf Chump. *Fish Feathers. Carnival Boat. Hold 'Em Jail! Westward Passage. Rockabye. The Penguin Pool Murder (GB: The Penguin Pool Mystery). Little Orphan Annie. 1933: *Kickin' the Crown Around. *Art in the Raw. *The Merchant of Menace. *Good Housewrecking. *Quiet, Please. *What Fur? *Grin and Bear It. Professional Sweetheart. Duck Soup. Tillie and Gus. Scarlet River. Crossfire. Son of the Border. 1934: *Wrong Direction. *In-Laws Are Out. *Love on a Ladder. *A Blasted Event. *Poisoned Ivory. Kid Millions. All of Me. Twentieth Century. Flirting with Danger. Heat Lightning. Murder on the Blackboard. The Silver Streak. We're Rich Again. Money Means Nothing. Gridiron Flash (GB: Luck of the Game). King Kelly of the USA. The Marines Are Coming. 1935: *A Night at the Biltmore Bowl. *Bric-a-Brac. *South Seasick-

ness. *Edgar Hamlet. *Sock Me to Sleep. *Happy Tho' Married. *In Love at 40. *Gobs of Trouble (GB: Navy Blues). The Cowboy Millionaire. Living on Velvet. Little Big Shot. Woman Wanted. In Person. $1,000 a Minute. The Bride Comes Home. Rendezvous at Midnight. 1936: *Gasoloons. *Will Power. *High Beer Pressure. Vocalising. *Dummy Ache. The Return of Jimmy Valentine. Three Men on a Horse. Small Town Girl. Mad Holiday. Fatal Lady. San Francisco. Yours for the Asking. Robin Hood of El Dorado. 1937: *Locks and Bonds. *Bad Housekeeping. *Dumb's the Word. *Hillbilly Goat. *Tramp Trouble. *Morning, Judge. *Edgar and Goliath. A Star is Born. When's Your Birthday? Super Sleuth. Double Wedding. True Confession. Hollywood Hotel. 1938: Hey! Hey! USA. Peck's Bad Boy with the Circus. The Black Doll. Scandal Street. *Beaux and Errors. *Ears of Experience. *False Roomers. *Kennedy's Castle. *Fool Coverage. *A Clean Sweep. 1939: *Maid to Order. *Kennedy the Great. *Clock Wise. *Baby Daze. *Feathered Pests. *Act Your Age. Little Accident. Everything's on Ice. Charlie McCarthy, Detective. Laugh It Off. It's a Wonderful World. 1940: *Mutiny in the County. *Slightly at Sea. *'Taint Legal. *Sunk by the Census. *Trailer Tragedy. *Drafted in the Depot. Dr Christian Meets the Women. Sandy is a Lady. The Quarterback. Margie. Who Killed Aunt Maggie? Remedy for Riches. Li'l Abner. Sandy Gets Her Man. 1941: *It Happened All Night. *Mad About Moonshine. *An Apple in His Eye. *Westward Ho-Hum. *I'll Fix That. *A Quiet Fourth. Public Enemies. Blondie in Society (GB: Henpecked). The Bride Wore Crutches. 1942: Snuffy Smith, Yard Bird (GB: Snuffy Smith). Pardon My Stripes. There's One Born Every Minute. In Old California. Hillbilly Blitzkrieg. *Cooks and Crooks. *Inferior Decorator. *Heart Burn. *Two for The Money. *Duck Soup (and 1933 feature). *Rough on Rents. 1943: Cosmo Jones - Crime Smasher (GB: Crime Smasher). The Falcon Strikes Back. Air Raid Wardens. Hitler's Madman. The Girl from Monterey. Crazy House. *Hold Your Temper. *Indian Signs. *Hot Foot. *Not on My Account. *Unlucky Dog. *Prunes and Politics. 1944: *Love Your Landlord. *Radio Rampage. *The Kitchen Cynic. *Feather Your Nest. It Happened Tomorrow. The Great Alaskan Mystery (serial). 1945: *Alibi Baby. *You Drive Me Crazy. *Sleepless Tuesday. *What? No Cigarettes? *It's Your Move. *The Big Beef. *Mother-in-Law's Day (remake) 1946: *Noisy Neighbors. *Wall Street Blues. *Motor Maniacs. *I'll Build It Myself. *Trouble or Nothing. *Social Terrors. The Sin of Harold Diddlebock (later and GB: Mad Wednesday). 1947: *Do or Diet. *Heading for Trouble. *Television Turmoil. *Mind over Mouse. *Host to a Ghost. Heaven Only Knows. 1948: Variety Time. Unfaithfully Yours. *No More Relatives. *Brother Knows Best. *How to Clean House. *Dig That Gold. *Home Canning. *Contest Crazy. 1949: My Dream is Yours.

**As director** (as E. Livingston Kennedy): 1925: †\*The Marriage Circus. \*Cupid's Boots. 1928: \*From Soup to Nuts. \*You're Darn Tootin' (GB: The Music Blasters).

†Co-directed.

### KERR, Bill 1922-

Deadpan, dark-haired, slightly gloomy-looking entertainer, born in South Africa. Moving with his show business parents to Australia, he became a child actor there, then stand-up comedian, at which he was a great success in post-war Britain, with such catch-phrases as 'Don't wanna worry yer' and 'I've only got four minutes'. Acting roles, both comic and dramatic, came either side of an extended radio and TV association with Tony Hancock, before Kerr returned to Australia - as a character actor - in the late 1970s.

1933: †Harmony Row. 1934: †The Silence of Dean Maitland. 1951: Penny Points to Paradise. 1952: My Death is a Mockery. Appointment in London. 1953: You Know What Sailors Are. 1954: The Dam Busters. 1955: The Night My Number Came Up. Port of Escape. 1957: The Shiralee. 1958: The Captain's Table. 1962: The Wrong Arm of the Law. 1963: Doctor in Distress. 1966: Doctor in Clover. A Funny Thing Happened on the Way to the Forum. 1973: Ghost in the Noonday Sun (unreleased). Tiffany Jones. 1975: Girls Come First. House of Mortal Sin (US: The Confessional). 1981: Deadline. Save the Lady. Gallipoli. 1982: The Pirate Movie. The Year of Living Dangerously. 1983: Razorback. 1984: Dusty. Vigil. The Coca Cola Kid. 1985: Relatives.

†As Billy Kerr

### KIBBEE, Guy 1882-1956

Bald-headed, beaming, pink-cheeked American actor. He started his film career as a ruthless killer (in City Streets), but soon developed into a kind of benevolent W. C. Fields, and he was in great demand for character roles throughout the 1930s. Later still he starred in the low-budget 'Scattergood Baines' comedy series as a do-gooding small-town busybody. Died from Parkinson's Disease.

1931: City Streets. Man of the World. Blonde Crazy (GB: Larceny Lane). Flying High (GB: Happy Landing). \*Position and Backswing. Laughing Sinners. Side Show. Stolen Heaven. The New Adventures of Get-Rich-Quick Wallingford. 1932: Fireman, Save My Child. Taxi! The Strange Love of Molly Louvain. Union Depot (GB: Gentleman for a Day). Crooner. Central Park. Week-End Marriage (GB: Working Wives). The Mouthpiece. High Pressure. Play Girl. The Crowd Roars. Two Seconds. Man Wanted. So Big. Winner Take All. The Dark Horse. Big City Blues. Rain. Scarlet Dawn. The Conquerors. 1933: 42nd Street. Gold Diggers of 1933. They Just Had to Get Married. The Life of Jimmy Dolan (GB: The Kid's Last Fight). Lady for a Day. The World Changes. Convention City. Girl Missing. Lilly Turner. The Silk Express. Footlight Parade. Havana Widows. 1934: Harold Teen (GB: The Dancing Fool). Big-Hearted Herbert. The Merry Wives of Reno. Babbitt. The Merry Frinks (GB: The Happy Family). Wonder Bar. Dames. Easy to Love. 1935: Mary Jane's Pa (GB: Wanderlust). While the Patient Slept. Don't Bet on Blondes. Going Highbrow. I Live for Love (GB: I Live for You). Captain Blood. Crashing Society. 1936: Captain January. Earthworm Tractors (GB: A Natural Born Salesman). Three Men on a Horse. M'Liss. Little Lord Fauntleroy. I Married a Doctor. The Big Noise (GB: Modern Madness). 1937: Mama Steps Out. Riding on Air. Jim Hanvey, Detective. Bad Man from Brimstone. The Captain's Kid. Don't Tell the Wife. The Big Shot. Mountain Justice. 1938: Three Comrades. Of Human Hearts. Rich Man, Poor Girl. Three Loves Has Nancy. Joy of Living. 1939: It's a Wonderful World. Bad Little Angel. Mr Smith Goes to Washington. Babes in Arms. Let Freedom Ring. Henry Goes Arizona (GB: Spats to Spurs). 1940: Our Town. Chad Hanna. Street of Memories. Scattergood Baines. 1941: It Started With Eve. Design for Scandal. Scattergood Pulls the Strings. Scattergood Meets Broadway. 1942: Sunday Punch. Scattergood Rides High. Tish. Whistling in Dixie. Scattergood Survives a Murder. Miss Annie Rooney. This Time for Keeps. 1943: Girl Crazy. Cinderella Swings It. Power of the Press. White Savage (GB: White Captive). 1944: Dixie

Jamboree. 1945: White Pongo (GB: Adventure Unlimited). The Horn Blows at Midnight. 1946: Singing on the Trail (GB: Lookin' for Someone). Cowboy Blues (GB: Beneath the Starry Skies). Gentleman Joe Palooka. Lone Star Moonlight (GB: Amongst the Thieves). 1947: Over the Santa Fé Trail (GB: No Escape). The Romance of Rosy Ridge. Red Stallion. 1948: Fort Apache. Three Godfathers.

### KIEL, Richard 1940-

Fearsome 7 ft. 2 in. American actor with light-coloured hair, handsome in a thick-featured way, but confined for many years to lumbering around as giants and monsters. After one or two minor leading roles in the mid-1970s, he hit pay dirt when cast as the villainous, steel-toothed killer Jaws in The Spy Who Loved Me, proving so popular that the character was reprised (as a semi-goodie) in another James Bond adventure Moonraker.

1961: The Phantom Planet. 1962: The Magic Sword. 1963: Eegah! House of the Damned. The Nutty Professor. 1964: The Human Duplicators. 1965: Brainstorm. 1967: A Man Called Dagger. 1968: Now You See It, Now You Don't (TV). Skidoo. 1970: The Boy Who Stole the Elephant (TV). 1974: The Longest Yard (GB: The Mean Machine). 1975: Barbary Coast (TV). Shadow in the Streets (TV). 1976: Silver Streak. Flash and the Firecat. 1977: The Spy Who Loved Me. 1978: They Went That-a-Way and That-a-Way. Force Ten from Navarone. 1979: Moonraker. The Humanoid. 1981: So Fine. 1982: Hysterical. 1983: Cannonball Run II. 1984: The Racketeers. 1985: Pale Rider.

### KILBRIDE, Percy 1888-1964

Thin, slightly stooping, flat-haired, tight-mouthed, gloomy-looking American actor, who came to Hollywood in middle age and made sporadic appearances there in cameos between stage engagements, mostly as rustics who were a good deal more calculating than they looked. He found a niche as Pa Kettle in the Universal-International comedy series opposite Marjorie Main, which he left to retire in 1955. Died from brain injuries sustained in a car accident.

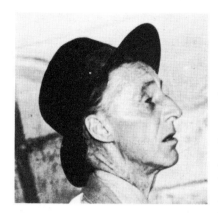

1933: White Woman. 1936: Soak the Rich. 1942: Keeper of the Flame. George Washington Slept Here. 1943: Crazy House. The Woman of the Town. 1944: The Adventures of Mark Twain. Guest in the House. Knickerbocker Holiday. 1945: State Fair. She Wouldn't Say Yes. Fallen Angel. 1946: The Well Groomed Bride. 1947: Welcome Stranger. Riffraff. The Egg and I. 1948: You Gotta Stay Happy. You Were Meant for Me. Black Bart (GB: Black Bart - Highwayman). Feudin', Fussin' and A-Fightin'. 1949: Ma and Pa Kettle. Mr Soft Touch (GB: House of Settlement). Free for All. The Sun Comes Up. Ma and Pa Kettle Go to Town (GB: Goin' to Town). 1950: Riding High. 1951: Ma and Pa Kettle Back on the Farm. 1952: Ma and Pa Kettle on Vacation (GB: Ma and Pa Kettle Go to Paris). Ma and Pa Kettle at the Fair. 1954: Ma and Pa Kettle at Home. 1955: Ma and Pa Kettle at Waikiki.

**KILIAN, Victor** 1891-1979
Hulkingly gaunt, arrow-nosed, cavern-cheeked, brown-haired, sometimes bearded American actor who looked perfect casting for Abraham Lincoln, and finally did get to play the role in 1940's *Virginia City*. Not too dissimilar to John Dierkes (*qv*), he was often cast as woodsmen, prospectors, sheriffs and fire-breathing preachers. At 85, he began a whole new career as the 'flashing' grandfather in the TV comedy show *Mary Hartman, Mary Hartman* but, sadly, three years later he was killed by burglars at his Hollywood apartment.

1929: Valley Forge. Gentlemen of the Press. 1932: The Wiser Sex. *Artistic Temper. 1935: Bad Boy. Air Hawks. After the Dance. Public Menace. The Girl Friend. Riffraff. 1936: I Loved a Soldier. The Music Goes 'Round. Adventure in Manhattan (GB: Manhattan Madness). Fair Warning. Shakedown. The Lady from Nowhere. The Road to Glory. Banjo on My Knee. Ramona. 1937: Seventh Heaven. It Happened in Hollywood. The League of Frightened Men. Tovarich. It's All Yours. 1938: The Adventures of Tom Sawyer. Marie Antoinette. Orphans of the Street. Prison Break. Boys' Town. Gold Diggers in Paris (GB: The Gay Imposters). 1939: Paris Honeymoon. Fighting Thoroughbreds. St Louis Blues. The Adventures of Huckleberry Finn. The Return of the Cisco Kid. Only Angels Have Wings. Never Say Die. Dust Be My Destiny. Blackmail. Young Tom Edison. 1940: Florian. Virginia City. My Favorite Wife. Dr Cyclops. The Mark of Zorro. Little Old New York. Till We Meet Again. King of the Lumberjacks. Gold Rush Maisie. All This and Heaven Too. The Return of Frank James. Torrid Zone. Barnyard Follies. Out West With the Peppers. They Knew What They Wanted. Tugboat Annie Sails Again. Chad Hanna. Santa Fé Trail. 1941: Western Union. Mob Town. I Was a Prisoner on Devil's Island. Blood and Sand. Secrets of the Lone Wolf (GB: Secrets). A Date with the Falcon. Sergeant York. 1942: Reap the Wild Wind. This Gun for Hire. Atlantic Convoy. The Ox-Bow Incident (GB: Strange Incident). 1943: Bomber's Moon. Hitler's Madman. Johnny Come Lately (GB: Johnny Vagabond). The Iron Major. 1944: Belle of the Yukon. The Adventures of Mark Twain. Uncertain Glory. Kismet. Barbary Coast Gent. Dangerous Passage. Meet Me in St Louis. 1945: Behind City Lights. The Spanish Main. Spellbound. The Fighting Guardsman. 1946: Little Giant (GB: On the Carpet). Smoky. The Yearling. Duel in the Sun. 1947: Gentleman's Agreement. 1948: Yellow Sky. Northwest Stampede. 1949: Madame Bovary. I Shot Jesse James. Rimfire. Colorado Territory. Wyoming Bandit. 1950: The Old Frontier. The Showdown. The Return of Jesse James. The Bandit Queen. The Flame and the Arrow. 1951: The Tall Target. One Too Many (GB: Killer with a Label).

**KINNEAR, Roy** 1934- 1988
Plump, florid, wheezy, wispy-haired British comic character actor, from the Theatre Workshop. Although his performances seem rather unvarying, his timing is undervalued, and, with the right director, he is sometimes consistently funny.

1962: Tiara Tahiti. The Boys. Sparrows Can't Sing. 1963: The Small Word of Sammy Lee. A Place to Go. The Informers. Heavens Above! 1964: French Dressing. 1965: The Hill. Help! 1966: The Deadly Affair. A Funny Thing Happened on the Way to the Forum. 1967: How I Won the War. Albert Carter Q.O.S.O. 1969: Lock Up Your Daughters! The Bed Sitting Room. 1970: Taste the Blood

of Dracula. Scrooge. Egghead's Robot. The Firechasers. On a Clear Day You Can See Forever. 1971: Melody (Later SWALK). Willy Wonka and the Chocolate Factory. Madame Sin (TV: GB cinemas). The Pied Piper. Raising the Roof. 1972: The Alf Garnett Saga. Alice's Adventures in Wonderland. That's Your Funeral. 1973: The Three Musketeers - The Queen's Diamonds. 1974: Juggernaut. Eskimo Nell. The Four Musketeers - The Revenge of Milady. The Amorous Milkman. Barry McKenzie Holds His Own. Three for All. 1975: Royal Flash. One of Our Dinosaurs is Missing. The Adventure of Sherlock Holmes' Smarter Brother. 1976: Not Now, Comrade. 1977: The Last Remake of Beau Geste. The Hound of the Baskervilles. Herbie Goes to Monte Carlo. 1978: Watership Down (voice only). 1979: The London Connection (US: The Omega Connection). *Mad Dogs and Cricketers. 1980: High Rise Donkey. *A Fair Way to Play. Hawk the Slayer. Dick Turpin (GB: TV). 1981: Hammett. 1983: The Boys in Blue. Pavlova - A Woman for All Time. 1984: Robin Hood (TV). 1985: Squaring the Circle. Pirates.

**KINSKEY, Leonid** 1903-
Lanky Russian eccentric comic actor with long, angular features, thick lips, low forehead, stick-out hair and wonderful fractured English. In numerous cameos from 1932 to 1944, Kinskey, who started out in grand opera in Russia, seemed all arms and legs as he capered on and off the screen as a quasi-mad music teacher or the

like. Seen only sporadically in post-war years, he made his latter-day living by staging industrial shows.

*1932: Trouble in Paradise. 1933: Three Cornered Moon. Duck Soup. Girl Without a Room. 1934: Goin' to Town. Hollywood Party. We Live Again. The Cat and the Fiddle. The Merry Widow. Fugitive Road. 1935: The Gilded Lily. Les Misérables. Peter Ibbetson. 1936: The Garden of Allah. Love on the Run. Next Time We Love (GB: Next Time We Live). Rhythm on the Range. The Road to Glory. The General Died at Dawn. 1937: Maytime. We're on the Jury. Make a Wish. Espionage. My Dear Miss Aldrich. Café Metropole. The Sheik Steps Out. Meet the Boy Friend. 100 Men and a Girl. 1938: The Big Broadcast of 1938. Outside of Paradise. The Great Waltz. Algiers. A Trip to Paris. Three Blind Mice. Flirting with Fate. Professor, Beware! 1939: The Story of Vernon and Irene Castle. Day-Time Wife. The Spellbinder. Exile Express. On Your Toes. Everything Happens at Night. 1940: He Stayed for Breakfast. Down Argentine Way. 1941: Lady for a Night. Ball of Fire. That Night in Rio. So Ends Our Night. Broadway Limited. Week-End in Havana. 1942: I Married an Angel. Brooklyn Orchid. Talk of the Town. Casablanca. 1943: Gildersleeve on Broadway. Let's Have Fun. Cinderella Swings It. Presenting Lily Mars. 1944: Can't Help Singing. The Fighting Seabees. That's My Baby. 1946: Monsieur Beaucaire. 1949: The Great Sinner. Alimony. 1951: Honeychile. 1952: Gobs and Gals (GB: Cruising Casanovas). 1955: The Man With the Golden Arm. 1956: Glory.*

**KINSKI, Klaus**
(Nikolaus Nakszynski) 1926- 1991
Stocky, fair-haired, blue-eyed actor born in Danzig (now in Poland), with carved lips, Frankenstein eyebrows and the kind of strained baby-face looks that peppered his early career with sadistic villains. An undisciplined talent in these days, he was already a great scene-stealer; too much so, it seems, for most directors, as he toured nightclubs with a one-man show before becoming a regular in West German (and soon international) films from the early 1960s. Later he mixed fanatics and bizarre

guest roles with impressive leading parts for director Werner Herzog. Something of a latter-day Peter Lorre, he is the father of actress Nastassja Kinski.

*1948: Morituri. 1951: Decision Before Dawn. 1954: Kinder, Mütter und ein General. Ludwig II. 1955: Um Thron und Liebe/Sarajewo. Hanussen. 1956: Waldwinter. Liebe Corinna. 1957: A Time to Love and a Time to Die. 1960: Der Rächer. 1961: Die toten Augen von London (and English-language version: Dead Eyes of London). Bankraub in der Rue Latour. Die seltsame Gräfin. The Counterfeit Traitor. Das Rätsel der roten Orchidee (and English-language version: The Puzzle of the Red Orchid). 1962: The Devil's Daffodil (US: Daffodil Killer). Der rote Rausch. Die Tür mit den sieben Schlössern. Das Gasthaus an der Themse. 1963: The Black Abbot. Der Zinker (US: The Squeaker). Scotland Yard jagt Doktor Mabuse (US: Dr Mabuse vs Scotland Yard). Die schwartze Kobra. Das indische Tuch. Das Geheimnis der schwarzen Witwe (US: Secret of the Black Widow). Piccadilly null Uhr zwölf. Kali-Yug, Goddess of Vengeance. Kali-Yug: The Mystery of the Indian Tomb (combined version shown in GB under former title). 1964: Last Stage to Santa Cruz. Estambul 65/That Man in Istanbul. Winnetou II (GB and US: Last of the Renegades). Die Gruft mit dem Rätselschloss. Wartezimmer zum Jenseits. Das Geheimnis der chinesischen Nelke. 1965: Traitor's Gate. The Pleasure Girls. The Dirty Game. Doctor Zhivago. For a Few Dollars More. Neues vom Hexer. 1966: Our Man in Marrakesh (US: Bang! Bang! You're Dead). Circus of Fear (US: Psycho-Circus). Quien sabe? (GB and US: A Bullet for the General). I bastardi (GB: Sons of Satan). Carnival of Killers. Das Geheimnis der gelben Mönche (GB: Target for Killing). 1967: Die blaue Hand (US: Creature with the Blue Hand). Sumuru (US: The 1,000,000 Eyes of Su-Muru). Coplan sauve sa peau (GB: Devil's Garden). Five Golden Dragons. Grand Slam. Carmen, Baby. L'uomo, l'orgoglio, la vendetta. †Jules Verne's Rocket to the Moon (US: Those Fantastic Flying Fools). Sigpress contro Scotland Yard. 1968: Cinque per l'inferno (GB: Five for Hell. US: Five into Hell). Marquis de Sade: Justine (GB: Justine and Juliet). Sam Cooper's Gold (US: The Ruthless Four). Sartana. Vatican Story. Due volte Giuda. Il grande silenzio. 1969: La peau de torpédo (GB: Pill of Death. US: Children of Mata Hari). Paroxismus (GB: Black Angel. US: Venus in Furs). Il dito nella piaga (US: The Dirty Two). Quintero. A doppia faccia (US: Puzzle of Horrors). I'll Dig Your Grave. E Dio disse a Caino ...(GB: And God Said to Cain). 1970: How Did a Nice Girl Like You Get into This Business? I leopardi di Churchill (GB: Commando Attack). El Conde Dracula (GB: Bram Stoker's Count Dracula. US: Count Dracula). Per una bara piena di dollari/Adios Compañeros! La belva. Prega il morte e ammazza il vivo. Giù le mani ... carogna. The Night of the Assassins. 1971: Dracula im Schloss des Schreckens*

*(US: Web of the Spider). L'occhio del ragno (US: Eye of the Spider). La bestia uccide a sangue freddo (GB: Cold-Blooded Beast. US: Slaughter Hotel). Lo chiamavano King (US: The Man Called King). Black Killer. Vengeance Trail. Il venditore di morte. 1972: Aguirre, Wrath of God. The Price of Death. Doppia taglia per Minnesota Stinky. Il ritorno di Clint il solitario. 1973: Il mio nome è Shanghai Joe (GB: To Kill or to Die. US: Shanghai Joe). La mano spietata della legge (GB: The Bloody Hands of the Law). La mano che nutre la morte. Sette strani cadaveri. Imperativo categorio: contro il crimine con rabbia. 1974: L'important c'est d'aimer (US: That Most Important Thing: Love). Footprints. Le amanti del mostro. Who Stole the Shah's Jewels? 1975: Lifespan. Un genio, due compari, un pollo (US: Nobody's the Greatest). Das Netz (US: The Web). 1976: Jack the Ripper. Madame Claude (US: The French Woman). 1977: Entebbe: Operation Thunderbolt. Nuit d'or. Mort d'un pourri. 1978: The Song of Roland. Zoo-Zéro. 1979: Nosferatu: Phantom der Nacht (GB and US: Nosferatu the Vampyre). Woyzeck. Haine/Hatred/Traquenard. 1980: Schizoid. Love and Money. 1981: Les fruits de la passion. Venom. Buddy Buddy. 1982: Fitzcarraldo. Burden of Dreams. Android. The Soldier (GB: Codename: The Soldier). 1983: Der Schatten des Wolfes (made in 1981). The Secret Diary of Sigmund Freud. 1984: Codename Wildgeese. The Little Drummer Girl. 1985: The Hitchhiker. Titan Find/Creature.*

†Scenes deleted from final release print

**KLEMPERER, Werner** 1919- 2000
Big, smooth German actor, shiningly bald from an early age, who moved to America in 1933 with his father, conductor Otto Klemperer; he became an actor in post-war years, coming to Hollywood to play villains in smart suits. From 1965, he became involved with villainy of a comic kind with his six-year stint as the camp commandant in *Hogan's Heroes*, a portrayal which won him two Emmy awards.

*1956: Five Steps to Danger. Flight to Hong Kong. Death of a Scoundrel. 1957: Istanbul. Kiss Them for Me. 1958: The Goddess. 1961: Operation Eichmann. Judgment at Nuremberg.*

*1962: Tunnel 28 (GB and US: Escape from East Berlin). 1964: Youngblood Hawke. 1965: Ship of Fools. 1968: The Wicked Dreams of Paula Schultz. 1969: Wake Me When the War Is Over (TV). 1972: Assignment Munich (TV). 1977: The Rhinemann Exchange (TV). 1981: The Return of the Beverly Hillbillies (TV).*

**KLUGMAN, Jack** 1922–
Dour-looking, watery-eyed, brown-haired American actor, in surprisingly few films, although enormously productive on television, and popular in two long-running series, *The Odd Couple* (for which he won two Emmys) and *Quincy*. His glum growl can be sinister, weak, cynical or wrily comic.

*1955: Timetable. 1956: Invasion of the Body Snatchers. 1957: 12 Angry Men. The Thundering Wave (TV). 1958: Cry Terror! The Time of Your Life (TV). 1959: The Velvet Alley (TV). 1961: The Million Dollar Incident (TV). 1962: Days of Wine and Roses. I Could Go On Singing. 1963: The Yellow Canary. Act One. 1966: Fame is the Name of the Game (TV). 1967: Hail Mafia! 1968: The Detective. The Split. 1969: Goodbye Columbus. 1971: Who Says I Can't Ride a Rainbow? 1976: Two-Minute Warning.*

**KOSLECK, Martin**
(Nicolai Yoshkin) 1907–1994
German actor who fled to America in 1933, but hardly got a nibble at Hollywood films

until World War II loomed. Suddenly Kosleck, with his sleek, dark evil looks, and narrow face and eyes, found himself in demand to portray Nazis and sinister villains generally - quite an irony for a Jewish player. Portrayed Goebbels ('like he was, without a single redeeming feature') several times. Demands for his services slackened after 1946.

*1930: Alraune. Der singende Stadt. 1933: Fashions of 1934 (GB: Fashions). 1939: Confessions of a Nazi Spy. Nurse Edith Cavell. Nick Carter, Master Detective. Espionage Agent. 1940: Calling Philo Vance. The Mad Doctor (GB: A Date with Destiny). Foreign Correspondent. 1941: International Lady. The Devil Pays Off. Underground. 1942: All Through the Night. Nazi Agent. Berlin Correspondent. Manila Calling. Fly by Night. 1943: Chetniks. North Star. Bombers' Moon. 1944: Secrets of Scotland Yard. The Hitler Gang. The Mummy's Curse. The Great Alaskan Mystery (serial). 1945: Pursuit to Algiers. Gangs of the Waterfront. The Spider. The Frozen Ghost. Strange Holiday (GB: The Day After Tomorrow). 1946: House of Horrors (GB: Joan Medford Is Missing). Just Before Dawn. Crime of the Century. The Wife of Monte Cristo. She-Wolf of London (GB: The Curse of the Allenbys). 1947: The Beginning or the End? 1948: Half Past Midnight. Smugglers' Cove. Assigned to Danger. 1961: Hitler. Something Wild. 1964: 36 Hours. 1965: Morituri (GB: The Saboteur, Code Name Morituri). 1966: Agent for HARM. 1967: The Flesh Eaters. 1969: Wake Me When the War is Over (TV). 1970: Which Way to the Front (GB: Ja, Ja, Mein General, But Which Way to the Front?). 1971: Longstreet (TV). 1973: A Day at the White House.*

**KOSSOFF, David** 1919–
Small, dapper, moustachioed British actor, a former draughtsman and interior designer who became a skilled, multi-voiced radio actor before coming to films in wise, often Jewish-slanted roles. Later he co-starred with Peggy Mount in an enormously popular TV series, *The Larkins* (which led to a film) and became famous for his readings of Bible stories on television. Often played older than his real age.

*1953: The Good Beginning. 1954: The Young Lovers (US: Chance Meeting). The Angel Who Pawned Her Harp. Svengali. 1955: A Kid for Two Farthings. *The Bespoke Overcoat. The Woman for Joe. Who Done It? 1956: Now and Forever. House of Secrets (US: Triple Deception). Wicked As They Come. The Iron Petticoat. 1958: Innocent Sinners. Count Five and Die. Indiscreet. 1959: Jet Storm. The House of the Seven Hawks. The Journey. The Mouse That Roared. Inn for Trouble. 1960: Conspiracy of Hearts. The Two Faces of Dr Jekyll (US: House of Fright). 1962: Freud/Freud - the Secret Passion. 1963: The Mouse on the Moon. Summer Holiday. Ring of Spies. 1970: The Private Life of Sherlock Holmes. 1979: The London Connection (US: The Omega Connection).*

**KOTTO, Yaphet** 1937–
Rock-like black American actor in aggressive, hard-man characters. After a tough climb to decent roles, he began to get continuous work in films and television from 1967 and burst through to top supporting parts following his assignment as the villain in the James Bond film *Live and Let Die*. The private Kotto is far from the tough public image: he's a lay reader with the Self Realization Fellowship, a Hindu sect.

*1964: Nothing But a Man. 1968: Five Card Stud. The Thomas Crown Affair. 1969: The Liberation of L. B. Jones. 1970: Night Chase (TV). 1972: Man and Boy. †The Limit/Speed Limit 65. Bone (GB: Dial Rat for Terror). Across 110th Street. 1973: Live and Let Die. 1974: Truck Turner. Sharks' Treasure. 1975: Report to the Commissioner. Friday Foster. 1976: Drum. Monkey Hustle. Raid on Entebbe (TV. GB: cinemas). 1978: Blue Collar. 1979: Alien. 1980: Brubaker. 1982: Fighting Back (GB: Death Vengeance). 1983: The Star Chamber. Women of San Quentin (TV). 1985: Playing With Fire (TV).*

†Also directed

**KOVE, Kenneth** 1893–
Monocled, round-faced 'silly ass' comic actor whose profitable stage career (from 1913) was interrupted by the cinema from

Kenneth **Kove** and Kay Hammond, here in a 1931 publicity shot, were popular comedy players of the early sound days. BIP studios wouldn't need the lifebelt until the end of the decade

1930 to 1936 when he dashed from one film to another during the 'quota' years. After that he went back to the theatre, with barely a handful of additional film appearances before his retirement in 1953. His son, John Kove (1921-), was briefly a child actor in the early 1930s.

*1930: Murder. The Great Game. 1931: Chance of a Night Time. Down River. Fascination. The Man at Six (US: The Gables Mystery). Almost a Divorce. Out of the Blue. M'Blimey (unreleased). Mischief. 1932: Two White Arms (US: Wives Beware). Help Yourself. Diamond Cut Diamond (US: Blame the Woman). Pyjamas Preferred. Her First Affaire. The Man from Toronto. 1933: Dora. Send 'Em Back Half Dead. Crime on the Hill. Song of the Plough. 1934: The Crimson Candle. The Life of the Party. Crazy People. Leave It to Blanche. The Scarlet Pimpernel. 1935: Radio Pirates. Marry the Girl. Look Up and Laugh. 1936: Don't Rush Me. Cheer Up! The Bank Messenger Mystery. 1937: Talking Feet. 1939: Black Eyes. 1942: Asking for Trouble. 1945: They Knew Mr Knight. 1949: The Golden Arrow (released 1952. US: Three Men and a Girl). 1952: Treasure Hunt. 1953: Innocents in Paris.*

**KREUGER, Kurt** 1916-
Blond Swiss-German actor with the handsomeness of a male model. He came to America in 1937 as a skiing instructor and broke into films in the war years, playing Nazi officers and playboy romeos. Too stiff to stay on the Hollywood scene for long, he drifted away from films after the 1950s, and went into business buying homes and remodelling them for rent. Later Kreuger wrote a book about his experiences entitled *Hollywood Landlord*, and made a couple of small film appearances in the 1960s, his last to date. Bears a close resemblance to the slightly younger American actor Peter Graves.

*1942: The Moon Is Down. 1943: Edge of Darkness. The Strange Death of Adolf Hitler. Sahara. The Purple V. 1944: None Shall Escape. Mademoiselle Fifi (later The Silent Bell). 1945: Hotel Berlin. Escape in the Desert. Paris Underground (GB: Madame Pimpernel). The Spider. 1946: Sentimental Journey.*

*The Dark Corner. 1948: Unfaithfully Yours. 1950: Spy Hunt (GB: Panther's Moon). 1954: La paura/Angst/Fear. 1957: The Enemy Below. 1958: Legion of the Doomed. 1966: What Did You Do in the War, Daddy? 1967: The St Valentine's Day Massacre.*

**KROEGER, Berry** 1912- 1991
Thick-lipped, evil-looking American actor with dark, receding, smarmed-across hair, whose speciality was villains so repulsive they deserved to be wiped from the face of the earth. Redeeming qualities were not in the Kroeger armoury, the grey bags under his eyes heightening the likeness to an eminently hissable silent villain. Such undiluted vitriol was too much, it seemed, to admit him to many films but, after a start in post-war years, his characters continued to surface, like scum on the water, until his retirement in the late 1970s.

*1948: The Iron Curtain. Cry of the City. The Dark Past. An Act of Murder. Act of Violence. 1949: Chicago Deadline. Gun Crazy. Black Magic. Fighting Man of the Plains. Down to the Sea in Ships. 1950: Guilty of Treason (GB: Treason). 1951: The Sword of Monte Cristo. 1953: Battles of Chief Pontiac. 1955: Yellowneck. Blood Alley. 1956: Man in the Vault. 1960: Seven Thieves. The Story of Ruth. The Walking Target. 1961: Atlantis the Lost Continent. Hitler. Womanhunt. 1963: Youngblood Hawke. 1966: Chamber of Horrors. Monster of the Wax Museum (GB: Nightmare in Wax). 1970: The Incredible Two-Headed Transplant. 1971: The Mephisto Waltz. The Seven Minutes. 1973: Pets (GB: Submission). 1975: The Man in the Glass Booth. 1977: Demon Seed.*

**KRUGER, Otto** 1885-1974
This long-faced, pale-eyed, most civilized and courteous of actors was almost entirely a stage star until his late forties, when he came to the screen to play lawyers, lovers, doctors, politicians both crooked and straight and, in the end, kindly uncles. Even his villains were always immaculately dressed and that deep, metallic voice exuded class. Died on his 89th birthday following a stroke. Filmed in Britain in the late 1930s.

*1915: When the Call Came. 1923: Under the Red Robe. 1928: *The Home Girl. 1929: *Mr Intruder. 1933: Beauty for Sale (GB: Beauty). Ever in My Heart. Gallant Lady. The Prizefighter and the Lady (GB: Everywoman's Man). The Women in His Life. Turn Back the Clock. 1934: Treasure Island. Chained. Springtime for Henry. The Crime Doctor. Men in White. Paris Interlude. 1935: Two Sinners. Vanessa - Her Love Story. 1936: Dracula's Daughter. Living Dangerously. Lady of Secrets. 1937: Glamorous Night. Counsel for Crime. They Won't Forget. The Barrier. 1938: Housemaster. Star of the Circus (US: Hidden Menace). I Am the Law. Thanks for the Memory. Exposed. 1939: Black Eyes. The Gang's All Here (US: The Amazing Mr Forrest). Another Thin Man. Zero Hour. A Woman Is the Judge. Disbarred. 1940: A Dispatch from Reuter's (GB: This Man Reuter). Dr Ehrlich's Magic Bullet (GB: The Story of Dr Ehrlich's Magic Bullet). Scandal Sheet. Seventeen. The Man I Married. 1941: The Men in Her Life. The Big Boss. Mercy Island. 1942: Friendly Enemies (released 1946). Saboteur. 1943: Hitler's Children. Secrets of a Co-Ed (GB: Silent Witness). Corregidor. Tarzan's Desert Mystery. Stage Door Canteen. Night Plane from Chungking. 1944: Cover Girl. Knickerbocker Holiday. Storm Over Lisbon. They Live in Fear. 1945: On Stage, Everybody! Murder, My Sweet (GB: Farewell, My Lovely). The Great John L (GB: A Man Called Sullivan). The Woman Who Came Back. Jungle Captive. The Chicago Kid. Wonder Man. Escape in the Fog. Allotment Wives (GB: Woman in the Case). Earl Carroll's Vanities. 1946: The Fabulous Suzanne. Duel in the Sun. 1947: Love and Learn. 1948: Lulu Belle. Smart Woman. 1950: 711 Ocean Drive. 1951: Payment on Demand. Valentino. 1952: High Noon. 1954: Magnificent Obsession. Black Widow. 1955: The Last Command. 1958: The Colossus of New York. 1959: Della (TV). The Young Philadelphians (GB: The City Jungle). Cash McCall. 1962: The Wonderful World of the Brothers Grimm. 1964: Sex and the Single Girl.*

**KRUSCHEN, Jack** 1922-
Canadian actor of burly build, with chubby face, bushy black (later grey) hair and

to films, where he played tough minor heavies, and equally tough good-hearted sergeants of army and cavalry alike. Profitably occupied on television from 1956, he died from a heart attack on the set of the *Voyage to the Bottom of the Sea* series in which he was a regular. He used to joke that his wrestling career had taught him all he ever needed to know about acting!

equally bushy brows. Mostly in comic supporting parts, such as eccentric, explosive professors, he was also a sturdy and sometimes stern dramatic player when the occasion demanded. Nominated for a best supporting actor Oscar in *The Apartment*. Started acting on radio at 16.

*1949: Red, Hot and Blue. 1950: Woman from Headquarters. Where Danger Lives. 1951: Cuban Fireball. The People against O'Hara. Comin' Round the Mountain. Meet Danny Wilson. 1952: Tropical Heatwave. Confidence Girl. Just across the Street. Ma and Pa Kettle on Vacation (GB: Ma and Pa Kettle Go to Paris). 1953: War of the Worlds. Blueprint for Murder. Money from Home. It Should Happen to You. Abbott and Costello Go to Mars. 1954: Untamed Heiress. Tennessee Champ. The Long, Long Trailer. 1955: Dial Red O. Carolina Cannonball. Soldier of Fortune. The Night Holds Terror. 1956: Outside the Law. Julie. 1957: Badlands of Montana. Reform School Girl. 1958: The Buccaneer. Cry Terror! Fraulein. The Decks Ran Red. 1960: The Apartment. The Last Voyage. The Angry Red Planet. Studs Lonigan. Seven Ways from Sundown. 1961: The Ladies' Man. Where the Boys Are. Lover Come Back. Cape Fear. 1962: Convicts Four (GB: Reprieve!). Follow That Dream. 1963: McLintock! 1964: The Unsinkable Molly Brown. 1965: Harlow (Carol Lynley version). 1966: Caprice. The Happening. 1968: Istanbul Express (TV. GB: cinemas). 1971: Million Dollar Duck. 1972: Emergency (TV). Deadly Harvest (TV). 1974: Freebie and the Bean. 1975: The Log of the Black Pearl (TV). 1976: The November Plan. Guardian of the Wilderness. 1977: Satan's Cheerleaders. The Incredible Rocky Mountain Race (TV). 1978: The Time Machine (TV). 1979: Sunburn. 1981: Legend of the Wild. Under the Rainbow. 1984: Dark Mirror (TV).*

## KULKY, Henry 1911-1965

Squat, hairy, dark, flat-nosed, cigar-chewing American actor whose battered features bore mute witness to scores of boxing and wrestling bouts as 'Bomber Kulkavich'. At one time, he was judo champion of South America, but in post-war years fellow exwrestler Mike Mazurki (*qv*) introduced him

*1947: Call Northside 777. A Likely Story. Northwest Outpost (GB: End of the Rainbow). 1949: Tarzan's Magic Fountain. The Red Danube. Bandits of El Dorado (GB: Tricked). South Sea Sinner (GB: East of Java). 1950: Jackpot Jitters (GB: Jiggs and Maggie in Jackpot Jitters). Wabash Avenue. Bodyhold. Jiggs and Maggie Out West. 1951: *Chinatown Chump. The Kid from Amarillo (GB: Silver Chains). The Guy Who Came Back. Love Nest. You Never Can Tell (GB: You Never Know). Fixed Bayonets. 1952: Gobs and Gals (GB: Cruising Casanovas). The World in His Arms. No Holds Barred. My Wife's Best Friend. Red Skies of Montana. What Price Glory? Target - Hong Kong. Down Among the Sheltering Palms. 1953: The Glory Brigade. Powder River. The Robe. The 5,000 Fingers of Dr T. The Charge at Feather River. 1954: A Star is Born. Hell and High Water. Fireman, Save My Child. Yukon Vengeance. Tobor the Great. The Steel Cage. 1955: Prince of Players. New York Confidential. Abbott and Costello Meet the Keystone Kops. To Hell and Back. Jail Busters. Illegal. 1956: The Girl Can't Help It. 1957: Sierra Stranger. 1959: Up Periscope. The Gunfight at Dodge City. Guns of the Timberland. 1962: All Fall Down. 1963: A Global Affair.*

## KWOUK, Burt 1930-

Britain's busiest 'oriental' actor from the past three decades, Manchester-born, Shanghai-raised Kwouk has rarely been off cinema and (mainly) television screens since his film debut in 1958. Best remembered as Peter Sellers' maniacal houseboy Cato in the 'Pink Panther' films, he has also become a familiar figure (and voice) in TV commercials and as the Japanese commandant in the long-running *Tenko* series on TV. An unmistakeable character with his attractively harsh tones and impassive stare.

*1958: The Inn of the Sixth Happiness. 1959: Once More with Feeling. Yesterday's Enemy. 1961: The Terror of the Tongs. The Sinister Man. 1962: 55 Days at Peking. The War Lover. The Devil Never Sleeps (US: Satan Never Sleeps). 1963: The Cool Mikado. 1964: Goldfinger. A Shot in the Dark. 1965: Curse of the Fly. 1966: Lost Command. The Sandwich Man. The Brides of Fu Manchu. 1967: You Only Live Twice. 1968: Nobody Runs Forever. The Shoes of the Fisherman. 1969: The Most Dangerous Man in the World (US: The Chairman). 1970: Deep End. 1971: Madame Sin (TV. GB: cinemas). 1974: The Return of the Pink Panther. 1975: Girls Come First. Rollerball. 1976: The Pink Panther Strikes Again. 1977: The Last Remake of Beau Geste. The Strange Case of the End of Civilization As We Know It (TV). 1978: The Revenge of the Pink Panther. 1980: The Fiendish Plot of Dr Fu Manchu. 1982: Trail of the Pink Panther. 1983: Curse of the Pink Panther.*

## KYDD, Sam 1915-1982

Slight built, but craggy-faced, Irish-born portrayer of resilient cockney types in British films. Just as likely to be friendly or antagonistic, straight or crooked. Before service in World War II, his show-business experience was mainly limited to a period as emcee for a dance band. Interned in a Polish P-o-W camp from 1941 to 1946, he quickly picked up his career in post-war years, appearing in scores of films and a popular TV series, *Crane*. A perfectly cast Sam

Weller in a TV version of *The Pickwick Papers*. Died from a respiratory ailment. His son, Jonathan Kydd, is also an actor.

1940: *They Came by Night*. 1941: *Penn of Pennsylvania* (US: *The Courageous Mr Penn*). 1946: *The Captive Heart*. 1947: *They Made Me a Fugitive* (US: *I Became a Criminal*). *Colonel Bogey*. 1948: *Trouble in the Air*. *Scott of the Antarctic*. *Portrait from Life* (US: *The Girl in the Painting*). *Fly Away Peter*. *Love in Waiting*. *A Song for Tomorrow*. *To the Public Danger*. *A Piece of Cake*. *Passport to Pimlico*. *Badger's Green*. *The Small Back Room* (US: *Hour of Glory*). *Vengeance Is Mine*. 1949: *Movie-Go-Round*. *Floodtide*. *Poet's Pub*. *Stop Press Girl*. *Saints and Sinners*. *Madness of the Heart*. *The Cure for Love*. *Trottie True* (US: *Gay Lady*). *The Blue Lamp*. *The Hasty Heart*. 1950: *Treasure Island*. *Cage of Gold*. *The Dark Man*. *Seven Days to Noon*. *The Magnet*. *The Second Mate*. *The Clouded Yellow*. *Pool of London*. 1951: *High Treason*. *Captain Horatio Hornblower RN*. *Cheer the Brave*. *The Galloping Major*. *Penny Points to Paradise*. *Assassin for Hire*. *Secret People*. *Brandy for the Parson*. 1952: *Hunted* (US: *The Stranger in Between*). *Sing Along with Me*. *The Voice of Merrill* (US: *Murder Will Out*). *Angels One Five*. *Trent's Last Case*. *Derby Day* (US: *Four Against Fate*). *The Brave Don't Cry*. *Hot Ice*. *The Lost Hours* (US: *The Big Frame*). *Appointment in London*. *The Hour of 13*. 1953: *The Cruel Sea*. *Time Bomb* (US: *Terror on a Train*). *The Runaway Bus*. *Death Goes to School*. *Single-Handed* (US: *Sailor of the King*). *They Who Dare*. *Malta Story*. *The Steel Key*. 1954: *Devil on Horseback*. *Radio Cab Murder*. *Final Appointment*. *Father Brown* (US: *The Detective*). *The Rainbow Jacket*. *The Embezzler*. *The End of the Road*. 1955: *Storm Over the Nile*. *The Dark Avenger* (US: *The Warriors*). *The Quatermass Experiment* (US: *The Creeping Unknown*). *Portrait of Alison* (US: *Postmark for Danger*). *The Constant Husband*. *The Ladykillers*. *Raising a Riot*. *Where There's a Will*. *A Kid for Two Farthings*. *Passage Home*. *You Can't Escape*. *Josephine and Men*. 1956: *Tiger in the Smoke*. *Soho Incident* (US: *Spin a Dark Web*). *The Hideout*. *Reach for the Sky*. *Circus Friends*. *Jacqueline*. *Ramsbottom Rides Again*. *The Baby and the Battleship*. *It's a Wonderful World*. *Home and Away*. 1957: *Yangtse Incident* (US: *Battle Hell*). *The Scamp*. *The Smallest Show on Earth*. *Barnacle Bill* (US: *All at Sea*). *Happy is the Bride!* *Carry On Admiral* (US: *The Ship Was Loaded*). *Just My Luck*. *Dangerous Exile*. *The Safecracker*. 1958: *Up the Creek*. *Orders to Kill*. *I Was Monty's Double* (US: *Monty's Double*). *Life Is a Circus*. *Carlton-Browne of the FO* (US: *Man in a Cocked Hat*). *Law and Disorder*. *The Captain's Table*. *Further Up the Creek*. *Too Many Crooks*. 1959: *The Hound of the Baskervilles*. *The Thirty Nine Steps*. *Libel*. *The Price of Silence*. *I'm All Right, Jack*. *Follow That Horse!* *Upstairs and Downstairs*. *Make Mine a Million*. 1960: *Sink the Bismarck*. *Dead Lucky*. *Suspect* (US: *The Risk*). *The House in Marsh Road*. *There Was a Crooked Man*. 1961: *The Treasure of Monte Cristo* (US: *The Secret of Monte Cristo*). *Clue of the Silver Key*. 1962: *The Iron Maiden* (US: *The Swingin' Maiden*). 1963: *The Young Detectives* (serial). 1964: *Smokescreen*. 1965: *Island of Terror*. 1966: *The Projected Man*. 1967: *Smashing Time*. 1968: *\*Gold is Where You Find It*. *The Killing of Sister George*. 1969: *Till Death Us Do Part*. *Moon Zero Two*. *The Magnificent Six and ½* (second series). *Too Late the Hero*. 1970: *10 Rillington Place*. 1971: *Dad's Army*. *Quest for Love*. *The Magnificent Six and ½* (third series). *Up the Chastity Belt*. 1973: *Steptoe and Son Ride Again*. 1974: *The Amorous Milkman*. *Confessions of a Window Cleaner*. *The Fire Fighters*. 1975: *Great Expectations* (TV. GB: cinemas). 1976: *The Chiffy Kids* (series). 1979: *Yesterday's Hero*. *The Shillingbury Blowers* (TV). 1980: *Danger on Dartmoor*. *High Rise Donkey*. 1981: *Eye of the Needle*.

**LAHR, Bert**
(Irving Lahrheim) 1895-1967
The Cowardly Lion in *The Wizard of Oz*, of course. Apart from that landmark, however, Hollywood hardly made the most of this moon-faced, brown-haired, ever-beaming vaudevillian, a popular figure with audiences and colleagues alike. Alas, his india-rubber features and gurgling laugh enlivened too few films, following long musical comedy experience. Died from an internal haemorrhage.

1929: *\*Faint Heart*. 1931: *Flying High* (GB: *Happy Landing*). 1933: *Mr Broadway*. 1934: *\*Hizzoner*. 1936: *\*Gold Bricks*. 1937: *Merry-Go-Round of 1938*. *Love and Hisses*. 1938: *Just Around the Corner*. *Josette*. 1939: *Zaza*. *The Wizard of Oz*. 1942: *Sing Your Worries Away*. *Du Barry Was a Lady*. *Ship Ahoy*. 1944: *Meet the People*. 1949: *Always Leave Them Laughing*. 1951: *Mr Universe*. 1954: *Rose Marie*. 1955: *The Second Greatest Sex*. *The Great Waltz* (TV). 1965: *The Fantasticks* (voice only). 1966: *Thompson's Ghost* (TV). 1968: *The Night They Raided Minsky's*.

**LAMBERT, Jack (1)** 1899-
Severe-looking Scottish actor who spent ten years on the amateur stage before deciding to turn professional in 1930. He played in several Ealing films of the 1940s, enjoying his finest hour as the tough sergeant in *Nine Men*. Could have had a Hollywood contract in the early 1930s but preferred to work in Britain.

1931: *A Honeymoon Adventure*. 1935: *The Ghost Goes West*. 1936: *House Broken*. 1938: *Thistledown*. *The Terror*. *Marigold*. 1939: *The Spider*. *The Outsider*. 1943: *Nine Men*. 1946: *The Captive Heart*. 1947: *Hue and Cry*. *The Brothers*. *Dear Murderer*. 1948: *Eureka Stockade* (US: *Massacre Hill*). 1949: *Floodtide*. 1952: *The Lost Hours* (US: *The Big Frame*). *The Great Game*. 1953: *The Master of Ballantrae*. *Twice Upon a Time*. *\*The Candlelight Murder*. 1954: *The Sea Shall Not Have Them*. *Track the Man Down*. *Companions in Crime*. *Out of the Clouds*. *Three Cases of Murder*. 1955: *Storm Over the Nile*. *The Dark Avenger* (US: *The Warriors*). *Cross Channel*. *Jumping for Joy*. *Lost* (US: *Tears for Simon*). 1956: *Reach for the Sky*. *The Last Man to Hang?* 1957: *The Little Hut*. 1958: *Son of Robin Hood*. 1959: *The Bridal Path*. *The Devil's Disciple*. 1960: *Greyfriars Bobby*. 1961: *Francis of Assisi*. *On the Fiddle* (US: *Operation Snafu*). 1963: *Bomb in the High Street* (shown 1961). 1965: *Cuckoo Patrol*. *Dracula—Prince of Darkness*. 1966: *Modesty Blaise*. *\*Miss Mactaggart Won't Lie Down*. 1967: *They Came from Beyond Space*. 1972: *Neither the Sea nor the Sand*.

came to films from repertory and was kept busy from 1950 on, mostly in support, but occasionally in minor leads. Memorable as the villain in *The Adventures of Quentin Durward*, battling it out in a bell-tower with Robert Taylor. Long-married to actress Patricia Driscoll.

1950: *Waterfront (US: Waterfront Women). The Woman in Question (US: Five Angles on Murder). She Shall Have Murder.* 1951: *The Galloping Major. The Man in the White Suit. Night Without Stars.* 1952: *Emergency Call (US: 100 Hour Hunt). The Lost Hours (US: The Big Frame). La carrozza d'oro (GB: The Golden Coach). The Night Won't Talk. Song of Paris (US: Bachelor in Paris).* 1953: *The Final Test. The Intruder. Meet Mr Malcolm.* 1954: *Burnt Evidence. Time Is My Enemy. The End of the Road. The Teckman Mystery. The Passing Stranger.* 1955: *Passage Home. The Adventures of Quentin Durward (US: Quentin Durward). The Quatermass Experiment.* 1956: *The Baby and the Battleship.* 1957: *High Flight.* 1958: *A Tale of Two Cities. I Was Monty's Double (US: Monty's Double).* 1959: *The 39 Steps. Ben-Hur. A Touch of Larceny.* 1960: *Circle of Deception. The Queen's Guards.* 1961: *Macbeth.* 1962: *Mutiny on the Bounty.* 1963: *Murder at the Gallop. The Scarlet Blade (US: The Crimson Blade). Panic. The Devil-Ship Pirates.* 1964: *The Evil of Frankenstein.* 1965: *The Brigand of Kandahar. The Murder Game.* 1966: *Arabesque. The Witches (US: The Devil's Own).* 1967: *Frankenstein Created Woman. Quatermass and the Pit (US: 5,000,000 Miles to Earth).* 1968: *Decline and Fall ... of a birdwatcher!* 1969: *Battle of Britain.* 1971: *Burke and Hare. Mary Queen of Scots.* 1972: *Pope Joan. Nothing But the Night.* 1976: *Escape from the Dark (US: The Littlest Horse Thieves).*

## LAMBERT, Jack (2) 1920-

Fair-haired, surly-looking, small-nosed American actor who studied to be an English professor but, after gaining his degree, took himself off to Hollywood and played some really nasty villains, often with a psychopathic streak, and not usually with too much brain. He was a man you loved to see bite the dust but, failing to get a wider range of roles, Lambert drifted away from films after 1963.

1943: *The Cross of Lorraine.* 1945: *The Hidden Eye. The Harvey Girls. Abilene Town.* 1946: *The Hoodlum Saint. The Killers. The Plainsman and the Lady.* 1947: *The Vigilantes Return. Dick Tracy's Dilemma (GB: Mark of the Claw). The Unsuspected.* 1948: *Belle Starr's Daughter. River Lady. Montana Belle (released 1952). Big Jack. Brimstone.* 1949: *Border Incident.* 1950: *Stars in My Crown. Dakota Lil. North of the Great Divide. The Enforcer (GB: Murder Inc).* 1951: *The Secret of Convict Lake.* 1952: *Blackbeard the Pirate. Bend of the River (GB: Where the River Bends).* 1953: *Scared Stiff. 99 River Street.* 1954: *Vera Cruz.* 1955: *Run for Cover. Kiss Me Deadly. At Gunpoint! (GB: Gunpoint!).* 1956: *Canyon River.* 1957: *Chicago Confidential.* 1958: *Hot Car Girl. Machine Gun Kelly. Party Girl.* 1959: *Day of the Outlaw. Alias Jesse James.* 1960: *Freckles.* 1961: *The George Raft Story (GB: Spin of a Coin).* 1962: *How the West Was Won.* 1963: *Four for Texas.* 1967: *Winchester '73 (TV).*

## LAMBLE, Lloyd 1914-

Sandy-haired Australian actor of quiet authority, in Britain from 1951, and quickly building up a gallery there of officers, inspectors, civil servants, concerned parents and the occasional highly placed, cultivated crook. Like so many of his contemporaries, Lamble found the cinema's requirements for his services consistently heavy through the 1950s. After 1962, he turned to TV and the theatre, becoming well-known as Mr Eliot in TV's *Crossroads*.

1951: *Saturday Island (US: Island of Desire).* 1952: *Lady in the Fog. (US: Scotland Yard Inspector). Come Back Peter. Curtain Up. Appointment in London.* 1953: *The Story of Gilbert and Sullivan (US: The Great Gilbert*

and Sullivan). *Background (US: Edge of Divorce). Street Corner (US: Both Sides of the Law). Mantrap (US: Woman in Hiding). Three Steps to the Gallows (released 1955. US: White Fire). The Straw Man.* 1954: *Profile. The Red Dress. *The Mirror and Markheim. The Green Buddha. Out of the Clouds. The Dam Busters. The Belles of St Trinian's. Track the Man Down. *Fatal Journey.* 1955: *The Man Who Never Was.* 1956: *The Gelignite Gang (US: The Dynamiters). Private's Progress. The Girl in the Picture. The Man Who Knew Too Much. *Person Unknown. The Good Companions. Suspended Alibi.* 1957: *Night of the Demon (US: Curse of the Demon). These Dangerous Years (US: Dangerous Youth). Quatermass II (US: Enemy from Space). Barnacle Bill (US: All at Sea). Sea Wife. There's Always a Thursday. Blue Murder at St Trinian's.* 1958: *Dunkirk. No Trees in the Street. The Man Who Wouldn't Talk. The Bank Raiders.* 1959: *The Heart of a Man. Our Man in Havana. The Challenge. Breakout. Expresso Bongo.* 1960: *The Pure Hell of St Trinian's. The Trials of Oscar Wilde (US: The Man With the Green Carnation).* 1962: *Tiara Tahiti. Term of Trial. The Boys.* 1973: *And Now the Screaming Starts. No Sex Please—We're British. On the Game.* 1974: *Eskimo Nell.*

## LAMONT, Duncan 1918-

Born in Portugal and raised in Scotland, this lowering, rugged actor with tousled brown hair and jutting lower lip was just as easily cast as gentle giant or cruel villain. He

## LANCHESTER, Elsa

(Elizabeth Sullivan) 1902- 1986

Bright, bird-like, chestnut-haired British leading lady whose heroines tended to be eccentric; later she became an attention-grabbing character actress after moving to Hollywood. In show business from 16 and originally a singer, she married Charles Laughton in 1929. Probably best remembered now as the creature's mate in *Bride of Frankenstein*. Twice nominated for Academy Awards.

*1927: One of the Best. The Constant Nymph. 1928: \*Bluebottles. \*The Tonic. \*Daydreams. 1929: \*Comets. \*Mr Smith Wakes Up. 1930: \*Ashes. The Love Habit. 1931: The Stronger Sex. Potiphar's Wife (US: Her Strange Desire). The Officer's Mess. 1933: The Private Life of Henry VIII. 1934: The Private Life of Don Juan. 1935: David Copperfield. Bride of Frankenstein. Naughty Marietta. \*Miss Bracegirdle Does Her Duty. The Ghost Goes West. 1936: Rembrandt. 1938: Vessel of Wrath (US: The Beachcomber). 1941: Ladies in Retirement. 1942: Son of Fury. Tales of Manhattan. 1943: Forever and a Day. Thumbs Up. Lassie Come Home. 1944: Passport to Adventure. 1945: The Spiral Staircase. 1946: The Razor's Edge. 1947: Northwest Outpost (GB: End of the Rainbow). The Bishop's Wife. 1948: The Big Clock. 1949: The Inspector-General. The Secret Garden. Come to the Stable. 1950: Buccaneer's Girl. Mystery Street. The Petty Girl (GB: Girl of the Year). Frenchie. 1951: Young Man with Ideas. 1952: Androcles and the Lion. Dreamboat. Les Miserables. 1953: The Girls of Pleasure Island. 1954: Hell's Half Acre. Three Ring Circus. The Glass Slipper. 1956: Stranger in the Night (TV). 1957: Witness for the Prosecution. 1958: Bell, Book and Candle. \*Fabulous Hollywood. 1964: Honeymoon Hotel. Mary Poppins. Pajama Party. 1965: That Darn Cat! 1966: Easy Come, Easy Go. 1967: Blackbeard's Ghost. 1969: Me, Natalie. My Dog, the Thief (TV. GB: cinemas). In Name Only (TV). Rascal. 1971: Willard. 1973: Arnold. Terror in the Wax Museum. 1976: Murder by Death. 1980: Die Laughing.*

### LANDAU, Martin 1931-

Spare, tall, sharp-faced, dark-haired American actor, reminiscent of Raymond Massey but with a more desperate look. He seemed set for a prolific film career after his second-lead villain in Hitchcock's *North by Northwest*, but in fact has made very few films, getting tied up in the television series *Mission Impossible* and *Space 1999*, in both of which he appeared with his wife Barbara Bain.

*1959: Pork Chop Hill. North by Northwest. The Sounds of Eden (TV). The Gazebo. 1962: Stagecoach to Dancer's Rock. 1963: Cleopatra. Decision at Midnight. 1965: The Hallelujah Trail. The Greatest Story Ever Told. 1966: Nevada Smith. 1969: Mission Impossible Versus The Mob (TV. GB: cinemas). 1970: They Call Me MISTER Tibbs! 1971: Welcome Home Johnny Bristol (TV). A Town Called Bastard (US: A Town Called Hell). 1972: Black Gunn. 1973: Savage (TV). 1976: Tony Saitta/Tough Tony. Blazing Magnum/Strange Shadows in an Empty Room. 1979: Meteor. The Last Word. 1980: Without Warning. 1981: Easter Sunday. The Return. 1982: Alone in the Dark. 1983: The Being. Trian by Terror (TV)*

### LANDIS, Jessie Royce
(J. R. Medbury) 1904-1972

Dark-haired American stage actress who came to her busiest time in films in her middle forties and played matrons both caustic and dizzy. Her most notable screen appearance was probably as Grace Kelly's mother in *To Catch a Thief*, when she stubs out her cigarette in a soft-boiled egg. Died from cancer.

*1930: Derelict. 1937: Oh! Doctor. 1939: First Love. 1949: My Foolish Heart. Mr Belvedere Goes to College. It Happens Every Spring. 1950: Mother Didn't Tell Me. 1952: Meet Me Tonight. 1953: She Couldn't Say No (GB: Beautiful But Dangerous). 1955: To Catch a Thief. 1956: The Girl He Left Behind. The Swan. 1957: My Man Godfrey. 1958: I Married a Woman. 1959: North by Northwest. A Private's Affair. 1961: Aimez-vous Brahms? (GB: Goodbye Again). 1962: Bon Voyage! Boys' Night Out. 1963: Critics' Choice. Gidget Goes to Rome. 1969: Airport. 1971: Mr and Mrs Bo Jo Jones (TV).*

### LANE, Charles
(C. Levison) 1899-

Tall, thin, scoop-nosed, long-faced, brown-haired, snoopy-looking American actor; one could think of no better choice to play the kind of 'peeper' a husband would hire to trail his wife with a view to grounds for divorce. Consequently he was cast as bailiffs, reporters, tax inspectors, debt

collectors and various shady characters in pin-stripe suits, trilby hats and (often) rimless spectacles, from behind which beady eyes fastened on their victim. Still acting into his eighties.

*1933: †42nd Street. 1934: †Twentieth Century. †Broadway Bill (GB: Strictly Confidential). 1935: †Here Comes the Band. †Two for Tonight. 1936: †Neighborhood House. †Mr Deeds Goes to Town. †The Milky Way. The Crime of Dr Forbes. Ticket to Paradise. Thirty-Six Hours to Kill. Three Men on a Horse. Band of Outlaws. 1937: We're on the Jury. River of Missing Men. Internes Can't Take Money (GB: You Can't Take Money). Trapped by G-Men. Danger, Love at Work! City Girl. Ali Baba Goes to Town. 1938: Always in Trouble. Inside Story. In Old Chicago. You Can't Take It With You. Cocoanut Grove. Thanks for Everything. Professor, Beware! Kentucky. 1939: The Flying Irishman. Rose of Washington Square. Boy Slaves. Second Fiddle. News Is Made at Night. They All Come Out. Lucky Night. Mr Smith Goes to Washington. The Cat and the Canary. 1940: Buck Benny Rides Again. Blondie Plays Cupid. The Crooked Road. Johnny Apollo. We Who Are Young. On Their Own. Queen of the Mob. The Great Profile. Rhythm on the River. The Leather Pushers. Ellery Queen, Master Detective. 1941: Repent at Leisure. Meet John Doe. Ellery Queen and the Perfect Crime (GB: The Perfect Crime). Hot Spot (GB: I Wake Up Screaming). Never Give a Sucker an Even Break (GB: What a Man!). Barnacle Bill. Buy Me That Town. Ball of Fire. Ellery Queen's Penthouse Mystery. Three Girls About Town. The Invisible Woman. Sealed Lips. Sing Another Chorus. The Crooked Road. Back Street. Ride 'Em Cowboy. The Big Store. 1942: A Gentleman at Heart. The Lady Is Willing. Dudes Are Pretty People. Tarzan's New York Adventure. Home in Wyomin'. Thru Different Eyes. Friendly Enemies. My Sarong. 1943: Arsenic and Old Lace. 1946: The Invisible Informer. A Close Call for Boston Blackie (GB: Lady of Mystery). Just Before Dawn. The Mysterious Intruder. Swell Guy. It's a Wonderful Life! 1947: The Farmer's Daughter. Louisiana. Intrigue. Roses Are Red. Call Northside 777. 1948: State of the Union (GB: The World and His Wife). The Gentleman from Nowhere. Apartment for Peggy. Out of the Storm. Race Street. 1949: Mother Is a Freshman (GB: Mother Knows Best). You're My Everything. Miss Grant Takes Richmond (GB: Innocence Is Bliss). 1950: Bannerline. Riding High. For Heaven's Sake. 1951: I Can Get It for You Wholesale (GB: This is My Affair). Here Comes the Groom. 1953: Remains To Be Seen. The Juggler. The Affairs of Dobie Gillis. 1956: The Birds and the Bees. 1957: Top Secret Affair (GB: Their Secret Affair). God Is My Partner. 1958: Teacher's Pet. 1959: The Mating Game. The Thirty-Foot Bride of Candy Rock. 1961: The Music Man. 1962: Papa's Delicate Condition. 1963: It's a Mad, Mad, Mad, Mad World. 1964: Good Neighbor*

*Sam. The New Interns. The Carpetbaggers. John Goldfarb, Please Come Home. 1965: Looking for Love. Billie. 1966: The Ugly Dachshund. The Ghost and Mr Chicken. 1967: The Gnome-Mobile. 1968: What's So Bad About Feeling Good? 1970: The Aristocats (voice only). 1980: The Little Dragons.*

†As Charles Levison

## LANG, Harold 1923-1970

Fair-haired, slim-faced, shady-looking British actor who, in dark shirt and light tie, leeringly menaced many a British 'B' hero of the 1950s before perhaps deciding that such conduct was unbecoming to a RADA gold medallist and concentrating on a stage career, notably touring a record number of countries, including Sweden, Italy, Germany, Switzerland, Turkey, Portugal, Sri Lanka, Pakistan and Egypt, where he died.

*1949: Floodtide. The Spider and the Fly. 1950: Cairo Road. The Franchise Affair. 1951: Calling Bulldog Drummond. Cloudburst. 1952: So Little Time. Wings of Danger (US: Dead on Course). It Started in Paradise. Folly to be Wise. The Long Memory. 1953: Counterspy (US: Undercover Agent). The Saint's Return (US: The Saint's Girl Friday). Laughing Anne. Street Corner (US: Both Sides of the Law). The Intruder. Star of My Night. A Day to Remember. 1954: The Case of the Bogus Count. Adventure in the Hopfields. Dance Little Lady. The Case of Diamond Annie. 36 Hours (US: Terror Street). The Passing Stranger. Men of Sherwood Forest. 1955: Murder by Proxy (completed 1953. US: Blackout). The Quatermass Experiment (US: The Creeping Unknown). 1956: It's a Wonderful World. The Hideout. 1957: The Flesh is Weak. 1958: Chain of Events. Man with a Gun. The Betrayal. Links of Justice. Carve Her Name with Pride. 1962: Paranoiac. 1963: West 11. 1964: Dr Terror's House of Horrors. 1965: The Nanny. 1966: The Psychopath. 1968: Two Gentlemen Sharing.*

## LANSING, Joi
(Joyce Wassmansdoff) 1928-1972

Buxom American blonde with attractive looks and silky hair, a minor-league Jayne Mansfield, but hotter on the wisecracks. She

probably had more talent than most of her rivals on the sexpot scene, but lacked an aura of innocence. She had one or two B-movie leads (the last as late as 1969), but was mostly confined to cameos and minor roles. Began as a singer. Actor Lance Fuller (1928- ) was the first (1951-3) of her three husbands. Cancer killed her at 44.

*1948: †Julia Misbehaves. †The Counterfeiters. †Easter Parade. 1949: *†Super Cue Men. †The Girl from Jones Beach. †Neptune's Daughter. Take Me Out to the Ball Game (GB: Everybody's Cheering). 1951: On the Riviera. Two Tickets to Broadway. Pier 23. 1952: The Merry Widow. Singin' in the Rain. 1953: The French Line. 1954: *So You Want to Go to a Nightclub. *So You're Taking in a Roomer. 1955: *So You Want to Be a VP. *So You Want to Be a Policeman. Son of Sinbad. 1956: *The Fountain of Youth. *So You Think the Grass is Greener. Hot Cars. The Brave One. Hot Shots. 1958: Touch of Evil. 1959: Atomic Submarine. A Hole in the Head. It Started With a Kiss. Who Was That Lady? 1965: Marriage on the Rocks. 1967: Hillbillys in a Haunted House. 1969: Bigfoot.*

†As Joyce Lansing

## LARCH, John 1924-

Light-haired, light-eyed, tall, cynical-looking American actor who came to Hollywood to play largely friendly types who couldn't be trusted; then he drifted off into television in the early 1960s, returning later for a few crooked businessmen and others who wore a crooked smile and didn't quite meet your gaze.

*1954: Bitter Creek. 1955: The Phenix City Story (GB: The Phoenix City Story). Tight Spot. 1956: The Killer is Loose. Written on the Wind. Behind the High Wall. Seven Men from Now. 1957: Gun for a Coward. Man in the Shadow (GB: Pay the Devil). The Careless Years. Quantez. 1958: The Saga of Hemp Brown. From Hell to Texas (GB: Manhunt). 1959: Stampede at Bitter Creek (TV. GB: cinemas). 1960: Hell to Eternity. 1962: Miracle of the White Stallions (GB: The Flight of the White Stallions). How the West Was Won. 1968: The Wrecking Crew. The House of Seven Joys. 1969: The Great Bank*

*Robbery. Hail Hero! 1970: Cannon for Cordoba. 1971: The City (TV). Dirty Harry. Play 'Misty' For Me. 1972: Santee. Madigan: The Park Avenue Beat (TV). 1974: The Chadwick Family (TV). Winterkill (TV). Bad Ronald (TV). Framed. 1975: The Desperate Miles (TV). Ellery Queen (TV). 1976: Future Cop (TV). 1978: The Critical List (TV). 1979: The Amityville Horror. 1982: Airplane II The Sequel.*

## LAURIE, John 1897-1980

Thin-headed, wild-eyed, frizzy-haired, bushy-browed, (very) Scottish actor, frequently seen in fanatical or eccentric roles. Although the earlier characters he created were often surrounded by gloom and doom, he also had a dry, faintly maniacal sense of humour, seen to good effect in his later years as one of the denizens of TV's *Dad's Army*. Originally planned to become an architect, but switched to an acting course in his early twenties.

*1929: Juno and the Paycock (US: The Shame of Mary Boyle). 1934: Red Ensign (US: Strike!). 1935: Her Last Affaire. The 39 Steps. 1936: Tudor Rose (US: Nine Days a Queen). As You Like It. East Meet West. Born That Way. 1937: The Edge of the World. Farewell Again (US: Troopship). The Windmill. Jericho (US: Dark Sands). There Was a Young Man. 1938: A Royal Divorce. The Claydon Treasure Mystery. 1939: The Ware Case. The Four Feathers. Q Planes (US: Clouds Over Europe). 1940: Convoy. Laugh It Off. Sailors Three (US: Three Cockeyed Sailors). 1941: Dangerous Moonlight (US: Suicide Squadron). Old Mother Riley's Ghosts. The Ghost of St Michael's. Ships with Wings. Old Mother Riley Cleans Up. 1943: The Demi-Paradise (US: Adventure for Two). The Lamp Still Burns. The Gentle Sex. The Life and Death of Colonel Blimp (US: Colonel Blimp). 1944: Fanny by Gaslight (US: Man of Evil). Medal for the General. The Way Ahead. Henry V. 1945: I Know Where I'm Going! The Agitator. Great Day. Caesar and Cleopatra. The World Owes Me a Living. 1946: School for Secrets (US: Secret Flight). Gaiety George (US: Showtime). 1947: Jassy. The Brothers. Uncle Silas (US: The Inheritance. Mine Own Executioner. 1948: Bonnie*

ABOVE Charles **Lane** (with trilby) and a couple of minions keep
Margaret Lindsay and Anna May Wong apart in *Ellery Queen's
Penthouse Mystery* (1941)

BELOW Unusual to find one of Harold **Lang**'s film characters
among the girls. But here he's with Maya Koumani (left) and
Mylene Demongeot in the 1956 film *It's a Wonderful World*

Prince Charlie. Hamlet. 1949: Floodtide. Madeleine. 1950: No Trace. Treasure Island. Trio. Happy Go Lovely. Pandora and the Flying Dutchman. 1951: Laughter in Paradise. Encore. Saturday Island (US: Island of Desire). 1952: *Potter of the Yard. Tread Softly. The Great Game. *Rig 20 (narrator only). 1953: The Fake. Too Many Detectives. Love in Pawn. Mr Beamish Goes South. Strange Stories. Johnny on the Run. 1954: Destination Milan. Devil Girl from Mars. Hobson's Choice. The Black Knight. 1955: Richard III. 1957: *Day of Grace. Campbell's Kingdom. Murder Reported. 1958: Rockets Galore! (US: Mad Little Island). Next to No Time! 1959: Kidnapped. 1961: Don't Bother to Knock! (US: Why Bother to Knock?). 1963: Ladies Who Do. Siege of the Saxons. 1964: Eagle Rock (voice only). 1966: Mr Ten Per Cent. The Reptile. 1971: Dad's Army. The Abominable Dr Phibes. 1975: One of Our Dinosaurs is Missing. 1978: Return to the Edge of the World. 1979: The Prisoner of Zenda.

**LAUTER, Ed** 1940-
Bald, tall, leering, long-jawed, villainous-looking American actor sometimes playing toughies whose yellow streak was revealed in the final reel. A former English graduate and stand-up comic, he came to films in his early thirties and was soon one of the few familiar character faces of the 1970s and beyond. He acquitted himself more than adequately as a private eye in the leading role of a TV movie, but was of more value in the supporting cast and has lodged at around fifth billing ever since.

1971: Hickey and Boggs. 1972: Dirty Little Billy. Rage. The Magnificent Seven Ride! The New Centurions (GB: Precinct 45—Los Angeles Police). Bad Company. 1973: The Last American Hero. Executive Action. Lolly Madonna XXX (GB: The Lolly Madonna War). Class of '63 (TV). 1974: The Longest Yard (GB: The Mean Machine). The Midnight Man. French Connection II (GB: French Connection No. 2). The Migrants (TV). The Godchild (TV). 1975: Satan's Triangle (TV). A Shadow in the Streets (TV). Breakheart Pass. Last Hours Before Morning (TV). 1976: King Kong. Family Plot. 1977: The Chicken

Chronicles. The White Buffalo. 1978: The Clone Master (TV). Magic. 1979: The Jericho Mile (TV. GB: cinemas). 1980: Death Hunt. 1981: Loose Shoes. The Amateur. 1982: Timerider: The Adventure of Lyle Swann. Eureka. 1983: Cujo. Lassiter. The Big Score. Hardcastle and McCormick (TV). 1984: Finders Keepers. The Cartier Affair (TV). 1985: Youngblood. Girls Just Want to Have Fun. Death Wish 3.

**LAUTER, Harry** 1920- 1990
Tall, fair-haired, blue-eyed, glum-looking American actor who played villains in serials, westerns and all kinds of low-budget adventure films, and had the height and looks to appear genuinely menacing. He actually got to play heroes in three mid-1950s' serials, but the genre was a dying breed, and he returned to secondary bad guys in minor movies and very small roles in major ones. Got out of the business in the early 1970s to concentrate on running an art and antique gallery and on his own secondary career as a painter.

1948: Moonrise. The Gay Intruders. A Foreign Affair. 1949: Prince of the Plains. White Heat. Tucson. Slattery's Hurricane. The Great Dan Patch. Zamba (GB: Zamba the Gorilla). 1950: Blue Grass of Kentucky. Experiment Alcatraz. Between Midnight and Dawn. I'll Get By. 1951: Silver City Bonanza. Roadblock. Thunder in God's Country. Let's Go Navy. Flying Disc Man from Mars (serial). Lorna Doone. Whirlwind. The Mob (GB: Remember That Face). Hills of Utah. The Day the Earth Stood Still. According to Mrs Hoyle. The Kid from Amarillo. Valley of Fire. The Racket. 1952: Night Stage to Galveston. This Woman Is Dangerous. Apache Country. The Sea Tiger. The Steel Fist. Talk About a Stranger. Yukon Gold. 1953: Canadian Mounties vs Atomic Invaders (serial). The Marshal's Daughter. Prince of Pirates. Topeka. The Big Heat. The Fighting Lawman. Forbidden. Fighter Attack. Pack Train. 1954: Dragonfly Squadron. Trader Tom of the China Seas (serial). Crime Wave (GB: The City is Dark). Yankee Pasha. The Bob Mathias Story (GB: The Flaming Torch). Return to Treasure Island. The Forty-Niners. 1955: It Came from Beneath the Sea. King of the Carnival (serial).

The Creature with the Atom Brain. Lord of the Jungle. The Crooked Web. At Gunpoint! (GB: Gunpoint!). 1956: Earth vs the Flying Saucers. The Werewolf. The Man in the Gray Flannel Suit. Miami Exposé. Dig That Uranium. 1957: The Women of Pitcairn Island. The Badge of Marshal Brennan. Hellcats of the Navy. Death in Small Doses. The Oklahoman. Raiders of Old California. 1958: Return to Warbow. Toughest Gun in Tombstone. Cry Baby Killer. Missile Monsters. Tarzan's Fight for Life. Good Day for a Hanging. 1959: The Gunfight at Dodge City. Louisiana Hussy (GB: Bad Girl). 1961: Posse from Hell. 1962: The Wild Westerners. 1965: Fort Courageous. Convict Stage. 1966: Ambush Bay. Fort Utah. 1967: Tarzan's Jungle Rebellion (TV. Released to cinemas 1970). 1968: More Dead Than Alive. Massacre Harbor. 1969: Barquero. Superbeast (released 1972). 1971: The Todd Killings. Escape from the Planet of the Apes.

**LAWRENCE, Marc**
(Max Goldsmith) 1910-
Dark-haired Italianate Hollywood actor, a former singer and stage actor who devoted himself almost exclusively to films from 1936. With his narrow head, hooded eyes and tight, humourless smile, Lawrence was a natural for gangsters—and very efficient at it too. As he grew older, his pock-marked face took on a mottled appearance, making him look like an ancient, but still very deadly cobra.

1933: Gambling Ship. White Woman. 1934: Death on the Diamond. 1935: Little Big Shot. Dr Socrates. Man of the Hour. G-Men. Don't Bet on Blondes. Go Into Your Dance. 1936: Trapped by Television (GB: Caught by Television). Counterfeit. Night Waitress. The Final Hour. Love on a Bet. Under Two Flags. Desire. The Cowboy Star. 1937: I Promise to Pay. Racketeers in Exile. San Quentin. Counsel for Crime. Murder in Greenwich Village. The Shadow (GB: The Circus Shadow). Charlie Chan on Broadway. Criminals of the Air. Motor Madness. What Price Vengeance? (GB: Vengeance). 1938: Penitentiary. Convicted. Adventure in Sahara. The Spider's Web (serial). There's That Woman Again (GB: What a Woman!) Charlie Chan in Honolulu. Who Killed Gail Preston? I Am the Law.

Squadron of Honor. While New York Sleeps. 1939: Romance of the Redwoods. Blind Alley. The Housekeeper's Daughter. Beware, Spooks! Homicide Bureau. SOS Tidal Wave (GB: Tidal Wave). Sergeant Madden. Ex-Champ (GB: Golden Gloves). The Lone Wolf Spy Hunt (GB: The Lone Wolf's Daughter). *Think First. Code of the Streets. Dust Be My Destiny. Invisible Stripes. 1940: Charlie Chan at the Wax Museum. Brigham Young—Frontiersman (GB: Brigham Young). Love, Honor and Oh, Baby! The Man Who Talked Too Much. Johnny Apollo. The Golden Fleecing. The Great Profile. 1941: A Dangerous Game. The Man Who Lost Himself. Lady Scarface. The Shepherd of the Hills. Public Enemies. The Monster and the Girl. Tall, Dark and Handsome. Blossoms in the Dust. Sundown. Hold That Ghost! 1942: Yokel Boy (GB: Hitting the Headlines). Call of the Canyon. This Gun for Hire. Nazi Agent. 'Neath Brooklyn Bridge. The Ox-Bow Incident (GB: Strange Incident). 1943: Hit the Ice. Calaboose. Submarine Alert. Eyes of the Underworld. 1944: Rainbow Island. Tampico. Dillinger. The Princess and the Pirate. 1945: Don't Fence Me In. Flame of the Barbary Coast. Club Havana. Life with Blondie. 1946: Blonde Alibi. The Virginian. Cloak and Dagger. The Big Sleep. 1947: I Walk Alone. Yankee Fakir. Unconquered. Captain from Castile. Joe Palooka in the Knock-Out. 1948: Out of the Storm. Key Largo. 1949: Jigsaw. Tough Assignment. Calamity Jane and Sam Bass. 1950: The Black Hand. Abbott and Costello in the Foreign Legion. The Asphalt Jungle. The Desert Hawk. 1951: Hurricane Island. My Favorite Spy. Vacanze col gangster (US: Gun Moll). 1953: I tre corsari. Foreign Legion/Legion straniera. Noi peccatori/Noi peccatini. La tratta della bianchi (GB: Girls Marked Danger). 1953: Il piu comico spettacolo del mondo. Fratelli d'Italia. Jolanda, la figlia del corsaro nero. 1954: Ballata tragica/Love without Tomorrow. Helen of Troy. 1956: Suor Maria. 1957: Kill Her Gently. 1962: Recoil (TV. GB: cinemas). 1963: Johnny Cool. †Nightmare in the Sun. 1964: Due mafiosi contro Al Capone. 1966: Savage Pampas. Johnny Tiger. Deux tueurs. 1967: Custer of the West. 1968: Eve, the Savage Venus. Krakatoa—East of Java. 1969: The Five Man Army. The Kremlin Letter. 1973: Frasier, the Sensuous Lion. Honor Thy Father (TV. GB: cinemas). 1974: The Man with the Golden Gun. 1976: Marathon Man. 1977: A Piece of the Action. 1978: Foul Play. 1979: Goin' Coconuts. 1980: Supersnooper (US: Super Fuzz). 1982: Cataclysm. †Pigs (later Daddy's Deadly Darling. Filmed 1972). 1985: Night Train to Terror.

† Also directed

## LEACHMAN, Cloris 1926-
Thin-faced blonde American actress, mostly in anguished roles, but no slouch in screwball comedy. Tremendously busy in television from the late 1940s, but hardly seen in the cinema at all until an Academy

Award for The Last Picture Show brought her wider recognition. Television called her back for featured (and sometimes starring) roles in many TV movies of the 1970s and 1980s.

1955: Kiss Me Deadly. 1956: The Rack. 1961: The Chapman Report. 1969: Butch Cassidy and the Sundance Kid. Silent Night, Lonely Night (TV). 1970: The People Next Door. WUSA. Lovers and Other Strangers. 1971: The Steagle. The Last Picture Show. Suddenly Single (TV). 1972: Haunts of the Very Rich (TV). Of Thee I Sing (TV). Of Men and Women (TV). A Brand New Life (TV). Crime Club (TV). 1973: Dying Room Only (TV). Dillinger. Charley and the Angel. Run, Stranger, Run/Happy Mother's Day ... Love George. 1974: Hitchhike! (TV). Daisy Miller. Death Sentence (TV). Young Frankenstein. The Migrants (TV). A Girl Named Sooner (TV). Thursday's Game (TV). 1975: Death Scream (TV). Someone I Touched (TV). Crazy Mama. The New Original Wonder Woman (TV). 1976: The Love Boat (TV). 1977: It Happened One Christmas (TV). High Anxiety. The Mouse and His Child (voice only). 1978: The Muppet Movie. The North Avenue Irregulars (GB: Hill's Angels). Foolin' Around (released 1980). Willa (TV). Long Journey Back (TV). 1979: SOS Titanic (TV. GB: cinemas). Mrs R's Daughter (TV). Scavenger Hunt. 1980: Scoring. The Acorn People (TV) Herbie Goes Bananas. 1981: History of the World Part One. Advice to the Lovelorn (TV). 1983: The Woman Who Willed a Miracle (TV) DIXIE: Changing Habits (TV). The Demon Murder Case (TV). 1984: Ernie Kovacs: Between the Laughter (TV).

## LEBEDEFF, Ivan 1894-1953
This brown-haired, pencil-moustached, Lithuanian-born actor was, in films, a real smoothie. A cigarette, a tan and a dazzling smile usually accompanied his romantic advances; for a few years, he became a Hollywood lothario par excellence after beginning his career in German and French films. This king of screen co-respondents did not enlarge his range, however, and in post-war years drifted away from the cinema. Died from a heart attack.

1923: Friedericus Rex. 1924: La mort fortunée. L'âme d'un artiste. 600,000 francs par mois. Le prince charmant. 1925: Les Doigts brûlés. 1926: The Sorrows of Satan. 1927: The Love of Sunya. The Angel of Broadway. The Forbidden Woman. Let 'Er Go Gallegher (GB: Gallegher). 1928: Walking Back. Sin Town. 1929: The Veiled Woman. Street Girl. They Had to See Paris. 1930: Half Shot at Sunrise. The Cuckoos. The Midnight Mystery. The Conspiracy. 1931: Bachelor Apartment. Deceit. Woman Pursued. The Lady Refuses. The Gay Diplomat. 1932: *Hollywood on Parade. *The Hollywood Handicap. Unholy Love. 1933: Bombshell (GB: Blonde Bombshell). Made on Broadway (GB: The Girl I Made). Laughing at Life. Sweepings. 1934: Kansas City Princess. The Merry Frinks (GB: The Happy Family). The Merry Widow. Moulin Rouge. 1935: China Seas. Goin' to Town. Sweepstake Annie (GB: Annie Doesn't Live Here). 1936: The Golden Arrow. Pepper. Love on the Run. 1937: Fair Warning. Conquest (GB: Marie Walewska). History is Made at Night. Atlantic Flight. Mama Steps Out. Angel. 1938: Straight, Place and Show (GB: They're Off!). Wise Girl. 1939: You Can't Cheat an Honest Man. Trapped in the Sky. The Mystery of Mr Wong. Elsa Maxwell's Hotel for Women/Hotel for Women. 1940: Public Deb No. 1. Passport to Alcatraz. 1941: The Shanghai Gesture. Blue, White and Perfect. 1942: Foreign Agent. Lure of the Islands. 1943: Mission to Moscow. Around the World. 1944: Oh, What a Night! Are These Our Parents? (GB: They Are Guilty). 1952: California Conquest. The Snows of Kilimanjaro.

## LEE, Bernard 1908-1981
Brown-haired British actor with large, honest, friendly face, a screen portrayer of solid, pleasant, dependable types. Never a star, but in demand for reliable character roles for 40 years—only effectively cast against type in 1963's Ring of Spies. Prolonged his screen presence past retirement with his long-running portrayal of James Bond's affable, humourless boss, 'M', an extension of his many film policemen. Died from cancer.

1934: The Double Event. 1935: The River House Mystery. 1936: Rhodes of Africa.

*1937: The Black Tulip. 1938: The Terror. Murder in Soho (US: Murder in the Night). 1939: Frozen Limits. The Outsider. 1940: Let George Do It. Spare a Copper. 1941: Once a Crook. 1946: This Man is Mine. 1947: Dusty Bates (serial). The Courtneys of Curzon Street (US: The Courtney Affair). 1948: The Fallen Idol. Quartet. Elizabeth of Ladymead. 1949: The Third Man. The Blue Lamp. 1950: Morning Departure (US: Operation Disaster). Odette. Last Holiday. Cage of Gold. The Adventurers (US: The Great Adventure). 1951: Calling Bulldog Drummond. White Corridors. Appointment with Venus (US: Island Rescue). Mr Denning Drives North. 1952: Gift Horse (US: Glory at Sea). The Yellow Balloon. 1953: Single-Handed (US: Sailor of the King). Beat the Devil. 1954: Father Brown (US: The Detective). Seagulls over Sorrento (US: Crest of the Wave). The Rainbow Jacket. The Purple Plain. 1955: Out of the Clouds. The Ship That Died of Shame (US: PT Raiders). 1956: The Battle of the River Plate (US: Pursuit of the Graf Spee). The Spanish Gardener. 1957: Fire Down Below. Across the Bridge. High Flight. Interpol (US: Pick-up Alley). 1958: Dunkirk. The Key. Nowhere to Go. The Man Upstairs. Danger Within (US: Breakout). 1959: Beyond This Place (US: Web of Evidence). Kidnapped. 1960: The Angry Silence. Cone of Silence (US: Trouble in the Sky). Clue of the Twisted Candle. 1961: Partners in Crime. Clue of the Silver Key. Fury at Smuggler's Bay. The Secret Partner. Whistle down the Wind. 1962: The Share Out. The L-Shaped Room. Dr No. Vengeance (US: The Brain). Two Left Feet. 1963: From Russia with Love. A Place to Go. Ring of Spies. Saturday Night Out. 1964: Who Was Maddox? Goldfinger. Dr Terror's House of Horrors. 1965: The Legend of Young Dick Turpin. Thunderball. The Amorous Adventures of Moll Flanders. The Spy Who Came in from the Cold. 1967: You Only Live Twice. Operation Kid Brother. 1969: Crossplot. On Her Majesty's Secret Service. 1970: 10 Rillington Place. The Man Who Died Twice (TV). The Raging Moon (US: Long Ago Tomorrow). 1971: Danger Point. Diamonds Are Forever. 1973: Live and Let Die. Frankenstein and the Monster from Hell. 1974: Percy's Progress. The Man with the Golden Gun. 1976: Beauty and the Beast.*

*1977: The Spy Who Loved Me. 1979: Moonraker. 1980: Dangerous Davies—The Last Detective (TV).*

## LEECH, Richard
(R. McClelland) 1922-

Flat-faced, snub-nosed, chunkily built, Irish-born actor with dark, crinkly hair and rich, fruity voice. His slightly self-satisfied looks often had him cast in British films as unsympathetic officers and gentlemen, or other men trying to woo the heroine from her husband. He had studied (successfully) to be a doctor, but practised for only a year before opting for an acting career. The first stage appearance of this most cultivated of actors was as a Nubian slave. He has an actress daughter, Eliza McClelland.

*1949: The Temptress. Morning Departure (US: Operation Disaster). 1952: Little Big Shot. Treasure Hunt. 1953: The Red Dress. 1954: Lease of Life. Children Galore. The Dam Busters. 1955: The Prisoner. 1956: It's Never Too Late. The Long Arm (US: The Third Key). The Feminine Touch (US: The Gentle Touch). The Iron Petticoat. The Good Companions. 1957: Yangtse Incident (US: Battle Hell). Night of the Demon (US: Curse of the Demon). These Dangerous Years (US: Dangerous Youth). The Birthday Present. The Moonraker. 1958: Dublin Nightmare. Gideon's Day (US: Gideon of Scotland Yard). Ice Cold in Alex (US: Desert Attack). A Night to Remember. The Horse's Mouth. The Wind Cannot Read. 1960: Tunes of Glory. 1961: The Terror of the Tongs. The Wild and the Willing. 1962: The War Lover. I Thank a Fool. 1963: Ricochet. Walk a Tightrope. 1965: Life at the Top. 1966: The Fighting Prince of Donegal. 1967: *Promenade. 1971: Young Winston. 1984: The Shooting Party.*

## LEIBER, Fritz 1882-1949

American Shakespearian actor with 'noble Roman' profile, very dark hair and piercing gaze. He played one or two distinguished roles in silents (including Julius Caesar in *Cleopatra*), then went back to the stage. He returned to Hollywood in 1935, white-haired but with profile intact, for 15 years of austere character roles as abbots, doctors, and assorted saintly characters east and

west with so many wise aphorisms to hand that it hurt. Died from a heart attack.

*1916: Romeo and Juliet. 1917: Cleopatra. 1920: If I Were King. 1921: The Queen of Sheba. 1935: A Tale of Two Cities. The Story of Louis Pasteur. 1936: Under Two Flags. Down to the Sea. Hearts in Bondage. Sins of Man. Anthony Adverse. Camille. 1937: Champagne Waltz. The Prince and the Pauper. The Great Garrick. 1938: Gateway. If I Were King (and earlier version). The Jury's Secret. Flight into Nowhere. 1939: Nurse Edith Cavell. Pack Up Your Troubles. They Made Her a Spy. The Hunchback of Notre Dame. 1940: All This and Heaven Too. The Sea Hawk. The Way of All Flesh. The Lady with Red Hair. The Mortal Storm. 1941: Aloma of the South Seas. 1942: Crossroads. 1943: First Comes Courage. The Phantom of the Opera. The Desert Song. 1944: Are These Our Parents? (GB: They Are Guilty). The Imposter. Cry of the Werewolf. 1945: The Cisco Kid Returns. The Spanish Main. This Love of Ours. Son of Lassie. 1946: Angel on My Shoulder. Humoresque. Thieves' Holiday (later and GB: A Scandal in Paris). Strange Journey. 1947: High Conquest. Bells of San Angelo. Monsieur Verdoux. Dangerous Venture. The Web. 1948: To the Ends of the Earth. Adventures of Casanova. Another Part of the Forest. Inner Sanctum. 1949: Bagdad. Bride of Vengeance. Samson and Delilah. Song of India. 1950: Devil's Doorway.*

## LEIGH-HUNT, Ronald 1916-

Tall, suave, sleek, authoritative-looking British actor probably still best remembered as King Arthur in the television series *The Adventures of Sir Lancelot*. His upright bearing testified to his former career in the British Army, and he was often cast as officers and policemen. Also took the title role in *Rogue Herries* on TV. His characters were almost always grim and determined and he has played little comedy.

*1950: Blackout. 1952: Tread Softly. Paul Temple Returns. 1953: The Broken Horseshoe. Colonel March Investigates. Flannelfoot. Three Steps to the Gallows (released 1955: US: White Fire). 1954: Shadow of a Man. 1955: Tiger by the Tail (US: Crossup). *The Man on the Cliff. 1956: Assignment Redhead (US:*

*Requirement for a Redhead).* 1957: *Hi-Jack* (unreleased). *Zoo Baby* (released 1960). 1959: *A Touch of Larceny.* 1960: *Sink the Bismarck! Piccadilly Third Stop. Oscar Wilde. The League of Gentlemen. The Hand.* 1961: *Very Important Person (US: A Coming Out Party).* 1962: *We Joined the Navy.* 1963: *The Invisible Asset. The Third Secret.* 1964: *70 Deadly Pills.* 1965: *Curse of Simba/Curse of the Voodoo. The Truth About Spring. The Liquidator.* 1966: *Where the Bullets Fly. Khartoum.* 1968: *Hostile Witness.* 1969: *Clegg. Le Mans.* 1971: *Universal Soldier.* 1972: *Baxter! (US: The Boy).* 1976: *The Message.*

### LEMBECK, Harvey 1923-1982
Shortish, bulky, black-haired, Brooklynese American actor, in good parts almost right away from 1950 after radio work, and at his most popular in the early 1950s, when he played with Tom Ewell in the 'Willie and Joe' army comedies; he had another good featured role in *Stalag 17.* Semi-leading roles in more dramatic vein were somewhat less successful, but Lembeck was in any case soon entrenched on TV as Rocco, Sergeant Bilko's sidekick, in the long-running comedy series *You'll Never Get Rich.* In later years, he ran The Comedy Workshop before his early death from a heart attack. His son Michael is also an actor.

1950: *USS Teakettle (later You're in the Navy Now).* 1951: *The Frogmen. Finders Keepers. Fourteen Hours.* 1952: *Back at the Front (GB: Willie and Joe in Tokyo). Just Across the Street.* 1953: *Girls in the Night (GB: Life After Dark). Stalag 17. Mission over Korea (GB: Eyes of the Skies).* 1954: *The Command.* 1956: *Between Heaven and Hell.* 1961: *Sail a Crooked Ship. A View from the Bridge. The Last Time I Saw Archie.* 1963: *Beach Party.* 1964: *Bikini Beach. The Unsinkable Molly Brown. Love With the Proper Stranger. Pajama Party. Sergeant Deadhead.* 1965: *How to Stuff a Wild Bikini. Beach Blanket Bingo. Dr Goldfoot and the Bikini Machine (GB: Dr G and the Bikini Machine).* 1966: *Fireball 500. The Spirit is Willing. The Ghost in the Invisible Bikini.* 1968: *Hello Down There. Lola in Lipstick (TV).* 1976: *There Is No 13. Raid on Entebbe (TV. GB: cinemas).* 1980: *The Gong Show Movie.*

### LE MESURIER, John 1912-1983
Brow-mopping, fretful-looking, (very) British actor, with long, equine features wryly resigned to disaster. He played dramatic roles at first, although his characters were equally as harassed as those in the comic gloom-and-doom which enveloped him from the mid-1950s on, when he became an ostensibly bewildered foil for some of Britain's best comedians. Later popular in the TV series *Dad's Army.* Married to Hattie Jacques (first of two—*qv*) from 1949 to 1965, he left an obituary at the time of his death from an abdominal illness, saying that he had 'conked out'. A human Eeyore.

1948: *Death in the Hand. Escape from Broadmoor.* 1949: *A Matter of Murder. Old Mother Riley's New Venture.* 1950: *Dark Interval.* 1951: *Never Take No for an Answer. Blind Man's Bluff.* 1952: *Mother Riley Meets the Vampire (US: Vampire over London).* 1953: *The Drayton Case. The Blue Parrot. Black 13. The Pleasure Garden.* 1954: *Dangerous Cargo. Beautiful Stranger (US: Twist of Fate).* 1955: *Police Dog. Josephine and Men. A Time to Kill.* 1956: *The Baby and the Battleship. The Battle of the River Plate (US: Pursuit of the Graf Spee). Private's Progress. Brothers in Law. The Good Companions.* 1957: *Happy is the Bride! These Dangerous Years (US: Dangerous Youth). High Flight. The Admirable Crichton (US: Paradise Lagoon). The Man Who Wouldn't Talk. The Moonraker.* 1958: *Law and Disorder. Another Time, Another Place. Operation Amsterdam. I Was Monty's Double (US: Monty's Double). Gideon's Day (US: Gideon of Scotland Yard). Blind Spot. Man with a Gun. The Lady is a Square. Blood of the Vampire. Too Many Crooks. Carlton-Browne of the FO (US: Man in a Cocked Hat). The Captain's Table.* 1959: *A Touch of Larceny. I'm All Right, Jack. The Wreck of the Mary Deare. The Hound of the Baskervilles. Our Man in Havana. Shake Hands With the Devil. Follow a Star. Desert Mice.* 1960: *Jack the Ripper. School for Scoundrels. The Day They Robbed the Bank of England. Let's Get Married. Never Let Go. Dead Lucky. Doctor in Love. The Night We Got the Bird. The Pure Hell of St Trinian's. The Bulldog Breed.* 1961: *Five Golden Hours. The Rebel (US: Call Me Genius). Very Important Person (US: A Coming Out Party). Don't Bother to Knock! (US: Why Bother to Knock?). Invasion Quartet. On the Fiddle (US: Operation Snafu). Village of Daughters. Mr Topaze (US: I Like Money).* 1962: *Jigsaw. Hair of the Dog. Go to Blazes. Flat Two. The Waltz of the Toreadors. Mrs Gibbons' Boys. Only Two Can Play. The Wrong Arm of the Law. We Joined the Navy. The Punch and Judy Man.* 1963: *The Pink Panther. In the Cool of the Day. Never Put It in Writing. Hot Enough for June (US: Agent 8¾). The Mouse on the Moon. The Main Attraction.* 1964: *The Moon-Spinners.* 1965: *The Early Bird. City Under the Sea (US: War Gods of the Deep). Cuckoo Patrol. Masquerade. Where the Spies Are. Those Magnificent Men in Their Flying Machines. The Liquidator.* 1966: *The Sandwich Man. Eye of the Devil. Finders Keepers. Mr Ten Per Cent. The Wrong Box. Our Man in Marrakesh (US: Bang! Bang! You're Dead).* 1967: *The 25th Hour. Casino Royale.* 1968: *Salt and Pepper.* 1969: *The Undertakers. The Italian Job. Midas Run (US: A Run on Gold). The Magic Christian.* 1970: *Doctor in Trouble. On a Clear Day You Can See Forever.* 1971: *Dad's Army.* 1972: *The Garnett Saga. Au Pair Girls.* 1974: *Confessions of a Window Cleaner. Barry McKenzie Holds His Own. Three for All. Brief Encounter (TV).* 1975: *The Adventure of Sherlock Holmes' Smarter Brother.* 1977: *Stand Up, Virgin Soldiers. Jabberwocky. What's Up Nurse?* 1978: *Rosie Dixon Night Nurse. Who Is Killing the Great Chefs of Europe? (GB: Too Many Chefs).* 1979: *The Spaceman and King Arthur (US: Unidentified Flying Oddball).* 1980: *The Fiendish Plot of Dr Fu Manchu. Late Flowering Love.*

### LEONARD, Sheldon
(S. L. Barshad) 1907-*1997*
Invaluable dark-haired American actor of vaguely shifty looks, a Macdonald Carey from the other side of the tracks and one of the cinema's shadiest characters. Rarely seen without a trilby, his Brooklynesque gangsters were equally divided between the comic and the serious. Left acting all too soon to turn to production, but was seen in the late 1970s in a few cameo roles.

1934: *Ouanga.* 1939: *Another Thin Man.* 1941: *Tall, Dark and Handsome. Buy Me That Town. Married Bachelor. Rise and Shine. Week-End in Havana. Private Nurse.* 1942: *Born to Sing. Tortilla Flat. Lucky Jordan. Pierre of the Plains. Tennessee Johnson (GB: The Man on America's Conscience). The McGuerins from Brooklyn. Street of Chance.* 1943: *Hit the Ice. Klondike Kate. City Without Men. Taxi, Mister. Passport to Suez. Harvest Melody.* 1944: *Uncertain Glory. To Have and Have Not. Timber Queen. The Falcon in Hollywood. Gambler's Choice. Trocadero.* 1945: *Why Girls Leave Home. Zombies on Broadway (GB: Loonies on Broadway). Shadow of Terror. Frontier Gal (GB: The Bride Wasn't Willing). Radio Stars on Parade. Captain Kidd. River Gang. Crime Inc.* 1946: *Decoy. Bowery Bombshell. The Last Crooked Mile. Somewhere in the Night. The Gentleman Misbehaves. It's a Wonderful Life! Her Kind of Man. Rainbow over Texas.* 1947: *Sinbad the Sailor. The Fabulous Joe. Violence. The Gangster.* 1948: *If You Knew Susie. Open Secret. Jinx Money. Joe Palooka in Winner Take All (GB: Winner Take All). Madonna of the Desert. Alias a Gentleman. Shep Comes Home.* 1949: *Take One False Step. My Dream is Yours. Daughter of the Jungle.* † *Two Knights in Brooklyn/Two Mugs from Brooklyn.* 1950: *The Iroquois Trail (GB: The Tomahawk Trail).* 1951: *Abbott and Costello Meet the Invisible Man. Behave Yourself! Come Fill the Cup. Young Man with Ideas.* 1952: *Here Come the Nelsons. Breakdown. Stop, You're Killing Me!* 1953: *Money from Home. Diamond Queen.* 1955: *Guys and Dolls.* 1961: *Pocketful of Miracles.* 1978: *The Brink's Job. The Islander (TV). Top Secret (TV).*

† Combined GB version of *The McGuerins from Brooklyn* and *Taxi, Mister*

**LEVANT, Oscar** 1906-1972
Shambling, worried-looking, thick-lipped American humorist and pianist who brightened up a number of films at Warners, Paramount, M-G-M and Fox in the forties and fifties. His subsequent TV show proved a treasury of insult as Oscar got the guests, describing himself as a verbal vampire. Died from a heart attack.

1929: *The Dance of Life.* 1935: *In Person.* 1940: *Rhythm on the River.* *Information, Please (series). Kiss the Boys Goodbye.* 1945: *Rhapsody in Blue.* 1946: *Humoresque.* 1948: *Romance on the High Seas (GB: It's Magic) You Were Meant for Me.* 1949: *The Barkleys of Broadway.* 1951: *An American in Paris.* 1952: *O. Henry's Full House (GB: Full House).* 1953: *The 'I Don't Care' Girl. The Band Wagon.* 1955: *The Cobweb.*

**LEVENE, Sam** 1905-1980
Thin, sardonic, moustachioed Brooklynesque American character actor, typically as sharpsters and not-too-menacing criminals, familiar in trilby and pin-stripe suit. Occasionally, as in *Crossfire* and *Boomerang*, in much more serious roles within social conscience thrillers. Stayed a working actor until his death from a heart attack.

1936: *After the Thin Man. Three Men on a Horse.* 1938: *Yellow Jack. The Shopworn Angel. The Mad Miss Manton.* 1939: *Golden Boy.* 1941: *Married Bachelor. Shadow of the Thin Man.* 1942: *Sing Your Worries Away. Sunday Punch. Grand Central Murder. The Big Street. Destination Unknown.* 1943: *I Dood It (GB: By Hook or By Crook). Action in the North Atlantic. Whistling in Brooklyn. Gung Ho!* 1944: *The Purple Heart.* 1946: *The Killers.* 1947: *Boomerang, Brute Force. Crossfire. A Likely Story. Killer McCoy.* 1948: *Leather Gloves (GB: Loser Take All). The Babe Ruth Story.* 1950: *Dial 1119 (GB: The Violent Hour). Guilty Bystander.* 1953:

*Three Sailors and a Girl.* 1956: *The Opposite Sex.* 1957: *Designing Woman. Sweet Smell of Success. Slaughter on 10th Avenue. A Farewell to Arms.* 1958: *Kathy O.* 1963: *Act One.* 1969: *A Dream of Kings.* 1972: *Such Good Friends.* 1976: *The Money. Demon/God Told Me To.* 1979: *Last Embrace... And Justice for All.*

**LEWIS, Geoffrey** 1935-
Sour-mouthed, creaking-voiced, dark-complexioned American actor of medium build who came lamentably late to films, but has since racked up 45 movies in 15 years—not bad going today. Usually plays wrong-headed moaners, or pains-in-the-neck who are hard to get rid of, and has been seen to great effect in several of Clint Eastwood's more light-hearted romps.

1971: *Welcome Home Johnny Bristol (TV).* 1972: *High Plains Drifter. Moon of the Wolf (TV). The Culpepper Cattle Co. Bad Company.* 1973: *Macon County Line. Dillinger. My Name Is Nobody.* 1974: *Honky Tonk (TV). Thunderbolt and Lightfoot. The Gun and the Pulpit (TV). The Great Waldo Pepper. The Great Ice Rip-Off (TV). Smile.* 1975: *The Wind and the Lion. Attack on Terror: The FBI versus the Ku Klux Klan (TV). Lucky Lady.* 1976: *The Return of a Man Called Horse. The New Daughters of Joshua Cabe (TV). The Great Houdinis (TV).* 1977: *The Deadly Triangle (TV). The Hunted Lady (TV).* 1978: *Every Which Way But Loose. Tilt. When Every Day Was the Fourth of July (TV).* 1979: *Human Experiments. The Jericho Mile (TV. GB: cinemas). Samurai (TV).* 1980: *Tom Horn. Bronco Billy. Any Which Way You Can. Heaven's Gate.* 1981: *I, the Jury.* 1982: *Life of the Party. The Story of Beatrice (TV). The Shadow Riders (TV).* 1983: *Return of the Man from UNCLE (TV). September Gun (TV). 10 to Midnight. Travis McGee (TV).* 1984: *Lust in the Dust. Night of the Comet.* 1985: *Stormin' Home (TV).*

**LEXY, Edward**
(E. Gerald Little) 1897-
Stocky, barrel-chested, tight-lipped, brown-haired, moustachioed, aggressive-looking British actor who made his name in the immediate pre-war cinema playing sergeant majors. Near the top of the cast from his 1937 debut until 1940; in smaller roles in post-war years, and progressively less often seen towards the end of the 1950s.

1937: *Knight Without Armour. Farewell Again (US: Troopship). Smash and Grab. Mademoiselle Docteur.* 1938: *The Drum (US: Drums). The Terror. South Riding. This Man is News. Kate Plus Ten. Second Best Bed. St Martin's Lane (US: Sidewalks of London). Many Tanks Mr Atkins. Night Journey.* 1939: *The Gang's All Here (US: The Amazing Mr Forrest). Too Dangerous to Live. The Outsider. This Man in Paris. Mrs Pym of Scotland Yard. The Spider. Traitor Spy (US: The Torso Murder Mystery). The Proud Valley.*

ABOVE A gaggle of gangsters. Geoffrey **Lewis** (second from left), John P. Ryan (*qv*), Warren Oates, John Martino and Harry Dean Stanton (*qv*) are five men the FBI would like to interview in the 1973 version of *Dillinger*

BELOW The truculent Inspector Hollis provided a juicy role for Edward Lexy (right) in two late 1930s comedy-thrillers. Here, he and Garry Marsh (*qv*, left) watch Barry K. Barnes phone in a story in *This Man is News* (1938)

*1940: Laugh It Off. Spare a Copper. \*Larceny Street. Convoy. 1944: Medal for the General. 1946: A Girl in a Million. Piccadilly Incident. School for Secrets (US: Secret Flight). 1947: While I Live. Captain Boycott. Temptation Harbour. The Ghosts of Berkeley Square. Blanche Fury. 1948: The Mark of Cain. The Winslow Boy. Bonnie Prince Charlie. It's Not Cricket. 1949: For Them That Trespass. Children of Chance. Golden Arrow (released 1952: US: Three Men and a Girl). 1950: The Twenty Questions Murder Mystery. 1951: Cloudburst. The Lady With a Lamp. Smart Alec. Night Was Our Friend. 1952: The Happy Family (US: Mr Lord Says No). You're Only Young Twice! Miss Robin Hood. 1954: The Golden Link. Orders Are Orders. 1955: Where There's a Will. 1956: Up in the World. 1957: The Rising of the Moon. The Man Who Wouldn't Talk.*

## LITHGOW, John 1946-

Big (6ft 4in), puffy-faced, small-eyed American actor who progressed only slowly to top supporting parts, but then worked prodigiously by modern standards, demonstrating considerable versatility. He can play broad or sensitive as the occasion demands, and has already been nominated for Oscars in *The World According to Garp* and *Terms of Endearment*, fearlessly taking on the portrayal of a transvestite in the former and creating a sympathetic character.

*1971: Dealing: or, the Berkeley-to-Boston-Forty-Brick-Lost Bag Blues. 1976: Obsession. 1978: The Big Fix. 1979: Rich Kids. All That Jazz. 1980: Mom, the Wolfman and Me (TV). 1981: Big Blonde (TV). Blow Out. 1982: The World According to Garp. I'm Dancing As Fast I Can. Not in Front of the Children (TV). 1983: The Twilight Zone (GB: Twilight Zone the Movie). Terms of Endearment. The Day After (TV). The Glitter Dome (cable TV. GB: cinemas). 1984: Footloose. 2010. The Adventures of Buckaroo Banzai: Across the Eighth Dimension. 1985: Mesmerized. Santa Claus The Movie. The Manhattan Project.*

## LLOYD, Norman 1914-

Narrow-featured American actor with receding fair hair and a hunted look. He is

probably still best remembered for his debut role—the spy who fell from the Statue of Liberty at the end of Hitchcock's *Saboteur*. Lloyd dropped out of acting in 1952 to become a producer (notably for Hitchcock himself on many of his TV shows) and sometime director, but returned to play a few cameo roles towards the end of the 1970s.

*1942: Saboteur. 1945: The Unseen. Within These Walls. The Southerner. A Walk in the Sun. 1946: A Letter for Evie. Spellbound. The Green Years. Young Widow. 1947: The Beginning or the End? 1948: No Minor Vices. 1949: Scene of the Crime. Calamity Jane and Sam Bass. Reign of Terror/The Black Book. 1950: Buccaneer's Girl. The Flame and the Arrow. 1951: The Light Touch. M. Flame of Stamboul. He Ran All the Way. 1952: Limelight. 1977: Audrey Rose. 1978: FM. The Dark Secret of Harvest Home (TV). 1979: King Cobra (later Jaws of Satan). 1980: The Nude Bomb.*

## LOCKE, Harry 1915-

Cheery, bustling, bouncy British actor of round face, dark hair and chunky build, a purveyor of 'lower rank' cameos—batmen, orderlies, porters, warders, cab-drivers and the like; in the immediate post-war period, he was also a popular stand-up comedian who told jokes about immigrants on buses getting themselves and the conductor hopelessly confused. A repertory actor at 16, he returned to the stage after the 1960s to round out his career.

*1946: Piccadilly Incident. 1948: Passport to Pimlico. Panic at Madame Tussaud's. No Room at the Inn. 1949: Private Angelo. 1950: The Naked Heart (Maria Chapdelaine/The Naked Earth). The Undefeated. Treasure Island. 1951: Judgment Deferred. 1952: Angels One Five. Father's Doing Fine. Tread Softly. Time Bomb (US: Terror on a Train). 1953: The Red Beret (US: Paratrooper). 1954: The Teckman Mystery. Doctor in the House. Devil on Horseback. 1955: A Kid for Two Farthings. A Yank in Ermine. 1956: Yield to the Night (US: Blonde Sinner). Reach for the Sky. The Baby and the Battleship. The Long Arm (US: The Third Key). Town on Trial! 1957: Doctor at Large. Woman in a Dressing Gown. Barnacle Bill (US: All at Sea). 1958: Nowhere to Go. The Captain's Table. Carlton-Browne of the F O (US: Man in a Cocked Hat). 1959: Upstairs and Downstairs. Carry on Nurse. I'm All Right, Jack. 1960: Light Up the Sky. Clue of the Twisted Candle. The Girl on the Boat. 1961: The Man in the Back Seat. Never Back Losers. In the Doghouse. Two and Two Make Six. On the Fiddle (US: Operation Snafu). Watch It Sailor! She'll Have to Go (US: Maid for Murder). The Wild and the Willing. 1962: Tiara Tahiti. Crooks Anonymous. Play It Cool. The Amorous Prawn. The L-Shaped Room. Kill or Cure. 1963: The Small World of Sammy Lee. Heavens Above! What a Crazy World. 1964: Go Kart Go! The Devil-Ship Pirates. A Home of Your Own. 1965: \*The Material Witness. The Legend of Young Dick Turpin. The Early Bird. 1966: Alfie. The Family Way. Arabesque. 1967: The Sky Bike. Mr Ten Per Cent. Half a Sixpence. 1968: Carry on Doctor. Subterfuge. 1969: Carry on Again, Doctor. On the Run. Oh! What a Lovely War. 1972: Tales from the Crypt. The Creeping Flesh.*

## LOCKHART, Gene

(Eugene Lockhart) 1891-1957

Light-haired, short, chubby-faced Canadian-born actor, somewhere between Charles Coburn and Cecil Kellaway, and one of Hollywood's most valuable character players from the 1930s to the 1950s. He started his career as a singer and songwriter, beginning his films in sly crookedness which, by the end of his career, had all but evaporated into crusty benevolence. Oscar nomination for his performance in *Algiers*. Died from a coronary thrombosis.

*1922: Smilin' Through. 1934: By Your Leave. The Gay Bride. Star of Midnight. 1935: Ah, Wilderness! Captain Hurricane. Thunder in the Night. Crime and Punishment. I've Been Around. Storm over the Andes. 1936: Brides Are Like That. Earthworm Tractors (GB: A Natural Born Salesman). Career Woman. The Gorgeous Hussy. Wedding Present. Come Closer, Folks. Times Square Playboy (GB: His Best Man). The First Baby. The Garden Murder Case. The Devil is a Sissy (GB: The Devil Takes the Count). Mind Your Own Business. 1937: Mama Steps Out. Make Way for Tomorrow. Something to Sing About. Too Many Wives. The Sheik Steps Out. 1938: Of Human Hearts. A Christmas Carol. \*Stocks and Blondes. Listen, Darling. Sweethearts. Men are Such Fools. Algiers. Meet the Girls. Penrod's Double Trouble. Blondie. Sinners in Paradise. 1939: I'm from Missouri. Our Leading Citizen. Tell No Tales. Blackmail. The Story of Alexander Graham Bell (GB: The Modern Miracle). Hotel Imperial. Geronimo. Bridal Suite. 1940: Edison the Man. We Who Are Young. South of Pago Pago. His Girl Friday. Abe Lincoln in Illinois (GB: Spirit of the People). Dr Kildare Goes Home. A Dispatch from Reuter's (GB: This Man Reuter). 1941: Billy the Kid. Meet John Doe. All That Money Can Buy/The Devil and Daniel Webster. Steel Against the Sky. They Died with Their Boots On. Keeping Company. The Sea Wolf. One Foot in Heaven. International Lady. 1942: The Gay Sisters. Juke Girl. You Can't Escape Forever. 1943: Hangmen Also Die! Find the Blackmailer. Madame Curie. Forever and a Day. Mission to Moscow. The Desert Song. Northern Pursuit. 1944: The White Cliffs of Dover. Action in Arabia. Going My Way. The Man from Frisco. 1945: The House on 92nd Street. That's the Spirit. Leave Her to Heaven. 1946: Meet Me on Broadway. Thieves' Holiday (GB: A Scandal in Paris). The Strange Woman. She-Wolf of London (GB: The Curse of the Allenbys). The Shocking Miss Pilgrim. 1947: The Foxes of Harrow. Cynthia (GB: The Rich, Full Life). Miracle on 34th Street (GB: The Big Heart). Honeymoon (GB: Two Men and a Girl). Her Husband's Affairs. 1948: The Inside Story. Joan of Arc. I, Jane Doe (GB: Diary of a Bride). That Wonderful Urge. Apartment for Peggy. 1949: Down to the Sea in Ships. Madame Bovary. The Inspector-General. The Red Light. 1950: The Big Hangover. Riding High. 1951: Hill Number One. The Sickle and the Cross. Seeds of Destruction. Rhubarb. I'd Climb the Highest Mountain. The Lady from Texas. Hoodlum Empire. 1952: A Girl in Every Port. Bonzo Goes to College. Face to Face. Androcles and the Lion. Apache War Smoke. 1953: Down Among the Sheltering Palms. The Lady Wants Mink. Francis Covers the Big Town. Confidentially Connie. 1954: World for Ransom. 1955: The Vanishing American. The Late Christopher Bean (TV. GB: cinemas). 1956:*

*Carousel. The Man in the Gray Flannel Suit. 1957: Jeanne Eagels.*

**LODGE, David 1921-**
Tough-looking, moustachioed, well-built British actor with dark, wavy hair whose aggressive Londoners were usually leavened with humour. After varied experience in Gang Shows, a circus and musichall, he moved into cinema character roles and, following an apprenticeship as tough, backstreet types, soon showed a penchant for comedy, making notable contributions to several Peter Sellers films. Broader comedy roles in later days were on the whole less successful but he has remained busy and proved a prodigious worker for charity.

*1955: Cockleshell Heroes. 1956: Women Without Men (US: Blonde Bait). Private's Progress. The Battle of the River Plate (US: Pursuit of the Graf Spee). The Intimate Stranger (US: Finger of Guilt). The Counterfeit Plan. 1957: Strangers' Meeting. These Dangerous Years (US: Dangerous Youth). The Naked Truth (US: Your Past is Showing!). The Safecracker. 1958: Up the Creek. No Time to Die! (US: Tank Force). The Silent Enemy. I Was Monty's Double (US: Monty's Double). Ice Cold in Alex (US: Desert Attack). \*The Crossroads Gallows. I Only Arsked! Further Up the Creek. Girls at Sea. 1959: Life in Emergency Ward 10. Bobbikins. Idle on Parade (US: Idol on Parade). I'm All Right, Jack. Yesterday's Enemy. The Ugly Duckling. Jazzboat. 1960: Two-Way Stretch. The League of Gentlemen. \*The Running, Jumping and Standing Still Film. Watch Your Stern. The Bulldog Breed. Never Let Go. 1961: The Hellfire Club. Yesterday's Enemy. No, My Darling Daughter! Raising the Wind (US: Roommates). Carry On Regardless. The Pirates of Blood River. 1962: Go to Blazes. Mrs Gibbons' Boys. The Dock Brief (US: Trial and Error). Captain Clegg (US: Night Creatures). Time to Remember. The Boys. On the Beat. Kill or Cure. 1963: Two Left Feet. 1964: The Long Ships. A Shot in the Dark. Guns at Batasi. Saturday Night Out. 1965: The Intelligence Men. The Amorous Adventures of Moll Flanders. Cup Fever. The Early Bird. San Ferry Ann. Catch Us If You Can (US: Having a Wild Week-End). The Alphabet*

*Murders/The ABC Murders. 1966: The Sandwich Man. Press for. Time. 1967: The Sky Bike. Smashing Time. 1968: The Fixer. Headline Hunters. 1969: The Smashing Bird I Used To Know. What's Good for the Goose. Crooks and Coronets (US: Sophie's Place). The Magic Christian. \*Bachelor of Arts (US: Durti Week-End). Oh! What a Lovely War. Scream and Scream Again. Corruption. 1970: Incense for the Damned. Scramble. Tomorrow. Crime Doesn't Pay. Hoffman. The Railway Children. 1971: Raising the Roof. On the Buses. Mr Horatio Knibbles. The Fiend. Nobody Ordered Love. 1972: Go for a Take. The Amazing Mr Blunden. Some Kind of Hero. Mutiny on the Buses. Hide and Seek. \*Always on Saturday. 1973: Carry On Girls. Charley One-Eye. 1974: Return of the Pink Panther. QB VII (TV). Carry On Dick. 1975: Carry On Behind. 1976: Carry On England. 1983: Sahara. Bloodbath at the House of Death.*

**LÖHR, Marie 1890-1975**
Although one remembers this puffy-faced, brown-haired Australian-born actress for her dragons and dowagers, she was on stage at four in her native Sydney and a London stage regular at 11, eventually running up one of the longest lists of credits ever recorded in the British theatre. Film appearances were understandably spasmodic, but hers were always performances to be reckoned with and she was still in leading character roles well into her sixties.

*1916: \*The Real Thing at Last. 1932: Aren't We All? 1934: Road House. My Heart Is Calling. Lady in Danger. 1935: Oh Daddy! Royal Cavalcade (US: Regal Cavalcade). Foreign Affaires. Fighting Stock. Cock o' the North. 1936: Whom the Gods Love (US: Mozart). It's You I Want. Dreams Come True. Reasonable Doubt. 1938: South Riding. Pygmalion. 1939: A Gentleman's Gentleman. 1940: George and Margaret. 1941: Major Barbara. 1942: Went the Day Well? (US: 48 Hours). 1944: Twilight Hour. Kiss the Bride Goodbye. 1945: The Rake's Progress (US: Notorious Gentleman). 1946: The Magic Bow. 1947: The Ghosts of Berkeley Square. 1948: Counterblast. Anna Karenina. The Winslow Boy. Silent Dust. 1952: Little Big Shot. Treasure Hunt. 1953: Always a Bride. 1954:*

*Out of the Clouds. 1955: Escapade. On Such a Night. 1956: A Town Like Alice. 1957: Seven Waves Away (US: Abandon Ship!). Small Hotel. 1958: Carlton-Browne of the F O (US: Man in a Cocked Hat). 1967: Great Catherine.*

## LOMAS, Herbert 1887-1961

Dour, grim-looking British actor with light brown hair, twisted expression and sepulchral tones, frequently cast as a prophet of doom. Had it not been for the slightness of his stature, he might have made a good Scrooge. Retired in 1952 and went to live in the Devon countryside, where he died.

*1931: Hobson's Choice. Many Waters. 1932: Frail Women. The Sign of Four. When London Sleeps. The Missing Rembrandt. The Man from Toronto. 1933: Daughters of Today. 1934: Java Head. The Phantom Light. Lorna Doone. 1935: Fighting Stock. The Black Mask. The Ghost Goes West. 1936: Fame. Rembrandt. 1937: Knight Without Armour. Over the Moon (released 1940). South Riding. 1939: Inquest. Jamaica Inn. The Lion Has Wings. Ask a Policeman. 1940: *Mr Borland Thinks Again. 1941: The Ghost Train. South American George. Penn of Pennsylvania (US: The Courageous Mr Penn). 1943: They Met in the Dark. 1944: Welcome Mr Washington. 1945: I Know Where I'm Going! 1946: The Man Within (US: The Smugglers). 1947: Master of Bankdam. 1948: The Guinea Pig. Bonnie Prince Charlie. 1951: The Magic Box. 1952: The Net (US: Project M7).*

## LONG, Walter 1879-1952

Bull-necked, barrel-chested, crop-haired, ferociously-scowling American tough-guy actor, who took over from the equally fearsome Noah Young whenever Laurel and Hardy needed an awesome opponent to threaten them with physical improbabilities. After blacking up for his first film, *The Birth of a Nation*, Long was almost always a villain, most notably as Stan Laurel's (cheating) boxing opponent in *Any Old Port*. More or less retired after 1942: died from a heart attack.

*1915: The Birth of a Nation. 1916: Intolerance. 1917: The Evil Eye. The Little American. 1918: The Queen of the Sea. 1919:*

*The Mother and the Law. Scarlet Days. 1920: The Fighting Shepherdess. What Women Love. Go and Get It. 1921: The Fire Cat. Tiger True. A Giant of His Race. The Sheik. White and Unmarried. 1922: Moran of the Lady Letty. Blood and Sand. Across the Continent. The Dictator. The Beautiful and the Damned. Omar the Tent-Maker. My American Wife. To Have and to Hold. Shadows. South of Suva. 1923: Kick In. Desire. The Broken Wing. The Call of the Wild. His Great Chance. The Last Hour. Little Church around the Corner. The Isle of Lost Ships. The Shock. A Shot in the Night. The Huntress. Quicksands. 1924: The Ridin' Kid from Powder River. Daring Love. Yankee Madness. White Man. Wine. Missing Daughters. 1925: Bobbed Hair. Soul-Fire. Raffles, the Amateur Cracksman. The Reckless Sex. The Verdict. The Lady. The Shock Punch. The Road to Yesterday. 1926: Red Dice. Eve's Leaves. The Highbinders. Steel Preferred. West of Broadway. 1927: White Pants Willie. The Yankee Clipper. Back to God's Country. Jim the Conqueror. Jewels of Desire. 1928: Forbidden Grass. The Thunder God. Gang War. Me, Gangster. 1929: The Black Watch (GB: King of the Khyber Rifles). Black Cargoes of the South Seas. 1930: Beau Bandit. Conspiracy. Moby Dick. 1931: Sea Devils. Larceny Lane/The Steel Highway. The Maltese Falcon. Pardon Us (GB: Jailbirds). *Taxi Troubles. Other Men's Women. Soul of the Slums (GB: The Samaritan). Dragnet Patrol (GB: Love Redeemed). 1932: Escapade (GB: Dangerous Ground). *Any Old Port. 1933: Women Won't Tell. 1934: Six of a Kind. Operator 13 (GB: Spy 13). *Three Little Pigskins. *The Live Ghost. Lightning Strikes Twice. *Going Bye Bye. 1935: Naughty Marietta. 1936: Drift Fence. Wedding Present. The Beloved Rogue. The Glory Trail. The Bold Caballero. 1937: Pick a Star. North of the Rio Grande. 1938: The Painted Trail. Six-Shootin' Sheriff. Man's Country. Bar 20 Justice. 1939: Wild Horse Canyon. 1940: Silver Stallion. 1941: Ridin' on a Rainbow. City of Missing Girls. 1948: *No More Relatives. 1950: Wabash Avenue.*

## LONSDALE, Michel 1931-

Sturdy, dark-haired, often moustachioed French actor, almost unknown outside the

Continent until his performance as the man pursuing Edward Fox in *The Day of the Jackal*. After that, he performed in several international films (often billed as Michael) although his choice of roles did not always seem wise, and he has been less frequently seen in movies in more recent times.

*1956: C'est arrivé à Aden. 1957: La main chaude. 1958: Une balle dans le canon. 1960: Les portes claquent. 1961: Adorable menteuse. Les snobs. La dénonciation (US: The Immoral Moment). 1962: The Trial. 1963: Tous les enfants du monde (unfinished). 1964: Behold a Pale Horse. Les Copains. Jaloux comme un tigre. 1965: Je vous salue, Mafia (GB and US: Hail! Mafia). La bourse et la vie. 1966: Les compagnons de la marguerite. Le judoka agent secret. 1967: L'homme à la Buick. L'authentique procès de Carl Emmanuel Jung. 1968: La mariée était en noir (GB and US: The Bride Wore Black). *La pince à ongles (GB: The Nail Clippers). Baisers volés (GB and US: Stolen Kisses). 1969: Hibernatus. Détruire, dit-elle (US: Destroy, She Said). L'hiver. 1970: L'étalon. Le printemps. La Rose et le revolver. 1971: Out One (unreleased). Le Souffle au coeur (GB: Dearest Love. US: Murmur of the Heart). Les assassins de l'ordre. Jaune le soleil. La vieille fille. L'automne. Papa, les petits bâteaux. 1972: Il était une fois un flic. The Lumière Years (narrator only). Chut! La grande Paulette. La raison du plus fou. 1973: La fille au violoncelle. The Day of the Jackal. Glissements progressifs du plaisir. Les grands sentiments font les bons gueuletons. Out One: Spectre. 1974: Stavisky. Le fantôme de la liberté (GB and US: The Phantom of Liberty). Galileo. Une baleine qui avait mal aux dents. Aloïse. Un linceul n'a pas de poches. Caravan to Vaccares. Sérieux comme le plaisir. Les suspects. India Song. 1975: The Romantic Englishwoman. Le téléphone rose (GB: The Pink Telephone). Section spéciale. Folle à tuer (GB: TV, as The Evil Trap). 1976: Le traqué. Mr Klein. Les oeufs brouillés. 1977: Le diable dans la boîte. Die linkshändige Frau (GB and US: The Left-Handed Woman). L'imprécateur. 1978: The Passage. 1979: Moonraker. 1980: Les jeux de la comtesse. 1981: Chariots of Fire. 1982: Enigma. 1984: Le bon roi Dagobert. 1985: The Holcroft Covenant.*

**LOO, Richard** 1903-1983
Hawaiian actor of Chinese parentage, who graduated from the University of California in business studies, and became an importer. When his business was hit by the Depression, he turned to acting. His roles in the 1930s were predictable and relatively few but, with the coming of World War II, he screwed his pleasant features into a merciless, humourless expression and played some memorable Japanese tormentors, especially in *The Purple Heart, China Sky* and, in post-war years, *I Was an American Spy*.

*1931: Dirigible. 1932: War Correspondent (GB: Soldiers of Fortune). Secrets of Wu Sin (GB: Secrets of Chinatown). The Bitter Tea of General Yen. 1934: Now and Forever. 1935: Stranded. East of Java (GB: Java Seas). 1936: Shadow of Chinatown (serial). 1937: The Good Earth. Lost Horizon. The Singing Marine. That Certain Woman. Thank You, Mr Moto. West of Shanghai. 1938: Shadows over Shanghai. Too Hot to Handle. Blondes at Work. 1939: Mr Wong in Chinatown. Daughter of the Tong. Island of Lost Men. Miracles for Sale. 1940: The Fatal Hour. 1941: Secrets of the Wasteland. They Met in Bombay. 1942: Little Tokyo USA. Bombs Over Burma. Across the Pacific. Star-Spangled Rhythm. 1943: Flight for Freedom. China. The Falcon Strikes Back. Yanks Ahoy. Jack London. 1944: The Keys of the Kingdom. The Story of Dr Wassell. The Purple Heart. 1945: Betrayal from the East. God is My Co-Pilot. Back to Bataan. Tokyo Rose. First Yank into Tokyo (GB: Mask of Fury). China Sky. Prison Ship. 1947: Seven Were Saved. Web of Danger. Women in the Night. 1948: Half Past Midnight. The Cobra Strikes. Rogues' Regiment. 1949: The Clay Pigeon. Malaya (GB: East of the Rising Sun). State Department— File 649 (GB: Assignment in China). 1950: The Steel Helmet. 1951: I Was an American Spy. 1952: Five Fingers. 1953: China Venture. Target Hong Kong. 1954: Hell and High Water. The Shanghai Story. Living It Up. The Bamboo Prison. 1955: Soldier of Fortune. Love Is a Many-Splendored Thing. 1956: The Conqueror. Around the World in 80 Days. Battle Hymn. 1958: The Quiet American. Hong Kong Affair. 1961: Seven*

*Women from Hell. 1962: Confessions of an Opium Eater (GB: Evils of Chinatown). A Girl Named Tamiko. 1966: The Sand Pebbles. 1969: A Matter of Humanities (TV). 1971: One More Train to Rob. Chandler. 1972: Kung Fu (TV). 1974: The Man With the Golden Gun.*

**LOVE, Montagu** 1877-1943
Hefty, square-faced, chunk-nosed British actor with thinning light-brown hair, in Hollywood from 1915 (after an early career as a newspaper cartoonist). Once into his stride, Love proved himself a thoroughly hissable villain, starring as Rasputin and other sinister historical figures. With the coming of sound, his unyielding features were seen in lesser, though still striking roles, often in period costume.

*1914: The Suicide Club. 1915: The Face in the Moonlight. The Antique Dealer. Hearts in Exile. A Royal Family. The Greater Will. A Woman's Way. Sunday. 1916: Friday the Thirteenth. Husband and Wife. The Scarlet Oath. The Gilded Cage. Bought and Paid For. The Hidden Scar. The Man She Married. The Challenge. 1917: Rasputin the Black Monk. Hands Up! The Brand of Satan. 1918: The Awakening. The Cross-Bearer. Vengeance. The Grouch. Stolen Orders. The Good For Nothing. 1919: The Hand Invisible. Three Green Eyes. A Broadway Saint. Rough Neck. To Him That Hath. Through the Toils. The Quickening Flame. The Steel King. 1920: Place of Honeymoons. The World and His Wife. 1921: Shams of Society. The Wrong Woman. Forever (GB: Peter Ibbetson). The Case of Becky. Love's Redemption. 1922: The Beauty Shop. Streets of Paris/Secrets of Paris. The Darling of the Rich. What's Wrong with Women? 1923: The Leopardess. The Eternal City. 1924: Roulette. A Son of the Sahara. Sinners in Heaven. Love of Women. Restless Wives. Who's Cheating? Week-End Husbands. 1925: The Desert's Price. The Ancient Highway. The Mad Marriage. 1926: Out of the Storm. The Social Highwayman. Brooding Eyes. Don Juan. The Silent Lover. Hands Up! (and 1917 film). The Son of the Sheik. 1927: The Night of Love. The King of Kings. Good Time Charley. The Haunted Ship. Jesse James. One Hour of Love. Rose of the Golden West. The Tender Hour.*

*1928: The Noose. The Devil's Skipper. The Hawk's Nest. The Haunted House. \*Character Studies. The Wind. Silks and Saddles (GB: Thoroughbreds). 1929: The Divine Lady. Synthetic Sin. The Last Warning. Her Private Life. Bulldog Drummond. Charming Sinners. Midstream. The Mysterious Island. The Voice Within. A Most Immoral Lady. 1930: A Notorious Affair. Double Cross Roads. Back Pay. Kismet. The Cat Creeps. Inside the Lines. Reno. Love Comes Along. Outward Bound. The Furies. 1931: Alexander Hamilton. The Lion and the Lamb. 1932: Silver Lining. Stowaway. Vanity Fair. Love Bound. Riding Tornado. Midnight Lady (GB: Dream Mother). Out of Singapore. Broadway Tornado. 1933: His Double Life. 1934: Limehouse Blues. Menace. 1935: Hi Gaucho. The Man Who Broke the Bank at Monte Carlo. Clive of India. The Crusades. 1936: The Country Doctor. Sutter's Gold. Sing, Baby, Sing. Reunion (GB: Hearts in Reunion). Lloyds of London. One in a Million. The White Angel. Champagne Charlie. 1937: The Prince and the Pauper. Parnell. The Life of Emile Zola. Tovarich. The Prisoner of Zenda. London by Night. A Damsel in Distress. Adventure's End. 1938: Professor, Beware! The Buccaneer. If I Were King. Kidnapped. The Adventures of Robin Hood. 1939: Gunga Din. Juarez. Rulers of the Sea. The Man in the Iron Mask. We Are Not Alone. 1940: Northwest Passage. The Son of Monte Cristo. All This and Heaven Too. The Sea Hawk. A Dispatch from Reuter's (GB: This Man Reuter). Dr Ehrlich's Magic Bullet (GB: The Story of Dr Ehrlich's Magic Bullet). The Lone Wolf Strikes: Private Affairs. North West Mounted Police. The Mark of Zorro. Hudson's Bay. 1941: The Devil and Miss Jones. Shining Victory. Lady for a Night. 1942: The Remarkable Andrew. Sherlock Holmes and the Voice of Terror. Tennessee Johnson (GB: The Man on America's Conscience). 1943: Forever and a Day. The Constant Nymph. Devotion (released 1946). Holy Matrimony. 1946: Thieves' Holiday (GB: A Scandal in Paris. Filmed 1943).*

**LOVELL, Raymond** 1900-1953
Portly Canadian actor, long in Britain, where he married actress Tamara Desni. He seemed to be forever playing plump princes and ranting regents, although his

florid features could also convey a very smooth brand of villainy indeed. Also directed stage plays.

*1934: Love, Life and Laughter. The Third Clue. Warn London! 1935: Some Day. The Case of Gabriel Perry. Crime Unlimited. Sexton Blake and the Mademoiselle. King of the Damned. 1936: Not So Dusty. Gaolbreak. Troubled Waters. Gypsy Melody. Fair Exchange. 1937: Glamorous Night. Secret Lives (US: I Married a Spy). Behind Your Back. Midnight Menace (US: Bombs over London). Mademoiselle Docteur. 1938: Murder Tomorrow. 1939: Q Planes (US: Clouds over Europe). 1940: Contraband (US: Blackout). 1941: He Found a Star. 49th Parallel (US: The Invaders). The Common Touch. The Young Mr Pitt. 1942: The Goose Steps Out. Uncensored. Alibi. 1943: Candlelight in Algeria. Warn That Man. The Man in Grey. 1944: Hotel Reserve. The Way Ahead. 1945: Caesar and Cleopatra. Night Boat to Dublin. 1946: Appointment with Crime. 1947: Edge of the River. Easy Money. 1948: Who Killed Van Loon? The Three Weird Sisters. Quartet. The Blind Goddess. But Not in Vain. My Brother's Keeper. The Calendar. Snowbound. So Evil My Love. The Bad Lord Byron. 1949: The Romantic Age (US: Naughty Arlette). Madness of the Heart. Once Upon a Dream. Fools Rush In. 1950: The Mudlark. 1952: Time Gentlemen Please! The Pickwick Papers. 1953: The Steel Key.*

**LOWE, Arthur** 1914-1982

Perceptive, stoutly built British actor who became a character star (via several television series) in his fifties: a supreme example of how even brilliant players can spend a lifetime wasting away in bit parts. But his bumbling, roly-poly characters with thoughts and emotions deeper than their outward pomposity would indicate deservedly brought him leading roles; and he subsequently enriched almost any assignment he was given. Died following a stroke.

*1948: London Belongs to Me (US: Dulcimer Street). 1949: Kind Hearts and Coronets. Stop Press Girl. Floodtide. The Spider and the Fly. Poets' Pub. 1950: Cage of Gold. 1953: Gilbert Harding Speaking of Murder. *The Mirror*

*and Markheim. 1954: Final Appointment. 1955: The Reluctant Bride (US: Two Grooms for a Bride). Windfall. One Way Out. The Woman for Joe. 1956: Breakaway. Who Done It? The High Terrace. The Green Man. 1957: Table in the Corner/Hour of Decision. Stranger in Town. 1958: Blind Spot. Stormy Crossing (US: Black Tide). 1959: The Boy and the Bridge. The Day They Robbed the Bank of England. 1960: Follow That Horse! 1961: Go to Blazes. 1962: Murder on Cloud Seven. This Sporting Life. 1965: You Must Be Joking! The White Bus (released 1967). 1968: If... 1969: *It All Goes to Show. The Bed Sitting Room. Spring and Port Wine. 1970: Some Will, Some Won't. The Rise and Rise of Michael Rimmer. *A Hole Lot of Trouble. *William Webb Ellis, Are You Mad? Fragment of Fear. 1971: Dad's Army. The Ruling Class. 1972: Adolf Hitler—My Part in His Downfall. 1973: O Lucky Man! Theatre of Blood. No Sex Please—We're British. 1974: Man About the House. 1975: Royal Flash. The Bawdy Adventures of Tom Jones. 1977: The Strange Case of the End of Civilization As We Know It (TV). 1979: The Lady Vanishes. The Lion, the Witch and the Wardrobe (TV. Voice only). Sweet William. 1982: Wagner (TV). Britannia Hospital.*

**LUKE, Keye** 1904- 1991

Slightly-built Hollywood oriental actor, born in China but raised in America. Films kept him busy from 1934 as assorted easterners, including two popular series characters— Charlie Chan's Number One Son in the detective thrillers about the slit-eyed sleuth, and Dr Lee Won How in M-G-M's Dr Gillespie hospital dramas.

*1934: The Painted Veil. Charlie Chan in Paris. 1935: Oil for the Lamps of China. Mad Love (GB: Hands of Orlac). King of Burlesque. Here's to Romance. Charlie Chan in Shanghai. Shanghai. Charlie Chan in Egypt. Eight Bells. The Casino Murder Case. 1936: Charlie Chan at the Circus. Charlie Chan at the Race Track. Anything Goes. Charlie Chan at the Opera. 1937: Charlie Chan on Broadway. The Good Earth. Charlie Chan at the Olympics. Charlie Chan at Monte Carlo. 1938: International Settlement. Mr Moto's Gamble.*

*1939: Barricade. Disputed Passage. North of Shanghai. 1940: Phantom of Chinatown. The Green Hornet (serial). No, No, Nanette. Sued for Libel. The Green Hornet Strikes Again (serial). 1941: The Gang's All Here. Bowery Blitzkrieg (GB: Stand and Deliver). Let's Go Collegiate (GB: Farewell to Fame). Mr and Mrs North. No Hands on the Clock. They Met in Bombay. Burma Convoy. Passage from Hong Kong. 1942: A Yank on the Burma Road (GB: China Caravan). Somewhere I'll Find You. North to the Klondike. Across the Pacific. The Falcon's Brother. Dr Gillespie's New Assistant. Adventures of Smilin' Jack (serial). Invisible Agent. Mexican Spitfire's Elephant. Spy Ship. A Tragedy at Midnight. Destination Unknown. Journey for Margaret. 1943: Salute to the Marines. Dr Gillespie's Criminal Case (GB: Crazy to Kill). 1944: Andy Hardy's Blonde Trouble. Three Men in White. 1945: First Yank into Tokyo (GB: Mask of Fury). Between Two Women. Tokyo Rose. How Do You Do? Secret Agent X-9 (serial). 1946: Lost City of the Jungle (serial). 1947: Dark Delusion (GB: Cynthia's Secret). 1948: Sleep My Love. Waterfront at Midnight. The Feathered Serpent. 1949: Sky Dragon. Young Man with a Horn (GB: Young Man of Music). 1953: South Sea Woman. Fair Wind to Java. 1954: Hell's Half Acre. World for Ransom. Bamboo Prison. 1955: Love is a Many-Splendored Thing. 1956: Around the World in 80 Days. 1957: Yangtse Incident (US: Battle Hell). 1958: The Hunters. 1968: Nobody's Perfect. 1969: The Chairman (GB: The Most Dangerous Man in the World). Project X. 1970: The Hawaiians (GB: Master of the Islands). 1971: Noon Sunday. 1973: The Cat Creature (TV). 1975: Won Ton Ton, the Dog Who Saved Hollywood. 1977: The Amsterdam Kill. 1979: Just You and Me, Kid. 1981: Fly Away Home (TV). 1982: They Call Me Bruce. 1984: Gremlins.*

**MacDONALD, J. Farrell**

(John F. MacDonald) 1875-1952

Burly (later positively portly), jovial, bull-necked, bald American actor, who was a singer in stage productions, then tried direction in early silents (among them a couple of Harold Lloyd comedies), before settling down to play scores of tough but

affable character roles, many of them for director John Ford. Equally happy with cops and prison wardens or outdoor types, his characters were sometimes thick-skulled but more often tinged with Irish humour.

*1911:* *IMP shorts (series). *1914:* The Last Egyptian. The Patchwork Girl of Oz. *1915:* Rags. The Heart of Maryland. *1918:* The Price of Power. $5,000 Reward. Fair Enough. Three Mounted Men. *1919:* Molly of the Follies. A Fight for Love. Riders of Vengeance. Charge It to Me. Roped. Trixie from Broadway. This Hero Stuff. A Sporting Chance. The Outcasts of Poker Flat. Marked Men. *1920:* Under Sentence. Bullet Proof. The Path She Chose. Hitchin' Posts. *1921:* The Freeze Out. Action. The Wallop. Desperate Youth. Bucking the Line. Trailin'. Little Miss Hawkshaw. Riding With Death. Sky High. *1922:* The Bachelor Daddy. Manslaughter. The Bonded Woman. Tracks. The Young Rajah. Come On Over. The Ghost Breaker. Over the Border. *1923:* While Paris Sleeps. The Age of Desire. Quicksands. Drifting. Racing Hearts. Fashionable Fakers. *1924:* The Brass Bowl. The Storm Daughter. Western Luck. Fair Week. The Signal Tower. Mademoiselle Midnight. General Cranston's Lady. The Iron Horse. *1925:* The Scarlet Honeymoon. The Fighting Heart. Thank You. Kentucky Pride. Let Women Alone. Lightnin'. The Lucky Horseshoe. *1926:* A Trip to Chinatown. The Dixie Merchant. Bertha, the Sewing Machine Girl. The Shamrock Handicap. The Family Upstairs. The First Year. Three Bad Men. The Country Beyond. *1927:* Ankles Preferred. The Cradle Snatchers. East Side, West Side. Love Makes 'Em Wild. Paid To Love. Rich But Honest. Colleen. Sunrise—A Song of Two Humans (GB: Sunrise). *1928:* Bringing Up Father. The Cohens and Kellys in Paris. Abie's Irish Rose. Riley the Cop. None But the Brave. Phantom City. *1929:* Masked Emotions. In Old Arizona. The Four Devils. South Sea Rose. Strong Boy. Masquerade. Happy Days. *1930:* Broken Dishes. Men Without Women. Song o' My Heart. Girl of the Golden West. Painted Angel. The Truth About Youth. Born Reckless. Woman Hungry (GB: The Challenge). *1931:* River's End. Leftover Ladies (GB: Broken Links). The Painted Desert. The Easiest Way. The Maltese Falcon. The Millionaire. Steel Highway. Other Men's Women. The Squaw Man (GB: The White Man). Too Young to Marry. The Brat. Spirit of Notre Dame (GB: Vigour of Youth). *The Stolen Jools (GB: The Slippery Pearls). Touchdown (GB: Playing the Game). Sporting Blood. *1932:* Hotel Continental. Under Eighteen. The Phantom Express. Discarded Lovers. Scandal for Sale. Probation. Week-End Marriage (GB: Working Wives). 70,000 Witnesses. The Thirteenth Guest. Me and My Gal. Steady Company. The Racing Strain. No Man of Her Own. Pride of the Legion (GB: The Big Pay-Off). The Vanishing Frontier. Hearts of Humanity. This Sporting Age. *1933:* The Working Man. Laughing at Life. Peg o' My Heart. The Power and the Glory. I Loved a Woman. The Iron Master. Myrt and Marge (GB: Laughter in the Air). Heritage of the Desert. Under Secret Orders. *1934:* Romance in Manhattan. Murder on the Campus (GB: On the Stroke of Nine). The Crime Doctor. Man of Two Worlds. Once to Every Woman. The Crosby Case (GB: The Crosby Murder Case). The Cat's Paw. Beggar's Holiday. The Whole Town's Talking (GB: Passport to Fame). *1935:* The Square Shooter. Northern Frontier. Let 'Em Have It (GB: False Faces). Star of Midnight. The Best Man Wins. The Healer. Swell Head. Maybe It's Love. Our Little Girl. The Irish in Us. Front Page Woman. Danger Ahead. Fighting Youth. Stormy. Waterfront Lady. Riffraff. *1936:* Hitch Hike Lady (GB: Eventful Journey). Florida Special. Exclusive Story. Showboat. *1937:* The Great Barrier (US: Silent Barriers). Shadows of the Orient. Maid of Salem. Mysterious Crossing. Roaring Timber. Slim. My Dear Miss Aldrich. The Hit Parade. County Fair. Slave Ship. Topper. The Game That Kills. Courage of the West. *1938:* My Old Kentucky Home. Numbered Woman. State Police. Gang Bullets. Flying Fists. There Goes My Heart. Extortion. White Banners. Come On, Rangers. Little Orphan Annie. The Crowd Roars. Submarine Patrol. *1939:* Susannah of the Mounties. Zenobia (GB: Elephants Never Forget). Mickey the Kid. East Side of Heaven. Conspiracy. The Gentleman from Arizona. Coast Guard. *1940:* The Light of Western Stars. Knights of the Range. Dark Command. I Take This Oath. Prairie Law. The Last Alarm. Untamed. Stagecoach War. Friendly Neighbors. *1941:* In Old Cheyenne. Meet John Doe. The Great Lie. Broadway Limited. Riders of the Timberline. *1942:* One Thrilling Night. Snuffy Smith—Yard Bird (GB: Snuffy Smith). Reap the Wild Wind. Sullivan's Travels. Phantom Killer. The Living Ghost. The Palm Beach Story. Bowery at Midnight. Little Tokyo USA. Captains of the Clouds. *1943:* The Ape Man. The Great Moment. Clancy Street Boys. True to Life. Tiger Fangs. *1944:* The Miracle of Morgan's Creek. Irish Eyes Are Smiling. Greenwich Village. Texas Masquerade. Follow the Boys. Hail the Conquering Hero. Shadow of Suspicion. A Tree Grows in Brooklyn. *1945:* Nob Hill. Johnny Angel. Pillow of Death. The Woman Who Came Back. Pardon My Past. Fallen Angel. *1946:* It's a Wonderful Life! Joe Palooka—Champ. Behind Green Lights. Smoky. My Darling Clementine. *1947:* Web of Danger. Thunder in the Valley (GB: Bob, Son of Battle). Keeper of the Bees. *1948:* Fury at Furnace Creek. Whispering Smith. Panhandle. Shep Comes Home. Belle Starr's Daughter. The Luck of the Irish. The Walls of Jericho. Sitting Pretty. *1949:* Streets of San Francisco. The Beautiful Blonde from Bashful Bend. Law of the Barbary Coast. You're My Everything. The Dalton Gang. Fighting Man of the Plains. *1950:* Dakota Lil. Hostile Country. Woman on the Run. *1951:* Elopement. Here Comes the Groom. Mr Belvedere Rings the Bell. Superman and the Mole Men (GB: Superman and the Strange People).

**As director:**
*1914:* The Patchwork Girl of Oz. And She Never Knew. The Tides of Sorrow. *1915:* Lorna Doone. Lonesome Luke. Lonesome Luke—Social Gangster.

**MacGINNIS, Niall** 1913-
Burly, round-faced Irish character actor with a wild mop of dark curly hair, which disappeared in the fifties, giving him a professorial look. Largely a support for the stars in literate action roles, with an occasional villain or semi-lead thrown in. In British films from the mid-thirties, he remained in demand for 35 years.

*1935:* Turn of the Tide. The Luck of the Irish. *1936:* Ourselves Alone (US: River of Unrest). The Crimson Circle. Debt of Honour. *1937:* The Edge of the World. The Last Adventurers. *1938:* Mountains o' Mourne. *1940:* East of Piccadilly (US: The Strangler). *1941:* 49th Parallel (US: The Invaders). *1942:* The Day Will Dawn (US: The Avengers). *1943:* We Dive at Dawn. Undercover (US: Underground Guerillas). The Hundred Pound Window. *1944:* Tawny Pipit. Henry V. *1947:* Captain Boycott. *1948:* Hamlet. No Room at the Inn. *1949:* Christopher Columbus. Down to the Sea in Ships. Which Will You Have? (US: Barabbas the Robber). Diamond City. *1950:* Chance of a Lifetime. *1951:* No Highway (US: No Highway in the Sky). Talk of a Million (US: You Can't Beat the Irish). *1952:* Murder in the Cathedral. *1953:* Hell Below Zero. *1954:* Conflict of Wings. Martin Luther.

Knights of the Round Table. Betrayed. Helen of Troy. 1955: Vom Himmel gefallen/Special Delivery. Alexander the Great. 1956: Lust for Life. 1957: The Shiralee. Night of the Demon (US: Curse of the Demon). 1958: She Didn't Say No! Behind the Mask. The Nun's Story. 1959: Shake Hands with the Devil. Tarzan's Greatest Adventure. This Other Eden. 1960: Never Take Sweets from a Stranger. Kidnapped. A Terrible Beauty (US: The Night Fighters). Foxhole in Cairo. Sword of Sherwood Forest. In the Nick. 1961: Johnny Nobody. 1962: The Prince and the Pauper. The Webster Boy. The Playboy of the Western World. Billy Budd. A Face in the Rain. The Devil's Agent. The Man Who Finally Died. 1963: Jason and the Argonauts. Becket. 1964: The Truth About Spring. 1965: The Spy Who Came in from the Cold. The War Lord. 1966: Island of Terror. A Man Could Get Killed. 1967: The Viking Queen. Torture Garden. 1968: The Shoes of the Fisherman. Krakatoa—East of Java. 1969: Sinful Davey. River of Mystery (TV). The Kremlin Letter. 1973: The Mackintosh Man. 1978: Crisis at Sun Valley (TV).

**MacGOWRAN, Jack** 1916-1973
Sharp-faced, ferret-like, Irish (very Irish), dark-haired purveyor of memorable character studies in British films—usually providing a malicious element in one way or another. His leprechauns looked harmless, and were sometimes comic too, but occasionally insidiously deadly. He began in small roles and worked his way up in films, without ever really deserting the stage. Died from complications following influenza. Father of actress Tara MacGowran.

1951: No Resting Place. 1952: The Quiet Man. The Gentle Gunman. The Titfield Thunderbolt. 1954: The Young Lovers (US: Chance Meeting). 1955: Dust and Gold. 1956: Raiders of the River (serial). Jacqueline. Sailor Beware! (US: Panic in the Parlor). 1957: The Rising of the Moon. Manuela (US: Stowaway Girl). 1958: Darby O'Gill and the Little People. She Didn't Say No! Rooney. 1959: The Boy and the Bridge. Blind Date. Behemoth the Sea Monster (US: The Giant Behemoth). 1961: Two and Two Make Six. Mix Me a Person. 1962: Vengeance (US: The Brain). Captain Clegg (US: Night

Creatures). 1963: Tom Jones. The Ceremony. 1964: Young Cassidy. Lord Jim. 1965: Doctor Zhivago. 1966: Cul-de-Sac. 1967: Dance of the Vampires (US: The Fearless Vampire Killers). How I Won the War. 1968: *Faithful Departed (narrator only). Wonderwall. 1969: Age of Consent. Start the Revolution Without Me. 1970: King Lear. 1973: The Exorcist.

**MACKAY, Fulton** 1920- 1987
Acidulous, slightly built, wry-mouthed Scottish actor who has played everything from ruthless detectives to whisky priests and is also a talented playwright. Somehow, Ealing Studies failed to pick up the ex-quantity surveyor and ex-soldier for their regional comedies and in consequence he has made too few films. Enormous personal success has come on television, however, especially through the series Special Branch and Porridge.

1952: I'm a Stranger. Laxdale Hall (US: Scotch on the Rocks). 1954: The Last Moment. 1961: A Prize of Arms. 1962: Mystery Submarine (US: Decoy). 1971: Gumshoe. 1972: Nothing but the Night. 1974: †The Wilby Conspiracy. 1979: Porridge. 1982: Britannia Hospital. 1983: Ill Fares the Land (TV). Local Hero. 1985: Water. Defence of the Realm.

† Scene deleted from final release print

**MacMAHON, Aline** 1899- 1991
Distinguished, dark-haired, tall American stage actress originally intended for stardom by Warners when they brought her to the screen. But her horsey, mournful face was obviously destined for more interesting things than straight leads, and she proved as adept with wisecracks as with wisdom. When her studio contract was over, she again devoted the majority of her time to the theatre. Nominated for an Academy Award for Dragon Seed.

1931: Five Star Final. The Mouthpiece. 1932: Heart of New York. Life Begins (GB: The Dawn of Life). Sign of the Cross. One-Way Passage. Week-End Marriage (GB: Working Wives). Once in a Lifetime. Silver Dollar. 1933: Heroes for Sale. Gold Diggers of 1933.

The World Changes. The Life of Jimmy Dolan (GB: The Kid's Last Fight). 1934: Big-Hearted Herbert. Heat Lightning. The Merry Frinks (GB: The Happy Family). Babbitt. Side Streets (GB: Woman in Her Thirties). 1935: I Live My Life. While the Patient Slept. Ah, Wilderness! Mary Jane's Pa (GB: Wanderlust). Kind Lady (GB: House of Menace). 1937: When You're in Love. 1939: Back Door to Heaven. 1941: Out of the Fog. 1942: Tish. The Lady is Willing. 1943: Stage Door Canteen. Seeds of Freedom (narrator only). 1944: Guest in the House. Dragon Seed. 1946: The Mighty McGurk. 1948: The Search. 1949: Roseanna McCoy. 1950: The Flame and the Arrow. 1953: The Eddie Cantor Story. 1955: The Man from Laramie. 1960: Cimarron. 1961: The Young Doctors. 1962: I Could Go On Singing. Diamond Head. 1963: All the Way Home.

**MACRAE, Duncan**
(John D. Macrae) 1905-1967
Gaunt, craggy, long-chinned Scottish actor who was a teacher for 20 years before switching careers during World War II. His cadaverous shape loomed memorably in a few films, almost all with a heavy Scottish slant. He was also chairman of the Scottish branch of Equity, the actors' union, and got too few chances at his favourite parts—'dignified fools'.

1947: The Brothers. 1948: Whisky Galore! (US: Tight Little Island). 1950: The Woman in Question (US: Five Angles on Murder). 1952: You're Only Young Twice! 1953: The

Kidnappers (US: The Little Kidnappers). The 'Maggie' (US: High and Dry). 1955: Geordie (US: Wee Geordie). 1957: Rockets Galore (US: Mad Little Island). 1958: The Bridal Path. 1959: Kidnapped. Our Man in Havana. 1960: Tunes of Glory. Greyfriars Bobby. 1961: The Best of Enemies. 1963: Girl in the Headlines (US: The Model Murder Case). A Jolly Bad Fellow (US: They All Died Laughing). 1967: Casino Royale. 30 is a Dangerous Age, Cynthia.

Caesar. 1954: Duffy of San Quentin (GB: Men Behind Bars). Vera Cruz. 1956: A Kiss Before Dying. Thunder Over Arizona. 1957: Paths of Glory. Gunfire at Indian Gap. The Abductors. 1958: Plunderers of Painted Flats. 1959: Jet over the Atlantic. The Alligator People. 1960: In the Presence of Mine Enemies (TV). Two Weeks in Another Town. Taras Bulba. 1964: Dead Ringer (GB: Dead Image). Where Love Has Gone. 1965: The Great Race. The Human Duplicators. 1966: Fame is the Name of the Game (TV). 1967: Asylum for a Spy (TV). 1969: The Young Lawyers (TV). Daughter of the Mind (TV). Night Gallery (TV). 1970: Tora! Tora! Tora! 1971: The Return of Count Yorga.

## MACREADY, George 1908-1973

One of America's most distinctive villains: a blond, blue-eyed death's head of a man with an aristocratic sneer on the upper lip, and skin drawn pellucidly over the features—a face that somehow went with his having run an art gallery before giving into the acting urge in the 1940s. Created a whole range of distinguished nasties and sadists, nearly all with a civilized veneer. An emphysema killed him just after retirement.

1942: Commandos Strike at Dawn. 1944: The Seventh Cross. The Story of Dr Wassell. Follow the Boys. Soul of a Monster. Wilson. The Conspirators. 1945: Don Juan Quilligan. The Missing Juror. I Love a Mystery. The Monster and the Ape (serial). A Song to Remember. The Fighting Guardsman. Counter-Attack (GB: One Against Seven). My Name is Julia Ross. 1946: The Man Who Dared. The Walls Came Tumbling Down. Gilda. The Bandit of Sherwood Forest. The Return of Monte Cristo (GB: Monte Cristo's Revenge). 1947: The Swordsman. Down to Earth. 1948: The Big Clock. The Black Arrow (GB: The Black Arrow Strikes). The Gallant Blade. Coroner Creek. Beyond Glory. Alias Nick Beal (GB: The Contact Man). 1949: Johnny Allegro (GB: Hounded). The Doolins of Oklahoma (GB: The Great Manhunt). Knock on Any Door. 1950: The Nevadan (GB: The Man from Nevada). Fortunes of Captain Blood. A Lady Without Passport. Rogues of Sherwood Forest. The Desert Hawk. 1951: Tarzan's Peril (GB: Tarzan and the Jungle Queen). Detective Story. The Golden Horde (GB: The Golden Horde of Genghis Khan). The Green Glove. The Desert Fox (GB: Rommel—Desert Fox). 1953: Treasure of the Golden Condor. The Golden Blade. The Stranger Wore a Gun. Julius

## MADDEN, Peter 1905-1976

Thin, hollow-cheeked British actor of menacing presence. Born in Malaya he was, at 16, 'assistant to a drunken magician', later a racing driver and stand-up comic before bringing his grim expression and deep bass voice to character roles. He once said: 'I'm generally cast as a baddie because I've got such a miserable bloody face. Thank God I never wanted to be a star'.

1943: Rhythm Serenade. 1947: Penny and the Pownall Case. 1948: Counterblast. 1949: A Matter of Murder. 1951: Tom Brown's Schooldays. 1958: Battle of the V1 (US: V1/Unseen Heroes). Fiend Without a Face. Floods of Fear. 1959: Hell Is a City. 1960: Saturday Night and Sunday Morning. Exodus. 1962: The Loneliness of the Long Distance Runner. The Road to Hong Kong. A Kind of Loving. 1963: The Very Edge. From Russia with Love. Nothing But the Best. 1964: Woman of Straw. 1965: Doctor Zhivago. 1966: He Who Rides a Tiger. 1967: The Magnificent Six and a Half (first series). 1972: Henry VIII and His Six Wives. Nearest and Dearest. 1975: One of Our Dinosaurs Is Missing. 1976: The Message.

## MADDERN, Victor 1926-

Lively British actor with expressive features and ready scowl. He made his debut as a cockney private soldier and made a good living from the part for the next ten years. Maddern could just as easily play jaunty, shifty or sympathetic, which made for one

or two interesting variations in his roles when not in uniform. Lately more often seen in theatre and TV productions and, in recent times, a diligent worker for religion-slanted charities.

1950: Seven Days to Noon. Morning Departure (US: Operation Disaster). Pool of London. 1951: His Excellency. The Franchise Affair. The House in the Square (US: I'll Never Forget You). 1952: Angels One Five. The Planter's Wife (US: Outpost in Malaya). Top Secret (US: Mr Potts Goes to Moscow). Time Bomb (US: Terror on a Train). 1953: Malta Story. Street of Shadows (US: Shadow Man). Single-Handed (US: Sailor of the King). The Good Beginning. 1954: Carrington VC (US: Court-Martial). Fabian of the Yard. Raising a Riot. The Sea Shall Not Have Them. The End of the Affair. 1955: The Night My Number Came Up. Footsteps in the Fog. Josephine and Men. Cockleshell Heroes. It's a Great Day. 1956: Private's Progress. Child in the House. The Last Man To Hang? A Hill in Korea (US: Hell in Korea). The Man in the Sky (US: Decision Against Time). 1957: Seven Waves Away (US: Abandon Ship!). Face in the Night. Saint Joan. Strangers' Meeting. Barnacle Bill (US: All at Sea). Happy is the Bride! Son of a Stranger. The Safecracker. 1958: The Square Peg. Blood of the Vampire. Dunkirk. Cat and Mouse/The Desperate Men. I Was Monty's Double (US: Monty's Double). Carve Her Name With Pride. 1959: I'm All Right, Jack. The Siege of Pinchgut. Please Turn Over. 1960: Sink the Bismarck! Let's Get Married. Light Up the Sky. Carry On Constable. Exodus. Watch Your Stern. Crossroads to Crime. 1961: Carry On Regardless. Raising the Wind. On the Fiddle (US: Operation Snafu). Petticoat Pirates. 1962: HMS Defiant (US: Damn the Defiant!). The Longest Day. 1964: Carry On Cleo. 1965: Rotten to the Core. Bunny Lake is Missing. Cuckoo Patrol. Circus of Fear (US: Psycho-Circus). 1966: Run Like a Thief. 1967: The Magnificent Two. *Talk of the Devil. 1968: The Lost Continent. Decline and Fall … of a Birdwatcher! Chitty Chitty Bang Bang. 1969: The Magic Christian. 1970: *A Hole Lot of Trouble. Cromwell. 1971: The Magnificent Six and a Half (third series). 1972: Steptoe and Son. 1973: Digby—the Biggest Dog in the

World. 1978: Carry On Emmannuelle. Death on the Nile.

## MADISON, Noel
(Nathaniel Moscovitch) 1898-1975
Very dark, sullen-looking American actor who almost always played a bad guy—often one who turned yellow in the end. The son of another character actor, Russian-born Maurice Moscovitch (1871-1940), he was billed in the theatre as Nat Madison, then came to Hollywood with the beginnings of sound. Fleeing from a run of evil gangsters, he made several films in Britain in the late 1930s, including three with Jessie Matthews.

1930: The Doorway to Hell (GB: Handful of Clouds). Sinner's Holiday. Little Caesar. 1931: The Star Witness. 1932: The Hatchet Man (GB: The Honourable Mr Wong). Hat Check Girl (GB: Embassy Girl). Me and My Gal (GB: Pier 13). Play Girl. Symphony of Six Million. Man About Town. The Trial of Vivienne Ware. The Last Mile. Laughter in Hell. 1933: Humanity. Destination Unknown. West of Singapore. Important Witness. 1934: I Like It That Way. Manhattan Melodrama. The House of Rothschild. Journal of a Crime. Four Hours to Kill. 1935: The Morals of Marcus. G Men. What Price Crime? The Girl Who Came Back. Three Kids and a Queen (GB: The Baxter Millions). My Marriage. Murder at Glen Athol. Woman Wanted. 1936: Muss 'Em Up (GB: House of Fate). Our Relations. Champagne Charlie. Straight from the Shoulder. Easy Money. Missing Girls. The Criminal Within. 1937: House of Secrets. Man of the People. Nation Aflame. Gangway. 1938: Sailing Along. Crackerjack (US: The Man with a Hundred Faces). Climbing High. Kate Plus Ten (US: Queen of Crime). Anything to Declare? Missing Evidence. 1939: Charlie Chan in City of Darkness. 1940: *Know Your Money. The Great Plane Robbery. 1941: Ellery Queen's Penthouse Mystery. *Sucker List. Footsteps in the Dark. Highway West. A Shot in the Dark. 1942: Bombs Over Burma. Secret Agent of Japan. Joe Smith, American (GB: Highway to Freedom). 1943: Miss V from Moscow. Jitterbugs. Shantytown. Forever and a Day. The Black Raven. 1948: The Gentleman from Nowhere.

## MAGEE, Patrick 1923-1982
Stooped, stocky, intense-looking Irish actor with unkempt silver hair, often in horror films, and almost always the man to send a shiver down your spine with his off-centre presence. Like most 'frighteners' Magee was the very opposite in real life. 'Even a person in a film standing in a high place', he once said, 'gives me the shivers.'

1960: The Criminal. 1961: Never Back Losers. Rag Doll. 1962: A Prize of Arms. The Boys. 1963: The Servant. Dementia 13 (GB: The Haunted and the Hunted). The Young Racers. Ricochet. The Very Edge. Zulu. 1964: The Masque of the Red Death. Seance on a Wet Afternoon. 1965: The Skull. Monster of Terror (US: Die, Monster, Die). 1966: The Persecution and Assassination of Jean Paul Marat ... (The Marat/Sade) 1968: Decline and Fall ... of a Birdwatcher! The Birthday Party. 1969: Hard Contract. Destiny of a Spy (TV). King Lear. 1970: Cromwell. You Can't Win 'Em All. 1971: The Fiend. A Clockwork Orange. The Trojan Women. Young Winston. 1972: Asylum. Beware of the Brethren. 1973: Lady Ice. And Now the Screaming Starts. The Final Programme (US: The Last Days of Man on Earth). Luther. 1974: Demons of the Mind. Galileo. 1975: Barry Lyndon. 1977: Telefon. 1980: Rough Cut. The Monster Club. 1981: Chariots of Fire. Dr Jekyll and the Women (GB: The Blood of Dr Jekyll).

## MAIN, Marjorie
(Mary Tomlinson) 1890-1975
Unique, crow-voiced American actress with bundled-up nest of dark hair and sack-of-potatoes figure who became a film regular after the early death of her husband and delighted audiences with a great series of haranguing harridans both comic and tragic; most memorably in partnership with Wallace Beery and, later, in the Ma and Pa Kettle series. Oscar-nominated for The Egg and I. Died from cancer.

1932: Hot Saturday. A House Divided. 1933: Take a Chance. 1934: Music in the Air. *New Deal Rhythm. Crime Without Passion. 1935: Naughty Marietta. 1937: City Girl. Boy of the Streets. Love in a Bungalow. Dead End. The Shadow (GB: The Circus Shadow). The Man Who Cried Wolf. Stella

Dallas. The Wrong Road. 1938: Penitentiary. Girls' School. Romance of the Limberlost. Under the Big Top (GB: The Circus Comes to Town). King of the Newsboys. Too Hot to Handle. Little Tough Guy. Three Comrades. Test Pilot. Prison Farm. There Goes My Heart. 1939: Angels Wash Their Faces. Another Thin Man. Lucky Night. They Shall Have Music (GB: Melody of Youth). The Women. Two Thoroughbreds. 1940: Women Without Names. Dark Command. Turnabout. Susan and God (GB: The Gay Mrs Trexel). Wyoming (GB: Bad Man of Wyoming). I Take This Woman. The Captain Is a Lady. 1941: The Wild Man of Borneo. The Trial of Mary Dugan. Honky Tonk. A Woman's Face. The Bugle Sounds. Shepherd of the Hills. Barnacle Bill. 1942: The Affairs of Martha (GB: Once Upon a Thursday). Jackass Mail. Tennessee Johnson (GB: The Man on America's Conscience). We Were Dancing. 1943: Heaven Can Wait. Woman of the Town. Johnny Come Lately (GB: Johnny Vagabond). 1944: Rationing. Meet Me in St Louis. Gentle Annie. 1945: Murder, He Says. The Harvey Girls. 1946: The Show-Off. Bad Bascomb. Undercurrent. 1947: The Wistful Widow of Wagon Gap (GB: The Wistful Widow). The Egg and I. 1948: Feudin', Fussin' and a-Fightin'. Ma and Pa Kettle. 1949: Big Jack. Ma and Pa Kettle Go to Town (GB: Going to Town). 1950: Summer Stock (GB: If You Feel Like Singing). Mrs O'Malley and Mr Malone. Mr Imperium (GB: You Belong to My Heart). 1951: It's a Big Country. Ma and Pa Kettle Back on the Farm. The Law and the Lady. 1952: The Belle of New York. Ma and Pa Kettle on Vacation (GB: Ma and Pa Kettle Go to Paris). Ma and Pa Kettle at the Fair. 1953: Fast Company. 1954: Ricochet Romance. Ma and Pa Kettle at Home. The Long, Long Trailer. Rose Marie. 1955: Ma and Pa Kettle at Waikiki. 1956: The Kettles in the Ozarks. Friendly Persuasion. 1957: The Kettles on Old MacDonald's Farm.

## MAITLAND, Marne 1920-
Dusky, hook-nosed, shady-looking Anglo-Indian actor, much in demand for shifty middle easterners in British films, from the moment he made an appropriate debut in Cairo Road. After that, his characters were to be discovered peddling drugs, smuggling diamonds, pinching curios, involved with refugees and generally making money from every dubious racket going.

1950: Cairo Road. 1951: His Excellency. Outcast of the Islands. 1952: South of Algiers (US: The Golden Mask). 1953: Beat the Devil. 1954: Father Brown (US: The Detective). Flame and the Flesh. Svengali. Diplomatic Passport. 1955: Break in the Circle. Dust and Gold. 1956: Bhowani Junction. Ramsbottom Rides Again. 1957: Hour of Decision/Table in the Corner. Interpol (US: Pickup Alley). Seven Thunders (US: The Beasts of Marseilles). Accused (US: Mark of the Hawk). 1958: I Was Monty's Double (US: Monty's Double). I Only Arsked! The Camp on Blood Island. Windom's Way. The

ABOVE Marjorie **Main** provided formidable opposition for Bud
Abbott and Lou Costello in *The Wistful Widow of Wagon Gap*
(1947). Here it's Costello who's looking wistful

BELOW We don't know what Marne **Maitland** (left) is up to
with Trevor Howard in this scene from *Interpol* (1957). But we
wouldn't mind betting he's trying to sell him something

Wind Cannot Read. Carlton-Browne of the F O (US: Man in a Cocked Hat). 1959: The Stranglers of Bombay. I'm All Right, Jack. 1960: Visa to Canton (US: Passport to China). Cone of Silence (US: Trouble in the Sky). Sands of the Desert. 1961: The Middle Course. Three on a Spree. The Terror of the Tongs. 1962: Phantom of the Opera. Nine Hours to Rama. 1963: Cleopatra. Master Spy. Panic. 1964: The First Men in the Moon. Lord Jim. 1965: The Return of Mr Moto. The Reptile. 1966: Khartoum. 1967: The Bobo. 1968: Duffy. Decline and Fall . . . of a Birdwatcher! The Bushbaby. The Shoes of the Fisherman. 1969: Anne of the Thousand Days. 1970: The Statue. 1972: Roma (GB: Fellini's Roma). Man of La Mancha. 1973: Shaft in Africa. Massacre in Rome. 1974: The Man With the Golden Gun. 1976: The Pink Panther Strikes Again. The Anonymous Avenger. 1977: March or Die. 1979: Ashanti. 1980: The Day Christ Died (TV). 1982: Trail of the Pink Panther. 1983: Memed My Hawk. 1984: The Assisi Underground.

**MAKEHAM, Eliot** 1882-1956
Brown-haired, inoffensive-looking British actor of small stature, often seen, bespectacled, in apologetic or downtrodden roles, sometimes as little men who triumphed in the end over nagging wives or bullying bosses. Played a few leading roles in the 1930s and made the most of them; otherwise in dozens of minor cameos as clerks, shopkeepers, auditors and the like. Known to his friends as Billy. Married (third of three) to fellow character player Betty Shale.

1932: Rome Express. 1933: Friday the Thirteenth. Forging Ahead. I'm an Explosive. Orders Is Orders. Britannia of Billingsgate. I Lived With You. The Lost Chord. Little Napoleon. Home Sweet Home. The Laughter of Fools. The Roof. 1934: By-Pass to Happiness. The Unfinished Symphony. The Crimson Candle. Lorna Doone. Once in a New Moon. 1935: The Last Journey. Peg of Old Drury. Two Hearts in Harmony. Her Last Affaire. 1936: To Catch a Thief. A Star Fell from Heaven. The Brown Wallet. Born That Way. Calling the Tune. Someone at the Door. All That Glitters. East Meets West. Tomorrow We

Live. The Mill on the Floss. 1937: Take My Tip. Racing Romance. East of Ludgate Hill. Dark Journey. Farewell Again (US: Troopship). Our Island Nation. Head Over Heels. (US: Head over Heels in Love). Storm in a Teacup. 1938: Coming of Age. Vessel of Wrath (US: The Beachcomber). Darts Are Trumps. Merely Mr Hawkins. Bedtime Story. You're the Doctor. Anything to Declare? The Citadel. Everything Happens to Me. 1939: What Men Live By. The Four Just Men (US: The Secret Four). The Nursemaid Who Disappeared. A Window in London (US: Lady in Distress). Inspector Hornleigh. Me and My Pal. Return to Yesterday. Spy for a Day. 1940: Saloon Bar. Spare a Copper. Night Train to Munich (US: Night Train). Busman's Honeymoon (US: Haunted Honeymoon). Pastor Hall. *All Hands. *Food for Thought. John Smith Wakes Up. 1941: The Common Touch. Facing the Music. They Flew Alone (US: Wings and the Woman). 1942: Let the People Sing. Suspected Person. Uncensored. 1943: Bell Bottom George. The Yellow Canary. 1944: A Canterbury Tale. Champagne Charlie. The Halfway House. Madonna of the Seven Moons. Candles at Nine. Give Us the Moon. 1945: I'll Be Your Sweetheart. Perfect Strangers (US: Vacation from Marriage). 1946: Daybreak. The Magic Bow. 1947: Frieda. The Little Ballerina. Jassy. Nicholas Nickleby. Call of the Blood. 1948: No Room at the Inn. Love in Waiting. Forbidden. Vote For Huggett. So Evil My Love. 1949: Murder at the Windmill (US: Murder at the Burlesque). Children of Chance. 1950: Trio. Night and the City. The Miniver Story. 1951: Green Grow the Rushes. Scrooge (US: A Christmas Carol). Scarlet Thread. 1952: Decameron Nights. The Yellow Balloon. The Crimson Pirate. 1953: The Fake. Always a Bride. Meet Mr Lucifer. Stryker of the Yard. The Million Pound Note (US: Man with a Million). The Weak and the Wicked. 1954: Doctor in the House. Fast and Loose. The Rainbow Jacket. Companions in Crime. 1956: Sailor Beware! (US: Panic in the Parlor).

**MALANDRINOS, Andrea** 1896-
Short, thick-set, dark-haired, bushily-moustached, bag-eyed Greek-born actor in British films. A former music-hall entertainer (billed as 'Malandrinos'), he became a supporting player in films in the boom

years of the early 1930s, and stayed to play dozens of waiters, hoteliers, curio shop owners and other huffly-snuffly foreign types, forever rubbing his hands together in anticipation, but mostly on the up and up. Generally seems to be billed as 'Andreas' from 1961 on.

1930: Raise the Roof. 1932: The Lodger (US: The Phantom Fiend). 1933: The Medicine Man. The Golden Cage. Two Wives for Henry. Send 'Em Back Half Dead. 1934: Broken Melody. How's Chances? The Admiral's Secret. Virginia's Husband. 1935: Midshipman Easy (US: Men of the Sea). The Invader (US: An Old Spanish Custom). Play Up the Band. Limelight (US: Backstage). Late Extra. The Improper Duchess. 1936: Under Proof. Prison Breaker. The Secret of Stamboul. The Amazing Quest of Ernest Bliss (US: Romance and Riches). Secret Agent. Tropical Trouble. 1937: The Price of Folly. The Show Goes On. Gypsy. A Romance in Flanders (US: Lost on the Western Front). Midnight Menace (US: Bombs Over London). The Sky's the Limit. Non Stop New York. Mad About Money (US: He Loved An Actress). 1938: The Last Barricade. *Take Cover. I See Ice. Crackerjack (US: The Man with a Hundred Faces). Sexton Blake and the Hooded Terror. 1939: Two Days to Live. What Would You Do Chums? 1940: Crooks' Tour. Room for Two. 1941: The Big Blockade. 1942: Flying Fortress. We'll Smile Again. Thunder Rock. 1943: Candlelight in Algeria. 1944: English Without Tears (US: Her Man Gilbey). Champagne Charlie. The Way Ahead (US: Immortal Battalion). 1946: While the Sun Shines. 1947: The End of the River. A Man About the House. My Brother Jonathan. 1948: Sleeping Car to Trieste. 1949: The Spider and the Fly. 1950: Cairo Road. 1951: Captain Horatio Hornblower RN. Chelsea Story. Salute the Toff. The Lavender Hill Mob. 1952: Paul Temple Returns. Hammer the Toff. 1953: The Captain's Paradise. Innocents in Paris. Gilbert Harding Speaking of Murder. 1954: The Love Lottery. The Teckman Mystery. Beautiful Stranger (US: Twist of Fate). *Night Plane to Amsterdam. 1955: Double Jeopardy. Dust and Gold. Cockleshell Heroes. Stolen Time (US: Blonde Blackmailer). 1956: Checkpoint. Ill-Met by Moonlight (US: Night Ambush). 1957: The Prince and the Showgirl. There's Always a Thursday. Seven Thunders (US: The Beasts of Marseilles). 1958: Orders To Kill. Links of Justice. No Time To Die! (US: Tank Force). 1959: The Angry Hills. Tommy the Toreador. The Boy and the Bridge. 1960: Sands of the Desert. Make Mine Mink. 1961: Tarnished Heroes. A Weekend With Lulu. The Boy Who Stole a Million. 1962: In the Cool of the Day. In Search of the Castaways. 1964: The Yellow Rolls Royce. 1965: San Ferry Ann. Joey Boy. 1966: The Mummy's Shroud. 1967: The Magnificent Two. Dance of the Vampires (US: The Fearless Vampire Killers). 1968: The Magus. Hammerhead. 1969: Hell Boats. 1970: Man of Violence/The Sex Racketeers. Underground.

**MALLALIEU, Aubrey** 1873-1948
Sleepy-looking, bespectacled, strongly-built British actor with thinning, pasted-across hair. Said to have played supporting roles in some silent films, he had a long theatrical career before embarking on sound film character roles in his sixties, and playing more than 100 of them as solicitors, vicars, school governors, judges and assorted senior citizens of some fussiness and dignity.

*1934: What Happened to Harkness? 1935: Cross Currents. Music Hath Charms. The Riverside Murder. 1936: Nothing Like Publicity. Prison Breaker. A Touch of the Moon. Such Is Life. All That Glitters. Once in a Million (US: Weekend Millionaire). A Star Fell from Heaven. The Tenth Man. Talk of the Devil. 1937: The Black Tulip. Holiday's End. Mayfair Melody. The Rat. Patricia Gets Her Man. Pearls Bring Tears. When the Devil Was Well. Keep Fit. The Strange Adventures of Mr Smith. Fifty Shilling Boxer. Change for a Sovereign. East of Ludgate Hill. 21 Days (released 1940. US: 21 Days Together). 1938: His Lordship Regrets. Thank Evans. Easy Riches. The Reverse Be My Lot. Paid in Error. Simply Terrific. Coming of Age. The Claydon Treasure Mystery. Dangerous Medicine. Almost a Honeymoon. The Gables Mystery. The Return of Carol Deane. Miracles Do Happen. The Return of the Frog. Save a Little Sunshine. You're the Doctor. His Lordship Goes to Press. 1939: So This Is London. Me and My Pal. Murder Will Out. Dead Men Are Dangerous. The Face at the Window. I Killed the Count (US: Who is Guilty?). All at Sea. The Stars Look Down. 1940: The Briggs Family. 'Bulldog' Sees It Through. The Girl in the News. Busman's Honeymoon (US: Haunted Honeymoon). The Door with Seven Locks. Spare a Copper. *Salvage with a Smile. 1941: *Mr Proudfoot Shows a Light. Atlantic Ferry (US: Sons of the Sea). Facing the Music. *The Fine Feathers. The Black Sheep of Whitehall. Gert and Daisy's Weekend. Breach of Promise. Hatter's Castle. The Young Mr Pitt. They Flew Alone (US: Wings and the Woman). Pimpernel Smith (US: Mister V). 1942: Uncensored. Unpublished Story. Let the People Sing. We'll Meet Again. Squadron Leader X. The Goose Steps Out. Asking for Trouble. 1943: The Lamp Still Burns. My Learned Friend. The Yellow Canary. The Demi-Paradise (US: Adventure for Two). Rhythm Serenade. 1944: Kiss the Bride Goodbye. He Snoops to Conquer. Champagne Charlie. 1945: I Live in Grosvenor Square (US: A Yank in London). 29 Acacia Avenue (US: The Facts of Love). A Place of One's Own. For You Alone. Murder in Reverse. 1946: Under New Management. Meet Me at Dawn. A Girl in a Million. Bedelia. School for Secrets (US: Secret Flight). I'll Turn to You. While the Sun Shines. 1947: Frieda. Master of Bankdam. The Ghosts of Berkeley Square. 1948: Counterblast. The Fatal Night. The Queen of Spades. The Winslow Boy. Calling Paul Temple. The Bad Lord Byron. Saraband for Dead Lovers (US: Saraband).*

**MALLESON, Miles**
(William M. Malleson) 1888-1969
Round-faced, fish-mouthed, jolly-looking, lovable British actor, a playwright (from 1913) and screenplay writer (1930-1944), who started by playing cameo roles in films that he had written. His stubby figure, double-jowls and tousled (disappearing) hair soon became an indispensable part of the British cinema. Only failing sight forced him to retire.

*1921: The Headmaster. 1930: The Yellow Mask. City of Song (US: Farewell to Love). 1931: Frail Women. 1932: The Sign of Four. The Love Contract. The Mayor's Nest. Love on Wheels. Money Means Nothing. 1933: Summer Lightning. Bitter Sweet. 1934: The Queen's Affair (US: Runaway Queen). Evergreen. Nell Gwyn. Lazybones. 1935: Vintage Wine. Peg of Old Drury. The Thirty Nine Steps. 1936: Tudor Rose (US: Nine Days a Queen). Secret Agent. 1937: The Rat. Victoria the Great. Knight Without Armour. 1938: Sixty Glorious Years. 1939: Q Planes (US: Clouds Over Europe). 1940: The Thief of Bagdad. Spellbound (US: The Spell of Amy Nugent). 1941: Major Barbara. This Was Paris. They Flew Alone (US: Wings and the Woman). 1942: Unpublished Story. Thunder Rock. The First of the Few (US: Spitfire). 1943: The Demi-Paradise (US: Adventure for Two). The Gentle Sex. I Want to Be an Actress. Adventures of Tartu (US: Tartu). The Yellow Canary. 1945: Dead of Night. Journey Together. 1946: While the Sun Shines. Beware of Pity. Land of Promise (voice only). 1947: The Mark of Cain. 1948: One Night with You. Idol of Paris. Saraband for Dead Lovers (US: Saraband). Woman Hater. Bond Street. 1949: The History of Mr Polly. Cardboard Cavalier. The Perfect Woman. The Queen of Spades. Kind Hearts and Coronets. Adam and Evelyne. Train of Events. 1950: Golden Salamander. Stage Fright. 1951: The Magic Box. Scrooge. The Man in the White Suit. The Woman's Angle. 1952: The Happy Family (US: Mr Lord Says No). Treasure Hunt. Venetian Bird (US: The Assassin). The Importance of Being Earnest. Folly to Be Wise. Trent's Last Case. 1953: The Captain's Paradise. 1955: Geordie (US: Wee Geordie). King's Rhapsody. 1956: Private's Progress. The Man Who Never Was. The Silken Affair. Three Men in a Boat. Dry Rot. Brothers in Law. 1957: Campbell's Kingdom. The Admirable Crichton (US: Paradise Lagoon). The Naked Truth (US: Your Past is Showing). Barnacle Bill (US: All at Sea). Happy is the Bride. 1958: Bachelor of Hearts. Behind the Mask. Gideon's Day (US: Gideon of Scotland Yard). The Captain's Table. 1959: Carlton-Browne of the FO (US: Man in a Cocked Hat). I'm All Right, Jack. Peeping Tom. The Hound of the Baskervilles. Kidnapped. 1960: And the Same to You. The Day They Robbed the Bank of England. The Brides of Dracula. 1961: Fury at Smuggler's Bay. The Hellfire Club. Double Bunk. 1962: Postman's Knock. Go to Blazes. The Phantom of the Opera. Vengeance (US: The Brain). 1963: Heavens Above! A Jolly Bad Fellow. 1964: First Men in the Moon. Circus World (GB: The Magnificent Showman). Murder Ahoy. 1965: You Must Be Joking!*

**MALTBY, H. F.** 1880-1963
Stout, puff-checked British actor, a prolific screenplay writer who also played comedy character roles from 1933 up to his retirement in 1945. As well as appearing as self-inflated judges, magistrates, politicians and military men, he still found time to write for the theatre and radio as well. The 'H' stood for Henry.

*1921: The Rotters. 1933: Facing the Music. I Spy. Home Sweet Home. A Political Party. 1934: Luck of a Sailor. Those Were the Days. Freedom of the Seas. Over the Garden Wall. Josser on the Farm. Falling in Love (US: Trouble Ahead). Lost in the Legion. Girls Will Be Boys. 1935: A Little Bit of Bluff. The Right Age to Marry. It Happened in Paris. The Morals of Marcus. Emil and the Detectives (US: Emil). King of the Castle. Vanity. 1936: Queen of Hearts. Jack of All Trades (US: The Two of Us). Not So Dusty. A Touch of the Moon. Trouble Ahead. Sweeney Todd the Demon Barber of Fleet Street. Fame. The Howard Case. The Crimes of Stephen Hawke. Calling the Tune. Everything Is Thunder. Nothing Like Publicity. To Catch a Thief. Where There's a Will. Busman's Holiday. Head Office. The Heirloom Mystery. Everything in Life. Secret Agent. Reasonable Doubt. 1937: Pearls Bring Tears. Song of the Road. Never Too Late to Mend. Wake Up Famous. Farewell to Cinderella. O Kay for Sound. Take My Tip. The Strange Adventures of Mr Smith. Paradise for Two (US: The Gaiety Girls). Young and Innocent (US: The Girl Was Young). Boys Will Be Girls. Why Pick on Me? Mr Smith Carries On. Sing As You Swing. Song of the Road. Live Wire. The Sky's the Limit. Captain's Orders. What a Man! Owd Bob (US: To the Victor). A Yank at Oxford. 1938: Paid in Error. Darts are Trumps. His Lordship Regrets. Pygmalion. Weddings Are Wonderful. You're the Doctor. Everything Happens to Me. His Lordship Goes to Press. 1939: The Good Old Days. The Gang's All Here (US: The Amazing Mr Forrest). Old Mother Riley Joins Up. 1940: Garrison Follies. Under Your Hat. Facing the Music (and 1933 film). 1941: Bob's Your Uncle. 1942: The Great Mr Handel. 1943: Old Mother Riley Detective. Somewhere in Civvies. 1944: A Canterbury Tale. Medal for the General. 1945: Home Sweet Home. Caesar and Cleopatra. The Trojan Brothers.*

the stage veteran for severe, sour, be-stern-with-the-children roles. She was still glooming about as Mrs Sketcher in 1943's *Jane Eyre* and only retired at 70.

*1931: Born to Love. 1932: Night Court (GB: Justice for Sale). The Wet Parade. Lovers Courageous. 1933: Looking Forward (GB: Service). Today We Live. 1934: The Little Minister. Romance in Manhattan. Forsaking All Others. His Greatest Gamble. Limehouse Blues. Great Expectations. 1935: Clive of India. The Florentine Dagger. The Flame Within. The Melody Lingers On. A Tale of Two Cities. The Widow from Monte Carlo. Stranded. Nina. Kind Lady (GB: House of Menace). 1936: Little Lord Fauntleroy. One Rainy Afternoon. Dracula's Daughter. The White Angel. A Woman Rebels. Anthony Adverse. Three Men on a Horse. Camille. Angel of Mercy. Cain and Mabel. Career Woman. God's Country and the Woman. 1937: Night Must Fall. Another Dawn. 1938: Rebecca of Sunnybrook Farm. Kidnapped. The Young in Heart. 1939: On Borrowed Time. The Hound of the Baskervilles. We Are Not Alone. The Little Princess. Confessions of a Nazi Spy. Barricade. 1940: Untamed. Foreign Correspondent. 1941: Young Tom Edison. Man Hunt. Hit the Road. Arkansas Judge (GB: False Witness). 1942: The Man in the Trunk. Scattergood Survives a Murder. I Married a Witch. The Undying Monster (GB: The Hammond Mystery). 1943: Above Suspicion. Shadow of a Doubt. Jane Eyre. 1944: Going My Way. The Seventh Cross. 1945: Roughly Speaking. Grissly's Millions. She Wouldn't Say Yes. Paris Underground (GB: Madame Pimpernel). Son of Lassie. 1946: The Secret Heart. Devotion (completed 1943). She Wolf of London (GB: The Curse of the Allenbys). 1948: The Challenge.*

all trades in the 1920s, acting, writing, producing and directing. Mander went to Hollywood in 1935, and was heavily in demand for foxy character parts, mostly in second-feature thrillers, when a heart attack killed him at 57.

*1918: †Once Upon a Time. 1920: †The Old Arm Chair. †Testimony. †The Children of Gideon. †A Rank Outsider. 1921: †Place of Honour. †The Road to London. *The Temporary Lady. 1922: Half a Truth. Open Country. 1924: Lovers in Araby. The Prude's Fall. 1925: *The Painted Lady. *The Lady in Furs. *Riding for a King. 1926: The Pleasure Garden (and German version). London Love. *Castles in the Air. 1927: *As We Lie. Tiptoes. The Fake. 1928: The Physician. The First Born. Balaclava (US: Jaws of Hell). Women of Paris. Dr Monnier und die Frauen. Der Faschingskönig. 1929: Meineid. The Crooked Billet. 1930: Loose Ends. Murder. 1931: Frail Women. 1932: The Missing Rembrandt. Lily Christine. *Lost: One Wife. That Night in London (US: Overnight). The Lodger (US: The Phantom Fiend). 1933: Don Quixote. Matinee Idol. Loyalties. The Private Life of Henry VIII. Bitter Sweet. 1934: Four Masked Men. The Case for the Crown. The Battle (US: Thunder in the East). 1935: Death Drives Through. The Three Musketeers. Here's to Romance. 1936: Lloyd's of London. 1937: Slave Ship. Youth on Parole. Wake Up and Live. 1938: Kidnapped. Suez. The Mad Miss Manton. 1939: The Three Musketeers (GB: The Singing Musketeer). Stanley and Livingstone. The Little Princess. Tower of London. The Man in the Iron Mask. Wuthering Heights. Daredevils of the Red Circle (serial). 1940: The Primrose Path. Road to Singapore. The House of Seven Gables. Captain Caution. Babies for Sale. Laddie. South of Suez. The Earl of Chicago. 1941: Dr Kildare's Wedding Day (GB: Mary Names the Day). Shadows on the Stairs. That Hamilton Woman (GB: Lady Hamilton). They Met in Bombay. 1942: Mrs Miniver (voice only). Fly By Night. A Tragedy at Midnight. Fingers at the Window. To Be or Not to Be. Somewhere I'll Find You. Lucky Jordan. A Yank on the Burma Road (GB: China Caravan). Journey for Margaret. Apache Trail. Tarzan's New York Adventure. This Above All. The War Against Mrs Hadley. You're Telling Me. 1943: The Fallen Sparrow. Assignment in Brittany. Five Graves to Cairo. Secrets of the Underground. Phantom of the Opera. Guadalcanal Diary. First Comes Courage. Madame Curie. The Return of the Vampire. 1944: The Pearl of Death. Four Jills in a Jeep. Enter Arsène Lupin. The Scarlet Claw. The White Cliffs of Dover. The Story of Dr Wassell. 1945: Murder, My Sweet (GB: Farewell, My Lovely). The Brighton Strangler. Week-End at the Waldorf. Confidential Agent. The Picture of Dorian Gray. The Crime Doctor's Warning (GB: The Doctor's Warning). Captain Kidd. 1946: Bandit of Sherwood Forest. The Walls Came Tumbling Down. The Imperfect Lady (GB: Mrs Loring's Secret).*

**MALYON, Eily**
(E. Lees-Craston) 1879-1961
Fair-haired, gloomy-looking British actress of strong features who came to Hollywood in the early 1930s, her almost weather-beaten face and sharp delivery qualifying

**MANDER, Miles**
(Lionel Mander) 1888-1946
Stocky, light-haired British actor-manager with military bark, plus moustache and bearing to match. Entered films after World War I (he was an aviator), often playing moustache-twirling villains—appropriately billed as Luther Miles. He became a jack of

**As director:**

*1926:\*The Fair Maid of Perth. \*The Whistler. \*The Sheik of Araby. \*Knee Deep in Daisies. 1927:\*As We Lie. \*The Sentence of Death. \*Packing Up. \*False Colours. 1928: The First Born. 1930: The Woman Between (US: The Woman Decides). 1934: Youthful Folly. 1935: The Morals of Marcus. 1936: The Flying Doctor.*

† As Luther Miles

**MARION CRAWFORD, Howard** 1914–1969

Burly, pale-eyed British actor with bristling moustache and ruddy complexion, usually in stolid roles as upper-crust officer types who could be affable or dyspeptic. His hearty but mellow tones made his a popular and prolific voice on radio productions, and he was nudging middle age before he entered the major part of his film career as a character player. Also a notable Dr Watson in a TV Sherlock Holmes series. Died from an overdose of sleeping pills.

*1935: Music Hath Charms. †Brown on Resolution (later For Ever England. US: Born for Glory). 1938: 13 Men and a Gun. 1940: \*Torpedo Raider. 1941: Freedom Radio (US: A Voice in the Night). 1945: The Rake's Progress (US: Notorious Gentleman). 1947: The Phantom Shot. 1948: Man on The Run. 1949: The Hasty Heart. 1950: Mr Drake's Duck. 1951: The Man in the White Suit. His Excellency. 1952: Where's Charley? Top of the Form. Rose of Baghdad (narrator only). 1953: Gilbert Harding Speaking of Murder. Don't Blame the Stork! 1954: West of Zanzibar. The Rainbow Jacket. Five Days (US: Paid To Kill). 1956: The Silken Affair. Reach for the Sky. The Man in the Sky (US: Decision against Time). 1957: Don Kikhot (dubbed) voice only). The Birthday Present. \*The Tyburn Case. 1958: Nowhere to Go. The Silent Enemy. Virgin Island (US: Our Virgin Island). Gideon's Day (US: Gideon of Scotland Yard). Next to No Time! 1959: Model for Murder. Life in Danger. 1960: Othello. Foxhole in Cairo. 1961: Carry on Regardless. 1962: Lawrence of Arabia. 1963: Tamahine. Man in the Middle. 1965: The Face of Fu Manchu. 1966: The Brides of Fu Manchu. The Singing Princess (voice only). Secrets of a Windmill Girl. 1967: Smashing Time. The Vengeance of Fu Manchu. 1968: Blood of Fu Manchu (US: Kiss and Kill). The Charge of the Light Brigade. The Castle of Fu Manchu.*

† As Marion Crawford.

**MARLEY, John** 1907–1984

Grey-haired, wise-looking American actor, a rather more handsome equivalent of Eduard Franz (qv), and in films from 1947. He was scarcely noticed by the paying public until nominated for an Oscar in 1970's *Love Story*, even though he had previously won the best actor award at the Venice Film Festival for his work in *Faces*. Marley started his show business career as half of a comedy team; strangely, there was very little comedy in most of his film roles, which were usually as senior sobersides. Died following open heart surgery.

*1947: Kiss of Death. 1948: The Naked City. 1951: The Mob (GB: Remember That Face). 1952: My Six Convicts. 1953: The Joe Louis Story. 1955: The Square Jungle. Timetable. 1957: Flood Tide (GB: Above All Things). 1958: I Want To Live! 1960: Pay or Die! 1962: A Child Is Waiting. 1963: America, America (GB: The Anatolian Smile). The Wheeler Dealers (GB: Separate Beds). 1965: Cat Ballou. 1966: The Etruscans. 1967: In Enemy Country. 1968: Faces. Istanbul Express (TV: GB: cinemas). 1970: Sledge/A Man Called Sledge. Love Story. 1971: Incident in San Francisco (TV). The Godfather. Clay Pigeon (GB: Trip to Kill). The Sheriff (TV). In Broad Daylight (TV). 1972: Images. Dead of Night. The Family Rico (TV). Jory. 1973: Blade. The Alpha Caper (TV. GB: cinemas, as Inside Job). 1974: Framed. 1975: The Dead Are Alive. 1976: W. C. Fields and Me. 1977: The Greatest. Telethon (TV). The Car. The Private Files of J. Edgar Hoover. Kid Vengeance. 1978: Hooper. It Lives Again. 1980: Tribute. 1981: Threshold. Utilities. The Amateur. 1983: Falcon's Gold (TV). Robbers of the Sacred Mountain. The Glitter Dome (cable TV. GB: cinemas). 1984: Mother Lode. Over the Edge.*

**MARMONT, Percy** 1883–1977

Lean, suave, weathered-looking, cultured British romantic lead—moustachioed in his

latter days as a character player—with one of the longest careers in the business. He made his stage debut at 17 and his first film in Australia, on his way to Hollywood, where the fair-haired Marmont proved himself a smooth, versatile leading man, soon in calm, pipe-smoking roles before his return to Britain in 1928 to play neckerchiefed charmers in early middle age. Largely returned to the theatre from 1933 on, giving his last film performance at 85. Actress Patricia Marmont is his daughter.

*1917: The Monk and the Woman. 1918: Rose of the World. The Lie. Turn of the Wheel. 1919: Three Men and a Girl. The Vengeance of Durand. The Climbers. 1920: Dead Men Tell No Tales. The Branded Woman. 1921: What's Your Reputation Worth? Love's Penalty. Wife against Wife. 1922: The First Woman. Married People. 1923: Broadway Broke. The Midnight Alarm. If Winter Comes. The Man Life Passed By. The Light That Failed. 1924: The Enemy Sex. The Shooting of Dan MacGrew. The Marriage Cheat. The Clean Heart. The Legend of Hollywood. K the Unknown. Broken Laws. Idle Tongues. 1925: Daddy's Gone a Hunting. Street of Forgotten Men. Lord Jim. Fine Clothes. Just a Woman. Infatuation. 1926: The Miracle of Life. Mantrap. Fascinating Youth. Aloma of the South Seas. 1927: The Stronger Will. 1928: Sir or Madam. San Francisco Nights (GB: Divorce). The Warning. Yellow Stockings. The Lady of the Lake. 1929: The Silver King. 1930: The Squeaker. Cross Roads. 1931: The Loves of Ariane (US: Ariane). The Written Law. Rich and Strange (US: East of Shanghai). 1932: The Silver Greyhound. Blind Spot. Say It with Music. 1933: Her Imaginary Lover. 1935: White Lilac. Vanity. 1936: David Livingstone. The Captain's Table. Secret Agent. Conquest of the Air (released 1940). 1937: Young and Innocent (US: The Girl Was Young). Action for Slander. Les perles de la couronne (GB and US: Pearls of the Crown). 1940: \*Bringing It Home. 1941: Penn of Pennsylvania (US: The Courageous Mr Penn). 1942: Those Kids from Town. 1943: I'll Walk Beside You. 1946: Loyal Heart. 1947: Swiss Honeymoon. 1948: No Orchids for Miss Blandish. 1949: Dark Secret. 1952: The Gambler and the Lady.*

1953: *Four-Sided Triangle. Thought to Kill.* 1954: *Knave of Hearts* (US: *Lovers, Happy Lovers*). 1955: *Footsteps in the Fog.* 1956: *Lisbon.* 1968: *Hostile Witness.*

**MARRIOTT, Moore**
(George Moore-Marriott) 1885-1949
Short, wiry British actor, from theatrical background. He was a star of the early British cinema before moving into disgruntled roles; but, while still in his forties, he began playing garrulous, sometimes toothless, but usually lovable old codgers and, had he lived longer, would have probably carried on doing so into his eighties. Chiefly now remembered as old Harbottle in the Will Hay comedies.

1908: *Dick Turpin.* 1912: *A Maid of the Alps.* 1914: *His Sister's Honour.* 1915: *By the Shortest of Heads.* 1920: *The Grip of Iron. Mary Latimer, Nun. The Winding Road.* 1921: *Four Men in a Van.* 1922: *The Head of the Family. The Skipper's Wedding.* 1923: *The Monkey's Paw. *An Odd Freak. *Lawyer Quince. *Dixon's Return.* 1924: *The Affair at the Novelty Theatre. The Conspirators. *The Clicking of Cuthbert. *The Long Hole. The Mating of Marcus. *Ordeal by Golf. Not for Sale.* 1925: *There's Many a Slip. King of the Castle. The Qualified Adventurer. *The Only Man. The Gold Cure. Every Mother's Son. *A Madonna of the Cells.* 1926: *The Happy Rascals. London Love. *Regaining the Wind. *Goose and Stuffing. *Mined and Counter-Mined. *The Little Shop in Fore Street. *Second to None. *Cash on Delivery. *The Greater War. The Conspirators (and 1924 film).* 1927: *Passion Island. The Silver Lining. Huntingtower. Carry On!* 1928: *Victory. Widdecombe Fair. *The Burglar and the Girl. Toni. *The King's Breakfast. Kitty. Sweeney Todd.* 1929: *Mr Smith Wakes Up. The Flying Scotsman. Lady from the Sea. Kitty* (sound version). 1930: *Kissing Cup's Race. Peace on the Western Front.* 1931: *Aroma of the South Seas. The Lyons Mail. Up for the Cup.* 1932: *Dance Pretty Lady. The Water Gipsies. Mr Bill the Conqueror* (US: *The Man Who Won*). *The Crooked Lady. Nine Till Six. Heroes of the Mine. The Little Waitress. The Wonderful Story.* 1933: *Money for Speed. A Moorland Tragedy. Dora. Lucky Blaze. A*

*Political Party. The Crime at Blossoms. Hawleys of High Street. Love's Old Sweet Song. The House of Trent. Faces. The Song of the Plough.* 1934: *The Black Skull. *The Unknown Warrior. Girls Please. The Scoop* (US: *A Political Scoop*). *Nell Gwyn. The Feathered Serpent.* 1935: *Dandy Dick. Drake of England* (US: *Drake the Pirate*). *Peg of Old Drury. *His Apologies. *The Half-Day Excursion. The Man Without a Face. Gay Old Dog. Turn of the Tide.* 1936: *Strange Cargo. What the Puppy Said. The Amazing Quest of Ernest Bliss* (GB: *Romance and Riches*). *Luck of the Turf. When Knights Were Bold. Windbag the Sailor. Wednesday's Luck. Accused. Talk of the Devil. As You Like It.* 1937: *Feather Your Nest. Fifty Shilling Boxer. The Fatal Hour. Night Ride. Oh, Mr Porter! Victoria the Great. Intimate Relations. Owd Bob* (US: *To the Victor*). *Dreaming Lips.* 1938: *Convict 99. Old Bones of the River.* 1939: *Ask a Policeman. Where's That Fire? The Frozen Limits. A Girl Must Live. Cheer Boys Cheer. The Band Waggon.* 1940: *Charley's (Big-Hearted) Aunt. Gasbags.* 1941: *I Thank You. Hi Gang!* 1942: *Back Room Boy.* 1943: *Millions Like Us. Time Flies.* 1944: *It Happened on Sunday. The Agitator. Don't Take It to Heart.* 1945: *A Place of One's Own. I'll Be Your Sweetheart.* 1946: *Green for Danger.* 1947: *Green Fingers. Jassy. The Root of All Evil. The Hills of Donegal.* 1949: *The History of Mr Polly. High Jinks in Society.*

**MARSH, Garry**
(Leslie March Geraghty) 1902-1981
Alphabetical order places two of the most prolific figures in British cinema next to each other. Garry Marsh was a big, burly, bustling, blustering character actor with beaming smile and a fine array of harassed looks that made him the forerunner of America's Fred Clark in exasperation, if not in waspish humour. Played some star roles in comedy-thrillers of the early thirties before giving up the battle with his receding hairline and settling down to dozens of frustrated figures of authority.

1930: *Night Birds. PC Josser.* 1931: *The Eternal Feminine/The Eternal Flame. Uneasy Virtue. Dreyfus* (US: *The Dreyfus Case*). *The Man They Could Not Arrest. Stranglehold. The*

*Star Reporter. Third Time Lucky. Keepers of Youth. The Professional Guest. Stamboul.* 1932: *After Office Hours. COD. Fires of Fate. Don't Be a Dummy. *Postal Orders. Number Seventeen. Maid of the Mountains.* 1933: *The Lost Chord. Falling for You. Taxi to Paradise. That's a Good Girl. Two Wives for Henry. Forging Ahead. The Love Nest. Ask Beccles. The Silver Spoon.* 1934: *It's a Cop. Warn London. Money Mad. Josser on the Farm. Rolling in Money. Gay Love. The Green Pack. Lord Edgware Dies. Bella Donna. Are You a Mason?* 1935: *Widow's Might. Three Witnesses. Mr What's-his-Name. Night Mail. Charing Cross Road. A Wife or Two. Death on the Set* (US: *Murder on the Set*). *Inside the Room. Full Circle. Bargain Basement (later Department Store). Scrooge.* 1936: *When Knights Were Bold. The Man in the Mirror. All In. The Amazing Quest of Ernest Bliss* (US: *Romance and Riches*). *Debt of Honour.* 1937: *It's a Grand Old World. Leave It to Me. Melody and Romance. The Vicar of Bray. A Romance in Flanders* (US: *Lost on the Western Front*). *Intimate Relations. The Dark Stairway. Bank Holiday* (US: *Three on a Week-End*). *Who Killed Fen Markham/The Angelus. Meet Mr Penny.* 1938: *I See Ice. Break the News. The Claydon Treasure Mystery. Convict 99. This Man is News. It's in the Air* (US: *George Takes the Air*). 1939: *Let's Be Famous. The Four Just Men* (US: *The Secret Four*). *Old Mother Riley Joins Up. Return to Yesterday. Trouble Brewing. This Man in Paris. Hoots Mon!* 1940: *Let George Do It.* 1945: *I'll Be Your Sweetheart. Dead of Night. Pink String and Sealing Wax. The Rake's Progress* (US: *Notorious Gentleman*). 1946: *I See a Dark Stranger* (US: *The Adventuress*). *The Shop at Sly Corner* (US: *The Code of Scotland Yard*). *A Girl in a Million. While the Sun Shines.* 1947: *Dancing with Crime. Frieda. Just William's Luck.* 1948: *Good Time Girl. Things Happen at Night. My Brother's Keeper. Badger's Green. William Comes to Town. Forbidden.* 1949: *Murder at the Windmill* (US: *Murder at the Burlesque*). *Paper Orchid. Miss Pilgrim's Progress.* 1950: *Someone at the Door. Something in the City. Mr Drake's Duck.* 1951: *Worm's Eye View. Old Mother Riley's Jungle Treasure. Madame Louise. The Magic Box.* 1952: *The Lost Hours* (US: *The Big Frame*). *The Voice of Merrill* (US: *Murder Will Out*). *Those People Next Door.* 1954: *Double Exposure. Aunt Clara.* 1955: *Man of the Moment. Johnny You're Wanted.* 1956: *Who Done It?* 1960: *Trouble with Eve.* 1963: *Ring of Spies.* 1966: *Where the Bullets Fly.* 1967: *Ouch! Camelot.*

**MARTIN, Edie** 1880-1964
Beak-nosed, sharp-chinned, bespectacled, beady-eyed, shrilly-spoken British actress usually seen in roles almost as tiny as herself, but so distinctive she could be picked out in a second. On stage at six, she remained busy in that medium throughout her working life, which went on into her eighties, although she did find time for

nearly 50 cameos in films, mostly as maids or frail but fierce old ladies.

*1936: Servants All. The Big Noise. 1937: Action for Slander. Under the Red Robe. Farewell Again (GB: Troopship). 1938: Bad Boy. A Spot of Bother. St Martin's Lane (US: Sidewalks of London). 1939: Old Mother Riley MP. 1940: Old Mother Riley in Business. 1942: Unpublished Story. 1943: The Demi-Paradise (US: Adventure for Two). It's in the Bag. 1944: Don't Take It to Heart. 1945: A Place of One's Own. They Were Sisters. Here Comes the Sun. 1946: Great Expectations. 1947: It Always Rains on Sunday. When the Bough Breaks. 1948: Another Shore. Oliver Twist. Cardboard Cavalier. The History of Mr Polly. 1949: Adam and Evelyne (US: Adam and Evalyn). 1950: Blackmailed. 1951: The Lady with a Lamp. The Lavender Hill Mob. The Man in the White Suit. Night Was Our Friend. 1952: Time Gentlemen Please! 1953: Genevieve. The Titfield Thunderbolt. Meet Mr Lucifer. 1954: Lease of Life. The End of the Road. *The Mysterious Bullet. 1955: The Ladykillers. As Long As They're Happy. Room in the House. 1956: Ramsbottom Rides Again. My Teenage Daughter (US: Teenage Bad Girl). Sailor Beware! (US: Panic in the Parlor). 1958: Too Many Crooks. 1959: Kidnapped. I'm All Right, Jack. 1961: A Weekend with Lulu. 1962: Sparrows Can't Sing.*

**MARTIN, Strother** 1919-1980
A rare latter-day character star in the best Hollywood tradition, at a time when there weren't too many around. Round-faced, fair-haired Martin first came to Hollywood as a swimming coach, but subsequently spent 20 years in small roles—often as cunning countrified whiners—before shuffling his way into a couple of leading parts. But he was still better employed in bolstering the supporting cast.

*1950: The Damned Don't Cry. The Asphalt Jungle. 1951: The People Against O'Hara. Rhubarb. 1952: Storm over Tibet. 1953: The Magnetic Monster. South Sea Woman. 1954: A Star is Born. Drum Beat. 1955: The Big Knife. Cowboy. Strategic Air Command. Kiss Me Deadly. Target Zero! 1956: Johnny Concho. The Black Whip. Attack! 1957: Copper Sky. Black Patch. 1959: The Shaggy Dog. The Wild and the Innocent. The Horse Soldiers. 1961: Sanctuary. The Deadly Companions. 1962: The Man Who Shot Liberty Valance. 1963: McLintock! Showdown. 1964: Invitation to a Gunfighter. 1965: Brainstorm. Shenandoah. The Sons of Katie Elder. 1966: Harper (GB: The Moving Target). An Eye for an Eye. 1967: The Flim Flam Man (GB: One Born Every Minute). Cool Hand Luke. 1969: True Grit. Butch Cassidy and the Sundance Kid. The Wild Bunch. 1970: The Brotherhood of Satan. The Ballad of Cable Hogue. 1971: Fool's Parade (GB: Dynamite Man from Glory Jail). Pocket Money. Hannie Caulder. 1973: Sssssss (GB: Sssnake). The Boy and the Bronc Buster (TV). 1975: Rooster Cogburn. Hard Times (GB: The Streetfighter). One of Our Own (TV). 1976: The Great Scout and Cathouse Thursday. 1977: Slap Shot. 1978: Up in Smoke. The Champ. Steel Cowboy (TV). Love and Bullets. The End. 1979: Nightwing. The Villain (GB: Cactus Jack). Better Late Than Never (TV). 1980: Hotwire. The Secret of Nikola Tesla.*

**MATTHEWS, A. E.** 1869-1960
Round-faced, owl-eyed, affectionately regarded British actor who moved from smooth leading men to character roles on stage, then enjoyed 20 years of fame in his last two decades as the British cinema's most famous crotchety and sometimes rascally old man. For many years Britain's oldest working actor, known to his friends as 'Matty'.

*1914: A Highwayman's Honour. 1916: Wanted a Widow. *The Real Thing at Last. The Lifeguardsman. 1918: Once Upon a Time. 1919: The Lackey and the Lady. Castle of Dreams. 1934: The Iron Duke. 1936: Men Are Not Gods. 1941: Pimpernel Smith (US: Mister V). Quiet Wedding. This England. *Surprise Broadcast. 1942: The Great Mr Handel. Thunder Rock. 1943: The Life and Death of Colonel Blimp (US: Colonel Blimp). Escape to Danger. The Man in Grey. 1944: The Way Ahead. They Came to a City. Love Story (US: A Lady Surrenders). Flight from Folly. Twilight Hour. 1946: Piccadilly Incident. 1947: The Ghosts of Berkeley Square.*

*Just William's Luck. 1948: William Comes to Town. 1949: Britannia Mews (US: Forbidden Street). Whisky Galore! (US: Tight Little Island). The Chiltern Hundreds (US: The Amazing Mr Beecham). Landfall. 1950: Mr Drake's Duck. 1951: The Galloping Major. Laughter in Paradise. The Magic Box. 1952: Penny Princess. Who Goes There! (US: The Passionate Sentry). Castle in the Air. Something Money Can't Buy. Made in Heaven. 1953: Skid Kids. The Million Pound Note (US: Man with a Million). The Weak and the Wicked. 1954: Happy Ever After (US: Tonight's the Night/O'Leary Night). Aunt Clara. 1955: Miss Tulip Stays the Night. 1956: Jumping for Joy. Loser Takes All. Three Men in a Boat. Around the World in 80 Days. 1957: Doctor at Large. Carry on Admiral (US: The Ship Was Loaded). 1960: Inn for Trouble.*

**MATTHEWS, Lester** 1900-1975
Tall, dark, saturnine British actor with receding hairline, slightly stooping gait, dashing moustache and faintly bad-tempered countenance. These attributes combined to have him cast as double-shaded characters in his days (1931-1934) as a popular leading man of early British sound films, before he went to Hollywood with his then-wife, actress Anne Grey. Here there were a couple of minor leads, but he always looked a little more than his real age, and soon settled into dozens of character parts, largely as military men or villains.

*1929: *Shivering Shocks. 1931: *The Lame Duck. Creeping Shadows (US: The Limping Man). The Man at Six (US: The Gables Mystery). The Wickham Mystery. Gypsy Blood (US: Carmen). The Old Man. 1932: Her Night Out. The Indiscretions of Eve. Fires of Fate. 1933: The Stolen Necklace. Called Back. On Secret Service (US: Secret Agent). House of Dreams. Their Night Out. Out of the Past. She Was Only a Village Maiden. The Melody Maker. Facing the Music. The Song You Gave Me. 1934: Borrowed Clothes. Boomerang. Song at Eventide. Blossom Time (US: April Romance). Irish Hearts (US: Norah O'Neale). The Poisoned Diamond. 1935: The Werewolf of London. The Raven. 1936: Thank You, Jeeves. Professional Soldier. Spy 77. Song and Dance Man. 15 Maiden Lane. Lloyds of London. Too Many Parents. Tugboat Princess. 1937: Crack Up. Lancer Spy. The Prince and the Pauper. 1938: There's Always a Woman. Three Loves Has Nancy. Mysterious Mr Moto. If I Were King. Time Out for Murder. The Adventures of Robin Hood. *Think It Over. I Am a Criminal. 1939: The Three Musketeers (GB: The Singing Musketeer). Susannah of the Mounties. Should a Girl Marry? Conspiracy. Rulers of the Sea. Everything Happens at Night. 1940: Northwest Passage. British Intelligence (GB: Enemy Agent). Gaucho Serenade. The Biscuit Eater. Women in War. Sing, Dance, Plenty Hot (GB: Melody Girl). 1941: Man Hunt. A Yank in The RAF. The Lone Wolf Keeps a Date. 1942: Son of Fury. Now,*

ABOVE A. E. **Matthews** (left) as the admiral carries on in style, while James Hayter (*qv*), Desmond Walter-Ellis and Eunice Gayson can only watch. From *Carry On Admiral* (1957)

RIGHT Lester **Matthews** and Anne Grey were a popular husband-and-wife team in early British sound films before Matthews made the greater part of his career in Hollywood. This is from *Borrowed Clothes* (1934)

Voyager. The Pied Piper. Across the Pacific. Desperate Journey. Manila Calling. London Blackout Murders (GB: Secret Motive). 1943: The Mysterious Doctor. Ministry of Fear. Corvette K-225 (GB: The Nelson Touch). Tonight We Raid Calais. 1944: Nine Girls. Four Jills in a Jeep. Between Two Worlds. The Story of Dr Wassell. The Invisible Man's Revenge. Shadows in the Night. Gaslight (GB: The Murder in Thornton Square). A Wing and a Prayer. 1945: The Beautiful Cheat (GB: What a Woman!). Objective Burma! Two O'Clock Courage. I Love a Mystery. Salty O'Rourke. 1947: Dark Delusion (GB: Cynthia's Secret). The Exile. Bulldog Drummond at Bay. 1948: Fighting Father Dunne. 1949: Free for All. 1950: Tyrant of the Sea. Her Wonderful Lie. Rogues of Sherwood Forest. Montana. 1951: Lorna Doone. The Son of Dr Jekyll. Anne of the Indies. Corky of Gasoline Alley (GB: Corky). The Lady and the Bandit (GB: Dick Turpin's Ride). Tales of Robin Hood. 1952: Jungle Jim in the Forbidden Land. Lady in the Iron Mask. Les Miserables. Savage Mutiny. The Brigand. Against All Flags. Stars and Stripes Forever (GB: Marching Along). Captain Pirate (GB: Captain Blood, Fugitive). 1953: Trouble Along the Way. Niagara. Young Bess. Fort Ti. Bad for Each Other. Jamaica Run. Rogue's March. Sangaree. 1954: Charge of the Lancers. Desiree. The Far Horizons. Jungle Man-Eaters. Moonfleet. King Richard and the Crusaders. Man in the Attic. 1955: Ten Wanted Men. Flame of the Islands. 1960: Song Without End. 1963: A Global Affair. 1964: Mary Poppins. 1966: Assault on a Queen. The Scorpio Letters (TV. GB: cinemas). 1968: Star! 1970: Comeback (later Hollywood Horror House).

**MAUR, Meinhart** 1891-1964
Short, shaven-headed, grinning gremlin of a man, a Hungarian from a small town near the Russian and Czech borders who took his career to Germany and became one of Berlin's leading Shakespearian actors. Crossing to Britain ahead of the Nazis in 1935, he played out the remainder of his career there in featured roles that gave him an assortment of villainous and kindly characters.

1919: Harakiri. Die Spinnen/The Spiders—Part I: Der goldene See. 1920: Die Spinnen/The Spiders—Part II: Das brillianten Schiff/The Diamond Ship. 1936: Rembrandt. Second Bureau. 1937: 21 Days (US: 21 Days Together. Released 1940). O Kay for Sound. Dr Syn. 1938: Who Goes Next? The Return of the Frog. The Last Barricade. 1939: An Englishman's Home (US: Madmen of Europe). 1940: Gasbags. Three Silent Men. Pack Up Your Troubles. 1941: Jeannie (US: Girl in Distress). 1942: We'll Smile Again. 1943: Candlelight in Algeria. 1948: It's Not Cricket. 1949: The Huggetts Abroad. 1950: Dick Barton at Bay. The Wooden Horse. 1951: The Tales of Hoffman. 1952: Decameron Nights. 1953: Never Let Me Go. 1954: Malaga (US: Fire Over Africa).

**MAY, Jack** 1922-
Tall, stern British actor well-employed in the theatre though only in sporadic cinema roles through the last 40 years. These were mostly of minor significance, or as upper-class neurotics, but he was quite extraordinary as the kinky judge who turns out to be the murderer in Night After Night After Night. His sardonic, rumbling tones are well-known to British radio listeners as those of Nelson Gabriel in the long-running farm/soap series The Archers.

1944: Give Me the Stars. 1945: Brief Encounter. 1948: No Room at the Inn. 1952: Time Gentlemen Please! The Oracle. 1953: Behind the Headlines. 1955: It's a Great Day. 1957: Cat Girl. 1958: The Silent Enemy. 1960: The Professionals. 1962: A Prize of Arms. Solo for Sparrow. 1966: A Funny Thing Happened on the Way to the Forum. 1967: How I Won the War. 1968: A Twist of Sand. 1969: Goodbye Mr Chips. Night After Night After Night. 1970: Trog. 1971: The Yes Girls. 1973: Big Zapper. 1975: The Man Who Would Be King. 1976: The Seven-Per-Cent Solution. 1978: Sammy's Super T-Shirt. 1982: The Return of the Soldier. 1983: A Swarm in May. 1984: The Bounty. The Shooting Party.

**MAYNE, Ferdy**
(Ferdinand Mayer-Börckel) 1916-
Dark-haired (now grey), lantern-faced, sardonic-looking German actor of sinister

charm who came to British films via radio and, from 1948 to 1963 in particular, must have menaced more British second-feature heroes than any other actor. His villains had a touch of class and exuded suave decadence. Billed as Ferdi on his first four British films, Ferdinand in the 1980s, otherwise as Ferdy throughout the remainder of his movie career.

1943: Old Mother Riley Overseas. Warn That Man. 1944: Meet Sexton Blake. 1945: The Echo Murders. Waltz Time. 1947: Broken Journey. 1949: Vote for Huggett. The Huggetts Abroad. Celia. The Temptress. 1950: Prelude to Fame. Cairo Road. 1951: Hotel Sahara. Encore. 1952: Venetian Bird (US: The Assassin). The Man Who Watched Trains Go By (US: Paris Express). Made in Heaven. 1953: The Captain's Paradise. The Case of the Second Shot. Desperate Moment. The Broken Horseshoe. All Hallowe'en. The Blue Parrot. Marilyn (later Roadhouse Girl). Three Steps to the Gallows (US: White Fire. Released 1955). You Know What Sailors Are. 1954: Malaga (US: Fire over Africa). Beautiful Stranger (US: Twist of Fate). The Divided Heart. Betrayed. 1955: *Crossroads. Third Party Risk (US: The Deadly Game). Storm over the Nile. Dust and Gold. Value for Money. The Glass Cage (US: The Glass Tomb). 1956: The Narrowing Circle. Gentlemen Marry Brunettes. Find the Lady. *The Magic Carpet. The Big Money (released 1958). The Baby and the Battleship. 1957: You Pay Your Money. The Big Chance. The End of the Line. Three Sundays to Live. Blue Murder at St Trinian's. The Safecracker. 1958: A Woman of Mystery. Next to No Time! 1959: Ben-Hur. Deadly Record. Third Man on the Mountain. Tommy the Toreador. Our Man in Havana. 1960: Crossroads to Crime. The Spider's Web. 1961: *Frederic Chopin. The Green Helmet. Highway to Battle. 1962: Three Spare Wives. The Password is Courage. Masters of Venus (serial). Freud (GB: Freud—the Secret Passion). The Story of Private Pooley. 1963: Shadow of Treason. 1964: Allez France (US: The Counterfeit Constable). 1965: Those Magnificent Men in Their Flying Machines. Promise Her Anything. 1967: Dance of the Vampires (US: The Fearless Vampire Killers). The Bobo. 1968: Gates to Paradise. The Limbo

Line. *Where Eagles Dare. The Best House in London.* 1969: *The Magic Christian.* 1970: *The Walking Stick. The Vampire Lovers. The Adventurers.* 1971: *When Eight Bells Toll. Vampire Happening. Jo. Les grandes vacances. The Blonde in the Blue Movie. Von Richthofen and Brown* (GB: *The Red Baron*). 1972: *Au Pair Girls. Innocent Bystanders. Il vichingo venuto del sud. Il terna di Marco.* 1973: *Idoo Mark Belehnung.* 1974: *Die Ameisen kommen/The Ants Are Coming. Journey to Vienna.* 1975: *Barry Lyndon. Floris. Call of Gold* (TV). *Das Schweigen im Walde/The Silent Forest.* 1976: \**Red.* 1978: *Revenge of the Pink Panther. Fedora. The Pirate* (TV). 1979: *The Music Machine. A Man Called Intrepid* (TV). 1980: *Hawk the Slayer. The Formula.* 1981: *Death of a Centerfold* (TV). 1982: *The Horror Star.* 1983: *The Secret Diary of Sigmund Freud. The Black Stallion Returns. Yellowbeard.* 1984: *Conan the Destroyer.* 1985: *Night Train to Terror. Howling II: Your Sister is a Werewolf.*

### MAZURKI, Mike

(Mikhail Mazurski) 1909- *1990*
Hulking Austrian-born actor; in America from an early age, he was a professional footballer and wrestler before taking his huge frame to Hollywood to play hoodlums' henchmen. Dim-looking (but actually well-educated), with hook nose, open mouth and aggressive, small-eyed stare, he would have done any Damon Runyon story proud, and became the definitive Moose Malloy in the 1945 version of Raymond Chandler's *Farewell, My Lovely.*

1934: *Belle of the Nineties.* 1935: *Black Fury.* 1938: *Mr Moto's Gamble.* 1941: *The Shanghai Gesture.* 1942: *Gentleman Jim. About Face. That Other Woman. The McGuerins from Brooklyn.* 1943: *Henry Aldrich Haunts a House* (GB: *Henry Haunts a House*). *Thank Your Lucky Stars. Taxi, Mister. Swing Fever. Lost Angel. It Ain't Hay* (GB: *Money for Jam*). *Mission to Moscow. Behind the Rising Sun. Bomber's Moon.* 1944: *The Missing Juror. Summer Storm. The Canterville Ghost. The Thin Man Comes Home. The Princess and the Pirate. Shine On, Harvest Moon.* 1945: *Bud Abbott and Lou Costello in Hollywood. Nob Hill. Murder, My*

Sweet (GB: *Farewell, My Lovely*). *Dick Tracy* (GB: *Split Face*). *Dakota. The Spanish Main. The Horn Blows at Midnight.* 1946: *Mysterious Intruder. Live Wires. The French Key.* 1947: *Sinbad the Sailor. Unconquered. Nightmare Alley. Killer Dill. I Walk Alone.* 1948: *The Noose Hangs High. Relentless.* 1949: *Abandoned. Come to the Stable. Two Knights in Brooklyn/Two Mugs from Brooklyn* (combined GB version of *The McGuerins from Brooklyn/Taxi, Mister*). *The Devil's Henchman. Neptune's Daughter. Rope of Sand. Samson and Delilah.* 1950: *Dark City. He's a Cockeyed Wonder. Night and the City.* 1951: *Criminal Lawyer. My Favorite Spy. The Light Touch. Pier 23. Ten Tall Men.* 1954: *The Egyptian.* 1955: *The Man from Laramie. New York Confidential. New Orleans Uncensored* (GB: *Riot on Pier 6*). *Blood Alley. Kismet. Davy Crockett—King of the Wild Frontier.* 1956: *Man in the Vault. Comanche. Around the World in 80 Days.* 1957: *Hell Ship Mutiny. The Buccaneer.* 1959: *Alias Jesse James. Some Like It Hot.* 1960: *The Schnook* (GB: *Double Trouble*). *The Facts of Life.* 1961: *The Errand Boy. Pocketful of Miracles.* 1962: *Zotz! Swingin' Along* (revised version of *The Schnook*). *Five Weeks in a Balloon.* 1963: *Donovan's Reef. Four for Texas. It's a Mad, Mad, Mad, Mad World.* 1964: *Cheyenne Autumn.* 1965: *The Adventures of Bullwhip Griffin. Requiem for a Gunfighter.* 1966: *Seven Women.* 1970: *Which Way to the Front?* (GB: *Ja! Ja! Mein General, But Which Way to the Front?*). 1972: *Challenge to Be Free.* 1974: *Centerfold Girls.* 1975: *Won Ton Ton, the Dog Who Saved Hollywood. The Wild McCullochs.* 1977: *The Incredible Rocky Mountain Race* (TV). *Mad Bull* (TV). 1978: *The Magic of Lassie.* 1979: *Gas Pump Girls. The Man with Bogart's Face.* 1980: *Alligator.* 1981: *All the Marbles ...* (GB: *The California Dolls*).

### McCARTHY, Neil 1935-

Tough-looking British actor whose jagged facial features and unruly, wispy dark hair confined him largely in films to thick-skulled minor heavies. Like so many film hard men, McCarthy, the son of a dentist, is the quiet type in real life, listing his hobbies as the piano and study of foreign languages.

TV and the classical theatre, though, gave him more rewarding roles.

1959: *Breakout.* 1960: *Sands of the Desert.* 1961: *Offbeat.* 1962: *The Pot Carriers.* 1963: *The Young Detectives* (serial). *Two Left Feet. The Cracksman. Zulu.* 1965: *The Hill. Cuckoo Patrol.* 1967: *Where Eagles Dare.* 1968: *Project Z* (serial). 1971: *Follow Me!* (US: *The Public Eye*). 1973: *The Zoo Robbery. Steptoe and Son Ride Again.* 1974: *The Nine Tailors* (TV). 1975: *Operation Daybreak. Side by Side.* 1976: *Trial by Combat* (US: *Dirty Knights' Work*). *The Incredible Sarah. Fern the Red Deer.* 1978: *The Thief of Baghdad.* 1980: *The Monster Club. Shōgun* (TV. GB: cinemas, in abbreviated version). *George and Mildred.* 1981: *Clash of the Titans. Time Bandits.*

### McCOWEN, Alec 1925-

Light-haired British actor with thin smile. His immense talent for sardonic humour was little used on screen, a medium in which his stocky stature kept him in star character roles. His dramatic characterizations in films—*Frenzy* apart—have seemed rather bloodless, but he has shone in witty cameos. The bulk of his work has been in the British theatre, where his reputation is justly high.

1953: \**A Midsummer Night's Dream. The Cruel Sea.* 1954: *The Divided Heart.* 1955: *The Deep Blue Sea.* 1956: *The Long Arm* (US: *The Third Key*). *Town on Trial!* 1957: *The Good Companions. Time Without Pity. The One That Got Away.* 1958: *The Silent Enemy. A Night to Remember. A Midsummer Night's Dream* (dubbed voice). 1959: *The Doctor's Dilemma.* 1962: *The Loneliness of the Long Distance Runner. In the Cool of the Day.* 1965: *The Agony and the Ecstasy.* 1966: *The Witches* (US: *The Devil's Own*). 1970: *The Hawaiians* (GB: *Master of the Islands*). 1972: *Frenzy. Travels with My Aunt.* 1978: *Stevie.* 1979: *Hanover Street.* 1983: *Never Say Never Again. Forever Young.* 1985: *The Assam Garden.*

### McDANIEL, Hattie 1895-1952

Big, beaming, much-loved black actress who was a vocalist with a dance band before taking up acting in her thirties. Won an Academy Award as best supporting actress in *Gone With the Wind*, and was a delight singing and dancing 'Ice Cold Katie' in *Thank Your Lucky Stars*, but retired because of ill-health in 1948. Sister of actress Etta McDaniel (1890-1946) and actor Sam McDaniel (1886-1962). The archetypal black lady's-maid.

1932: Hypnotized. The Washington Masquerade (GB: Mad Masquerade). Blonde Venus. The Golden West. 1933: The Story of Temple Drake. I'm No Angel. 1934: Operator 13 (GB: Spy 13). Lost in the Stratosphere. Judge Priest. Babbitt. Little Men. *The Chases of Pimple Street. *Fate's Fathead. Imitation of Life. 1935: Music is Magic. Alice Adams. Traveling Saleslady. The Little Colonel. Another Face. *Anniversary Trouble. *Four Star Boarder. *Okay Toots! China Seas. 1936: Gentle Julia. Next Time We Love (GB: Next Time We Live). Show Boat. High Treason. The Postal Inspector. The Singing Kid. Reunion (GB: Hearts in Reunion). Libeled Lady. The First Baby. Hearts Divided. Star for a Night. The Bride Walks Out. Valiant is the Word for Carrie. Can This Be Dixie? *Arbor Day. *Big Time Vaudeville. 1937: Racing Lady. The Crime Nobody Saw. Saratoga. True Confession. 45 Fathers. Nothing Sacred. The Wildcatter. Over the Goal. Don't Tell the Wife. Merry-Go-Round of 1938. 1938: Battle of Broadway. The Shining Hour. The Mad Miss Manton. Carefree. The Shopworn Angel. 1939: Zenobia (GB: Elephants Never Forget). Gone With the Wind. Everybody's Baby. 1940: Maryland. 1941: Affectionately Yours. The Great Lie. They Died with their Boots On. 1942: The Male Animal. Reap the Wild Wind. In This Our Life. George Washington Slept Here. 1943: Johnny Come Lately (GB: Johnny Vagabond). Thank Your Lucky Stars. 1944: Since You Went Away. Three Is a Family. Janie. Hi, Beautiful (GB: Pass to Romance). 1946: Janie Gets Married. Margie. Song of the South. Never Say Goodbye. 1947: The Flame. 1948: Mickey. Mr Blandings Builds His Dream House. Family Honeymoon. 1949: The Big Wheel.

## McGIVER, John

(George Morris) 1913-1975
American character actor who came to films in his forties and quickly proved a

treasure. Instantly identifiable with his pinkly plump features, bald head, tiny eyes and lips pursed in anticipation of some new problem, he was one of the most astute scene-stealers around in the late fifties and early sixties. Died from a heart attack.

1956: L'homme à l'imperméable. 1957: Love in the Afternoon. 1958: I Married a Woman. Once upon a Horse. 1959: The Gazebo. 1960: Love in a Goldfish Bowl. 1961: Bachelor in Paradise. Breakfast at Tiffany's. 1962: Period of Adjustment. Mr Hobbs Takes a Vacation. The Manchurian Candidate. Who's Got the Action? 1963: Take Her, She's Mine. Johnny Cool. Who's Minding the Store? A Global Affair. My Six Loves. 1964: Man's Favorite Sport? 1965: Marriage on the Rocks. Made in Paris. 1966: The Glass Bottom Boat. 1967: Fitzwilly (GB: Fitzwilly Strikes Back). The Spirit is Willing. The Pill Caper (TV). 1969: Midnight Cowboy. 1970: The Feminist and the Fuzz (TV). Lawman. 1971: Sam Hill: Who Killed the Mysterious Mr Foster? (TV). The Great Man's Whiskers (TV). 1974: The Apple Dumpling Gang. 1975: Tom Sawyer (TV).

## McHUGH, Frank

(Francis McHugh) 1898-1981
Stocky American actor of Irish extraction, with light wavy hair and an almost permanent look of amiable bafflement on his face. A regular member of the Warner repertory company from 1930 to 1942 usually as the not-too-bright but true-blue loyal friend of

the intrepid hero.

1926: Mademoiselle Modiste. 1928: *If Men Played Cards As Women Do. 1930: College Lovers. The Dawn Patrol. Top Speed. Bright Lights. Little Caesar. The Widow from Chicago. 1931: Corsair. *The Big Scoop. *That's News to Me. *The Hot Spot. Traveling Husbands. Going Wild. Bad Company. Up for Murder. The Front Page. Fires of Youth. Millie. Men of the Sky. Kiss Me Again (GB. The Toast of the Legion). 1932: One Way Passage. Blessed Event. *The News Hound. *Pete Burke, Reporter. *Extra, Extra. High Pressure. Union Depot (GB: Gentleman for a Day). The Strange Love of Molly Louvain. Life Begins (GB: The Dawn of Life). The Dark Horse. The Crowd Roars. 1933: Parachute Jumper. The Mystery of the Wax Museum. Grand Slam. Private Jones. Telegraph Trail. Convention City. Lilly Turner. Footlight Parade. Professional Sweetheart (GB: Imaginary Sweetheart). Hold Me Tight. The House on 56th Street. Elmer the Great. Son of a Sailor. Havana Widows. Tomorrow at Seven. The Mad Game. Ex-Lady. 42nd Street. 1934: Maybe It's Love. Fashions of 1934. Heat Lightning. Here Comes the Navy. Return of the Terror. Happiness Ahead. Merry Wives of Reno. Smarty (GB: Hit Me Again). Let's Be Ritzy (GB: Millionaire for a Day). Six Day Bike Rider. *Not Tonight, Josephine. 1935: A Midsummer Night's Dream. Stars over Broadway. The Irish In Us. Page Miss Glory. Devil Dogs of the Air. Gold Diggers of 1935. Three Kids and a Queen (GB: The Baxter Millions). 1936: Snowed Under. Freshman Love (GB: Rhythm on the River). Stage Struck. Moonlight Murder. Three Men on a Horse. Bullets or Ballots. 1937: Mr Dodd Takes the Air. Marry the Girl. Ever Since Eve. Submarine D-1. 1938: Little Miss Thoroughbred. Swing Your Lady. Four Daughters. He Couldn't Say No. Boy Meets Girl. Valley of the Giants. 1939: Indianapolis Speedway (GB: Devil on Wheels). Dust Be My Destiny. Daughters Courageous. Four Wives. Dodge City. The Roaring Twenties. On Your Toes. 1940: Saturday's Children. The Fighting 69th. 'Til We Meet Again. City for Conquest. Virginia City. 1941: Four Mothers. Back Street. Manpower. I Love You Again. 1942: Her Cardboard Lower. All Through the Night. 1944: Marine Raiders. Bowery to Broadway. Going My Way. 1945: A Medal for Benny. State Fair. 1946: Deadline for Murder. Little Miss Big (GB: Baxter's Millions). The Hoodlum Saint. The Runaround. 1947: Easy Come, Easy Go. Carnegie Hall. 1948: The Velvet Touch. 1949: Mighty Joe Young. Miss Grant Takes Richmond (GB: Innocence is Bliss). 1950: Paid in Full. The Tougher They Come. 1952: My Son John. The Pace That Thrills. 1953: A Lion is in the Streets. It Happens Every Thursday. 1954: There's No Business Like Show Business. 1957: Three Men on a Horse (TV). 1958: The Last Hurrah. 1959: Career. Say One for Me. 1963: A Tiger Walks. 1967: Easy Come, Easy Go.

## McINTIRE, John 1907- *1991*

Dark-haired American actor with tightly concentrated features, a taller, thinner-faced version of Barry Fitzgerald. He looked as if he ought to be wearing rimless spectacles even when he wasn't and could play wily villains and caring professional men with equal facility. McIntire often didn't get the billing he deserved during his 1950s' stay in Hollywood, and was largely lost to long-running western series on TV after 1961. Married to actress Jeanette Nolan (1911-  ). Actor Tim McIntire is their son.

*1947: Call Northside 777. 1948: Black Bart (GB: Black Bart—Highwayman). River Lady. An Act of Murder. The Street with No Name. Command Decision. 1949: Down to the Sea in Ships. Ambush. Red Canyon. Johnny Stoolpigeon. Top of the Morning. Francis. Scene of the Crime. 1950: The Asphalt Jungle. No Sad Songs for Me. Shadow on the Wall. Winchester 73. Saddle Tramp. Under the Gun. USS Teakettle (later You're in the Navy Now). 1951: The Raging Tide. That's My Boy. Westward the Women. 1952: The World in His Arms. Glory Alley. Horizons West. Sally and Saint Anne. The Lawless Breed. 1953: The President's Lady. Mississippi Gambler. A Lion is in the Streets. War Arrow. 1954: The Far Country. The Yellow Mountain. Four Guns to the Border. There's No Business Like Show Business. Apache. 1955: Stranger on Horseback. The Kentuckian. The Phenix City Story (GB: The Phoenix City Story). The Scarlet Coat. To Hell and Back (narrator only). The Spoilers. 1956: World in My Corner. Away All Boats. Backlash. I've Lived Before. 1957: The Tin Star. 1958: Sing, Boy, Sing. Mark of the Hawk/Accused. The Light in the Forest. The Gunfight at Dodge City. 1959: Who Was That Lady? 1960: Psycho. Elmer Gantry. Seven Ways from Sundown. Flaming Star. 1961: Two Rode Together. Summer and Smoke. 1967: Rough Night in Jericho. 1970: Powderkeg (TV. GB: cinemas). 1973: Linda (TV). Herbie Rides Again. 1974: The Healers (TV). 1975: Rooster Cogburn. 1976: The New Daughters of Joshua Cabe (TV). 1977: The Rescuers (voice only). 1978: Crisis at Sun Valley (TV). The Jordan Chance (TV). 1981: American Dream (TV). The Fox and the Hound (voice only). 1983: Honkytonk Man. 1984: Cloak and Dagger.*

## McKERN, Leo
(Reginald McKern) 1920-

Rotund, florid, dark-haired Australian—an engineer turned commercial artist turned actor. Brought his distinctive throaty tones and aggressive approach to Britain in 1946, and was briefly in star roles in the early sixties. Had great personal success in the seventies in the TV comedy-drama series *Rumpole of the Bailey.*

*1952: Murder in the Cathedral. 1955: All for Mary. 1956: X the Unknown. 1957: Time Without Pity. A Tale of Two Cities. 1959: Beyond This Place (US: Web of Evidence). The Mouse That Roared. Yesterday's Enemy. Jazzboat. 1960: Mikhali (narrator only). Scent of Mystery (GB: Holiday in Spain). \*The Running, Jumping and Standing Still Film. 1961: The Day the Earth Caught Fire. Mr Topaze (US: I Like Money). 1962: The Inspector (US: Lisa) The Horse Without a Head (US: TV). 1963: Doctor in Distress. A Jolly Bad Fellow. Hot Enough for June (US: Agent 8¾). 1964: King and Country. 1965: Help. The Amorous Adventures of Moll Flanders. 1966: A Man for All Seasons. 1967: Assignment K. 1968: Nobody Runs Forever. The Shoes of the Fisherman. Decline and Fall ... of a Birdwatcher! 1970: Ryan's Daughter. 1973: Massacre in Rome. 1975: The Adventure of Sherlock Holmes' Smarter Brother. 1976: The Omen. 1977: Candleshoe. 1978: Damien—Omen II. The Nativity (TV). 1979: The House on Garibaldi Street (TV. GB: cinemas). The Last Tasmanian (narrator only). The Lion, the Witch and the Wardrobe (TV. Voice only). 1980: The Blue Lagoon. 1981: The French Lieutenant's Woman. 1984: Ladyhawke. The Voyage of Bounty's Child (Narrator only). 1985: The Chain. Murder With Mirrors (TV).*

## McLAUGHLIN, Gibb 1884-1960

Thin, haggard-looking British actor with more wrinkles than a prune. In his earlier days a gloomy comic monologuist on stage, he came to films to lend his own touch of gleeful ghoulishness and mastery of disguise to everything from ancient retainers to oriental fiends. By the time he reached his sixties, he could easily have passed for the world's oldest man and the cinema seized his unusual talents to keep him frantically busy, especially in the 1930s.

*1920: Beyond the Dreams of Avarice. 1921: Carnival. The Road to London. 1922: The Bohemian Girl. The Pointing Finger. 1923: Three to One Against. 1925: The Only Way. Somebody's Darling. 1926: Nell Gwyn. London. The House of Marney. 1927: Madame Pompadour. The Arcadians/Land of Heart's Desire. Poppies of Flanders. 1928: The White Sheik. The Farmer's Wife. Glorious Youth/ Eileen of the Trees. The Price of Divorce. 1929: Kitty. The Silent House. Power Over Men. The Woman from China. 1930: The 'W' Plan. The Brat/The Nipper. The School for Scandal. 1931: Third Time Lucky. Sally in Our Alley. Lloyd of the CID (serial. US: Detective Lloyd). My Old China. Such is the Law. Jealousy. The Temperance Fete. Congress Dances. 1932: The Love Contract. Goodnight Vienna (US: Magic Night). Whiteface. Money Means Nothing. Where is This Lady? Atlantide. 1933: The Thirteenth Candle. King of the Ritz. No Funny Business. High Finance. Britannia of Billingsgate. The Private Life of Henry VIII. Bitter Sweet. Dick Turpin. Friday the Thirteenth. 1934: Catherine the Great/The Rise of Catherine the Great. The Church Mouse. Blossom Time. Little Friend. The Queen's Affair (US: Runaway Queen). Jew Süss (US: Power). There Goes Susie. The Old Curiosity Shop. The Scarlet Pimpernel. 1935: The Love Affair of the Dictator (US: The Loves of a Dictator). The Iron Duke. Swinging the Lead. Bulldog Jack (US: Alias Bulldog Drummond). Drake of England (US: Drake the Pirate). Me and Marlborough. I Give My Heart. Hyde Park Corner. 1936: Two's Company. Where There's a Will. Broken Blossoms. All In. Juggernaut. Irish for Luck. 1937: You Live and Learn. 1938: Hey! Hey! USA (shown 1937). Almost a Gentleman. Break the News. Hold My Hand. Thirteen Men and a Gun. The Loves of Madame DuBarry. 1939: Come on George. Inspector Hornleigh. Confidential Lady. Spy for a Day. 1940: Spellbound (US: The Spell of Amy Nugent). 1941: Freedom Radio (US: A Voice in the Night). Penn of Pennsylvania (US: The Courageous Mr Penn). The Young Mr Pitt. 1942: Much Too Shy. Tomorrow We Live (US: At Dawn We Die). 1943: My Learned Friend. 1944: Give Us the Moon. 1945: Caesar and Cleopatra. 1947: Jassy. 1948: Oliver Twist. No Orchids for Miss Blandish. The Queen of Spades. Once Upon a Dream. 1950: Night and the City. The Black Rose. 1951: The Lavender Hill Mob. The House in the Square (US: I'll Never Forget You). 1952: The Card (US: The Promoter). The Pickwick Papers. The Man Who Watched Trains Go By (US: Paris Express). 1953: Grand National Night (US: Wicked Wife). 1954: Hobson's Choice. The Brain Machine. 1955: The Deep Blue Sea. The Man Who Never Was. 1956: Who Done It? 1957: Sea Wife.*

ABOVE Gibb **McLaughlin** (centre), in familiar winged collar, harangues Nora Swinburne and Leslie Perrins (*qv*) in *Whiteface* (1932)

BELOW Gordon **McLeod** (right), an expert at expressing exasperation, got plenty of chance in *The Squeaker* (1937), especially when confronted by Alastair Sim as an eager reporter on the trail of a jewel thief

## McLEOD Gordon 1889-1961

Dark-haired, stern-looking, moustachioed British actor who came from repertory work in his native Devon to become a character star of the London stage. Regular film work came along in the 1930s, usually in humourless, villainous or exasperated roles. Retired in 1954. At his best as Alastair Sim's cigar-chewing editor in *The Squeaker*, but in much smaller roles from the 1940s on.

*1925: The Only Way. 1928: David Garrick. 1932: There Goes the Bride. 1933: Chelsea Life. Mixed Doubles. 1934: Lucky Loser. The Primrose Path. Brides to Be. The Case for the Crown. Borrow a Million. 1935: The Silent Passenger. 1936: To Catch a Thief. The Crimson Circle. Nothing Like Publicity. Not Wanted on Voyage. Talk of the Devil. 1937: The Squeaker (US: Murder on Diamond Row). The Frog. Victoria the Great. The Rat. 1938: Sixty Glorious Years (US: Queen of Destiny). Thistledown. I See Ice. Double or Quits. Dangerous Medicine. 1939: Confidential Lady. Q Planes (US: Clouds Over Europe). Hoots Mon! The Saint in London. 1940: Crooks' Tour. That's the Ticket. Two for Danger. 1941: The Patient Vanishes/This Man is Dangerous. The Saint's Vacation. The Prime Minister. Facing the Music. The Saint Meets the Tiger. Banana Ridge. Hatter's Castle. 1942: The Balloon Goes Up. The First of the Few (US: Spitfire). We'll Smile Again. 1943: The Yellow Canary. 1944: Meet Sexton Blake. He Snoops to Conquer. 1945: I Didn't Do It. Night Boat to Dublin. 1946: Under New Management. 1947: Easy Money. 1948: Corridor of Mirrors. The Winslow Boy. 1949: Floodtide. The Twenty Questions Murder Mystery. 1950: Chance of a Lifetime. Once a Sinner. 1951: A Case for PC 49. Four Days. 1953: The Triangle. Johnny on the Run. 1954: The Diamond (US: Diamond Wizard). A Tale of Three Women. The House across the Lake (US: Heatwave).*

## McMAHON, Horace 1906-1971

Flat-nosed, wry-mouthed, dark-haired American actor whose frankly homely features were seen as a variety of chisellers and sharpies until stage and film success as the hard-pressed police lieutenant in *Detective Story* left him equally typed as the hard-nosed but basically sympathetic sergeant or senior detective, a role he also played with great success in the TV series *Naked City*. Long married to lovely red-haired actress Louise Campbell from the Bulldog Drummond films—a true mating of Beauty and the Beast. Died from a heart ailment.

*1937: The Wrong Road. Navy Blues. Exclusive. A Girl with Ideas. Double Wedding. Paid to Dance. The Last Gangster. They Gave Him a Gun. Kid Galahad. 1938: Tenth Avenue Kid. When G-Men Step In. I Am the Law. Fast Company. Ladies in Distress. King of the Newsboys. Secrets of a Nurse. Broadway Musketeers. Pride of the Navy. Alexander's Ragtime Band. Gangs of New York. Marie Antoinette. Federal Man Hunt (GB: Flight from Justice). 1939: Rose of Washington Square. Sergeant Madden. The Gracie Allen Murder Case. I Was a Convict. Big Town Czar. Laugh It Off (GB: Lady Be Gay). Quick Millions. Sabotage (GB: Spies at Work). She Married a Cop. For Love or Money (GB: Tomorrow at Midnight). That's Right—You're Wrong. Newsboys' Home. Pirates of the Skies. Another Thin Man. 60,000 Enemies. Calling Dr Kildare. 1940: Gangs of Chicago. Dr Kildare's Crisis. The Marines Fly High. I Can't Give You Anything But Love, Baby. Margie. Millionaires in Prison. Oh Johnny, How You Can Love. Dr Kildare's Strangest Case. The Leather Pushers. Melody Ranch. We Who Are Young. Dr Kildare Goes Home. My Favourite Wife. 1941: Come Live with Me. Rookies on Parade. Lady Scarface. The Bride Wore Crutches. Birth of the Blues. The Stork Pays Off. Buy Me That Town. 1942: Jail House Blues. 1944: The Navy Way. Timber Queen. Roger Touhy, Gangster (GB: The Last Gangster). 1946: 13 Rue Madeleine. 1948: Fighting Mad (GB: Joe Palooka in Fighting Mad). The Return of October (GB: Date with Destiny). Smart Woman. Waterfront at Midnight. 1951: Detective Story. 1953: Abbott and Costello Go to Mars. Fast Company. Champ for a Day. Man in the Dark. 1954: Duffy of San Quentin (GB: Men Behind Bars). Susan Slept Here. 1955: My Sister Eileen. Blackboard Jungle. Texas Lady. 1957: Beau James. The Delicate Delinquent. 1959: Never Steal Anything Small. 1966: The Swinger. 1968: The Detective.*

## McNAUGHTON, Gus
(Augustus Howard) 1884-1969

Hollywood had dozens of drily comic sidekicks and fast-talking reporters. But McNaughton was one of the few British character men who fitted into those categories. Originally a stand-up music hall comic, he could do a double-take with the best of them. Small-chinned, large-nosed, thin-lipped and wrinkle-browed, he talked the comedy hero out of more than one tight situation (and, on occasions, into them) and was an enjoyable foil in several George Formby comedies.

*1929: Comets. 1930: Murder. Children of Chance. 1932: The Last Coupon. Lucky Girl. Money Talks. Maid of the Mountains. His Wife's Mother. 1933: Radio Parade. Their Night Out. Leave It to Me. Heads We Go (US: The Charming Deceiver). The Love Nest. Song Birds. Crime on the Hill. 1934: Happy. Bagged. Master and Man. Seeing is Believing. Luck of a Sailor. There Goes Susie. Crazy People. Spring in the Air. Barnacle Bill. 1935: Royal Cavalcade (US: Regal Cavalcade). The 39 Steps. Joy Ride. Music Hath Charms. Invitation to the Waltz. The Crouching Beast. 1936: Not So Dusty. Keep Your Seats Please. Southern Roses. The Heirloom Mystery. Busman's Holiday. You Must Get Married. 1937: The Strange Adventures of Mr Smith. Storm in a Teacup. Action for Slander. Keep Fit. South Riding. 1938: The Divorce of Lady X. We're Going to be Rich. St Martin's Lane (US: Sidewalks of London). You're the Doctor. Keep Smiling (US: Smiling Along). Easy Riches. 1939: All at Sea. What Would You Do Chums? Blind Folly. Q Planes (US: Clouds over Europe). Trouble Brewing. I Killed the Count (US: Who is Guilty?). There Ain't No Justice! 1940: Two for Danger. George and Margaret. That's the Ticket. Old Bill and Son. 1941: Facing the Music. Jeannie (US: Girl in Distress). South American George. Penn of Pennsylvania (US: The Courageous Mr Penn). 1942: Let the People Sing. Much Too Shy. Rose of Tralee. The Day Will Dawn (US: The Avengers). 1943: The Shipbuilders. 1944: Demobbed. 1945: A Place of One's Own. Here Comes the Sun. The Trojan Brothers. 1947: The Turners of Propect Road. 1948: This Was a Woman. Lucky Mascot/Brass Monkey.*

## MEDWIN, Michael 1923-

Cheery-looking, sandy-haired British actor of youthful aspect and pronounced lower lip. Usually seen as brash young men, cockney crooks or soldiers up to all the dodges, he sprinkled these characterizations later with a few lounge-suited wiseacres. Rattled up nearly 70 films before becoming a successful producer. Now only occasionally seen as an actor, although he made a welcome reappearance in a running role in the TV series *Shoestring* in the early 1980s.

1946: *Piccadilly Incident. The Root of All Evil.* 1947: *Just William's Luck. The Courtneys of Curzon Street (US: The Courtney Affair). Black Memory. An Ideal Husband.* 1948: *Call of the Blood. Anna Karenina. William Comes to Town. Night Beat. Woman Hater. My Sister and I. Another Shore. Look Before You Love. Operation Diamond. Forbidden.* 1949: *The Queen of Spades. For Them That Trespass. Trottie True (US: Gay Lady). Boys in Brown. Helter Skelter.* 1950: *Someone at the Door. Trio. Shadow of the Past. Four in a Jeep. The Lady Craved Excitement.* 1951: *The Long Dark Hall.* 1952: *Hindle Wakes (US: Holiday Week). Curtain Up. Top Secret (US: Mr Potts Goes to Moscow). Love's a Luxury (US: The Caretaker's Daughter). Miss Robin Hood. The Oracle (US: The Horse's Mouth).* 1953: *Genevieve. Street Corner. Malta Story. Spaceways. The Intruder.* 1954: *Bang! You're Dead (US: Game of Danger). The Green Scarf. The Teckman Mystery. The Harassed Hero. Conflict of Wings.* 1955: *Above Us the Waves. Doctor at Sea.* 1956: *\*A Man on the Beach. Charley Moon. A Hill in Korea (US: Hell in Korea). Checkpoint. The Man in the Road.* 1957: *The Steel Bayonet. Doctor at Large.* 1958: *The Duke Wore Jeans. The Wind Cannot Read. I Only Arsked!* 1959: *Carry on Nurse. Heart of a Man.* 1962: *The Longest Day. Crooks Anonymous.* 1963: *It's All Happening. Night Must Fall. Kali-Yug—Goddess of Vengeance. Kali-Yug: the Mystery of the Indian Tomb.* 1964: *Rattle of a Simple Man. I've Gotta Horse.* 1965: *24 Hours to Kill. The Sandwich Man.* 1966: *A Countess from Hong Kong.* 1970: *Scrooge.* 1973: *O Lucky Man!* 1974: *Law and Disorder.* 1980: *The Sea Wolves.* 1982: *Britannia Hospital.* 1983: *Never Say Never Again.* 1984: *The Jigsaw Man.*

## MEEK, Donald 1880-1946

Dumpy, bald, Scottish-born actor in Hollywood films. With sad eyes, long, thin mouth petering out in the folds of his chubby cheeks, little nose and blinky gaze, he was constantly in employment from the coming of sound until his death, almost always in roles that matched his name—although he could play a nice variety of tunes on the one fiddle. Died from leukaemia.

1923: *Six Cylinder Love.* 1929: *The Hole in the Wall.* 1930: *The Love Kiss.* 1931: *Personal Maid. The Girl Habit. \*The Clyde Mystery. \*The Wall Street Mystery. \*The Weekend Mystery.* 1932: *\*The Babbling Book. \*The Symphony Murder Mystery. \*The Skull Murder Mystery. \*Murder in the Pullman. \*The Side Show Mystery. \*The Crane Poison Case. \*The Campus Mystery. Wayward.* 1933: *College Coach (GB: Football Coach). Love, Honor and Oh! Baby.* 1934: *The Defense Rests. Romance in Manhattan. Bedside. Mrs Wiggs of the Cabbage Patch. Hi, Nellie! Murder at the Vanities. What Every Woman Knows. The Captain Hates the Sea. The Last Gentleman. The Merry Widow. Only Eight Hours. The Whole Town's Talking (GB: Passport to Fame).* 1935: *Biography of a Bachelor Girl. The Return of Peter Grimm. Village Tale. Old Man Rhythm. Accent on Youth. Society Doctor. Baby Face Harrington. Barbary Coast. Captain Blood. Peter Ibbetson. China Seas. Happiness COD. Top Hat. The Informer. The Gilded Lily. The Bride Comes Home. Mark of the Vampire. Kind Lady (GB: House of Menace). She Couldn't Take It.* 1936: *Pennies from Heaven. Everybody's Old Man. Three Wise Guys. Love on the Run. Two in a Crowd. And So They Were Married. One Rainy Afternoon. Old Hutch. Three Married Men.* 1937: *Artists and Models. Maid of Salem. Double Wedding. Behind the Headlines. Make a Wish. You're a Sweetheart. Parnell. Three Legionnaires. The Toast of New York.* 1938: *Breakfast for Two. Adventures of Tom Sawyer. Double Danger. Little Miss Broadway. You Can't Take It with You. Hold That Co-Ed (GB: Hold That Girl). Having Wonderful Time. Goodbye Broadway.* 1939: *Hollywood Cavalcade. Jesse James. Stagecoach. Blondie Takes a Vacation. The Housekeeper's Daughter. Young Mr Lincoln. Nick Carter, Master Detective.* 1940: *Dr Ehrlich's Magic Bullet (GB: The Story of Dr Ehrlich's Magic Bullet). The Man from Dakota (GB: Arouse and Beware). The Ghost Comes Home. Phantom Raiders. Third Finger, Left Hand. Turnabout. Star Dust. Hullabaloo. Sky Murder. The Return of Frank James. My Little Chickadee. Oh Johnny, How You Can Love.* 1941: *A Woman's Face. Design for Scandal. Blonde Inspiration. Rise and Shine. The Feminine Touch. Wild Man of Borneo. Come*

Live with Me. Babes on Broadway. Barnacle Bill. 1942: *Seven Sweethearts. Tortilla Flat. The Omaha Trail. Maisie Gets Her Man (GB: She Got Her Man). Keeper of the Flame. They Got Me Covered.* 1943: *Air Raid Wardens. DuBarry Was a Lady. Lost Angel.* 1944: *Maisie Goes to Reno (GB: You Can't Do That to Me). Rationing. Bathing Beauty. Two Girls and a Sailor. The Thin Man Goes Home. Barbary Coast Gent.* 1945: *State Fair. Colonel Effingham's Raid (GB: Man of the Hour).* 1946: *Janie Gets Married. Affairs of Geraldine. Because of Him.* 1947: *The Fabulous Joe. Magic Town.*

## MEILLON, John 1933- 1989

Fair-haired, plump-cheeked Australian actor who came to Britain for a few years in the early 1960s to play scruffy servicemen and slightly down-at-heel figures in crime stories, then returned 'down under' to play ruddy-cheeked, hard-drinking, trilby-hatted businessmen. His son, John Meillon Jr, is also a film actor.

1959: *On the Beach.* 1960: *The Sundowners. Offbeat. The Long and the Short and the Tall.* 1961: *Watch It Sailor! The Valiant.* 1962: *Operation Snatch. Billy Budd. Death Trap.* 1963: *Cairo. The Running Man.* 1964: *633 Squadron. Guns at Batasi.* 1965: *Dead Man's Chest.* 1966: *They're a Weird Mob.* 1970: *Outback. Walkabout.* 1972: *Sunstruck.* 1974: *The Cars That Ate Paris. Sidecar Racers.* 1975: *Ride a Wild Pony.* 1977: *The Picture Show Man. Born to Run.* 1978: *The Fourth Wish (TV).* 1981: *Heatwave.* 1984: *The Camel Boy (voice only).*

## MELVIN, Murray 1932-

Long-faced, snooty-looking, dark-haired, at times sensitive British actor who scored as the sympathetic young homosexual in *A Taste of Honey*, but has since been less successfully cast in more extravagant roles, doing his best work in other media.

1960: *Suspect (US: The Risk). The Criminal (US: The Concrete Jungle).* 1961: *A Taste of Honey. Petticoat Pirates.* 1962: *HMS Defiant (US: Damn the Defiant!). Solo for Sparrow. Sparrows Can't Sing.* 1963: *The Ceremony.* 1966: *Alfie. Kaleidoscope.* 1967: *Smashing Time.* 1968: *The Fixer.* 1969: *Start the*

*Revolution Without Me. 1971: The Devils. The Boy Friend. A Day in the Death of Joe Egg. 1973: Ghost in the Noonday Sun (unreleased). Gawain and the Green Knight. 1974: Ghost Story. 1975: Lisztomania. Barry Lyndon. The Bawdy Adventures of Tom Jones. 1976: Shout at the Devil. Joseph Andrews. Gulliver's Travels (voice only). 1977: The Prince and the Pauper (US: Crossed Swords). 1979: Stories from a Flying Trunk. 1982: Nutcracker. 1985: Sacred Hearts.*

**MERCER, Beryl** (1939)
See Herbert, Holmes

**MERKEL, Una** 1903- 1986
Prettily pixieish American actress with dimpled cheeks and red-gold hair, sometimes in leading roles in the thirties, but more often as the heroine's wisecracking friend or characters called Tootsie, Trixie and the like. In post-war years, looking more sprite-like than ever, she turned up as maiden aunts and sassy spinsters. Oscar nominee for *Summer and Smoke.*

*1920: Way Down East. 1923: The White Rose. 1924: †World Shadows. *Love's Old Sweet Song. The Fifth Horseman. 1930: Abraham Lincoln. The Bat Whispers. Eyes of the World. 1931: Six Cylinder Love. The Maltese Falcon. Command Performance. Wicked. Secret Witness/Terror by Night. Don't Bet on Women. Daddy Long Legs. The Bargain. Private Lives. 1932: Red-Headed Woman. She Wanted a Millionaire. Man*

*Wanted. They Call It Sin (GB: The Way of Life). Huddle (GB: Impossible Lover). Impatient Maiden. Men Are Such Fools. 1933: Reunion in Vienna. Whistling in the Dark. Beauty for Sale (GB: Beauty). Bombshell. Her First Mate. The Women in His Life. 42nd Street. Midnight Mary. Broadway to Hollywood (GB: Ring Up the Curtain). Day of Reckoning. Clear All Wires. The Secret of Madame Blanche. 1934: Paris Interlude. This Side of Heaven. Murder in the Private Car (GB: Murder on the Runaway Train). The Cat's Paw. The Merry Widow. Bulldog Drummond Strikes Back. Have a Heart. Evelyn Prentice. 1935: Biography of a Bachelor Girl. One New York Night (GB: The Trunk Mystery). Murder in the Fleet. Baby Face Harrington (GB: Baby Face). It's in the Air. Riffraff. The Night is Young. Broadway Melody of 1936. Speed. We Went to College (GB: The Old School Tie). *How to Stuff a Goose. Born to Dance. 1937: Don't Tell the Wife. Good Old Soak. Saratoga. True Confession. Checkers. 1938: Test Pilot. 1939: Four Girls in White. On Borrowed Time. Destry Rides Again. Some Like It Hot. 1940: Saturday's Children. Comin' Round the Mountain. The Bank Dick (GB: The Bank Detective). Sandy Gets Her Man. 1941: Cracked Nuts. Double Date. Road to Zanzibar. 1942: Twin Beds. The Mad Doctor of Market Street. 1943: This is the Army. *Quack Service. 1944: *To Heir is Human. *Bachelor Daze. Sweethearts of the USA (GB: Sweethearts on Parade). 1947: Its a Joke, Son. 1948: The Bride Goes Wild. The Man from Texas. 1950: Kill the Umpire. My Blue Heaven. Emergency Wedding (GB: Jealousy). 1951: Rich, Young and Pretty. A Millionaire for Christy. Golden Girl. 1952: With a Song in My Heart. The Merry Widow (remake). 1953: I Love Melvin. 1955: The Kentuckian. 1956: Bundle of Joy. The Kettles in the Ozarks. 1957: The Greer Case (TV). The Fuzzy Pink Nightgown. The Girl Most Likely. 1959: The Mating Game. 1961: The Parent Trap. 1963: Summer Magic. A Tiger Walks. 1966: Spinout (GB: California Holiday)*
† Unreleased.

**MERRITT, George** 1890–1977
Solid, dependable, fair-haired British actor, on the short side but built like a barn door, who maximized his long career with nearly

80 London theatrical appearances, more than 100 films, and translations and adaptations of several European plays for the London stage. He first trod the boards at 19, but had the misfortune to be studying theatre in Germany at the outbreak of World War I and was interned for the next four years in a prisoner-of-war camp. In films he usually played upholders of the law who were often by no means as dense as they seemed.

*1930: Thread o' Scarlet. The 'W' Plan. 1931: A Gentleman of Paris. Bracelets. Dreyfus (US: The Dreyfus Case). 1932: The Blind Spot. The Lodger (US: The Phantom Fiend). Little Fella. 1933: FP 1. White Face. Mr Quincy of Monte Carlo. I Was a Spy. Double Bluff. Going Straight. The Fire Raisers. The Ghost Camera. Crime on the Hill. 1934: Jew Süss (US: Power). No Escape. My Song for You. The Silver Spoon. Nine Forty-Five. 1935: Emil and the Detectives (US: Emil). Mr Cohen Takes a Walk. Brown on Resolution (later For Ever England. US: Born for Glory). Ten Minute Alibi. Me and Marlborough. Drake of England (US: Drake the Pirate). Crime Unlimited. Line Engaged. Ticket of Leave. 1936: Rembrandt. Windbag the Sailor. Everything is Thunder. Spy of Napoleon. Prison Breaker. The Man Behind the Mask. Educated Evans. Love at Sea. 1937: Dr Syn. Young and Innocent (US: The Girl Was Young). The Rat. The Vicar of Bray. The Compulsory Wife. Wife of General Ling. The Vulture. Dangerous Fingers. The Return of the Scarlet Pimpernel. 1938: The Gaunt Stranger (US: The Phantom Strikes). Mr Reeder in Room 13 (US: Mystery of Room 13). No Parking. 1939: All at Sea. Q Planes (US: Clouds over Europe). Meet Maxwell Archer (US: Maxwell Archer, Detective). The Proud Valley. 1940: The Frightened Lady (US: The Case of the Frightened Lady). Two for Danger. They Came by Night. The Four Just Men (US: The Secret Four). Spare a Copper. Gasbags. 1941: Breach of Promise (US: Adventure in Blackmail). The Ghost Train. He Found a Star. The Black Sheep of Whitehall. Hatter's Castle. They Flew Alone (US: Wings and the Woman). 1942: Back Room Boy. Let the People Sing. Women Aren't Angels. Asking for Trouble. Alibi. We'll Smile Again. 1943: I'll Walk Beside You. Undercover (US: Underground Guerillas). Escape to Danger. 1944: A Canterbury Tale. Demobbed. The Way Ahead. Don't Take It to Heart. Waterloo Road. Give Me the Stars. 1945: For You Alone. Don Chicago. Home Sweet Home. The Voice Within. 1946: I'll Turn to You. Quiet Weekend. 1947: Nicholas Nickleby. The Man Within (US: The Smugglers). The Root of All Evil. The Upturned Glass. Daughter of Darkness. 1948: Love in Waiting. Good Time Girl. My Brother's Keeper. Calling Paul Temple. Quartet. 1949: Marry Me! Dark Secret. 1950: Something in the City. Pool of London. 1953: Small Town Story. Noose for a Lady. 1954: Night of the Full Moon. The Green Scarf. The End of the Road. 1957: Quatermass II (US: Enemy from*

*Space). 1958: Dracula (US: The Horror of Dracula). Tread Softly, Stranger. 1960: The Full Treatment. The Hands of Orlac. 1962: What Every Woman Wants. 1970: I, Monster. Cromwell. 1973: Gawain and the Green Knight.*

## MERVYN, William
(W. M. Pickwood) 1912-1976
Generously girthed, double-chinned, hail-fellow-well-met British actor whose portentously plummy voice made him a favourite on radio before and during World War II. Film roles were very few and far between, but he became immensely popular in television series (latterly perfectly cast as a bishop in *All Gas and Gaiters*) and also worked prodigiously in the theatre. Born in Nairobi, Kenya.

*1947: The Loves of Joanna Godden. The Mark of Cain. 1949: That Dangerous Age (US: If This Be Sin). Stop Press Girl. Marry Me! Helter Skelter. The Blue Lamp. 1954: Conflict of Wings (US: Fuss over Feathers). 1956: The Long Arm (US: The Third Key). 1958: Carve Her Name With Pride. 1959: Upstairs and Downstairs. The Battle of the Sexes. A Touch of Larceny. 1960: Circus of Horrors. 1961: Invasion Quartet. 1963: Hot Enough for June (US: Agent 8¾). 1964: Murder Ahoy. 1965: The Legend of Young Dick Turpin. Up Jumped a Swagman. 1966: The Jokers. 1967: Deadlier Than the Male. Follow That Camel. 1968: Salt and Pepper. Hammerhead. 1970: Incense for the Damned. Carry on Henry. The Railway Children. 1971: The Ruling Class. The Magnificent Six and ½ (third series). 1972: Up the Front. 1973: Charley One-Eye. 1975: The Bawdy Adventures of Tom Jones.*

## MEYER, Emile 1908- *1987*
It's always something of a shock to realize that someone you thought had appeared in hundreds of films hasn't made anywhere near that number. And, even though this big, burly, disgruntled-looking American actor, who always looked about 48, did make almost 50, that's fewer than one had imagined. His drawn-back dark hair and furrowed brows were seen as prison wardens, sheriffs, fight managers and cops and

administrators both crooked and straight. Began acting in repertory, but films drew him from 1950 and he also did much character work on TV.

*1950: Panic in the Streets. Cattle Queen (GB: Queen of the West). 1951: The Big Night. The Guy Who Came Back. The People against O'Hara. The Mob (GB: Remember That Face). 1952: Bloodhounds of Broadway. Hurricane Smith. We're Not Married. 1953: Shane. 1954: Drums across the River. Shield for Murder. Silver Lode. Riot in Cell Block 11. The Human Jungle. 1955: Blackboard Jungle. Stranger on Horseback. White Feather. The Man With the Gun (GB: The Trouble Shooter). The Girl in the Red Velvet Swing. The Man with the Golden Arm. The Tall Men. 1956: The Maverick Queen. Raw Edge. Gun the Man Down. 1957: Sweet Smell of Success. Baby Face Nelson. Paths of Glory. Badlands of Montana. 1958: The Case Against Brooklyn. The Fiend Who Walked the West. The Lineup. 1959: The Girl in Lovers' Lane. King of the Wild Stallions. Revolt in the Big House. 1960; The Threat. Young Jesse James. 1964: Young Dillinger. 1965: Taggart. 1967: Hostile Guns. A Time for Killing (GB: The Long Ride Home). 1968: Buckskin. More Dead Than Alive. 1969: A Time for Dying. 1973: The Blue Knight (TV. GB: cinemas [abridged]). The Outfit. Macon County Line.*

## MIDDLETON, Charles 1878-1949
American actor with black hair, reptilian eyes and cruel, shifty looks—a perfect

murder case suspect, in fact, or out-and-out villain, most memorably as Ming the Merciless in the three Flash Gordon serials. In his youth a circus ringmaster, then vaudevillian, he came to Hollywood at 50, although he never looked his age, and racked up almost 150 films in the 20 years remaining to him. Also notable as the harsh fort commandant in both Laurel and Hardy's Foreign Legion films. He married Leora Spellman, an actress 13 years his junior, but she died from a heart attack at 54.

*1928: \*A Man of Peace. The Farmer's Daughter. 1929: The Bellamy Trial. The Far Call. Welcome Danger. 1930: East Is West. \*The Frame. Beau Bandit. Way Out West. \*Christmas Knight. \*More Sinned Against Than Usual. Framed. 1931: An American Tragedy. Ship of Hate. Beau Hunks (GB: Beau Chumps). Safe in Hell (GB: The Lost Lady). Caught Plastered. The Miracle Woman. Palmy Days. Alexander Hamilton. Sob Sister (GB: The Blonde Reporter). A Dangerous Affair. 1932: The Hatchet Man (GB: The Honourable Mr Wong). High Pressure. A House Divided. Manhattan Parade. The Sign of the Cross. I Am a Fugitive from a Chain Gang. The Strange Love of Molly Louvain. Pack Up Your Troubles. Hell's Highway. Mystery Ranch. Kongo. The Phantom President. Silver Dollar. Breach of Promise. Rockabye. Tomorrow at Seven. 1933: Pickup. Sunset Pass. Destination Unknown. Disgraced. This Day and Age. Big Executive. Duck Soup. White Woman. Lone Cowboy. 1934: When Strangers Meet. Nana. The Last Round Up. Murder at the Vanities. Behold My Wife! Whom the Gods Destroy. David Harum. Broadway Bill (GB: Strictly Confidential). Mrs Wiggs of the Cabbage Patch. Massacre. Red Morning. 1935: Special Agent. Steamboat 'Round the Bend. The Fixer-Uppers. The Frisco Kid. The County Chairman. Hop-a-Long Cassidy. The Square Shooter. In Spite of Danger. The Virginia Judge. Reckless. The Miracle Rider (serial). 1936: Flash Gordon (serial). Trail of the Lonesome Pine. Road Gang. Empty Saddles. Sunset of Power. Showboat. Wedding Present. Jailbreak. Song of the Saddle. A Son Comes Home. The Texas Rangers. Space Soldiers. Ramona. Career Woman. 1937: John Meade's Woman. Last Train from Madrid. We're on the Jury. Two-Gun Law. Slave Ship. Hollywood Cowboy/Wings Over Wyoming. Souls at Sea. The Good Earth. The Yodelin' Kid from Pine Ridge (GB: The Hero of Pine Ridge). Stand In. 1938: Dick Tracy Returns (serial). Outside the Law. Flaming Frontiers (serial). Strange Faces. Flash Gordon's Trip to Mars (serial). Kentucky. Law West of Tombstone. 1939: Captain Fury. Jesse James. Blackmail. Daredevils of the Red Circle (serial). The Oklahoma Kid. Allegheny Uprising (GB: The First Rebel). Wyoming Outlaw. Cowboys from Texas. Juarez. The Flying Deuces. $1,000 a Touchdown. Way Down South. \*One Against the World. 1940: Chad Hanna. Abe Lincoln in*

Illinois. (GB: Spirit of the People). Thou Shalt Not Kill. The Grapes of Wrath. Rangers of Fortune. Flash Gordon Conquers the Universe (serial). Shooting High. Charlie Chan's Murder Cruise. Virginia City. Brigham Young—Frontiersman (GB: Brigham Young). Santa Fé Trail. Island of Doomed Men. 1941: Wild Geese Calling. Sergeant York. Bad Men of Missouri. Shepherd of the Hills. Western Union. Belle Starr. Jungle Man. Wild Bill Hickok Rides. 1942: The Mystery of Marie Roget. Tombstone—the Town Too Tough to Die. Men of San Quentin. Perils of Nyoka (serial). 1943: Two Weeks To Live. The Black Raven. Hangmen Also Die. *Oklahoma Outlaws. Batman (serial). *Wagon Wheels West. The Black Arrow (serial). 1944: The Town Went Wild. Kismet. 1945: Captain Kidd. How Do You Do? Hollywood and Vine (GB: Daisy (the Dog) Goes Hollywood). Our Vines Have Tender Grapes. Strangler of the Swamp. Northwest Trail. Who's Guilty? 1946: Spook Busters. The Killers. 1947: The Pretender. Welcome, Stranger. Road to Rio. Jack Armstrong (serial). Wyoming. Unconquered. Sea of Grass. 1948: Station West. Jiggs and Maggie in Court. The Black Arrow (GB: The Black Arrow Strikes. And 1943 serial). Mr Blandings Builds His Dream House. Feudin', Fussin' and A-Fightin'. 1949: The Last Bandit.

**MIDDLETON, Guy**
(G. Middleton-Powell) 1906-1973
Brown-haired British actor with RAF-style moustache. Came late to acting after a stock exchange career, but soon became one of the cinema's most familiar faces—initially as the most hissable villain, comic or serious, in British films. Subsequently spent a fruitful 25 years playing cads, bounders, officer-types and men-from-the-ministry, with an occasional leading role thrown in.

1935: Jimmy Boy. Trust the Navy. Two Hearts in Harmony. 1936: Under Proof. The Gay Adventure. A Woman Alone (US: Two Who Dared). Take a Chance. The Mysterious Mr Davis. Fame. 1937: Keep Fit. 1938: Break the News. 1939: Goodbye Mr Chips! French Without Tears. 1940: For Freedom. 1941: Dangerous Moonlight (US: Suicide Squadron). 1942: Talk about Jacqueline. 1943: The Demi-Paradise (US: Adventure

for Two). 1944: Halfway House. English Without Tears (US: Her Man Gilbey). Champagne Charlie. 1945: 29 Acacia Avenue (US: The Facts of Love). The Rake's Progress (US: Notorious Gentleman). Night Boat to Dublin. 1946: The Captive Heart. 1947: The White Unicorn (US: Bad Sister). A Man About the House. 1948: Snowbound. One Night with You. 1949: Once Upon a Dream. Marry Me. No Place for Jennifer. 1950: The Happiest Days of Your Life. 1951: The Third Visitor. Laughter in Paradise. Young Wives' Tale. 1952: Never Look Back. 1953: The Fake. Albert RN (US: Break to Freedom). Front Page Story. 1954: The Harassed Hero. Conflict of Wings. Malaga (US: Fire Over Africa). The Belles of St Trinian's. Make Me an Offer. The Sea Shall Not Have Them. Alive on Saturday (released 1957). 1955: Break in the Circle. A Yank in Ermine. Gentlemen Marry Brunettes. 1956: Now and Forever. 1957: Doctor at Large. Let's Be Happy. Light Fingers. 1958: The Passionate Summer. 1960: Escort for Hire. 1962: Waltz of the Toreadors. What Every Woman Wants. The Fur Collar. 1965: Lady L. 1969: Oh! What a Lovely War. The Magic Christian.

**MIDDLETON, Robert**
(Samuel Messer) 1911-1977
Glowering, hulking (20 stone), balding, beetle-browed American portrayer of oily villains. Quit his job as a radio announcer in his late thirties to try the stage. Only had around ten years in the cinema, but they were memorable ones, as he ran up as repulsive a gallery of nasties as one could wish to relish.

1954: The Silver Chalice. 1955: The Big Combo. The Court Jester. The Desperate Hours. Trial. 1956: Red Sundown. Friendly Persuasion. The Proud Ones. Love Me Tender. 1957: The Lonely Man. The Tarnished Angels. 1958: Day of the Bad Man. No Place to Land (GB: Man Mad). The Law and Jake Wade. 1959: Don't Give Up the Ship. Career. 1960: Hell Bent for Leather. 1961: Gold of the Seven Saints. The Great Imposter. 1963: Cattle King (GB: Guns of Wyoming). 1964: For Those Who Think Young. 1966: A Big Hand for the Little Lady (GB: Big Deal at Dodge City). 1970: Company of Killers. Which Way to the

Front? (GB: Ja, Ja, Mein General, But Which Way to the Front?). 1973: The Harrad Experiment. Anche gli angeli mangiano fagioli. 1974: The Mark of Zorro (TV). Remember When (TV). 1977: The Lincoln Conspiracy.

**MILES, Sir Bernard**
(Lord Miles) 1907-1991
Dark-haired, oval-faced British character-creator with distinctive scowling smile. On stage since 1930, he played supporting roles in films since 1933—but gained his real fame as a comic monologuist, portraying knowing rustics. In films, he was mainly cast as simple folk, but he was always well in character in Dickensian parts and, after he became passionately involved with his own London theatre (the Mermaid), it was inevitable that he should move on to a ripe Long John Silver. Knighted in 1969. Created Lord Miles in 1978.

1933: Channel Crossing. 1934: The Love Test. 1935: Late Extra. 1936: Twelve Good Men. Crown v Stevens. Midnight at Madame Tussaud's (US: Midnight at the Wax Museum). 1937: Kew Gardens (narrator only). 1938: The Citadel. The Challenge. Convict 99. 13 Men and a Gun. The Rebel Son/Taras Bulba. 1939: Q Planes (US: Clouds Over Europe). The Four Feathers. The Spy in Black (US: U-Boat 29). The Lion Has Wings. Band Waggon. The Stars Look Down. 1940: Pastor Hall. *Dawn Guard. *Sea Cadets (narrator only). Contraband (US: Blackout). 1941: Freedom Radio (US: A Voice in the Night). This Was Paris. Quiet Wedding. *Home Guard. The Common Touch. The Big Blockade. 1942: One of Our Aircraft Is Missing. The Day Will Dawn (US: The Avengers). In Which We Serve. The First of the Few (US: Spitfire). 1943: Tunisian Victory (voice only). 1944: †Tawny Pipit. *The Two Fathers. 1946: Carnival. Great Expectations. 1947: Nicholas Nickleby. Fame is the Spur. 1948: The Guinea Pig. 1949: *Bernard Miles on Gun Dogs. 1950: †Chance of a Lifetime. 1951: The Magic Box. 1953: *River Ships (narrator only). Never Let Me Go. 1956: Moby Dick. Tiger in the Smoke. Zarak. The Man Who Knew Too Much. 1957: Fortune is a Woman (US: She Played with Fire). The Smallest Show on Earth. Saint Joan. 1958:

*The Vision of William Blake (narrator only). tom thumb. 1959: Sapphire. 1961: *A Flourish of Tubes (narrator only). 1963: Heavens Above! 1965: *The Specialist. 1969: Run Wild, Run Free. 1983: Treasure Island—the Musical (TV).

† And co-directed

### MILJAN, John 1892-1960

Appropriate that John Miljan and Charles Middleton should be close together in this book—as two of the slimiest villains that ever graced the screen. Miljan's villains were perhaps more dangerous, since he also had, under that curly hair and smooth moustache, a wolfish smile that oozed charm over many a poor, unfortunate heroine. He had some memorable exchanges with Mae West in Belle of the Nineties, and was still being principal nasty as late as 1955 in Pirates of Tripoli.

1923: Love Letters. 1924: Lone Chance. The Painted Lady. On the Stroke of Three. The Lone Fighter/The Lone Wolf. Empty Hearts. Romance Ranch. 1925: The Unnamed Woman. Sackcloth and Scarlet. † The Phantom of the Opera. Wreckage. The Unholy Three. Overland Limited. Silent Sanderson. Flaming Waters. Morals for Men. The Unchastened Woman. Sealed Lips. 1926: The Devil's Circus. My Official Wife. Brooding Eyes. Unknown Treasures. Race Wild. Footloose Widows. The Amateur Gentleman. Devil's Island. Almost a Lady. 1927: Wolf's Clothing. The Clown. Husbands for Rent. Salor Izzy Murphy. Final Extra. What Happened to Father? Quarantined Rivals. The Satin Woman. Lovers? Paying the Price. Rough House Rosie. The Ladybird. The Silver Slave. Stranded. Desired Woman. A Sailor's Sweetheart. The Slaver. Ham and Eggs at the Front (GB: Ham and Eggs). Framed. The Yankee Clipper. In Old San Francisco. 1928: Tenderloin. The Little Snob. The Crimson City. Lady Be Good. Glorious Betsy. Women They Talk About. The Terror. Land of the Silver Fox. The Home Towners. *The Beast. *His Night Out. Devil-May-Care. 1929: Innocents of Paris. Fashions inLove. Queen of the Night Clubs. Times Square (GB: The Street of Jazz). The Desert Song. Hard-Boiled Rose. Speedway. The Voice of the City. Stark Mad. Eternal Woman.

Untamed. The Unholy Night. *Gossip. 1930: The Unholy Three. The Sea Bat. The Woman Racket. Show Girl in Hollywood. War Nurse. Our Blushing Brides. Paid (GB: Within the Law). His Night Out. Remote Control. Not So Dumb. Free and Easy. Lights and Shadows. 1931: Politics. Inspiration. Iron Man. The Secret Six. A Gentleman's Fate. Son of India. The Great Meadow. Hell Drivers. Susan Lenox, Her Fall and Rise (GB: The Rise of Helga). Possessed. The Green Meadow. War Nurse. 1932: Emma. Sky Devils. West of Broadway. Beast of the City. Arsène Lupin. The Wet Parade. Are You Listening? Grand Hotel. The Rich Are Always with Us. Flesh. Night Court (GB: Justice for Sale). Prosperity. The Kid from Spain. The Nuisance (GB: Accidents Wanted). Unashamed. 1933: What! No Beer? King for a Night. Blind Adventure. The Way to Love. Whistling in the Dark. The Sin of Nora Moran. The Mad Game. 1934: The Line-Up (GB: Identity Parade). Unknown Blonde. The Poor Rich. Madame Spy. Whirlpool. Belle of the Nineties. Young and Beautiful. The Ghost Walks. Twin Husbands. 1935: Under the Pampas Moon. Tomorrow's Youth. Mississippi. Charlie Chan in Paris. Murder at Glen Athol (GB: The Criminal Within). Three Kids and a Queen (GB: The Baxter Millions). 1936: North of Nome. Sutter's Gold. Private Number. The Gentleman from Louisiana. The Plainsman. Arizona Mahoney. 1938: Border G-Man. Pardon Our Nerve. Man-Proof. Ride a Crooked Mile. If I Were King. *Miracle Money. 1939: Juarez. The Oklahoma Kid. Torchy Runs for Mayor. Fast and Furious. Emergency Squad. 1940: Queen of the Mob. New Moon. Women Without Names. Young Bill Hickok. Texas Rangers Ride Again. 1941: The Cowboy and the Blonde. The Deadly Game. Forced Landing. Riot Squad. Double Cross. 1942: True to the Army. The Big Street. Scattergood Survives a Murder. Boss of Big Town. Criminal Investigator. North of the Rockies. 1943: Bombardier. The Fallen Sparrow. Submarine Alert. The Iron Major. 1944: Bride By Mistake. I Accuse My Parents. The Merry Monahans. It's in the Bag! (GB: The Fifth Chair). 1945: Wildfire. Back to Bataan. 1946: The Last Crooked Mile. White Tie and Tails. The Killers. 1947: Sinbad the Sailor. Unconquered. In Self Defense. Queen of the Amazons. That's My Man (GB: Will Tomorrow Ever Come?). The Flame. 1948: Perilous Waters. 1949: Stampede. Mrs Mike. Adventure in Baltimore (GB: Bachelor Bait). Samson and Delilah. 1950: Mule Train. 1951: M. 1952: The Savage. Bonzo Goes to College. 1955: Pirates of Tripoli. Run for Cover. 1956: The Ten Commandments. The Wild Dakotas. The Gentle Stranger (TV). 1957: Apache Warrior. 1958: The Lone Ranger and the Lost City of Gold.

† Scenes deleted from final release print.

### MILLER, Dick (Richard) 1928-

Tough-looking, jut-jawed, black haired native New Yorker with 'street corner' good

looks and beefy build, he looked as though he would be more at home in boiler suit and tin helmet than on a film set and was, in his younger days. boxing champion, commercial artist, psychologist and dis jockey before turning to acting. He is also said to have done the first ever late-night chat show on TV. After starting as Brooklynese leads in Z-grade horrors and teenpix—one of them was the now-legendary Walter Paisley in A Bucket of Blood, a role he has reprised in other movies—he proved something of a good luck charm for the Roger Corman/American-International/New World dynasty, appearing in a good percentage of their exploitation films, latterly in (largely comic) cameos. Billed as Richard in some early roles.

1955: Apache Woman. The Oklahoma Woman. 1956: Gunslinger. Not of This Earth. Thunder Over Hawaii. Rock All Night. Attack of the Crab Monsters. Naked Paradise. It Conquered the World. 1957: The Undead. Sorority Girl (GB: The Bad One). Carnival Rock. 1958: War of the Satellites. 1959: A Bucket of Blood. 1960: The Little Shop of Horrors. 1961: The Intruder (GB: The Stranger). 1963: The Terror. 1965: Ski Party. 1967: The St Valentine's Day Massacre. The Trip. A Time for Killing (GB: The Long Ride Home). The Dirty Dozen. 1968: Targets. The Legend of Lylah Clare. 1969: TNT Jackson (unreleased). Four Rode Out. 1970: Which Way to the Front? (GB: Ja! Ja! Mein General, But Which Way to the Front?). 1971: The Grissom Gang. 1972: Ulzana's Raid. 1973: Executive Action. The Slams. The Student Teachers. 1974: Big Bad Mama. Candy Stripe Nurses. Truck Turner. Night Call Nurses. 1975: Hustle. White Line Fever. Capone. Crazy Mama. Summer School Teachers. Darktown Strutters. 1976: Cannonball (GB: Carquake). Moving Violation. Hollywood Boulevard. 1977: Mr Billion. Grand Theft Auto. Game Show Models. 1978: I Wanna Hold Your Hand. Piranha. Starhops. New York, New York. Corvette Summer (GB: The Hot One). 1979: The Lady in Red. Rock 'n' Roll High School. 1980: The Howling. Dr Heckyl and Mr Hype. Used Cars. 1981: Heartbeeps. 1982: White Dog. 1983: The Twilight Zone (GB: Twilight Zone The

Movie). *Heart Like a Wheel. Lies. All the Right Moves. Space Raiders. 1984: Gremlins. The Terminator. 1985: Explorers. After Hours.*

## MILLER, Martin

(Rudolf Müller) 1899- *1969*

Short, studious-looking, bespectacled, jutting-lipped, latterly white-haired Czechoslovakian-born actor in British films, often as professors, technicians, chemists and benevolent old buffers with attractively fractured English. He fled from Berlin to Britain in 1939, founding the Little Viennese Theatre there. In the early 1950s, he played in more than 1000 performances of the record-breaking whodunnit *The Mousetrap.*

*1942: Squadron Leader X. 1943: The Adventures of Tartu (GB: Tartu). 1944: Hotel Reserve. English Without Tears (US: Her Man Gilbey). 1945: Latin Quarter. Night Boat to Dublin. 1946: Woman to Woman. 1947: The Ghosts of Berkeley Square. Mine Own Executioner. 1948: Counterblast. The Blind Goddess. Bond Street. Bonnie Prince Charlie. Man on the Run. 1949: The Huggetts Abroad. The Third Man. Don't Ever Leave Me. 1951: Encore. I'll Get You for This (US: Lucky Nick Cain). 1952: Where's Charley? 1953: Twice Upon a Time. Front Page Story. The Genie. You Know What Sailors Are. 1954: To Dorothy a Son (US: Cash on Delivery). Mad About Men. 1955: The Woman for Joe. An Alligator Named Daisy. Man of the Moment. The Gamma People. 1956: A Child in the House. The Baby and the Battleship. 1957: Seven Thunders (US: The Beasts of Marseilles). 1958: Mark of the Phoenix 1959: Violent Moment. The Rough and the Smooth. Libel. Expresso Bongo. Peeping Tom. 1960: Exodus. 1962: The Phantom of the Opera. 55 Days at Peking. 1963: Incident at Midnight. The VIPs. The Pink Panther. 1964: The Yellow Rolls-Royce. Children of the Damned. 1965: Up Jumped a Swagman.*

## MILLICAN, James 1910-1955

Sandy-haired Millican's laconic line in villainy really should have brought him to the fore earlier, but he became bogged down in small roles after several efforts to break into Hollywood films of the early 1930s

ended in failure. He acted at the University of Southern California, but it was Broadway experience that got him regular work in movies from the late 1930s on. He was just moving into a better class of roles at the time of his early death.

*1932: The Sign of the Cross. 1933: Mills of the Gods. 1936: Mr Deeds Goes to Town. Panic on the Air. 1938: You Can't Take It with You. I Am the Law. Annabel Takes a Tour. Who Killed Gail Preston? 1939: Mr Smith Goes to Washington. *The Sap Takes a Wrap. The Lone Wolf Spy Hunt (GB: The Lone Wolf's Daughter). Only Angels Have Wings. Coastguard. 1940: Golden Gloves. The Phantom Submarine. A Chump at Oxford. The Mortal Storm. 1941: Barnacle Bill. The Bugle Sounds. Love Crazy. You'll Never Get Rich. I Wanted Wings. Meet John Doe. Down in San Diego. Here Comes Mr. Jordan. 1942: The Remarkable Andrew. Star Spangled Rhythm. The Glass Key. The Wife Takes a Flyer (GB: A Yank in Dutch). Take a Letter, Darling (GB: The Green-Eyed Woman). My Favorite Blonde. Nazi Agent. 1943: So Proudly We Hail! Thousands Cheer. Air Force. A Guy Named Joe. Northern Pursuit. 1944: The Story of Dr Wassell. The Sign of the Cross (revised version of 1932 film). Practically Yours. I Love a Soldier. 1945: Bring On the Girls. Tokyo Rose. The Affairs of Susan. Love Letters. Duffy's Tavern. Incendiary Blonde. The Lost Weekend. The Trouble with Women (released 1947). 1946: The Tender Years. Stepchild. Rendezvous with Annie. To Each His Own. The Blue Dahlia. The Well-Groomed Bride. Our Hearts Were Growing Up. The Bride Wore Boots. 1947: Suddenly It's Spring. 1948: Mr Reckless. Hazard. Let's Live Again. Disaster. Man from Colorado. The Return of Wildfire (GB: BlackStallion). Adventures of Gallant Bess. Rogues' Regiment. In This Corner. 1949: Last of the Wild Horses. Command Decision. The Dalton Gang. Fighting Man of the Plains. The Gal Who Took the West. Grand Canyon. Rimfire. 1950: Beyond the Purple Hills. Devil's Doorway. The Gunfighter. Military Academy with That 10th Avenue Gang (GB: Sentence Suspended). Mister 880. Winchester '73. Convicted. 1951: Al Jennings of Oklahoma. Cavalry Scout. Fourteen Hours. The Great Missouri Raid. I*

*Was a Communist for the FBI. Missing Women. Rawhide/Desperate Siege. Warpath. Scandal Sheet (GB: The Dark Page). 1952: High Noon. Bugles in the Afternoon. Carson City. Diplomatic Courier. Springfield Rifle. The Winning Team. Torpedo Alley. 1953: Cow Country. Gun Belt. The Silver Whip. A Lion Is in the Streets. Crazylegs. The Stranger Wore a Gun. 1954: Dawn at Socorro. Jubilee Trail. The Long Wait. The Outcast (GB: The Fortune Hunter). Riding Shotgun. 1955: Las Vegas Shakedown. Top Gun. The Vanishing American. Strategic Air Command. The Man from Laramie. The Big Tip Off. Chief Crazy Horse (GB: Valley of Fury). I Died a Thousand Times. 1956: Red Sundown.*

## MILNER, Martin 1927-

Fresh-faced, cherub-cheeked, blond, bland American actor who played clean-cut young sons, boy friends, college kids and servicemen without ever becoming a name most people would recognize. From 1953 he became involved in several long-running television programmes, almost one on top of another. The last of these, *Adam 12*, finished in 1975 and Milner has been less regularly seen since that time.

*1947: Life With Father. 1948: The Wreck of the Hesperus. 1949: Sands of Iwo Jima. 1950: Louisa. Halls of Montezuma. Cheaper by the Dozen. Our Very Own. 1951: Fighting Coast Guard. Smuggler's Island. I Want You. Operation Pacific. 1952: Belles on Their Toes. The Captive City. My Wife's Best Friend. Springfield Rifle. Battle Zone. Last of the Comanches (GB: The Sabre and the Arrow). 1953: Destination Gobi. 1954: The Long Gray Line. 1955: Francis in the Navy. Pete Kelly's Blues. Mister Roberts. 1956: On the Threshold of Space. Screaming Eagles. Pillars of the Sky (GB: The Tomahawk and the Cross). 1957: Gunfight at the OK Corral. Sweet Smell of Success. Man Afraid. 1958: Marjorie Morningstar. Too Much, Too Soon. 1959: Compulsion. 1960: 13 Ghosts. Sex Kittens Go to College. The Private Lives of Adam and Eve. 1965: Zebra in the Kitchen. 1967: Sullivan's Empire (TV. GB: cinemas). Valley of the Dolls. 1968: Three Guns for Texas (TV. GB: cinemas). 1969: Ski Fever. 1972: Emergency (TV). 1973: Runaway*

(GB: TV, as The Runaway Train). 1976: Flood (TV. GB: cinemas).

**MITCHELL, Grant** 1874-1957
Small, pale-faced, fair-haired American actor with very tiny eyes and mouth, square face and little neck. He often played meek and henpecked types who were suckers for the attentions of vamps and golddiggers, but could also project malevolence with some force and was occasionally the unexpected villain of the piece in a whodunnit.

1923: Radio Mania. 1930: Man to Man. 1931: The Star Witness. 1932: Three on a Match. The Famous Ferguson Case. Big City Blues. No Man of Her Own. A Successful Calamity. Week-End Marriage. 20,000 Years in Sing Sing. 1933: He Learned About Women. Central Airport. Lilly Turner. I Love Tha Man. Heroes for Sale. Dinner at Eight. The Stranger's Return. Tomorrow at Seven. Saturday's Millions. Dancing Lady. King for a Night. Wild Boys of the Road (GB: Dangerous Days). Our Betters. Convention City. Shadows of Sing Sing. 1934: The Poor Rich. The Show-Off. Gridiron Flash (GB: Luck of the Game). Twenty Million Sweethearts. We're Rich Again. The Secret Bride (GB: Concealment). The Cat's Paw. The Case of the Howling Dog. 365 Nights in Hollywood. One Exciting Adventure. 1935: One More Spring. Traveling Saleslady. Gold Diggers of 1935. Men Without Names. Staight from the Heart. Broadway Gondolier. In Person. A Midsummer Night's Dream. It's in the Air. Seven Keys to Baldpate. 1936: The Garden Murder Case. Next Time We Love (GB: Next Time We Live). Moonlight Murder. Piccadilly Jim. The Devil Is a Sissy (GB: The Devil Takes the Count). Her Master's Voice. Parole! My American Wife. The Ex-Mrs Bradford. 1937: The Life of Emile Zola. First Lady. The Last Gangster. Music for Madame. Hollywood Hotel. Lady Behave. 1938: Women Are Like That. The Headleys at Home (GB: Among Those Present). Peck's Bad Boy with the Circus. Reformatory. Youth Takes a Fling. That Certain Age. 1939: 6,000 Enemies. Juarez. Hell's Kitchen. Mr Smith Goes to Washington. On Borrowed Time. The Secret of Dr Kildare. 1940: The Grapes of Wrath. It All Came True. Edison, the Man. New Moon. My Love

Came Back. Castle on the Hudson (GB: Years Without Days). Father Is a Prince. We Who Are Young. 1941: The Bride Wore Crutches. Tobacco Road. One Foot in Heaven. Skylark. The Feminine Touch. Nothing But the Truth. Footsteps in the Dark. The Penalty. The Great Lie. The Man Who Came to Dinner. 1942: Larceny Inc. Meet the Stewarts. The Gay Sisters. My Sister Eileen. Cairo. Orchestra Wives. 1943: The Amazing Mrs Holliday. Dixie. All by Myself. *The Gold Tower. Arsenic and Old Lace. 1944: Laura. Step Lively. See Here, Private Hargrove. And Now Tomorrow. When the Lights Go On Again. The Impatient Years. 1945: Bedside Manner. A Medal for Benny. Crime Inc. Conflict. Guest Wife. Bring on the Girls. Leave Her to Heaven. Colonel Effingham's Raid (GB: Man of the Hour). 1946: Easy to Wed. Cinderella Jones. 1947: Blondie's Holiday. Blondie's Anniversary. Honeymoon. It Happened on Fifth Avenue. The Copse Came C.O.D. 1948: Who Killed Doc Robbin? (GB: Sinister House).

**MITCHELL, Millard** 1900-1953
Rasp-voiced, short-haired Cuban-born American actor with sharp, rat-trap, cynical-looking facial features. His image as an acid, but likeable world-weary type had taken him into top featured film roles (like the producer in Singin' in the Rain) at the time of his death from lung cancer.

1931: Secrets of a Secretary. 1940: Mr and Mrs North. 1941: Mr and Mrs Smith. 1942: Grand Central Murder. Little Tokyo USA. Get Hep to Love (GB: She's My Lovely). The Mayor of 44th Street. The Big Street. 1943: Slightly Dangerous. 1946: Swell Guy. 1947: Kiss of Death. A Double Life. 1948: A Foreign Affair. 1949: Twelve O'Clock High. Everybody Does It. Thieves' Highway. 1950: The Gunfighter. Mr 880. Winchester '73. Convicted. USS Teakettle (later You're in the Navy Now). 1951: Strictly Dishonorable. 1952: My Six Convicts. Singin' in the Rain. 1953: The Naked Spur. Here Come the Girls.

**MITCHELL, Thomas** 1892-1962
Stubby, fleshy-faced, small-eyed American actor who gave deeply-thought, richly enjoyable, often Irish-tinged performances, and was for many years one of Hollywood's

best actors and top character stars. Took an Academy Award as best supporting actor in Stagecoach. Also wrote several plays. Died from cancer.

1923: Six Cylinder Love. 1934: *Cloudy with Showers. 1936: Craig's Wife. Adventure in Manhattan (GB: Manhattan Madness). Theodora Goes Wild. 1937: Lost Horizon. Man of the People. When You're in Love. I Promise to Pay. The Hurricane. Make Way for Tomorrow. 1938: Love, Honor and Behae. Trade Winds. 1939: Mr Smith Goes to Washington. Only Angels Have Wings. Gone with the Wind. The Hunchback of Notre Dame. Stagecoach. 1940: Our Town. Swiss Family Robinson. Angels over Broadway. The Long Voyage Home. Three Cheers for the Irish. 1941: Out of the Fog. Flight from Destiny. *Cavalcade of the Academy Awards. 1942: This Above All. Moontide. The Black Swan. Tales of Manhattan. Joan of Paris. Song of the Islands. 1943: The Immortal Sergeant. Bataan. The Outlaw. Flesh and Fantasy. 1944: Dark Waters. The Sullivans. The Keys of the Kingdom. Wilson. Buffalo Bill. 1945: Within These Walls. Captain Eddie. Adventure. 1946: Three Wise Fools. The Dark Mirror. It's a Wonderful Life! Swell Guy. 1947: High Barbaree. The Romance of Rosy Ridge. 1948: Silver River. Alias Nick Beal (GB: The Contact Man). 1949: The Big Wheel. 1951: Journey into Light. 1952: High Noon. 1953: Tumbleweed. 1954: Secret of the Incas. Destry. 1956: Miracle on 34th Street (TV. GB: cinemas). While the City Sleeps. 1958: Natchez (TV). Handle with Care. 1960: The Right Man (TV). 1961: Pocketful of Miracles. By Love Possessed.

**MITCHELL, Warren** 1926-
Balding British actor who, once started in films in earnest at 31, busily built up a formidable list of Jewish cockneys and other ethnic types, before creating a series of suburban monsters that culminated in the long-running, multi-prejudiced Alf Garnett of the TV series Till Death Us Do Part, the forerunner of America's All in the Family. Recently spending more time on stage.

1954: The Passing Stranger. 1957: Manuela (US: Stowaway Girl). Barnacle Bill (US: All

at Sea). 1958: Girls at Sea. The Trollenberg Terror (US: The Crawling Eye). Man With a Gun. Three Crooked Men. 1959: Tommy the Toreador. Hell Is a City. 1960: Surprise Package. Two-Way Stretch. The Pure Hell of St Trinians. 1961: The Boy Who Stole a Million. The Curse of the Werewolf. Don't Bother to Knock! (US: Why Bother to Knock?). The Silent Invasion (released 1967). Postman's Knock. Village of Daughters. The Roman Spring of Mrs Stone. 1962: Incident at Midnight. *The King's Breakfast. We Joined the Navy. The Main Attraction. Operation Snatch. 1963: The Small World of Sammy Lee. Calculated Risk. Unearthly Stranger. 70 Deadly Pills. 1964: Where Has Poor Mickey Gone? The Sicilians. Carry On Cleo. The Intelligence Men. 1965: San Ferry Ann. The Spy Who Came In from the Cold. Help! Promise Her Anything. The Night Caller (US: Blood Beast from Outer Space). 1966: The Sandwich Man. The Jokers. Drop Dead Darling (US: Arrivederci, Baby!). 1967: Dance of the Vampires (US: The Fearless Vampire Killers. Voice only). 1968: Diamonds for Breakfas. Till Death Us Do Part. The Assassination Bureau. The Best House in London. 1969: Moon Zero Two. All the Way Up. 1972: The Alf Garnett Saga. Innocent Bystanders. 1974: What Changed Charley Farthing? 1977: Jabberwocky. Stand Up Virgin Soldiers. 1982: Norman Loves Rose. The Plague Dogs (voice only). 1985: The Chain. Knights and Emeralds.

## MOFFATT, Graham 1919-1965

Insolence was in the very bearing of this roly-poly British actor's film fat boys. Not much of an actor, he only had one role, but it dovetailed perfectly with those of Will Hay (dithering incompetence) and Moore Marriott (bewhiskered cunning) in a memorable series of comedy films in the late thirties. When Hay decided to go solo, Moffatt and Marriott made a few films with other comedians, then Moffatt left films to run a pub. Died from a heart attack.

1934: A Cup of Kindness. 1935: Stormy Weather. The Clairvoyant. 1936: Where There's a Will. Windbag the Sailor. Good Morning, Boys. 1937: Okay for Sound. Dr Syn. Gangway. Oh, Mr Porter! Owd Bob

(US: To the Victor). 1938: Convict 99. Old Bones of the River. 1939: Ask a Policeman. Cheer Boys Cheer. Where's That Fire? 1940: Charley's (Big-Hearted) Aunt. 1941: I Thank You. Hi Gang! 1942: Back Room Boy. 1943: Dear Octopus (US: The Randolph Family). 1944: Time Flies. Welcome Mr Washington. A Canterbury Tale. 1945: I Know Where I'm Going!1946: The Voyage of Peter Joe (serial). 1947: Stage Frights. 1948: Woman Hater. 1949: Three Bags Full (serial). 1950: The Dragon of Pendragon Castle. The Second Mate. 1952: Mother Riley Meets the Vampire (US: Vampire over London). 1960: Inn for Trouble. 1963: 80,000 Suspects.

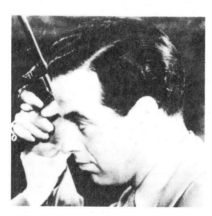

## MOHR, Gerald 1914-1968

Slim, dark, swarthy, treacherous-looking American actor with narrowed eyes, close-cropped hair and wolfish smile. His laconic voice made him an ideal choice to portray Chandler's Philip Marlowe on radio, but he played mostly charming villains in (largely co-feature) films, apart from a stint as the gentleman crook, The Lone Wolf, in the 1940s. Died from a heart attack while in Sweden.

1939: Panama Patrol. Love Affair. Charlie Chan at Treasure Island. 1940: The Sea Hawk. Catman of Paris (released 1946). 1941: We Go Fast. The Monster and the Girl. Jungle Girl (serial). The Reluctant Dragon. Adventures of Captain Marvel (serial. Voice only). Woman of the Year (voiceonly). 1942: The Lady Has Plans. 1943: Murder in Times

Square. Lady of Burlesque (GB: Striptease Lady). One Dangerous Night. The Desert Song. King of the Cowboys. Redhead from Manhattan. 1945: A Guy Could Change. 1946: Gilda. The Notorious Lone Wolf. Passkey to Danger. Dangerous Business. Young Widow. The Truth About Murder (GB: The Lie Detector). The Invisible Informer. 1947: The Lone Wolf in Mexico. The Magnificent Rogue. Heaven Only Knows. The Lone Wolf in London. 1948: The Emperor Waltz. Two Guys from Texas (GB: Two Texas Knights). 1949: The Blonde Bandit. 1950: Hunt the Man Down. Undercover Girl. 1951: Sirocco. Detective Story. Ten Tall Men. 1952: The Duel at Silver Creek. Son of Ali Baba. The Sniper. The Ring. 1953: Raiders of the Seven Seas. Invasion USA. The Eddie Cantor Story. Money from Home. 1954: Dragonfly Squadron. 1957: The Buckskin Lady. 1958: Guns, Girls and Gangsters. My World Dies Screaming (GB: Terror in the Haunted House). 1959: A Date With Death. The Angry Red Planet. 1960: This Rebel Breed. 1964: Wild West Story. 1968: Funny Girl.

## MOODY, Ron

(Ronald Moodnick) 1924-

Mournful-looking British tragi-comedian who looks perfect casting for the clown that cried, and indeed has played Grimaldi (a pet role) on stage. Unlike Sir Alec Guinness, who won stardom with the kind of star character roles in which Moody excels, Moody has never found his niche in the cinema, although he repeated his great personal stage success as Fagin in Oliver! (ironically, also a Guinness role) in the musical film version.

1957: Davy. 1959: Follow a Star. 1960: Make Mine Mink. 1961: Five Golden Hours. 1962: A Pair of Briefs. Summer Holiday. 1963: The Mouse on the Moon. Ladies Who Do. 1964: Murder Most Foul. Every Day's a Holiday (US: Seaside Swingers). 1965: San Ferry Ann. 1966: The Sandwich Man. 1968: Oliver! 1969: David Copperfield (TV. GB: cinemas). 1970: The Twelve Chairs. 1971: Flight of the Doves. 1974: Legend of the Werewolf. Dogpound Shuffle (GB: Spot). 1978: Dominique. 1979: The Spaceman and King Arthur (US: Unidentified Flying Oddball). 1981: Dial M for Murder (TV). 1982: Wrong Is Right (GB: The Man with the Deadly Lens). 1984: Where Is Parsifal?

## MOORE, Alvy 1925-

Skinny, crew-cut, cheerful, light-haired American actor who was briefly popular in the early 1950s. From the mid-1960s, he became increasingly interested in production, forming a company with L.Q. Jones (qv) and returning to acting in cameo roles in several 'in-house' productions on which he customarily also acted as executive producer. Played brash, bright young types in his earlier days.

1952: Okinawa. 1953: The Glory Brigade. China Venture. Susan Slept Here. 1954: Riot in Cell Block 11. Return from the Sea. 1955: Annapolis Story (GB: The Blue and the Gold). Five Against the House. 1956: Screaming Eagles. 1957: Designing Woman. The Persuader. 1958: The Perfect Furlough (GB: Strictly for Pleasure). 1960: The Wackiest Ship in the Army. 1961: Everything's Ducky. Twist around the Clock. 1963: For Love or Money. Move Over, Darling. 1964: Three Nuts in Search of a Bolt. 1965: Love and Kisses. 1966: The Gnome-Mobile. 1967: One Way Wahini. 1970: The Brotherhood of Satan. 1974: A Boy and His Dog. Herbie Rides Again. 1975: The Specialist. Dr Minx. 1978: Lacy and the Mississippi Queen (TV). 1979: Cotton Candy (TV). 1980: Ms 45 (GB: Angel of Vengeance). 1985: Here Come the Littles (voice only).

## MOORE, Ida 1883-1964

Of all the many scene-stealers who appear in this book, this tiny American actress with the 'pixilated' features was one of the most incorrigible. A dear little old lady who played dear little old ladies, she appeared as a comedienne on Broadway in her younger days, when she also made a couple of silents. Nearly always peddled sweetness and light, and could get away with murder; clearly relished her role as Needle Nellie in 1951's Scandal Sheet.

1925: Thank You. The Merry Widow. 1943: *Cutie on Duty. 1944: Reckless Age. Riders of the Santa Fé (GB: Mile a Minute). Hi, Beautiful (GB: Pass to Romance). The Ghost Walks Alone. Once Upon a Time. She's a Soldier, Too. 1945: Girls of the Big House. Rough, Tough and Ready (GB: Men of the Deep). Her Lucky Night. She Wouldn't Say Yes. Easy to Look At. I'll Tell the World. 1946: Cross My Heart. To Each His Own. The Show-Off. I'll Be Yours. From This Day Forward. The Bride Wore Boots. The Dark Mirror. 1947: *Host to a Ghost. Easy Come, Easy Go. It's a Joke, Son. Dream Girl. The Egg and I. High Barbaree. 1948: Money Madness. Good Sam. Johnny Belinda. Return of the Bad Men. Rusty Leads the Way. 1949: Dear Wife. Manhattan Angel. Roseanna McCoy. Ma and Pa Kettle. Hold That Baby. Rope of Sand. Leave It to Henry. The Inspector General. The Sun Comes Up. 1950: Paid in Full. Mother

Didn't Tell Me. Harvey. Backfire. Mr Music. Let's Dance. Fancy Pants. 1951: The Lemon Drop Kid. Comin' Round the Mountain. Double Dynamite. Show Boat. Leave It to the Marines. Honeychile. Scandal Sheet (GB: The Dark Page). 1952: Rainbow 'Round My Shoulder. Scandal at Scourie. Something to Live For. The First Time. Carson City. 1954: The Country Girl. The Long, Long Trailer. 1955: Ma and Pa Kettle at Waikiki. 1957: Desk Set (GB: His Other Woman). 1958: Rock-a-Bye Baby.

## MOOREHEAD, Agnes 1906-1974

Doughty red-haired American actress who came to the screen with Orson Welles' Mercury Players, and proceeded to play stern figures of power—not always with a heart of gold either. Memorable as the sophisticated murderess in Dark Passage, and four times nominated for an Academy Award, her distinctively strong face cropped up in later years as pioneers, harridans, witches and even nuns. Died from cancer.

1941: Citizen Kane. 1942: The Magnificent Ambersons. The Big Street. Journey into Fear. 1943: Government Girl. The Youngest Profession. Jane Eyre. 1944: Since You Went Away. The Seventh Cross. Dragon Seed. Tomorrow the World. Mrs Parkington. 1945: Keep Your Powder Dry. Her Highness and the Bellboy. Our Vines Have Tender Grapes. 1946: Summer Holiday (released 1948). 1947: The Beginning or the End? The Lost Moment. Dark Passage. 1948: The Woman in White. Johnny Belinda. Station West. 1949: Without Honor. The Great Sinner. The Stratton Story. 1950: Caged. Blackjack (US: Captain Blackjack). The Adventures of Captain Fabian. 1951: The Blue Veil. Show Boat. Fourteen Hours. 1952: The Blazing Forest. 1953: The Story of Three Loves. Main Street to Broadway. Scandal at Scourie. Those Redheads from Seattle. 1954: Magnificent Obsession. 1955: Untamed. The Left Hand of God. 1956: All That Heaven Allows. Meet Me in Las Vegas (GB: Viva Las Vegas!). The Revolt of Mamie Stover. The Swan. The Conqueror. Pardners. The Opposite Sex. 1957: The True Story of Jesse James (GB: The James Brothers). Raintree County. Jeanne Eagels. 1958: The

Dungeon (TV). Tempest. 1959: The Bat. Night of the Quarter Moon. 1960: Pollyanna. 1961: Bachelor in Paradise. Twenty Plus Two (GB: It Started in Tokyo). 1962: How the West Was Won. 1963: Who's Minding the Store? 1964: Hush ... Hush, Sweet Charlotte. 1966: The Singing Nun. 1969: The Ballad of Andy Crocker (TV). 1970: Marriage: Year One (TV). 1971: Suddenly Single (TV). What's the Matter with Helen? 1972: Rolling Man (TV). Night of Terror (TV). Dear Dead Delilah. Charlotte's Web (voice only). 1973: Frankenstein: The True Story (TV. GB: cinemas). 1974: Three Faces of Love (TV).

## MORELAND, Mantan 1901-1973

Solidly built, balding American actor who ran away to join a circus at 12, then spent many years in vaudeville before coming to Hollywood to star in black-only films, also appearing in a stream of mainline studio films as the archetypal panicky manservant who found everything but his eyes transfixed in times of terror ('Feet—do your thing!'). The ongoing role of Birmingham Brown, Charlie Chan's chauffeur in the Monogram series of the 1940s, allowed the Moreland sense of (dry) humour often to peep through.

1936: Lucky Ghost. 1937: Spirit of Youth. Two-Gun Man from Harlem. Gang Smashers. 1938: Harlem on the Prairie. Next Time I Marry. Frontier Scout. There's That Woman Again. 1939: One Dark Night. Tell No Tales. Irish Luck (GB: Amateur Detective). Riders of the Frontier. 1940: Chasing Trouble. Pier 13. Millionaire Playboy. The City of Chance. Four Shall Die. While Thousands Cheer. Lady Luck. Mr Washington Goes to Town. Professor Creeps (shown 1942). The Girl in 313. Star Dust. The Man Who Wouldn't Talk. Viva Cisco Kid. On the Spot. Maryland. Laughing at Danger. Drums of the Desert. 1941: Four Jacks and a Jill. Marry the Boss's Daughter. Up Jumped the Devil. Ellery Queen's Penthouse Mystery. Cracked Nuts. Bachelor Daddy. It Started With Eve. Up in the Air. Accent on Love. King of the Zombies. The Gang's All Here. Hello, Sucker. Dressed to Kill. Footlight Fever. You're Out of Luck. Sign of the Wolf. Sleepers West. Let's Go Collegiate (GB: Farewell to Fame). World Premiere. 1942: A-Haunting We Will Go.

ABOVE Alvy **Moore** (second from right) is little remembered by most of today's filmgoers. But in 1955, the chirpy, crewcut player was rubbing shoulders with Brian Keith, Guy Madison, Kim Novak and Kerwin Mathews in *Five Against the House*

BELOW Tiny Ida **Moore** (left) never needed to hold centre stage to steal a scene. And, in the low-budget musical *Rainbow Round My Shoulder* (1952), she had one of her biggest roles. The nominal stars are Arthur Franz and Charlotte Austin

Freckles Comes Home. Andy Hardy's Double
Life. The Strange Case of Dr RX. The Palm
Beach Story. Treat 'Em Rough. Mexican
Spitfire Sees a Ghost. Footlight Serenade. The
Phantom Killer. Eyes in the Night. Tarzan's
New York Adventure. Girl Trouble. It Comes
Up Love (GB: A Date with an Angel). 1943:
Hit the Ice. Sarong Girl. Cabin in the Sky.
Revenge of the Zombies. Cosmo Jones—Crime
Smasher (GB: Crime Smasher). Melody
Parade. She's for Me. He Hired the Boss. My
Kingdom for a Cook. Slightly Dangerous.
Swing Fever. You're a Lucky Fellow, Mr
Smith. We've Never Been Licked (GB: Texas
to Tokyo). 1944: The Mystery of the River
Boat (serial). This Is the Life. The Chinese Cat.
Moon Over Las Vegas. Chip Off the Old Block.
Pin-Up Girl. South of Dixie. Black Magic.
Bowery to Broadway. Charlie Chan in the
Secret Service. See Here, Private Hargrove.
1945: The Scarlet Clue. She Wouldn't Say
Yes. The Jade Mask. The Shanghai Cobra. The
Spider. Captain Tugboat Annie. 1946: Man-
tan Messes Up. Dark Alibi. Shadows Over
Chinatown. Mantan Runs for Mayor. River-
boat Rhythm. Tall, Tan and Terrific. The Trap
(GB: Murder at Malibu Beach). What a Guy.
1947: The Red Hornet. Ebony Parade. The
Chinese Ring. 1948: The Mystery of the
Golden Eye. Docks of New Orleans. The
Feathered Serpent. The Shanghai Chest. Come
on, Cowboy. Best Man Wins. The Dreamer.
She's Too Mean to Me. Return of Mandy's
Husband. 1949: Sky Dragon. 1956: Rockin'
the Blues. Rock 'n' Roll Revue. 1957: Rock 'n'
Roll Jamboree. 1967: Enter Laughing. 1968:
Spider Baby/Cannibal Orgy. 1970: Water-
melon Man. 1971: Marriage: Year One
(TV). 1972: The Biscuit Eater. 1973: The
Young Nurses.

**MORGAN, Frank**
(Francis Wupperman) 1890-1949
Had this square-faced, crusty-looking—
somewhere between Will Hay and Adolphe
Menjou—light-haired American character
star not saddened Hollywood by dying in
his sleep at 59, there is little doubt that he
would have served 20 years at M-G-M,
seen the downfall of the studio system, and
gracefully retired. Although his performances were unvarying, mostly as blustering buffoons, and sometimes seem rushed,

he carved his own niche of immortality by
playing the title role in The Wizard of Oz.
Oscar nominee for Tortilla Flat.

1916: The Suspect. 1917: A Modern Cinder-
ella. The Daring of Diana. Who's Your
Neighbor? Baby Mine. Light in the Darkness.
The Girl Phillippa. A Child of the Wild. Raffles,
the Amateur Cracksman. 1918: At the Mercy
of Men. The Knife. 1919: The Golden Shower.
Gray Towers of Mystery. 1924: Born Rich.
Manhandled. 1925: The Scarlet Saint. The
Crowded Hour. The Man Who Found Himself.
1927: Love's Greatest Mistake. 1930: *Belle
of the Night. Laughter. Dangerous Nan
McGrew. Fast and Loose. Queen High. 1932:
Secrets of the French Police. The Half-Naked
Truth. 1933: Luxury Liner. Hallelujah, I'm a
Bum (GB: Hallelujah, I'm a Tramp). Reunion
in Vienna. The Kiss Before the Mirror. The
Best of Enemies. Bombshell (GB: Blonde
Bombshell). Billion Dollar Scandal. When
Ladies Meet. The Nuisance (GB: Accidents
Wanted). Broadway to Hollywood (GB: Ring
Up the Curtain). 1934: Affairs of Cellini. The
Cat and the Fiddle. A Lost Lady (GB:
Courageous). There's Always Tomorrow. Sis-
ters Under the Skin. Success at Any Price. By
Your Leave. The Mighty Barnum. 1935:
Enchanted April. Naughty Marietta. The
Perfect Gentleman. The Good Fairy. Escapade.
I Live My Life. 1936: Trouble for Two (GB:
The Suicide Club). Piccadilly Jim. The Great
Ziegfeld. Dimples. The Dancing Pirate. 1937:
The Last of Mrs Cheyney. Beg, Borrow or Steal.
Saratoga. The Emperor's Candlesticks. Rosalie.
1938: Port of Seven Seas. Paradise for Three
(GB: Romance for Three). Sweethearts. The
Crowd Roars. 1939: Balalaika. Broadway
Serenade. The Wizard of Oz. Henry Goes
Arizona (GB: Spats to Spurs). 1940: The
Shop Around the Corner. Hullabaloo. Boom
Town. The Mortal Storm. Broadway Melody
of 1940. The Ghost Comes Home. 1941:
Keeping Company. The Vanishing Virginian.
Washington Melodrama. Honky Tonk. Wild
Man of Borneo. 1942: White Cargo. Tortilla
Flat. 1943: A Stranger in Town. Thousands
Cheer. The Human Comedy. 1944: The White
Cliffs of Dover. Casanova Brown. 1945:
Yolanda and the Thief. 1946: The Great
Morgan. The Cockeyed Miracle (GB: Mr
Griggs Returns). Courage of Lassie. Lady Luck.
Summer Holiday (released 1948). 1947:
Green Dolphin Street. 1948: The Three
Musketeers. 1949: Any Number Can Play.
The Great Sinner. The Stratton Story. 1950:
Key to the City.

**MORGAN, Henry 'Harry'**
(Harry Bratsburg) 1915-
Small, weasel-faced, light-haired American
character actor who through the forties and
early fifties played bad guys, losers and
worms that sometimes turned. His prominent performance in The Glenn Miller Story
changed the course of his career, and his
characters became much more likeable.
Recently seen in considerably broader
comic roles. Billed as 'Harry' from 1958.

1942: The Loves of Edgar Allan Poe. The
Omaha Trail. To the Shores of Tripoli.
Orchestra Wives. Crash Dive. The Ox-Bow
Incident (GB: Strange Incident). A-Haunting
We Will Go. 1943: Happy Land. 1944:
Wing and a Prayer. Roger Touhy—Gangster
(GB: The Last Gangster). The Eve of St
Mark. Gentle Annie. 1945: A Bell for Adano.
State Fair. 1946: It Shouldn't Happen to a
Dog. Dragonwyck. Johnny Comes Flying
Home. Somewhere in the Night. From This Day
Forward. 1947: The Gangster. 1948: Race
Street. The Big Clock. The Saxon Charm. All
My Sons. Yellow Sky. Moonrise. 1949: Red
Light. Down to the Sea in Ships. Strange
Bargain. Holiday Affair. Madame Bovary.
1950: Outside the Wall. The Showdown. Dark
City. 1951: Appointment with Danger. The
Blue Veil. Belle le Grand. When I Grow Up.
The Well. The Highwayman. Scandal Sheet
(GB: The Dark Page). 1952: My Six
Convicts. Boots Malone. Bend of the River
(GB: Where the River Bends). High Noon.
What Price Glory? Apache War Smoke. Stop,
You're Killing Me. Toughest Man in Arizona.
1953: Thunder Bay. Torch Song. Arena.
Champ for a Day. The Glenn Miller Story.
1954: The Forty-Niners. The Far Country.
About Mrs Leslie. Prisoner of War. 1955: Not
As a Stranger. Strategic Air Command. 1956:
The Bottom of the Bottle (GB: Beyond the
River). Backlash. The Teahouse of the August
Moon. 1957: Under Fire. 1959: It Started
with a Kiss. 1960: Cimarron. Inherit the Wind.
The Mountain Road. 1962: How the West Was
Won. 1964: John Goldfarb, Please Come
Home. 1966: Frankie and Johnny. What Did
You Do in the War, Daddy? 1967: The Flim
Flam Man (GB: One Born Every Minute).
1969: Dragnet (TV). Support Your Local
Sheriff. 1970: But I Don't Want to Get
Married (TV). Viva Max! The Feminist and
the Fuzz (TV). 1971: The Barefoot Executive.
Support Your Local Gunfighter. Scandalous
John. 1972: Jeremiah Johnson. 1973: Snow-
ball Express. Charley and the Angel. 1974: The
Apple Dumpling Gang. Sidekicks (TV). 1976:
The Shootist. 1977: The Magnificent Magical
Magnet of Santa Mesa/Adventures of Freddie
(TV). Exo-Man (TV). 1978: The Cat from
Outer Space. Kate Bliss and the Ticker Tape
Kid (TV). Maneaters Are Loose! (TV).
Murder at the Mardi Gras (TV). 1979: Better

Late Than Never (TV). You Can't Take It with You (TV). The Apple Dumpling Gang Rides Again. The Wild Wild West Revisited (TV). 1980: Scout's Honor (TV). 1981: Rivkin: Bounty Hunter (TV). 1983: Sparkling Cyanide/Agatha Christie's Sparkling Cyanide (TV).

## MORGAN, Ralph

(Raphael Wuppermann) 1883-1956
Recognizably the brother of Frank Morgan (qv), but quieter and more introspective in performance, this short, sturdy, moustachioed American actor with light-brown hair had squarely handsome features but shifty eyes that often caused him to be cast as suspects in cinematic murder cases. A former lawyer, he could bring great strength to less usual roles, such as the czar in *Rasputin and the Empress*, which combined the sinister and avuncular sides of his personality. Played a few old codgers, too, in his twilight years.

1923: Penny Philanthropist. 1925: The Man Who Found Himself. 1930: *Excuse the Pardon. 1931: Honor Among Lovers. Charlie Chan's Chance. 1932: Strange Interlude (GB: Strange Interval). Dance Team. Cheaters at Play. Disorderly Conduct. The Son-Daughter. The Devil's Lottery. 1933: Humanity. Rasputin and the Empress (GB: Rasputin—the Mad Monk). The Power and the Glory. Trick for Trick. Shanghai Madness. Walls of Gold. The Mad Game. The Kennel Murder Case. Dr Bull. 1934: Transatlantic Merry-Go-Round. The Last Gentleman. Hell in the Heavens. Their Big Moment (GB: Afterwards). No Greater Glory. Orient Express. Little Men. Stand Up and Cheer. Girl of the Limberlost. She Was a Lady. The Cat and the Fiddle. 1935: Condemned to Live. Star of Midnight. Unwelcome Stranger. Calm Yourself. I've Been Around. Magnificent Obsession. 1936: Muss 'Em Up (GB: House of Fate). Little Miss Nobody. Yellowstone. Human Cargo. Speed. General Spanky. The Ex-Mrs Bradford. Anthony Adverse. Crack-Up. 1937: The Life of Emile Zola. Exclusive. Wells Fargo. The Man in Blue. Behind Prison Bars. Orphans of the Street. The Outer Gate. 1938: Out West With the Hardys. Army Girl (GB: The Last of the Cavalry). Love is a Headache. Wives Under

Suspicion. Mother Carey's Chickens. Shadows Over Shanghai. That's My Story. Barefoot Boy. Mannequin. 1939: Fast and Loose. Man of Conquest. Off the Record. Way down South. Smuggled Cargo. Trapped in the Sky. The Lone Wolf Spy Hunt (GB: The Lone Wolf's Daughter). Geronimo. 1940: Forty Little Mothers. I'm Still Alive. *Soak the Old. Wagons Westward. The Mad Doctor (GB: A Date With Destiny). 1941: Dick Tracy vs Crime Inc (serial). Adventure in Washington (GB: Female Correspondent). 1942: Gang Busters (serial). A Close Call for Ellery Queen (GB: A Close Call). Klondike Fury. The Traitor Within. Night Monster (GB: House of Mystery). 1943: Hitler's Madman. Jack London. Stage Door Canteen. 1944: Double Furlough. The Monster Maker. I'll Be Seeing You. Weird Woman. Trocadero. The Impostor. The Great Alaskan Mystery (serial). 1945: Black Market Babies. This Love of Ours. Hollywood and Vine (GB: Daisy (the Dog) Goes Hollywood). The Monster and the Ape. 1947: Mr District Attorney. The Last Roundup. Song of the Thin Man. 1948: Sleep My Love. Sword of the Avenger. The Creeper. 1950: Blue Grass of Kentucky. 1951: Heart of the Rockies. 1953: Gold Fever.

## MORTON, Clive 1904-1975

Dark-haired, oval-headed, aristocratic British actor often seen in arrogant or supercilious roles. In business with the East India dock company for four years before switching to an acting career. Popular on TV in postwar years, but rarely played more than 'clubman'-type cameos in films. Married to actresses Joan Harben (1909-1962) and Fanny Rowe.

1932: Fires of Fate. 1933: The Blarney Stone (US: The Blarney Kiss). 1934: The Great Defender. Evergreen. 1936: The Man Who Changed His Mind. 1938: Dead Men Tell No Tales. 1946: While the Sun Shines. 1947: Jassy. This Was a Woman. Mine Own Executioner. 1948: Here Come the Huggetts. The Blind Goddess. Scott of the Antarctic. Quartet. Vote for Huggett. 1949: Kind Hearts and Coronets. A Run for Your Money. The Blue Lamp. Traveller's Joy (released 1951). 1950: Trio. 1951: His Excellency. The Lavender Hill Mob. Night Without Stars.

1952: Castle in the Air. 1953: Turn the Key Softly. All Hallowe'en. 1954: The Harassed Hero. Orders Are Orders. Carrington VC (US: Court Martial). 1955: Richard III. 1956: Beyond Mombasa. 1957: Seven Waves Away (US: Abandon Ship!). Lucky Jim. After the Ball. The Safecracker. The Moonraker. 1958: The Duke Wore Jeans. Next to No Time! 1959: Shake Hands with the Devil. The Navy Lark. Make Mine a Million. 1960: The Pure Hell of St Trinian's. 1961: Clue of the New Pin. 1962: Lawrence of Arabia. A Matter of WHO. I Thank a Fool. 1964: *All in Good Time. 1965: The Alphabet Murders/The ABC Murders. 1967: Stranger in the House (US: Cop-Out). 1969: Lock Up Your Daughters! Goodbye Mr Chips. 1970: Jane Eyre (TV. GB: cinemas). 1971: Zeppelin. Young Winston. 1972: *The Man and the Snake. 1974: 11 Harrowhouse.

## MOWBRAY, Alan 1893-1969

Dark-haired, heavy-set British actor, good-looking despite a large nose and ruddy complexion, who went to America in 1923, arrived in Hollywood in 1931, and found himself typecast in pompous or lofty roles, with an occasional break as a strong, understanding confidant. His imperious style and 'distinguished' manner soon steered him into butler roles, and he became one of the screen's most peerless manservants from the mid-1930s on. Died from a heart attack.

1931: Leftover Ladies (GB: Broken Links). Guilty Hands. God's Gift to Women. Alexander Hamilton. The Honor of the Family. The Man in Possession. 1932: Lovers Courageous. The Silent Witness. Nice Women. Ladies Courageous. The World and the Flesh. *Two Lips and Juleps. *Snake in the Grass. Man about Town. Winner Take All. Jewel Robbery. The Man Called Back. Two Against the World. Sherlock Holmes. Hotel Continental. The Man from Yesterday. The Phantom President. 1933: Berkeley Square. The World Changes. Peg o' My Heart. A Study in Scarlet. Voltaire. Midnight Club. Roman Scandals. Our Betters. Her Secret. 1934: Long Lost Father. Where Sinners Meet (GB: The Dover Road). The Girl from Missouri (GB: 100 Per Cent Pure). Charlie Chan in London. The House of

Rothschild. Cheaters. Little Man, What Now? One More River (GB: Over the River). Embarrassing Moments. 1935: Lady Tubbs (GB: The Gay Lady). Becky Sharp. Night Life of the Gods. The Gay Deception. In Person. She Couldn't Take It. 1936: Rose Marie. Muss 'Em Up (GB: House of Fate). Rainbow on the River. Ladies in Love. Mary of Scotland. Desire. Give Us This Night. The Case Against Mrs Ames. Fatal Lady. My Man Godfrey. 1937: As Good as Married. Topper. Four Days' Wonder. Stand-In. On Such a Night. Music for Madame. Vogues of 1938. On the Avenue. The King and the Chorus Girl (GB: Romance is Sacred). Marry the Girl. Hollywood Hotel. 1938: Merrily We Live. There Goes My Heart. 1939: Topper Takes a Trip. The Llano Kid. Never Say Die. Way Down South. 1940: The Villain Still Pursued Her. Music in My Heart. Curtain Call. The Quarterback. The Boys from Syracuse. Scatterbrain. 1941: Ice-Capades. The Perfect Snob. I Wake Up Screaming (GB: Hot Spot). That Hamilton Woman (GB: Lady Hamilton). That Uncertain Feeling. Footlight Fever. The Cowboy and the Blonde. Moon Over Her Shoulder. 1942: A Yank at Eton. We Were Dancing. Panama Hattie. Isle of Missing Men. So This is Washington. Yokel Boy (GB: Hitting the Headlines). The Devil With Hitler. The Mad Martindales. 1943: The Powers Girl (GB: Hello! Beautiful). Slightly Dangerous. His Butler's Sister. Holy Matrimony. Stage Door Canteen. *Screen Snapshots No 108. 1944: The Doughgirls. My Gal Loves Music. Ever Since Venus. 1945: The Phantom of 42nd Street. Bring on the Girls. Men in Her Diary. Earl Carroll Vanities. Sunbonnet Sue. Tell It to a Star. Where Do We Go from Here? 1946: Idea Girl. Terror by Night. My Darling Clementine. 1947: The Pilgrim Lady. Lured (GB: Personal Column). Merton of the Movies. Man About Town. Captain from Castile. 1948: The Main Street Kid. My Dear Secretary. Prince of Thieves. Don't Trust Your Husband/An Innocent Affair. Every Girl Should Be Married. 1949: You're My Everything. The Lovable Cheat. The Lone Wolf and His Lady. Abbott and Costello Meet the Killer Boris Karloff. 1950: Wagonmaster. The Jackpot. 1951: The Lady and the Bandit (GB: Dick Turpin's Ride). Crosswinds. 1952: Androcles and the Lion. Blackbeard the Pirate. 1954: Ma and Pa Kettle At Home. The Steel Cage. 1955: The King's Thief. 1956: The King and I. Around the World in 80 Days. The Man Who Knew Too Much. 1961: A Majority of One.

## MULLARD, Arthur 1912-

Raucous-voiced, gap-toothed, ever-smiling British cockney player, whose round and battered features bear witness to his bouts as a boxer. Mullard was also a bouncer and a rag-and-bone merchant before getting into post-war films as an extra and stuntman. In the 1970s his roly-poly figure and rough-and-ready delivery broke into more prominent comedy roles on television. Says he has been in more than 100 films, but if you can

spot him in any more than the 30-odd listed below, you're a better man than I am....

1946: The Captive Heart. School for Secrets (US: Secret Flight). 1948: Oliver Twist. Operation Diamond. 1949: Skimpy in the Navy. 1950: There Is Another Sun (US: Wall of Death). 1951: The Man in the White Suit. The Lavender Hill Mob. 1952: The Pickwick Papers. 1954: One Good Turn. The Belles of St Trinian's. 1956: Brothers in Law. 1957: The Long Haul. Happy Is the Bride! 1958: The Man Who Liked Funerals. 1959: And the Same to You. 1960: Two-Way Stretch. 1962: The Wrong Arm of the Law. The Loneliness of the Long-Distance Runner. 1963: Ladies Who Do. Father Came Too. 1965: Cuckoo Patrol. 1966: The Great St Trinian's Train Robbery. *Fish and Milligan. 1967: Smashing Time. 1968: Chitty Chitty Bang Bang. 1969: Lock Up Your Daughters! Crooks and Coronets (US: Sophie's Place). 1973: Vault of Horror. Holiday on the Buses. 1974: Three for All. 1978: Adventures of a Plumber's Mate.

## MULLIGAN, Richard 1932- 2000

Tall, toothy television star and occasional migrant to the cinema as a character player. Around for years before he made his name on TV as Bert in Soap. Always seen in faintly hysterical roles or as off-centre characters who set their fellows on edge. It's hard to imagine him in anything but comedy, especially with those fruity tones, but he did do a few straight roles in his early years.

1964: One Potato, Two Potato. 1966: The Group. 1969: The Undefeated. 1970: Little Big Man. *Arthur Penn—the Director. 1973: From the Mixed-Up Files of Mrs Basil E. Frankweiler (GB: The Hideaways). 1974: Visit to a Chief's Son. 1976: The Big Bus. 1978: Having Babies III (TV). 1979: Scavenger Hunt. 1980: SOB. 1982: Trail of the Pink Panther. 1983: Jealousy (TV). 1984: Teachers. 1985: The Heavenly Kid. Quicksilver. Micki & Maude. Doin' Time. A Fine Mess (The Music Box.)

## MUNDIN, Herbert 1898-1939

Short, dumpy, dark-haired, often moustachioed British actor with the common touch, facially not unlike the present-day British comedian Ronnie Corbett. A concert-party and music-hall comedian, he soon won popularity in early British talkies and decided to go to Hollywood, which kept him equally busy, most notably as the manservant in Cavalcade, Barkis in David Copperfield and the chirpy Much the Miller in The Adventures of Robin Hood. Killed in a car crash.

1930: *Ashes. Enter the Queen. 1931: Immediate Possession. The Wrong Mr Perkins. We Dine at Seven. Peace and Quiet. East Lynne on the Western Front. 1932: The Devil's Lottery. Life Begins (GB: The Dawn of Life). The Trial of Vivienne Ware. The Silent Witness. Love Me Tonight. Almost Married. Bachelor's Affairs. One Way Passage. Chandu the Magician. Sherlock Holmes. 1933: Cavalcade. Dangerously Yours. Pleasure Cruise. Adorable. It's Great to be Alive. Arizona to Broadway. The Devil's in Love. Shanghai Madness. Hoop-La. 1934: Such Women Are Dangerous. Call It Luck. Ever Since Eve. Hell in the Heavens. Orient Express. Bottoms Up. All Men Are Enemies. Springtime for Henry. Love Time. 1935: David Copperfield. The Widow from Monte Carlo. Mutiny on the Bounty. Ladies Love Danger. The Perfect Gentleman. Black Sheep. King of Burlesque. 1936: A Message to Garcia. Under Two Flags. Charlie Chan's Secret. Champagne Charlie. Tarzan Escapes! 1937: You Can't Beat Love. Angel. Another Dawn. 1938: Invisible Enemy. Exposed. Lord Jeff (GB: The Boy from Barnardo's). The Adventures of Robin Hood. 1939: Society Lawyer.

**MUNSHIN, Jules** 1915-1970
Dark-haired, long-faced, tall, indiarubber-limbed American comedian and dancer with moony smile—the sailor who *wasn't* Gene Kelly or Frank Sinatra in *On the Town.* Worked his way up from small-town nightclubs and vaudeville to Broadway success, but only made a few films for M-G-M before returning to the stage. Died from a heart attack at 54.

*1948: Easter Parade. 1949: Take Me Out to the Ball Game (GB: Everybody's Cheering). On the Town. That Midnight Kiss. 1951: Nous irons à Monte Carlo (GB and US: Monte Carlo Baby). 1957: Silk Stockings. Ten Thousand Bedrooms. 1963: Wild and Wonderful. 1966: Monkeys Go Home!*

**MURTON, Lionel** 1915-
London-born, Canada-raised, long-headed actor and entertainer whose eyebrow-raising expression of cheerful surprise had him cast almost constantly in comedy. He came into prominence with the Canadian Navy show, *Meet the Navy,* during World War II and was seen from time to time in post-war British films as affable but often none-too-bright officials or friends. Also played one or two leading roles in minor films.

*1946: Meet the Navy. 1948: Trouble in the Air. 1949: I Was a Male War Bride (GB: You Can't Sleep Here). 1950: The Girl Is Mine. Dangerous Assignment. 1951: The Long Dark Hall. 1952: The Pickwick Papers.*

*1953: The Runaway Bus. Our Girl Friday (US: The Adventures of Sadie). 1954: Night People. 1955: Raising a Riot. 1956: The Battle of the River Plate (US: Pursuit of the Graf Spee). 1957: Interpol (US: Pickup Alley). Fire Down Below. Carry on Admiral (US: The Ship Was Loaded). 1958: Up the Creek. The Captain's Table. Further Up the Creek. 1959: Northwest Frontier (US: Flame Over India). Make Mine a Million. Our Man in Havana. 1960: Surprise Package. 1961: Petticoat Pirates. Hamilton in the Music Festival (narrator only). 1962: The Main Attraction. Summer Holiday. 1963: Man in the Middle. 1965: The Truth about Spring. 1966: Doctor in Clover. 1967: The Dirty Dozen. 1968: The Last Shot You Hear. 1969: Patton (GB: Patton: Lust for Glory). 1970: Zeta One. The Revolutionary. Welcome to the Club. 1974: Confessions of a Window Cleaner. 1977: Twilight's Last Gleaming.*

**MUSE, Clarence** 1889-1979
Pleasant black American actor who found himself typecast as a handyman or other menial, although he was a law graduate who later moved to acting, writing and composing. The role of Jim in the 1931 version of *Huckleberry Finn* established him in Hollywood, and he made films there for 50 years, as well as founding, or co-founding black theatre groups in New York. His star roles were confined to all-black productions, although he was delightful singing the Oscar-winning *Sunshine Cake* with Bing Crosby and Coleen Gray in *Riding High.* Died from a cerebral haemorrhage.

*1929: Hearts in Dixie. 1930: A Royal Romance. Guilty? Rain or Shine. 1931: Safe in Hell (GB: The Lost Lady). Dirigible. The Last Parade. The Fighting Sheriff. Huckleberry Finn. Secret Witness/Terror By Night. Secret Service. 1932: Lena Rivers. The Woman from Monte Carlo. Prestige. Night World. The Wet Parade. Winner Take All. Attorney for the Defense. Is My Face Red? Big City Blues. White Zombie. Hell's Highway. Cabin in the Cotton. Washington Merry-Go-Round (GB: Invisible Power). Laughter in Hell. Man Against Woman. 1933: From Hell to Heaven. The Mind Reader. Flying Down to Rio. 1934: Fury of the Jungle. Massacre. Broadway Bill (GB: Strictly Confidential).*

*Black Moon. Kid Millions. The Personality Kid. The Count of Monte Cristo. 1935: Alias Mary Dow. O'Shaughnessy's Boy. So Red the Rose. East of Java. Harmony Lane. 1936: Muss 'Em Up (GB: House of Fate). Laughing Irish Eyes. Follow Your Heart. Daniel Boone. Showboat. Spendthrift. 1937: Spirit of Youth. Mysterious Crossing. 1938: The Toy Wife (GB: Frou Frou). Secrets of a Nurse. Prison Train. 1939: Broken Earth. Way Down South. 1940: Zanzibar. Sporting Blood. That Gang of Mine. Murder Over New York. Broken Strings. Maryland. Chad Hanna. 1941: Flame of New Orleans. Adam Had Four Sons. The Invisible Ghost. Love Crazy. Gentleman from Dixie. Among the Living. Belle Starr. Kisses for Breakfast. 1942: The Talk of the Town. Sin Town. The Black Swan. Tales of Manhattan. 1943: Watch on the Rhine. Shadow of a Doubt. Heaven Can Wait. Honeymoon Lodge. Flesh and Fantasy. Johnny Come Lately (GB: Johnny Vagabond). The Sky's the Limit. 1944: In the Meantime, Darling. The Soul of a Monster. Follow the Boys. The Racket Man. The Thin Man Goes Home. Jam Session. Double Indemnity. San Diego, I Love You. 1945: Scarlet Street. The Lost Weekend. Without Love. God is My Co-Pilot. 1946: She Wouldn't Say Yes. Two Smart People. Night and Day. 1947: Joe Palooka in The Knock-Out. A Likely Story. Welcome, Stranger. Unconquered. My Favorite Brunette. 1948: An Act of Murder. 1949: The Great Dan Patch. 1950: Riding High. County Fair. 1951: My Forbidden Past. Apache Drums. 1952: Caribbean (GB: Caribbean Gold). The Las Vegas Story. 1953: Jamaica Run. The Sun Shines Bright. She Couldn't Say No (GB: Beautiful But Dangerous). 1956: The First Travelling Saleslady. 1959: Porgy and Bess. 1971: Buck and the Preacher. 1973: The World's Greatest Athlete. A Dream for Christmas (TV). 1976: Car Wash. 1977: Passing Through. 1979: The Black Stallion.*

**NAISH, J. Carrol**
(Joseph C. Naish) 1897-1973
You could never tell what this swarthy, black-haired American actor would turn up as next. He played Italians, Indians, Red Indians, Orientals, Spaniards, Greeks, Mexicans and dozens of others, besides ape-men, hunchbacks and various fiends (or

comic characters) of vague foreign backgrounds. Almost always hidden beneath make-up; people would have been hard-put to recognize Naish as himself. Virtually lost to films after starting to play Charlie Chan on TV in 1958. Oscar nominations for *Sahara* and *A Medal for Benny*.

*1926: What Price Glory? 1930: Cheer Up and Smile. Good Intentions. Scotland Yard (GB: 'Detective Clive', Bart). Double Crossroads. 1931: Tonight or Never. Homicide Squad (GB: The Lost Men). Gun Smoke. Kick In. Ladies of the Big House. The Royal Bed (GB: The Queen's Husband). 1932: The Mouthpiece. Week-End Marriage (GB: Working Wives). The Conquerors. The Kid from Spain. Big City Blues. Two Seconds. Tiger Shark. Washington Merry-Go-Round (GB: Mad Masquerade). The Hatchet Man (GB: The Honourable Mr Wong). Cabin in the Cotton. Beast of the City. It's Tough to be Famous. The Famous Ferguson Case. Crooner. No Living Witness. 1933: The Mystery Squadron (serial). The Devil's in Love. Elmer the Great. Arizona to Broadway. The Whirlwind. Notorious But Nice. Captured. Frisco Jenny. Ann Vickers. Central Airport. The Mad Game. The World Gone Mad (GB: The Public Be Hanged). The Past of Mary Holmes. The Avenger. Silent Men. No Other Woman. The Big Chance. The Infernal Machine. The Last Trail. 1934: Murder in Trinidad. What's Your Racket? The Hell Cat. Return of the Terror. British Agent. The Defense Rests. Marie Galante. Upper World. One Is Guilty. Sleepers East. Bachelor of Arts. Girl in Danger. Hell in the Heavens. 1935: Behind Green Lights. The President Vanishes (GB: Strange Conspiracy). *Spilled Salt. Black Fury. Under the Pampas Moon. Little Big Shot. The Crusades. The Lives of a Bengal Lancer. Captain Blood. Confidential. Front Page Woman. Special Agent. 1936: We Who Are About to Die. Two in the Dark. The Return of Jimmy Valentine. Robin Hood of El Dorado. Absolute Quiet. Ramona. The Charge of the Light Brigade. Special Investigator. Exclusive Story. The Leathernecks Have Landed (GB: The Marines Have Landed). Moonlight Murder. Charlie Chan at the Circus. Anthony Adverse. Crack-Up. 1937: Border Café. Think Fast, Mr Moto. Sea Racketeers. Thunder Trail. Daughter of Shanghai (GB:*

*Daughter of the Orient). Song of the City. Hideaway. Bulldog Drummond Comes Back. Night Club Scandal. 1938: Hunted Men. Tip-Off Girls. Bulldog Drummond in Africa. Illegal Traffic. King of Alcatraz (GB: King of the Alcatraz). Her Jungle Love. Prison Farm. Persons in Hiding. 1939: Undercover Doctor. Beau Geste. Hotel Imperial. King of Chinatown. Island of Lost Men. 1940: Golden Gloves. Typhoon. Down Argentine Way. A Night at Earl Carroll's. Queen of the Mob. 1941: Blood and Sand. That Night in Rio. Forced Landing. The Corsican Brothers. Mr Dynamite. Accent on Love. Birth of the Blues. 1942: Jackass Mail. A Gentleman at Heart. Tales of Manhattan. Dr Renault's Secret. Dr Broadway. The Pied Piper. The Man in the Trunk. Sunday Punch. 1943: Batman (serial). Harrigan's Kid. Sahara. Calling Dr Death. Good Morning, Judge. Behind the Rising Sun. Gung Ho! 1944: Waterfront. The Monster Maker. Two-Man Submarine. Nabonga (GB: The Jungle Woman). Enter Arsene Lupin. The Whistler. Voice in the Wind. Dragon Seed. House of Frankenstein. Mark of the Whistler (GB: The Marked Man). 1945: *Star in the Night. Strange Confession. The Southerner. A Medal for Benny. Getting Gertie's Garter. 1946: Bad Bascomb. Humoresque. The Beast With Five Fingers. 1947: The Fugitive. Carnival in Costa Rica. Road to Rio. 1948: Joan of Arc. The Kissing Bandit. 1949: That Midnight Kiss. Canadian Pacific. 1950: Rio Grande. The Toast of New Orleans. Annie Get Your Gun. The Black Hand. Please Believe Me. 1951: Across the Wide Missouri. Mark of the Renegade. Bannerline. 1952: Clash by Night. Woman of the North Country. Denver and Rio Grande. Ride the Man Down. 1953: Beneath the 12-Mile Reef. Fighter Attack. 1954: Saskatchewan (GB: O'Rourke of the Royal Mounted). Sitting Bull. 1955: New York Confidential. Violent Saturday. Hit the Deck. The Last Command. Rage at Dawn. Desert Sands. 1956: Yaqui Drums. Rebel in Town. 1957: The Young Don't Cry. This Could Be the Night. 1961: Force of Impulse. 1964: The Hanged Man (TV. GB: cinemas). 1970: Blood of Frankenstein (GB: Dracula vs Frankenstein). Cutter's Trail (TV).*

## NAISMITH, Laurence

(Lawrence Johnson) 1908- 1992

Big, benign, thick-necked British actor with thinning cotton-wool hair; he played clerics, administrators and sympathetic senior citizens. A merchant seaman in his younger days, he joined Bristol Repertory Company in 1930. World War II (he served for seven years in the Royal Artillery) changed the pattern of his career and he became a welcome and reliable film performer in post-war years; despite his turned-down mouth his characters were usually kindly and rarely on the wrong side of the law.

*1948: Trouble in the Air. A Piece of Cake. Badger's Green. 1949: Dark Secret. Train of Events. Room to Let. 1950: The Happiest Days of Your Life. Pool of London. There Is Another Sun (US: Wall of Death). 1951:*

*High Treason. Chelsea Story. Hell Is Sold Out. His Excellency. I Believe in You. Whispering Smith Hits London (US: Whispering Smith versus Scotland Yard). 1952: A Killer Walks. Penny Princess. The Happy Family (US: Mr Lord Says No). Rough Shoot (US: Shoot First). The Beggar's Opera. Cosh Boy (US: The Slasher). The Long Memory. 1953: Love in Pawn. The Flanagan Boy (US: Bad Blonde). Gilbert Harding Speaking of Murder. Mogambo. The Million Pound Note (US: Man With a Million). 1954: The Black Knight. The Dam Busters. Carrington VC (US: Court Martial). 1955: The Final Column. Josephine and Men. Richard III. The Man Who Never Was. 1956: Tiger in the Smoke. The Weapon. The Extra Day. Lust for Life. The Barretts of Wimpole Street. 1957: Seven Waves Away (US: Abandon Ship!). Boy on a Dolphin. Robbery Under Arms. I Accuse! The Gypsy and the Gentleman. 1958: The Two-Headed Spy. Gideon's Day (US: Gideon of Scotland Yard). The Naked Earth. A Night to Remember. Tempest. 1959: Third Man on the Mountain. Solomon and Sheba. 1960: The Angry Silence. The Singer Not the Song. The Criminal (US: The Concrete Jungle). Sink the Bismarck! The Trials of Oscar Wilde (US: The Man with the Green Carnation). The World of Suzie Wong. Village of the Damned. 1961: Greyfriars Bobby. The Valiant. 1962: The 300 Spartans. We Joined the Navy. I Thank a Fool. The Prince and the Pauper. 1963: Cleopatra. Jason and the Argonauts. The Three Lives of Thomasina. 1965: Sky West and Crooked (US: Gypsy Girl). 1966: The Scorpio Letters (TV. GB: cinemas). Deadlier Than the Male. 1967: Camelot. Fitzwilly (GB: Fitzwilly Strikes Back). The Long Duel. 1968: The Bushbaby. 1969: The Valley of Gwangi. Eye of the Cat. Run a Crooked Mile (TV). 1970: Scrooge. 1971: Quest for Love. Diamonds Are Forever. Young Winston. 1972: The Amazing Mr Blunden.*

## NAPIER, Alan

(A. Napier-Clavering) 1903- 1988

Extremely tall, distinguished-looking, somewhat gaunt, moustachioed performer of very British aspect. Born in Birmingham, he was mainly a stage player until going to Hollywood in 1939, where he played noblemen, butlers, senior officers and aristocrats. In the 1960s he became familiar as Alfred, the manservant in television's *Batman* series.

*1930: Caste. 1931: Stamboul. 1932: In a Monastery Garden. 1933: Loyalties. Bitter Sweet. 1936: Wings Over Africa. 1937: For Valour. 1938: Wife of General Ling. 1939: The Four Just Men (US: The Secret Four). We Are Not Alone. 1940: The Invisible Man Returns. The House of the Seven Gables. 1941: Confirm or Deny. 1942: A Yank at Eton. Random Harvest. Cat People. Eagle Squadron. 1943: Lassie Come Home. The Song of Bernadette. Madame Curie. Assignment in Brittany. The Ministry of Fear. Appointment in Berlin. The Uninvited. 1944: Lost Angel. Action in Arabia. The Hairy Ape. Thirty Seconds Over Tokyo. Dark Waters. 1945: Mademoiselle Fifi. Hangover Square. Isle of the Dead. 1946: A Scandal in Paris. Three Strangers. High Conquest. House of Horrors (GB: Joan Medford is Missing). The Strange Woman. 1947: Driftwood. Adventure Island.*

*The Lone Wolf in London. Sinbad the Sailor. Forever Amber. Ivy. Fiesta. Unconquered. 1948: Joan of Arc. Hills of Home (GB: Master of Lassie). Macbeth. Johnny Belinda. 1949: Criss Cross. The Red Danube. Tarzan's Magic Fountain. My Own True Love. A Connecticut Yankee in King Arthur's Court (GB: A Yankee in King Arthur's Court). Manhandled. Master Minds. 1950: Double Crossbones. Challenge to Lassie. Tripoli. 1951: Tarzan's Peril (GB: Tarzan and the Jungle Queen). The Great Caruso. Across the Wide Missouri. The Blue Veil. The Strange Door. The Highwayman. 1952: Big Jim McLain. 1953: Young Bess. Julius Caesar. 1954: Desiree. Moonfleet. 1955: The Court Jester. 1956: Miami Exposé. The Mole People. 1957: Until They Sail. 1959: Journey to the Center of the Earth. 1961: Tender is the Night. 1962: The Premature Burial. 1964: My Fair Lady. Marnie. 36 Hours. Signpost to Murder. 1965: The Loved One. 1966: Batman.*

**NAPIER, Russell** 1910-1974
Hook-nosed, intent-looking Australian actor who struggled at first on coming to Britain, then found a running role as the dogged, authoritative policeman (usually

called Duggan) in charge of numerous cases in the 30-minute series of 'Scotland Yard' featurettes, in which he could be seen, on and off, from 1953 to 1962.

*1947: The End of the River. 1951: Blind Man's Bluff. Death of an Angel. 1952: Stolen Face. 1953: Black Orchid. The Saint's Return (US: The Saint's Girl Friday). *The Dark Stairway. 1954: Conflict of Wings (US: Fuss Over Feathers). Companions in Crime. The Stranger Came Home (US: The Unholy Four). *The Strange Case of Blondie. The Brain Machine. Little Red Monkey (US: The Case of the Little Red Monkey). 36 Hours (US: Terror Street). 1955: A Time to Kill. Out of the Clouds. The Blue Peter. 1956: The Narrowing Circle. The Man in the Road. *Destination Death. Guilty? The Last Man to Hang? *Distant Neighbours (narrator only). A Town Like Alice. *Person Unknown. *The Lonely House. 1957: *The Case of the Smiling Widow. The Shiralee. *The White Cliffs Mystery. Robbery Under Arms. *Night Crossing. 1958: Tread Softly, Stranger. *Crime of Honour. A Night To Remember. Son of Robin Hood. 1959: *The Unseeing Eye. The Witness. *The Ghost Train Murder. Hell is a City. 1960: The Angry Silence. Sink the Bismarck! *The Last Train. *Evidence in Concrete. 1961: The Mark. *The Grand Junction Case. Francis of Assisi. *The Never Never Murder. Barabbas. 1962: Mix Me a Person. HMS Defiant (US: Damn the Defiant!). *Fire Below. 1963: Man in Middle. 1966: It (US: Return of the Golem). 1967: The Blood Beast Terror. 1968: Nobody Runs Forever. Twisted Nerve. 1974: The Black Windmill.*

**NATWICK, Mildred** 1908- *1994*
One look at sharp-faced, dark-haired American actress Mildred Natwick, and you knew that here was a lady who had a sense of humour but would stand no nonsense. In character roles on stage from an early age, she usually played bird-like eccentrics in films, but could be very droll — especially as Jane Fonda's mother in *Barefoot in the Park*, the role for which she was nominated for an Academy Award.

*1940: The Long Voyage Home. 1945: The Enchanted Cottage. Yolanda and the Thief. 1946: The Late George Apley. 1947: A*

*Woman's Vengeance. 1948: Three Godfathers. The Kissing Bandit. 1949: She Wore a Yellow Ribbon. 1950: Cheaper by the Dozen. 1952: The Quiet Man. Against All Flags. 1955: The Trouble With Harry. The Court Jester. 1956: Teenage Rebel. Eloise (TV). 1957: Tammy and the Bachelor (GB: Tammy). 1967: Barefoot in the Park. 1969: If It's Tuesday, This Must Be Belgium. Trilogy. The Maltese Bippy. 1971: Do Not Fold, Spindle or Mutilate (TV). 1972: The Female Instinct (TV. GB: The Snoop Sisters). The House Without a Christmas (TV). 1974: Money to Burn (TV). Daisy Miller. 1975: At Long Last Love. 1979: You Can't Take It With You (TV). 1982: Maid in America (TV).*

**NEDELL, Bernard** 1898-1972
Dark, dapper, smooth, moustachioed American actor whose suavely crooked countenance had him type-cast as charming gangsters, even in British films, where he spent a long sojourn from 1929 to 1938. Hollywood called him back, but his roles there, though no less shady, were not so interesting and his film career had all but petered out by the late 1940s. Married to actress Olive Blakeney (1903-1963) who left him a widower. A second marriage ended in divorce.

*1916: The Serpent. 1929: Eine Nacht in London/A Knight in London. The Silver King. The Return of the Rat. 1930: The Call of the Sea. The Man from Chicago. 1931: Shadows. 1932: Innocents of Chicago (US: Why Saps Leave Home). 1933: Her Imaginary Lover. 1934: The Girl in Possession. 1935: Lazybones. Heat Wave. 1936: The Man Who Could Work Miracles. First Offence/Bad Blood. Terror on Tiptoe. 1937: The Live Wire (US: Plunder in the Air). 1938: Oh Boy! Mr Moto's Gamble. *Come Across. Exposed. 1939: Secret Service of the Air. Lucky Night. Angels Wash Their Faces. They All Come Out. Those High Gray Walls (GB: The Gates of Alcatraz). Some Like It Hot. Fast and Furious. Slightly Honorable. 1940: Rangers of Fortune. Strange Cargo. So You Won't Talk. 1941: Ziegfeld Girl. 1942: Ship Ahoy. 1943: The Desperadoes. Northern Pursuit. 1944: Maisie Goes to Reno (GB: You Can't Do That To Me). One Body Too Many. *Lucky Cowboy.*

1945: *Allotment Wives*. 1946: *Crime Doctor's Man Hunt. Behind Green Lights*. 1947: *Monsieur Verdoux*. 1948: *Albuquerque (GB: Silver City). The Loves of Carmen*. 1960: *Heller in Pink Tights*. 1972: *Hickey and Boggs*.

## NICHOLS, Barbara
(B. Nickerauer) 1929-1976

This tall, blonde American actress with the 'Watch it, buster' face seems to be many people's favourite film floozie, and she certainly made her presence felt in most of her roles. A pity that her later life was dogged by illness; she was little seen, even on TV, after the late 1960s, and died following a long coma after liver complications. A striptease girl before she started an acting career.

1955: *Miracle in the Rain*. 1956: *Manfish (GB: Calypso). Beyond a Reasonable Doubt. The King and Four Queens*. 1957: *Sweet Smell of Success. The Pajama Game. Pal Joey*. 1958: *Ten North Frederick. The Naked and the Dead*. 1959: *Woman Obsessed. That Kind of Woman. The Scarface Mob (TV. GB: cinemas). Who Was That Lady?* 1960: *Where the Boys Are*. 1961: *The George Raft Story (GB: Spin of a Coin)*. 1962: *House of Women*. 1963: *Looking for Love*. 1964: *Dear Heart. The Disorderly Orderly*. 1965: *The Loved One. The Human Duplicators*. 1966: *The Swinger*. 1967: *The Power*. 1968: *Sette uomini e un cervello*. 1973: *Charley and the Angel*. 1975: *Won Ton Ton, the Dog Who Saved Hollywood*.

## NICHOLS, Dandy 1907- 1986

Dark-haired, pudge-faced British actress whose apologetic manner turned to truculence with the passing of the years as her characters began to stand up for themselves. She started off as maids, chars and housewives that you could almost see doffing their forelocks, but her image changed especially with her long-running TV role as Else the 'silly old moo' wife of the monstrous Alf Garnett in *Till Death Us Do Part*, and she was allowed some abrasive dialogue and more interesting roles in her declining years.

1947: *Hue and Cry. Nicholas Nickleby*. 1948: *The Fallen Idol. The Winslow Boy. Here Come the Huggetts. The History of Mr Polly. Scott of the Antarctic*. 1949: *Don't Ever Leave Me. Now Barabbas was a Robber* ... 1950: *Tony Draws a Horse. Dance Hall. The Clouded Yellow*. 1951: *White Corridors*. 1952: *The Holly and the Ivy. The Happy Family (US: Mr Lord Says No). Mother Riley Meets the Vampire (US: Vampire Over London). Emergency Call (US: Hundred Hour Hunt). The Pickwick Papers. Women of Twilight (US: Twilight Women)*. 1953: *Street Corner (US: Both Sides of the Law). The Wedding of Lilli Marlene. Meet Mr Lucifer. The Intruder*. 1954: *Time Is My Enemy. The Crowded Sky. Mad About Men*. 1955: *Where There's a Will. The Deep Blue Sea. A Time To Kill. Lost (US: Tears for Simon)*. 1956: *Not So Dusty. The Feminine Touch (US: The Gentle Touch). Yield to the Night (US: Blonde Sinner)*. 1958: *The Strange World of Planet X (US: Cosmic Monsters). Carry on Sergeant. A Cry from the Streets*. 1962: *Don't Talk to Strange Men*. 1963: *Ladies Who Do. The Leather Boys*. 1964: *Act of Murder*. 1965: *Help! The Amorous Adventures of Moll Flanders. The Knack ... and how to get it. The Early Bird*. 1966: *Doctor in Clover. Georgy Girl*. 1967: *How I Won the War*. 1968: *Carry On Doctor. Till Death Us Do Part*. 1969: *The Bed Sitting Room*. 1973: *O Lucky Man!* 1974: *Confessions of a Window Cleaner. Three for All*. 1982: *The Plague Dogs (voice only). Britannia Hospital*.

## NIMMO, Derek 1931-

Tall, dark, neat British comic actor with mouth as round as his eyes and plummy, upper-class tones; an entertainer born out of his time. Thirty years earlier, he would have been snapped up for leading roles in 'silly ass' comedies. As it was, he only decorated the fringes of a few 1960s' offerings before devoting the major part of his energies to radio (where he became an expert in panel games), TV (especially in the series *All Gas and Gaiters*) and farces in the theatre. Famous for comic clerics.

1960: *The Millionairess*. 1961: *Go to Blazes*. 1962: *It's Trad, Dad! The Amorous Prawn*. 1963: *Tamahine. Hot Enough for June (US:*

*Agent 8¾). The Small World of Sammy Lee. Heavens Above!* 1964: *The Bargee. Murder Ahoy! Coast of Skeletons*. 1965: *Joey Boy. The Liquidator*. 1966: *The Yellow Hat. Mr Ten Per Cent*. 1967: *Casino Royale*. 1969: *A Talent for Loving*. 1975: *One of Our Dinosaurs Is Missing*.

## NORTON, Jack
(Mortimer J. Naughton) 1889-1958

This affectionately regarded American ex-vaudevillian with dark, crinkly hair and up-tilted pencil moustache staggered in a state of blissful screen inebriation through more than 100 film roles as amiable alcoholics before disappearing to (in real life, teetotal) early retirement at 60. With Arthur Housman (qv), he was one of Hollywood's two busiest film 'drunks', and a perfect member for Preston Sturges' 'Ale and Quail Club' in *The Palm Beach Story*. Died from a respiratory ailment.

1934: *Cockeyed Cavaliers.* *Fixing a Stew.* *Super Snooper.* *One Too Many. One Hour Late.* *Woman Haters.* *Counsel on De Fence. Death on the Diamond. Sweet Music. Now I'll Tell (GB: When New York Sleeps)*. 1935: *She Gets Her Man. Calling All Cars. The Gilded Lily. Dante's Inferno. Front Page Woman. Stolen Harmony. Page Miss Glory. One More Spring. Doctor Socrates. The Girl from 10th Avenue (GB: Men on Her Mind). Alibi Ike. Going Highbrow. Don't Bet on Blondes. Miss Pacific Fleet. His Night Out. Bordertown. Broadway Gondolier. Ship Café. Ruggles of Red Gap*. 1936: *The Moon's Our Home.* *Down the Ribber. After the Thin Man. The Preview Murder Mystery. Gold Diggers of 1937. Too Many Parents*. 1937: *Marked Woman. Time Out for Romance. The Great Garrick. Pick a Star. A Day at the Races. My Dear Miss Aldrich. Married Before Breakfast. Meet the Missus.* *Swing Fever*. 1938: *The Awful Tooth. Man Proof. Arsene Lupin Returns. Strange Faces. Meet the Girls. Jezebel. Thanks for the Memory. King of Alcatraz (GB: King of the Alcatraz)*. 1939: *Grand Jury Secrets. The Roaring Twenties. Joe and Ethel Turp Call on the President. Laugh It Off. Society Smugglers. The Lone Wolf Spy Hunt (GB: The Lone Wolf's Daughter). It's a Wonderful World*. 1940: *The Farmer's Daughter. The*

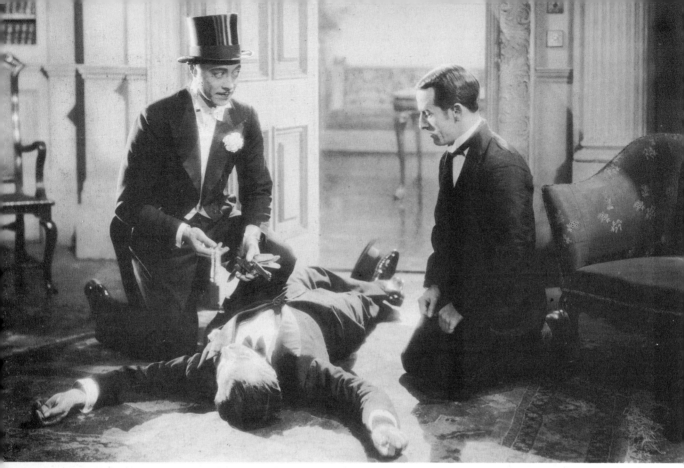

ABOVE Spider (Bernard **Nedell**, left) removes valuable evidence from a dead man (Harold Huth), watched by Donald Stuart, in the 1929 British silent *The Silver King*

BELOW Barbara **Nichols** (blonde) in a 'happier times' scene from *That Kind of Woman* (1959), with Jack Warden (*qv*), Sophia Loren and (back to camera) Tab Hunter

Villain Still Pursued Her. Opened by Mistake. A Night at Earl Carroll's. The Bank Dick (GB: The Bank Detective). The Ghost Breakers. Road Show. 1941: You Belong to Me (GB: Good Morning, Doctor). Down in San Diego. No Greater Sin (GB: Social Enemy No.1). *Crazy Like a Fox. Louisiana Purchase. 1942: The Spoilers. Ice-Capades Revue (GB: Rhythm Hits the Ice). Moonlight in Havana. Dr Renault's Secret. The Palm Beach Story. My Favorite Spy. Tennessee Johnson (GB: The Man on America's Conscience). The Fleet's In. Roxie Hart. Brooklyn Orchid. The McGuerins from Brooklyn. 1943: Taxi, Mister. Assignment in Brittany. It Ain't Hay (GB: Money for Jam). So's Your Uncle. Thank Your Lucky Stars. The Falcon Strikes Back. Gildersleeve On Broadway. Lady Bodyguard. Prairie Chickens. 1944: *His Tale is Told. Ghost Catchers. Once Upon a Time. The Story of Dr Wassell. Here Come the Waves. The Chinese Cat/Charlie Chan in The Chinese Cat. The Miracle of Morgan's Creek. Cover Girl. And the Angels Sing. Shine On Harvest Moon. Hail the Conquering Hero. Make Your Own Bed. The Big Noise. Barbary Coast Gent. Going My Way. 1945: Hold That Blonde. Her Highness and the Bellboy. Wonder Man. Fashion Model. The Naughty Nineties. The Scarlet Clue. Flame of the Barbary Coast. The Horn Blows at Midnight. Man Alive. Strange Confession. Lady on a Train. Two O'Clock Courage. Captain Tugboat Annie. A Guy, A Gal, A Pal. *Double Honeymoon. 1946: *Rhythm and Weep. The Strange Mr Gregory. No Leave, No Love. Blue Skies. Lady Luck. The Hoodlum Saint. Nocturne. The Sin of Harold Diddlebock (later and GB: Mad Wednesday). The Kid from Brooklyn. Rendezvous 24. Shadows Over Chinatown. Bringing Up Father. 1947: Linda Be Good. Down to Earth. Variety Girl. *The Hired Husband. 1948: Variety Time. Alias a Gentleman. 1949: ††Two Knights in Brooklyn/Two Mugs from Brooklyn.

††Combined GB version of The McGuerins from Brooklyn/Taxi, Mister.

busy in films until 1966, and then increasingly tied up in television to the end of his career. Died from cancer.

1938: Tenth Avenue Angel. Flirting With Fate. 1939: Calling All Marines. The Girl from Havana. The Border Legion. 1940: Outside the 3-Mile Limit (GB: Mutiny on the Seas). 1941: Robin Hood of the Pecos. Two-Gun Sheriff. Sheriff of Tombstone. They Met in Bombay. The Great Train Robbery. Citadel of Crime (GB: Outside the Law). Bad Man of Deadwood. 1942: Dr Broadway. Sleepytime Gal. Swamp Woman. 1943: The Man from Music Mountain. Phantom Lady. 1945: Passport to Suez. Hotel Berlin. The Bullfighters. The Chicago Kid. 1946: Perilous Holiday. 1948: Port Said. Kiss the Blood off My Hands (GB: Blood on My Hands). 1949: Tell It to the Judge. 1951: Smuggler's Island. Sirocco. 1952: The Sniper. Captain Pirate (GB: Captain Blood, Fugitive). The Iron Mistress. The Miracle of Our Lady of Fatima (GB: The Miracle of Fatima). Cattle Town. Operation Secret. Ma and Pa Kettle On Vacation (GB: Ma and Pa Kettle Go to Paris). 1953: The Hindu (GB: Sabaka). Diamond Queen. The Robe. Beneath the 12-Mile Reef. Crime Wave (GB: The City Is Dark). 1954: The Mad Magician. The Gambler from Natchez. 1955: The Prodigal. Bengazi. Son of Sinbad. 1956: Jaguar. Lisbon. The Pride and the Passion. 1958: The Perfect Furlough (GB: Strictly for Pleasure). 1959: Execution Night. 1960: Zorro the Avenger (TV. GB: cinemas). This Rebel Breed. The Lost World. 1961: Atlantis the Lost Continent. Pocketful of Miracles. Escape from Zahrain. 1962: The Sutton Story. 1963: The Man from the Diners' Club. 1965: Sylvia. Zebra in the Kitchen. The Art of Love. A Very Special Favor. Harum Scarum (GB: Harem Holiday). 1966: What Did You Do in The War, Daddy? The Caper of the Golden Bulls (GB: Carnival of Thieves). 1969: The Comic. 1971: Powderkeg (TV. GB: cinemas). 1976: The Domino Principle (GB: The Domino Killings. Released 1978).

1958: The Brothers Karamazov. I Want to Live! 1959: Who Was That Lady? The Rise and Fall of Legs Diamond. 1960: Psycho. Murder Inc. 1961: West Side Story. 1962: Hemingway's Adventures of a Young Man (GB: Adventures of a Young Man). Follow That Dream. One Third of a Man. 1963: Wall of Noise. 1964: The Raiders. Ready for the People. The Satan Bug. 1966: The Plainsman. The Sand Pebbles. 1967: Tony Rome. Chubasco. 1968: Bullitt. 1970: On a Clear Day You Can See For Ever. 1971: The Hunting Party. Scandalous John. The Night Stalker (TV). Chato's Land. 1972: The Night Strangler (TV). Toma (TV. GB: Man of Many Faces). 1973: Emperor of the North Pole (GB: Emperor of the North). Happy Mother's Day . . . Love George/Run, Stranger, Run. 1978: Evening in Byzantium (TV).

**O'BRIEN, Virginia** 1921-
Dark-haired, deadpan singer and comedienne who joined M-G-M after Broadway success, but never proved more than an added attraction in several of their musicals, most notably The Harvey Girls. Married (first of two) to actor Kirk Alyn, one of the screen portrayers of Superman, from 1942 to 1955. Niece of film director Lloyd Bacon.

1940: Hullabaloo. Sky Murder. 1941: Ringside Maisie. Lady Be Good. The Big Store. 1942: Ship Ahoy! Panama Hattie. 1943: Du Barry Was a Lady. Thousands Cheer. 1944: Two Girls and a Sailor. Meet the People.

**NOVELLO, Jay** 1904-1982
Dark, scurrying, usually moustachioed little American actor, just as likely to be a dapper crook or the unkempt Arab in the market-place trying to sell you his wares. Fairly

**OAKLAND, Simon** 1922-1983
Thick-faced, black-haired, gravel-voiced, square-built American actor with Edward G Robinson lips, usually seen as cigar-puffing crook or politician, his sharkish grin marking him out as 'up to no good'. Started his career as a violinist. TV almost totally took over his acting output after 1973. Died from cancer.

*Ziegfeld Follies (released 1946). 1945: The Harvey Girls. 1946: The Show-Off. Till the Clouds Roll By. 1947: Merton of the Movies. 1955: Francis in the Navy.*

## O'CONNELL, Arthur 1908-1981

American actor with tousled light-brown hair, owlish, worried-looking face and fluffy, drooping moustache. He got nowhere very fast in films until he received a showy role in *Picnic* (1955), grabbed the chance with both hands, and suddenly became a man in demand, working steadily for 20 years. Film debut in Britain. Oscar-nominated for *Picnic* and *Anatomy of a Murder*. Died from a brain disease.

*1938: Murder in Soho (US: Murder in the Night). Freshman Year. 1940: And One Was Beautiful. *'Taint Legal. Dr Kildare Goes Home. Two Girls on Broadway (GB: Choose Your Partner). The Leather Pushers. *Bested by a Beard. *He Asked for It. 1941: Citizen Kane. Lucky Devils. 1942: Blondie's Blessed Event (GB: A Bundle of Trouble). Man from Headquarters. Fingers at the Window. Canal Zone. Shepherd of the Ozarks (GB: Susanna). Yokel Boy (GB: Hitting the Headlines). Law of the Jungle. 1944: It Happened Tomorrow. 1948: The Naked City. State of the Union (GB: The World and His Wife). One Touch of Venus. Homecoming. Open Secret. Force of Evil. Countess of Monte Cristo. 1950: Love That Brute. 1951: The Whistle at Eaton Falls (GB: Richer Than the Earth). 1955: Picnic. 1956: The Proud Ones. The Solid Gold Cadillac. The Man in the Gray Flannel Suit. Bus Stop. The Monte Carlo Story. 1957: April Love. Operation Mad Ball. The Violators. 1958: Man of the West. Voice in the Mirror. 1959: Hound Dog Man. Gidget. Anatomy of a Murder. Operation Petticoat. 1960: Cimarron. The Great Imposter. 1961: Pocketful of Miracles. A Thunder of Drums. Misty. 1962: Follow That Dream. 1963: Nightmare in the Sun. The Third Secret. Kissin' Cousins. The Seven Faces of Dr Lao. Your Cheatin' Heart. 1965: The Monkey's Uncle. The Third Day. The Great Race. 1966: Ride Beyond Vengeance. Birds Do It. The Silencers. Fantastic Voyage. A Covenant With Death. 1967: The Reluctant Astronaut. The Power. 1968: If He Hollers, Let Him Go! 1969: Seven in*

*Darkness (TV). 1970: There Was a Crooked Man. Suppose They Gave a War and Nobody Came? 1971: A Taste of Evil (TV). 1972: Ben. The Poseidon Adventure. They Only Kill Their Masters. 1973: Shootout in a One-Dog Town (TV). Wicked, Wicked. 1974: Huckleberry Finn (TV). The Hiding Place (released 1977).*

## O'CONNOR, Carroll 1922- 2001

Round-faced, curly-haired American actor of Irish extraction who began his acting career in Ireland. Returning to America, he began playing in films and TV from 1960, usually as blustering, apoplectic, bull-at-a-gate types, but his film career as a character star was all but wiped out by his role as Archie Bunker (based on Britain's Alf Garnett) which ran on television from 1971 to 1982.

*1960: Sacco and Vanzetti (TV). A Fever in the Blood. 1961: By Love Possessed. Parrish. Lad: a Dog. 1962: Lonely Are the Brave. Belle Sommers. 1963: Cleopatra. 1965: In Harm's Way. 1966: What Did You Do in the War, Daddy? Not With My Wife, You Don't! Hawaii. Warning Shot. 1967: Waterhole Number 3 (GB: Waterhole 3). Point Blank. 1968: The Devil's Brigade. For Love of Ivy. A Walk in the Night (TV). 1969: Fear No Evil (TV). Ride a Northbound Horse (TV. GB: cinemas). Death of a Gunfighter. Marlowe. 1970: Kelly's Heroes. Doctors' Wives. 1974: Law and Disorder. 1977: The Last Hurrah (TV).*

## O'CONNOR, Una
(Agnes McGlade) 1880-1959

Twittering, pinch-featured, black-haired Irish actress of pale complexion, darting eyes and birdlike movements. Starting in British films (after an early career with the Abbey Theatre, Dublin), she moved to Hollywood to recreate her stage role (Ellen Bridges) in *Cavalcade*, and was soon launched into a succession of maids, crones, chaperones and nagging wives — mostly less warm-hearted versions of characters played in Britain by Kathleen Harrison.

*1929: Dark Red Roses. 1930: Murder. To Oblige a Lady. Timbuctoo. 1933: Cavalcade. The Invisible Man. Mary Stevens MD.*

*Pleasure Cruise. 1934: The Poor Rich. The Barretts of Wimpole Street. Stingaree. All Men Are Enemies. Orient Express. Chained. *Horse Play. 1935: David Copperfield. Father Brown, Detective. The Informer. Bride of Frankenstein. Thunder in the Night. The Perfect Gentleman. 1936: The Plough and the Stars. Rose Marie. Little Lord Fauntleroy. Suzy. Lloyds of London. 1937: Personal Property. Call It A Day. 1938: The Return of the Frog. The Adventures of Robin Hood. 1939: We Are Not Alone. All Women Have Secrets. 1940: It All Came True. The Sea Hawk. Lillian Russell. He Stayed for Breakfast. Kisses for Breakfast. 1941: The Strawberry Blonde. How Green Was My Valley. Her First Beau. Three Girls About Town. 1942: Always in My Heart. Random Harvest. My Favorite Spy. This Land is Mine! 1943: Forever and a Day. Holy Matrimony. Government Girl. 1944: The Canterville Ghost. My Pal Wolf. 1945: *Whispering Walls. Christmas in Connecticut. The Bells of St Mary's. 1946: The Return of Monte Cristo (GB: Monte Cristo's Revenge). Banjo. Child of Divorce. Cluny Brown. Of Human Bondage. Unexpected Guest. 1947: Ivy. Lost Honeymoon. The Corpse Came COD. 1948: Fighting Father Dunne. The Adventures of Don Juan. 1957: Witness for the Prosecution.*

## OLIVER, Edna Mae
(E. M. Nutter) 1883-1942

One of Hollywood's invaluable horse-faced character actresses: Edna May Oliver's characters possessed arched eyebrows, a purposeful stare and a disapproving sniff, and stood no nonsense from anyone. A delight as a spinster schoolteacher sleuth in three mid-thirties whodunnits. Died from an intestinal disorder on her 59th birthday. Oscar nominee for *Drums Along the Mohawk*.

*1923: Wife in Name Only. Three O'Clock in the Morning. Icebound. Restless Wives. 1924: Manhattan. 1925: Lovers in Quarantine. The Lady Who Lied. The Lucky Devil. 1926: The American Venus. Let's Get Married. 1929: The Saturday Night Kid. 1930: Half Shot at Sunrise. Hook, Line and Sinker. 1931: Fanny Foley Herself (GB: Top of the Bill). Newly Rich (GB: Forbidden Adventure). Cimarron. Cracked Nuts. Laugh and Get Rich. 1932: Hold 'em Jail. Lost Squadron. The Conquerors. Ladies of the Jury. Penguin Pool Murder (GB: The Penguin Pool Mystery). 1933: It's Great to be Alive. The Great Jasper. Only Yesterday. Little Women. Alice in Wonderland. Ann Vickers. Strawberry Roan (GB: Flying Fury). Meet the Baron. 1934: We're Rich Again. The Poor Rich. Murder on the Blackboard. The Last Gentleman. 1935: David Copperfield. A Tale of Two Cities. No More Ladies. Murder on a Honeymoon. 1936: Romeo and Juliet. 1937: My Dear Miss Aldrich. Parnell. Rosalie. 1938: Little Miss Broadway. Paradise for Three (GB: Romance for Three). 1939: The Story of Vernon and Irene Castle. Drums Along the Mohawk. Second Fiddle. Nurse Edith Cavell. 1940: Pride and Prejudice. 1941: Lydia.*

## OLSEN, Moroni 1889-1954

Big, bluff, balding, often moustachioed American actor of immense experience with touring companies, heading his own playhouse until lured to Hollywood in 1935. Here he played dominant, larger-than-life characters (Robert E. Lee, Sam Houston, Porthos — twice — and Buffalo Bill included), as well as governors, inspectors, generals and no-nonsense fathers. In his last film, he played a pope.

*1935: The Three Musketeers. Annie Oakley. Seven Keys to Baldpate. 1936: We're Only Human. The Farmer in His Dell. Yellow Dust. Two in the Dark. Mary of Scotland. The Witness Chair. Two in Revolt. The Plough and the Stars. Mummy's Boys. Grand Jury. M'Liss.*

*1937: Adventure's End. Manhattan Merry-Go-Round (GB: Manhattan Music Box). 1938: Gold Is Where You Find It. Kentucky. Kidnapped. Submarine Patrol. 1939: Rose of Washington Square. The Three Musketeers (GB: The Singing Musketeer). Code of the Secret Service. Homicide Bureau. Allegheny Uprising (GB: The First Rebel). Susannah of the Mounties. Barricade. That's Right, You're Wrong. Dust Be My Destiny. Invisible Stripes. 1940: Brother Rat and a Baby (GB: Baby Be Good). East of the River. If I Had My Way. Brigham Young — Frontiersman (GB: Brigham Young). Santa Fé Trail. Virginia City. 1941: One Foot in Heaven. Three Sons o' Guns. Dive Bomber. Life with Henry. Dangerously They Live. 1942: Sundown Jim. Reunion/Reunion in France (GB: Mademoiselle France). Nazi Agent. My Favorite Spy. Mrs Wiggs of the Cabbage Patch. The Glass Key. Air Force. 1943: Mission to Moscow. The Song of Bernadette. Ali Baba and the 40 Thieves. 1944: Roger Touhy, Gangster (GB: The Last Gangster). Buffalo Bill. Cobra Woman. 1945: Week-End at the Waldorf. Pride of the Marines (GB: Forever in Love). Don't Fence Me In. Mildred Pierce. Behind City Lights. 1946: A Night in Paradise. Boys' Ranch. The Walls Came Tumbling Down. Notorious. From This Day Forward. The Strange Woman. 1947: The Beginning or the End? That Hagen Girl. Possessed. Life With Father. Black Gold. High Wall. The Long Night. Call Northside 777. 1948: Up in Central Park. Command Decision. 1949: The Fountainhead. Samson and Delilah. Task Force. 1950: Father of the Bride. 1951: No Questions Asked. Father's Little Dividend. Payment on Demand. Submarine Command. At Sword's Point (GB: Sons of the Musketeers). 1952: The Washington Story (GB: Target for Scandal). Lone Star. 1953: Marry Me Again. So This Is Love (GB: The Grace Moore Story). 1954: The Long, Long Trailer. Sign of the Pagan.*

## O'NEILL, Henry 1891-1961

Playing figures of authority must have come as second nature to this distinguished, thoughtful-looking American actor whose fair hair went grey early in his career. After 20 years of playing judges, lawyers, officers and doctors in more than

150 films, he probably found it quite a relief to play the occasional murder suspect or villain. But his quiet dignity usually decreed he would be on the right side of the law.

*1930: *The Strong Arm. 1933: The World Changes. I Loved a Woman. Lady Killer. Ever in My Heart. The Kennel Murder Case. From Headquarters. The House on 56th Street. Footlight Parade. 1934: Side Streets (GB: Woman in Her Thirties). Fog Over Frisco. Murder in the Clouds. The Key. Wonder Bar. Journal of a Crime. Twenty Million Sweethearts. Upper World. The Personality Kid/Information, Please. The Man With Two Faces. Gentlemen Are Born. The Secret Bride (GB: Concealment). Fashions/Fashions of 1934. 1934: Flirtation Walk. Massacre. Bedside. I've Got Your Number. The Big Shakedown. Now I'll Tell (GB: While New York Sleeps). Madame Du Barry. Midnight Alibi. Big-Hearted Herbert. Midnight. 1935: The Florentine Dagger. Living on Velvet. The Man Who Reclaimed His Head. While the Patient Slept. Dinky. Alias Mary Dow. Oil for the Lamps of China. The Case of the Lucky Legs. Dr Socrates. Sweet Music. Bordertown. The Great Hotel Murder. Black Fury. Bright Lights (GB: Funny Face). Stranded. We're in the Money. Special Agent. 1936: The Story of Louis Pasteur. Freshman Love (GB: Rhythm on the River). The Walking Dead. Two Against the World (GB: The Case of Mrs Pembrook). The Golden Arrow. The White Angel. Rainbow on the River. Boulder Dam. Road Gang (GB: Injustice). Bullets or Ballots. The Big Noise (GB: Modern Madness). Anthony Adverse. Draegerman Courage (GB: The Cave-In). 1937: The Go-Getter. The Great O'Malley. Mr Dodd Takes the Air. First Lady. Wells Fargo. Marked Woman. The Green Light. The Life of Emile Zola. The Singing Marine. The Great Garrick. Submarine D-1. 1938: Jezebel. The Amazing Dr Clitterhouse. Yellow Jack. The Chaser. Brother Rat. Racket Busters. Gold Is Where You Find It. White Banners. Girls on Probation. 1939: Confessions of a Nazi Spy. Torchy Blane in Chinatown. Lucky Night. Angels Wash Their Faces. Dodge City. Juarez. Four Wives. Wings of the Navy. *Young America Flies. The Man Who Dared. Everybody's Hobby. Invisible Stripes. 1940: A Child Is Born. Calling Philo Vance. Castle on the Hudson (GB: Years Without Days). 'Til We Meet Again. Santa Fé Trail. Knute Rockne — All American (GB: A Modern Hero). They Drive by Night (GB: The Road to Frisco). Dr Ehrlich's Magic Bullet (GB: The Story of Dr Ehrlich's Magic Bullet). The Fighting 69th. Money and the Woman. 1941: The Bugle Sounds. Honky Tonk. Men of Boys' Town. Blossoms in the Dust. Down in San Diego. Shadow of the Thin Man. Billy The Kid. The Trial of Mary Dugan. The Get-Away. Whistling in the Dark. Johnny Eager. 1942: White Cargo. Tortilla Flat. This Time for Keeps. Stand By for Action! (GB: Cargo of Innocents). Born to Sing. 1943: Dr Gillespie's Criminal Case (GB: Crazy to Kill). Whistling in Brooklyn. Air Raid Wardens. The Human*

Comedy. Best Foot Forward. Girl Crazy. The Heavenly Body. Lost Angel. A Guy Named Joe. 1944: Barbary Coast Gent. *Dark Shadows. Airship Squadron No.4. Rationing. Two Girls and a Sailor. Nothing But Trouble. 1945: This Man's Navy. Keep Your Powder Dry. Dangerous Partners. Anchors Aweigh. 1946: Three Wise Fools. The Virginian. Little Mr Jim. The Green Years. Bad Bascomb. The Hoodlum Saint. 1947: The Beginning or the End? This Time for Keeps. 1948: The Return of October (GB: A Date With Destiny). Leather Gloves (GB: Loser Takes All). Alias Nick Beal (GB: The Contact Man). Holiday Affair. You're My Everything. Strange Bargain. The Reckless Moment. 1950: The Flying Missile. Convicted. The Second Woman (GB: Ellen). No Man of Her Own. The Milkman. 1951: The People Against O'Hara. The Family Secret. Scandal Sheet (GB: The Dark Page). 1952: Scarlet Angel. 1953: The Sun Shines Bright. 1955: Untamed. 1957: The Wings of Eagles.

**OSCAR, Henry** (H. O. Wale) 1891-1969
Light-haired British actor, usually seen in films in meek, wheedling or vindictive 'subservient' roles. His extraordinarily varied and prolific career outside the cinema included touring British camps in World War I, staging numerous plays from the 1930s to the 1950s, being the first actor to receive a BBC Radio contract (1922), writing books, directing in repertory, being an active actors' trade unionist from 1919, becoming drama director of ENSA in World War II, playing more than 100 TV and theatrical roles and earning a reputation as a painter. An excellent sardonic villain for the cinema when the right part came along.

1932: After Dark. 1933: I Was a Spy. 1934: Red Ensign (US: Strike!). Brides to Be. The Man Who Knew Too Much. 1935: Me and Marlborough. The Tunnel (US: Transatlantic Tunnel). Sexton Blake and the Bearded Doctor. The Case of Gabriel Perry. Father O'Flynn. Night Mail. 1936: The Man Behind the Mask. Seven Sinners (US: Doomed Cargo). Dishonour Bright. Love in Exile. No Escape. Spy of Napoleon. Fire Over England. 1937: Sensation. Who Killed John Savage? Dark Journey.

The Academy Decides. The Return of the Scarlet Pimpernel. 1938: Luck of the Navy (US: North Sea Patrol). The Terror. Black Limelight. 1939: Hell's Cargo (US: Dangerous Cargo). Dead Man's Shoes. On the Night of the Fire (US: The Fugitive). The Four Feathers. The Saint in London. Spies of the Air. 1940: Two for Danger. The Flying Squad. Tilly of Bloomsbury. Mein Kampf My Crimes. 1941: The Seventh Survivor. Hatter's Castle. Atlantic Ferry (US: Sons of the Sea). Penn of Pennsylvania (US: The Courageous Mr Penn). 1942: The Day Will Dawn (US: The Avengers). Squadron Leader X. 1947: They Made Me a Fugitive (US: I Became a Criminal). The Upturned Glass. Mrs Fitzherbert. 1948: The Idol of Paris. Bonnie Prince Charlie. House of Darkness. It Happened in Soho. The Greed of William Hart. The Bad Lord Byron. 1949: The Man from Yesterday. Which Will You Have? (US: Barabbas the Robber). 1950: Prelude to Fame. The Black Rose. 1953: Martin Luther. Knights of The Round Table. 1954: *Men at Work. Diplomatic Passport. Beau Brummell. Three Cases of Murder. 1955: Portrait of Alison (US: Postmark for Danger). It's a Great Day. 1956: Private's Progress. 1957: The Little Hut. 1958: The Spaniard's Curse. The Secret Man. 1959: Beyond This Place (US: Web of Evidence). 1960: Oscar Wilde. Brides of Dracula. Foxhole in Cairo. 1962: Lawrence of Arabia. 1963: The Long Ships. 1964: Murder Ahoy. 1965: City Under the Sea (US: War Gods of the Deep).

**O'SHEA, Milo** 1925-
Black-browed, smiling-faced Irish actor, often in slightly eccentric roles. On stage in Dublin at 10, he was 'discovered' by John Gielgud, and eventually became a popular British TV star, although efforts to make him a star in movies, as opposed to a top character player, never quite gelled. Still busy in the theatre, often in ingratiating roles.

1951: Talk of a Million (US: You Can't Beat the Irish). 1959: This Other Eden. 1962: Mrs Gibbons' Boys. 1963: Carry On Cabby. 1964: *Down Boy! Never Put It in Writing. 1967: Ulysses. Barbarella. 1968: Romeo and Juliet. 1969: The Adding Machine. 1970: Paddy.

The Angel Levine. Loot. 1971: Sacco and Vanzetti. 1972: The Love Ban (originally It's a Two-Foot-Six-Inch-Above-the-Ground-World). 1973: The Hebrew Lesson. And No One Could Save Her (TV). Theatre of Blood. Steptoe and Son Ride Again. 1974: Digby the Biggest Dog in the World. QB VII (TV). Percy's Progress (US: It's Not the Size That Counts). 1977: Peter Lundy and the Medicine Hat Stallion (TV). 1979: Arabian Adventure. The Pilot. 1981: Portrait of a Rebel (TV). 1982: The Verdict. 1985: The Purple Rose of Cairo.

**OSMOND, Hal** 1919-1959
Short, small-nosed, dark-haired, narrow-eyed, rat-like British supporting actor who played cloth-capped criminals, small-time safecrackers and the like. One would have expected more comedy roles in his 60-film career, which was entirely packed into the years 1948 to 1959 before his early death.

1948: Here Come the Huggetts. Miranda. Once Upon a Dream. Quartet. It's Not Cricket. Vote for Huggett. A Boy, a Girl and a Bike. 1949: Helter Skelter. Diamond City. Marry Me! The Spider and the Fly. Stop Press Girl. 1950: Double Confession. Last Holiday. There Is Another Sun (US: Wall of Death). Treasure Island. Your Witness (US: Eye Witness). 1951: Hell Is Sold Out. Death of an Angel. 1952: The Story of Robin Hood and His Merrie Men. The Happy Family (US: Mr Lord Says No). Stolen Face. The Brave Don't Cry. Top Secret (US: Mr Potts Goes to Moscow). The Net (US: Project M7). 1953: The Steel Key. The Dog and the Diamonds. Love in Pawn. The Sword and the Rose. Rob Roy the Highland Rogue. Three Steps to the Gallows (released 1955. US: White Fire). You Know What Sailors Are. 1954: Forbidden Cargo. To Dorothy A Son (US: Cash on Delivery). 1955: Value for Money. Simon and Laura. You Can't Escape. 1956: Bond of Fear. *Dick Turpin—Highwayman. It's A Wonderful World. The Last Man to Hang? Loser Takes All. Three Men in a Boat. 1957: The Depraved. High Flight. Murder Reported. The Truth About Women. 1958: Blood of the Vampire. The Great Van Robbery. Innocent Meeting. Links of Justice. No Safety Ahead. Tread Softly, Stranger. 1959: Crash Drive.

*Top Floor Girl. Upstairs and Downstairs. Jack the Ripper. Web of Suspicion.*

**OTTIANO, Rafaela** 1894-1942
Dark-haired, sharp-faced, pop-eyed Italian actress who came to America and played dangerously hysterical characters. Her menials, from maids to housekeepers, were not to be relied upon, and she was a formidable adversary for Mae West in *She Done Him Wrong.* Died from a heart attack.

*1924: The Law and the Lady. 1925: Married? 1932: Washington Masquerade (GB: Mad Masquerade). As You Desire Me. Grand Hotel. 1933: Her Man. Bondage. She Done Him Wrong. Female. Ann Vickers. 1934: A Lost Lady (GB: Courageous). Mandalay. All Men Are Enemies. The Last Gentleman. Great Expectations. 1935: Lottery Lover. Remember Last Night? Enchanted April. The Florentine Dagger. Curly Top. One Frightened Night. Crime and Punishment. 1936: Riffraff. Anthony Adverse. That Girl from Paris. Devil Doll. Mad Holiday. We're Only Human. 1937: Seventh Heaven. Maytime. The League of Frightened Men. 1938: I'll Give a Million. Suez. 1939: Paris Honeymoon. 1940: Victory. The Long Voyage Home. 1941: Topper Returns. 1942: The Adventures of Martin Eden. I Married an Angel.*

**OULTON, Brian** 1908- *1992*
Tallish, dark-haired, hesitant, dubious-looking British actor, often as prim-and-

proper, milk-and-water, easily-scandalized characters. Primarily a man of the theatre (for which he also wrote and directed), he was at first seen in quasi-romantic leads, but soon settled into (mainly comic) character roles for the post-war British cinema.

*1938: Too Many Husbands. 1948: Miranda. It's Not Cricket. Panic at Madame Tussaud's. Warning to Wantons. 1949: The Huggetts Abroad. Helter Skelter. Paper Orchid. 1950: Last Holiday. 1951: Young Wives' Tale. Quo Vadis? 1952: Castle in the Air. 1953: Will Any Gentleman?... The Dog and the Diamonds. The Million Pound Note (US: Man With a Million). 1954: Devil on Horseback. The Crowded Day. Doctor in the House. 1955: The Reluctant Bride (US: Two Grooms for a Bride). The Deep Blue Sea. The Man Who Never Was. 1956: Private's Progress. Charley Moon. Brothers in Law. The Good Companions. 1957: Happy Is the Bride! 1958: The Spaniard's Curse. The Silent Enemy. 1959: Carry On Nurse. The Devil's Disciple. The Thirty-Nine Steps. I'm All Right, Jack. 1960: There Was a Crooked Man. The Bulldog Breed. Carry On Constable. A French Mistress. No Kidding (US: Beware of Children). Suspect (US: The Risk). 1961: The Damned (US: These Are the Damned). No Love for Johnnie. Very Important Person (US: A Coming-Out Party). Raising the Wind (US: Roommates). 1962: Kiss of the Vampire. Hair of the Dog. The Iron Maiden (US: The Swingin' Maiden). Jigsaw. 1964: Carry On Cleo. Devils of Darkness. 1965: The Intelligence Men. 1969: Carry On Camping. Some Will, Some Won't. 1971: On the Buses. Mr Forbush and the Penguins (US: Cry of the Penguins). 1972: Ooh... You Are Awful (US: Get Charlie Tully). 1982: Gandhi. 1985: Young Sherlock Holmes.*

**OUSPENSKAYA, Maria** 1876-1949
Wizened, beetle-faced, tiny Russian actress who came to America in the early 1930s to set up an acting school in New York. Despite playing a wide range of diminutive dynamos of varying nationalities (she was twice Oscar-nominated, in *Dodsworth* and *Love Affair*), film buffs remember her best as the gypsy woman who teaches poor Lon

Chaney the werewolf rhyme in *The Wolf Man.* Tragically burned to death in her Los Angeles apartment.

*1915: Sverchok na Pechi/The Cricket on the Hearth. 1916: Nichtozniye/Worthless. 1917: Dr Torpokov. 1918: Zazhivo Pogrebenni/Buried Alive. 1923: Khveska. 1929: Tanka Traktirschitsa. Protiv Otsa. 1936: Dodsworth. 1937: Conquest (GB: Marie Walewska). 1939: Love Affair. The Rains Came. Judge Hardy and Son. 1940: Dance, Girl, Dance. Dr Ehrlich's Magic Bullet (GB: The Story of Dr Ehrlich's Magic Bullet). The Mortal Storm. Waterloo Bridge. Beyond Tomorrow. The Man I Married. 1941: The Shanghai Gesture. The Wolf Man. Kings Row. 1942: The Mystery of Marie Roget. 1943: Frankenstein Meets the Wolf Man. 1945: Tarzan and the Amazons. 1946: I've Always Loved You. 1947: Wyoming. 1949: A Kiss in the Dark.*

**OVERMAN, Lynne** 1887-1943
Grizzled, flat-faced Hollywood veteran (once a jockey) who, after many years of struggle in the theatre, made a few early sound shorts, and then brought his dry wit and even drier, mulish voice to character roles, usually as friendly, fast-talking types from lower-class background. Enjoyed 10 good film years before his death from a heart attack.

*1929: *Kisses. 1930: *Five Minutes from the Station. *Horseshoes. *A Sure Cure. 1933: *Poor Fish. 1934: *Around the Clock. Broadway Bill (GB: Strictly Confidential). Little Miss Marker (GB: Girl in Pawn). The Great Flirtation. Midnight. You Belong to Me. Enter Madame! She Loves Me Not. 1935: Men Without Names. Rumba. Paris in Spring (GB: Paris Love Song). Two for Tonight. 1936: Three Married Men. Poppy. Yours for the Asking. The Jungle Princess. Collegiate (GB: The Charm School). 1937: *Nobody's Baby. Blonde Trouble. Murder Goes to College. Hotel Haywire. True Confession. Partners in Crime. Don't Tell the Wife. Wild Money. Night Club Scandal. 1938: Hunted Men. The Big Broadcast of 1938. Sons of the Legion. Ride a Crooked Mile (GB: Escape from Yesterday). Persons in Hiding. Her Jungle Love. Spawn of the North. Men With Wings. 1939: Union*

Pacific. Death of a Champion. 1940: Safari. Edison the Man. Typhoon. North West Mounted Police. 1941: New York Town. Aloma of the South Seas. Caught in the Draft. There's Magic in Music. 1942: The Forest Rangers. Roxie Hart. Star Spangled Rhythm. Reap the Wild Wind. Silver Queen. 1943: Dixie. The Desert Song.

**OWEN, Bill** (William Rowbotham) 1914-
Short, dark, pale-faced, bright-eyed British character actor who started in show business as a holiday camp entertainer, turned to acting in films after World War II as forthright cockney types and created a series of real-life people, stamped with the brightness of his own personality, that almost elevated him to stardom in the mid 1950s. Very much a part of the British cinema of that time: less effective after 1960.

1945: †*Song of the People. †The Way to the Stars (US: Johnny in the Clouds). †Perfect Strangers (US: Vacation from Marriage). 1946: †School for Secrets. Daybreak. 1947: †Dancing with Crime. When the Bough Breaks. Holiday Camp. Easy Money. 1948: Trouble in the Air. My Brother's Keeper. The Weaker Sex. Once a Jolly Swagman (US: Maniacs on Wheels). 1949: Trottie True (US: Gay Lady). Diamond City. The Girl Who Couldn't Quite. 1951: Hotel Sahara. 1952: The Story of Robin Hood and his Merrie Men. There Was a Young Lady. 1953: The Square Ring. A Day to Remember. Thought to Kill. 1954: The Rainbow Jacket. 1955: The Ship That Died of Shame (US: PT Raiders). 1956: Not So Dusty. 1957: Davy. 1958: Carve Her Name with Pride. Carry on Sergeant. 1959: Carry on Nurse. The Shakedown. 1961: The Hellfire Club. On the Fiddle (US: Operation Snafu). Carry on Regardless. 1963: Carry on Cabby. 1964: The Secret of Blood Island. 1966: Georgy Girl. The Fighting Prince of Donegal. 1968: Headline Hunters. 1969: Mischief. 1972: Kadoyng. 1973: O Lucky Man! 1974: In Celebration. 1975: Smurfs and the Magic Flute (voice only). 1977: The Comeback. 1984: Laughterhouse. 1985: Uncle of the Bride (TV).

†As Bill Rowbotham

**PAIVA, Nestor** 1905-1966
Bald, bushy-browed American actor, built like a barn door, with square features, staring eyes and inverted Joe E. Brown mouth. Mostly in aggressive roles, his long radio experience gave him an ear for accents that he quickly turned to his advantage on arriving in Hollywood in 1938. Playing Russians, Mexicans, Red Indians, Arabs, South Americans, Spaniards, Italians and half-castes in general, he soon became one of the cinema's 'familiar faces' to whom it was most difficult to pin a name.

1938: Prison Train. Ride a Crooked Mile (GB: Escape from Yesterday). 1939: Midnight. Another Thin Man. Bachelor Mother. Union Pacific. The Magnificent Fraud. Beau Geste. 1940: Dark Streets of Cairo. The Primrose Path. The Devil's Pipeline. Phantom Raiders. The Sea Hawk. They Knew What They Wanted. North West Mounted Police. He Stayed for Breakfast. Santa Fé Trail. Arise, My Love. The Marines Fly High. 1941: Hold Back the Dawn. Hold That Ghost! Tall, Dark and Handsome. Meet Boston Blackie. Pot o' Gold (GB: The Golden Hour). The Kid from Kansas. Wild Geese Calling. Johnny Eager. Rise and Shine. Flame of New Orleans. 1942: Broadway. Reap the Wild Wind. Road to Morocco. The Lady Has Plans. Fly-by-Night. Flying Tigers. Jail House Blues. The Girl from Alaska. Timber. Pittsburgh. King of the Mounties (serial). The Hard Way. 1943: The Dancing Masters. The Crystal Ball. Rhythm of the Islands. The Desert Song. The Fallen Sparrow. The Song of Bernadette. Tornado. Background to Danger. True to Life. 1944: The Purple Heart. Kismet. Tampico. Shine On, Harvest Moon. The Falcon in Mexico. 1945: Along the Navajo Trail. A Medal for Benny. The Southerner. Nob Hill. Salome, Where She Danced. Cornered. The Trouble With Women (released 1947). A Thousand and One Nights. Fear. Road to Utopia. 1946: Humoresque. Suspense. Sensation Hunters. The Well-Groomed Bride. The Last Crooked Mile. Badman's Territory. 1947: Ramrod. Carnival in Costa Rica. Shoot to Kill. A Likely Story. Robin Hood of Monterey. The Lone Wolf in Mexico. Road to Rio. Angels' Alley. 1948: Adventures of Casanova. Mr Reckless. The Paleface. Joan of Arc. Mr Blandings Builds

His Dream House. Alias Nick Beal (GB: The Contact Man). 1949: Bride of Vengeance. Mighty Joe Young. Follow Me Quietly. Oh, You Beautiful Doll. Young Man With a Horn (GB: Young Man of Music). The Inspector General. 1950: The Desert Hawk. I Was a Shoplifter. The Great Caruso. 1951: Flame of Stamboul. Jim Thorpe —All American (GB: Man of Bronze). A Millionaire for Christy. The Lady Pays Off. Double Dynamite. My Favorite Spy. On Dangerous Ground. 1952: Phone Call from a Stranger. April in Paris. Split Second. Five Fingers. Viva Zapata! With a Song in My Heart. South Pacific Trail. Mara Maru. The Fabulous Senorita. 1953: The Bandits of Corsica (GB: Return of the Corsican Brothers). Prisoners of the Casbah. Killer Ape. Jivaro (GB: Lost Treasure of the Amazon). Casanova's Big Night. Call Me Madam. 1954: Thunder Pass. Four Guns to the Border. The Cowboy. The Creature from the Black Lagoon. The Desperado. 1955: New York Confidential. Hell on Frisco Bay. Tarantula! Revenge of the Creature. All That Heaven Allows. 1956: Comanche. The Mole People. Ride the High Iron. The Wild Party. Scandal Inc. 1957: The Guns of Fort Petticoat. Les Girls. 10,000 Bedrooms. The Lady Takes a Flyer. 1958: The Deep Six. Outcasts of the City. The Left-Handed Gun. The Case Against Brooklyn. 1959: The Nine Lives of Elfego Baca (TV. GB: cinemas). Pier 5—Havana. Vice Raid. Alias Jesse James. 1960: The Purple Gang. Can-Can. Frontier Uprising. 1961: The Four Horsemen of the Apocalypse. 1962: The Three Stooges in Orbit. Girls! Girls! Girls! The Wild Westerners. California. 1964: Madman of Mandoras. Ballad of a Gunfighter. 1965: Jesse James Meets Frankenstein's Daughter. 1966: The Spirit Is Willing. Let's Kill Uncle.

**PALLETTE, Eugene** 1889-1954
Squat, dark, gravel-voiced American actor, who looked like some huge black beetle, but for all his girth was almost always dressed in immaculately cut suits. A busy man from 1915 onwards, but especially popular as a character actor of the 1930s, usually as fathers or figures of authority who proved to be neither as dumb nor as grouchy as they looked.

1913: The Tattooed Arm. When Jim Returned. Broken Nose Bailey. Monroe. 1914: The Peach Brand. The Beat of the Year. *The Gunman. The Sheriff's Prisoner. The Horse Wranglers. The Burden. On the Border. 1915: The Birth of a Nation. The Story of a Story. After 20 Years. The Highbinders. The Death Doll. The Penalty. When Love is Mocked. Isle of Content. How Hazel Got Even. Spell of the Poppy. The Emerald Brooch. The Ever-Living Isles. The Scarlet Lady. 1916: Hell-to-Pay Austin. Intolerance. Gretchen the Greenhorn. Children in the House. Whispering Smith. His Guardian Angel. Going Straight. Sunshine Dad. Runaway Freight. Diamond in the Rough. 1917: The Purple Scar. Lonesome Chap. The Winning of Sally Temple. The Victim. Heir of

ABOVE Nestor **Paiva** (balding, second from left) finds himself in heavy company in this scene from *Johnny Eager* (1942). His co-players include Lana Turner, Robert Taylor and Van Heflin (who won an Oscar for the film)

BELOW Smoothly-clad as ever, Eugene **Pallette** (left) holds court – indeed it was difficult for him not to – in *The Ghost Goes West* (1935) with Robert Donat (right) and Herbert Lomas (*qv*)

the Ages. Ghost House. The Bond Between. The Marcellini Millions. World Apart. A Man's Man. Each of His Kind. 1918: His Robe of Honor. Madame Who. Tarzan of the Apes. Vivette. The Turn of a Card. Breakers Ahead. No Man's Land. 1919: Be a Little Sport. The Amateur Adventuress. Fair and Warmer. Words and Music By... 1920: Terror Island. Alias Jimmy Valentine. Parlor, Bedroom and Bath. 1921: The Three Musketeers. Fine Feathers. 1922: Without Compromise. Two Kinds of Women. 1923: The Ten Commandments. Hell's Hole. A Man's Man. To the Last Man. North of Hudson Bay. 1924: The Wolf Man. The Cyclone Rider. The Galloping Fish. Wandering Husbands. 1925: The Light of Western Stars. Ranger of the Big Pines. Without Mercy. Wild Horse Mesa. 1926: Mantrap. Desert Valley. Rocking Moon. Whispering Smith (remake). Yankee Senor. The Fighting Edge. Whispering Canyon. 1927: Moulders of Men. Chicago. *Sugar Daddies. *The Second Hundred Years. *Battle of the Century. 1928: *Don't Be Jealous. *How's Your Stock? Out of the Ruins. The Good-bye Kiss. The Red Mark. Lights of New York. His Private Life. 1929: The Greene Murder Case. The Canary Murder Case. The Studio Murder Mystery. Pointed Heels. The Dummy. The Love Parade. The Virginian. 1930: Follow Thru. *The Dancing Instructor. The Kibitzer (GB: The Busybody). Slightly Scarlet. The Border Legion. Sea Legs. Santa Fé Trail. The Benson Murder Case. The Sea God. Let's Go Native. Men Are Like That. Paramount on Parade. Playboy of Paris. 1931: Gun Smoke. Fighting Caravans. The Adventures of Huckleberry Finn. Dude Ranch. Girls About Town. *It Pays to Advertise. 1932: Tom Brown of Culver. Shanghai Express. Strangers of the Evening. Wild Girl (GB: Salomy Jane). Dancers in the Dark. Thunder Below. The Night Mayor. *Off His Base. *A Hockey Hick (GB: Ice Hockey Hick). *The Stolen Jools (GB: The Slippery Pearls). The Half-Naked Truth. *The Pig Boat. 1933: Storm at Daybreak. Made on Broadway (GB: The Girl I Made). Mr Skitch. From Headquarters. Hell Below. Shanghai Madness. The Kennel Murder Case. Phantom Fame. *Meet the Champ. *One Awful Night. 1934: Friends of Mr Sweeney. Caravan. The Dragon Murder Case. One Exciting Adventure. Cross Country Cruise. I've Got Your Number. Strictly Dynamite. *News Hounds. 1935: Baby Face Harrington (GB: Baby Face). Steamboat 'round the Bend. Bordertown. Black Sheep. All the King's Horses. The Ghost Goes West. 1936: The Golden Arrow. My Man Godfrey. Stowaway. Easy to Take. Dishonour Bright. The Luckiest Girl in the World. 1937: Song of the City. Topper. Clarence. One Hundred Men and a Girl. She Had to Eat. The Crime Nobody Saw. 1938: The Adventures of Robin Hood. There Goes My Heart. 1939: First Love. Wife, Husband and Friend. Mr Smith Goes to Washington. 1940: Sandy is a Lady. Young Tom Edison. He Stayed for Breakfast. It's a Date. A Little Bit of Heaven. The Mark of Zorro. 1941:

Unfinished Business. Ride, Kelly, Ride. World Premiere. The Bride Came COD. The Lady Eve. Appointment for Love. Swamp Water. (GB: The Man Who Came Back). 1942: Almost Married. The Male Animal. Are Husbands Necessary? Tales of Manhattan. The Big Street. Lady in a Jam. The Forest Rangers. Silver Queen. 1943: It Ain't Hay (GB: Money for Jam). The Gang's All Here (GB: The Girls He Left Behind). The Kansan (GB: Wagon Wheels). Slightly Dangerous. Heaven Can Wait. 1944: Pin-Up Girl. In the Meantime, Darling. Heavenly Days. Step Lively. Sensations of 1945. The Laramie Trail. Lake Placid Serenade. 1945: The Cheaters. 1946: Suspense. In Old Sacramento. 1948: Silver River.

**PANGBORN, Franklin** 1893-1958
Pangborn was the dark-haired American character comedian who always looked as though he had detected a bad smell in the room, and frequently behaved as if whatever he was doing was beneath him. The height of prissiness as hotel manager, banker, dress-shop manager or floorwalker, he had his routine to perfection, and could make audiences laugh even in the midst of a bad film. Unbelievably, in his early theatrical days, he was once typed as a villain.

1926: Exit Smiling. 1927: Getting Gertie's Garter. The Cradle Snatchers. My Friend from India. The Rejuvenation of Aunt Mary. The Night Bridge. The Girl in the Pullman. Fingerprints. 1928: On Trial. Blonde for a Night. The Rush Hour. 1929: The Sap. *The Crazy Nut. Watch Out. Lady of the Pavements (GB: Lady of the Night). *Who's the Boss? *Happy Birthday. 1930: Not So Dumb. A Lady Surrenders (GB: Blind Wives). Cheer Up and Smile. Her Man. *The Doctor's Wife. *Poor Aubrey. *The Chumps. *Reno or Bust. 1931: A Woman of Experience. *Against the Rules. *Rough House Rhythm. *Torchy Passes the Buck. 1932: A Fool's Advice. *Torchy Raises the Auntie. *Doctor's Orders. *Tee for Two. *Torchy's Two Toots. *Torchy's Busy Day. *The Giddy Age. *Torchy Turns the Trick. *Torchy's Night Cap. The Half-Naked Truth. *Torchy's Vocation. *What Price, Taxi? *The Candid Camera. *Torchy Rolls His Own. Meet the Mayor (released 1938).

1933: Professional Sweetheart (GB: Imaginary Sweetheart). International House. Flying Down to Rio. The Important Witness. Design for Living. Headline Shooters (GB: Evidence in Camera). Only Yesterday. *Torchy Turns Turtle. *Torchy's Loud Spooker. *Blue of the Night. *Easy on the Eyes. *Wild Poses. *Art in the Raw. *Torchy's Kitty Coup. Bed of Roses. 1934: Strictly Dynamite. Manhattan Love Song. Many Happy Returns. Stand Up and Cheer. Imitation of Life. That's Gratitude. Young and Beautiful. Unknown Blonde. King Kelly of the USA. Cockeyed Cavaliers. College Rhythm. 1935: $1,000 a Minute. Headline Woman (GB: The Woman in the Case). Eight Bells. Flirtation. Tomorrow's Youth. She Couldn't Take It. *The Captain Hits the Ceiling. *Ye Old Saw Mill. 1936: Three Smart Girls. Mr Deeds Goes to Town. Don't Gamble with Love. To Mary—With Love. Hats Off. Doughnuts and Society (GB: Stepping into Society). The Luckiest Girl in the World. My Man Godfrey. The Mandarin Mystery. Tango. 1937: *Bad Housekeeping. *Bridal Griefs. They Wanted to Marry. Step Lively, Jeeves. She Had to Eat. It Happened in Hollywood. High Hat. Easy Living. We Have Our Moments. When Love Is Young. Dangerous Number. Hotel Haywire. All Over Town. Stage Door. I'll Take Romance. The Lady Escapes. Swing High, Swing Low. Danger! Love at Work. Turn Off the Moon. Thrill of a Lifetime. A Star Is Born. She's Dangerous. Dangerous Holiday. The Life of the Party. Living on Love. 1938: Rebecca of Sunnybrook Farm. Vivacious Lady. Always Goodbye. Just Around the Corner. Bluebeard's Eighth Wife. Love on Toast. Topper Takes a Trip. The Girl Downstairs. She Married an Artist. It's All Yours. Three Blind Mice. Joy of Living. Carefree. Dr Rhythm. Mad About Music. Four's a Crowd. 1939: Fifth Avenue Girl. Broadway Serenade. 1940: Public Deb. No.1. The Bank Dick (GB: The Bank Detective). Turnabout. The Villain Still Pursued Her. Christmas in July. Spring Parade. Hit Parade of 1941. 1941: Flame of New Orleans. Where Did You Get That Girl? Bachelor Daddy. Tillie the Toiler. A Girl, a Guy and a Gob (GB: The Navy Steps Out). Never Give a Sucker an Even Break (GB: What a Man!). Week-End for Three. Mr District Attorney in the Carter Case (GB: The Carter Case). Sullivan's Travels. Obliging Young Lady. Sandy Steps Out. 1942: Moonlight Masquerade. George Washington Slept Here. Now, Voyager. Call Out the Marines. Strictly in the Groove. What's Cookin'? (GB: Wake Up and Dream). The Palm Beach Story. 1943: Reveille With Beverly. Honeymoon Lodge. His Butler's Sister. Never a Dull Moment. Stage Door Canteen. Two Weeks to Live. Crazy House. Holy Matrimony. *Slick Chick. The Great Moment. 1944: Hail the Conquering Hero. The Reckless Age. Allergic to Love. My Best Gal. 1945: The Horn Blows at Midnight. *Hollywood Victory Caravan. Hollywood and Vine (GB: Daisy (the Dog) Goes Hollywood). See My Lawyer. Tell It to a Star. You Came Along. 1946: Lover Come Back. Two Guys *from Milwaukee (GB: Royal Flush). The Sin of Harold Diddlebock (later and GB: Mad Wednesday). I'll Be Yours. 1947: Calendar Girl. Addio Mimi (GB and US: Her Wonderful Lie). 1948: Romance on the High Seas (GB: It's Magic). 1949: Down Memory Lane. My Dream Is Yours. 1957: The Story of Mankind. Oh, Men! Oh, Women!*

### PARKE, (J.) MacDonald 1891-1960

Rotund, bald, bespectacled, back-slapping American-born actor of Scots-Canadian parentage whose salty tones made him the Walter Brennan-cum-Eugene Pallette of British pictures. He was even better known on TV and radio, winning nationwide popularity in the latter medium in the western series *Riders of the Range*. In films he played mostly gullible millionaire Americans being sold imaginary assets.

*1939: Shipyard Sally. 1943: Candlelight in Algeria. 1947: Teheran (US: The Plot To Kill Roosevelt). 1948: No Orchids for Miss Blandish. The Fool and the Princess. 1950: Dangerous Assignment. Night and the City. 1951: A Tale of Five Cities (US: A Tale of Five Women). Saturday Island (US: Island of Desire). 1952: Penny Princess. Babes in Baghdad. The Man Who Watched Trains Go By (US: Paris Express). 1953: Is You Honeymoon Really Necessary? Innocents in Paris. 1954: The Good Die Young. The Red Dress. 1955: Summer Madness (US: Summertime). 1956: The March Hare. 1957: Beyond Mombasa. 1958: I Was Monty's Double (US: Monty's Double). 1959: A Touch of Larceny. The Battle of the Sexes. The Mouse That Roared. 1960: Never Take Sweets from a Stranger (US: Never Take Candy from a Stranger).*

### PARNELL, Emory 1894-1979

Rotund American actor with receding brown hair, a big demon imp of a man with a neck that stretched from the point of his jaw to his chest, and just as likely to turn up in a lunatic comedy part or as a prison warden. He also played a large number of policemen—frequently baffled by the hero or the case. A former vaudevillian, he made scores of Hollywood films before venturing into television in the 1950s, becoming familiar to viewers as the bartender in the

long-running western series *Lawman*. Died from a heart attack.

*1938: Call of the Yukon. Doctor Rhythm. Arson Racket Squad. King of Alcatraz (GB: King of the Alcatraz). I Am the Law. The Mad Miss Manton. Girls on Probation. Sweethearts. Angels With Dirty Faces. 1939: Pacific Liner. The Star Maker. You Can't Get Away With Murder. *Tiny Troubles. At the Circus. One Hour to Live. Winter Carnival. Little Accident. The House of Fear. St Louis Blues. They Shall Have Music (GB: Melody of Youth). The Roaring Twenties. I Stole a Million. East Side of Heaven. Off the Record. Union Pacific. Let Freedom Ring. Invisible Stripes. 1940: Stranger on the Third Floor. Sued for Libel. If I Had My Way. Out West With the Peppers. Northwest Mounted Police. Foreign Correspondent. Blondie on a Budget. 1941: Young Tom Edison. The Case of the Black Parrot. Sullivan's Travels. So Ends Our Night. The Lady from Cheyenne. *All the World's a Stooge. The Maltese Falcon. A Shot in the Dark. Kiss the Boys Goodbye. Unholy Partners. The Blonde from Singapore (GB: Hot Pearls). Louisiana Purchase. Johnny Eager. Mr and Mrs Smith. 1942: Cadets on Parade. Wings for the Eagle. They All Kissed the Bride. Over My Dead Body. Arabian Nights. I Married a Witch. Saboteur. The Major and the Minor. The Pride of the Yankees. The Remarkable Andrew. Obliging Young Lady. Kings Row. Once Upon a Honeymoon. Larceny Inc. All Through the Night. The Hard Way. 1943: Mission to Moscow. The Outlaw. That Nazty Nuisance. The Dancing Masters. This Land Is Mine! Young Ideas. The Unknown Guest. Two Senoritas from Chicago. Government Girl. Mr Lucky. The Human Comedy. Let's Face It. You're a Lucky Fellow, Mr Smith. It's a Great Life. 1944: Address Unknown. And Now Tomorrow. *Love Your Landlord. *Radio Rampage. *The Kitchen Cynic. *He Forgot to Remember. *Feather Your Nest. *Tripe Trouble. The Falcon in Hollywood. Casanova Brown. The Falcon in Mexico. Gildersleeve's Ghost. The Miracle of Morgan's Creek. A Night of Adventure. Seven Days Ashore. Tall in the Saddle. Wilson. Once Upon a Time. It's in the Bag! (GB: The Fifth Chair). 1945: *Alibi Baby. *The Big Beef. Crime Doctor's Courage. (GB: The Doctor's*

*Courage). *You Drive Me Crazy. *What, No Cigarettes? Mama Loves Papa. Sing Your Way Home. Two O'Clock Courage. What a Blonde. Colonel Effingham's Raid (GB: Man of the Hour). State Fair. Having Wonderful Crime. 1946: It Shouldn't Happen to a Dog. The Falcon's Alibi. Deadline for Murder. Queen of Burlesque. Little Iodine. Strange Triangle. Abie's Irish Rose. The Show Off. Deadline at Dawn. Badman's Territory. Summer Holiday (released 1948). 1947: The Guilt of Janet Ames. Calendar Girl. Violence. Gas House Kids Go West. Crime Doctor's Gamble (GB: The Doctor's Gamble). Stork Bites Man. 1948: Suddenly It's Spring. Song of Idaho. Assigned to Danger. Blonde Ice. Mr Blandings Builds His Dream House. Here Comes Trouble. You Gotta Stay Happy. Strike It Rich. Words and Music. 1949: A Woman's Secret. Hellfire. The Beautiful Blonde from Bashful Bend. Ma and Pa Kettle. Hideout. Rose of the Yukon. Alaska Patrol. Massacre River. Ma and Pa Kettle Go to Town (GB: Going to Town). 1950: Key to the City. Rock Island Trail (GB: Transcontinent Express). County Fair. Unmasked. Beware of Blondie. Chain Gang. To Please a Lady. 1951: My True Story. Trail of Robin Hood. Ma and Pa Kettle Back on the Farm. Footlight Varieties. All That I Have. Golden Girl. Let's Go Navy. Honeychile. Belle le Grand. Show Boat. Boots Malone. *Deal Me In. 1952: When in Rome. Oklahoma Annie. Ma and Pa Kettle at the Fair. The Fabulous Senorita. Gobs and Gals (GB: Cruising Casanovas). Macao. Dreamboat. Lost in Alaska. The Yellow-Haired Kid (TV. GB: cinemas). Has Anybody Seen My Gal? The Lawless Breed. 1953: Call Me Madam. Sweethearts on Parade. Safari Drums (GB: Bomba and the Safari Drums). Fort Vengeance. Shadow of Tombstone. The Band Wagon. Easy to Love. The Girl Who Had Everything. 1954: Battle of Rogue River. Ma and Pa Kettle At Home. Pride of the Blue Grass (GB: Prince of the Blue Grass). The Rocket Man. Sabrina (GB: Sabrina Fair). The Long, Long Trailer. 1955: You're Never Too Young. The Looters. How to Be Very, Very Popular. Artists and Models. 1956: That Certain Feeling. Pardners. *So You Think the Grass is Greener. *So Your Wife Wants To Work. 1957: The Delicate Delinquent. 1958: The Notorious Mr Monks. Man of the West. The Hot Angel. 1959: Alias Jesse James. A Hole in the Head. This Earth Is Mine! 1961: The Two Little Bears. Ada. 1965: Git! The Bounty Killer.*

### PARSONS, Nicholas 1928-

Tall, cheerful-looking British actor with light, wavy hair who played handsome but sometimes lamebrained types in a few British comedy films before his genial tones and easy-going manner launched him into new careers as straight man for TV comedians, and as quizmaster for radio and TV game shows, notably the perennial *Just a Minute*. Made his film debut at 19 while in repertory in Glasgow after an engineering apprenticeship on Clydebank. Married actress Denise Bryer.

1947: *Master of Bankdam.* 1954: *To Dorothy a Son* (US: *Cash on Delivery*). 1956: *Eyewitness. The Long Arm* (US: *The Third Key*). *Brothers in Law.* 1957: *Happy is the Bride!* 1958: *Too Many Crooks. Carleton-Browne of the 'F O* (US: *Man in a Cocked Hat*). 1959: *Upstairs and Downstairs.* 1960: *Doctor in Love. Let's Get Married.* 1961: *Carry On Regardless.* 1966: *The Wrong Box.* 1968: *Don't Raise the Bridge, Lower the River.* 1971: *Danger Point!* 1974: *The Best of Benny Hill.*

## PATCH, Wally
(Walter Vinnicombe) 1888-1970
Stoutly built, dark-haired (vanishing from a high forehead), massive-headed British cockney portrayer of working-class types from dustmen to foremen with a good few sergeant-majors in between. He was a sandblaster, a bookmaker, a boxing promoter, a dentist, a nightclub proprietor and a music-hall entertainer before coming to films in 1926 and staying for more than 40 years, starring in a few minor comedies to which he often contributed script material, or standing solidly around as a cheery support to the stars.

1926: *Boadicea.* 1927: *The Luck of the Navy. Carry On! The King's Highway. Blighty. Shooting Stars.* 1928: *The Guns of Loos. Balaclava* (US: *The Jaws of Hell*). *Dr Sin Fang (and ensuing series). A Reckless Gamble. You Know What Sailors Are. Warned Off. The Woman in White.* 1929: *Dick Turpin (and

ensuing series). High Treason.* 1930: *The Great Game. Kissing Cup's Race. Thread o' Scarlet.* 1931: *The Sport of Kings. Shadows. Tell England* (US: *The Battle of Gallipoli*). *Never Trouble Trouble. The Great Gay Road.* 1932: *Castle Sinister. Little Waitress. Heroes of the Mine. Here's George.* 1933: *The Crime at Blossoms. The Good Companions. Don Quixote. Britannia of Billingsgate. Orders Is Orders. Tiger Bay. Channel Crossing. Marooned. Sorrell and Son. Trouble. The Scotland Yard Mystery* (US: *The Living Dead*). 1934: *The Man I Want. Those Were the Days. Passing Shadows. Music Hall. The Perfect Flaw. What Happened to Harkness. Virginia's Husband. Badger's Green. Crazy People. The Scoop. The Old Curiosity Shop. A Glimpse of Paradise. Borrow a Million. Lost Over London. Once in a New Moon/Once in a Blue Moon.* 1935: *His Majesty and Co. Death on the Set* (US: *Murder on the Set*). *Dandy Dick. The Public Life of Henry the Ninth. That's My Wife. Street Song. Off the Dole. Marry the Girl. Half Day Excursion. Where's George?* (US: *The Hope of His Side*). *What the Parrot Saw. While Parents Sleep. Old Faithful. Get Off My Foot. A Wife or Two. Ticket of Leave. A Fire Has Been Arranged.* 1936: *On Top of the World. King of the Castle. Excuse My Glove. What the Puppy Said. Prison Breaker. A Touch of the Moon. Not So Dusty. Interrupted Honeymoon. Apron Fools. The Man Who Could Work Miracles. Luck of the Turf. Hail and Farewell. Busman's Holiday. Men Are Not Gods. The Scarab Murder Case. You Must Get Married.* 1937: *The Inspector. The Price of Folly. Holiday's End. The High Command. The Street Singer. Farewell Again* (US: *Troopship*). *Dr Syn. Missing — Believed Married. Night Ride. The Sky's the Limit. Captain's Orders. Owd Bob* (US: *The Victor*). *Bank Holiday* (US: *Three on a Weekend*). 1938: *Quiet Please. On Velvet. Almost a Honeymoon. Break the News. Alf's Button Afloat. 13 Men and a Gun. A Night Alone. Pygmalion. The Ware Case.* 1939: *The Mind of Mr Reeder* (US: *The Mysterious Mr Reeder*). *Inspector Hornleigh. Home from Home. Sword of Honour. Poison Pen. Down Our Alley. What Would You Do Chums? The Lion Has Wings. *Hospital Hospitality. Inspector Hornleigh on Holiday. Return to Yesterday. Laugh It Off. Band Waggon.* 1940: *They Came by Night. Charley's (Big-Hearted) Aunt. Pack Up Your Troubles. Night Train to Munich* (US: *Night Train*). *Two Smart Men. Old Mother Riley in Business. Gasbags. Neutral Port.* 1941: *Quiet Wedding. Inspector Hornleigh Goes to It* (US: *Mail Train*). *Jeannie* (US: *Girl in Distress*). *Once a Crook. Facing the Music. Cottage To Let* (US: *Bombsight Stolen*). *I Thank You. The Seventh Survivor. Gert and Daisy's Weekend. The Common Touch. Bob's Your Uncle. Banana Ridge. Major Barbara.* 1942: *Let the People Sing. Sabotage at Sea. We'll Smile Again. Unpublished Story. Asking for Trouble. In Which We Serve. Much Too Shy.* 1943: *Death by Design. *Strange to Relate. *Women in Bondage. The Life and Death of Colonel Blimp* (US: *Colonel Blimp*). *Get

Cracking. The Butler's Dilemma.* 1945: *Old Mother Riley at Home. Don Chicago. I Didn't Do It. Dumb Dora Discovers Tobacco.* 1946: *A Matter of Life and Death* (US: *Stairway to Heaven*). *Gaiety George* (US: *Showtime*). *Appointment with Crime. George in Civvy Street. Wanted for Murder.* 1947: *Green Fingers. The Ghosts of Berkeley Square. Dusty Bates (serial). Brighton Rock* (US: *Young Scarface*). 1948: *River Patrol. A Date With a Dream. The Guinea Pig. Calling Paul Temple. The History of Mr Polly.* 1949: *Helter Skelter. The Adventures of Jane. Marry Me! Stop Press Girl.* 1950: *The Twenty Questions Murder Mystery.* 1951: *Salute the Toff.* 1952: *Hammer the Toff.* 1953: *Will Any Gentleman?... Thought to Kill. The Wedding of Lilli Marlene.* 1955: *Josephine and Men.* 1956: *Private's Progress. Not So Dusty (and 1936 film). Suspended Alibi.* 1957: *Morning Call* (US: *The Strange Case of Dr Manning*). *The Naked Truth* (US: *Your Past is Showing!*). 1958: *Too Many Crooks.* 1959: *I'm All Right, Jack. Operation Cupid. The Challenge* (US: *It Takes a Thief*). 1960: *The Millionairess. The Night We Got the Bird.* 1961: *The Damned* (US: *These Are the Damned*). *Nothing Barred.* 1962: *Serena. Sparrows Can't Sing. Danger by My Side.* 1963: *A Jolly Bad Fellow* (US: *They All Died Laughing*). *The Comedy Man.* 1964: *The Bargee.* 1967: *Poor Cow.*

## PATE, Michael 1920-
There can't be many Australian actors who went to Hollywood and played Red Indians. Pate began performing on stage and radio as a child and grew to be dark and handsome in a sullen-looking way, going to the States in 1951 and portraying period villains (often with moustache and beard) as well as Redskins. In 1968, he returned to Australia, where he concentrated on the production side, with the occasional foray into direction. Also wrote books (*The Film Actor, The Director's Eye*) and made a TV series, *Hondo* —as an Indian chief.

1940: *40,000 Horsemen.* 1949: *Sons of Matthew* (GB and US: *The Rugged O'Riordans*). 1950: *Bitter Springs.* 1951: *Thunder on the Hill* (GB: *Bonaventure*). *The Strange Door. Ten Tall Men.* 1952: *Five Fingers. The Black Castle. Face to Face. Target Hong Kong.*

Scandal at Scourie. 1953: Julius Caesar. The Desert Rats. Rogue's March. Houdini. The Maze. All the Brothers Were Valiant. Royal African Rifles (GB: Storm Over Africa). El Alamein (GB: Desert Patrol). Hondo. 1954: The Silver Chalice. Secret of the Incas. King Richard and the Crusaders. 1955: A Lawless Street. African Fury (narrator only). The Court Jester. 1956: The Killer Is Loose. The Revolt of Mamie Stover. Congo Crossing. 7th Cavalry. Reprisal! 1957: Something of Value. The Oklahoman. The Tall Stranger. 1958: Desert Hell. Hong Kong Confidential. 1959: Green Mansions. Curse of the Undead. Westbound. 1960: Zorro the Avenger (TV. GB: cinemas). Walk Like a Dragon. 1962: Tower of London. Sergeants Three. Beauty and the Beast. California. PT109. 1963: Drums of Africa. McLintock! Advance to the Rear (GB: Company of Cowards). 1964: Major Dundee. 1965: Brainstorm. The Great Sioux Massacre. The Singing Nun. 1966: Return of the Gunfighter. Willie and the Yank (TV. GB: cinemas, as Mosby's Marauders). Hondo and the Apaches. 1970: The Little Jungle Boy. 1976: Mad Dog. 1982: The Return of Captain Invincible.

**As director:**
1978: Tim.

**PATON, Charles** 1886-1950
Strong-featured, pale-eyed, British supporting player who came to films at the very beginnings of sound. Played respected figures—citizens, councillors, businessmen and the like although often with a quaint, quizzical quality. In progressively smaller roles towards the end of his career.

1928: In Borrowed Plumes. Two of a Trade. 1929: Piccadilly. The Feather. Blackmail. 1930: A Sister To Assist 'Er. The 'W' Plan. 1931: Stepping Stones. The Sleeping Cardinal (US: Sherlock Holmes' Fatal Hour). My Wife's Family. Glamour. What a Night. The Speckled Band. Contraband Love. The Other Mrs Phipps. Rynox. 1932: The Spare Room. Bachelor's Baby. The Third String. A Letter of Warning. Josser Joins the Navy. The Iron Stair. 1933: This Acting Business. The Love Nest. 1934: Freedom of the Seas. Song at Eventide. Girls Will Be Boys. The Girl in Possession. 1935: Royal Cavalcade (US: Regal Cavalcade). Music Hath Charms. No

Monkey Business. Jury's Evidence. 1936: Rembrandt. When Knights Were Bold. The Vandergilt Diamond Mystery. The Marriage of Corbal (US: The Prisoner of Corbal). Pal o' Mine. 1937: Museum Mystery. The Dominant Sex. The Last Chance. Old Mother Riley. 1938: A Sister to Assist 'Er (and 1930 film). Double or Quits. Mother of Men. Sailing Along. Convict 99. The Ware Case. 1939: Men Without Honour. Old Mother Riley MP. 1940: The Briggs Family. 1941: South American George. Pimpernel Smith (US: Mister V). Old Mother Riley's Ghosts. 1942: The Young Mr Pitt. Uncensored. Old Mother Riley Detective. 1943: The Demi-Paradise (US: Adventure for Two). 1944: A Canterbury Tale. Give Us the Moon. He Snoops to Conquer. Strawberry Roan. 1945: Waltz Time. Caesar and Cleopatra. 1946: Bedelia. London Town (US: My Heart Goes Crazy). Spring Song (US: Springtime). 1947: Green Fingers. 1948: Miranda. 1949: Celia. 1950: The Adventurers. Once a Sinner.

**PATRICK, Lee** 1906-1982
Long-faced, fair-haired, plain but peppy American actress, hard on the heels of Veda Ann Borg (qv) and Gladys George in the shop-soiled blonde stakes, although not quite in the same mould, being just as likely to turn up as secretary (supremely as girl-Friday Effie in The Maltese Falcon, a role she amusingly reprised 34 years later in The Black Bird), or confidante. Died from a heart attack.

1929: Strange Cargo. 1937: Danger Patrol. Music for Madame. Border Café. 1938: Maid's Night Out. Crashing Hollywood. Law of the Underworld. Night Spot. Condemned Women. The Sisters. 1939: Fisherman's Wharf. Invisible Stripes. 1940: City for Conquest. Strange Cargo. Money and the Woman. Father is a Prince. South of Suez. Saturday's Children. Ladies Must Live. 1941: Footsteps in the Dark. The Maltese Falcon. Honeymoon for Three. The Smiling Ghost. Million Dollar Baby. Kisses for Breakfast. The Nurse's Secret. Dangerously They Live. 1942: In This Our Life. George Washington Slept Here. Now, Voyager. Somewhere I'll Find You. A Night to Remember. 1943: Nobody's Darling. Larceny With Music. Jitterbugs.

1944: Gambler's Choice. Mrs Parkington. Faces in the Fog. Moon Over Las Vegas. 1945: Keep Your Powder Dry. Mildred Pierce. Over 21. 1946: The Walls Came Tumbling Down. Strange Journey. Wake Up and Dream. 1947: Mother Wore Tights. 1948: Singing Spurs. Inner Sanctum. The Snake Pit. 1949: The Doolins of Oklahoma (GB: The Great Manhunt). 1950: The Lawless (GB: The Dividing Line). The Fuller Brush Girl (GB: The Affairs of Sally). Caged. 1951: Tomorrow Is Another Day. 1953: Take Me to Town. 1954: There's No Business like Show Business. 1958: Auntie Mame. Vertigo. 1959: Pillow Talk. 1960: A Visit to a Small Planet. 1961: Goodbye Again. Summer and Smoke. 1962: A Girl Named Tamiko. 1963: Wives and Lovers. 1964: The Seven Faces of Dr Lao. The New Interns. 1975: The Black Bird.

**PATTERSON, Elizabeth** 1874-1966
American actress with scruffed-back brown hair, shuffling gait, scrawny neck, dumpy figure and take-it-all-in gaze. She came to Hollywood sound films at 55 to bring her Tennessee accent to portraits of down-to-earth country spinsters and maiden aunts and continued doing it for another 30 years. Had a rare leading role as Charley Grapewin's worn-out wife in Tobacco Road.

1926: The Boy Friend. The Return of Peter Grimm. 1929: South Sea Rose. Timothy's Quest. Words and Music. 1930: The Lone Star Ranger. Harmony at Home. The Big Party. The Cat Creeps. 1931: Tarnished Lady. Husband's Holiday. Daddy Long Legs. The Smiling Lieutenant. Penrod and Sam. 1932: Love Me Tonight. Miss Pinkerton. The Expert. Play Girl. Two Against the World. New Morals for Old. Breach of Promise. So Big. No Man of Her Own. The Conquerors. A Bill of Divorcement. Guilty As Hell (GB: Guilty As Charged). Life Begins (GB: The Dawn of Life). They Call It Sin (GB: The Way of Life). Dangerous Brunette. 1933: Doctor Bull. They Just Had to Get Married. Golden Harvest. Dinner at Eight. The Infernal Machine. Hold Your Man. The Story of Temple Drake. The Secret of the Blue Room. 1934: Hide-Out. 1935: Men Without Names. So Red the Rose. Mississippi. Chasing Yesterday. 1936: Timothy's Quest (and 1929 film). The Return of

Sophie Lang. Three Cheers for Love. Go West, Young Man. Small Town Girl. Her Master's Voice. Old Hutch. 1937: A Night of Mystery. Hold 'Em Navy. High, Wide and Handsome. Night Club Scandal. 1938: Scandal Street. Bulldog Drummond's Peril. Bluebeard's Eighth Wife. Sing, You Sinners. The Adventures of Tom Sawyer. Sons of the Legion. 1939: The Story of Alexander Graham Bell (GB: The Modern Miracle). Bulldog Drummond's Bride. Our Leading Citizen. Bad Little Angel. The Cat and the Canary. Bulldog Drummond's Secret Police. 1940: Remember the Night. Anne of Windy Poplars (GB: Anne of Windy Willows). Adventure in Diamonds. Michael Shayne, Private Detective. Who Killed Aunt Maggie? Earthbound. 1941: Belle Starr. Kiss the Boys Goodbye. Tobacco Road. The Vanishing Virginian. 1942: Almost Married. Her Cardboard Lover. Beyond the Blue Horizon. My Sister Eileen. Lucky Legs. I Married a Witch. 1943: The Sky's the Limit. 1944: Follow the Boys. Together Again. Hail the Conquering Hero. 1945: Lady on a Train. Colonel Effingham's Raid (GB: Man of the Hour). 1946: The Secret Heart. I've Always Loved You (GB: Concerto). The Shocking Miss Pilgrim. 1947: Welcome, Stranger. Out of the Blue. 1948: Miss Tatlock's Millions. 1949: Little Women. Song of Surrender. Intruder in the Dust. 1950: Bright Leaf. 1951: Katie Did It. 1952: Washington Story (GB: Target for Scandal). 1955: Las Vegas Shakedown. 1957: Mr and Mrs McAdam (TV). Pal Joey. 1958: Portrait of a Murderer (TV). 1959: The Oregon Trail. 1960: Tomorrow (TV). Tall Story.

**PEARCE, Alice** 1913-1966
Short, beaky, brown-haired American comic actress with receding chin and protruding lips, who made the most of her caricature of a face to create the unforgettably sinus-ridden Lucy Schmeeler in the stage and film versions of On the Town. A popular Broadway and nightclub comedienne following her stage debut in New Faces of 1943, she found too little time to provide films with enough gems to follow the toothy and far from juicy Lucy, everyone's idea of the blind date they'd rather not see. Died from cancer.

1949: On the Town. 1952: Belle of New York. 1955: How to Be Very, Very Popular. 1956: The Opposite Sex. 1962: Lad: a Dog. 1963: My Six Loves. The Thrill of It All. Tammy and the Doctor. Beach Party. 1964: The Disorderly Orderly. Dear Heart. Kiss Me Stupid. 1965: That Darn Cat! Dear Brigitte.... Bus Riley's Back in Town. 1966: The Glass Bottom Boat.

**PEARSON, Richard** 1918-
Tubby, worried-looking Welsh-born actor with a shock of unruly wavy hair, seen as a range of mild-mannered professional men during his infrequent appearances in British films. Much busier in TV and on the stage, where he made his debut at London's Collins Music Hall when only 18. Almost a dead ringer for Britain's Foreign Secretary Sir Geoffrey Howe. 1985: Water. Reunion at Fairborough (TV).

1938: *An Act of Mercy. 1950: The Woman in Question (US: Five Angles on Murder). The Girl Is Mine. The Woman With No Name (US: Her Paneled Door). 1951: Scrooge. 1953: The Blue Parrot. 1954: Dangerous Cargo. Svengali. 1958: The Crowning Touch. Sea Fury. 1959: Life in Danger. Libel. 1961: The Man in the Moon. Attempt to Kill. 1962: Guns of Darkness. 1963: *The King's Breakfast. 1964: The Yellow Rolls-Royce. One-Way Pendulum. 1965: The Legend of Young Dick Turpin. The Agony and the Ecstasy. 1967: Charlie Bubbles. How I Won the War. 1968: The Strange Affair. Inspector Clouseau. 1970: The Rise and Rise of Michael Rimmer. 1971: Macbeth. Sunday Bloody Sunday. Catch Me a Spy. 1972: Pope Joan. 1974: Love Among the Ruins (TV). 1975: Royal Flash. One of Our Dinosaurs is Missing. 1976: The Blue Bird. It Shouldn't Happen to a Vet (US: All Things Bright and Beautiful). 1978: She Fell Among Thieves (TV). 1979: Tess. 1980: Masada (TV. GB: cinemas (abridged) as The Antagonists). The Mirror Crack'd.

**PENDLETON, Nat** 1895-1967
'Playing dumb' made Pendleton one of the most popular American supporting actors of the 1930s. Tall, dark and handsome in a faintly bemused-looking way, Pendleton, brother of actor Gaylord Pendleton, was in reality an Olympic wrestling champion and

all-round smart guy with a college degree. In films, however, he was soon playing dim hoodlums and other characters with more brawn than brain to whom the truth dawned but slowly. When demands for his services declined in the post-war period, he slipped away from show business into early retirement. Died from a heart attack.

1912: The Battle of Gettysburg. 1924: Monsieur Beaucaire. The Hoosier Schoolmaster (GB: The Schoolmaster). 1926: Let's Get Married. 1929: The Laughing Lady. 1930: The Big Pond. The Big Trail. Last of the Duanes. The Sea Wolf. Liliom. 1931: The Star Witness. Spirit of Notre Dame (GB: Vigour of Youth). The Seas Beneath. Blonde Crazy (GB: Larceny Lane). Mr Lemon of Orange. The Ruling Voice. Fair Warning. The Secret Witness/Terror by Night. Cauliflower Alley. *Pottsville Paluka. 1932: Taxi! Play Girl. Attorney for the Defense. Exposure. Hell Fire Austin. Beast of the City. State's Attorney (GB: Cardigan's Last Case). The Sign of the Cross. Manhattan Parade. By Whose Hand? Horse Feathers. Night Club Lady. You Said a Mouthful. *A Fool's Advice. 1933: College Coach (GB: Football Coach). Parachute Jumper. Baby Face. Whistling in the Dark. The White Sister. Goldie Gets Along. Lady for a Day. Deception. Penthouse (GB: Crooks in Clover). I'm No Angel. The Chief (GB: My Old Man's a Fireman). 1934: Fugitive Lovers. Death On the Diamond. The Defense Rests. The Cat's Paw. Manhattan Melodrama. Lazy River. The Thin Man. The Gay Bride. Sing and Like It. The Girl from Missouri (GB: 100 Per Cent Pure). Straight Is the Way. 1935: Reckless. Times Square Lady. Baby Face Harrington. Murder in the Fleet. Calm Yourself. It's in the Air. Here Comes the Band. 1936: Trapped by Television (GB: Caught by Television). Two in a Crowd. The Garden Murder Case. The Great Ziegfeld. Sworn Enemy. The Luckiest Girl in the World. Sing Me a Love Song. 1937: Gangway. Under Cover of Night. Song of the City. Life Begins in College (GB: The Joy Parade). 1938: Meet the Mayor (filmed 1932). Shopworn Angel. Arsene Lupin Returns. Swing Your Lady. Fast Company. Young Dr Kildare. The Crowd Roars. The Chaser. 1939: Calling Dr Kildare. Burn 'Em Up O'Connor. It's a Wonderful

World. 6,000 Enemies. At the Circus. On
Borrowed Time. Another Thin Man. The
Secret of Dr Kildare. 1940: The Ghost Comes
Home. Northwest Passage. Dr Kildare's Stran-
gest Case. Phantom Raiders. The Golden
Fleecing. Dr Kildare's Crisis. Flight Command.
Dr Kildare Goes Home. 1941: Buck Privates
(GB: Rookies). Dr Kildare's Wedding Day
(GB: Mary Names the Day). Top Sergeant
Mulligan. The Mad Doctor of Market Street.
†Dr Kildare's Victory (GB: The Doctor and
the Debutante). 1942: Calling Dr Gillespie.
Jail House Blues. Dr Gillespie's New Assistant.
1943: Swing Fever. Dr Gillespie's Criminal
Case (GB: Crazy to Kill). 1946: Death
Valley. 1947: Buck Privates Come Home
(GB: Rookies Come Home). Scared to Death.

†Scene deleted from final release print

**PERCIVAL, Lance** 1933-
Toothy, fair-haired, languorous-looking,
Scots-born satirist, entertainer, revue star,
comic actor and light singer. He came to
prominence in London cabaret and the
trailblazing TV satire programme That Was
the Week That Was. The cinema generally
asked him to play comedy roles rather too
broad for his talents. His laconic voice was
often heard telling TV stories or in unseen
narration.

1961: What a Whopper! On the Fiddle (US:
Operation Snafu). Raising the Wind (US:
Roommates). 1962: Postman's Knock. The
Devil's Daffodil. Twice Round the Daffodils.
Carry On Cruising. 1963: *The Sure Thing
(voice only). The VIPs. Hide and Seek. It's All
Over Town. 1964: The Yellow Rolls-Royce.
1965: The Big Job. Joey Boy. 1968: Yellow
Submarine (voice only). Mrs Brown, You've
Got a Lovely Daughter. 1969: Darling Lili.
Too Late the Hero. 1970: There's a Girl in My
Soup. Concerto per pistola solista (GB: The
Weekend Murders). 1971: The Magnificent
Six and a ½ (third series). Up Pompeii. Up the
Chastity Belt. 1972: Up the Front. Our Miss
Fred. 1974: The Boy with Two Heads (serial).
1977: Confessions from a Holiday Camp.
1978: The Water Babies (voice only). Rosie
Dixon Night Nurse.

**PERRINS, Leslie** 1902-1962
Dark-haired, moustachioed, full-faced British actor, a very smooth and professional

villain, charming the heroine up the wrong
path, and so good at it that the British
cinema pigeonholed him in the role and
kept him frantically busy throughout the
1930s. From 1940 on, his sharply cultured
tones were heard rather more often on
radio, several times as police inspectors in
long-running series. A dominant personality; didn't often play comedy.

1928: *Silken Threads. *The Clue of the
Second Goblet. *Blake the Lawbreaker. 1930:
Immediate Possession. 1931: The Sleeping
Cardinal (US: Sherlock Holmes' Fatal Hour).
The Rosary. The Calendar (US: Bachelor's
Folly). We Dine at Seven. The House of Unrest.
1932: Betrayal. Whiteface. 1933: The Lost
Chord. Early to Bed. Just Smith (US: Leave It
to Smith). The Roof. The Pointing Finger. The
Scotland Yard Mystery (US: The Living
Dead). Lily of Killarney (US: Bride of the
Lake). 1934: Lord Edgware Dies. The Man
Who Changed His Name. The Lash. Song at
Eventide. Gay Love. Open All Night. Woman-
hood. D'Ye Ken John Peel? (US: Captain
Moonlight). 1935: The Rocks of Valpré (US:
High Treason). The Shadow of Mike Emerald.
The Triumph of Sherlock Holmes. The Village
Squire. White Lilac. The Silent Passenger.
Lucky Days. Expert's Opinion. Line Engaged.
Sunshine Ahead. 1936: They Didn't Know.
Tudor Rose (US: Nine Days a Queen).
Rhythm in the Air. Southern Roses. The
Limping Man. No Escape. Sensation. 1937:
The Price of Folly. Bulldog Drummond at Bay.
Secret Lives (US: I Married a Spy). The High
Command. Dangerous Fingers (US: Wanted
by Scotland Yard). 1938: Mr Reeder in Room
13 (US: Mystery of Room 13). Romance à la
Carte. The Gables Mystery. No Parking.
Calling All Crooks. His Lordship Goes to Press.
Luck of the Navy (US: North Sea Patrol). Old
Iron. 1939: I Killed the Count (US: Who is
Guilty?). The Gang's All Here (US: The
Amazing Mr Forrest). All at Sea. Blind Folly.
1940: John Smith Wakes Up. 1941: The
Prime Minister. 1942: Suspected Person.
Women Aren't Angels. 1944: Heaven Is
Round the Corner. 1946: I'll Turn to You.
1947: The Turners of Prospect Road. 1948:
Idol of Paris. Man on the Run. 1949: A Run
for Your Money. 1950: Midnight Episode.
1952: The Lost Hours (US: The Big Frame).

1956: Guilty? 1958: Grip of the Strangler
(US: The Haunted Strangler).

**PERSOFF, Nehemiah** 1920-
Powerful, stockily built, squat-faced Israeli-
born actor with dark, fuzzy hair. In America
from the age of nine, he worked at one time
as a subway electrician, but in post-war
years, he enrolled at the Actors' Studio,
emerging in the late 1940s and becoming a
film regular from the mid-1950s, often in
intense, aggressive roles, but later in more
routine 'guest star'-type spots as professors,
elders and the like.

1948: The Naked City. A Double Life. 1954:
On the Waterfront. 1956: The Wild Party.
The Harder They Fall. The Wrong Man.
1957: Men in War. Street of Sinners. 1958:
The Badlanders. This Angry Age (GB: The
Sea Wall). Never Steal Anything Small.
1959: Al Capone. Some Like It Hot. Green
Mansions. Day of the Outlaw. 1961: The
Comancheros. The Big Show. 1963: The Hook.
A Global Affair. 1964: Fate Is the Hunter.
1965: The Greatest Story Ever Told. 1966:
The Dangerous Days of Kiowa Jones (TV.
GB: cinemas). Too Many Thieves (TV. GB:
cinemas). 1967: The Power. Panic in the City.
1968: The Money Jungle. Escape to Minda-
nao (TV). Il giorno della civetta. The Girl Who
Knew Too Much. 1970: Cutter's Trail (TV).
Mrs Pollifax—Spy. The People Next Door.
Red Sky at Morning. 1972: Lieutenant
Schuster's Wife (TV). 1974: The Stranger
Within (TV). The Sex Symbol (TV. GB:
cinemas). 1975: Eric (TV). Psychic Killer.
1976: Voyage of the Damned. 1978: Stone/
Killing Stone (TV). Ziegfeld: the Man and
His Women (TV). FDR: the Last Year (TV).
The Henderson Monster (TV). 1981: St
Helens/Killer Volcano. O'Hara's Wife. 1983:
Yentl.

**PERTWEE, Jon** 1917-
Tall, long-striding, red-headed (now
white), beaky-nosed British comic actor
with burbling tones whose chief claim to
fame in the post-war years was as a radio
voice, especially in the series Waterlogged
Spa and The Navy Lark, sadly not transfer-
ring his character in the latter to the film
version. He was also popular on television as
one of the personalities of Dr Who. A sort of

minor-key British Danny Kaye, an actor for whom, strangely, Pertwee 'stood in' on the London location scenes of Kaye's *Knock on Wood*. Son of playwright and screenwriter Roland Pertwee, and brother of another, Michael Pertwee.

*1937: A Yank at Oxford. Dinner at the Ritz. 1939: Young Man's Fancy. The Four Just Men (US: The Secret Four). There Ain't No Justice! 1947: Penny and the Pownall Case. 1948: William Comes to Town. Trouble in the Air. A Piece of Cake. 1949: Murder at the Windmill (US: Murder at the Burlesque). Helter Skelter. Stop Press Girl. Dear Mr Prohack. Miss Pilgrim's Progress. 1950: The Body Said No. Mr Drake's Duck. 1953: Will Any Gentleman?... 1954: The Gay Dog. Knock on Wood (stand-in). 1955: A Yank in Ermine. 1956: It's a Wonderful World. 1958: The Ugly Duckling. 1959: Just Joe. 1960: Not a Hope in Hell. 1961: Nearly a Nasty Accident. 1963: Ladies Who Do. 1964: Carry On Cleo. 1965: Carry On Cowboy. How To Undress in Public Without Undue Embarrassment. I've Gotta Horse. 1966: Carry On Screaming. A Funny Thing Happened on the Way to the Forum. 1969: Up in the Air. Under the Table You Must Go. 1970: The House That Dripped Blood. 1974: Four Against the Desert. 1975: One of Our Dinosaurs Is Missing. 1977: Adventures of a Private Eye. Wombling Free (voice only). No.1 of the Secret Service. 1978: The Water Babies (voice only). 1983: The Boys in Blue.*

## PETRIE, Hay

(David H. Petrie) 1895-1948
Short, scuttling Scottish actor who specialized in eccentric characterizations. In his element as The MacLaggan in *The Ghost Goes West*, although probably his biggest role was as the avaricious Quilp in the 1934 version of Dickens' *The Old Curiosity Shop*. Otherwise cast as an assortment of tiny terrors, from stagedoor-keepers to spies, who could give anyone as good as they got in the verbal stakes.

*1930: Suspense. Night Birds. 1931: Gipsy Blood (US: Carmen). Many Waters. 1932: Help Yourself. 1933: The Private Life of Henry VIII. Daughters of Today. Lucky Number. Song of the Plough. Crime on the Hill.*

*Matinee Idol. Red Wagon. Colonel Blood. 1934: Nell Gwyn. The Old Curiosity Shop. The Queen's Affair (US: Runaway Queen). The Private Life of Don Juan. Blind Justice. 1935: Peg of Old Drury. The Ghost Goes West. Moscow Nights (US: I Stand Condemned). Invitation to the Waltz. I Give My Heart. The Silent Passenger. Koenigsmark. 1936: Men of Yesterday. The House of the Spaniard. Conquest of the Air (released 1940). Hearts of Humanity. Forget-Me-Not (US: Forever Yours). Rembrandt. No Escape. Not Wanted on Voyage (US: Treachery on the High Seas). 1937: Secret Lives (US: I Married a Spy). Knight Without Armour. 21 Days (released 1940. US: 21 Days Together). 1938: The Last Barricade. Consider Your Verdict. Keep Smiling (US: Smiling Along). The Loves of Madame Du Barry. 1939: Ten Days in Paris (US: Missing Ten Days). The Four Feathers. Q Planes (US: Clouds Over Europe). The Spy in Black (US: U-Boat 29). Jamaica Inn. Inquest. Trunk Crime (US: Design for Murder). Spy for a Day. 1940: Contraband (US: Blackout). Spellbound (US: The Spell of Amy Nugent). Convoy. Pastor Hall. The Thief of Baghdad. Crimes at the Dark House. 1941: \*Rush Hour. Quiet Wedding. Freedom Radio (US: A Voice in the Night). Turned Out Nice Again. The Ghost of St Michael's. Cottage to Let. (US: Bombsight Stolen). They Flew Alone (US: Wings and the Woman). This Was Paris.*

*1942: Hard Steel. The Great Mr Handel. One of Our Aircraft Is Missing. 1943: Battle for Music. Escape to Danger. The Demi-Paradise (US: Adventure for Two). 1944: A Canterbury Tale. On Approval. Kiss the Bride Goodbye. 1945: The Voice Within. Waltz Time. Night Boat to Dublin. For You Alone. 1946: The Laughing Lady. Great Expectations. Under New Management. 1948: The Monkey's Paw. The Red Shoes. The Guinea Pig. The Lucky Mascot/Brass Monkey. The Fallen Idol. Noose (US: The Silk Noose). The Queen of Spades.*

## PETTINGELL, Frank 1891-1966

Beefy, phlegmatic, dark-haired British actor who brought his good-humoured north country-men to sound films after 20 years' experience on stage. He made his debut as Will Mossop in the first sound version of *Hobson's Choice* and was thereafter mostly in

stout supporting roles, though none more effective than the justice-seeking policeman in the British version of *Gaslight*. Also wrote and adapted a number of historical plays for the theatre.

*1931: Hobson's Choice. Jealousy. Frail Women. 1932: In a Monastery Garden. The Crooked Lady. Once Bitten. Double Dealing. Tight Corner. The Medicine Man. Yes, Madam. The Good Companions. Excess Baggage. That's My Wife. Lucky Number. This Week of Grace. A Cuckoo in the Nest. Red Wagon. 1934: Keep It Quiet. Sing As We Go. My Old Dutch. 1935: Say It With Diamonds. The Big Splash. The Right Age to Marry. Where's George? (US: The Hope of His Side). The Last Journey. The Amateur Gentleman. 1936: On Top of the World. Fame. Millions. 1937: It's a Grand Old World. Take My Tip. Spring Handicap. 1938: Queer Cargo (US: Pirates of the Seven Seas). Sailing Along. 1939: Return to Yesterday. 1940: Busman's Honeymoon (US: Haunted Honeymoon). Gaslight (US: Angel Street). 1941: This England. Kipps (US: The Remarkable Mr Kipps). Once a Crook. The Seventh Survivor. Ships With Wings. 1942: The Young Mr Pitt. When We Are Married. The Goose Steps Out. 1943: Get Cracking. The Butler's Dilemma. 1946: Gaiety George (US: Showtime). 1948: No Room at the Inn. Escape. 1951: The Magic Box. 1952: The Card (US: The Promoter). The Crimson Pirate. The Great Game. Meet Me Tonight. 1953: Meet Mr Lucifer. 1955: Value for Money. 1958: Up the Creek. Corridors of Blood. 1962: Term of Trial. The Dock Brief (US: Trial and Error). 1963: Becket.*

## PHILLPOTTS, Ambrosine 1912-1980

Forthright, forceful, dark-haired British actress who was a formidable stage Lady Macbeth at 19 and has made scores of subsequent appearances in the theatre, far too many alas, to allow this distinctive actress to carve out a film career as well. Often in aristocratic or bitchy roles, or in fact anything with a bit of bite.

*1946: This Man Is Mine! 1950: The Franchise Affair. Happy Go Lovely. 1951: Mr Denning Drives North. 1952: Stolen Face. Father's Doing Fine. 1953: The Captain's*

*Paradise. 1956: Up in the World. 1957: The Truth About Women. 1958: The Reluctant Debutante. The Duke Wore Jeans. Room at the Top. 1959: Operation Bullshine. Expresso Bongo. 1960: Doctor in Love. 1961: Carry On Regardless. 1962: Two and Two Make Six. 1963: Carry On Cabby. 1965: Life at the Top. 1967: Berserk! 1972: Diamonds on Wheels. Ooh... You Are Awful (US: Get Charlie Tully). 1980: The Wildcats of St Trinian's.*

### PHIPPS, Nicholas 1913-1980

Tall, dark-haired, heavily-moustachioed, wolfish-looking British comedy actor likely to be remembered for his successful screenplays rather than his (nonetheless enjoyable) performances. He wrote or co-wrote many of the Anna Neagle-Michael Wilding romances, as well as the later 'Doctor' films from the books by Richard Gordon. An elegant light comedian in the theatre, both in revue and straight plays. In films, often had an eye for the heroine but rarely got her.

*1940: You Will Remember. Old Bill and Son. 1946: Piccadilly Incident. 1947: The Courtneys of Curzon Street (US: The Courtney Affair). 1948: Spring in Park Lane. 1949: Maytime in Mayfair. Elizabeth of Ladymead. Madeleine. 1951: Appointment With Venus (US: Island Rescue). 1953: The Captain's Paradise. The Intruder. 1954: Doctor in the House. Mad About Men. Out of the Clouds. 1955: Doctor at Sea. All for Mary. 1956:*

*Who Done It? The Iron Petticoat. 1957: Doctor at Large. 1958: Orders to Kill. Rockets Galore (US: Mad Little Island). The Captain's Table. 1959: The Navy Lark. Don't Panic, Chaps! 1960: The Pure Hell of St Trinian's. Doctor in Love. 1961: No Love for Johnnie. A Pair of Briefs. 1962: The Wild and the Willing. Summer Holiday. 1963: Doctor in Distress. 1967: Charlie Bubbles. 1969: Some Girls Do. Monte Carlo or Bust! 1970: The Rise and Rise of Michael Rimmer.*

### PICKENS, Slim
(Louis Lindley) 1919-1983

Pickens' rather grand real name certainly hardly suited the beak-nosed, buck-toothed, bright-eyed, no-chinned 'B' western sidekicks he played in the early 1950s, coming to films after years as a rodeo clown. Later put on weight and became a quite formidable character player, in both comic and dramatic roles. Despite the twangy drawl, he came from California.

*1950: Rocky Mountain. 1951: Colorado Sundown. 1952: The Last Musketeer. Old Oklahoma Plains. Border Saddlemates. Thunderbirds. South Pacific Trail. The Story of Will Rogers. 1953: Old Overland Trail. Iron Mountain Trail. Down Laredo Way. Shadows of Tombstone. Red River Shore. The Sun Shines Bright. 1954: The Boy from Oklahoma. The Phantom Stallion. The Outcast (GB: The Fortune Hunter). 1955: The Last Command. Santa Fé Passage. 1956: Stranger at My Door. When Gangland Strikes. The Great Locomotive Chase. Gun Brothers. 1957: Gunsight Ridge. 1958: Tonka. The Sheepman. 1959: Escort West. 1960: Chartroose Caboose. 1961: One-Eyed Jacks. A Thunder of Drums. 1963: Savage Sam. Dr Strangelove, or: How I Learned to Stop Worrying and Love the Bomb. Stampede at Bitter Creek (TV. GB: cinemas). 1965: Major Dundee. Up from the Beach. In Harm's Way. The Glory Guys. 1966: An Eye for an Eye. Stagecoach. 1967: The Flim Flam Man (GB: One Born Every Minute). Rough Night in Jericho. Will Penny. Never a Dull Moment. 1968: Skidoo. 1969: Eighty Steps to Jonah. 1970: The Ballad of Cable Hogue. Savage Season. The Deserter. 1971: J.C. The Devil and Miss Sarah (TV). Hitched (TV. GB: Westward the Wagon). The*

*Cowboys. 1972: Rolling Man (TV). The Honkers. The Getaway. Outdoor Rambling. 1973: Pat Garrett and Billy the Kid. Ginger in the Morning (GB: TV). 1974: Bootleggers. Twice in a Lifetime (TV). The Legend of Earl Durand. Blazing Saddles. Poor Pretty Eddie. The Apple Dumpling Gang. 1975: Rancho DeLuxe. Babe (TV). White Line Fever. 1976: Pony Express Rider. Hawmps. The Gun and the Pulpit (TV). Banjo Hackett (TV). 1977: Mr Billion. The Shadow of Chikara. The White Buffalo. 1978: The Swarm. Good Time Outlaws/The Sweet Creek County War. The Freedom Riders (TV). My Undercover Years With the Ku Klux Klan (TV). Charlie and the Great Balloon Chase (TV). 1979: The Sacketts (TV). Swan Song (TV). 1941. Beyond the Poseidon Adventure. 1980: Tom Horn. Spirit of the Wind. The Howling. Honeysuckle Rose. 1981: High Country Pursuit. This House Possessed (TV). 1982: Christmas Mountain. Pink Motel (GB: Motel).*

### PIPER, Frederick 1902-1979

Probably one of the most anonymous of those British actors who played men in the street. Dark-haired, medium-built, ferret-faced Piper, a former tea merchant who switched to acting, turned up in dozens of pictures just flashing through a scene—as bus conductors, milkmen, postmen, policemen or neighbours. He also worked in many television series from as far back as 1938, including one called, appropriately, *Down Our Street*. The loss of his hair in later years only accentuated the image of the working man *par excellence*.

*1933: The Good Companions. 1935: The 39 Steps. 1936: Jack of All Trades (US: The Two of Us). Crown v Stevens. Sensation. Where There's A Will. Fame. Sabotage (US: The Woman Alone). 1937: Feather Your Nest. Non-Stop New York. Oh, Mr Porter! 1939: Jamaica Inn. The Four Just Men (US: The Secret Four). 1940: Spare a Copper. East of Piccadilly (US: The Strangler). 1941: The 49th Parallel (US: The Invaders). The Big Blockade. 1942: In Which We Serve. 1943: San Demetrio London. Nine Men. The Bells Go Down. 1944: Fiddlers Three. Return of the Vikings. It Happened One Sunday. Champagne Charlie.*

1945: *Johnny Frenchman. Pink String and Sealing Wax.* 1947: *Hue and Cry. The October Man. The Loves of Joanna Godden. Master of Bankdam. It Always Rains on Sunday. Penny and the Pownall Case. Easy Money.* 1948: *Fly Away Peter. My Brother's Keeper. To the Public Danger. Look Before You Love. Escape. Vote for Huggett. It's Not Cricket.* 1949: *Passport to Pimlico. Don't Ever Leave Me. The Blue Lamp.* 1950: *Your Witness (US: Eye Witness).* 1951: *The Lavender Hill Mob. Home at Seven. Brandy for the Parson.* 1952: *Hunted (US: The Stranger in Between). The Story of Robin Hood and His Merrie Men. Escape Route (US: I'll Get You). Cosh Boy (US: The Slasher).* 1954: *Conflict of Wings (US: Fuss over Feathers). The Rainbow Jacket. Lease of Life. Devil on Horseback.* 1955: *Doctor at Sea.* 1956: *The Man in the Road. The Passionate Stranger (US: A Novel Affair). Suspended Alibi.* 1957: *Doctor at Large. Second Fiddle. The Birthday Present. Barnacle Bill (US: All at Sea).* 1958: *Dunkirk. Violent Moment.* 1959: *A Touch of Larceny.* 1960: *Dead Lucky. The Day They Robbed the Bank of England. The Monster of Highgate Ponds (completed 1957).* 1961: *The Frightened City. What a Carve Up! (US: Home Sweet Homicide). Very Important Person (US: A Coming-Out Party). The Piper's Tune. Return of a Stranger. Only Two Can Play.* 1962: *Postman's Knock.* 1963: *Reach for Glory. Ricochet. Becket.* 1964: *Catacombs (US: The Woman Who Wouldn't Die). One Way Pendulum.* 1965: *He Who Rides a Tiger.*

## PITHEY, Wensley 1914–

Thick-set, brown-haired, often moustachioed South African-born actor in British films, latterly well known for his portrayals of Sir Winston Churchill. He began his career in his native country when, at 23, he won a nationwide contest for a radio announcer. Came to British films in postwar days, and usually tackled parts—often policemen or minor figures of authority—that were older than his years.

1947: *The October Man. The Mark of Cain.* 1948: *It's Hard To Be Good. London Belongs to Me (US: Dulcimer Street). Cardboard Cavalier.* 1950: *Guilt Is My Shadow. Your Witness (US: Eye Witness).* 1951: *Brandy for the Parson.* 1952: *The Woman's Angle. Lady in the Fog (US: Scotland Yard Inspector). Father's Doing Fine. The Titfield Thunderbolt. Isn't Life Wonderful! The Story of Robin Hood and His Merrie Men.* 1955: *The Dark Avenger (US: The Warriors). You Can't Escape.* 1956: *Moby Dick. Tiger in the Smoke.* 1957: *Kill Me Tomorrow. The Long Haul. Blue Murder at St Trinian's. Doctor at Large. Hell Drivers.* 1959: *Serious Charge (US: A Touch of Hell).* 1960: *Make Mine Mink. Snowball. The Pure Hell of St Trinian's.* 1962: *The Barber of Stamford Hill. The Boys. *The Guilty Party.* 1965: *The Knack... and how to get it.* 1968: *Oliver!* 1969: *Oh! What a Lovely War.* 1975: *One of Our Dinosaurs Is Missing.* 1979: *Ike (TV).* 1980: *FDR: the Last Year (TV).*

## PITTS, ZaSu 1898-1963

Bird-like, dark-haired, slender American actress with thin upper lip and large, dark, darting eyes. At first in vulnerable roles, most notably in Von Stroheim's *Greed*, she later took to comedy in early sound two-reelers with various partners, then played equally vulnerable spinsterish character parts. Died from cancer.

1917: *Why They Left Home. *Uneasy Money. The Little Princess. A Modern Musketeer. Rebecca of Sunnybrook Farm.* 1918: *How Could You, Jean? As the Sun Went Down. A Society Sensation.* 1919: *Better Times. The Other Half. Men, Women and Money.* 1920: *Poor Relations. Bright Skies. Seeing It Through. Heart of Twenty.* 1921: *Patsy.* 1922: *Youth to Youth. For the Defense. Is Matrimony a Failure? A Daughter of Luxury.* 1923: *Poor Men's Wives. The Girl Who Came Back. Tea With a Kick. West of the Water Tower. Mary of the Movies. Souls for Sale. Three Wise Fools.* 1924: *Triumph. Daughters of Today. The Legend of Hollywood. The Fast Set. Greed. The Goldfish. Changing Husbands. Wine of Youth.* 1925: *The Great Love. The Business of Love. Old Shoes. The Re-Creation of Brian Kent. Thunder Mountain. A Woman's Faith. What Happened to Jones? The Great Divide. Lazybones. Pretty Ladies. Secrets of the Night. Wages for Wives. Mannequin.* 1926: *Monte Carlo (GB: Dreams of Monte Carlo). Early to Wed. Risky Business. Sunny Side Up. Her Big Night.* 1927: *Casey at the Bat.* 1928: *13 Washington Square. Buck Privates. The Wedding March. Wife Savers. Sins of the Fathers.* 1929: *Her Private Life. The Argyle Case. The Dummy. Oh, Yeah! (GB: No Brakes). The Locked Door. Paris. This Thing Called Love. The Squall. Twin Beds.* 1930: †*All Quiet on the Western Front. Honey. The Lottery Bride. No, No, Nanette. River's End. The Squealer. The Devil's Holiday. Little Accident. Monte Carlo (and 1926 film). Passion Flower. Sin Takes a Holiday. War Nurse.* 1931: *Finn and Hattie. Beyond Victory. Their Mad Moment. Bad Sister. The Big Gamble. Seed. A Woman of Experience. Penrod and Sam. The Guardsman.* *The Secret Witness. *Let's Do Things. *Catch As Catch Can. *The Pajama Party. *War Mamas.* 1932: *Seal Skins. *On the Loose. *Red Noses. *The Old Bull. *Strictly Unreliable. *Show Business. *Alum and Eve. *The Soilers. Shopworn. Steady Company. The Trail of Vivienne Ware. Unexpected Father. Westward Passage. Blondie of the Follies. Make Me a Star. The Crooked Circle. Once in a Lifetime. Broken Lullaby (GB: The Man I Killed). Destry Rides Again. Strangers of the Evening. Speak Easily. Is My Face Red? Roar of the Dragon. Vanishing Frontier. Madison Square Garden. Back Street. They Just Had to Get Married.* 1933: *Hello, Sister! Professional Sweetheart (GB: Imaginary Sweetheart). Love, Honor and Oh, Baby! *Sneak Easily. *Asleep in the Fleet. *Maids à la Mode. *One Track Minds. *The Bargain of the Century. Aggie Appleby, Maker of Men (GB: Cupid in the Rough). Mr Skitch. Out All Night. Her First Mate. Meet the Baron.* 1934: *Two Alone. The Meanest Gal in Town. Three on a Honeymoon. Mrs Wiggs of the Cabbage Patch. Their Big Moment (GB: Afterwards). Sing and Like It. Love Birds. Private Scandal. The Gay Bride. Dames.* 1935: *Hot Tip. Ruggles of Red Gap. The Affairs of Susan. Going Highbrow. She Gets Her Man. Spring Tonic.* 1936: *Thirteen Hours by Air. The Plot Thickens (GB: The Swinging Pearl Mystery). Sing Me a Love Song. Mad Holiday.* 1937: *Forty Naughty Girls. 52nd Street. Wanted. Merry Comes to Town.* 1938: *So's Your Aunt Emma (later Meet the Mob).* 1939: *Naughty But Nice. The Lady's from Kentucky. Mickey the Kid. Nurse Edith Cavell. Eternally Yours.* 1940: *No, No, Nanette (remake). It All Came True.* 1941: *Niagara Falls. Broadway Limited. The Mexican Spitfire's Baby. Miss Polly. Week-End for Three.* 1942: *Tish. Mexican Spitfire at Sea. The Bashful Bachelor.* 1943: *Let's Face It.* 1946: *The Perfect Marriage. Breakfast in Hollywood (GB: The Mad Hatter).* 1947: *Life with Father. *A Film Goes to Market.* 1949: *Francis.* 1951: *Denver and Rio Grande.* 1954: *Francis Joins the WACs.* 1956: *Mr Belvedere (TV. GB: cinemas).* 1957: *This Could Be the Night.* 1959: *The Gazebo.* 1961: *Teenage Millionaire.* 1963: *It's a Mad, Mad, Mad, Mad World. The Thrill of It All.*

†Silent version only

## PLATT, Edward C. 1916-1974

Neat, sturdy, waspish American actor with greying hair and trim moustache (he looked skull-like when clean-shaven), a former dance-band vocalist who turned to acting in his thirties. Became a more than useful support—for some, perhaps, too useful!—to the stars of minor 'A' budget studio (mainly Universal) films of the 1950s before drifting into television and a long run (as Ed Platt) as the spy chief in the comedy series *Get Smart*. Died from a heart attack.

1953: *Stalag 17.* 1955: *The Shrike. The Private War of Major Benson. Rebel Without a Cause. Cult of the Cobra. Illegal. Sincerely*

RIGHT ZaSu **Pitts** in one of her typical spinster roles of the mid-1930s, here in *Mrs Wiggs of the Cabbage Patch*, with Virginia Weidler (*qv*)

BELOW Edward C. **Platt** (full length visible) backs Jeanne Crain and Jeff Chandler on the courthouse steps in the 1957 film *The Tattered Dress*

*Yours. 1956: Serenade. Written on the Wind. The Proud Ones. Backlash. Storm Center. The Unguarded Moment. The Lieutenant Wore Skirts. The Great Man. Reprisal! Rock, Pretty Baby. 1957: The Tattered Dress. Designing Woman. Omar Khayyam. House of Numbers. The Helen Morgan Story (GB: Both Ends of the Candle). Damn Citizen! 1958: The Gift of Love. Oregon Passage. Summer Love. Last of the Fast Guns. The High Cost of Loving. Gunman's Walk. 1959: North by Northwest. They Came to Cordura. Inside the Mafia. The Rebel Set. Cash McCall. 1960: Pollyanna. 1961: Atlantis, the Lost Continent. The Explosive Generation. The Fiercest Heart. Cape Fear. 1962: Black Zoo. 1963: A Ticklish Affair. 1964: Man from Button Willow (voice only). Bullet for a Badman.*

## POHLMANN, Eric

(Erich Pohlmann) 1913-1979
Austrian actor who came to Britain in 1938 and, after World War II, became familiar in British crime thrillers as the fat, oily, moustachioed villain with the thick cigar and carnation in lapel, never doing his own dirty work and vying with Ferdy Mayne (qv) as the treacherous charming foreigner behind most crooked night-clubs and river-side rackets in the business. Returned to Austria and Germany for a few films towards the end of his days.

*1948: Portrait from Life (US: The Girl in the Painting). 1949: Children of Chance. The Third Man. Marry Me! Traveller's Joy (released 1951). 1950: Blackout. Highly Dangerous. Cairo Road. Chance of a Lifetime. State Secret (US: The Great Manhunt). The Clouded Yellow. There Is Another Sun (US: Wall of Death). 1951: The Long Dark Hall. Hell Is Sold Out. His Excellency. The Woman's Angle. 1952: Emergency Call (US: Hundred Hour Hunt). Penny Princess. Venetian Bird (US: The Assassin). Top Secret (US: Mr Potts Goes to Moscow). Moulin Rouge. The Gambler and the Lady. Monsoon. The Man Who Watched Trains Go By (US: Paris Express). 1953: Blood Orange. Mogambo. Rob Roy the Highland Rogue. 1954: They Who Dare. Knave of Hearts (US: Lovers, Happy Lovers). Forbidden Cargo. 36 Hours (US: Terror Street). The*

*Flame and the Flesh. The Belles of St Trinian's. 1955: A Prize of Gold. The Constant Husband. Gentlemen Marry Brunettes. The Glass Cage (US: The Glass Tomb). The Adventures of Quentin Durward (US: Quentin Durward). Break in the Circle. Dust and Gold. 1956: The Gelignite Gang. Reach for the Sky. Anastasia. Let's Be Happy. Zarak. The High Terrace. Lust for Life. House of Secrets (US: Triple Deception). The Counterfeit Plan. 1957: Interpol (US: Pickup Alley). Fire Down Below. Not Wanted on Voyage. Across the Bridge. Barnacle Bill (US: All at Sea). I Accuse! 1958: The Duke Wore Jeans. Nor the Moon by Night (US: Elephant Gun). The Man Inside. A Tale of Two Cities. Three Crooked Men. Further Up the Creek. The Mark of the Phoenix. Alive and Kicking. Life Is a Circus. 1959: Upstairs and Downstairs. The House of the Seven Hawks. Expresso Bongo. John Paul Jones. 1960: Snowball. Sands of the Desert. Surprise Package. The Man Who Couldn't Walk. Visa to Canton (US: Passport to China). No Kidding (US: Beware of Children). The Singer Not the Song. 1961: The Kitchen. Village of Daughters. Carry On Regardless. 1962: Mrs Gibbons' Boys. 55 Days at Peking. The Devil's Agent. 1963: Cairo. Shadow of Fear. Dr Syn—Alias the Scarecrow. Hot Enough for June (US: Agent 8 ¾). Follow the Boys. The Million Dollar Collar. 1964: Carry On Spying. The Sicilians. Night Train to Paris. 1965: Joey Boy. Those Magnificent Men in Their Flying Machines. Where the Spies Are. 1968: Mit Eichenlaub und Feigenblatt. Inspector Clouseau. 1969: Foreign Exchange (TV). 1970: The Horsemen. 1973: Tiffany Jones. 1974: The Return of the Pink Panther. 1976: Auch Mimosen wollen blühen. 1979: Ashanti. Tales from the Vienna Woods.*

## POLLARD, Michael J.

(M. J. Pollack) 1939-
Diminutive American actor with light curly hair, cherubic face and demonic smile. An Actors' Studio graduate, he shot to fame as *Bonnie and Clyde*'s accomplice in 1967 (he was nominated for an Oscar), but, as the leading actor he briefly became, he proved difficult to cast and his films were not too successful. Recently he has returned to character roles.

*1962: Hemingway's Adventures of a Young Man (GB: Adventures of a Young Man). The Stripper (GB: Woman of Summer). Summer Magic. 1966: The Russians Are Coming, the Russians Are Coming. Caprice. 1967: The Wild Angels. Enter Laughing. Bonnie and Clyde. 1968: Hannibal Brooks. The Smugglers (TV). Jigsaw (TV). 1970: Little Fauss and Big Halsy. 1971: Les pétroleuses/The Legend of Frenchie King. 1972: Dirty Little Billy. 1974: Sunday in the Country. 1977: Between the Lines. 1980: Melvin and Howard. 1985: The American Way. Heated Vengeance.*

## POLLOCK, Ellen 1903-

Black-haired, green-eyed British actress (born in Heidelberg, Germany) of long, strong facial features and predatory look. Her relatively few films through the years have tended to cast her as harpies and other women, but in the theatre she has gained a reputation as a formidable interpreter of George Bernard Shaw (she is also a long-time president of the Shaw Society). Runs her own street market antique stall. Her second husband was the painter James Proudfoot.

*1928: Moulin Rouge. 1929: Piccadilly. The Informer. 1930: Too Many Crooks. Night Birds. 1931: Midnight. My Wife's Family. Let's Love and Laugh (US: Bridegroom for Two). 1932: The First Mrs Fraser. The Last Coupon. Down Our Street. 1933: Heads We Go (US: The Charming Deceiver). Channel Crossing. 1934: Mr Cinders. Lord Edgware Dies. 1935: I Give My Heart. It's a Bet. Royal Cavalcade (GB: Regal Cavalcade). 1936: The Happy Family. Millions. Aren't Men Beasts! 1937: The Street Singer. Non-Stop New York. Splinters in the Air. 1939: *Shadow of Death. Sons of the Sea. 1940: Spare a Copper. 1942: Soldiers Without Uniform. 1944: Kiss the Bride Goodbye. 1945: Don Chicago. 1946: Bedelia. 1948: Warning to Wantons. 1950: Something in the City. To Have and to Hold. 1951: The Galloping Major. 1953: The Fake. 1954: The Golden Link. 1955: The Time of His Life. 1956: Not So Dusty. 1957: The Hypnotist (US: Scotland Yard Dragnet). 1958: The Long Knife. 1973: Horror Hospital. 1983: The Wicked Lady.*

## POWER, Hartley 1894-1966

Big, bald, explosive, full-faced American actor of genial expression. He acted on stage in America, Australia, England and Ireland before settling in England and bringing his booming tones to a handful of films from 1931 on, sometimes as con-man, agent, American officer, impresario or out-and-out crook. Married British actress-singer Betty Paul.

*1931: Down River. 1933: Aunt Sally (US: Along Came Sally). Just Smith (US: Leave It to Smith). Friday the Thirteenth. Yes Mr Brown. 1934: Road House. Evergreen. The Camels Are Coming. 1935: Jury's Evidence. 1936: Where There's a Will. Living Dangerously. 1938: The Return of the Frog. Just Like a Woman. 1939: Murder Will Out. A Window in London (US: Lady in Distress). Return to Yesterday. 1941: Atlantic Ferry (US: Sons of the Sea). 1942: Alibi. 1945: The Man from Morocco. The Way to the Stars (US: Johnny in the Clouds). Dead of Night. 1946: A Girl in a Million. 1951: The Armchair Detective. 1952: The Net (US: Project M7). 1953: Roman Holiday. The Million Pound Note (US: Man With a Million). 1954: To Dorothy a Son (US: Cash on Delivery). 1957: Island in the Sun.*

## PRICE, Nancy
(Lillian N. Price) 1880-1970

Formidable doyenne British actress with long nose and strong, stern facial features. Especially in the latter half of her long career (first stage appearance 1899), she appeared in dominant and sinister roles in which one could almost see the malevolence flashing from the eyes and the cobwebs trailing behind. In real life, this remarkable woman was a musicologist, painter, author, climber, naturalist, world-wide traveller and quasi-mystic. Her daughter, Joan Maude (Nancy Price married Charles Maude, who predeceased her) is also an actress.

*1916: The Lyons Mail. 1921: Belphegor the Mountebank. 1923: Love, Life and Laughter (US: Tip Toes). Comin' thro' the Rye. The Woman Who Obeyed. Bonnie Prince Charlie. 1927: Huntingtower. 1928: His House in Order. The Price of Divorce. 1929: The American Prisoner. The Doctor's Secret. Three Live Ghosts. 1930: The Loves of Robert Burns. 1931: The Speckled Band. 1932: Down Our Street. 1934: The Crucifix. 1939: The Stars Look Down. Dead Man's Shoes. 1942: Secret Mission. 1944: Madonna of the Seven Moons. 1945: I Live in Grosvenor Square (US: A Yank in London). I Know Where I'm Going! 1946: Carnival. 1947: Master of Bankdam. 1948: The Three Weird Sisters. 1950: The Naked Heart (Maria Chapdelaine/The Naked Earth). 1952: Mandy (US: Crash of Silence).*

## PURCELL, Noel 1900-1985

Lugubrious, bewhiskered Irish actor, the life and soul of many a British comedy of the forties, fifties and sixties. His tall, shambling figure was seen for many years in Irish stage classics at Dublin theatres before he became a film regular.

*1934: Jimmy Boy. 1938: Blarney (US: Ireland's Border Line). 1947: Captain Boycott. 1949: Saints and Sinners. The Blue Lagoon. 1951: Talk of a Million (GB: You Can't Beat the Irish). No Resting Place. Appointment with Venus (US: Island Rescue). Encore. 1952: Father's Doing Fine. The Pickwick Papers. Decameron Nights. The Crimson Pirate. 1953: Grand National Night (US: Wicked Woman). Doctor in the House. 1954: The Seekers (US: Land of Fury). Mad About Men. Svengali. 1955: Doctor at Sea. 1956: Jacqueline. Lust for Life. Moby Dick. 1957: Doctor at Large. The Rising of the Moon. 1958: Merry Andrew. Rooney. The Key. Rockets Galore (US: Mad Little Island).*

*1959: Tommy the Toreador. \*Seven Wonders of Ireland (narrator only). Shake Hands With the Devil. 1960: Make Mine Mink. Watch Your Stern. Man in the Moon. The Millionairess. No Kidding (US: Beware of Children). 1961: Double Bunk. Johnny Nobody. 1962: The Iron Maiden. Nurse on Wheels. Mutiny on the Bounty. 1963: The List of Adrian Messenger. The Ceremony. The Running Man. Zulu. 1964: Lord Jim. 1966: Doctor in Clover. Drop Dead Darling (US: Arrivederci Baby). 1969: Sinful Davey. Where's Jack? The Violent Enemy. 1970: The MacKenzie Break. 1971: Flight of the Doves. 1973: The Mackintosh Man.*

## PURDELL, Reginald
(R. Grasdorf) 1896-1953

Cheerful, chunky, ebullient, dark-haired British stage and radio comedian, screenplay writer and comic actor, often in 'ordinary man' roles, occasionally at the head of the cast, more often bolstering the support. Wrote the script for the 1933 version of *Three Men in a Boat* and many other minor film comedies.

*1930: The Middle Watch. 1931: Congress Dances. A Night in Montmartre. 1933: My Lucky Star. Strictly in Confidence. Up to the Neck. Crime on the Hill. 1934: On the Air. The Queen's Affair (US: Runaway Queen). Luck of a Sailor. The Old Curiosity Shop. What's in a Name? 1935: Key to Harmony. Royal Cavalcade (GB: Regal Cavalcade). Get Off My Foot. 1936: Crown v Stevens. Debt of Honour. Where's Sally? Hail and Farewell. 1937: Side Street Angel. Ship's Concert. The Dark Stairway. 1938: Quiet Please. Simply Terrific. Many Tanks Mr Atkins. 1939: The Missing People. The Middle Watch (and 1930 version). Q Planes (US: Clouds Over Europe). His Brother's Keeper. Pack Up Your Troubles. 1940: Busman's Honeymoon (US: Haunted Honeymoon). Fingers. 1943: Variety Jubilee. Bell Bottom George. We Dive at Dawn. It's in the Bag. 1944: Candles at Nine. 2,000 Women. Love Story (US: A Lady Surrenders). 1946: London Town (US: My Heart Goes Crazy). 1947: Brighton Rock (US: Young Scarface). Holiday Camp. Captain Boycott. The Root of All Evil. Man About the House. 1951: Files from Scotland Yard.*

**As director:**
1937: Patricia Gets Her Man.

**PYLE, Denver** 1920- 1997
Sharp-featured American actor with Donald Sutherland mouth, in later years buried beneath a bushy beard. Almost entirely cast in westerns (the name may have had something to do with it: he was christened after the capital of the state, Colorado, in which he was born), he at first played lean, mean and sneaky characters. But, after his vengeful sheriff in *Bonnie and Clyde*, he got away from all that, helped by a stint in TV's *The Doris Day Show*, and reappeared as benevolent westerners, in harmony with their surroundings. Had his first leading role in 1976 in *Guardian of the Wilderness*.

1947: Devil Ship. 1948: Where the North Begins. Train to Alcatraz. The Man from Colorado. Marshal of Amarillo. 1949: Hellfire. Flame of Youth. Streets of San Francisco. Too Late for Tears. Red Canyon. 1950: Dynamite Pass. Federal Agent at Large. The Flying Saucer. Customs Agent. The Old Frontier. Jet Pilot (released 1957). 1951: Rough Riders of Durango. Million Dollar Pursuit. Hills of Utah. 1952: Oklahoma Annie. Desert Passage. Fargo. Man from the More Plains. The Maverick. 1953: Texas Bad Man. Vigilante Terror. Canyon Ambush. Rebel City. Topeka. Goldtown Ghost Riders. A Perilous Journey. 1954: Ride Clear of Diablo. Johnny Guitar. The Forty-Niners. Crime Squad. 1955: To Hell and Back. Rage at Dawn. Run for Cover. Ten Wanted Men. Top Gun. 1956: Please Murder Me. The Naked Hills. 7th Cavalry. Yaqui Drums. 1957: The Lonely Man. Gun Duel in Durango. Destination 60,000. Domino Kid. 1958: The Left-Handed Gun. Fort Massacre. The Party Crashers. China Doll. Good Day for a Hanging. 1959: King of the Wild Stallions. Cast a Long Shadow. 1960: The Alamo. 1962: Geronimo. Terrified. This Rugged Land (TV. GB: cinemas). The Man Who Shot Liberty Valance. 1963: Mail Order Bride (GB: West of Montana). 1964: The Rounders. 1965: Mara of the Wilderness. Shenandoah. The Great Race. Incident at Phantom Hill. Gunpoint. 1966: Welcome to Hard Times. 1967: Bonnie and Clyde. Tammy and the Millionaire.

1968: Bandolero! Five Card Stud. 1971: Something Big. 1973: Hitched (TV. GB: Westward the Wagon). Cahill, United States Marshal (GB: Cahill). 1974: Sidekicks (TV). Murder or Mercy (TV). The Life and Times of Grizzly Adams (GB: TV). Escape to Witch Mountain. 1975: Death Among Friends (TV). Winterhawk. 1976: Buffalo Bill and the Indians, or: Sitting Bull's History Lesson. Hawmps. Welcome to LA. Guardian of the Wilderness. The Adventures of Frontier Fremont (GB: Spirit of the Wild). 1978: Return from Witch Mountain.

**QUAID, Randy** 1948-
Tall, strapping American actor with light, curly hair, 'simple' looks and idiot grin. A former stand-up nightclub comic who worked as a cartoonist and painter in his spare time, Quaid was brought to films by Peter Bogdanovich, and was especially well-cast in *The Last Detail*; his moving performance was nominated for an Oscar. His female impersonation in *Breakout* was amusing and clearly relished, but (he's six-feet-five) unlikely to fool anyone. Brother of actor Dennis Quaid.

1971: The Last Picture Show. 1972: What's Up Doc? Getting Away from It All (TV). 1973: Paper Moon. The Last Detail. Lolly Madonna XXX (GB: The Lolly Madonna War). 1974: The Apprenticeship of Duddy Kravitz. The Great Niagara (TV). 1975: Breakout. 1976: The Missouri Breaks. Bound

for Glory. 1977: The Choirboys. Three Warriors. 1978: Midnight Express. 1979: Foxes. Guyana Tragedy (TV). 1980: The Raid on Coffeyville/The Last Ride of the Dalton Gang (TV). The Long Riders. 1981: Of Mice and Men (TV). Heartbeeps. 1983: Cowboy (TV). National Lampoon's Vacation. 1984: The Slugger's Wife. A Streetcar Named Desire (TV). The Wild Life. 1985: Sweet Country. Fool for Love.

**QUALEN, John** (J. Oleson) 1899- 1987
Sad-looking little actor, born in Canada of Norwegian parents (his father was a minister) and Hollywood's resident Scandinavian (often put-upon, occasionally sinister) from the mid-1930s. After his excellent performance as Axel in *The Long Voyage Home*, his mournful, oval, moustachioed features were seen in several more John Ford films through the years. Also a talented musician; plays piano, flute and saxophone.

1931: Street Scene. Arrowsmith. 1933: The Devil's Brother (GB: Fra Diavolo). Counsellor at Law. 1934: Let's Fall in Love. Upper World. He Was Her Man. Servants' Entrance. Hi, Nellie! Sing and Like It. Straight Is the Way. Private Scandal. Our Daily Bread. 365 Nights in Hollywood. 1935: Charlie Chan in Paris. One More Spring. Orchids to You. The Farmer Takes a Wife. Black Fury. Chasing Yesterday. Cheers of the Crowd. The Great Hotel Murder. Doubting Thomas. Thunder in the Night. The Silk Hat Kid. The Three Musketeers. Man of Iron. 1936: The Road to Glory. The Country Doctor. Wife versus Secretary. Whipsaw. Reunion (GB: Hearts in Reunion). Meet Nero Wolfe. Ring Around the Moon. Girls' Dormitory. 1937: Fifty Roads to Town. Nothing Sacred. She Had to Eat. Bad Man from Brimstone. Seventh Heaven. Angel's Holiday. Fit for a King. 1938: Five of a Kind. The Texans. Outside the Law. The Chaser. The Mad Miss Manton. Joy of Living. 1939: Career. Stand Up and Fight. Let Us Live. Thunder Afloat. Mickey the Kid. Honeymoon in Bali (GB: Husbands or Lovers). Four Wives. 1940: Angels Over Broadway. His Girl Friday. On Their Own. Brother Orchid. The Long Voyage Home. Ski Patrol. Blondie on a Budget. The Grapes of Wrath. Youth Will Be Served. Knute Rockne—All American (GB: A Modern Hero). Saturday's Children.

1941: Shepherd of the Hills. Million Dollar Baby. All That Money Can Buy/The Devil and Daniel Webster/Daniel and the Devil. New Wine (GB: The Great Awakening). Out of the Fog. Model Wife. 1942: Tortilla Flat. Larceny Inc. Jungle Book. Arabian Nights. Casablanca. 1943: Swing Shift Maisie (GB: The Girl in Overalls). 1944: An American Romance. Dark Waters. The Impostor. 1945: Roughly Speaking. River Gang (GB: Fairy Tale Murder). Captain Kidd. Adventure. 1947: High Conquest. Song of Scheherezade. The Fugitive. 1948: My Girl Tisa. Hollow Triumph (GB: The Scar). A Miracle Can Happen (later and GB: On Our Merry Way). Sixteen Fathoms Deep. Alias a Gentleman. 1949: The Big Steal. Captain China. Buccaneer's Girl. 1950: The Jackpot. Woman on the Run. 1951: Belle le Grand. Goodbye, My Fancy. The Flying Missile. 1952: Hans Christian Andersen. . . and the dancer. 1953: I, the Jury. Ambush at Tomahawk Gap. 1954: The High and the Mighty. Passion. The Student Prince. The Other Woman. 1955: Unchained. The Sea Chase. At Gunpoint (GB: Gunpoint!). 1956: Johnny Concho. The Searchers. 1957: The Big Land (GB: Stampeded!). 1958: The Gun Runners. Revolt in the Big House. 1959: Anatomy of a Murder. 1960: Elmer Gantry. North to Alaska. Hell Bent for Leather. 1961: Two Rode Together. The Comancheros. 1962: The Man Who Shot Liberty Valance. 1963: The Prize. 1964: Cheyenne Autumn. The Seven Faces of Dr Lao. Those Calloways. 1965: I'll Take Sweden. A Patch of Blue. The Sons of Katie Elder. 1966: A Big Hand for the Little Lady (GB: Big Deal at Dodge City). 1967: PJ (GB: New Face in Hell). Firecreek. 1969: Hail, Hero! 1971: Getting Away from It All (TV). 1973: Frasier, the Sensuous Lion.

## QUILLAN, Eddie 1907- 1990

Bright-eyed, dark-haired, effervescent American juvenile lead, well at home in collegiate comedies, who later developed into a useful supporting player, at home in both comedy and drama. On stage with his family's vaudeville act at seven, he came to Hollywood at 19 to feature in comedy shorts, but it was in 1940 that he got one of his best roles, as Connie Rivers in The Grapes of Wrath. Played increasingly smaller roles in post-war years, but kept acting up to the early 1980s. Has never married.

1922: Up and At 'Em! 1926: *A Love Sundae. *Her Actor Friend. 1927: *College Kiddo. *The Bullfighter. *The Plumber's Daughters. *Love in a Police Station. 1928: Show Folks. 1929: The Godless Girl. The Sophomore. Geraldine. Noisy Neighbors. Hot and Bothered. 1930: Night Work. Big Money. A Little Bit of Everything. 1931: Looking for Trouble. Sweepstakes. Tip Off. The Big Shot (GB: The Optimist). 1932: Girl Crazy. Easy Money. 1933: Strictly Personal. Broadway to Hollywood (GB: Ring Up the Curtain). 1934: Gridiron Flash (GB: Luck of the Game). Hollywood Party. 1935: Mutiny on the

Bounty. 1936: The Gentleman from Louisiana. The Mandarin Mystery. 1937: London by Night. Big City. 1938: Swing Sister Swing! The Family Next Door. 1939: The Flying Irishman. Allegheny Uprising (GB: The First Rebel). Young Mr Lincoln. Made for Each Other. 1940: La Conga Nights. Margie. The Grapes of Wrath. Hawaiian Nights. Dark Streets of Cairo. 1941: Six Lessons from Madame La Zonga. Where Did You Get That Girl? Dancing on a Dime. Flame of New Orleans. Too Many Blondes. Flying Blind. 1942: Kid Glove Killer. Priorities on Parade. 1943: Hi Ya Sailor! It Ain't Hay (GB: Money for Jam). Follow the Band. Melody Parade. Here Comes Kelly. 1944: Dark Mountain. Dixie Jamboree. Hi Good Lookin'. The Impostor. Moonlight and Cactus. Mystery of the River Boat (serial). Slightly Terrific. This Is the Life. Twilight on the Prairie. 1945: Jungle Queen (serial). Jungle Raiders (serial). Song of the Sarong. 1946: A Guy Could Change. Sensation Hunters. 1950: Sideshow. 1954: Brigadoon. 1963: Promises! Promises! Move Over, Darling. 1965: The Ghost and Mr Chicken. The Bounty Hunter. 1967: Did You Hear the One About the Traveling Saleslady? 1969: Angel in My Pocket. 1971: How to Frame a Figg. 1972: The Judge and Jake Wyler (TV). 1973: She Lives (TV). 1974: Hitchhike! (TV). Melvin Purvis, G-Man (TV. GB: cinemas, as The Legend of Machine-Gun Kelly). 1975: The Strongest Man in the World. 1977: Mad Bull (TV). 1979: The Darker Side of Terror (TV). 1981: White Mama (TV).

## QUINN, Tony (T. Quin) 1899-1967

Small, shuffling, fair-haired (soon grey) Irish actor who, after a long stage career in Ireland (from 1919) and England (from 1927), popped in and out of dozens of British films as briefly glimpsed ushers, guides, drivers, neighbours and manual workers. Moved to London (where he died) and became an expert on military history, building up a huge collection of toy soldiers.

1934: Lest We Forget. 1937: Non-Stop New York. 1941: The Saint Meets the Tiger. Danny Boy. 1942: Squadron Leader X. Thunder Rock. 1943: It's in the Bag. 1944: Welcome Mr Washington. 1946: I See a Dark Stranger (US: The Adventuress). Hungry Hill. 1947: Uneasy Terms. 1948: Bond Street. 1949: Saints and Sinners. The Strangers Came (US: You Can't Fool an Irishman). Diamond City. Boys in Brown. 1950: Never Say Die/Don't Say Die. 1951: Talk of a Million (US: You Can't Beat the Irish). The Long Dark Hall. High Treason. The Lavender Hill Mob. 1952: Treasure Hunt. Gift Horse (US: Glory at Sea). 1954: The Beachcomber. 1955: Shadow of a Man. See How They Run. 1956: Not So Dusty. The Last Man To Hang? Tons of Trouble. Satellite in the Sky. Operation Murder. 1957: The Story of Esther Costello (US: Golden Virgin). The Man Without a Body. Booby Trap. Undercover Girl. The Rising of the Moon. 1958: Life in

Emergency Ward 10. Alive and Kicking. 1959: The Great Van Robbery. Trouble With Eve (US: In Trouble With Eve). 1960: Circle of Deception. The Unstoppable Man. 1961: The Trunk. The Golden Rabbit. 1962: The Durant Affair. Out of the Fog. 1963: Hide and Seek. 1964: The Runaway. Murder Ahoy.

## RAGLAN, Robert 1906-

Heavy-set, moustachioed British actor of flat nose and choleric complexion. Usually to be seen as the trilby-hatted, raincoated police sergeant or inspector called to the scene of the crime. Once reckoned to have played 27 different policemen, of all ranks, in one year's television work alone.

1953: The Good Beginning. Recoil. 1954: The Yellow Robe. 1955: Handcuffs London. 1956: Brothers in Law. 1957: Man from Tangier (US: Thunder Over Tangier). There's Always a Thursday. Count Five and Die. Undercover Girl. Zoo Baby (released 1960). 1958: The Great Van Robbery. Hidden Homicide. Innocent Meeting. Corridors of Blood (released 1961). 1959: An Honourable Murder. 'Beat' Girl (US: Wild for Kicks). Web of Suspicion. A Woman's Temptation. 1960: Dead Lucky. A Taste of Money. 1965: Where the Spies Are. 1966: Slave Girls. 1967: The Magnificent Six and a ½ (first series). 1968: Subterfuge. 1969: The Magic Christian. The Haunted House of Horror. 1970: Tomorrow. Loot. The Rise and Rise of Michael Rimmer. 1971: Dad's Army. Catch Me a Spy.

ABOVE Eddie **Quillan** (foreground, in shirtsleeves) looks condemned by forensic evidence in *Kid Glove Killer* (1942). Lee Bowman (with moustache), the real killer, offers mock sympathy. Scientists Marsha Hunt and Van Heflin (left) will sort it out

BELOW Tony **Quinn** comes into possession of a priceless book in *Not So Dusty* (1956), confounding sneaky Ellen Pollock and watched by Bill Shine, and (background) Bill Owen and Leslie Dwyer (all *qv*)

**RALPH, Jessie** (Jessica R. Chambers) 1864-1944

One of those 'stately as a galleon' ladies, this dark-haired American actress brought a touch of warmth and dignity to everything she tackled — nurses, governesses, companions and dowagers. At one end of the scale, she was a good fairy in *The Blue Bird*, then in the same year enjoyed a rare chance to play the harridan as W.C. Fields' mother-in-law in *The Bank Dick*. Forced to give up acting only after the amputation of a leg in 1941.

*1916: New York. 1921: Such a Little Queen. 1933: Elmer the Great. Child of Manhattan. Cocktail Hour. Ann Carver's Profession. 1934: Nana (GB: Lady of the Boulevards). Coming-Out Party. One Night of Love. We Live Again. Evelyn Prentice. Murder at the Vanities. The Affairs of Cellini. 1935: David Copperfield. Les Misérables. Paris in Spring (GB: Paris Love Song). Enchanted April. Vanessa: Her Love Story. Mark of the Vampire. Jalna. I Live My Life. Metropolitan. Captain Blood. I Found Stella Parish. 1936: The Garden Murder Case. San Francisco. Bunker Bean (GB: His Majesty Bunker Bean). The Unguarded Hour. After the Thin Man. Camille. Little Lord Fauntleroy. Yellow Dust. Walking on Air. 1937: Double Wedding. The Last of Mrs Cheyney. The Good Earth. 1938: Hold That Kiss. Love Is a Headache. Port of Seven Seas. 1939: St Louis Blues. Mickey the Kid. Café Society. Four Girls in White. The Kid from Texas. Drums Along the Mohawk. 1940: Star Dust. The Girl from Avenue A. I Can't Give You Anything But Love, Baby. The Blue Bird. The Bank Dick (GB: The Bank Detective). I Want a Divorce. 1941: The Lady from Cheyenne. They Met in Bombay.*

**RAMBEAU, Marjorie** 1889-1970

Handsome, sunny-dispositioned American actress with light-brown hair, on the stage at 12, a star of silents by 1916. With sound, she came back as a character actress, often as discarded mistresses, but in as many high- as low-society roles in post-war years. She made a few raucous comedies opposite Wallace Beery, rather ironically in the light of the fact that her character in *Min and Bill*

had been killed off by Beery's most famous partner Marie Dressler, and was twice nominated for the Best Supporting Actress Oscar, in *The Primrose Path* and *Torch Song*. Her characters were perhaps summed up by the title of her 1931 release *Leftover Ladies*.

*1916: The Dazzling Miss Davison. Motherhood. The Greater Woman. 1917: Mary Moreland. The Mirror. The Debt. 1918: The Common Cause. 1920: The Fortune Teller. 1926: Syncopating Sue. 1930: Her Man. Min and Bill. 1931: Son of India. Inspiration. The Easiest Way. Silence. A Tailor-Made Man. Strangers May Kiss. Leftover Ladies (GB: Broken Links). This Modern Age. The Secret Six. Laughing Sinners. Hell Divers. 1933: The Warrior's Husband. Strictly Personal. A Man's Castle. 1934: Ready for Love. A Modern Hero. Palooka (GB: The Great Schnozzle). Grand Canary. 1935: Under Pressure. Dizzy Dames. 1937: First Lady. 1938: Merrily We Live. Woman Against Woman. 1939: Sudden Money. The Rains Came. Heaven With a Barbed-Wire Fence. Laugh It Off. 1940: Santa Fé Marshal. Twenty-Mule Team. The Primrose Path. East of the River. Tugboat Annie Sails Again. 1941: Three Sons o' Guns. Tobacco Road. So Ends Our Night. 1942: Broadway. 1943: In Old Oklahoma (later and GB: War of the Wildcats). 1944: Oh, What a Night! Army Wives. 1945: Salome, Where She Danced. 1948: The Walls of Jericho. 1949: The Lucky Stiff. Abandoned. Any Number Can Play. 1953: Bad for Each Other. Forever Female. Torch Song. 1955: A Man Called Peter. The View from Pompey's Head (GB: Secret Interlude). 1956: Slander. 1957: Man of a Thousand Faces.*

**RATOFF, Gregory** 1897-1960

Heavy-set, scruffy-looking, big-nosed, brown-haired Russian-born actor with delightfully thick Slavic accent. He was always welcome as arm-waving impresarios and the like, having come to America in the late 1920s; but, from the late 1930s, he began to concentrate on direction and became, for a while, one of 20th Century-Fox's leading directors. His returns to acting were infrequent and he died in Switzerland at 63.

*1929: \*For Sale. 1932: Roar of the Dragon. Skyscraper Souls. Deported. Once in a Lifetime. Symphony of Six Million (GB: Melody of Life). Secrets of the French Police. Undercover Man. What Price Hollywood? Thirteen Women. 1933: Headline Shooter (GB: Evidence in Camera). Professional Sweetheart (GB: Imaginary Sweetheart). I'm No Angel. Sweepings. Girl Without a Room. Sitting Pretty. Broadway Thru a Keyhole. 1934: The Forbidden Territory. Falling in Love (US: Trouble Ahead). George White's Scandals. The Great Flirtation. Let's Fall in Love. 1935: Hello Sweetheart/The Butter and Egg Man. King of Burlesque. Remember Last Night? 1936: Here Comes Trouble. Sins of Man. Under Two Flags. Sing, Baby, Sing. The Road to Glory. Under Your Spell. 1937: Top of the Town. Seventh Heaven. Café Metropole. 1938: Sally, Irene and Mary. Gateway. 1940: The Great Profile. 1950: All About Eve. 1952: O. Henry's Full House (GB: Full House). 1957: The Sun Also Rises. 1960: Once More With Feeling. Exodus. 1961: The Big Gamble.*

**As director:**

*1933: †Sins of Man. 1937: Lancer Spy. 1938: Wife, Husband and Friend. 1939: Rose of Washington Square. Barricade. Day-Time Wife. Intermezzo: A Love Story (GB: Escape to Happiness). Hotel for Women/Elsa Maxwell's Hotel for Women. 1940: I Was an Adventuress. Public Deb No.1. 1941: Adam Had Four Sons. The Men in Her Life. The Corsican Brothers. 1942: Two Yanks in Trinidad. Footlight Serenade. 1943: Something to Shout About. The Heat's On (GB: Tropicana). 1944: Song of Russia. Irish Eyes Are Smiling. 1945: Paris Underground (GB: Madame Pimpernel). Where Do We Go from Here? 1946: Do You Love Me? 1947: Carnival in Costa Rica. Moss Rose. 1949: Black Magic. That Dangerous Age (US: If This Be Sin). 1950: My Daughter Joy (US: Operation X). 1953: Taxi. 1954: Abdullah's Harem (GB: Abdullah the Great). 1960: Oscar Wilde.*

**RAYMOND, Cyril** 1895-1973

Affable, dark-haired, moustachioed British actor of ruddy complexion and solid, pipe-smoking image. An actor since he was 19,

he was quietly professional in many 'reliable' roles, such as doctors, police inspectors or family solicitors, but probably most memorably as the 'dull', sit-by-the-fire husband of Celia Johnson in *Brief Encounter*; this beautifully understated performance is one of his best. Retired at 70. Married to actresses Iris Hoey and Gillian Lind.

*1916: The Hypocrites. Disraeli. 1919: His Last Defence. I Will. 1920: The Scarlet Kiss. Wuthering Heights. 1921: Moth and Rust. Sonia. 1922: The Norwood Builder. Cocaine. The Faithful Heart. 1931: These Charming People. The Happy Ending. Man of Mayfair. The Ghost Train. Condemned to Death. 1932: The Frightened Lady (US: Criminal at Large). 1933: The Shadow. Mixed Doubles. Home Sweet Home. Strike It Rich. The Lure. The Man Outside. 1934: Keep It Quiet. 1935: The Tunnel (US Transatlantic Tunnel). 1936: It's Love Again. Accused. Tomorrow We Live. Thunder in the City. 1937: Stardust. Dreaming Lips. 1938: Night Alone. 1939: The Spy in Black (US: U-Boat 29). Come On George. 1940: Saloon Bar. 1945: Brief Encounter. 1946: Men of Two Worlds (US: Kisenga). 1947: This Was a Woman. 1948: Quartet. The Jack of Diamonds. 1952: Angels One Five. Rough Shoot (US: Shoot First). 1953: The Heart of the Matter. 1954: The Crowded Day. Lease of Life. The Gay Dog. 1955: One Just Man. 1956: Charley Moon. The Baby and the Battleship. 1958: Dunkirk. 1960: No Kidding (US: Beware of Children). 1962: Don't Talk to Strange Men. 1964: Night Train to Paris.*

## REDMOND, Liam 1913-

Burly, dark-but-balding, full-faced Irish actor, often in angry or aggressive roles, who divided his time between the English, Irish and American stages, squeezing in nearly 50 film assignments as well. A master of dialect who often didn't sound Irish at all, he's best remembered as the chief saboteur in *High Treason*. Made several trips to Hollywood.

*1946: I See a Dark Stranger (US: The Adventures). 1947: Captain Boycott. 1948: Daughter of Darkness. 1949: Saints and Sinners. Sword in the Desert. The Twenty*

*Questions Murder Mystery. 1951: High Treason. 1952: The Gentle Gunman. 1953: The Cruel Sea. 1954: Devil on Horseback. Final Appointment. The Passing Stranger. The Divided Heart. Happy Ever After (US: Tonight's the Night/O'Leary Night). 1955: The Glass Cage (US: The Glass Tomb). 1956: Jacqueline. Yield to the Night (US: Blonde Sinner). 23 Paces to Baker Street. Safari. 1957: The Long Haul. Night of the Demon (US: Curse of the Demon). 1958: Rooney. Ice-Cold in Alex (US: Desert Attack). Diplomatic Corpse. She Didn't Say No! Alive and Kicking. No Trees in the Street. 1959: The Boy and the Bridge. 1960: Scent of Mystery (GB: Holiday in Spain). Under Ten Flags. 1961: The Valiant. 1962: Phantom of the Opera. The Playboy of the Western World. Kid Galahad. 1964: The Luck of Ginger Coffey. 1965: The Ghost and Mr Chicken. The Amorous Adventures of Moll Flanders. The Adventures of Bullwhip Griffin. 1966: Tobruk. 1967: The 25th Hour. The Last Safari. The Sky Bike. 1969: David Copperfield (TV. GB: cinemas). 1972: The Alf Garnett Saga (US: Alf 'n' Family). 1973: And No One Could Save Her (TV). 1975: Barry Lyndon.*

## REEVES, (P) Kynaston 1893-1971

Tall, stork-like, beaky British actor with high forehead disappearing into fuzzy, receding hair; almost always in learned roles: deans, professors, ministers, clerics and the like. After an army career, he turned to the theatre at 27 and ran up a huge list of credits, as well as making over 70 films and appearing frequently on TV. Seemed to become increasingly emaciated in later years. The P. stood for Philip. The Kynaston came from his mother's maiden name.

*1919: His Last Defence. 1932: The Sign of Four. The Lodger (US: The Phantom Fiend). 1933: Puppets of Fate. 1934: Broken Melody. The Crimson Candle. Jew Süss (US: Power). 1935: Vintage Wine. Dark World. 1936: Take a Chance. 1937: A Romance in Flanders (US: Lost on the Western Front). 1938: Housemaster. 1939: The Outsider. Dead Men Are Dangerous. The Stars Look Down. Sons of the Sea. Inspector Hornleigh on Holiday (US: Inspector Hornleigh on Leave). 1940: Two for Danger. The Flying Squad. 1941: The Prime Minister. This England. 1942: The Young Mr Pitt. The Night Invader. 1944: Strawberry Roan. 1945: The Rake's Progress (US: Notorious Gentleman). The Echo Murders. Murder in Reverse. 1947: This Was a Woman, Vice Versa. 1948: The Winslow Boy. Counterblast. The Guinea Pig. The Weaker Sex. Badger's Green. 1949: Madness of the Heart. Madeleine. The Twenty Questions Murder Mystery. 1950: Tony Draws a Horse. Blackout. The Mudlark. The Undefeated. Trio. 1951: Captain Horatio Hornblower RN. Smart Alec. 1952: Top Secret (US: Mr Potts Goes to Moscow). Penny Princess. Top of the Form. Laxdale Hall (US: Scotch on the Rocks). Four-Sided Triangle. 1954: Eight O'Clock Walk. Burnt Evidence. The Crowded Day. 1955: Touch and Go (US: The Light Touch). Fun at St Fanny's. 1956: Guilty? Brothers-in-Law. 1957: High Flight. 1958: Fiend Without a Face. Family Doctor (US: RX Murder). A Question of Adultery. Carleton-Browne of the FO (US: Man in a Cocked Hat). 1959: In the Nick. 1960: School for Scoundrels. The Night We Got the Bird. 1961: Shadow of the Cat. Carry On Regardless. In the Doghouse. Don't Bother To Knock! (US: Why Bother to Knock?). 1962: Go to Blazes. 1963: Hide and Seek. 1968: Hot Millions. 1969: Anne of the Thousand Days.*

## REICHER, Frank

(Franz Reicher) 1875-1965

German-born actor in Hollywood whose small chin, high forehead, pointed nose and crow's-feet eyes gave the impression that he was forever leaning intently forward. He had begun his film career as a director of silents, but in sound films concentrated on acting, mostly as professors, doctors, surgeons and small-town officials. Usually in kind or gentle parts, occasionally victims or suspicious figures of authority, he was intensely busy throughout the latter stages of his career.

*1921: Behind Masks. Out of the Depths. Wise Husbands. Idle Hands. 1926: Her Man o' War. 1928: Beau Sabreur. Four Sons. The Blue Danube. The Masks of the Devil. *Napoleon's Barber. Sins of the Fathers. Someone to Love. The Masked Angel (GB: Her Love Cottage). 1929: Mister Antonio. His Captive Woman. Strange Cargo. Her Private Affair. Big News. Black Waters. Paris Bound. The Changeling. 1930: Die Sehnsucht Jeder Frau. The Grand Parade. Girl of the Port. 1931: A Gentleman's Fate. Beyond Victory. Suicide Fleet. Mata Hari. 1932: A Woman Commands. Scarlet Dawn. The Crooked Circle. 1933: Jennie Gerhardt. Captured. After Tonight. King Kong. Ever in My Heart. Before Dawn. Topaze. Employees' Entrance. Rasputin and the Empress (GB: Rasputin — the Mad Monk). Son of Kong. 1934: I Am a Thief. Journal of a Crime. Hi, Nellie! Countess of Monte Cristo. Little Man, What Now? Let's Talk It Over. No Greater Glory. Return of the Terror. The Fountain. The Case of the Howling Dog. 1935: A Dog of Flanders. Mills of the Gods. Star of Midnight. Charlie Chan in Egypt. The Florentine Dagger. Kind Lady. Remember Last Night. Rendezvous. Straight from the Heart. Life Returns. The Man Who Broke the Bank at Monte Carlo. The Great Impersonation. Magnificent Obsession. The Story of Louis Pasteur. 1936: Sutter's Gold. The Country Doctor. Under Two Flags. The Invisible Ray. The Murder of Dr Harrigan. Girls' Dormitory. Along Came Love. Old Hutch. Star for a Night. 'Til We Meet Again. Murder on a Bridle Path. The Ex-Mrs Bradford. Second Wife. Camille. Anthony Adverse. Stolen Holiday. 1937: Westbound Limited. Laughing at Trouble. The Great O'Malley. Midnight Madonna. The Mighty Treve. Under Cover of Night. Espionage. Stage Door. The Road Back. The Emperor's Candlesticks. Prescription for Romance. Fit for a King. Lancer Spy. Night Key. On Such a Night. Beg, Borrow or Steal. 1938: Rascals. City Streets. Letter of Introduction. Of Human Hearts. Prison Nurse. I'll Give a Million. The Storm. Torchy Gets Her Man. Suez. 1939: Unexpected Father (GB: Sandy Takes a Bow). Mystery of the White Room. Juarez. Woman Doctor. The Magnificent Fraud. Society Smugglers. Ninotchka. Our Neighbors, the Carters. The Escape. South of the Border. Never Say Die. Everything Happens at Night. 1940: The Man I Married. All This, and Heaven Too. Dr Cyclops. Typhoon. Devil's Island. South to Karanga. The Lady in Question. Sky Murder. 1941: They Dare Not Love. Underground. Flight from Destiny. Shining Victory. Father Takes a Wife. The*

*Nurse's Secret. Dangerously They Live. 1942: Nazi Agent. Salute to Courage. To Be or Not To Be. The Mystery of Marie Roget. Secret Enemies. Beyond the Blue Horizon. The Gay Sisters. The Mummy's Tomb. Scattergood Survives a Murder. I Married an Angel. Night Monster (GB: House of Mystery). 1943: Yanks Ahoy! The Song of Bernadette. Mission to Moscow. Tornado. Watch on the Rhine. 1944: The Canterville Ghost. In Our Time. Scattergood's Ghost. The Adventures of Mark Twain. The Mummy's Ghost. Address Unknown. The Hitler Gang. Mrs Parkington. The Conspirators. House of Frankenstein. The Big Bonanza. 1945: A Medal for Benny. *Phantoms Inc. Voice of the Whistler. The Jade Mask. Hotel Berlin. Rhapsody in Blue. Blonde Ransom. The Tiger Woman. 1946: The Shadow Returns. The Strange Mrs Gregory. Home in Oklahoma. My Pal Trigger. Sister Kenny. 1947: Mr District Attorney. Violence. Yankee Fakir. Escape Me Never. The Secret Life of Walter Mitty. 1948: Carson City Raiders. I, Jane Doe. Fighting Mad. 1949: Barbary Pirate. Samson and Delilah. 1950: Cargo to Capetown. The Arizona Cowboy. The Happy Years. Kiss Tomorrow Goodbye. 1951: The Lady and the Bandit (GB: Dick Turpin's Ride). Superman and the Mole Men (GB: Superman and the Strange People).*

**As director:**

*1915: The Chorus Lady. The Case of Becky. The Secret Orchard (GB: The Secret Garden). The Secret Sin. 1916: For the Defense. The Love Mask. Witchcraft. The Dupe. The Victory of Conscience. Puddin' Head Wilson. Alien Souls. The Black Wolfe. 1917: Castles for Two. The Eternal Mother. Lost and Won. Sacrifice. The Inner Shrine. Unconquered. An American Widow. 1918: The Claim. The Only Road. Suspense. The Treasure of the Sea. The Prodigal Wife. The Trap. 1919: The American Way. The Battler. 1920: The Black Circle. Empty Arms. 1921: Behind Masks. Idle Hands. Wise Husbands. Out of the Depths. 1929: †Paris Bound. †Big News. †Mister Antonio. 1930: †The Grand Parade.*

†Co-directed

**REID, Beryl** 1918-
Purse-lipped, round-faced, light-haired British radio comedienne who amused

audiences through three decades with her impersonations of lisping schoolgirls with such names as Marlene and Monica, before unexpectedly becoming a star character actress of considerable impact, mostly in comic roles, but most noticeably with the tragi-comic *The Killing of Sister George*, a film repeat of her stage triumph. Latterly in 'guest star' roles.

*1940: Spare a Copper. 1954: The Belles of St Trinian's. 1956: The Extra Day. 1960: Two-Way Stretch. 1962: The Dock Brief (US: Trial and Error). 1968: Inspector Clouseau. The Assassination Bureau. Star! The Killing of Sister George. 1970: Entertaining Mr Sloane. The Beast in the Cellar. 1972: Dr Phibes Rises Again. Father Dear Father. Psychomania. 1973: No Sex Please — We're British. 1976: Joseph Andrews. 1978: Rosie Dixon Night Nurse. Carry On Emmannuelle. 1980: *Late Flowering Love. 1983: Yellowbeard. 1985: The Doctor and the Devils.*

**REID, Carl Benton** 1893-1973
Distinguished-looking, authoritative, sometimes moustachioed American actor with long theatrical experience. He came to Hollywood to recreate his stage role of the conniving Oscar Hubbard in *The Little Foxes* and his squatly handsome features remained near the top of Hollywood casts for the next 20 years as doctors, wardens, Cavalry captains, businessmen and lawyers, never over-playing his hand in any guise.

*1941: The Little Foxes. 1942: Tennessee Johnson (GB: The Man on America's Conscience). 1943: The North Star (later Armored Attack). Mission to Moscow. 1949: The Doctor and the Girl. 1950: The Fuller Brush Girl (GB: The Affairs of Sally). The Killer That Stalked New York (GB: The Frightened City). Stage to Tucson (GB: Lost Stage Valley). In a Lonely Place. Convicted. The Flying Missile. 1951: The Family Secret. The Great Caruso. Lorna Doone. Smuggler's Gold. Criminal Lawyer. Boots Malone. 1952: Carbine Williams. The Brigand. The First Time. The Story of Will Rogers. Indian Uprising. 1953: Escape from Fort Bravo. Main Street to Broadway. 1954: The Command. Broken Lance. Athena. The Egyptian. 1955: One Desire. The Spoilers. Wichita. The Left Hand of God. 1956: A Day of Fury. The First Texan. The Last Wagon. Strange Intruder. Battle Hymn. 1957: Time Limit. Spoilers of the Forest. 1958: Tarzan's Fight for Life. Last of the Fast Guns. The Trap (GB: The Baited Trap). 1960: The Bramble Bush. The Gallant Hours. 1962: Underwater City. Pressure Point. 1963: The Ugly American. 1965: Madame X.*

**REID, Milton** 1917-
Massively-built, shaven-headed, India-born ex-wrestler who entered the British entertainment arena in his late thirties and played sadistic villains, mutes, mulattoes, genies, Thuggees and other exotic characters, mostly of the menacing variety. Just the sort of man to turn up in James Bond

films, he did eventually make one, remaining active in films and (especially) television into his early sixties, still often playing muscular heavies.

*1957: Undercover Girl. 1958: The Camp on Blood Island. Blood of the Vampire. 1959: Ferry to Hong Kong. Our Man in Havana. Swiss Family Robinson. 1960: Visa to Canton (US: Passport to China). 1961: The Terror of the Tongs. Follow That Man! The Wonders of Aladdin. 1962: Captain Clegg (US: Night Creatures). 1963: Panic. 1964: Ursus. Spartacus and the Ten Gladiators. 1965: Monster! Cimbro. 1966: Deadlier Than the Male. 1967: Berserk! Great Catherine. Casino Royale. 1968: The Assassination Bureau. 1969: How To Make It (GB: Target: Harry). 1970: The Horsemen. 1971: Blinker's Spy Spotter. 1972: Dr Phibes Rises Again. 1974: The Return of the Pink Panther. 1977: Come Play With Me. The Spy Who Loved Me. The People That Time Forgot. No 1 of the Secret Service. 1978: Terror. What's Up Superdoc? 1979: Arabian Adventure. Confessions from the David Galaxy Affair. Queen of the Blues.*

**RELPH, George** 1888-1960
Dark, moustachioed, amiable British actor with hound-like face who, unfortunately for filmgoers, decided to spend almost his entire career on stage after film experience in Hollywood in the early silent days. Now best remembered on film as the vicar in *The Titfield Thunderbolt.* Father of producer and sometime director Michael Relph.

*1916: Paying the Price. 1921: Candytuft, I Mean Veronica. The Door That Has No Key. 1939: Too Dangerous to Live. 1944: Give Us the Moon. 1947: Nicholas Nickleby. 1951: I Believe in You. 1953: The Final Test. The Titfield Thunderbolt. 1957: Doctor at Large. Davy. 1959: Ben-Hur.*

**REVERE, Anne** 1903- )990
Fresh-faced, dark-haired, old-looking American character actress who looked set for a record number of hard-working, worldly-wise mothers and sympathetic if sharp-tongued friends, before the McCarthy blacklistings stopped her career. Academy Award as Elizabeth Taylor's

mother in *National Velvet* (plus two more nominations).

*1934: Double Door. 1940: The Howards of Virginia (GB: The Tree of Liberty). One Crowded Night. 1941: The Devil Commands. Men of Boys' Town. HM Pulham Esq. Remember the Day. Design for Scandal. The Flame of New Orleans. 1942: The Falcon Takes Over. The Gay Sisters. Meet the Stewarts. Star Spangled Rhythm. Are Husbands Necessary? 1943: Old Acquaintance. The Song of Bernadette. The Meanest Man in the World. Shantytown. 1944: The Keys of the Kingdom. Standing Room Only. Sunday Dinner for a Soldier. The Thin Man Goes Home. Rainbow Island. National Velvet. 1945: Don Juan Quilligan. Fallen Angel. 1946: Dragonwyck. The Shocking Miss Pilgrim. 1947: Gentleman's Agreement. Carnival in Costa Rica. Forever Amber. Body and Soul. 1948: Deep Waters. Secret Beyond the Door. Scudda-Hoo! Scudda-Hay! (GB: Summer Lightning). 1949: You're My Everything. 1950: The Great Missouri Raid. 1951: A Place in the Sun. 1969: Deadlock (TV). Tell Me That You Love Me, Junie Moon. 1970: Macho Callahan. 1972: Two for the Money (TV). 1976: Birch Interval.*

**REVILL, Clive** 1930-
Fair-haired, barrel-shaped, parrot-like New Zealand-born actor attracting attention with scene-stealing performances in British films from the mid-1960s. Later worked much in America, especially from

the late 1970s, when films, plays and television kept him working hard in both comic and dramatic roles, in which his slightly off-centre characterizations proved equally effective.

*1956: Reach for the Sky. 1959: The Headless Ghost. 1965: Bunny Lake Is Missing. 1966: Modesty Blaise. Kaleidoscope. A Fine Madness. 1967: The Double Man. Italian Secret Service. Fathom. 1968: Nobody Runs Forever (US: The High Commissioner). The Shoes of the Fisherman. The Assassination Bureau. 1970: The Private Life of Sherlock Holmes. The Buttercup Chain. A Severed Head. Boulevard du rhum (US: Rum Runner). 1972: Avanti! Escape to the Sun. 1973: The Legend of Hell House. Ghost in the Noonday Sun (unreleased). 1974: The Boy With Two Heads (serial. Voice only). The Black Windmill. Galileo. The Little Prince. 1975: One of Our Dinosaurs Is Missing. 1976: The Great Houdinis (TV). 1977: Pinocchio (TV). 1978: Matilda. Once Upon a Brothers Grimm (TV). 1979: TR Sloane of the Secret Service (TV). She's Dressed to Kill (TV. GB: Somebody's Killing the World's Greatest Models). Charlie Muffin (TV). 1980: The Empire Strikes Back (voice only). 1981: Zorro the Gay Blade. 1984: Samson and Delilah (TV).*

**REY, Fernando**
(F. Casado d'Arambillet) 1915- 1994
Kindly-looking in a rather haggard way, this Spanish actor has popped up here, there and everywhere over the past 40 years. Every time a British or American company made a film in Spain, it has seemed that Rey was in it. He has made much international co-production rubbish, but has also been associated with Oscar-winning films and was regularly hired by Spain's most famous director, Luis Buñuel. As a young man, Rey fought in the Spanish Civil War against the Frangistes and was captured. In the 1940s, he dubbed British and American films into Spanish while building his own screen career. He is particularly grateful for the association with Buñuel — 'Something in my cadaverous expression must have caught his eye' — but probably best-known to international audiences as the smooth mastermind in the 'French Connection' films.

*1939: Los cuatros Robinsons. 1940: La gitanilla. 1944: Eugenia de Montijo. 1945: Tierra sediata. Los ultimos de Filipinas. Misión blanca. 1947: Locura de amor (US: The Mad Queen). Don Quijote de la Mancha (US: Don Quixote). 1949: Du sang à l'aube/Mare nostrum. Los aventuras de Juan Lucas. 1950: Agustina de Aragon. 1951: Cielo negro. Esa pareja feliz/Cet heureux couple. La senora de Fatima. 1952: Bienvenido Mr Marshall! (GB and US: Welcome Mr Marshall!). 1953: Cómicos. En alcalde de Zalamea. Rebeldia. 1955: Marcelino. Don Juan (GB and US: Pantaloons). Un marido de ida y vuelta. Tangier Assignment. Les aventures de Gil Blas de Santillane. 1957: La venganza/Vengeance. Les bijoutiers du clair de lune (GB: Heaven Fell That Night. US: The Night Heaven Fell). 1958: Culpables. Parque de Madrid. Los habitants de la casa deshabitada. 1959: The Last Days of Pompeii. Sonatas. Operación Relampage. 1960: Fabiola. Don Lucio y el hermano pio. 1961: The Revolt of the Slaves. Viridiana. 1962: The Savage Guns. Face of Terror. Shéhérazade (GB: Scorching Sands). 1963: The Castilian. El espontanes. Dios eligio sus viajeros. The Running Man. The Ceremony. El diablo también llora. 1964: Los palomas. Son of a Gunfighter. Echappement libre (US: Backfire). El señor de la salle. Le nueva cenicienta. 1965: El hijo de pistolero. Cards on the Table. España insolita. Misión Lisboa. Zampo y yo. 1966: Chimes at Midnight (US: Falstaff). Run Like a Thief. Navajo Joe. Return of the Seven. Don Quijote. Dulcinea del Tobosco. Das Vermachtnis des Inka. Los jeuces de la Biblia. 1967: The Viscount. Amor en el aire. Cervantes/Cervantes, The Young Rebel. Mas alla de los montañas. 1968: Villa Rides! Guns of the Magnificent Seven. The Immortal Story. 1969: Fellini-Satyricon. Un sudario a la Medira. Land Raiders. Il prezzo de potere (GB: The Price of Power). Candidate for a Killing. 1970: Tristana. The Adventurers. Muerte de un presidente. Compañeros! 1971: A Town Called Bastard (US: A Town Called Hell). The Light at the Edge of the World. Los frios ojos del miedo. Historia de una traición. The French Connection. 1972: Antony and Cleopatra. Le charme discret de la bourgeoisie (GB and US: The Discreet Charm of the Bourgeoisie). Chicas de club. I due volti della paura (GB: The Two Faces of Fear). 1973: La polizia incrimma, la legge assolve (GB: High Crime). White Sister. One Way. 1974: Tarots. White Fang. La femme aux bottes rouges. Corruzione al Palazzo di Giustizia. Fatti di gente perbene (GB: Drama of the Rich). 1975: French Connection II (GB: French Connection No. 2). Pasqualino settebelleze (GB and US: Seven Beauties). Il contesto. Cadaveri eccellenti (GB and US: Illustrious Corpses). Le originia della Mafia. 1976: A Matter of Time. Le désert des Tartars/Desert of the Tartars. Voyage of the Damned. 1977: Elisa vida mia. L'uomo del 4 piano. Cet obscur objet du désir (GB and US: That Obscure Object of Desire). The Assignment. La grande bourgeoise. 1978: El segundo poder. Le dernier amant romantique. 1979: Le grand embouteillage. Cabo Blanco. Quintet. Vestire gli ignudi. 1980: La dame aux camélias (US: Camille — The True Story). 1981: Confessions of Felix Krull. Casta e pura. Meile di donna. 1982: Monsignor. 1984: The Hit. Saving Grace. The Black Arrow. (Cable TV) Nicolo', ou l'enfant trouve'. 1985: Padre Nuestro. Rustlers' Rhapsody.*

**RHODES, Erik** 1906- 1990
Pale-faced, frequently moustachioed American musical-comedy actor, handsome in an alarmed-looking sort of way, who played the unsuccessful Italian suitor in a couple of Astaire-Rogers musicals of the 1930s during his brief five-year tenure in Hollywood. After 1939, he returned to the stage, his excitable lotharios no longer in demand.

*1934: Give Her a Ring. The Gay Divorcee (GB: The Gay Divorce). 1935: A Night at the Ritz. The Nitwits. Charlie Chan in Paris. Old Man Rhythm. Another Face. Top Hat. 1936: One Rainy Afternoon. Special Investigator. Second Wife. Chatterbox. Two in the Dark. The Smartest Girl in Town. 1937: Criminal Lawyer. Fight for Your Lady. Music for Madame. Beg, Borrow or Steal. Woman Chases Man. 1938: Meet the Girls. Dramatic School. Say It in French. Mysterious Mr Moto. 1939: On Your Toes.*

**RHODES, Marjorie**
(M.R. Wise) 1902-1979
Marjorie Rhodes played the kind of women whose daughter you hoped your son wouldn't marry. One can picture the flowered hat, the print dress and the coverall coat. Her mothers could have lashing tongues or loving natures, but whether from London or her native Yorkshire, they were all thoroughly working class. Occasionally she broke out of the mould to play something like the wardress in *Yield to the Night*, but generally shabbiness and homeliness prevailed.

*1939: Poison Pen. 1941: Love on the Dole. The Black Sheep of Whitehall. World of Plenty. 1942: Squadron Leader X. When We Are Married. 1943: Old Mother Riley Detective. Theatre Royal. Escape to Danger. The Butler's Dilemma. 1944: Tawny Pipit. On Approval. It Happened One Sunday. 1945: Great Day. 1946: School for Secrets (US: Secret Flight). 1947: Uncle Silas (US: The Inheritance). The Silver Darlings. This Was a Woman. 1948: Escape. Enchantment. 1949: Private Angelo. The Cure for Love. 1951: A Tale of Five Cities (US: A Tale of Five Women). 1952: Time Gentlemen Please! The Yellow Balloon. Decameron Nights. Those People Next Door. 1953: Street Corner (US: Both Sides of the Law). The Weak and the Wicked. The Girl on the Pier. 1954: To Dorothy a Son (US: Cash on Delivery). Children Galore. The Case of Diamond Annie. 1955: Footsteps in the Fog. Room in the House. Where There's a Will. Lost (US: Tears for Simon). It's a Great Day (and 1945 film of similar title). 1956: Yield to the Night (US: Blonde Sinner). The Good Companions. Now and Forever. It's Great to be Young! 1957: Hell Drivers. The Passionate Stranger (US: A Novel Affair). After the Ball. These Dangerous Years (US: Dangerous Youth). No Time for Tears. There's Always a Thursday. Just My Luck. The Naked Truth (US: Your Past Is Showing!). 1958: Gideon's Day (US: Gideon of Scotland Yard). A Tale of Two Cities. Alive and Kicking. 1960: Over the Odds. 1961: Watch It Sailor! 1965: Those Magnificent Men in Their Flying Machines. I've Gotta Horse. 1966: The Family Way. 1968: Mrs Brown, You've Got a Lovely Daughter. 1969: Spring and Port Wine. 1971: Hands of the Ripper.*

**RIDGELY, John** (J. Rea) 1909-1968
Plum-nosed American actor of set expression, dark hair and strikingly pale blue eyes.

Born in Chicago, he was trained in industry but became interested in acting while working in California, and work at the Pasadena Community Playhouse led to a film contract with Warners. Ridgely's tall, faintly menacing figure moved into its best roles there in the 1940s, notably in Hawks' *Air Force*, and as Eddie Mars, chief menace to Humphrey Bogart, in Hawks' *The Big Sleep*. Declining to smaller roles, his later acting days were spent in stock and TV. Died from a heart ailment at 58.

1937: *Larger Than Life. They Won't Forget. Submarine D-1. Kid Galahad. Hollywood Hotel.* 1938: *Forbidden Valley. The Invisible Menace. Torchy Gets Her Man. Crime School. Secrets of an Actress. The Patient in Room 18. He Couldn't Say No. Blondes at Work. Torchy Blane in Panama* (GB: *Trouble in Panama*). *Little Miss Thoroughbred. White Banners. Cowboy from Brooklyn* (GB: *Romance and Rhythm*). *My Bill. Going Places. Hard to Get. Broadway Musketeers. Boy Meets Girl. Western Trails. Garden of the Moon. Crime School.* 1939: *Angels Wash Their Faces. The Cowboy Quarterback. Torchy Runs for Mayor. Nancy Drew and the Hidden Staircase. Kid Nightingale. Dark Victory. Secret Service of the Air. Everybody's Hobby. Indianapolis Speedway* (GB: *Devil on Wheels*). *Women in the Wind. Torchy Plays with Dynamite. They Made Me a Criminal. You Can't Get Away with Murder. King of the Underworld. Private Detective. Wings of the Navy. The Return of Dr X. The Kid from Kokomo* (GB: *Orphan of the Ring*). *Smashing the Money Ring. Naughty But Nice. Each Dawn I Die. The Roaring Twenties. Confessions of a Nazi Spy. Invisible Stripes.* 1940: *River's End. Father Is a Prince. The Man Who Talked Too Much. Saturday's Children. Flight Angels. Torrid Zone. Brother Orchid. They Drive by Night* (GB: *The Road to Frisco*). *The Letter. The Fighting 69th. 'Til We Meet Again. Knute Rockne — All-American* (GB: *A Modern Hero*). *No Time for Comedy. The Lady With Red Hair. A Child Is Born.* 1941: *The Wagons Roll at Night. Million Dollar Baby. International Squadron. The Great Mr Nobody. The Man Who Came to Dinner. Here Comes Happiness. Strange Alibi. Navy Blues. Highway West. They Died With Their Boots On. Nine Lives Are Not Enough. Knockout/Right to the Heart. The Bride Came COD.* 1942: *Bullet Scars. Wings for the Eagle. The Big Shot. Secret Enemies. Dangerously They Live.* 1943: *Air Force. Northern Pursuit. Arsenic and Old Lace.* 1944: *Destination Tokyo. Hollywood Canteen. The Doughgirls.* 1945: *Pride of the Marines* (GB: *Forever in Love*). *God Is My Co-Pilot. Danger Signal.* 1946: *The Big Sleep. My Reputation. Two Guys from Milwaukee* (GB: *Royal Flush*). 1947: *High Wall. The Man I Love. That's My Man/Will Tomorrow Ever Come? Nora Prentiss. That Way With Women. Cheyenne. Cry Wolf. Possessed.* 1948: *Night Winds. Luxury Liner. Sealed Verdict. Trouble Makers. The Iron Curtain.* 1949: *Command Decision. Once More, My Darling. Border Incident.*

*Task Force. Tucson. South Sea Sinner* (GB: *East of Java*). 1950: *Backfire. The Lost Volcano/Bomba and the Lost Volcano. The Petty Girl* (GB: *Girl of the Year*). *Rookie Fireman. Saddle Tramp. Edge of Doom* (GB: *Stronger Than Fear*). 1951: *The Last Outpost. When the Redskins Rode. Thunder in God's Country. Half Angel. Al Jennings of Oklahoma. The Blue Veil. A Place in the Sun. As You Were.* 1952: *Room for One More. The Greatest Show on Earth. The Outcasts of Poker Flat. Off Limits* (GB: *Military Policemen*). *Fort Osage.*

RIDGES, Stanley 1891-1951
One of Hollywood's most underrated players, a tall, heavy-set British-born actor whose dark-brown wig hid thinning, greying hair, but suited his strong features and commanding presence. In America from 1920, he was mainly a stage actor until 1938, coming too late to Hollywood to make the impact he deserved, but offering some startlingly good performances, particularly in the dual role he inherited from Bela Lugosi on *Black Friday*.

1923: *Success.* 1930: *\*Let's Merge. \*For Two Cents.* 1934: *Crime Without Passion.* 1935: *The Scoundrel.* 1936: *Winterset.* 1937: *Internes Can't Take Money* (GB: *You Can't Take Money*). 1938: *\*They're Always Caught. Yellow Jack. There's That Woman Again* (GB: *What a Woman*). *The Mad Miss Manton. If I Were King.* 1939: *Let Us Live! I Stole a Million. Confessions of a Nazi Spy. Union Pacific. Each Dawn I Die. Silver on the Sage. Dust Be My Destiny. Espionage Agent. Nick Carter, Master Detective.* 1940: *Black Friday.* 1941: *Mr District Attorney. Sergeant York. They Died With Their Boots On. The Sea Wolf.* 1942: *To Be or Not To Be. Eyes in the Night. The Big Shot. Eagle Squadron. The Lady Is Willing. Air Force.* 1943: *Tarzan Triumphs. This Is the Army.* 1944: *The Sign of the Cross* (new prologue to 1932 feature). *The Story of Dr Wassell. The Master Race. Wilson.* 1945: *The Suspect. God Is My Co-Pilot. Captain Eddie. The Phantom Speaks.* 1946: *Mr Ace. Because of Him. Canyon Passage.* 1947: *Possessed.* 1948: *An Act of Murder.* 1949: *You're My Everything. Streets of Laredo. Thelma Jordon* (GB: *The File on Thelma Jordon*). *There's a Girl in My*

*Heart. Task Force.* 1950: *No Way Out. Paid in Full.* 1951: *The Groom Wore Spurs.*

RIGBY, Edward (E. Coke) 1879-1951
Stocky, knowing-looking British character actor who led a full stage career before coming to films in his mid-fifties and becoming the British cinema's best-loved old buffer, often in near-star roles, for 18 years.

1907: *The Man Who Fell by the Way.* 1910: *The Blue Bird.* 1934: *Lorna Doone.* 1935: *Gay Old Dog. Windfall. No Limit. Queen of Hearts.* 1936: *Land Without Music* (US: *Forbidden Music*). *This Green Hell. Irish for Luck. Accused. The Heirloom Mystery.* 1937: *The Fatal Hour. Jump for Glory* (US: *When Thief Meets Thief*). *Mr Smith Carries On. The Show Goes On. Under a Cloud. Young and Innocent* (US: *The Girl Was Young*). 1938: *Keep Smiling* (US: *Smiling Along*). *A Yank at Oxford. The Ware Case. Yellow Sands. Kicking the Moon Around.* 1939: *Young Man's Fancy. The Four Just Men* (US: *The Secret Four*). *There Ain't No Justice. The Proud Valley. Poison Pen. The Stars Look Down.* 1940: *Convoy. Fingers. The Farmer's Wife. Sailors Don't Care. The Girl in the News.* 1941: *The Common Touch. Kipps* (US: *The Remarkable Mr Kipps*). *Penn of Pennsylvania* (US: *The Courageous Mr Penn*). *Major Barbara.* 1942: *Flying Fortress. Let the People Sing. Salute John Citizen. Went the Day Well?* (US: *48 Hours*). 1943: *Get Cracking. They Met in the Dark.* 1944: *A Canterbury Tale. Don't Take It to Heart. The Agitator.* 1945: *I Live in Grosvenor Square* (US: *A Yank in London*). *Perfect Strangers* (US: *Vacation from Marriage*). *Murder in Reverse.* 1946: *Piccadilly Incident. Quiet Weekend. The Years Between. Daybreak.* 1947: *The Loves of Joanna Godden. Temptation Harbour. Easy Money. Green Fingers. The Courtneys of Curzon Street* (US: *The Courtney Affair*). 1948: *It's Hard to be Good. The Three Weird Sisters. Rover and Me. Noose* (US: *The Silk Noose*). *All Over the Town.* 1949: *Christopher Columbus. Don't Ever Leave Me. A Run for Your Money.* 1950: *The Happiest Days of Your Life. Double Confession. Tony Draws a Horse. What the Butler Saw. Into the Blue* (US: *The Man in the Dinghy*). *The Mudlark.* 1951: *Circle of Danger.*

## RILLA, Walter 1895-

Tall, eminent, rather grim-looking German actor with very black eyebrows. In international (mainly British) films from 1934, he played evil, sinister criminals and megalomaniac statesmen. Also directed one film and a number of television plays. His son is the director Wolf Rilla.

*1922: Hanneles Himmelfahrt. 1923: Alles für Geld (US: Fortune's Fool). 1924: Der Spring ins Leben. 1926: Der Geiger von Florenz. 1927: Der gefährliche Alter. 1928: Revolutionshochzeit (US: The Last Night). Prinzessin Olala (GB and US: Princess Olala). 1929: Vererbte Triebe. Sajenko der Soviet. 1930: Kommt mit mir zum Rendezvous (US: Rendezvous). 1931: Zirkuz Leben/Schatten der Manege (US: Circus Life). 1932: Namensheirar. 1933: Ein Gewisser Herr Gran. La voce del sangue. 1934: Lady Windermeres Fächer (GB and US: Lady Windermere's Fan). The Scarlet Pimpernel. 1935: Abdul the Damned. 1937: Victoria the Great. 1938: Sixty Glorious Years (US: Queen of Destiny). 1939: At the Villa Rose. Hell's Cargo. The Gang's All Here (US: The Amazing Mr Forrest). Black Eyes. 1943: The Adventures of Tartu (US: Tartu). Candlelight in Algeria. 1944: Mr Emmanuel. 1946: Lisbon Story. 1949: Golden Salamander. 1950: State Secret (US: The Great Manhunt). My Daughter Joy (US: Operation X). Shadow of the Eagle. 1951: I'll Get You For This (US: Lucky Nick Cain). 1952: Venetian Bird (US: The Assassin). 1953: Desperate Moment. Senza bandiera. Star of India. 1954: The Green Buddha. Track the Man Down. 1956: The Gamma People. Die Bekenntnisse des Hochstaplers Felix Krull (GB and US: The Confessions of Felix Krull). 1958: The Girl Rosemarie. 1960: Song Without End. 1961: The Secret Ways. Cairo (released 1963). 1962: Room 13. The Testament of Dr Mabuse. The Wonderful World of the Brothers Grimm. 1963: Death Drums Along the River. 1964: Der Fall X701 (GB and US: Frozen Alive). Code 7, Victim 5 (US: Victim Five). 1965: The Face of Fu Manchu. The Four Keys. 1966: Martin Soldat. 1967: I giorni dell' ira (GB and US: Day of Anger).*

**As director:**
*1951: Behold the Man.*

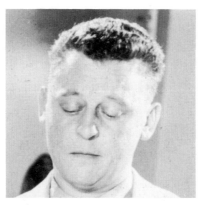

## RIPPER, Michael 1913-

Bright, jaunty, brown-haired British actor, mostly seen as minor crooks, comedy relief or oppressed little men until the mid-1950s, from which time he gradually became the favourite prey of the screen's monsters, particularly those from the Hammer vaults. As if aggrieved by all this horror, his own film characters grew less good-tempered as he got older. Drifted away from the cinema and into the theatre in the late 1970s.

*1935: Twice Branded. 1936: Prison Breaker. A Touch of the Moon. Not So Dusty. To Catch a Thief. Nothing Like Publicity. Busman's Holiday. The Heirloom Mystery. All That Glitters. 1937: Pearls Bring Tears. Farewell to Cinderella. The Strange Adventures of Mr Smith. Fifty Shilling Boxer. Father Steps Out. Why Pick on Me? Racing Romance. Easy Riches. 1938: Merely Mr Hawkins. Paid in Error. Luck of the Navy. Romance à la Carte. If I Were Boss. Coming of Age. His Lordship Regrets. Weddings Are Wonderful. His Lordship Goes to Press. You're the Doctor. Miracles Do Happen. 1939: Blind Folly. 1947: Captain Boycott. The Dark Road. 1948: Noose (US: The Silk Noose). Oliver Twist. 1949: The History of Mr Polly. The Adventures of PC 49. The Rocking Horse Winner. 1950: The Undefeated. Your Witness (US: Eye Witness). 1951: Old Mother Riley's Jungle Treasure. A Case for PC 49. Lady Godiva Rides Again. 1952: Secret People. Derby Day (US: Four Against Fate). Treasure Hunt. Alf's Baby. Folly to be Wise. Appointment in London. 1953: The Story of Gilbert and Sullivan (US: The Great Gilbert and Sullivan). The Intruder. Blood Orange. 1954: The Rainbow Jacket. The Belles of St Trinian's. A Tale of Three Women. The Sea Shall Not Have Them. 1955: Geordie (US: Wee Geordie). Secret Venture. The Constant Husband. Richard III. 1984. 1956: Reach for the Sky. The Green Man. *A Man on the Beach. Yield to the Night (US: Blonde Sinner). X the Unknown. 1957: The Steel Bayonet. These Dangerous Years (US: Dangerous Youth). Not Wanted on Voyage. Woman in a Dressing Gown. The One That Got Away. Blue Murder at St Trinian's. The Naked Truth (US: Your Past is Showing!). Quatermass II (US: Enemy from Space). 1958: The Changing Years. Up the Creek. The Camp on Blood Island. I Only Arsked! The Revenge of Frankenstein. Further Up the Creek. Girls at Sea. 1959: The Man Who Could Cheat Death. Bobbikins. The Ugly Duckling. The Mummy. 1960: Sink the Bismarck! Jackpot. The Pure Hell of St Trinian's. Dead Lucky. Macbeth. Circle of Deception. The Brides of Dracula. 1961: The Curse of the Werewolf. Petticoat Pirates. A Matter of WHO. The Pirates of Blood River. 1962: The Amorous Prawn. Captain Clegg (US: Night Creatures). The Punch and Judy Man. The Phantom of the Opera. Out of the Fog. A Prize of Arms. Two Left Feet. 1963: The Scarlet Blade (US: The Crimson Blade). What a Crazy World. The Devil-Ship Pirates. 1964: The Curse of the Mummy's Tomb. Every Day's a Holiday (US: Seaside Swingers). The Secret of Blood Island. 1965: The Spy Who Came in from the Cold. The Plague of the Zombies. The Reptile. 1966: Where the Bullets Fly. The Great St Trinian's Train Robbery. 1967: The Mummy's Shroud. The Deadly Bees. Torture Garden. 1968: Inspector Clouseau. The Lost Continent. Dracula Has Risen from the Grave. 1969: Moon Zero Two. Mumsy, Nanny, Sonny and Girly. 1970: Taste the Blood of Dracula. The Scars of Dracula. 1972: The Creeping Flesh. That's Your Funeral. 1973: No Sex, Please — We're British. 1974: Legend of the Werewolf. 1977: The Prince and the Pauper (US: Crossed Swords). 1978: Sammy's Super T-Shirt. 1980: Danger on Dartmoor.*

## RITTER, Thelma 1905-1969

With a face best described as homely, brown hair scruffed back (you could almost see the curlers), plaintive, nasal tones and a figure usually tied up like a sack of potatoes, Brooklyn's Thelma Ritter, arms akimbo, ruined more than one star's chance of being the thing most remembered from a film. She was a character comedienne on radio who quickly established herself in top-billed supporting roles in post-war years, being nominated six times for the Best Supporting Actress Oscar between 1950 and 1962 without winning. Died from a heart attack.

*1947: Miracle on 34th Street (GB: The Big Heart). Call Northside 777. 1949: A Letter to*

*Three Wives. City Across the River. Father Was a Fullback. 1950: Perfect Strangers (GB: Too Dangerous to Love). All About Eve. I'll Get By. 1951: The Mating Season. The Model and the Marriage Broker. As Young As You Feel. 1952: With a Song in My Heart. 1953: Titanic. Pick Up on South Street. The Farmer Takes a Wife. 1954: Rear Window. 1955: Lucy Gallant. The Late Christopher Bean (TV. GB: cinemas). Daddy Long Legs. 1956: The Proud and Profane. 1959: A Hole in the Head. Pillow Talk. 1961: The Misfits. The Second Time Around. 1962: Bird Man of Alcatraz. How the West Was Won. 1963: A New Kind of Love. For Love or Money. Move Over, Darling. 1965: Boeing-Boeing. 1967: The Incident.*

**ROBARDS, Jason Sr** 1892-1963

Erect, dark-haired, rather sad-looking American actor, father of Jason Robards Jr. He achieved theatrical prominence before coming to Hollywood silents as a leading man. With the advent of sound, he soon slipped into character roles, making dozens for RKO in the 1940s as figures of some authority — with the occasional villain *mis*using authority thrown in. Died from a heart attack.

*1921: The Land of Hope. The Gilded Lily. 1925: Paris. Stella Maris. 1926: The Cohens and the Kellys. The Third Degree. Footloose Widows. Honeymoon Express. 1927: Hearts of Maryland. A Bird in the Hand. Hills of Kentucky. White Flannels. Tracked by the Police. Irish Hearts. Jaws of Steel. Wild Geese. Streets of Shanghai. Polly of the Movies. 1928: Casey Jones. The Death Ship. On Trial. 1929: Gamblers. Isle of Lost Ships. Trial Marriage. Paris (and 1925 film).* \*A Bird in Hand. Some Mother's Boy. Pain. Flying Marine. 1930: Peacock Alley. Crazy That Way. The Last Dance. Abraham Lincoln. Jazz Cinderella. Lightnin'.* \*Trifles. Sisters. 1931: Charlie Chan Carries On. Subway Express. Salvation Nell. Men Women Love). Ex-Bad Boy. Caught Plastered. Full of Notions. Law of the Tongs. 1932: Discarded Lovers. Docks of San Francisco. Unholy Love (GB: Deceit). Klondike. The White Eagle. The Pride of the Legion. The Conquerors. Slightly Married. 1933: Strange Adventure. Corruption. Only Yesterday. The Way to Love. Dance Hall Hostess.*

*The Devil's Mate (GB: He Knew Too Much). Ship of Wanted Men. Carnival Lady. Public Stenographer (GB: Private Affairs). 1934: All of Me.* \*Super Snooper. Broadway Bill *(GB: Strictly Confidential). The Merry Widow. Woman Unafraid. Take the Stand (GB: The Great Radio Mystery). The Crimson Romance. One Exciting Adventure. A Woman Condemned. Burn 'Em Up Barnes (GB: Devils on Wheels). 1935: The President Vanishes (GB: Strange Conspiracy). The Last Days of Pompeii. Break of Hearts. Ladies Crave Excitement. The Crusades. The Miracle Rider (serial). 1936: The White Legion. San Francisco. Laughing at Death (GB: Laughing at Trouble). 1937: Sweethearts of the Navy. Damaged Lives. The Firefly. Zorro Rides Again (serial). The Man Who Cried Wolf. 1938: The Adventures of Marco Polo. Clipped Wings. Cipher Bureau. Flight to Fame. Little Tough Guy. 1939: Mystery Plane. The Mad Empress/Juarez and Maximilian (GB: Carlotta, The Mad Empress). Stunt Pilot. Range War. Sky Patrol. Scouts to the Rescue (serial). Zorro's Fighting Legion (serial). Danger Flight (GB: Scouts of the Air). I Stole a Million. 1940: The Fatal Hour (GB: Mr Wong at Headquarters). I Love You Again. 1941: San Antonio Rose. 1942: Joan of Ozark (GB: Queen of Spies). Give Out, Sisters. Silver Queen. 1944: Bermuda Mystery. Sing a Jingle (GB: Lucky Days). Mademoiselle Fifi. The Master Race. Music in Manhattan. 1945: What a Blonde. Betrayal from the East. Isle of the Dead. Ding Dong Williams (GB: Melody Maker).* \*Let's Go Stepping.* \*It Shouldn't Happen to a Dog. Man Alive. Wander of the Wasteland. The Falcon in San Francisco. Radio Stars on Parade. Johnny Angel. A Game of Death.* \*What, No Cigarettes? Dick Tracy (GB: Split Face). 1946: The Falcon's Alibi. Bedlam. Step by Step. Vacation in Reno. Deadline at Dawn.* \*Twin Husbands.* \*I'll Take Milk.* \*I'll Build It Myself. The Falcon's Adventure.* \*Follow That Music. The Bamboo Blonde. 1947:* \*Do or Diet. The Farmer's Daughter. Trail Street. Desperate. Seven Keys to Baldpate. Riffraff. Under the Tonto Rim. Thunder Mountain. Wild Horse Mesa. Born to Kill (GB: Lady of Deceit). A Likely Story. 1948: Western Heritage. If You Knew Susie. Smoky Mountain Melody. Race Street. Mr Blandings Builds His Dream House. Fighting Father Dunne. Return of the Bad Men. Guns of Hate. Son of God's Country. 1949: Riders of the Whistling Pines. Rimfire. Post Office Investigator. South of Death Valley (GB: River of Poison). Feudin' Rhythm (GB: Ace Lucky). Horsemen of the Sierras (GB: Remember Me). Impact. Alaska Patrol. Haunted Trails. 1950: The Second Woman (GB: Ellen). 1961: Wild in the Country.*

**ROBSON, May** (Mary Robison) 1858-1942

One of Australia's most valuable exports to Hollywood: a light-haired, round-as-a-dumpling lady who took to acting when widowed at 25, and soon found herself in demand for strong-willed character roles.

She came to Hollywood from the stage for good in 1931 to play very human doyennes from both sides of the tracks, who had a flinty exterior and usually took a firm hand with the juveniles, but were good for a tear at the end. Had a few leading roles in an appropriate batch of titles: *Lady for a Day, You Can't Buy Everything, Grand Old Girl* and *Granny Get Your Gun*. For her Apple Annie in *Lady for a Day*, she was nominated for an Oscar.

*1915: How Molly Made Good. 1916: A Night Out. 1919: A Broadway Saint. His Bridal Night. The Lost Battalion. 1926: Pals in Paradise. 1927: A Harp in Hock. Rubber Tires. The Angel of Broadway. The King of Kings. Chicago. Turkish Delight. The Rejuvenation of Aunt Mary. 1928: The Blue Danube. 1931: The She-Wolf of Wall Street (later and GB: Mother's Millions). Red-Headed Woman. 1932: Letty Lynton. Strange Interlude (GB: Strange Interval). Little Orphan Annie. Two Against the World. If I Had a Million.* \*The Engineer's Daughter. 1933: Reunion in Vienna. Dinner at Eight. Broadway to Hollywood (GB: Ring Up the Curtain). Solitaire Man. Dancing Lady. Beauty for Sale (GB: Beauty). One Man's Journey. Alice in Wonderland. Lady for a Day. Men Must Fight. The White Sister. 1934: Straight is the Way. You Can't Buy Everything. Lady by Choice. 1935: Grand Old Girl. Vanessa: Her Love Story. Mills of the Gods. Three Kids and a Queen (GB: The Baxter Millions). Strangers All. Anna Karenina. Reckless. Age of Indiscretion. 1936: The Captain's Kid. Wife vs Secretary. Rainbow on the River. 1937: A Star is Born. Woman in Distress. The Perfect Specimen. Top of the Town. 1938: The Texans. Bringing Up Baby. The Adventures of Tom Sawyer. Four Daughters. 1939: Yes, My Darling Daughter. The Kid from Kokomo (GB: The Orphan of the Ring). Daughters Courageous. That's Right, You're Wrong. Nurse Edith Cavell. Four Wives. They Made Me a Criminal. 1940: The Texas Rangers Ride Again. Irene. Granny Get Your Gun. 1941: Four Mothers. Million Dollar Baby. Playmates. 1942: Joan of Paris.*

**ROSE, George** 1920-*1988*

Stocky, fuzzily dark-haired British actor with ready grin, adept at characters whose

surface bonhomie dissolved speedily into panic at the first signs of crisis. Turned from farming to acting in his mid-twenties and popped up regularly in British films of the 1950s. After 1961, he was seen mainly in America, principally on the New York stage.

1952: The Pickwick Papers. The Beggar's Opera. 1953: Grand National Night (US: Wicked Wife). The Square Ring. 1954: Devil on Horseback. The Sea Shall Not Have Them. Track the Man Down. 1955: The Night My Number Came Up. 1956: The Last Wagon. The Long Arm (US: The Third Key). The Good Companions. Brothers in Law. Sailor Beware! (US: Panic in the Parlour). 1957: No Time for Tears. The Shiralee. Barnacle Bill (US: All at Sea). 1958: A Night to Remember. Cat and Mouse/The Desperate Ones. 1959: Jack the Ripper. The Devil's Disciple. The Heart of a Man. The Flesh and the Fiends (US: Mania). Macbeth. Desert Mice. 1964: Hamlet. 1966: Hawaii. 1967: The Pink Jungle. 1971: A New Leaf. 1973: From the Mixed-Up Files of Mrs Basil E Frankweiler (GB: The Hideaways). 1982: The Pirates of Penzance.

light-heavyweight champion of the world in 1932, a title he held for three years. In films, he played dim hoodlums and, after he left Warners, where he had some of his best roles, there was a brief attempt to make him and Billy Gilbert (qv) into a low-budget comedy team. The cumulative effect of batterings in the ring took its toll in later years, and he was much in hospital after 1970, dying from Paget's Disease.

1933: Mr Broadway. King for a Night. 1936: Muss 'Em Up (GB: House of Fate). Kelly the Second. 1937: Nothing Sacred. Two Wise Maids. Big City. The Kid Comes Back (GB: Don't Pull Your Punches). 1938: Submarine Patrol. Mr Moto's Gamble. His Exciting Night. The Amazing Dr Clitterhouse. Gangs of New York. 1939: Women in the Wind. Naughty But Nice. The Kid from Kokomo (GB: The Orphan of the Ring) Private Detective. 20,000 Men a Year. Each Dawn I Die. Public Deb No. 1/Elsa Maxwell's Public Deb No. 1. Grandpa Goes to Town. Passport to Alcatraz. 1941: The Stork Pays Off. Ringside Maisie. Louisiana Purchase. Harvard, Here I Come (GB: Here I Come). 1942: To the Shores of Tripoli. The Yanks Are Coming. Smart Alecks. The Boogie Man Will Get You. 1943: Swing Fever. My Son the Hero. Here Comes Kelly. 1944: Three of a Kind. Follow the Boys. Ghost Crazy. Slick Chick. Irish Eyes Are Smiling. Crazy Knights. Allergic to Love. Night Club Girl. 1945: Men in Her Diary. Penthouse Rhythm. Trouble Chasers. 1948: Hazard. 1950: Mr Universe. 1951: Skipalong Rosenbloom. 1955: Abbott and Costello Meet the Keystone Kops. Guys and Dolls. 1956: Hollywood or Bust. 1958: I Married a Monster from Outer Space. 1959: The Beat Generation. 1963: Follow the Boys (and 1944 film). 1966: The Spy in the Green Hat (TV. GB: cinemas). Don't Worry, We'll Think of a Title. 1967: Cottonpickin' Chickenpickers. 1969: My Side of the Mountain.

at working-class accents from broad cockney to his native Liverpudlian.

1955: Keep It Clean. 1956: Three Men in a Boat. 1957: The Long Haul. Strangers' Meeting. The One That Got Away. Saint Joan. 1958: A Night to Remember. I Only Arsked! Carry On Sergeant. 1959: Carry On Nurse. 1960: The League of Gentlemen. Saturday Night and Sunday Morning. 1961: Carry On Regardless. 1962: Go to Blazes. Lawrence of Arabia. The Longest Day. Crooks Anonymous. 1963: Nurse On Wheels. The Comedy Man. 1964: A Hard Day's Night. Daylight Robbery. 1965: Cup Fever. Joey Boy. Those Magnificent Men in Their Flying Machines. 1966: The Wrong Box. Double Trouble. Tobruk. 1968: The Charge of the Light Brigade. Negatives. 1969: The Adventures of Gerard. 1970: The Rise and Rise of Michael Rimmer. *Simon, Simon. The Engagement. 1971: Man in the Wilderness. Young Winston. 1972: Death Line/Raw Meat. Go for a Take. 1973: Digby the Biggest Dog in the World. 1976: Joseph Andrews. 1979: The Prisoner of Zenda. SOS Titanic. 1982: House of the Long Shadows.

### ROSSITER, Leonard 1927–1984

Lugubrious, beaky, dark-haired British player, established on the stage as a straight dramatic actor before a succession of situation comedy television series in the 1970s revealed his talents as a comic star, mostly as complaining charlatans. Through twisted mouth, he played it straight and got the laughs — continuing to win leading roles in the theatre although he did not emerge as a consistent star attraction at the cinema box-office. Died from a heart attack in the interval of a play.

1962: A Kind of Loving. This Sporting Life. 1963: Billy Liar! A Jolly Bad Fellow. 1965: King Rat. 1966: The Wrong Box. Hotel Paradiso. The Witches (US: The Devil's Own). Deadlier Than the Male. The Whisperers. 1967: Deadfall. 1968: 2001: A Space Odyssey. Oliver! Otley. Diamonds for Breakfast. 1973: Luther. Butley. 1975: Barry Lyndon. 1976: The Pink Panther Strikes Again. Voyage of the Damned. 1978: *The Waterloo Bridge Handicap. 1980: Rising Damp. 1982: Britannia Hospital. 1985: Water.

### ROSENBLOOM, (Slapsie) Maxie 1903–1976

Big, friendly, plug-ugly American boxer and, later, actor. A cross between Mike Mazurki and Dan Seymour (both qv), his gnarled features were a legacy of many years in the ring, during which he became

### ROSSINGTON, Norman 1928–

Stocky, bouncy British actor with dark, curly hair. He made his name as one of the bone-idle soldiers in the TV comedy series The Army Game, and was thereafter frequently seen in films, almost always as the ebullient but none-too-bright sidekick of the hero, or an inept comic crook. An expert

(GB: Meet Whiplash Willie). Last of the Secret Agents? Way ... Way Out.

## ROYLE, Selena 1904-1983

Gracious-looking, fair-haired American actress with beautiful light-skinned complexion. After a long stage career, she was drafted into Hollywood in the war years to play mothers. Although she proved she could handle superbly a major role such as the mother of *The Sullivans*, she gained a reputation for being outspoken about anomalies in the film city, and never rose above supporting roles. Married (second) to fellow character player George Renavent (1896-1969), she lived in Mexico after 1955, and later wrote *A Gringa's Guide to Mexican Cooking* there.

*1932: The Misleading Lady. 1943: Stage Door Canteen. *Paddy Rollers. 1944: Main Street After Dark. The Sullivans. Mrs Parkington. Thirty Seconds Over Tokyo. 1945: This Man's Navy. The Harvey Girls. 1946: The Green Years. Courage of Lassie. Gallant Journey. No Leave, No Love. Night and Day. Till the End of Time. Summer Holiday (released 1948). 1947: Cass Timberlane. The Romance of Rosy Ridge. Wild Harvest. 1948: Smart Woman. You Were Meant for Me. A Date With Judy. Joan of Arc. Moonrise. 1949: Bad Boy. My Dream Is Yours. You're My Everything. The Heiress. 1950: The Big Hangover. Branded. The Damned Don't Cry. 1951: Come Fill the Cup. He Ran All the Way. 1953: Robot Monster. 1955: Murder Is My Beat.*

## RUMANN, Siegfried or Sig 1884-1967

German-born actor often seen as eccentric professors, idiot saboteurs and moronic megalomaniacs. He never lost the thick continental accent that was part of his splutteringly excitable personality and helped him make a brilliant and explosive foil for comedians with wild senses of humour, notably The Marx Brothers, Jack Benny and Jerry Lewis. His pop eyes and manic smile were never seen to better advantage than as 'Concentration Camp' Erhardt in *To Be or Not To Be*. Surname sometimes spelled Ruman. Died from a heart attack.

*1929: The Royal Box. 1934: Servants' Entrance. The World Moves On. Marie Galante. 1935: East of Java (GB: Java Seas).*

*Under Pressure. Spring Tonic. The Farmer Takes a Wife. The Wedding Night. A Night at the Opera. 1936: The Beloved Rogue. The Bold Caballero. The Princess Comes Across. I Loved a Soldier. 1937: Seventh Heaven. Midnight Taxi. On the Avenue. Thin Ice. (GB: Lovely to Look At). Think Fast, Mr Moto. This Is My Affair (GB: His Affair). Love Under Fire. Lancer Spy. Heidi. Maytime. Thank You, Mr Moto. The Great Hospital Mystery. A Day at the Races. Nothing Sacred. Dead Yesterday. 1938: I'll Give a Million. Paradise for Three (GB: Romance for Three). Suez. The Great Waltz. The Saint in New York. Girls on Probation. 1939: Ninotchka. Honolulu. Remember? Only Angels Have Wings. Never Say Die. Confessions of a Nazi Spy. 1940: Dr Ehrlich's Magic Bullet (GB: The Story of Dr Ehrlich's Magic Bullet). Outside the 3-Mile Limit (GB: Mutiny on the Seas). Four Sons. I Was an Adventuress. Comrade X. Bitter Sweet. Victory. 1941: So Ends Our Night. Love Crazy. Shining Victory. This Woman Is Mine. The Man Who Lost Himself. World Premiere. That Uncertain Feeling. The Wagons Roll at Night. 1942: Crossroads. Remember Pearl Harbor. Enemy Agents Meet Ellery Queen (GB: The Lido Mystery). To Be or Not To Be. China Girl. Berlin Correspondent. Desperate Journey. 1943: Tarzan Triumphs. They Came To Blow Up America. Sweet Rosie O'Grady. The Song of Bernadette. Government Girl. 1944: The Hitler Gang. It Happened Tomorrow. Summer Storm. House of Frankenstein. 1945: The Dolly Sisters. A Royal Scandal (GB: Czarina). The Men in Her Diary. She Went to the Races. 1946: A Night in Casablanca. Faithful in My Fashion. Night and Day. 1947: Mother Wore Tights. 1948: Give My Regards to Broadway. The Emperor Waltz. If You Knew Susie. 1949: Border Incident. 1950: Father Is a Bachelor. 1951: On the Riviera. 1952: The World in His Arms. O. Henry's Full House (GB: Full House). Ma and Pa Kettle on Vacation (GB: Ma and Pa Kettle Go to Paris). 1953: Houdini. Stalag 17. The Glenn Miller Story. 1954: White Christmas. Living It Up. Three-Ring Circus. 1955: Many Rivers to Cross. Spy Chasers. Carolina Cannonball. 1957: The Wings of Eagles. 1961: The Errand Boy. 1964: Robin and the Seven Hoods. 36 Hours. 1966: The Fortune Cookie*

## RUYSDAEL, Basil 1888-1960

Relaxed, wise-looking, brown-haired American actor, often as judges, lawyers and senior officers. A prominent opera singer (he appeared with Caruso) in his younger days, Ruysdael turned first to straight acting, then became a radio announcer in the 1930s. In post-war years, he moved to Hollywood character roles to play out the remainder of his long and varied career.

*1929: The Cocoanuts. 1934: Dealers in Death (narrator only). 1949: Pinky. Colorado Territory. Come to the Stable. Thelma Jordon (GB: The File on Thelma Jordon). The Doctor and the Girl. Task Force. 1950: One Way Street. Broken Arrow. Gambling House. The Dungeon. Raton Pass (GB: Canyon Pass). 1951: The Scarf. My Forbidden Past. Half Angel. People Will Talk. Boots Malone. Hoodlum Empire. 1952: Carrie. 1954: The Shanghai Story. Prince Valiant. The Violent Men (GB: Rough Company). Davy Crockett — King of the Wild Frontier. 1955: Pearl of the South Pacific. Blackboard Jungle. Diane. 1956: Jubal. These Wilder Years. 1958: The Last Hurrah. 1959: The Horse Soldiers. 1960: The Story of Ruth.*

## RYAN, John (P.) 1938-

Full-faced American actor with distinctive thin mouth and pale eyes. This 'Irish'-style countenance carried such natural toothy menace that he has often been cast as especially mean and vicious criminals whose calm exteriors barely concealed the explosive violence beneath. But he also did extremely well when given the rare opportunity to play for sympathy — as with the leading role of the father to the monster baby in *It's Alive!* Hasn't been seen enough in films.

*1967: The Tiger Makes Out. 1968: A Lovely Way to Die (GB: A Lovely Way to Go). 1970: Five Easy Pieces. 1972: The Legend of Nigger Charley. Shamus. The King of Marvin Gardens. 1973: Cops and Robbers. Dillinger. It's Alive! 1974: Target Risk (TV). 1976: The Missouri Breaks. Futureworld. 1978: It Lives Again! 1980: The Last Flight of Noah's Ark. 1981: The Postman Always Rings Twice. 1982: One from the Heart. The Escape Artist. 1983: Breathless. The Right Stuff. Rumble Fish. Shooting Stars (TV). 1984: Bearn. The Cotton Club.*

**SAKALL, S. Z. 'Cuddles'**
(Eugene Sakall) 1884-1955
Roly-poly Hungarian character actor, seen initially in Hungarian and German silent and early sound films, but remembered only from his Hollywood period as a white-haired, beaming, bespectacled, multi-jowled fractured-English flapper and forehead-mopper, just about everybody's favourite uncle. Died from a heart attack.

*1916: †Süszterherceg. †Ujszulott Apa. 1918: †Az Onkéntes Tüzoltó. 1922: †Die Stumme von Portici/The Dumb Girl of Portici. 1926: †Wenn das Herz der Jugend spricht. 1927: †Familientag in Hause Prellstein. †Der fidele Bauer. †Der Himmel auf Erden. 1928: †Mary Lou. †Ratschbahn. 1929: †Grossstadt-schmetterling. †Wer wird denn weinen, wenn man auseinandergeht. 1930: †Der Hempel-mann. †Kam zu mir zum Rendezvous. †Susanne macht Ordnung. †Zweimal Hoch-zeit. †Zwei Herzen im ¾ Takt. 1931: †Der unbekannte Gast. †Der Zinker. †Die Fasching-see. †Die Frau, von der man spricht. †Die schwebende Jungfrau. †Ich heirate meinen Mann. †Ihr Junge. †Ihre Majestät der Liebe (German version of Her Majesty Love). †Kopfüber ins Glück. †Meine Cousine aus Warschau. †Walzerparadies. 1932: †Eine Stadt steht Kopf. †Glück über Nacht. †Gräfin Mariza. †Ich will nicht wissen, wer du bist. †Kaiserwalzer. †Mädchen zum Heiraten. †Melodie der Liebe (GB: The Right to Happiness). †Muss man sich gleich scheiden lassen. 1933: †Eine Frau wie Du. †Es war einmal ein Musikus. †Gross fürstin Alexandra. †Skandal in Budapest. †Mindent a Nort. †Az Ellopot Szerda. 1934: †Frühlingstimmen. †Helvet az Oregeknek. 1935: †Harom es Fel Musketas/4½ Musketeers. †Tagebuch der Ge-liebten. †Barátsagos Arcot Kerek. †Smile, Please. 1936: †Mircha. †Fräulein Lilly. 1937: †The Lilac Domino. 1938: †Les affaires de Maupassant. 1940: It's a Date. Spring Parade. My Love Came Back. Florian. 1941: The Devil and Miss Jones. The Man Who Lost Himself. Ball of Fire. That Night in Rio. 1942: Seven Sweethearts. Yankee Doodle Dandy. Broadway. Casablanca. 1943: Thank Your Lucky Stars. Wintertime. The Human Comedy. 1944: Hollywood Canteen. Shine on Harvest Moon. 1945: The Dolly Sisters. Wonder Man. San Antonio. Christmas in Connecticut. 1946: Cinderella Jones. Never Say Goodbye. The Time, the Place and the Girl. Two Guys from Milwaukee (GB: Royal Flush). 1947: Cynthia (GB: The Rich, Full Life). 1948: April Showers. Whiplash. Em-braceable You. Romance on the High Seas (GB: It's Magic). 1949: My Dream Is Yours. It's a Great Feeling. Oh, You Beautiful Doll! Look for the Silver Lining. 1950: Tea for Two. Montana. The Daughter of Rosie O'Grady. *A Swing of Glory. 1951: Sugarfoot. Lullaby of Broadway. Painting the Clouds with Sunshine. It's a Big Country. 1952: *Screen Snapshots No.205. 1953: Small Town Girl. 1954: The Student Prince.*
†As Szöke Sakall

**SALEW, John** 1897-
Despite his meek and mild-mannered appearance, this chubby British supporting actor, bald from an early age, was often cast as minor villains. Although one of the most difficult 'familiar faces' to put a name to, he nonetheless built up a formidable list of credits after switching from a theatrical to a movie career when the demand for non-serving actors in Britain became acute at

the onset of World War II. A weightier actor in his later years, he also made many episodes of television drama series.

*1939: The Silent Battle (US: Continental Express). A Window in London (US: Lady in Distress). 1940: Sailors Don't Care. The Briggs Family. Neutral Port. 1941: The Saint Meets the Tiger/Meet the Tiger. Turned Out Nice Again. 1942: The Young Mr Pitt. One of Our Aircraft Is Missing. Suspected Person. Secret Mission. Back Room Boy. Squadron Leader X. Tomorrow We Live (US: At Dawn We Die). 1943: Warn That Man. The Night Invader. We Dive at Dawn. The Hundred Pound Window. Millions Like Us. Time Flies. 1944: Tawny Pipit. The Way Ahead. Give Us the Moon. Candles at Nine. Don't Take It to Heart. 1945: Murder in Reverse. The Rake's Progress (US: Notorious Gentleman). Bothered by a Beard. 1946: Wanted for Murder. I See a Dark Stranger (US: The Adventuress). Bede-lia. Caravan. Beware of Pity. Meet Me at Dawn. A Girl in a Million. 1947: Uncle Silas (US: The Inheritance). Dancing With Crime. Anna Karenina. Nicholas Nickleby. Tempta-tion Harbour. The October Man. It Always Rains on Sunday. My Brother Jonathan. 1948: Counterblast. Noose (US: The Silk Noose). All Over the Town. The Bad Lord Byron. London Belongs to Me (US: Dulcimer Street). Quartet. Lucky Mascot/Brass Monkey. Cardboard Cavalier. 1949: Kind Hearts and Coronets. For Them That Trespass. The Astonished Heart. The Spider and the Fly. No Way Back. Dark Secret. Don't Ever Leave Me. Diamond City. The Blue Lamp. The Twenty Questions Murder Mystery. 1950: *Help Yourself. 1951: Green Grow the Rushes. Hotel Sahara. The Lavender Hill Mob. Night Was Our Friend. Mystery Junction. His Excellency. 1952: The Happy Family (US: Mr Lord Says No). 1953: Stryker of the Yard. 1954: Face the Music (US: The Black Glove). Father Brown (US: The Detective). Duel in the Jungle. The Red Dress. Lease of Life. 1955: Dust and Gold. Three Cases of Murder. 1956: It's Great to be Young! Rogue's Yarn. The Good Companions. 1957: Night of the Demon (US: Curse of the Demon). Alive on Saturday (completed 1954). 1958: Tread Softly, Stranger. The Gypsy and the Gentleman. Alive and Kicking. 1959: Left, Right and Centre. 1960: The Shakedown. Too Hot To Handle (US: Playgirl After Dark). 1961: The Impersonator. Three on a Spree.*

**SALLIS, Peter** 1921-
Dark-haired, diffident, thin-mouthed, often bespectacled British actor; frequently seen in sneaky roles in the early part of his career, he has latterly become more asso-ciated with comedy through his participa-tion in the long-running British television series *Last of the Summer Wine*. Started life as a bank clerk, but after some amateur acting in the RAF during World War II, he enrolled at RADA on leaving the service.

*1954: Child's Play. 1956: Anastasia. Julie. 1958: The Scapegoat. The Doctor's Dilemma.*

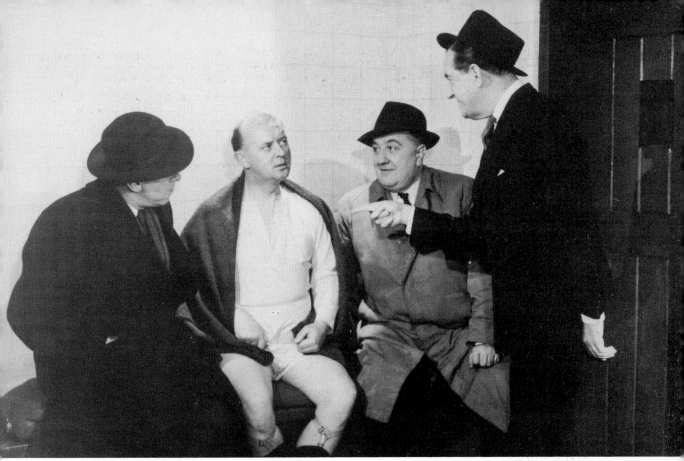

ABOVE John **Salew** is reduced to his underwear when quizzed by detectives Ben Williams, Robert Adair and (standing) Stanley Holloway during the 1948 thriller *Noose*

LEFT Albert **Salmi** (right) was a regular on the 1964 TV series *Daniel Boone*, along with Ed Ames (left) and star Fess Parker

*1960: Saturday Night and Sunday Morning. Doctor in Love. 1961: Curse of the Werewolf. 1962: I Thank a Fool. 1963: Clash by Night. The VIPs. Mouse on the Moon. 1964: The Third Secret. 1965: Rapture. 1967: Charlie Bubbles. 1968: Inadmissible Evidence. 1969: Scream and Scream Again. My Lover, My Son. The Reckoning. 1970: Taste the Blood of Dracula. Wuthering Heights. 1971: The Night Digger. 1973: Frankenstein: The True Story (TV. GB: cinemas in abridged version). 1976: Full Circle. The Incredible Sarah. 1978: Who Is Killing the Great Chefs of Europe? (GB: Too Many Chefs). 1979: Dracula. 1983: Last of the Summer Wine (TV). 1985: Uncle of the Bride.*

## SALMI, Albert 1928-1990

Heavy-set, tow-haired, thick-faced American actor, usually seen in sweaty, forceful roles, and a typical graduate of the Actors' Studio in the 1950s. After war service, Salmi worked for a detective agency, but quit when the agency decided its operatives would carry guns, and enrolled in a drama workshop instead. At first in prestigious supporting roles in films, he later played more routine stuff, including a stint as Barry Newman's 'leg-man' in the popular TV series *Petrocelli*, which gave him a more sympathetic role than the rednecks he often played. Married to actress Peggy Ann Garner (first of two) from 1956 to 1963.

*1956: The Open Door (TV). 1958: The Brothers Karamazov. Man Under Glass (TV). The Bravados. 1959: The Unforgiven. 1960: Wild River. 1964: The Outrage. 1966: The Flim Flam Man (GB: One Born Every Minute). 1967: Hour of the Gun. The Ambushers. 1968: Three Guns for Texas (TV. GB: cinemas). 1969: Four Ride Out. 1970: The Deserter. Lawman. Menace on the Mountain (TV. GB: cinemas). 1971: Escape from the Planet of the Apes. Something Big. 1972: Kung Fu (TV). 1973: Female Artillery (TV). 1974: The Take. Night Games (TV). 1975: Truckin'. The Legend of Earl Durand. 1976: The Manhunter (TV). 1977: Viva Knievel! Black Oak Conspiracy. Empire of the Ants. Moonshine County Express. 1978: Love and Bullets. The Sweet Creek County War/Good Time Outlaws. 1979: Steel. Cloud Dancer.*

*1980: Key West Crossing. Brubaker. The Great Cash Giveaway Getaway (TV). Caddyshack. 1981: Dragonslayer. The Guns and the Fury. St Helens/Killer Volcano. 1985: Superstition (made 1981). The Witch. Arctic Heat.*

## SAWYER, Joe (Joseph Sauers) 1901-1982

Tough-looking, square-faced, fair-haired, large-headed, solidly-built American actor who played top sergeants, taxi-drivers, crooks, sailors and sundry denizens of working-class districts. The scourge of the rookie serviceman, Sawyer was a sort of B-picture William Bendix who could play straight or comic. He actually teamed with Bendix in a few rough-and-ready comedies of the 1940s. Died from cancer of the liver.

*1929: †*Campus Sweethearts. 1931: †Surrender. 1932: †Huddle (GB: Impossible Lover). †Forgotten Commandments. 1933: †College Humor. †*Saturday's Millions. †Three-Cornered Moon. †College Coach (GB: Football Coach). †Blood Money. †The Stranger's Return. †Ace of Aces. †Son of a Sailor. 1934: †Death on the Diamond. †Looking for Trouble. †Behold My Wife! †College Rhythm. †The Prescott Kid. †The Band Plays On. †Stamboul Quest. †Jimmy the Gent. †The Notorious Sophie Lang. †The Westerner. †The Whole Town's Talking (GB: Passport to Fame). 1935: †Broadway Gondolier. †Car 99. †Special Agent. †The Arizonian. †The Informer. I Found Stella Parish. Little Big Shot. Man of Iron. Frisco Kid. Moonlight on the Prairie. The Man on the Flying Trapeze (GB: The Memory Expert). The Revenge Rider. 1936: Big Brown Eyes. The Petrified Forest. And Sudden Death. Murder With Pictures. Crash Donovan. The Leathernecks Have Landed (GB: The Marines Have Landed). Two in a Crowd. Freshman Love (GB: Rhythm on the River). The Country Doctor. The Last Outlaw. The Walking Dead. High Tension. Special Investigator. Pride of the Marines. Black Legion. 1937: Great Guy (GB: Pluck of the Irish). Slim. Midnight Madonna. *Behind the Criminal. The Lady Fights Back. They Gave Him a Gun. Navy Blues. Reported Missing. Motor Madness. San Quentin. 1938: Always in Trouble. Tarzan's Revenge. Stolen Heaven. Gambling Ship. Heart of the North. The Storm. Passport*

*Husband. 1939: You Can't Get Away With Murder. The Lady and the Mob. I Stole a Million. Union Pacific. Sabotage (GB: Spies at Work). Inside Information. Confessions of a Nazi Spy. Frontier Marshal. The Roaring Twenties. 1940: The Man from Montreal. The Grapes of Wrath. King of the Lumberjacks. Women Without Names. The Long Voyage Home. Border Legion. Santa Fé Trail. The House Across the Bay. Dark Command. Lucky Cisco Kid. Melody Ranch. Wildcat Bus. 1941: Tanks a Million. The Lady from Cheyenne. Last of the Duanes. Down in San Diego. Swamp Water (GB: The Man Who Came Back). You're in the Army Now. Sergeant York. Belle Starr. Down Mexico Way. They Died With Their Boots On. 1942: The McGuerins from Brooklyn. *A Letter from Bataan. Wrecking Crew. Sundown Jim. Hay Foot. Brooklyn Orchid. 1943: Buckskin Frontier (GB: The Iron Road). Fall In. Prairie Chickens. Taxi, Mister. Yanks Ahoy. Let's Face It. Tarzan's Desert Mystery. The Outlaw. Cowboy in Manhattan. Hit the Ice. Tornado. Alaska Highway. Sleepy Lagoon. 1944: Moon Over Las Vegas. Hey, Rookie. Raiders of Ghost City (serial). The Singing Sheriff. South of Dixie. 1945: The Naughty Nineties. High Powered. Brewster's Millions. 1946: Joe Palooka—Champ. Deadline at Dawn. GI War Brides. The Runaround. Gilda. Inside Job. 1947: Big Town After Dark. Christmas Eve. A Double Life. Roses are Red. 1948: Half Past Midnight. If You Knew Susie. Fighting Back. Coroner Creek. The Untamed Breed. Here Comes Trouble. Fighting Father Dunne. 1949: The Gay Amigo. Deputy Marshal. And Baby Makes Three. Curtain Call at Cactus Creek (GB: Take the Stage). Kazan. The Lucky Stiff. The Stagecoach Kid. Tucson. ‡Two Knights in Brooklyn/Two Mugs from Brooklyn. 1950: Blondie's Hero. Operation Haylift. The Traveling Saleswoman. The Flying Missile. 1951: Pride of Maryland. Comin' Round the Mountain. As You Were. 1952: Red Skies of Montana. Indian Uprising. Mr Walkie Talkie. 1953: It Came from Outer Space. 1954: Taza Son of Cochise. Johnny Dark. Riding Shotgun. 1955: The Kettles in the Ozarks. 1956: The Killing. 1960: North to Alaska. 1962: How the West Was Won. 1973: Harry in Your Pocket (GB: Harry Never Holds).*

† As Joseph Sauer

‡ Combined GB version of *The McGuerins from Brooklyn/Taxi, Mister*

## SCHILDKRAUT, Joseph 1895-1964

Dashing, moustachioed, dark-haired Austrian-born actor with flashing smile. Came to Hollywood in the early twenties, and played lithe heroes. Sound films cast him mainly as suave, irritable villains — although there were also some good character roles, and for one of them, Captain Dreyfus in *The Life of Emile Zola*, he won an Academy Award. Died from a heart attack.

*1915: Arpád Szomory Schlemihil. 1916: Schweigepflich. 1918: Die Leben von Theodore Herzl. 1920: Der Roman der Komtesse*

*Orth. 1922: Orphans of the Storm. 1923: Dust of Desire. 1924: The Song of Love. 1925: The Road to Yesterday. 1926: Young April. Meet the Prince. Shipwrecked. 1927: His Dog. The King of Kings. The Heart Thief. The Forbidden Woman. 1928: The Blue Danube. Tenth Avenue. 1929: Mississippi Gambler. Show Boat. 1930: Die Sehnsucht jeder Frau. Cock o' the Walk. Night Ride. 1931: Carnival (US: Venetian Nights). The Blue Danube (remake). 1934: Viva Villa! Cleopatra. Sisters Under the Skin. 1935: The Crusades. 1936: The Garden of Allah. 1937: Souls at Sea. Slave Ship. Lady Behave. The Life of Emile Zola. Lancer Spy. 1938: Suez. The Baroness and the Butler. Marie Antoinette. 1939: The Man in the Iron Mask. Idiot's Delight. Lady of the Tropics. Barricade. The Three Musketeers (GB: The Singing Musketeer). Mr Moto Takes a Vacation. The Rains Came. Pack Up Your Troubles (GB: We're in the Army Now). 1940: Rangers of Fortune. The Shop Around the Corner. Phantom Raiders. Meet the Wildcat. 1941: The Parson of Panamint. *The Tell Tale Heart. 1945: Flame of the Barbary Coast. The Cheaters. 1946: Monsieur Beaucaire. The Plainsman and the Lady. 1947: Northwest Outpost (GB: End of the Rainbow). 1948: Gallant Legion. Old Los Angeles. 1959: The Diary of Anne Frank. 1961: King of the Roaring Twenties (GB: The Big Bankroll). 1965: The Greatest Story Ever Told.*

**SCHOFIELD, Johnnie** 1889-1961
Chunky, chirpy, brown-haired, dark-eyed Londoner with cheery face. From panto-

mime, revue and musical comedy, he was an assistant director looking to move his career backstage when sound films grabbed him for light supporting roles, of which he would play almost 100 before his retirement in 1954. Many of his appearances are fleeting, but he drove cabs, coaches, ambulances and lorries, served drinks at cafés and nightclubs, attended lifts and played orderlies, workmen, servicemen and generally men with their sleeves rolled up. Appropriate that he should have played in *Millions Like Us*; in the same year (1943), he had his only leading role, in *Down Melody Lane.*

*1933: Hawleys of High Street. The Pride of the Force. 1934: Josser on the Farm. The Outcast. Lost in the Legion. Doctor's Orders. 1935: Cock o' the North. Father O'Flynn. Jimmy Boy. The Mystery of the Marie Celeste/The Mystery of the Mary Celeste (US: Phantom Ship). A Real Bloke. Sexton Blake and the Bearded Doctor. Variety. 1936: The End of the Road. Melody of My Heart. One Good Turn. Song of Freedom. 1937: Rhythm Racketeer. Sam Small Leaves Town. Song of the Road. Talking Feet. Make-Up. 1938: Lassie from Lancashire. Mountains o' Mourne. Night Journey. Special Edition. *Receivers. I See Ice. 1939: The Arsenal Stadium Mystery. Down Our Alley. The Middle Watch. 1940: The Briggs Family. Two Smart Men. Spare a Copper. Convoy. Let George Do It. 1941: Bob's Your Uncle. Sheepdog of the Hills. 1942: The Young Mr Pitt. In Which We Serve. Old Mother Riley Detective. Uncensored. Went the Day Well? (US: 48 Hours). The Goose Steps Out. Next of Kin. Squadron Leader X. 1943: The Bells Go Down. The Demi-Paradise (US: Adventure for Two). Down Melody Lane. Millions Like Us. We Dive at Dawn. The Gentle Sex. *Welcome to Britain. 1944: English Without Tears (US: Her Man Gilbey). Give Me the Stars. Tawny Pipit. Waterloo Road. The Way Ahead. Welcome Mr Washington. They Came to a City. 1945: The Echo Murders. The Way to the Stars (US: Johnny in the Clouds). The Wicked Lady. The Voice Within. The Rake's Progress (US: Notorious Gentleman). 1946: The Shop at Sly Corner (US: The Code of Scotland Yard). This Man Is Mine! I See a Dark Stranger (US: The Adventuress). Wanted for Murder. 1947: The Mark of Cain. My Brother Jonathan. While I Live. Dancing With Crime. 1948: Love in Waiting. Mr Perrin and Mr Traill. So Evil My Love. 1949: Adam and Evelyne (US: Adam and Evalyn). Dark Secret. Train of Events. 1950: Blackmailed. The Reluctant Widow. The Second Mate. 1951: Appointment With Venus (US: Island Rescue). The Browning Version. White Corridors. 1952: Home at Seven (US: Murder on Monday). The Net (US: Project M7). Something Money Can't Buy. The Voice of Merrill (US: Murder Will Out). 1953: The Saint's Return (US: The Saint's Girl Friday). Solution by Phone. Small Town Story. Three Steps to the Gallows (released 1955. US: White Fire). Wheel of Fate. 1954: Carrington VC (US: Court-Martial).*

**SCOTT, Terry** 1927- 1994
Plump, dark-haired British comedian who moved from spluttering schoolboys to indignant adults before success in television series led him to comedy roles in films. These series, mostly in collaboration, included *Great Scott It's Maynard, Hugh and I, Happy Ever After* and *Terry and June.* Perhaps not quite enough of an actor to settle down to leading comedy roles in the cinema, he remained largely in cameos. Originally studied to be an accountant. Survived a major brain operation in 1979.

*1957: Blue Murder at St Trinian's. 1958: Carry On Sergeant. Too Many Crooks. 1959: The Bridal Path. I'm All Right, Jack. And the Same to You. 1960: The Night We Got the Bird. 1961: Nothing Barred. Double Bunk. Mary Had a Little.... Nearly a Nasty Accident. No, My Darling Daughter! What a Whopper! 1964: Murder Most Foul. 1965: Gonks Go Beat. 1966: The Great St Trinian's Train Robbery. Doctor in Clover. 1968: Carry On Up the Khyber. 1969: Carry On Camping. Carry On Up the Jungle. 1970: Carry On Henry. Carry On Loving. 1982: The Pantomime Dame.*

**SETON, Sir Bruce** 1909-1969
Tall, sour-looking, narrow-eyed, dark-haired (greying in his forties) British actor who had a military career before switching to show business and becoming a dancer in the Drury Lane Theatre chorus. As a speciality dancer in partnership with Betty

Astell (later a queen of British 'quota quickies') he broke into films, mixing straight dramas with small-scale musicals. He was relegated to minor roles in post-war years, but his career received an enormous boost with his long-running portrayal of a real-life detective in TV's *Fabian of the Yard* series. Returned to lesser roles in the latter stages of his career. Married to actresses Tamara Desni and Antoinette Cellier. Never used his (hereditary) title in films.

*1935: Blue Smoke. Flame in the Heather. The Shadow of Mike Emerald. Sweeney Todd the Demon Barber of Fleet Street. The Vanderbilt Diamond Mystery. 1936: Melody of My Heart. \*The Beauty Doctor. Wedding Group (US: Wrath of Jealousy). Jack of All Trades (US: The Two of Us). The Man Who Changed His Mind. \*Cocktail. Annie Laurie. The End of the Road. Café Colette (US: Danger in Paris). Love from a Stranger. 1937: Racing Romance. Song of the Road. Fifty Shilling Boxer. Father Steps Out. The Green Cockatoo (US: Four Dark Hours). 1938: If I Were Boss. Weddings Are Wonderful. You're the Doctor. Miracles Do Happen. 1939: Old Mother Riley Joins Up. The Middle Watch. Lucky to Me. 1946: The Curse of the Wraydons. 1948: The Story of Shirley Yorke. Scott of the Antarctic. Look Before You Love. Whisky Galore! (US: Tight Little Island). 1949: The Blue Lamp. 1950: Portrait of Clare. Paul Temple's Triumph. Blackmailed. Take me to Paris. 1951: White Corridors. High Treason. Worm's Eye View. 1952: Emergency Call (US: Hundred Hour Hunt). The Second Mrs Tanqueray. Rough Shoot (US: Shoot First). 1953: The Cruel Sea. 1954: Eight O'Clock Walk. Delayed Action. Fabian of the Yard. 1955: Man of the Moment. 1956: Breakaway. West of Suez (GB: Fighting Wildcats). 1957: There's Always a Thursday. Morning Call (US: The Strange Case of Dr Manning). The Crooked Sky. Zoo Baby (released 1960). Undercover Girl. 1958: Violent Moment. Hidden Homicide. 1959: Make Mine a Million. John Paul Jones. Life in Danger. Strictly Confidential. Operation Cupid. Trouble With Eve (US: In Trouble With Eve). 1960: Carry On Constable. Just Joe. Greyfriars Bobby. 1961: The Frightened City. Gorgo. Freedom To Die. 1962: Ambush in Leopard Street. Dead Man's Evidence. The Pot Carriers. 1963: Dr Syn Alias the Scarecrow.*

## SEYLER, Athene 1889- 1990

Light-haired, charmingly pug-faced, plump British actress, second only to Dame Margaret Rutherford in endearing qualities, and seen in her heyday as maiden aunts and loveable old dears from all walks of life. Played quite prominent film roles into her early seventies, having made her stage debut in 1908. Although no-one seemed more at home among the raspberry jam and Royal Doulton teacups, she could also convincingly play pioneer ladies of indomitable spirit.

*1921: The Adventures of Mr Pickwick. 1923: This Freedom. 1931: The Perfect Lady. 1932: Tell Me Tonight (US: Be Mine Tonight). 1933: Early to Bed. 1934: Blossom Time (US: April Romance). The Rocks of Valpré (US: High Treason). The Private Life of Don Juan. 1935: Scrooge. Royal Cavalcade (US: Regal Cavalcade). Drake of England (US: Drake the Pirate). Moscow Nights (US: I Stand Condemned). D'Ye Ken John Peel? (US: Captain Moonlight). 1936: Irish for Luck. It's Love Again. The Mill on the Floss. Sensation. Southern Roses. 1937: The Sky's the Limit. The Lilac Domino. Non Stop New York. 1938: Sailing Along. Jane Steps Out. The Citadel. The Ware Case. 1939: The Saint in London. Young Man's Fancy. 1940: Tilly of Bloomsbury. The House of the Arrow (US: Castle of Crimes). 1941: Quiet Wedding. 1943: Dear Octopus (US: The Randolph Family). 1947: Jassy. Nicholas Nickleby. 1948: The First Gentleman (US: Affairs of a Rogue). 1949: The Queen of Spades. 1951: The Franchise Affair. Young Wives' Tale. No Highway (US: No Highway in the Sky). Secret People. 1952: Treasure Hunt. Made in Heaven. The Pickwick Papers. 1953: The Beggar's Opera. The Weak and the Wicked. 1954: For Better, For Worse (US: Cocktails in the Kitchen). 1955: As Long As They're Happy. 1956: Yield to the Night (US: Blonde Sinner). 1957: Campbell's Kingdom. Doctor at Large. How to Murder a Rich Uncle. Night of the Demon (US: Scream of the Demon). 1958: The Inn of the Sixth Happiness. A Tale of Two Cities. Happy is the Bride! 1960: Make Mine Mink. A French Mistress. Passport to China (US: Visa to Canton). The Girl on the Boat. 1961: Francis of Assisi. Two and Two Make Six. 1962: I Thank a Fool. The Devil Never Sleeps (US: Satan Never Sleeps). 1963: Nurse on Wheels.*

## SEYMOUR, Anne 1909- 1988

Knowing-looking, tough-but-tender, light-haired American actress with droll tones who dispensed wit and wisdom in brittle Hollywood comedies and dramas, mainly in the 1957-1968 period, outside which she was much more often seen in theatre and TV. Made a good lady judge.

*1931: Aloha (GB: No Greater Love). 1949: All the King's Men. 1951: The Whistle at Eaton Falls (GB: Richer Than the Earth). 1957: Four Boys and a Gun. Desire Under the Elms. Man on Fire. 1958: The Gift of Love. Handle With Care. 1959: Home From the Hill. 1960: All the Fine Young Cannibals. The Subterraneans. Pollyanna. 1961: Misty. 1962: This Rugged Land (TV. GB: cinemas). 1964: Good Neighbor Sam. Stage to Thunder Rock. Where Love Has Gone. 1965: Blindfold. Mirage. 1966: How To Succeed in Business Without Really Trying. Waco. 1967: Fitzwilly (GB: Fitzwilly Strikes Back). 1968: Stay Away Joe. 1973: So Long Blue Boy. 1974: A Tree Grows in Brooklyn (TV). A Cry in the Wilderness (TV). 1975: The Gemini Affair. The Last Survivors (TV). 1976: Dawn: Portrait of a Teenage Runaway (TV). 1980: The Miracle Worker (TV). Angel on My Shoulder (TV). 1981: Never Never Land. 1982: Triumphs of a Man Called Horse. 1984: Gemini Affair II — a Diary. Trancers. 1985: A Future Cop.*

## SEYMOUR, Dan 1915-1982

Dark, plump, crunch-faced, blue-jowled Seymour was one of the slimiest Hollywood villains of the 1940s, his 'inverted' mouth twisting frequently into a scowl, as he contemplated committing some new and more painful mayhem on the hero, most notably Humphrey Bogart and his associates in *To Have and Have Not*. Although only 29 at the time of this film, Seymour, a former nightclub entertainer, always looked around (a very round) 40. Occasionally relaxed and played a comic hoodlum instead; was too little seen after the end of the 1950s.

*1942: Cairo. Road to Morocco. Bombs Over Burma. Casablanca. 1943: Tahiti Honey. Rhythm of the Islands. Klondike Kate. Tiger Fangs. 1944: †Rainbow Island. Kismet. It's in the Bag! (GB: The Fifth Chair). To Have and Have Not. 1945: The Spanish Main. Confidential Agent. 1946: A Night in Casablanca. Cloak and Dagger. 1947: Slave Girl. Hard Boiled Mahoney. The Searching Wind. Philo Vance's Gamble. Intrigue. 1948: Highway 13. Johnny Belinda. Unfaithfully Yours. Key Largo. 1949: Trail of the Yukon. 1950: Joe Palooka in the Squared Circle (GB: The Squared Circle). Abbott and Costello in the Foreign Legion. Young Man with a Horn (GB: Young Man of Music). 1951: The Blue Veil. 1952: Rancho Notorious. Mara Maru. Glory Alley. Face to Face. 1953: The System. Second Chance. Tangier Incident. The Big Heat. 1954: Moonfleet. Human Desire. 1955: While the City Sleeps. Abbott and Costello Meet the Mummy. 1956: Beyond a Reasonable Doubt. 1957: The Buster Keaton Story. The Sad Sack. Undersea Girl. 1959: The Return of the Fly. Watusi. 1973: The Way We Were. 1974: Escape to Witch Mountain. Center Fold Girls (GB: Centrefold Girls).*

†Scenes deleted from final release print

**SHAUGHNESSY, Mickey**
(Joseph Shaughnessy) 1920-1985
Bullet-headed, snub-nosed, button-eyed, crop-haired, fast-talking, aggressive American actor, built like a little tank. After war service, he became a nightclub singer, then mixed comedy with the singing. Became a well-known film face as the serviceman who has his swear-words 'fluffed out' on the soundtrack in *Don't Go Near the Water*. Disappeared into television after 1970. Died from lung cancer.

*1952: The Marrying Kind. Last of the Comanches (GB: The Sabre and the Arrow). 1953: From Here to Eternity. 1955: The Burglar. Conquest of Space. 1956: Don't Go Near the Water. 1957: Slaughter on 10th Avenue. Designing Woman. Until They Sail.*

*Jailhouse Rock. 1958: The Sheepman. Gunman's Walk. A Nice Little Bank That Should Be Robbed (GB: How to Rob a Bank). 1959: Don't Give Up the Ship. Edge of Eternity. The Hangman. 1960: The Adventures of Huckleberry Finn. Sex Kittens Go to College. North to Alaska. College Confidential. Dondi. 1961: King of the Roaring Twenties (GB: The Big Bankroll). Pocketful of Miracles. 1962: How the West Was Won. 1963: A Global Affair. 1964: A House Is Not a Home. 1967: Never a Dull Moment. A Boy Called Nuthin' (TV). 1969: My Dog, the Thief. 1970: The Boatniks.*

**SHAW, Denis** 1921-1971
Bulky British actor with a shock of dark wavy hair whose simian features consigned him to 'heavy' roles in more ways than one, although his portrayal of a judo-throwing Interpol detective in one minor thriller was engaging enough to make one regret the lack of a follow-up. But his slit eyes and outsize frame moved back into greasy-villain roles. Died from a heart attack at 49.

*1952: The Long Memory. 1953: House of Blackmail. The Case of Soho Red. 1954: The Colditz Story. 1955: Keep It Clean. 1956: Port Afrique. Who Done It? The Weapon. 1957: Seven Thunders (US: The Beasts of Marseilles). The Flesh Is Weak. The Depraved. 1958: Blood of the Vampire. A Woman Possessed. Soap Box Derby. Moment of Indiscretion. Links of Justice. The Great Van Robbery. 1959: Passport to Shame (US: Room 43). Innocent Meeting. The Bandit of Zhobe. No Safety Ahead. Jack the Ripper. The Mummy. The Man Who Could Cheat Death. The Night We Dropped a Clanger. Naked Fury. 1960: Beyond the Curtain. The Misfits. The Two Faces of Dr Jekyll (US: House of Fright). The Night We Got the Bird. Make Mine Mink. 1961: Ticket to Paradise. Curse of the Werewolf. The Hellfire Club. A Weekend With Lulu. Nothing Barred. The Pirates of Blood River. Carry On Regardless. 1962: The Day of the Triffids. 1964: The Runaway. 1966: The Deadly Affair. 1967: The Viking Queen. The Magnificent Six and a ½ (first series). 1969: The File of the Golden Goose. The Magnificent Six and a ½ (second series).*

**SHEPLEY, Michael** (M. Shepley-Smith) 1907-1961
Brown-haired, solidly built, moustachioed, myopically peering British actor who played amiable buffoons through three decades of films; the sort of chap you'd expect to find asleep at the club behind his newspaper. It comes as no surprise to learn that his principal interest outside show-business was cricket.

*1931: Black Coffee. 1933: A Shot in the Dark. 1934: Are You a Mason? Bella Donna. Tangled Evidence. Lord Edgware Dies. The Green Pack. Open All Night. 1935: Lazybones. Vintage Wine. The Rocks of Valpré (US: High Treason). The Ace of Spades. The Lad. Squibs. Jubilee Window. Private Secretary. The Triumph of Sherlock Holmes. That's My Uncle. 1936: In the Soup. 1937: Beauty and the Barge. 1938: Crackerjack (US: The Man With a Hundred Faces). Housemaster. It's in the Air (US: George Takes the Air). 1939: Goodbye Mr Chips! 1941: Quiet Wedding. 1942: The Great Mr Handel. Women Aren't Angels. 1943: The Demi-Paradise (US: Adventure for Two). 1944: Henry V. 1945: A Place of One's Own. I Live in Grosvenor Square (US: A Yank in London). 1947: Nicholas Nickleby. Mine Own Executioner. 1949: Maytime in Mayfair. Elizabeth of Ladymead. 1951: Mr Denning Drives North. Secret People. 1952: Home at Seven (US: Murder on Monday). 1953: You Know What Sailors Are. 1954: Trouble in the Glen. Happy Ever After (US: Tonight's the Night/O'Leary Night). 1955: Where There's a Will. An Alligator Named Daisy. Doctor at Sea. 1956: My Teenage Daughter (US: Teenage Bad Girl). Dry Rot. The Passionate Stranger (US: A Novel Affair). 1957: Not Wanted on Voyage. 1958: Gideon's Day (US: Gideon of Scotland Yard). 1960: Just Joe. 1961: Don't Bother to Knock! (US: Why Bother to Knock?). Double Bunk.*

**SHEYBAL, Vladek** (Wladislaw Sheybal) 1932-
Polish actor with dark hair and pinched, cunning-looking features. Twice escaped from concentration camps during World War II, then, after one Polish film, came to England and became a TV director. He

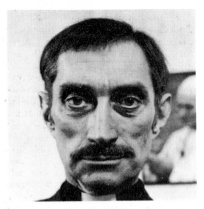

returned to acting in 1965 and has been seen occasionally in British and international films, usually in eccentric or menacing roles. Married/divorced Polish actress Irena Aklarovna.

*1957: Kanal. 1965: Return from the Ashes. 1967: Billion Dollar Brain. 1968: Deadfall (shown 1967). Mosquito Squadron. 1969: Leo the Last. Women in Love. 1970: The Last Valley. Puppet on a Chain. 1971: *The Spy's Wife. The Boy Friend. 1972: Innocent Bystanders. Scorpio. 1973: Pilatus und andere. Un baccio di una morte. 1974: S*P*Y*S. QB VII (TV). 1975: Bordella. The Wind and the Lion. The Sellout. 1976: Gulliver's Travels (voice only). Hamlet. 1977: Exorcist II The Heretic (voice only). 1979: The Lady Vanishes. Avalanche Express. 1980: Shogun (TV. GB: cinemas in abbreviated version). The Apple (GB: Star Rock). 1983: Memed My Hawk. 1984: Red Dawn.*

**SHIELDS, Arthur** 1895-1970
Light-haired, wistful-looking Irish actor, recognizably the brother of character superstar Barry Fitzgerald. Shields (the real family name) played much smaller roles than his brother after their arrival in Hollywood in the 1930s, but nonetheless etched some sharp studies. Often seen in rimless spectacles, usually dispensing wisdom to those more headstrong than himself. Died from an emphysema.

*1918: Rafferty's Rise. 1936: The Plough and the Stars. 1939: Drums along the Mohawk. 1940: The Long Voyage Home. Little Nellie*

Kelly. *1941: How Green Was My Valley. The Gay Falcon. Lady Scarface. Confirm or Deny. 1942: Pacific Rendezvous. Gentleman Jim. This Above All. Broadway. Nightmare. Random Harvest. The Black Swan. 1943: Lassie Come Home. The Man from Down Under. Madame Curie. Above Suspicion. 1944: The Keys of the Kingdom. The Sign of the Cross (new prologue to 1932 feature). The White Cliffs of Dover. Youth Runs Wild. National Velvet. 1945: *Phantoms Inc. Too Young to Know. The Corn Is Green. The Valley of Decision. The Picture of Dorian Gray. Roughly Speaking. 1946: Three Strangers. Gallant Journey. Never Say Goodbye. The Verdict. The Shocking Miss Pilgrim. 1947: Easy Come, Easy Go. Seven Keys to Baldpate. The Fabulous Dorseys. 1948: Fighting Father Dunne. Tap Roots. My Own True Love. 1949: Red Light. Challenge to Lassie. The Fighting O'Flynn. She Wore a Yellow Ribbon. 1950: Tarzan and the Slave Girl. 1951: Sealed Cargo. Apache Drums. Blue Blood. The People Against O'Hara. A Wonderful Life. The River. The Barefoot Mailman. 1952: The Quiet Man. Scandal at Scourie. 1953: South Sea Woman. Main Street to Broadway. 1954: Pride of the Blue Grass (GB: Prince of the Blue Grass). World for Ransom. River of No Return. 1955: Lady Godiva (GB: Lady Godiva of Coventry). 1956: The King and Four Queens. 1957: Daughter of Dr Jekyll. 1958: Enchanted Island. 1959: Night of the Quarter Moon. 1960: For the Love of Mike (GB: None But the Brave). 1961: King of the Roaring Twenties (GB: The Big Bankroll). 1962: The Pigeon That Took Rome.*

**SHINE, Bill** (Wilfred Shine Jr) 1911-
Tall, light-haired, sleepy-eyed, thin British supporting actor with handlebar moustache; you were prepared for the upper-crust accent before it came and he fitted in well as well-meaning but addle-brained officer or aristocrat. He was also seen as the hero's friend or slightly inefficient official. The son of actor Wilfred Shine, who appeared in early British sound films, Bill (billed as Billy until 1940) made his first appearance on stage at six, playing a stork. Hobbies: ridin', fishin' and racin' (what about the shootin'?). Splendidly cast in one film as 'Flying Officer Prang'.

*1929: High Seas. The Flying Scotsman. Under the Greenwood Tree. 1930: The Last Hour. The Yellow Mask. Harmony Heaven. 1931: These Charming People. Money for Nothing. Many Waters. 1932: Verdict of the Sea. The Man from Toronto. 1934: My Old Dutch. Waltzes from Vienna (US: Strauss's Great Waltz). The Scarlet Pimpernel. 1935: Blue Smoke. It Happened in Paris. Late Extra. 1936: Highland Fling. Find the Lady. Servants All. Gaolbreak. To Catch a Thief. Sensation. 1937: The Strange Adventures of Mr Smith. Farewell Again (US: Troopship). Young and Innocent (US: The Girl Was Young). The Last Adventurers. The Green Cockatoo (US: Four Dark Hours). Over the Moon (released 1940). The Compulsory Wife. 1938: The Villiers Diamond. Second Thoughts. You're the Doctor. 1939: The Face at the Window. 1940: Let George Do It. Crooks' Tour. 1941: Inspector Hornleigh Goes to It (US: Mail Train). Turned Out Nice Again. 1944: Champagne Charlie. 1945: Perfect Strangers (US: Vacation from Marriage). For You Alone. 1946: Wanted for Murder. 1947: Captain Boycott. Vice Versa. 1948: The Red Shoes. The Winslow Boy. The Small Voice (US: Hideout). Another Shore. Passport to Pimlico. 1949: Private Angelo. Under Capricorn. The Chiltern Hundreds (US: The Amazing Mr Beecham). 1950: Something in the City. The Woman with No Name (US: Her Paneled Door). Old Mother Riley's Jungle Treasure. 1951: Talk of a Million (US: You Can't Beat the Irish). 1952: Love's a Luxury (US: The Caretaker's Daughter). The Woman's Angle. Never Look Back. Hot Ice. No Haunt for a Gentleman. Mother Riley Meets the Vampire (US: Vampire Over London). There Was a Young Lady. 1953: Melba. Innocents in Paris. The Blakes Slept Here. The Clue of the Missing Ape. 1954: Knave of Hearts (US: Lovers, Happy Lovers). Father Brown (US: The Detective). Duel in the Jungle. Devil on Horseback. Happy Ever After (US: Tonight's the Night/O'Leary Night). 1955: As Long as They're Happy. An Alligator Named Daisy. The Adventures of Quentin Durward (US: Quentin Durward). The Deep Blue Sea. Richard III. Raising a Riot. Where There's a Will. John and Julie. 1956: Bond of Fear. Not So Dusty. Women Without Men (US: Blonde Bait). The Last Man to Hang? 1957: The House in the Woods. Blue Murder at St Trinian's. 1958: Diplomatic Corpse. 1959: Make Mine a Million. Left, Right and Centre. Jack the Ripper. The Boy and the Bridge. The Challenge. Trouble With Eve (US: In Trouble With Eve). 1960: The Pure Hell of St Trinian's. 1961: Double Bunk. 1963: The Rescue Squad. 1965: Joey Boy. 1966: Bindle (One of Them Days). 1967: *Ouch! The Sky Bike. 1971: Not Tonight Darling! 1985: The McGuffin (TV).*

**SHOWALTER, Max** 1917-
Fair-haired, pale-eyed American actor who changed his name to Casey Adams when with 20th Century-Fox in 1952 and played

glib charmers and light romantic leads. He reverted to his real name during 1962, but has preferred to concentrate in his secondary career as a composer of background scores for the theatre and cinema. He also composed the title song for *Vicki*, in which he had one of his best roles.

1949: *Always Leave Them Laughing.* 1952: *With a Song in My Heart.* †*What Price Glory?* †*My Wife's Best Friend.* 1953: †*Niagara.* †*Destination Gobi.* †*Dangerous Crossing.* †*Vicki.* 1954: †*Night People.* †*Naked Alibi.* †*Down Three Dark Streets.* 1955: †*The Return of Jack Slade (GB: Texas Rose).* 1956: †*Never Say Goodbye.* †*The Indestructible Man.* †*Bus Stop.* 1957: †*Dragoon Wells Massacre.* †*The Monster That Challenged the World.* †*Designing Woman.* 1958: †*The Female Animal.* †*Voice in the Mirror.* †*The Naked and the Dead.* 1959: †*It Happened to Jane.* 1960: †*Elmer Gantry.* 1961: †*Return to Peyton Place.* †*Summer and Smoke.* †*The Music Man.* 1962: †*Bon Voyage!* *Smog.* 1963: *My Six Loves. Move Over, Darling.* 1964: *Fate Is the Hunter. Sex and the Single Girl.* 1965: *How to Murder Your Wife. Lord Love a Duck.* 1969: *A Talent for Loving.* 1970: *The Moonshine War.* 1971: *The Anderson Tapes.* 1972: *Bonnie's Kids.* 1978: *Sergeant Pepper's Lonely Hearts Club Band.* 1979: *'10'.* 1984: *Racing With the Moon.*

†As Casey Adams

**SIKKING, James B.** 1934-
Tall, dark, dour American actor with a

passing resemblance to Roy Scheider. Playing officers, detectives and businessmen, he seemed to escape the public eye until pitched into the limelight with his running role as Hunter in the popular TV series *Hill Street Blues*. Sometimes bespectacled in recent years, he continues to achieve a good range of roles, and one also suspects a dry sense of comedy. The 'B' stands for Barrie (named after his parents' favourite author).

1963: *The Strangler.* 1964: *The Americanization of Emily.* 1965: *Von Ryan's Express.* 1967: *Point Blank.* 1969: *Charro! Daddy's Gone a-Hunting.* 1971: *The Night God Screamed (GB: Scream). Chandler.* 1972: *The Astronaut (TV). Man on a String (TV). Brother on the Run. The Magnificent Seven Ride! Boots Turner. Family Flight (TV). Scorpio. The New Centurions (GB: Precinct 45—Los Angeles Police).* 1973: *The Alpha Caper (TV. GB: cinemas, as Inside Job). Coffee, Tea or Me? (TV).* 1974: *The FBI versus Alvin Karpis, Public Enemy Number One (TV).* 1977: *Capricorn One. Young Joe, the Forgotten Kennedy (TV). The Last Hurrah (TV).* 1978: *A Woman Called Moses (TV).* 1979: *The Electric Horseman.* 1980: *Ordinary People. The Competition.* 1981: *Outland.* 1983: *The Star Chamber.* 1984: *Star Trek III: The Search for Spock.* 1985: *Morons from Outer Space. First Steps (TV).*

**SILVA, Henry** 1928-
Cold-eyed, impassive, scowling, slightly oriental-looking, dark-haired American actor (of Puerto Rican parentage) who often plays emotionless killers. If you saw Silva coming down a street towards you, the odds are that you would cross to the other side. An attempt to install him in leading roles in the early sixties was not successful and, although he has continued with bad guys, they have often been too silly for him to make an impact. Much in Italy from the mid-sixties.

1952: *Viva Zapata!* 1956: *Crowded Paradise.* 1957: *A Hatful of Rain. The Tall T.* 1958: *The Law and Jake Wade. The Bravados. Ride a Crooked Trail.* 1959: *Green Mansions. The Jayhawkers.* 1960: *Cinderfella. Ocean's Eleven.* 1962: *Sergeants Three. The*

*Manchurian Candidate.* 1963: *A Gathering of Eagles. Johnny Cool.* 1964: *The Secret Invasion.* 1965: *The Reward. The Return of Mr Moto. Je vous salue Mafia (US: Hail Mafia).* 1966: *Matchless. The Plainsman. Un fiume di dollari (GB: The Hills Run Red).* 1967: *Assassination. Never a Dull Moment.* 1968: *Quella carogna dell' Ispettore Sterling (US: Blood Money).* 1969: *Probabilità zero. Drive Hard, Drive Fast (TV).* 1970: *The Animals (GB: Five Savage Men).* 1971: *Black Noon (TV). Man and Boy.* 1972: *La 'mala' ordina (GB: Manhunt in Milan). L'insolent. Les hommes.* 1973: *Il boss (GB: Murder Inferno). Zinksärge für die Goldjungen.* 1974: *Cry of a Prostitute. Milano odia: la polizia non puo' sparare (US: Almost Human).* 1975: *The Kidnap of Mary Lou. L'uomo della strada fa giustizia.* 1976: *Shoot. Eviolenti.* 1977: *Fox Bat. Contract on Cherry Street (TV).* 1978: *Love and Bullets.* 1979: *Buck Rogers in the 25th Century (TV. GB: cinemas).* 1980: *Thirst. Virus. Alligator.* 1981: *Sharky's Machine. Trapped.* 1982: *Wrong Is Right (GB: The Man With the Deadly Lens). Megaforce.* 1983: *Chained Heat. Violent Breed. Cannonball Run II.* 1984: *Crossfire. Man Hunt Warning.* 1985: *Code of Silence. Quatermain.*

**SILVERHEELS, Jay** (Harold J. Smith) 1918-1980
One of the few Red Indian actors to play 'normal' acting roles, round-faced, cheerful-looking Silverheels, the son of a Canadian Mohawk chief, came to films as an extra and stuntman in 1938, in the days when he was a budding boxing and lacrosse star in real life. His best film roles came after his television success as Tonto in the long-running western series *The Lone Ranger*. In later years, he combined acting with a career in harness-racing, but died at 62 as a result of complications from pneumonia.

1940: *Too Many Girls.* 1945: †*Song of the Sarong.* 1946: †*Canyon Passage.* 1947: †*The Last Round-Up. Captain from Castile. Northwest Outpost (GB: End of the Rainbow).* 1948: *Indian Agent. The Feathered Serpent. Key Largo. Fury at Furnace Creek. The Prairie. Singing Spurs. Yellow Sky. Family Honeymoon.* 1949: *Will James' Sand (GB:*

Sand). *Trail of the Yukon. For Those Who Dare. Lust for Gold. Laramie. The Cowboy and the Indians. 1950: Broken Arrow. 1951: Red Mountain. The Wild Blue Yonder (GB: Thunder Across the Pacific). 1952: Brave Warrior. The Battle at Apache Pass. Yankee Buccaneer. The Will Rogers Story (GB: The Story of Will Rogers). The Pathfinder. Last of the Comanches (GB: The Sabre and the Arrow). 1953: War Arrow. Jack McCall—Desperado. The Nebraskan. 1954: The Black Dakotas. Masterson of Kansas. Drums across the River. Four Guns to the Border. Saskatchewan (GB: O'Rourke of the Royal Mounted). 1955: The Vanishing American. 1956: Walk the Proud Land. The Lone Ranger. 1958: Return to Warbow. The Lone Ranger and the Lost City of Gold. 1959: Alias Jesse James. 1962: Geronimo's Revenge (TV: GB: cinemas). 1964: Indian Paint. 1969: Smith! True Grit. The Phynx. 1972: Santee. 1973: One Little Indian. The Man Who Loved Cat Dancing.*

†As Silverheels Smith

### SIM, Gerald 1925-

Light-haired British actor with friendly, open face, often cast in well-meaning roles, such as probation officers, social workers or helpful civil servants. After an effective appearance in *The Angry Silence*, he was seen in almost all of the films made by its co-producers, Bryan Forbes and Richard Attenborough.

*1947: Fame Is the Spur. 1960: The Angry Silence. Cone of Silence (US: Trouble in the Sky). 1961: Whistle Down the Wind. 1962: Flat Two. The Amorous Prawn. The Wrong Arm of the Law. The L-Shaped Room. 1963: I Could Go On Singing (shown 1962). Heavens Above! 1964: The Pumpkin Eater. Seance on a Wet Afternoon. 1965: King Rat. 1966: The Murder Game. The Wrong Box. The Whisperers. 1967: Our Mother's House. 1969: Mischief. The Madwoman of Chaillot. Oh! What a Lovely War. The Last Grenade (US: Grigsby). 1970: Ryan's Daughter. The Man Who Haunted Himself. Doctor in Trouble. The Raging Moon (US: Long Ago Tomorrow). 1971: Dr Jekyll and Sister Hyde. Young Winston. 1972: Dr Phibes Rises Again. Frenzy. Kadoyng. 1973: No Sex Please—*

*We're British. 1976: The Slipper and the Rose. 1977: A Bridge Too Far. 1982: Gandhi.*

### SIMS, Joan 1930-

Cheery-looking, fair-haired British actress with distinctive light voice and pinched lips. Almost entirely in comedy parts, at first as curvaceous, man-hungry cockneys, sometimes with assumed upper-class accents, and later, with added weight, a key member of the 'Carry On' comedy team, usually playing nagging wives. Vanished from the cinema with the demise of that series.

*1953: Will Any Gentleman? The Square Ring. Colonel March Investigates. Trouble in Store. Meet Mr Lucifer. 1954: Doctor in the House. What Every Woman Wants. The Belles of St Trinian's. To Dorothy a Son (US: Cash on Delivery). The Sea Shall Not Have Them. 1955: As Long As They're Happy. Doctor at Sea. Lost (US: Tears for Simon). 1956: Keep It Clean. The Silken Affair. Stars in Your Eyes. Dry Rot. 1957: Just My Luck. Davy. Carry On Admiral (US: The Ship Was Loaded). No Time for Tears. The Naked Truth (US: Your Past is Showing). 1958: The Captain's Table. 1959: Passport to Shame (US: Room 43). Carry On Nurse. Life in Emergency Ward 10. Carry On Teacher. Upstairs and Downstairs. Please Turn Over. 1960: Carry On Constable. Doctor in Love. Watch Your Stern. His and Hers. 1961: Carry On Regardless. Mr Topaze (US: I Like Money). No, My Darling Daughter! 1962: Twice Round the Daffodils. A Pair of Briefs. The Iron Maiden. Nurse On Wheels. 1963: Strictly for the Birds. 1964: Carry On Cleo. 1965: The Big Job. San Ferry Ann. Carry On Cowboy. Doctor in Clover. 1966: Carry On Screaming. Don't Lose Your Head. 1967: Follow That Camel. Carry On Doctor. 1968: Carry On Up the Khyber. 1969: Carry On Camping. Carry On Again, Doctor. Carry On Up the Jungle. 1970: Doctor in Trouble. Carry On Loving. Carry On Henry. 1971: The Magnificent Seven Deadly Sins. Carry On at Your Convenience. 1972: Carry On Matron. The Alf Garnett Saga. Carry On Abroad. Not Now Darling. 1973: Carry On Girls. Don't Just Lie There, Say Something! 1974: Carry On Dick. Love Among the Ruins (TV). 1975: Carry On Behind. One of Our Dinosaurs is Missing. 1976: Carry On England. 1978: Carry On Emmannuelle.*

### SINGER, Campbell 1909-1976

Dark-haired, lively, moustachioed British actor whose oval features could easily express such disparate emotions as hopefulness, friendliness, grouchiness and resolution. He was generally cast as hard workers—police sergeants, railwaymen, labourers or forces types. Born in London, he was raised in South Africa, where he made his stage debut in 1928 before returning to England in the early 1930s. A busy employee of the British cinema (usually lending a friendly hand to the hero) from 1947 to 1962; after that he devoted his talents mainly to television. Mainly in minor parts, but had a good leading role in *The Young and the Guilty.*

*1938: Premiere (US: One Night in Paris). 1947: The Woman in the Hall. Take My Life. Jim the Penman. 1948: Operation Diamond. Woman Hater. 1949: Rover and Me. The Blue Lamp. Hangman's Wharf. 1950: Dick Barton at Bay. Cage of Gold. Pool of London. The Quiet Woman. 1951: The Man With the Twisted Lip. A Case for PC 49. 1952: Emergency Call (US: Hundred Hour Hunt). The Happy Family (US: Mr Lord Says No). Lady in the Fog (US: Scotland Yard Inspector). Home at Seven (US: Murder on Monday). The Yellow Balloon. The Ringer. Appointment in London. The Titfield Thunderbolt. Time Bomb (US: Terror on a Train). 1953: Street Corner (US: Both Sides of the Law). The Girl on the Pier. The Intruder. 1954: Simba. Forbidden Cargo. Conflict of Wings (US: Fuss over Feathers). To Dorothy a Son (US: Cash on Delivery). 1956: Ramsbottom Rides Again. Reach for the Sky. Town on Trial! 1957: Davy. 1958: The Young and the Guilty. No Trees in the Street. The Square Peg. 1960: The Hands of Orlac. The Trials of Oscar Wilde (US: The Man with the Green Carnation). Sands of the Desert. 1961: No, My Darling Daughter! 1962: The Devil's Daffodil (US: The Daffodil Killer). The Wild and the Willing. The Fast Lady. On the Beat. Flat Two. The Pot Carriers. 1964: Go Kart Go! 1966: †The Collector.*

†Scenes delected from final release print

### SKIPWORTH, Alison (née Groom) 1863-1952

Brown-haired, heavy-featured, slightly menacing British actress, a heavy-weight who looked built for stern dramatics, but more often scored in comedy. Married to the artist Frank Markam Skipworth, she didn't become an actress until she was 30 and went to America two years later, gradually becoming a solid player on Broadway. In Hollywood from 1930, she never looked her real age, and people were amazed to find she was 75 when she finally retired. More than a match for W. C. Fields and even Mae West, she had a couple of vehicles of her own (*A Lady's Profession, Madame Racketeer*) as well as taking the Sydney Greenstreet role in *Satan Met a Lady*, the second verson of *The Maltese Falcon!*

ABOVE Campbell **Singer** (second from left) shown here with
Alan MacNaughtan, Arnold Diamond and R. Meadows White
in *Night of the Reckoning*, a British television drama from the
1960s

BELOW Alison **Skipworth** (left) didn't have to do very much to
dominate a scene in a film, as Susan Fleming finds out here in
*He Learned About Women* (1933)

1921: *Handcuffs or Kisses.* 1930: *Du Barry, Woman of Passion* (GB: *Du Barry*). *Oh! For a Man. Outward Bound. Raffles. Strictly Unconventional.* 1931: *Devotion. The Virtuous Husband* (GB: *What Wives Don't Want*). *The Road to Singapore. Tonight or Never. Night Angel. Sinners in the Sun.* 1932: *High Pressure. Madame Racketeer* (GB: *The Sporting Widow*). *Unexpected Father. Night After Night. If I Had a Million.* 1933: *Tonight Is Ours. He Learned About Women. A Lady's Profession. Song of Songs. Tillie and Gus. Midnight Club. Alice in Wonderland.* 1934: *Six of a Kind. Wharf Angel. The Notorious Sophie Lang. Here in My Heart. Shoot the Works* (GB: *Thank Your Stars*). *Coming-Out Party. The Captain Hates the Sea.* 1935: *Shanghai. The Devil Is a Woman. The Casino Murder Case. Becky Sharp. The Girl from 10th Avenue* (GB: *Men On Her Mind*). *Doubting Thomas. Dangerous.* 1936: *Hitch Hike Lady* (GB: *Eventful Journey*). *The Princess Comes Across. Satan Met a Lady. The Gorgeous Hussy. Two in a Crowd. White Hunter. Stolen Holiday.* 1937: *Two Wise Maids.* 1938: *King of the Newsboys. Wide Open Faces. Ladies in Distress.*

*Music. The Common Touch. Penn of Pennsylvania* (US: *The Courageous Mr Penn*). *They Flew Alone* (US: *Wings and the Woman*). 1942: *The Young Mr Pitt. Uncensored. Went the Day Well?* (US: *48 Hours*). *The Day Will Dawn* (US: *The Avengers*). 1943: *We Dive at Dawn. Candlelight in Algeria. Deadlock. Millions Like Us. The Hundred Pound Window.* 1944: *A Canterbury Tale. *Unity is Strength. For Those in Peril.* 1945: *I Live in Grosvenor Square* (US: *A Yank in London*). *Murder in Reverse. The Seventh Veil.* 1946: *Othello.* 1947: *Teheran* (US: *The Plot to Kill Roosevelt*). *It Always Rains on Sunday.* 1948: *Against the Wind. Noose* (US: *The Silk Noose*). *Escape.* 1949: *Passport to Pimlico.* 1950: *Prelude to Fame.* 1951: *The Third Visitor.* 1952: *The Ringer. Faithful City. The Long Memory. *Dark London (narrator only).* 1953: *The Flanagan Boy* (US: *Bad Blonde*). *The Million Pound Note* (US: *Man With a Million*). *Strange Stories (narrator only). Star of India.* 1955: *Dollars for Sale. Johnny You're Wanted. *Puzzle Corner No.17. *Puzzle Corner No.18.* 1956: *Do You Remember?* 1957: *The Devil's Pass. Violent Playground.* 1960: *The Night We Got the Bird.* 1961: *Three on a Spree. Nothing Barred.* 1962: *Pig Tales (narrator only).* 1963: *A Place to Go.* 1966: *The Yellow Hat. *Germany Today (narrator only).*
†As B. John Slater

*Blut. Marccos tollste Wette. Der Seekadett. Wie bliebe ich jung und schön.* 1927: *Der Fahnenträger von Sedan. Die grosse Rause. Liebe geht seltsame Wege. Die Lorelei.* 1928: *Das Hannerl vom Rolandsbogen. Einen Jux will er sich machen. Ledige Mütter. Addio. Glovinezza.* 1932: *Spione am Savoy Hotel.* 1942: *Once Upon a Honeymoon.* 1943: *This Land Is Mine. The Fallen Sparrow.* 1944: *Step Lively. Lifeboat. Till We Meet Again. And Now Tomorrow. The Princess and the Pirate.* 1945: *The Spanish Main. Salome, Where She Danced. Cornered.* 1947: *Born to Kill* (GB: *Lady of Deceit*). *Riffraff. Sinbad the Sailor.* 1948: *The Pirate.* 1949: *The Inspector General.* 1950: *The Yellow Cab Man. Spy Hunt* (GB: *Panther's Moon*). *Abbott and Costello in the Foreign Legion.* 1951: *Bedtime for Bonzo. People Will Talk.* 1953: *Confidentially Connie. White Witch Doctor. Call Me Madam.* 1954: *The Steel Cage.* 1956: *The Last Patriarch* (TV). *Deadlier Than the Male.* 1957: *Ten Thousand Bedrooms.* 1958: *The Gentleman from Seventh Avenue* (TV). 1959: *The Miracle.* 1961: *Come September.* 1962: *The Wonderful World of the Brothers Grimm.* 1964: *Emil and the Detectives. Wonderful Life* (US: *Swingers' Paradise*). 1965: *24 Hours to Kill. Der Kongress amüsiert sich.* 1966: *Coppelius.* 1967: *The Caper of the Golden Bulls* (GB: *Carnival of Thieves*). 1968: *Legend of Robin Hood* (TV). *Heidi Comes Home* (US: *Heidi*). 1971: *Black Beauty. Treasure Island.* 1972: *The Mysterious House of Dr C.*

## SLATER, John (B. John Slater) 1916-1975

Dark-haired British actor of thin lips and shadowed aspect — from the narrowness of his projecting features—who usually found himself cast as down-to-earth working types. Sometimes he would don a scowl and play a crook. His beetle brows were much in evidence in British films from 1941 to 1957 (although his career was temporarily slowed when he was injured in an air crash in 1946), after which he was mainly on stage and TV. Also for many years the narrator of the *Mining Review* documentary shorts. He suffered from ill-health later in his career, although he did become popular as Sgt Stone in TV's *Z Cars*. Died from a heart attack.

1938: †*Alf's Button Afloat.* 1941: †*Love on the Dole.* †*The Patient Vanishes (later This Man is Dangerous). *The Harvest Shall Come. Gert and Daisy's Weekend. Hatter's Castle. *Shunter Black's Night Off (narrator only). Pimpernel Smith* (US: *Mister V*). *Facing the*

## SLEZAK, Walter 1902-1983

Tubby, moustachioed Austrian actor, just as likely to be affable or menacing (but probably most memorable as the German on Hitchcock's *Lifeboat*) and a welcome part of any film. He had two bursts of intense film activity, in Germany from 1924 to 1928 and in Hollywood from 1942 to 1954, having been in America since the early 1930s. Otherwise mostly on stage. Also a writer and humorist. Retired in 1972, but in 1983 committed suicide by shooting himself.

1921: *Sodom and Gomorrah.* 1924: *Mein Leopold. Michael.* 1925: *Die gefundene Braut. Grüss mir das blonde Kind am Rhein. O alte Burschenherrlichkeit. Sumpf und Moral.* 1926: *Aus des Rheinlands Schicksalstagen. Das war in Heidelberg in blauer Sommernacht. Junges*

## SLOANE, Everett 1909-1965

Small, hard-hitting American actor with receding gingery hair and weasel-like face, often bespectacled. Made his initial impact in films with Orson Welles, his Mercury Theatre colleague, then rather faded away before *The Big Knife* and *Patterns* deservedly restored him to prominence among in-demand character stars. But in 1965 he committed suicide with sleeping pills.

1941: *Citizen Kane.* 1942: *Journey into Fear.* 1945: *We Accuse (narrator only).* 1948: *The Lady from Shanghai.* 1949: *Prince of Foxes.* 1950: *The Men. The Enforcer* (GB: *Murder Inc.*). *The Prince Who Was a Thief.* 1951: *Sirocco. The Desert Fox* (GB:

Rommel—Desert Fox). Bird of Paradise. The Blue Veil. The Sellout. 1952: Way of a Gaucho. 1955: The Big Knife. 1956: Patterns (GB: Patterns of Power). Child of the Regiment (TV). Lust for Life. Somebody Up There Likes Me. Massacre at Sand Creek (TV). 1958: Marjorie Morningstar. The Gun Runners. 1959: The Sounds of Eden (TV). 1960: Home from the Hill. Alas, Babylon (TV). 1961: By Love Possessed. 1962: Brushfire! 1963: The Man from the Diners' Club. 1964: Ready for the People. The Disorderly Orderly. The Patsy.

### SLOANE, Olive 1896-1963

British actress who should have gone to Hollywood, where frowzy blondes of the type she portrayed so expertly were much more in demand. As it was, she stayed in the British cinema (and theatre) and had to be content with a couple of decent film roles in the early 1950s. Began as a child entertainer, singer and clog dancer, making a few silent films as a leading lady before coming back to sound films in her late thirties.

1921: Greatheart. The Door That Has No Key. 1922: Lonesome Farm. Trapped by the Mormons. 1923: Rogues of the Turf. The Dream of Eugene Aram. 1925: Money Isn't Everything. 1933: The Good Companions. Soldiers of the King (US: The Woman in Command). Lily of Killarney (US: Bride of the Lake). 1934: Sing As We Go. Faces. Brides To Be. Music Hall. 1935: Key to Harmony. Alibi Inn. 1936: In the Soup. The Howard Case. Café Colette (US: Danger in Paris). 1937: Overcoat Sam. Dreaming Lips. Mad About Money/Stardust (US: He Loved an Actress). 1938: Consider Your Verdict. Make-Up. Make It Three. 1939: Inquest. 1941: The Tower of Terror. 1942: Thunder Rock. Those Kids from Town. Let the People Sing. 1945: They Knew Mr Knight. The Voice Within. 1946: Send for Paul Temple. 1947: Bank Holiday Luck. 1948: The Guinea Pig. Counterblast. 1949: Under Capricorn. 1950: Waterfront (US: Waterfront Women). Seven Days to Noon. Once a Sinner. The Franchise Affair. 1952: Tall Headlines. Curtain Up! My Wife's Lodger. 1953: Alf's Baby. Meet Mr

Lucifer. The Weak and the Wicked. 1954: The Golden Link. 1955: A Prize of Gold. 1956: The Man in the Road. The Last Man to Hang? Brothers in Law. 1959: Serious Charge (US: A Touch of Hell). Wrong Number. Your Money or Your Wife. The Price of Silence. 1960: The House in Marsh Road.

### SMITH, Sir C. Aubrey

(Charles A. Smith) 1863-1948

Tall, stately, aristocratic-looking English actor with bristling moustache. Went to Hollywood in 1931, and became the doyen of the English colony there, organizing their cricket in between a hectic acting life. Died (from pneumonia) with his boots on at 85, his last film still to be shown. Known to his friends as 'Round-the-Corner Smith', from the way he bowled at cricket. Knighted in 1944.

1915: Builder of Bridges. 1916: The Witching Hour. 1918: Red Pottage. 1920: The Face at the Window. Castles in Spain. *The Bump. The Shuttle of Life. 1922: Flames of Passion. The Bohemian Girl. 1923: The Temptation of Carlton Earlye. 1924: The Unwanted. The Rejected Woman. 1930: Birds of Prey (US: The Perfect Alibi). Such Is the Law. 1931: Contraband Love. Bachelor Father. Trader Horn. Daybreak. Never the Twain Shall Meet. Just a Gigolo (GB: The Dancing Partner). Man in Possession. Guilty Hands. Son of India. Phantom of Paris. Surrender. 1932: But the Flesh is Weak. Polly of the Circus. Trouble in Paradise. They Just Had to Get Married. Tarzan the Ape Man. Love Me Tonight. No More Orchids. 1933: The Barbarian (GB: A Night in Cairo). Luxury Liner. The Monkey's Paw. Bombshell (GB: Blonde Bombshell). Secrets. Adorable. Morning Glory. Queen Christina. 1934: Curtain at Eight. The House of Rothschild. Cleopatra. One More River (GB: Over the River). The Firebird. Gambling Lady. Bulldog Drummond Strikes Back. Madame Du Barry. Caravan. We Live Again. Riptide. The Scarlet Empress. 1935: The Florentine Dagger. The Right to Live (GB: The Sacred Flame). Clive of India. Jalna. The Tunnel (US: Transatlantic Tunnel). Lives of a Bengal Lancer. The Gilded Lily. China Seas. The Crusades. 1936:

*The Story of Papworth. The Garden of Allah. Little Lord Fauntleroy. Romeo and Juliet. Lloyds of London. 1937: Wee Willie Winkie. The Hurricane. The Prisoner of Zenda. Thoroughbreds Don't Cry. 1938: Sixty Glorious Years (US: Queen of Destiny). Four Men and a Prayer. Kidnapped. 1939: The Four Feathers. The Sun Never Sets. East Side of Heaven. The Under-Pup. Another Thin Man. Eternally Yours. Five Came Back. Balalaika. 1940: A Bill of Divorcement. Rebecca. Beyond Tomorrow. City of Chance. Waterloo Bridge. A Little Bit of Heaven. 1941: Maisie Was a Lady. Dr Jekyll and Mr Hyde. Free and Easy. 1943: Two Tickets to London. Forever and a Day. Flesh and Fantasy. Madame Curie. 1944: They Shall Have Faith (GB: The Right to Live). Secrets of Scotland Yard. The White Cliffs of Dover. The Adventures of Mark Twain. Sensations of 1945. 1945: And Then There Were None (GB: Ten Little Niggers). Scotland Yard Investigator. 1946: Cluny Brown. Rendezvous With Annie. 1947: Unconquered. High Conquest. An Ideal Husband. 1949: Little Women.

### SMITH, Charlie Martin 1954-

Baby-faced, earnest-looking, light-haired American actor blinking his way into film roles while still at college. A must for guys who got pushed around because of his youthful looks and small stature, he shot to prominence as one of the boys in American Graffiti; but rewarding follow-up roles have seemed hard to find.

1972: The Rookies (TV). The Culpepper Cattle Co. Fuzz. 1973: Pat Garrett and Billy the Kid. American Graffiti. 1974: The Spikes Gang. 1975: Rafferty and the Gold Dust Twins. 1976: No Deposit, No Return. 1977: The Hazing. 1978: The Buddy Holly Story. 1979: Cotton Candy (TV). More American Graffiti/The Party's Over/Purple Haze. 1980: Herbie Goes Bananas. 1983: Never Cry Wolf. 1984: Starman.

### SMITH, Cyril (C. Bruce-Smith)

1892-1963

Shortish, dark-haired, dark-eyed, slightly-built, crestfallen-looking British actor who

*Vampire Over London). The Lost Hours (US: The Big Frame). Women of Twilight (US: Twilight Women). Hindle Wakes (US: Holiday Week). 1953: Innocents in Paris. Wheel of Fate. 1954: Burnt Evidence. The Angel Who Pawned Her Harp. \*The Strange Case of Blondie. Svengali. The Brain Machine. 1955: John and Julie. Value for Money. \*The Silent Witness. 1956: Sailor Beware! (US: Panic in the Parlor). 1959: The Rough and the Smooth (US: Portrait of a Sinner). 1960: Light Up the Sky. 1961: Watch It Sailor! Over the Odds. On the Fiddle (US: Operation Snafu). 1962: She Knows Y'Know.*

played dozens of working-class types and penny-ante crooks without finding the limelight until towards the end of his life, when he repeated his stage success as Pa Hornett in *Sailor Beware!* — the henpecked husband to end them all. Born in Scotland. Worked in America (mainly on stage) from 1921 to 1930.

*1908: The Great Fire of London. 1914: Old St Paul's. 1919: Pallard the Punter. 1920: Walls of Prejudice. Sweep. On the Reserve. Cupid's Cardinal. Run! Run! A Broken Contract. Cousin Ebenezer. Souvenirs. A Little Bet. A Pair of Gloves. Home Influence. The Lightning Liver Cure. The Fordington Twins. 1921: The Way of a Man. Class and No Class. 1923: Fires of Fate. 1924: The Desert Sheik. 1930: His First Car. 1932: The Mayor's Nest. The Maid of the Mountains. The Innocents of Chicago (US: Why Saps Leave Home). 1933: The Good Companions. Friday the Thirteenth. Channel Crossing. The Roof. The Black Abbot. 1934: Waltzes from Vienna (US: Strauss's Great Waltz). It's a Cop! The Iron Duke. Wild Boy. Evergreen. 1935: Hello Sweetheart. Key to Harmony. Mr What's His Name. Lend Me Your Wife. Brown On Resolution (later For Ever England. US: Born for Glory). Bulldog Jack (US: Alias Bulldog Drummond). 1936: Pot Luck. OHMS (US: You're in the Army Now). 1937: Storm in a Teacup. The Frog. 1938: No Parking. The Challenge. The Return of the Frog. St Martin's Lane (US: Sidewalks of London). 1939: Sword of Honour. Traitor Spy (US: The Torso Murder Mystery). 1940: Law and Disorder. The Flying Squad. 1941: This England. 1943: When We Are Married. 1944: One Exciting Night (US: You Can't Do Without Love). Meet Sexton Blake. 1945: The Echo Murders. Don Chicago. Murder in Reverse. 1946: School for Secrets (US: Secret Flight). Appointment With Crime. 1948: Escape. No Room at the Inn. It's Hard to be Good. The History of Mr Polly. 1949: The Rocking Horse Winner. Conspirator. 1950: The Body Said No! Old Mother Riley Headmistress. The Dark Man. 1951: Green Grow the Rushes. Mystery Junction. The Third Visitor. Night Was Our Friend. Judgment Deferred. 1952: Stolen Face. Mother Riley Meets the Vampire (US:*

**SOFAER, Abraham** 1896- 1988
Dark-haired, long-faced Burmese actor of austere aspect, often in sinister roles. A teacher in Rangoon, then London, he turned to acting in his mid-twenties, his sombre tones and commanding presence soon getting him important, often foreign-slanted roles. Also a respected Shakespearian and a popular voice on radio. British film roles were few and far between and since 1955 he has lived in Hollywood. His last film part was as a Red Indian!

*1931: Dreyfus (US: The Dreyfus Case). 1936: Rembrandt. Things to Come. 1940: Crook's Tour. 1941: Freedom Radio (US: A Voice in the Night). 1946: A Matter of Life and Death (US: Stairway to Heaven). Dual Alibi. 1947: The Ghosts of Berkeley Square. 1948: Calling Paul Temple. 1949. The Green Promise (GB: Raging Waters). Christopher Columbus. 1950: Cairo Road. Pandora and the Flying Dutchman. 1951: Quo Vadis? Judgment Deferred. 1953: His Majesty O'Keefe. 1954: Elephant Walk. The Naked Jungle. Out of the Clouds. 1956: Bhowani Junction. The First Texan. 1957: Omar Khayyam. The Story of Mankind. 1958: The Sad Sack. 1961: King of Kings. 1963: Taras Bulba. Twice-Told Tales. Captain Sindbad. 1965: The Greatest Story Ever Told. 1967: Journey to the Center of Time. 1968: Head. 1969: Justine. Che! 1970: Chisum.*

**SOKOLOFF, Vladimir** (V. Sokolov) 1889-1962
Impassive, diminutive, brown-haired Russian actor with sneaky eyes and (often)

goatee beard. He usually played the evil brains behind the muscle, but occasionally got a more sympathetic role. Sokoloff portrayed almost as many nationalities as J. Carrol Naish (*qv*), following his arrival in Hollywood late in 1936 after a career in German and French films. Continued acting until his death from a stroke.

*1926: Die Abenteuer eines Zehnmarkscheines nehmer antwortet nicht. Gehetzte Menschen/ Liebe der Jeanne Ney (GB and US: The Love of Jeanne Ney). Der Sohn der Hoger (US: Out of the Mist). 1928: Die weisse Sonate. 1929: Das Schiff der verlorenen Menschen. Sensation im Wintergarten. 1930: Liebling der Götter/ Der grosse Tenor (US: Darling of the Gods). Moral im Mitternacht. Abschied. Westfront 1914. Die heilige Flamme. Das Flotenkonzert. L'opéra de quat-sous. 1931: Niemandsland (US: Hell on Earth). Kismet. Die Dreigroschenoper (GB: The Threepenny Opera. US: The Beggar's Opera). 1932: Die Herrin von Atlantis (and French-language version). Teilnehmer nicht antwortet. Gehetzte Menschen/ Steckbrief Z. Strafsache von Geldern. 1933: Dans les rues (US: Song of the Street). Du haut en bas. Don Quichotte. 1934: Le lac aux dames. Le secret de Waronzeff. Napoléon Bonaparte (revised version of 1926 film with sound added). 1935: Mayerling. 1936: Mister Flow (US: Compliments of Mr Flow). Sous les jeux d'accident. Les bas-fonds (GB and US: The Lower Depths). La vie est à nous. 1937: The Life of Emile Zola. Conquest (GB: Marie Walewska). West of Shanghai. Tovarich. Expensive Husbands. Beg, Borrow or Steal. The Prisoner of Zenda. 1938: Alcatraz Island. Arsène Lupin Returns. Spawn of the North. Blockade. Ride a Crooked Mile. The Amazing Dr Clitterhouse. 1939: Juarez. The Real Glory. 1940: Comrade X. 1941: Love Crazy. 1942: Crossroads. Road to Morocco. 1943: Mission to Moscow. Song of Russia. Mr Lucky. For Whom the Bell Tolls. 1944: Passage to Marseille (GB: Passage to Marseilles). Till We Meet Again. The Conspirators. 1945: The Blonde from Brooklyn. Paris Underground (GB: Madame Pimpernel). Back to Bataan. A Royal Scandal (GB: Czarina). Scarlet Street. 1946: Two Smart People. Cloak and Dagger. Thieves' Holiday (later and GB: A Scandal in Paris). 1948: To the Ends of the Earth. 1950:*

The Baron of Arizona. 1952: Macao. 1956: While the City Sleeps. Istanbul. 1957: Sabu and the Magic Ring. I Was a Teenage Werewolf. The Monster from Green Hell. 1958: Twilight for the Gods. 1960: Man on a String (GB: Confessions of a Counterspy). Beyond the Time Barrier. The Magnificent Seven. Cimarron. 1961: Mr Sardonicus (GB: Sardonicus). The Judas Goat (TV. GB: cinemas). Escape from Zahrain. 1962: Taras Bulba.

### SOLON, Ewen 1923–1985

New Zealand actor with fine-boned face, slightly menacing smile, gravel tones and dark complexion, in roles of gradually increasing importance in the British cinema until swallowed up for several years by his part as Lucas in TV's *Maigret* series, which began in 1961. He was seen little in film parts since, with less hair and in more fragile roles.

*1948: London Belongs to Me (US: Dulcimer Street). 1949: Vengeance Is Mine. 1950: The Naked Heart (Maria Chapdelaine/The Naked Earth). The Rossiter Case. 1951: Valley of Eagles. Assassin for Hire. Mystery Junction. 1952: The Story of Robin Hood and His Merrie Men. Crow Hollow. 1953: The Sword and the Rose. Rob Roy the Highland Rogue. 1954: \*Night Plane to Amsterdam. The End of the Road. The Dam Busters. 1955: \*Murder Anonymous. The Dark Avenger (US: The Warriors). Jumping for Joy. Lost (US: Tears for Simon). 1956: Behind the Headlines. 1984. 1957: Yangtse Incident (US: Battle Hell). The Story of Esther Costello (US: Golden Virgin). Murder Reported. There's Always a Thursday. Account Rendered. Black Ice. Mark of the Hawk/Accused. 1958: The Silent Enemy. 1959: The Hound of the Baskervilles. The White Trap. The Stranglers of Bombay. Jack the Ripper. 1960: Tarzan the Magnificent. The Sundowners. 1961: The Terror of the Tongs. Curse of the Werewolf. 1962: Mystery Submarine (US: Decoy). 1966: \*Infamous Conduct. 1976: The Message (US: Mohammed Messenger of God). 1979: The Spaceman and King Arthur (US: Unidentified Flying Oddball). 1982: Nutcracker. 1983: The Wicked Lady.*

### SONDERGAARD, Gale

(Edith Sondergaard) 1899– 1985

Tall, dark, stern-looking American actress who, after winning an Academy Award in her first feature, *Anthony Adverse* (she was nominated again for *Anna and the King of Siam*), went on to corner the market, with Dame Judith Anderson (*qv*), in sinister housekeepers, domineering mothers and femmes very fatale. Career wrecked by the McCarthy witch-hunts (her second husband, writer-director Herbert Biberman, was one of the 'Hollywood 10').

*1936: Anthony Adverse. 1937: The Life of Emile Zola. Maid of Salem. Seventh Heaven. 1938: Lord Jeff (GB: The Boy from Barnardo's). Dramatic School. 1939: Juarez. Never Say Die. The Cat and the Canary. \*Sons of Liberty. 1940: The Llano Kid. The Mark of Zorro. The Blue Bird. The Letter. 1941: The Black Cat. Paris Calling. 1942: Enemy Agents Meet Ellery Queen (GB: The Lido Mystery). My Favorite Blonde. A Night To Remember. 1943: Isle of Forgotten Sins. Appointment in Berlin. The Strange Death of Adolf Hitler. Sherlock Holmes and Spider Woman (GB: Spider Woman). 1944: Follow the Boys. Christmas Holiday. The Invisible Man's Revenge. Enter Arsène Lupin. The Climax. Gypsy Wildcat. 1946: Anna and the King of Siam. Spider Woman Strikes Back. The Time of Their Lives. A Night in Paradise. 1947: Road to Rio. Pirates of Monterey. 1949: East Side, West Side. 1969: Slaves. 1970: Comeback (later copyrighted 1973 as Savage Intruder). 1973: The Cat Creature. 1976: The Return of a Man Called Horse. Pleasantville. 1977: Hollywood on Trial. 1980: Echoes.*

### SPARKS, Ned (Edward Sparkman) 1883–1957

Thin, dark-haired, fast-talking, darting-eyed Canadian actor who once sold patent medicines in a carnival and, when into Hollywood sound films, harangued his audiences with the same unique style that had once held customers in thrall. With his incisive nasal tones, he became one of filmdom's most imitated actors and, in between a legion of reporters, press agents and con-men, all of whom seemed to live life on a nervous edge, he made a marvellous caterpillar in the 1933 *Alice in Wonderland*. Died from a blocked intestine.

*1919: A Virtuous Vamp. 1922: A Wide-Open Town. The Bond Boy. 1925: Bright Lights. His Supreme Moment. Faint Perfume. The Boomerang. Seven Keys to Baldpate. The Only Thing. Soul Mates. 1926: Mike. Love's Blindness. The Hidden Way. Oh, What a Night! Money Talks. When the Wife's Away. The Auction Block (GB: Lock, Stock and Barrel). 1927: Alias the Deacon. The Small Bachelor. The Secret Studio. Alias the Lone Wolf. 1928: The Big Noise (GB: Nine Days' Wonder). The Magnificent Flirt. On to Reno. 1929: The Canary Murder Case. Strange Cargo. Nothing But the Truth. Street Girl. 1930: The Fall Guy (GB: Trust Your Wife). Love Comes Along. Double Crossroads. The Devil's Holiday. Conspiracy. Leathernecking (GB: Present Arms). 1931: The Iron Man. Corsair. The Secret Call. Kept Husbands. 1932: The Miracle Man. Big City Blues. Blessed Event. The Crusader. 1933: 42nd Street. Lady for a Day. Too Much Harmony. Gold Diggers of 1933. Alice in Wonderland. The Kennel Murder Case. Going Hollywood. Secrets. 1934: Servants' Entrance. Marie Galante. Hi, Nellie! Private Scandal. Sing and Like It. Down to Their Last Yacht (GB: Hawaiian Nights). Imitation of Life. 1935: George White's Scandals of 1935. Sweet Adeline. Sweet Music. 1936: Collegiate (GB: The Charm School). The Bride Walks Out. One in a Million. Two's Company. 1937: Wake Up and Live. This Way, Please. 1938: Hawaii Calls. 1939: The Star Maker. 1941: For Beauty's Sake. 1943: Stage Door Canteen. 1947: Magic Town.*

### SPINETTI, Victor 1932–

Dark-haired, Welsh-born actor (of Italian father) with distinctive very dark, very short, receding hair and pained expression. Usually plays head waiters, TV directors, impresarios or avant-garde friends, much given to arm-waving, sarcasm and/or panic. He came to the fore in London revue but film roles, on the whole, provided him with too little subtlety, and he has preferred television and the theatre.

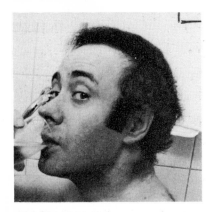

1961: The Gentle Terror. 1963: Becket. 1964: *I Think They Call Him John (narrator only). The Wild Affair. A Hard Day's Night. 1965: Help! 1966: The Taming of the Shrew. 1967: The Biggest Bundle of Them All. 1968: Can Hieronymous Merkin Ever Forget Mercy Humppe and Find True Happiness? 1969: A Promise of Bed. Start the Revolution Without Me. 1971: Unman, Wittering and Zigo. Under Milk Wood. 1972: The 500-Pound Jerk (TV). 1973: Digby the Biggest Dog in the World. 1974: The Little Prince. Return of the Pink Panther. The Great McGonagall. 1975: Dick Deadeye (voice only). 1976: Emily. Voyage of the Damned. 1977: The Rise and Rise of Casanova. Hardcore (US: Fiona).

**SQUIRE, Ronald** (R. Squirl) 1886-1958
Bald, burly, affable British actor with beaming smile and splendid moustache. He found himself billed above the title in middle age, following many years on stage as actor, producer and director, having started his long career with seaside concert parties. Continued to be popular in film roles up to his death.

1916: Whoso Is Without Sin. 1934: The Unfinished Symphony. Wild Boy. Forbidden Territory. 1935: Come Out of the Pantry. 1936: Love in Exile. Dusty Ermine (US: Hideout in the Alps). 1937: Action for Slander. 1941: Freedom Radio (US: A Voice in the Night). Major Barbara. 1943: The Flemish Farm. 1944: Don't Take It to Heart.

1945: Journey Together. 1946: While the Sun Shines. 1948: The First Gentleman (US: Affairs of a Rogue). Woman Hater. 1949: The Rocking Horse Winner. 1951: No Highway (GB: No Highway in the Sky). Encore. 1952: It Started in Paradise. My Cousin Rachel. 1953: Laxdale Hall (US: Scotch on the Rocks). Always a Bride. The Million Pound Note (US: Man With a Million). 1955: Raising a Riot. Josephine and Men. Footsteps in the Fog. 1956: Now and Forever. The Silken Affair. Around the World in 80 Days. 1957: Seawife. Island in the Sun. 1958: The Sheriff of Fractured Jaw. Law and Disorder. The Inn of the Sixth Happiness. 1959: Count Your Blessings.

**STANDER, Lionel** 1908- *1994*
Fuzzy-haired, gravel-voiced New Yorker much in demand for comic gangsters and other side-of-the-mouth types before the McCarthy blacklist halted his career in 1948. After a spell as a Wall Street broker, he played many character roles in Britain and Italy before going back to Hollywood and finding a secure slot with the five-season-long TV series Hart to Hart. Six times married, he has six daughters.

1926: Men of Steel. 1935: *The Old Grey Mayor. The Gay Deception. The Scoundrel. Hooray for Love. If You Could Only Cook. Page Miss Glory. We're in the Money. I Live My Life. 1936: Meet Nero Wolfe. The Music Goes Round. The Milky Way. They Met in a Taxi. Mr Deeds Goes to Town. More than a Secretary. Soak the Rich. 1937: The Last Gangster. The League of Frightened Men. A Star Is Born. 1938: The Crowd Roars. No Time To Marry. Professor Beware! 1939: Ice Follies of 1939. What a Life. 1941: The Bride Wore Crutches. 1943: Tahiti Honey. Guadalcanal Diary. Hangmen Also Die. 1945: A Boy, a Girl and a Dog (GB: Lucky). The Big Show-Off. 1946: Specter of the Rose. The Kid from Brooklyn. Gentleman Joe Palooka. In Old Sacramento. The Sin of Harold Diddlebock (later and GB: Mad Wednesday). 1947: Call Northside 777. 1948: Unfaithfully Yours. Trouble Makers. 1951: St Benny the Dip (GB: Escape If You Can). 1961: Blast of Silence (narrator only). 1963: The Moving Finger. 1965: The Loved One. Promise Her

Anything. 1966: Cul-de-Sac. 1967: Al di la della legge/Beyond the Law. 1968: The Gates to Paradise. A Dandy in Aspic. Sette volte sette. Once Upon a Time in the West. H2S. Die letzte Rechnung zählst du selbst. 1969: Casanova. La collina degli stivali (US: Boot Hill). Zenabel. 1970: Room 17. Mir hat es immer Spass gemacht. How Did a Nice Girl Like You Get into This?... 1971: Treasure Island. The Gang That Couldn't Shoot Straight. Le président aime les femmes. Per grazia ricevuta (US: The Cross-Eyed Saint). 1972: La dove volano le pallotole. Milano calibro 9 (GB: The Contract). Pulp. Don Camillo e i Giovanni d'Oggi. Siamo tutti in libertà provvisoria. Tutti fratelli nel West ... per parte di padre. 1973: Crescete e moltiplicatevi. Mordi e fuggi (US: Bite and Run). The Black Hand. Paolo il caldo/The Sensual Man/Sensuous Sicilian. Te Deum (GB: The Con Men). Piazzi pulita (GB: Pete, Pearl and the Pole). Partirono preti, tornarono curati. 1975: The Black Bird. San Pasquale Baillone, protettore delle donne (GB: Sex for Sale). Giubbe rosse. Ah si? ... e io lo dico a Zorro. 1976: The Cassandra Crossing. 1977: New York, New York. 1978: Matilda. Cyclone. The Big Rip-Off (US: The Squeeze). 1979: 1941. Hart to Hart (TV).

**STANTON, Harry Dean** 1926-
Considered by many to be the best Hollywood character actor of recent times, Stanton found that his dark, lean and hungry-looking features confined him for many years to psychos, vicious villains and (often mean-tempered) 'countrified' characters. Nobody's idea of a native New Yorker or Californian, Stanton was born in Kentucky and took up acting after wartime service with the US Navy. For years he toured with a children's theatre company before beginning to pick up film and television work in the late 1950s. In recent times, his shadowed unsmiling face has belatedly appeared with success in demanding lead roles, and he has even tried comedy. Billed as Dean Stanton until 1968.

1956: The Wrong Man. 1957: Revolt at Fort Laramie. The Tomahawk Trail. 1958: The Proud Rebel. 1959: Pork Chop Hill. A Dog's Best Friend. 1960: The Adventures of Huckleberry Finn. 1961: Hero's Island. 1962: How the West Was Won. 1963: The Man from the Diners' Club. 1966: The Hostage. The Dangerous Days of Kiowa Jones (TV. GB: cinemas). 1967: A Time for Killing (GB: The Long Ride Home). Cool Hand Luke. 1968: Day of the Evil Gun. The Mini-Skirt Mob. 1970: Rebel Rousers. The Intruders (TV). Kelly's Heroes. 1971: Two-Lane Blacktop. 1972: Count Your Bullets/Face to the Wind. (GB: Naked Revenge). Cisco Pike. Pat Garrett and Billy the Kid. Apache Massacre. 1973: Dillinger. Where the Lilies Bloom. 1974: Born to Kill (later and GB: Cockfighter). Another Day at the Races (GB: Win, Place or Steal). Rancho de Luxe. The Godfather Part II. Zandy's Bride. 1975: Farewell, My Lovely. Rafferty and the Gold Dust Twins. 92 in the Shade. 1976: The Missouri Breaks. 1977: Straight Time. Renaldo and Clara. 1978: Flatbed Annie and Sweetiepie: Lady Truckers (TV. GB: Girls of the Road). 1979: Alien. The Rose. Death Watch. Wise Blood. 1980: Private Benjamin. The Black Marble. 1981: Escape from New York. 1982: Tough Enough/Tough Dreams. One from the Heart. Young Doctors in Love. 1983: I Want to Live! (TV). Christine. 1984: Uforia 84 (filmed 1980). Paris, Texas. Red Dawn. Repo Man. 1985: The Bear. Father Christmas. The Care Bears Movie (voice only). Fool for Love. 1986: Pretty in Pink.

**STAPLETON, Maureen** 1925-
Dumpy but dynamic American actress, equally successful at being lonely or companionable, snobbish or down-to-earth, aggressive or vulnerable. Despite motherly looks, in fact, she played a wide variety of roles from her 1946 Broadway debut onwards, making occasional but memorable forays into films. After being three times nominated for the best supporting actress Oscar (in Lonelyhearts, Airport, and Interiors), she finally won it for Reds.

1959: For Whom the Bell Tolls (TV). Lonelyhearts. 1960: The Fugitive Kind. 1961: A View from the Bridge. 1963: Bye Bye Birdie. 1967: Among the Paths to Eden (TV). 1969: Airport. Trilogy. 1970: Cold Turkey. Plaza Suite. 1974: Tell Me Where It Hurts (TV). 1975: Queen of the Stardust Ballroom (TV). 1976: Cat on a Hot Tin Roof

**STARK, Graham** 1922-
Dapper, dark-haired British comedian, scriptwriter, sometime director and general contributor of comic cameos, with Mr Punch-like facial features which made him look as if he was always about to laugh. A minor member of The Goons who gradually assumed greater familiarity and importance, he built up his early experience with a mixture of straight and comic film roles and funny voices in radio comedy. Attempts to direct comedy were less successful and he returned to the front of the camera.

1952: Emergency Call (US: Hundred Hour Hunt). Down Among the Z Men. 1953: *The Super Secret Service. Forces' Sweetheart. Flannelfoot. 1954: Johnny on the Spot. 1955: *Song of Norway. 1956: They Never Learn. 1959: Inn for Trouble. 1960: *The Running, Jumping and Standing Still Film. The Millionairess. Sink the Bismarck! 1961: Dentist on the Job (US: Get On With It!). Watch It Sailor! She'll Have to Go (US: Maid for Murder). A Weekend With Lulu. Double Bunk. Only Two Can Play. On the Fiddle (US: Operation Snafu). Village of Daughters. A Pair of Briefs. 1962: Operation Snatch. The Wrong Arm of the Law. Lancelot and Guinevere. 1963: The Mouse on the Moon. Ladies Who Do. Strictly for the Birds. The Pink Panther. Becket. 1964: Guns at Batasi. A Shot in the Dark. Go Kart Go! 1965: Runaway Railway. San Ferry Ann. Those Magnificent Men in Their Flying Machines. 1966: Alfie. Finders Keepers. The Wrong Box. 1967: Casino Royale. The Plank. Jules Verne's Rocket to the Moon (US: Those Fantastic Flying Fools). 1968: Salt and Pepper. Ghost of a Chance. 1969: Start the Revolution Without Me. The Magic Christian. 1970: *Simon Simon. Scramble. Doctor in Trouble. Rhubarb. 1972: Hide and Seek. 1973: Secrets of a Door-to-Door Salesman. 1974: Where's Johnny? Return of the Pink Panther. 1975: I'm Not Feeling Myself Tonight. 1976:

(TV). 1977: The Gathering (TV). 1978: Interiors. 1979: Lost and Found. The Runner Stumbles. 1981: The Fan. Reds. On the Right Track. 1984: Johnny Dangerously. 1985: Cocoon. Private Lessons (TV). The Money Pit.

Gulliver's Travels (voice only). The Pink Panther Strikes Again. 1977: The Prince and the Pauper (US: Crossed Swords). Hardcore (US: Fiona). What's Up Nurse? Let's Get Laid. 1978: Revenge of the Pink Panther. 1979: There Goes the Bride. The Prisoner of Zenda. 1980: Hawk the Slayer. The Sea Wolves. 1982. Trail of the Pink Panther. Victor/Victoria. 1983: Superman III. Curse of the Pink Panther. Bloodbath at the House of Death.

**As director:**
1970: *Simon Simon. 1971: The Magnificent Seven Deadly Sins.

**STEELE, Bob** (Robert Bradbury Jr) 1906- *1988*
Dark-haired American cowboy star of slight stature but whirlwind acting style. His smile turned so readily to a distinctive scowl that he was soon seen in the occasional double-shaded role, after starting in films directed by his father, Robert North Bradbury, a western specialist, and developing into a two-fisted star of 'B' westerns and minor action films. As the 1930s ebbed, he won some interesting character roles, such as Curly in Of Mice and Men and Canino in The Big Sleep, and went over to character acting altogether in the mid-1940s. In some ways, his career pattern was similar to that of Tim Holt, another small-scale cowboy hero, although Steele's roles grew very minor as his career drew towards its close.

1920: The Adventures of Bob and Bill (series). 1926: The Border Sheriff. The Fighting Doctor. Davy Crockett at the Fall of the Alamo. 1927: Sitting Bull at the Spirit Lake Massacre. The Mojave Kid. 1928: Man in the Rough. Spirit of Youth. Crooks Can't Win. Breed of the Sunsets. Driftin' Sands. Riding Renegade. Lightning Speed. Captain Careless. Headin' for Danger. Trail of Courage. Come and Get It! 1929: The Amazing Vagabond. Laughing at Death. The Invaders. The Cowboy and the Outlaw. 1930: Land of Missing Men. Breezy Hill. Oklahoma Cyclone. Near the Rainbow's End. Hunted Men. Headin' North. Western Honor. Texas Cowboy. The Man from Nowhere. The Oklahoma Sheriff. 1931: The

Ridin' Fool. Sunrise Trail. Nevada Buckaroo. Law of the West. 1932: South of Santa Fé. Near the Trail's End. Riders of the Desert. The Man from Hell's Edges. Son of Oklahoma. Texas Buddies. Hidden Valley. The Fighting Champ. 1933: Mystery Squadron (serial). Young Blood. Breed of the Border. California Trail. Trailin' North. The Gallant Fool. Rangers' Code. Galloping Romeo. 1934: Demon for Trouble. Brand of Fate. 1935: Kid Courageous. No Man's Range. Big Calibre. Rider of the Law. The Ridin' Fool†. Alias John Law. Powdersmoke Range. 1936: Sundown Saunders. The Kid Ranger. Cavalry. Trail of Terror. Brand of Outlaws. Arizona Gunfighter. Last of the Warrens. 1937: Gun Lords of Stirrup Basin. Border Phantom. Doomed at Sundown. The Red Rope. Ridin' the Lone Trail. The Trusted Outlaw. The Gun Ranger. The Colorado Kid. Lightnin' Crandall. 1938: Desert Patrol. Thunder in the Desert. Paroled to Die. 1939: Smoky Trail. El Diablo Rides. Of Mice and Men. 1940: The Carson City Kid. Lone Star Raiders. City for Conquest. 1941: The Great Train Robbery. Billy the Kid's Fighting Pals. Prairie Schooners (GB: Through the Storm). Saddlemates. Pals of the Pecos. Gangs of Sonora. Outlaws of Cherokee Trail. Gauchos of Eldorado. West of Cimarron. 1942: Raiders of the Range. Code of the Outlaws. Westward Ho! Prairie Pioneers. The Phantom Plainsmen. Valley of Haunted Men. 1943: Shadows on the Sage. Riders of the Rio Grande. Blocked Trail. Revenge of the Zombies (GB: The Corpse Vanished). Santa Fé Scouts. 1944: Sonora Stagecoach. Westward Bound. The Utah Kid. Marked Trails. The Outlaw Trail. Arizona Whirlwind. Trigger Law. 1945: The Navajo Kid. Northwest Trail. 1946: Sheriff of Redwood Valley. Thunder Town. Six Gun Man. Rio Grande Raiders. The Big Sleep. Ambush Trail. 1947: Killer McCoy. Exposed. Six Guns for Hire. Bandits of Dark Canyon. Cheyenne. Twilight on the Rio Grande. 1949: South of St Louis. 1950: The Savage Horde. The Enforcer (GB: Murder Inc). 1951: Silver Canyon. Cattle Drive. Fort Worth. 1952: Rose of Cimarron. Bugles in the Afternoon. The Lion and the Horse. 1953: Island in the Sky. Savage Frontier. San Antone. Column South. 1954: The Outcast (GB: The Fortune Hunter). Drums Across the River. 1955: The Spoilers. The Fighting Chance. 1956: The Steel Jungle. Pardners. Gun for a Coward. 1957: Duel at Apache Wells. The Parson and the Outlaw. Band of Angels. Decision at Sundown. 1958: Once Upon a Horse. Giant from the Unknown. 1959: Atomic Submarine. Rio Bravo. Pork Chop Hill. 1960: Hell Bent for Leather. 1961: The Comancheros. Six Black Horses. 1962: The Wild Westerners. 1963: McLintock! 1964: Bullet for a Badman. Taggart. 1965: Outlaw Trail. Town Tamer. Requiem for a Gunfighter. The Bounty Killer. Shenandoah. 1967: Hang 'Em High. 1969: The Great Bank Robbery. 1971: Something Big. 1972: Nightmare Honeymoon.

†Remake of 1931 film.

**STEPANEK, Karel** 1899-1980
Crafty-looking, thin-mouthed Czech actor. In German films through the thirties, he fled to England with the outbreak of World War, and quickly became that country's answer to Eduardo Ciannelli. He was not too keen on playing Nazis, but was inevitably seen as villainous foreigners of one kind or another. Later made a few films in Hollywood.

1928: †Ein Lieb, ein Dieb, ein Warenhaus. 1931: †Berlin—Alexanderplatz. 1932: †Fünf von der Jazzband. †Hallo Hallo! Hier Spricht Berlin. †Spione im Savoy-Hotel. 1933: †Ein Lied Für Dich. †Walzerkrieg. 1934: †Hermine und die sieben Aufrechten. 1935: †Aussenseiter. †Die Werft zum grauen Hecht. 1936: †Die Unbekannte. †Stärker als Paragraphen. 1937: †Die Fledermaus. †Signal in der Nacht. 1938: †Es leuchten die Sterne. †Narren im Schnee. †War es dem in dreiter Stock? 1939: †Jede Frau hat ein süsses Geheimnis. †Der Florentiner Hut/The Italian Straw Hat. †Die kluge Schwiegermutter. †Drei Väter um Anna. †Hotel Sacher. †Alles Schwindel. 1942: Our Film. Secret Mission. Tomorrow We Live (US: At Dawn We Die). 1943: Escape to Danger. They Met in the Dark. 1946: The Captive Heart. 1948: Counterblast. 1949: Conspirator. Give Us This Day (US: Salt to the Devil). The Golden Arrow. 1950: State Secret (US: The Great Manhunt). Cairo Road. 1951: The Third Visitor. 1952: Walk East on Beacon! (GB: Crime of the Century). Affair in Trinidad. 1953: City Beneath the Sea. Never Let Me Go. Rough Shoot (US: Shoot First). 1954: A Tale of Three Women. Dangerous Cargo. 1955: Secret Venture. A Prize of Gold. Man of the Moment. Cockleshell Heroes. 1956: The Man in the Road. Anastasia. 1957: West of Suez (US: Fighting Wildcats). The Traitors (US: The Accused). 1959: Our Man in Havana. Sink the Bismarck! 1960: Schachnovelle (GB: Three Moves to Freedom. US: The Royal Game). I Aim at the Stars. 1961: *Johann Sebastian Bach. 1962: Neunzig Minuten nach Mitternacht. 1963: The Devil Doll. 1965: Licensed to Kill (US: The Second Best Secret Agent in the Whole Wide World). Sperrbezirk. The Heroes of Telemark. 1966: The Frozen Dead. Der Mörderclub von

Brooklyn. 1968: The File of the Golden Goose. 1969: Before Winter Comes. The Games.

†As Karl Stepanek.

**STEPHENSON, Henry**
(H. S. Garroway) 1871-1956
Tall, elegant, moustachioed, jut-jawed British actor with firm gaze, a key member of Hollywood's prominent British community of the 1930s. Long in America, after considerable experience on the London and New York stages, he was often cast in lordly roles, as historical figures or the hero's aristocratic friend. Born in Grenada.

1917: The Spreading Dawn. 1921: The Black Panther's Cub. 1925: Men and Women. Wild, Wild Susan. 1932: Red-Headed Woman. Cynara. The Animal Kingdom (GB: The Woman in His House). Guilty As Hell (GB: Guilty as Charged). A Bill of Divorcement. 1933: Little Women. Tomorrow at Seven. Queen Christina. Blind Adventure. Double Harness. My Lips Betray. If I Were Free. 1934: One More River (GB: Over the River). Man of Two Worlds. Outcast Lady (GB: A Woman of the World). Stingaree. The Richest Girl in the World. Thirty Day Princess. What Every Woman Knows. The Mystery of Mr X. She Loves Me Not. All Men Are Enemies. 1935: The Flame Within. Vanessa: Her Love Story. O'Shaughnessy's Boy. Mutiny on the Bounty. The Night Is Young. Rendezvous. Reckless. The Perfect Gentleman. Captain Blood. 1936: Little Lord Fauntleroy. Half Angel. Walking on Air. Hearts Divided. Beloved Enemy. Give Me Your Heart. The Charge of the Light Brigade. 1937: The Prince and the Pauper. When You're in Love. The Emperor's Candlesticks. Conquest (GB: Marie Walewska). Wise Girl. 1938: Marie Antoinette. The Young in Heart. Dramatic School. Suez. The Baroness and the Butler. 1939: The Private Lives of Elizabeth and Essex. Tarzan Finds a Son! The Adventures of Sherlock Holmes. 1940: Spring Parade. It's a Date. Little Old New York. Down Argentine Way. 1941: The Lady from Louisiana. The Man Who Lost Himself. 1942: Rings On Her Fingers. This Above All. Half Way to Shanghai. 1943: The Man Trap. Mr Lucky. 1944: Secrets of Scotland Yard. The Hour Before the Dawn. The Reckless Age. Two Girls and a Sailor. 1945: Tarzan and the Amazons. 1946: The Green Years. Her Sister's Secret. The Return of Monte Cristo (GB: Monte Cristo's Revenge). Heartbeat. Night and Day. The Locket. Of Human Bondage. 1947: The Homestretch. Dark Delusion (GB: Cynthia's Secret). Ivy. Time Out of Mind. Song of Love. 1948: Julia Misbehaves. Enchantment. Oliver Twist. 1949: Challenge to Lassie.

**STEVENS, Onslow** (O. Stevenson)
1902-1977
Dark, serious-looking, taciturn, long-faced American actor, the son of Houseley Stevenson (qv). In occasional leads, few of which have survived in the memory, save perhaps his mad scientist in House of

ABOVE Having cracked the case, Henry **Stephenson** (second left, with moustache) is congratulated by Lloyd Corrigan, Dorothy Lovett, Alice Fleming and Joseph Allan Jr in *The Man Trap* (1943)

BELOW Onslow **Stevens** (left) and Walter Connolly (*qv*) as prison surgeons in *Those High Gray Walls* (1939)

*Dracula*, but more often phlegmatic character parts as sobersides lawyers, prison officers, policemen and politicians. Directed many plays in the theatre, but never a film. Murdered by persons unknown in a convalescent home.

*1932: Once in a Lifetime. Okay America (GB: Penalty of Fame). Heroes of the West (serial). Radio Patrol (serial). Jungle Mystery (serial). The Golden West. Born to Fight. 1933: Peg o' My Heart. Nagana. Secret of the Blue Room. Counsellor at Law. Only Yesterday. Grand Exit. Yellow Dust. 1934: Bombay Mail. This Side of Heaven. House of Danger. The Crosby Case (GB: The Crosby Murder Case). In Love With Life (GB: Re-Union). Life Returns. Affairs of a Gentleman. The Vanishing Shadow (serial). I'll Tell the World. I Can't Escape. 1935: The Three Musketeers. A Notorious Gentleman. Born to Gamble. F Man. Bridge of Sighs. Three on a Trail. Forced Landing. 1936: Under Two Flags. Straight from the Shoulder. Murder With Pictures. Easy Money. 1937: You Can't Buy Luck. Flight from Glory. There Goes the Groom. 1939: Those High Gray Walls (GB: The Gates to Alcatraz). When Tomorrow Comes. 1940: Mystery Sea Raider. Who Killed Aunt Maggie? The Man Who Wouldn't Talk. 1941: The Monster and the Girl. Go West, Young Lady. 1942: Sunset Serenade. 1943: Appointment in Berlin. Idaho. Hands Across the Border. 1945: House of Dracula. 1946: Angel on My Shoulder. Canyon Passage. OSS. 1948: The Gallant Blade. The Night Has a Thousand Eyes. The Creeper. Walk a Crooked Mile. 1949: Red, Hot and Blue. Bomba the Jungle Boy. 1950: Mark of the Gorilla. State Penitentiary. Revenue Agent. Motor Patrol. Lonely Hearts Bandits (GB: Lonely Heart Bandits). 1951: Lorna Doone. One Too Many (GB: Killer With a Label). All That I Have. The Hills of Utah. The Family Secret. Sirocco. Sealed Cargo. 1952: The San Francisco Story. 1953: A Lion Is in the Streets. The Charge at Feather River. 1954: Fangs of the Wild. Them! They Rode West. 1955: New York Confidential. 1956: Tribute to a Bad Man. Outside the Law. Kelly and Me. 1958: The Buccaneer. Tarawa Beachhead. Lonelyhearts. The Party Crashers. 1960: All the Fine Young Cannibals. 1962: The Couch. Geronimo's Revenge (TV. GB: cinemas).*

## STEVENS, Ronnie 1925-

Breezy, light-haired British light comedian who came to films from revue success and proved a polished foil and semi-straight man in a number of British comedies from the early 1950s. After the 1960s he was much busier in the theatre and on TV.

*1952: Top Secret (US: Mr Potts Goes to Moscow). Made in Heaven. 1953: Love in Pawn. 1954: The Scarlet Web. For Better, For Worse (US: Cocktails in the Kitchen). The Embezzler. 1955: The Narrowing Circle. An Alligator Named Daisy. As Long As They're Happy. The Hornet's Nest. 1957: Doctor at Large. 1958: Bachelor of Hearts. I Was*

*Monty's Double (US: Monty's Double). Danger Within (US: Breakout). 1959: I'm All Right, Jack. 1960: Doctor in Love. Dentist in the Chair. 1961: Dentist on the Job (US: Get On With It!). Very Important Person (US: A Coming-Out Party). Nearly a Nasty Accident. A Pair of Briefs. 1962: It's Trad Dad. On the Beat. 1963: Doctor in Distress. 1964: A Home of Your Own. 1965: San Ferry Ann. Those Magnificent Men in Their Flying Machines. 1966: Doctor in Clover. The Sandwich Man. Give a Dog a Bone. 1967: Smashing Time. 1969: Some Girls Do. Goodbye, Mr Chips. 1980: Twelfth Night. 1982: Captain Stirrick. 1985: Morons from Outer Space.*

## STEVENSON, Houseley 1879-1953

Bony, sharp-featured British-born actor who made no films anywhere until he was pushing 60, but enjoyed a hectic few postwar Hollywood years up to his death playing cantankerous old codgers, often unshaven, hollow-cheeked westerners. Father of actors Onslow Stevens (*qv*) and Houseley Stevenson Jr.

*1936: Law in Her Hands. Isle of Fury. 1937: Once a Doctor. 1942: Native Land. 1943: Happy Land. 1945: Dakota. 1946: Little Miss Big (GB: The Baxter Millions). Somewhere in the Night. 1947: The Brasher Doubloon (GB: The High Window). Dark Passage. Thunder in the Valley (GB: Bob, Son of Battle). Ramrod. Time Out of Mind. 1948: Four Faces West (GB: They Passed This*

*Way). The Challenge. Smart Woman. The Paleface. Secret Beyond the Door. Casbah. Kidnapped. Joan of Arc. Moonrise. Apartment for Peggy. 1949: Colorado Territory. Leave It to Henry. Bride of Vengeance. Calamity Jane and Sam Bass. Knock on Any Door. The Lady Gambles. Masked Raiders. Sorrowful Jones. You Gotta Stay Happy. Take One False Step. The Walking Hills. The Gal Who Took the West. All the King's Men. 1950: Edge of Doom (GB: Stronger than Fear). Sierra. The Gunfighter. The Sun Sets at Dawn. 1951: All That I Have. Cave of Outlaws. Hollywood Story. The Secret of Convict Lake. As Young As You Feel. Darling, How Could You? (GB: Rendezvous). 1952: The Atomic City. The Wild North. Oklahoma Annie.*

## STEWART, Paul 1908- 1986

Cold-eyed, heavy-eyebrowed American actor of set, rather menacing features; a leading member of Orson Welles' Mercury Theatre group who only gradually became a Hollywood film regular, in villainous (often callously so) roles. Stewart went grey early, and in any case always looked older than his years. Since 1955, he has directed a large number of productions and episodes for television, as well as continuing a sporadic acting career.

*1941: Citizen Kane. Johnny Eager. 1942: The World at War (narrator only). 1943: Government Girl. Mr Lucky. 1949: The Window. Illegal Entry. Easy Living. Champion. Twelve O'Clock High. 1950: Walk Softly, Stranger. Edge of Doom (GB: Stronger than Fear). 1951: Appointment With Danger (completed 1949). 1952: Carbine Williams. Deadline USA (GB: Deadline). Loan Shark. We're Not Married. The Bad and the Beautiful. 1953: The Juggler. The Joe Louis Story. 1954: Deep in My Heart. Prisoner-of-War. 1955: Chicago Syndicate. Kiss Me Deadly. Hell on Frisco Bay. The Cobweb. 1956: The Wild Party. Confession (TV). 1957: Top Secret Affair (GB: Their Secret Affair). 1958: King Creole. 1962: A Child Is Waiting. 1965: The Greatest Story Ever Told. 1967: In Cold Blood. 1969: How to Commit Murder. Jigsaw. 1973: F for Fake. 1974: The Day of the Locust. Murph the Surf (GB: Love a Little, Steal a Lot). 1975: Bite the*

Bullet. 1976: W. C. Fields and Me. 1977:
Opening Night. 1978: The Revenge of the
Pink Panther. The Nativity (TV). 1981:
SOB. Nobody's Perfekt. 1982: Tempest.

**As director:**
1956: Lady in Fear (TV. GB: cinemas).

**STOCK, Nigel** 1919- *1986*
Light-haired, pugnacious British actor
(born in Malta) who lived up to his name by
being stocky and square-built. Mostly on
stage (where he first performed as a boy of
12), he gave a number of determined screen
performances that were often better than
those billed above him. Also a first-class Dr
Watson in a TV Sherlock Holmes series
featuring Peter Cushing.

1937: Lancashire Luck. 1938: Break the
News! Luck of the Navy (GB: North Sea
Patrol). 1939: Goodbye Mr Chips! Sons of the
Sea. 1944: *Victory Wedding. 1947: It
Always Rains on Sunday. Brighton Rock.
1951: The Lady With a Lamp. 1952: Derby
Day (US: Four Against Fate). 1953: Malta
Story. 1954: Aunt Clara. The Dam Busters.
1955: The Night My Number Came Up.
1956: *The Gentle Corsican (narrator only).
Eyewitness. Battle of the River Plate (US:
Pursuit of the Graf Spee). 1958: The Silent
Enemy. 1960: Never Let Go. 1961: Victim.
1962: The Password Is Courage. 1963: The
Great Escape. To Have and to Hold. Nothing
But the Best. 1964: Weekend à Zuyd-
coote/Weekend at Dunkirk. The High Bright
Sun (US: McGuire Go Home!). 1966: The
Night of the Generals. 1968: The Lost
Continent. The Lion in Winter. 1970: Crom-
well. 1973: Bequest to the Nation (US: The
Nelson Affair). 1975: Russian Roulette. Oper-
ation Daybreak. 1977: *When I'm Rich (voice
only). 1979: A Man Called Intrepid (TV).
1980: The Mirror Crack'd. 1983: Red
Monarch (TV, but first shown in cinemas).
Yellowbeard.

**STONE, George E.** (Georgy Stein)
1903-1967
Small (5ft 3½in) Polish-born actor with dark
hair and droopy moustache, who could be
furtive or forlorn and whose Brooklynese
gangsters were alternately vicious or
broadly comic. He was The Sewer Rat in

Seventh Heaven and The Runt in the Boston
Blackie films—two 'monickers' that
summed up his screen characters. A close
friend of author Damon Runyon, he played
Runyon's Society Max in Guys and Dolls.
Died following a stroke.

1915: *The Baby. *The Rivals. *The Little
Cupids. *Little Dick's First Case/Little Dick's
First Adventure. *The Straw Man. *Her
Filmland Hero. *Pirates Bold. *Dirty Face
Dan. *The Ash Can. *The Kid Magicians. *A
Ten Cent Adventure. *The Runaways. *The
Doll-House Mystery. Let Katy Do It. Martha's
Vindication. 1916: The Children in the House.
Children of the Feud. Going Straight. Gretchen
the Greenhorn. The Little Schoolma'am. 1917:
Sudden Jim. 1918: 'Till I Come Back to
You. Six Shooter Andy. The Scoffer.
1919: The Speed Maniac. 1920: Just Pals.
1921: Penny of Top Hill Trail. Jackie.
Desperate Trails. White and Unmarried. The
Whistle. 1923: The Fourth Musketeer. 1927:
Seventh Heaven. Brass Knuckles. 1928: San
Francisco Nights (GB: Divorce). Turn Back
the Hours (GB: The Badge of Courage).
Clothes Make the Woman. State Street Sadie
(GB: The Girl from State Street). Walking
Back. Beautiful But Dumb. The Racket.
Tenderloin. 1929: The Redeeming Sin. Skin
Deep. Weary River. Naughty Baby (GB:
Reckless Rosie). The Girl in the Glass Cage.
Two Men and a Maid. Melody Lane. 1930:
The Medicine Man. Under a Texas Moon.
Little Caesar. The Stronger Sex. *So This is
Paris Green. 1931: *The Stolen Jools (GB:
The Slippery Pearls). The Front Page. Five
Star Final. Cimarron. The Spider. Sob Sister
(GB: The Blonde Reporter). 1932: The Last
Mile. Taxi! File No. 113. The Woman from
Monte Carlo. The World and the Flesh. The
Phantom of Crestwood. 1933: 42nd Street.
King for a Night. Vampire Bat. Sailor Be
Good. Song of the Eagle (GB: The Beer
Baron). Emergency Call. The Big Brain (GB:
Enemies of Society). Sing, Sinner, Sing.
Penthouse (GB: Crooks in Clover). Ladies
Must Love. He Couldn't Take It. 1934:
The Return of the Terror. Viva Villa!
The Dragon Murder Case. Embarrassing
Moments. One Hour Late. Frontier Mar-
shal. Secret of the Chateau. 1935: Make a
Million. Hold 'Em Yale (GB: Uniform

Lovers). Moonlight on the Prairie. Frisco Kid.
Public Hero No. 1. Million Dollar Baby.
1936: Freshman Love (GB: Rhythm on the
River). King of Hockey (GB: King of the Ice
Rink). Jailbreak. Polo Joe. Rhythm on the
Range. Man Hunt. Anthony Adverse. Bullets
or Ballots. Here Comes Carter (GB: The Voice
of Scandal). The Captain's Kid. 1937: Don't
Get Me Wrong. Clothes and the Woman. Back
in Circulation. The Adventurous Blonde/
Torchy Blane the Adventurous Blonde. 1938:
Alcatraz Island. A Slight Case of Murder. Over
the Wall. Mr Moto's Gamble. You and Me.
The Long Shot. Submarine Patrol. 1939: You
Can't Get Away With Murder. The Night of
Nights. The Housekeeper's Daughter. 1940:
Island of Doomed Men. I Take This Woman.
North West Mounted Police. Slightly Tempted.
Cherokee Strip (GB: Fighting Marshal). Road
Show. 1941: Broadway Limited. Last of the
Duanes. The Face Behind the Mask (GB:
Behind the Mask). Confessions of Boston
Blackie (GB: Confessions). 1942: The Affairs
of Jimmy Valentine. The Lone Star Ranger.
Little Tokyo USA. Boston Blackie Goes
Hollywood (GB: Blackie Goes Hollywood).
The Devil With Hitler. Alias Boston Blackie.
1943: After Midnight With Boston Blackie
(GB: After Midnight). The Chance of a
Lifetime. 1944: Strangers in the Night. Timber
Queen. My Buddy. One Mysterious Night.
Roger Touhy, Gangster (GB: The Last
Gangster). 1945: Boston Blackie Booked on
Suspicion (GB: Booked on Suspicion). Boston
Blackie's Rendezvous (GB: Blackie's Rendez-
vous). Scared Stiff. Nob Hill. Midnight
Manhunt. 1946: One Exciting Week. Doll
Face (GB: Come Back to Me). Boston Blackie
and the Law (GB: Blackie and the Law). A
Close Call for Boston Blackie (GB: Lady of
Mystery). The Phantom Thief. Suspense. Senti-
mental Journey. Abie's Irish Rose. 1947: Daisy
Kenyon. 1948: Trapped by Boston Blackie.
The Untamed Breed. 1949: Dancing in the
Dark. 1952: Bloodhounds of Broadway. A
Girl in Every Port. 1953: The Robe. Pickup on
South Street. Combat Squad. 1954: The
Miami Story. The Steel Cage. Broken Lance.
Three-Ring Circus. Woman's World. 1955:
Guys and Dolls. The Man With the Golden
Arm. 1956: Slightly Scarlet. The Conqueror.
1957: The Story of Mankind. Sierra Stranger.
Baby-Face Nelson. Calypso Heat Wave. The
Tijuana Story. 1958: Some Came Running.
1959: Some Like It Hot. Alias Jesse James.
Night of the Quarter Moon. 1960: Ocean's
Eleven. 1961: Pocketful of Miracles.

**STONE, Harold J.** 1911-
Heavy-set, thick-lipped, intense American
actor with black, curly hair. Trained at the
Actors' Studio, he became briefly very
popular in the mid-1950s with personable
performances that earned him marquee
billing and saw him as high as third on the
cast list. After this initial surge, however, he
was more often seen on Broadway and
television, although he has continued to
appear from time to time in (smaller) roles
in films.

1956: Slander. The Harder They Fall. Somebody Up There Likes Me. The Wrong Man. 1957: House of Numbers. The Garment Jungle. Man Afraid. The Invisible Boy. 1959: These Thousand Hills. Stampede at Bitter Creek. 1960: Spartacus. 1961: The Chapman Report. 1962: Recoil (TV. GB: cinemas). 1963: Showdown. 'X'—The Man With the X-Ray Eyes (GB: The Man With the X-Ray Eyes). 1965: Girl Happy. The Greatest Story Ever Told. 1967: The St Valentine's Day Massacre. The Big Mouth. 1970: Breakout (TV). Which Way to the Front? (GB: Ja! Ja! Mein General, But Which Way to the Front?). 1971: The Seven Minutes. 1972: Pickup on 101 (GB: Echoes of the Road). 1975: The Legend of Valentino (TV). 1977: Mitchell.

**STONE, Marianne** 1924-

Dark-haired, dark-eyed, ultra-slim British actress whose rather downcast looks got her cast, after beginnings as a leading lady, in serious, scarf-over-the-head roles; land-ladies, working wives and slum mums. She played more comedy in the 1970s, by which time she had become Britain's most prolific supporting actress of the post-war period. Long married to show business columnist Peter Noble.

1947: Brighton Rock (US: Young Scarface). Escape Dangerous. When the Bough Breaks. 1949: A Run for Your Money. Miss Pilgrim's Progress. Marry Me! 1950: The Clouded Yellow. Blackmailed. Seven Days to Noon.

1951: The Magic Box. Appointment With Venus (US: Island Rescue). Home to Danger. 1952: Angels One Five. The Pickwick Papers. The Net (US: Project M7). Venetian Bird (US: The Assassin). Time Gentlemen Please! 1953: A Day to Remember. The Runaway Bus. Spaceways. You Know What Sailors Are. 1954: The Dog and the Diamonds. The Good Die Young. Beautiful Stranger (US: Twist of Fate). 36 Hours (US: Terror Street). Dance Little Lady. Mad About Men. 1955: Barba-dos Quest. Simon and Laura. Fun at St Fanny's. Lost (US: Tears for Simon). Cloak Without Dagger (US: Operation Conspiracy). The Quatermass Experiment (US: The Creep-ing Unknown). 1956: *Person Unknown. Passport to Treason. Yield to the Night (US: Blonde Sinner). The Long Arm (US: The Third Key). A Touch of the Sun. Private's Progress. The High Terrace. Eyewitness. Bond of Fear. The Good Companions. The Intimate Stranger (US: Finger of Guilt). Brothers in Law. 1957: Quatermass II (US: Enemy from Space). Man from Tangier. Time Lock. Hell Drivers. Woman in a Dressing Gown. Just My Luck. The Good Companions. 1958: The Golden Disc (US: The Inbetween Age). Inno-cent Sinners. A Night to Remember. At the Stroke of Nine. A Cry from the Streets. *Man With a Dog. No Trees in the Street. Carlton-Browne of the F O (US: Man in a Cocked Hat). 1959: Carry On Nurse. Tiger Bay. Jack the Ripper. The Man from Tangier. Operation Bullshine. I'm All Right, Jack. The Man Who Liked Funerals. Please Turn Over. Follow a Star. The Heart of a Man. 1960: The Big Day. The Angry Silence. Doctor in Love. 1961: Double Bunk. Five Golden Hours. Two and Two Make Six. Watch It Sailor! Lolita. The Frightened City. On the Fiddle (US: Operation Snafu). The Day the Earth Caught Fire. 1962: The Wild and the Willing. The Fast Lady. Night of the Prowler. Jigsaw. The Wrong Arm of the Law. Paranoiac. Play It Cool. Crooks Anonymous. 1963: Return to Sender. The Marked One. Echo of Diana. Carry On Jack (US: Carry On Venus). The Hi-Jackers. Heavens Above! The Victors. Blind Corner. West 11. The World 10 Times Over (US: Pussycat Alley). Ladies Who Do. Stolen Hours. Nothing But the Best. 1964: Hysteria. A Hard Day's Night. Rattle of a Simple Man. The Beauty Jungle (US: Contest Girl). We Shall See. The Curse of the Mummy's Tomb. The Intelligence Men. Act of Murder. Witchcraft. Devils of Darkness. 1965: Catch Us If You Can (US: Having a Wild Weekend). You Must Be Joking! Traitor's Gate. The Night Caller (US: Blood Beast from Outer Space). Strangler's Web. 1966: The Wrong Box. The Spy With a Cold Nose. Carry On Screaming. The Sandwich Man. A Count-ess from Hong Kong. Don't Lose Your Head. The Long Duel. To Sir with Love. 1967: Berserk! The Jokers. Carry On Doctor. Here We Go Round the Mulberry Bush. 1968: Twisted Nerve. The Best House in London. The Bliss of Mrs Blossom. Otley. The Games. 1969: Lock Up Your Daughters! Oh! What a Lovely War. All the Right Noises. 1970: Doctor in

Trouble. Scrooge. The Raging Moon (US: Long Ago Tomorrow). Assault. Countess Dra-cula. Every Home Should Have One. The Firechasers. Hoverbug. There's a Girl in My Soup. 1971: Mr Forbush and the Penguins (US: Cry of the Penguins). Carry On at Your Convenience. Whoever Slew Auntie Roo? (US: Who Slew Auntie Roo?) Danny Jones. All Coppers Are... 1972: Carry On Matron. Tower of Evil (US: Horror of Snape Island). Bless This House. The Cherry Picker. The Creeping Flesh. The Love Ban (originally It's a Two-Foot-Six-Inch-Above-the-Ground World). Baxter! (US: The Boy). 1973: Penny Gold. Vault of Horror. Carry On Girls. Mistress Pamela. Craze. 1974: Carry On Dick. Dead of Night (TV). Confessions of a Window Cleaner. Percy's Progress. 1975: That Lucky Touch. Carry On Behind. I'm Not Feeling Myself Tonight. 1976: The Incredible Sarah. The Chiffy Kids (series). 1977: Confes-sions from a Holiday Camp. The Great Snail Race. 1978: Sammy's Super T-Shirt. What's Up Superdoc? The Class of Miss MacMichael. 1979: The Human Factor. A Man Called Intrepid (TV). 1980: Dangerous Davies the Last Detective (TV). Little Lord Fauntleroy. 1982: Funny Money. 1984: Always.

**STONE, Milburn** 1904-1980

Stocky, moustachioed American actor with dark wavy hair who alternated as hero and villain of low-budget action films and serials, then moved into character roles as bankers, crooks, wardens, doctors and officers. He found a permanent home on television with the role of the grouchy Doc Adams in Gunsmoke, a role in which the quizzical Stone features were seen from 1955 to 1972. Died from a heart attack.

1935: The Fighting Marines (serial). Ladies Crave Excitement. Rendezvous. The Three Mesquiteers. 1936: The Milky Way. China Clipper. The Princess Comes Across. Two in a Crowd. 1937: A Doctor's Diary. Atlantic Flight. Federal Bullets. Wings Over Honolulu. Blazing Barriers. Music for Madame. Swing It, Professor. Youth on Parole. The Thirteenth Man. The Man in Blue. Port of Missing Girls. Mr Boggs Steps Out. 1938: Wives Under Suspicion. The Storm. Sinners in Paradise. Crime School. Paroled from the Big House.

California Frontier. 1939: Mystery Plane/Sky Pilot. King of the Turf. Society Smugglers. Fighting Mad. Blind Alley. Young Mr Lincoln. Tail Spin. Tropic Fury. Stunt Pilot. When Tomorrow Comes. Sky Patrol. Made for Each Other. Danger Flight. Nick Carter, Master Detective. Crashing Through. Charlie McCarthy, Detective. 1940: Chasing Trouble. Enemy Agent (GB: Secret Enemy). Johnny Apollo. An Angel from Texas. Framed. Give Us Wings. Lillian Russell. Colorado. The Great Plane Robbery. 1941: The Phantom Cowboy. The Great Train Robbery. Death Valley Outlaws. 1942: Reap the Wild Wind. Eyes in the Night. Rubber Racketeers. Invisible Agent. Frisco Lil. Police Bullets. Pacific Rendezvous. 1943: Keep 'em Slugging. You Can't Beat the Law. Get Going. Sherlock Holmes Faces Death. Captive Wild Woman. Corvette K-225 (GB: The Nelson Touch). Gung Ho! The Mad Ghoul. 1944: The Imposter. Hi, Good Looking. Hat Check Honey. Moon Over Las Vegas. Jungle Woman. Phantom Lady. Twilight on the Prairie. The Great Alaskan Mystery (serial). 1945: The Master Key (serial). The Beautiful Cheat (GB: What a Woman!). The Daltons Ride Again. The Frozen Ghost. I'll Remember April. On Stage, Everybody. She Gets Her Man. Strange Confession. Swing Out, Sister. The Royal Mounted Rides Again (serial). 1946: Danger Woman. Inside Job. Smooth As Silk. Little Miss Big (GB: Baxter's Millions). Spider Woman Strikes Back. Strange Conquest. Her Adventurous Night. 1947: Cass Timberlane. Killer Dill. The Michigan Kid. Headin' for Heaven. Buck Privates Come Home (GB: Rookies Come Home). 1948: Train to Alcatraz. The Judge (GB: The Gamblers). 1949: The Green Promise (GB: Raging Waters). Calamity Jane and Sam Bass. Sky Dragon. 1950: No Man of Her Own. The Fireball. Snow Dog. Branded. 1951: The Racket. Road Block. Flying Leathernecks. 1952: The Atomic City. The Savage. 1953: The Sun Shines Bright. Invaders from Mars. Second Chance. Arrowhead. Pickup on South Street. 1954: The Siege at Red River. Black Tuesday. The Long Gray Line. 1955: White Feather. Smoke Signal. The Private War of Major Benson. 1957: Drango. 1972: The World of Sport Fishing (documentary).

**STRANGE, Glenn** (George G. Strange) 1899-1973

Massive American actor with square, solid, moustachioed features that betrayed his part-Cherokee Indian ancestry. A promising heavy-weight boxer until he developed trouble with his hands, Strange tried ranching and rodeo riding (he was even once a deputy sheriff) before drifting into show business as one of the Arizona Wranglers group on radio, playing fiddle, composing songs and joining in the chorus. After playing dozens of minor heavies in low-budget westerns, Strange won a measure of fame with three portrayals of the Frankenstein monster in the 1940s. Died from cancer.

1931: Border Law. The Range Feud. Wild Horse. Hard Hombre. 1932: McKenna of the Mounted. Hurricane Express (serial). 1933: The Thrill Hunter. The Sundown Rider. 1934: The Law of the Wild (serial). The Star Packer (GB: He Wore a Star). 1935: The New Frontier. Stormy. Border Vengeance. Westward Ho. His Fighting Blood. Moonlight on the Prairie. Lawless Range. The Gallant Defender. The Law of the 45s (GB: The Mysterious Mr Sheffield). 1936: Flash Gordon (serial). Avenging Waters. Sunset of Power. The Cattle Thief. The Fugitive Sheriff (GB: Law and Order). The California Mail. Trailin' West (GB: On Secret Service). Song of the Gringo (GB: The Old Corral). Guns of the Pecos. 1937: Arizona Days. Adventure's End. Singing Outlaw. Trouble in Texas. Land Beyond the Law. Cherokee Strip (GB: Strange Laws). Blazing Sixes. Empty Holsters. The Devil's Saddle Legion. Danger Valley. Courage of the West. A Tenderfoot Goes West. 1938: Pride of the West. In Old Mexico. Sunset Trail. The Spy Ring. The Mysterious Rider. Black Bandit. Border Wolves. Forbidden Valley. Guilty Trails. The Last Stand. Prairie Justice. Prison Break. California Frontier. Whirlwind Horseman. Ghost Town Riders. The Painted Trail. Six-Shootin' Sheriff. Call of the Rockies. Gunsmoke Trail. Gun Packer. 1939: Law of the Pampas. Range War. The Lone Ranger Rides Again (serial). The Night Riders. Honor of the West. The Phantom Stage. Blue Montana Skies. Arizona Legion. Rough Riders' Round Up. Across the Plains. Oklahoma Terror. *Cupid Rides the Range. Overland Mail. The Fighting Gringo. The Llano Kid. Days of Jesse James. 1940: Wyoming (GB: Bad Man of Wyoming). Dark Command. Land of the Six-Guns. Pioneer Days. San Francisco Docks. Rhythm of the Rio Grande. Covered Wagon Trails. Pals of the Silver Sage. The Cowboy from Sundown. Stage to Chino. Triple Justice. Wagon Train. *Bar Buckaroos. Three Men from Texas. The Fargo Kid. 1941: Riders of Death Valley (serial). In Old Colorado. Wide Open Town. Arizona Cyclone. Badlands of Dakota. Forbidden Trails. *Westward Ho-Hum. The Kid's Last Ride. Billy the Kid Wanted. Saddlemates. The Bandit Trail. The Driftin' Kid. *California or Bust. Lone Star Law Men. Dude Cowboy. Billy the Kid's Round Up. The Ghost of Frankenstein. Come

On, Danger! 1942: Juke Girl. Little Joe, the Wrangler. Stagecoach Buckaroo. Romance on the Range. Down Texas Way. The Lone Rider and the Bandit. Western Mail. Raiders of the West. Billy the Kid Trapped. Sunset on the Desert. Boot Hill Bandits. Rolling Down the Great Divide. Billy the Kid's Smoking Guns (GB: Smoking Guns). Texas Trouble Shooters. Prairie Gunsmoke. Bandit Ranger. Overland Stagecoach. The Mad Monster. The Mummy's Tomb. 1943: The Lone Rider in Border Roundup (GB: Border Roundup). False Colors. Mission to Moscow. The Black Raven. Arizona Trail. The Woman of the Town. Wild Horse Stampede. Death Valley Rangers. Black Market Rustlers (GB: Land and the Law). The Kid Rides Again. Haunted Ranch. Western Cyclone. The Desperadoes. The Kansan (GB: Wagon Wheels). The Return of the Rangers. Action in the North Atlantic. Bullets and Saddles (GB: Vengeance in the Saddle). 1944: Knickerbocker Holiday. Forty Thieves. Trail to Gunsight. Sonora Stagecoach. Renegades of the Rio Grande (GB: Bank Robbery). Valley of Vengeance (GB: Vengeance). The Silver City Kid. San Antonio Kid. The Monster Maker. Alaska. Harmony Trail (GB: White Stallion). The Contender. House of Frankenstein. 1945: Saratoga Trunk. House of Dracula. Bad Men of the Border. 1946: Up Goes Maisie (GB: Up She Goes). Devil's Playground. Beauty and the Bandit. 1947: Brute Force. The Wistful Widow of Wagon Gap (GB: The Wistful Widow). Sea of Grass. Sinbad the Sailor. Wyoming. The Fabulous Texan. Frontier Fighters. 1948: Red River. Abbott and Costello Meet Frankenstein (GB: Abbott and Costello Meet the Ghosts). The Gallant Legion. Silver Trails. The Far Frontier. Montana Belle (released 1952). 1949: Master Minds. The Gal Who Took the West. Rimfire. Roll, Thunder, Roll. 1950: Comanche Territory. Surrender. Double Crossbones. 1951: Comin' Round the Mountain. The Red Badge of Courage. Texas Carnival. Vengeance Valley. Callaway Went Thataway (GB: The Star Said No). 1952: The Lusty Men. The Lawless Breed. 1953: Escape from Fort Bravo. The Great Sioux Uprising. All the Brothers Were Valiant. Veils of Bagdad. Devil's Canyon. Born to the Saddle. 1954: Jubilee Trail. 1955: The Kentuckian. The Vanishing American. The Road to Denver. 1956: Backlash. The Fastest Gun Alive. 1957: The Halliday Brand. Last Stagecoach West. Gunfire at Indian Gap. 1958: Quantrill's Raiders. 1959: Last Train from Gun Hill. Alias Jesse James.

**STRAUSS, Robert** 1913-1975

This gloweringly round-faced, dark-haired, solid-featured American actor was near the top of the character tree following his stage and film performances as Animal in *Stalag 17*, for the latter of which he was nominated for an Academy Award. But he slid steadily down the cast after that, revealing a certain monotony of performance, and ended up in some fairly bizarre exploitation films before

his early death from complications following a stroke.

*1942: Native Land. 1950: The Sleeping City. 1951: Sailor Beware. 1952: The Redhead from Wyoming. Jumping Jacks. 1953: Stalag 17. Act of Love. Money from Home. Here Come the Girls. 1954: The Atomic Kid. The Bridges at Toko-Ri. 1955: The Seven-Year Itch. The Man With the Golden Arm. 1956: Attack! 1958: Frontier Gun. I, Mobster. 1959: Li'l Abner. The 4-D Man (GB: The Evil Force). Inside the Mafia. 1960: Wake Me When It's Over. September Storm. 1961: The Last Time I Saw Archie. Dondi. The George Raft Story (GB: Spin of a Coin). Twenty Plus Two (GB: It Started in Tokyo). 1962: Girls! Girls! Girls! 1963: The Wheeler Dealers (GB: Separate Beds). The Thrill of It All. 1964: Stage to Thunder Rock. 1965: Harlow (Carol Lynley version). That Funny Feeling. The Family Jewels. Frankie and Johnny. 1966: Fort Utah. Movie Star, American Style, or: LSD, I Hate You. 1971: Dagmar's Hot Pants Inc.*

veteran, but still acting in small featured roles.

*1941: Sundown. 1942: Star Spangled Rhythm. 1951: Lion Hunters (GB: Bomba and the Lion Hunters). 1952: Bomba and the African Treasure. Caribbean (GB: Caribbean Gold). 1953: City Beneath the Sea. 1954: The Gambler from Natchez. Demetrius and the Gladiators. Jungle Gents. 1955: Son of Sinbad. 1956: The Ten Commandments. 1958: The Buccaneer. Tarzan's Fight for Life. 1959: Pork Chop Hill. 1960: Spartacus. The Last Voyage. Sergeant Rutledge. 1961: Two Rode Together. The Sins of Rachel Cade. 1962: The Man Who Shot Liberty Valance. 1963: Tarzan's Three Challenges. 1965: Seven Women. Genghis Khan. 1966: The Professionals. Daniel Boone—Frontier Trail Rider (TV. GB: cinemas). 1967: Tarzan's Deadly Silence (TV. GB: cinemas). 1968: Shalako. Once Upon a Time in the West. Seduto alla sua destra (GB: Out of Darkness. US: Black Jesus). 1969: King Gun. Che! Ciak Mull, l'uomo della vendetta (GB: The Unholy Four). La collina degli stivali (US: Boot Hill). 1970: Breakout (TV). The Deserter. 1971: The Last Rebel. The Gatling Gun. 1972: La 'mala' ordina (GB: Manhunt in Milan. US: The Italian Connection). Black Rodeo (narrator only). The Revengers. 1973: Key West (TV). 1974: Colpo in canna (GB: Stick 'em Up, Darlings!). 1975: Winterhawk. Oil: The Billion Dollar Fire. 1976: Loaded Guns. Keoma (GB: The Violent Breed). 1977: Kingdom of the Spiders. 1979: Jaguar Lives. Ravagers. 1980: Key West Crossing. 1982: Vigilante. 1983: The Black Stallion Returns. 1984: Lust in the Dust. The Cotton Club. Jungle Warriors.*

*1967: The Ballad of Josie. Games. Banning. Journey to Shiloh. 1968: Madigan. What's So Bad About Feeling Good? Coogan's Bluff. Something for a Lonely Man (TV). 1969: Bloody Mama. . . .tick . . .tick . . .tick. Explosion. 1970: Angel Unchained. Breakout (TV). 1971: The DA: Conspiracy to Kill (TV). Von Richthofen and Brown (GB: The Red Baron). 1972: The Daughters of Joshua Cabe (TV). The Deadly Dream (TV). Rolling Man (TV). Joe Kidd. 1973: Scalawag. The Nightmare Step (TV). Slaughter's Big Rip Off. 1974: Murph the Surf (GB: Live a Little, Steal a Lot). 1975: The Killer Inside Me. The Return of Joe Forrester (TV). 1976: The House by the Lake (GB: Death Weekend). High Risk (TV). Death Threat. 1977: Sudden Death. The Choirboys. 1978: Katie: Portrait of a Centerfold (TV). The Buddy Holly Story. 1979: The Amityville Horror. Supertrain (TV. GB: Express to Terror). Search and Destroy. 1981: The Night the Lights Went Out in Georgia. 1983: Murder Me, Murder You (TV). I Want to Live (TV).*

**STRODE, Woody/Woodrow** 1914-*1994*
Strapping (6ft 5in), muscly, soon shaven-headed black American actor with granite-carved features. A former professional footballer and all-round athlete, it took Strode a long time to prove himself a good actor as well, but he took the chance in the title role of John Ford's *Sergeant Rutledge*, and went on to a series of hard action-men in continental adventure films. Now a

**STROUD, Don** 1937-
Pugnacious, strongly built, fair-haired American actor who only came to films and television at 30, but was quickly in demand, mostly as wild-eyed, violent types, although he could handle quieter roles extremely effectively. He seemed about to become a star at the beginning of the 1970s, but did not quite make it, returning to playing characters destined to be troublemakers beneath a barely-calm surface.

**SULLIVAN, Francis L.** 1903-1956
Heavyweight British actor with stern, forbidding face, the epitome of pompous portliness. Almost always cast as either prosecuting counsels or villains, he had made his name in Shakespeare (1921-1931) before bringing his massive presence and withering gaze to the cinema. Also filmed in Hollywood, especially towards the end of his life—but mostly in unworthy roles.

*1932: When London Sleeps. The Missing Rembrandt. The Chinese Puzzle. 1933: The Right to Live. The Stickpin. Called Back. FP1. The Fire Raisers. The Wandering Jew. Red Wagon. 1934: Chu Chin Chow. Princess Charming. What Happened Then? The Return of Bulldog Drummond. Great Expectations. 1935: The Mystery of Edwin Drood. Her Last Affaire. 1936: Spy of Napoleon. The Interrupted Honeymoon. The Limping Man. A Woman Alone (US: Two Who Dared). 1937: Fine Feathers. Dinner at The Ritz. Action for Slander. Non-Stop New York. 1938: The Drum (US: Drums). The Gables Mystery. *First at the Post. Kate Plus Ten. Climbing High. The Ware Case. The Citadel. 1939: The Four Just Men (US: The Secret Four). Young*

Man's Fancy. 1940: The Briggs Family. 1941: Pimpernel Smith (US: Mister V). 1942: ‡The Foreman Went to France (US: Somewhere in France). The Day Will Dawn (US: The Avengers). Lady from Lisbon. 1943: The Butler's Dilemma. 1944: Fiddlers Three. 1945: Caesar and Cleopatra. 1946: The Laughing Lady. Great Expectations (remake). 1947: The Man Within (US: The Smugglers). Take My Life. Broken Journey. 1948: Oliver Twist. The Winslow Boy. Joan of Arc. 1949: Christopher Columbus. The Red Danube. 1950: Night and the City. 1951: My Favorite Spy. Behave Yourself! 1952: Caribbean (GB: Caribbean Gold). 1953: Sangaree. Plunder of the Sun. 1954: Drums of Tahiti. 1955: Hell's Island. The Prodigal.

‡As François Sully

## SUMMERFIELD, Eleanor 1921-

Blonde, blue-eyed British actress with soaraway eyebrows and shopgirl looks. After winning a gold medal at the Royal Academy of Dramatic Art, she began her film career in straight roles, sometimes minor leads. It soon became evident, however, that her personality was more suited to bright and chatty comedy roles, and she was often the woman you couldn't get away from. A vivacious real-life personality, she was popular for years on radio panel games, especially Many a Slip. Married actor Leonard Sachs.

1947: Take My Life. 1948: London Belongs to Me (US: Dulcimer Street). The Weaker Sex. The Story of Shirley Yorke. Man on the Run. All Over the Town. 1949: No Way Back. 1951: The Third Visitor. Laughter in Paradise. Scrooge (GB: A Christmas Carol). 1952: Mandy (US: Crash of Silence). Top Secret (US: Mr Potts Goes to Moscow). The Last Page (US: Manbait). Isn't Life Wonderful! 1953: Street Corner (US: Both Sides of the Law). 1954: Face the Music (US: The Black Glove). Final Appointment. 1955: Murder by Proxy (completed 1953. US: Blackout). Lost (US: Tears for Simon). 1956: It's Great to be Young! Odongo. No Road Back. 1958: A Cry from the Streets. 1960: Dentist in the Chair. The Millionairess. 1961: Spare the Rod. Don't Bother to Knock! (US: Why Bother to Knock?). Petticoat Pirates. On

the Fiddle (US: Operation Snafu). 1962: Act of Mercy. On the Beat. Guns of Darkness. 1963: The Running Man. 1965: The Yellow Hat. 1969: Foreign Exchange (TV). Some Will, Some Won't. 1981: The Watcher in the Woods.

## SUMMERVILLE, Slim
(George Summerville) 1892-1946

Very tall, gangling, brown-haired, big-nosed American comedy actor with clown's smile that made him look as if he never had any teeth, and an unmistakeable slow, drawling voice. An amiable foil for such distinctively different scene-stealers as Shirley Temple and ZaSu Pitts, he also directed a number of early comedy shorts. Died after a stroke.

1914: *A Rowboat Romance. *Gentlemen of Nerve. *The Knock-Out. *Mabel's Busy Day. Tillie's Punctured Romance. *Laughing Gas. *Cursed by His Beauty. *Dough and Dynamite. *Ambrose's First Falsehood. 1915: *Caught in the Act. *Her Winning Punch. *Other People's Wives/The Home Breakers. *Their Social Splash. *Gussie's Day of Rest. *The Great Vacuum Robbery. *His Bitter Half. *Her Painted Hero. *A Game Old Knight. *Beating Hearts and Carpets. Those College Girls. 1916: *Bucking Society. *His Bread and Butter. *Her Busted Trust. *The Three Slims. Cinders of Love. 1917: *A Dog Catcher's Love. The Winning Punch. Villa of the Movies. Are Witnesses Safe? *Her Fame and Shame. *His Precious Life. *A Pullman Bride. *Mary's Little Lobster. *Roping Her Romeo. *Hold That Line. *It Pays to Exercise. *The Kitchen Lady. *High Diver's Last Kiss. *Ten Nights Without a Barroom. 1918: The Beloved Rogue. 1921: Skirts. 1926: The Texas Steer. The Texas Streak. 1927: The Denver Dude. The Beloved Rogue (remake). Hey Hey Cowboy. Painted Ponies. The Chinese Parrot. The Wreck of the Hesperus. 1928: Riding for Fame. 1929: King of the Rodeo. The Shannons of Broadway. The Last Warning. Strong Boy. Tiger Rose. 1930: Under Montana Skies. *Voice of Hollywood No. 2. One Hysterical Night. King of Jazz. Her Man. See America Thirst. Troopers Three. All Quiet on the Western Front. Little Accident. The Spoilers. Free Love. *Parlez-vous. *Hello

Russia! *We! We! Marie. 1931: Reckless Living. Heaven on Earth. Many a Slip. Bad Sister. The Front Page. Lasca of the Rio Grande. *Arabian Knights. *Bless the Ladies. *First to Fight. *Hotter than Haiti. *Let's Play. *Royal Bluff. *Parisian Gaieties. *Sarge's Playmates. *Here's Luck. 1932: Tom Brown of Culver. Unexpected Father. They Just Had to Get Married. Airmail. Racing Youth. *Eyes Have It. *In the Bag. *Kid Glove Kisses. 1933: Love, Honor and Oh! Baby. Her First Mate. Out All Night. *Early to Bed. *Meet the Princess. *See Soldier's Sweeties. 1934: Their Big Moment (GB: Afterwards). The Love Birds. *Horse Play. 1935: Way Down East. Life Begins at 40. The Farmer Takes a Wife. 1936: The Country Doctor. Captain January. Pepper. Reunion (GB: Hearts in Reunion). Can This Be Dixie? White Fang. 1937: The Road Back. Off to the Races. Fifty Roads to Town. Love Is News. 1938: Up the River. Kentucky Moonshine (GB: Three Men and a Girl). Five of a Kind. Rebecca of Sunnybrook Farm. Submarine Patrol. 1939: Charlie Chan in Reno. Jesse James. Winner Take All. Henry Goes Arizona (GB: Spats to Spurs). 1940: Anne of Windy Poplars (GB: Anne of Windy Willows). Gold Rush Maisie. 1941: Miss Polly. Puddin' Head (GB: Judy Goes to Town). Niagara Falls. Highway West. Tobacco Road. Western Union. 1942: The Valley of Vanishing Men (serial). 1944: I'm from Arkansas. Bride by Mistake. Swing in the Saddle (GB: Swing and Sway). 1945: Sing Me a Song of Texas (GB: Fortune Hunter). 1946: The Hoodlum Saint.

As director (all shorts):

1920: †Hold Me Tight. 1921: Pardon Me. One Moment Please. 1922: Hold the Line. Ranch Romeos. The Eskimo. High and Dry. The Barnstormer. 1923: The Cyclist. The Five Fifteen. The Artist. The Riding Master. Rough Sailing. 1924: Why Wait? The Green Grocers. Hello, 'Frisco! Her Ball and Chain. Keep Healthy. The Orphan. The Pinhead. Ship Ahoy! The Very Bad Man. Case Dismissed. 1925: When Dumb Bells Ring. Absent Minded. All Out. All Tied Up. Back to Nature. Faint Heart. Happy Go Lucky. Kick Me Again. 1926: The Village Cut Up. Wanted a Bride. Badly Broke. A Bedtime Story. Business Women. Don't Be a Dummy. A Dumb Friend. Hearts for Rent. The Honeymoon Quickstep. Oprey House Tonight. Papa's Mama. A Perfect Lie. A Swell Affair. Switching Sleepers. Tune Up! Too Much Sleep. 1927: Hop Along. Jailhouse Blues. In Again, Out Again. Meet the Husband. The Midnight Bum. A Run for His Money. 1929: Don't Say Ain't. Who's the Boss?

†Co-directed

## SUMNER, Geoffrey 1908-

Round-faced, dark-haired, pop-eyed, pipe-smoking British comedy actor with thick, short moustache and 'I say, old boy' voice. He began his career as a newsreel commentator, then switched to acting, portraying mostly affable asses, notably in TV's *The Army Game*. From 1958 to 1962 he became a producer/writer/reporter on documentary films; was also managing director of the company that made them.

*1938: Premiere (US: One Night in Paris). Too Many Husbands. 1939: She Couldn't Say No. 1940: Law and Disorder. 1946: While the Sun Shines. 1947: Mine Own Executioner. 1949: Helter Skelter. Traveller's Joy (released 1951). Dark Secret. 1950: The Dark Man. 1951: A Tale of Five Cities (US: A Tale of Five Women). Appointment With Venus (US: Island Rescue). 1952: Top Secret (US: Mr Potts Goes to Moscow). The Happy Family (US: Mr Lord Says No). 1953: Always a Bride. The Dog and the Diamonds. Those People Next Door. 1954: Doctor in the House. Five Days (US: Paid to Kill). 1955: The Flying Eye. 1958: I Only Arsked! 1962: Band of Thieves. 1964: \*All in Good Time. 1966: Cul-de-Sac. 1975: Side by Side. 1979: There Goes the Bride.*

## SUNDBERG, Clinton 1906- 1987

Po-faced American actor with sleek dark hair who played fusspots, worriers and assiduous assistants. He began his career as a teacher, but turned to acting and in 1946 was put under contract by M-G-M as a supporting player, turning in effective cameos for them for the next eight years, but almost entirely on television after leaving the studio. His best role was probably on loan-out to Universal-International as the right-hand man of the title detective in *The Fat Man*.

*1946: The Mighty McGurk. Love Laughs at Andy Hardy. Undercurrent. 1947: Living in a Big Way. The Song of Love. Undercover Maisie (GB: Undercover Girl). The Hucksters. Good News. 1948: The Kissing Bandit. Good Sam. Easter Parade. Mr Peabody and the Mermaid. A Date With Judy. Words and Music. Command Decision. 1949: Big Jack. In the Good Old Summertime. The Barkleys of Broadway. 1950: Annie Get Your Gun. Key to the City. Father is a Bachelor. Duchess of Idaho. The Toast of New Orleans. Two Weeks With Love. Mrs O'Malley and Mr Malone. 1951: On the Riviera. The Fat Man. As Young as You Feel. 1952: The Belle of New York. 1953: The Girl Next Door. Main Street to Broadway. Sweethearts on Parade. The Caddy. 1956: The Birds and the Bees. 1961: Bachelor in Paradise. 1962: The Wonderful World of the Brothers Grimm. How the West Was Won. 1967: Hotel. 1968: Shadow Over Elveron (TV).*

## SUTTON, Dudley 1933-

British actor with a mass of tight, fair curls and impish, puck-like face beneath. He tended to play smiling neurotics in his younger days but, with the passing years, his villains became scruffier and less menacing. Can still occasionally be nasty to great effect.

*1961: Go to Blazes. 1962: The Boys. 1963: The Leather Boys. 1965: Rotten to the Core. 1969: Crossplot. 1970: The Walking Stick. One More Time. A Town Called Bastard (US: A Town Called Hell). 1971: The Devils. Mr Forbush and the Penguins (US: Cry of the Penguins). 1972: Diamonds on Wheels. 1973: Paganini Strikes Again. 1974: The Stud. 1975: Cry Terror. Great Expectations (TV. GB: cinemas). 1976: The Pink Panther Strikes Again. One Hour to Zero. 1977: Fellini's Casanova. Valentino. The Prince and the Pauper (US: Crossed Swords). No. 1 of Secret Service. 1978: The Big Sleep. The Playbirds. 1979: The London Connection (US: TV, as The Omega Connection). 1980: George and Mildred. The Island. 1982: Brimstone and Treacle. 1983: Those Glory, Glory Days (originally TV). 1984: The House (TV).*

## SUTTON, Grady 1908- 1995

Tall, dark-haired, damply plump, dumpling-cheeked, shyly smiling American actor who played faintly effete suitors doomed not to get the girl, or victims of verbal venom. His small features could explode into a marvellous array of surprised, outraged or anguished expressions, and he remained well in demand for cameos and amusing supporting parts from the beginning of sound until the end of the 1940s, when he became heavily (!) involved in television. Notable quailing from the acid tongue of W. C. Fields, he is still occasionally glimpsed in cinema and TV.

*1925: The Mad Whirl. Skinner's Dress Suit. The Freshman. 1926: The Boy Friend. 1928: The Sophomore. 1929: Tanned Legs. 1930: Wild Company. Let's Go Native. Hit the Deck. \*Blood and Thunder. \*Ladies Last. 1931: \*Air Tight. \*High Gear. \*Call a Cop! \*The Kick-Off! \*Mama Loves Papa. 1932: \*Boys Will Be Boys. \*You're Telling Me. \*Family Troubles. \*Who, Me? Movie Crazy. This Reckless Age. Are These Our Children?/Age of Consent. Hot Saturday. Pack Up Your Troubles. 1933: The Story of Temple Drake. College Humor. \*The Pharmacist. Ace of Aces. The Sweetheart of Sigma Chi (GB: Girl of My Dreams). Only Yesterday. 1934: Bachelor Bait. Gridiron Flash (GB: Luck of the Game). 1935: Stone of Silver Creek. Laddie. \*A Night at the Biltmore Bowl. Alice Adams. The Man on the Flying Trapeze (GB: The Memory Expert). Dr Socrates. 1936: Palm Springs (GB: Palm Springs Affair). King of the Royal Mounted. She's Dangerous. The Singing Kid. Valiant is the Word for Carrie. Pigskin Parade (GB: The Harmony Parade). My Man Godfrey. 1937: Waikiki Wedding. Stage Door. We Have Our Moments. Dangerous Holiday. Love Takes Flight. Turn Off the Moon. Behind the Mike. Two Minutes to Play. 1938: Vivacious Lady. Having Wonderful Time. Alexander's Ragtime Band. Joy of Living. Hard to Get. Three Loves Has Nancy. The Mad Miss Manton. 1939: You Can't Cheat an Honest Man. It's a Wonderful World. In Name Only. Naughty But Nice. Blind Alley. Blondie Meets the Boss. They Made Her a Spy. Angels Wash Their Faces. Three Sons. Three Smart Girls Grow Up. The Flying Irishman. 1940: Anne of Windy Poplars (GB: Anne of Windy Willows). Lucky Partners. Sky Murder. Torrid Zone. Too Many Girls. The Bank Dick (GB: The Bank Detective). City of Chance. We Who Are Young. Millionaire Playboy. He Stayed for Breakfast. Millionaires in Prison. 1941: She Knew All the Answers. Blondie in Society. Father Takes a Wife. Four Jacks and a Jill. Penny Serenade. Bedtime Story. Flying Blind. Doctors Don't Tell. You Belong to Me (GB: Good Morning, Doctor). Three Girls About Town. 1942: Whispering Ghosts. Dudes Are Pretty People. The Affairs of Martha (GB: Once Upon a Thursday). The Bashful Bachelor. Somewhere I'll Find You. 1943: The More the Merrier. A Lady Takes a Chance. What a Woman! (GB: The Beautiful Cheat). The Great Moment. 1944: Johnny Doesn't Live Here Anymore. Week-End Pass. Nine Girls. Allergic to Love. Goin' to Town. Since You Went Away. Hi, Beautiful (GB: Pass to Romance). Casanova Brown. 1945: Grissly's Millions. A Royal Scandal (GB: Czarina). Three's a Crowd. On Stage, Everybody. Her Lucky Night. Captain Eddie. The Stork Club. A Bell for Adano. Anchors Aweigh. Pillow to Post. Brewster's Millions. 1946: Ziegfeld Follies (completed 1944). The Fabulous Suzanne. My Dog Shep. Hit the Hay. It's Great to be Young. Nobody Lives Forever. Idea Girl. The Plainsman and the Lady. The Magnificent Rogue. Partners in Time. The Show Off. Susie Steps Out. Dragonwyck. Two Sisters from*

RIGHT Geoffrey **Sumner** and his wife Mary at home on their Surrey farm in the early 1960s, at the time of his great success as Major Upshott-Bagley in the television comedy series *The Army Game*

BELOW Clinton **Sundberg** (centre) played so many waiters and butlers that he still looks like one here, as a detective's assistant in *The Fat Man* (1951), with Jayne Meadows and J. Scott Smart

Boston. No Leave, No Love. Dead Reckoning. 1947: Beat the Band. My Wild Irish Rose. Philo Vance's Gamble. Love and Learn. Always Together. 1948: Romance on the High Seas (GB: It's Magic). Jiggs and Maggie in Court. Last of the Wild Horses. My Dear Secretary. 1949: Grand Canyon. Air Hostess. 1954: Living It Up. A Star Is Born. White Christmas. 1961: Madison Avenue. The Chapman Report. 1962: Jumbo/Billy Rose's Jumbo. 1963: Come Blow Your Horn. 1964: My Fair Lady. 1965: Tickle Me. The Chase. The Bounty Killer. Paradise, Hawaiian Style. 1968: I Love You, Alice B. Toklas. Something for a Lonely Man (TV). 1969: The Great Bank Robbery. Suppose They Gave a War and Nobody Came? 1970: Myra Breckinridge. Dirty Dingus Magee. 1971: Support Your Local Gunfighter. 1979: Rock 'n' Roll High School.

**TAFLER, Sydney** 1916-1979
British actor with receding dark hair and 'working-class' looks. In occasional star roles in early 1950s' thrillers, he was more likely to turn up, cigarette dangling from his mouth, as smooth-talking sharpsters or thieves. On stage from the age of 20, he became an indelible part of the British cinema scene, as probably the character you'd least want to buy a second-hand car from. Married to Joy Shelton (1922- ) from 1944. Died from cancer.

1942: The Young Mr Pitt. 1943: The Bells Go Down. 1946: I See a Dark Stranger (US: The Adventuress). 1947: The Little Ballerina.

It Always Rains on Sunday. 1948: London Belongs to Me (US: Dulcimer Street). The Monkey's Paw. Calling Paul Temple. Uneasy Terms. No Room at the Inn. 1949: Passport to Pimlico. 1950: Dance Hall. Once a Sinner. 1951: Assassin for Hire. The Lavender Hill Mob. The Galloping Major. Scarlet Thread. Hotel Sahara. Chelsea Story. Mystery Junction. Blind Man's Bluff. There is Another Sun (US: Wall of Death). 1952: Secret People. Emergency Call (US: Hundred Hour Hunt). Wide Boy. Venetian Bird (US: The Assassin). Time Gentlemen Please! There Was a Young Lady. 1953: The Floating Dutchman. Operation Diplomat. Johnny on the Run. The Square Ring. The Saint's Return (US: The Saint's Girl Friday). 1954: The Crowded Day. The Sea Shall Not Have Them. 1955: A Kid for Two Farthings. The Glass Cage (US: The Glass Tomb). Dial 999 (US: The Way Out). The Woman for Joe. Cockleshell Heroes. 1956: Guilty? Reach for the Sky. The Long Arm (US: The Third Key). Fire Maidens from Outer Space. The Counterfeit Plan. Booby Trap. 1957: Interpol (US: Pickup Alley). The Surgeon's Knife. 1958: Carve Her Name With Pride. The Bank Raiders. 1959: Too Many Crooks. Tommy the Toreador. The Crowning Touch. Follow a Star. 1960: Sink the Bismarck! Make Mine Mink. Let's Get Married. Bottoms Up! Light Up the Sky. No Kidding (US: Beware of Children). The Bulldog Breed. 1961: Five Golden Hours. A Weekend With Lulu. Carry On Regardless. 1964: The Seventh Dawn. 1965: Runaway Railway. Promise Her Anything. 1966: Alfie. The Sandwich Man. 1967: Berserk! 1969: The Birthday Party. 1970: The Adventurers. 1971: Danger Point. 1977: The Spy Who Loved Me.

**TALMAN, William** 1915-1968
Tall, cold-eyed, unsmiling American actor with crinkly blond-auburn hair who switched from writing (and playing pro. tennis) to acting, and was building up a nice line in film villainy when sidetracked into television where, from 1957 to 1965, he was internationally known as the DA who lost every case to Perry Mason in the last reel. Married/divorced actress Barbara Read, who died at 45 in 1963, five years before Talman's death from cancer.

1949: I Married a Communist (GB: The Woman on Pier 13). Red, Hot and Blue. The Kid from Texas (GB: Texas Kid — Outlaw). 1950: Armored Car Robbery. 1951: The Racket. 1952: One Minute to Zero. 1953: The Hitch-Hiker. City That Never Sleeps. 1955: Big House, USA. Smoke Signal. Crashout. 1956: The Man Is Armed. Two Gun Lady. Uranium Boom. 1957: The Persuader. Hell on Devil's Island. 1967: The Ballad of Josie.

**TAMIROFF, Akim** 1898-1972
One can still see Tamiroff in that white trilby, moustache glistening with sweat, white handkerchief mopping the brow, cooking up some new double-deal. Nearly all the characters created by this Russian-born actor (in America since the early twenties) were disreputable, whether in filthy sweat-shirt or lurking beneath semi-respectable clothes. Small, round and beetle-like, he was invaluable to any film. Academy Award nominations for *The General Died at Dawn* and *For Whom the Bell Tolls*.

1932: Okay America (GB: Penalty of Fame). 1933: Storm at Daybreak. Gabriel Over the White House. Fugitive Lovers. Queen Christina. The Devil's in Love. 1934: The Great Flirtation. Wonder Bar. Now and Forever. The Merry Widow (and French version). Here is My Heart. The Winning Ticket. Sadie McKee. Whom the Gods Destroy. Chained. The Captain Hates the Sea. Lives of a Bengal Lancer. The Scarlet Empress. Murder in the Private Car (GB: Murder on the Runaway Train). 1935: Black Fury. Rumba. Paris in Spring (GB: Paris Love Song). The Gay Deception. Two Fisted. Naughty Marietta. Go into Your Dance (GB: Casino de Paree). China Seas. The Last Outpost. The Big Broadcast of 1936. Reckless. Black Sheep. 1936: The Story of Louis Pasteur. Anthony Adverse. Woman Trap. The Jungle Princess. The General Died at Dawn. Desire. 1937: King of Gamblers. Her Husband Lies. High, Wide and Handsome. The Soldier and the Lady (GB: Michael Strogoff). The Great Gambini. This Way Please. 1938: Dangerous to Know. Spawn of the North. Ride a Crooked Mile (GB: Escape from Yesterday). The Buccaneer. Paris Honeymoon. 1939: The Magnificent Fraud. King of Chinatown. Disputed Passage. Union Pacific. Honeymoon in

*Bali (GB: Husbands or Lovers). Geronimo. 1940: The Great McGinty (GB: Down Went McGinty). The Way of All Flesh. Texas Rangers Ride Again. Northwest Mounted Police. Untamed. 1941: New York Town. The Corsican Brothers. 1942: Tortilla Flat. Are Husbands Necessary? 1943: His Butler's Sister. Five Graves to Cairo. For Whom the Bell Tolls. 1944: The Miracle of Morgan's Creek. Dragon Seed. The Bridge of San Luis Rey. Can't Help Singing. 1945: Pardon My Past. 1946: A Scandal in Paris. 1947: The Gangster. Fiesta. 1948: Relentless. My Girl Tisa. Tenth Avenue Angel. 1949: Black Magic. Outpost in Morocco. 1953: Desert Legion. You Know What Sailors Are. 1954: Cartouche. They Who Dare. 1955: La vedova (US: The Widow). The Black Forest. Confidential Report (US: Mr Arkadin). 1956: The Black Sleep. Anastasia. 1957: The Miracle Worker (TV). Yangtse Incident (US: Battle Hell). †Don Quixote. 1958: Touch of Evil. Me and the Colonel. 1959: Desert Desperadoes/The Sinner. 1960: Les bacchantes/Le baccanti. Ocean's Eleven. 1961: Romanoff and Juliet. I briganti italiani/Seduction of the South. With Fire and Sword. Il giudizio universale (US: The Last Judgment). Ursus e la ragazza tartara (GB: The Savage Hordes. US: Tartar Invasion). La moglie di mio marito. 1962: The Reluctant Saint. A Queen for Caesar. The Trial. 1963: The Black Tulip. Panic Button. 1964: La bambole (GB: Four Kinds of Love). Topkapi. Spirit Elf. The Fabulous Adventures of Marco Polo (GB: Marco the Magnificent). 1965: Lord Jim. Marie-Chantal contre le docteur Kah. The Liquidator. Chimes at Midnight (US: Falstaff). The Blue Panther. Par un beau matin d'été (US: Crime on a Summer Morning). 1966: Alphaville. The Happening. Lt. Robin Crusoe U.S.N. After the Fox. I nostri mariti. Adultery Italian Style. Hotel Paradiso. The Vulture. Every Man's Woman/A Rose for Everyone. 1967: Great Catherine. 1968: Justine and Juliet/Marquis de Sade: Justine. Tenderly (GB and US: The Girl Who Couldn't Say No). 1969: The Great Bank Robbery. Sabra. Then Came Bronson (TV: GB. cinemas).*

†Unfinished.

## TANDY, Jessica 1909- 1994

Petite, whippy, dark-haired British actress, in America since 1940. A powerful character star, she was often seen in crafty or neurotic roles, but has remained largely a stage actress. Her second husband (since 1942) is the Canadian actor Hume Cronyn (qv); their daughter, Tandy Cronyn, is also an actress. Her first husband (1932-1942) was the British star Jack Hawkins.

*1932: The Indiscretions of Eve. 1938: Murder in the Family. 1944: The Seventh Cross. 1945: The Valley of Decision. 1946: The Green Years. Dragonwyck. 1947: Forever Amber. A Woman's Vengeance. 1950: September Affair. 1951: The Desert Fox (GB: Rommel — Desert Fox). 1958: The Light in the Forest. 1962: Hemingway's Adventures of*

*a Young Man (GB: Adventures of a Young Man). 1963: The Birds. 1973: Butley. 1985: Cocoon.*

## TAPLEY, Colin 1911-

Tall, good-looking, light-haired, pale-eyed, often moustachioed New Zealand actor who played strong, silent types in Hollywood after winning a contract in a Paramount talent contest. He never became a star personality, and came to Britain to make his career from 1950.

*1934: Double Door. Search for Beauty. Murder at the Vanities. The Pursuit of Happiness. 1935: The Black Room. The Lives of a Bengal Lancer. Becky Sharp. Peter Ibbetson. The Last Outpost. The Crusades. 1936: The Return of Sophie Lang. Early to Bed. Till We Meet Again. The Sky Parade. Thank You, Jeeves. 1937: The Crime Nobody Saw. Night of Mystery. King of Gamblers. Booloo. 1938: If I Were King. Storm Over Bengal. 1939: The Light That Failed. 1940: Women in War. 1941: Arizona. 1949: Samson and Delilah. 1951: Cloudburst. 1952: Wings of Danger (US: Dead on Course). Angels One Five. Wide Boy. 1953: Strange Stories. The Steel Key. Noose for a Lady. Three Steps to the Gallows (released 1955. US: White Fire). 1954: The Diamond (US: Diamond Wizard). *Late Night Final. The Dam Busters. Little Red Monkey (US: The Case of the Red Monkey). 1955: Barbados Quest (US: Murder on Approval). 1957: Stranger in Town. The Safecracker. 1958:*

*Blood of the Vampire. High Jump. 1959: Innocent Meeting. Man Accused. An Honourable Murder. Night Train for Inverness. 1960: Compelled. 1961: So Evil, So Young. Strongroom. 1962: Emergency. The Lamp in Assassin Mews. Gang War. Paranoiac. 1963: Shadow of Fear. 1968: Fraulein Doktor.*

## TAYLOR, Dub (Walter Taylor) 1908-

Shortish, dumpy, wisp-haired American supporting actor with happily apologetic air, a former saxophonist given his first acting chance by director Frank Capra, who used him several times in featured roles over the years. In the 1940s, Taylor became a 'B' western sidekick, a sort of poor man's Smiley Burnette (qv), to such stars as Bill Elliott, Russell Hayden, Charles Starrett and singing cowboy Jimmy Wakely. More recently, he has been playing old-timers in westerns and hillbilly capers.

*1938: You Can't Take It with You. 1939: Mr Smith Goes to Washington. Taming of the West. 1940: One Man's Law. The Return of Wild Bill (GB: False Evidence). Beyond the Sacramento (GB: Power of Justice). The Wildcat of Tucson (GB: Promise Fulfilled). Pioneers of the Frontier (GB: The Anchor). Prairie Schooners (GB: Through the Storm). The Man from Tumbleweeds. 1941: The Son of Davy Crockett (GB: Blue Clay). Across the Sierras (GB: Welcome Stranger). North from the Lone Star. Hands across the Rockies. King of Dodge City. The Return of Daniel Boone (GB: The Mayor's Nest). Roaring Frontiers. 1942: The Lone Prairie. Inside Information). A Tornado in the Saddle (GB: Ambushed). 1943: What's Buzzin' Cousin? Silver City Raiders (GB: Legal Larceny). Saddles and Sagebrush (GB: The Pay-Off). The Vigilantes Ride (GB: Hunted). Cowboy in the Clouds. Riders of the Northwest Mounted. 1944: Cowboy Canteen (GB: Close Harmony). Wyoming Hurricane (GB: Proved Guilty). Marshal of Gunsmoke. Cowboy from Lonesome River (GB: Signed Judgment). Saddle Leather Law (GB: The Poisoner). Sundown Valley. The Last Horseman. Hidden Valley Outlaws. Cyclone Prairie Rangers. 1945: Both Barrels Blazing (GB: The Yellow Streak). Lawless Empire (GB: Power of Possession). Blazing the Western Trail (GB:*

Who Killed Waring?). Rough Ridin' Justice (GB: Decoy). Rustlers of the Badlands (GB: By Whose Hand?). Outlaws of the Rockies (GB: A Roving Rogue). Texas Panhandle. 1946: Frontier Gun Law (GB: Menacing Shadows). 1947: †Ridin' Down the Trail. 1948: †Song of the Drifter. †Oklahoma Blues. †Partners of the Sunset. †Range Renegades. †Silver Trails. †The Rangers Ride. †Outlaw Brand. †Courtin' Trouble. †Cowboy Cavalier. 1949: †Gun Runner. †Gun Law Justice. †Across the Rio Grande. †Brand of Fear. †Roaring Westward. †Lawless Code. 1950: Riding High. 1952: The Will Rogers Story (GB: The Story of Will Rogers). 1953: ††Crime Wave (GB: The City Is Dark). 1954: A Star is Born. The Bounty Hunter. 1955: I Died a Thousand Times. 1956: You Can't Run Away from It. 1958: No Time for Sergeants. 1959: A Hole in the Head. 1961: Sweet Bird of Youth. Pocketful of Miracles. 1962: The Mooncussers (TV. GB: cinemas). Black Gold. 1963: Spencer's Mountain. 1964: Major Dundee. 1965: The Hallelujah Trail. The Adventures of Bullwhip Griffin. 1967: Don't Make Waves. Bonnie and Clyde. The Shakiest Gun in the West. 1968: Bandolero! Something for a Lonely Man. 1969: The Reivers. Ride a Northbound Horse (TV. GB: cinemas). Death of a Gunfighter. The Undefeated. ... tick... tick... tick. The Liberation of L. B. Jones. 1970: A Man Called Horse. The Wild Country. 1971: Support Your Local Gunfighter. Evel Knievel. Wild in the Sky. Sam Hill: Who Killed the Mysterious Mr Foster? (TV). 1972: The Delphi Bureau (TV). Menace on the Mountain. Junior Bonner. The Getaway. 1973: Brock's Last Case (TV). Shoot-Out in a One-Dog Town (TV). Tom Sawyer. This is a Hijack. 1974: Honky Tonk (TV). Thunderbolt and Lightfoot. The Fortune. 1975: Flash and the Firecat. The Daughters of Joshua Cabe Return (TV). Hearts of the West (GB: Hollywood Cowboy). 1976: Gator. The Treasure of Matecumbe. Burnt Offerings. 1977: The Rescuers (voice only). Moonshine County Express. 1978: They Went That-a-Way and That-a-Way. 1979: 1941. Wolf Lake. 1980: Used Cars. 1983: Cannonball Run II. 1984: The Outlaws (TV).

†As Dub 'Cannonball' Taylor
††As Walter Dub Taylor

**TAYLOR, Vaughn** 1910-1983
Slight, balding American actor with pencil moustache and waspish delivery of a line, just as likely to turn up as an avuncular adviser or a crooked attorney. Mainly on stage, he became a semi-regular in films from the 1950s, returning to Broadway between Hollywood assignments. Forced to retire in the mid-1970s with crippling spinal deterioration, he died from a cerebral haemorrhage.

1932: Lawyer Man. 1951: Up Front. Francis Goes to the Races. Meet Danny Wilson. Hoodlum Empire. 1952: Back at the Front (GB: Willie and Joe in Tokyo). 1953: It Should Happen to You. 1957: This Could Be

the Night. Jailhouse Rock. Decision at Sundown. Cowboy. 1958: Screaming Mimi. Cat on a Hot Tin Roof. Gunsmoke in Tucson. Andy Hardy Comes Home. Party Girl. The Lineup. 1959: Blue Denim (GB: Blue Jeans). Warlock. 1960: The Wizard of Baghdad. The Plunderers. The Gallant Hours. Psycho. 1962: FBI Code 98. Diamond Head. 1963: The Carpetbaggers. The Wheeler Dealers (GB: Separate Beds). 1964: The Unsinkable Molly Brown. 1965: Dark Intruder. Zebra in the Kitchen. 1966: The Russians Are Coming, the Russians Are Coming. The Professionals. 1967: In Cold Blood. The Shakiest Gun in the West. The Power. 1968: Fever Heat. 1969: My Dog the Thief. Set This Town on Fire (TV. Not shown until 1973). 1970: The Ballad of Cable Hogue. 1971: Million Dollar Duck. 1973: Brock's Last Case (TV). 1974: Winterkill (TV). 1975: Eleanor and Franklin (TV). 1976: The Gumball Rally.

**TEAL, Ray** 1902-1976
Solidly-built, moustachioed, bullet-headed, pointed-nosed American 'western' actor with thinning brown hair. Teal played saxophone in dance bands for 20 years, then drifted into films and ended up as the screen's best-known sheriff, whose friendly smile was often a mask for graft and corruption. Largely lost to the long-running western TV series Bonanza after 1961, in which he played — the sheriff.

1937: Zorro Rides Again (serial). 1938: Western Jamboree. 1939: Edison the Man. 1940: Pony Post. Cherokee Strip (GB: Fighting Marshal). Strange Cargo. Kitty Foyle. The Adventures of Red Ryder (serial). Northwest Passage. The Trail Blazers. New Moon. I Love You Again. Prairie Schooners (GB: Through the Storm). Third Finger, Left Hand. Florian. 1941: Billy the Kid. Shadow of the Thin Man. They Met in Bombay. They Died With Their Boots On. Wild Bill Hickok Rides. Bad Men of Missouri. Honky Tonk. Ziegfeld Girl. Outlaws of the Panhandle (GB: Faro Jack). The Bugle Sounds. Woman of the Year. 1942: Tennessee Johnson (GB: The Man on America's Conscience). Juke Girl. Apache Trail. Prairie Chickens. Nazi Agent. Secret Enemies. Captain Midnight (serial). Northwest Rangers. 1943: Lost Angel. Madame Curie. The Youngest Profession. North Star (later Armored Attack). Chance of a Lifetime. Thousands Cheer. 1944: Maisie Goes to Reno (GB: You Can't Do That to Me). Strange Affair. Hollywood Canteen. The Princess and the Pirate. A Wing and a Prayer. None Shall Escape. Nothing But Trouble. The Thin Man Goes Home. Slightly Dangerous. Once Upon a Time. Barbary Coast Gent. Ziegfeld Follies (released 1946). 1945: Circumstantial Evidence. Wonder Man. The Clock (GB: Under the Clock). Sudan. The Fighting Guardsman. Strange Voyage. Anchors Aweigh. Captain Kidd. Adventure. Along Came Jones. Gentle Annie. *A Gun in His Hand. Keep Your Powder Dry. Back to Bataan. The Harvey Girls. 1946: Blondie Knows Best. Pursued.

Blonde Alibi. The Best Years of Our Lives. Decoy. Deadline for Murder. Till the Clouds Roll By. The Bandit of Sherwood Forest. Canyon Passage. The Missing Lady. Dead Reckoning. 1947: The Michigan Kid. Ramrod. Cheyenne. The Long Night. Unconquered. Brute Force. Driftwood. Deep Valley. High Wall. Road to Rio. Desert Fury. The Sea of Grass. The Fabulous Texan. Northwest Passage (GB: End of the Rainbow). 1948: Raw Deal. Roadhouse. The Man from Colorado. The Black Arrow (GB: The Black Arrow Strikes). The Countess of Monte Cristo. Joan of Arc. I Wouldn't Be in Your Shoes. Daredevils of the Clouds. Black Bart (GB: Black Bart — Highwayman). One Sunday Afternoon. Fury at Furnace Creek. Tenth Avenue Angel. The Miracle of the Bells. Whispering Smith. Montana Belle (released 1952). 1949: Blondie Hits the Jackpot (GB: Hitting the Jackpot). Rusty's Birthday. Streets of Laredo. Scene of the Crime. Ambush. Kazan. Once More, My Darling. Samson and Delilah. It Happens Every Spring. The Kid from Texas (GB: Texas Kid — Outlaw). 1950: No Way Out. Where Danger Lives. The Redhead and the Cowboy. Our Very Own. The Petty Girl (GB: Girl of the Year). The Men. Convicted. Davy Crockett — Indian Scout (GB: Indian Scout). Harbor of Missing Men. When You're Smiling. Winchester '73. Edge of Doom (GB: Stronger than Fear). 1951: Tomorrow Is Another Day. Fort Worth. The Big Carnival (later and GB: Ace in the Hole). Lorna Doone. The Secret of Convict Lake. Along the Great Divide. Flaming Feather. Distant Drums. 1952: The Turning Point. The Lion and the Horse. Jumping Jacks. Hangman's Knot. Cattle Town. The Wild North. The Captive City. Carrie. 1953: Ambush at Tomahawk Gap. 1954: The Command. Lucky Me. Rogue Cop. About Mrs Leslie. 1955: The Man from Bitter Ridge. Rage at Dawn. The Indian Fighter. The Desperate Hours. Apache Ambush. Run for Cover. 1956: The Burning Hills. The Young Guns. Canyon River. 1957: Phantom Stagecoach. Band of Angels. The Wayward Girl. Decision at Sundown. The Oklahoman. The Tall Stranger. The Guns of Fort Petticoat. Girl on the Run. Utah Blaine. 1958: Saddle the Wind. Gunman's Walk. 1960: Home from the Hill. One-Eyed Jacks. 1961: Posse from Hell. Judgment at Nuremberg. Ada. 1963: Cattle King (GB: Guns of Wyoming). 1964: Taggart. Bullet for a Badman. 1970: The Liberation of L. B. Jones. Chisum. 1974: The Hanged Man (TV).

**THATCHER, Heather** 1897- *1987*
Sparkling, long-nosed, blue-eyed blonde British musical comedy star of the theatre who led a sporadic career in home grown features, then went to Hollywood in the 1930s and came into demand for eccentric characterizations lent strength and animation by her off-centre features and stylish delivery. Returned to Britain in the late 1940s to round out her career with a few sharply witty character roles.

ABOVE Vaughn **Taylor** shows his alligator smile as he enters the scene in *Cat on a Hot Tin Roof* (1958). With him are Judith Anderson (*qv*) and Madeleine Sherwood

BELOW Ray **Teal** (extreme left) is part of a disbelieving group listening to one of Hoagy Carmichael's stories in *Canyon Passage* (1946). Also in the crowd: Lloyd Bridges, Dana Andrews and Brian Donlevy

*1915: The Prisoner of Zenda. 1916: Altar Chains. 1918: The Key of the World. 1919: Pallard the Punter. The First Men in the Moon. The Green Terror. 1920: \*A Little Bet. \*Home Influence. \*A Pair of Gloves. The Little Hour of Peter Wells. 1925: \*Stage Stars Off Stage. 1926: The Flag Lieutenant. \*Gaumont Mirror No. 2. 1929: The Plaything. \*Express Love. Comets. 1930: A Warm Corner. 1931: Stepping Stones. 1932: But the Flesh Is Weak. 1933: Loyalties. It's a Boy! 1934: The Private Life of Don Juan. 1935: The Dictator (US: The Loves of a Dictator). 1937: Tovarich. The Thirteenth Chair. Mama Steps Out. 1938: Fools for Scandal. If I Were King. 1939: Girls' School. Beau Geste. 1940: Scotland Yard. 1941: Man Hunt. 1942: We Were Dancing. Son of Fury. The Moon and Sixpence. This Above All. The Undying Monster (GB: The Hammond Mystery). 1943: Journey for Margaret. Flesh and Fantasy. Above Suspicion. 1944: Gaslight (GB: The Murder in Thornton Square). The Conspirators. 1948: Anna Karenina. 1949: Trottie True (US: Gay Lady). Dear Mr Prohack. 1951: Encore. 1952: The Hour of 13. Father's Doing Fine. 1953: Will Any Gentleman...? 1954: Duel in the Jungle. 1955: The Deep Blue Sea. Josephine and Men.*

**THATCHER, Torin** (Torren Thatcher) 1905-1981
Tall, burly, dark-haired, strong-looking, India-born actor, in British films off and on for 20 years before going to Hollywood, where he played villains in westerns,

swashbucklers, comedies and thrillers, without ever quite making star billing. Began his career as a schoolmaster (and enthusiastic amateur boxer) before going on the stage. Retired at the end of 1969. Died from cancer.

*1932: But the Flesh Is Weak. 1933: General John Regan. Red Wagon. 1934: Irish Hearts (US: Norah O'Neale). 1935: Drake of England (US: Drake the Pirate). School for Stars. 1936: Sabotage (US: The Woman Alone). Well Done Henry. The Man Who Could Work Miracles. 1937: The Return of the Scarlet Pimpernel. Young and Innocent (US: The Girl Was Young). Knight Without Armour. 1938: Climbing High. 1939: Old Mother Riley MP. The Spy in Black (US: U-Boat 29). The Lion Has Wings. Too Dangerous to Live. 1940: Let George Do It. Law and Disorder. Night Train to Munich (US: Night Train). Gasbags. The Case of the Frightened Lady (US: The Frightened Lady). Saloon Bar. 1941: Major Barbara. 1942: Next of Kin. Saboteur. 1946: The Captive Heart. I See a Dark Stranger (US: The Adventuress). Great Expectations. 1947: Jassy. The End of the River. The Man Within (US: The Smugglers). When the Bough Breaks. 1948: Bonnie Prince Charlie. The Fallen Idol. Lost Illusion. 1949: Which Will You Have? (US: Barabbas the Robber). 1950: The Black Rose. 1952: Affair in Trinidad. The Snows of Kilimanjaro. The Crimson Pirate. Blackbeard the Pirate. 1953: The Desert Rats. Houdini. The Robe. 1954: Knock on Wood. Bengal Brigade (GB: Bengal Rifles). The Black Shield of Falworth. Helen of Troy. 1955: Lady Godiva (US: Lady Godiva of Coventry). Love Is a Many-splendored Thing. Diane. Yacht on the High Sea (TV. GB: cinemas). 1957: Istanbul. Witness for the Prosecution. Band of Angels. So Soon to Die (TV). Darby's Rangers (GB: The Young Invaders). 1958: The 7th Voyage of Sinbad. 1959: The Miracle. 1961: Jack the Giant Killer. The Canadians. 1962: Mutiny on the Bounty. The Sweet and the Bitter. 1963: Decision at Midnight. Drums of Africa. 1964: From Hell to Borneo. 1965: The Sandpiper. 1966: Hawaii. 1967: The King's Pirate. 1968: Dr Jekyll and Mr Hyde (TV). 1976: Brenda Starr/Brenda Starr — Girl Reporter (TV).*

**THESIGER, Ernest** 1879-1961
Eccentric British character actor, as emaciated as he was animated, who carved out some memorably grotesque and sometimes quite frightening figures, most notably his Dr Praetorius, the scientist who kept miniature beings in bottles, in *Bride of Frankenstein*. Later in more routine roles in post-war Britain, although each had the distinctive Thesiger touch.

*1916: \*The Real Thing at Last. 1918: Nelson. The Life Story of David Lloyd George. 1919: A Little Bit of Fluff. 1921: The Adventures of Mr Pickwick. The Bachelor Club. †Number Thirteen. 1928: Weekend Wives. 1929: The Vagabond Queen. 1930:*

*\*Ashes. 1932: The Old Dark House. 1933: The Only Girl (US: Heart Song). The Ghoul. 1934: My Heart Is Calling. The Night of the Party. 1935: Bride of Frankenstein. 1936: The Man Who Could Work Miracles. 1938: The Ware Case. They Drive by Night. Lightning Conductor. 1943: The Lamp Still Burns. My Learned Friend. 1944: Don't Take It to Heart. Henry V. 1945: A Place of One's Own. Caesar and Cleopatra. 1946: Beware of Pity. 1947: The Man Within (US: The Smugglers). Jassy. The Ghosts of Berkeley Square. 1948: The Winslow Boy. Portrait from Life. (US: The Girl in the Painting). The Bad Lord Byron. Quartet. The Brass Monkey/Lucky Mascot. 1950: Last Holiday. 1951: The Man in the White Suit. Laughter in Paradise. Scrooge (US: A Christmas Carol). The Magic Box. The Woman's Angle. 1953: Thought to Kill. Meet Mr Lucifer. The Robe. The Million Pound Note (US: Man With a Million). 1954: Father Brown (US: The Detective). Make Me an Offer. 1955: Value for Money. An Alligator Named Daisy. The Adventures of Quentin Durward (US: Quentin Durward). 1956: Who Done It? Three Men in a Boat. 1957: Doctor at Large. 1958: The Truth About Women. The Horse's Mouth. 1959: Battle of the Sexes. 1960: Sons and Lovers. 1961: The Roman Spring of Mrs Stone.*
†Unfinished.

**THORNTON, Frank** 1921-
Erect, dark-haired British actor whose expression of impending outrage or horror

came in useful in comedy after he had proved himself as a distinguished Shakespearian actor without quite making his mark in films. In the 1970s, he became a nationally known figure for his portrayal of Captain Peacock in the long-running TV comedy programme *Are You Being Served?*, also starring in the spin-off film.

1954: *Radio Cab Murder.* 1955: *Cloak Without Dagger* (US: *Operation Conspiracy*). *Johnny You're Wanted. Portrait of Alison* (US: *Postmark for Danger*). *Stock Car.* 1961: *Tarnished Heroes.* 1962: *It's Trad Dad. The Dock Brief* (US: *Trial and Error*). *Doomsday at Eleven.* 1964: *The Tomb of Ligeia. The Wild Affair.* 1965: *The Murder Game. Gonks Go Beat. The Early Bird.* 1966: *Carry On Screaming. A Funny Thing Happened on the Way to the Forum.* 1967: *Danny the Dragon. 30 Is a Dangerous Age, Cynthia.* 1968: *A Flea in Her Ear. The Assassination Bureau. The Bliss of Mrs Blossom. Crooks and Coronets* (US: *Sophie's Place*). 1969: *The Bed Sitting Room. The Magic Christian. Till Death Us Do Part. Some Will, Some Won't.* 1970: *The Private Life of Sherlock Holmes. All the Way Up. The Rise and Rise of Michael Rimmer.* 1971: *Up the Chastity Belt.* 1972: *Our Miss Fred. Bless This House. That's Your Funeral.* 1973: *No Sex Please — We're British. Digby the Biggest Dog in the World. Steptoe and Son Ride Again. Keep It Up, Jack!* 1974: *The Three Musketeers (The Queen's Diamonds). Vampira* (US: *Old Dracula*). 1975: *Spanish Fly. Side by Side. The Bawdy Adventures of Tom Jones.* 1977: *Are You Being Served?* 1981: *The Taming of the Shrew* (TV).

**TOBIAS, George** 1901-1980
Tall, lumpy, small-eyed, affable-looking American supporting actor whose homely pan decorated Warner films for most of the 1940s, mostly as the hero's loyal, but not-too-bright sidekick, but sometimes in juicier and more interesting roles. Hung around in films as a freelance for a few years afterwards, but was mostly seen on television after 1958. Died from cancer.

1939: *They All Came Out. Maisie. The Hunchback of Notre Dame. Balalaika. Ninotchka.* 1940: *The Man Who Talked Too*

*Much. Music in My Heart. Saturday's Children. City for Conquest. Calling All Husbands. River's End. Torrid Zone. They Drive By Night* (GB: *The Road to Frisco*). *South of Suez. East of the River.* 1941: *The Strawberry Blonde. The Bride Came C.O.D. Affectionately Yours. You're in the Army Now. Sergeant York. Out of the Fog.* 1942: *Wings for the Eagle. My Sister Eileen. Yankee Doodle Dandy. Juke Girl. Captains of the Clouds.* 1943: *Mission to Moscow. Thank Your Lucky Stars. This Is the Army. Air Force.* 1944: *Make Your Own Bed. The Mask of Dimitrios. Passage to Marseille. Between Two Worlds.* 1945: *Mildred Pierce. Objective Burma!* 1946: *Her Kind of Man. Nobody Lives Forever. Gallant Bess.* 1947: *My Wild Irish Rose. Sinbad the Sailor.* 1948: *The Adventures of Casanova. The Judge Steps Out* (GB: *Indian Summer*). 1949: *Everybody Does It. The Set-Up.* 1950: *Southside 1-1000* (GB: *Forgery*). 1951: *Rawhide. Mark of the Renegade. The Tanks Are Coming. The Magic Carpet. Ten Tall Men.* 1952: *Desert Pursuit.* 1953: *The Glenn Miller Story.* 1955: *The Seven Little Foys.* 1957: *The Tattered Dress. Silk Stockings.* 1958: *Marjorie Morningstar.* 1963: *A New Kind of Love. Nightmare in the Sun.* 1964: *Bullet for a Badman.* 1966: *The Glass Bottom Boat.* 1969: *The Phynx.*

**TOMBES, Andrew** 1889-
Bald American actor, a great gnome of a man whose upper lip was almost non-existent, dwarfed by a distance between nose and mouth that gave him an aspect of Macchiavellian glee. Following World War I he became a vaudeville and musical-comedy entertainer then, with the approach of middle-age, moved into film character roles in which he was equally likely to be genial or grasping as undertaker, insurance man, school governor or policeman, giving many of his characterizations a faintly zany slant.

1933: *The Bowery.* 1934: *Moulin Rouge. Born to be Bad.* 1935: *Doubting Thomas. Here Comes Cookie* (GB: *The Plot Thickens*). *Music is Magic. Thanks a Million.* 1936: *King of Burlesque. The Country Beyond. Here Comes Trouble. Stage Struck. Ticket to Paradise. It Had to Happen.* 1937: *Big City. Meet*

*the Boy Friend. Charlie Chan at the Olympics. Turn Off the Moon. Easy Living. Sing and Be Happy. The Holy Terror. Time Out for Romance.* 1938: *Sally, Irene and Mary. Battle of Broadway. Everybody Sing. Romance on the Run. A Desperate Adventure* (GB: *It Happened in Paris*). *Always in Trouble. Five of a Kind. One Wild Night. Thanks for Everything.* 1939: *What a Life! Too Busy to Work. Boy Trouble.* 1940: *Captain Caution. Wolf of New York. Money to Burn. Village Barn Dance. Third Finger, Left Hand. In Old Missouri. Charter Pilot.* 1941: *Sis Hopkins. Meet the Chump. Melody for Three. Wild Man of Borneo. Lady Scarface. World Premiere. A Dangerous Game. Mountain Moonlight. Louisiana Purchase. Bedtime Story. Meet John Doe. Texas. The Obliging Young Lady. The Last of the Duanes. Caught in the Draft. Down Mexico Way. Double Date. Hellzapoppin'.* 1942: *Blondie Goes to College. Larceny Inc. My Gal Sal. They All Kissed the Bride. Road to Morocco. Between Us Girls. Hi-Ya Chum* (GB: *Everything Happens to Us*). *Don't Get Personal. A Close Call for Ellery Queen* (GB: *A Close Call*). 1943: *The Meanest Man in the World. Coney Island. Hi Diddle Diddle. I Dood It* (GB: *By Hook or By Crook*). *His Butler's Sister. A Stranger in Town. Swing Fever. Let's Face It. Riding High* (GB: *Melody Inn*). *DuBarry Was a Lady. Phantom Lady. San Fernando Valley. Crazy House. Reveille With Beverly. Honeymoon Lodge. It Ain't Hay* (GB: *Money for Jam*). *It's a Great Life. The Mad Ghoul.* 1944: *Lake Placid Serenade. Goin' to Town. Murder in the Blue Room. Night Club Gal. Bathing Beauty. Show Business. Something for the Boys. Can't Help Singing. Reckless Age. The Singing Sheriff. Week-End Pass.* 1945: *Don't Fence Me In. Frontier Gal* (GB: *The Bride Wasn't Willing*). *GI Honeymoon. Rhapsody in Blue. You Came Along. Bring on the Girls. Incendiary Blonde. Patrick the Great.* 1946: *Badman's Territory. Sing While You Dance.* 1947: *Hoppy's Holiday. Beat the Band. Copacabana. The Devil Thumbs a Ride. The Fabulous Dorseys. Christmas Eve.* 1948: *Two Guys from Texas* (GB: *Two Texas Knights*). 1949: *Oh! You Beautiful Doll.* 1950: *Joe Palooka in Humphrey Takes a Chance* (GB: *Humphrey Takes a Chance*). *The Jackpot.* 1951: *A Wonderful Life. Belle le Grand.* 1952: *Oklahoma Annie. I Dream of Jeanie.* 1955: *How to be Very, Very Popular.*

**TOMELTY, Joseph** 1910-
Thick-set Irish actor with a bush of silver hair. He played whimsical roles in British films from 1952 to 1960, mostly as helpful old codgers in shabby waistcoats and rolled-up sleeves. Apart from this period, however, he remained largely on the stages of theatres in Ireland. Began his career as a playwright.

1946: *Odd Man Out.* 1952: *Treasure Hunt. You're Only Young Twice! The Sound Barrier* (US: *Breaking the Second Barrier*). *The Gentle Gunman.* 1953: *Meet Mr Lucifer.*

Melba. The Oracle. Hell Below Zero.
1954: Devil Girl from Mars. The Young
Lovers. Front Page Story. The Death of
Michael Turbin. Happy Ever After (US:
Tonight's the Night/O'Leary Night). Hobson's
Choice. Simba. A Prize of Gold. 1955: A Kid
for Two Farthings. Timeslip. Bedevilled. John
and Julie. 1956: Moby Dick. 1958: A Night
to Remember. Life Is a Circus. Tread Softly,
Stranger. The Captain's Table. 1959: Upstairs
and Downstairs. Hell Is a City. 1960: The Day
They Robbed the Bank of England. 1962:
Lancelot and Guinevere. 1964: The Black
Torment.

**TOWB, Harry** 1925–
Roughly-spoken, tough-looking Irish portrayer of aggressive characters in British
films. His sleepy-eyed, jut-lipped, tousle-
headed features were mostly seen as thugs
and lower ranks, but mellowed as the years
went by. Has kept very busy in television
and the theatre; still pops up occasionally in
films too.

1950: The Quiet Woman. 1951: Reluctant
Heroes. 1952: Gift Horse (US: Glory at Sea).
1954: The Sleeping Tiger. Knave of Hearts
(US: Lovers, Happy Lovers). A Prize of Gold.
1955: Above Us the Waves. The Time of His
Life. 1956: Eyewitness. Doublecross. The
March Hare. 1959: The Thirty Nine Steps.
1960: Crossroads to Crime. 1961: All Night
Long. 1963: The Scarlet Blade (US: The
Crimson Blade). 1966: The Blue Max. 1967:
30 Is a Dangerous Age, Cynthia. 1968:

Prudence and the Pill. The Bliss of Mrs
Blossom. All Neat in Black Stockings. 1971:
Carry On at Your Convenience. 1972: Some
Kind of Hero. 1973: Digby the Biggest Dog in
the World. 1974: Sex Play/The Bunny Caper.
1975: Barry Lyndon. 1978: Rosie Dixon
Night Nurse. 1983: Lassiter.

**TOWNLEY, Toke** 1912–1984
With his clown's face and high forehead
topped by a frizz of hair, Townley was
impossible to miss in a film. The son of a
vicar, this British actor was working as a
clerk in a factory when he became interested in amateur dramatics and, at 32, decided
to throw his job up to go on a stage tour.
Turning professional, he quickly found
regular employment in small roles, often as
country bumpkins and slow-witted menials.
Lost to the cinema after 1972, when he
became a regular in the long-running TV
series Emmerdale Farm, in which he played
Sam Pearson, a role which, the frizz of hair
now disappeared, he played until his death
from a heart attack.

1951: Lady Godiva Rides Again. 1952:
Meet Me Tonight. Time Gentlemen Please!
Cosh Boy (US: The Slasher). 1953: Innocents
in Paris. The Broken Horseshoe. Meet Mr
Lucifer. The Runaway Bus. 1954: Fast and
Loose. Men of Sherwood Forest. Bang! You're
Dead (US: Game of Danger). 1955: John and
Julie. Doctor at Sea. The Quatermass Experi-
ment (US: The Creeping Unknown). 1956:
Three Men in a Boat. Now and Forever.
1957: The Admirable Crichton (US: Para-
dise Lagoon). Carry On Admiral (US: The
Ship Was Loaded). 1958: Law and Disorder.
A Cry from the Streets. 1959: Look Back in
Anger. Libel. 1962: HMS Defiant (US:
Damn the Defiant!). 1963: Doctor in Distress.
1964: The Chalk Garden. 1965: The Legend
of Young Dick Turpin. 1970: The Scars of
Dracula.

**TRAVERS, Henry** (T. Heagerty) 1874–
1965
British-born actor, in America from the
turn of the century, whose long, thin mouth
only added to his benign expression. Came
to films when almost 60 and specialized in
wisdom and whimsicality, combining both

in memorable fashion as Clarence the
Angel in Capra's It's a Wonderful Life!
Died from complications following arter-
iosclerosis. Oscar nomination for Mrs
Miniver.

1933: Reunion in Vienna. My Weakness.
Another Language. The Invisible Man. 1934:
Ready for Love. The Party's Over. Death Takes
a Holiday. Born to be Bad. 1935: Escapade.
Maybe It's Love. Captain Hurricane. Four
Hours to Kill. After Office Hours. Pursuit.
Seven Keys to Baldpate. 1936: Too Many
Parents. 1938: The Sisters. 1939: Dodge City.
Remember? Dark Victory. You Can't Get
Away with Murder. On Borrowed Time.
Stanley and Livingstone. The Rains Came.
1940: Edison the Man. The Primrose Path.
Anne of Windy Poplars (GB: Anne of Windy
Willows). 1941: A Girl, a Guy and a Gob
(GB: The Navy Steps Out). Ball of Fire. I'll
Wait for You. High Sierra. The Bad Man
(GB: Two-Gun Cupid). 1942: Pierre of the
Plains. Random Harvest. Mrs Miniver. The
Moon is Down. 1943: Madame Curie.
Shadow of a Doubt. 1944: The Very Thought
of You. Dragon Seed. None Shall Escape.
1945: The Bells of St Mary's. Thrill of a
Romance. The Naughty Nineties. 1946: The
Yearling. It's a Wonderful Life! Gallant
Journey. 1947: The Flame. 1948: Beyond
Glory. 1949: The Girl from Jones Beach.

**TREACHER, Arthur**
(A. Veary) 1894–1975
Tall, dark-haired, long-faced, rather dis-
dainful British actor who came to America

in 1926 and in the next decade became Hollywood's perfect butler, complete with upper-crust voice and unflappable manner. He actually played P.G. Wodehouse's Jeeves twice but from 1940 was less busy, and began to devote more time to television and outside interests, having built up a chain of up-market fish-and-chip shops in America at the time of his death from a heart ailment.

*1929: The Battle of Paris. 1933: Alice in Wonderland. 1934: Fashions of 1934/Fashions. Madame Du Barry. Riptide. The Key. Gambling Lady. Desirable. Here Comes the Groom. The Captain Hates the Sea. Forsaking All Others. Hollywood Party. Viva Villa! Student Tour. 1935: Bordertown. David Copperfield. The Nitwits. No More Ladies. Orchids to You. The Woman in Red. Magnificent Obsession. Cardinal Richelieu. I Live My Life. Bright Lights (GB: Funny Face). Personal Maid's Secret. Curly Top. Let's Live Tonight. Remember Last Night? The Daring Young Man. Splendor. A Midsummer Night's Dream. Go Into Your Dance. Vanessa: Her Love Story. The Winning Ticket. 1936: Mister Cinderella. Hitch Hike Lady (GB: Eventful Journey). Stowaway. The Case Against Mrs Ames. Hearts Divided. Under Your Spell. Anything Goes. Satan Met a Lady. Thank You, Jeeves. Hard Luck Dame. 1937: You Can't Have Everything. Thin Ice (GB: Lovely to Look At). She Had to Eat. Heidi. Step Lively, Jeeves. 1938: Mad About Music. My Lucky Star. Up the River. Always in Trouble. 1939: Bridal Suite. The Little Princess. Barricade. 1940: Irene. Brother Rat and a Baby (GB: Baby Be Good). 1942: Star Spangled Rhythm. 1943: Forever and a Day. The Amazing Mrs Holliday. 1944: Chip Off the Old Block. In Society. National Velvet. 1945: Delightfully Dangerous. Swing Out, Sister. That's the Spirit. 1947: Slave Girl. Fun on a Weekend. 1948: The Countess of Monte Cristo. 1949: That Midnight Kiss. 1950: Love That Brute. 1964: Mary Poppins.*

America and, after World War I service, played with the Rhine Army Dramatic Company in Cologne. This cosmopolitan upbringing led to his becoming a formidable interpreter of foreign accents and, with the coming of sound, he was much in demand for the portrayal of continental detectives, including A.E.W. Mason's Inspector Hanaud and Agatha Christie's Hercule Poirot, his meticulous acting style rounding off the characterization. Later seen as affable aristocrats in more routine roles.

*1930: Escape. At the Villa Rose. The 'W' Plan. The Man from Chicago. 1931: Alibi. A Night in Montmartre. Black Coffee. 1932: The Chinese Puzzle. The Crooked Lady. A Safe Proposition. 1933: On Secret Service (US: Secret Agent). 1934: The Broken Melody. Lord Edgware Dies. Death at Broadcasting House. 1935: Inside the Room. Royal Cavalcade (US: Regal Cavalcade). Mimi. The Silent Passenger. 1936: As You Like It. La vie Parisienne. Spy 77. The Beloved Vagabond. Dusty Ermine (US: Hideout in the Alps). Rembrandt. Sabotage (US: The Woman Alone). Thunder in the City. 1937: Dark Journey. Knight Without Armour. 1939: Goodbye Mr Chips! The Lion Has Wings. 1940: The Briggs Family. Law and Disorder. Under Your Hat. Night Train to Munich (US: Night Train). 1941: The Seventh Survivor. The Big Blockade. 1942: The Young Mr Pitt. 1944: Heaven is Round the Corner. Champagne Charlie. 1946: Lisbon Story. 1947: Anna Karenina. 1948: Bonnie Prince Charlie. The Red Shoes. 1950: So Long at the Fair. 1954: Father Brown (US: The Detective). To Paris with Love. 1956: Tons of Trouble. 1957: Dangerous Exile. Seven Waves Away (US: Abandon Ship!). 1959: Horrors of the Black Museum. 1961: Konga. The Day the Earth Caught Fire. The Court Martial of Major Keller. 1962: Never Back Losers. 1965: The Alphabet Murders.*

years, was drawn to the film capital from 1941. Although appearing with some irregularity in films, he became a prolific performer on TV, at first as Slavic menaces, but in later times as scientists and professors. Died from heart failure.

*1941: The Girl from Leningrad. Out of the Fog. 1943: Mission to Moscow. Song of Russia. Cry of the Werewolf. Days of Glory. The Black Parachute. 1944: The Mummy's Ghost. In Our Time. Uncertain Glory. The Hitler Gang. 1945: A Song to Remember. Counter-Attack (GB: One Against Seven). Escape in the Fog. 1946: Crime Doctor's Manhunt. Notorious. The Return of Monte Cristo (GB: Monte Cristo's Revenge). 1947: The Crimson Key. Golden Earrings. 1948: To the Ends of the Earth. 1949: Johnny Allegro (GB: Hounded). Home in San Antone. 1950: Kim. Jet Pilot (released 1957). Spy Hunt (GB: Panther's Moon). 1951: My True Story. The Desert Fox (GB: Rommel — Desert Fox). The Lady and the Bandit (GB: Dick Turpin's Ride). 1952: Five Fingers. The Bad and the Beautiful. Ma and Pa Kettle on Vacation (GB: Ma and Pa Kettle Go to Paris). 1953: Young Bess. How to Marry a Millionaire. Desert Legion. 1954: Border River. Charge of the Lancers. The Gambler from Natchez. Her Twelve Men. 1955: The Girl in the Red Velvet Swing. 1957: Silk Stockings. The Buster Keaton Story. 1958: Fraulein. The Young Lions. 1959: The Amazing Transparent Man. 1960: Cimarron. 1961: Barabbas. It Happened in Athens. 1962: The 300 Spartans. Escapade in Florence. 1965: Von Ryan's Express. Morituri (GB: The Saboteur — Code Name 'Morituri'). 1966: Batman. 1967: Search for the Evil One.*

**TROUGHTON, Patrick** 1920-*1987*
Squat, stern-looking, dark-haired British actor who, after acting training in America, war service at sea and theatrical experience with the Old Vic, scurried from role to role on radio and TV in the post-war years. He never really settled in films, but became nationally known on British television as one of the portrayers of science-fiction time traveller Dr Who.

*1948: Hamlet. Escape. Cardboard Cavalier. Badger's Green. 1950: Treasure Island. The*

**TREVOR, Austin**
(A.T. Schilsky) 1897-1978
Neat, latterly moustachioed, tiny-mouthed, Irish-born, Swiss-educated actor in British films who made his stage debut in

**TRIESAULT, Ivan** 1900-1980
Brown-haired Estonian actor with strained, lined features and darting eyes. He came to America in 1920 to pursue his career as a ballet dancer and mime artist, but became interested in acting and, with the call for foreign types in Hollywood films of the war

*Franchise Affair. Chance of a Lifetime. The Woman with No Name (US: Her Panelled Door). Waterfront (US: Waterfront Women). 1951: White Corridors. 1954: The Black Knight. 1955: Richard III. 1957: The Curse of Frankenstein. The Moonraker. 1962: The Phantom of the Opera. 1964: The Black Torment. The Gorgon. 1966: The Viking Queen. 1967: Witchfinder-General (US: The Conqueror Worm). 1970: Scars of Dracula. 1973: Frankenstein and the Monster from Hell. 1976: The Omen. 1977: Sinbad and the Eye of the Tiger. 1978: A Hitch in Time.*

### TRUBSHAWE, Michael 1905-1985

Gangling, very tall, dark-haired British actor whose rather gloomy features were lightened by the addition of a huge handlebar moustache. A close friend of David Niven since their days together in the British Army of the late 1920s, he drifted into acting following Niven's joke of trying to mention the name Trubshawe in all his films. The real Trubshawe soon became established as hearty officer types and played around 40 film roles before his retirement in 1970.

*1950: They Were Not Divided. Dance Hall. 1951: The Lavender Hill Mob. Encore. The Magic Box. Brandy for the Parson. 1952: The Card (US: The Promoter). Meet Me Tonight. Something Money Can't Buy. The Titfield Thunderbolt. 1954: Orders Are Orders. The Rainbow Jacket. 1955: You Lucky People. 1956: Private's Progress. The Passionate Stranger (US: A Novel Affair). 1957: The Rising of the Moon. Doctor at Large. I Accuse! 1958: Gideon's Day (US: Gideon of Scotland Yard). Law and Disorder. 1960: Scent of Mystery (GB: Holiday in Spain). 1961: The Guns of Navarone. The Best of Enemies. 1962: Operation Snatch. Reach for Glory. 1963: The Mouse on the Moon. The Pink Panther. 1964: A Hard Day's Night. The Runaway. 1965: Those Magnificent Men in Their Flying Machines. The Amorous Adventures of Moll Flanders. 1968: The Sandwich Man. The Spy with a Cold Nose. 1967: Bedazzled. 1968: Salt and Pepper. A Dandy in Aspic. 1969: Monte Carlo or Bust. The Magic Christian. 1970: The Rise and Rise of Michael Rimmer.*

### TRUMAN, Ralph 1900-1977

Tall, dark-haired, genial-looking British actor with distinctive long, oval face, a superstar of radio who never quite made the same impact in films, although seen as a good variety of solid, reliable types. Once estimated to have made more than 5,000 broadcasts since his radio debut in 1925.

*1930: City of Song (GB: Farewell to Love). 1931: The Bells. 1932: Partners Please. Called Back. 1934: The Perfect Flaw. 1935: That's My Uncle. The Lad. The Case of Gabriel Perry (Wild Justice). Three Witnesses. Late Extra. The Silent Passenger. Jubilee Window. Lieutenant Daring RN. Mr Cohen Takes a Walk. Father O'Flynn. 1936: The Crimson Circle. East Meets West. The Marriage of Corbal (US: The Prisoner of Corbal). The Gay Adventure. 1937: Under the Red Robe. It's a Grand Old World. Change for a Sovereign. Dinner at the Ritz. 1938: Just Like a Woman. The Challenge. Many Tanks Mr Atkins. 1939: The Outsider. The Saint in London. 1941: The Seventh Survivor. 1942: Sabotage at Sea. 1943: The Butler's Dilemma. 1944: Henry V. 1946: Beware of Pity. Lisbon Story. The Laughing Lady. 1947: Mrs Fitzherbert. The Man Within (US: The Smugglers). 1948: Eureka Stockade (US: Massacre Hill). Oliver Twist. Mr Perrin and Mr Traill. 1949: Christopher Columbus. The Interrupted Journey. 1950: Treasure Island. The Reluctant Widow. 1951: Quo Vadis? 1953: The Master of Ballantrae. 1954: Beau Brummell. 1955: The Night My Number Came Up. The Ship That Died of Shame (US: PT Raiders). 1956: The Man Who Knew Too Much. The Long Arm (US: The Third Key). The Black Tent. Wicked As They Come. The Good Companions. Tons of Trouble. 1957: Yangtse Incident (US: Battle Hell). 1958: The Spaniard's Curse. 1959: Beyond This Place (US: Web of Evidence). 1960: Exodus. Under Ten Flags. 1961: El Cid. 1971: Nicholas and Alexandra. 1972: Lady Caroline Lamb.*

### TULLY, Tom 1896-1982

Big, beefy, brown-haired American actor with a face that looked as though he had gone many rounds in the ring rather than had a career as a reporter, served in the US

Navy and made a name for himself on Broadway. He came to films in the war years in tough-but-tender roles that suited his volcanic features and gruffly kindly personality. Nominated for an Oscar in *The Caine Mutiny*, after which he did have one leading role, as the prison warden, opposite Sylvia Sidney, in *Behind the High Wall*. Very busy on TV until the end of the 1960s, when he slowed his work rate.

*1938: Carefree. 1943: Mission to Moscow. Northern Pursuit. Destination Tokyo. 1944: Secret Command. The Sign of the Cross (new prologue to 1932 feature). The Town Went Wild. I'll Be Seeing You. 1945: The Unseen. Kiss and Tell. Adventure. 1946: The Virginian. Lady in the Lake. Till the End of Time. 1947: Intrigue. Killer McCoy. Scudda Hoo! Scudda Hay! (GB: Summer Lightning). 1948: Blood on the Moon. June Bride. Rachel and the Stranger. 1949: The Lady Takes a Sailor. A Kiss for Corliss. Illegal Entry. 1950: Where the Sidewalk Ends. Branded. Tomahawk (GB: The Battle of Powder River). 1951: The Lady and the Bandit (GB: Dick Turpin's Ride). Texas Carnival. Love is Better than Ever (GB: The Light Fantastic). Return of the Texan. 1952: Lure of the Wilderness. The Turning Point. Ruby Gentry. 1953: Trouble Along the Way. Sea of Lost Ships. The Moon is Blue. The Jazz Singer. 1954: Arrow in the Dust. The Caine Mutiny. 1955: Love Me or Leave Me. Soldier of Fortune. 1956: Behind the High Wall. 1958: Ten North Frederick. 1960: The Wackiest Ship in the Army. 1963: The Carpetbaggers. 1965: McHale's Navy Joins the Air Force. 1968: Coogan's Bluff. 1969: Any Second Now (TV). 1973: Charley Varrick. Hijack! (TV).*

### TURNBULL, John 1880-1956

Burly, bull-headed, light-haired Scottish actor in stalwart roles. Played schoolmasters, statesmen, policemen and officers for years, finally getting his first leading role at 67 in his third-last film. He was a medical student and a purser before deciding on an acting career, also dabbling in stage direction, and producing ENSA shows during World War II. A lifelong cricket fanatic, he was a Lords Taverners and MCC member and long-time president of the Stage Cricket Club.

1913: *The Good Samaritan. The Star and Crescent.* 1930: *Tons of Money.* 1931: *77 Park Lane. Rodney Steps In. Keepers of Youth. The Man at Six (US: The Gables Mystery). Lloyd of the CID (serial. US: Detective Lloyd). The Wickham Mystery.* 1932: *Murder on the Second Floor. A Voice Said Goodnight. The Midshipmaid (US: Midshipmaid Gob). Puppets of Fate (US: Wolves of the Underworld). The Iron Stair.* 1933: *The Man Outside. The Medicine Man. The Umbrella. Ask Beccles. The Private Life of Henry VIII. The Black Abbot. The Shadow. The Lady is Willing.* 1934: *The Case for the Crown. Badger's Green. Lord Edgware Dies. What Happened to Harkness. Passing Shadows. Warn London! The Girl in the Flat. It's a Cop! Tangled Evidence. The Night of the Party. The Scarlet Pimpernel. Once in a New Moon.* 1935: *The Lad. A Real Bloke. Sexton Blake and the Bearded Doctor. Radio Pirates. Black Mask. Line Engaged. Music Hath Charms. The Passing of the Third Floor Back.* 1936: *The Limping Man. Conquest of the Air (released 1940). Tudor Rose (US: Nine Days a Queen). Rembrandt. His Lordship (US: Man of Affaires). Shipmates o' Mine. Where There's a Will. Hearts of Humanity. The Amazing Quest of Ernest Bliss (US: Romance and Riches).* 1937: *It's a Grand Old World. Song of the Road. Make Up. Silver Blaze (US: Murder at the Baskervilles). Talking Feet. Saturday Night Revue. Who Killed Fen Markham?/The Angelus. Death Croons the Blues.* 1938: *The Terror. Stepping Toes. Star of the Circus (US: Hidden Menace). Night Alone. Strange Boarders.* 1939: *Inspector Hornleigh on Holiday (US: Inspector Hornleigh on Vacation). Return to Yesterday. Dead Men Are Dangerous. Spies of the Air.* 1940: *Three Silent Men. Spare a Copper.* 1941: *The Common Touch. Old Mother Riley's Circus.* 1942: *Hard Steel.* 1943: *There's a Future in It.* 1944: *Don't Take It to Heart. Fanny by Gaslight (US: Man of Evil).* 1945: *A Place of One's Own.* 1946: *Daybreak.* 1947: *The Hangman Waits. So Well Remembered.* 1950: *The Happiest Days of Your Life.*

**TYNER, Charles** 1925-

No doubt he has a full set of molars and wouldn't hurt a fly but this dark, taciturn, 'countrified' American actor looked tooth-

less and dangerous. With his familiar big black floppy hat, unkempt clothes and wad of chewing tobacco, he was just as likely to shoot the hero (or worse) before asking questions, and the only surprise about his brief flowering in the cinema was that he didn't turn up in *Deliverance.* Brought by Paul Newman from Broadway for a typically sadistic role, in *Cool Hand Luke,* he was less effective outside this image, and has been mainly back in the theatre since 1977.

1967: *Cool Hand Luke.* 1968: *The Stalking Moon.* 1969: *The Reivers. Gaily, Gaily (GB: Chicago, Chicago).* 1970: *The Moonshine War. The Cheyenne Social Club. Monte Walsh. The Traveling Executioner.* 1971: *Lawman. The Cowboys. Sometimes a Great Notion (GB: Never Give an Inch).* 1972: *Harold and Maude. Fuzz. Bad Company.* 1973: *The Emperor of the North Pole (GB: Emperor of the North). The Stone Killer.* 1974: *The Longest Yard (GB: The Mean Machine). The Midnight Man. The Greatest Gift (TV).* 1976: *Family Plot. The Young Pioneers (TV).* 1977: *Pete's Dragon. Peter Lundy and the Medicine Hat Stallion (TV).* 1979: *The Incredible Journey of Dr Meg Laurel (TV).* 1981: *Evilspeak.* 1985: *Deadly Messages (TV). Hamburger—The Motion Picture.*

**URECAL, Minerva** (M. Holzer)
1894-1966

Formidable, square-jawed, hook-nosed, raucous-voiced American actress with brown hair, a cross between Marjorie Main and Hope Emerson (both *qv*) and usually seen in roles calling for explosive emotional reaction of one kind or another, often cruelty or indignation, but sometimes turned to good comedy effect. Her character names—Death Watch Mary in *Oh, Doctor,* and Hatchet-Faced Woman in *The Doughgirls*—give a good impression of what to expect from this radio-trained player. Her stage name was sort-of-an-anagram from Eureka, California, her birthplace. She died from a heart attack.

1934: *Sadie McKee. Student Tour.* 1935: *Bonnie Scotland.* 1936: *Fury. God's Country and the Woman.* 1937: *Live, Love and Learn. Behind the Mike. Her Husband's Secretary. Mountain Justice. Love in a Bungalow. Life Begins with Love. Oh, Doctor. Exiled to Shanghai. The Go Getter. Ever Since Eve.* 1938: *Start Cheering. Lady in the Morgue (GB: Case of the Missing Blonde). Wives under Suspicion. Prison Nurse. Frontier Scout. Air Devils. She Loved a Fireman. Dramatic School. In Old Chicago.* 1939: *\*Maid to Order. Dancing Co-Ed (GB: Every Other Inch a Lady). Destry Rides Again. Golden Boy. Little Accident. Second Fiddle.* 1940: *You Can't Fool Your Wife. The Sagebrush Family Trails West. Boys of the City. No, No, Nanette. San Francisco Docks.* 1941: *Arkansas Judge (GB: False Witness). The Cowboy and the Blonde. Man at Large. Accent on Love. They Died With Their Boots On. Murder by Invitation. Never Give a Sucker an Even Break (GB: What a Man!). Billy the Kid. Skylark. Lady for a Night. Six Lessons from Madame La Zonga. The Trial of Mary Dugan.* 1942: *Sweater Girl. In Old California. Henry and Dizzy. The Corpse Vanishes. Quiet Please, Murder. My Favorite Blonde. That Other Woman. The Living Ghost. Sons of the Pioneers. Man in the Trunk.* 1943: *The Ape Man. Wagon Tracks West. Riding Through Nevada. The Powers Girl (GB: Hello, Beautiful). Kid Dynamite. Ghosts on the Loose. Hit the Ice. So This is Washington. Keep 'em Slugging. White Savage (GB: White Captive). The Song of Bernadette. Shadow of a Doubt.* 1944: *The Doughgirls. Block Busters. Music in Manhattan. Irish Eyes Are Smiling. Louisiana Hayride. Moonlight and Cactus. Crazy Knights. County Fair. The Bridge of San Luis Rey. Kismet. Man from Frisco. Mr Skeffington. And Now Tomorrow. When Strangers Marry.* 1945: *\*Alibi Baby. Who's Guilty? (serial). A Medal for Benny. A Bell for Adano. Wanderer of the Wasteland. Men in Her Diary. The Kid Sister. State Fair. Mr Muggs Rides Again. George White's Scandals. The Bells of St Mary's. Colonel Effingham's Raid (GB: Man of the Hour).* 1946: *Wake Up and Dream. Sioux City Sue. Crime Doctor's Manhunt. The Virginian. Rainbow Over Texas. The Dark Corner. Sensation Hunters. The Trap (GB: Murder at Malibu Beach). Without Reservations. California. The Bride Wore Boots. The Well-Groomed Bride. Little Miss Big (GB: The Baxter Millions).* 1947: *Saddle Pals. The Lost Moment. \*Hired*

Husband. Ladies' Man. Apache Rose. Bowery Buckaroos. Blaze of Noon. The Secret Life of Walter Mitty. 1948: Variety Time. The Snake Pit. Good Sam. Marshal of Amarillo. Secret Service Investigator. Sitting Pretty. Sundown at Santa Fé. The Noose Hangs High. Family Honeymoon. The Night Has a Thousand Eyes. Carson City Raiders. Fury at Furnace Creek. 1949: Holiday in Havana. The Lovable Cheat. Master Minds. Outcasts of the Trail. Take One False Step. Song of Surrender. Scene of the Crime. The Traveling Saleswoman. Big Jack. 1950: The Arizona Cowboy. Quicksand. My Blue Heaven. The Jackpot. Side Street. Harvey. Mister 880. 1951: Stop That Cab. *Blonde Atom Bomb. Texans Never Cry. Mask of the Avenger. 1952: Aaron Slick from Punkin Crick (GB: Marshmallow Moon). Gobs and Gals (GB: Cruising Casanovas). Anything Can Happen. Lost in Alaska. †Two Gun Marshal (TV). Oklahoma Annie. Harem Girl. 1953: The Woman They Almost Lynched. Niagara. By the Light of the Silvery Moon. She's Back on Broadway. 1955: Sudden Danger. *So You Want to Be a VP. A Man Alone. Miracle in the Rain. 1956: Crashing Las Vegas. 1960: The Adventures of Huckleberry Finn. 1962: Mr Hobbs Takes a Vacation. 1964: The Seven Faces of Dr Lao. 1965: That Funny Feeling.

†Shown in cinemas outside US

**VALK, Frederick** (Fritz Valk) 1901-1956
Imposing, hugely headed, brown-haired Czechoslovakian actor with a mouth like a gaping wound, a menacing figure in British films after his flight from Germany in the late 1930s. A favourite for Nazi roles at the onset of the 1940s, he is best remembered as the sceptical Dr Van Straaten from Ealing's chiller compendium Dead of Night. Briefly in international roles in his last years.

1939: Traitor Spy (US: The Torso Murder Mystery). 1940: Neutral Port. Gasbags. Night Train to Munich (US: Night Train). 1941: This Man is Dangerous/The Patient Vanishes. Dangerous Moonlight (US: Suicide Squadron). The Young Mr Pitt. 1942: Thunder Rock. 1944: Hotel Reserve. 1945: Dead of Night. Latin Quarter. 1947: Mrs Fitzherbert. 1948: Saraband for Dead Lovers (US:

Saraband). 1949: Dear Mr Prohack. 1951: The Magic Box. Outcast of the Islands. 1952: Top Secret (US: Mr Potts Goes to Moscow). 1953: Never Let Me Go. The Flanagan Boy (US: Bad Blonde). Albert RN (US: Break to Freedom). 1954: The Colditz Story. Secret Venture. 1955: I Am a Camera. Double Jeopardy. 1956: Magic Fire. Wicked As They Come. Zarak.

**VAN FLEET, Jo** 1919-
Incisive, fiercely dominant blonde American stage actress of waspishly attractive features who made her name by playing women older than herself. Almost entirely a stage personality, she stopped off in Hollywood just long enough to win an Academy Award for her first screen role—as James Dean's mother (at 35) in East of Eden.

1954: East of Eden. 1955: The Rose Tattoo. I'll Cry Tomorrow. Heidi (TV). 1956: The King and Four Queens. Gunfight at the OK Corral. 1958: This Angry Age/The Sea Wall. 1960: Wild River. 1967: Cool Hand Luke. 1968: I Love You, Alice B Toklas. 1969: 80 Steps to Jonah. 1971: The Gang That Couldn't Shoot Straight. 1972: The Family Rico (TV). 1976: The Tenant.

**VAN SLOAN, Edward** 1881-1964
Eagle-nosed, hawk-eyed, fair-haired American actor (once a commercial artist) who came to films with the beginning of sound, and spent much of his time in the cinema as the voice of science and reason, meddling with a motley of monsters and sporting a variety of guttural accents. Retired in 1948.

1930: Dracula. 1931: Frankenstein. 1932: Play Girl. The Infernal Machine. Man Wanted. Thunder Below. The Last Mile. Manhattan Parade. Billion Dollar Scandal. Behind the Mask. Forgotten Commandments. The Mummy. The Death Kiss. 1933: Silk Express. Trick for Trick. The Deluge. Infernal Machine. The World Gone Mad (GB: The Public Be Hanged). The Working Man. It's Great to be Alive. 1934: Murder on the Campus (GB: On the Stroke of Nine). Death Takes a Holiday. The Scarlet Empress. Manhattan Melodrama. The Crosby Case (GB: The Crosby Murder Case). The Man Who Reclaimed His Head. The Life of Vergie Winters. I'll Fix It. 1935: The Woman in Red. Grand Old Girl. The Last Days of Pompeii. The Black Room. Mills of the Gods. A Shot in the Dark. Air Hawks. Grand Exit. 1936. The Story of Louis Pasteur. Dracula's Daughter. Sins of Man. Road Gang (GB: Injustice). 1937: The Man Who Found Himself. 1938: Danger on the Air. Penitentiary. Storm over Bengal. 1939: The Phantom Creeps (serial). Honeymoon in Bali (GB: Husbands or Lovers). 1940: Abe Lincoln in Illinois (GB: Spirit of the People). The Secret Seven. The Doctor Takes a Wife. Before I Hang. 1941: Love Crazy. 1942: Valley of Hunted Men. A Man's World. 1943: Submarine Alert. Mission to Moscow. Riders of the Rio Grande. End of the Road. 1944: The Conspirators. Captain America. Wing and a Prayer. 1945. I'll Remember April. 1946: The Mask of Diijon. Betty Co-Ed (GB: The Melting Pot). 1948: A Foreign Affair. Sealed Verdict.

**VAN ZANDT, Phil(ip)** 1904-1958
Big, burly, florid, dark-haired, moustachioed Dutch actor who came to America in the late 1920s and had practically lost his accent by the time he started making Hollywood films in 1939. Often a sinister villain, especially in the war years, he played many broad comedy roles too, several of them in shorts with The Three Stooges. Died from an overdose of barbiturates at 53.

ABOVE Kent Taylor gets The Look from Minerva **Urecal**, one of the cinema's most formidable harridans, in *Four Girls in White* (1939)

BELOW Frederick **Valk** (left), Roland Culver, Mervyn Johns, Antony Baird and Googie Withers in the 'framework' story from Ealing Studios' masterly chiller compendium *Dead of Night* (1945)

1939: *Those High Gray Walls* (GB: *The Gates of Alcatraz*). 1940: *The Lady in Question.* *Boobs in Arms.* 1941: *In Old Colorado. City of Missing Girls. Ride on Vaquero. Citizen Kane. So Ends Our Night. Paris Calling. Invisible Woman.* 1942: *Sherlock Holmes and the Secret Weapon. Reunion/Reunion in France* (GB: *Mademoiselle France*). *Commandos Strike at Dawn. Wake Island. Northwest Rangers. All Through the Night. Invisible Agent. Desperate Journey. The Hard Way. Nazi Agent.* 1943: *Tarzan Triumphs. Murder on the Waterfront. Air Raid Wardens. The Deerslayer. Hangmen Also Die. Hostages. Tarzan's Desert Mystery. Old Acquaintance. Hit Parade of 1943. A Guy Named Joe. Always a Bridesmaid.* 1944: *America's Children. Call of the Jungle. The Black Parachute. The Big Noise. Swing Hostess. The Unwritten Code. The Conspirators. Dragon Seed. Till We Meet Again. House of Frankenstein.* 1945: *Outlaws of the Rockies* (GB: *A Roving Rogue*). *Sudan. Counter-Attack* (GB: *One Against Seven*). *I Love a Bandleader* (GB: *Memory for Two*). *A Thousand and One Nights. Boston Blackie's Rendezvous* (GB: *Blackie's Rendezvous*). 1946: *Night and Day. Monsieur Beaucaire. Gilda. The Avalanche. Below the Deadline. Joe Palooka, Champ. Don't Gamble with Strangers. The Bandit of Sherwood Forest. California. Somewhere in the Night. Decoy.* 1947: *Slave Girl. Last Frontier Uprising. Life with Father.* 1948: *Embraceable You. Alias Nick Beal* (GB: *The Contact Man*). *The Shanghai Chest. The Vicious Circle. Walk a Crooked Mile. The Loves of Carmen. The Night Has a Thousand Eyes. The Street with No Name.* *Fiddlers Three.* *Mummy's Dummies.* *Squareheads of the Round Table. April Showers. The Saxon Charm. The Big Clock. The Lady from Shanghai.* 1949: *The Blonde Bandit. Red, Hot and Blue.* *Fuelin' Around. The Lady Gambles. The Lone Wolf and His Lady.* 1950: *Between Midnight and Dawn. Indian Territory. The Petty Girl* (GB: *Girl of the Year*) *Dopey Dicks. Copper Canyon. Where Danger Lives. Cyrano de Bergerac. The Jackpot.* 1951: *Submarine Command. At Sword's Point* (GB: *Sons of the Musketeers*). *Ghost Chasers. Ten Tall Men. His Kind of Woman.* *Three Arabian Nuts. Mask of the Avenger. Two Dollar Bettor* (GB: *Beginner's Luck*). *Target Unknown.* 1952: *Viva Zapata! Yukon Gold. Macao. Because of You. Son of Ali Baba. Thief of Damascus. The Pride of St Louis.* 1953: *Love's a-Poppin'.* *So You Want to be a Musician. Three Sailors and a Girl.* *So You Want a Television Set.* *Spooks.* *So You Want to be an Heir. Prisoners of the Casbah. Clipped Wings. The Girl Who Had Everything. Ride Vaquero! Perilous Journey. Captain John Smith and Pocahontas* (GB: *Burning Arrows*). 1954: *Yankee Pasha. Playgirl. Gog. Three-Ring Circus. The High and the Mighty.* *So You Want to Go to a Nightclub.* *Musty Musketeers.* *Knutzy Knights.* *Scotched in Scotland.* 1955: *So You Want to be a Gladiator.* *So You Want to be a VP.* *Bedlam in Paradise. Untamed. I Cover the Underworld.*

*To Catch a Thief. The Big Combo.* 1956: *Hot Stuff. Our Miss Brooks. Around the World in 80 Days. Uranium Boom. The Pride and the Passion.* 1957: *Outer Space Jitters. The Crooked Circle. Man of a Thousand Faces. Shoot-Out at Medicine Bend. The Lonely Man.* 1958: *Fifi Blows Her Top.*

**VARCONI, Victor** (Mihaly Varkonyi) 1891-1976
Brown-haired, smoothly handsome Hungarian matinée idol of silent days in Hungary, Germany and then Hollywood. With the coming of sound, his lips tightened and he took on a more sinister look as suave continentals who often proved to be on the other side of the fence from that they first pretended. Died from a heart attack.

1913: *Sarga csiko/The Yellow Colt. Marta.* 1914: *Bank bán. Tetemtrahivas.* 1915: *Talkoas. A tanitono. Havasi Magdolna.* 1916: *Baccarat. Hotel Imperial. A riporter kiraly. Magia.* 1918: *Szent Peter esernyoje. Sapho. A skorpio. '99'. Varazskeringo.* 1919: *Jenseits von Gott und Rose.* 1921: *Die sonne Asiens.* 1922: *Herrin der Meere. Eine versunkene Welt* (*Herrin der Meere II*). *Sodom und Gomorra.* 1924: *The Dancers. Poisoned Paradise. Changing Husbands. Triumph. Feet of Clay. Worldly Goods.* 1925: *L'uomo più allegro di Vienna.* 1926: *Die Warshauer Zitadelle. The Last Days of Pompeii. The Volga Boatman. For Wives Only. Silken Shackles.* 1927: *The King of Kings. The Angel of Broadway. Fighting Love. The Forbidden Woman. Chicago. The Little Adventuress.* 1928: *Sinners' Parade. Tenth Avenue* (GB: *Hell's Kitchen*). 1929: *The Divine Lady. Eternal Love. Kult ciala.* 1930: *Captain Thunder.* 1931: *Doctors' Wives. Safe in Hell. Men in Her Life. The Black Camel.* 1932: *The Doomed Battalion. The Rebel* (and German version). 1933: *The Song You Gave Me.* 1935: *A Feather in Her Hat. Mister Dynamite. Roberta.* 1936: *Dancing Pirate. The Plainsman.* 1937: *Trouble in Morocco. Big City. Men in Exile.* 1938: *King of the Newsboys. Suez. Submarine Patrol.* 1939: *Mr Moto Takes a Vacation. The Story of Vernon and Irene Castle. Disputed Passage. Everything Happens at Night.* 1940: *The Sea Hawk.*

*Pound Foolish. Strange Cargo.* 1941: *Federal Fugitives. Forced Landing.* 1942: *My Favorite Blonde. Reap the Wild Wind. They Raid by Night.* 1943: *For Whom the Bell Tolls.* 1944: *The Story of Dr Wassell. The Hitler Gang.* 1945: *Scotland Yard Investigator.* 1947: *Unconquered. Where There's Life. Pirates of Monterey.* 1949: *Samson and Delilah.* 1950: *Once a Gentleman* (TV). 1951: *My Favorite Spy.* 1953: *The Roman Kid* (TV). 1957: *The Man Who Turned to Stone.* 1959: *Atomic Submarine.*

**VARDEN, Norma** 1898- *1989*
Tall, dignified, blonde British actress, attractive in a supercilious kind of way, who began her career as a concert pianist. She became a butt for the gags of the Aldwych farceurs, much as Margaret Dumont with the Marx Brothers, and moved with them into films in 1932. She went to Hollywood in 1939 and played largely sniffy aristocrats until her retirement at 70.

1932: *A Night Like This.* 1933: *Turkey Time. Happy.* 1934: *The Iron Duke.* 1935: *Foreign Affaires. Boys Will Be Boys. Music Hath Charms. Get Off My Foot.* 1936: *East Meets West. Where There's a Will. Windbag the Sailor.* 1937: *Wanted! The Strange Adventures of Mr Smith. Make Up. Rhythm Racketeer.* 1938: *You're the Doctor. Everything Happens to Me. Fools for Scandal.* 1939: *Home from Home. Shipyard Sally.* 1940: *The Earl of Chicago.* 1941: *Scotland Yard. Road to Zanzibar.* 1942: *Random Harvest. The Major and the Minor. We Were Dancing. Casablanca.* 1943: *Dixie. What a Woman!* (GB: *The Beautiful Cheat*). *Sherlock Holmes Faces Death.* 1944: *The White Cliffs of Dover. National Velvet.* 1945: *Bring on the Girls. Those Endearing Young Charms. Hold That Blonde. The Trouble with Women* (released 1947). 1946: *The Searching Wind. The Green Years.* 1947: *The Senator Was Indiscreet* (GB: *Mr Ashton Was Indiscreet*). *Thunder in the Valley* (GB: *Bob, Son of Battle*). *Where There's Life. Forever Amber. Ivy.* 1948: *Let's Live a Little. My Own True Love. Hollow Triumph* (GB: *The Scar*). 1949: *The Secret Garden. Adventure in Baltimore* (GB: *Bachelor Bait*). 1950: *Fancy Pants.* 1951: *Thunder on the Hill* (GB: *Bonaventure*). *Strangers on a Train.* 1952: *Les Miserables. Something for the Birds.* 1953:

Loose in London. Young Bess. Gentlemen Prefer Blondes. Elephant Walk. 1955: Jupiter's Darling. 1956: The Birds and the Bees. 1957: Witness for the Prosecution. 1958: The Buccaneer. In the Money. 1963: 13 Frightened Girls! 1965: A Very Special Favor. The Sound of Music. 1966: Door-to-Door Maniac. 1967: Doctor Dolittle. 1968: Istanbul Express (TV. GB: cinemas).

Joy. 1956: The Feminine Touch (US: The Gentle Touch). Tiger in the Smoke. The Good Companions. 1957: Sea Wife. Hell Drivers. The Surgeon's Knife. 1958: Room at the Top. Bachelor of Hearts. 1959: The Rough and the Smooth (US: Portrait of a Sinner). Horrors of the Black Museum. 1960: *Identity Unknown. 1961: Echo of Barbara. 1962: Night Without Pity.

### VARLEY, Beatrice 1896-1969

Careworn-looking, grey-eyed, brown-haired British actress whose low eyebrows, downturned mouth and narrow, wrinkled forehead consigned her for years to downtrodden women who, one felt, had perhaps come from slightly better stock than those who ill-treated them. Also played maids, housekeepers and glum aunts and was certainly memorable in one film, *Hatter's Castle*, as the cancer- and husband-ridden Mrs Brodie, a role that set the pattern for her career.

1937: Spring Handicap. Young and Innocent (US: The Girl Was Young). 1939: Poison Pen. 1941: Kipps (US: The Remarkable Mr Kipps). South American George. *Rush Hour. Hatter's Castle. 1942: Secret Mission. Talk about Jacqueline. Squadron Leader X. 1943: We Dive at Dawn. The Bells Go Down. The Man in Grey. *There's a Future in It. I'll Walk Beside You. Welcome to Britain. 1944: Bees in Paradise. Welcome Mr Washington. Love Story (US: A Lady Surrenders). *Victory Wedding. Waterloo Road. 1945: The Wicked Lady. The Agitator. The Seventh Veil. Great Day. Johnny Frenchman. 1946: Send for Paul Temple. Bedelia. 1947: The Upturned Glass. So Well Remembered. Jassy. Holiday Camp. The Little Ballerina. Master of Bankdam. My Brother Jonathan. 1948: No Room at the Inn. Good Time Girl. My Brother's Keeper. 1949: Marry Me! Adam and Evelyne (US: Adam and Evalyn). 1950: Paul Temple's Triumph. She Shall Have Murder. Gone to Earth (US revised version: The Wild Heart). 1951: Out of True. 1952: Hindle Wakes (US: Holiday Week). 1953: Melba. Death Goes to School. 1954: Bang! You're Dead (US: Game of Danger). The Black Rider. 1955: Jumping for

### VAUGHAN, Peter (P. Ohm) 1923-

British actor of massive menace, with very thin lips and small eyes set deep inside a large head topped by close-cropped fair hair. Also a useful leading actor and quite busily employed by the British cinema until the mid-1970s, when he became the powerful leading figure in some successful television series. Married/divorced actress Billie Whitelaw.

1959: Sapphire. 1960: Make Mine Mink. Village of the Damned. 1961: Two Living, One Dead. The Court Martial of Major Keller. 1962: The Punch and Judy Man. The Devil's Agent. 1963: The Horse Without a Head. The Victors. 1964: Smokescreen. 1965: Fanatic (US: Die, Die, My Darling). Rotten to the Core. 1967: The Man Outside. The Naked Runner. A Twist of Sand. 1968: The Bofors Gun. Hammerhead. 1969: Taste of Excitement. Alfred the Great. 1970: Eyewitness (US: Sudden Terror). 1971: Straw Dogs. The Pied Piper. 1972: Savage Messiah. Madigan: The Lisbon Beat (TV). 1973: The Blockhouse. Massacre in Rome. The Seaweed Children. (later Malachi's Cove). 1974: Symptoms. 11 Harrowhouse. 1975: Intimate Reflections. 1977: Valentino. 1979: Porridge. Zulu Dawn. 1981: Time Bandits. The French Lieutenant's Woman. 1982: The Missionary. 1984: The Razor's Edge. 1985: Brazil.

### VENESS, Amy 1876-1960

Fair-haired, pleasantly plump British actress with rosy cheeks and beaming face. Her housekeepers were always well-scrubbed and usually ready with a cheery word of advice. She was middle-aged when she came to sound film roles; but stayed for 25 years, having begun her long stage

career in the chorus of a George Edwardes musical show in the 1890s.

1931: Murder on the Second Floor. My Wife's Family. Hobson's Choice. Money for Nothing. 1932: Pyjamas Preferred. The Marriage Bond. Flat No.9. Let Me Explain, Dear. Self-Made Lady. Tonight's the Night. 1933: Hawleys of High Street. Their Night Out. A Southern Maid. The Love Nest. Red Wagon. 1934: The Old Curiosity Shop. Brewster's Millions. Lorna Doone. 1935: Play Up the Band. Royal Cavalcade (US: Regal Cavalcade). Drake of England (US: Drake the Pirate). Joy Ride. Did I Betray? 1936: King of Hearts. The Beloved Vagabond. Windbag the Sailor. Skylarks. The Mill on the Floss. Aren't Men Beasts! 1937: Who Killed Fen Markham?/The Angelus. The Show Goes On. 1938: Thistledown. Yellow Sands. 1939: Just William. Flying Fifty-Five. 1940: John Smith Wakes Up. 1941: This England. The Saint Meets the Tiger. 1943: Millions Like Us. The Man in Grey. 1944: Fanny by Gaslight (US: Man of Evil). Madonna of the Seven Moons. This Happy Breed. Don't Take It to Heart. The World Owes Me a Living. 1945: Don Chicago. They Were Sisters. 1946: Carnival. 1947: The Turners of Prospect Road. The Woman in the Hall. Blanche Fury. 1948: My Brother's Keeper. Good Time Girl. Oliver Twist. Here Come the Huggetts. Vote for Huggett. A Boy, a Girl and a Bike. 1949: The Huggetts Abroad. Madeleine. 1950: The Woman with No Name (US: Her Paneled Door). Chance of a Lifetime. The Astonished Heart. Portrait of Clare. 1951: Captain Horatio Hornblower RN. Tom Brown's Schooldays. The Magic Box. 1952: Angels One Five. 1954: Doctor in the House. 1955: The Woman for Joe.

### VERNO, Jerry 1895-1975

Chirpy British cockney, slightly built, who moved from music-hall comedian to minor leading roles in early low-budget British comedy-musicals, then settled down as a 'second banana' through the 1930s. His film career became distinctly spotty after 1940, although he continued to be busy in the theatre, appearing in pantomimes, musicals and straight drama, ending on the New York stage in the mid-1960s. Also well-

known as the voice of 'Shorty' in the long-running (1941-52) radio series *Taxi*. Began his career as a boy singer in 1907.

*1931: Two Crowded Hours. My Friend the King. The Beggar Student. 1932: Hotel Splendide. His Lordship. His Wife's Mother. There Goes the Bride. 1934: The Life of the Party. 1935: Lieutenant Daring RN. The 39 Steps. Royal Cavalcade (US: Regal Cavalcade). 1936: Ourselves Alone. Broken Blossoms. Gypsy Melody. Pagliacci. Sweeney Todd the Demon Barber of Fleet Street. Annie Laurie. Sensation! 1937: Farewell Again (US: Troopship). River of Unrest. Non-Stop New York. Young and Innocent (US: The Girl Was Young). 1938: Queer Cargo (US: Pirates of the Seven Seas). Oh, Boy! The Gables Mystery. Mountains o' Mourne. Old Mother Riley in Paris. Anything to Declare? *Take Cover. 1939: The Chinese Bungalow. 1940: The Girl in the News. 1941: The Common Touch. 1945: Bothered by a Beard. 1948: My Brother's Keeper. The Red Shoes. 1949: Dear Mr Prohack. 1954: The Belles of St Trinian's. 1957: After the Ball. 1963: A Place to Go.*

**VERNON, John** 1932-
Heavy-headed, light-eyed, soft-voiced Canadian actor, who has played a rare old melange of movie roles since he provided the voice of Big Brother in the original *1984* soon after completing his studies at RADA in London. He has combined prestigious Italian, Yugoslav and Canadian films with chores for Hitchcock, Don Siegel and Clint Eastwood and a considerable slice of Hollywood rubbish. Despite his good looks, films have often seen him as a frazzle-nerved villain; he has also adapted a slightly over-the-top style easily to comedy.

*1956: 1984 (voice only). 1964: Nobody Waved Goodbye. 1967: Point Blank. 1969: Trial Run (TV). Justine. Tell Them Willie Boy is Here. Topaz. 1971: Escape (TV). One More Train to Rob. Dirty Harry. 1972: Cool Million (TV). Fear is the Key. 1973: Charley Varrick. 'W'. Hunter (TV). 1974: The Questor Tapes (TV). The Virginia Hill Story (TV). Sweet Movie. Mousey (TV. GB: cinemas, as Cat and Mouse). The Black Windmill. 1975: Angela. Brannigan. The Imposter (TV). The Swiss Family Robinson (TV). Barbary Coast (TV). Matt Helm (TV). 1976: The Outlaw Josey Wales. 1977: The Uncanny. Golden Rendezvous. Una giornata particolara (GB and US: A Special Day). Mary Jane Harper Cried Last Night (TV). 1978: National Lampoon's Animal House. 1979: It Rained All Night the Day I Left. The Sacketts (TV). Crunch. 1980: Herbie Goes Bananas. 1981: Heavy Metal (voice only). Kinky Coaches and the Pom Pom Pussycats. 1982: Curtains. Airplane II The Sequel. 1984: Savage Streets. Jungle Warriors. 1985: Fraternity Vacation. Doin' Time.*

**VERNON, Richard** 1907-
Tall, distinguished-looking, moustachioed British actor of somewhat shambling gait and harassed air, often seen as magistrates, officers or (faintly seedy) aristocrats. Films have generally taken second place to his successes on television (especially the series *Upstairs, Downstairs, Edward the Seventh* and *The Duchess of Duke Street*) and in the theatre.

*1936: Conquest of the Air (released 1940). 1949: Stop Press Girl. 1958: Indiscreet. 1959: The Siege of Pinchgut. 1960: Clue of the Twisted Candle. Foxhole in Cairo. 1962: The Share-Out. Reach for Glory. Cash on Demand. 1963: The Servant. Hot Enough for June (US: Agent 8¾). Accidental Death. Just for Fun. 1964: The Yellow Rolls Royce. Goldfinger. A Hard Day's Night. Allez France! (US: The Counterfeit Constable). The Tomb of Ligeia. 1965: The Intelligence Men. The Secret of My Success. The Early Bird. 1969: One Brief Summer. 1970: Song of Norway. 1973: The Satanic Rites of Dracula. 1976: The Pink Panther Strikes Again. 1978: Sammy's Super T-Shirt. 1979: The Human Factor. 1980: Oh Heavenly Dog. 1981: Evil Under the Sun. 1982: La Traviata (voice only). Gandhi. 1985: Lady Jane. Paradise Postponed.*

**VICTOR, Charles** (C.V. Harvey) 1896-1965
Stubby, brown-haired British actor with crooked eyebrows, plum nose and battered, homely features. It's surprising to find that this portrayer of down-to-earth Londoners was a dancer in his early days (1917-1929) before turning to straight dramatic acting. From the early 1950s, he made numerous stage appearances as Alfred Doolittle in *Pygmalion* and *My Fair Lady* and took several minor leading character roles in films in the Eliot Makeham/Edmund Gwenn tradition of downtrodden little men seeking their own salvation. Also perfectly cast as Inspector Teal in *The Saint's Return*.

*1935: The 39 Steps. Me and Marlborough. 1937: The Academy Decides. Song of the Road. 1938: Stepping Toes. 1939: Hell's Cargo (US: Dangerous Cargo). Laugh It Off. Dr O'Dowd. 1940: Contraband (US: Blackout). Old Mother Riley in Society. You Will Remember. East of Piccadilly (US: The Strangler). Old Mother Riley in Business. 1941: 49th Parallel (US: The Invaders). Ships With Wings. *Rush Hour. The Common Touch. This England. Atlantic Ferry (US: Sons of the Sea). He Found a Star. The Saint Meets the Tiger. *You're Telling Me. Love on the Dole. Breach of Promise (US: Adventure in Blackmail). They Flew Alone (US: Wings and the Woman). 1942: Seven Days' Leave. Those Kids from Town. The Missing Million. The Foreman Went to France. (US: Somewhere in France). Next of Kin. The Peterville Diamond. Lady from Lisbon. Squadron Leader X. 1943: Undercover (US: Underground Guerillas). The Silver Fleet. When We Are Married.*

Escape to Danger. Rhythm Serenade. My Learned Friend. The Shipbuilders. They Met in the Dark. San Demetrio, London. The Bells Go Down. 1944: It Happened One Sunday. 1945: The Man from Morocco. The Way to the Stars (US: Johnny in the Clouds). I Live in Grosvenor Square (US: A Yank in London). Caesar and Cleopatra. The Rake's Progress (US: Notorious Gentleman). 1946: Woman to Woman. Gaiety George (US: Showtime). While the Sun Shines. This Man is Mine! The Magic Bow. Meet Me at Dawn. 1947: While I Live. Green Fingers. Broken Journey. Temptation Harbour. 1948: The Calendar. Vote for Huggett. Fools Rush In. 1949: Landfall. The Cure for Love. 1950: Waterfront (US: Waterfront Women). The Elusive Pimpernel (US: The Fighting Pimpernel). The Woman in Question (US: Five Angles on Murder). 1951: The Magic Box. Calling Bulldog Drummond. The Galloping Major. Encore. 1952: Something Money Can't Buy. Made in Heaven. The Frightened Man. The Ringer. Appointment in London. Those People Next Door. 1953: Street Corner (US: Both Sides of the Law). The Girl on the Pier. Meet Mr Lucifer. The Love Lottery. The Saint's Return (US: The Saint's Girl Friday). 1954: Fast and Loose. The Rainbow Jacket. For Better, For Worse (US: Cocktails in the Kitchen). The Embezzler. 1955: Police Dog. Value for Money. An Alligator Named Daisy. Dial 999 (US: The Way Out). Now and Forever. 1956: The Extra Day. Charley Moon. Eyewitness. Tiger in the Smoke. Home and Away. The Prince and the Showgirl. 1957: There's Always a Thursday. After the Ball. 1966: The Wrong Box.

**VILLIERS, James** 1933–
Tall, dark, snooty-looking British actor with plummy voice, long typecast in snobby, arrogant or obnoxious roles, but now beginning to move into more interesting characters. Also plays villains, both sinister and slightly comic. Began his career at 21 in a London West End production of Toad of Toad Hall.

1960: The Entertainer. 1961: Clue of the New Pin. The Damned (US: These Are the Damned). Petticoat Pirates. 1962: Operation Snatch. Eva. 1963: Bomb in the High Street (shown 1961). Murder at the Gallop. Nothing But the Best. Father Came Too. Girl in the Headlines (US: The Model Murder Case). 1964: King and Country. Daylight Robbery. 1965: The Alphabet Murders. Repulsion. You Must Be Joking! The Nanny. 1966: The Wrong Box. 1967: Half a Sixpence. 1968: Otley. The Touchables. 1969: A Nice Girl Like Me. Some Girls Do. 1970: Blood from the Mummy's Tomb. 1971: The Ruling Class. 1972: Asylum. The Amazing Mr Blunden. 1975: The Double Kill (TV). 1976: Joseph Andrews. Seven Nights in Japan. 1977: Spectre (TV). 1979: Saint Jack. 1981: For Your Eyes Only. 1983: Mantrap. 1984: Under the Volcano.

**VINSON, Helen** (H. Rulfs) 1907–
Attractive American actress with fluffy blonde hair, mean lips and long, pencilled eyebrows. In Hollywood from 1932, she quickly became the 'other woman' par excellence, although she fought against the typecasting and in the mid-1930s went to Britain in search of a wider range of leading roles. She left films in the post-war years to concentrate on a stage career. Briefly (second of three husbands) married to British tennis star Fred Perry in 1935.

1932: They Call It Sin (GB: The Way of Life). Lawyer Man. Jewel Robbery. Two Against the World. The Crash. I Am a Fugitive from a Chain Gang. Second-Hand Wife (GB: The Illegal Divorce). 1933: As Husbands Go. The Power and the Glory. Midnight Club. Little Giant. Grand Slam. The Kennel Murder Case. 1934: The Gift of Gab. Broadway Bill (GB: Strictly Confidential). Let's Try Again. The Life of Vergie Winters. The Captain Hates the Sea. 1935: The Wedding Night. A Notorious Gentleman. Private Worlds. Age of Indiscretion. The Tunnel (US: Transatlantic Tunnel). King of the Damned. 1936: Love in Exile. Reunion (GB: Hearts in Reunion). 1937: Vogues of 1938. Live, Love and Learn. 1939: In Name Only. 1940: The Bowery Boy. Curtain Call. Enemy Agent (GB: Secret Enemy). Married and in Love. Torrid Zone. Beyond Tomorrow. 1941: Nothing But the Truth. 1944: Chip Off the Old Block. The Lady and the Monster. The Thin Man Goes Home. Are These Our Parents? (GB: They Are Guilty).

**WAKEFIELD, Hugh** 1888–1971
Light-haired, moustachioed, tall, dandified British actor, often in monocled, aristocratic or regal roles. He began on stage as a boy actor of 10 and continued his career unbroken in the theatre and cinema until his retirement in 1954. Films saw the most of him in the 1930s, when he played character leads and roguish rakes in some light-hearted entertainments.

1930: City of Song (US: Farewell to Love). 1931: The Sport of Kings. The Man They Could Not Arrest. 1932: Aren't We All? Life Goes On. Women Who Play. 1933: The Crime at Blossom's. King of the Ritz. The Fortunate Fool. 1934: Luck of a Sailor. My Heart Is Calling. Lady in Danger. The Man Who Knew Too Much. 1935: Marry the Girl. 18 Minutes. No Monkey Business. Runaway Ladies. 1936: The Improper Duchess. The Crimson Circle. Forget-Me-Not (US: Forever Yours). The Interrupted Honeymoon. It's You I Want. The Limping Man. Dreams Come True. 1937: The Live Wire. The Street Singer. Death Croons the Blues. 1938: Make It Three. 1945: Journey Together. 1948: Blithe Spirit. One Night With You. 1951: No Highway (US: No Highway in the Sky). 1952: Love's a Luxury (US: The Caretaker's Daughter). 1953: The Million Pound Note (US: Man With a Million).

**WALBURN, Raymond** 1887–1969
Round-faced, brown-haired, moustachioed, pop-eyed American actor, a favourite comic

character star of the 1930s and 1940s, often seen as phony military types and jovial confidence tricksters, and constantly surprised at the pricking of his own pomposity or bogusness. Excelled in the low-budget 'Henry' comedies of the late 1940s and early 1950s. A most likeable rogue.

1916: The Scarlet Runner (serial). 1929: The Laughing Lady. 1934: Lady by Choice. The Great Flirtation. Broadway Bill (GB: Strictly Confidential). The Defense Rests. Jealousy. The Count of Monte Cristo. 1935: Mills of the Gods. Thanks a Million. It's a Small World. She Married Her Boss. Society Doctor. Death Flies East. I'll Love You Always. Welcome Home. Redheads on Parade. 1936: The Lone Wolf Returns. The Great Ziegfeld. They Met in a Taxi. The King Steps Out. Craig's Wife. Mr Deeds Goes to Town. Absolute Quiet. Three Wise Guys. Mr Cinderella. Born to Dance. 1937: High, Wide and Handsome. Breezing Home. Thin Ice (GB: Lovely to Look At). Murder in Greenwich Village. Let's Get Married. It Can't Last Forever. Broadway Melody of 1938. 1938: The Battle of Broadway. Sweethearts. Professor Beware! Gateway. Start Cheering. The Under-Pup. Let Freedom Ring. It Could Happen to You. Heaven With a Barbed-Wire Fence. Eternally Yours. 1940: Flowing Gold. Dark Command. Christmas in July. San Francisco Docks. Millionaires in Prison. Third Finger, Left Hand. 1941: Bachelor Daddy. Kiss the Boys Goodbye. Rise and Shine. Louisiana Purchase. Puddin' Head (GB: Judy Goes to Town). Confirm or Deny. 1942: The Man in the Trunk. 1943: Let's Face It. Dixie. Lady Bodyguard. The Desperadoes. Dixie Dugan. 1944: Heavenly Days. And the Angels Sing. Music in Manhattan. Hail the Conquering Hero. 1945: I'll Tell the World. The Cheaters. Honeymoon Ahead. 1946: Breakfast in Hollywood (GB: The Mad Hatter). Rendezvous With Annie. The Plainsman and the Lady. Lover Come Back. The Affairs of Geraldine. The Sin of Harold Diddlebock (later and GB: Mad Wednesday). 1948: State of the Union (GB: The World and His Wife). 1949: Leave It to Henry. Red, Hot and Blue. Riding High. Henry the Rainmaker. 1950: Key to the City. Father Makes Good. Short Grass. Father's Wild Game. 1951: Excuse My Dust. Father Takes the Air.

Golden Girl. 1953: She Couldn't Say No (GB: Beautiful But Dangerous). 1955: The Spoilers.

**WALSH, M. Emmet** 1935-
Bulky American small-part player with large face and thinning gingery hair, a kind of more serious-looking Roy Kinnear (qv). Despite graduating from college with a degree in business administration, Walsh was drawn to acting, although he found himself cast in mostly very minor beastly roles as bullying sheriffs and interfering officials, following his arrival in Hollywood in 1968. Recently 'hot' after his excellent portrayal of a seedy amoral private eye in Blood Simple, he is now beginning to command juicier roles.

1969: Stiletto. Midnight Cowboy. End of the Road. Alice's Restaurant. 1970: Loving. The Traveling Executioner. Cold Turkey. Little Big Man. 1971: They Might Be Giants. Escape from the Planet of the Apes. 1972: Get to Know Your Rabbit. What's Up, Doc! 1973: Kid Blue/Dime Box. Serpico. 1974: The Gambler (TV). Sara T: Portrait of a Teenage Alcoholic (TV). 1975: The Prisoner of Second Avenue. At Long Last Love. Crime Club (TV). 1976: Bound for Glory. Mikey and Nicky. The Invasion of Johnson County (TV). 1977: Straight Time. Slap Shot. Airport 1977. Red Alert (TV). Superdome (TV). 1978: A Question of Guilt (TV). 1979: Mrs R's Daughter (TV). No Other Love (TV). The Gift (TV). The Jerk. The Fish That Saved Pittsburgh. 1980: Brubaker. Raise the Titanic. Ordinary People. Hellinger's Law (TV). High Noon Part Two (TV). City in Fear/Panic on Page One (TV). 1981: Back Roads. Reds. Fast-Walking. Skag/The Wildcatters (TV). 1982: The Escape Artist. Cannery Row. Blade Runner. 1983: Silkwood. Scandalous. Night Partners (TV). 1984: The Pope of Greenwich Village. Blood Simple. Missing in Action. Grandview USA. Courage. 1985: Fletch. The Best of Times.

**WALSTON, Ray** 1917- 2001
Slight, energetic American actor whose film roles have been few but almost always ripe and juicy. A theatre player until the early 1950s, the light-haired, fizzy Walston was older than he looked and began to appear

like a wizened hobgoblin with the advent of the 1970s. Also very popular as the extra-terrestrial visitor in TV's long-running My Favorite Martian. Still around in spiky cameos.

1957: Kiss Them for Me. 1958: Damn Yankees (GB: What Lola Wants). South Pacific. Shadows Tremble (TV). 1959: Say One for Me. 1960: The Apartment. Portrait in Black. Tall Story. 1962: Convicts Four (GB: Reprieve!). 1963: Who's Minding the Store. Wives and Lovers. 1964: Kiss Me, Stupid. 1967: Caprice. 1969: Paint Your Wagon. 1970: Viva Max! 1973: The Sting. 1976: Silver Streak. 1977: The Happy Hooker Goes to Washington. 1978: Institute for Revenge (TV). 1981: Galaxy of Terror. O'Hara's Wife. 1982: Fast Times at Ridgemont High (GB: Fast Times). 1983: The Jerk, Too (TV). 1984: Johnny Dangerously.

**WALTERS, Hal** 1892-1940
Hook-nosed, fast-talking, dark-haired British comedian and comic actor, a whipper-snapper of a man fond of loud suits and an ideal foil for Max Miller (and other British comedians) in crazy, rough-edged comedies of the 1930s. After running up 55 films in nine years, Walters was killed by a bomb in a wartime air raid.

1931: Tonight's the Night — Pass It On. 1932: Come into My Parlour. Old Spanish Customers. On the Air. Little Fella. The River House Ghost. Women Are That Way. 1933: Great Stuff. Yes, Madam. Going Straight. That's My Wife. Long Live the King. I'll Stick to You. Enemy of the Police. Strike it Rich. Marooned. 1934: The Man I Want. Bagged. The Perfect Flaw. Virginia's Husband. Crazy People. Big Business. 1935: Department Store. Death on the Set (US: Murder on the Set). A Fire Has Been Arranged. The Right Age to Marry. Blue Smoke. Can You Hear Me Mother? Don't Rush Me! 1936: The Interrupted Honeymoon. Where There's a Will. Apron Fools. Educated Evans. 1937: The Vulture. Pearls Bring Tears. Song of the Forge. The Strange Adventures of Mr Smith. Keep Fit. Little Miss Somebody. Televison Talent. 1938: The Viper. Double or Quits. Meet Mr Penny. Thank Evans. Everything Happens to Me. Ghost Tales Retold (series). 1939: The

ABOVE Hal **Walters** (left) usually played fast-talking men on the make. Here he is competing in loudness of ties with Max Miller in the 1938 British comedy *Thank Evans*

BELOW Diplomat Thorley **Walters** samples the local delicacies in the Boulting brothers' 1958 comedy *Carlton-Browne of the FO*

*Good Old Days.* \**Pandamonium. Hoots Mon!
The Four Feathers. Spies of the Air. 1940:
They Came by Night. That's the Ticket.*

## WALTERS, Thorley 1913- *1991*

Brown-haired British actor with square face
and trim moustache, angry-looking in an
ineffectual way, often seen in British
comedy films as aggressive buffoons or
ministerial bunglers. The son of a priest, he
began in Shakespearian roles and essayed
the occasional light leading role in films.
But he was seen in increasingly comic and
light-hearted parts on stage, and his cinema
career as a featured player took off in the
mid-1950s with his association with the
Boulting Brothers and Launder-Gilliat
teams, as he frowned alternately in suspicion and bemusement at the misfortunes
that befell him.

*1934: The Love Test. His Majesty and Co.
Once in a New Moon. 1939: Trunk Crime.
Secret Journey (US: Among Human Wolves).
1940: Gentleman of Venture (US: It Hap-
pened to One Man). 1944: Medal for the
General. 1945: Waltz Time. They Were
Sisters. 1955: Josephine and Men. 1956: You
Can't Escape. Who Done It? Private's Progress.
The Baby and the Battleship. The Passionate
Stranger (US: A Novel Affair). 1957:
Second Fiddle. The Birthday Present. Blue
Murder at St Trinian's. Happy Is the Bride!
The Truth About Women. 1958: A Lady
Mislaid. Carlton-Browne of the FO (US: Man
in a Cocked Hat). 1959: Don't Panic Chaps!
1960: Two Way Stretch. Suspect (US: The
Risk). A French Mistress. The Pure Hell of St
Trinian's. 1961: Invasion Quartet. Petticoat
Pirates. Murder She Said. 1962: The Phan-
tom of the Opera. 1963: Sherlock Holmes und
das Halsband des Todes (GB and US:
Sherlock Holmes and the Deadly Necklace).
Ring of Spies. Heavens Above! 1964: The
Earth Dies Screaming. A Home of Your Own.
1965: Joey Boy. Rotten to the Core. A Study in
Terror (US: Fog). The Psychopath. 1966:
Dracula Prince of Darkness. The Family Way.
The Wrong Box. 1967: Frankenstein Created
Woman. 1968: Twisted Nerve. Crooks and
Coronets (US: Sophie's Place). The Last Shot
You Hear. 1969: Oh! What a Lovely War.
Frankenstein Must Be Destroyed. 1970:
Bartleby. The Man Who Haunted Himself.
Trog. There's a Girl in My Soup. 1971:
Vampire Circus. Mr Forbush and the Penguins
(US: Cry of the Penguins). Young Winston.
1973: Death in Small Doses (TV). Soft Beds,
Hard Battles (US: Undercovers Hero). 1975:
The Adventure of Sherlock Holmes' Smarter
Brother. 1977: The People That Time Forgot.
1980: The Wildcats of St Trinian's. 1983:
The Sign of Four. 1984: The Little Drummer
Girl.*

## WARD, Michael 1915-

Thin, long-faced British actor with light
crinkly hair, often in fey or sourpuss roles
and a master of flappability. Usually

impeccably dressed, his characters were the
inevitable targets for 'idiot' comedians,
especially Norman Wisdom, with whom he
appeared five times. He played a number of
straight roles, but comedy gradually took
over his career. Once took three years off
acting and became a qualified statistician.

*1947: An Ideal Husband. 1948: Sleeping
Car to Trieste. 1949: Hi Jinks in Society. Stop
Press Girl. Helter Skelter. Marry Me! 1950:
What the Butler Saw. So Long at the Fair.
Tony Draws a Horse. Trio. Pool of London. No
Trace. Lilli Marlene. 1951: Tom Brown's
Schooldays. Cheer the Brave. Chelsea Story.
Appointment With Venus (US: Island Res-
cue). The Galloping Major. Whispering Smith
Hits London (US: Whispering Smith versus
Scotland Yard). 1952: Tall Headlines. The
Happy Family (US: Mr Lord Says No). The
Frightened Man. 13 East Street. Tread Softly.
1953: The Fake. Street Corner (US: Both
Sides of the Law). Trouble in Store. The Love
Lottery. 1955: Man of the Moment. Josephine
and Men. Lost (US: Tears for Simon).
Jumping for Joy. 1956: Private's Progress.
The Intimate Stranger (US: Finger of Guilt).
Up in the World. Brothers in Law. 1958:
Carlton-Browne of the FO (US: Man in a
Cocked Hat). 1959: Just My Luck. The Ugly
Duckling. I'm All Right, Jack. The Rough and
the Smooth (US: Portrait of a Sinner). Follow
a Star. 1960: Doctor in Love. 1961: Mary
Had a Little... A Pair of Briefs. Carry On
Regardless. 1963: Father Came Too. Carry
On Cabby. 1964: Carry On Cleo. 1965: The
Big Job. 1966: Carry On Screaming. Don't
Lose Your Head. 1967: \*Ouch! Smashing
Time. 1973: Frankenstein and the Monster
from Hell. 1974: Man About the House. \*The
Walker. 1978: Revenge of the Pink Panther.*

## WARDEN, Jack 1920-

Ginger-haired, ruddy-complexioned, ebullient American actor whose forceful personality and barking tones first brought him
to the fore as one of the jurors in *Twelve
Angry Men*. He was a top featured player
after that, often third or fourth on the cast
list, but rarely the villain. More recently he
has taken to playing eccentrics, sometimes
apoplectic senior officials. He was unlucky
in the 1970s when two good TV 'pilots'

failed to lead to successful series. Nominated for Oscars in *Shampoo* and *Heaven
Can Wait*.

*1950: The Asphalt Jungle. USS Teakettle
(later You're in the Navy Now). 1951: The
Frogmen. The Man With My Face. 1952: Red
Ball Express. 1953: From Here to Eternity.
1956: Edge of the City (GB: A Man Is Ten
Feet Tall). 1957: Twelve Angry Men. The
Bachelor Party. Darby's Rangers (GB: The
Young Invaders). 1958: Run Silent, Run
Deep. 1959: The Sound and the Fury. That
Kind of Woman. 1960: Wake Me When It's
Over. The Lawbreakers (TV. GB: cinemas).
1961: Escape from Zahrain. 1963: Dono-
van's Reef. 1964: The Thin Red Line. 1965:
Mirage. 1966: Blindfold. Fame Is the Name of
the Game (TV). 1968: Bye Bye Braverman.
1970: The Sporting Club. Wheeler and
Murdoch (TV). 1971: Man on a String (TV).
Summertree. Brian's Song (TV). Who Is
Harry Kellerman and Why Is He Saying
These Terrible Things About Me? Welcome to
the Club. The Face of Fear (TV). 1972: Lt
Schuster's Wife (TV). 1973: Remember
When? (TV). What's a Nice Girl Like You?...
(TV). The Man Who Loved Cat Dancing.
Billy Two Hats. 1974: The Godchild (TV).
The Apprenticeship of Duddy Kravitz. 1975:
Journey from Darkness (TV). Shampoo. Jigsaw
John (TV). 1976: Raid on Entebbe (TV. GB:
cinemas). All the President's Men. †Voyage of
the Damned. 1977: The White Buffalo. 1978:
Death on the Nile. Heaven Can Wait. The
Champ. 1979: ...and Justice for All. Beyond the
Poseidon Adventure. Being There. Dreamer.
Topper (TV). 1980: Used Cars. A Private
Battle (TV). Chu Chu and the Philly Flash.
Carbon Copy. So Fine. The Great Muppet
Caper. 1982: The Verdict. 1983: Helen and
Teacher. Hobson's Choice (TV). Crackers.
1984: Aviator.*

†Scenes deleted from final release print.

## WARNER, H. B.

(Henry Byron Warner-Lickford)
1876-1958
Tall, skeletal, dignified, light-haired, moustachioed British actor who went to Hollywood in 1914 and spent more than 40 years
in films playing men whose opinion had to
be respected, even when, as was often the

case, they were under pressure. He kept acting almost to the end of his long life. Nominated for an Academy Award for his performance in the 1937 version of *Lost Horizon*.

*1900: English Nell. 1914: The Ghost Breaker. Your Ghost and Mine. Lost Paradise. 1915: The Beggar of Cawnpore. The Raiders. 1916: The Vagabond Prince. The Market of Vain Desire. The House of 1,000 Candles. Shell 43. A Wife's Sacrifice. 1917: The Danger Trail. The Seven Deadly Sins. God's Man. 1919: The Man Who Turned White. A Fugitive from Matrimony. Uncharted Channels. For a Woman's Honor. The Pagan God. Maruja. 1920: Grey Wolf's Ghost. Hunting Shadows. Once a Plumber. Dice of Destiny. The White Dove. One Hour Before Dawn. Felix O'Day. Below the Deadline. 1921: When We Were Twenty-One. 1923: Zaza. 1924: Is Love Everything? The Lone Fighter. The Dark Swan. 1926: The Temptress. Silence. Whispering Smith. 1927: King of Kings. French Dressing (GB: Lessons for Wives). Sorrell and Son. 1928: Conquest. The Romance of a Rogue. The Naughty Duchess. Man-Made Woman. 1929: The Doctor's Secret. The Divine Lady. The Gamblers. The Show of Shows. The Green Goddess. The Trial of Mary Dugan. The Argyle Case. Stark Mad. Tiger Rose. 1930: The Second Floor Mystery. Wedding Rings. On Your Back. The Princess and the Plumber. The Furies. Wild Company. Liliom. 1931: Woman of Experience. Expensive Women. Five Star Final. The Reckless Hour. 1932: A Woman Commands. The Menace. Charlie Chan's Chance. The Crusader. The Son-Daughter. Tom Brown of Culver. Cross Examination. Unholy Love (GB: Deceit). The Phantom of Crestwood. 1933: Sorrell and Son (GB remake). Supernatural. Jennie Gerhardt. Justice Takes a Holiday. Christopher Bean (GB: The Late Christopher Bean). 1934: Night Alarm. Grand Canary. Behold My Wife. In Old Santa Fé. 1935: Born to Gamble. A Tale of Two Cities. 1936: Moonlight Murder. The Garden Murder Case. Blackmailer. Rose of the Rancho. Mr Deeds Goes to Town. Along Came Love. 1937: Our Fighting Navy (US: Torpedoed!). Victoria the Great. Lost Horizon. 1938: The Toy Wife (GB: Frou Frou). The Adventures of Marco Polo. Bulldog Drummond in Africa. You Can't Take It With You. Girl of the Golden West. Kidnapped. Army Girl (GB: The Last of the Cavalry). 1939: Arrest Bulldog Drummond! The Rains Came. Bulldog Drummond's Secret Police. The Gracie Allen Murder Case. Bulldog Drummond's Bride. Nurse Edith Cavell. Mr Smith Goes to Washington. Let Freedom Ring. 1940: New Moon. 1941: All That Money Can Buy/The Devil and Daniel Webster. Ellery Queen and the Perfect Crime (GB: The Perfect Crime). City of Missing Girls. Topper Returns. The Corsican Brothers. South of Tahiti (GB: White Savage). 1942: Crossroads. A Yank in Libya. Boss of Big Town. Hitler's Children. 1943: Woman in Bondage. 1944: Faces in the Fog. Action in Arabia. Enemy of Women. 1945: Captain Tugboat Annie. Rogues' Gallery. 1946: Gentleman Joe Palooka. Strange Impersonation. It's a Wonderful Life! 1947: Driftwood. The High Wall. Bulldog Drummond Strikes Back. 1948: The Prince of Thieves. The Judge Steps Out (GB: Indian Summer). 1949: El Paso. Hellfire. 1950: Sunset Boulevard. 1951: The First Legion. Journey into Light. Savage Drums. Here Comes the Groom. 1956: The Ten Commandments. 1957: Darby's Rangers (GB: The Young Invaders).*

**WARREN, C. Denier** 1889-1971

Tubby, balding American-born comedy actor in British films—often cast as explosive and excitable Americans in spite of the fact that he lived mainly in Britain from the age of eight. Busy in character roles through the major part of the 1930s, he then devoted himself to writing and appearing in the popular wartime 'Kentucky Minstrels' programmes on radio. Still popped up occasionally in films, but semi-retired after 1961. Often billed in his earlier films without the 'C', which stood for Charles.

*1932: Let Me Explain, Dear. 1933: Counsel's Opinion. Prince of Arcadia. Channel Crossing. 1934: The Great Defender. Two Hearts in Waltztime. Music Hall. Kentucky Minstrels. 1935: Temptation. A Fire Has Been Arranged. The Small Man. The Clairvoyant. Heat Wave. A Real Bloke. Be Careful, Mr Smith. Charing Cross Road. Heart's Desire. Birds of a Feather. 1936: A Star Fell from Heaven. They Didn't Know. The Big Noise. It's in the Bag. Spy of Napoleon. The Beloved Vagabond. Everybody Dance. You Must Get Married. Café Colette (US: Danger in Paris). 1937: Good Morning, Boys. Cotton Queen. Song of the Forge. Rose of Tralee. Keep Fit. Me and My Pal. A Romance in Flanders (US: Lost on the Western Front). Change for a Sovereign. Little Miss Somebody. Who Killed John Savage? Melody and Romance. Captain's Orders. Second Best Bed. 1938: Make It Three. Strange Boarders. Kicking the Moon Around (US: The Playboy). Break the News. Old Mother Riley in Paris. My Irish Molly (US: Little Miss Molly). The Challenge. Take Off That Hat. It's in the Air (US: George Takes the Air). 1939: Trouble Brewing. The Body Vanishes. Come On George. A Gentleman's Gentleman. Secret Journey (US: Among Human Wolves). 1942: We'll Smile Again. 1943: The Hundred Pound Window. The Shipbuilders. 1944: Twilight Hour. Kiss the Bride Goodbye. Candles at Nine. 1945: Don Chicago. 1949: Old Mother Riley's New Venture. 1950: Old Mother Riley Headmistress. The Dragon of Pendragon Castle. 1953: Alf's Baby. House of Blackmail. 1955: Handcuffs London. 1960: A Taste of Money. Escort for Hire. Bluebeard's Ten Honeymoons. 1961: Return of a Stranger. So Evil, So Young. The Silent Invasion. Lolita. Two Wives at One Wedding. The Treasure of Monte Cristo (US: The Secret of Monte Cristo). 1969: The Adding Machine.*

**WARREN, Kenneth J.** 1926-1973

Burly, balding (later shaven-headed) Australian actor in British films, frequently playing aggressive, tough-guy roles. In private life an enthusiastic gourmet cook and talented painter, he made his name in stage productions of *Summer of the Seventeenth Doll*, and stayed in Britain from 1959 after being in the Australian production of the play there.

*1959: I'm All Right, Jack. A Woman's Temptation. The Siege of Pinchgut. The Navy Lark. 1960: The Criminal (US: The Concrete Jungle). Danger Tomorrow. 1961: On the Fiddle (US: Operation Snafu). Strip Tease Murder. Part Time Wife. 1962: The Boys. 1963: The Small World of Sammy Lee. The*

*Informers.* *The Invisible Asset. 1965: A High Wind in Jamaica. 1966: The 25th Hour. 1967: The Double Man. 1968: Decline and Fall...of a Birdwatcher! 1970: Leo the Last. I, Monster. The Revolutionary. 1971: Demons of the Mind. 1972: The Creeping Flesh. 1973: Digby the Biggest Dog in the World. 1974: S\*P\*Y\*S.*

**WARWICK, John** (J. Beattie) 1905-1972
Australian actor with fuzzy brown hair and vindictive eyes who starred in and produced films in his native country before coming to Britain in 1936. Here the shiftiness in his makeup seemed to pigeonhole him as a natural successor to Donald Calthrop (*qv*) and he played an equal number of good and bad guys before war service disrupted the pattern of his career. In post-war years, he was seen in much smaller roles, often as policemen, before returning to Australia in the mid-1960s, dying there from a heart attack.

*1933: In the Wake of the Bounty. The Squatter's Daughter. 1934: The Silence of Dean Maitland. 1935: Down on the Farm. 1936: Orphan of the Wilderness. Find the Lady. 1937: Lucky Jade. Double Alibi. Catch as Catch Can. When the Poppies Bloom Again. 21 Days (released 1940. US: 21 Days Together). Passenger to London. The Ticket-of-Leave Man. Riding High. A Yank at Oxford. 1938: John Halifax — Gentleman. This Man Is News. Bad Boy. 1939: Me and My Pal. Dead Men Are Dangerous. The Mind of Mr Reeder (US: The Mysterious Mr Reeder). The Face at the Window. Flying Fifty-Five. All at Sea. 1940: The Case of the Frightened Lady (US: The Frightened Lady). Spare a Copper. 1941: Danny Boy. My Wife's Family. 1942: The Missing Million. The Day Will Dawn. Talk About Jacqueline. 1946: Woman to Woman. 1947: Dancing With Crime. Teheran (US: The Plot to Kill Roosevelt). While I Live. 1950: The Franchise Affair. 1951: The Lavender Hill Mob. 1952: Never Look Back. Circumstantial Evidence. Escape Route (US: I'll Get You). 1953: Thought to Kill. The Accused. Street Corner (US: Both Sides of the Law). Trouble in Store. 1954: Up to His Neck. The Red Dress. Bang! You're Dead (US: Game of Danger). Dangerous Voyage. 1955:*

*Contraband Spain. One Just Man.* *The Mysterious Bullet. 1956: The Long Arm (US: The Third Key). 1957: *The Tyburn Case. Just My Luck. 1958: *Print of Death. *The Crossroad Gallows. Law and Disorder. The Square Peg. 1959: The Desperate Man. Horrors of the Black Museum. Murder at Site Three. 1961: The Fourth Square. Go to Blazes. 1969: Adam's Woman.*

**WASHBOURNE, Mona** 1903- *1988*
Brown-haired, round-faced, dumpy, like-able British actress who played 'dear old things' from her forties, mostly on stage but with a good sprinkling of films thrown in, with characters that could be forthright or querulous. Her two most striking film performances—in *Night Must Fall*, as the pathetic Mrs Bramson, and in *Stevie*, as the 'lion Aunt' (the latter winning her a British Oscar)—were both from plays. Originally trained as a concert pianist.

*1948: Once Upon a Dream. The Winslow Boy. 1949: Maytime in Mayfair. Adam and Evelyne (US: Adam and Evalyn). 1950: Double Confession. Dark Interval. 1952: The Gambler and the Lady. Wide Boy. 1953: Johnny on the Run. Star of My Night. 1954: Adventure in the Hopfields. Doctor in the House. Child's Play. To Dorothy a Son (US: Cash On Delivery). The Yellow Robe. 1955: Cast a Dark Shadow. Lost (US: Tears for Simon). Triple Blackmail. John and Julie. Count of Twelve. The Diamond Expert. 1956: It's Great to be Young. Alias John Preston. Yield to the Night (US: Blonde Sinner). 1957: The Good Companions. Stranger in Town. Three Sundays to Live. Son of a Stranger. 1958: A Cry from the Streets. 1959: Count Your Blessings. 1960: Brides of Dracula. 1963: Billy Liar! Night Must Fall. 1964: My Fair Lady. Ferry 'Cross the Mersey. One Way Pendulum. 1965: The Third Day. The Collector. 1967: Mrs Brown, You've Got a Lovely Daughter. If... 1969: The Games. The Bed Sitting Room. 1970: Fragment of Fear. 1971: What Became of Jack and Jill? (US: Romeo and Juliet '71). 1973: O Lucky Man! 1974: Mister Quilp. The Driver's Seat/Identi-kit. 1976: The Blue Bird. 1978: Stevie. 1979: The London Affair/The London Connection (US: The Omega Connection). 1982: Charles and Diana, a Royal Love Story (TV).*

**WATERS, Russell** 1908-
Stocky, inoffensive-looking, brown-haired Scottish-born actor who made a start in British films as the hapless hero of director Richard Masingham's highly rated comedy shorts of the 1930s. After war service, he settled down to play dozens of mildly authoritative, not-to-be-feared official figures and kept busy on television as well.

*1934: *Tell Me If It Hurts. 1936: *And So to Work. 1937: *The Daily Round. 1947: The Woman in the Hall. 1948: *What a Life! London Belongs to Me (US: Dulcimer Street). Obsession (US: The Hidden Room). The Blue Lagoon. 1949: Dear Mr Prohack. The Chiltern Hundreds (US: The Amazing Mr Beecham). Marry Me! Stop Press Girl. Helter Skelter. 1950: Chance of a Lifetime. *The Cure. State Secret (US: The Great Manhunt). The Happiest Days of Your Life. The Wooden Horse. The Magnet. Seven Days to Noon. 1951: The Browning Version. Mr Denning Drives North. Captain Horatio Hornblower RN. Green Grow the Rushes. The Man in the White Suit. Lady Godiva Rides Again. Death of an Angel. Saturday Island (US: Island of Desire). 1952: Castle in the Air. The Brave Don't Cry. Angels One Five. You're Only Young Twice! The Long Memory. Miss Robin Hood. Isn't Life Wonderful! The Story of Robin Hood and His Merrie Men. 1953: The Cruel Sea. Turn the Key Softly. Rob Roy the Highland Rogue. The 'Maggie' (US: High and Dry). Street Corner (US: Both Sides of the Law). The Sword and the Rose. Grand National Night (US: Wicked Wife). 1954: The Sleeping Tiger. Lease of Life. Adventure in the Hopfields. The Passing Stranger. The Love Match. The Case of the Pearl Payroll. 1955: John and Julie. Third Party Risk (US: The Deadly Game). Now and Forever. 1956: It's Great to be Young! Reach for the Sky. Man in the Sky (US: Decision Against Time). 1957: The Little Hut. Interpol (US: Pick-Up Alley). Let's Be Happy. 1958: The Key. 1959: Yesterday's Enemy. Left, Right and Centre. The Bridal Path. 1960: The Man in the Moon. Danger Tomorrow. Marriage of Convenience. 1962: Flat Two. Bomb in the High Street. The Punch and Judy Man. The Longest Day. Play It Cool! 1963: I Could Go On Singing (shown 1962). The Flood. Crooks* in Cloisters. Heavens Above! 1965: The Heroes of Telemark. 1966: The Trygon Factor. 1967: The Devil Rides Out. 1971: Kidnapped. 1972: Endless Night. That's Your Funeral. 1973: The Wicker Man. 1979: Black Jack.

## WATTSON, Jack 1921-

Craggy, rugged-looking, ginger-haired Londoner who so firmly established himself as a character actor in the 1960s (sergeant-majors and similarly gruff types) that few now remember that he was a brisk and funny music-hall comedian and monologuist for 15 years, in succession to his comedian father Nosmo King, to whom he was stooge in his first variety experience. A part in TV's Z Cars launched him on his second career. In real life an outdoor sports fanatic.

1960: The Man Who Was Nobody. Peeping Tom. The Queen's Guards. 1961: Konga. 1962: Time to Remember. Fate Takes a Hand. Out of the Fog. This Sporting Life. 1963: Five to One. Master Spy. 1964: The Gorgon. 1965: The Hill. The Night Caller (US: Blood Beast from Outer Space). 1966: The Idol. Grand Prix. Tobruk. 1967: The Strange Affair. 1968: The Devil's Brigade. Decline and Fall...of a Birdwatcher! 1969: Midas Run (US: A Run on Gold). 1970: Every Home Should Have One. The Mackenzie Break. 1971: Kidnapped. 1972: Tower of Evil (US: Horror of Snape Island). 1973: From Beyond the Grave. 1974: The Four Musketeers (The Revenge of Milady). Juggernaut. 11 Harrowhouse. 1975: Brannigan. 1976: Treasure Island. 1977: The Wild Geese. 1978: Schizo. 1979: North Sea Hijack (US: ffolkes). 1980: The Sea Wolves. Masada (TV. GB: abridged for cinemas as The Antagonists).

## WATTSON, Wylie (John Wylie Robertson) 1889-1966

Small, slightly built, dark-haired, moustachioed Scottish actor who played wily, henpecked or mealy-mouthed little men. A member of a family variety act, he started his career before the turn of the century, as a boy vocalist singing 15 times a day in a waxworks. He is said to have made his film

debut in a 1928 Hollywood film while on a trip to America, but became a British film regular after his role as Mr Memory in Hitchcock's 1935 version of The 39 Steps. Went to Australia in the early 1950s.

1932: For the Love of Mike. 1933: Leave It to Me. Hawleys of High Street. 1934: Road House. 1935: The 39 Steps. Black Mask. 1936: Radio Lover. 1937: Please Teacher. Why Pick On Me? Paradise for Two (US: The Gaiety Girls). 1938: Queer Cargo (US: Pirates of the Seven Seas). Yes, Madam? 1939: Jamaica Inn. She Couldn't Say No. 1940: Pack Up Your Troubles. 'Bulldog' Sees It Through. 1941: Danny Boy. My Wife's Family. The Saint Meets the Tiger. *Mr Proudfoot Shows a Light. 1943: The Lamp Still Burns. The Flemish Farm. 1944: Tawny Pipit. Kiss the Bride Goodbye. Waterloo Road. Don't Take It to Heart. Strawberry Roan. The World Owes Me a Living. 1945: Don Chicago. Waltz Time. Murder in Reverse. The Trojan Brothers. 1946: The Years Between. A Girl in a Million. 1947: Brighton Rock (US: Young Scarface). Fame Is the Spur. Temptation Harbour. My Brother Jonathan. 1948: London Belongs to Me (US: Dulcimer Street). No Room at the Inn. Things Happen at Night. Whisky Galore! (US: Tight Little Island). The History of Mr Polly. 1949: Train of Events. 1950: Your Witness (US: Eye Witness). Morning Departure (US: Operation Disaster). Shadow of the Past. The Magnet. Happy Go Lovely. 1960: The Sundowners.

## WATTIS, Richard 1912-1975

Bespectacled, heron-like British supporting actor whose neat light-brown hair concealed an unexpected bald patch at the back and whose thin, elongated lips could open wide and screw themselves into expressions of Donald Duck-like outrage, while the plaintively light, upper-class Wattis tones complained of some new affront. He was the happy butt of many British comedians, often as salesmen, butlers, solicitors and teachers. Died from a heart attack.

1937: A Yank at Oxford. 1949: Marry Me! Helter Skelter. Stop Press Girl. 1950: The Happiest Days of Your Life. The Clouded Yellow. 1951: Appointment With Venus (US:

Island Rescue). Lady Godiva Rides Again. 1952: Song of Paris (US: Bachelor in Paris). The Happy Family (US: Mr Lord Says No). Mother Riley Meets the Vampire (US: Vampire Over London). Made in Heaven. The Importance of Being Earnest. Stolen Face. Penny Princess. Derby Day (US: Four Against Fate). Top Secret (US: Mr Potts Goes to Moscow). Appointment in London. 1953: The Intruder. The Final Test. Background (US: Edge of Divorce). Top of the Form. Innocents in Paris. Colonel March Investigates. Small Town Story. Blood Orange. Park Plaza 605 (US: Norman Conquest). 1954: The Belles of St Trinian's. Doctor in the House. Lease of Life. Hobson's Choice. The Crowded Day. The Colditz Story. 1955: See How They Run. The Time of His Life. I Am a Camera. A Yank in Ermine. An Alligator Named Daisy. Simon and Laura. Jumping for Joy. The Man Who Never Was. 1956: The Silken Affair. Around the World in 80 Days. The Man Who Knew Too Much. A Touch of the Sun. Eyewitness. It's a Wonderful World. The Green Man. The Iron Petticoat. 1957: The Prince and the Showgirl. The Abominable Snowman. Second Fiddle. Barnacle Bill (US: All at Sea). High Flight. Blue Murder at St Trinian's. 1958: The Inn of the Sixth Happiness. The Captain's Table. Ten Seconds to Hell. 1959: The Ugly Duckling. Libel. Left, Right and Centre. Your Money or Your Wife. Follow a Star. Follow That Horse! 1961: Very Important Person (US: A Coming Out Party). Dentist On the Job (US: Get On With It!). 1962: Play It Cool. I Thank a Fool. Bon Voyage! The Longest Day. Come Fly With Me. 1963: The VIPs. 1964: Carry On Spying. 1965: The Amorous Adventures of Moll Flanders. The Battle of the Villa Fiorita. Up Jumped a Swagman. You Must Be Joking! Bunny Lake Is Missing. The Alphabet Murders. Operation Crossbow (US: The Great Spy Mission). The Liquidator. 1966: The Great St Trinian's Train Robbery. 1968: Wonderwall. Chitty Chitty Bang Bang. 1969: Monte Carlo or Bust. 1970: Games That Lovers Play. Egghead's Robot. 1971: Tam Lin/The Devil's Widow. The Troublesome Double. 1972: Sex and the Other Woman. That's Your Funeral. Diamonds On Wheels. 1973: Take Me High (US: Hot Property). 1974: Confessions of a Window Cleaner.

**WEBBER, Robert 1924-** *1989*

Smooth, handsome (a kind of cross between Richard Arlen and Bruce Cabot), dark-haired American actor who started as a leading man, but seemed to prefer character roles, often turning up as plausible charmers or executives with feet of clay. He began acting in the US Marines during his war service, but didn't settle in films until the mid-1960s. Says he likes playing 'the antagonist' and has also shown a penchant for fairly broad comedy.

*1951: Highway 301. 1957: 12 Angry Men. 1962: The Nun and the Sergeant. 1963: The Stripper (GB: Woman of Summer). Hysteria. 1965: The Sandpiper. The Third Day. Tecnida di un omicidio (GB: No Tears for a Killer. US: Hired Killer). 1966: Dead Heat on a Merry-Go-Round). Harper (GB: The Moving Target). The Silencers. 1967: Don't Make Waves. The Dirty Dozen. 1968: The Big Bounce. 1970: The Great White Hope. The Movie Murderer (TV). Hauser's Memory (TV). 1971: Thief (TV). $ (GB: The Heist). 1973: Death and the Maiden (TV). Double Indemnity (TV). 1974: Bring Me the Head of Alfredo Garcia. Murder or Mercy (TV). 1975: Death Stalk (TV). 1976: Passi di morte perduti nel buio. Madame Claude. Midway (GB: Battle of Midway). 1977: Casey's Shadow. L'imprecateur. The Choirboys. 1978: Revenge of the Pink Panther. Gardenia. 1979: '10'. Streets of LA (TV). Courage fuyons. 1980: Les séducteurs/Sunday Lovers. Private Benjamin. 1981: S.O.B. 1982: Starflight One (TV. GB: cinemas). Wrong Is Right (GB: The Man With the Deadly Lens). Who Dares Wins. 1983: Cocaine: One Man's Seduction (TV). 1984: No Man's Land (TV). Getting Physical (TV). 1985: Wild Geese II. Half Nelson (TV).*

**WEIDLER, Virginia 1927-1968**

Not many screen children really qualify as character players, but bumpy-nosed Virginia Weidler was definitely one of them. The dark-haired Californian tot had homely, inquisitive features, could sing a bit (her mother was an opera singer) and was usually seen as the kid told to scram because she bothered the adults. One director went on record as saying she would never really get anywhere as a juvenile because 'all she can do is act'. He was right. Despite spells at Paramount and M-G-M, the 'little horror' was washed up at 18. She married happily, but died from a heart attack at 41.

*1931: Surrender. 1933: After Tonight. 1934: Long Lost Father. Stamboul Quest. Mrs Wiggs of the Cabbage Patch. 1935: Freckles. Laddie. The Big Broadcast of 1936. Peter Ibbetson. 1936: Trouble for Two (GB: The Suicide Club). Timothy's Quest. Girl of the Ozarks. The Big Broadcast of 1937. 1937: Maid of Salem. Souls at Sea. The Outcasts of Poker Flat. 1938: Scandal Street. Out West With the Hardys. Love Is a Headache. Mother Carey's Chickens. Men With Wings. Too Hot to Handle. 1939: Fixer Dugan. The Lone Wolf Spy Hunt (GB: The Lone Wolf's Daughter). The Under-Pup. Bad Little Angel. The Women. The Great Man Votes. The Spellbinder. The Rookie Cop (GB: Swift Vengeance). Henry Goes Arizona (GB: Spats to Spurs). 1940: All This and Heaven Too. Gold Rush Maisie. The Philadelphia Story. 1941: Young Tom Edison. I'll Wait for You. Barnacle Bill. Keeping Company. Babes on Broadway. 1942: The Affairs of Martha (GB: Once Upon a Thursday). This Time for Keeps. Born to Sing. 1943: The Youngest Profession. Best Foot Forward.*

**WEIR, Molly 1920-**

One of the best-known voices on British radio over the past 40 years belongs to this diminutive Scots woman who has also, in recent times, become well-known on TV commercials. Despite a 1944 film debut, she has rarely ventured into films, but has become a 'home' expert on cookery, gardening and knitting. Her distinctive Glaswegian tones became nationally famous as Tattie in *ITMA* and Aggie in *Life With the Lyons*—two long-running British radio shows.

*1944: 2,000 Women. 1951: Flesh and Blood. Cheer the Brave. 1954: Life With the Lyons. The Lyons in Paris. 1955: John and Julie. *The Silent Witness. 1957: Let's Be Happy. 1959: The Bridal Path. 1961: Carry On Regardless. What a Whopper! 1968: The Prime of Miss Jean Brodie. 1970: Scrooge. 1971: Hands of the Ripper. The Magnificent Six and a ⅓ (third series). 1972: Bless This House. 1975: One of Our Dinosaurs Is Missing. 1978: Mr Selkie.*

**WELDEN, Ben 1901-**

Short, stockily built, round-faced, wary-looking, dark-haired American-born actor popular in early British sound films as tough-talking gangsters and sharpies, even having a leading role or two. He went to Hollywood in late 1936 and, after a good start as Humphrey Bogart's henchman in *Kid Galahad*, declined to fairly minor mobster roles.

*1930: The Man from Chicago. Big Business. 1931: Who Killed Doc Robin? 77 Park Lane. 1932: The Missing Rembrandt. His Lordship (US: Man of Affaires). The Innocents of Chicago (US: Why Saps Leave Home). Born Lucky. Puppets of Fate (US: Wolves of the Underworld). 1933: Home Sweet Home. Send 'Em Back Half Dead. The Medicine Man. Mr Quincey of Monte Carlo. Their Night Out. His Grace Gives Notice. Pride of the Force. General John Regan. This Is the Life. Mannequin. 1934: Aunt Sally (US: Along Came Sally). The River Wolves. The Black Abbot. The Man Who Changed His Mind. Gay Love. The Medium. 1935: Death on the Set (US: Murder on the Set). Annie, Leave the Room! Royal Cavalcade (US: Regal Cavalcade). The Big Splash. Admirals All. Come Out of the Pantry. The Mystery of the Marie Celeste/The Mystery of the Mary Celeste (US: Phantom Ship). The Triumph of Sherlock Holmes. Trust the Navy. Alibi Inn. 1936: The Avenging*

Hand. Hot News. The Improper Duchess. She Knew What She Wanted. 1937: The Great Barrier (US: Silent Barriers). Maytime. Kid Galahad. Marked Woman. The King and the Chorus Girl. Another Dawn. The Great Garrick. Confession. Varsity Show. That Certain Woman. Back in Circulation. Alcatraz Island. The Missing Witness. Love Is on the Air (GB: The Radio Murder Mystery). 1938: Crime Ring. Happy Landing. Prison Nurse. The Saint in New York. Always Goodbye. Mystery House. Little Miss Broadway. The Night Hawk. Little Orphan Annie. Smashing the Rackets. Tenth Avenue Kid. Straight, Place and Show (GB: They're Off!). Federal Man Hunt (GB: Flight from Justice). 1939: The Lone Wolf Spy Hunt (GB: The Lone Wolf's Daughter). Hollywood Cavalcade. Fugitive at Large. I Was a Convict. Sergeant Madden. Boys' Reformatory. The Roaring Twenties. The Star Maker. Rose of Washington Square. 1940: Outside the 3-Mile Limit (GB: Mutiny on the Seas). Wolf of New York. Strange Cargo. South of Pago Pago. City for Conquest. 1941: Men of Boys' Town. Strange Alibi. I'll Wait for You. Manpower. Right to the Heart/Knockout. Nine Lives Are Not Enough. 1942: All Through the Night. Dangerously They Live. Maisie Gets Her Man (GB: She Gets Her Man). A Close Call for Ellery Queen (GB: A Close Call). Bullet Scars. Stand By for Action! (GB: Cargo of Innocents). 1943: Appointment with Murder. Here Comes Elmer! Dr Gillespie's Criminal Case (GB: Crazy to Kill). 1944: The Fighting Seabees. Shadows in the Night. It's in the Bag! (GB: The Fifth Chair). 1945: Follow That Woman. Circumstantial Evidence. The Missing Corpse. Angel on My Shoulder. 1946: Mr Hex (GB: Pride of the Bowery). The Big Sleep. The Last Crooked Mile. Anna and the King of Siam. 1947: Sinbad the Sailor. Killer Dill. The Pretender. Heading for Heaven. 1948: Jinx Money. Trapped by Boston Blackie. The Noose Hangs High. The Vicious Circle. Appointment with Murder (and 1943 film). A Song is Born. Lady at Midnight. Smart Girls Don't Talk. 1949: Search for Danger. Impact. Tough Assignment. Sorrowful Jones. Fighting Fools. Riders in the Sky. Mary Ryan, Detective. 1950: Buccaneer's Girl. On the Isle of Samoa. The Desert Hawk. 1951: The Lemon Drop Kid. My True Story. Tales of Robin Hood. 1953: The Veils of Baghdad. All Ashore. 1954: Killers from Space. The Steel Cage. 1955: Ma and Pa Kettle at Waikiki. 1956: Hidden Guns. Hollywood or Bust. 1957: Spook Chasers.

## WELSH, John 1914-1985

Tall, lean, austere, balding, slightly snooty-looking Irish actor, often cast as people of authority, sometimes with feet of clay. After years of theatrical experience at the Gate Theatre, Dublin, he moved to London, entering the theatre there in 1950 and films two years later. Much television work followed (and a spell with the Royal Shakespeare Company) often playing decaying aristocrats. Died from cancer.

1952: Isn't Life Wonderful! 1953: The Case of Soho Red. The Clue of the Missing Ape. 1954: Diplomatic Passport. Track the Man Down. An Inspector Calls. The Divided Heart. 1955: Confession (US: The Deadliest Sin). The Dark Avenger (US: The Warriors). Lost (US: Tears for Simon). The Man Who Never Was. 1956: The Long Arm (US: The Third Key). Women Without Men (US: Blonde Bait). The Secret Place. Brothers in Law. 1957: Lucky Jim. The Counterfeit Plan. Man in the Shadow. The Long Haul. The Surgeon's Knife. The Safecracker. The Birthday Present. The Man Who Wouldn't Talk. 1958: Behind the Mask. The Revenge of Frankenstein. Next to No Time! Room at the Top. Nowhere to Go. 1959: The Rough and the Smooth (US: Portrait of a Sinner). Bobbikins. The Night We Dropped a Clanger (US: Make Mine a Double). Operation Bullshine. Follow That Horse! 1960: Konga. The Trials of Oscar Wilde (US: The Man with the Green Carnation). Beyond the Curtain. Snowball. 1961: Circle of Deception. Francis of Assisi. The Mark. *The Square Mile Murder. Johnny Nobody. Go to Blazes. 1962: Playboy of the Western World. Number Six. The Quare Fellow. The Inspector (US: Lisa). Out of the Fog. 1963: Nightmare. 1964: Dead End Creek. 1965: Rasputin—The Mad Monk. 1967: Attack on the Iron Coast. 1968: Subterfuge. 1970: The Man Who Haunted Himself. Cromwell. 1971: The Pied Piper of Hamelin (TV). 1973: Yellow Dog. A Story of Tutenkhamun (TV. US: cinemas). 1978: Grayeagle. The Thirty-Nine Steps. 1983: Krull.

## WENGRAF, John (Johannes Wenngraft) 1897-1974

Scraggy, dark-haired, bush-browed Viennese-born actor with unusually long space between nose and lip; it gave him lowering looks which he would adapt equally to the kindly or sinister. He was almost entirely a stage actor before flight from the Nazis took him first to Britain, then to Hollywood. Inevitably at first cast as Nazis himself, he later played more than a fair share of professors and ambivalent advisers.

1922: Homo sum. 1940: †Night Train to Munich (US: Night Train). †Convoy. †Sailors Three (US: Three Cockeyed Sailors).

1941: *†All Hands. 1942: Lucky Jordan. 1943: Mission to Moscow. Paris After Dark (GB: The Night Is Ending). Sahara. Song of Russia. 1944: The Seventh Cross. Till We Meet Again. U-Boat Prisoner (GB: Dangerous Mists). The Thin Man Goes Home. Strange Affair. 1945: Week-End at the Waldorf. 1946: Tomorrow is Forever. The Razor's Edge. 1947: T-Men. 1948: Sofia. 1949: The Loveable Cheat. 1951: Belle le Grand. 1952: Five Fingers. Tropic Zone. 1953: The Desert Rats. Flight to Tangier. The French Line. Call Me Madam. 1954: Hell and High Water. The Gambler from Natchez. Paris Playboys. Gog. 1955: The Racers (GB: Such Men Are Dangerous). 1956: The Pride and the Passion. 1957: Valerie. Oh Men! Oh Women! The Disembodied. 1958: The Return of Dracula (GB: The Fantastic Disappearing Man). 1960: Portrait in Black. 12 to the Moon. 1961: Judgment at Nuremberg. Hitler. 1963: The Prize. 1965: Ship of Fools.

†As Hans Wengraf

## WESSON, Dick 1919-1979

Toothy, mule-faced, crew-cut American nightclub comedian, often in endearingly panicky roles in his brief (10-film) contract years with Warner Brothers, during which his most successful part was as Francis Fryer in Calamity Jane. He provided likeable comedy relief in other films, and it was a surprise when he returned to radio, TV and nightclub work in the mid-1950s. Cropped up a couple of times on screen in 1977, looking the same as 20 years before; but then, within three weeks of his 60th birthday, Wesson shot himself. Not to be confused with thick-set American supporting actor Dick Wessel (1910-1965), in dozens of films from 1934 on.

1949: Destination Moon. 1950: Breakthrough. 1951: Inside the Walls of Folsom Prison. Sunny Side of the Street. Starlift. Force of Arms. Jim Thorpe—All American (GB: Man of Bronze). 1952: About Face. The Man Behind the Gun. 1953: The Desert Song. Calamity Jane. 1954: The Charge at Feather River. 1955: Paris Follies of 1956. 1961: The Errand Boy. 1977: Dog and Cat (TV). Rollercoaster.

## WEST, Lockwood 1905- 1989

Balding, sharp-eyed, crane-like British actor with friendly air; equally likely to turn up in amiable or ghoulish roles. Once employed by a north of England collieries' association, he determined to be an actor, and made his debut on the London stage in 1931, appearing exclusively in the theatre until the late 1940s, when his fish-eye lens features began to crop up in the occasional film.

1949: No Place for Jennifer. Celia. 1950: Last Holiday. 1951: High Treason. 1952: Hammer the Toff. The Oracle. 1953: Single-Handed (US: Sailor of the King). 1954: Lease of Life. 1955: Touch and Go (US: The Light Touch). 1956: Private's Progress. 1957:

ABOVE John **Wengraf** (second left, with moustache), John Abbott (light suit, *qv*) and their men clearly have Bruce Bennett at a disadvantage in this scene from *U-Boat Prisoner* (1944)

RIGHT Dick **Wesson** (left) assumes the rumpled expression familiar to 1950s' filmgoers, as William Tracy gives him some unpalatable information in 1951's *Sunny Side of the Street*

*Accused/Mark of the Hawk. The Birthday Present. 1959: The Man Who Could Cheat Death. 1960: Tunes of Glory. 1961: Strongroom. 1963: The Leather Boys. The Running Man. 1965: Game for Three Losers. Life at the Top. 1967: Bedazzled. Up the Junction. 1968: A Dandy in Aspic. 1969: One Brief Summer. 1970: Jane Eyre (TV. GB: cinemas). 1973: Clouds of Witness (TV). The Satanic Rites of Dracula. 1983: The Dresser. 1984: The Shooting Party.*

## WESTERFIELD, James 1912-1971

Big, beaming Jim Westerfield was the perfect screen incarnation of the slightly comic, frequently nonplussed New York cop. One can still see him taking off the peaked cap and scratching the balding head. There was a lot of this Tennessee-born actor at 6ft 1in and 200 lbs-plus, and much of the big face seemed to be teeth and eyebrows. Westerfield may have looked thick-skulled, but it was far from the truth. As a man of the theatre—the reason he didn't make more films—he was at various times set designer, producer and director and won two New York Drama Critics' awards for his acting. Died from a heart attack.

*1941: Highway West. 1942: The Magnificent Ambersons. 1943: Around the World. 1946: The Chase. Undercurrent. 1950: Side Street. 1951: The Whistle at Eaton Falls (GB: Richer than the Earth). 1954: The Human Jungle. Three Hours to Kill. On the Waterfront.*

*The Violent Men (GB: Rough Company). 1955: Chief Crazy Horse (GB: Valley of Fury). The Cobweb. The Scarlet Coat. The Man With the Gun (GB: The Trouble Shooter). Lucy Gallant. 1956: Away All Boats. 1957: Jungle Heat. Three Brave Men. Decision at Sundown. 1958: Cowboy. The Proud Rebel. 1959: The Shaggy Dog. The Gunfight at Dodge City. The Scarface Mob (TV. GB: cinemas). 1960: Wild River. The Plunderers. 1961: The Absent-Minded Professor. Homicidal. 1962: Birdman of Alcatraz. 1963: Son of Flubber. Man's Favorite Sport? 1964: Bikini Beach. 1965: The Sons of Katie Elder. That Funny Feeling. 1966: Dead Heat on a Merry-Go-Round. Scalplock (TV. GB: cinemas). 1967: Hang 'Em High. 1968: Blue. Now You See It, Now You Don't (TV). A Man Called Gannon. Burn! (GB: Queimada!). 1969: Smith! The Love God? True Grit. Set This Town on Fire (TV. Shown 1973).*

## WESTMAN, Nydia 1902-1970

Fair-haired, palely attractive, stocky little American actress who had spinsters-on-the-shelf down to a T, and could make them comic, pathetic, twittering or fey. From theatrical parents, she made her Broadway debut at 16, alternating plays with films from the early 1930s. Left films in the late 1940s, but came back years later for a few old maids. Died from cancer.

*1932: Strange Justice. Manhattan Towers. 1933: Bondage. The Way to Love. Little Women. The Cradle Song. King of the Jungle. From Hell to Heaven. 1934: Success at Any Price. Two Alone. Ladies Should Listen. Manhattan Love Song. The Trumpet Blows. One Night of Love. 1935: Dressed to Thrill. A Feather in Her Hat. Captain Hurricane. Sweet Adeline. 1936: Rose Bowl (GB: O'Riley's Luck). The Gorgeous Hussy. Craig's Wife. The Invisible Ray. Pennies from Heaven. Three Live Ghosts. 1937: Bulldog Drummond's Revenge. When Love is Young. 1938: The Goldwyn Follies. The First Hundred Years. Bulldog Drummond's Peril. 1939: When Tomorrow Comes. The Cat and the Canary. 1940: Hullabaloo. Forty Little Mothers. 1941: The Bad Man (GB: Two-Gun Cupid). The Chocolate Soldier. 1942: They All Kissed*

*the Bride. The Remarkable Andrew. 1943: Hers to Hold. Princess O'Rourke. 1944: Her Primitive Man. 1947: The Late George Apley. 1948: The Velvet Touch. 1962: Don't Knock the Twist. 1963: For Love or Money. 1965: The Chase. 1966: The Ghost and Mr Chicken. The Swinger. 1967: The Reluctant Astronaut. 1968: The Horse in the Gray Flannel Suit. 1970: Flap (GB: The Last Warrior). Rabbit Run.*

## WESTON, Jack (J. Weinstein) 1925- *1996*

Tubby, balding American actor sometimes seen as not-too-serious crooks or bungling, would-be helpful friends. He had a hard struggle to establish himself near the top of the supporting actors' league, taking menial work while fighting for a foothold in TV (which began to happen from the early 1950s) and films, to which he has remained only an occasional, but distinctive visitor. Married to actress Marge Redmond, he lists his hobbies as acting, films and lying down.

*1958: Stage Struck. 1960: Please Don't Eat the Daisies. 1961: The Honeymoon Machine. All in a Night's Work. 1962: It's Only Money. 1963: Palm Springs Weekend. The Incredible Mr Limpet. 1965: Mirage. The Cincinnati Kid. 1966: Fame is the Name of the Game (TV). 1967: Wait Until Dark. I Love a Mystery (TV. Shown 1973). 1968: Now You See It, Now You Don't (TV). The Thomas Crown Affair. The Counterfeit Killer (TV. GB: cinemas). 1969: The April Fools. Cactus Flower. 1971: A New Leaf. 1972: Fuzz. 1973: Deliver Us from Evil (TV). Marco. 1976: Gator. The Ritz. 1979: Cuba. 1980: Can't Stop the Music. 1981: The Four Seasons. 1983: High Road to China.*

## WHEATLEY, Alan 1907- *1991*

Supercilious, dark-haired (soon greying), shifty-eyed British actor with neat moustache and cutting, upper-class tones. Often the smooth villain whose surface coolness (and hair) was dishevelled by the hero before the end. An industrial psychologist who gradually veered away into acting, he was a newsreader for BBC radio in World War II. Gained greatest national fame in the 1950s as the Sheriff of Nottingham in the popular TV series *Robin Hood*.

1936: *Conquest of the Air* (released 1940). 1945: *Caesar and Cleopatra. The Rake's Progress* (US: *Notorious Gentleman*). 1946: *Spring Song* (US: *Springtime*). *Appointment with Crime.* 1947: *Brighton Rock* (US: *Young Scarface*). *Jassy. End of the River.* 1948: *Calling Paul Temple. Counterblast. Corridor of Mirrors. Sleeping Car to Trieste. It's Not Cricket.* 1949: *For Them That Trespass.* 1951: *Home to Danger. Whispering Smith Hits London* (US: *Whispering Smith versus Scotland Yard*). 1952: *The Pickwick Papers.* 1953: *Spaceways. Small Town Story. The Limping Man.* 1954: *The House across the Lake* (US: *Heatwave*). *The Diamond* (US: *Diamond Wizard*). *Delayed Action.* 1955: *Simon and Laura.* 1958: *The Duke Wore Jeans.* 1959: *Inn for Trouble.* 1961: *Shadow of the Cat. Checkmate.* *Frederic Chopin.* 1962: *Tomorrow at Ten.* 1963: *Clash by Night. A Jolly Bad Fellow* (US: *They All Died Laughing*).

**WHILEY, Manning** 1915-
British actor with dark hair and complexion, usually in neurotic or villainous roles. Despite something of a *tour de force* in the leading role of his second film, *Trunk Crime*, he soon slipped into routinely bad-tempered parts, and had faded from the show business scene by the early 1950s.

1938: *Consider Your Verdict.* 1939: *Trunk Crime. The Four Just Men* (US: *The Secret Four*). 1940: *Contraband* (US: *Blackout*). *Gasbags. Pastor Hall. The Flying Squad.*

*Saloon Bar. Pack Up Your Troubles. Sailors Three* (US: *Three Cockeyed Sailors*). *Old Bill and Son.* 1941: *Freedom Radio* (US: *A Voice in the Night*). *Mr Proudfoot Shows a Light. Pimpernel Smith* (US: *Mister V*). *The Ghost of St Michael's. The Saint's Vacation. Penn of Pennsylvania* (US: *The Courageous Mr Penn*). 1943: *Bell Bottom George. The Dummy Talks.* 1944: *Meet Sexton Blake.* 1945: *The Seventh Veil. For You Alone.* 1946: *The Shop at Sly Corner* (US: *The Code of Scotland Yard*). 1947: *Teheran* (US: *The Plot to Kill Roosevelt*). *Uncle Silas* (US: *The Inheritance*). 1949: *Children of Chance.* 1952: *Little Big Shot.*

**WHITE, Jesse** (J. Wiedenfeld) 1918-
Pug-faced, plug-ugly, beaky-nosed, brown-haired, cigar-chewing, stoutly built American actor who might have stepped straight out of the pages of Damon Runyon. Usually spoke out of the side of his mouth, wore a pin-striped suit and was on the make. Also a favourite for taxi-drivers, but always an eye-catching performer.

1947: *Kiss of Death.* 1948: *Texas, Brooklyn and Heaven* (GB: *The Girl from Texas*). 1950: *Harvey.* 1951: *Death of a Salesman. Katie Did It. Bedtime for Bonzo. Francis Goes to the Races. Callaway Went Thataway* (GB: *The Star Said No!*). *The Raging Tide.* 1952: *The Girl in White* (GB: *So Bright the Flame*). *Million Dollar Mermaid* (GB: *The One Piece Bathing Suit*). 1953: *Gunsmoke. Forever Female. Champ for a Day.* 1954: *Hell's Half Acre. Witness to Murder.* 1955: *Not As a Stranger. The Girl Rush.* 1956: *The Come On. The Bad Seed. Back from Eternity. The Hefferan Family* (TV. GB: *cinemas*). *He Laughed Last.* 1957: *Designing Woman. Johnny Trouble. God is My Partner.* 1958: *Country Music Holiday. Marjorie Morningstar.* 1959: *The Rise and Fall of Legs Diamond.* 1960: *The Big Night. Three Blondes in His Life.* 1961: *Tomboy and the Champ. A Fever in the Blood. On the Double. The Right Approach. Sail a Crooked Ship.* 1962: *It's Only Money.* 1963: *The Yellow Canary. It's a Mad, Mad, Mad, Mad World.* 1964: *Pajama Party. A House is Not a Home. Looking for Love.* 1965: *Dear Brigitte ...* 1966: *The Spirit is Willing. The Ghost in the Invisible*

*Bikini.* 1967: *The Reluctant Astronaut.* 1970: *Togetherness.* 1971: *Bless the Beasts and Children.* 1973: *The Brothers O'Toole.* 1975: *Las Vegas Lady. Return to Campus. Won Ton Ton, the Dog Who Saved Hollywood.* 1976: *New Girl in Town. Nashville Girl.* 1978: *The Cat from Outer Space.*

**WHITMORE, James** 1921-
Solidly built American actor with homely, philosophical face and crinkly sandy hair. Utterly reliable in performance, he was sort of a supporting players' Spencer Tracy. A solid bulwark to M-G-M films of the early 1950s, Whitmore was usually to be found in sincere dramatic roles, but could also be delightfully comic, as demonstrated by his singing/clowning partnership with Keenan Wynn (*qv*) in *Kiss Me, Kate!* When films failed to make the most of him, he toured America with one-man shows. Twice nominated for an Oscar, in *Battleground* and *Give 'Em Hell Harry.*

1949: *The Undercover Man. Battleground.* 1950: *The Asphalt Jungle. Please Believe Me. The Outriders. Mrs O'Malley and Mr Malone. The Next Voice You Hear.* 1951: *Across the Wide Missouri. The Red Badge of Courage* (narrator only). *Shadow in the Sky.* 1952: *Because You're Mine. Above and Beyond.* 1953: *The Girl Who Had Everything. Kiss Me, Kate! All the Brothers Were Valiant. The Great Diamond Robbery.* 1954: *The Command. Them!* 1955: *The McConnell Story* (GB: *Tiger in the Sky*). *Battle Cry. The Last Frontier. Oklahoma!* 1956: *The Eddy Duchin Story. Crime in the Streets.* 1957: *Deep Water* (TV. GB: *cinemas*). *The Young Don't Cry. Galvanized Yankee* (TV). 1958: *The Deep Six. The Restless Years* (GB: *The Wonderful Years*). *Free Week-End* (TV). 1959: *Face of Fire. Who Was That Lady? Dark December* (TV). *The Sounds of Eden* (TV). 1964: *The Tenderfoot* (TV. GB: *cinemas*). *Black Like Me.* 1967: *Chuka. Nobody's Perfect. Waterhole No. 3* (GB: *Waterhole 3*). *Planet of the Apes.* 1968: *Madigan. The Split.* 1969: *Guns of the Magnificent Seven.* 1970: *Tora! Tora! Tora!* 1971: *If Tomorrow Comes* (TV). 1972: *Chato's Land. The Lost World of Libra.* 1973: *The Harrad Experiment. High Crime.* 1974: *Where the Red Fern Grows. Calling*

Crime Command. The Challenge (TV). Venditore di Palloncini (GB: Last Moments. US: The Last Circus Show). 1975: I Will Fight No More Forever (TV). Give 'Em Hell Harry. 1977: The Serpent's Egg. 1978: Bully. 1980: The First Deadly Sin. Mark, I Love You (TV). The Rage (TV). 1985: Mark Twain (voice only).

**WHITNEY, Peter** (P. Engle) 1916-1972
Chunky, powerful, full-faced, dark-haired American actor, often seen as men of inbred violence from the wrong side of the tracks. As far as producers were concerned he was nearly always 'in the ranks' and his best roles in an in-and-out film career proved to be as twins in *Murder He Says* and as Anthony Quinn's adversary in *The Man from Del Rio*. Died from a heart attack.

1941: Nine Lives Are Not Enough. Blues in the Night. Underground. 1942: Rio Rita. Valley of the Sun. Busses Roar. Spy Ship. Whistling in Dixie. Reunion/Reunion in France (GB: Mademoiselle France). 1943: Action in the North Atlantic. Destination Tokyo. 1944: Mr Skeffington. 1945: Murder He Says. Hotel Berlin. Bring on the Girls. 1946: The Notorious Lone Wolf. Blonde Alibi. The Brute Man. Canyon Passage. Three Strangers. 1947: Northwest Outpost (GB: End of the Rainbow). Violence. 1948: The Iron Curtain. 1953: The Great Sioux Uprising. The Big Heat. All the Brothers Were Valiant. 1954: Superman's Peril. Day of Triumph. The Black Dakotas. Gorilla at Large. 1955: The Sea Chase. The Last Frontier. 1956: Man from Del Rio. Great Day in the Morning. The Cruel Tower. 1957: The Domino Kid. 1958: Buchanan Rides Alone. 1962: The Wonderful World of the Brothers Grimm. 1965: The Sword of Ali Baba. 1967: In the Heat of the Night. Chubasco. 1969: The Great Bank Robbery. 1970: The Ballad of Cable Hogue.

**WHITTY, Dame May** 1865-1948
Small, neat, plump-cheeked, brown-haired British actress who, after a distinguished stage career, made her first Hollywood film at 72, and largely stayed there for the last 11 years of her life, exuding kindliness, resourcefulness and British common sense. Most memorable as the disappearing Miss Fray in Hitchcock's *The Lady Vanishes*.

Created Dame in 1918. Academy Award nominations for *Night Must Fall* and *Mrs Miniver*.

1914: Enoch Arden. 1915: The Little Minister. 1920: Col. Newcome the Perfect Gentleman. 1937: Night Must Fall. Conquest (GB: Marie Walewska). The Thirteenth Chair. 1938: I Met My Love Again. The Lady Vanishes. 1939: Return to Yesterday. 1940: Raffles. A Bill of Divorcement. 1941: Suspicion. One Night in Lisbon. 1942: Thunder Birds. Mrs Miniver. Crash Dive. 1943: The Constant Nymph. Slightly Dangerous. Forever and a Day. Lassie Come Home. Stage Door Canteen. Madame Curie. Devotion (released 1946). 1944: The White Cliffs of Dover. Gaslight (GB: The Murder in Thornton Square). 1945: My Name is Julia Ross. 1947: This Time for Keeps. Green Dolphin Street. If Winter Comes. 1948: The Sign of the Ram. The Return of October (GB: Date with Destiny).

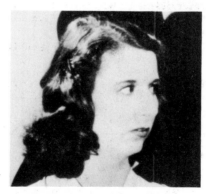

**WICKES, Mary** (M. Wickenhauser) 1912- 1995
Tallish, beaky, angular, chestnut-haired, bony-fingered American actress with the look of a startled but aggressive bird. She played people looking after other people, or busybodies, or do-gooders, and would stand no shenanigans from any of her elderly or variously eccentric charges. The original Mary Poppins in a TV production of 1949.

1938: Too Much Johnson (unreleased). 1941: The Man Who Came to Dinner. 1942: Private Buckaroo. Now, Voyager. Blondie's Blessed Event (GB: A Bundle of Trouble).

Who Done It? The Mayor of 44th Street. 1943: My Kingdom for a Cook. Rhythm of the Islands. Happy Land. Higher and Higher. 1948: The Decision of Christopher Blake. June Bride. 1949: Anna Lucasta. 1950: The Petty Girl (GB: Girl of the Year). Ma and Pa Kettle at Home. 1951: On Moonlight Bay. I'll See You in My Dreams. 1952: The Will Rogers Story (GB: The Story of Will Rogers). Young Man with Ideas. Bloodhounds of Broadway. 1953: By the Light of the Silvery Moon. Half a Hero. The Actress. 1954: Destry. White Christmas. 1953: Good Morning, Miss Dove. 1956: Dance with Me, Henry. 1957: Don't Go Near the Water. 1959: It Happened to Jane. 1960: Cimarron. 1961: The Sins of Rachel Cade. 101 Dalmatians (voice only). The Music Man. 1964: Fate is the Hunter. Dear Heart. 1965: How to Murder Your Wife. The Trouble with Angels. 1966: The Spirit is Willing. 1967: Where Angels Go . . . Trouble Follows. 1969: The Monk (TV). 1971: Napoleon and Samantha. 1973: Snowball Express. 1979: Willa (TV). 1980: Touched by Love.

**WILKE, Robert J.** 1911-
Tall, broad-shouldered, light-haired American actor with fleshy lips, icy eyes and taut features. A former stuntman, Wilke looked ill-at-ease in a suit and was almost always cast as western villains. He proved towards the end of his career that he could handle *bona-fide* character roles as well. Also billed variously as Robert Wilkie, Robert Wilke and Bob Wilke.

1936: San Francisco. 1938: Come On Rangers! Under Western Stars. 1939: Rough Riders' Round-Up. In Old Monterey. 1940: The Adventures of Red Ryder (serial). King of the Royal Mounted (serial). 1943: California Joe. 1944: Captain America (serial). The San Antonio Kid. Call of the Rockies. Vigilantes of Dodge City. Sheriff of Las Vegas. Beneath Western Skies. The Cowboy and the Senorita. Yellow Rose of Texas. Marshal of Reno. Bordertown Trail. Cheyenne Wildcat. Sheriff of Sundown. 1945: Sunset in El Dorado. Topeka Terror. Sheriff of Cimarron. Santa Fé Saddlemates. Rough Riders of Cheyenne. Corpus Christi Bandits. Trail of the Badlands. The Man from Oklahoma. Bandits of the Badlands.

1946: *The Phantom Rider* (serial). *The El Paso Kid. Out California Way. Roaring Rangers* (GB: *False Hero*). *The Inner Circle. King of the Texas Rangers. Haunted Harbor. Traffic in Crime. Dick Tracy versus Crime Inc.* 1947: *Buck Privates Come Home* (GB: *Rookies Come Home*). *The Michigan Kid. The Vigilantes Return. West of Dodge City* (GB: *The Sea Wall*). *Law of the Canyon* (GB: *The Price of Crime*). 1948: *River Lady. Last Days of Boot Hill. Six Gun Law. Daredevils of the Clouds. Carson City Raiders. West of Sonora. Trail to Laredo* (GB: *Sign of the Dagger*). 1949: *The Wyoming Bandit. Laramie. Frontier Outpost.* 1950: *Outcast of Black Mesa* (GB: *The Clue*). *The Desert Hawk. Mule Train. Kill the Umpire! Across the Badlands* (GB: *The Challenge*). 1951: *Beyond the Purple Hills. Best of the Badmen. Gunplay. Saddle Legion. Pistol Harvest. Hot Lead. Cyclone Fury. Overland Telegraph.* 1952: *High Noon. The Las Vegas Story. Frontier Outpost. Laramie Mountains* (GB: *Mountain Desperadoes*). *Hellgate. Fargo. Road Agent. The Maverick. Cattle Town. Wyoming Roundup.* 1953: *From Here to Eternity. Powder River. War Paint. Arrowhead. Cow Country.* 1954: *Black Widow. 20,000 Leagues Under the Sea. The Lone Gun. Son of Sinbad. The Far Country. Two Guns and a Badge.* 1955: *Strange Lady in Town. Wichita. Smoke Signal. Shotgun. The Rawhide Years.* 1956: *The Lone Ranger. Backlash. Raw Edge. Canyon River. Gun the Man Down. Written on the Wind. Mountain Fortress* (TV. GB: cinemas). 1957: *The Tarnished Angels. Night Passage. Hot Summer Night.* 1958: *Man of the West. Return to Warbow. Never Steal Anything Small.* 1960: *The Magnificent Seven. Texas John Slaughter. Spartacus.* 1961: *A Blueprint for Robbery. The Long Rope.* 1963: *The Gun Hawk.* 1964: *Fate is the Hunter. Shock Treatment.* 1965: *The Hallelujah Trail.* 1966: *Smoky.* 1967: *Tony Rome.* 1968: *Joaquin Murieta* (released only on TV, in 1975, as *Desperate Mission*). 1970: *The Cheyenne Social Club. A Gunfight.* 1971: *They Call It Murder* (TV). *The Resurrection of Zachary Wheeler.* 1972: *Santee. The Rookies* (TV). 1973: *The Boy Who Cried Werewolf.* 1978: *Days of Heaven. Wild and Wooly* (TV). *The Sweet Creek County War/Good Time Outlaws.* 1981: *Stripes.*

**WILLES, Jean** (J. Donahue) 1922-1988
Tall, dark, strongly built American actress of handsome looks and forceful style. She had a couple of minor leading roles in the 1950s, but was usually seen either as a saloon girl or an officer in the forces, and never broke into the upper echelon of roles that her ability seemed to warrant.

1943: *So Proudly We Hail!* 1948: *The Winner's Circle.* 1949: *Chinatown at Midnight.* 1950: *A Woman of Distinction. Revenue Agent. The Fuller Brush Girl* (GB: *The Affairs of Sally*). *Emergency Wedding* (GB: *Jealousy*). 1952: *Gobs and Gals* (GB: *Cruising Casanovas*). *The First Time. Son of*

*Paleface. The Sniper. Jungle Jim in the Forbidden Land. A Yank in Indo-China* (GB: *Hidden Secret*). 1953: *All Ashore. From Here to Eternity. Abbott and Costello Go to Mars.* 1954: *Masterson of Kansas. Bowery to Baghdad.* 1955: *Bobby Ware is Missing. Five Against the House. Count Three and Pray.* 1956: *Invasion of the Body Snatchers. The Revolt of Mamie Stover. The King and Four Queens. The Lieutenant Wore Skirts. The Man Who Turned to Stone.* 1957: *Hear Me Good. The Tijuana Story.* 1958: *Desire Under the Elms. No Time for Sergeants.* 1959: *The FBI Story. These Thousand Hills.* 1960: *Ocean's 11. The Crowded Sky.* 1961: *By Love Possessed.* 1962: *Gun Street. Gypsy.* 1964: *McHale's Navy.* 1970: *The Cheyenne Social Club.* 1975: *Bite the Bullet.*

**WILLIAMS, Guinn 'Big Boy'**
1899-1962
Big, hunkish, light-haired, small-eyed American actor who began in tiny roles, won feature billing in a series of 1920s' westerns then, with the coming of sound, settled down to more than 20 years of being the big, loyal, but not-too-bright friend of the hero, mostly in vigorous action pictures. A former baseball pro in his youth, he died from uraemic poisoning.

1919: *Soapsuds and Sapheads. Almost a Husband. Jubilo.* 1920: *Jes' Call Me Jim. Cupid the Cowpuncher.* 1921: *Western Firebrands. The Jack Rider. The Vengeance Trail. Doubling for Romeo.* 1922: *Trail of Hate.*

Blaze Away. The Freshie (GB: *Life Begins at 17*). *The Cowboy King. Across the Border. Rounding Up the Law.* 1923: *$1,000 Reward. Cyclone Jones. Riders at Night. End of the Rope.* 1924: *The Avenger. The Eagle's Claw.* 1925: *The Big Stunt. Black Cyclone. Fangs of Wolfheart. Riders of the Sandstorm. Sporting West. Wolfheart's Revenge. Bad Man from Bodie. Courage of Wolfheart* (GB: *Lone Bandit*). *Red Blood and Blue. Rose of the Desert. Whistling Jim.* 1926: *Brown of Harvard. The Desert's Toll.* 1927: *Arizona Bound. The Down Grade. Babe Comes Home. Backstage. Slide, Kelly, Slide* (GB: *They All Cheered for Kelly*). *The Woman Who Did Not Care. The College Widow. Quarantined Rivals. Lightning. Snowbound.* 1928: *Ladies' Night in a Turkish Bath* (GB: *Ladies' Night*). *Beggars of Life. Burning Daylight. Lucky Star. Vamping Venus. My Man.* 1929: *From Headquarters. Forward Pass. Noah's Ark.* 1930: *College Lovers. The Big Fight. City Girl. The Bad Man. Liliom.* 1931: *Bachelor Father. The Great Meadow. The Phantom.* *Catch As Catch Can.* *War Mamas.* 1932: *70,000 Witnesses. Polly of the Circus. The Devil is Driving. Ladies of the Jury. Drifting Souls. Heritage of the Desert. You Said a Mouthful.* 1933: *Mystery Squadron* (serial). *The Phantom Broadcast* (GB: *Phantom of the Air*). *Laughing at Life. Man of the Forest. College Coach* (GB: *Football Coach*). 1934: *Half a Sinner. Rafter Romance. The Cheaters. Flirtation Walk. Thunder over Texas. Palooka* (GB: *The Great Schnozzle*). *Our Daily Bread. Romance in the Rain. Here Comes the Navy. Silver Streak.* 1935: *Private Worlds. One in a Million. Village Tale. Gun Play. Danger Trail. The Law of the .45s* (GB: *The Mysterious Mr Sheffield*). *Miss Pacific Fleet. Cowboy Holiday. The Glass Key. Society Fever. Powdersmoke Range. Big Boy Rides Again. The Littlest Rebel.* 1936: *The Big Game. Muss 'Em Up* (GB: *House of Fate*). *End of the Trail. Career Woman. The Vigilantes Are Coming* (serial). *The Champ's a Chump. Grand Jury. Kelly the Second. North of Nome* (GB: *Alaska Bound*). 1937: *A Star is Born. You Only Live Once. The Singing Marine. She's No Lady. My Dear Miss Aldrich. Bad Man from Brimstone. Girls Can Play. Don't Tell the Wife. Dangerous Holiday. Big City. Wise Girl.* 1938: *Down in Arkansaw. Everybody's Doing It. Professor, Beware. I Demand Payment. Flying Fists. Army Girl* (GB: *The Last of the Cavalry*). *You and Me. Hold That Co-Ed* (GB: *Hold That Gal*). *The Marines Are Here. Crashin' Through Danger.* 1939: *6,000 Enemies. Pardon Our Nerve. Fugitive at Large. Mutiny on the Blackhawk. Bad Lands. Dodge City. Blackmail. Street of Missing Men. Legion of Lost Flyers.* 1940: *Virginia City. The Fighting 69th. Santa Fé Trail. Dulcy. Castle on the Hudson* (GB: *Years Without Days*). *Money and the Woman. Alias the Deacon. Wagons Westward.* 1941: *Billy the Kid. Six Lessons from Madame La Zonga. Swamp Water* (GB: *The Man Who Came Back*). *Riders of Death Valley* (serial). *Country Fair. You'll Never Get Rich. The Bugle Sounds.* 1942: *American*

Empire (GB: My Son Alone). Mr Wise Guy. Lure of the Islands. Between Us Girls. Silver Queen. 1943: Buckskin Frontier (GB: The Iron Road). The Desperadoes. Hands Across the Border. Minesweeper. 1944: Swing in the Saddle (GB: Swing and Sway). Belle of the Yukon. The Cowboy and the Senorita. Nevada. Thirty Seconds Over Tokyo. Cowboy Canteen (GB: Close Harmony). 1945: The Man Who Walked Alone. Rhythm Roundup (GB: Honest John). Sing Me a Song of Texas (GB: Fortune Hunter). Song of the Prairie (GB: Sentiment and Song). 1946: Throw a Saddle on a Star. Cowboy Blues (GB: Beneath the Starry Skies). That Texas Jamboree (GB: Medicine Man). Singing on the Trail (GB: Lookin' for Someone). 1947: King of the Wild Horses (GB: King of the Wild). Singin' in the Corn (GB: Give and Take). Road to the Big House. Over the Santa Fé Trail (GB: No Escape). 1948: Bad Men of Tombstone. Station West. Smoky Mountain Melody. 1949: Brimstone. 1950: Hoedown. Rocky Mountain. 1951: Al Jennings of Oklahoma. Man in the Saddle (GB: The Outcast). 1952: Springfield Rifle. Hangman's Knot. 1954: Southwest Passage. (GB: Camels West). Massacre Canyon. The Outlaw's Daughter. 1956: Hidden Guns. The Man from Del Rio. 1957: The Hired Gun. 1959: Five Bold Women. 1960: Home from the Hill. The Alamo. 1961: The Comancheros.

**WILLIAMS, John** 1903-1983
Tall, stately, sandy-haired, moustachioed British actor who never lost his essential Englishness despite living almost entirely in America from 1924. His film appearances are minor apart from his famous running role as Inspector Hubbard in *Dial M for Murder*, which he played on stage, in film and on television. He began on stage as a boy of 13, playing John in *Peter Pan*; during World War II he served with the RAF and made a couple of movies in England. The John Williams who appears in 1935's *Emil and the Detectives* (US: *Emil*) is not the same actor.

1942: The Foreman Went to France (US: Somewhere in France). Next of Kin. 1947: A Woman's Vengeance. The Paradine Case. 1949: The Dancing Years. 1950: Kind Lady. 1951: The Lady and the Bandit (GB: Dick Turpin's Ride). Thunder in the East (released 1953). 1954: Dial M for Murder. The Student Prince. Sabrina (GB: Sabrina Fair). 1955: To Catch a Thief. 1956: D-Day the Sixth of June. The Solid Gold Cadillac. 1957: Will Success Spoil Rock Hunter? (GB: Oh! For a Man!). Island in the Sun. Witness for the Prosecution. 1959: The Young Philadelphians (GB: The City Jungle). 1960: Visit to a Small Planet. Midnight Lace. 1965: Dear Brigitte.... Harlow (Carol Lynley version). 1966: The Last of the Secret Agents? 1967: Double Trouble. The Secret War of Harry Frigg. 1968: A Flea in Her Ear. 1972: The Hound of the Baskervilles (TV). 1974: Lost in the Stars. 1976: No Deposit, No Return. 1978: Hot Lead and Cold Feet. The Swarm.

## WILLIAMS, Rhys 1897-1969
Barrel-shaped Welsh-born actor with small facial features beneath a bald head, with two bushes of black hair at the sides. He never lost the Welsh lilt in his voice despite being in America since boyhood. He was a stage player until going to Hollywood in 1941 to work as a dialogue coach and technical adviser on *How Green Was My Valley*. Director John Ford asked him to play a role in the film and Hollywood found it had an efficient and likeable new character player in its hands. Williams stayed there for the remainder of his career, playing preachers, doctors and other anxious-looking professional men.

1941: How Green Was My Valley. 1942: This Above All. Remember Pearl Harbor. Mrs Miniver. Cairo. Eagle Squadron. Gentleman Jim. Random Harvest. 1943: No Time for Love. 1945: The Corn is Green. The Bells of St Mary's. You Came Along. Blood on the Sun. The Spiral Staircase. The Trouble with Women (released 1947). 1946: The Imperfect Lady (GB: Mrs Loring's Secret). Cross My Heart. So Goes My Love (GB: A Genius in the Family). Easy Come, Easy Go. The Strange Woman. Voice of the Whistler. 1947: The Farmer's Daughter. Moss Rose. If Winter Comes. 1948: Hills of Home (GB: Master of Lassie). The Black Arrow (GB: The Black Arrow Strikes). Tenth Avenue Angel. 1949: Bad Boy. The Crooked Way. Tokyo Joe. The Inspector General. Fighting Man of the Plains. 1950: Devil's Doorway. Kiss Tomorrow Goodbye. California Passage. The Showdown. Tyrant of the Sea. 1951: Lightning Strikes Twice. One Too Many (GB: Killer with a Label). The Son of Dr Jekyll. The Sword of Monte Cristo. Never Trust a Gambler. The Law and the Lady. The Light Touch. Million Dollar Pursuit. 1952: Okinawa. Mutiny. Carbine Williams. Plymouth Adventure. Les Miserables. The World in his Arms. Scandal at Scourie. Meet Me at the Fair. 1953: Julius Caesar. Bad for Each Other. 1954: Johnny Guitar. Man in the Attic. The Black Shield of Falworth. Crime Squad. There's No Business Like Show Business. 1955: Battle Cry. How to Be Very, Very Popular. The Scarlet Coat. Mohawk. The King's Thief. The Kentuckian.

1956: Nightmare. The Fastest Gun Alive. The Desperadoes Are in Town. The Boss. 1957: Raintree County. The Restless Breed. Lure of the Swamp. 1958: Merry Andrew. 1960: Midnight Lace. 1965: The Sons of Katie Elder. Our Man Flint. 1969: Skullduggery.

## WILLMAN, Noel 1918- 1988
Soft-spoken, short-haired Irish actor, often in roles of quietly chilling menace. On stage in London at 20, he apeared in a few British films in post-war years, floating through the more sinister ones like some ethereal death's head moth. A certain lack of warmth may have limited these appearances, but he has been kept working hard in the theatre, directing as well as acting.

1952: The Pickwick Papers. Androcles and the Lion. 1953: The Net (US: Project M7). Malta Story. 1954: Beau Brummell. 1955: The Dark Avenger (US: The Warriors). 1956: The Man Who Knew Too Much. 1957: Seven Waves Away (US: Abandon Ship!). Across the Bridge. 1958: Carve Her Name with Pride. 1960: Cone of Silence (US: Trouble in the Sky). The Criminal (US: The Concrete Jungle). Never Let Go. The Girl on the Boat. 1961: Two Living, One Dead. 1962: Kiss of the Vampire (US: Kiss of Evil). 1965: Doctor Zhivago. The Reptile. 1968: The Vengeance of She. 1974: The Odessa File. 1976: 21 Hours at Munich (TV. GB: cinemas).

**WILLS, Chill** 1903-1978
Amiable, scrape-voiced, frog-faced American actor who played mainly folksy western roles. He began as an equally wheezy country-and-western singer (with his group, the Avalon Boys; they formed a memorable background to Laurel and Hardy's soft-shoe number in *Way Out West*), but graduated to small acting roles in the late 1930s and remained a popular, colourful support. Almost never a villain. Later the voice of Francis the Talking Mule in Universal-International's comedy series. Nominated for an Oscar in *The Alamo*.

1933: Bar 20 Rides Again. 1936: *At Sea Ashore. Anything Goes. Nobody's Baby. The Call of the Prairie. 1937: Hideaway Girl. Way

LEFT Rhys **Williams** (left) looks his usual reliable self in this scene from 1951's *The Law and the Lady*, with Greer Garson and Michael Wilding

BELOW Looking as forbidding as ever, Noel **Willman** (left) lurks behind William Holden and Georg Marischka in *21 Hours at Munich* (1976), his last film work to date

Out West. 1938: Lawless Valley. 1939:
Racketeers of the Range. Arizona Legion.
Allegheny Uprising (GB: The First Rebel).
Sorority House (GB: That Girl from College).
Timber Stampede. Trouble in Sundown.
1940: The Westerner. Boom Town. Sky
Murder. Wyoming (GB: Bad Man of Wyom-
ing). Tugboat Annie Sails Again. 1941: Billy
the Kid. Western Union. The Bugle Sounds.
Belle Starr. Honky Tonk. The Bad Man (GB:
Two Gun Cupid). 1942: Apache Trail.
Tarzan's New York Adventure. Stand by for
Action! (GB: Cargo of Innocents). The Omaha
Trail. Her Cardboard Lover. 1943: Best Foot
Forward. A Stranger in Town. 1944: See
Here, Private Hargrove. Rationing. *The
Immortal Blacksmith. Barbary Coast Gent.
Sunday Dinner for a Soldier. Meet Me in St
Louis. I'll Be Seeing You. 1945: What Next,
Corporal Hargrove? Leave Her to Heaven.
The Harvey Girls. 1946: The Yearling.
Gallant Bess. 1947: Heartaches. High Bar-
baree. 1948: The Sainted Sisters. That
Wonderful Urge. Family Honeymoon. Raw
Deal. The Saxon Charm. Northwest Stampede.
1949: Tulsa. *The Grass is Always Greener.
*Trailin' West. Loaded Pistols. Red Canyon.
Francis (voice only). The Sundowners (GB:
Thunder in the Dust). 1950: Rio Grande. Rock
Island Trail (GB: Transcontinent Express).
Stella. High Lonesome. 1951: Cattle Drive.
The Sea Hornet. Oh! Susanna. Francis Goes
to the Races (voice only). 1952: Bronco Buster.
Francis Goes to West Point (voice only). Ride
the Man Down. 1953: City That Never Sleeps.
The Man from the Alamo. Small Town Girl.
Francis Covers the Big Town (voice only).
Tumbleweed. 1954: Francis Joins the WACs.
Ricochet Romance. 1955: Hell's Outpost.
Timberjack. Francis in the Navy (voice only).
1956: Santiago (GB: The Gun Runner).
Giant. Kentucky Rifle. Francis in the Haunted
House (voice only). Gun for a Coward. 1957:
Gun Glory. 1958: From Hell to Texas (GB:
Manhunt). 1959: The Sad Horse. 1960: The
Alamo. Tomorrow (TV). 1961: Gold of the
Seven Saints. Where the Boys Are. The Little
Shepherd of Kingdom Come. The Deadly
Companions. 1962: Young Guns of Texas.
1963: The Wheeler Dealers (GB: Separate
Beds). McLintock! The Cardinal. 1964: The
Rounders. 1966: Fireball 500. 1969: The
Over-the-Hill Gang (TV). 1970: The Libera-
tion of L B Jones. The Over-the-Hill Gang
Rides Again (TV). 1971: The Steagle. 1973:
Pat Garrett and Billy the Kid. Guns of a
Stranger. 1975: Big Daddy. 1977: Poco —
Little Dog Lost. Mr Billion.

## WILSON, Dooley (Arthur D Wilson)
1894-1953
Small black actor and entertainer with sad
eyes but massive smile. A singing drummer
and nightclub owner in his early years, he
took up acting in 1930, won praise for the
leading role in the stage production of Cabin
in the Sky, and then brought his warm
personality to films, most notably as Sam,
the pianist in Rick's Cafe Americain in

Casablanca. Ironically, this was easily his
best-remembered role; in real life, he could
not play a note, and was dubbed for the film.

1941: Take a Letter, Darling (GB: The
Green-Eyed Woman). 1942: Cairo. A Night
in New Orleans. Casablanca. My Favorite
Blonde. 1943: Stormy Weather. Two Tickets
to London. Higher and Higher. 1944: Seven
Days Ashore. 1948: Triple Threat. Racing
Luck. 1949: Free for All. Come to the Stable.
1950: No Man of Her Own. 1951: Passage
West (GB: High Venture).

## WILSON, Ian 1902-
Small, dark-haired, bespectacled British
actor with disapproving mouth, the archetypal fussy little man of the British cinema
through five decades, seen in most of the
films from the Boulting Brothers, for whom
he seemed to be something of a good luck
charm.

1922: The Master of Craft. 1923: Through
Fire and Water. 1924: The Cavern Spider.
1926: The Fighting Gladiator. 1927: Shoot-
ing Stars. 1928: What Next? 1930: Bed and
Breakfast. The Dizzy Limit. 1931: Splinters
in the Navy. 1932: Heroes of the Mine. Double
Dealing. Little Waitress. *The Bailiffs. 1933:
Oh For a Plumber! Facing the Music. Lucky
Blaze. 1934: The Unholy Quest. The Broken
Rosary. The Merry Men of Sherwood. Those
Were the Days. Song at Eventide. Love, Life
and Laughter. 1935: Father O'Flynn. Birds of
Feather. Play Up the Band. The City of
Beautiful Nonsense. *Polly's Two Fathers. Joy

Ride. 1936: Melody of My Heart. Pal
O'Mine. Apron Fools. 1937: Song of the Forge.
The Vicar of Bray. 1941: Quiet Wedding.
1943: The Dummy Talks. 1948: My Sister
and I. 1950: Seven Days to Noon. The Lady
Craved Excitement. 1951: The Magic Box.
Whispering Smith Hits London (US: Whisper-
ing Smith versus Scotland Yard). 1952: The
Last Page (US: Manbait). Mother Riley Meets
the Vampire (US: Vampire over London).
Treasure Hunt. Meet Me Tonight. Hindle
Wakes (US: Holiday Week). 1953: The
Floating Dutchman. Trouble in Store. 1954:
*The Strange Case of Blondie. The Brain
Machine. Radio Cab Murder. Seagulls over
Sorrento (US: Crest of the Wave). Time is My
Enemy. 1955: See How They Run. 1956:
Brothers in Law. The Good Companions. My
Wife's Family. Up in the World. 1957: The
Key Man. Just My Luck. Lucky Jim. Happy is
the Bride! 1958: Carlton-Browne of the F O
(US: Man in a Cocked Hat). 1959: Idle on
Parade (US: Idol on Parade). The Ugly
Duckling. I'm All Right, Jack. Top Floor Girl.
A Woman's Temptation. 1960: Suspect (US:
The Risk). Two-Way Stretch. Feet of Clay. A
French Mistress. 1961: Raising the Wind
(GB: Roommates). 1962: Phantom of the
Opera. Carry On Cruising. 1963: Carry On
Cabby. Heavens Above! 1964: The Runaway.
Carry On Jack. Carry On Cleo. 1965: Rotten
to the Core. San Ferry Ann. 1966: The
Sandwich Man. 1967: *Ouch! The Plank.

## WINNINGER, Charles
(Karl Winninger) 1884-1969
Chubby, loveable, round-faced, usually
moustachioed American character actor
and entertainer, from a family of vaudevil-
lians with whose act he stayed for many
years, on and off, until films claimed him as
a regular after his role as Cap'n Andy in the
1936 Show Boat. He was a top featured
attraction after that until the early fifties,
almost equalling his earlier success when he
played the father of the family in the 1945
version of State Fair.

1915: The Doomed Groom. 1924: Pied Piper
Malone. 1926: The Canadian. Summer
Bachelors. 1930: Soup to Nuts. 1931: Flying
High (GB: Happy Landing). Bad Sister. The
Sin of Madelon Claudet (GB: The Lullaby).

*Fighting Caravans. Children of Dreams. Night Nurse. God's Gift to Women (GB: Too Many Women). Gun Smoke. 1932: Husband's Holiday. 1934: Social Register. 1936: White Fang. Show Boat. 1937: Woman Chases Man. Three Smart Girls. Café Metropole. The Go-Getter. You're A Sweetheart. Nothing Sacred. You Can't Have Everything. Every Day's a Holiday. 1938: Hard to Get. Goodbye Broadway. 1939: Babes in Arms. Destry Rides Again. Barricade. Three Smart Girls Grow Up. 1940: Beyond Tomorrow. If I Had My Way. My Love Came Back. Little Nellie Kelly. 1941: The Get-Away. When Ladies Meet. Ziegfeld Girl. My Life with Caroline. Pot o' Gold (GB: The Golden Hour). 1942: Friendly Enemies. 1943: Coney Island. A Lady Takes a Chance. Hers to Hold. Flesh and Fantasy. 1944: Sunday Dinner for a Soldier. Broadway Rhythm. Belle of the Yukon. 1945: State Fair. She Wouldn't Say Yes. 1946: Lover Come Back. 1947: Living in a Big Way. Something in the Wind. 1948: The Inside Story. Give My Regards to Broadway. 1950: Father is a Bachelor. 1953: The Sun Shines Bright. Torpedo Alley. Champ for a Day. A Perilous Journey. 1955: Las Vegas Shakedown. 1960: Raymie.*

**WINTERS, Roland** 1904-*1989*

Bulkily-built, florid-featured, moustachioed American actor with light, crinkly hair. In Hollywood, he played mostly minor figures of authority with gruff good humour, plus a three-year stint as the cinema's third, last and, to be honest, least charismatic Charlie Chan — although he was hardly ideal casting as the oriental sleuth. With his Chan chore over, Winters looked more relaxed playing his sometimes oily wheeler-dealers and father figures.

*1946: 13 Rue Madeleine. 1947: The Chinese Ring. The Red Hornet. 1948: The Return of October (GB: Date with Destiny). Mystery of the Golden Eye. Kidnapped. Cry of the City. The Feathered Serpent. Docks of New Orleans. The Shanghai Chest. 1949: Once More, My Darling. Tuna Clipper. Sky Dragon. A Dangerous Profession. Abbott and Costello Meet the Killer, Boris Karloff. Malaya (GB: East of the Rising Sun). Captain Carey, USA (GB: After Midnight). 1950: Guilty of*

*Treason (GB: Treason). The West Point Story (GB: Fine and Dandy). Killer Shark. Convicted. Between Midnight and Dawn. To Please a Lady. Raton Pass (GB: Canyon Pass). 1951: Follow the Sun. Inside Straight. Sierra Passage. 1952: She's Working Her Way Through College. 1953: So Big. 1956: Bigger Than Life. 1957: Jet Pilot (filmed 1950). Top Secret Affair (GB: Their Secret Affair). 1959: Never Steal Anything Small. Cash McCall. 1961: Everything's Ducky. Blue Hawaii. 1962: Follow That Dream. 1970: Loving. 1973: Miracle on 34th Street (TV). 1978: The Dain Curse (TV). 1979: You Can't Go Home Again (TV).*

**WINWOOD, Estelle,** (E. Goodwin) 1882-1984

Angular, twittering, bird-like, amazingly long-lived British-born actress, who completed a remarkable 80 years on stage (she made her theatrical debut at 16) and played a leading role in a film at the age of 94. Largely in America from 1916, with occasional returns to the London stage. Her film appearances were far too few, but almost all memorable as she click-clacked, like knitting needles on legs, through one eccentric characterisation after another.

*1933: The House of Trent. 1937: Quality Street. 1953: The Glass Slipper. 1956: The Swan. 23 Paces to Baker Street. 1957: This Happy Feeling. 1958: Alive and Kicking. Darby O'Gill and the Little People. 1960: Sergeant Rutledge. 1961: The Misfits. 1962: The Cabinet of Caligari. The Notorious Landlady. 1964: Dead Ringer (GB: Dead Image). 1967: Games. Camelot. 1968: The Producers. 1969: Jenny. 1976: Murder by Death.*

**WISEMAN, Joseph** 1919-

Dark-haired, cruel-looking Canadian actor with sharply defined features who has been providing uncompromising and humourless villainy for more than 30 years. His crook in *Detective Story* and title character from *Dr No* were only two of some memorably etched portraits. But his bad men became less rooted in reality with the passing years, and he has done most of his best work in the theatre.

*1950: With These Hands. 1951: Detective Story. 1952: Viva Zapata! Les Miserables. 1953: Champ for a Day. 1954: The Silver Chalice. 1955: Mella (narrator only). The Prodigal. 1957: Three Brave Men. Eliahu (narrator only). The Garment Jungle. 1959: The Unforgiven. 1962: The Happy Thieves. Dr No. 1967: The Outsider (TV). The Counterfeit Killer. 1968: Bye Bye Braverman. The Night They Raided Minsky's. 1969: Stiletto. 1971: Lawman. 1972: Pursuit (TV). The Valachi Papers. 1973: The Suicide Club (TV). 1974: The Apprenticeship of Duddy Kravitz. Men of the Dragon (TV). 1976: Journey into Fear. 1978: The Betsy. Homage to Chagall (narrator only). Jaguar Lives. 1979: Buck Rogers in the 25th Century (TV. GB: cinemas).*

**WITHERS, Grant** (Granville G. Withers) 1904-1959

Thick-set, aggressively handsome, dark-haired American tough-guy actor who gave up a career as a reporter to become the rugged lead of minor action films and romantic dramas in the 1920s and 1930s. After 1935 he was mainly seen taking leading roles in serials, or secondary roles in tough outdoor dramas. Rarely looking at home on screen in collar and tie, Withers was in real life five times married and divorced, including actresses Loretta Young (second 1930-1) and Estelita Rodriguez (fifth 1953-8). Committed suicide with sleeping pills.

1926: *The Gentle Cyclone*. 1927: *The Final Extra*. *College*. *Upstream*. *In a Moment of Temptation*. 1928: *Golden Shackles*. *The Road to Ruin*. *Bringing Up Father*. *Tillie's Punctured Romance*. 1929: *Saturday's Children*. *Hearts in Exile*. *Greyhound Limited*. *Tiger Rose*. *The Madonna of Avenue A*. *The Show of Shows*. *The Time, the Place and the Girl*. *In the Headlines*. *So Long, Letty*. 1930: *Broken Dishes*. *Back Pay*. *The Second Story Murder* (later and GB: *The Second Floor Mystery*). *Scarlet Pages*. *Soldiers and Women*. *The Other Tomorrow*. *Dancing Sweeties*. *Sinners' Holiday*. 1931: *First Aid* (GB: *In Strange Company*). *Too Young to Marry*. *Swanee River*. *Other Men's Women/The Steel Highway*. 1932: *Gambling Sex*. *Red-Haired Alibi*. 1933: *Secrets of Wu Sin*. 1934: *The Red Rider* (serial). *Tailspin Tommy* (serial). *Goin' to Town*. 1935: *Rip Roaring Riley* (GB: *The Mystery of Diamond Island*). *Hold 'Em Yale* (GB: *Uniform Lovers*). *Waterfront Lady*. *Storm Over the Andes*. *Fighting Marines* (serial). *Ship Café*. *Valley of Wanted Men*. *Skybound*. *Society Fever*. 1936: *Border Flight*. \**Three on a Limb*. *Lady, Be Careful*. *The Sky Parade*. *Let's Sing Again*. *Arizona Raiders*. 1937: *Jungle Jim* (serial). *Bill Cracks Down* (GB: *Men of Steel*). *Hollywood Roundup*. *Radio Patrol* (serial). *Paradise Express*. 1938: *Held for Ransom*. *Telephone Operator*. *The Secret of Treasure Island* (serial). *Touchdown Army* (GB: *Generals of Tomorrow*). *Mr Wong, Detective*. *Three Loves Has Nancy*. 1939: *Navy Secrets*. *Irish Luck* (GB: *Amateur Detective*). *Mr Wong in Chinatown*. *Boys' Reformatory*. *Mutiny in the Big House*. *Mystery of Mr Wong*. *Daughter of the Tong*. *Mexican Spitfire*. 1940: *Son of the Navy*. *The Fatal Hour*. *On the Spot*. *Men against the Sky*. *Tomboy*. *Mexican Spitfire Out West*. *Doomed to Die* (GB: *The Mystery of the Wentworth Castle*). *Phantom of Chinatown*. 1941: *Let's Make Music*. *Country Fair*. *Father Takes a Wife*. *You'll Never Get Rich*. *Billy the Kid*. *Swamp Water* (GB: *The Man Who Came Back*). *The Bugle Sounds*. *The Get-Away*. *Parachute Battalion*. *The Masked Rider*. *Woman of the Year*. 1942: *Butch Minds the Baby*. *Tennessee Johnson* (GB: *The Man on America's Conscience*). *Northwest Rangers*. *Apache Trail*. *Between Us Girls*. *Lure of the Islands*. 1943: *In Old Oklahoma* (later and GB: *War of the Wildcats*). *Captive Wild Woman*. *A Lady Takes a Chance*. *Gildersleeve's Bad Day*. *Petticoat Larceny*. *No Time for Love*. 1944: *The Girl Who Dared*. *The Yellow Rose of Texas*. *Cowboy Canteen* (GB: *Close Harmony*). *The Cowboy and the Senorita*. *Goodnight, Sweetheart*. *The Fighting Seabees*. *Roger Touhy, Gangster* (GB: *The Last Gangster*). *Silent Partner*. 1945: *Road to Alcatraz*. *The Vampire's Ghost*. *Dakota*. *China's Little Devils*. *Bells of Rosarita*. *Utah*. *Bring on the Girls*. *Dangerous Partners*. 1946: *Cowboy Blues* (GB: *Beneath the Starry Skies*). *Singing on the Trail* (GB: *Lookin' for Someone*). *Throw a Saddle on a Star*. *In Old Sacramento*. *My Darling Clementine*. *Affairs of Geraldine*. *Singin' in the Corn* (GB: *Give

and Take*). *That Texas Jamboree* (GB: *Medicine Man*). 1947: *Gunfighters* (GB: *The Assassin*). *The Trespasser*. *Wyoming*. *The Ghost Goes Wild*. *King of the Wild Horses*. *Over the Santa Fé Trail*. *Tycoon*. *Blackmail*. 1948: *Bad Men of Tombstone*. *Station West*. *Old Los Angeles*. *Fort Apache*. *Wake of the Red Witch*. *Gallant Legion*. *Daredevils of the Clouds*. *Sons of Adventure*. *Angel in Exile*. *The Plunderers*. *Homicide for Three*. *Nighttime in Nevada*. 1949: *Brimstone*. *Hellfire*. *The Duke of Chicago*. *The Last Bandit*. *The Fighting Kentuckian*. 1950: *Tripoli*. *Bells of Coronado*. *Trigger Jr*. *The Savage Horde*. *Rock Island Trail* (GB: *Transcontinent Express*). *Rio Grande*. *Hit Parade of 1951*: *Hoedown*. *Rocky Mountain*. 1951: *The Sea Hornet*. *Million Dollar Pursuit*. *Spoilers of the Plains*. *Utah Wagon Train*. *Man in the Saddle* (GB: *The Outcast*). *Al Jennings of Oklahoma*. *Hoodlum Empire*. 1952: *Captive of Billy the Kid*. *Woman of the North Country*. *Leadville Gunslinger*. *Tropical Heat Wave*. *Springfield Rifle*. *Hangman's Knot*. *Oklahoma Annie*. 1953: *Champ for a Day*. *Tropic Zone*. *The Sun Shines Bright*. *Iron Mountain Trail*. *Fair Wind to Java*. 1954: *Southwest Passage* (GB: *Camels West*). *Massacre Canyon*. *The Outlaw's Daughter*. 1955: *Lady Godiva* (GB: *Lady Godiva of Coventry*). *Run for Cover*. 1956: *The White Squaw*. *Hidden Guns*. *The Man from Del Rio*. 1957: *The Hired Gun*. *Hell's Crossroads*. *The Last Stagecoach West*. 1958: *I, Mobster*.

**WOLFE, Ian** 1896- *1992*

Slight, gaunt, light-haired, mean-looking American actor who might have been born to play landlords who foreclose the mortgage and throw the heroine out in the snow. His characters, though mostly minor, frequently carried a quiet menace that sent a shiver down the spine. He came to films in his late thirties (almost always in humourless supporting roles), but certainly made up for the late start. Over 140 films later, he was still acting, only retiring at 85.

1934: *The Fountain*. *The Barretts of Wimpole Street*. *The Mighty Barnum*. 1935: *Clive of India*. *The Raven*. *Mad Love* (GB: *Hands of Orlac*). *Mutiny on the Bounty*. *$1,000 a Minute*. 1936: *The Leavenworth Case*. *Romeo

and Juliet*. *The Last of the Mohicans*. *The Bold Caballero*. 1937: *The Prince and the Pauper*. *The Firefly*. *The Devil is Driving*. *Maytime*. *The Emperor's Candlesticks*. *The League of Frightened Men*. *Conquest* (GB: *Marie Walewska*). 1938: *Orphans of the Street*. *Blondie*. *Marie Antoinette*. *Arsene Lupin Returns*. *You Can't Take It With You*. 1939: *Fast and Loose*. *Society Lawyer*. *On Borrowed Time*. *Tell No Tales*. *Blondie Brings Up Baby*. *The Return of Dr X*. *The Great Commandment*. *Allegheny Uprising* (GB: *The First Rebel*). 1940: *Son of Monte Cristo*. *Earthbound*. *We Who Are Young*. *Hudson's Bay*. *The Earl of Chicago*. *Abe Lincoln in Illinois* (GB: *Spirit of the People*). *Foreign Correspondent*. 1941: *The Trial of Mary Dugan*. *Love Crazy*. *Paris Calling*. *Bombs Over Burma*. 1942: *Secret Agent of Japan*. *We Were Dancing*. *Eagle Squadron*. *Mrs Miniver*. *Now, Voyager*. *Random Harvest*. *Nightmare*. *The Moon Is Down*. \**Keep 'Em Sailing*. *Saboteur*. \**Famous Boners*. 1943: *Government Girl*. *Sherlock Holmes in Washington*. *Flesh and Fantasy*. *Sherlock Holmes Faces Death*. *Corvette K-225* (GB: *The Nelson Touch*). *The Falcon in Danger*. *Holy Matrimony*. *The Iron Major*. *The Falcon and the Co-Eds*. *The Song of Bernadette*. 1944: *The Impostor*. *Seven Days Ashore*. *The Invisible Man's Revenge*. *Are These Our Parents?* (GB: *They Are Guilty*). *Her Primitive Man*. *Once Upon a Time*. *Babes on Swing Street*. *In Society*. *Mystery of the River Boat* (serial). *The Reckless Age*. *Pearl of Death*. *The Merry Monahans*. *The Scarlet Claw*. *Murder in the Blue Room*. 1945: *Zombies on Broadway* (GB: *Loonies on Broadway*). *The Brighton Strangler*. *Counter-Attack* (GB: *One Against Seven*). *Blonde Ransom*. *Love Letters*. *Confidential Agent*. *The Fighting Guardsman*. *Tomorrow is Forever*. *A Song to Remember*. *This Love of Ours*. *Confidential Agent*. 1946: *Three Strangers*. *The Notorious Lone Wolf*. *The Searching Wind*. *The Bandit of Sherwood Forest*. *Gentleman Joe Palooka*. *Without Reservations*. *Dressed to Kill* (GB: *Sherlock Holmes and the Secret Code*). *Pursued*. *The Falcon's Adventure*. *Bedlam*. *California*. 1947: *That Way With Women*. *Unexpected Guest*. *Wild Harvest*. *The Marauders*. *They Live by Night* (released 1949). *If Winter Comes*. 1948: *The Twisted Road*. *Mr Blandings Builds His Dream House*. *Johnny Belinda*. *Julia Misbehaves*. *Angel in Exile*. *The Judge Steps Out* (GB: *Indian Summer*). *Silver River*. *Three Daring Daughters* (GB: *The Birds and the Bees*). 1949: *Bride of Vengeance*. *The Younger Brothers*. *Colorado Territory*. *Joe Palooka in The Counterpunch*. 1950: *Please Believe Me*. *Emergency Wedding* (GB: *Jealousy*). *Copper Canyon*. *The Petty Girl* (GB: *Girl of the Year*). *The Magnificent Yankee* (GB: *The Man with Thirty Sons*). 1951: *The Great Caruso*. *On Dangerous Ground*. *Mask of the Avenger*. *A Place in the Sun*. *Here Comes the Groom*. 1952: *The Captive City*. *Les Miserables*. *Captain Pirate* (GB: *Captain Blood, Fugitive*). *Something for the Birds*. *Scandal at Scourie*. 1953: *99 River Street*. *Houdini*. *Julius Caesar*. *The Actress*. *Young Bess*. 1954: *Her

*Twelve Men. About Mrs Leslie. Seven Brides for Seven Brothers. The Steel Cage. The Silver Chalice. Moonfleet. 1955: The King's Thief. Rebel Without a Cause. Sincerely Yours. The Court Martial of Billy Mitchell (GB: One Man Mutiny). Diane. 1956: Gaby. 1957: Witness for the Prosecution. 1960: Pollyanna. The Lost World. 1961: All in a Night's Work. 1962: The Wonderful World of the Brothers Grimm. 1963: Diary of a Madman. 1964: One Man's Way. 1967: Games. 1971: THX 1138. 1972: The Devil's Daughter (TV). 1973: Homebodies. 1974: The Fortune. The Terminal Man. 1975: The New Original Wonder Woman (TV). Mr Sycamore. 1976: Dynasty (TV). 1978: Seniors. Mean Dog Blues. 1979: The Frisco Kid. 1980: Up the Academy. 1981: Reds. 1982: Jinxed. Mae West (TV).*

**WOODBRIDGE, George** 1907-1973
Big, jovial British actor with ruddy, countryman's complexion (he came from Devon), always likely to be one of the locals you saw in film taverns, whether pulling pints, swapping stories, scared of the vampire or just having a drink after a day's farming. He also played policemen — most notably the sergeant in the 'Stryker of the Yard' featurettes of the 1950s.

*1941: The Black Sheep of Whitehall. The Tower of Terror. The Big Blockade. 1943: The Life and Death of Colonel Blimp (US: Colonel Blimp). 1946: Green for Danger. I See a Dark Stranger (US: The Adventuress). 1947: The October Man. Temptation Harbour. My Brother Jonathan. Blanche Fury. 1948: Bonnie Prince Charlie. Escape. The Queen of Spades. The Fallen Idol. Silent Dust. 1949: Children of Chance. 1950: The Naked Heart (Maria Chapdelaine/The Naked Earth). Double Confession. The Black Rose. 1951: Cloudburst. 1952: Isn't Life Wonderful! Murder in the Cathedral. The Crimson Pirate. 1953: The Story of Gilbert and Sullivan (US: The Great Gilbert and Sullivan). Stryker of the Yard. The Flanagan Boy (US: Bad Blonde). The Bosun's Mate. The Case of Express Delivery. The Case of Soho Red. The Case of Canary Jones. The Case of Gracie Budd. The Case of the Black Falcon. The Case of the Last Dance. The Case of the Marriage Bureau. 1954: Companions in Crime. The Case of the*

*Second Shot. Conflict of Wings (US: Fuss over Feathers). The Case of the Bogus Count. The Green Buddha. The Case of Diamond Annie. An Inspector Calls. The Case of Uncle Henry. For Better, For Worse (US: Cocktails in the Kitchen). The Case of the Pearl Payroll. Mad About Men. 1955: Third Party Risk. The Constant Husband. An Alligator Named Daisy. Richard III. Passage Home. A Yank in Ermine. Lost (US: Tears for Simon). 1956: Eyewitness. The Good Companions. Three Men in a Boat. The Passionate Stranger (US: A Novel Affair). Now and Forever. 1957: Day of Grace. High Flight. A King in New York. The Moonraker. 1958: The Revenge of Frankenstein. Dracula (US: The Horror of Dracula). Son of Robin Hood. 1959: Breakout. The Mummy. Jack the Ripper. The Flesh and the Fiends (US: Mania). 1960: Two-Way Stretch. Brides of Dracula. 1961: Curse of the Werewolf. Only Two Can Play. The Piper's Tune. What a Carve-Up! (US: No Place Like Homicide). Raising the Wind (US: Roommates). 1962: Out of the Fog. The Iron Maiden (US: The Swingin' Maiden). The Amorous Prawn. 1963: Nurse On Wheels. Carry On Jack (US: Carry On Venus). Heavens Above! 1964: Dead End Creek. 1965: Dracula — Prince of Darkness. 1966: The Reptile. 1967: The Magnificent Six and a ½ (first series). 1969: Where's Jack? *Bachelor of Arts (US: Durti Weekend). Take a Girl Like You. 1970: David Copperfield (TV. GB: cinemas. Shown 1969). All the Way Up. 1971: Up Pompeii. 1972: Doomwatch. Along the Way. Diamonds on Wheels.*

**WRIGHT, Will** 1891-1962
Tall, slightly stooping, long-faced American supporting actor with a slick of dark hair and a hangdog look. Quite unmistakeable in appearance, but rarely rose above minor roles; a happy exception was his seedy apartment house detective in *The Blue Dahlia*. His credits are sometimes confused with those of a younger actor, William Wright, but the films given here should all belong to the correct actor! Died from cancer.

*1936: China Clipper. 1939: Silver on the Sage. 1940: Blondie Plays Cupid. 1941: Rookies on Parade. *The Tell Tale Heart.*

*Honky Tonk. Cracked Nuts. Shadow of the Thin Man. Blossoms in the Dust. World Premiere. The Richest Man in Town. 1942: The Postman Didn't Ring. True to the Army. Shut My Big Mouth. Lucky Legs. Tennessee Johnson (GB: The Man on America's Conscience). Parachute Nurse. Wildcat. Night in New Orleans. Sweetheart of the Fleet. Saboteur. The Daring Young Man. The Major and the Minor. Tales of Manhattan. *A Letter from Bataan. 1943: Murder in Times Square. In Old Oklahoma (later and GB: War of the Wildcats). Cowboy in Manhattan. Sleepy Lagoon. Reveille with Beverly. Saddles and Sagebrush (GB: The Pay Off). So Proudly We Hail! Here Comes Elmer. 1944: Practically Yours. One Mysterious Night. The Town Went Wild. Wilson. 1945: Eadie Was a Lady. Eve Knew Her Apples. State Fair. Salome, Where She Danced. Road to Utopia. Grissly's Millions. Scarlet Street. The Strange Affair of Uncle Harry/Uncle Harry. Rhapsody in Blue. Gun Smoke. Bewitched. You Came Along. 1946: Lover Come Back. The Blue Dahlia. Without Reservations. Johnny Comes Flying Home. One Exciting Week. The Inner Circle. The Madonna's Secret. Rendezvous with Annie. Hot Cargo. The Hoodlum Saint. The Jolson Story. Blue Skies. Nocturne. Down Missouri Way. California. 1947: Along the Oregon Trail. Blaze of Noon. Mother Wore Tights. Cynthia (GB: The Rich, Full Life). Keeper of the Bees. Wild Harvest. The Trouble with Women. They Live by Night (released 1949). 1948: An Act of Murder. Mr Blandings Builds His Dream House. The Inside Story. Disaster. Black Eagle. Act of Violence. Relentless. Green Grass of Wyoming. The Walls of Jericho. Whispering Smith. *California's Golden Beginning (narrator only). 1949: Lust for Gold. Little Women. Big Jack. Adam's Rib. Miss Grant Takes Richmond (GB: Innocence Is Bliss). Mrs Mike. Impact. Brimstone. All the King's Men. 1950: Dallas. No Way Out. The Savage Horde. Sunset in the West. Mister 880. The House by the River. A Ticket to Tomahawk. 1951: Excuse My Dust. My Forbidden Past. Vengeance Valley. The Tall Target. People Will Talk. 1952: Holiday for Sinners. The Las Vegas Story. Paula (GB: The Silent Voice). O. Henry's Full House (GB: Full House). Lydia Bailey. The Happy Time. Lure of the Wilderness. 1953: Niagara. The Last Posse. The Wild One. 1954: River of No Return. The Raid. Johnny Guitar. 1955: The Tall Men. The Kentuckian. The Man with the Golden Arm. The Court Martial of Billy Mitchell (GB: One Man Mutiny). Not As a Stranger. 1956: These Wilder Years. 1957: The Iron Sheriff. Johnny Tremain. The Wayward Bus. Jeanne Eagels. 1958: The Missouri Traveler. Quantrill's Raiders. Gunman's Walk. 1959: Alias Jesse James. The 30-Foot Bride of Candy Rock. 1961: The Deadly Companions. Twenty Plus Two (GB: It Started in Tokyo). Cape Fear. 1964: Fail Safe.*

**WYNN, Ed** (Isaiah Edwin Leopold, later legally changed) 1886-1966
Dark-haired, inimitably Jewish (although

he married a Catholic), bespectacled American comedian, known in his wildly successful, baggy-panted vaudeville days as 'The Perfect Fool'. His early film sound comedies were not successful, but he returned to Hollywood in his seventies with his gurgling voice intact and found himself in demand to play eccentric old gentlemen, especially in Walt Disney productions. Father of Keenan Wynn (qv). Nominated for an Oscar in The Diary of Anne Frank. Died from cancer.

1927: Rubber Heels. 1930: Follow the Leader. Manhattan Mary. 1933: The Chief. 1943: Stage Door Canteen. 1951: Alice in Wonderland (voice only). 1956: The Great Man. Requiem for a Heavyweight (TV). 1957: The Great American Hoax (TV). 1958: Marjorie Morningstar. 1959: The Diary of Anne Frank. Miracle on 34th Street (TV). 1960: The Absent Minded Professor. Cinderfella. 1961: Babes in Toyland. 1962: The Golden Horseshoe Revue. 1963: Son of Flubber. 1964: Those Calloways. Mary Poppins. The Patsy. 1965: That Darn Cat! Dear Brigitte... The Greatest Story Ever Told. 1966: The Daydreamer (voice only). 1967: The Gnome-Mobile. Warning Shot.

WYNN, Keenan (Francis K. Wynn) 1916- 1986
Dark-haired, often moustachioed American actor with faintly dejected air, rough-edged voice and energetic character. At his best during his long association with M-G-M,

specifically from 1945 to 1955, he provided more useful back-up for the stars than some of them could handle, notably in comedy. He might well have been nominated for an Oscar for his best performances, in Holiday for Sinners and Kiss Me, Kate!, although later portrayals were more extravagant and less enjoyable. Son of Ed Wynn (qv); father of screenwriter Tracy Keenan Wynn.

1934: Chained (as stunt double). 1942: For Me and My Gal (GB: For Me and My Girl). Somewhere I'll Find You. Northwest Rangers. 1943: Lost Angel. 1944: Marriage is a Private Affair. See Here, Private Hargrove. Since You Went Away. Ziegfeld Follies (released 1946). 1945: Between Two Women. Without Love. Week-End at the Waldorf. The Clock (GB: Under the Clock). 1946: The Thrill of Brazil. The Cockeyed Miracle (GB: Mr Griggs Returns). Easy to Wed. No Leave, No Love. 1947: Song of the Thin Man. The Hucksters. 1948: My Dear Secretary. BF's Daughter (GB: Polly Fulton). The Three Musketeers. 1949: Neptune's Daughter. That Midnight Kiss. 1950: Love That Brute. Annie Get Your Gun. Royal Wedding (GB: Wedding Bells). Three Little Words. 1951: Texas Carnival. Kind Lady. It's a Big Country. Angels in the Outfield (GB: Angels and the Pirates). The Belle of New York. 1952: Phone Call from a Stranger. Fearless Fagan. Sky Full of Moon. Desperate Search. Holiday for Sinners. 1953: All the Brothers Were Valiant. Battle Circus. Code Two. Kiss Me, Kate! 1954: Men of the Fighting Lady. Tennessee Champ. The Long, Long Trailer. The Glass Slipper. 1955: The Marauders. Running Wild. Shack Out on 101. 1956: The Naked Hills. The Man in the Gray Flannel Suit. Johnny Concho. Requiem for a Heavyweight (TV). 1957: Joe Butterfly. The Great Man. The Last Tycoon (TV). Don't Go Near the Water. The Fuzzy Pink Nightgown. The Troublemakers (TV). 1958: Touch of Evil. A Time to Love and a Time to Die. The Deep Six. No Time at All (TV). The Perfect Furlough (GB: Strictly for Pleasure). 1959: A Hole in the Head. The Scarface Mob (originally TV). That Kind of Woman. 1960: The Absent-Minded Professor. 1961: The Power and the Glory (TV. GB: cinemas). Il re di poggioreale. King of the Roaring Twenties (GB: The Big Bankroll). 1963: The Bay of St Michel (US: Pattern for Plunder). Son of Flubber. Dr Strangelove, or: How I Learned to Stop Worrying and Love the Bomb. Man in the Middle. Nightmare in the Sun. 1964: Stage to Thunder Rock. Honeymoon Hotel. The Americanization of Emily. The Patsy. Bikini Beach. 1965: The Great Race. Promise Her Anything. 1966: Around the World Under the Sea. Night of the Grizzly. Stagecoach. Welcome to Hard Times (GB: Killer on a Horse). Run Like a Thief. 1967: Warning Shot. Point Blank. The War Wagon. 1968: Spara, Gringo, spara (GB: and US: The Longest Hunt). Finian's Rainbow. Blood Holiday. Once Upon a Time in the West. 1969: Smith! McKenna's Gold. The Young Lawyers (TV).

The Monitors. 80 Steps to Jonah. 1970: Viva Max! Loving. Assault on the Wayne (TV). The House on Greenapple Road (TV). Battle at Gannon's Ridge (TV). The Animals (GB: Five Savage Men). 1971: L'uomo dagli occhi di ghiaccio. Terror in the Sky (TV). BJ Presents. Pretty Maids All in a Row. The Falling Man. 1972: Padella calibro 38/Panhandle Calibre 38 (released 1975). Assignment Munich (TV). The Artist. Wild in the Sky. Cancel My Reservation. The Mechanic (later Killer of Killers). 1973: Snowball Express. Hijack (TV). Hit Lady (TV). Hollywood Knight. Night Train to Terror. Herbie Rides Again. 1974: The Internecine Project. 1975: The Devil's Rain. The Man Who Would Not Die. Nashville. He Is My Brother. The Killer Inside Me. 1976: The Lindbergh Kidnapping Case (TV). Twenty Shades of Pink (TV). The Shaggy DA. High Velocity. 1977: Orca... Killer Whale. The Thoroughbreds (later Treasure Seekers). Kino, the Padre on Horseback. Sex and the Married Woman (TV). Laserblast. 1978: Coach. The Dark. Piranha. The Bushido Blade (released 1982). Touch of the Sun. 1979: Monster. The Billion Dollar Threat (TV. GB: cinemas). Supertrain (TV. Later: Express to Terror). The Clonus Horror. Just Tell Me What You Want. The Glove (released 1981). Sunburn. 1980: Mom, the Wolfman and Me (TV). The Monkey Mission (TV). 1981: A Piano for Mrs Cimino (TV). The Capture of Grizzly Adams (TV). The Last Unicorn (voice only). 1982: Wavelength. Best Friends. Hysterical. 1983: Boomerang. Return of the Man from UNCLE (TV). 1984: Prime Risk. 1985: Black Moon Rising. Tales from the Darkside.

YARDE, Margaret 1878-1944
Formidable Britsh actress who had many years of theatrical experience behind her before she came to British films to play mothers, landladies and nagging wives. This Kathleen Harrison of her day began her career as an opera singer — then turned to straight acting with the accent on comedy.

1913: A Cigarette Maker's Romance. 1922: The Unwanted Bride. 1923: *Falstaff the Tavern Knight. *Madame Recamier — or The Price of Virtue. 1925: *The Weakness of Men. *Red Lips. *Sables of Death. *Hearts Trump Diamonds. *Heel Taps. *The Leading

Man. 1926: London. 1929: The Crooked Billet. 1930: Night Birds. 1931: Michael and Mary. Let's Love and Laugh. Third Time Lucky (US: Bridegroom for Two). Uneasy Virtue. The Woman Between (US: The Woman Decides). 1932: The Man from Toronto. 1933: The Good Companions. A Shot in the Dark. Tiger Bay. Matinee Idol. Enemy of the Police. Trouble in Store. 1934: Nine Forty-Five. Father and Son. Sing As We Go. A Glimpse of Paradise. The Broken Rosary. Quest of Honour. 1935: That's My Uncle. Scrooge. Widows Might. It Happened in Paris. The Crouching Beast. Who's Your Father? Squibs. 18 Minutes. Jubilee Window. Full Circle. The Deputy Drummer. Handle With Care. 1936: Queen of Hearts. Faithful. What the Puppy Said. Gypsy Melody. No Escape/No Exit. Fame. 1937: Beauty and the Barge. The Compulsory Wife. The Biter Bit/Calling All Ma's. French Leave. You Live and Learn. 1938: You're the Doctor. Prison Without Bars. 1939: The Face at the Window. French Without Tears. 1940: Crimes at the Dark House. Two Smart Men. George and Margaret. Henry Steps Out. 1942: Tomorrow We Live (US: At Dawn We Die). 1943: Thursday's Child. It's in the Bag. 1944: *The Two Fathers.

## YOUNG, Burt 1940-

Fat-lipped, bulbous-eyed, round-faced, stockily built aggressive little American actor with rapidly disappearing dark curly hair. An ex-prizefighter who also writes screenplays, he has mostly appeared in streetwise roles (notably as the brother of Talia Shire in the Rocky films) where, between tiptilted trilby and grubby collar, he seemed more at home with modern scatological dialogue than most. Nominated for a best supporting Oscar in Rocky.

1970: Carnival of Blood. 1971: Born to Win. The Gang That Couldn't Shoot Straight. 1972: Across 110th Street. 1973: Cinderella Liberty. 1974: The Great Niagara (TV). Chinatown. Murph the Surf (GB: Live a Little, Steal a Lot). The Gambler. 1975: Hustling (TV). The Killer Elite. 1976: Harry and Walter Go to New York. Rocky. Serpico: The Deadly Game (TV). Woman of the Year (TV). 1977: Twilight's Last Gleaming. The Choirboys. 1978: Convoy. Daddy, I Don't Like It Like This (TV). 1979: Rocky II. Uncle Joe Shannon. 1980: Blood Beach (filmed 1978). Murder Can Hurt You! (TV). Lookin' to Get Out (released 1982). 1981: All the Marbles... (GB: The California Dolls). 1982: Rocky III. Amityville II: The Possession. 1983: Over the Brooklyn Bridge. Once Upon a Time in America. 1984: The Pope of Greenwich Village. 1985: A Summer to Remember (TV). Rocky IV.

## YURKA, Blanche (B. Jurka) 1887-1974

Strong Hollywood actress of Bohemian parentage (brought to America in infancy), with inimitably mellow voice and hollow-set eyes. A former opera singer, she made her name on the Broadway stage in the early 1920s, and became a Hollywood character actress with her memorably brooding Madame DeFarge ('I was the 67th actress to test for the part') in A Tale of Two Cities. Died from arteriosclerosis.

1935: A Tale of Two Cities. 1940: Queen of the Mob. City for Conquest. Escape. 1941: Ellery Queen and the Murder Ring (GB: The Murder Ring). 1942: Pacific Rendezvous. A Night to Remember. Lady for a Night. Keeper of the Flame. 1943: Hitler's Madman. The Song of Bernadette. Tonight We Raid Calais. 1944: One Body Too Many. The Bridge of San Luis Rey. Cry of the Werewolf. 1945: The Southerner. 1946: 13 Rue Madeleine. 1947: The Flame. 1950: The Furies. 1951: At Sword's Point (GB: Sons of the Musketeers). 1953: Taxi. 1959: Thunder in the Sun.

## ZERBE, Anthony 1936-

Solidly built American actor with thick brown wavy hair, square face and slight scowl, faintly reminiscent of Britain's Victor Maddern (qv). Hitchhiking to New York to become an actor, he broke into television from 1965 and films from 1967. At first, he was (frequently) seen in violent or bigoted roles; he estimates that in one early year he killed or was killed 119 times, mostly in TV, a medium in which his long-running role as the police lieutenant in the Harry O series gave him a chance to pitch a quieter, more laconic note.

1967: Cool Hand Luke. Will Penny. 1969: The Molly Maguires. The Liberation of L B Jones. 1970: Cotton Comes to Harlem. They Call Me MISTER Tibbs! 1971: The Omega Man. The Priest Killer (TV). 1972: The Life and Times of Judge Roy Bean. The Strange Vengeance of Rosalie. The Hound of the Baskervilles (TV). 1973: Snatched (TV). She Lives (TV). The Laughing Policeman (GB: An Investigation of Murder). Papillon. 1974: The Parallax View. The Healers (TV). 1975: Rooster Cogburn. Farewell, My Lovely. 1977: In the Glitter Palace (TV). The Turning Point. 1978: Who'll Stop the Rain? (GB: Dog Soldiers). Attack of the Phantoms/KISS Meets the Phantom of the Park (TV). 1979: The Chisholms (TV). 1980: The First Deadly Sin. 1983: The Dead Zone. The Return of the Man from UNCLE (TV). 1985: Clay Pigeons.

**ZUCCO, George** 1886-1960

Staring-eyed, bushy-browed British actor who played uninteresting supporting roles in early British sound films and went to Hollywood in 1936, where his deep, mellifluous voice and air of faintly seedy upper-class menace very soon made him the Boris Karloff of the 'B' feature. His characters frequently dabbled in things best left alone, and from 1938 (*Charlie Chan in Honolulu*) to 1948 (*Who Killed 'Doc' Robbin?*), he became associated with a whole run of doomed medical ventures. Died from pneumonia.

1931: *Dreyfus* (US: *The Dreyfus Case*). 1932: *There Goes the Bride. The Midshipmaid* (US: *Midshipmaid Gob*). *The Man from Toronto*. 1933: *The Good Companions. The Roof*. 1934: *Autumn Crocus. What Happened Then? What's in a Name?* 1935: *It's a Bet. Abdul the Damned*. 1936: *The Man Who Could Work Miracles. After the Thin Man. Sinner Take All*. 1937: *Saratoga. Parnell. The Firefly. Madame X. Conquest* (GB: *Marie Walewska*). *Souls at Sea. London by Night. The Bride Wore Red. Rosalie*. 1938: *Lord Jeff* (GB: *The Boy from Barnardo's*). *Arsene Lupin Returns. Vacation from Love. Suez. Marie Antoinette. Fast Company. Three Comrades. Charlie Chan in Honolulu*. 1939: *Arrest Bulldog Drummond! The Adventures of Sherlock Holmes* (GB: *Sherlock Holmes*). *The Magnificent Fraud. The Cat and the Canary. Captain Fury. Here I Am, a Stranger. The Hunchback of Notre Dame*. 1940: *Dark Streets of Cairo. New Moon. Arise My Love. The Mummy's Hand*. 1941: *International Lady. The Monster and the Girl. Ellery Queen and the Murder Ring* (GB: *The Murder Ring*). *A Woman's Face. Topper Returns*. 1942: *Dr Renault's Secret. Half Way to Shanghai. My Favorite Blonde. The Mummy's Tomb. The Mad Monster. The Black Swan*. 1943: *The Black Raven. Sherlock Holmes in Washington. Holy Matrimony. The Mad Ghoul. Song of Russia. Dead Men Walk. Never a Dull Moment*. 1944: *The Devil's Brood. The Mummy's Ghost. One Body Too Many. The Seventh Cross. The Voodoo Man. Shadows in the Night. House of Frankenstein*. 1945: *Sudan. Hold That Blonde. Confidential Agent. Week-End at the Waldorf. Midnight Manhunt. Having Wonderful Crime. Fog Island. One Exciting Night. The Woman in Green*. 1946: *The Imperfect Lady* (GB: *Mrs Loring's Secret*). *The Flying Serpent*. 1947: *Captain from Castile. Scared to Death. Where There's Life. Lured* (GB: *Personal Column*). *Desire Me. Moss Rose*. 1948: *Secret Service Investigator. Tarzan and the Mermaids. The Pirate. Joan of Arc. Who Killed 'Doc' Robbin?* (GB: *Sinister House*). 1949: *The Barkleys of Broadway. Madame Bovary. The Secret Garden*. 1950: *Let's Dance. Harbor of Missing Men*. 1951: *David and Bathsheba. The First Legion. Flame of Stamboul*.

# Bibliography

Of the many magazines used in the compilation of this book, listings, reviews and casts published by the following between 1925 and 1985 have proved especially useful:

*Film, Film Dope, Film in Review, Films and Filming, Hollywood Reporter, Monthly Film Bulletin, The Movie, New York Times, Picturegoer, Picture Show* and *Variety.*

My thanks go also to the authors of the following books which provided so many of the fragments that went towards building up what I hope are mounds of information.

AARONSON, Charles S. (and others, eds). *International Motion Picture Almanac.* 1933-1984. Quigley Publications, dates as given.

ADAMS, Les, and RAINEY, Buck. *Shoot-em-Ups.* Arlington House, 1980.

BARBOUR, Alan G. *Cliffhanger, a Pictorial History of the Motion Picture Serial.* A & W Publishers/BCW Publishing, 1977.

BAXTER, John. *The Hollywood Exiles.* Macdonald and Jane's, 1976.

BLUM, Daniel. *A Pictorial History of the Silent Screen.* Spring Books, 1953.

BLUM, Daniel. *A Pictorial History of the Talkies.* Spring Books, 1958. (Revised) Grosset and Dunlap, 1970.

BODEEN, DeWitt. *From Hollywood.* Barnes, 1976.

BODEEN, DeWitt. *More from Hollywood.* Barnes/Tantivy, 1977.

BROWN, Geoff. *Launder and Gilliat.* British Film Institute, 1977.

BROWNLOW, Kevin. *The War, the West and the Wilderness.* Secker and Warburg, 1978.

CAMERON, Ian and Elisabeth. *Heavies.* Studio Vista, 1967.

CAMERON, Ian and Elisabeth. *Broads.* Studio Vista, 1969.

COPYRIGHT Entries, 1912-1960. Washington DC: Copyright Office of the Library of Congress.

CORNEAU, Ernest N. *The Hall of Fame of Western Film Stars.* Christopher Publishing, 1969.

COWIE, Peter, ed. *International Film Guide.* 1948 through 1984. Tantivy Press, dates as given.

DIMMITT, Richard Bertrand. *An Actor Guide to the Talkies* (two vols). The Scarecrow Press, 1968.

EISNER, Lotte. *Fritz Lang.* Secker and Warburg, 1976.

EVERSON, William K. *The Bad Guys.* Citadel, 1964.

EYLES, Allen. *The Western.* Barnes/Tantivy, 1975.

FILMLEXICON *degli autori e delle opera* (six vols). Bianco e Nero, 1958, 1962.

FITZGERALD, Michael V. *Universal Pictures.* Arlington House, 1977.

GERTNER, Richard, (and others, eds). *International Motion Picture Almanac,* 1929 through 1984. Quigley Publishing Company, dates as given.

GIFFORD, Denis. *Catalogue of British Films,* 1895-1970. David and Charles, 1971.

GIFFORD, Denis. *The Illustrated Who's Who in British Films.* B.T. Batsford, 1978.

HALLIWELL, Leslie. *The Filmgoer's Companion* (eight editions). MacGibbon and Kee/Hart–Davis—MacGibbon/Granada Publishing. Dates various, 1965-1984.

HERBERT, Ian, (and others, eds). *Who's Who in the Theatre* (17 editions), Pitman Publishing. Dates various, 1929-1984.

JONES, Ken D., McCLURE, Arthur F. and TWOMEY, Alfred E. *Character People,* Citadel Press, 1976.

KATZ, Ephraim. *The International Film Encyclopedia.* Macmillan, 1980.

KULIK, Karol. *Alexander Korda.* W.H. Allen, 1975.

LAMPARSKI, Richard. *Whatever Became Of...?* (eight volumes). Crown Publishing, various dates, 1967 through 1982.

LAMPRECHT, Gerhardt. *Deutsche Stummfilm* (nine volumes). Deutsche Kinemathek, 1967.

LOW, Rachael. *The History of the British Film* (six volumes to date; Vol 1 written with Roger Manvell). Unwin Brothers/George Allen and Unwin. Various dates, 1948-1979.

MALTIN, Leonard, and others. *The Real Stars* (two volumes). Signet Books, 1969 and 1972.

MALTIN, Leonard, and BANN, Richard W. *Our Gang.* Crown Publishing, 1977.

MARILL, Alvin H. *Motion Pictures Made for Television 1964–1979*. BCW Publishing, 1980.

McCLURE, Arthur F, and JONES, Ken D. *Heroes, Heavies and Sagebrush*. Barnes, 1972.

MEYERS, Warren B. *Who Is That?* Production Design Associates, 1967.

NOBLE, Peter, ed. *International Film and TV Yearbook*. 1946 through 1984. British and American Film Press/Holdings Ltd/Screen International dates as given.

PALMER, Scott. *A Who's Who of British Film Actors*. The Scarecrow Press, 1981.

PARISH, James Robert. *Actors' Television Credits, 1950-1972*. The Scarecrow Press, 1973.

PARISH, James Robert. *Film Actors' Guide – Western Europe*. The Scarecrow Press, 1977.

PARISH, James Robert. *Hollywood Character Actors*. Arlington House, 1978.

PARISH, James Robert, and BOWERS, Ronald L. *The MGM Stock Company*, Ian Allan, 1973.

PARISH, James Robert, and DeCARL, Lennard. *Hollywood Players: The Forties*. Arlington House, 1976.

PARISH, James Robert, and LEONARD, William T. *Hollywood Players – The Thirties*. Arlington House, 1976.

PARISH, James Robert, and STANKE, Don E. *The Leading Ladies*. Rainbow Books, 1979.

PERRY, George. *Forever Ealing*. Pavilion/Michael Joseph, 1981.

PERRY, George. *Hitchcock*. Macmillan, 1975.

PICKARD, Roy. *The Oscar Movies* (two editions). Muller, 1977 and 1982.

PICTURE SHOW *Who's Who on the Screen*. The Amalgamated Press, 1956.

PICTUREGOER *British Film and TV Who's Who*. Published with magazine, Odhams Press, 1953.

PICTUREGOER *Hollywood Who's Who*. Published with magazine. Odhams Press, 1953.

QUINLAN, David. *British Sound Films: The Studio Years 1928-1959*. B.T. Batsford, 1984.

RAGAN, David. *Who's Who in Hollywood 1900-1976*. Arlington House, 1976.

READE, Eric. *The Australian Screen*. Lansdowne Press/BCW Publishing, 1975.

ROTHEL, David. *The Singing Cowboys*. Barnes, 1978.

ROUD, Richard, ed. Cinema: a Critical Dictionary (two volumes). Secker and Warburg, 1980.

SILVER, Alain, and WARD, Elizabeth, eds. *Film Noir*. Secker and Warburg, 1980.

SPEED, F. Maurice. *Film Review*. Various editions. 1947-1984. MacDonald and Co/W.H. Allen.

THOMAS, Tony. *Cads and Cavaliers*. Barnes, 1973.

THOMAS, Tony. *The Films of the Forties*. Citadel Press, 1975.

TRUITT, Evelyn Mack. *Who Was Who on Screen* (three editions). R.R. Bowker Co, 1973, 1977 and 1984.

TV Feature Film *Source Book*, 1985 edition. Broadcast Information Bureau, date as given.

TWOMEY, Alfred E. and McCLURE, Arthur, F. *The Versatiles*. Barnes, 1969.

VERMILYE, Jerry. *The Great British Films*. Citadel Press, 1978.

WEAVER, John T. *Forty Years of Screen Credits* (two volumes). The Scarecrow Press, 1970.

WEAVER, John T. and JOHNSON, A. Collins. *Twenty Years of Silents*. The Scarecrow Press, 1971.

WILLIAMS, Mark. *Road Movies*. Proteus, 1978.

WILLIS, John. *Screen World* (32 editions, to 1984). Muller.

WITCOMBE, R. T. *The New Italian Cinema*. Secker and Warburg, 1982.

ZIEROLD, Norman J. *The Child Stars*. MacDonald, 1965.

TOM TYLER
VICTOR JORY
BRUE CABOT